COST ACCOUNTING

Michael Chatfield
California State University, Fresno

Denis Neilson
University of San Francisco

HARCOURT BRACE JOVANOVICH, INC.
New York   San Diego   Chicago   San Francisco   Atlanta
London   Sydney   Toronto

Printed in the United States of America
Library of Congress Catalog Card Number: 82–082703
ISBN: 0–15–514140–6

PREFACE

Cost accounting has the reputation of being hard to teach and hard to learn. Most current texts in the area have done little to alleviate this problem. This book takes a new approach to the subject: teaching by example. The discussion of each topic that involves conceptual or computational difficulties is immediately followed by a numerical illustration. This method of instruction is reinforced by a solved comprehensive review problem at the end of most chapters.

This book is divided into three parts. Parts One and Two (Chapters 1–14) deal with cost accumulation and the use of cost information for planning and control purposes. These chapters are meant to be covered sequentially and comprise the basic materials for a one-term cost accounting course for undergraduate accounting majors. The more computationally challenging topics in Part Three (Chapters 15–22) may be covered at the instructor's discretion or as time permits. Alternatively, the entire text can be taught in a two-term sequence, with the first course providing coverage of those topics needed by all undergraduate business students and the second term devoted to the more specialized and technical subjects needed by accounting undergraduates. Finally, selective coverage of appropriate chapters provides a text suitable for the introductory managerial accounting course taken by graduate students entering an MBA program.

In this book, we cover a specified and "generally accepted" body of knowledge, and support approved accounting methods with citations from authority. Our discussion of the various aspects of cost accounting combines practice, theory, and authoritative statements of best practice—and, where such exist, statements of required practice. This is the essential format of nearly all intermediate and advanced financial accounting texts. Recent efforts to regulate and standardize cost accounting procedures parallel financial accounting developments of the 1930s and 1940s, and seem to call for a similar pedagogical response.

Although this text covers more topics and offers a wider range of quantitative analysis than many cost accounting books, the level of discussion is not beyond the abilities of most accounting undergraduates. We assume that the student has already taken an introductory course in financial accounting but has no cost accounting background. Those attempting Part Three will find it easier if they have had some previous exposure to basic college algebra and elementary statistics. However, the problem materials are arranged in order of difficulty, allowing the more quantitative chapters to be taught either comprehensively or on a survey basis.

Assignment materials are an important component of any textbook. The questions, exercises, cases, and problems contribute significantly to the strength of this text as a total teaching–learning package. All assignment materials have been written entirely by the authors, and are, therefore, fully coordinated and consistent with the techniques, concepts, and terminology presented in the chapters.

These assignment materials have been successfully class tested for more than four years in accounting courses at the University of California, Berkeley; University of San Francisco; California State University, Hayward; San Francisco State University; Saint Mary's College; and College of Marin. To those students who used these materials in their developmental form, we express our sincere thanks for their numerous suggestions, comments, and criticisms.

Many colleagues also provided suggestions and encouragement during the development and writing of this text. In particular, our personal thanks to Dean Bernard L. Martin, McLaren College of Business Administration, University of San Francisco; Richard Bagozzi, Massachusetts Institute of Technology; Greg Buckman, California State University, Hayward; Alan P. Johnson, California State University, Hayward; Frank Lowenthal, California State University, Hayward; and John Grant Rhode, McLaren College of Business Administration, University of San Francisco. Robert H. Trezevant, College of Marin, has been of invaluable assistance in contributing a substantial amount of the material incorporated into the instructor's Solutions Manual. The following professors provided helpful reviews of the manuscript as it developed: Alison Hubbard Ashton, New York University; James Bedingfield, University of Maryland, College Park; Charles Brandon, Rollins College; William Call, New Mexico State University; John A. Caspari, Bradley University; Joseph R. Curran, Northeastern University; Carl Dennler, Florida Atlantic University; Joseph Goetz, Jr., Iowa State University; Lawrence A. Gordon, University of Maryland, College Park; Michael Haselkorn, Bentley College; Ronald W. Hilton, Cornell University; Robert R. Irish, University of Toledo; Robert S. Main, Butler University; Charles D. Mecimore, University of North Carolina, Greensboro; Ronald Pawliczek, Boston College; Gordon Pirrong, Boise State University; and Harry Wolk, Drake University.

Financial assistance was provided by the Accountancy Council of McLaren College of Business Administration at the University of San Francisco. Secretarial, reproduction, and inspirational assistance were provided by the following people at various stages of the project: Sandy Anderson, Anita Doleman, Gini Ferguson, Barbara Gunderson, Sharon Kwiatkowski, M. Kaye Long, Patricia G. Murphy, Kiyo Noji, Hannah Peña, Peggy L. Renk, Gloria Rodriguez, Barbara Rothman, Nancy Six, and Connie Wong. We also wish to acknowledge the editorial assistance of Steve Dowling and Karen Bierstedt, both formerly part of the College Department of Harcourt Brace Jovanovich.

We appreciate the help received from all of these individuals. However, they are absolved from responsibility for what appears in the text. Any errors remaining are the property of the authors. Comments from users are welcome.

Finally, a word of personal thanks from one of the authors to some very special people—John, Joe, Jaime, Jeff, and Sweetie Pie. In the words of a prominent spokesman from another field, "Thank you for making this whole thing necessary!"

Michael Chatfield
Denis Neilson

CONTENTS

PART TWO
COST INFORMATION FOR PLANNING AND CONTROL

PART THREE
COST INFORMATION FOR SPECIALIZED DECISION MAKING

x   Contents

PART ONE
COST ACCUMULATION

1

ACCOUNTING INFORMATION FOR MANAGEMENT

LEARNING OBJECTIVES

After studying Chapter 1, you should be able to:

1. Describe the principal management tasks and explain how top managers delegate authority to perform those tasks.
2. Explain the nature and purposes of financial accounting and management accounting.
3. Discuss how cost accounting is related to both financial and management accounting.
4. Identify three purposes of management accounting.
5. Prepare an income statement for a manufacturing business.
6. Explain the basic uses of budgets in a management accounting system.
7. Describe the role of a controller in a modern business.
8. Distinguish between line and staff functions and the duties of line and staff managers.
9. Understand the differentiation of detail in reports prepared for top-level, middle-level, and low-level managers.
10. Describe the role of the Cost Accounting Standards Board and its effects on management accounting procedures.

Introductory accounting textbooks may briefly discuss *management accounting,* which provides information for use by decision makers within an organization. But they emphasize *financial accounting,* which provides information to stockholders, creditors, and others outside the organization.

In the real world of operating businesses, these priorities tend to be reversed. A company's audited financial statements *must* be prepared—they are required by state law, by such regulatory agencies as the Securities and Exchange Commission, and by the stock exchanges as a condition for trading the firm's securities. On the other hand, no business is legally required to produce accounting information for use by its executives. Management accounting data is expected to justify its cost by providing benefits that exceed the expense of producing the information. It does so by helping managers plan for the future, control operations, reduce costs and waste, and generally by improving performance and increasing profits. As one management accountant said, pointing to his company's published financial statements, "Those are the things we *have* to do, and these"—indicating a stack of managerial accounting reports—"are the things we *want* to do."

This chapter first outlines the managerial functions that require accounting information. It then defines the major purposes of management accounting and illustrates accounting reports prepared for managers at different operating levels. Finally, it traces the development of management accounting procedures and describes the sources of authority underlying those procedures.

MANAGEMENT TASKS

Management is the art of getting things done. More specifically, business management involves setting company goals and directing human and physical resources to achieve those goals. A study of management accounting logically begins with a survey of basic management functions:

1. *Policymaking*—deciding in general what should be done.
2. *Goal Setting*—specifying the firm's short- and long-run objectives.
3. *Planning* to reach those objectives.
4. *Staffing*—finding the right person to do each job.
5. *Organizing* economic and human resources in accordance with the plans made.
6. *Coordinating* the efforts of employees whose duties are interrelated.
7. *Directing* the conduct of day-to-day operations by giving subordinates sufficiently detailed instructions so that they always know what is expected of them.

8. *Controlling* operations by taking corrective action when needed to see that plans are carried out, goals are reached, and jobs are done in the best possible way.
9. *Evaluating* the performance of responsible individuals and groups.

The president of a company, as chief executive, has overall management authority. But no individual can personally supervise all the activities of a large business. Effective management requires that the company be divided into operating units, that authority be delegated to the managers of those units, and that managers at all levels be held responsible for their performance. This delegation of management tasks may be based on functions to be performed, such as production, sales, or research. Authority may also be delegated on the basis of product lines, sales territories, geographic areas, or any combination of these.

Each such operating unit is a **decision center**—a department or other company segment headed by a manager who has the *authority* to make decisions and the *responsibility* for the results of those decisions. This is an important management accounting concept because internal accounting information is gathered, processed, interpreted, and distributed according to the activities and needs of these decision centers.

Managers need accounting information that is relevant to their particular interests and responsibilities. Consequently, in designing the accounting reports required for different managers, it is first necessary to specify what those interests and responsibilities are.

THE ORGANIZATION CHART

An **organization chart** identifies each manager's areas of authority, responsibility, and accountability. Every box on the chart represents an individual or group with a job to do—in other words, a defined responsibility. The lines connecting these boxes show the responsibilities of managers to each other and the delegations of authority that created those responsibilities.

In Figure 1–1, for example, the line connecting the president and the manufacturing vice president indicates that the latter is responsible to the president and reports directly to him. The chart also shows that the president has delegated authority over major company functions to five vice presidents. The manufacturing vice president has delegated operating authority to a production superintendent, who in turn has given control of day-to-day operations to managers of the two factories, and so on. The whole organization chart resembles a multilayered pyramid, with executives at each lower level given certain rights in exchange for performing certain duties.

ACCOUNTING INFORMATION AND MANAGEMENT DECISIONS

All management tasks involve making decisions. Managers need accounting information to estimate the costs and benefits of alternative courses of action, to implement decisions, and to evaluate the results of past decisions. By requiring

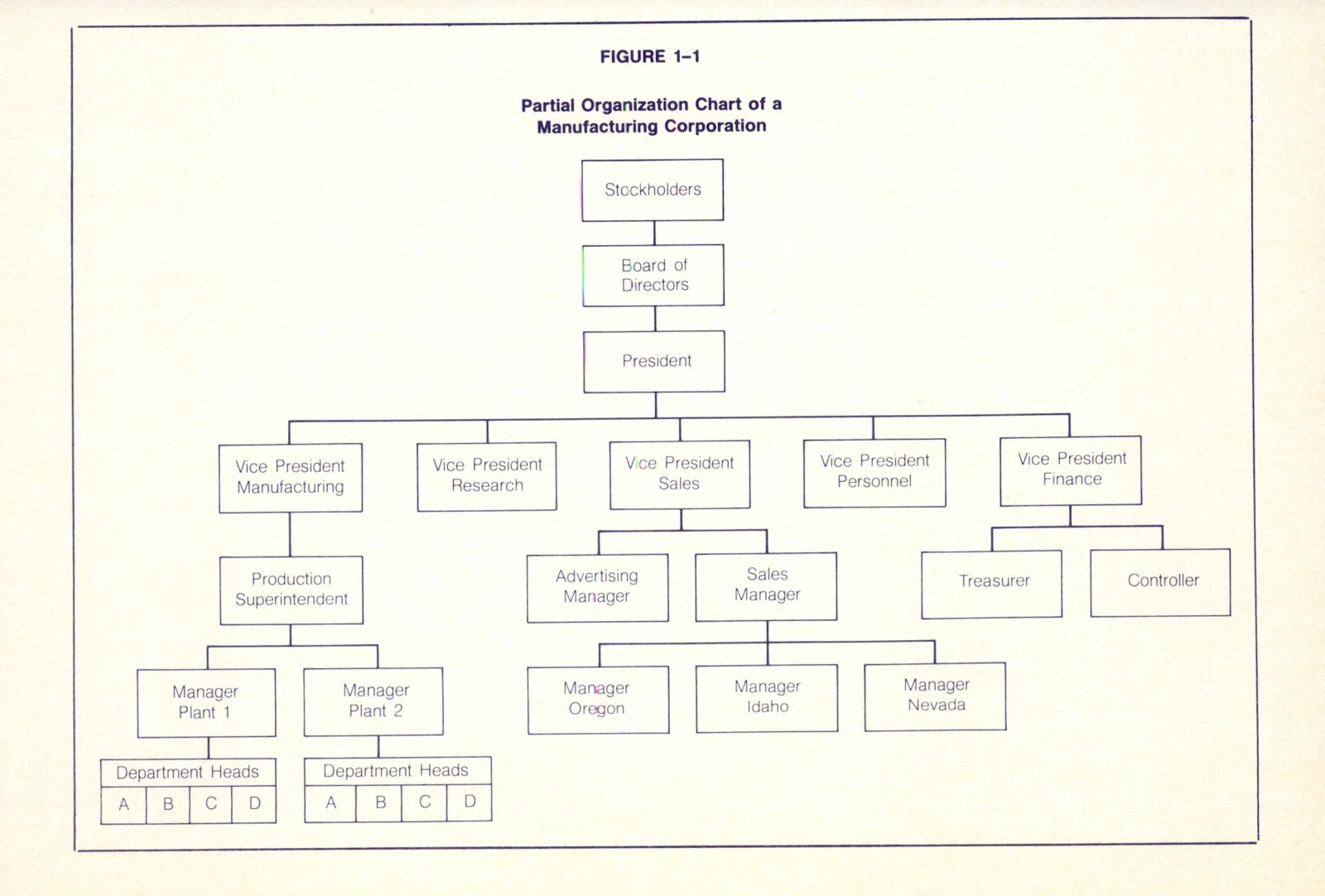

FIGURE 1–1

Partial Organization Chart of a Manufacturing Corporation

that certain information be made available, the managerial decision process helps to structure the accounting system. The output from that system influences managerial perceptions of reality and, in doing so, affects the decisions finally taken.

The extent of the information needed depends on both the decision to be made and the size of the business. In very small firms, where managers are in personal contact with operations, the information processing methods can be quite simple. In larger companies, a formal accounting system becomes a practical necessity. In all cases, the amount of information to be supplied should be determined through a comparison of its estimated cost with the benefits to be derived from it.

Information for managers is provided by financial accountants as well as by management accountants. These two types of accounting should be viewed as parts of a company-wide **accounting information system.** Both financial and managerial accounting employ the double entry system, use broadly similar terminology and account classifications, and record essentially the same transactions. They also have common output; although a company's financial statements are intended primarily for stockholders, they always include inventory, profit, and other performance measures originally prepared for use by managers. The two systems differ chiefly in the needs of their users, in the types of information they provide, and in the rules under which that information is produced.

FINANCIAL ACCOUNTING

Financial accounting primarily reports the results of transactions with outsiders. Its end products are financial statements that serve as communication devices between the managers who run a company and the stockholders who own it. When a corporation's stock is publicly held, its balance sheet, income statement, and statement of changes in financial position are made available to anyone who wants them. These statements summarize the entire company's financial position and operating results. Their broad scope is intended to satisfy the information needs of stockholders, creditors, financial analysts, regulatory agencies, customers, suppliers, and others who must make decisions about the company *as a whole.* Investors must buy shares in the entire corporation; creditors can only lend to the company as a whole; the government normally taxes and regulates each firm as a single entity.

MANAGEMENT ACCOUNTING

Management accounting tends to focus on *segments* of a business. Typical managerial decisions concern the operations of a particular department—a choice between two products, or the replacement or retention of an individual machine. General purpose financial statements sometimes provide starting points for such analyses. For example, an income statement might raise questions about the profitability of certain divisions within a company. However, most managerial decisions require more detailed information about company segments. Such information can only be found in specialized management accounting reports.

Financial accountants in publicly owned corporations must adopt only those accounting methods that conform to the "generally accepted accounting principles" established by the accounting profession. Financial accountants must also comply with disclosure requirements set by federal and state regulatory agencies. In contrast, the selection of management accounting procedures is rarely governed by standards set outside the company. Except when government contracts are involved, every business is free to adopt whatever internal accounting methods it finds most useful. Any procedure that improves operating efficiency reflects good management accounting.

COST ACCOUNTING

Cost accounting includes the recording, classifying, analysis, and reporting of all cost aspects of company performance. Manufacturing as well as merchandising businesses must determine the costs of products sold and on hand. Cost accounting is chiefly concerned with a company's internal events, such as the usage of raw materials, analysis of labor costs, and the distribution of costs to various products and departments. Cost accounting is therefore a vital part of the total management accounting system. Cost accounts are the principal sources of management accounting information. As its title suggests, this text is primarily concerned with *how* and *why* management accountants produce measures of cost performance.

THREE PURPOSES OF MANAGEMENT ACCOUNTING

The discussions in this book center around three purposes of management accounting: *performance measurement, planning,* and *control.*

PERFORMANCE MEASUREMENT

Profit is the crucial accounting indicator. Usually, it is the entrepreneur's primary motive. Profit reflects the essence of successful operations. Without income, a business cannot remain strong, nor can it easily raise new capital from investors. However, determining *past* profits for inclusion in financial statements is much less important to management accountants than helping managers reach *future* profit targets. These future profits are the main incentive to managerial action in a commercial business. Implicitly or explicitly, profit performance is the yardstick used in planning future operations, in controlling costs, and in deciding what products to make, how to price them, and where and how to sell them.

Profit measurement is more complicated in a manufacturing company than it is in a merchandising business. The Cost of Goods Sold figure that appears on a merchandising company's income statement is simply the net purchase cost of items sold during the period. Similarly, the retailer's inventories of unsold

FIGURE 1–2

Income Statements of Merchandising and Manufacturing Companies

ABC Retailers Income Statement For the Year Ended December 31, 19X8 (in thousands)		
Sales		$500
Less: Cost of Goods Sold		
Inventory, January 1	$ 20	
Net Purchases	275	
Freight In	10	
	$305	
Inventory, December 31	25	
Cost of Goods Sold		280
Gross Profit		$220
Operating Expenses		60
Net Income		$160

XYZ Manufacturing Company Income Statement For the Year Ended December 31, 19X8 (in thousands)			
Sales			$750
Less: Cost of Goods Sold			
Finished Goods Inventory, January 1			$ 50
Cost of Goods Manufactured:			
Work in Process, January 1	$ 30		
Raw Materials Inventory, January 1	$ 10		
Raw Materials Purchases	240		
	$250		
Raw Materials Inventory, December 31	15		
Raw Materials Used in Production		235	
Factory Labor Cost		145	
Manufacturing Overhead Costs (Rent, Depreciation, Repairs, Power, Supervision)		125	
Total Manufacturing Costs		$535	
Less: Work in Process, December 31		35	
Cost of Goods Manufactured		500	
		$550	
Less: Finished Goods Inventory, December 31		75	
Cost of Goods Sold			475
Gross Profit			$275
Operating Expenses			75
Net Income			$200

goods are valued at their net acquisition prices. But in a manufacturing business, the costs of products sold and on hand include the firm's total expenditures for raw materials, factory labor, and all other production costs. Each of these costs must first be measured, then accumulated, and finally distributed to raw materials, partly completed products, fully completed products, and cost of goods sold. Consequently, the amount of profit reported by a manufacturing firm depends on the accuracy of its product cost calculations.

In Figure 1–2, the income statement of a merchandising company is compared with that of a manufacturing company. Notice the greater length and complexity of the manufacturing income statement. The manufacturer must determine Cost of Goods Sold by measuring product costs. The retailer typically buys merchandise in salable form and knows its cost when the goods are purchased.

PLANNING

In a competitive business environment, not every firm can raise prices or increase its sales volume. But any company can try to increase profits by reducing costs. Systematic cost control requires a detailed cost accounting system. Management must understand the nature and behavior of particular costs, know when and where they are incurred and who is responsible for them. It must be able to incorporate cost expectations into its plans for future operations, compare planned costs with actual costs as operations proceed, analyze differences to find their causes, and take corrective action to eliminate such differences when possible.

Planning is the process of setting goals and allocating resources to achieve those goals. **Budgets** express the expected financial outcomes of planned actions. The **master budget** typically includes projections of all aspects of operating performance for the coming year. Besides specifying profit objectives, the master budget coordinates company-wide operations and fixes departmental and individual responsibilities for achieving the planned results. The master budget is supported by detailed budgets that show planned revenues, expenses, cash flows, and other financial projections for each segment of the company.

CONTROL

Having established budget targets for production, sales, financial, and other activities, management requires continuous accounting feedback to ensure that actual operations conform to plans—in other words, that the company's goals are being reached. **Control** consists of managerial action taken to correct conditions that cause actual performance to deviate from planned performance. As operations proceed, accountants accumulate information about the outcomes of overall operations and compare these actual results with budgeted estimates of planned performance. If significant differences arise, a responsible manager can often take corrective action to bring operations back in line with plans. Similar comparisons are used to evaluate the performance of individuals.

A good control system allocates each manager's time in the most productive way. Comparisons between actual and budgeted costs will identify poor or superior performance as well as operations that have gone out of control. By reporting only those operations that deviate from plan—ignoring all others—accountants direct managers' attention to areas that urgently require investigation. This type of control procedure is called **management by exception.**

THE CONTROLLER

The chief accountant, or **controller,** is responsible for collecting, interpreting, and reporting all types of accounting information. The controller must design an accounting system to meet both financial and managerial accounting needs. He must also supervise tax administration and reporting, internal audit, budgeting, and internal control. However, the controller is first of all an advisor to management. His department not only compiles the accounting reports needed for performance measurement, planning, and control, but assists managers by organizing and interpreting the data in these reports.

The organizational structure of all but quite small firms is divided between line and staff functions. Line departments produce and sell the company's goods or services. **Line managers** are directly responsible for guiding operations to attain company goals. Staff departments—such as engineering, accounting, and public relations—support the activities of line departments. **Staff managers** provide advice and assistance to line managers and sometimes to each other.

As a staff officer, the controller makes specialized studies and recommendations for line executives, but has no authority to order changes in ongoing company activities. In other words, the controller does not actually control operations, except within his own department. However, he is not subordinate to the line officers he advises. He holds delegated authority as the representative of top management and carries out policy directives in terms prescribed by them. He consults with managers concerning particular operations, policy effectiveness, and decision making. He assesses the performance of individuals and company units, indicating where corrective action should be taken by line managers. He also exerts considerable indirect influence on operations through his choice of what and how he reports and to whom.

The controller must be an expert accounting technician, because accounting measures of performance are the tools of his trade as management consultant. He must have sufficient executive ability to coordinate the activities of his own department. He must have enough detailed knowledge of every facet of company operations—production, sales, finance, research, advertising, and so on—to advise the managers of those areas. Most important, he must work closely with line managers at all levels and be effective in face to face contacts with them. Not many accountants combine the technical and human engineering skills needed to handle the controller's job. Those who do have often made the controllership position a steppingstone to the presidency of major corporations.

Figure 1–3 shows the functional organization chart of a controller's department, setting out the chief accounting officer's typical areas of responsibility.

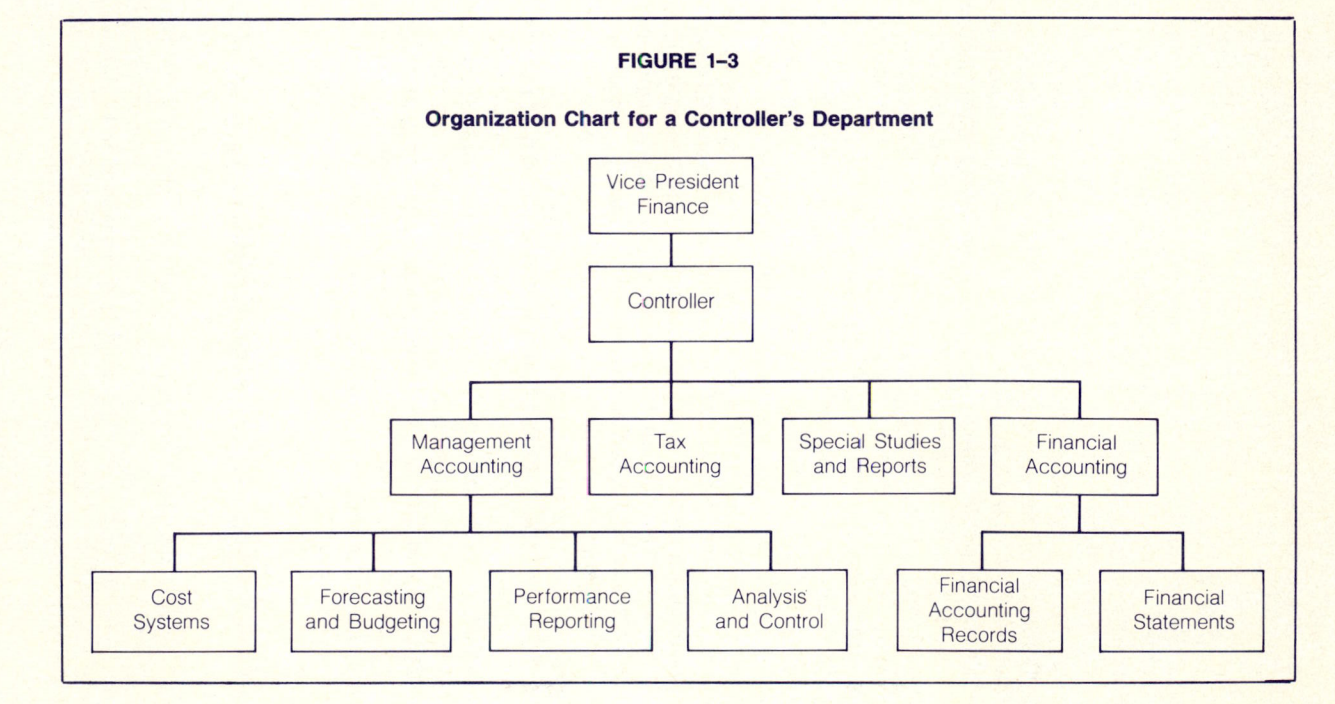

FIGURE 1–3

Organization Chart for a Controller's Department

ACCOUNTING REPORTS FOR MANAGEMENT

Published financial statements contain summarized operating results and financial position data for an entire company. They are prepared for the widest possible audience—not only for investors, but for the interested public. These statements appear in standardized formats, use a specified range of approved accounting methods, and conform to generally accepted accounting principles that are intended to make reported results comparable among firms.

In reporting to management, the tendency is toward diversity rather than uniformity. Each manager's information needs, and his scope of authority and responsibility, should determine what accounting data he receives. Every executive has a unique set of tasks that may affect the form and frequency of reports prepared for him. Managers controlling current operations must receive reports more often than the public does—and with less delay after the event. Such statements might be prepared monthly, weekly, or even daily, depending on the manager's needs. The guiding principle is that they should focus on those aspects of operations for which the particular executive is responsible and which he has the authority to control. Then, when a report indicates that a process is out of control, corrective action can be taken quickly. This reporting of performance according to managerial responsibility is called **responsibility accounting.**

Performance reports typically compare goals and accomplishments. Reports for *top-level managers* are often summaries of overall operating performance broken down by departments or divisions. Statements for *middle-level supervisors* might compare a department's actual and budgeted expenditures for one month, or planned versus actual progress on a special project for which the supervisor is responsible. Detailed breakdowns showing actual and budgeted costs of materials used, direct labor cost, and specific items of manufacturing overhead are often prepared for *lower-level managers*.

Figures 1–4, 1–5, and 1–6 illustrate this differentiation of detail in reporting to managers at different levels. Hayward Oddments Company's total direct labor cost is shown as one line item in Figure 1–4, the report for top management. These same direct labor costs are the total labor costs of Departments A, B, C, and D, as shown in Figure 1–5, which is prepared for the superintendent of the Milling Division. In Figure 1–6, the direct labor cost for Department A is shown as part of a monthly report prepared for the head of that department.

FOUNDATIONS OF MANAGEMENT ACCOUNTING

Cost accounting and double entry bookkeeping originated in Renaissance Italy in response to many of the same business needs. Although they originated at about the same time, the two disciplines developed quite differently. Since the Industrial Revolution, financial accountants have had to meet demands for published, audited financial statements to inform investors about corporate affairs. On the other hand, because the public interest was not involved, there seemed no reason for manufacturers to disclose internal accounting data. Many nineteenth century corporations published annual balance sheets, but guarded their cost accounting methods as industrial secrets. Because bookkeeping texts

FIGURE 1–4

Report for Top Management

Hayward Oddments Company
Cost of Goods Manufactured
Month of April, 19X7

	Costs in April		This Year to Date		Last Year to Date		
	Actual	Budget	Actual	Budget	Actual	Budget	
Raw Materials Cost	$12,720	$11,500	$ 55,290	$ 54,300	$ 52,550	$ 51,500	
Direct Labor Cost	26,730	24,150	98,250	96,000	84,300	82,500	← Refer to Figure 1–5
Manufacturing Overhead Cost	16,325	15,000	67,350	65,000	59,210	58,500	
Total Current Costs	$55,775	$50,650	$220,890	$215,300	$196,060	$192,500	
Add: Beginning Work in Process	18,600	18,600	18,600	18,600	16,300	16,300	
	$74,375	$69,250	$239,490	$233,900	$212,360	$208,800	
Less: Ending Work in Process	21,200	20,000	21,200	20,000	16,150	15,000	
Cost of Goods Manufactured	$53,175	$49,250	$218,290	$213,900	$196,200	$193,800	

FIGURE 1–5

Report for a Divisional Superintendent

Hayward Oddments Company
Direct Labor Costs—Milling Division
Month of April, 19X7

Department	Costs in April		This Year to Date		Last Year to Date		
	Actual	Budget	Actual	Budget	Actual	Budget	
A	$ 2,520	$ 2,400	$10,800	$10,000	$ 9,350	$ 9,000	← Refer to Figure 1–6
B	6,240	6,500	24,900	24,000	21,050	21,000	
C	5,850	4,000	20,270	20,000	17,450	17,000	
D	12,120	11,250	42,280	42,000	36,450	35,500	
	$26,730	$24,150	$98,250	$96,000	$84,300	$82,500	← Refer to Figure 1–4

FIGURE 1–6

Report for a Department Head

Hayward Oddments Company
Summary of Costs
Department A, Milling Division
Month of April, 19X7

	Costs in April		This Year to Date		Last Year to Date		
	Actual	Budget	Actual	Budget	Actual	Budget	
Materials Used	$ 1,560	$ 1,600	$ 3,580	$ 4,000	$ 3,350	$ 4,000	
Direct Labor.....................	2,520	2,400	10,800	10,000	9,350	9,000	← Refer to Figure 1–5
Variable Overhead:							
Indirect Labor..................	3,010	2,800	6,050	6,000	6,100	6,000	
Supplies	1,210	1,100	2,400	2,500	1,150	1,200	
Maintenance	2,550	2,800	5,250	4,000	4,720	5,000	
Power and Heat	750	600	1,500	1,200	1,100	1,100	
	$11,600	$11,300	$29,580	$27,700	$25,770	$26,300	

generally ignored management accounting, the art of cost finding progressed largely through the accident of employees changing jobs and taking their knowledge with them. Cost accounting practice in the 1870s was only marginally better than it had been four hundred years earlier.[1]

Large scale industrialization created a demand for people whose managerial skills allowed them to make use of cost information. In the early 1900s, a new generation of "scientific" managers made cost finding an integral part of daily planning and control rather than a subject for analysis weeks or months after the fact. Attempts were made to predict what costs *should be* under normal operating conditions. Accountants who had been trained to develop historical cost summaries were reluctant to estimate a product's cost *before* it had been manufactured. Engineers and efficiency experts had no such inhibitions. Predetermined **standard costs** were a natural outgrowth of the production standards and work routines developed by Frederick Taylor and his followers.[2] In their efforts to increase output and reduce expenses, industrial engineers found that information available before the event was far more valuable than historical data.

Recent developments in management techniques and management-related technology have significantly broadened the practice of management accounting. Advances in management science, particularly in the areas of operations research, mathematical and statistical decision analysis, and the behavioral sciences, have produced new management procedures which in turn have created demands for more and different accounting information. Other disciplines, especially economics, computer science, and engineering, have also stimulated management accounting practice.[3]

Though these developments have received attention in the periodical accounting literature, they have been less adequately treated at the instructional level. This text addresses both their technical and conceptual aspects and places them in their proper context within the management accounting discipline.

SOURCES OF AUTHORITY IN MANAGEMENT ACCOUNTING

American management accounting practices have been influenced by a number of organizations. By setting rules for inventory valuation and profit measurement, the **Financial Accounting Standards Board** has helped to standardize cost accounting procedures. Certain rulings by the Securities and Exchange Commission and the Internal Revenue Service have produced a similar effect. The National Association of Accountants has published many special studies in the areas of cost and management accounting.

---

[1] S. Paul Garner, *Evolution of Cost Accounting to 1925* (Alabama: University of Alabama Press, 1954), pp. 9, 27.
[2] Daniel A. Wren, *The Evolution of Management Thought* (New York: Ronald Press, 1972), pp. 128–32.
[3] R. H. Parker, *Management Accounting: An Historical Perspective* (New York: Augustus M. Kelley, 1969), pp. 15–72.

THE COST ACCOUNTING STANDARDS BOARD

The strongest pressure for standardizing cost accounting methods has come from the federal government. Admiral Hyman Rickover, testifying before the Senate Housing and Banking Committee in 1963, called the lack of uniform cost accounting standards the most serious deficiency in government procurement. Each year the Department of Defense placed orders for billions of dollars worth of military hardware, usually at contracted prices set in relation to estimated production costs, sometimes on a cost-plus-fixed-fee basis. But the accounting systems used by civilian contractors and subcontractors varied so widely that it was almost impossible to compare contracts, set fair prices, determine defense equipment costs, or assess true defense industry profits. Rickover added that defense contractors had no interest in changing this situation and that the accounting profession had had ample time and opportunity to do something about it, but "pays only lip service to the concept." He felt that if uniform cost standards were ever to be implemented, the federal government would have to take the initiative.

In 1970, Congress established the **Cost Accounting Standards Board** (CASB). The Board was responsible for developing cost accounting standards that would promote uniformity and consistency in the cost methods used by federal defense contractors. During its lifetime, from 1970 to 1980, the CASB promulgated eighteen cost accounting standards:

401. *Consistency in Estimating, Accumulating, and Reporting Costs*
402. *Consistency in Allocating Costs Incurred for the Same Purpose*
403. *Allocation of Home Office Expenses to Segments*
404. *Capitalization of Tangible Assets*
405. *Accounting for Unallowable Costs*
406. *Cost Accounting Period*
407. *Use of Standard Costs for Direct Material and Direct Labor*
408. *Compensated Personal Absence*
409. *Depreciation of Tangible Assets*
410. *Allocation of Business Unit General and Administrative Expense to Cost Objectives*
411. *Accounting for Acquisition Cost of Material*
412. *Composition and Measurement of Pension Cost*
414. *Cost of Money as an Element of the Cost of Facilities Capital*
415. *Accounting for the Cost of Deferred Compensation*
416. *Accounting for Insurance Costs*
417. *Cost of Money as an Element of the Cost of Capital Assets Under Construction*
418. *Allocation of Direct and Indirect Costs*
420. *Accounting for Independent Research and Development Costs and Bid and Proposal Costs*

As a government agency, the Cost Accounting Standards Board had the narrow purpose of standardizing the rules under which payments are made from the Treasury to civilian defense contractors. The Board had no authority over management accounting methods unless federal defense contracts were involved. But within its jurisdiction, the Board's rulings had the force of law; it tended to prescribe accounting methods without reference to general principles, and without allowing alternative procedures.

THE CERTIFICATE IN MANAGEMENT ACCOUNTING

Management accountants have recently gained increased recognition as a distinct professional group with its own "common body of knowledge" and its own program of certification. In 1972 the National Association of Accountants, acting through its Institute of Management Accounting, established the **Certificate in Management Accounting** (CMA) program.[4] A certificate is awarded to aspirants with two years' working experience in management accounting who have successfully completed a comprehensive examination in the following subject areas:

1. Economics and business finance.
2. Organization and behavior, including ethical considerations.
3. Public reporting standards, auditing, and taxes.
4. Periodic reporting for internal and external purposes.
5. Decision analysis, including modeling and information systems.

SUMMARY

1. The common denominator of all managerial tasks is decision making. Managers need accounting data to improve, implement, and evaluate decisions.
2. Financial accounting provides information about a whole company's operations, mainly for use by stockholders and others outside the firm.
3. Management accounting supplies information about segments of company activities, primarily for use by the firm's own executives.
4. Cost accounting, which deals specifically with the cost aspects of managerial performance, contributes to both of these functions. It serves financial accounting by accumulating the unit costs needed to value inventories and determine Cost of Goods Sold on the income statement. Within the company, cost data provide a rational basis for performance measurement, planning, and control.
5. The controller, in charge of all accounting operations, is primarily an advisor to management.
6. Published financial statements are general-purpose reports prepared under uniform standards for distribution to stockholders and the general public.

---

[4] Detailed information about the CMA Examination can be obtained from the Institute of Management Accounting, 570 City Center Building, Ann Arbor, Michigan, 48104.

7. In contrast, each management accounting report should be tailored to fit the needs of particular operating units or even the requirements of individual managers. The goal of internal reporting should be to give each manager exactly the information he needs to make informed decisions within his span of authority and responsibility.

8. Historically, there has been little uniformity in cost accounting methods. In recent years the Cost Accounting Standards Board and other accounting organizations have attempted to standardize cost accounting procedures.

KEY WORDS AND PHRASES

Decision Center (4)
Organization Chart (4)
Accounting Information System (6)
Financial Accounting (6)
Management Accounting (6)
Cost Accounting (7)
Budget (9)
Master Budget (9)
Control (9)
Management by Exception (10)
Controller (10)
Line Managers (10)
Staff Managers (10)
Responsibility Accounting (12)
Standard Costs (16)
Financial Accounting Standards Board (16)
Cost Accounting Standards Board (17)
Certificate in Management Accounting (18)

Questions

1. Distinguish between financial accounting and management accounting in terms of (a) their users and (b) the necessity for each.
2. What are the fundamental tasks of management? Why is accounting information needed to perform these tasks?
3. What is a decision center and why is it an important concept in management accounting?
4. Explain the relationship between a firm's organization chart and its management accounting system.
5. What is the connection between accounting information and management decision making?
6. Is management accounting practice required to comply with any externally set guidelines? Why or why not?
7. Identify three basic objectives of management accounting. Why are they important?
8. Explain the basic difference between the income statement of a manufacturing business and the income statement of a merchandising business.
9. What is a budget and why is it an important feature of management accounting systems?
10. What role does the controller play in an organization? Why is the controller's position important?
11. Why do management accounting reports tend to be less standardized than financial accounting reports?
12. What basic principle underlies a system of responsibility accounting? How does the concept of a managerial hierarchy fit into responsibility accounting procedures?
13. What was the major reason for the development of management and cost accounting in the nineteenth and twentieth centuries?
14. From what disciplines have contemporary management accounting practices been derived?
15. What sources of authoritative support exist for management accounting practices? Why are they less pervasive and authoritative than their counterparts in financial accounting?

2
COST CONCEPTS, OBJECTS, AND CLASSIFICATIONS

LEARNING OBJECTIVES

After studying Chapter 2, you should be able to:

1. Explain why costs should be classified and describe the most important methods for classifying costs.
2. Calculate unit costs, average costs, marginal costs, incremental costs, and total costs.
3. Specify how each of these cost measures might be useful in decision analysis.
4. Describe the purposes of decision centers and activity centers and distinguish between cost centers, profit centers, and investment centers.
5. Explain why objects of costing are needed and list the three major types of cost objects.
6. Identify particular costs that fit each of the following cost classifications:
    a. Expired and unexpired costs
    b. Product and period costs
    c. Fixed and variable costs
    d. Direct and indirect costs
    e. Common and separable costs
7. Explain how the chart of accounts facilitates each of the cost classifications in objective 6.
8. Make the calculations to divide a mixed cost into its separate fixed and variable portions.
9. Describe how direct materials costs and direct labor costs are attached to units in process.
10. Describe how manufacturing overhead costs are attached to units in process.

This chapter defines accounting concepts of cost, identifies three major cost objects that serve as focal points for cost accumulation and measurement, and introduces many of the terms and cost classifications that will be expanded on in later technical discussions.

BASIC CONCEPTS OF COST

The word **cost** is popularly understood to mean the sacrifice of something valuable to achieve a particular goal. The monetary cost of purchasing a restaurant meal, the time cost of attending a public lecture, the energy cost of running five miles, or the personnel cost of trading one professional baseball player for another—all involve the exchange of scarce resources, either commodities or services.

This condition of scarcity—limited supply—is central to business decision making. Because they never have sufficient resources to take advantage of all opportunities, managers must choose among alternative courses of action that arise. The essence of successful decision making is the ability to select those alternatives that improve resource holdings. *Business costs represent the value of economic resources that are sacrificed to obtain more desirable resources.*

COSTS REPRESENT RESOURCE FLOWS

Resource management is a vital concern of decision makers in every type of organization. Managers continually make decisions regarding the acquisition, use, and disposal of resources. In a manufacturing business, monetary resources are acquired and exchanged for physical resources (raw materials), for the services of employees, and for other supplies and services. These are combined during the production process to create output resources (finished goods) which, by means of sale, are exchanged for other financial resources, and so on.

The common element in all these steps is **resource transformation**—the flow of resources from one form into another. Cost is a yardstick that enables accountants to meter resource levels and flows at various points during production. In other words, the cost concept helps identify, classify, and measure resource transformations as they occur.

IDENTIFYING AND CLASSIFYING COSTS

Before resources can be transformed, they must be identified and described. Costs can be classified in many ways, each of which is relevant to particular decision situations. Costs may be grouped according to their *natural characteris-*

tics (materials, labor), their *intended function* (manufacturing, marketing, administration), their *association with a product* (direct, indirect), their *tendency to vary with activity level changes* (fixed, variable), or in any other way that aids analysis.

In general, costs should be classified according to the types of information desired by decision makers. However, no single arrangement of costs can satisfy every managerial decision need. A cost accountant, asked to determine the cost of a product or activity, might first inquire what the cost figure will be used for, then produce a number tailored to the user's needs. There is never one universally correct cost of anything. The phrase "different costs for different purposes" expresses a basic concept of management accounting.

Information requirements are also affected by the particular **decision models** (decision making rules and criteria) used by different managers. An effective cost classification system must therefore be sufficiently extensive to fit a wide range of decision situations, yet flexible enough to respond to the problem solving approaches of individual executives.

COST MEASUREMENTS

Once a resource transformation has been identified, it must be assigned a numerical value as the measure of its cost. In deciding which attributes of the resource transformation process are to be measured, financial accountants use a system of measurement based on the *acquisition costs* of resources transformed. Economists often measure costs in terms of the value of *alternative resources foregone* as a result of committing resources to a particular transformation process.

In this text, the *prices paid for resources transformed* will be used as the primary measure of their cost. Later, as more complex techniques of cost analysis are examined, appropriate alternative measures will be introduced.

UNIT COSTS

The concept of cost developed to this point centers around events described as resource transformations. Raw materials are purchased, wages are paid, materials and supplies are used in production, a machine is repaired, an advertising bill is paid. In each case, resources are acquired or consumed. It is often useful to measure the *cost per unit of each input* to the production process. (The raw material costs $10 per ton. The labor cost is $7.50 per hour.) The *cost per unit of each output* is also an important measure. (One fully completed chair costs $87.50 to manufacture.) In this text, you will frequently encounter **unit costs** as aids in the decision making process. They are convenient common denominators in production planning, product pricing, as well as in the measurement, evaluation, and control of performance.

AVERAGE COSTS

A unit cost is normally thought of as the cost of an *identifiable* unit of input or output. Sometimes a particular production order results in a custom made or even a unique product, the cost of which can be identified and accounted for individually. This situation is the basis for the discussion of job order costing procedures in Chapter 4.

However, it is usually physically impossible or uneconomical to measure separately the individual cost of each item manufactured. In most cases, unit costs must be calculated for an *average* or *representative unit.* For example, suppose a firm uses materials costing $50,000, pays $30,000 in wages to factory workers, and incurs other manufacturing costs of $20,000 during a month when 10,000 items are produced. The *average cost per unit* of output is $10 [($50,000 + $30,000 + $20,000) ÷ 10,000].

Averaging methods are described in Chapter 3, "Cost Allocation" and Chapter 5, "Process Cost Systems." In addition to simple averaging, other approximation techniques are used to measure unit costs. FIFO and LIFO inventory valuation procedures are familiar examples of approximations based on assumptions concerning the physical flow of resources.

MARGINAL AND INCREMENTAL COSTS

Marginal cost is the cost added when one additional unit of output is produced. **Incremental cost** is the change in total cost resulting from decisions to operate at higher or lower activity levels. Continuing the previous example, if output in the following month increases from 10,000 to 11,000 units and costs rise from $100,000 to $115,500, the *incremental cost* of the 1,000 additional units is $15,500 ($115,500 − $100,000). If the total cost of 11,001 units is $115,512, then the *marginal cost* of that 11,001st unit is $12 ($115,512 − $115,500). Both of these concepts are developed further in Chapter 9, "Incremental Analysis for Short-run Decision Making," and permeate much of the discussion of planning and control in Part Three of this book.

TOTAL COSTS

The same basic concept of cost applies to situations that involve a group of resource transformations. The group may be defined in terms of a total quantity of output, a time period, a physical location, or a decision making entity—all of which provide a basis for accumulating and measuring **total costs.** In the preceding example, the costs of resource transformations were accumulated in various ways: the cost of the *10,000 or 11,000 units* (quantity of output), produced by the *firm* (decision making entity, physical location), were collected for the *month* (time period). This notion of collecting and grouping costs is fundamental to the idea of cost objects, which will be considered next.

OBJECTS OF COSTING

Costs result from the choices of decision makers and provide much of the information on which future decisions will be based. To make rational choices, managers must predict the cost of each alternative being considered. Sometimes the connections between costs incurred and results attained are direct and obvious. Often they can only be estimated. In either case, cost data must be collected and organized so that they will be readily available when a decision must be made. To do this, accountants begin by associating costs with particular *objects*—such as products, departments, jobs, or sales territories—which then become focal points for cost accumulation and evaluation.

Objects of costing include every "function, organizational subdivision, contract or other work unit"[1] for which costs are separately determined. A cost object may be a single unit of output or a single decision situation. It may be a long-term construction project or the activities of a production department, a marketing area, or an administrative unit.

Cost information is usually organized around three types of cost objects:

1.   Units of output produced.
2.   Decision centers within an organization.
3.   Accounting time periods.

UNITS OF OUTPUT

A *unit of output,* whether it is a tangible commodity or a service, clearly qualifies as an object for which costs may be gathered. In a manufacturing firm, the resource transformations that help create units of output are called *product costs*. Figure 2–1 illustrates the process of transforming resources to create an output unit.

Although a unit of output is an easily understood cost object, many practical difficulties arise in identifying and measuring the outputs of actual businesses. Units of output in most manufacturing companies are not hard to identify; they consist of such things as automobiles, steel, furniture, and houses. But identifying units of output in a service-oriented business can pose problems. Consider for example a bank, an accounting firm, a computer service bureau, a hospital, or an insurance company. What are their units of output?

In a service business, the item requiring identification as a unit of output is usually the service being marketed. A bank's output might be identified as "financial services," "banking services," "loans," or simply "accounts." The output of a CPA firm could be called "client engagements" or "audits." Hospital services might be described as "mended bodies" or "remedied illnesses." However, a more useful unit of output can be developed by using some commonly held feature of the services as a substitute cost object—for example, "billable hours" for CPA firms, "dollar-loan days" for banks, and "patient-care days" for hospitals.

Because commodity outputs can usually be identified in some physical sense (number, size, weight), the association of costs with output units might seem to be a fairly straightforward task. However, **indirect product costs**—such as depreciation, rent, repairs, and insurance—that can be readily associated with a company's *total output,* may not be directly identifiable with *individual units of output*. Consequently, accountants must calculate unit costs without knowing exactly how indirect costs relate to each of the items being manufactured.

Although cost information is often organized according to the *outcomes* of resource transformations, *input-oriented* figures are also necessary. Cost

---

[1] Cost Accounting Standards Board, *Standards, Rules, and Regulations as of June 30, 1975,* Subchapter G, § 400.1, p. 192.

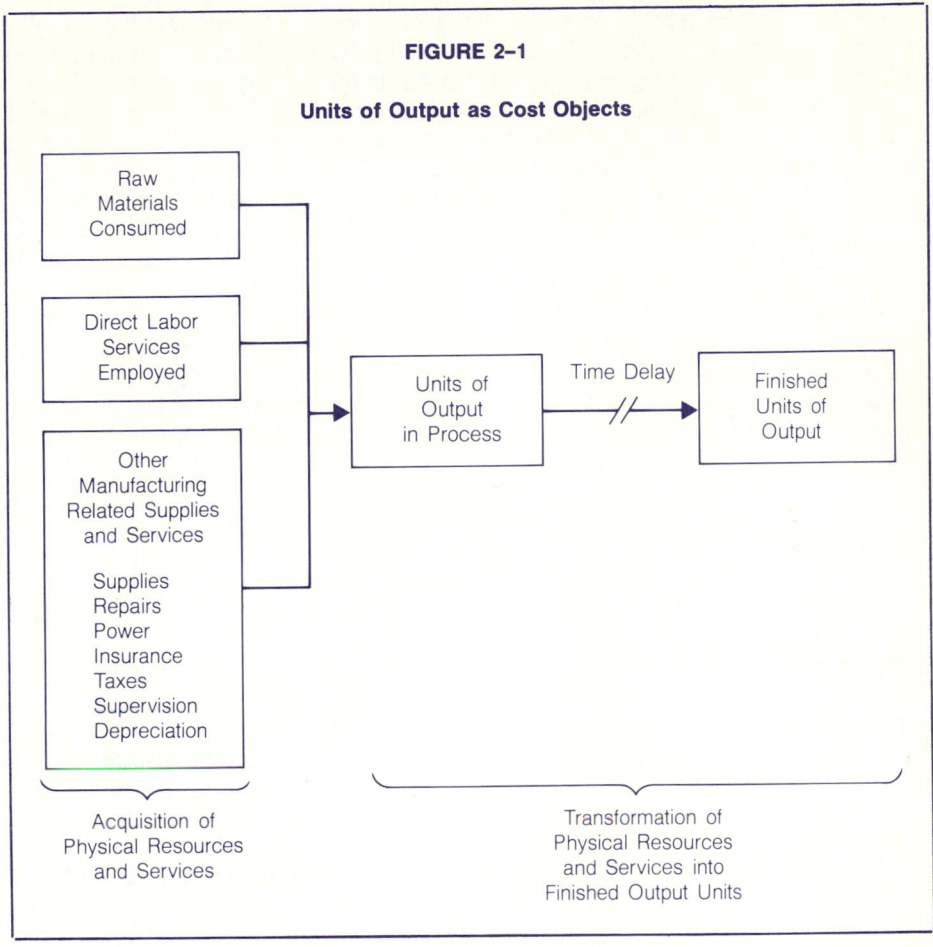

FIGURE 2–1

Units of Output as Cost Objects

objects based on *units of input* are especially useful in showing how particular resources were utilized. Most balance sheet and income statement classifications are input-oriented. The objects represented are groupings of similar resources, either held (as assets) or consumed (as expenses). For example, in the income statement, Cost of Goods Sold represents the cost of inventory items that have been disposed of. Sales Salaries Expense measures the consumptions of sales personnel services, and Office Supplies Expense measures the use of office supplies. In the balance sheet, Land, Buildings, and Inventory are examples of accounts that represent resources held for use as inputs to the firm's total operating processes. Such input-oriented cost objects are useful in performance evaluation and control; moreover, they are contributing factors in pricing and activity level decisions.

Cost objects often represent the pooling of many resource transformations. Cost of Goods Manufactured is a composite of resource flows combined according to their functional classifications: raw materials, labor, and manufacturing overhead. Cost of Goods Sold is also a composite of resource flows, often including costs of goods manufactured during different accounting periods. These objects of costing are relevant to decision making situations in which information is needed about *total costs.* Note that a unit of output is also an aggregated cost object, because it is composed of all the resources added to it during the manufacturing process.

Geographical groupings of resource flows can also be objects of costing. In a large business, cost performance often must be measured at a number of different locations. Production facilities at separate plants, distribution activities at various sales outlets, and administrative operations of regional offices and headquarters create situations in which the performance of company segments must be monitored individually. Similarly, the resource flows related to physically separate groups of customers (sales territories) or groups of suppliers (supply regions) are important objects of costing. In all these cases, the physical location of activities is the common characteristic that identifies a cost object.

DECISION CENTERS

A company's organizational structure can be described in terms of the human relationships involved in its decision making processes. The organization chart on page 5 depicts these **decision centers** as the intersections of the flows of authority (downward) and of responsibility (upward). When authority is delegated, information must be communicated downward in the form of budgets that help managers plan for the acquisition and use of resources. The outcomes of decisions made by subordinates to whom authority has been delegated must be communicated upward in the form of performance and control reports.

Decision centers are therefore important cost objects. The formal relationships among managers largely determine which aspects of company performance will be subject to measurement and who will be held responsible for the resulting performance measures. Such a structure, in turn, depends on which resource flows are identifiable as being controlled by particular decision centers.

Cost classifications based on managerial relationships are typically made in terms of **activity centers**—groupings of activities with a common purpose. A company's Sales Division, Manufacturing Division, and General Administrative Office are rather broadly defined activity centers.

The way in which planning and performance evaluation then proceed will depend on whether the activity center is treated as a **cost center,** where only cost performance is measured; a **profit center,** where profit margins are the object of performance measurement; or an **investment center,** where both profit and the investment base underlying it are considered in performance analysis.

Narrowly specified decision centers are usually the most useful cost objects. Within a manufacturing division, the separate production facilities controlled by a plant manager are one such subclassification. The activities of a single production foreman or department head provide an even narrower focus for cost analysis. Cost objects such as these underlie the systems of responsibility accounting that will be discussed throughout this text.

Special Purpose Decisions   Authority–responsibility relationships are a permanent part of existing company structures. Occasionally situations arise in which less formally structured relationships become the focus of decision makers. A typical example is a one-time, special purpose decision for which temporary managerial coalitions are formed. These unique decision situations must be treated as cost objects. Managers concentrate on the decision rules and alternative actions pertinent to one specific decision situation, organizing all relevant cost information around that particular decision. The resulting cost measures may cut across established authority–responsibility relationships. They will almost certainly include cost data that has already been organized around units of output and decision center objects of costing.

For example, cost estimates might be developed for a proposed long-term investment in plant and equipment. Information is needed on all aspects of the proposal. What will be its initial cost? How much revenue will it earn? How long will it take to complete? What is its expected rate of return compared with alternative investments? Much of this information—such as the costs and revenues of the product to be manufactured or the operating costs of the department that will use the equipment—can normally be derived from data that has been previously accumulated for existing output units or decision centers.

Certain short-run, special purpose decision situations also qualify for treatment as cost objects. Common examples involve deciding whether or not to produce additional units of output, whether or not to expand production capacity beyond current operating requirements, and whether or not to manufacture product components now purchased from outsiders. When such problems are structured so that an incremental approach can be adopted, the best way to accumulate cost information is to treat the decision itself as a cost object.

TIME PERIODS

Accounting periods are the primary cost objects for financial reporting purposes. A firm's financial statements are normally prepared at regular calendar intervals. The revenue realization and accrual principles provide a basis for measuring the total income that results from all the resource transformations which occur during each month, quarter, or year.

In measuring income, the essential problem is to associate resource transformations with accounting periods. Accounting principles require that each period's revenues be matched with related expenses. The shorter the time interval, the more difficult it becomes to identify revenues earned and expenses incurred during that particular period. As will be seen, it is important to distinguish product costs from period costs and expired from unexpired costs, because they allow expenses to be associated with the appropriate time period for purposes of income measurement.

COST CLASSIFICATION SYSTEMS

Cost classification involves grouping costs that have similar characteristics. Accumulating costs in this way facilitates analysis of cost behavior and the preparation of accounting reports. The previous discussion introduced a number of bases for cost classification systems: products, functions, responsibilities, time periods, activity centers, and reference to particular decisions. Costs may be classified according to whether they are:

1. Expired costs or unexpired costs.
2. Product costs or period costs.
3. Fixed costs, variable costs or mixed costs.
4. Direct costs or indirect costs.
5. Common costs or separable costs.

THE CHART OF ACCOUNTS

The **chart of accounts** is a table of contents to the general ledger and a starting point for the development of all cost classification systems. Ledger accounts are statistical sorting devices, in that they first classify each transaction according to its effect on resource flows, then tabulate the results of all transactions so that financial statements can be prepared.

Figure 2–2 is an abbreviated chart of accounts for a manufacturing business. The *asset* sections represent resources presently held. The *expense* categories reflect resources consumed in the current period. The *revenue* section lists the sources of resources from the sale of outputs. The *liability* and *stockholder's equity* sections summarize claims on company resources.

UNEXPIRED COSTS AND EXPIRED COSTS

The asset and expense sections of the chart of accounts correspond to two general cost categories: unexpired and expired costs. Sometimes the resources represented by cost items have the potential to provide future service benefits. These **unexpired costs** are classified as *assets*. In other cases, the resources underlying recorded costs have already been used up in the revenue producing process and consequently retain no future service potential. These **expired costs** are classified as *expenses*. Accountants must measure the expiration of service potentials because they calculate income by matching expired costs with revenues.

PRODUCT COSTS AND PERIOD COSTS

Costs that contribute to the manufacturing of a firm's products must be classified separately from costs that relate directly to periodic sales performance. **Product costs** are capitalized as inventory costs. **Period costs** are expensed and matched with periodic revenues.

This distinction is especially important in manufacturing firms that store their products prior to sale. Whereas period costs such as sales commissions are charged to expense and thereby become expired costs immediately on incurrence, costs of raw materials and other manufacturing inputs "attach" to products and are reported in the balance sheet as part of manufacturing inventory.

FIGURE 2–2

Chart of Accounts for a Manufacturing Corporation

Assets (100–299)

Current Assets (100–199)

101	Cash in Bank
102	Change Fund Cash
111	Accounts Receivable
112	Allowance for Bad Debts
113	Notes Receivable
121	Inventory—Raw Materials
122	Inventory—Work in Process
123	Inventory—Finished Goods
124	Inventory—Factory Supplies
125	Inventory—Office Supplies
131	Prepaid Insurance

Long-term Assets (200–299)

201	Land
202	Factory Buildings
203	Office Buildings
211	Factory Equipment
212	Office Equipment
221	Delivery Vehicles
222	Administrative Vehicles

Liabilities (300–499)

Current Liabilities (300–399)

301	Notes Payable
311	Accounts Payable
321	Wages Payable
331	Taxes Payable

Long-term Liabilities (400–499)

401	Bonds Payable
411	Other Long-term Debt

Stockholder's Equity (500–599)

501	Capital Stock
511	Contributed Capital
521	Retained Earnings

Revenues (600–699)

601	Sales
602	Sales Returns and Allowances
611	Rental Income
621	Miscellaneous Income

Expenses (700–999)

Cost of Goods Sold (700–799)

701	Raw Materials
702	Freight In
711	Direct Labor
721	Factory Supplies
722	Plant Supervision
723	Power and Heating—Plant
724	Repairs and Maintenance—Plant
725	Plant Security Service
726	Plant Property Taxes
731	Depreciation Expense—Plant

Selling and Distribution Expense (800–899)

801	Sales Salaries
802	Sales Commissions
811	Depreciation—Delivery Vehicles
821	Advertising
831	Entertainment
836	Travel Expense
841	Telephone and Telegraph
851	Stationery and Printing
852	Postage

General and Administrative Expense (900–999)

901	Office Salaries
902	Office Supplies
911	Depreciation—Office Equipment
912	Depreciation—Administrative Vehicles
921	Miscellaneous Expense
931	Rent
941	Accounting and Auditing
951	Telephone and Telegraph
961	Stationery and Postage

These costs will only become expired costs when the inventory items that they represent have been sold. This will occur irregularly, depending on the company's seasonal patterns of purchasing, production, and sales. The timing of such conversions—from the acquisition of raw materials, to work in process, finished goods, and cost of goods sold—can significantly affect reported income.

In a manufacturing company, product costs include all resources consumed

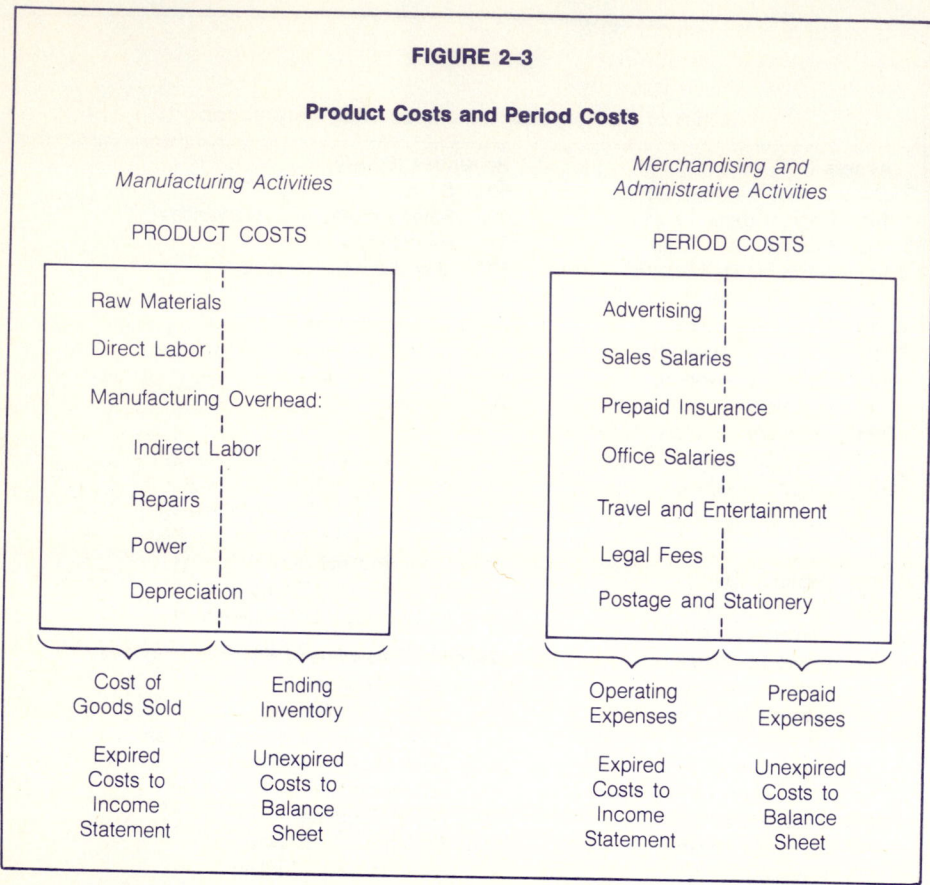

FIGURE 2–3

Product Costs and Period Costs

Manufacturing Activities

PRODUCT COSTS

| Raw Materials |
| Direct Labor |
| Manufacturing Overhead: |
| Indirect Labor |
| Repairs |
| Power |
| Depreciation |

| Cost of Goods Sold | Ending Inventory |

| Expired Costs to Income Statement | Unexpired Costs to Balance Sheet |

Merchandising and Administrative Activities

PERIOD COSTS

| Advertising |
| Sales Salaries |
| Prepaid Insurance |
| Office Salaries |
| Travel and Entertainment |
| Legal Fees |
| Postage and Stationery |

| Operating Expenses | Prepaid Expenses |

| Expired Costs to Income Statement | Unexpired Costs to Balance Sheet |

in order to create a salable commodity. Clearly, the costs of materials that make up finished products qualify as product costs. So do the wages of production workers who manufacture the product. These two categories are usually called **direct materials costs** and **direct labor costs.**

Many other expenditures support manufacturing operations. The third broad grouping of product costs is **manufacturing overhead** (or simply overhead). It includes all incidental materials and supplies used in manufacturing, other than those physically incorporated as major components of final products. It also includes the cost of all factory labor, except for payments to people directly engaged in manufacturing. Overhead also includes all other services without which factory assets could not operate, such as plant heating, power, rent, repairs and maintenance, depreciation, insurance, and property taxes.

Figure 2–3 depicts graphically this separation of period and product costs and, simultaneously, the separation of expired and unexpired costs.

FIXED COSTS AND VARIABLE COSTS

Every cost classification system is designed to depict cost behavior as a response to those events that produced the costs. Accountants often analyze costs in relation to activity level changes, letting units of output represent activity and classifying costs according to their tendency to be either fixed or variable. **Fixed costs** are those for which the total amount does not change in response to activity level changes during a given time period. This group normally includes such items as rent, property taxes, insurance, and supervisory salaries. **Variable costs** are those for which the total amount increases or decreases in response to changes in the number of units produced. Examples include the cost of raw materials, direct labor, factory supplies, and payroll taxes.

Costs cannot be effectively budgeted or controlled until their behavior pattern has been determined. However, cost behavior also depends on the conditions prevailing in particular manufacturing situations. Certain costs may be fixed in one case and variable in another. A classification system will produce consistent results only when the environment in which cost behavior is studied has been specified in detail. Fixed–variable classification requires careful definition of the boundaries of the particular decision situation and also of the time span to which the analysis applies.

Many costs will be fixed when production levels are relatively stable, because in the short run these costs are unaffected by small changes in activity levels. Examples are supervisory and support salaries, rental charges, depreciation, and capacity-related components of expenditures for power and heating, facilities maintenance, and equipment repairs. Over longer time periods and over a wider range of output variations, most of these costs will become variable.

Figures 2–4 and 2–5 show examples of the behavior of (1) *total fixed cost,* (2) *unit fixed cost,* (3) *total variable cost,* and (4) *unit variable cost,* over a range of output levels.

Total fixed costs will remain the same no matter how many units are produced. *Fixed costs per unit* will decrease as output levels increase. If the equation for total fixed costs is TFC = $10,000, then the equation for unit fixed cost must be UFC = $10,000 ÷ Q, because UFC = TFC ÷ Q.

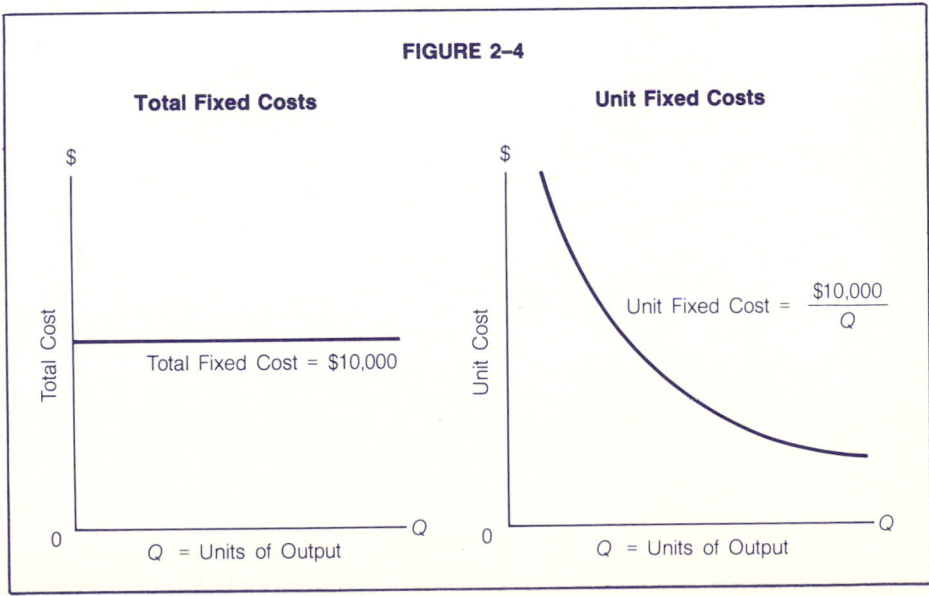

FIGURE 2–4

Total Fixed Costs

Total Fixed Cost = $10,000

Total Cost · $ · 0

Q = Units of Output

Unit Fixed Costs

$$\text{Unit Fixed Cost} = \frac{\$10,000}{Q}$$

Unit Cost · $ · 0

Q = Units of Output

In Figure 2–5, *total variable cost* increases at a constant rate as output rises, whereas *variable cost per unit* remains the same. If the equation for total variable cost is TVC = $5 × Q, then the equation for unit variable cost must be UVC = ($5 × Q) ÷ Q = $5, because UVC = TVC ÷ Q.

Of the four cost relationships illustrated, the *unit fixed cost* is the only non-linear relationship. In later discussions of cost planning, analysis, and control techniques, unit fixed costs frequently will be the stumbling block, point of exception, or source of confusion. As will be seen, these problems arise because the value of a unit fixed cost is only valid for the particular activity level for which it was calculated. On the other hand, because *total fixed costs* and *unit variable costs* are constant amounts, and because *total variable cost* changes at a constant rate, these cost functions are valid over a wide range of activity levels.

Mixed Costs   Figures 2–4 and 2–5 and all the previous discussion of fixed and variable costs assume that costs are either completely fixed or vary at a constant rate over the entire range of output. **Mixed costs** include both fixed and variable elements. They vary in response to activity level changes, but include a fixed cost component that remains constant. Power and heating, equipment repairs, and building maintenance are examples of costs that respond to production volume changes in this way.

Figure 2–6 is a diagram of a mixed cost that combines the fixed and variable costs shown previously in Figures 2–4 and 2–5.

Total mixed cost will be at least $10,000 regardless of the number of units produced. Above that $10,000 level, total costs will increase at a constant rate of $5 for each additional unit manufactured. As output quantities increase,

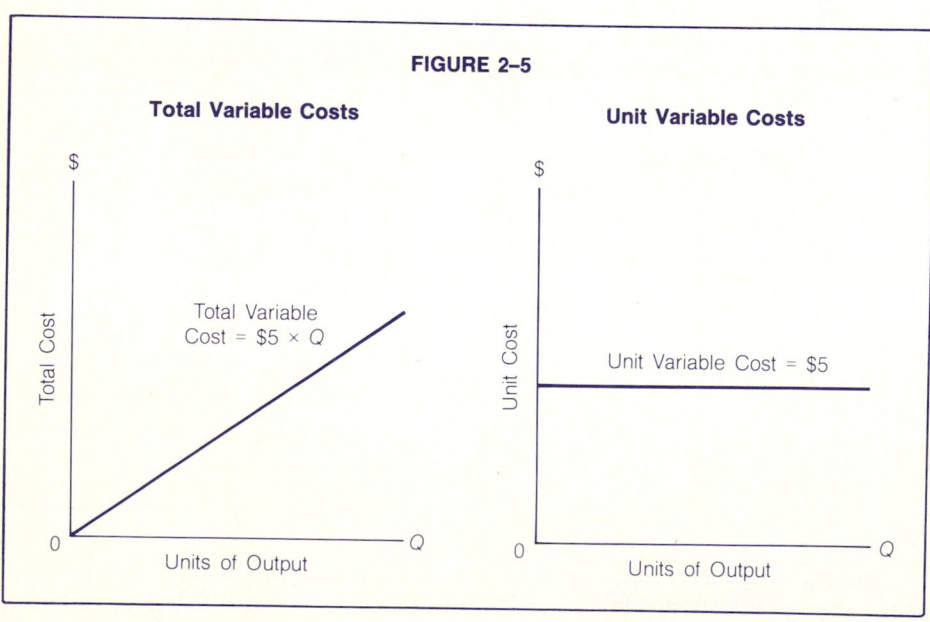

FIGURE 2–5

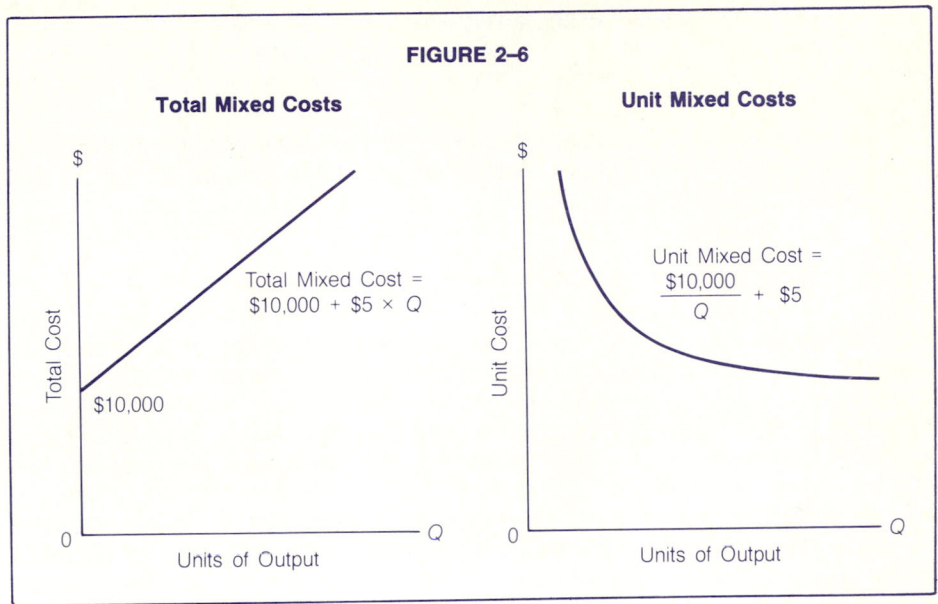

FIGURE 2-6

Total Mixed Costs

Total Mixed Cost = $10,000 + $5 × Q

$10,000

Total Cost

Units of Output

Unit Mixed Costs

Unit Mixed Cost = $\frac{\$10,000}{Q}$ + $5

Unit Cost

Units of Output

mixed cost per unit will decline at a decreasing rate. If the equation for total mixed cost is TMC = $10,000 + (5 × Q), then the equation for unit mixed cost must be UMC = ($10,000 ÷ Q) + $5, because UMC = TMC ÷ Q.

This simple mixed cost pattern is often used to analyze cost behavior when several individual costs are being considered as a group. For analytical purposes, it may be necessary to divide a mixed cost into its fixed and variable portions. If the amounts of total mixed cost at several output levels are known, a method of interpolation can be used to isolate the fixed and variable cost elements.

Example: The following monthly figures are available for Andrews Company:

Units of Output	Repair and Maintenance Cost
10,000	$ 8,000
15,000	10,500

As output increased by 5,000 units (from 10,000 to 15,000 units), total cost increased by $2,500 (from $8,000 to $10,500). This suggests that *average variable cost per unit* in that output range is 50¢, determined as follows:

$$UVC\ (15,000) - UVC\ (10,000) = \$10,500 - \$8,000$$
$$5,000\ UVC = \$2,500$$
$$UVC = 50¢$$

Substituting this result into the original relationship between cost and output permits the calculation of the *total fixed cost* component:

$$(\$.50)\ 10{,}000 + \text{TFC} = \$8{,}000$$
$$\text{TFC} = \$8{,}000 - \$5{,}000$$
$$\text{TFC} = \$3{,}000$$

Based on the observed data, repair and maintenance cost appears to consist of a fixed amount of $3,000 per month and a variable amount of 50¢ per unit of output.

DIRECT COSTS AND INDIRECT COSTS

Cost classification is also needed to determine which costs are to be attached to which cost objects. Cause–effect relationships are the logical basis for such attachments, but there may never be complete certainty as to the nature of those relationships. For example, exactly how does the use of power and heating interact with production volume? It is necessary to distinguish between relationships in which there is a *direct* link to a cost object and those in which only an *indirect* association exists. The choice of a cost object is vitally important, because costs that are directly linked to one cost object may be only indirectly linked to another.

Direct costs can be identified specifically with one final cost object.[2] If output units are the objects of costing, then direct costs represent resources that become identifiable and measurable components of the finished product. *Direct materials costs* represent the raw materials physically present in the end product in easily determined amounts. *Direct labor costs* represent the labor services of employees who perform physical manufacturing operations that are readily monitored in relation to units of output produced.

Indirect costs are identified with two or more final cost objects or at least one intermediate cost object.[3] Certain types of materials costs (nails, screws, glue, paint) and some categories of labor cost (materials handling, tool and die making, machine setup) are clearly costs of producing final products. But to associate them with particular units of output is impossible, inconvenient, or simply not worthwhile. For practical reasons, they are usually classified as *indirect materials costs* and *indirect labor costs* and are included in manufacturing overhead.

Manufacturing overhead costs must usually be treated as indirect costs in relation to units of output. The overhead category includes all costs of supplies and services that support the production process without necessarily becoming part of the final product. In addition to indirect materials and indirect labor, manufacturing overhead includes such items as power and heat, repairs and maintenance, building occupancy costs, depreciation, insurance, property taxes, and costs of supervision. Overhead costs seldom meet all three requirements for direct costs; that is, they are seldom (1) traceable, (2) measurable, and (3) material in amount. Although it might be theoretically possible to measure the exact amount of electricity, rent, or insurance needed to produce one unit of output, in practice, approximation methods are used to attach overhead costs to products.

[2] Cost Accounting Standards Board, *Standards, Rules, and Regulations as of June 30, 1975*, Subchapter G, § 400.1, p. 192.
[3] Ibid., p. 193.

Manufacturing overhead costs must be associated with units of output indirectly, through the use of **intermediate activity measures.** An index chosen to assign overhead costs to products should be representative of the way in which total overhead costs are incurred; it should also directly reflect changes in levels of manufacturing activity. Direct labor hours is often used as an index. Many overhead costs tend to vary proportionally with the number of direct labor hours worked, which in turn often fluctuate in proportion to the number of units produced. Given this two-stage association pattern, indirect costs can be allocated to units of output by means of an overhead application rate. This process is explained in detail in Chapter 3.

Decision Centers as Cost Objects   Besides output units, other cost objects must be analyzed to identify the costs that are directly and indirectly traceable to them. In particular, costs must be associated with the decision centers that gave rise to those costs. In this context, direct costs are those that can be traced directly to managerial decisions made in a particular decision center.

For example, the *direct costs* of a manufacturing firm's machining division include all costs that result from decisions made by that division's manager. The machining division may also cause or contribute to costs incurred in other activity centers. It might use services provided by the building maintenance department, for which direct costs have already been identified and measured. These service costs can then be passed on to the machining division and to other activity centers that benefit from them. They will be treated as *indirect costs* by the machining division, because that division's manager has only partial and indirect control over their incurrence.

Figure 2–7 shows how certain costs may be classified either as direct or indirect, depending on whether *units of output* or a *decision center* is the object of costing.

FIGURE 2–7				
Direct Costs and Indirect Costs				
Cost Item	**Units of Output as Cost Objects**		**Machining Division as Cost Object**	
	Direct	Indirect	Direct	Indirect
Wages of Machine Operators..................	X		X	
Factory Rent		X		X
Freight In on Materials Purchased	X		X	
Labor Costs of Idle Time Due to Machine Breakdown		X	X	
Tools and Dies Used		X	X	
Factory Power (from own Power Plant)		X		X
Raw Materials Consumed	X		X	
Machining Division Manager's Salary		X	X	
Overtime Premium Paid to Machinists		X	X	
Cost of Janatorial Services		X		X
Depreciation of Machinery		X	X	
Lubricants Used in Machining Operations		X	X	

Time Periods as Cost Objects   When a time period is the primary cost object, costs are classified according to their identification with resource transformations during that period of time. Most resource transformations are easy to identify with accounting periods, unless the periods are very short. Raw materials used, labor services utilized, and factory supplies consumed are direct costs of the time period in which the resource use occurs. Certain other resource uses are not as easily identified with a specific time interval because they occur fairly continuously, possibly over several accounting periods. Depreciation, for example, involves an indirect allocation of asset cost to the various time periods during which the asset is used. The flow of costs through the Raw Materials, Work in Process and Finished Goods inventory accounts into Cost of Goods Sold also depends on the association of costs with specific time periods. Depending on the inventory method used, this occurs either directly (specific identification) or indirectly (FIFO, LIFO, average cost).

COMMON COSTS AND SEPARABLE COSTS

Often several types of products are made from the same group of input resources. Input costs that cannot be traced directly to particular products are considered **common costs;** they can only be associated as a group with the **joint outputs** that emerge from a series of common processing operations. For example, all costs of raising, feeding, transporting, and slaughtering a steer to the point at which sectioning occurs are common costs that are identifiable with all the final products from the carcass and must be apportioned among them. But any costs incurred during the subsequent processing and marketing of the different cuts of beef are considered **separable costs** of those individual products. Accounting for multiple and joint outputs is explored more fully in Chapter 6.

COST CONCEPTS AND TERMINOLOGY ILLUSTRATED: THE BETTER-BILT BAT COMPANY

The following example illustrates the basic cost concepts and terminology introduced in this chapter. The Better-Bilt Bat Company manufactures a single product—fiberglass baseball bats—which it sells to a distributor for $6 per bat.

During December, 19X6, 100,000 bats were sold. Inventories of 15,000 finished bats were on hand at the beginning and at the end of the month. The company's December income statement appears in Figure 2–8.

The primary *cost object* in this income statement is the *time period*—the month of December—for which the various performance measures (revenues, expenses, income) are presented. Supporting cost objects are (1) the aggregate *decision centers,* represented by the performance measures of Sales, Cost of Goods Sold, Selling and Distribution Expenses, and General and Administrative Expenses, and (2) *output units,* represented by production cost measures of beginning and ending inventories, Cost of Goods Manufactured, and Cost of Goods Sold.

FIGURE 2–8

Better-Bilt Bat Company
Income Statement
For the Month Ended December 31, 19X6

Sales (100,000 units @ $6.00)			$600,000
Less: Cost of Goods Sold:			
Inventory, December 1, 19X6			
(15,000 units @ $3.20)		$ 48,000	
Cost of Goods Manufactured			
(100,000 units @ $3.20)		320,000	
		$368,000	
Less: Inventory, December 31, 19X6			
(15,000 units @ $3.20)		48,000	320,000
Gross Profit			$280,000
Operating Expenses:			
Selling and Distribution Expenses:			
Fixed:			
Salaries	$48,000		
Depreciation: Vehicles	24,000	$72,000	
Variable:			
Sales Commissions	$50,000		
Sundry Selling Expenses	20,000	70,000	$142,000
General and Administrative Expenses:			
Fixed:			
Salaries	$12,000		
Depreciation: Furniture	6,000	$18,000	
Variable:			
Office Supplies	$20,000		
Sundry Administrative Expenses . . .	10,000	30,000	48,000
Total Expenses			190,000
Net Income			$ 90,000

This income statement also illustrates the separation of *period costs* and *product costs.* The Cost of Goods Sold and Operating Expense categories are *period costs,* consisting of the expenses being matched with periodic sales revenues. Cost of Goods Manufactured, together with beginning and ending inventories, are *product costs* that are attached to the output of baseball bats.

These product costs are subdivided into two categories: *expired costs* (Cost of Goods Sold) and *unexpired costs* (Inventories). In this example, only *expired period costs* (Selling and Administrative Expenses) are included, because no detail is given of any *unexpired period costs* (prepaid expenses).

The statement of cost of goods manufactured in Figure 2–9 shows in detail the materials, labor, and overhead costs that make up the $320,000 Cost of Goods Manufactured in the income statement.

To simplify calculations, it is assumed that there are no beginning or ending work in process inventories. This is not a realistic assumption, but it is useful in demonstrating several basic relationships and cost concepts. Also, because

---

FIGURE 2–9

Better-Bilt Bat Company
Statement of Cost of Goods Manufactured
For the Month Ended December 31, 19X6

Current Manufacturing Costs:		
Raw Materials Used		$50,000
Direct Labor		75,000
		$125,000
Manufacturing Overhead:		
Fixed:		
Factory Supervision	$50,000	
Depreciation: Factory	25,000	
Factory Rent	45,000	120,000
Variable:		
Indirect Materials	$25,000	
Indirect Labor	20,000	
Power	15,000	
Supplies	15,000	75,000
Cost of Goods Manufactured		$320,000

---

beginning and ending finished goods inventories are equal in amount, Cost of Goods Manufactured is equal to Cost of Goods Sold. Again, this is not to be expected; it is done here only to simplify the statement and supporting calculations.

The cost of goods manufactured statement can be reformulated as shown in Figure 2–10, with costs separated into *fixed* and *variable* categories according to how each item responds to production level changes during the current period.

The fixed and variable *unit cost* measures in Figure 2–10 will behave differently as output levels change. If production technology, raw materials input combinations, and input prices are stable, the *unit variable cost* and each of its components will remain constant as production increases or decreases.

However, only the *total fixed cost* of $120,000 is likely to remain constant, given the same assumptions about production characteristics and volume. *Unit fixed costs* will not remain the same at different production levels. The unit fixed cost of $1.20 in the preceding example is a valid measure only when the output level is 100,000 units per month. This can be demonstrated by examining the effects on fixed and variable costs of a production increase to 120,000 units per month (Figure 2–11).

As 20,000 additional units are produced, *total variable costs* increase from $200,000 to $240,000 and *unit fixed cost* decreases from $1.20 to $1.00. On the other hand, *unit variable cost* and *total fixed costs* remain unchanged at $2.00 and $120,000 respectively. These effects are shown graphically in Figure 2–12.

FIGURE 2–10

Better-Bilt Bat Company
Statement of Cost of Goods Manufactured
For the Month Ended December 31, 19X6
(100,000 Units Produced)

	Total Costs		Unit Costs	
Variable Costs:				
Raw Materials Used	$50,000		$ .50	
Direct Labor	75,000		.75	
Indirect Materials	25,000		.25	
Indirect Labor	20,000		.20	
Power	15,000		.15	
Supplies	15,000	$200,000	.15	$2.00
Fixed Costs:				
Factory Supervision	$48,000		$ .48	
Depreciation: Factory	24,000		.24	
Factory Rent	48,000	120,000	.48	1.20
Total Cost of Goods Manufactured		$320,000		$3.20

FIGURE 2–11

Better-Bilt Bat Company
Statement of Cost of Goods Manufactured
For the Month Ended December 31, 19X6
(120,000 Units Produced)

	Total Costs		Unit Costs	
Variable Costs:				
Raw Materials Used	$60,000		$ .50	
Direct Labor	90,000		.75	
Indirect Materials	36,000		.25	
Indirect Labor	24,000		.20	
Power	18,000		.15	
Supplies	12,000	$240,000	.15	$2.00
Fixed Costs:				
Factory Supervision	$48,000		$ .40	
Depreciation: Factory	24,000		.20	
Factory Rent	48,000	120,000	.40	1.00
Total Cost of Goods Manufactured		$360,000		$3.00

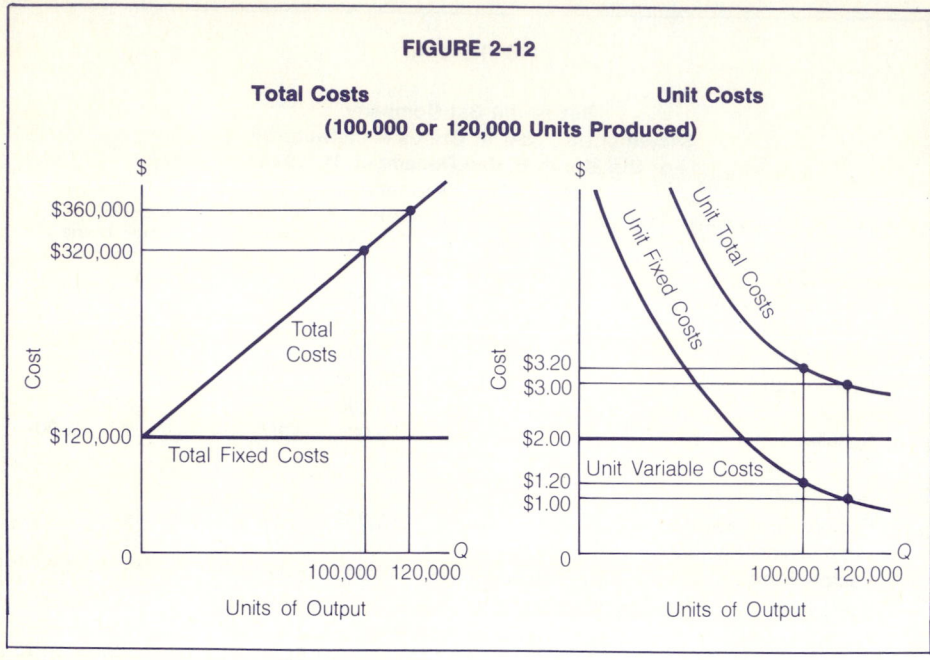

FIGURE 2–12

Total Costs **Unit Costs**

(100,000 or 120,000 Units Produced)

FIGURE 2–13

Better-Bilt Bat Company
Income Statement
Month of December, 19X6, and Projection

	December, 19X6 100,000 Units		Projection 120,000 Units	
	Total Costs	Unit Cost	Total Costs	Unit Cost
Sales	$600,000	$6.00	$720,000	$6.00
Variable Expenses:				
Production	$200,000	$2.00	$240,000	$2.00
Selling and Distribution	70,000	.70	84,000	.70
General and Administrative	30,000	.30	36,000	.30
	$300,000	$3.00	$360,000	$3.00
Fixed Expenses:				
Production	$120,000	$1.20	$120,000	$1.00
Selling and Distribution	72,000	.72	72,000	.60
General and Administrative	18,000	.18	18,000	.15
	$210,000	$2.10	$210,000	$1.75
Total Expenses	$510,000	$5.10	$570,000	$4.75
Net Income	$ 90,000	$ .90	$150,000	$1.25

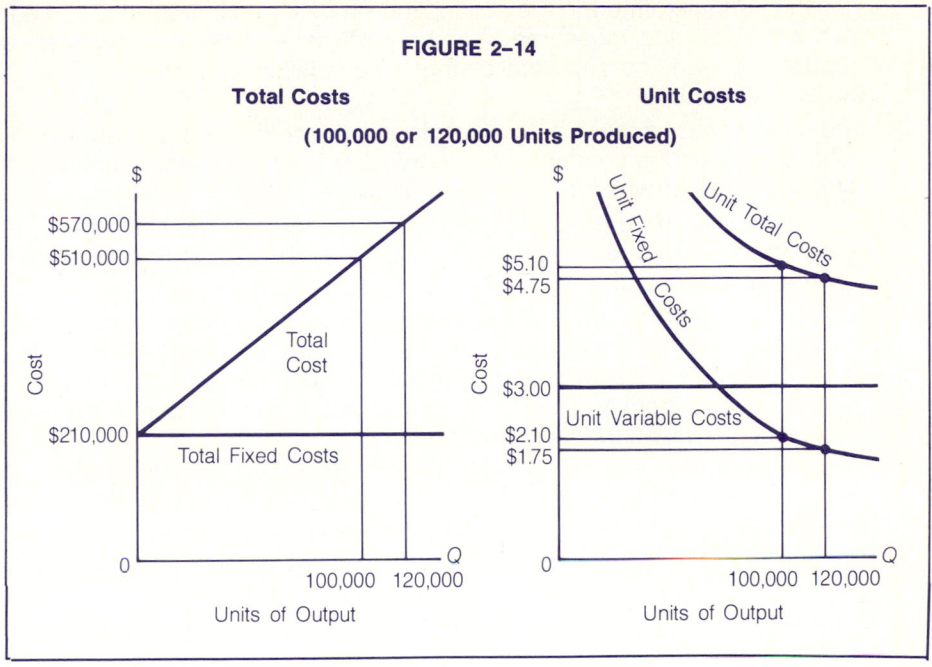

FIGURE 2–14

The *incremental cost* of manufacturing an additional 20,000 units is $40,000, which increases total cost from $320,000 to $360,000. Because it is assumed that *unit variable costs* and *total fixed costs* will remain constant over this range of activity levels, the *marginal cost* of each of those additional 20,000 units will be $2—the amount by which total manufacturing cost increases as output is expanded by each additional unit.

In Figure 2–13, the income statement is recast in a format that divides nonmanufacturing expenses as well as manufacturing costs into fixed and variable categories.

The revised income statement data are shown graphically in Figure 2–14 to demonstrate the behavior of total and unit cost components when *all costs,* not just *manufacturing costs,* are divided into their fixed and variable elements.

As before, *total variable costs* increase, while *unit fixed cost* declines. The *incremental cost* of producing an additional 20,000 units, including manufacturing, selling, and administrative expenses, is $60,000 ($570,000 − $510,000). The *marginal cost* of each of those 20,000 additional units is $3.

SUMMARY

1. The popular concept of cost implies a sacrificing of scarce resources. Business costs represent resource transformations resulting from the decisions of managers who seek to improve resource holdings.

2. Resources transformed in the production process must first be identified, then classified and measured. A variety of measurement procedures is needed to provide cost information that is compatible with the classification system adopted.

3. The cost concept applies both to single and multiple resource transformations, producing the concepts of unit, average, marginal, incremental, and total costs—all of which are useful in particular decision situations.

4. A cost object can be any item, activity, or relationship for which the cost is separately calculated. Objects of costing include output units, decision centers, and accounting time periods.

5. Units of output (products or services) are the most widely used cost objects. Decision centers, originating in authority–responsibility relationships within the firm, provide a framework for the cost measurement process. Accounting time periods identify groups of output units and decision center activities for which cost measurements are made.

6. Cost classification involves grouping costs according to their similarities. The conventional chart of accounts is a functional classification system designed to assist the preparation of accounting reports.

7. Costs included in financial statements must be classified either as unexpired costs (assets) or as expired costs (expenses).

8. The costs that facilitate production (product costs) are separated from those that support selling, distributive, and administrative activities (period costs).

9. Cost behavior is described primarily in terms of the response of resource flows to decision alternatives. Total variable costs change in response to fluctuations in activity levels. Total fixed costs do not vary with activity level changes (within the context of a specified time period and a particular decision situation).

10. Costs are identified with cost objects either directly or indirectly. Direct costs can be traced to one final cost object on the basis of an easily measurable relationship. Indirect costs are usually traceable only by way of some intermediate relationship between the cost object and the initiating resource flow. This classification of costs as direct or indirect applies to all cost objects: output units, decision centers, and time periods.

KEY WORDS AND PHRASES

Cost (25)
Resource Transformation (25)
Decision Model (26)
Unit Cost (26)
Average Cost (26)
Marginal Cost (27)
Incremental Cost (27)
Total Costs (27)
Objects of Costing (28)
Indirect Product Costs (28)
Decision Center (30)
Activity Center (30)
Cost Center (30)
Profit Center (30)
Investment Center (30)
Cost Classifications (31)
Chart of Accounts (32)
Unexpired Costs (32)
Expired Costs (32)
Product Costs (32)
Period Costs (32)
Direct Materials Cost (34)
Direct Labor Cost (34)
Manufacturing Overhead (34)
Fixed Costs (35)
Variable Costs (35)
Mixed Costs (36)
Direct Costs (38)
Indirect Costs (38)
Intermediate Activity Measure (39)
Common Costs (40)
Joint Outputs (40)
Separable Costs (40)

Questions

1. Explain in your own words the concept of cost.
2. Why is the notion of scarcity important in relation to the cost concept?
3. Give five examples, different from those in the text, of transactions that involve the transformation of resources.
4. Why is information about resource flows so important for managerial decision making?
5. "Costs are *representations* of resource flows." How does the *identification, classification,* and *measurement* of cost items contribute to this procedure?
6. Discuss the meaning of the phrase "different costs for different purposes."
7. List five alternative types of cost measurements.
8. Why is historical acquisition cost the most commonly used method of measuring costs?
9. Explain the concepts of (1) unit cost, (2) average cost, (3) marginal cost, (4) incremental cost, and (5) total cost.
10. Identify the three major categories of cost objects. Give specific examples of each and state the circumstances in which each would be a pertinent object of costing.
11. "Units of output are easily identified." When is this statement correct and when is it incorrect? Give specific examples of each situation.
12. What collections or groups of resource transformations constitute important cost objects? Why?
13. "Costs arise as a result of the choices made by decision makers." Why is this an important concept for cost measurement and control?
14. Give three examples of decision centers in an electrical appliance firm. Explain why they are important objects of costing.
15. Explain how the concept of *marginal cost* differs from that of *incremental cost.* Give an example.
16. Explain how the concept of *average unit cost* differs from that of *marginal cost.* Give an example.
17. Does the use of historical monetary measures simplify the process of cost measurement? Why or why not?
18. Why is it important to classify costs as either *period costs* or *product costs?*
19. Why is the distinction between *direct costs* and *indirect costs* necessary? Why is it so important?
20. "Fixed costs are always a varying amount, but variable costs never change." Explain.

Exercises

E 2–1   Cost Classification—Fixed Costs/Variable Costs

It is not always possible to classify manufacturing costs as strictly fixed or variable according to the definition given in this chapter. However, classify each of the following items as a *fixed, variable,* or *mixed* (partly fixed, partly variable) cost, in terms of its behavior over a predetermined (relevant) range of activity levels.

(a) Repairs and Maintenance
(b) Power and Heating (own generating plant)
(c) Factory Cafeteria Deficit
(d) Factory Clerical Salaries
(e) Rent—Factory Premises
(f) Depreciation—Equipment (machine hours basis)
(g) Depreciation—Factory Buildings (straight line basis)
(h) Factory Supplies
(i) F.I.C.A. Tax—Employer's Contribution (*all* factory employees)
(j) Raw Materials Used
(k) Overtime Premiums—Production Workers
(l) Workman's Compensation Insurance (all factory employees)

E 2–2 Cost Classification—Direct Costs/Indirect Costs

Alfa-Delta Corporation manufactures three products: frabbles, blimpies, and squongs. For each of the following factory costs, indicate whether the item is a *direct cost,* an *indirect cost,* or an *unrelated cost* of manufacturing *blimpies.*

(a) Factory Supervisory Salaries
(b) Janitorial Supplies
(c) Raw Materials Usage—Blimpies
(d) Factory Supplies Usage
(e) Property Tax
(f) Direct Labor—Frabbles
(g) Depreciation—General Purpose Factory Equipment
(h) Packaging Costs—Squongs
(i) Repair Costs (A machine broke down while blimpies were being processed on this piece of general purpose equipment.)
(j) Overtime Premium—(Only frabbles happened to be being processed during this overtime period. Overtime is frequently incurred.)

E 2–3 Total Cost, Unit Costs, Average Costs, Fixed Costs, and Variable Costs

From past performance records, Brown Corporation's management has determined that monthly manufacturing overhead costs are composed of a constant $8,000 amount and a variable amount equal to 50¢ for every direct labor hour worked. Four hours of direct labor are needed to produce one unit of output.

Required:
(a) During September, 10,000 units of output were produced. What should be the total amount of manufacturing overhead costs incurred?
(b) For September, what should be the *average* manufacturing overhead cost of one unit of output? How much of that is *fixed* and how much is *variable?*

(c) The corporation plans to produce only 8,000 units during October. What will be (1) the *total* manufacturing overhead cost and (2) the *average cost* of one unit of output for that month?

(d) Tabulate the average costs for September and October, showing the fixed and variable components. Explain the different patterns of cost behavior that you observe in this table.

E 2–4   Incremental Cost, Marginal Cost, and Average Cost

Garcia Company prepared the following production and cost figures from its records:

Units of Output	Total Cost	Fixed Cost	Variable Cost
2000	$3,000.00	$1,000.00	$2,000.00
2001	3,000.90	1,000.00	2,000.90
3000	4,100.00	1,200.00	2,900.00
3001	4,100.80	1,200.00	2,900.00
4000	5,300.00	1,600.00	3,700.00
4001	5,300.75	1,600.00	3,700.75

Required:

(a) What is the *average unit cost* at the 2,000, 3,000, and 4,000 unit levels? Explain how this is composed of unit fixed cost and unit variable cost amounts.

(b) Why is the average unit cost different at each of the three activity levels?

(c) What is the *marginal cost* of producing one unit at the 2,000, 3,000, or 4,000 unit levels?

(d) What is the *incremental cost* of (1) the first 2,000 units of output, (2) the next 1,000 units, and (3) the next 1,000 units?

(e) Explain why the total amount of "fixed" costs might not be constant at all levels of output production in this situation.

(f) Explain why the *unit* amount of "variable" costs might not be constant at all levels of output production in this situation.

E 2–5   Product Cost/Period Costs

Flanagan Manufacturing Company's chart of accounts includes the following categories. Indicate (1) those items that should be treated as *product costs* (and inventoried), (2) those that should be treated as *period costs* (and expensed in the current period), and (3) those that will probably need to be *apportioned* between the product and period cost groups:

(a) Advertising
(b) Plant Supervisory Salaries
(c) Salespersons' Commissions
(d) Depreciation—Delivery Trucks
(e) Accounting and Audit Fees
(f) Power and Heating (all premises)
(g) Property Taxes (all premises)

(h)   Packaging Supplies
 (i)   Federal Income Taxes
 (j)   Office Stationery Supplies
(k)   Tools, Dies, and Jigs
 (l)   Direct Labor
(m)   Repairs and Maintenance (all property)
(n)   Patent Amortization

Case

C 2–1   Total Cost, Average Cost, and Incremental Cost

Buckman Brewing Company operates its plant two shifts per day during five days of each week. To meet increased demand for its products, the company is considering changing either to (1) three shifts per day for five days, or (2) two shifts per day for seven days, plus an extra shift on Wednesday.
   The following cost information is available:

> Raw Materials .... $200 per 1,000 gallons of output
> Direct Labor .... $1,000 per regular shift
> Variable Overhead .... $50 per 1,000 gallons of output
> Fixed Overhead .... $10,000 per week

The plant produces 10,000 gallons per shift. Shift premiums will be incurred as follows: 50 percent for the third shift on weekdays, 100 percent for all shifts on weekends.
   Fixed costs will increase to $14,000 if the five-day, three-shift plan is adopted. All other cost behavior patterns and amounts will remain unchanged.

Required:
(a)   Compute the *total cost* of the two production alternatives.
(b)   What are the *incremental costs* of changing from the present shift arrangement to either of the two proposed alternatives? What are the *incremental revenues,* assuming that all output can be sold for $480 per 1,000 gallons?
(c)   What is the *average cost* of 1,000 gallons of output under each of the three situations?
(d)   Is it worthwhile to consider either of the changes? Why or why not? Which of the three alternatives will be most profitable?

Problems

P 2–1   Cost Classification—Period Costs/Product Costs

The following list of cost items is classified functionally. Each represents a resource flow in a typical manufacturing and distributing firm that produces electrical lighting fixtures.

Advertising
Cost of Goods Sold
Depreciation—Factory Equipment
Depreciation—Delivery Vehicles
Freight In
Factory Supplies
Insurance on Factory Equipment
Interest
Inventory—Finished Goods

Janitorial Supplies—Factory
Power and Light—Factory
Power and Light—Office
Research and Development—New
    Products
Raw Materials Used
Salaries—Plant Foremen
Sales Commissions
Telephone
Work in Process—End of Period

Required:

(a) Which of these items would usually be identified as *period costs* for income measure-ment purposes?

(b) Which of these items would usually be identified as *product costs* for inventory determination purposes?

(c) State the general criteria to be applied in making the identifications in parts (a) and (b).

(d) Do any items in the list appear *both* as *product costs* and as *period costs*? If so, why?

P 2–2 Cost Classification—Direct/Indirect, Product/Period, Fixed/Variable/Mixed

The following are included in the cost items that relate to the operations of DEF Corpora-tion:

Administrative Salaries
Advertising
Buildings and Grounds—Salaries
Depreciation—Machining Department
Factory Supplies (Oils and Greases)—
    Machining Department
Insurance—Plant
Office Supplies
Power and Heat—Plant
Production Scheduling—Salaries

Direct Labor—Machining Department
Property Tax—Plant
Raw Materials Used—Machining
    Department
Rework Costs—Machining Department
Sales Commissions
Sales Salaries
Supervisory Salaries—Plant
Telephone
Tools and Dies—Tool and Die Department

Required:

(a) Which of these would be classified as *product costs* and which would be classified as *period costs?*

(b) From the viewpoint of the foreman responsible for cost incurrence in the Machining Department, identify those items that are:
 (1) *Direct costs* of operating the Machining Department.
 (2) *Indirect costs* of operating the Machining Department.
 (3) Costs *not to be associated* with the Machining Department.

(c) Assuming a reasonable range of potential activity levels for a one-year period, divide the list of items between those that will be *fixed costs*, those that will be *variable costs*, and those that will be *mixed costs*.

(d) Review your answers to parts (a), (b), and (c) and comment on any pattern that appears to be present.

P 2-3 Cost Classification and Analysis—Total Unit/Fixed/Variable/Mixed—Incremental

During the months of March and April, ABC Company reported the following departmental cost and production results:

	Department C	
	March 8,000 Units	April 10,000 Units
Cleaning Supplies	$ 400	$ 500
Depreciation—Machinery	8,000	8,000
Direct Labor	20,000	25,000
Factory Power	2,400	2,700
Insurance—Plant	1,500	1,500
Materials Handling.............	800	1,000
Property Tax...................	2,000	2,000
Raw Materials	80,000	100,000
Repairs and Maintenance	3,600	4,000
Supervisory Salaries	15,300	15,300
	$134,000	$160,000

Required:
(a) What was the *total cost* of production in Department C in March? In April?
(b) What was the *average unit cost* of one unit of output in March? In April?
(c) What was the *incremental cost* of the change in the output level from 8,000 units in March to 10,000 in April?
(d) Inspect the amounts for each of the ten individual cost items. Indicate whether each is a *fixed, variable,* or *mixed cost.*
(e) From the answer to (d), determine (1) the *total amount* of *fixed costs per month* and (2) the *variable cost per unit.*
(f) Explain why your answers in *part (b)* are different from the answer in *part (e) (2).*
(g) Within the range of activity levels from 8,000 to 10,000 units per month what was the *marginal cost* of each individual unit?

P 2-4 Cost Behavior—Activity Level Changes, Fixed/Variable Costs, Total/Unit Costs

The Welco Division of H.N. Corporation manufactures automobile batteries. Unit costs of direct materials and direct labor in this division have been relatively stable at $9 and $5 per battery, respectively. During 19X6, manufacturing overhead costs associated with the production of 400,000 batteries were as follows:

	Variable Portion	Fixed Portion	Total
Supervisory Salaries	—	$625,000	$625,000
Indirect Labor.....................	$240,000	430,000	670,000
Overtime Premiums	40,000	—	40,000
Repairs	20,000	50,000	70,000
Power and Heat	200,000	50,000	250,000
Depreciation—Equipment	—	180,000	180,000
Rent—Plant	—	125,000	125,000
Factory Supplies	200,000	—	200,000
Property Tax—Plant	—	25,000	25,000
Insurance—Plant and Inventory	20,000	30,000	50,000
Materials Handling	80,000	25,000	105,000
Factory Clerical Salaries	—	60,000	60,000
	$800,000	$1,600,000	$2,400,000

Required:
(a) What was the *total cost* of manufacturing activities during 19X6? Divide this amount between *total fixed costs* and *total variable costs*.

(b) What was the *average cost* of producing one battery in 19X6? How much of this is the *unit fixed cost* and how much of that is the *unit variable cost?*

(c) To meet production schedules and sales forecasts for 19X7, 500,000 batteries must be manufactured. Assuming that all costs continue to display the same fixed or variable behavior with respect to activity levels as in 19X6, prepare a schedule of manufacturing costs for 19X7, using separate columns for the variable and fixed cost portions of each item.

(d) What is the estimated *total cost* of manufacturing batteries in 19X7?

(e) What are the *unit variable cost* and *unit fixed cost* components of the *average cost* of producing one battery in 19X7? Why are these either the same as or different from the results for 19X6?

(f) If actual output in 19X7 were only 200,000 batteries, what would be the *average unit cost* and its fixed and variable components?

P 2–5 Activity Level Changes—Fixed Costs/Variable Costs

MND Corporation manufactures a single product that sells for $20 per unit. Variable manufacturing costs are $12 per unit. Capacity-related fixed manufacturing costs are $100,000 per year in the normal operating range of 40,000 to 60,000 units of output. The company's fixed marketing costs are $45,000 per year. Sales commissions amount to 10 percent of sales revenue.

Required:
(a) What are the *total* annual costs of *manufacturing* (1) 40,000 units, (2) 50,000 units, and (3) 60,000 units?

(b) What is the *total* annual cost of *manufacturing and marketing* (1) 40,000 units, (2) 50,000 units, and (3) 60,000 units?

(c) What are the *average* unit costs of *manufacturing and marketing* (1) 40,000 units, (2) 50,000 units, and (3) 60,000 units?

(d)   What *net income* will be earned from manufacturing and marketing (1) 45,000 units, (2) 50,000 units, and (3) 55,000 units?

P 2-6   Cost Behavior—Fixed/Variable/Mixed

During the past two years, the following selected monthly production costs have been observed at various activity levels. It is anticipated that monthly manufacturing requirements should remain in the range of 30,000 to 45,000 units, barring unusual circumstances such as strikes or power shortages.

Output (units)	Direct Materials	Direct Labor	Repairs	Power and Heat	Supervision
10,000	$ 20,000	$15,000	$ 8,000	$4,000	$15,000
20,000	40,000	30,000	10,000	5,000	15,000
30,000	60,000	45,000	12,000	6,000	15,000
40,000	80,000	60,000	14,000	7,000	15,000
50,000	100,000	75,000	16,000	8,000	15,000

Required:
(a)   Examine the behavior of each cost item within the range of 30,000 to 45,000 units per month. Identify each as being either a *fixed, variable,* or *mixed* cost.

(b)   What are the amounts of *total fixed cost* and *unit variable cost* in the range of activity levels?

(c)   If the activity level for the month of April is 42,500 units, estimate the *total cost* for all five items. What will *total cost* be for 36,000 units?

(d)   What will the *average unit cost* be at 36,000 and 42,500 units? Why is average unit cost different at each level?

(e)   If power is rationed, output may have to be cut back to the 10,000 to 25,000 unit range. What is the *average unit cost* at the 20,000 unit activity level?

(f)   Describe the behavior of each of the five cost items represented in the table. Why is it reasonable to expect that each item will display either fixed, variable, or mixed cost behavior patterns?

P 2-7   Fixed Costs/Variable Costs—Substitution Effects

PQR Company makes a single product and incurs the following total manufacturing costs:

	Variable	Fixed
Materials Costs	$ 8 per unit	0
Labor Costs	10 per unit	0
Manufacturing Overheads	6 per unit	$24,000 per month

These costs will prevail for activity levels between 2,000 and 4,000 units per month.

The company is considering acquiring automated machinery that will replace much of the labor now required to produce its product. The equipment will result in additional monthly fixed overhead costs of $21,000 and additional variable overhead costs of $1 per unit. Direct labor costs will be reduced to $3 per unit.

Required:
(a) Complete the following table, showing the costs of operating at the indicated output levels under both the existing and the proposed production arrangements.

	Comparison of Total Manufacturing Costs					
	2,000 units		3,000 units		4,000 units	
	Original	Proposed	Original	Proposed	Original	Proposed
Materials	$16,000					
Labor	20,000					
Manufacturing Overhead:						
Variable	12,000					
Fixed.................	24,000					
	$72,000					

(b) What are the *average unit costs* of producing at each of the three activity levels mentioned (1) under the original production arrangement and (2) under the proposed arrangement?

(c) At what activity level would the two alternative plans be equally attractive with regard to total cost of production?

(d) If monthly activity levels are likely to be stable at 3,000 units per month, which alternative production arrangement would you recommend? Why?

P 2–8   Cost Behavior—Incremental Costs, Fixed Costs/Variable Costs

SK Corporation is confronted with the following decision situation. Regular sales and production have been stable at 50,000 units per month, with a sales price of $10 per unit and monthly costs as follows:

Variable Costs	$100,000
Fixed Costs	300,000
Total Costs	$400,000

During August, 19X8, an unusual opportunity occurs to increase sales from 50,000 to 100,000 units per month. A new customer offers to buy 50,000 units each month at $8 per unit.
Estimates of operating costs at the 100,000 unit per month level are as follows:

Variable Costs	$200,000
Fixed Costs	550,000
Total Costs	$750,000

Fixed costs increase because of additional salary and equipment-related items needed to manufacture the additional output.
The decision is made to *accept* the order, because the average cost per unit will then be $7.50 ($750,000 ÷ 100,000), which is less than both the original selling price of $10, and the $8 selling price of the additional units.

Required:

(a) Is this decision correct? Why or why not? (Hint: Consider the *incremental* costs and revenues involved.)

(b) What if the effect of accepting the extra order is to force a reduction of the selling price of *all* output to $8? Would the answer to part (a) change? Why?

(c) Assume that at the 100,000 unit level fixed costs change to $700,000 and variable costs to $150,000 (because of increased use of automated equipment and savings in direct labor costs). Should the original extra order be accepted in this case? Why or why not?

P 2–9   Statement of Cost of Goods Manufactured—Cost of Goods Sold, Product Costs, and Period Costs

The records of the SRQ Company on December 31, 19X8 included the following account balances:

Advertising Expense	$ 24,000
Depreciation—Machinery	36,000
Depreciation—Office Equipment	8,000
Direct Labor	124,000
Factory Power and Heat	31,000
Interest Expense	7,000
Inventories, January 1, 19X8	
Raw Materials	3,000
Work in Process	15,000
Finished Goods	31,000
Inventories, December 31, 19X8	
Raw Materials	2,000
Work in Process	18,000
Finished Goods	27,000
Raw Materials Purchased	115,000
Rent—Factory	36,000
Salaries—Plant Supervisors	45,000
Sales Commissions	15,000
Telephone Expense	2,000

Required:

(a) Prepare a statement of cost of goods manufactured for the year ended December 31, 19X8.

(b) Prepare a statement of cost of goods sold for the year ended December 31, 19X8.

(c) Which items in the list did *not* appear either in the answers to (a) or (b)? Why?

P 2–10   Statement of Cost of Goods Manufactured—Cost of Goods Sold, Product Costs, and Period Costs

Some of the account balances in the records of KML Corporation on December 31, 19X9 are as follows:

Administrative Salaries............................	$15,000
Bad Debt Expense	1,000
Depreciation—Plant and Equipment	18,000
Depreciation—Delivery Vehicles	3,000
Direct Labor	64,000
Factory Supplies Used.............................	5,000
Finished Goods—January 1, 19X9	
(1,500 units)	30,000
Finished Goods—December 31, 19X9	
(1,000 units)	?
Insurance—Plant..................................	8,000
Interest Expense	7,000
Power and Heat	12,000
Property Tax—Plant and Equipment	6,000
Raw Materials Inventory—January 1, 19X9	3,000
Raw Materials Inventory—December 31, 19X9	4,000
Raw Materials Purchases	83,000
Rent—Plant Premises	16,000
Repairs and Maintenance—Plant	9,000
Sales Commissions	12,000
Work in Process—January 1, 19X9..................	0
Work in Process—December 31, 19X9	0

Required:

(a) Prepare a statement of cost of goods manufactured for the year ended December 31, 19X9.

(b) Assume that 10,000 units were manufactured during 19X9, and that 10,500 units were sold. What was the *average cost* of a unit manufactured during the year?

(c) Prepare a statement of cost of goods sold for the year ended December 31, 19X9. (Assume a FIFO cost flow.)

(d) How much of the *average manufacturing cost* of a unit during the current year represents:
  (1) Raw Materials
  (2) Direct Labor
  (3) Depreciation—Plant
  (4) Property Taxes—Plant

(e) Assume that during the next year the number of units manufactured increases to 12,000 and that all cost items continue to behave in the same manner as they did in 19X9. What will be the *total cost* of the 12,000 units manufactured in terms of:
  (1) Raw Materials
  (2) Direct Labor
  (3) Depreciation—Plant
  (4) Property Taxes—Plant

(f) What will be the *average cost* of a unit manufactured in the next year, with regard to the four items in part (e)?

P 2-11   Statement of Cost of Goods Manufactured—Cost of Goods Sold—Income Statement, Correction of Improperly Prepared Statements, and Product/Period Costs

The following income statement was prepared by an inexperienced assistant in the Controller's Department from information in the records of DPQ Corporation.

DPQ Corporation
Income Statement for 19X7

Sales		$1,150,000
Expenses:		
Selling Expenses	$ 62,000	
Raw Materials Purchased	346,000	
Wages and Salaries Paid	232,000	
Rent Paid	56,000	
Equipment Purchased	20,000	
Utilities Paid	35,000	
Insurance Premiums	12,000	
Administrative Expenses	45,000	
Interest Paid	10,000	818,000
Net Income		$ 332,000

A review of supporting records discloses that the following data were overlooked:

(1) Inventory Records:

	January 1, 19X7	December 31, 19X7
Raw Materials	$ 4,000	$ 6,000
Work in Process	7,000	8,000
Finished Goods	24,000	16,000

(2) Wages payable on December 31, 19X7 were $6,000.

(3) Insurance premiums were paid on January 1, 19X7 for two years in advance.

(4) Rent paid included $8,000 for January and February, 19X8.

(5) Utilities unpaid at December 31, 19X7 totaled $2,000.

(6) Equipment costing $20,000 was purchased on January 1, 19X7. It had an expected useful life of five years and no salvage value.

(7) Payroll analysis showed that total wages and salaries expense was distributed as follows:

	Percent
Manufacturing	75
Selling	15
Administrative	10

(8) Rent Expense and Utilities Expense were for factory premises exclusively.

(9) In addition to the equipment purchased on January 1, 19X7, other equipment costing $80,000 had been acquired previously. These items had an expected useful life of six years and expected disposal value of $8,000.

(10) Insurance expense is to be allocated 60 percent to manufacturing and 40 percent to selling activities.

(11) Interest accrued at December 31, 19X7 amounted to $4,000.

(12) Corporate income tax is payable at the rate of 50 percent of net income.

Required:
Prepare a revised income statement and a statement of cost of goods manufactured.

P 2–12 Cost of Goods Manufactured—Total Cost/Average Cost, Income Statement, and Balance Sheet

On December 31, 19X8, at the end of QOP Corporation's first year of operations, its preclosing trial balance was as follows:

	Debit	Credit
Accounts Payable		$ 18,000
Accounts Receivable	$ 32,000	
Accumulated Depreciation		100,000
Administrative Expense	114,000	
Bonds Payable		200,000
Buildings and Equipment	800,000	
Capital Stock		400,000
Cash	16,000	
Direct Labor	280,000	
Manufacturing Overhead	160,000	
Raw Materials Purchases	430,000	
Sales		1,200,000
Selling Expense	86,000	
Work in Process, December 31, 19X8	0	
	$1,918,000	$1,918,000

During this first year of operations 22,000 units of output were produced; 20,000 units were sold at an average price of $60 each. There was no work in process inventory on December 31, 19X8. Ending inventories of raw materials were $40,000 and ending inventories of finished goods were $80,000.

Required:
(a) What was the *total cost* of output manufactured during 19X8?
(b) What was the *average unit cost* of output manufactured during 19X8?
(c) Prepare a statement of cost of goods manufactured, an income statement, and a balance sheet for the year ended December 31, 19X8.

3

COST ALLOCATION

LEARNING OBJECTIVES

After studying Chapter 3, you should be able to:

1. Explain how materials, labor, and overhead costs are accumulated in ledger accounts.
2. Define cost allocation, explain why it is needed, and describe four bases for allocating costs.
3. Compare and contrast full absorption costing with variable costing.
4. Describe how direct raw materials costs are measured.
5. Measure direct labor costs by the base pay rate method and by the effective gross pay rate method.
6. Use the Manufacturing Overhead Control account to accumulate overhead costs and apply them to products.
7. Calculate a predetermined overhead application rate and use it to apply overhead costs to products.
8. Calculate plant-wide and departmental overhead application rates.
9. Describe three methods for disposing of underapplied or overapplied overhead costs and make the necessary journal entries.
10. Analyze underapplied or overapplied overhead costs to determine their causes.
11. Reallocate service department overhead costs to production departments using the direct method and the step method.
12. Reallocate service department overhead costs to production departments using dual allocation rates.
13. Make a partial reallocation of variable service department costs to production departments.

The definition of *cost* given in Chapter 2 emphasized the identification and measurement of resource flows. Physical resources and services are acquired and combined to form a final product. The costs of these inputs are first *accumulated,* then *allocated* to cost objects in order to measure the cost of the resulting outputs.

This chapter demonstrates how manufacturing costs are allocated for purposes of inventory measurement and income determination. It includes descriptions of the bases for cost allocation and the methods by which materials, labor, and overhead costs are allocated to output units and decision centers.

COST ACCUMULATION

A cost accounting system accumulates measures of resource flows in various general ledger accounts. The movement of cost measures through these accounts should reflect the flow of resources through a manufacturing company's production and distribution operations. Such accounts as Raw Materials, Wages and Salaries, Factory Rent, Power and Heating, and Repairs and Maintenance represent *inputs* acquired and/or consumed for purposes indicated by the respective account titles.

Each of these **input accounts** can be subdivided to provide a more sophisticated cost accumulation structure. For example, Raw Materials can be divided into separate accounts for each type of input commodity. Wages and Salaries can be broken down to reflect each category of labor service input. The other functionally classified inputs can also be subclassified—Repairs by type and area of occurrence, Power and Heating by area of usage, and so on.

The account classifications in the general ledger provide a basis for accumulating measures of input costs. The basic general ledger account categories (Materials, Wages, Repairs, and so on) usually permit a direct identification and measurement of costs. Materials are purchased, wages and salaries are paid, and repair costs are incurred in specific and easily identifiable transactions. But once production begins, these costs must be transferred to Work in Process accounts so that they will reflect the combining of materials and services during processing. A secondary classification system is then needed to attach materials, labor, and overhead costs to products as manufacturing operations proceed.

COST ALLOCATION

Cost allocation is the process of attaching costs to particular cost objects—products, decision centers, and accounting periods. Materials, labor, and overhead costs must first be allocated to *units of output* in Work in Process accounts, before Finished Goods Inventory and Cost of Goods Sold can be calculated. These costs must also be allocated to *decision center* cost objects, to permit measurement of departmental costs. Finally, cost allocations are needed to separate expired costs from unexpired costs. This requires allocating the costs of resource flows to different *accounting periods* so that expired costs can be matched with revenues to determine income.

Five bases for making cost allocations will be examined:

1. Cause–effect relationships
2. Decision centers
3. Benefits produced by the cost
4. Ability to bear the cost
5. Controllability of costs

CAUSE–EFFECT RELATIONSHIPS

Cause–effect relationships are the natural basis for allocating costs to units of output. Manufacturing operations often exhibit obvious and physically determinable cause–effect patterns. For example, it may be possible to verify that 50 square feet of $\frac{1}{16}''$ sheet steel is used in constructing a refrigerator. It is then feasible to trace the cost of that steel directly to each refrigerator produced.

In other cases, a cause–effect relationship exists, but cannot as easily be identified or measured. For example, although power and heating costs must be incurred during manufacturing operations, it is difficult to determine how much power and heating cost is attributable to any particular refrigerator.

If a cost cannot be traced directly to a cost object, an *intermediate activity index* that is connected to the cause–effect pattern and is common to both the input resources and the cost object must be found. For example, over a period of time and a given activity range, total power and heating costs may tend to vary in proportion to changes in the number of hours of machine usage. If the number of machine hours used to produce each refrigerator can be measured, then power and heating costs, expressed as an amount per machine hour, can be *indirectly allocated* to refrigerators according to the number of machine hours used per refrigerator. If this rate is 2½¢ per machine hour, a product that requires 100 hours of machine usage to manufacture would have attached to it $2.50 of power and heating cost. The notion of indirect cost allocations will be explored more fully in later sections of this chapter.

DECISION CENTERS

Cause–effect relationships should also govern cost allocations to decision centers. Costs should be associated with the department, manager, or other area of responsibility where the cost-causing decision occurred. Many decisions have only a local impact. Materials requisitioned and used by a particular department are clearly traceable to that department. Similarly, labor services, supplies, and repair costs can usually be traced directly to the decision centers that incur the costs and benefit from them.

BENEFITS PRODUCED

But what if the department that caused the cost is not the one that benefits from it? The cause of equipment-related costs such as depreciation, insurance, and property taxes can be traced to the decision center that authorized equipment purchases. However, the equipment may be used in production departments the managers of which did not participate in the purchase decision. In that case, a direct allocation of equipment-related costs on a causal basis is not justified, because cause and effect are separated.

When cause–effect relationships are not immediately evident or measurable, some other basis must be used to allocate costs. Often the product or decision center that *benefits* from a cost incurrence is easier to identify than are the factors that *cause* the cost. Although depreciation may be traceable to a decision center outside the area in which the depreciable asset is used, for product costing purposes it should be allocated to the department that is actually using the asset.

ABILITY TO BEAR

Costs may also be allocated according to the ability of different outputs to absorb those costs. Cost allocations based on cause–effect relationships sometimes produce misleading information. For example, cost must often be allocated among several types of outputs that are produced jointly by two or more departments. In such cases, a cause–effect relationship exists between costs incurred and items manufactured. But if one type of output sells for much more than the others, allocating an equal amount of cost to each output unit may distort product costs. One alternative is to allocate common processing costs according to the expected sales revenues from each product. By matching costs with anticipated revenues, an **ability to bear** allocation basis generates product costs that are appropriate for income measurement, but may be of limited value for pricing or control purposes.

A similar situation exists when several departments share the use of equipment, work facilities, or supervisory and administrative personnel. The *common costs* of these shared resources cannot be traced directly to any particular decision center. Each department's ability to bear the common costs affects the allocation of those costs to final products.

Allocation problems also arise when production difficulties in one decision center contribute to the incurrence of costs elsewhere. For example, if a production department fails to produce its quota of acceptable outputs, idle time costs may occur in subsequent processing departments. In theory, these idle time costs should be allocated to the "bottleneck" department whose inefficiency caused them. The political realities of a company's management environment—and perhaps the inefficient department's inability to bear all the idle time costs —typically prevent such a cause–effect allocation.

CONTROLLABILITY OF COSTS

When cost measures are to be used for performance evaluation and control, *controllability of costs* should be the primary basis for allocation. Decision center managers should be held accountable only for the incurrence of costs that they can control. This principle of *responsibility accounting* underlies a major purpose of cost allocations—the assessment of managerial performance.

ALTERNATIVE COST ALLOCATION MODELS: FULL ABSORPTION COSTING AND VARIABLE COSTING

There are two major cost allocation models: the **full absorption cost** model and the **variable cost** model.

Variable cost measures of product cost include only the *direct materials* that form part of the finished product, the *direct labor services* of workers involved in its physical creation, and any *manufacturing overheads* that vary in response to changes in output quantities. This model treats fixed manufacturing costs as expenses of the period in which they are incurred.

Full absorption measures of product cost include all costs associated with the creation of a product. This model therefore treats as product costs all the preceding variable costs, plus fixed manufacturing costs.

Example: Goldsmith Roofers incurs the following costs in producing 10,000 batches of asbestos shingles:

Materials	$5,250	
Direct Labor	2,500	$ 7,750
Variable Manufacturing Costs:		
Supplies	$ 500	
Power	750	1,250
Total Variable Costs		$ 9,000
Fixed Manufacturing Costs:		
Rent	$ 700	
Depreciation	300	
Supervisor's Salary	1,000	2,000
Total Costs		$11,000

The *full absorption cost* per batch is $1.10 ($11,000 ÷ 10,000). The *variable cost* per batch is 90¢ ($9,000 ÷ 10,000).

These alternative costing models are discussed more fully in Chapter 14. They are introduced here because they represent a choice between partial and full allocation of costs to products. Full absorption costing provides a complete allocation of product costs for inventory valuation and income measurement. Variable costing is preferable for short-run decision making, as well as for control and performance evaluation.

MEASURING PRODUCT COSTS

Because cost accounting functions within the framework of a firm's general accounting system, cost measures are dependent on the data available in that system. *Acquisition cost* measures will be used in this chapter. They are relevant for basic cost accounting purposes—measurement of actual product costs, decision center performance measures, and periodic income determination. Estimated costs, standard costs, replacement costs, opportunity costs, discounted future costs, and price level adjusted costs will be introduced at appropriate points later in the text. The three major categories of product cost are *direct materials, direct labor,* and *manufacturing overhead.*

DIRECT MATERIALS

Direct materials include those physical resources that are observably present in end products, and for which quantities and unit costs can be conveniently measured and traced to output units.

Direct materials cost measurements should realistically depict the attachment of materials inputs to units of output. Raw materials acquisitions are recorded at their actual purchase prices. Issues of materials to production can be recorded in various ways. *Specific identification* and *first-in, first-out* (FIFO) are the inventory flow assumptions that best reflect the pattern of raw materials usage in most manufacturing operations. *Weighted average cost* is a compromise method that is often used to simplify unit cost calculations. The *last-in, first-out* (LIFO) and *lower of cost or market* methods may be adopted because of their tendency to minimize taxable income when prices and inventory levels are increasing. *Replacement cost,* now being adopted for external reporting purposes, produces particularly useful cost measures for managerial planning and control.

Each of these methods results in a different measure of product cost. Financial reporting requirements may favor the adoption of one method, data processing costs may be minimized under another, and tax considerations may dictate the use of a third. A combination of methods is sometimes used. For example, a firm might use LIFO for calculating taxable income, but use replacement costs for internal management purposes.

Example: Gillian Company purchased raw materials costing $86,450 during June, 19X8. Requisitions for materials issued to production departments in June totaled $79,355. Unused materials that cost $4,325 were returned to inventory. Net materials usage for June equaled requisitions of $79,355 less returns of $4,325. Therefore, $75,030 in raw materials costs can be traced to June outputs.

Raw Materials	86,450	
Accounts Payable		86,450
Purchased raw materials.		
Work in Process	79,355	
Raw Materials		79,355
Issued materials to production.		

Raw Materials   4,325
    Work in Process   4,325
    Unused materials returned.

The movement of resources between the Raw Materials account and Work in Process is diagrammed as follows:

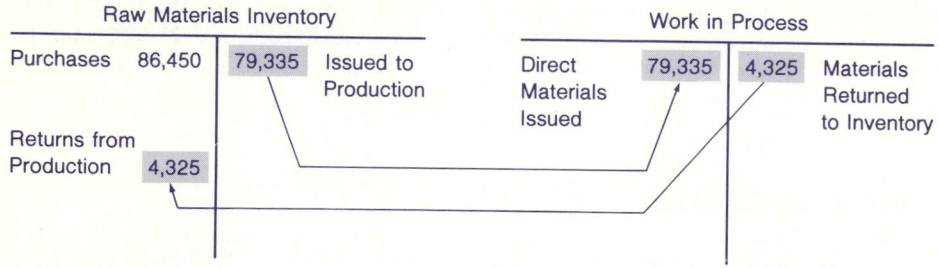

DIRECT LABOR

Direct labor consists of the services of employees who are engaged directly in the manufacture of products—for example, the services of machinists, fitters, carpenters, boilermakers, and other workers in manufacturing operations where specific outputs can be clearly identified with the labor inputs that created them.

However, employees who are normally engaged in manufacturing operations typically spend some of their working hours in activities that do not lead directly to the creation of specific products. Machine or work station setup time, normal idle time, and cleanup time are part of the total time for which these workers are paid. The cost of such nonproductive activities should be separated from direct labor costs and accounted for as *indirect labor,* which becomes part of manufacturing overhead.

There are many ways to compute the rate at which direct labor costs are attached to products. Most production workers are paid at a specified *base rate* per hour. They may also receive fringe benefits, such as health plan and pension fund contributions, which add to their total earnings. In addition, employers are subject to payroll-related costs, such as their contribution to FICA taxes and to state and federal unemployment insurance funds. All these costs can be combined with the **base pay rate** to arrive at an **effective gross pay rate** for production workers. If this rate can be calculated accurately and conveniently, the direct labor cost assigned to products can be determined simply by multiplying the effective gross pay rate by the number of direct labor hours worked. The alternative is to charge to products only the base pay rate multiplied by the number of direct labor hours worked; all other payroll-related costs are then charged to manufacturing overhead.

Example: Gillian Company recorded the following payroll-related transactions during June, 19X8:

Total Manufacturing Wages, @ $10 per hour	$50,000
FICA Tax (6%)...	3,000
Federal and State Unemployment Insurance	1,000
Health Plan Contributions	1,000
Effective Gross Pay	$55,000

The company's payroll records show that manufacturing employees worked 4,500 hours of direct labor and 500 hours of indirect labor during June. The $55,000 of June payroll costs can be assigned to direct labor and manufacturing overhead by using either a base pay rate or an effective gross pay rate.

Base Pay Rate Method:		
To Direct Labor: 4,500 hours @ $10		$45,000
To Manufacturing Overhead:		
Indirect Labor, 500 hours @ $10	$5,000	
FICA Tax	3,000	
Federal and State Unemployment Insurance	1,000	
Health Plan Contribution	1,000	10,000
Total Manufacturing Payroll Cost		$55,000

Effective Gross Pay Rate Method:

$$\text{Effective Gross Pay Rate} = \frac{\text{Total Labor Related Costs}}{\text{Total Labor Hours}} = \frac{\$55,000}{5,000} = \$11 \text{ per hour}$$

To Direct Labor: 4,500 hours @ $11...	$49,500
To Manufacturing Overhead: 500 hours of Indirect Labor @ $11	5,500
Total Manufacturing Payroll Cost	$55,000

The following journal entries are made to record and allocate manufacturing payroll cost using the effective gross pay method:

Manufacturing Payroll Control	55,000	
Wages Payable[1]		50,000
FICA Tax Payable		3,000
Federal and State Unemployment Taxes Payable		1,000
Health Plan Contributions Payable		1,000
To record manufacturing payroll cost.		
Work in Process	49,500	
Manufacturing Overhead Control	5,500	
Manufacturing Payroll Control		55,000
To allocate manufacturing payroll cost.		

[1] Payroll deductions are ignored in this example.

The movement of allocated labor costs to Work in Process and Manufacturing Overhead is diagrammed in the following ledger accounts:

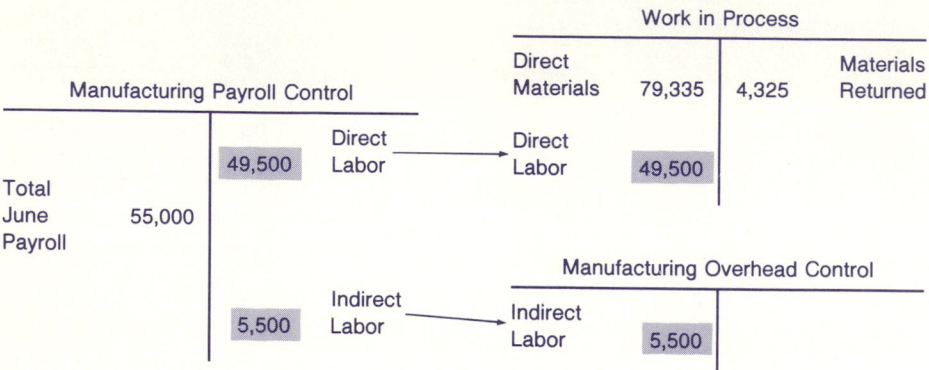

MANUFACTURING OVERHEAD

Apart from direct materials and direct labor, all costs that can be identified with the manufacture of products are classified as **manufacturing overhead.** Overhead costs are usually divided into two major groups. **Variable manufacturing overheads** can be identified with particular products; their amounts tend to vary in response to changes in activity levels. Examples of variable manufacturing overhead include indirect materials, most types of indirect labor, and factory supplies. **Fixed manufacturing overheads** are usually capacity-related, tend not to vary in response to changes in activity levels, and are only indirectly allocable to particular outputs. Typical fixed manufacturing overheads are depreciation, rent, property taxes, and supervisory salaries. Many overhead costs are **mixed,** combining both fixed and variable elements. Utilities and repairs and maintenance are cost items that usually have some components that vary with changes in activity levels and other components that do not.

As mentioned in Chapter 2, some materials and labor costs are more conveniently handled as manufacturing overheads. Nails, glue, labels, and other minor materials might possibly be traced to each product, but the inconvenience of doing so would outweigh any possible benefit. Imagine how time consuming it would be to keep records showing how many screws or rivets of each size were used in each item manufactured! The accounting principle of materiality determines whether materials inputs will be treated as direct costs or as components of manufacturing overhead.

Many indirect labor costs, such as supervision, materials handling, factory clerical salaries, and storekeeping, could in theory be metered out to particular products. But this would require elaborate timekeeping records, the cost of which would probably exceed the value of any increase in the accuracy of the resulting information. For example, to require stock clerks to keep track of the exact time spent in handling each materials requisition is clearly impractical and potentially attention-diverting.

Similarly, for certain variable overhead items, metering systems might be established to monitor the exact amount of resource usage allocable to particular units of output. Heating and lighting, electric power, and factory supplies could possibly be handled as direct charges to products. However, as a matter of convenience, these items, like indirect materials and indirect labor, are nearly always accounted for as indirect manufacturing costs and are assigned ratably to products.

Capacity-related manufacturing costs are also hard to identify with individual outputs. Factory rent, property taxes, insurance, and depreciation of factory buildings and equipment are examples. All products made during a period will benefit from these costs, which must be included in calculations of the full absorption cost of products. Yet these costs usually remain the same regardless of changes in production volume. For example, property taxes remain the same whether a factory works one shift or three. This makes cost allocation difficult because there is no direct connection between the amount of costs incurred and the quantity of output.

In other cases, a direct relationship may seem to exist between a cost item (say, repairs to a particular machine) and the cost object (a product being processed on the machine). However, this direct physical relationship may have to be ignored for cost allocation purposes. Although repairs to the machine might have been made while a particular product was being manufactured on it, a single unit of output should not be penalized by having to bear the total cost of repairs. Previously manufactured outputs were processed on the same machine and presumably contributed to the wear and tear that finally caused it to break down. It is fairer that all units produced during the period should bear some share of the repair costs.

Overtime pay should receive similar treatment. When overtime is routinely worked to achieve the desired rate of production, items processed during the overtime period should not bear the total direct labor cost incurred during those particular hours. Instead, all output should be allocated some share of the over-time premiums paid. The direct labor cost of units produced during overtime should be calculated in terms of the base pay rate only, with all additional labor costs treated as overhead. An exception to this treatment of overtime pay may occur if overtime work is required solely to complete a specific order.

Finally, many costs exhibit combinations of these characteristics. The cost of power and lighting (1) could potentially be measured precisely for each output unit, if elaborate metering systems were installed; (2) is at least partially capacity-related, because a certain amount of power is needed no matter how many items are manufactured; and (3) could be traced directly to output units, but would penalize those units that happen to be processed in cold weather or during non-daylight hours when more power and heat are required.

Summary   The circumstances in which manufacturing overheads arise are important. Many different types of costs are involved. Some overhead costs are materials-related. Others are labor-related, equipment-related, or service-related. In addition, a variety of cost behavior patterns is likely, because overhead costs may be fixed, variable, or mixed. It is therefore much more difficult to establish appropriate accounting procedures for overhead items than for direct materials or direct labor costs.

ACCOUNTING FOR OVERHEAD COSTS

INTRODUCTION: A PHYSICAL ANALOGY

The accounting treatment of manufacturing overhead costs can be illustrated through the analogy suggested in Figure 3–1. A pool or storage receptacle is used to collect inflows from various sources. Inputs to this pool originate in dissimilar forms and arrive at irregular intervals and in nonuniform amounts. Once in the pool, they are blended into a homogeneous mixture. The outflows from this pool are controlled by a switching and regulatory mechanism that allows quantities of mixture to flow to several destinations at predetermined rates. This regulatory mechanism channels appropriate amounts of mixture to each destination and maintains an equilibrium in the system so that the long-run average level in the pool will be zero.

In accounting terms, the "dissimilar forms of inputs" are the resources consumed *indirectly* during the production process. These consist of such items as **indirect materials, indirect labor,** repairs, depreciation, and insurance. These resources are converted into a "homogeneous form" when dollar values are assigned to each resource usage. The "pool" is a control or clearing account. The "inflows" to it are actual overhead costs incurred and charged to the **Manufacturing Overhead Control** account. The "outflows" credited to this account are overhead costs applied to individual cost objects, or "destinations."

The regulatory and switching mechanism that maintains this system in balance is its most critical component. In accounting terms, it consists of an **overhead application rate** ("regulator") and the process of **overhead application**

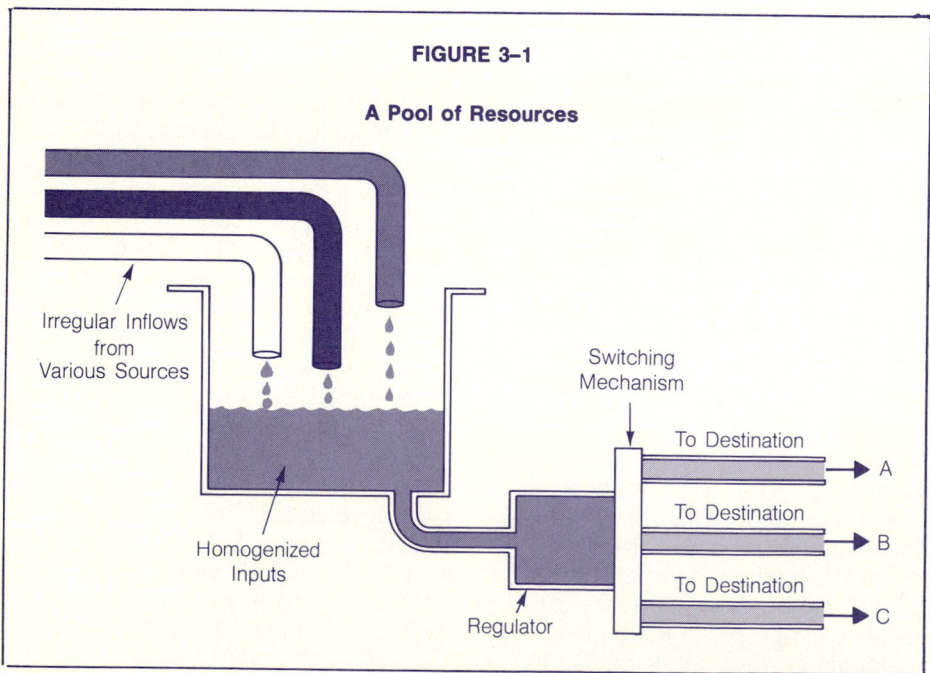

FIGURE 3–1

A Pool of Resources

Irregular Inflows from Various Sources

Switching Mechanism

To Destination → A

To Destination → B

To Destination → C

Homogenized Inputs

Regulator

to cost objects ("switching mechanism"). This mechanism serves two purposes. First, it must maintain long-run equilibrium in the overhead control account, so that the amounts of overhead applied to products tend to equal the actual overhead costs incurred. Second, the application rate must ensure that overhead costs are allocated in appropriate amounts to output units, so that reliable and relevant cost data will be forthcoming.

Example: Gillian Company incurred the following manufacturing overhead costs during June, 19X8:

Variable Manufacturing Overheads:		
Factory Supplies Used	$7,375	
Indirect Labor	5,500	$12,875
Mixed Manufacturing Overheads:		
Equipment Repairs	$2,250	
Power and Heating	3,250	5,500
Fixed Manufacturing Overheads:		
Property Taxes	$4,100	
Depreciation—Equipment	2,745	
Janitorial Services	780	7,625
Total Manufacturing Overhead Costs		$26,000

The following journal entries are made to record the $26,000 of overhead cost incurred and to apply $24,750 of overhead cost to Work in Process, based on an application rate of 50 percent of direct labor cost (.50 × $49,500).

Manufacturing Overhead Control	26,000	
Cash, Accounts Payable, Payroll Control		26,000
Overhead costs incurred during June.		
Work in Process	24,750	
Manufacturing Overhead Control		24,750
Overhead costs applied to work in process.		

The application of incurred overhead costs to Work in Process is diagrammed in the following ledger accounts:

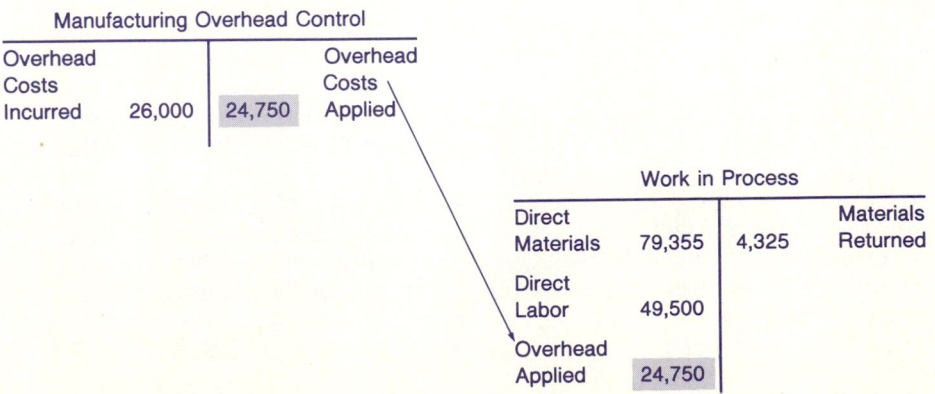

CHOOSING AN INTERMEDIATE ACTIVITY INDEX

As the Gillian Company example shows, the accounting treatment of overhead costs requires:

1. Accumulating incurred overhead costs in a Manufacturing Overhead Control account.
2. Setting an overhead application rate based on an appropriate intermediate activity index.
3. Applying overhead costs ratably to Work in Process.

An *intermediate activity index* should respond consistently both to changes in the quantity of output produced and to the total amount of overhead cost incurred. To find a suitable index, accountants examine the cost behavior patterns of the components of Manufacturing Overhead Control. Sometimes a clear overall pattern emerges. In firms with relatively labor-intensive production operations, most manufacturing overhead costs tend to vary in response to changes in the number of direct labor hours worked. In equipment-intensive production settings, manufacturing overhead cost may vary in response to changes in machine use (machine hours worked or number of machine operations). Other widely used intermediate activity indexes are direct materials cost or quantities, direct labor cost, and total materials and labor costs.

When a variety of materials, labor, and equipment-related overhead costs are combined in the Manufacturing Overhead Control account, it may be necessary to use statistical analysis to select the most accurate indicator of overhead cost behavior. In general, the activity index chosen should be supported by statistical evidence of its superior ability to reflect relationships between overhead costs incurred and output units produced. Statistical applications of this type will be discussed in Chapter 15.

CALCULATING OVERHEAD APPLICATION RATES

Determining the *overhead application rate* is as important as choosing an activity index. If total direct labor hours is to be used as an index, how much overhead cost should be allocated to products for each hour of direct labor spent in manufacturing those products? To answer this question, accountants must measure both the period's total overhead costs and the level of the activity index during that period.

The easiest solution would be to allocate overhead costs to products *after the period's costs had been accumulated.* It would be a simple matter to total the amount of overhead cost incurred during a given period, divide it by the actual index of activity for that period, and use the resulting figure as an application rate. After the fact allocations of overhead costs are an acceptable way to develop the product cost measures used in income determination for external reporting. But after the fact rates are inappropriate for planning and control, because historical overhead costs and activity levels might be obsolete before managers could act on them. Decision makers can control only the future, not the past.

FORECASTING OVERHEAD COSTS AND ACTIVITY LEVELS

In practice, overhead allocation requires **predetermined application rates** which are based on forecasts of total overhead costs and total activity levels for a particular accounting period. The essential problem is to develop reliable and coordinated estimates of these two items. First, a total activity index must be predicted for the forthcoming period; then an estimate must be made of the total overhead costs likely to be incurred at that operating level.

Example: Mister Manufacturing Company produces custom built hulls for sail-boats, using manual production techniques to the virtual exclusion of powered machinery. When operating at its estimated normal capacity level of 50,000 direct labor hours per year, the company expects to incur the following manufacturing overhead costs:

Supervision	$ 85,000
Indirect Labor	70,000
Supplies	10,000
Payroll Taxes	16,000
Insurance	7,500
Janitorial Services	5,000
Power and Heating	2,500
Property Taxes	2,500
Repairs and Maintenance	1,000
Depreciation—Equipment	500
Total Forecast Overhead Costs	$200,000

Using direct labor hours as the activity index results in an overhead application rate of $4 per direct labor hour ($200,000 ÷ 50,000 hours = $4 per hour). Each unit of output is then charged with $4 of overhead cost for every hour of direct labor worked on it. The choice of a labor hours basis in this case is supported by the nature of production activities and by the composition of overhead costs. Most of the firm's significant overhead costs are directly related to the amount of production labor used in manufacturing. Other types of costs (repairs, power, depreciation) are present, but only in small amounts.

The specific techniques used in estimating activity levels and overhead costs will be discussed in Chapter 15. At this point, it is sufficient to recognize that accurate forecasts of overhead costs and activity levels are critical to manufacturing overhead allocations. If actual activity levels or actual overhead costs deviate from the predicted amounts, the overhead cost applied to products will be more or less than the total overhead costs incurred.

MONTHLY OR ANNUAL OVERHEAD APPLICATION RATES?

The *length of the accounting period* for which a predetermined overhead application rate is established can influence the resulting cost allocations. Accountants must choose between the risk that cost measures may be distorted during a short period and the even greater risk of forecasting over longer periods.

The shorter the time period, the more likely there are to be fluctuations in the total amount of overhead costs and activity levels from one period to the next. Activity levels may vary between seasons of the year (as in the food processing industry) or in response to demand variations (summer and Christmas sales peaks). *Total* overhead, consisting of fixed and variable costs, tends to move in the same direction as activity levels from month to month. But *per unit* overhead costs tend to be higher during periods of low activity, and vice versa. This is because during slack periods the fixed cost element of overhead is spread over proportionally fewer units of activity, resulting in a higher overhead application rate per unit.

Example: Punchbowl Corporation forecasts the following overhead costs and activity levels for the coming year and for selected months:

Month	Direct Labor Hours	Variable Overheads	Fixed Overhead	Total Overhead	Application Rate
January	10,000	5,000	25,000	30,000	$ 3.00
April	25,000	12,500	25,000	37,500	1.50
July	2,500	1,250	25,000	26,250	10.50
October	5,000	2,500	25,000	27,500	5.50
Year	100,000	50,000	300,000	350,000	3.50

The annual rate of $3.50 per direct labor hour results in a uniform allocation of overhead costs to production throughout the year. In contrast, notice how the monthly application rates vary as activity levels change. If rates are set on a monthly basis, the units produced in July will bear disproportionately heavy amounts of overhead cost ($10.50 per hour) compared with units manufactured in April, for example, when the rate is only $1.50 per hour.

In this example, the fixed and variable overhead costs were presented as being "perfectly behaved." However, fixed costs frequently vary from month to month; variable costs, too, may be incurred at different rates during the year, even though activity levels remain fairly constant. Such variations may be caused by fluctuations in the demand for overhead items (lighting, heating), by the irregular behavior of some costs (repairs), by seasonal price variations of inputs (indirect materials, supplies), or by the tendency of certain costs to increase or decrease in steps rather than proportionally with activity level changes (supervisor's salaries, indirect labor).

The following table compares Punchbowl Corporation's monthly and annual overhead application rates. Note that monthly fixed overhead costs change during the year and that variable overhead costs do not fluctuate in proportion to changes in direct labor hours.

Month	Direct Labor Hours	Variable Overhead	Fixed Overhead	Total Overhead	Application Rate
February	10,000	5,000	15,000	20,000	$2.00
May	8,000	11,000	25,000	36,000	4.50
August	12,000	10,000	20,000	30,000	2.50
November	10,000	10,000	20,000	30,000	3.00
Year	100,000	50,000	300,000	350,000	3.50

Although activity levels do not change radically during the four months shown in this example, variations in the amounts of fixed and variable overhead costs incurred each month are sufficient to produce fluctuations in the monthly application rates.

The drawbacks resulting from the volatility of monthly overhead application rates usually outweigh the shortcomings of rates based on annual periods. The use of annual predetermined rates increases the likelihood of estimation errors, because it is harder to predict activity levels and costs accurately for a year than for a month. Monthly rates usually lead to a better matchup between overhead costs incurred and overhead costs applied, but the cost measures produced by annual rates are more useful for product costing because they smooth out short-run fluctuations in costs and activity levels. In general, annual overhead application rates are preferable to monthly rates.

PLANT-WIDE OR DEPARTMENTAL OVERHEAD APPLICATION RATES?

A wide variety of manufacturing activities contribute to overhead costs. Although some production departments are highly labor-intensive, other departments in the same factory may be equipment-intensive and have a completely different pattern of overhead incurrence. Under what circumstances is it appropriate to calculate product costs using a single, **plant-wide overhead application rate,** as opposed to using separate rates for identifiable segments of the manufacturing process?

Using a single plant-wide rate obviously simplifies calculations of applied overhead costs. For example, if a direct labor hour rate is used, overhead cost is allocated to all products according to the total number of direct labor hours needed to manufacture each product. This is appropriate only if (1) overhead costs in all production areas vary in response to the number of direct labor hours worked, and (2) all products require direct labor, although not necessarily in the same proportions.

When a firm's production departments incur overhead costs that relate to different activity indexes, **departmental overhead application rates** are preferable. If in addition the firm's products require significantly different amounts of processing in each department, then overhead costs should be applied on a differentiated basis that reflects the varying amounts of overhead incurred in each department.

Example: Siebert Corporation has two production operations—machining and assembly. Activity levels and overhead costs for the year have been forecast as follows:

	Machining	Assembly	Total
Overhead Costs	$240,000	$360,000	$600,000
Direct Labor Hours	20,000	60,000	80,000
Machine Hours	80,000	20,000	100,000

The possible overhead allocation rates that could be used on a plant-wide or departmental basis include:

1.	Entire Plant	Direct Labor Hours:	$\dfrac{\$600,000}{80,000} = \$7.50$
2.	Entire Plant	Machine Hours:	$\dfrac{\$600,000}{100,000} = \$6.00$
3.	Machining Department	Direct Labor Hours:	$\dfrac{\$240,000}{20,000} = \$12.00$
4.	Machining Department	Machine Hours:	$\dfrac{\$240,000}{80,000} = \$3.00$
5.	Assembly Department	Direct Labor Hours:	$\dfrac{\$360,000}{60,000} = \$6.00$
6.	Assembly Department	Machine Hours:	$\dfrac{\$360,000}{20,000} = \$18.00$

Overhead costs will probably vary in relation to both the use of machinery in the Machining Department and the use of labor in the Assembly Department. Therefore, options (3) and (6) are not acceptable because they do not reflect departmental cost behavior as accurately as, say, options (4) and (5). Alternatives (1) and (2) will tend to distort product costs if the number of direct labor hours or machine hours needed to manufacture a particular product differs from the number required to make the "average product" calculated using these plant-wide application rates.

In this company, departmental rates—rather than a single plant-wide rate—are desirable because of the varied composition of departmental overhead costs. Products that require different amounts of processing in the two departments should be assigned overhead costs in a way that reflects, as accurately as possible, the different cost structures in those departments. This suggests that options (4) and (5) are the best, because they reflect the separate types of cost behavior patterns to be expected in each department.

Summary   The choice between plant-wide or departmental rates should therefore depend on (1) the composition of overhead costs in different production areas, and (2) the degree to which products vary in their usage of the equipment, labor, or other input resource or activity that is adopted as the basis for applying overhead costs.

DISPOSING OF UNDERAPPLIED OR OVERAPPLIED OVERHEAD COST

Ideally, the total amount of overhead cost applied to products during each period should exactly equal the amount of overhead incurred during the period. In practice, this is unlikely. Predetermined overhead application rates are based on estimates of future overhead costs and activity levels. If actual results differ from these estimates, too much or too little overhead cost will be applied to units of output. When the amount of overhead cost applied to products *exceeds* the amount of actual overhead cost, the difference is called **overapplied overhead.** When the amount applied is *less* than the actual amount incurred, the difference is called **underapplied overhead.**

Example: Gillian Company (from the earlier example) incurred $26,000 in actual manufacturing overhead costs during June, 19X8, and applied $24,750 to products using a predetermined overhead application rate. The difference of $1,250 is the *underapplied overhead* for the month. At the end of June, the company must do one of three things:

1. Charge the $1,250 against Cost of Goods Sold.
2. Prorate it among the Cost of Goods Sold, Finished Goods Inventory, and Work in Process accounts, so that they will reflect the actual overheads incurred.
3. Carry it forward to the next accounting period.

The *amount* to be adjusted and the *frequency* with which the adjustment is to be made are the determining factors in deciding which of the three methods is preferable. The shorter the accounting period, the more reasonable it is to carry the underapplied balance forward to the next accounting period, anticipating that the balance will be offset in future months. Prorating the difference is the best treatment for large underapplied or overapplied balances, but it requires a recalculation of product costs. Charging the difference against Cost of Goods Sold, the method most commonly used, is appropriate when the adjustment is small.

The following journal entries illustrate the three alternative methods of disposing of the balance in the Manufacturing Overhead Control account. The June 30 balances in the Work in Process, Finished Goods Inventory, and Cost of Goods Sold accounts are $5,000, $20,000, and $100,000 respectively. Under the second method, these accounts absorb proportional shares of the $1,250 underapplied overhead.

Method 1:

Cost of Goods Sold	1,250	
Manufacturing Overhead Control		1,250
To write off underapplied manufacturing overhead to Cost of Goods Sold.		

Method 2:

Work in Process	50	
Finished Goods Inventory	200	
Cost of Goods Sold	1,000	
Manufacturing Overhead Control		1,250
To prorate underapplied manufacturing overhead on the basis of Cost of Goods Sold and inventory account balances.		

Method 3:
No entry required. The $1,250 underapplied overhead balance is carried forward to July.

INTERPRETING UNDERAPPLIED OR OVERAPPLIED OVERHEAD COST

What causes underapplied or overapplied overhead? The obvious answer is that because all the events affecting overhead costs cannot be accurately predicted, actual costs and activity levels will nearly always differ from the forecast amounts. Important control information can be derived by isolating, analyzing, and interpreting the differences between incurred and applied overhead cost.

The *activity level* of the period for which an application rate is established is a key forecast element. Most overhead costs include both fixed and variable elements. Activity level forecasts materially affect the amount of fixed overhead cost that is applied to each unit of output. If the level of actual operations differs from the predicted level, underapplied or overapplied overhead cost will result from the distortion in fixed overhead application rates, even if all overhead components behave exactly as anticipated.

Example: Horeiro Company forecasts an activity level of 100,000 direct labor hours during 19X5. Total overhead at that level is expected to include $200,000 of fixed costs and $400,000 of variable costs. Therefore, the overhead application of $6 per direct labor hour is composed of $2 per hour for fixed overhead cost and $4 per hour for variable overhead cost.

However, if only 80,000 hours are actually worked, overhead cost *applied* will be $480,000 (80,000 hours multiplied by $6 per hour). If at the same time all overhead items behave as expected, total *actual* overhead cost will be $520,000. The fixed component will be $200,000 as forecast, and the variable component will be $320,000 (the estimated $4 per hour multiplied by 80,000 hours).

Overhead costs will then be underapplied by $40,000 ($520,000 − $480,000). This is the amount of fixed overhead cost that was not applied to products *because of the activity level variation.*

One way to interpret the $40,000 underapplied overhead cost is to compare the actual and predetermined overhead rates. The actual overhead rate is $6.50 per direct labor hour ($520,000 ÷ 80,000 hours). The predetermined rate is $6 per direct labor hour ($600,000 ÷ 100,000 hours). So there is an underapplication of 50¢ per hour for every hour worked [($6.50 − $6.00) × 80,000 = $40,000].

Another way to analyze the variation is to separate the predetermined rate into its two parts—the fixed amount of $2 per hour and the variable amount of $4 per hour. Although the *variable overhead rate* is accurate, the *fixed overhead rate* should have been $2.50 per hour ($200,000 ÷ 80,000 hours). Consequently, overhead is underapplied by $40,000 [($2.50 − $2.00) × 80,000].

A third and more common way to explain this underapplication is to say that because 20,000 hours of anticipated activity *did not occur,* $40,000 (20,000 hours × $2) of fixed overhead costs were not applied to outputs.

Note that all three of these explanations focus on the treatment of the *fixed* component of manufacturing overhead. This example shows how significantly the accounting treatment of fixed costs can affect any analysis of product costs made for planning and control purposes. Usually it is potentially misleading to calculate fixed product costs on a per unit basis, as was done in the preceding discussion of overhead application. The value of a unit fixed cost is valid only for the particular activity level for which it is calculated. Expressing fixed overhead as a unit amount is appropriate for certain purposes—as in this case, to calculate the full absorption cost of products—but it produces measurements that can be misinterpreted unless they are handled carefully. The $40,000 underapplication in the preceding example reflects nothing more than the fact that the expected activity level was not achieved.

Other combinations of events can cause an overapplication or underapplication of overhead costs. These include any variation in the composition, rate of incurrence, or price of actual overheads compared with forecasts. Errors in using estimation techniques, changes in manufacturing methods, and substitutions among inputs (more equipment, less labor) can also produce underapplied or overapplied overhead costs.

Summary   The overhead application method presented here allows product costs to be determined for income measurement purposes. Its main shortcoming is the use of a predetermined rate, which usually leads to a mismatch between incurred and applied overhead costs. To facilitate preparation of financial statements, an expedient rather than a conceptually correct method is normally used to dispose of underapplied or overapplied overhead costs—that is, they are closed into the Cost of Goods Sold account rather than being prorated over all the affected accounts.

DECISION CENTER COST MEASUREMENT

To this point, the discussion has considered accounting treatments of situations in which *products* were the primary cost objects. But total product costs can only be determined after costs have been allocated to all the departments and decision centers that directly or indirectly participate in the production process. In addition, because management control focuses on the authority–responsibility relationships associated with decision centers, decision center costs are an essential part of any performance evaluation and control system.

ALLOCATING DECISION CENTER COSTS FOR PRODUCT COSTING

Product costing is essentially a process of combining costs that have been accumulated in the decision centers where actual production operations occur. Functionally classified costs—such as materials, labor, depreciation, and repairs—should first be traced directly to the decision centers that incurred them. Later, some or all of these costs may be reallocated to other decision centers, leading eventually to the association of costs only with those centers responsible for physical manufacturing operations.

This requires separating decision centers into two categories—**service departments** and **production departments**. Service department costs are reallocated and added to the total overhead costs of production departments.

Production departments and service departments are usually differentiated according to the nature of their outputs. If a decision center contributes directly and physically to the creation of end products, it is classified as a production department. If the center only supports or facilitates manufacturing operations, it is a service department. The machining department, foundry, and assembly department are typical production departments. The tool and die shop, factory personnel department, production scheduling department, janitorial services, and factory cafeteria are service departments.

The procedures for reallocating service department costs are similar to those for normal overhead allocation. Each service department's costs are applied to production departments according to an intermediate activity index that is representative of cost behavior patterns in the service department and the usage of service department outputs by the production department.

Direct Cost Reallocations   There are two major cost reallocation methods—(1) the *direct method,* and (2) the *indirect method,* which has several variations. When the **direct method of reallocation** is used, the costs of each service department are allocated *only* to production departments.

Example: Hoagland Company has three service departments—Factory Personnel, Buildings and Grounds, and Power Plant—and two production departments—Machining and Assembly. Service department costs are reallocated on the following bases:

1.   *Factory Personnel*—based on the number of employees in each production department.
2.   *Buildings and Grounds*—based on floor space occupied by each production department.
3.   *Power Plant*—based on kilowatt hours of power usage in each production department.

Costs of operating each department during June, 19X4, together with relevant activity measures, were as follows:

Department	Costs	Number of Employees	Floor Space	Kilowatt Hours
Factory Personnel	$ 3,600	5	1,500	—
Buildings and Grounds	2,000	4	2,500	—
Power Plant	1,000	2	4,000	—
	$ 6,600	11	8,000	–0–
Machining	11,800	10	10,000	700
Assembly	8,600	20	10,000	300
	$27,000	41	28,000	1,000

Direct allocations of service department costs to the Machining and Assembly departments can be made on the following bases:

	Machining	Assembly	Total
Factory Personnel:			
Number of Employees	10	20	30
Buildings and Grounds:			
Square Feet of Floor Space	10,000	10,000	20,000
Power Plant:			
Kilowatt Hours of Power Used	7,000	3,000	10,000

FIGURE 3–2

Hoagland Company
Direct Allocation of Service Department Overhead Costs
Month of June, 19X4

Department	Cost	Proportion	Machining	Proportion	Assembly
Factory Personnel	$ 3,600	$\frac{10}{30}$	$ 1,200	$\frac{20}{30}$	$ 2,400
Buildings and Grounds ...	2,000	$\frac{10,000}{20,000}$	1,000	$\frac{10,000}{20,000}$	1,000
Power Plant	1,000	$\frac{7,000}{10,000}$	700	$\frac{3,000}{10,000}$	300
	$ 6,600		$ 2,900		$ 3,700
Total Direct Costs	20,400		11,800		8,600
	$27,000		$14,700		$12,300

Figure 3–2 shows the direct allocation of service department costs to the Machining and Assembly departments. As a result of this allocation, $14,700 and $12,300 of service department costs will be applied to the outputs of the Machining and Assembly departments respectively.

Indirect Cost Reallocations   Indirect allocation methods trace service department cost to *all* user departments, including other service departments. Two indirect allocation methods will be considered: the *step method* and the *reciprocal method.*

The Step Method   The step method causes the costs of each service department to be reallocated one at a time, usually in decreasing order according to the amount of direct services it provides to other departments for which costs have not yet been allocated. Because this allocation sequence is somewhat arbitrary, a ranking of this type cannot always be made accurately. However, suppose the step method is applied to the data in the previous illustration, using the following sequence of allocations and the same allocation bases as before:

1. *Factory Personnel*—number of employees.
2. *Buildings and Grounds*—square feet of floor space.
3. *Power Plant*—kilowatt hours of power used.

Figure 3–3 shows that the direct method and the step method produce roughly similar overhead cost allocations to Hoagland Company's Machining and Assembly departments. The simpler direct method is most often used in practice, although the step method is more conceptually correct.

FIGURE 3–3

Hoagland Company
Step Method Allocation of Service Department Overhead Costs
Month of June, 19X4

	Direct Dept. Cost	Allocated Costs				
Dept.		Factory Personnel	Buildings & Grounds	Power Plant	Machining	Assembly
Factory Personnel	$ 3,600	$(3,600)	$400 [4/36]	$200 [2/36]	$1,000 [10/36]	$2,000 [20/36]
Buildings & Grounds	2,000	—	(2,400)	400 $\left[\frac{4000}{24,000}\right]$	1,000 $\left[\frac{10,000}{24,000}\right]$	1,000 $\left[\frac{10,000}{24,000}\right]$
Power Plant	1,000	—	—	(1,600)	$1,120 $\left[\frac{7,000}{10,000}\right]$	480 $\left[\frac{3,000}{10,000}\right]$
	$ 6,600	–0–	–0–	–0–	$ 3,120	$ 3,480
Machining	11,800	—	—	—	11,800	—
Assembly	8,600	—	—	—	—	8,600
	$27,000	–0–	–0–	–0–	$14,920	$12,080

The Reciprocal Method The most comprehensive and accurate reallocation technique is the **reciprocal method.** It not only requires that each service
department's overhead costs be allocated to all departments that use its services,
but that cost allocations received from other service departments be included
in the calculation of costs to be allocated. In the previous example, the Factory
Personnel Department's costs would be allocated to all other departments, but
the Buildings and Grounds and Power Plant costs would also be simultaneously
allocated to all other departments. And all three departments would include in
their allocations an allocation of "inputs" received from the other departments.
This requires the solution of a set of simultaneous equations to determine the
amounts that are finally allocated to the Machining and Assembly departments.

ALLOCATING DECISION CENTER COSTS
FOR PERFORMANCE EVALUATION AND CONTROL

The three cost reallocation methods just described are appropriate when
full absorption costing is used. This method, which assigns all manufacturing
costs to products, is useful in determining departmental overhead application
rates for purposes of product costing and income measurement. After being
reallocated, service department costs become part of the total manufacturing
overhead cost that is applied to the outputs of each production department.

Such reallocations of service department costs are not helpful for managerial decision making purposes. The arbitrary nature of the reallocation calculations and the progressive disassociation of the cost measures from their decision center sources make the resulting product cost measures unreliable for performance evaluation and cost control.

Multiple Reallocation Rates   Service department overhead costs can be reallocated according to their fixed or variable behavior patterns. This requires the use of **multiple reallocation rates,** with one allocation rate used to allocate the variable cost portion of service department costs and another rate used to allocate the fixed cost portion.

This method more accurately reflects the cost behavior patterns of each service department. Production departments benefit from the variable part of service department operations in proportion to activity levels or *usage rates.* The demand they place on the service department's fixed facilities is proportional to their own *capacity requirements.* Therefore, when variable overhead costs are allocated on the basis of *usage* and fixed overhead costs are allocated on the basis of *capacity,* the total costs reallocated to each production department give managers a better indication of how the capacity and operations of production departments affect service department costs.

Example: Assume that in the Hoagland Company example the $1,000 of power plant costs includes $600 of fixed costs and $400 of variable costs. The *variable costs* can be allocated between the Machining and Assembly departments as before, on the basis of *kilowatt hours of electricity used.* The Machining Division then receives 7,000 ÷ 10,000 of the $400 variable costs, or $280. The Assembly Division receives 3,000 ÷ 10,000 of $400, or $120.

The $600 of *fixed costs* can be logically allocated on the basis of the *capacity requirements* of the two departments. If the Machining Department has a potential capacity of 2,000 hours per month, and the Assembly Department has a capacity of 400 hours per month, the fixed power plant costs would be allocated as follows:

$$\text{Machining:}\quad \frac{2,000}{2,400} \times \$600 = \$500$$

$$\text{Assembly:}\quad \frac{400}{2,400} \times \$600 = \$100$$

The final result of this two-stage reallocation is that the Machining Department receives $780 of power plant overhead costs ($280 + $500) and the Assembly Department receives $220 ($120 + $100). This distribution is different from the reallocations under the direct method as shown in Figure 3–2, in which $700 of power plant costs were allocated to the Machining Department and $300 to the Assembly Department.

Partial Reallocation   Partial reallocation of service department costs— basically a variation of the multiple reallocation method—is another alternative. A partial reallocation transfers only *variable costs* to production departments. *Fixed costs* are not reallocated. This method has two advantages: (1) It facilitates use of the variable cost model in measuring product costs and (2) it provides better information for control and performance evaluation.

Reallocated variable costs reflect the amount of service department outputs used by production departments. The disadvantage of partial reallocation is that there may be no direct relationship between the amounts of variable cost incurred in the service departments and the activity levels in the production departments. For example, the variable costs of operating Hoagland Company's Buildings and Grounds Department will not always be directly related to the services provided by the Machining Department.

However, partial reallocations do avoid the potentially misleading effects of arbitrarily reallocating all costs and using the resulting cost measures to evaluate the performance of production departments. Allocating only variable costs is consistent with the principle of **responsibility accounting** introduced in Chapter 2. Under this concept, the costs reported to decision center managers should be those for which they are responsible and over which they have authority. In evaluating managerial performance, it is pointless to allocate the fixed costs of service departments to production departments in which managers have little effective control over the incurrence of those fixed costs.

This notion of allocating and analyzing costs in different ways for different purposes permeates the discussion in the remaining chapters of this text. The broader issues—including the disposition of production department costs, divisional performance measurement, internal transfer pricing systems, and cost control—all draw on the basic concepts of cost accumulation and allocation that have been presented in this chapter.

SUMMARY

1. Costs must be associated with objects of costing—output units, decision centers, or time periods.
2. Whenever possible, direct cause–effect relationships should be the basis for allocating costs to cost objects. If this is not possible, indirect relationships must be employed.
3. Application rates based on an intermediate activity index are used to apply manufacturing overhead costs to output units. These may be departmental or plant-wide rates, depending on the cost structures and behavior patterns of overhead items.
4. The use of predetermined overhead application rates facilitates short-run cost estimating and price setting decisions. But such rates nearly always result in underapplied or overapplied overhead costs, which must be disposed of before income is calculated.
5. When decision centers are the principal cost objects, direct cause–effect relationships are the basis for allocating overhead costs to the centers responsible for incurring those costs. To facilitate product cost determination, the costs of service departments are then reallocated to production departments.

KEY WORDS AND PHRASES

Cost Accumulation (63)
Input Accounts (63)
Cost Allocation (63)
Cause–effect Relationships (64)
Indirect Cost Allocations (64)
Ability to Bear (65)
Full Absorption Costing (66)
Variable Costing (66)
Direct Materials (67)
Direct Labor (68)
Base Pay Rate (68)
Effective Gross Pay Rate (68)
Manufacturing Overhead Cost (70)
Variable Manufacturing Overhead (70)
Fixed Manufacturing Overhead (70)
Mixed Costs (70)
Indirect Materials (72)
Indirect Labor (72)
Manufacturing Overhead Control Account (72)
Overhead Application Rate (72)
Overhead Application (72)
Intermediate Activity Index (74)
Predetermined Application Rates (75)
Plant-wide Overhead Application Rates (77)
Departmental Overhead Application Rates (77)
Overapplied Overhead Cost (78)
Underapplied Overhead Cost (78)
Service Departments (81)
Production Departments (81)
Direct Method of Reallocation (82)
Indirect Cost Reallocation (83)
Step Method (83)
Reciprocal Method (84)
Multiple Reallocation Rates (85)
Partial Reallocation (85)
Responsibility Accounting (86)

Questions

1. What are the main reasons for accumulating and allocating costs?
2. Distinguish between *cost accumulation* and *cost allocation.*
3. Explain how input–output analysis is a basic feature of accounting systems for cost accumulation.
4. "The cost of a product includes everything that goes into making it." What accounting problems arise in attempting to measure the cost of "what goes into a product"? How can these problems be solved?
5. Can the principle of causality be used to allocate costs to decision centers in all instances? Why or why not?
6. Give some examples (different from that in the text) of situations in which it would be difficult to make a direct allocation of a cost item to a single decision center.
7. Why is "ability to bear" or "benefits derived" a compromise as a basis for allocating costs?
8. Explain the basic difference between the *full cost model* and the *variable cost model.* Why are the two models important?
9. Describe several ways that the direct materials cost of a product can be measured. Why do so many alternatives exist?
10. "Every cent paid to each production worker in the factory adds to the cost of the products they turn out." Describe the accounting problems involved in making the measurements alluded to in this statement. How can they be solved?
11. How do *manufacturing overheads* differ from raw materials and direct labor costs with regard to traceability?
12. How are *indirect* materials and *indirect* labor distinguished from direct materials and direct labor? Why?
13. Give three examples of capacity-related manufacturing overhead costs. Give three examples of manufacturing overhead costs that are likely to be incurred very unevenly over an annual accounting period.
14. What purposes does an overhead application procedure serve?
15. Why is it necessary to choose an intermediate activity index? What factors should be considered in making that choice?
16. What are the advantages and disadvantages of *predetermined* overhead rates as compared with *historical actual* overhead rates?
17. Compare *short-term* (monthly) to *long-term* (annual) overhead application rates.
18. Compare plant-wide to departmental overhead application rates.
19. Why does underapplied or overapplied overhead usually arise?
20. What accounting treatments of underapplied or overapplied overhead are possible? Which treatment is preferable?
21. How does the allocation of costs to decision centers parallel the allocation of costs to products or output units? How does it differ?
22. Give three examples of *production* departments and three examples of *service* departments in a typical manufacturing business.

23. Explain the differences *in principle* between the *direct* method, the *step* method, and the *reciprocal* method for allocating service department costs.

24. Why might departmental costs be reallocated differently for product costs than for control purposes? How can this be done?

Exercises

E 3-1 Full Absorption Cost Model versus Variable Cost Model

Freeman Corporation manufactures valve casings. During 19X8, the following cost information was collected:

Direct Materials Used	$160,000
Indirect Materials Used	9,000
Direct Labor	120,000
Indirect Labor	24,000
Foremen's Salaries	50,000
Depreciation—Equipment	20,000
Factory Rent	15,000
Property Tax	5,000
Repairs	12,000
Power and Heat	28,000

Output was 80,000 units. It was observed that $8,000 of the repair costs and $12,000 of the power and heating cost were for fixed items. All other costs are either fixed or variable, according to the general cost behavior pattern expected of each item.

Required:
(a) Prepare a table to show the cost of one unit of output (1) using the full absorption cost model, and (2) using the variable cost model.
(b) If 60,000 units were sold (and assuming that there was no beginning inventory), what would be the cost of goods sold under (1) the full absorption cost model and (2) the variable cost model?
(c) List all of the manufacturing overhead items and, for each, suggest an appropriate intermediate activity index that could be used to explain its cost behavior pattern. If no intermediate activity index exists, explain why.

E 3-2 Decision Center Costs

The department heads of each production department of Langer Corporation have been authorized to make all acquisition and usage decisions with regard to each of the following resource items in their own departments:

Labor—all hourly rate employees.
Supplies—purchase and use.
Repairs—requisitioned from Repairs and Maintenance Department.
Raw Material—purchase and use.

The Metal Stamping Department received the following cost report:

Raw Material	$24,000
Direct Labor	36,000
Foreman's Salary	1,800
Plant Supervision	2,100
Indirect Labor:	
Idle Time	1,500
Rework	450
Power and Heating	2,450
Repairs and Maintenance	750
Payroll Taxes	420
Depreciation—Equipment	1,500
Depreciation—Building	750
Factory Personnel Services	250
Factory Supplies	1,125
Property Taxes	375
Total	$73,470

Required:

(a) Prepare a schedule showing which of the costs in this list are *direct costs* of the Metal Stamping Department. State briefly the basis for each direct relationship.

(b) Prepare a separate schedule showing which of the costs are *indirect costs* of the Metal Stamping Department. Suggest a possible basis of allocation for each of these indirect costs.

(c) State which cost items are probably *controllable* by the department head of the Metal Stamping Division.

(d) Make a list of all of the cost items that are likely to be fixed costs. Compare this list to your answer to part (b). What do you notice? Comment.

E 3–3   Labor Costs—Direct Costs and Indirect Costs

Two employees, Fred and Barney, of the Bedrock Manufacturing Company had the following payroll data for a typical week:

	Fred	Barney
Total Hours Worked	52	48
Overtime Hours	12	12
Hours Absent	0	4
Idle Time	6	4
Hourly Rate	$10.00	$8.00

Overtime premiums are paid at the rate of 50 percent of the regular hourly rate for hours worked in excess of the normal eight-hour work day. Vacation pay accrues at the rate of 4 percent of the normal 40-hour weekly pay of each employee. Payroll taxes are an average of 4 percent of the gross weekly pay of each employee. Pension fund and health plan contributions are 2 percent of the regular weekly pay of each employee.

Required:

(a) Allocate Fred's and Barney's *wages* between *direct labor* and *manufacturing overhead*.

(b) What other payroll-related costs would need to be accounted for with respect to Fred and Barney this week? How much is involved for each item? How would these costs usually be accounted for?

(c) Compute an *effective hourly wage* rate for Fred and Barney for all hours worked, taking into account all payroll-related costs.

(d) Using the rate calculated in part (c), allocate *all* payroll-related costs between direct labor and manufacturing overhead. Explain how each allocation was made.

(e) Compare your answer in part (d) with the combined answer to parts (a) and (b). What differences do you observe? How significant are they? In what circumstances might they be important?

E 3–4   Establishing Overhead Application Rates

The following table shows the 19X9 estimated costs and operating data for three independent companies, X, Y, and Z.

	X	Y	Z
Machine Hours	40,000	40,000	50,000
Direct Labor Hours	24,000	30,000	40,000
Direct Labor Cost	$96,000	$150,000	$240,000
Raw Materials Usage			
(tons)	20,000	10,000	12,000
Manufacturing Overhead:			
Fixed	$60,000	$200,000	$60,000
Variable	$120,000	$40,000	$240,000

Required:
(a) Using all four possible bases, calculate *total* overhead application rates for each company.

(b) Compute separate fixed and variable overhead application rates for each company as follows:

X—Direct Labor Cost
Y—Machine Hours
Z—Raw Materials Usage

(c) In 19X9, actual results were as follows:

	X	Y	Z
Actual Overhead			
Fixed	$60,000	$210,000	$50,000
Variable	$100,000	$50,000	$210,000
Machine Hours	40,000	45,000	45,000
Direct Labor Hours	23,000	32,000	36,000
Direct Labor Cost	$92,000	$160,000	$216,000
Raw Materials Usage			
(tons)	18,000	10,500	11,000

Calculate the amount of *applied* overhead for each company using the *predetermined rates* established in part (b).

E 3–5   Overhead Application—Overapplied and Underapplied Overhead

Kilgore Corporation has made the following estimates of operating data for 19X7, during which 100,000 machine hours is the predicted activity level.

Variable Overheads:		
Indirect Materials	$80,000	
Supplies	40,000	
Other Items	60,000	$180,000
Fixed Overheads:		
Rent	$40,000	
Depreciation	50,000	
Other Items	30,000	120,000
Total Estimated Overhead		$300,000

During 19X7, actual overheads were incurred as follows:

Indirect Materials	$74,000
Supplies	37,500
Other Variable Items	55,500
Rent	42,000
Depreciation	50,000
Other Fixed Items	28,000
Total Actual Overhead	$287,000

Actual machine hours worked amounted to 90,000.

Required:

(a) Using a machine-hour basis, calculate the predetermined overhead application rate for 19X7; show the variable and fixed components separately.

(b) How much overhead would be applied to the 19X7 output? Show the fixed and variable amounts separately.

(c) Calculate the total of underapplied or overapplied overhead for 19X7, showing the fixed and variable amounts separately.

(d) Comment on the possible interpretation of the calculations in part (c).

(e) What accounting treatment would you suggest for the overapplied or underapplied overhead in this case?

E 3–6   Service Department Cost Reallocation—Alternative Bases for Reallocation

Cheit Corporation operates its own power plant to generate electrical power for use by other departments. For 19X7, the following forecast data were prepared. (KWH stands for kilowatt hours.)

Power Plant:	
Variable Costs	$120,000
Fixed Costs	$210,000
Capacity (Normal Operations)	50,000 KWH
19X7 Forecast Usage	30,000 KWH

User Departments:	P	Q	R
Normal Operating Capacity (KWH)	10,000	15,000	25,000
19X7 Forecast Usage (KWH)	5,000	12,500	12,500

Required:

(a) Establish allocation rates for the cost of the power plant using the following methods:
   (1) Total Costs—Normal capacity
   (2) Total Costs—19X7 forecast usage
   (3) Variable Cost—19X7 forecast usage
       Fixed Cost—Normal capacity

(b) Comment on the relative usefulness of each of these methods. Which would you recommend? Why?

(c) During April of 19X7, actual usage of power by the three departments was as follows:

P	500 KWH
Q	500 KWH
R	1,000 KWH

Power plant costs for April were $9,000 variable and $16,500 fixed.

How much of the power plant costs should be allocated to P, Q, and R based on your answer to part (b)?

(d) How much of the power plant costs would be allocated if Cheit Corporation allocated exactly the amount of the costs incurred by the power plant during April? Explain the difference, if any, between the two answers.

E 3-7 Service Department Cost Reallocation—Establish Overhead Application Rate

Kamp Corporation has three service departments and two production departments. Forecast operating data for 19X1 are as follows:

	Number of Employees	Floor Space (sq. ft.)	Materials Purchases (tons)	Machine Hours
Service Departments:				
Plant Personnel	—	10,000	—	—
Building Maintenance	20	10,000	—	—
Materials Handling	20	30,000	—	—
Production Departments:				
Machining	100	40,000	$ 70,000	100,000
Assembly	60	30,000	30,000	80,000
	200	120,000	$100,000	180,000

Overhead costs directly traceable to each department were estimated as follows:

Plant Personnel	$ 200,000
Equipment Maintenance	160,000
Materials Handling	126,000
Machining	588,000
Assembly	146,000
	$1,220,000

Plant Personnel Department costs are to be reallocated first on the basis of number of employees. Building Maintenance Department costs are to be allocated next on a floor space basis. Finally, Materials Handling Department costs are to be reallocated on the basis of quantities of materials purchased.

Required:
(a) Reallocate the service department costs to the production departments according to the preceding instructions.
(b) Calculate departmental overhead application rates for the Machining and Assembly Departments based on machine hours.

E 3–8 Service Department Costs—Alternative Allocation Methods

Sherman Company is considering alternative methods of allocating the costs of its service departments for the purposes of determining overhead application rates in its production departments. The following estimates of the directly allocated costs of each department have been prepared, together with estimates of the proportions of the amount of services derived by each department from the service departments.

	Buildings and Grounds	Factory Clerical	Power Plant	Cutting	Finishing
Directly Allocated Costs	$500,000	$200,000	$800,000	$900,000	$1,000,000
Service Distribution					
Buildings and Grounds	0	.15	.25	.2	.4
Factory Clerical	.15	0	.25	.4	.2
Power Plant	.2	.1	0	.5	.2

Required:
(a) Prepare a schedule to allocate the service department costs *directly* to the two production departments.
(b) Prepare a schedule to allocate the service department costs to the production departments using the *step method.* Allocate in the following order: Buildings and Grounds, Factory Clerical, Power Plant.
(c) Compare your answers to parts (a) and (b); comment on the difference, if any. Which method would you recommend in this case? Why?

E 3–9 Departmental Overhead Rates—Service Department Reallocation—Full Cost versus Variable Cost

Production Departments A and B are two of several production departments that use the maintenance services provided by Department C. In a typical month, Department A uses 800 hours of Department C services and Department B uses 1,200 hours. The normal monthly volume of activity for Department A is 40,000 direct labor hours and for Department B, 120,000 pounds of raw material processed.

Department C, which serves several production departments, has the following monthly budget at its normal activity level of 6,000 service hours:

Service Labor	$15,000
Supervision	3,000
Supplies	1,500
Depreciation	9,000
Other Costs	1,500
	$30,000

All of these items, except Supervision and Depreciation, vary proportionately with changes in activity levels. Product M is processed by both Department A and Department B, with one unit of Product M requiring 10 direct labor hours in Department A and 20 pounds of raw materials in Department B.

Required:
How much of Department C cost should be allocated to one unit of Product M for (a) pricing purposes, (b) income measurement (assuming variable costing is being used), and (c) control of costs in *Department C?* Give supporting explanations for your answer in each case.

Cases

C 3-1   Direct and Indirect Costs—Materials and Labor

(a) The Mascot Wire Works manufactures an assortment of wire and metal products (cages, baskets, shelving, and so on). The major material inputs are wire, welding rods, and various chemical treating agents. The wire (in various diameters) is fabricated into mesh on automatic welding machines, requiring the use of the welding rods and chemicals.

   What accounting treatment of the costs of the three material inputs would you suggest with regard to the measurement of product costs? Discuss all alternative treatments fully. Consider also the accounting treatment of the offcuts of wire that are not used but are sold to scrap metal dealers.

(b) The company employs several categories of workers including equipment operators, fork-lift truck drivers, janitors (who are paid on an hourly rate basis) and production schedulers (who receive fixed monthly salaries).

   Discuss fully the accounting treatment of the wages and salaries of all four groups of workers with regard to measuring costs of products. Consider also the vacation pay, sick pay, and overtime premiums paid to each, as well as the payroll tax and pension fund contributions the company makes on behalf of each employee.

C 3-2   Direct and Indirect Costs—Overhead

(a) It is inconsistent to treat a foreman's salary as the *direct cost* of the department she works in. It should be an *indirect cost* of the products her department helps to produce. Discuss fully.

(b) Why has the traditional cost accounting emphasis on simply measuring the cost of products in great detail come to be inadequate for managerial purposes? What other cost measurements need to be attempted?

(c) "Since all costs of manufacturing, including materials, labor and overhead, end up as cost of goods sold in the long run, why bother to allocate them at all?" Do you agree? Why or why not?

(d) A department manager commented as follows: "When you accountants allocate materials and labor costs, you use a micrometer and slide rule, but when it comes to overhead, you get out your shovels and spread it around!" Respond to this comment as an accountant.

(e) "No matter what cost object is involved, be it product, decision center or time period, it is virtually impossible to measure directly the real cost of that object." Do you agree? Why or why not?

C 3–3   Overhead Application Rates

(a) "Why go to all the trouble of trying to estimate overhead costs and set predetermined application rates when you know full well that you will end up with either underapplied or overapplied overhead anyway? Why not just wait until the end of the year when you know what overhead costs really are and then allocate them?" Do you agree? Why or why not?

(b) "The purpose of departmental overhead application rates is to allow the total cost of manufacturing operations to be accurately distributed among units of output. A plant-wide overhead application rate should accomplish the same purpose. Then, why go to the trouble and expense of establishing departmental rates?" Do you agree? Why or why not?

(c) A plant manager came up with the following observation. "Actual overheads last month were really only 150 percent of direct labor cost, but we overapplied $50,000 of overhead because the annual rate set last December was 200 percent of direct labor cost. Don't you think we should adjust it for months like this when volume is up? After all, we're probably scaring off some potential customers by continuing to price our products based on the 200 percent rate." Give an accounting response to this comment.

(d) "The hardest part of handling overhead costs is finding an allocation base that does the job it has to do." Do you agree? Why or why not? Be sure to discuss all relevant problems in establishing an overhead application rate.

C 3–4   Service Department Reallocations

(a) "All overhead costs—service department and production department alike—should be thrown into a single pool and allocated to output on the basis of a single rate. That's all that is needed for product costing or anything!" Do you agree? Why or why not?

(b) "For most purposes, you don't really have to allocate service department overhead costs to other departments. Just let them stay where they belong." Do you agree? Why or why not?

(c) "The fact that some service department costs tend to be fixed costs and others tend to be variable costs is sufficient to suggest that only the variable costs should be allocated to other departments. The fixed costs will be the same no matter how you allocate them!" Do you agree? Why or why not?

C 3-5   Direct Costs and Indirect Costs—Service Department Allocation

Alfonso Corporation operates its manufacturing plant with three departments: Blending, Packaging, and Factory Services. Operating data for the month of August, 19X8, included the following data:

	Variable Costs	Fixed Costs	Total
Blending...............	$400,000	—	$400,000
Packaging	200,000	—	200,000
Factory Services	40,000	$240,000	280,000
	$640,000	$240,000	$880,000

The corporation allocates the costs of the Factory Services Department to the production departments on the basis of total variable costs incurred in each production department. Output of the final product during August, 19X8, was 10,000 units.

Required:
(a) Prepare a schedule showing the allocation of costs to the output of the two production departments and the calculation of unit costs for each of the production departments and for the firm as a whole.
(b) During the month of September, 19X8, output increased to 15,000 units and costs were as follows:

Blending	$ 600,000
Packaging	300,000
Factory Services:	
Variable	60,000
Fixed	240,000
	$1,200,000

It was proposed that the Factory Services costs now be divided equally between the two departments. Calculate the unit product costs in the two production departments and for the firm as a whole under this new arrangement for the month of September.
(c) The manager of the Blending Department is pleased with the results of the preceding change, but the manager of the Packaging Department is not. Is the new allocation procedure more appropriate than the original one? Why or why not?
(d) What additional information would you require to make a definite recommendation of how to allocate the Factory Services costs to the production departments?
(e) Perhaps the costs of the Factory Services Department should not be allocated at all. Under what circumstances would you agree with this contention?

Problems

P 3-1   Direct Costs and Indirect Costs—Product Costs and Decision Center Costs

During 19X7, Culhause Corporation had the following results of operations in Department X, which is one of five production departments:

Units Produced	200,000
Raw Materials Used	$460,000
Direct Labor	320,000
Factory Supplies Used	18,000
Indirect Labor	42,000
Department X—Supervisor's Salary	21,000
Plant Supervision	15,000
Power and Heat	12,500
Repairs and Maintenance	7,500
Insurance	4,000
Depreciation—Equipment	10,000
Rent	8,000
Property Tax	6,500
Telephone	2,000
Buildings and Grounds Department Services	18,500
	$945,000

The following additional information is available:

(1) The supervisor of Department X is authorized to make decisions with regard to acquisition and usage of materials and supplies, hiring, scheduling of production workers, and usage and upkeep of all physical facilities and equipment in the department.

(2) The following items have been charged to Department X on the basis of the relationships indicated:

Item	Allocation Basis
Plant Supervision	Number of Departmental Employees
Power and Heat	Hours of Machine Usage
Insurance	Total Departmental Payroll Charges
Rent	Floor Space
Property Tax	Departmental Property Value
Depreciation	Departments Depreciable Assets
Telephone	Number of Departmental Employees

(3) All repairs and maintenance transactions were made with outside contractors and suppliers. Building and Grounds services are allocated on the basis of a fixed monthly charge of $15,000 plus additional amounts for any work requested by Department X over and above the basic services provided by Buildings and Grounds. Those additional amounts are computed on the basis of the average hourly cost of services in the Buildings and Grounds Department.

(4) If Department X were eliminated, the plant-wide costs of rent, property taxes, depreciation, and plant supervision would continue at the same level. In addition, the salary of the Department X supervisor would continue because he would be transferred to another department. The fixed portion of the Buildings and Grounds charge would be absorbed by other departments.

Required:

(a) What was the total of the *direct costs of operating Department X* during 19X7? List the items included.

(b) What was the total *direct cost of 200,000 units of output* produced in the department during 19X7? List the items included.

(c) Comment on the relationship of the answers to parts (a) and (b). Are they the same or different? Why?

(d) What was the total amount of costs that were *directly controllable* by the supervisor of Department X? List the items included. Discuss any items that are difficult to classify as being controllable or uncontrollable.

(e) Why is it probably necessary to use an indirect allocation procedure to charge each of the individual items in section (2) to departments? How else might these items have been allocated to Department X and other departments?

(f) Consider your answers to parts (a), (b), and (d). Suggest situations in which each of the three cost measures would be useful and explain why. For example, in deciding whether to continue to keep Department X in operation, would any of the three cost measures be at all relevant?

P 3-2   Labor Costs—Direct Costs and Indirect Costs

The following information relates to the 100 production workers in Aaker Paint Company. The regular hourly rate is $9.00 per hour for a 35-hour week. Overtime premiums are paid at time-and-a-half for hours in excess of seven hours per day. Each employee is entitled to a three-week vacation and one week of sick leave, both at full pay.

The employer's contribution to federal and state payroll taxes amounts to an average of $1,500 per employee per year. The company operates a pension plan that requires it to make contributions equal to two percent of the annual regular gross pay (52 weeks at 35 hours per week) of each employee. Finally, employees are members of a major medical and dental insurance plan that costs the company an average of $1,800 per employee per year.

Required:
(a) Prepare a schedule showing the total amounts of each payroll-related item for a typical year. Assume (1) that all employees take their allotted vacation, (2) that on average only one-half of the available sick leave is claimed, and (3) that on average each employee works a total of 150 overtime hours per year.

(b) How much of the total payroll cost represents *direct labor cost* and how much is manufacturing overhead? (Do *not* calculate an effective all-inclusive hourly rate for production labor.)

(c) Based on your answer to part (b), if manufacturing overhead is to be applied to output using a direct labor hour rate, how much would payroll-related overhead costs contribute to that rate?

(d) During August of 19X6, production workers were paid for a total of 16,000 hours, including 1,250 hours of overtime, 700 hours of vacation pay, and 100 hours of sick pay. All other payroll-related costs are equal to one-twelfth of their annual amounts. Calculate the amounts of *direct labor cost* and *payroll-related manufacturing overhead* for August, using the separate direct labor cost and overhead rates as in your answers to (b) and (c).

P 3-3   Product Costs—Direct and Indirect Costs

During February of 19X1, Hinton Corporation prepared the following summary data regarding its manufacturing operations:

Units Produced		10,000
Materials Usage:		
Materials Issued to Production	$25,000	
Materials Used—Supplies and		
Indirect Materials	6,250	$31,250
Total Factory Payroll:		
Direct Labor	$37,500	
Indirect Labor	4,500	
Idle Time	3,500	
Rework	4,500	
Supervision	4,000	
Overtime Premiums.................	10,500	$64,500
Other Overhead Costs:		
Power and Heating	$ 3,500	
Depreciation—Equipment	2,000	
Depreciation—Building	2,500	
Janitorial Supplies Used.............	750	
Insurance—Property	250	
Insurance—Workers Compensation	1,000	
Property Tax.......................	1,200	
Repairs and Maintenance	6,800	$18,000

During the month, some extraordinary repairs were required and overtime was three times the usual monthly amount. In addition, rework costs were high due to the repairs to the machinery that broke down.

Required:

(a) From the preceding information, prepare a schedule showing the total cost of goods manufactured in February. (Assume that there were no balances of partly completed items at either the beginning or the end of the month.) Show separately the items that are *direct* costs of the output of the month and those that are *indirect* costs. (Use the *actual* costs in the original data and do not attempt to use an overhead application rate.)

(b) Indicate why each indirect cost in your list should *not* be considered a direct cost of the month's output.

(c) What are the shortcomings of the answer to part (a) as a measure of the total (and average) cost of output units produced? How might these shortcomings be overcome?

(d) Assume that the company has established an annual predetermined overhead rate of 100 percent of direct labor costs. If this rate were used to apply overhead costs during February, what would have been the cost of units produced? Show calculations. Comment on the difference between this answer and your answer to part (a).

(e) Assume that the company uses the variable product cost model. It has been determined that Depreciation, Property Tax, and Insurance—Property are the only fixed manufacturing overhead items. A predetermined annual variable overhead application rate of 85 percent of direct labor has been established.

Show calculations for the cost of units of output produced during February. Explain the treatment of the fixed manufacturing overhead items in this case. Comment on the difference (if any) between this answer and the answers to parts (a) and (b).

P 3-4   Establishing Overhead Application Rates

The manufacturing overhead budget for Hirsch Corporation for 19X5 at its budgeted capacity level of 50,000 labor hours and 30,000 machine hours included the following items:

	Variable	Fixed	Total
Indirect Materials..................	$ 52,000	$ —	$ 52,000
Indirect Labor	145,000	30,000	175,000
Idle Time	12,500	—	12,500
Factory Supplies	4,500	—	4,500
Power & Heating.................	8,000	17,000	25,000
Repairs & Maintenance	3,000	5,000	8,000
Insurance	—	2,000	2,000
Depreciation....................	—	16,000	16,000
Property Tax	—	5,000	5,000
	$225,000	$75,000	$300,000

Required:

(a) Calculate predetermined annual overhead application rates under the following circumstances:

(1) Total Overhead—Machine hours
(2) Total Overhead—Labor hours
(3) Variable Overhead—Machine hours
(4) Variable Overhead—Labor hours
(5) Fixed Overhead—Machine hours
(6) Fixed Overhead—Labor hours

(b) Assume that during the year 52,000 actual labor hours are worked, and 28,600 actual machine hours are used. Calculate the amount of overhead that would be applied under each of the six alternative rates in part (a).

(c) Assume that actual overheads amounted to $244,000 variable and $76,000 fixed. Compare your answers in part (b) with these numbers. Comment on this comparison.

P 3-5   Establishing Overhead Application Rates

Elliott Corporation has estimated its factory overhead for 19X7 to include the following:

Variable Overhead:		
Indirect Labor	$76,000	
Factory Supplies	36,000	
Sundry Items	24,000	
		$136,000

Fixed Overhead:		
Depreciation	$12,000	
Supervision	36,000	
Sundry Items	16,000	
		64,000
Total Estimated Factory Overhead		$200,000

The corporation expects to produce 20,000 units of output, each requiring 4 direct labor hours. It has been observed in the past that variations in the total amount of factory overhead tend to follow reasonably closely the variations in the number of labor hours worked.

Required:
(a) Calculate predetermined rates for applying overhead during 19X7 based on (1) units of output and (2) direct labor hours.
(b) Comment on the need for an overhead application rate and evaluate the relative usefulness of the two rates mentioned in part (a).
(c) During 19X7, 19,000 units are produced and 78,000 direct labor hours were worked. Calculate the amount of overhead that would have been applied to output using (1) the units of output rate, and (2) the labor hours rate.
(d) For 19X7, actual overheads were as follows: fixed, $70,000; variable, $132,500. What would the amounts of underapplied or overapplied overhead be for the two methods used in part (a)?
(e) What are the probable reasons for the underapplied or overapplied amounts in part (d)?

P 3-6   Overhead Application—Selection of Basis for Application Rate

For the past few years, Mays Company has applied overhead to its output using an annual predetermined rate based on direct labor cost in all three of its manufacturing departments. The rate has been 100 percent of direct labor cost. For the coming year, the following forecasts have been made:

	Cutting	Polishing	Assembly
Machine Hours	20,000	500	250
Direct Labor Hours	50,000	125,000	25,000
Direct Labor Cost	$700,000	$600,000	$200,000
Manufacturing Overhead	$900,000	$550,000	$ 50,000

Production operations involve the following sequence of steps:

(1) Products are first processed in the Cutting Department, where a large amount of overhead cost results from the special purpose equipment used in that department.
(2) Products are then transferred to the Polishing Department, where the equipment is much less expensive and where the major direct cost is the labor cost of polishing. Wage rates are relatively constant in this department.
(3) Finally, the product components are assembled. This is largely a manual operation. Because a wide range of skills and labor are used, wage rates vary considerably.

Required:
(a) Comment on the overhead application rate presently being used.
(b) Based on the information provided, and using the most appropriate application basis, calculate *separate* rates for each department. Explain your choices.
(c) Suggest the most appropriate application basis if a uniform rate is to be established for all three departments. Explain your choice.
(d) Which solution would you prefer, part (b), or part (c)? Why?

P 3–7 Overhead Application—Selection of Activity Level and Basis for Application Rate

Findlay Foundry operates a plant that produces metal castings. For 19X7, the following forecast data has been prepared:

	Full Capacity	Normal Capacity	Expected 19X7 Capacity
Direct Labor Hours	100,000	80,000	75,000
Direct Labor Costs	$ 750,000	$ 600,000	$ 550,000
Direct Materials Costs	$2,000,000	$1,680,000	$1,500,000
Foundry Operating Hours	180,000	150,000	140,000
Direct Materials Used (tons)......	5,000	4,000	3,500
Indirect Labor	$ 75,000	$ 60,000	$ 55,000
Indirect Materials	$ 300,000	$ 240,000	$ 210,000
Other Variable Overheads	$ 30,000	$ 25,000	$ 22,500
Fixed Overheads	$ 200,000	$ 200,000	$ 200,000

The capacity levels represent the following: (a) *full capacity*—100 percent utilization of all facilities at maximum level of efficiency; (b) *normal capacity*—long-run, average utilization under normal operating conditions of the facilities—that is, the activity level that would allow the firm to have average production costs (per unit of output) that are competitive with other similar firms; and (c) *expected 19X7 capacity*—the forecast level of production operations for 19X7 consistent with marketing estimates of sales volumes.

Production in the foundry requires varying amounts of labor on different types of castings, but the wage rates paid to foundry employees do not vary greatly. Foundry operating hours tend to depend on the size of each product (that is, the quantity of direct materials included). Fixed overheads are mainly equipment-related items (depreciation, maintenance, property tax).

Required:

(a) Calculate predetermined overhead rates for 19X7 on the basis of (1) direct labor hours, (2) direct labor cost, (3) foundry hours, and (4) direct materials usage.

(b) What *activity level* did you use in setting the rates in part (a)? Why?

(c) Which of the four rates calculated in part (a) would you recommend and why?

(d) During January of 19X7, actual operating data were as follows:

Manufacturing Overhead Incurred	$ 45,000
Direct Labor Cost......................	$ 48,000
Direct Material Cost....................	$140,000
Direct Labor Hours	6,500
Direct Material Used (tons)	325
Foundry Hours	12,500

What would the amount of overhead *applied* to output have been under each of the four rates calculated in part (a)? Does this information change your answer to part (c)? Why?

P 3–8   Overhead Application—Choice of Activity Level and Basis for Establishing Application Rate

Marconi Corporation is forecasting its operations for 19X4. Previously it has manufactured only a single type of product, and overhead has been applied on the basis of units of output. Preliminary estimates indicate the following:

Product A	19X4 Estimate	Normal Capacity
Sales (units)	80,000	100,000
Production (units)	50,000	100,000
Inventory (ending)	5,000	10,000
Overhead	$162,500	$200,000

Under normal long-run operating conditions, plant capacity is 100,000 units per year and the corporation has had a policy of maintaining a 10,000 unit inventory. However, at the end of 19X3, inventories had grown to 35,000 because sales had not kept pace with previous production levels of 100,000 units per year.

It was also decided to reduce inventory of this product to 5,000 units because of the decline in sales volume. Manufacturing overhead costs have averaged $200,000 per year recently, with fixed costs of $125,000 and variable costs of $75,000. Annual machine hours have been at the 50,000 hour level at normal capacity.

Management notes that the 19X4 forecasts show average overhead cost per unit increasing from $2.00 to $3.25. They propose to introduce a new product, B, to take advantage of the idle productive capacity. Estimates show that this new product will require ¼ machine hour for every unit produced; additional fixed overhead costs of $25,000 per year will be incurred. Variable overhead costs will continue at the same rate per machine hour as before. The extended capacity (which caused the increase in fixed overhead costs) will allow a total of 60,000 machine hours to be worked under normal operating conditions. Sales forecasts for product B are 120,000 units in 19X4, with a long-run average of 140,000 units annually. Production of product B will be 120,000 units in 19X4.

Required:
(a)   Prepare a schedule showing all relevant forecast data for 19X4.
(b)   Can the existing overhead application procedure be continued? Why or why not?
(c)   Assume that management requests a change in the overhead application rate for 19X4. What rate(s) would you select and why? Show all calculations.

P 3–9   Overhead Application—Selection of Activity Level in Establishing Application Rate

Schelling Corporation is developing its factory overhead application rate for the coming year, 19X2. The following data are available:

	Practical Capacity	Normal Capacity	19X2 Estimated Capacity
Sales (units)	40,000	36,000	32,000
Production (units)	40,000	36,000	30,000
Variable Overhead	$200,000	$180,000	$150,000
Fixed Overhead	$240,000	$240,000	$240,000
Direct Labor Hours	200,000	180,000	150,000

Required:

(a) Calculate predetermined overhead application rates for 19X2 on a direct labor hour basis at (1) practical (100 percent) capacity, (2) normal (long-run average) capacity, and (3) 19X2 estimated capacity.

(b) Compare the results derived in part (a) and explain the relative usefulness of each measure.

(c) Select one rate to be used for 19X2 and defend your choice.

(d) Actual results for 19X2 were:

Production	35,000 units
Labor Hours	180,000
Overhead Incurred	$415,000

In light of this information, evaluate the results of using the rate you chose in part (c).

P 3–10 Overhead Application—Annual Rates versus Quarterly Rates

The plant Confield Cannery Corporation operates in Salinas experiences wide variations in quarterly production volume due to the seasonal nature of the canning industry. The following table shows operating data for the Green Beans Division for a typical year:

	1st Quarter	2nd Quarter	3rd Quarter	4th Quarter
Direct Materials	$ 22,500	$ 7,500	$ 15,000	$ 30,000
Direct Labor	30,000	10,000	20,000	40,000
Variable Overhead	7,500	2,500	5,000	10,000
Fixed Overhead	60,000	60,000	60,000	60,000
	$120,000	$80,000	$100,000	$140,000
Machinery Hours	15,000	5,000	10,000	20,000
Tons Processed	600	200	400	800
Average Cost per Ton	$ 200	$ 400	$ 250	$ 175

Required:

(a) How has the average cost per ton been derived in this table?

(b) Calculate an annual overhead application rate.

(c) Calculate the average cost per ton using your answer to part (b).

(d) Evaluate the usefulness of your answer to parts (b) and (c) with regard to (1) pricing decisions, (2) income measurement, and (3) cost control.

P 3–11 Overhead Application Rates—Full Absorption Costing versus Variable Costing

Greenhorn Corporation has prepared the following estimates of operating data for 19X3.

Direct Labor Hours	100,000
Machine Hours	160,000
Variable Overheads	$400,000
Fixed Overheads	$320,000

Required:

(a) Calculate overhead application rates under the following assumptions:

(1) Full absorption costing—direct labor basis.

(2) Full absorption costing—direct labor hours for variable overheads and machine hours for fixed overheads.

(3) Variable costing—machine-hour basis.

(4) Variable costing—direct labor-hour basis.

(b) Compare your answers in part (a) and discuss the advantages and weaknesses of each solution.

(c) What additional information would you require in order to select the most appropriate rate?

(d) If the variable costing approach is adopted, what happens to the fixed overheads? Evaluate this method of allocating overhead costs to product units.

P 3–12 Underapplied or Overapplied Overhead—Interpretation and Disposition

For 19X3, estimated cost and operating data for the Omega, Epsilon, and Delta Corporations were as follows:

	Omega	Epsilon	Delta
Estimated Overhead	$300,000	$300,000	$300,000
Direct Labor Hours	16,000	15,000	24,000
Direct Labor Cost	$ 96,000	$120,000	$240,000
Machine Hours	100,000	20,000	15,000
Output (units)	10,000	10,000	10,000

The companies have decided to use the following predetermined overhead rates:

Omega	Machine Hours Basis
Epsilon	Direct Labor Hours Basis
Delta	Direct Labor Cost Basis

During 19X3, operating results for the three companies were as follows:

	Omega	Epsilon	Delta
Output	8,000	10,000	12,000
Overhead Incurred	$290,000	$320,000	$340,000
Machine Hours	95,000	N/A	N/A
Direct Labor Hours	N/A	16,000	N/A
Direct Labor Cost	N/A	N/A	$350,000

Required:

(a) Calculate the predetermined overhead application rates for each company in accordance with the preceding information.

(b) Comment on the appropriateness of the rates selected, based on the information available.

(c) How much overhead would be applied to output in each company during 19X3?

(d) Compute the amount of underapplied or overapplied overhead for each company.

(e) Comment on the various underapplied or overapplied overhead amounts. Suggest possible reasons for them. What accounting disposition of the amounts seems appropriate? Why?

P 3–13   Underapplied or Overapplied Overhead—Alternative Dispositions

Thor Corporation decided to use a predetermined overhead rate based on direct labor hours to apply overhead to its output. For 19X6, its first year of operation, the following forecast data was obtained:

Output (units)	100,000
Direct Labor Hours	50,000
Variable Overheads	$150,000
Fixed Overheads	$250,000

The operating results for 19X6 were as follows:

Direct Materials Used	$560,000
Direct Labor Costs	$340,000
Direct Labor Hours	42,000
Variable Overhead Incurred	$139,000
Fixed Overhead Incurred	$260,000

It was further determined that the distribution of the cost of output between partly finished items, finished items in inventory, and items that had already been sold was as follows:

	Items in Process	Finished Goods Inventory	Items Sold
Direct Materials	$25,000	$60,000	$475,000
Direct Labor	$20,000	$40,000	$280,000
Direct Labor Hours	2,500	5,000	35,000

Required:

(a) Calculate the predetermined overhead application rate for 19X6. Show the variable and fixed components separately.

(b) How much overhead would have been applied to total output for 19X6? Show the fixed and variable portions separately.

(c) Calculate the amount of underapplied or overapplied overhead. Show the fixed and variable portions separately. Comment on possible reasons for these amounts.

(d) Show three different accounting dispositions of the underapplied or overapplied overhead amounts. Show all calculations. Which treatment would you recommend in this case? Why?

P 3–14   Reallocation of Service Department Costs— Step Method/Direct Method

Vance Company uses the step method to allocate the costs of its service departments to its production departments. For 19X0, the following forecasts have been prepared:

Department	Directly Allocated Costs	Machine Hours	Employees	Square Feet
Equipment Maintenance	$ 57,800	2,000	20	1,000
Buildings & Grounds	109,400	1,000	140	3,000
Power Plant	140,000	6,000	80	2,000
Plant Personnel	40,000	2,000	200	1,000
Mixing...........................	200,100	14,000	200	6,000
Baking	72,700	8,000	210	4,000
Polishing	120,000	15,000	150	4,000
	$740,000	48,000	1,000	21,000

Service Department costs are to be reallocated in the following order and using the allocation base as indicated:

1. Plant Personnel   Number of Employees
2. Power Plant   Machine Hours
3. Buildings and Grounds   Floor Space
4. Equipment Maintenance   Machine Hours

Required:
(a) Prepare a schedule showing the reallocation of service department costs, using the step method and observing the instructions above.
(b) Calculate a predetermined overhead application rate for each of three production departments using a machine hours basis.
(c) Allocate the service department costs *directly* to the production departments, using the same allocation basis as in part (a). Calculate the overhead application rates for each of the three production departments. Compare these answers to part (b) and comment on any differences.

P 3–15 Service Department Allocation—Alternative Methods—Establish Overhead Application Rate

Brown Company has two service departments, Buildings and Grounds and Equipment Maintenance, and two production departments, Stamping and Packaging. The effects of alternative methods of allocating service department costs are being compared. The following estimated cost and operating data are available.

	Buildings and Grounds	Equipment Maintenance	Stamping	Packaging
Directly Allocated Overheads	$42,000	$84,000	$372,000	$248,000
Floor Space (square feet)	750	2,000	10,000	8,000
Equipment (cost)	$48,000	$31,100	$120,000	$ 72,000
Direct Labor Hours	—	—	50,000	30,000
Direct Labor Cost.................	—	—	$180,000	$100,000

Allocation Basis:
Buildings and Grounds .... Floor Space
Equipment Maintenance .... Equipment Cost

Required:
(a) Allocate service department costs *directly* to production departments.
(b) Allocate service department costs to production departments, using the *step method*—Buildings and Grounds first and Equipment Maintenance second.

(c) Allocate service department costs to production departments, using the *step method,* but reversing the order of allocation used in part (b).

(d) Prepare a schedule showing the results of the three alternative methods. Use these results to establish overhead application rates for the Stamping and Packing Departments, based on (1) direct labor hours, and (2) direct labor cost.

(e) Comment on the different answers in part (d). Which method would you recommend. Why?

P 3–16 Service Department Costs—Reallocation Methods, Predetermined Overhead Application Rates, and Analysis of Actual Costs

Boyd Corporation has three service departments and three production departments. For 19X1, the following forecast data was prepared:

Forecast Directly Allocable Overhead Costs

Machining	$298,200
Polishing	217,960
Assembly	28,820
Materials Handling	17,000
Factory Personnel	60,000
Buildings and Grounds	34,500
	$656,480

Other Operating Data

	Machining	Polishing	Assembly	Materials Handling	Factory Personnel	Buildings & Grounds
Floor Space (sq. ft.)	20,000	20,000	10,000	20,000	4,000	6,000
Direct Materials Usage	$44,000	$12,000	$ 4,000	—	—	—
Number of Employees	20	30	4	2	10	4
Direct Labor Hours	60,000	50,000	20,000	—	—	—

Required:

(a) Prepare a schedule to show the allocation of service department costs to production departments, using the *step method* in the following order:

(1) Factory Personnel   Number of Employees
(2) Buildings and Grounds   Square Footage Occupied
(3) Materials Handling   Direct Materials Usage

(b) Compute the predetermined overhead application rates for the production departments on a direct labor-hours basis.

(c) During March of 19X1, operating results included:

	Machining	Polishing	Assembly
Direct Materials Usage	$ 3,500	$ 900	$ 300
Direct Labor Hours..........	5,200	4,500	2,000
Overhead Incurred	$25,750	$19,750	$4,850

	Materials Handling	Factory Personnel	Buildings and Grounds
Overhead Incurred	$ 2,100	$ 4,800	$3,400

Calculate the total amount of underapplied or overapplied overhead in each production department for March.

(d) Discuss the usefulness of the predetermined overhead application rate calculated in part (b).

P 3–17   Service Department Costs—Fixed and Variable Components

Hertel Corporation manufactures two products, Alphas and Betas, in the two production divisions of its plant. A service department for equipment and facilities maintenance services both production departments. For 19X7, the following forecasts were prepared:

Equipment and Facilities Overhead

Fixed..................	$140,000
Variable	20,000
	$160,000

Capacity and Activity Levels
(machine hours)

	Normal Capacity	19X7 Estimated Activity
Alpha	10,000	8,000
Beta	10,000	8,000
	20,000	16,000

The corporation has previously allocated the Equipment and Facilities overhead to production departments on the basis of the actual machine hours usage for each department. For 19X7, actual results were as follows:

Alpha	5,000 machine hours
Beta	8,000 machine hours
	13,000

Total costs incurred in the Equipment and Facilities Department were $160,000.

Required:

(a) How much of the Equipment and Facilities overhead was allocated to each of the production departments for 19X7 under the existing procedure?

(b) How much would have been allocated if the 19X7 *estimated* activity level had actually occurred?

(c) The manager of the Beta Division observes the difference between parts (a) and (b) and expresses concern for the way in which the costs allocated to her division were affected by the failure of the Alpha Division to meet its forecast activity level. Explain this situation fully. Do you share her concern?

(d) What revisions in the procedure to reallocate the service department costs would you recommend? Why?

(e) Show how your recommendation in part (d) would affect the amount of costs allocated to each department in 19X7.

P 3–18 Overhead Application—Departmental Rates versus Plant-wide Rates/Service Department Reallocation

Williams Company is considering alternative ways of setting overhead application rates for 19X8. Forecast data include the following:

	Machining	Assembly	Personnel	Building Maintenance
Directly Allocated Overhead	$90,000	$30,000	$20,000	$80,000
Direct Labor Hours	30,000	20,000	—	—
Floor Space (square feet)	50,000	40,000	10,000	20,000
Number of Employees	20	15	5	5

Required:
(a) Calculate a plant-wide overhead application rate based on direct labor hours to be used in the production departments.
(b) Calculate separate departmental overhead application rates for the production methods: (1) Allocating service department costs *directly* to production departments on the basis of direct labor hours and (2) allocating service department costs using the *step method*—Personnel Department first, on the basis of number of employees, and Building and Maintenance next, on the basis of floor space.
(c) Compare the answers to parts (a) and (b). What conclusions can you make concerning the method that should be used here? Why?

4

JOB ORDER COST SYSTEMS

LEARNING OBJECTIVES

After studying Chapter 4, you should be able to:

1. Explain the differences between job order and process systems of cost accumulation and identify the types of production situations in which each is appropriate.
2. Trace the movement of raw material costs from acquisition to sale of the finished goods, making the journal entries at each stage.
3. Describe how labor costs are accumulated and distributed to jobs, and prepare the necessary journal entries.
4. Make the journal entries to transfer indirect materials and labor to the Manufacturing Overhead Control account and from there to jobs in process.
5. Explain the commonly used bases for overhead application, and the production circumstances in which each is suitable.
6. Describe the process of overhead application and the use of predetermined overhead rates, and explain why such a process is necessary.
7. Explain why underapplied or overapplied overhead costs are almost certain to occur and describe three ways to dispose of them.
8. Prepare the journal entries needed to transfer completed jobs from Work in Process if production is to order or for future sale.
9. Describe the contents and uses of the following documents:
   a. Materials requisition form
   b. Materials credit slip
   c. Labor time ticket
   d. Labor cost summary
   e. Job cost sheet
10. Explain the uses and limitations of job order cost information for income measurement, pricing decisions, and control evaluation.

TWO METHODS OF COST ACCUMULATION

Manufacturers must accumulate the materials, labor, and overhead costs of production and attach those costs to units of output. Product costs are needed to value ending inventories so that a firm's periodic income can be calculated and its balance sheet prepared. Knowing how much it costs to make a product is essential to setting retail prices for a company's products and to determining whether or not the business can sell its output profitably at established market prices.[1] Product costs are the basic ingredients in many types of short-run decision situations, because they are used to control operations and measure efficiency through comparisons between actual and estimated costs.

Two basic methods are used to assign costs to units of output. **Job order cost systems** associate costs with individual production orders, which might consist of a single item (a custom built yacht) or a number of similar items (four small sailboats) manufactured as a group. **Process cost systems** are appropriate when production involves a continuous flow rather than a series of separate jobs, and when costs can be identified with groups of items passing through standardized production processes (television sets, pocket calculators, boxes of cereal).

JOB ORDER COSTING

When products are manufactured individually or in distinct lots or batches, with each job requiring different amounts of materials and labor, costs should be recorded separately for every job produced. Such individual record keeping is possible only if the various inputs to a job can be conveniently identified. Detailed cost records must be kept for each job and updated as work progresses, sometimes for months or even years, until the job is finished. These records accumulate the direct materials cost of particular jobs and the direct labor costs incurred. Manufacturing overhead costs must be assigned to jobs indirectly—that is, they must be based on some measure of productive activity, such as the number of hours spent on a job by production workers, direct labor cost, or the number of machine hours required for processing.

Job order costing is typically used by producers of expensive, one-of-a-kind items—for example, building contractors, shipbuilders, and motion picture companies. Other types of businesses—job printers, machine shops, foundries, and design engineers, for example—adopt job order costing because of the diversity of their products, especially when items are made to order for customers. A job order system is often employed when products are manufactured

---

[1] Most manufacturers probably base selling prices on their costs. See R.C. Skinner, "The Determination of Selling Prices," *Journal of Industrial Economics,* vol. 8 (July 1970), pp. 201–17.

in separate batches and held in inventory awaiting sale or use. Job order costing may also be appropriate in manufacturing situations in which selling price depends on a close reading of production costs, as in the aerospace industry.[2]

Many service businesses also use job order costing. Lawyers and accountants, for example, normally bill their clients on the basis of accumulated employee hours spent on each client engagement. An auto repair shop itemizes the parts used in repairing a customer's car and adds a charge per hour for labor (a rate which includes overhead and a profit margin). Hospitals accumulate the costs of services provided to each patient and bill accordingly. In each case, the basic principles of job order costing are followed, even though no physical product is manufactured.

PROCESS COSTING

When identical products pass continuously through uniform production processes, product cost measurement is simplified. It is not necessary or useful to find the cost of *any particular* sack of flour or gallon of gasoline. A process cost system accumulates costs by departments or other stages of production through which the products move. An *average cost per unit* is obtained by dividing each period's total manufacturing cost by the number of units produced during that period. Because all items manufactured during a given accounting period are essentially alike, each of them is assigned the same unit cost. Process costing provides less specific information than a job order system, but makes record keeping comparatively simple and economical. Naturally, process costing becomes unworkable if finished products are so dissimilar that an average cost figure cannot reasonably be associated with every item produced. Process cost systems are discussed in Chapter 5.

COMPOSITE PRODUCT COST SYSTEMS

A company need not limit itself to one method of product cost measurement. Manufacturers sometimes use different product costing methods for different products, or even for the same product. Automakers employ job order cost systems in their engineering departments, but use process costing on their main assembly lines. Heavy equipment manufacturers often use job order costing to accumulate the total cost of a large machine, whereas the costs of mass produced machine components (motor subassemblies, switches, valves) are first determined by the process cost method.

THE COST ACCOUNTING CYCLE FOR JOBS

The flow of costs in a job order system is diagrammed in Figure 4–1. A manufacturer buys raw materials and disperses them to various jobs (Work in Process). Wages are paid to production workers and direct labor cost is assigned

[2] Surveys indicate that "cost-plus" pricing predominates among job order manufacturers. See Skinner, *op. cit.*, pp. 202–204; see also "Product Costs for Pricing Purposes," National Association of Accountants Research Report No. 24, pp. 5–6.

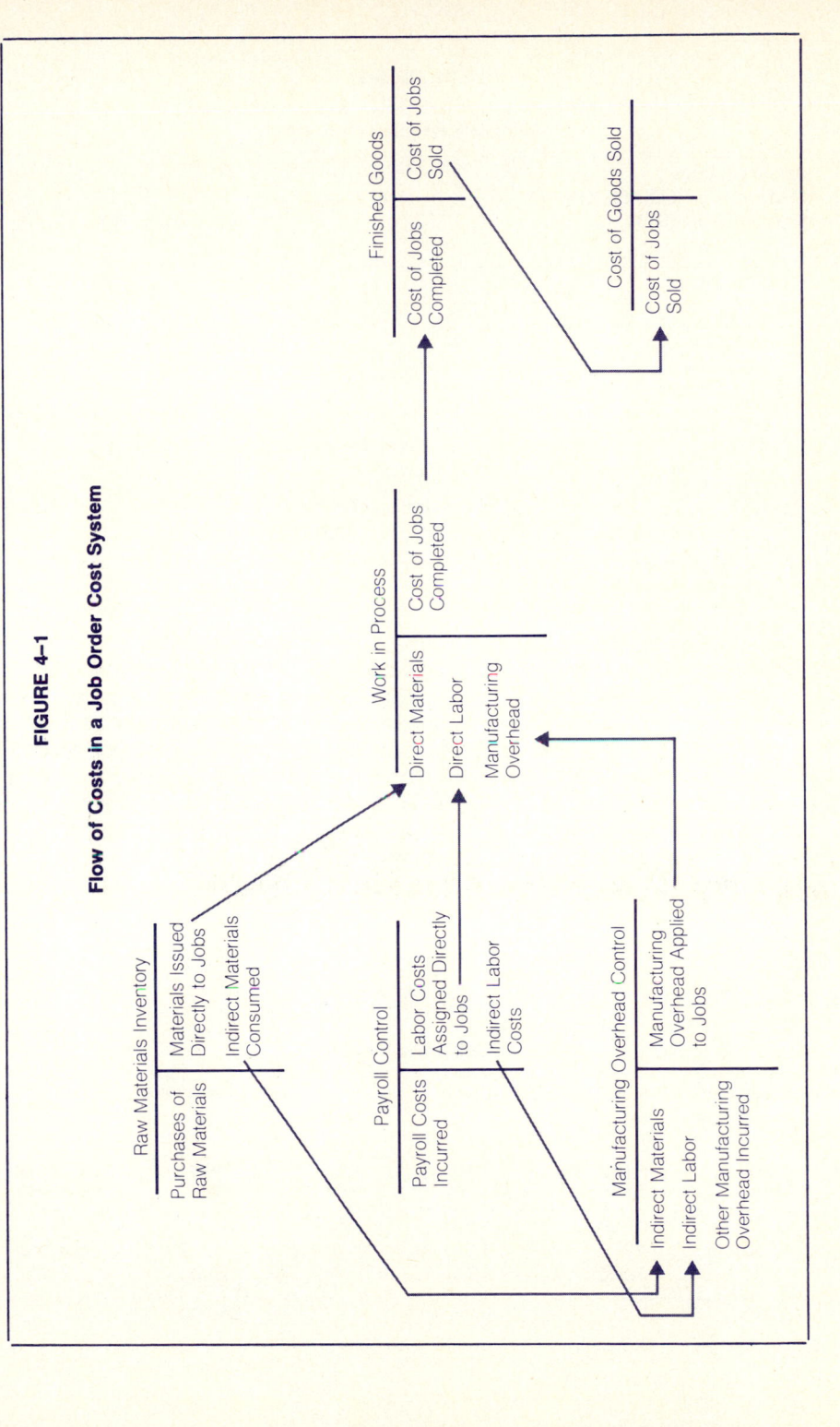

FIGURE 4-1

Flow of Costs in a Job Order Cost System

FIGURE 4–2

Materials Requisition Form

Assembly Dept.
MATERIALS REQUISITION NO. 247
REQUISITIONED BY:

DATE ISSUED: 11–16
CHARGE TO:
Job Order No: 2466

Quantity	Item	Unit Cost	Amount
100	Part #1743Q	$ 2.50	$250
10	Part #2487R	30.00	300

Approved by _____   Signed _____

Filled by _____ _____ Received by _____
                                   Date

Costed by _____ Entered Requisition Summary _____
Posted: Stores _____ Job Order _____ Indirect Mfg. Cost _____

---

to jobs. Manufacturing overhead, including the cost of materials and labor not traceable to particular jobs, is accumulated in a Manufacturing Overhead Control account and allocated to jobs. As each job is completed, its total cost is transferred from the Work in Process account to the Finished Goods account, where it remains until that job is sold. Study this diagram carefully; the remainder of this chapter is a detailed description of the procedures by which materials, labor, and overhead costs are incurred, accumulated, and assigned to jobs.

Underlying these general ledger accounts is a subsidiary record system designed to identify the costs of individual jobs. Every job order is given a number. A **job cost sheet** bearing that number is maintained for each job put

---

FIGURE 4–3

Job Time Ticket

Employee R.V. Asher   **Department** Cutting
Operation No.   16W   **Date**   June 28

Time Begun	Time Ended	Time Elapsed	Pay Rate	Total Amount	Job Order Number
8:00	11:00	3.0	$5	$15.00	714
11:00	12:00	1.0	5	5.00	cleanup
1:00	5:00	4.0	5	20.00	716
Totals		8.0		$40.00	

into production. **Materials requisition forms** and **labor time tickets** specify by job number the materials and labor costs incurred on particular jobs. These costs are then transferred to the job cost sheets, which eventually accumulate all the materials, labor, and overhead costs that have been attached to each job as it moves through various stages of production.

In physical appearance, these subsidiary cost records can be anything from hand- or typewritten forms to manual entries at a terminal device connected to a computer system. However, the essential accounting procedures are the same in all cases—the only variation is the extent of automation in the data processing activities. For the sake of simplicity, all forms described in this chapter are of the type appropriate to a manual data processing system. A job cost sheet (Figure 4–6) is illustrated on page 137. A materials requisition form (Figure 4–2) and a labor time ticket (Figure 4–3) appear on page 118.

ACCOUNTING FOR RAW MATERIALS

PURCHASE OF MATERIALS

The primary components of most manufacturing jobs are the materials (steel, timber, rubber, glass, chemicals) which make up the physical form of the product. Certain raw materials may be purchased to meet the specifications of particular jobs, to which they are immediately issued. More basic materials, used regularly on a number of jobs, are acquired and held in inventory. Purchases of raw materials by a manufacturing firm receive the same accounting treatment as inventory purchases in a merchandising business. The total cost of materials acquired is recorded in a Raw Materials Inventory account. It is also entered in the subsidiary **stores ledger,** in which a separate record for each type of material provides a perpetual inventory of materials costs and quantities on hand.

Example: A building contractor purchases 1,000 units of Metal Bracket Type 1743Q for $2,500 and 100 units of Switch Assembly 2487R for $3,000.

General Journal Entry			*Stores Ledger*		
Raw Materials Inventory 5,500			Item 1743Q		
Accounts Payable	5,500			Qty.	Amt.
Purchased raw materials.			Purchases *(Dr.)*	1,000	$2,500
			Item 2487R		
				Qty.	Amt
			Purchases *(Dr.)*	100	$3,000

MATERIALS ISSUED TO JOBS

A *materials requisition form* authorizes the storekeeper to issue specified materials to production workers. This requisition form identifies the job order number and lists the type and quantity of materials drawn from inventory.

When materials are issued to jobs, a journal entry is made to record the transfer of costs from the Raw Materials Inventory to the Work in Process account.

Work in Process	550	
Raw Materials Inventory		550
Issued materials to jobs.		

The quantities and total costs of materials issued must also be recorded in the subsidiary stores ledger and on the job cost sheet.

Stores Ledger Accounts			*Job Cost Sheet*		
Item 1743Q			**Job 2466**		
	Qty.	Amt.		Qty.	Amt.
Issued to Job 2466 (*Cr.*)	100	$250	Material #1743Q	100	$250
			Material #2487R	10	300
Item 2487R					
	Qty.	Amt.			
Issued to Job 2466 (*Cr.*)	10	$300			

Any materials not used in producing the job for which they were requisitioned should be returned to inventory. A **materials credit slip** is then prepared and the following journal entry is made:

Raw Materials Inventory	35	
Work in Process		35
Surplus materials returned to stores.		

The subsidiary stores ledger and the job cost sheet are adjusted to show the return of unused materials.

MEASURING UNIT COSTS OF MATERIALS ISSUED

If identical materials are bought at varying prices during an accounting period, a choice among inventory costing methods is necessary to determine the unit costs at which materials are issued to jobs. When raw materials are purchased for use on specific jobs, costing on a *specific identification* basis is feasible. This is the preferred method because it allows the flow of costs to coincide as precisely as possible with the physical movement of materials. *First-in, first-out* is the next most logical approach, because manufacturing operations usually exhibit some degree of FIFO flow as purchased materials are incorporated into finished products. The *moving average* cost of raw materials may be assigned to jobs when the more conceptually correct FIFO or specific identification methods cannot easily be applied. Job order costs should be accumulated on a perpetual inventory basis so that issues of materials to jobs can be recorded as they occur.

INDIRECT MATERIALS

Often it is not worthwhile to assign costs of very small items directly to the jobs in which they are used. Their value is immaterial compared to the total cost of the job. To save accounting effort, costs of such items as nails, screws, glue, and labels are usually treated as indirect rather than direct materials costs.

The *acquisition* of indirect materials is normally recorded in the same way as direct materials purchases—as a debit to the Raw Materials Inventory account. However, their *issue* to production is treated as an addition to indirect manufacturing cost and is charged to the Manufacturing Overhead Control account. Indirect materials costs are then allocated to jobs through an overhead application procedure that will be described later in this chapter.

Example: A construction company buys ten kegs of nails for $25 each and issues two kegs to the carpenter's shop. The following journal entries are made:

Raw Materials Inventory	250	
Accounts Payable		250
Purchased 10 kegs of nails at $25 each.		
Manufacturing Overhead Control	50	
Raw Materials Inventory		50
Issued 2 kegs of nails to carpenter's shop.		

SUBCONTRACTS IN JOB ORDER COSTING

Job order manufacturers often subcontract parts of the work to be done on particular jobs. This means that not all manufacturing activities will be performed by the firm's own employees using purchased raw materials. Subassemblies at some stage of completion may be acquired from an outside supplier or specialized manufacturing services may be performed by other firms. Subcontracting might also be done to reduce costs or because particular labor skills or production facilities are not available within the firm.

Job order cost systems treat subcontracted items basically the same as raw materials, though the inventorying and requisitioning phases may be bypassed. Invoices and vouchers should indicate the specific job or jobs for which subcontracted materials or services were acquired. Unless it is company practice to subcontract supplies before jobs begin, the cost of each subcontracted item will immediately be released into the flow of job costs. At that time it should be recorded as part of the direct materials cost of a particular job. When subcontracting is a normal practice, job cost records should include separate sections for subcontracted items and raw materials issues. This segregation is important for evaluation and control purposes.

Example: A manufacturer of customized motor homes subcontracts all seat upholstery work. Invoices received from the subcontractor for work done on Jobs 187, 189, and 192 totalled $150, $225, and $110, respectively. The manufacturer makes this journal entry:

Work in Process	485	
Accounts Payable		485
Subcontracted seat upholstery on jobs 187, 189, and 192.		

Separate entries for the cost of upholstery work performed on each of the three motor homes would be made on the job cost sheets for Jobs 187, 189, and 192, under the category of *Subcontracted Components*.

ACCOUNTING FOR DIRECT LABOR COSTS

The second component of manufacturing jobs is the labor expended in physically creating products. In job order costing, **direct labor costs** are payments for the services of employees directly engaged in manufacturing activities on jobs in progress—for example, wages paid to machinists, drill press operators, welders, and assemblers.

However, not all payments to production workers can be assigned directly to jobs. Costs of idle time, machine setup time, and rework time should be treated as **indirect labor costs** and charged to Manufacturing Overhead Control. So should supervisors' salaries and the wages paid for such support activities as janitorial services, materials handling, and factory clerical services. Overtime premium pay, when overtime is a normal feature of operations, is also excluded from the computation of direct labor costs.

Production workers are sometimes given *time tickets* on which they record the number of hours spent on each job during a working day. The direct labor cost of any job is found by multiplying the hours worked on that job by the employee's hourly pay rate. In computerized accounting systems, this labor cost data can be entered in various ways, including work station terminal devices and precoded work tickets. A job time ticket is illustrated in Figure 4–3.

A **labor cost summary** is prepared each pay period to tabulate total labor costs and show the distribution of direct labor costs to jobs.

Each time wages are paid, journal entries are needed to:

1. Accrue the total payroll liability.
2. Record payments to employees.
3. Distribute payroll costs to jobs and to manufacturing overhead.
4. Accrue the employer's payroll taxes.

Example: Assuming a weekly payroll of $6,000 as detailed in Figure 4–4, federal income tax withholdings of $950, FICA contributions by employees of

---

FIGURE 4–4

Labor Cost Summary
Week Ended July 30, 19X7

Total Labor Costs:		Direct Labor Costs by Jobs:	
Direct Labor	$3,200	Job 714—200 hours @ $5....	$1,000
Indirect Labor....	1,000	Job 715—200 hours @ $8....	1,600
Supervision......	1,800	Job 716—120 hours @ $5....	600
	$6,000		$3,200

$350 (5.85 percent of gross wages),[3] and no other deductions, the following entries would be made to accrue, pay, and distribute labor costs:

Payroll Control	6,000	
Wages Payable		4,700
Income Tax Withheld		950
FICA Tax Payable		350
Weekly payroll liability.		

Wages Payable	4,700	
Cash		4,700
Paid weekly payroll.		

Work in Process	3,200	
Manufacturing Overhead Control	2,800	
Payroll Control		6,000
Weekly payroll cost distributed to jobs and to manufacturing overhead.		

Periodically—usually at the end of each payroll period—accumulated direct labor costs are posted from the labor cost summary to the individual job cost sheets. The $3,200 of direct labor costs summarized in Figure 4–4 would be assigned to jobs as follows:

Job Cost Sheets		
Job 714:	Job 715:	Job 716:
200 hours @ $5 = $1,000	200 hours @ $8 = $1,600	120 hours @ $5 = $600

The employees' payroll taxes may be accrued each payday or at the end of every month. They include an FICA tax that matches the employee's contribu-

---

[3] Both FICA (Social Security) tax rates and the base earnings to which they apply have been increased several times in recent years and are scheduled to increase in the future.

tion, a federal unemployment tax of 0.4 percent of gross wages, and a state unemployment tax of 2.7 percent of gross wages. Assuming these taxes are treated as manufacturing overhead costs, the entry to record employer's payroll tax liability is:

Manufacturing Overhead Control	536	
FICA Tax Payable		350
State Unemployment Tax Payable		162
Federal Unemployment Tax Payable		24
Employer's payroll tax liability.		

ACCOUNTING FOR MANUFACTURING OVERHEAD COSTS

DIRECT OVERHEAD COSTS

Job order manufacturers often incur costs that cannot be classified as direct materials or direct labor, but can be assigned directly to specific jobs. Such **direct overhead costs** might involve:

- Rental of a crane, forklift, compressor, high speed drill, or other equipment expressly for work on a particular job.
- Purchase for use on a job of small tools that would normally be charged to expense rather than being capitalized and depreciated.
- Manufacture of a special die or casting blank for use on a certain job.
- Payment of wage rate premiums for heat, dirt, height, or danger to high-risk workers on a job.
- Payment of overtime premiums, if the overtime is required to complete the contract terms of a specific job.

The accounting treatment of direct overhead items is similar to that for subcontracts. Direct overhead costs should be charged to the Work in Process account as they are incurred.

Example: A plumbing contractor must rent a forklift truck for $250 to complete a job. Another of his jobs requires the purchase of special left-hand thread dies costing $175; these are not likely to be used on any other project in the foreseeable future. He makes the following journal entry:

Work in Process	425	
Accounts Payable		425
Incurred direct overhead costs.		

Separate entries for $250 and $175 are recorded on the job cost sheets for the two jobs, under the category of *Direct Overhead*.

INDIRECT OVERHEAD COSTS

Most manufacturing overhead costs are indirect—that is, they do not readily "attach" to any job. In this group are indirect materials and labor and all production-facilitating and production-supporting costs, such as factory rent, power and heating, depreciation, repairs and maintenance, insurance, and property taxes. Tracing these costs to particular jobs is either impossible or uneconomic. Yet because each job requires the services represented by indirect overhead, it should be charged with its fair share of **indirect overhead costs.**

Assigning indirect overhead costs to jobs is the hardest task in job order costing. The cost of services that benefit the factory environment as a whole, such as insurance, must be divided among every job worked on in that factory. Certain overhead costs, such as power and heating, vary according to the amount of work done; others, such as property taxes, are fixed in amount regardless of the number of jobs produced. Applying overhead costs to jobs is further complicated by the fact that jobs are completed and sold at various times during an accounting period, but the actual amounts of most overhead costs are not known until the end of each period.

Accounting for overhead costs is most easily understood as a three part sequence of events:

1. As indirect overhead costs are incurred they are accumulated in a Manufacturing Overhead Control account.
2. While operations proceed, overhead costs are removed from Manufacturing Overhead Control and assigned to jobs through a process of *overhead application,* at a rate determined by an activity index that is selected before production begins.
3. Any difference between overhead costs incurred and overhead costs applied to jobs is either disposed of at the end of the accounting period or is carried forward into the next period.

RECORDING INCURRED OVERHEAD COSTS

All indirect overhead costs are charged to the **Manufacturing Overhead Control account** as they are incurred.

Example: During September of the current year, a factory manager makes the following payments: supervisory salaries, $10,000; heat and power, $7,000; rent, $4,000; and janitorial supplies, $500. Indirect materials costing $3,000 are used during the month. Property taxes of $1,200 and insurance expense of $750 are accrued. Equipment depreciation for September is calculated at $3,500. Entries are made to record manufacturing overhead incurred as follows:

Manufacturing Overhead Control	29,950	
Cash		21,500
Raw Materials Inventory		3,000
Property Taxes Payable		1,200
Insurance Payable		750
Accumulated Depreciation—Equipment		3,500
Incurred manufacturing overhead costs.		

The Manufacturing Overhead Control account should be supported by a subsidiary ledger system that groups overhead costs either by functions (repairs, insurance, property taxes) or by departments (Buildings and Grounds, Janitorial Services, Materials Handling). These subsidiary cost classifications make it possible to develop cost data for a variety of purposes, especially for control.

APPLYING OVERHEAD COSTS TO JOBS

As discussed in Chapter 3, indirect costs are usually associated with a cost object by way of an *intermediate index*. That index must first be a measure of some easily identified and quantified *attribute* of the cost object. Secondly, it must reflect the indirect cost's *behavior* in response to variations in the attribute being measured. In job order costing, accountants must find some directly measurable component of each job that tends to vary in relation to changes in the amount of overhead costs incurred.

If a firm's manufacturing activities are labor intensive and require little equipment use, a large proportion of overhead costs will be attributable to the amount of direct labor used. In such cases, an allocation of overhead cost to jobs based on *direct labor hours worked* or *direct labor cost* may be appropriate. The number of direct labor hours worked on each job is conveniently measured (indeed must be measured) and is a basic element of that job's direct cost. Direct labor cost is an acceptable index in any job order situation in which total overhead costs vary in proportion to the direct labor cost incurred on each job.

If production requires extensive use of machinery, overhead may consist largely of equipment-related costs and the allocation of overhead costs may be based on *machine hours worked* or *units-of-machine-output*. Other frequently used indexes are *direct materials cost* and *direct prime costs* (materials plus labor). Under appropriate circumstances, each of these indexes permits accountants to establish a connection between the amount of overhead cost incurred and the productive effort made on particular jobs.

To keep the cost records up to date, frequent entries must be made to apply overhead costs to jobs. This requires a transfer of overhead costs from the Manufacturing Overhead Control account to the Work in Process account in the general ledger.

Example: Continuing the previous illustration, assume that Jobs 2478, 2479, and 2480 were in process during the month of September. Incurred overhead costs are applied to jobs on a direct labor hours basis. At the start of the current year, an overhead application rate of $5 per direct labor hour was calculated by dividing the expected overhead costs for the year by the expected number of direct labor hours. Direct labor hours spent on each job during September were:

Job	Hours Worked
2478	1,350
2479	2,200
2480	2,150
	5,700

A journal entry is made to apply 5,700 hours of overhead at $5 per hour to jobs in process:

Work in Process	28,500	
Manufacturing Overhead Control		28,500
Manufacturing overhead cost applied to jobs.		

The amount of overhead cost applied to each job is then entered in the overhead section of the individual job cost sheets:

Job Number	Hours Worked	Hourly Rate	Overhead Applied
2478	1,350	$5.00	$ 6,750
2479	2,200	5.00	11,000
2480	2,150	5.00	10,750
	5,700		$28,500

DISPOSING OF UNDERAPPLIED OR OVERAPPLIED OVERHEAD COSTS

The two preceding journal entries show how Manufacturing Overhead Control acts as a clearing account. Actual overhead costs are debited to Manufacturing Overhead Control as they are incurred. Periodically these costs are applied to jobs according to a predetermined overhead rate based on direct labor hours worked or some other index of activity.[4]

Ideally, the Manufacturing Overhead Control account should balance out to zero at the end of each accounting period. In practice, this is unlikely to happen, because the application rate is based on estimates of future overhead costs and future activity levels. If actual results differ from these estimates, either too much or too little overhead cost will be applied to Work in Process.

A *debit* balance remaining in Manufacturing Overhead Control represents an *underapplication* of overhead cost, whereas a *credit* balance represents an *overapplication*. At the end of each accounting period, underapplied or overapplied overhead balances must be treated in one of three ways:

1. Written off against Cost of Goods Sold.
2. Prorated between the Cost of Goods Sold, Finished Goods Inventory, and Work in Process accounts.
3. Carried forward to the next accounting period.

Example: To conclude the previous illustration, at the end of September the Manufacturing Overhead Control account has a debit balance of $1,450:

---

[4] Many firms credit a separate account called Manufacturing Overhead Applied when overhead costs are applied to Work in Process.

Actual Overhead Costs }   Manufacturing Overhead Control   { Applied Overhead Costs

	Manufacturing Overhead Control	
29,950		28,500
Underapplied Balance	1,450	

If method 1 is used, the $1,450 underapplied balance is simply charged to Cost of Goods Sold—the justification being that prorating underapplied overhead cost among finished and unfinished jobs would not materially affect their final cost or the company's reported income.

Cost of Goods Sold   1,450
    Manufacturing Overhead Control   1,450
    Disposed of underapplied manufacturing overhead cost.

Method 2 prorates the $1,450 between jobs that have been sold, completed jobs, and jobs in process. This treatment suggests that the underapplied balance is large enough to justify correcting the costs of jobs worked on during September.[5] The firm applies overhead costs to jobs on a direct labor hours basis. Analysis of the job cost sheets shows that the direct labor hours worked in September were distributed among jobs sold, finished jobs, and unfinished jobs as shown at the left in the following table. This distribution is the basis for the proration of underapplied overhead cost shown at the right.

	Direct Labor Hours Worked	Proration of Underapplied Overhead Cost
Cost of Goods Sold	20,000	$\frac{20}{32} \times \$1,450 = \$ \ 906.25$
Finished Goods	2,000	$\frac{2}{32} \times \$1,450 = \ 90.63$
Work in Process	10,000	$\frac{10}{32} \times \$1,450 = \ 453.12$
	32,000	$1,450.00

The following entry is made to close the Manufacturing Overhead Control account:

Cost of Goods Sold   906.25
Finished Goods   90.63
Work in Process   453.12
    Manufacturing Overhead Control   1,450.00
    Prorated underapplied manufacturing overhead cost.

This proration also affects the subsidiary accounting records. The job cost sheets for every job, whether completed or in process, will be charged an

---

[5] This method of disposing of underapplied or overapplied overhead cost is required by the Cost Accounting Standards Board for use by contractors and subcontractors who deal with the Department of Defense.

additional overhead cost of 4.53 cents for each direct labor hour worked on that job during September.

$$\frac{\$1,450}{32,000 \text{ hours}} = 4.53\text{¢ per hour}$$

Method 3 leaves the $1,450 balance in the Manufacturing Overhead Control account in the expectation that it will be offset by overapplied balances in later accounting periods.

MONTHLY OR ANNUAL OVERHEAD APPLICATION RATES?

The production volume of firms using job order costing often varies considerably from month to month. Manufacturers who produce in response to customer orders have on the average a less stable pattern of activity than have manufacturers of standardized products, who can use finished goods inventories as a buffer against variations in demand. For this reason, and also because of seasonal, cyclical, and random fluctuations in incurred overhead costs, it is appropriate for job order manufacturers to use *annual* rather than *monthly* overhead application rates.

PLANT-WIDE OR DEPARTMENTAL OVERHEAD APPLICATION RATES?

Overhead applications to jobs should reflect as accurately as possible the amount of overhead cost that each job causes or requires in each production area. The issue of departmental versus plant-wide overhead application rates, discussed in Chapter 3, applies to job order cost systems. If production is such that different jobs require widely varying quantities of direct labor hours or other primary activities in different departments, there is a case for calculating separate overhead application rates for each department. The case is even stronger if, in addition, the overhead costs incurred in different departments are closely related to different primary activities. On the other hand, if overhead costs are fairly homogeneous throughout a factory (for example, mostly labor-related or mostly equipment-related), and if all jobs require about the same use of departmental facilities, then a single plant-wide overhead application rate should produce acceptable job cost measurements.

ACCOUNTING FOR COSTS OF COMPLETED JOBS

PRODUCTION TO ORDER

Job order manufacturers normally expect that when a job is finished it will immediately be sold and delivered to a customer. At the time of completion, all Work in Process account balances pertaining to that job are transferred directly to Cost of Goods Sold.

Example: A job order has been completed and delivered to a contracting customer at a price of $10,000. The job cost sheet for this order shows the following balances:

Direct Materials	$2,500
Direct Labor	2,250
Manufacturing Overhead	2,250
Subcontracts	750
Total Costs	$7,750

Two journal entries are made to record the job's completion and sale.

Cost of Goods Sold	7,750	
Work in Process		7,750
Completed Job 1379.		
Accounts Receivable	10,000	
Sales		10,000
Sold Job 1379.		

The subsidiary job cost sheet for Job 1379 is removed from the job cost ledger and placed in a finished jobs file.

PRODUCTION FOR FUTURE SALE

Exceptions to this treatment occur when production anticipates customer demand and jobs are produced for inventory rather than for specific customers. **Example:** If Job 1379 is completed but not immediately sold, the following journal entry is made:

Finished Goods Inventory	7,750	
Work in Process		7,750
Completed Job 1379.		

Two entries are made when Job 1379 is sold:

Accounts Receivable	10,000	
Sales		10,000
Sold Job 1379.		
Cost of Goods Sold	7,750	
Finished Goods Inventory		7,750
Job costs removed from inventory.		

NONMANUFACTURING COSTS IN JOB ORDER COSTING

The manufacturing costs assigned to jobs represent materials, labor and overhead needed to complete those jobs in salable form. All other costs are usually treated as operating expenses of the period in which they are incurred.

However, nonmanufacturing costs—for example, sales commissions, freight and delivery charges, and product warranty and guarantee costs—can sometimes be traced directly to specific jobs. Because these costs are incurred after a job has been completed, they should not be classified as costs of production. Instead, the subsidiary job cost sheets can be modified to add nonmanufacturing costs to the costs of individual jobs, while keeping them segregated from materials, labor, and overhead costs. The result is more complete information about the direct costs of selling, distributing, and servicing particular jobs. This information is useful in estimating future job costs and in bidding on jobs.

COST CONTROL IN JOB ORDER SYSTEMS

The methods described in this chapter are primarily concerned with determining the *actual costs* of jobs. These methods also provide a foundation for the more difficult tasks of estimating costs, evaluating performance, and controlling costs. Because the individual job is the principal cost object, *estimating the costs of prospective jobs* is the critical first step in any control process. Estimates of future job costs serve as a basis for bidding and price setting, as well as a standard for measuring efficiency through comparisons with actual costs incurred. Direct materials, direct labor, and other costs directly traceable to specific jobs must be forecast as separate identifiable amounts. Comparisons between anticipated and actual job costs can then proceed on an item by item basis. Indirect costs assigned to particular jobs are less easily handled because they require the use of overhead application procedures. Consequently, direct evaluation of such costs cannot easily be made on a job by job basis.

JOB ORDER COSTING ILLUSTRATED: KARTER KUSTOM BODY COMPANY

The operation of a job order cost system will now be demonstrated by summarizing a single month's activity for a manufacturer of custom-made camper vans.

Karter Kustom Body Company accumulates costs by individual jobs. As each job is started, it receives a number. When materials needed for that job are issued from stores, their quantity, cost, and the job's number are recorded on materials requisition forms. The information on these forms is summarized by job number in the job cost ledger, making it possible to determine the total direct materials cost of every job.

Foremen keep a daily record of the time spent by production workers on each job. At the end of each month, the Payroll Department prepares a labor cost summary from these time tickets and converts the total hours worked to a dollar cost that is charged either to jobs in process or to indirect labor.

Overhead costs that cannot be associated directly with particular jobs are allocated among all jobs on the basis of direct labor hours worked. It is estimated that during the current year indirect manufacturing costs will total $120,000 and that 30,000 direct labor hours will be worked. Each job will therefore be allocated $4 of manufacturing overhead cost for every direct labor hour spent on it.

Karter Company's accounting records include the following documents:

1. General Journal
2. General Ledger
3. Subsidiary Ledgers:
   a. Stores Ledger
   b. Job Cost Ledger
   c. Manufacturing Overhead Ledger
   d. Finished Goods Ledger
   e. Accounts Receivable Ledger
4. Ancillary Records:
   a. Materials Requisition Forms
   b. Materials Credit Slips
   c. Time Tickets
   d. Labor Cost Summary

Figure 4–5 shows the company's trial balance at the beginning of December. The following entries summarize transactions that occurred during December. *General Journal entries* are on the *left. Subsidiary ledger postings* are on the *right.*

FIGURE 4–5

Karter Kustom Body Company
Trial Balance
December 1, 19X7

	Debit	Credit
Cash	$ 9,000	$
Accounts Receivable	6,500	
Raw Materials Inventory	6,500	
Work in Process	18,850	
Land	24,000	
Building	35,500	
Accumulated Depreciation—Building		6,500
Factory Equipment	12,600	
Accumulated Depreciation—Equipment		5,600
Office Furniture	2,300	
Accumulated Depreciation—Furniture		1,600
Accounts Payable		5,050
Customers' Deposits		7,500
Wages Payable		300
Sales		325,750
Cost of Goods Sold	241,450	
Manufacturing Overhead Control	2,655	
Operating Expenses	57,945	
Capital Stock		40,000
Retained Earnings		25,000
	$417,300	$417,300

(1) *Purchased Materials*   Assorted truck body materials costing $18,000 were purchased; $12,000 cash was paid.

Raw Materials Inventory 18,000		*Stores Ledger:*	
Cash	12,000	Individual Raw Materials	
Accounts Payable	6,000	Cards (Dr.)	18,000
Purchased raw materials.			

(2) *Materials Issued to Jobs*   Raw materials were requisitioned from stores and issued to jobs as follows: Job 121, $1,250; Job 122, $2,250; Job 123, $6,000. In addition, $900 worth of materials drawn from stores were not assigned to any particular job. Their cost was charged to the Manufacturing Overhead Control account, where it will remain with other overhead costs until they are allocated to individual jobs by means of the predetermined overhead application rate.

Work in Process	9,500		(a)	*Stores Ledger:*
Manufacturing Overhead				Individual Raw Materials
Control	900			Cards (Cr.) 10,400
Raw Materials Inventory		10,400		
Issued materials from stores.			(b)	*Job Cost Ledger:*
				Individual Job Cost
				Sheets (Dr.) 9,500
			(c)	*Manufacturing Overhead Ledger:*
				Indirect Materials Used
				Account (Dr.) 900

(3) *Materials Returned to Stores*   Materials costing $600, assigned to Job 123, were not needed and were returned to stores.

Raw Materials Inventory	600	(a)	*Stores Ledger:*
Work in Process	600		Individual Raw Materials
Surplus materials returned to stores.			Cards (Dr.) 600
		(b)	*Job Cost Ledger:*
			Job Cost Sheet—Job 123 (Cr.) . 600

(4) *Wages and Salaries Accrued*   Direct labor cost during December was $14,100, and indirect labor cost was $3,900. FICA taxes at 5.85 percent and federal income taxes of $3,097 were withheld from employee wages.

Payroll Control	18,000	
Wages Payable		13,850
Income Tax Withheld		3,097
FICA Taxes Payable		1,053
December payroll liability.		

(5) *Wages and Salaries Paid*   Checks totaling $12,750 were issued in payment of wages and salaries due all employees. Accrued wages payable were $300 on December 1 and $1,400 on December 31.

Wages Payable	12,750	
Cash		12,750
Paid December payroll		
($13,850 + $300 − $1,400).		

(6) *Employer's Payroll Taxes*   Karter Company matches the amounts of FICA taxes deducted from workers' paychecks. It must also pay an amount equal to 3.1 percent of the gross payroll as unemployment insurance. This includes state unemployment compensation tax of 2.7 percent and federal unemployment compensation tax of 0.4 percent. These taxes are considered part of the cost of employing labor, but for convenience they are classified as overhead costs.

Manufacturing Overhead			*Manufacturing Overhead Ledger:*
Control	1,611		Payroll Tax Control (Dr.) 1,611
FICA Taxes Payable		1,053	
State Unemployment			
Taxes Payable		486	
Federeral Unemployment			
Taxes Payable		72	
Employer's payroll tax liability.			

(7) *Payroll Costs Distributed to Jobs*   On December 31, payroll costs for direct and indirect labor are distributed to jobs and to the Manufacturing Overhead Control account.

Distributed to:	Job 120	$ 2,200
	Job 121	3,100
	Job 122	5,600
	Job 123	3,200
Direct Cost to Jobs............................		$14,100
Indirect Payroll Cost, to Manufacturing Overhead....		3,900
Total Payroll Cost		$18,000

Work in Process	14,100		(a)	Job Cost Ledger:	
Manufacturing Overhead				Individual Job Cost	
Control	3,900			Sheets (Dr.)	14,100
Payroll Control		18,000			
December payroll cost distributed to			(b)	Manufacturing Overhead Ledger:	
jobs and to manufacturing overhead.				Indirect Labor (Dr.)	3,900

(8) *Manufacturing Overhead Costs Incurred*   Invoices received in December for manufacturing overhead items totaled $5,600. This amount included power and heating costs, repairs, janitorial supplies, security service fees, factory insurance, and property taxes. During December, $4,000 of these costs were paid.

Manufacturing Overhead			Manufacturing Overhead Ledger:	
Control	5,600		Various Overhead: Accounts (Dr.) .	5,600
Cash		4,000		
Accounts Payable		1,600		
Incurred manufacturing overhead costs.				

(9) *Fixed Overhead Costs Accrued*   On December 31, an entry was made to record depreciation on buildings and factory equipment.

Manufacturing Overhead			Manufacturing Overhead Ledger:	
Control	1,160		Depreciation—Factory	
Accumulated			Equipment (Dr.)	160
Depreciation—			Depreciation—Building (Dr.)	1,000
Factory Equipment		160		
Accumulated Depreci-				
ation—Buildings		1,000		
Depreciation for December.				

(10) *Manufacturing Overhead Costs Applied*   Manufacturing overhead cost is applied to jobs in proportion to the number of direct labor hours incurred on each job. The predetermined rate is $4 of overhead applied for every direct labor hour worked. The number of hours worked on each job during December and the overhead cost applied to each job were as follows:

Job Number	Direct Labor Hours	Overhead Applied
	440	$ 1,760
121	620	2,480
122	1,120	4,480
123	640	2,560
	2,820	$11,280

Work in Process	11,280		(a) *Job Cost Ledger:*
Manufacturing Over-			Individual Job Cost
head Control		11,280	Sheets (Dr.) 11,280
Manufacturing overhead cost			
applied to jobs			(b) *Manufacturing Overhead Ledger:*
			Overhead Summary
			Account (Cr.) 11,280

(11) *Jobs Completed*   Jobs 120 and 121 were finished during December. (The detailed job cost sheet for Job 121 is shown in Figure 4–6.) A summary of their job cost sheets showed these accumulated costs.

	Job 120	**Job 121**	**Total**
Materials	$ 2,850	$ 2,850	$ 5,700
Labor	5,200	5,600	10,800
Overhead	4,160	4,480	8,640
	$12,210	$12,930	$25,140

The following entry was made to transfer the costs of jobs completed in December from Work in Process to Finished Goods.

Finished Goods			(a) *Job Cost Ledger:*
Inventory	25,140		Individual Job Cost
Work in Process		25,140	Sheets (Cr.) 25,140
Completed Jobs 120 and 121.			
			(b) *Finished Goods Ledger:*
			Inventory Cards (Dr.) 25,140

(12) *Sales*   Job 120 was sold during December for $17,500. The customer had previously paid a deposit of $7,500.

Accounts Receivable	10,000		(a) *Accounts Receivable Ledger:*
Customer Deposits	7,500		Customer's Account (Dr.) ... 10,000
Sales		17,500	
Sold Job 120.			
			(b) *Finished Goods Ledger:*
Cost of Goods Sold	12,210		Inventory Card (Cr.) 12,210
Finished Goods			
Inventory		12,210	
Costs of Job 120 removed			
from inventory.			

FIGURE 4–6

Karter Kustom Body Company
Job Cost Sheet—Job 121

Job 121   **Item:** Custom Camper Model 87Q
Customer: Fenwick Motors
                  134 Main St.
                  Centerville, Ca.
Start Date: November 10   **Estimated Cost:** $12,500
Delivery Date: January 4   **Contract Price:** $17,500

Materials Requisitions:		**Labor Costs:**	
Nov. Sundry Items	$1,600	Nov. 500 Hours @ $5	$2,500
Dec. Sundry Items	1,250	Dec. 620 Hours @ $5	3,100
	$2,850		$5,600

Manufacturing Overhead Applied:		**Cost Summary:**	
Nov. 500 Hours @ $4	$2,000	Materials	$ 2,850
Dec. 620 Hours @ $4	2,480	Labor	5,600
	$4,480	Manufacturing Overhead	4,480
			$12,930

---

(13) *Disposition of Underapplied Overhead Cost*   Actual manufacturing overhead costs of $125,646 were incurred during the year. At year end, all individual accounts in the subsidiary Manufacturing Overhead Ledger are closed to the Overhead Summary account, which then has the same balance as the Manufacturing Overhead Control account in the general ledger.

On December 1, the Manufacturing Overhead Control account had a debit balance of $2,655. December transactions affected this account as follows:

Manufacturing Overhead Control

Dec.	1	Balance	2,655	Dec. 31	Overhead Applied	
	31	Indirect Materials	900		to Work in Process	11,280
	31	Indirect Labor	3,900			
	31	Payroll Taxes	1,611			
	31	Sundry Overhead	5,600			
	31	Depreciation	1,160			
			15,826			11,280

The ending balance in the Manufacturing Overhead Control account of $4,546 ($15,826 − $11,280) is the total underapplied overhead cost for the year. Karter Company's policy is to transfer such balances directly to Cost of Goods Sold at year end.

Cost of Goods Sold 4,546	Manufacturing Overhead Ledger:
Manufacturing Over-	Overhead Summary
head Control 4,546	Account 125,646
Disposed of underapplied	Various Overhead
overhead.	Accounts 125,646
	Overhead Summary
	Account (Cr.) 4,546

The following partial listing of general ledger accounts includes only those directly involved in the preceding analysis:

Raw Materials Inventory

Dec.	1	Balance	6,500	Dec. 31	Issued to Jobs	10,400
	31	Purchases	18,000			
	31	Returns	600			

Work in Process

Dec.	1	Balance	18,850	Dec. 30	Materials Returned	500
	31	Materials Issued to Jobs	9,500	31	Finished Goods	25,140
	31	Labor Costs	14,100			
	31	Overhead Applied	11,280			

Finished Goods Inventory

| Dec. 31 | Completions, from | | Dec 31 | Cost of Goods Sold | 12,210 |
| | Work in Process | 25,140 | | | |

Cost of Goods Sold

Dec.	1	Balance	241,450
	31	Sales	12,210
	31	Overhead Adjustment	4,546

Manufacturing Overhead Control

Dec.	1	Balance	2,655	Dec. 31	Work in Process	11,280
	31	Various	13,171	31	Cost of Goods Sold	4,546
			15,826			15,826

Sales

| | Dec. | 1 | Balance | 325,750 |
| | | 31 | December Sales | 17,500 |

FIGURE 4–7

Karter Kustom Body Company
Manufacturing Statement
For the Year Ended December 31, 19X7

	Eleven Months Ended November 30	Month of December	Year of 19X7
Beginning Work in Process	$ 11,245	$18,850	$ 11,245
Add: Direct Materials Used	72,500	8,900	81,400
Direct Labor Cost	78,385	14,100	92,485
Applied Manufacturing Overhead	60,100	11,280	71,380
	$222,230	$53,130	$256,510
Less: Ending Work in Process	18,850	27,990	27,990
Cost of Goods Manufactured	$203,380	$25,140	$228,520

FIGURE 4–8

Karter Kustom Body Company
Income Statement
For the Year Ended December 31, 19X7

	Eleven Months Ended November 30	Month of December	Year of 19X7
Sales	$325,750	$17,500	$343,250
Less: Cost of Goods Sold	241,450	12,210	253,660
Unadjusted Gross Profit	$ 84,300	$ 5,290	$ 89,590
Less: Underapplied Overhead	2,655	1,891	4,546
Adjusted Gross Profit	$ 81,645	$ 3,399	$ 85,044
Less Operating Expenses	57,945	5,149	63,094
Net Profit from Operations	$ 23,700	$(1,750)	$ 21,950

SUMMARY

1. Manufacturers use two systems for accumulating the materials, labor, and overhead costs of production and attaching those costs to units of output.
2. Job order costing traces costs to individual units of output that are physically segregated during production.
3. Process costing is appropriate for manufacturing situations in which units of output are interchangable.
4. This chapter describes accounting methods that permit accumulation of costs by individual jobs.

5. Direct materials and direct labor costs are traced to jobs by means of materials requisition forms and time tickets.
6. Manufacturing overhead costs are applied to jobs on the basis of predetermined application rates.
7. Underapplied or overapplied overhead costs may be (1) prorated among the inventory and Cost of Goods Sold accounts, (2) closed out to Cost of Goods Sold, or (3) carried forward to the next accounting period.
8. Job cost measures are useful for inventory measurement and periodic income determination; they provide a basis for cost control, product pricing, cost estimating, and bidding on prospective jobs.

KEY WORDS AND PHRASES

Job Order Cost System (115)
Process Cost System (116)
Composite Process Cost System (116)
Direct Materials (117)
Job Cost Sheet (118)
Materials Requisition Form (119)
Labor Time Ticket (119)
Stores Ledger (119)
Materials Credit Slip (120)
Indirect Materials (121)
Direct Labor Cost (122)
Indirect Labor Cost (122)
Labor Cost Summary (122)
Direct Overhead Cost (124)
Indirect Overhead Cost (125)
Overhead Application (125)
Manufacturing Overhead Control Account (125)
Underapplied or Overapplied Overhead Cost (127)

Questions

1. Identify the two major product costing systems.
2. Under what circumstances would a job order costing system be more useful than a process costing system?
3. List *six* types of businesses that should use a job order costing system.
4. Why is the *average cost concept* more relevant to process cost systems than to job order cost systems?
5. "A company can use only one method of costing its products—the job order method or the process method." Do you agree? Why or why not?
6. What special problems arise in applying job order costing to a firm that produces a service rather than a physical commodity?
7. What are the major steps in the flow of job order costs?
8. "All materials that become physically attached to the final product are a part of direct materials cost." Evaluate this statement.
9. Which inventory costing method of measuring the cost of materials used on a job is (a) most correct conceptually and (b) most practically convenient? Why?
10. Explain the differences and similarities that exist between accounting for subcontracts and accounting for direct and indirect materials.
11. What source documentation is needed to allow the measurement of the direct labor costs of a job?
12. "All of the 36 hours that each factory employee works each week should be costed to specific jobs." Do you agree? Why or why not?
14. List five different activity indexes that may be used to set overhead application rates.
15. Why should accounts be maintained for each separate overhead item (repairs, power, property tax, and so on) while at the same time a Manufacturing Overhead Control account is being used?
16. At the end of January, the Manufacturing Overhead Control account had a *credit* balance of $4,250. Has too much or too little overhead cost been assigned to jobs in January? Discuss all the possible reasons for this credit balance.
17. Under what conditions would *departmental* overhead application rates be appropriate in a job order cost system?
18. How should nonmanufacturing costs (such as delivery expenses, advertising, office salaries, and sales commissions) be treated in a job order cost system?
19. What basic techniques can be incorporated into a job order cost system to facilitate cost control?
20. What are the major uses of job cost information?
21. How does the treatment of manufacturing overhead cost affect the periodic measurement of income in a job order cost system?
22. "Bidding on a job that is dissimilar to any job previously produced requires a complete understanding of the likely behavior of all overhead items." Comment on this statement.

23. "Calculating the cost of each order in a job lot printing shop is not at all useful for control purposes." Do you agree? Why or why not?

Exercises

E 4–1   Calculation of Job Costs—Job Cost Sheet

Acme Building Corporation uses a job order cost system for each construction project it undertakes. Cost and operating data for Project 5277 are as follows:

(1) Materials Requisitioned for Use $39,600
(2) Excess Materials Returned $ 1,200
(3) Direct Labor Costs:

April 3	650 hours	$ 5,300
April 10	1040 hours	9,250
April 17	710 hours	6,550
April 24	400 hours	3,700
	2800 hours	$24,800

(4) Other Direct Costs:

Equipment Rentals	$ 4,500
Subcontracts	12,700
	$17,200

(5) Manufacturing Overhead: Applied at the rate of $5 per direct labor hour.
(6) Sales Price of Project 5277—$140,000.
(7) Estimated Selling, Administrative, and General Expenses—10 percent of Sales Price.

Required:
(a) Prepare a job cost sheet showing the total job cost of Project 5277.
(b) Prepare an income statement showing the profit or loss attributable to Project 5277.

E 4–2   Job Cost Calculation—Bid Price Selection

Mark Sharkz Pool Company is considering a customer's request for a customized swimming pool. Analysis of the requirements of the job show the following:

(1) Construction materials $4,300
(2) Excavation (to be handled by subcontractor) $1,800
(3) Construction labor:
       200 hours @ $15
       100 hours @ $10
(4) Overhead costs are estimated to be $5 per labor hour.
(5) The company's practice is to prepare bids based on materials and subcontracts cost plus 50 percent, and labor and overhead costs plus 100 percent.

Required:
Prepare a job cost sheet estimate and calculate the bid price.

E 4–3 Job Order Cost System—Journal Entries

The following summary data relate to HRN Corporation for the month of April, 19X7:

(1)	Raw materials purchased	$200,000
(2)	Raw materials issued to jobs in process	180,000
(3)	Total factory payroll accrued for month	120,000
(4)	Payroll analysis:	
	Direct Labor (8,000 hours)	80,000
	Indirect Labor	15,000
	Supervision	25,000
(5)	Other manufacturing overhead incurred (excluding labor)	67,500
(6)	The overhead application rate is $12 per direct labor hour.	
(7)	Total cost of jobs completed during the month	320,000
(8)	All completed jobs were shipped to customers at cost plus 50%.	

Required:

(a) Prepare general journal entries to record these summary transactions.

(b) If the balance in Work in Process on April 1 was $15,000, what would the April 30 Work in Process balance be?

E 4–4 Flow of Costs in a Job Order Cost System Documentation—Basic Interrelationships in an Accounting System

The following chart represents the general ledger accounts of Terrace Building Company as they relate to manufacturing transactions.

Required:

(a) Explain each of the separate flows of cost items represented by the arrows A, B, C, D, E, F, G.

(b) Describe the documentation necessary to authorize and evidence items A, B, C, and D.

(c) How is the flow labeled E measured?

(d) Which of the accounts in this system will normally have end-of-period balances? Describe what each account balance represents.

(e) Classify all of the accounts in this system according to the following groups:

    (1) Asset accounts

    (2) Expense accounts

    (3) Clearing or control accounts

E 4–5 Job Order Costs—Departmental Overhead Application Rates

Lucerne Machinery Overhaul Company uses departmental manufacturing overhead application rates. In Department 1, rates are based on labor hours and in Department 2 they are based on machine hours. The following estimates were obtained for 19X7:

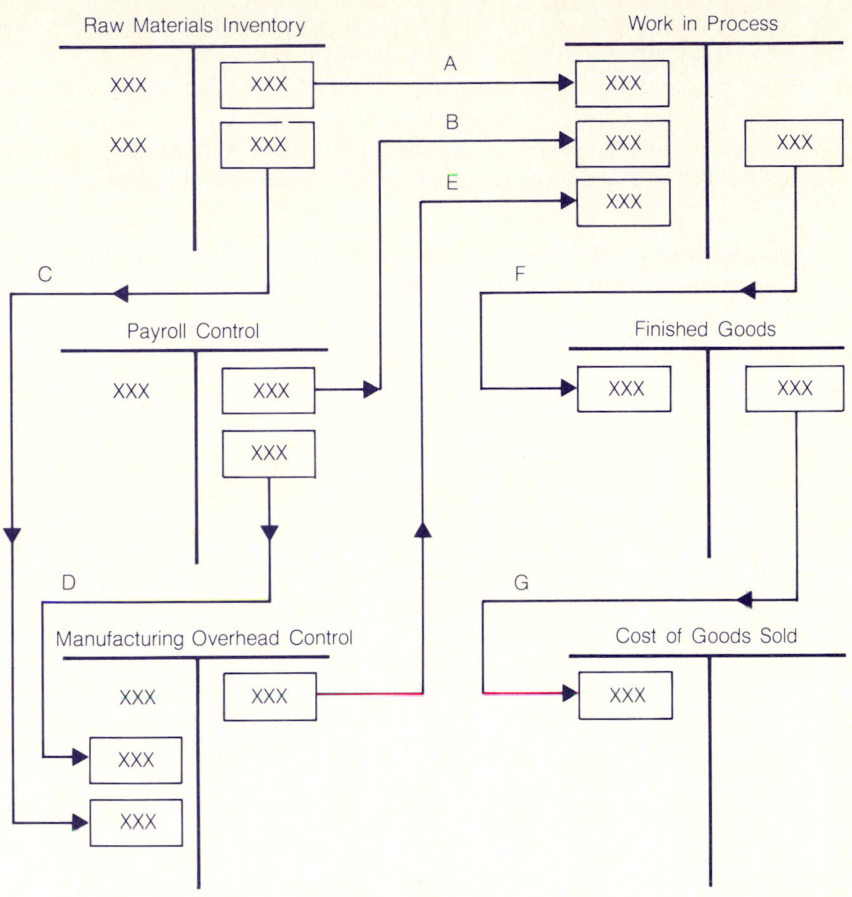

	Dept. 1	Dept. 2	Total
Manufacturing Overhead	$160,000	$240,000	$400,000
Direct Labor Hours	40,000	10,000	50,000
Machine Hours	40,000	120,000	160,000

The job cost sheet for order P807 included the following details:

	Dept. 1	Dept. 2	Total
Materials Used	$ 600	$3,000	$3,600
Direct Labor Cost	$1,000	$ 250	$1,250
Direct Labor Hours	200	50	250
Machine Hours	260	500	760

Required:
(a) Calculate the total cost of job P807, using the departmental labor hours and machine hours application rates.

(b) Recompute the total cost of job P807, using (1) a plant-wide labor hour application rate and (2) a plant-wide machine hour application rate.

(c) Comment on the differences between the answers in part (b) and the answer in part (a).

(d) If the company bases its bid prices for jobs on a cost-plus formula, what recommendations would you make regarding the choice of an overhead basis?

E 4–6   Disposition of Underapplied or Overapplied Manufacturing Overhead in Job Order Cost Systems

Rinder Construction Company uses a job order cost system. Manufacturing overhead is applied to all production activities at the rate of $7 per direct labor hour based on predetermined annual estimates. The following information was available for the year ended December 31, 19X8:

Direct Materials Usage	$2,500,000
Direct Labor	3,000,000
Indirect Labor and Supervision	60,000
Rent—Factory Premises	600,000
Indirect Materials Usage	80,000
Other Manufacturing Overheads	400,000
Direct Labor Hours Worked	160,000

There were no work in process inventories or finished job inventories at either the beginning or end of the year.

Required:

(a) What was the total manufacturing overhead *incurred* for the year?

(b) How much manufacturing overhead was *applied* to jobs completed during the year?

(c) Was manufacturing overhead underapplied or overapplied during the year?

(d) How much would the Cost of Goods Sold be for the year, based on the applied overhead?

(e) What disposition of the underapplied or overapplied overhead would be feasible in this case?

Cases

C 4–1   Job Order Production Lots

Coyote Dress Company schedules its production in lots by dress style. Approximately 25 different styles of dresses are usually in current production. Because production is organized this way, the controller has decided to use a job order cost system. Discuss the advantages and disadvantages of such a system.

C 4–2   Overhead Allocation Bases

"What differences does it make whether one allocation basis or another is used to assign overhead to jobs? In the long run, all overheads are charged into Cost of Goods Sold anyway." Comment on this statement.

C 4–3   Job Order Cost and Pricing Strategies

The Vogue Fashion Company has developed a revolutionary new garment. It is intended to be marketed in two phases:

(1) Produce a small number, advertise extensively, and set a high market price to capture a high profit return before the product can be imitated by competitors.
(2) Then produce the product at high volume and cut the price to dominate the market. Would a job order cost system be useful in either phase (1), phase (2), or both? Why or why not?

C 4–4   Allocating Costs of Reprocessing

Anita Machine Tool Company uses highly specialized equipment in manufacturing custom designed tools, dies, and jigs. An analysis reveals that Job 6437 incurred a significant loss. While that job was processed, one machine developed a problem that required the job to be reprocessed several times, overtime to be incurred, and additional materials and factory supplies to be consumed. All of these cost items were charged directly to Job 6437. The machine was not repaired completely until Job 6437 was completed.

Do you agree with the accounting methods employed? Why or why not? How would you modify them?

C 4–5   Departmentalized Job Order Costing

Gray Manufacturing Corporation produces items to customer specifications. At the end of each month there is usually a large volume of production in process, but all such items can be identified with the sales orders of particular customers.

All manufacturing, sales, and administrative functions have been departmentalized. A job order cost system is used. This system has the following features:

(1) Materials requisition forms and daily time cards are used to record direct materials and direct labor associated with jobs in process.
(2) All overhead costs are first traced to factory service, selling, and administrative departments.
(3) The costs in feature (2) are then reallocated to all productive factory departments and, in turn, are charged to jobs passing through each department using a departmental, labor hour based application rate. This rate is computed every month on the basis of actual hours worked and total costs incurred.

Each month, therefore, all costs of the firm are charged to jobs in process during that month.

Required:
(a) Critically evaluate this costing system.
(b) How does it affect monthly inventory valuation and income measurement?
(c) Are there any circumstances that would justify the use of such a system?
(d) Suggest an alternative system that remedies any defects mentioned in your answers to parts (a) and (b).

C 4–6   Overhead Cost Allocations

Sommers Manufacturing Company has three production departments, W, X, and Y. Most customer orders are processed through all three departments, but the amount of processing in the separate departments varies from order to order. During a typical 12 month period, the following cost and operating data were collected:

	Dept. W	Dept. X	Dept. Y	Total
Materials Used	$180,000	$240,000	$300,000	$ 720,000
Direct Labor	160,000	80,000	120,000	360,000
Actual Overhead	80,000	160,000	120,000	360,000
	$420,000	$480,000	$540,000	$1,440,000

For purposes of analysis, the Job Cost Sheet for Job 7474 was examined. It showed the following information:

Job 7474	Dept. W	Dept. X	Dept. Y	Total
Materials	$1,000	$1,500	$1,500	$4,000
Labor	480	1,120	800	2,400
Overhead				2,400
				$8,800

Required:
(a) What overhead application rate is apparently being used? Show supporting calculations.
(b) If direct labor cost is in fact the appropriate basis for allocating factory overhead, is there anything wrong with the particular method being used?
(c) Revise the costing of Job 7474, using a more appropriate overhead allocation procedure.
(d) What incorrect decisions might management make if it continued to use the original overhead application procedure? Why?

C 4–7   Cost of Goods Sold Statement

For the year ended December 31, 19X7, the accountant for Johnstone Corporation prepared the following statement of cost of goods sold:

Johnstone Corporation
Cost of Goods Sold
Year Ended December 31, 19X7

Materials		$126,000
Direct Labor		360,000
Manufacturing Overhead Costs		240,000
		$726,000
Less: Jobs in Process, December 31, 19X7:		
Materials	$12,000	
Direct Labor	27,000	
Manufacturing Overhead Costs	18,000	
		57,000
Cost of Goods Sold		$669,000

The president of the corporation requests clarification of some of the terminology used and the basis for some of the calculations included in the above statement. The following additional information is available:

(1) There were no jobs in process on January 1, 19X7.

(2) Manufacturing activities take place in two departments: (a) Cutting and Grinding, and (b) Assembling.

(3) The Cutting and Grinding Department has several machines and operators supervise more than one machine. Customer orders are quite likely to require widely varying amounts of machine time. The Assembly Department is entirely a series of manual operations.

(4) Labor rates were $16 per hour in the Cutting and Grinding, and $8 per hour in Assembly.

(5) Jobs in process at December 31, 19X7 had the following entries in the job cost record:

	Cutting and Grinding	Assembly	Total
Materials	$12,000	0	$12,000
Direct Labor Hours	1,500	375	1,875
Machine Hours	4,000	0	4,000

(6) Cost data for the year 19X7 included:

	Cutting and Grinding	Assembly	Total
Materials	$126,000	$ 0	$126,000
Direct Labor	120,000	240,000	360,000
Indirect Materials	6,000	300	6,300
Indirect Labor	30,000	15,000	45,000
Depreciation	30,000	3,000	33,000
Other Overhead Costs	114,000	41,700	155,700
	$426,000	$300,000	$726,000
Labor Hours	7,500	30,000	37,500
Machine Hours	60,000	0	60,000

Required:
(a) Criticize the cost of goods sold statement as originally prepared.
(b) Prepare a revised statement to remedy the shortcomings identified in part (a).

Problems

P 4–1 Job Cost Calculation—Unit Costs
Price Determination Based on Cost

Osgood's Custom Crafts builds customized recreational vehicles. Currently its three most popular models are the Hairy Hustler, the Diamond Duster, and the Rocky Rover. Operating and total cost data for these models for a typical month are as follows:

	Hairy Hustler	Diamond Duster	Rocky Rover
Materials			
Chassis, Engine, and Transmission	$45,000	$36,000	$54,000
Other Components	$25,000	$24,000	$26,400
Direct Labor Cost	$12,500	$ 9,400	$10,800
Direct Labor Hours	1,000	720	960
Units Produced	10	8	12

Manufacturing overhead cost for the year was estimated to total $150,000, and total direct labor hours for the year were estimated to be 30,000. Overhead is applied to jobs on a direct labor hour basis.

Required:
(a) What was the total cost of all jobs produced this month?
(b) What was the unit cost of each of the three models?
(c) If sales prices are set at an amount equal to manufacturing cost plus 80 percent, at what price would each model be sold?

P 4–2 Job Cost Sheets—Job Order Cost Calculation

During the month of May, Cauthen Manufacturing Company had two projects under construction, Job 247 and Job 248. The following transaction data are available:

(1) Purchased construction materials for $10,000.
(2) Requisitions of materials were $3,500 for Job 247 and $5,900 for Job 248.
(3) Factory payroll for the month of May was $8,000, of which $3,500 was directly allocated to Job 247, and $3,000 to Job 248. The remainder represented general factory supervision.
(4) Materials returned to inventory from Job 248 amounted to $250.
(5) Miscellaneous construction supplies purchased and used amounted to $300. These were not specifically traced to either of the two jobs.
(6) Subcontractors performed services on Job 247 at a cost of $750.
(7) Various overhead costs, including power, maintenance, and insurance, amounted to $3,400 during the month.

(8) Depreciation on factory buildings and equipment for the month was $600.

(9) Overhead is charged to jobs at the rate of 100 percent of direct labor cost.

(10) Job 247 was completed and delivered to the customer, but Job 248 was still in progress at the end of the month.

Required:

(a) Prepare job cost sheets for Job 247 and Job 248.

(b) Assuming that no other jobs were in process, and that no other materials were on hand at the start of the month, what would be the end of the month balances in:

   (1) Raw Materials Inventory account?

   (2) Work in Process account?

   (3) Cost of Goods Sold account?

(c) What source documents would support each entry made on the job cost sheets?

P 4–3   Job Order Cost System—Journal Entries

SEG Corporation uses a job order cost system for its manufacturing activities. During the month of June, 19X7, the following transaction data were assembled:

(1) Jobs in Process, June 1:

Job 473	$ 2,000
Job 474	6,000
	$ 8,000

(2) Raw Materials Purchased $72,000

(3) Raw Materials and Supplies requisitioned from inventory:

Job 473	$10,000
Job 474	22,000
Job 475	24,000
General Factory Usage	4,000
	$60,000

(4) Total Factory Payroll:

Direct Labor	$62,000
Indirect Labor	6,000
	$68,000

(5) Depreciation on factory equipment and machinery for June, $6,000.

(6) Other overhead costs incurred included repairs, insurance, and power, $34,000.

(7) Manufacturing overhead is applied to jobs at the rate of 100 percent of direct labor cost.

(8) During the month, Job 473 and Job 474 were completed.

(9) Job 473 was delivered and billed to the customer for $90,000.

(10) Job 474 will be delivered and billed in July.

Required:

(a) Prepare general journal entries for these transactions.

(b) Calculate the balance in Work in Process on June 30, 19X7.

P 4–4 Flow of Costs in Job Order Cost System—General Ledger Relationships

Pedro & Pablo Constructions, Inc. uses a job order cost system. The company's trial balance prepared at the end of December, 19X7 included the following accounts:

	Total Debit Entries	Total Credit Entries
Raw Materials Inventory	$200,000	$180,000
Work in Process	660,000	640,000
Factory Payroll Control	200,000	200,000
Manufacturing Overhead Control	315,000	300,000
Finished Goods Inventory	640,000	630,000
Cost of Goods Sold	630,000	0

The totals in the preceding schedule included the following items:

(1) January 1, 19X7 balances:
  Raw Materials $15,000
  Work in Process   30,000
  Finished Goods   0

(2) Factory payroll included 75 percent direct labor, 15 percent indirect labor, and 10 percent supervision.

(3) Overhead was applied to jobs on the basis of direct labor cost.

(4) There were no returns of merchandise to suppliers and no excess materials requisitions.

Required:

(a) Using T-accounts for each of the six accounts listed above, reconstruct all entries that occurred during the year.

(b) Key each entry and give a brief explanation of each.

(c) List the balances of each account and explain its relationship to the preparation of 19X7 financial statements.

P 4–5 Flow of Costs in a Job Order Cost System—Analysis of General Ledger Relationships

The following information was obtained from the general ledger of Burnaby Builders, Inc., for the year ended December 31, 19X6. Entries (A) through (Q) are those that would be normally found in these accounts.

Raw Materials					Jobs In Process			
1/1/X6 Bal.	10,000	(B)	85,000	1/1/X6 Bal.	10,000	(G)		XXX
(A)	XXX	(C)	5,000	(D)	85,000			
				(E)	XXX			
				(F)	120,000			

Cost of Goods Sold			Manufacturing Overhead Control			
(H)	XXX		(I)	XXX	(L)	XXX
			(J)	10,000		
			(K)	XXX		

Payroll Control				Finished Goods			
(M)	90,000	(N)	XXX	1/1/X6 Bal.	10,000	(Q)	XXX
		(O)	10,000	(P)	XXX		

Additional Information:

Ending balances in the accounts were as follows:

Raw Materials	$ 5,000
Jobs in Process	25,000
Manufacturing Overhead Control	5,000 (Cr.)
Payroll Control	0
Finished Goods	20,000

Manufacturing overhead is applied to jobs in proportion to direct labor cost.

Required:

(a) What was the amount of raw materials purchases for 19X6?

(b) How much materials costs were charged directly to jobs and how much was treated as factory supplies?

(c) What was the total amount of direct labor costs charged to jobs?

(d) What other factory labor costs were accounted for besides those in part (c)?

(e) What was the total of manufacturing overhead *incurred* during the year?

(f) How much manufacturing overhead was *applied* to jobs during the year?

(g) What was the overhead application rate?

(h) The cost of jobs in process on December 31, 19X6 included materials of $5,000. What were the labor and overhead amounts involved?

(i) Finished Goods on December 31, 19X6 included labor cost of $5,000. What were the materials and overhead amounts?

(j) Was manufacturing overhead overapplied or underapplied during the year?

(k) What was the total cost of jobs *completed* during 19X6?

(l) What was the total cost of jobs *sold* during 19X6?

P 4–6 Job Order Costs—Departmental versus Plant-wide Overhead Application

Schaefer Corporation produces specialty packaging machines, which pass through three manufacturing departments. During 19X9, the estimated activity levels and manufacturing overheads for these departments were as follows:

	Dept. A	Dept. B	Dept. C
Manufacturing Overhead	$300,000	$200,000	$500,000
Total Direct Labor Cost	$240,000	$200,000	$250,000
Total Machine Hours	5,000	8,000	25,000
Total Direct Labor Hours	30,000	20,000	25,000

Job 763 was completed during the year. Direct costs and other details of that job were as follows:

Materials		$5,000
Labor:		
Dept. A	100 hours	$ 800
Dept. B	50 hours	$ 500
Dept. C	250 hours	$2,500
Machine Time:		
Dept. A	0 hours	
Dept. B	10 hours	
Dept. C	250 hours	

Required:

(a) Calculate plant-wide overhead application rates based on:
   (1) Direct labor cost
   (2) Machine hours
   (3) Direct labor hours

(b) Calculate separate departmental overhead application rates based on:
   (1) Direct labor cost
   (2) Machine hours
   (3) Direct labor hours

(c) Evaluate the answers obtained in parts (a) and (b) and suggest what might be the most appropriate rate(s) to use. Support your choice with appropriate analysis.

(d) Compute the total cost of Job 763, using:
   (1) A plant-wide machine hour rate.
   (2) The rate(s) proposed in part (c).

(e) If Job 763 consisted of a batch of 100 units, compare the effects on the measurement of average unit costs of the two solutions in part (d).

P 4–7 Job Cost Calculation—Departmental Overhead Application Rates

Fidelity Furnace Repair Company repairs furnace systems. It uses a job order cost system and has until now employed a plant-wide labor hours overhead application rate. It is considering changing to departmental rates, based on an investigation of factory overhead costs which disclosed the following annual forecast data:

	Dept. X	Dept. Y	Dept. Z	Total
Manufacturing Overhead	$200,000	$160,000	$40,000	$400,000
Direct Labor Hours	40,000	20,000	4,000	64,000

Depending on the requirements of each job accepted, varying amounts of work are required in each of the three departments. Three typical jobs were selected for analysis: Job 807, Job 943, and Job 972.

Labor Hours Required

	Dept. X	Dept. Y	Dept. Z	Total
Job 807	150	150	100	400
Job 943	0	100	300	400
Job 972	300	100	0	400

Required:

(a) Calculate the amount of manufacturing overhead that would be assigned to each job under the present plant-wide rate method.

(b) Calculate the amount of manufacturing overhead that would be assigned to each job using the proposed departmental rate method.

(c) Comment on the differences between the answers in part (a) and part (b).

(d) Discuss the effect of using the departmental rate on (1) measurement of Work in Process inventories and (2) pricing decisions based on job costs.

P 4–8 Disposition of Underapplied or Overapplied Manufacturing Overhead in Job Order Cost Systems—Effects of Alternative Methods on Income Measurement

Cox Construction Company uses a job order cost system and applies manufacturing overhead costs to jobs in process on the basis of direct labor hours. The following estimates of production and cost data were made for the year 19X9:

Total Estimated Manufacturing Overhead	$480,000
Total Estimated Direct Labor Cost	$360,000
Total Estimated Direct Labor Hours	40,000 hours

There were no inventories of raw materials or jobs in process on January 1, 19X9. For the year ended December 31, 19X9, the following actual operating results and cost data were accumulated:

Manufacturing Overhead Incurred	$396,000
Direct Labor Cost	$256,000
Raw Materials Purchased	$270,000
Direct Labor Hours Worked	32,000 hours

Inventory Data on December 31, 19X9

	Raw Materials	Direct Labor	Labor Hours
Raw Materials	$ 10,000	—	—
Work in Process	20,000	$ 16,000	2,000
Finished Jobs*	240,000	240,000	30,000
	$270,000	$256,000	32,000

* All finished jobs have been delivered to customers.

Required:

(a) What was the predetermined overhead rate for 19X9?

(b) What was the total of underapplied or overapplied overhead for 19X9?

(c) What will be the cost of goods sold figure based on the predetermined overhead rate?

(d) What will be the adjusted cost of goods sold figure:
  (1) If the company writes off the full amount of overapplied or underapplied overhead against cost of goods sold?
  (2) If the company allocates underapplied or overapplied overhead on the basis of direct labor hours?
  (3) If the company allocates the underapplied or overapplied overhead on the basis of total production costs?
(e) Prepare a schedule to show the differences in reported net income under the three alternatives in part (d). Assume that sales were $1,200,000, and that all expenses other than cost of goods sold totaled $340,000.
(f) Included in the completed jobs was Job 747, which had the following cost data:

Materials	$1,000
Direct Labor	$ 800
Labor Hours	100

  (1) How would Job 747 be costed under the original predetermined overhead rate method?
  (2) How would Job 747 be recosted under the method specified in part (d)(2)?
(g) Suggest possible explanations for the total amount of underapplied or overapplied manufacturing overhead in this problem.

P 4–9 Disposition of Underapplied or Overapplied Manufacturing Overhead in Job Order Costing—Annual versus Monthly Application Rates

On June 1, 19X5, selected account balances in the records of the Tobin Engineering Company were as follows:

Raw Materials Inventory	$40,000
Job 808 in Process:	
Materials	$ 4,000
Direct Labor	2,000
Overhead	1,800
	$ 7,800
Manufacturing Overhead Control	$ 2,100 (Dr.)

During the month, Jobs 808, 809 and 810 were completed. Job 811 was still in process at the end of the month. Details of costs charged to these jobs during the month (excluding previous month costs) were as follows:

	808	809	810	811
Materials	$12,000	$20,000	$14,000	$10,000
Direct Labor	8,000	12,000	8,000	4,000
Overhead	7,200	10,800	7,200	3,600
	$27,200	$42,800	$29,200	$17,600

Other operating data included the following:

Total Direct Labor Hours	3200 hours
Manufacturing Overhead Incurred	$26,900
Raw Materials Purchased	$36,000

Required:

(a) What overhead application rate appears to be in use?

(b) Determine all inventory account balances at June 30 and cost of goods sold for June, using the predetermined rate selected in part (a).

(c) What was the amount of overhead underapplied or overapplied for the month of June?

(d) What is the unadjusted balance in the Manufacturing Overhead Control account on June 30, 19X5?

(e) The company closes its books on December 31. What disposition of the June 30 balance in the Manufacturing Overhead Control account would you recommend? Why?

(f) If the company's fiscal year ends on June 30, would your answer to part (e) be different? Why?

(g) Jobs 809 and 810 were completed entirely during the month of June. Considering that the predetermined overhead application rate was used, was too much or too little overhead applied to these jobs in relation to the manufacturing overhead incurred during June? Why?

(h) Job 808 was produced partly in May and partly in June. Should it be costed to reflect its share of the amount of overhead costs incurred only in those two months, or should it be costed on the basis of estimated average overhead costs over the whole year? Why?

P 4–10 Comprehensive Review—Journal Entries
—Job Cost Records—Cost of Goods Manufactured
Income Statement

Johnson Manufacturing Corporation uses a job order cost system. The company's trial balance as of May 1, 19X5 included the following accounts:

Raw Materials Inventory	$45,500
Jobs in Process	$25,400
Finished Jobs Inventory (Job 810)	$28,800
Manufacturing Overhead Control	$ 4,300 (Cr.)

Job order cost sheets for jobs in process on May 1 showed the following:

	Job 809	Job 811
Materials	$ 2,500	$ 6,700
Labor	4,000	3,200
Overhead	5,000	4,000
	$11,500	$13,900

Transactions for the month of May, 19X5 were as follows:

(1) Raw materials purchased $136,000
(2) Total factory payroll $180,000
(3) Manufacturing overhead incurred and accrued:

Power and Heat	$ 35,500
Repairs	24,000
Other Manufacturing Overhead	39,000
Depreciation—Plant	60,000
	$158,500

(4) Materials requisitioned for use:

Job 809	$ 14,000
Job 811	32,000
Job 812	34,000
Job 813	33,500
Factory Supplies	15,500
	$129,000

(5) Payroll analysis—direct labor:

	Hours	Amount
Job 809	8,000	$ 64,000
Job 811	4,000	32,000
Job 812	4,500	36,000
Job 813	3,000	24,000
Indirect Factory Labor	500	4,000
Supervision	0	20,000
	20,000 hours	$180,000

(6) Overhead is applied to jobs in process at a predetermined rate of $10 per direct labor hour.

(7) Jobs 809, 811, and 812 were completed during the month.

(8) Jobs 809, 810, and 811 were sold to customers during the month. The prices of these jobs were $225,000, $37,500, and $150,000, respectively.

(9) Total operating expenses (selling, distribution, general, and administrative) were $74,500 for the month.

Required:
(a) Prepare general journal entries to record these transactions.
(b) Prepare job order cost sheets for all jobs worked on during the month.
(c) Prepare a cost of goods manufactured statement for the month of May.
(d) Prepare an income statement for the month of May.
(e) Prepare a schedule of inventory balances on May 31, 19X5.
(f) What is the balance in the Manufacturing Overhead Control account on May 31, 19X5? How should it be reported in the May 31 financial statements?

5

PROCESS COST SYSTEMS

LEARNING OBJECTIVES

After studying Chapter 5, you should be able to:

1. Identify the types of production situations in which process costing is appropriate.
2. Describe four significant uses of process cost information.
3. Explain the concept of equivalent units of output.
4. Calculate equivalent units of output processed for the weighted average cost method and equivalent units of output produced for the FIFO cost method.
5. Prepare journal entries to record the incurrence of materials, labor, and overhead costs, and to allocate them to work in process.
6. Calculate the cost of equivalent units of output by both the weighted average cost method and the FIFO cost method.
7. Calculate the cost of units completed and transferred to the next processing department or to Finished Goods Inventory.
8. Calculate the cost of ending Work in Process inventories.
9. Make the journal entry to transfer cost of completed units from one processing department to the next, and to Finished Goods Inventory.
10. Describe the contents and use of a production cost report.
11. Contrast and evaluate process cost data derived using the full absorption cost model and the variable cost model.
12. Explain the advantages and disadvantages of using weighted average costs and FIFO costs in process cost calculations.

Mass production does not permit or require cost measurements of individual output units. It is either too expensive or simply not feasible to measure the cost of producing each loaf of bread, hairpin, ballpoint pen, gallon of paint, or bag of fertilizer. These are outputs of continuous or process-oriented manufacturing operations.

In contrast to job order costing, for which it is possible to measure the cost of an identifiable item or group of items, product costs in a **process costing system** must be average rather than unique measures. The cost of a finished unit is determined by dividing the total manufacturing costs incurred by the number of units completed.

Process costing is appropriate when there exists:

1. *Homogeneity of outputs*—each unit of output is produced in the same way.
2. *Continuity of production*—output occurs in a fairly continuous flow, making it difficult to trace particular units as they move through each stage of production.
3. *Production in anticipation of sale*—units of output usually cannot be identified with any particular customer or sales order.
4. *Manufacturing operations divided into separate processes or departments*— costs of segments of the total production effort can be measured.

USES OF PROCESS COST INFORMATION

Unit process costs are primarily useful for inventory measurement and periodic income determination. If interpreted correctly, they may also be helpful in pricing products and controlling operations.

Both job order and process cost systems are designed to accumulate materials, labor, and overhead costs during each accounting period. These cost measures are then attached to physical quantities of output as they move from partly finished items (Work in Process) to fully completed units (Finished Goods Inventory), and finally to Cost of Goods Sold. Assigning the cost of each manufacturing process to the inventory items passing through that process is a necessary first step in asset valuation and income measurement.

Process costing provides unit cost measures that are helpful in establishing selling prices. Unit product costs are especially important when a firm has significant control over the market prices of its products and uses "cost-plus" or some other type of cost-based product pricing. In more competitive market situations, in which individual firms are less able to influence prices, product cost information is needed to assess whether or not products can be sold profitably at prevailing market prices.

The unit costs of production processes are also valuable control devices. Each process takes place within a decision center in which authority–responsibility relationships are defined and exercised. Measuring the unit costs of process outputs provides a basis for performance evaluation, particularly if all the components of process costs are controllable within the decision center.

Basic control and evaluation techniques that can be used with process cost measures include:

1. Comparison of unit process costs and their materials, labor, and overhead components from period to period.
2. Comparison of actual unit costs with budgeted or planned costs.
3. Use of unit cost information in departmental incentive plans.
4. Use of unit process costs as part of a formal standard cost system.

WHAT IS A PROCESS?

The term **process** applies to production departments that mass produce uniform outputs, either of finished products or their components. Process costing techniques can also be applied to service departments, if the services they provide for the company's other departments are sufficiently uniform (for example, electricity generated by a power plant).

A manufacturing company could treat its entire production activity as a single process, but doing so would restrict the detailed cost information that would otherwise be available. For product costing purposes, subgroups of production activities should be identified and treated as processes if they possess common characteristics. Processes may be defined on the basis of:

1. *Geographic location*—Pittsburgh plant, Los Angeles assembly division, building A.
2. *Functional specialization*—foundry, machine shop, paint shop, wiring department.

Other processes often can be identified within these two major categories, especially when a firm's manufacturing departments have significantly different physical outputs and/or cost structures. A machining department may work simultaneously on several different but standard products, each of which must be costed as a separate process output. The same may be true of successive steps in an assembly operation if they require widely varying amounts of labor or equipment use. The spraying, baking, and drying sections of a paint shop, for example, might be treated as separate processes.

This chapter describes the cost methods used to account for processes that have *single* or *separable outputs*. Chapter 6 will explore the more challenging situations which arise when processes have *multiple* and *joint outputs*.

ASSIGNING PROCESS COSTS
TO COMPLETED UNITS

Consider the simplest possible case—a firm that makes a single type of product and has only one processing department. When no partly completed units are in process either at the beginning or end of the company's accounting period, the period's manufacturing costs can be allocated to products simply by dividing total processing costs by the number of units produced. Because all units of output are assumed to be physically identical, it is reasonable that each unit should bear an equal amount of product cost.

Example: Ajax Corporation produces 10,000 fully complete output units during June, while incurring materials costs of $35,000, direct labor costs of $25,000, and overhead costs of $50,000, for a total manufacturing cost of $110,000.

Total Manufacturing Costs:	
Direct Materials	$ 35,000
Direct Labor	25,000
Manufacturing Overhead	50,000
	$110,000
Units Completed	10,000

$$\text{Average Cost per Unit} = \frac{\$110,000}{10,000} = \$11$$

Each fully completed unit costs $11 to manufacture. The separate elements of this cost are $3.50 for materials, $2.50 for labor, and $5 for overhead.

Assume now that 8,000 of these units are sold during June, but the other 2,000 remain in inventory. Because there was no beginning inventory of completed units, the total manufacturing cost of $110,000 is divided between finished goods inventory and cost of goods sold, using the average unit cost previously calculated:

Units Completed and Transferred to Finished Goods Inventory:	
10,000 @ $11	$110,000
Less: Cost of Goods Sold during June:	
8,000 @ $11	88,000
Finished Goods Inventory on June 30:	
2,000 @ $11	$ 22,000

EQUIVALENT UNITS: AN AVERAGING TECHNIQUE

The preceding example assumes that every unit put into process in June was fully completed during the month. But what if some units are still being processed on June 30? Inventories of partly finished items are usually described in such terms as "4,000 units, half completed," meaning that 4,000 units are currently at some stage in the production process and that these units are, *on the average,* 50 percent complete. This is necessarily an estimate rather than an exact measure, because the 4,000 units probably include products at several different stages of completion.

When some units are incomplete at the beginning and/or the end of an accounting period, manufacturing costs must be associated with products on the basis of **equivalent units of output.** For costing purposes, any number of partly completed units is treated as being equivalent to a proportionally smaller number of fully completed units—hence, the term *equivalent units.* Therefore, the 4,000 units that are half complete would be treated as 2,000 fully complete units. An average cost per equivalent unit of output is then calculated by dividing total manufacturing costs by the number of equivalent units manufactured during the period.

Example: Assume the same facts as in the example involving Ajax Corporation, except that in addition to the 10,000 units started and completed during June, 2,500 units are in process on June 30; these units are on the average 40 percent complete.

Total Manufacturing Costs:	
Direct Materials	$ 35,000
Direct Labor	25,000
Manufacturing Overhead	50,000
	$110,000
Units Completed	10,000
Plus Equivalent Units in Process:	
2,500 × 40%	1,000
Total Equivalent Units Completed	11,000 units

$$\text{Average Cost per Equivalent Unit} = \frac{\$110,000}{11,000} = \$10$$

The ending Work in Process inventory of 2,500 units that are 40 percent complete is considered equivalent to 1,000 (2,500 × 40 percent) fully completed units. Accordingly, the same amount of cost that would be allocated to 1,000 fully completed units is allocated to 2,500 units that are 40 percent complete. This is accomplished by adding 1,000 units of equivalent output to the 10,000 units of physical output that were started and completed during June. Total manufacturing costs of $110,000 are then averaged over.11,000 units of equivalent production. Each fully completed unit and each equivalent unit is allocated $10 of manufacturing cost.

As in the first example, assume that 8,000 completed units are sold during June and that 2,000 remain in finished goods inventory. The total manufacturing cost of $110,000 is divided among cost of goods sold, finished goods inventory, and work in process inventory as follows:

Cost of Goods Sold during June:	
8,000 × $10	$ 80,000
Finished Goods Inventory on June 30:	
2,000 × $10	20,000
Work in Process Inventory on June 30:	
1,000 (2,500 × 40%) × $10	10,000
	$110,000

The **percentage of completion** measure is affected by the amount of processing done as well as by the sequence in which materials, labor, and overhead are added to units in process. Raw materials usage typically occurs at the start of processing. When it does, units at any stage of processing can be considered 100 percent complete with respect to their raw materials content.

In contrast, labor and overhead costs are usually incurred gradually during production, though not necessarily at a constant rate. For convenience in calculation, it is often assumed that labor and overhead—referred to as **conversion costs**—are added to units in process at the same rate. This assumption permits such statements as "400 units, 30 percent complete with regard to conversion costs"—which means that on average the 400 units in process have had added to them 30 percent of the required labor and overhead processing.

There are many variations on these basic situations. Materials are sometimes added to units in process at intermediate points during production, and must be accounted for accordingly—for example, "6,000 units in process, complete with respect to raw materials A and B, but with no content of raw materials C, D, and E." Similarly, if different types of labor are required within a process, they should be accounted for separately if they are incurred at different stages in the process or at different hourly rates. Overhead should be accounted for separately from labor costs if a machine base rather than a labor base is used in the application rate.[1]

COST ACCUMULATION IN PROCESS COSTING

In a job order system, materials, labor, and overhead costs are associated with particular units of output. In a process cost system, the costs of each process or department are first accumulated in accounts that reflect their functional purpose. Processing costs might be collected in accounts such as Raw Materials Used—Grinding Department, Direct Labor—Assembly Department, or Manufacturing Overhead—Machining Department. The total costs of each department can then be accumulated in summary or control accounts such as Work in Process—Grinding Department, or Work in Process—Assembly Department Operation No. 3.

Direct materials and direct labor costs are allocated to departmental work in process accounts, using materials requisition forms and labor time records as source documents. Separate work in process accounts should be established for each type of product manufactured in each department. Whenever possible, direct materials and direct labor costs should be identified with the individual outputs of each process.

Factory overhead costs should be allocated to the outputs of each process on the basis of a predetermined application rate. This rate should be calculated separately for each department, because process costing stresses the measurement of departmental performance. The use of predetermined rates avoids minor short-run cost fluctuations that would occur if actual overhead costs were applied to work in process. Because process costs are most useful when calculated frequently, it is desirable to have the more reliable information provided by predetermined overhead application rates.

Applied overhead normally includes both fixed and variable manufacturing costs. It should also include reallocated overhead costs that were initially assigned to the company's service departments. The total cost of process outputs

---

[1] Many firms simply ignore unfinished items for costing purposes and apply total manufacturing costs only to fully completed units. This is feasible when beginning or ending work in process inventories are negligible or when work in process is fairly constant in quantity and type from one period to the next. See R.C. Skinner, "Process Costing," *Abacus,* Spring, 1978, pp. 160–70.

therefore incorporates all manufacturing costs that are directly or indirectly related to the outputs of that process. The following example demonstrates how
process costs are accumulated in the Work in Process account.

Example: Akron Company maintains two process cost centers: a Machining
Department and an Assembly Department. During December, 19X4, the Machining Department consumed raw materials costing $7,800 and incurred direct
labor costs of $8,000 and manufacturing overhead costs of $9,500. Manufacturing overhead cost is applied to departments at a rate of 125 percent of direct
labor cost. The general journal entries to accumulate Machining Department
process costs are:

Work in Process—Machining Department	7,800	
Raw Materials Inventory		7,800
Materials put into process.		
Work in Process—Machining Department	8,000	
Wages Payable		8,000
Direct labor cost incurred.		
Manufacturing Overhead Control—Machining Department	9,500	
Various Accounts		9,500
Overhead costs incurred.		
Work in Process—Machining Department	10,000	
Manufacturing Overhead Control—		
Machining Department		10,000

Overhead costs applied: 125% × $8,000 = $10,000.

CALCULATING UNIT PROCESS COSTS: WEIGHTED AVERAGE COST METHOD

After accumulating a department's total costs for an accounting period,
accountants must allocate those costs to the department's output. The first step
in process cost allocation is to calculate the materials, labor, and overhead
costs of *one unit of output*. When the **weighted average cost method** is used,
unit process costs are derived as follows:

1. Calculate the total materials, labor, and overhead costs incurred during
    the current period and add to them the materials, labor, and overhead
    costs of any units that were in process at the beginning of the period.
2. Calculate the number of physical units completed during the current period
    and add to them the number of equivalent units represented by the ending
    work in process inventory.
3. Divide the total cost from step one by the total number of equivalent units
    from step two to obtain the weighted average cost of an equivalent unit
    of process output.

Example: Akron Company's Machining Department reported the December
operating results shown in Figure 5–1.

FIGURE 5–1

Akron Company
Machining Department Operating Results
For the Month of December, 19X4

Units in Process—December 1	6,000
Materials: 100% Complete (6,000 equivalent units)	
Conversion Costs: 50% Complete (3,000 equivalent units)	
Cost of Units in Process—December 1:	
Materials	$ 3,000
Conversion Costs	$ 3,000
Processing Costs—December:	
Raw Materials Usage	$ 7,800
Conversion Costs	$18,000
Units Completed and Transferred to Assembly Department	10,000
Units in Process—December 31	8,000
Materials: 100% Complete (8,000 equivalent units)	
Conversion Costs: 62½% Complete (5,000 equivalent units)	

These operating results are used to calculate the *number of equivalent units processed* and the *weighted average cost per equivalent unit processed,* as shown in Figure 5–2, which can be summarized as follows: The weighted

FIGURE 5–2

Akron Company—Machining Department
Weighted Average Cost per Equivalent Unit Processed
For the Month of December, 19X4

	Materials	Conversion (Labor and Overhead)
Number of Equivalent Units Processed:		
Units Completed and Transferred to		
Assembly Department	10,000 units	10,000 units
Add: Units in Process, December 31	8,000	5,000
Number of Equivalent Units Processed	18,000 units	15,000 units
Weighted Average Cost per Equivalent Unit Processed:		
Processing Costs:		
Costs in Process on December 1	$ 3,000	$ 3,000
Costs Incurred in December	7,800	18,000
Total Processing Costs	$10,800	$21,000
Equivalent Unit Costs:		
$\dfrac{\text{Total Processing Costs}}{\text{Number of Equivalent Units Processed}} =$	$10,800 / 18,000	$21,000 / 15,000
Weighted Average Cost per Equivalent		
Unit Processed	$ .60	$ 1.40

average cost of one equivalent unit of output processed by the Machining Department in December was $2. This consisted of 60¢ in materials cost and $1.40 in labor and overhead cost.

TRANSFERRING COSTS TO SUBSEQUENT PROCESSING DEPARTMENTS

As products are manufactured, they typically pass through several processing departments. The output of each department normally includes units that have been processed in that department and transferred to subsequent processes as well as partially processed units that remain in the department. The costs of partially processed units are accumulated in the department's Work in Process account. The costs of fully processed units are transferred to the Work in Process account of the next processing department, or to the Finished Goods Inventory account.

In Akron Company, the cost of the 10,000 units that were completed and transferred from the Machining Department to the Assembly Department is $20,000 [10,000 × (60¢ + $1.40)]. The following journal entry is made to record this transfer:

Work in Process—Assembly Department	20,000	
Work in Process—Machining Department		20,000
To transfer costs of 10,000 units @ $2 per unit from		
the Machining Department to the Assembly Department.		

The 8,000 units that make up the Machining Department's ending work in process inventory are assigned costs of $11,800, calculated as follows:

Materials (8,000 Equivalent Units @ 60¢)	$ 4,800
Labor and Overhead Costs (5,000 Equivalent Units @ $1.40)	7,000
Total Cost of Work in Process on December 31	$11,800

The general ledger account for Work in Process—Machining Department appears as follows:

Work in Process—Machining Department

19X4				19X4		
Dec. 1	Balance	6,000		Dec. 31	Completed Units to	
Dec. 31	Materials	7,800			Assembly Department	20,000
31	Labor and Overhead	18,000			Balance	11,800
		31,800				31,800
19X5						
Jan. 1	Balance	11,800				

THE PRODUCTION COST REPORT

A **production cost report,** prepared at the end of every accounting period, summarizes the production activity and costs of each process or department. This information is used to calculate the number of equivalent units processed, the cost per equivalent unit of output, and the quantity and cost of ending work in process inventories and of units completed and transferred to subsequent processing departments.

A production cost report for Akron Company's Machining Department can be constructed in the following sequence of steps:

1. Account for all physical units in process during the period.
2. Calculate the number of equivalent units in the beginning and ending work in process inventories.
3. Calculate the total number of equivalent units processed.
4. Reconcile the sources and dispositions of equivalent units processed.
5. Calculate the weighted average cost per equivalent unit of output processed.
6. Allocate the total cost of processing to ending work in process and to units completed and transferred.

(1) *Account for all physical units in process during the period:*

	Physical Units
In Process, Dec. 1	6,000
Units Started	12,000
Production and Costs in Current Month	—
Units Processed	18,000
Units Completed and Transferred	10,000
In Process, Dec. 31	8,000
Units Processed	18,000

(2) *Calculate the number of equivalent units in the beginning and ending work in process inventories:*

Beginning and ending inventories were complete with regard to materials inputs. Beginning inventory was 50 percent complete with regard to conversion processing (labor and overhead), whereas ending inventory was 62½ percent complete in this respect. Completed units, of course, always contain 100 percent of materials and conversion processing.

	Physical Units	Equivalent Units	
		Materials	Conversion
In Process, Dec. 1	6,000	6,000	3,000
Units Started	12,000		
Production and Costs in Current Month	—		
Units Processed	18,000		

	Physical Units	Equivalent Units Materials	Equivalent Units Conversion
Units Completed and Transferred	10,000	10,000	10,000
In Process, Dec. 31	8,000	8,000	5,000
Units Processed	18,000		

(3) *Calculate the total number of equivalent units processed:*
The number of units completed and transferred during December, plus the number of equivalent units of work in process on December 31, equals *the number of equivalent units processed.* The 18,000 equivalent units of materials and 15,000 equivalent units of conversion processing represent all the Machining Department output that must be accounted for in the current period.

	Physical Units	Equivalent Units Materials	Equivalent Units Conversion
In Process, Dec. 1	6,000	6,000	3,000
Units Started	12,000		
Production and Costs in Current Month	—		
Units Processed	18,000		
Units Completed and Transferred	10,000	10,000	10,000
In Process, Dec. 31	8,000	8,000	5,000
Units Processed	18,000	18,000	15,000

(4) *Reconcile the sources and dispositions of equivalent units processed:*
The number of equivalent units processed by the Machining Department was calculated in terms of the *disposition* of units passing through the Department (completed units plus ending work in process). This number must be reconciled with the *sources* of those units, which must have come either from work done during December or from the partially completed units in process at the beginning of the month. Therefore, the next step is to balance the top half of the equivalent units section of the production cost report with the corresponding lower half.

The only equivalent units figures still missing are the number of equivalent units of materials and conversion processing that were *produced exclusively during the current month.* They are derived by subtracting the equivalent units in the December 1 work in process inventory from the total number of equivalent units processed. As will be shown, these figures for *equivalent units produced* in the current month are especially important when FIFO or standard costing methods are used to calculate unit processing costs.

	Physical Units	Equivalent Units Materials	Equivalent Units Conversion
In Process, Dec. 1	6,000	6,000	3,000
Units Started	12,000	—	—
Production and Costs in Current Month	—	12,000	12,000
Units Processed	18,000	18,000	15,000

	Physical Units	Equivalent Units Materials	Equivalent Units Conversion
Units Completed and			
Transferred	10,000	10,000	10,000
In Process, Dec. 31	8,000	8,000	5,000
Units Processed	18,000	18,000	15,000

(5) *Calculate the weighted average cost per equivalent unit of output processed:*

The costs of beginning units in process and of current period production have been accumulated in the Machining Department's Work in Process account (see page 168). These costs are now entered in the top right section of the production cost report. The column totals for materials and conversion costs are then divided by the corresponding totals of equivalent units processed, to obtain the Machining Department's average processing costs per equivalent unit of output in December.

	Physical Units	Equivalent Units Materials	Equivalent Units Conversion	Costs Materials	Costs Conversion	Total
In Process, Dec. 1 ...	6,000	6,000	3,000	$ 3,000	$ 3,000	$ 6,000
Units Started	12,000					
Production and Costs in Current Month ..		12,000	12,000	7,800	18,000	25,800
Units Processed	18,000	18,000	15,000	$10,800	$21,000	$31,800
Cost per Equivalent Unit				$10,800 / 18,000	$21,000 / 15,000	
				60¢	$1.40	
Units Completed and Transferred ...	10,000	10,000	10,000			
In Process, Dec. 31 ..	8,000	8,000	5,000			
Units Processed	18,000	18,000	15,000			

(6) *Allocate the total cost of processing to ending work in process and to units completed and transferred:*

The cost of ending work in process inventory and of units completed and transferred can now be found by multiplying the unit costs of materials and conversion processing by the corresponding number of equivalent units of output. Note that, as indicated in Figure 5-3, the costs of beginning units in process ($6,000) plus costs incurred during December ($25,800) reconcile to the cost of completed units ($20,000) plus the cost of ending units in process ($11,800).

This production cost report contains all the analysis of costs and output quantities needed to prepare journal entries to accumulate process costs and transfer them to subsequent processing departments. As will be demonstrated, the basic format of this report can easily be modified to permit the use of FIFO and standard costing methods of deriving unit process costs as well as to account for multiple input categories, units transferred from other processes, and (in Chapter 6) units spoiled, lost, or damaged in processing.

FIGURE 5–3

Akron Company—Machining Department
Production Cost Report
For the Month of December, 19X4
Weighted Average Cost Method

	Physical Units	Equivalent Units		Costs		
		Materials	Conversion	Materials	Conversion	Total
In Process, Dec. 1	6,000	6,000	3,000	$ 3,000	$ 3,000	$ 6,000
Units Started	12,000					
Production and Costs in Current Month		12,000	12,000	7,800	18,000	25,800
Units Processed	18,000	18,000	15,000	$10,800	$21,000	$31,800
Cost per Equivalent Unit				$10,800	$21,000	
				18,000	15,000	
				60¢	$1.40	
Units Completed and Transferred	10,000	10,000	10,000	$ 6,000	$14,000	$20,000
In Process, Dec. 31 ...	8,000	8,000	5,000	4,800	7,000	11,800
Units Processed	18,000	18,000	15,000	$10,800	$21,000	$31,800

CALCULATING UNIT PROCESS COSTS: FIFO COST METHOD

The most widely used alternative to weighted average calculation of unit processing costs is the **first-in, first-out cost method.** FIFO is applied in a process cost system in the same way that it is used to value purchased merchandise. Completed units transferred out of a department are assigned costs according to the sequence in which "layers" of units are processed through that department. The FIFO cost method usually requires unit cost calculations for at least two cost layers during each accounting period: first, the cost of beginning inventory items that were partly processed in earlier periods, and second, the cost of the current period's production.

FIFO cost calculations are based on the number of **equivalent units produced** during the current period, which is defined as the total number of equivalent units processed minus any equivalent units in process at the beginning of the period. In the preceding example, equivalent units produced were calculated as part of step (4) in developing the production cost report. For Akron Company's Machining Department, the equivalent units produced during December were determined as follows:

	Materials	Conversion
Equivalent Units Processed	18,000	15,000
Less: Equivalent Units in Process at Beginning of the Period	(6,000)	(3,000)
Equivalent Units Produced During the Current Period	12,000	12,000

The next step in FIFO process cost calculation is to determine the unit costs of (1) beginning inventories and (2) current period equivalent production.

Figure 5–4 shows that the cost of an equivalent unit of output from the work in process at the beginning of December was $1.50, consisting of 50¢ for raw materials and $1 for conversion costs. During December, an equivalent unit of production cost $2.15, consisting of 65¢ in materials and $1.50 in conversion costs.

The final step is to assign these separate unit costs to the output processed. Because the FIFO method assumes that the first items put into process are the first ones completed, the unit costs of beginning work in process are the first costs assigned to units finished during the current period. The remaining completed units are then assigned the current period's unit costs. Ending work in process inventories are also usually assigned the current period's unit costs.

For Akron Company, the assignment of unit costs to completed units and to ending units in process is summarized in the production cost report shown as Figure 5–5.

The use of FIFO causes the 10,000 units completed and transferred from the Machining Department to absorb first the entire cost of the units in beginning work in process inventory (materials cost, 6,000 units at 50¢; conversion cost, 3,000 units at $1). The remainder of the units that were completed during December are assigned the current period's unit costs (materials cost, 4,000 units at 65¢; conversion cost, 7,000 units at $1.50). Ending work in process inventory is measured entirely in terms of these current period unit costs.

The following journal entry records the transfer of 10,000 units from the Machining Department to the Assembly Department, using FIFO cost calculations.

Work in Process—Assembly Department	19,100	
Work in Process—Machining Department		19,100
To transfer costs of 10,000 units from the Machining Department to the Assembly Department		

THE COST FLOW ASSUMPTIONS COMPARED

The weighted average cost method of inventory valuation combines all costs incurred during the current period with the costs already incurred on units in process at the beginning of the period. The total of these costs is then applied *equally* to all equivalent units processed, including those that were partly complete at the beginning of the period. In the Akron Company example, 18,000 units were processed with respect to materials at a total cost of $10,800; the

FIGURE 5–4

Akron Company—Machining Department
Unit Costs
For the Month of December, 19X4

	Materials	Conversion
(1) Units in Process on December 1—6,000	$3,000	$3,000
Materials (100% complete)	6,000 Equivalent Units	
Conversion (50% complete)		3,000 Equivalent Units
Costs per Equivalent Unit	$\dfrac{\$3,000}{6,000} = 50\cancel{c}$	$\dfrac{\$3,000}{3,000} = \$1$
(2) Current Period Production:		
Total Costs	$7,800	$18,000
Equivalent Units Produced	12,000 Equivalent Units	12,000 Equivalent Units
Costs per Equivalent Unit	$\dfrac{\$\,7,800}{12,000} = 65\cancel{c}$	$\dfrac{\$18,000}{12,000} = \$1.50$

FIGURE 5–5

Akron Company—Machining Department
Production Cost Report
For the Month of December, 19X4
FIFO Cost Method

	Physical Units	Equivalent Units		Costs		
		Materials	Conversion	Materials	Conversion	Total
In Process, Dec. 1	6,000	6,000	3,000	$ 3,000	$ 3,000	$ 6,000
Unit Costs:				(50¢)	($1.00)	—
Units Started	12,000					
Current Costs and						
Production		12,000	12,000	$ 7,800	$ 18,000	$25,000
Unit Costs				(65¢)	($1.50)	—
Units Processed	18,000	18,000	15,000	$ 10,800	$ 21,000	$31,800
Units Completed and						
Transferred	10,000	10,000	10,000	$ 5,600	$ 13,500	$19,100
				$\left(\begin{array}{c}6,000\\@\ 50¢\end{array}\right)$	$\left(\begin{array}{c}3,000\\@\ \$1.\end{array}\right)$	
				$+\left(\begin{array}{c}4,000\\@\ 65¢\end{array}\right)$	$+\left(\begin{array}{c}7,000\\@\ \$1.50\end{array}\right)$	
In Process, Dec. 31	8,000	8,000	5,000	$ 5,200	$ 7,500	$12,700
				$\left(\begin{array}{c}8,000\\@\ 65¢\end{array}\right)$	$\left(\begin{array}{c}5,000\\@\ \$1.50\end{array}\right)$	
Units Processed	18,000	18,000	15,000	$ 10,800	$ 21,000	$31,800

average unit cost was 60¢ per unit. No attempt was made to distinguish the separate costs of any of the 18,000 units processed.

The FIFO method separates the beginning units in process and their costs incurred during the previous period from the equivalent units of output produced and the costs incurred during the current period. Consequently, when FIFO is adopted, at least two separate unit costs must be calculated—the cost of equivalent units of output produced in both the previous and current periods.

FIFO therefore provides more current information on changes in the level of unit process costs from period to period. The average cost method tends to smooth out and conceal interperiod variations in unit costs, because some older costs are always carried forward into subsequent periods. The separate unit cost measures obtained using FIFO will be more pertinent and useful when accounting periods are short. If the period is lengthy and partly completed units are only a small proportion of the number of units processed, the two methods will tend to produce similar overall results.

A FIFO flow of costs also gives a better representation of the way in which products absorb resources during processing. As partly finished items move through a department, materials, labor, and other manufacturing service inputs are physically added to them in a definite sequence. A FIFO measurement of the costs of these resource flows conforms to the physical movement of goods through the typical standardized, continuous production process.

However, it can become quite cumbersome to trace the costs of each period's output on a FIFO basis as it moves through successive stages of a multiprocess production operation. When inventories of several types of products are passing through a number of production departments, an accurate application of FIFO involves a large number of separate cost layers, especially when accounting periods are short. The intricate data processing needed to support such a system has often been cited as a disadvantage of the FIFO cost method. Under such conditions, FIFO's greater detail and accuracy may not justify the additional expense and inconvenience of making the necessary calculations.

In the past, these computational drawbacks provided an incentive to forego FIFO in favor of average cost inventory valuations.[2] Computer-based data processing has made FIFO process cost procedures more feasible. Prompt, accurate computation of current period production costs and the maintenance of FIFO process cost systems are well within the capabilities of computerized accounting systems.

One way to simplify FIFO cost calculations is to record the unit cost of items transferred into a process at the *average* amount of all FIFO costs transferred out of the preceding process. This eliminates the need to keep track of an increasing number of cost layers as units move through successive processes. The $19,100 total FIFO cost of the 10,000 units transferred out of Akron Company's Machining Department is composed of four separate cost layers: $5,600 and $4,000 for materials, and $13,500 and $7,000 for conversion costs. When transferred to the Assembly Department, these units could simply be treated as having an average unit cost carried forward from the Machining Department of $1.91 ($19,100 ÷ 10,000), rather than having four separate unit cost components (50¢ and 65¢ for materials, and $1 and $1.50 for conver-

---

[2] Charles T. Horngren, "Process Costing in Perspective: Forget FIFO," *The Accounting Review,* July, 1967.

sion) carried forward separately through the Assembly Department and all subsequent processes.

Other cost flow assumptions are generally inappropriate for process costing. **Specific identification** is not a logical alternative because it contradicts the basic principle that process costs cannot be associated with particular units of output. The **last-in, first-out cost method** does not normally coincide with the physical flow of manufacturing activities. Because assembly lines do not run backwards, it is hard to defend the assumption that partly finished units at the beginning of a period remain unfinished at the end of that period. LIFO's tendency to approximate the current replacement cost of products is possibly a desirable effect. However, the same data processing complexities that beset FIFO operate to the disadvantage of LIFO. In practice, LIFO is rarely used to measure short-run process costs for internal management purposes, but it is often used to value raw materials and finished goods inventory for external reporting. This hybrid treatment avoids some of the logical deficiencies of LIFO, but preserves its ability to reduce income tax payments under inflationary conditions and when physical inventories are increasing.

PROCESS COSTS AND INTERDEPARTMENTAL TRANSFERS

When several successive production processes are needed to complete a product, the output costs of each process are passed on to succeeding departments to reflect the physical movement of units from one process to the next. In the Akron Company example, using the weighted average cost method, the Assembly Department records the $20,000 cost of 10,000 units received from the Machining Department as one of its input costs for the current period. The process costs of units transferred from the Assembly Department to Finished Goods inventory then include these Machining Department costs, plus all processing costs incurred within the Assembly Department.

Assume that the Assembly Department had the December operating results shown in Figure 5–6.

These operating results provide a basis for calculating the Assembly Department's December process costs, as shown in Figure 5–7 (page 179).

INPUTS TRANSFERRED FROM MORE THAN ONE DEPARTMENT

When a department receives inputs from more than one other department, the foregoing process costing techniques require only minor adjustments. The unit being accounted for in each process is an equivalent unit of *output* of that process. Inputs from other departments must be restated in terms of equivalent output units of the receiving department.

Example: Rykin Company maintains four production departments, A, B, C, and D. During April, 19X8, 10,000 units from Department A and 24,000 units from Department B were transferred to Department C. Costs of processing these units were $10,000 in Department A and $16,000 in Department B. Department C had no beginning Work in Process inventory. During April, 4,000 units

---

FIGURE 5–6

Akron Company—Assembly Department
Operating Results
For the Month of December, 19X4

Units in Process on December 1:
  8,000 Units:
    Machining Department Costs (100% Complete) $12,400
    Materials Costs (100% Complete) $10,200
    Conversion Costs (25% Complete) . . . . $ 2,000
Units Transferred from the Machining Department:
  10,000 Units @ $2 . . . . $20,000
December Production Costs:
  Materials Costs $15,000
  Conversion Costs $10,000
Units Completed and Transferred to Finished Goods . . . .   12,000 Units
Units in Process on December 31:
  6,000 Units:
    Machining Department Costs . .   (100% Complete)
    Materials Costs . . . .   (100% Complete)
    Conversion Costs . . . .   (50% Complete)

---

of Department C output were completed and sent to Department D, and another 1,000 units were in process on April 30, 50 percent complete with respect to conversion costs. Department C adds no materials to the subassemblies received from Departments A and B. Each unit of Department C output requires two units of Department A output and three units of Department B output. Conversion costs in Department C during April were $2,250. The production cost report in Figure 5–8 (page 180) summarizes Department C inputs, operations, and outputs.

THE PROCESS COSTING PERIOD

The calculation of process costs is affected by the length of a company's accounting period. If the period is short (a day or a week), the number of units in process at the beginning and end of that period is likely to be a significant proportion of the total number of units completed during the period. In that case, calculations of the number of units in process and estimates of the stage of completion for materials, labor, and overhead inputs become vitally important. On the other hand, if the accounting period is longer (a month or more), inventories of partly finished goods will be a much smaller fraction of total units produced and will have less impact on measures of equivalent units and product costs.

The length of the accounting period also affects certain of the averaging assumptions used in process costing. The assumption that each unit of output should bear an equal (average) cost is more reasonable when that average is computed over a relatively short period of time. Unit costs are sure to vary over longer periods, as input prices, productivity, and other production conditions

FIGURE 5-7

Akron Company—Assembly Department
Production Cost Report
For the Month of December, 19X4
Weighted Average Cost Method

	Physical Units	Equivalent Units			Costs			
		Machining Department	Materials	Conversion	Machining Department	Materials	Conversion	Total
In Process, Dec. 1	8,000	8,000	8,000	2,000	$12,400	$10,200	$ 2,000	$24,600
Units Transferred In	10,000	10,000	—	—	20,000	—	—	20,000
Production and Costs During Month			10,000	13,000	—	15,000	10,000	25,000
Units Processed	18,000	18,000	18,000	15,000	$32,400	$25,200	$12,000	$69,600
Equivalent Unit Costs					$32,400	$25,200	$12,000	—
					18,000	18,000	15,000	
(Average)					$1.80	$1.40	$0.80	$4.00
Units Completed and Transferred to Finished Goods	12,000	12,000	12,000	12,000	$21,600	$16,800	$ 9,600	$48,000[a]
In Process, Dec. 31	6,000	6,000	6,000	3,000	10,800	8,400	2,400	21,600[b]
Units Processed	18,000	18,000	18,000	15,000	$32,400	$25,200	$12,000	$69,600

Supporting Calculations:

[a] Cost of 12,000 Units Completed and Transferred to Finished Goods Inventory:

Machining Department Costs (12,000 @ $1.80)	$21,600
Materials (12,000 @ $1.40)	16,800
Conversion (12,000 @ $0.80)	9,600
	$48,000

[b] Cost of 6,000 Units in Process at End of Month:

Matching Department Costs (6,000 @ $1.80)	$10,800
Materials (6,000 @ $1.40)	8,400
Conversion (50% complete) (3,000 @ $0.80)	2,400
	$21,600

FIGURE 5–8

Rykin Company—Department C
Production Cost Report
For the Month of April, 19X8
Weighted Average Cost Method

	Physical Units	Equivalent Units			Costs			
		Dept. A	Dept. B	Conver-sion	Dept. A	Dept. B	Conver-sion	Total
In Process, April 1	0	0	0	0	—	—	—	—
Transferred In		5,000c	8,000c	—	$10,000	$16,000	—	$26,000
Units Started	5,000a							
Production and Cost in the Current Month	—	—	—	4,500	—	—	$2,250	2,250
Units Processed	5,000	5,000	8,000	4,500	$10,000	$16,000	$2,250	$28,250
Equivalent Unit Costs					$10,000 / 5,000	$16,000 / 8,000	$2,250 / 4,500	—
(Average)					$2.00	$2.00	$0.50	$4.50
Units Completed and Transferred to D	4,000	4,000	4,000	4,000	$ 8,000	$ 8,000	$2,000	$18,000
In Process, April 30 Partly Complete	1,000	1,000	1,000	500	2,000	2,000	250	4,250
In Process, Components Only	—	—	3,000	—	—	6,000	—	6,000b
Units Processed	5,000	5,000	8,000	4,500	$10,000	$16,000	$2,250	$28,250

a Entries to be made in this column only for *units of output of Dept. C* that have begun to be processed.
b The ending Work in Process inventory of Department C will also include the *unprocessed* components from Department B—in this example, sufficient for 3,000 units of Department C output at $2 each. In this way they are viewed as 3,000 equivalent units of output of Department C that are complete only with respect to their Department B content.
c Entries in this row show the equivalent number of units of Department C output represented by the units transferred from Departments A and B. Department A transferred 10,000 units of its output, which correspond to 5,000 units of Department C output. Department B transferred 24,000 output units, which correspond to 8,000 units of Department C output.

change. It is therefore much less reasonable to expect that the cost of each unit of process output will remain constant over such longer periods.

Unit costs computed as averages over longer periods are less useful for control and evaluation than are the unit costs of shorter production periods. The more often unit costs are measured, the more promptly control action can be taken in response to that information. Clearly, quarterly measures of unit production costs are less useful than are monthly measures, which in turn are not as good as weekly figures. It would be futile to wait two or three months to discover what it costs to produce an item that takes only one or two days to manufacture. In such a case, weekly process cost reports are much more valuable.

PROCESS COSTING AND THE VARIABLE COST MODEL

The preceding discussion of process costing assumes the use of a **full absorption cost model,** in which unit costs include both the fixed and variable costs of process outputs. Process cost techniques are the same when a **variable cost model** is used, except that fixed manufacturing costs are charged to expense instead of being included in work in process and finished goods inventories.

Only the *variable* components of unit process costs (direct materials, direct labor, and variable overhead) are appropriate for comparative purposes. Using *fixed* costs expressed as unit amounts for comparison and evaluation invites misinterpretation when there is significant variation in process output levels from period to period. Moreover, variable process costs give a measure of performance that is more representative of items usually controllable by decision makers within the process or department.

Variable unit process costs are also relevant for certain types of pricing decisions. Because they reasonably approximate the marginal cost of producing a unit, they may be used for incremental short-run price–quantity decisions.

PROCESS COSTING ILLUSTRATED: PRESTO PRODUCTS CORPORATION

The operation of a process cost system will now be demonstrated via a summary of one month's activity for Presto Products Corporation, manufacturer of presto clips, an all-purpose fastening device. Manufacturing operations are fairly simple and are handled by two production departments, Stamping and Packing. A process cost system is used to accumulate product cost data.

Materials are requisitioned for use at the start of production in the Stamping Department. In the Packing Department, the wrapping and packing materials are added in such a way that it can be conveniently assumed that materials usage occurs continuously as the products move through that department.

In both departments, conversion costs (direct labor and manufacturing overhead) are treated as though they were incurred uniformly and continuously. In the Stamping Department, overhead is applied at the rate of $6 per machine hour; in the Packing Department, it is applied at the rate of 150 percent of direct labor costs. The weighted average cost method is used to calculate unit product costs in both departments. There is no monthly disposition of underapplied or overapplied overhead costs, but an annual adjustment is made.

The following cost and production figures were available at the beginning of June, 19X7:

	Stamping	Packing
Units in Process, June 1, 19X7	6,000 Units	8,000 Units
Completion Status and Costs:		
Materials	100%—$6,000	25%—$1,000
Conversion Costs	50%—$4,500	75%—$4,500
Stamping Department Costs	—	100%—$19,000

There was also a beginning inventory of 10,000 fully completed presto clips, for which recorded cost was $34,000. On June 1, the company's general ledger inventory accounts showed the following balances:

Work in Process—Stamping

June 1	Balance	10,500	

Work in Process—Packing

June 1	Balance	24,500	

Finished Goods Inventory

June 1	Balance	34,000	

During the month of June, 38,000 units were sold and the following production figures were collected:

	Stamping	Packing
Raw Materials Purchased	$62,500	$31,200
Raw Materials Requisitioned	$53,400	$26,600
Direct Labor Costs	$36,300	$13,680
Manufacturing Overhead Incurred	$31,250	$19,750
Machine Hours Worked	6,000 hours	—
Production Starts	48,000 units	44,000 units
Units Completed	44,000 units	40,000 units
Units in Process at End of Month	10,000 units	12,000 units
Completion Status:		
Materials	100%	50%
Conversion Costs	40%	25%
Stamping Department Costs	—	100%

Departmental operations during June are summarized in the following five entries:

Raw Materials Inventory—Stamping	62,500	
Raw Materials Inventory—Packing	31,200	
Accounts Payable		93,700
Raw Materials purchases.		

Payroll Control—Stamping	36,300	
Payroll Control—Packing	13,680	
Vouchers Payable		49,980
Payroll payable.		

Manufacturing Overhead Control—Stamping	31,250	
Manufacturing Overhead Control—Packing	19,750	
Accounts Payable		
Cash		51,000
Accumulated Depreciation		
Manufacturing overhead incurred.		

Work in Process—Stamping	125,700	
Raw Materials Inventory—Stamping		53,400
Payroll Control—Stamping		36,300
Manufacturing Overhead Control—Stamping		36,000
Materials used, payroll disposition, and overhead		
application in Stamping Department.		

Work in Process—Packing	60,800	
Raw Materials Inventory—Packing		26,600
Payroll Control—Packing		13,680
Manufacturing Overhead Control—Packing		20,520
Materials used, payroll disposition, and overhead		
application in Packing Department.		

At this point, production cost reports may be started in both departments, using these journal entries as a source of data for physical units of output and processing costs incurred.

FIGURE 5–9

Presto Products Corporation—Stamping Department
Production Cost Report
For the Month of June, 19X7
Weighted Average Cost Method

	Physical Units	Equiv. Units		Costs		
		Mtls.	Conv.	Mtls.	Conv.	Total
Units in Process on June 1	6,000	6,000	3,000	$6,000	$4,500	$10,500
Units Started During June	48,000	—	—	—	—	—
Current Costs and Production	—	?	?	53,400	72,300	125,700
Units Processed	54,000	?	?	59,400	76,800	136,200

The next step in preparing the production cost report is to calculate the equivalent units of materials and conversion processed. Stamping Department units in process on June 30 had all materials inputs added and 40 percent of conversion processing completed. The lower part of the production cost report can now be filled in as follows:

	Physical Units	Equiv. Units		Costs		
		Mtls.	Conv.	Mtls.	Conv.	Total
Units Completed in June	44,000	44,000	44,000			
Units in Process on June 30	10,000	10,000	4,000			
Units Processed	54,000	54,000	48,000			

Equivalent unit costs for the materials and conversion components of Stamping Department output can now be calculated:

$$\textbf{Raw Materials Unit Cost} = \frac{\text{Total Raw Materials Usage}}{\text{Equivalent Units Processed}} = \frac{\$59,400}{54,000} = \$1.10 \text{ per unit}$$

$$\textbf{Conversion Unit Cost} = \frac{\text{Total Conversion Costs}}{\text{Equivalent Units Processed}} = \frac{\$76,800}{48,000} = \$1.60 \text{ per unit}$$

Total Cost of One Equivalent Unit Processed in Stamping Department in June
$= \$1.10 + \$1.60 = \$2.70$

These unit costs are multiplied by the number of equivalent units processed to determine (1) the cost of units completed and transferred to the Packing Department and (2) the cost of units in process in the Stamping Department on June 30.

Units Completed and Transferred to Packing:
Materials Component (44,000 @ $1.10) . . . . $ 48,400
Conversion Component (44,000 @ $1.60)   70,400
    Total Cost of Units Completed $118,800
Units in Process on June 30:
Materials Component (10,000 @ $1.10) $11,000
Conversion Component (4,000 @ $1.60)   6,400
    Total Cost of Units in Process $17,400

The production cost report for the Stamping Department can now be completed, as shown in Figure 5–10.

FIGURE 5–10

Presto Products Corporation—Stamping Department
Production Cost Report
For the Month of June, 19X7
Weighted Average Cost Method

	Physical Units	Equivalent Units		Costs		
		Materials	Conversion	Materials	Conversion	Total
Units in Process on June 1	6,000	6,000	3,000	$ 6,000	$ 4,500	$ 10,500
Units Started During June	48,000	—	—	—	—	—
Current Costs and Production	—	48,000	45,000	53,400	72,300	125,700
Units Processed	54,000	54,000	48,000	$59,400	$76,800	$136,200
Units Completed in June	44,000	44,000	44,000	$48,400	$70,400	$118,800
Units in Process on June 30	10,000	10,000	4,000	11,000	6,400	17,400
Units Processed	54,000	54,000	48,000	$59,400	$76,800	$136,200

The Packing Department's production cost report will already have been developed to the point shown in Figure 5–11, on Packing Department operating results and on information in the Stamping Department's production cost report.

Equivalent unit costs for materials and conversion costs in the Packing Department can now be calculated:

Stamping Department Unit Cost Component

$$\frac{\text{Total Cost of Units Transferred from Stamping Department}}{\text{Total Units Transferred}} = \frac{\$19,000 + \$118,000}{8,000 + \quad 44,000} = \frac{\$137,800}{52,000} = \$2.65 \text{ per unit}$$

Raw Material Unit Cost

$$\frac{\text{Total Raw Materials Usage}}{\text{Equivalent Units Processed}} = \frac{\$1,000 + \$26,600}{46,000} = 60\text{¢ per unit}$$

Conversion Unit Cost

$$\frac{\text{Total Conversion Costs}}{\text{Equivalent Units Processed}} = \frac{\$4,500 + \$34,200}{43,000} = 90\text{¢ per unit}$$

Total Unit Cost = $2.65 + 60¢ + 90¢ = $4.15 per unit.

These unit costs are then multiplied by the number of equivalent units of Packing Department output to measure (1) the cost of units completed and transferred to finished goods inventory and (2) the cost of Packing Department units in process at the end of the month.

FIGURE 5–11

Presto Products Corporation—Packing Department
Production Cost Report
For the Month of June, 19X7
Weighted Average Cost Method

	Physical Units	Equivalent Units — Stamping Department	Equivalent Units — Materials	Equivalent Units — Conversion	Costs — Stamping Department	Costs — Materials	Costs — Conversion	Total
Units in Process on June 1	8,000	8,000	2,000	6,000	$ 19,000	$ 1,000	$ 4,500	$ 24,500
Transfers In	44,000	44,000	—	—	118,800	—	—	118,800
Current Costs and Production	—	—	44,000	37,000	—	26,600	34,200	60,800
Units Processed	52,000	52,000	46,000	43,000	$137,800	$27,600	$38,700	$204,100
Units Completed in June	40,000	40,000	40,000	40,000				
Units in Process on June 30	12,000	12,000	6,000	3,000				
Units Processed	52,000	52,000	46,000	43,000				

Units Completed and Transferred to Finished Goods:		
Stamping Department Costs	(40,000 @ $2.65)	$106,000
Materials Component	(40,000 @ $0.60)	24,000
Conversion Component	(40,000 @ $0.90)	36,000
Total Cost of Units Completed and Transferred	(40,000 @ $4.15)	$166,000
Units in Process on June 30:		
Stamping Department Costs	(12,000 @ $2.65)	$ 31,800
Materials Component	(6,000 @ $0.60)	3,600
Conversion Component	(3,000 @ $0.90)	2,700
Total Cost of Units in Process on June 30		$ 38,100

The Packing Department's production cost report is now completed as shown in Figure 5–12.

The final step is to calculate the cost of goods sold for the month, again using the weighted average cost method:

Finished Goods on June 1	10,000 @ $3.40	$ 34,000
Completed During June	40,000 @ $4.15	166,000
Total Cost of Goods Available	50,000 Units	$200,000

$$\text{(Unit Cost} = \frac{200,000}{50,000} = \$4.00 \text{ per unit)}$$

Cost of Goods Sold	38,000 @ $4.00	$152,000
Finished Goods on June 30	12,000 @ $4.00	48,000
Total Cost of Goods Available for Sale		$200,000

The preceding cost transfers affecting work in process and finished goods are reflected in the following journal entries:

Work in Process—Packing	118,800	
Work in Process—Stamping		118,800
44,000 units were completed at $2.65 per unit and transferred to Packing.		
Finished Goods Inventory	166,000	
Work in Process—Packing		166,000
40,000 units were completed at $4.15 per unit and transferred to Finished Goods Inventory.		
Cost of Goods Sold	152,000	
Finished Goods Inventory		152,000
Cost of 38,000 units sold at $4.00 per unit.		

FIGURE 5–12

Presto Products Corporation—Packing Department
Production Cost Report
For the Month of June, 19X7
Weighted Average Cost Method

| | Physical Units | Equivalent Units | | | Costs | | | |
		Stamping Department	Materials	Conversion	Stamping Department	Materials	Conversion	Total
Units in Process								
June 1	8,000	8,000	2,000	6,000	$ 19,000	$ 1,000	$ 4,500	$ 24,500
Transfers In	44,000	44,000	—	—	118,800	—	—	118,800
Current Costs								
and Production . . .	—	—	44,000	37,000	—	26,600	34,200	60,800
Units Processed	52,000	52,000	46,000	43,000	$137,800	$27,600	$38,700	$204,100
Units Completed	40,000	40,000	40,000	40,000	$106,000	$24,000	$36,000	$166,000
Units in Process								
June 30	12,000	12,000	6,000	3,000	31,800	3,600	2,700	38,100
Units Processed	52,000	52,000	46,000	43,000	$137,800	$27,600	$38,700	$204,100

The general ledger accounts affected by the month's activity can be summarized as follows:

Work in Process—Stamping

June 1	Balance	10,500	June 30	Units Transferred	118,800
30	Materials	53,400			
	Conversion	72,300		Balance	17,400
		136,200			136,200
July 1	Balance	17,400			

Work in Process—Packing

June 1	Balance	24,500	June 30	Units Completed	166,000
30	Materials	26,600			
	Conversion	38,700		Balance	38,100
	Units Transferred	118,800			
		204,100			204,100
July 1	Balance	38,100			

Finished Goods

June 1	Balance	34,000	June 30	Cost of Goods Sold	152,000
30	Completions	166,000		Balance	48,000
		200,000			200,000
July 1	Balance	48,000			

SUMMARY

1. Process costing systems typically measure product costs under conditions of continuous production, sequential processing, and uniform outputs.

2. The process cost procedure essentially involves averaging the total costs of a process or department over the equivalent number of output units it processed or produced during a period.

3. An equivalent unit is a hypothetical measure of accomplishment. It is based on the assumption that a number of partly completed units are the cost equivalents of a proportionally smaller number of fully completed units.

4. Weighted average and FIFO are the most commonly used methods of accounting for the costs of process outputs.

5. The weighted average cost per unit is obtained by dividing the number of equivalent units processed during a period into the combined total of beginning work in process costs and costs incurred during the period.

6. The FIFO method requires that separate unit costs be calculated for the beginning units in process and for the equivalent units produced during the current period.

7. A production cost report is prepared at the end of each accounting period. It summarizes the number of equivalent units processed during the period, the cost per equivalent unit of output, and the quantity and cost of ending work in process inventories and of units completed and transferred to subsequent processing departments.

KEY WORDS AND PHRASES

Process Cost System (161)
Process (162)
Equivalent Units of Output (163)
Percentage of Completion (164)
Conversion Costs (165)
Weighted Average Cost Method (166)
Equivalent Units of Output Processed (167)
Production Cost Report (169)
First-in, First-out Cost Method (172)
Equivalent Units of Output Produced (172)
Specific Identification Cost Method (177)
Last-in, First-out Cost Method (177)
Interdepartmental Transfers (177)
Full Absorption Process Cost Model (181)
Variable Process Cost Model (181)

Questions

1. What distinguishes a process-oriented production operation from a job-oriented one? Give examples of the former.
2. What is a process? Why is it an important concept for cost accounting procedures?
3. What are the main purposes of measuring process costs?
4. What is an equivalent unit?
5. What purpose does the equivalent unit concept serve in process cost accounting?
6. Is the measurement of equivalent units a precise or an approximate procedure? Why?
7. Distinguish between "equivalent units *processed*" and "equivalent units *produced*." Why is this distinction important?
8. Why may it be necessary to make separate equivalent units calculations for the materials, labor, and overhead inputs to products being processed?
9. What effect does the length of the accounting period have on the measurement of process costs?
10. Why has the weighted average method been used in preference to the FIFO method in measuring unit costs in a process? Is this preference reasonable?
11. How are *direct* manufacturing costs treated in a process cost system compared with *indirect* manufacturing costs?
12. What disposition of the costs incurred in a process must be made at the end of each accounting period? Why?
13. What is a production cost report? What purpose does it serve?
14. Explain briefly how equivalent units are computed when the FIFO cost method is used. Compare this to the weighted average cost method of calculating equivalent units.
15. "Transfer of completed units from one process to another is accompanied by a transfer of costs between those same processes." Explain.
16. Why might some manufacturing operations require a combined job order/process cost accounting system? Give examples.
17. What are the uses of the unit costs generated by a process cost system?
18. How can a process cost system be adapted for use with a variable cost model rather than a full absorption cost model?
19. Is it important to separate costs transferred from a prior process from materials costs incurred in the subsequent process? Why or why not?
20. What simplifying assumptions that are made in the weighted average cost method can be questioned? On what grounds?
21. What source documents are appropriate for cost data collection in a process cost system for each of the following?
    (a) Raw materials
    (b) Direct labor
    (c) Manufacturing overhead

22. How do the data requirements for a process cost system differ from those for a job order cost system? Why are they different?

23. "Output units in a process cost system are anonymous." Explain.

24. *"All* continuous manufacturing activities, especially those that use mechanized production lines, must use process costing." Do you agree? Why or why not?

25. "General Motors still doesn't know how much it really costs to produce one Chevrolet!" Evaluate this statement.

26. Why are predetermined departmental overhead application rates useful in a process costing system?

Exercises

E 5-1   Flow of Costs in a Process Cost System

Burnstein Manufacturing Company has three process cost centers, Department A, Department B, Department C. Output of Department A is transferred to Department B. Output of Department B is transferred to Department C. Output of Department C is sold to customers. During July, 19X7, the following cost and operating data were available from production cost reports:

	Department A	Department B	Department C
Cost of Units in Process—July 1	$10,000	$12,400	$ 7,400
Materials Used	$32,000	$29,000	$43,000
Direct Labor	$17,500	$21,000	$32,000
Cost of Units in Process—July 31	$12,000	$ 8,400	$11,400
Number of Units Transferred During July	8,250	9,000	9,000

Required:

(a) Prepare a set of T-accounts to show the flow of costs through the various departmental Work in Process accounts during the month of July.

(b) For the month of July, what was the average cost of completed units
   (1) transferred from Department A to Department B?
   (2) transferred from Department B to Department C?
   (3) transferred from Department C to finished goods?

E 5-2   Equivalent Units Calculations

	Production Situation			
	A	B	C	D
Beginning Inventory:				
Units	20,000	44,000	?	24,000
Percent Complete	20%	50%	40%	10%
Started During Period	160,000	120,000	136,000	?
Transferred Out	?	144,000	104,000	100,000
Ending Inventory:				
Units	20,000	?	56,000	30,000
Percent Complete	10%	30%	25%	80%

Required:

For each of the four production situations, calculate:

(a)   the number of equivalent units *processed* during the period.

(b)   the number of equivalent units *produced* during the period.

E 5–3   Production Cost Report—Weighted Average Cost

Shelly Shingle Manufacturing Company produces a single type of output, has only one manufacturing department, and uses a process costing system. For August, 19X9, the company's Work in Process account appeared as follows:

Work in Process

August 1 Balance	12,000	
30 Materials	46,000	
Labor	39,000	
Overhead	39,000	

The August 1 inventory consisted of 3,000 units that were fully complete with respect to materials and one-third complete with respect to conversion costs. Of the $12,000 cost of that inventory, $6,000 represented materials and $6,000 represented conversion costs. During the month, 10,000 units were put into process. The ending inventory consisted of 2,000 units fully complete in terms of materials inputs but only half complete in terms of conversion processing.

Required:

(a)   Prepare a production cost report for August. Use the weighted average cost method to calculate unit costs.

(b)   Prepare the journal entry to account for (1) costs charged to Work in Process and (2) cost of completed units transferred to Finished Goods Inventory.

E 5–4   Production Cost Report—FIFO Cost

Hoggatt Corporation, which uses a process cost system for its manufacturing activities, recorded the following operating and cost data during September, 19X4.

September 1 Inventory—15,000 Units:	
Materials—100% Complete	$30,000
Conversion—50% Complete	$ 7,500
Production Costs—September:	
Materials	$55,000
Conversion	$28,800
Units Completed and Transferred	30,000
September 30 Inventory—10,000 Units:	
Materials—100% Complete	
Conversion—15% Complete	

Required:

(a)   Prepare a production cost report for September, 19X4. Use the FIFO cost method to measure the cost of units produced.

(b) Prepare the journal entry to account for completed units transferred out.

(c) Evaluate the unit cost measures that were obtained using the FIFO method.

E 5–5   Process Cost System—Comprehensive Review

Reynolds Corporation manufactures a single type of product and uses a process cost system. The firm has two manufacturing departments, Pressing and Folding. The following cost and operating figures were available for January, 19X5:

		Pressing	Folding
(1)	January 1 Inventories:		
	Units	10,000	0
	Materials—100% Complete....	$10,000	0
	Conversion—50% Complete ...	$ 8,000	0
(2)	January Production:		
	Raw Materials Usage	$56,000	$36,000
	Direct Labor	$47,000	$27,840
	Overhead Incurred	$44,500	$41,500
	Units Completed	60,000	50,000
(3)	January 31 Inventories:		
	Units	0	10,000
	Materials—100% Complete		
	Conversion—80% Complete		

(4) Overhead application rates are 100 percent of direct labor in Pressing and 150 percent of direct labor in Folding.

(5) There were no finished products on hand on January 1, 19X5. Of the 50,000 units completed during the month, 45,000 were sold for $5.50 apiece.

(6) The weighted average method is used in the company's process cost system.

Required:
(a) Prepare process cost reports for both the Pressing and Folding Departments.

(b) Prepare journal entries to record all of the preceding transactions for January.

(c) Prepare a schedule to show how the unit cost of items in Cost of Goods Sold was determined.

(d) What inventory balances would be present on January 31, 19X5?

Cases

C 5–1   Job Order or Process Costing?

Watov Corporation produces a limited range of industrial alarm systems. Five basic models, each with standard components, are manufactured in batches and stored until customer orders are received. At that time, other components are added and modifications are made to meet each customer's specifications and the systems are sold in an installed and tested condition. On average, it takes three weeks to manufacture a basic system. It takes an average of ten additional weeks to modify, install, and test a system. The same factory personnel and production facilities are used for both model production and product modification.

Required:

Assuming that the corporation wishes to prepare monthly performance reports, what method of costing manufacturing activities would you recommend? Why? Discuss the product cost measurement problems that will be encountered in the system you have proposed.

C 5-2   FIFO or Weighted Average Cost?

Spreading Chestnut Corporation has been using a process cost system for its manufacturing cost centers. This process cost system has been considered suitable because production operations are continuous, with products passing through several departments and receiving uniform inputs.

However, the unit production costs reported under this system have sometimes varied significantly from month to month. The marketing manager who is responsible for quoting sales prices based on production costs has expressed concern over these variations. Observing that the company's FIFO unit costs lead to variability in short-run cost measures, he proposes switching to the weighted average cost method, which he claims will dampen some of the cost fluctuations. He also suggests a two-month costing period instead of a one-month period, so that some of the short-run cost fluctuations will cancel out.

However, the production manager argues that FIFO is a more accurate method of determining short-run period costs, especially because the company's production volume varies from month to month. He proposes to abandon the practice of allocating manufacturing overhead costs on the basis of a plant-wide monthly rate, and to set departmental application rates based on expected annual overheads.

Required:

Evaluate these two proposals and recommend what should be done.

C 5-3   Cost Methods and Cost Objects

What cost accounting method would be most appropriate in each of the following separate situations? What cost objects would be most critical in each case?

(a)   A company buys junked automobile bodies from used parts dealers who have removed all parts that are likely to be salable. The stripped auto bodies are run through a compressing machine that converts them into cubes of scrap steel, which are then sold to steel mills.

(b)   A similar company also operates a compressing machine, but purchases automobiles with all parts still attached. It discards all non-metal items (glass, fabric, upholstery, and so on), then selects any salable parts (transmission, motors, brake parts, accessories) and stores them for resale by its used parts division. The amount of scrap steel recovered per automobile from the compressing operation is reasonably constant, but the amount and value of used parts varies considerably, depending on the condition of the junked automobile.

(c)   A textile mill processes both natural fabrics (cotton, wool) and synthetics (rayon, dacron). The mill has three operating departments: Spinning, Dyeing, and Weaving. Final output is produced to meet customer orders with regard to color, pattern, and size of bolts. However, within each of the three departments, processing operations are relatively continuous and uniform, with only slight changes needed to set up for each different order. Orders are usually for large amounts and an average order requires approximately three weeks to produce. In addition, the company manufactures a few standard lines of fabric that it produces only when there is idle capacity in the plant.

(d) A company produces "antique" furniture for sale to furniture dealers. Basic frames are manufactured from low-grade unfinished wood acquired from lumber dealers in large lots. Finishing is performed by covering the frames with specially treated panels to produce an "antique" effect. This requires much manual processing because each batch of products (one hundred are produced at a time) is varied so that no two units look alike. Most sales are to dealers who specify in advance the general type of antique item they wish to purchase. Inventories of finished items are usually minimal.

Problems

P 5-1   Process Cost System—Flow of Costs

Malm Manufacturing Company began operations in February, 19X6, during which the following costs were incurred:

Raw Materials Usage	$ 60,000
Factory Labor—Direct	100,000
Factory Labor—Indirect	35,000
Depreciation—Equipment	15,000
Other Manufacturing Overhead	55,000

Output included 3,000 fully completed units and another 3,000 units to which all material components had been added but which were only one-third complete with respect to other manufacturing operations. Overhead cost is applied to the company's output at the rate of 100 percent of direct labor cost. Sales for the month were 2,500 units.

Required:
Record the preceding events in T-accounts. Label all entries and use arrows to show the flow of costs through the various accounts in this process cost system.

P 5-2   Equivalent Units

One of Irwin Corporation's manufacturing departments has the following production characteristics. Raw materials are added at two separate points to units passing through the department. Half the raw materials are added when the units have been 25 percent processed; the other half are added when the units are 75 percent complete. Processing costs are considered to be incurred at a uniform rate throughout the department.

Required:
In each of the following independent situations, determine the number of equivalent units *produced* during the period (a) with regard to their *materials content* and (b) with regard to their *conversion content*. Assume that the FIFO cost method is used.

	Production Situation		
	A	B	C
Beginning Inventory:			
Units	20,000	10,000	?
Percent Processed	80%	10%	50%
Units Transferred In	?	60,000	100,000
Units Transferred Out	80,000	?	120,000
Ending Inventory:			
Units	12,000	15,000	15,000
Percent Processed	40%	80%	50%

P 5–3   Equivalent Units

A process cost system is used by Filbert Filter Company, which has three process cost centers: Cutting, Assembling, and Boxing. In the Cutting Department, all raw materials are issued as soon as products are put into process. In the Assembly Department, the only additional materials are added when the product is halfway through that process. The final step in the Boxing Department, after the product has been fully processed, is to place it in its shipping container.

The following information was obtained for March of 19X0:

	Cutting	Assembling	Boxing
March 1 Inventories:			
Units	2,000	4,000	1,000
Percent Processed	75%	40%	100%
Units Completed in March	12,000	13,000	10,000
March 30 Inventories:			
Units	3,000	3,000	4,000
Percent Processed	20%	60%	75%

Required:

(a) Determine the number of equivalent units *processed* (weighted average cost method) in each department for the month (1) with regard to *materials content* and (2) with regard to *conversion content*.

(b) Repeat the calculations to determine the number of equivalent units *produced* (FIFO cost method).

P 5–4   Production Cost Report, One Department—Weighted Average Cost Method

Allen Manufacturing Company makes skateboards and uses a process cost system with the weighted average cost method. During December, 19X3, 70,000 skateboard components were completed by the Cutting and Sanding Department. Other information from that department for December included:

(1)	December 1	December 31
Inventories in Process:		
Units	5,000	10,000
Materials Components:		
Percent Complete	75%	80%
Cost to Date	$8,000	?
Conversion Cost Components:		
Percent Complete	40%	20%
Cost to Date	$7,200	?

(2) Costs incurred by the Cutting and Sanding Department in December were:

Materials Purchased...............	$172,500
Materials Issued to Production......	$156,500
Materials Returned to Inventory.....	$ 700
Factory Payroll:	
Direct Labor....................	$ 80,000
Indirect Labor	$ 50,000
Other Manufacturing Overhead	
Incurred	$ 57,200

(3) Overhead cost is applied to the output of this department at the rate of 125 percent of direct labor cost.

Required:
(a) Prepare a production cost report for the Cutting and Sanding Department for the month of December.

(b) Prepare journal entries to record all of the preceding events.

(c) Explain the balance that would appear in the Cutting and Sanding Department—Work in Process Account on December 31, 19X3.

(d) What was the cost of units transferred out of the Cutting and Sanding Department in December?

P 5–5 Production Cost Report, One Department—Weighted Average Cost Method

McGraw Manufacturing Company produces industrial lenses for which components and operations are as follows:

(1) (a) Component Part A is purchased and subjected to grinding and polishing operations.

(b) Upon completion of grinding and polishing, component Part B is added and the product is assembled and tested.

(c) All production occurs in a single process cost center.

(d) Labor cost distribution in this cost center consists of 40 percent grinding, 30 percent polishing, 20 percent assembly, and 10 percent testing.

(e) Overhead is applied to products at the rate of 150 percent of direct labor cost.

Operating and cost data for the month of November, 19X1, were as follows:

(2) Inventory in process on
November 1, 19X1—9,000 units $34,475

4,000 units ground	
2,000 units ground and polished	
3,000 units ground, polished, and assembled	
Cost of inventory in process on November 1:	
Component A	$12,150
Component B	4,500
Conversion costs	17,825
	$34,475

(3) Units started in production
     during November   31,000

(4) Inventory in process on
     November 30, 19X1—4,000 units .... $?
       1,000 units ground
       3,000 units ground and polished

(5) Finished Goods Inventory:
       November 1, 19X1—1,000 units .... $ 4,500
       November 30, 19X1—2,000 units .... $?

(6) Purchases:
       Component A $52,500
       Component B $31,500

(7) Materials Usage:
       Component A $47,850
       Component B $34,500

(8) Direct Labor Costs $23,670

(9) Manufacturing Overhead Incurred $43,200

(10) Sales—____?____ units @ $6 each.

Required:
(a) Calculate the number of equivalent units processed during the month with respect
     to:
     (1) Component A
     (2) Component B
     (3) Conversion costs
     Hint: First determine the equivalent unit content of ending inventory with regard
     to conversion. For example, if 2,000 units have been ground and polished, they
     represent 1,400 equivalent units with regard to conversion—that is, 1,400 = 2,000
     × (40% + 30%).
(b) Prepare a production cost report for November, using the weighted average unit
     cost method. Show separate calculations of unit costs with regard to Component
     A, Component B, and conversion cost.
(c) What was the cost of goods manufactured during November, 19X1?
(d) What was the cost of goods sold during November, 19X1?
(e) What are the inventory balances on November 30, 19X1?

P 5–6 Production Cost Report—Variable Cost Model—Weighted Average Cost Method

Refer to the information in Problem 5–4. An analysis of manufacturing overhead costs
reveals the following:

	Fixed Cost	Variable Cost	Total Cost
Indirect Labor	$45,000	$ 5,000	$ 50,000
Other Manufacturing Cost	42,200	15,000	57,200
Total Manufacturing Cost	$87,200	$20,000	$107,200

A variable overhead application rate equal to 25 percent of direct labor cost is established
and the cost of units processed through the Cutting and Sanding Department is to be

determined using the *variable cost model*. The cost of units in process at the beginning of the month is $12,000, consisting of $8,000 in materials, $3,200 in labor, and $800 in variable overhead cost.

Required:
(a) Prepare a production cost report for December.
(b) What balance will appear in the Cutting and Sanding Department—Work in Progress Account on December 31, 19X3? What does this balance represent?
(c) What was the variable cost of units transferred out of the Cutting and Sanding Department in December?
(d) What treatment will be given to the $87,200 of fixed manufacturing overhead cost incurred in December?
(e) Prepare journal entries for all December transactions.

P 5-7   Production Cost Report, One Department—FIFO Cost Method

Winslow Corporation uses a process cost system and employs the FIFO cost method. The following operating and cost data were obtained for one of its process cost centers, Department A, for March of 19X5:

Inventory, March 1, 19X5:	
Units in Process	12,000
Materials (100% complete)......	$ 8,000
Labor (66⅔% complete)	4,800
Overhead (66⅔% complete)	2,400
Production Costs Incurred:	
Materials	$58,500
Direct Labor Costs	48,000
Manufacturing Overhead Incurred ..	25,000
Units Completed and Transferred to	
Department B	70,000
Inventory, March 30, 19X5:	
Units in Process	20,000
Materials (100% complete)	
Labor (50% complete)	
Overhead (50% complete)	

Manufacturing overhead is applied to production in Department A at the rate of 50 percent of direct labor costs.

Required:
(a) Prepare a production cost report for Department A for March.
(b) Prepare a journal entry to record disposition of Department A production costs for March.
(c) Prepare a supporting schedule showing in detail the cost of units transferred to Department B in part (b).
(d) Evaluate the various unit cost measures developed for Department A for March. Compare them with February cost units.

P 5–8   Production Cost Report, One Department—FIFO Cost Method

Kauth Corporation employs a process cost system and uses the FIFO cost method. Manufacturing overhead is charged to production at predetermined rates. For Department X, this rate is $12 per direct labor hour. The normal activity level in Department X is 5,000 labor hours per month.

During May, 19X0, materials used in Department X cost $54,000; $39,600 was spent on direct labor at an average hourly rate of $8. Manufacturing overhead costs of $61,500 were incurred. Units transferred to Department X from Department W during the month totaled 10,000 at a unit cost of $5. Department X completed 9,000 units during May and transferred these to Department Y at full unit cost using the FIFO method.

On May 1, 19X0, 3,000 units were in process in Department X. They had been received from Department W during April at a cost of $4.50 per unit and had incurred materials costs of $15,000 and processing costs of $20,000. These units were fully complete with regard to material, but only two-thirds complete with regard to processing.

At the end of May, the remaining units in process in Department X were 75 percent complete with regard to materials and 50 percent complete with regard to processing.

Required:
(a) (1)   Prepare a production cost report for Department X.
     (2)   What was the cost of the 9,000 units transferred to Department Y during the month? Show separate calculations for all cost components using the FIFO method.
(b)   Calculate and explain the balance in the Department X—Work in Process account on May 31, 19X0.
(c)   Evaluate the differences between April and May unit costs in Department X.

P 5–9   Production Cost Report, One Department—FIFO Cost Method— Variable Cost Model

Using the information in Problem 5–8, assume that the predetermined variable overhead rate is $6 per hour. Also, assume that the total actual overhead for May of $61,500 included $41,000 of fixed overhead cost and $20,500 of variable overhead cost. Finally, the unit cost of items transferred from Department W included a 50¢ fixed cost element in both April and May and the beginning work in process conversion in Department X included $6,000 in fixed overhead at predetermined rates. This means that the units in process on May 1 were carried at $16 per unit, including $12,000 of Department W variable costs, $15,000 materials cost, and $14,000 of variable conversion costs ($20,000 total conversion − $6,000 fixed).

Required:
(a)   Prepare a production cost report for May of 19X0, using FIFO and the variable cost model.
(b)   Prepare the journal entry to transfer units from Department X to Department Y.
(c)   Evaluate the treatment of all aspects of manufacturing overhead costs in Department X for May.
(d)   Explain the balance in the Department X—Work in Process account on May 31, 19X0.

P 5-10 Production Cost Report—Comparison of FIFO and Weighted Average Cost Methods

Murphy Manufacturing Company is concerned that its present process cost system, which uses the weighted average cost method, does not give it accurate enough weekly cost information. It intends to change to the FIFO cost method for all cost centers in its plant.

The following information was available from the records of Department K for the first week of October, 19X2:

	Percent Complete	Costs
Start of Week		
Units in Process—5,000		
Units from Prior Departments	100	$26,500
Materials from Department K	80	10,000
Conversion—Department K	50	25,000
End of Week		
Units in Process—3,000		
Units from Prior Departments	100	
Materials—Department K	100	
Conversion—Department K	50	

During the week, 9,000 units were received from Department J at a unit cost of $6 each. The following costs were incurred in Department K:

Materials Used	$32,000
Direct Labor	62,500
Manufacturing Overhead......	57,000

Department K has a departmental overhead rate of 100 percent of direct labor cost. On completion, all of its output is transferred to Department L.

Required:
(a) Prepare two separate weekly production cost reports for Department K, first using the weighted average method, then using the FIFO method.
(b) Prepare a schedule that shows the differences between the two methods with regard to the cost of units transferred and the cost of units in process.
(c) Is the company's reason for changing to FIFO correct? Explain fully, using information from parts (a) and (b).

P 5-11 Process Cost System—Multiple Department Model—Weighted Average Cost Method

Ellison Electronics, Inc. uses a process cost system for its two manufacturing departments, Stamping and Assembly. In Stamping, all materials are issued to production as soon as processing begins; in Assembly, materials are not issued until the units are 50 percent complete with regard to processing in that department. Processing costs are incurred uniformly in both departments. Each unit of final output in the Assembly Department makes use of two units of the Stamping Department's output. Although they can be distinguished physically, the two different types of output of the Stamping Department are assigned the same amount of costs and are produced in equal quantities.

The following performance data are available for January of 19X8:

	Stamping	Assembly	Finished Goods
(1) Inventory January 1, 19X8:			
Units	15,000	12,000	15,000
Materials Costs	$ 18,000	$ 3,600	—
Conversion—Percent Complete	80%	75%	—
Conversion Costs	$ 7,400	$ 7,000	—
Prior Department Costs	—	$40,800	$65,600
(2) Inventory, January 31, 19X8:			
Units	10,000	8,000	19,000
Materials Costs	?	?	—
Conversion—Percent Complete	40%	25%	—
Prior Department Costs	—	?	?
(3) Units Completed	120,000	64,000	—
(4) Units Sold	—	—	?
(5) Production Costs:			
Materials	$164,000	$15,600	—
Conversion	$ 67,000	$39,200	—

Required:

(a) Prepare weighted average production cost reports for both departments for January of 19X8.

(b) Prepare journal entries to reflect all cost dispositions for January of 19X8.

(c) What was the cost of goods sold for January, 19X8?

(d) Explain in detail the January 31, 19X8 balances in all inventory accounts.

(e) Identify and evaluate the simplifying assumptions that are implicit in the various *unit cost* calculations made in this problem.

P 5–12   Process Cost System—Multiple Department Model—FIFO Cost Method

Sharon's Sweets, Inc. uses a process cost system and the FIFO unit cost method. The company maintains two process cost centers, Cooking and Packaging. In the Cooking Department, all materials are added to units in process at the beginning of processing, but in the Packaging Department no materials are added until all processing has been completed. Processing costs are assumed to be incurred at a uniform rate in both departments.

During July of 19X4, 50,000 boxes of candy were transferred from Cooking to Packaging and 60,000 boxes of packaged candy were moved to the Finished Goods inventory. Materials consumed during July in the Cooking Department cost $54,000; materials consumed in the Packaging Department cost $15,000. Labor and overhead costs were $82,500 in the Cooking Department and $42,750 in Packaging.

On July 1, the 8,000 boxes of candy in Finished Goods inventory had a total accumulated cost of $28,000. The Packaging Department had 15,000 boxes in process, 40 percent complete as to packaging. Costs already incurred on those boxes included $3,750 of labor and overhead in the Packaging Department and $35,250 of Cooking

Department costs. On July 1, enough candy to fill 6,000 boxes was 50 percent complete in the Cooking Department, where materials costing $6,600 and labor and overhead costs of $3,900 had already been incurred.

At the end of the month, 6,000 boxes of candy were in Finished Goods inventory, 10,000 boxes were being processed in Cooking and were 80 percent complete, and the boxes in Packaging were 60 percent complete as to processing.

Required:
(a) Using the FIFO cost method, prepare production cost reports for the Cooking and Packaging Departments for July.
(b) Prepare journal entries for all cost dispositions during July.
(c) Prepare a schedule of ending inventories on July 31, 19X4. Show all cost components.
(d) What might have caused the variations between the June and July unit costs?

P 5–13   Composite Costing System—Process Costs and Job Order Costs

Johnson Stereophonics Corporation manufactures and sells customized stereo sets. All units are first processed through a standardized sequence of production and assembly operations, after which each order is processed separately to customer specifications. The following production and cost data were available for August of 19X3:

(1) Basic Components Completed—1200 units
(2) Basic Components in Process on August 1—300 units:

Materials (80% completed)	$12,500
Conversion (50% completed)	5,625
	$18,125

(3) Basic Components in Process on August 30—500 units
    Materials (100% complete)
    Conversion (60% complete)
(4) Direct Production Costs Incurred During August:

	Basic Components	Job 751	Job 752	Other Jobs
Materials Used	$72,500	$1,500	$4,500	$18,500
Direct Labor	27,500	2,500	6,500	24,000

(5) Manufacturing Overhead Cost Incurred $68,000

Jobs 751 and 752 were started and finished during August. Job 751 required 100 basic component units, whereas Job 752 required 200. Overhead application rates are 125 percent of direct labor cost in basic processing and 100 percent of direct labor cost in customizing.

Required:
(a) Using the weighted average method, prepare a production cost report for August for the basic processing department.
(b) Prepare job cost sheets for Job 751 and Job 752.

(c) Explain the disposition of the cost of basic component units completed during August.

(d) What inventory accounts would have balances on August 30? Give as much detail as possible.

(e) Should the company use a job order cost system for *all* of its manufacturing operations? Why or why not?

P 5–14   Process Costs—Overhead Reallocation—Production Cost Report

Anita's Armatures, Inc. uses a process cost system and the weighted average cost method. The firm has two production cost centers, the Machining Department and the Winding Department. There is also a factory Service Department. Actual production costs (materials, labor, and overhead) are allocated to the output of the production centers each month. The Service Department's costs are allocated to production departments as follows:

> Personnel Costs . . . . . .   Number of employees
> Maintenance . . . .   Floor space
> Repairs . . . .   Machine hours
> Other Costs . . . .   Units of output

In the Winding Department, completed units received from the Machining Department are processed at a uniform rate with regard to labor and overhead, but additional materials are not added until the units are 50 percent complete in the Winding Department.

For February of 19X7, the Winding Department reported costs and production as follows:

(1) Units Completed and Transferred to Finished Goods Inventory—50,000 Units

(2) Units in Process on February 1—5,000 Units
> Machining Department Costs $40,750
> Materials (100% complete) $15,000
> Labor and Overhead (60% complete) . . . . . . $ 6,240

(3) Units in Process on February 28—15,000 Units

(4) Cost of Units Transferred from Machining Department during February—$450,000

(5) Costs Incurred in the Winding Department during February:
> Materials Consumed $130,500
> Direct Labor   65,500
> Factory Overhead   54,900
> $250,900

(6) Costs Incurred in the Service Department during February:
> Maintenance $25,000
> Repairs   15,000
> Personnel   6,000
> Other Items   11,000
> $57,000

(7) The two production cost centers use the following allocation bases:

	Machining Department	Winding Department
Floor Space	30,000 square feet	20,000 square feet
Machine Hours	5,000 hours	2,500 hours
Units of Output	60,000 units	50,000 units
Number of Employees	10 employees	20 employees

Required:

(a) Calculate the amount of overhead to be applied to units in process for February.

(b) Prepare a production cost report for February for the Winding Department.

(c) What is the balance in Work in Process—Winding Department on February 28? What does it represent?

(d) Were production costs higher in January or February in the Winding Department? In the Machining Department? Answer in as much detail as possible with regard to the individual cost components.

(e) If production volume tends to vary significantly from month to month in both the Winding and Machining Departments, evaluate the appropriateness of the costing methods presently being used. Would you suggest changing them? If so, in what way?

P 5–15   Production Cost Report, One Department—Multiple Unit Inputs, Multiple Outputs—Weighted Average Cost Method

Kimberlee Corporation is a multiproduct firm with several production departments, all of which use process costing systems. The Blending Department receives partly finished components from both the Rolling Department and the Shaping Department. In turn, the output of Blending, which is uniform, is transferred either to the Curing Department or to the Baking Department.

Two units of Rolling Department output are combined with three units of Shaping Department output to produce one unit of Blending Department output. Additional raw materials are added to units in process only at the halfway point through Blending, but conversion costs are incurred at a uniform rate.

The following Blending Department production and cost data are available for October, 19X8:

(1) Units in Process on October 1	10,000 units

Rolling Department Costs	$15,000
Shaping Department Costs	16,000
Raw Materials	4,500
Conversion Costs (60% complete)	8,750
	$44,250

(2) Units in Process on October 31 . . . . Conversion (40% complete with respect to conversion in Blending Department).	5,000 units

(3) Units Received from Rolling Department (in Rolling Department Units):	
240,000 units	$264,000

(4) Units Received from Shaping Department (in Shaping Department Units):	
255,000 units	$155,000

(5) October Production Costs—Blending Department:

Raw Materials used	$35,500
Direct Labor	37,500
Manufacturing Overhead	52,500
	$125,500

(6) Overhead Cost is applied at the rate of 150 percent of Blending Department direct labor cost.

(7) October Blending Department Output:

To Curing	50,000 units
To Baking	30,000 units

(8) Additional Information: On October 1, the Blending Department had on hand an additional 20,000 units of output from the Rolling Department that had been received in September at a cost of $15,000, but had not yet received any processing in the Blending Department. At the end of October, the Blending Department had on hand units from both the Rolling and Shaping Departments, received during October, that likewise had not been processed at all in the Blending Department.

Required:

(a) Using the weighted average cost method, prepare a production cost report for the Blending Department for October of 19X8.

(b) Prepare journal entries for all transactions relating to the Blending Department in October.

(c) Explain in detail the balance in the Blending Department—Work in Process account on October 31, 19X8.

(d) Did unit costs of production increase or decrease in October compared with previous months? Evaluate as many different cost components as possible.

P 5–16 Process Cost System, One Department, Two Periods—FIFO Cost Method

Noji Manufacturing Company uses a process cost system and the FIFO method for its production departments. For May and June of 19X2, the following performance and cost data were available for the Molding Department, which is the first stage in the production cycle.

		May	June
(1)	Units in Process: Beginning	10,000	5,000
	Materials (percent complete)	80%	60%
	Cost	$16,000	?
	Conversion (percent complete)	75%	40%
	Cost	$18,000	?
(2)	Units in Process: Ending	5,000	15,000
	Materials (percent complete)	60%	40%
	Conversion (percent complete)	40%	20%
(3)	Units Completed	40,000	70,000
(4)	Production Costs:		
	Materials	$78,750	$153,300
	Labor	34,500	71,000
	Overhead	103,500	106,500

Unit process costs are calculated on the FIFO basis, and actual overhead costs are charged to monthly production.

Required:

(a) Prepare production cost reports for May and June for the Molding Department. Show separate computations of unit costs for *labor* and *overhead*. The conversion cost of the $18,000 worth of work in process at the beginning of May, 19X2 included $7,500 for labor and $10,500 for overhead.

(b) What might have caused the variations in unit cost components between May and June?

(c) Discuss the costing method being used. What changes would you suggest? Why?

P 5–17 Comprehensive Review Problem

Scotten, Incorporated manufactures bakery products that pass through two process cost centers, Mixing and Baking. On January 1, 19X4, balances in the accounts were as follows:

Work in Process—Mixing		8,000 units
Materials	$15,000	
Labor and Overhead	12,500	
	$27,500	
Work in Process—Baking		5,000 units
Materials	$ 3,750	
Labor and Overhead	7,500	
Mixing Department Costs	20,000	
	$31,250	
Finished Goods:		
10,000 units @ $5.00	$50,000	
2,000 units @ $7.00	14,000	
	$64,000	
Raw Materials Inventory	$11,520	
Factory Overhead Control	$ 2,450 (Dr.)	

The Mixing Department inventory was complete with respect to materials, but only 50 percent complete with respect to processing. The Baking Department inventory was 75 percent complete with respect to both materials and processing.

During January, the following transactions occurred:

(1) Raw Materials Purchased $131,500

(2) Materials Issued:

Mixing	$ 78,500
Baking	$ 43,175

(3) Materials Returned Because of Excess Requisitions:

Mixing	$ 1,500

(4) Payroll Analysis:

Direct Labor:

Mixing	$ 38,000
Baking	$ 62,800

Indirect Labor	....	$ 21,500
Supervision	....	$ 10,250
(5) Other Overhead Costs Incurred	......	$ 56,250

During the month, 40,000 units were completed in the Mixing Department and 35,000 in the Baking Department. Sales were 36,000 units at $10 per unit. Overhead costs are applied to production using predetermined departmental application rates of 150 percent of direct labor cost in Mixing and 50 percent of direct labor cost in Baking.

At the end of January, 6,000 units in process in the Mixing Department were 100 percent complete with respect to materials, but only 50 percent complete with respect to processing. Units in process in Baking were 80 percent complete with respect to materials and processing.

In the Mixing Department, the weighted average cost method is used. FIFO is used in the Baking Department, but LIFO is used for the Finished Goods Inventory. However, to simplify cost calculating, units transferred *into* a department are measured at the *average unit cost* represented by the total measure of costs attaching from prior departments.

Required:

(a) Prepare schedules to show the calculation of unit costs in the two departments during January. A process cost report can be used.

(b) Prepare schedules to show the cost of all units transferred during the month, as well as schedules showing the determination of balances in all inventory accounts on January 31, 19X4. A process cost report can be used.

(c) Prepare journal entries for all transactions during January.

6

JOINT PRODUCTS, BY-PRODUCTS, AND PRODUCTION IRREGULARITIES

LEARNING OBJECTIVES

After studying Chapter 6, you should be able to:

1. Explain the averaging and other assumptions on which process costing is based and the circumstances that often invalidate these assumptions.
2. Describe the allocation problem that arises when joint outputs result from common processing efforts.
3. List four methods of allocating common processing costs among joint outputs. Under what conditions is each of these methods appropriate? What are the strengths and weaknesses of each method?
4. Explain how multiple splitoff points affect the allocation of common processing costs to joint outputs.
5. Evaluate the specific uses of joint product costs that include allocated common processing costs.
6. Describe two methods of accounting for by-products.
7. Describe how shrinkage or expansion of units in process should be accounted for in process costing systems.
8. Distinguish between normal and abnormal spoilage and explain how each is calculated and accounted for in process costing systems.
9. Explain how the choice between weighted average and FIFO cost flow assumptions affects the calculation of spoilage quantities and costs.
10. Describe the accounting treatment of reworked units, including the way in which original costs and rework costs are handled during the physical rerouting of the units being reworked.
11. Describe three methods of handling cost recoveries from the sale of defective units or scrap.

Most manufacturing operations do not conform exactly to the single output, uniform processing situations described in Chapter 5. The following variations on those elementary process costing procedures will be examined in this chapter:

A. Multiple Outputs
    1. Joint products
    2. By-products
B. Production Irregularities
    1. Shrinkage or expansion of units in process
    2. Spoiled or defective units in process
    3. Reworked units
    4. Disposal of defective units and raw materials scrap

JOINT PRODUCTS

MULTIPLE OUTPUTS

When a department produces more than one type of output, separate work in process accounts must be kept and separate unit costs must be calculated for each type of output. When possible, the costs of direct materials and labor should be assigned directly to particular types of output. Total departmental overhead costs must also be allocated to each type of output on some consistent basis.

One multiple output situation occurs in production departments where the same workers and equipment process many different kinds of products. For example, if a machining department processes ten different types of valve casings, the direct materials and labor costs of each type of casing should be measured separately. The machining department's overhead costs will have to be distributed to each of the ten different kinds of output, perhaps according to the number of machine hours worked on each type of casing.

This treatment of multiple outputs really amounts to a refined definition of cost objects for process costing purposes. The cost object is no longer a decision center with a single output. Instead, the individual identifiable outputs within each decision center must be treated as separate cost objects.

A second multiple output situation occurs when a manufacturing department produces physically similar items that are later transferred to other departments for processing into different types of finished products. If the items are identical up to the **splitoff point,** at which separate processing begins, each unit processed can be assigned an equal amount of the material, labor, and overhead costs incurred to that point. At the splitoff point, new cost streams begin for the individual products, each carrying its assigned share of the previously incurred **common processing costs.**

Example: Lolita Candy Company produces chocolate-covered cherries. At the end of the cooling operation—after mixing, cooking, and dipping—some chocolate-covered cherries are transferred to the firm's Bulk Sales Division and sold in plain 100-pound boxes; some are transferred to Boxed Candy Sales and sold in fancy 2-pound boxes; and some are transferred to Specialty Sales and wrapped individually for sale at premium prices. One work in process account accumulates costs of the common output (chocolate-covered cherries) up to the splitoff point, after which three separate work in process accounts are needed to accumulate subsequent processing costs of the three individual products.

JOINT OUTPUTS

The most complex multiple output situations occur when a sequence of processing operations results in several physically different outputs to which the process inputs cannot be directly and separately traced. When a combination of inputs is necessary for the production of *all* the outputs, the resulting products are known as *joint outputs.*

Production configurations of this kind are common in many industries, including lumber processing, meat packing, steel making, and chemical and oil refining. A significant part of manufacturing operations in such industries involves *common or joint processing.* Separate, salable products typically do not emerge until fairly late in the production cycle. Partly milled lumber before grading or cutting, slaughtered carcasses of beef before sectioning and grading, partly processed chemicals before final separation and purification, and partly refined oil before gasoline and other final products are extracted—all are outputs of

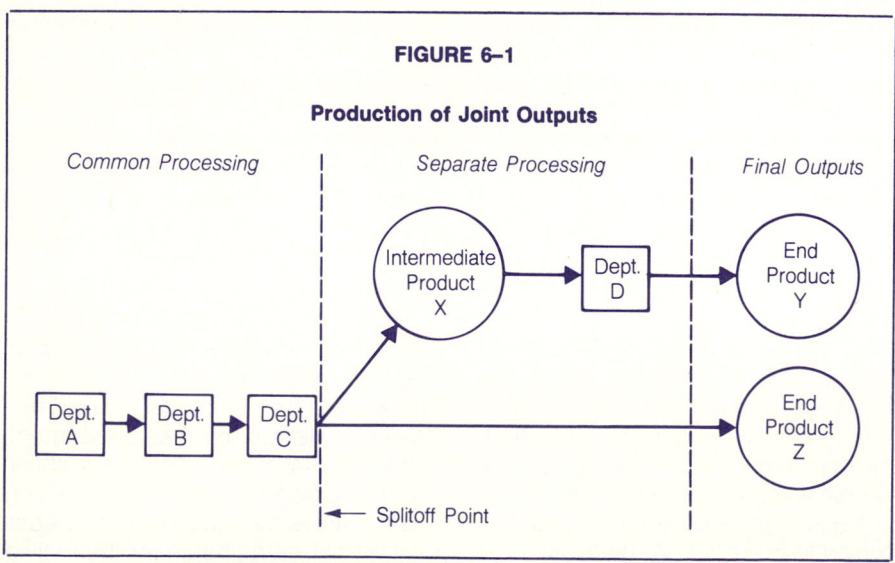

FIGURE 6–1

Production of Joint Outputs

common production processes. Figure 6–1 shows a typical production sequence involving common processing that leads to joint product outputs.

Common processing of inputs takes place in Departments A, B, and C, leading to the creation of *joint products* X and Z. The *splitoff point* occurs at the end of processing in Department C, at which time the total costs of these three departments become *joint costs* to be allocated to joint products X and Z. Product X receives additional processing in Department D. End products Y and Z are then sold.

Joint processing usually applies to physical outputs, such as different grades and sizes of lumber plus chips and sawdust, various shapes and types of steel plus slag and coke, chemical compounds that emerge from a refining process, or assorted cuts of meat plus hide, bones, and tallow from a carcass of beef. But jointly produced outputs are also common in service industries such as commercial banks (checking accounts, passbook savings accounts, certificates of deposit, loan services, trust arrangements, safe deposit rentals); insurance companies (fire, accident, and life insurance policies, tax sheltered annuities); and real estate brokers (property sales, property management, and investment services).

ACCOUNTING FOR JOINT COSTS

Ordinary process cost methods can be used in any production center in which the separate outputs of joint processing operations are not yet identifiable—for example, in costing batches of partly refined phosphates or mixes of molten steel. But at the splitoff point, when the separate outputs become identifiable, all accumulated processing costs must be allocated among these new, individual outputs. After this allocation is made, conventional process cost techniques can again be used to account for subsequent processing of the individual outputs.

Therefore, the critical problem in accounting for joint products is that of allocating common processing costs among the separate outputs that emerge from the joint process. Allocation is necessary because some of those outputs will probably be sold during the current period, whereas others will remain in inventory. The allocation method used will determine the amount of common processing costs allocated to each of the joint outputs. It will also affect the valuation of ending inventories, the calculation of cost of goods sold and annual income, and the amount of income tax liability.

Remember that although joint cost allocation is necessary, it is also an inherently arbitrary process. The following discussion of allocation methods is directed mainly at the need to determine periodic income. In decision making situations—such as budgetary planning, cost control, and short-run or incremental analysis—the allocation of common processing is rarely useful and can easily be misleading.

Commonly used methods for allocating joint processing costs include:

1. Physical units of output
2. Common physical input content
3. Market value of intermediate outputs

4. Net realizable value of end products
5. No allocation

Physical Units of Output   Some joint outputs are similar enough to be measured in terms of a common physical unit—for example, tons of copper, gallons of paint, pounds of beef, or board feet of lumber. The *physical units method* of allocation simply distributes common processing costs among the joint outputs in proportion to the number of physical units of each type of output that are produced.

Example: McGough Company manufactures chemicals. After a series of common processing operations, the product mix is divided into three separate items: Alpho, Beto, and Gammo. During a typical week of operations, common processing costs totaled $120,000; the total output of 6,000 tons consisted of 3,000 tons of Alpho, 2,000 tons of Beto, and 1,000 tons of Gammo. The average cost per ton is therefore $120,000 ÷ 6,000 = $20. Common processing costs can be allocated to the three products on a physical basis by multiplying the tons of each product manufactured by the average cost per ton.

$$
\begin{array}{lr}
\text{Alpho: 3,000 tons @ \$20} = & \$\ 60,000 \\
\text{Beto: 2,000 tons @ \$20} = & 40,000 \\
\text{Gammo: 1,000 tons @ \$20} = & \underline{20,000} \\
\text{Common Processing Costs} & \underline{\underline{\$120,000}}
\end{array}
$$

This method's usefulness lies in its directness and simplicity. Its chief drawback is that it can only be used when a common physical denominator exists and when it is reasonable to associate equal amounts of cost with equal physical quantities of output. Because it is based entirely on physical quantities, this allocation method ignores other potentially important factors, such as the relative sales prices of the joint products.

Common Physical Input Content   Certain joint outputs are somewhat similar physically, but not similar enough to permit the use of a common physical measuring unit. In such cases, the quantity of the *most important input* added to each type of product may be used as a substitute measure for physical units of output. Common costs can then be allocated in proportion to the amount of that key input used in each product.

Example: Waller Company makes three grades of industrial filters in a series of common processing operations. Common processing costs during December were $300,000. Output consisted of 25,000 mild, 30,000 strong, and 10,000 premium filters. The key input to the filter processing operations is a chemical compound that determines the strengths of the different types of filters. The required input quantities of this chemical are:

$$
\begin{array}{lcl}
\text{Mild} & = & \text{2 lbs. per filter} \\
\text{Strong} & = & \text{5 lbs. per filter} \\
\text{Premium} & = & \text{10 lbs. per filter}
\end{array}
$$

Figure 6–2 shows common processing costs allocated according to the amount of chemical needed to produce each type of filter. First the total quantity

---

FIGURE 6–2

Waller Company
Physical Input Allocation of Common Costs
Month of December, 19X2

	Units	Input Content Per Unit	Total Input Content	Percent	Common Costs	Cost Allocation
Mild	25,000 ×	2 lbs. =	50,000	16⅔% ×	$30,000 =	$ 5,000
Strong	30,000 ×	5 lbs. =	150,000	50 ×	30,000 =	15,000
Premium	10,000 ×	10 lbs. =	100,000	33⅓ ×	30,000 =	10,000
			300,000	100%		$30,000

---

of inputs needed to manufacture each kind of filter is calculated. Then the proportion of the total input quantity used in each filter is multiplied by total common costs to determine how much of those costs will be applied to each type of filter.

Market Value of Intermediate Products   Often the joint outputs of common processing are physically dissimilar—for example, when solids, liquids, and gases result from a series of chemical refining processes. The market value of each type of output at the splitoff point is a measure of that output's ability to help recover the processing costs incurred to that point. This suggests that when joint outputs are not physically similar, common processing costs can be allocated in proportion to the *relative market values* of the products at the splitoff point.

Example: Long Company processes a combination of ingredients that generate three products—Sigmo (a compound), Epso (a fluid), and Xeno (a gas). During February, common processing costs totaled $200,000. Output consisted of 5,000 tons of Sigmo, 10,000 gallons of Epso, and 4,000,000 cubic feet of Xeno. Market prices of the three products in their current state are respectively $48 per ton, $12 per gallon, and $10 per 1,000 cubic feet. Figure 6–3 shows the allocation of common costs that would be made according to the relative market values of the three products.

One disadvantage of the market value method is that it allocates costs according to each product's ability to bear those costs. This prevents any direct measure of a product's individual profitability, because each type of output is required to absorb an amount of common processing cost proportional to its market value. This method also requires that market prices of the joint outputs be determinable. However, some or all of the joint products may be subjected to further processing that alters their market value. In such cases, market prices at the splitoff point are less likely to indicate the contribution that each product will eventually make to total net income.

Net Realizable Value Method   This method is intended to overcome problems that arise in costing outputs that have different physical characteristics

FIGURE 6–3

Long Company
Market Value Allocation of Common Costs
Month of February, 19X3

	Quantity Processed		Market Price per Unit		Total Market Value	Percent		Common Costs		Allocated Costs
Sigmo	5,000 tons	×	$48	=	$240,000	60%	×	$200,000	=	$120,000
Epso	10,000 gals.	×	$12	=	120,000	30	×	200,000	=	60,000
Xeno	4,000,000 cu. ft.	×	1¢	=	40,000	10	×	200,000	=	20,000
					$400,000	100%				$200,000

and require additional processing after the splitoff point. The basis for allocation is the *net realizable value* of each type of output at the splitoff point. This amount is calculated by subtracting subsequent processing costs from the sales revenue ultimately earned by each product.

Example: Assume that in the preceding example Long Company subjects its three products to further refining, with no change in physical inputs or outputs, to obtain new end products—Sigmo II, Epso III, and Xeno IV.

	Sales Price per Unit	Subsequent Processing Costs
Sigmo II	$60 per ton	$100,000
Epso III	$20 per gallon	25,000
Xeno IV	2¢ per 1,000 cu. ft.	5,000

The net realizable value method produces the allocation of common processing costs shown in Figure 6–4.

Like the market value method, the net realizable value method creates a circularity in the income determination process by allocating costs to joint outputs on the basis of their ability to bear those costs.

No Allocation   Allocating common processing costs to products in order to measure periodic income is only necessary when there are ending inventories of the joint products. If all joint outputs are sold during the period, total income will not be affected by the method used to allocate common processing costs. In that case, allocation merely measures the profitability of each joint product— an exercise in futility, given the inherent arbitrariness of the four allocation methods previously described. Nonallocation is also preferable when decisions involving short-run incremental analysis are required or when planning and control of common costs is the primary concern.

MULTIPLE SPLITOFF POINTS

In a complex series of processing operations, there is often more than one splitoff point. Cost allocations then become even more arbitrary, not only because several allocations are required, but because different allocation methods may be appropriate at the different splitoff points. For example, early in the manufacturing process, while there is still sufficient commonality in the joint outputs, the physical units basis of allocation may be appropriate. Later, as the process becomes more physically differentiated, sales value-related methods may be preferable.

Example: Lopez Metal Products Company buys sheet steel, which it fabricates into metal ductwork, awnings, and metal toys. The sheet steel is cut and shaped on a special machine that simultaneously turns out several products. Materials, labor, and overhead for this operation during March totaled $80,000. In terms of sheet steel processed, the product mix was as follows:

Ductwork......	50,000 sq. ft.
Awnings	45,000 sq. ft.
Toys..........	5,000 sq. ft.
	100,000 sq. ft.

After being cut to shape, the awnings and toys are dipped in a rust-resistant solution. The total monthly cost of this operation is $10,000. Toys are then painted at a cost of $500 per 1,000. On average, 1,000 toys are obtained from each 1,000 square feet of sheet steel. Sales prices are as follows:

Ductwork......	$1.50 per sq. ft.
Awnings	$2.00 per sq. ft.
Toys..........	$2,500.00 per 1,000 items

Figure 6-5 shows how common processing costs are distributed to the three end products, assuming that the cost of rust-resistant treatment is allocated on a *net realizable value* basis and that the cutting and shaping costs are allocated on a *physical units processed* basis.

The partial income statement shows *net realizable values* for ducts, awnings, and toys of $75,000, $90,000, and $10,000 respectively. This suggests that awnings are the strongest sales performers, followed by ducts, and then toys. The three products contribute $175,000 ($75,000 + $90,000 + $10,000) toward common processing costs of $90,000 ($80,000 + $10,000), but these figures do not clearly indicate each product's *relative profitability,* because the $10,000 rust treatment cost was allocated only to the awnings and toys. The *net income contribution* of each product line ($35,000, $45,000, and $5,000 respectively) should not be used to evaluate profit performance for the following reasons:

1. The common processing costs of cutting and shaping were arbitrarily allocated according to the quantity processed of each product.
2. The common processing costs of rust-resistant coating were allocated to products on a net realizable value basis that anticipates and prejudges the relative profitability of the three joint outputs.

FIGURE 6–5

Lopez Metal Products Company
Multiple Splitoff Point Allocation of Common Processing Costs
Month of March, 19X5

(1) Rust-Resistant Coating Costs:

	Sales Price	Units Pro-cessed	Sales Value	Separa-ble Costs	Net Realiz-able Value	Per-cent	Com-mon Costs	Allo-cated Costs
Awnings	$2.00 ×	45,000 =	$90,000 −	0	=$ 90,000	90% ×	$10,000 =	$ 9,000
Toys ...	2.50 ×	5,000 =	12,500 −	$2,500 =	10,000	10 ×	10,000 =	1,000
					$100,000	100%		$10,000

(2) Cutting and Shaping Costs:

	Quantity Processed	Per-cent	Common Costs	Allo-cated Costs
Ducts	50,000 sq. ft.	50% ×	$80,000 =	$40,000
Awnings.....	45,000 sq. ft.	45 ×	80,000 =	36,000
Toys	5,000 sq. ft.	5 ×	80,000 =	4,000
	100,000	100%		$80,000

(3) Partial Income Statement:

	Ducts	Awnings	Toys	Total
Sales	$75,000	$90,000	$12,500	$177,500
Less: Separable Costs	—	—	2,500	2,500
Net Realizable Value	$75,000	$90,000	$10,000	$175,000
Less: Rust Treatment Costs	—	9,000	1,000	10,000
	$75,000	$81,000	$ 9,000	$165,000
Less: Cutting and Shaping Costs	40,000	36,000	4,000	80,000
Net Contribution	$35,000	$45,000	$ 5,000	$ 85,000

3. Because of the preceding allocations, the unit costs of these joint outputs are not independent of each other.

HOW USEFUL ARE JOINT PRODUCT COSTS?

In a manufacturing environment where joint products are the rule rather than the exception, allocation of common processing costs among joint outputs is necessary for inventory measurement and for periodic income determination. The previously described allocation methods fulfill this basic task of assigning joint costs to products. This allocation process is important: The amount of reported annual income can be influenced by choosing an allocation method that shifts inventoriable costs to or away from particular joint products. But there can never be a universally "correct" method of making joint cost allocations. Because common processing costs cannot be traced directly to particular joint outputs, all allocation methods are inherently arbitrary.

It is generally not appropriate to allocate common processing costs for decision making purposes. The resulting product costs are usually not helpful for product pricing or for performance evaluation and control. Because of the arbitrary nature of these allocations, any attempt to use them as a basis for internal accounting analysis is likely to produce irrelevant information and may lead to incorrect decisions.

In particular, any assessment of the relative profitability of joint products is of doubtful value. As the Lopez Metal Products example demonstrated, analysis based on the net incomes generated by sales of the joint products is questionable because it requires allocations of common costs. Profit comparisons are especially dangerous if the net realizable values of joint outputs were used as the basis for allocation, because the common costs have been allocated in accordance with each product's ability to help cover those costs.

Profitability analysis of joint outputs should be limited to determining (1) whether each product has a positive or negative net realizable value, and (2) how large the *total* net realizable value is for a particular quantity of joint products in relation to *total* common processing costs. Per unit amounts of net income or net realizable value are not valid for purposes of profitability analysis, because the output quantity of each joint product is necessarily interrelated with the output quantities of the other joint products.

BY-PRODUCTS

The allocation problem can sometimes be avoided by identifying multiple outputs of common processing operations as **main products** and **by-products,** rather than simply as joint products. It then becomes more manageable to measure income from joint outputs and make certain types of price and activity-related decisions.

A *by-product* is an output the total market value of which does not contribute materially to company revenues. A by-product may also be an output which is produced simply to obtain the product or products that represent the company's main business. Chemical residuals, sawdust and shavings, slag, and bones are typical by-products in the chemical, lumber, steel, and meat processing industries.

By-products can be accounted for in many ways, but the discussion that follows will be limited to two basic approaches.

(1) *The revenues derived from by-product sales, less any directly attributable disposal costs, can be reported as incidental revenue.* This treatment requires no allocation of common processing costs between main products and by-products. In the fortunate situation in which there is only one main product, this method allows costing procedures, price–quantity decision making, and income measurement to proceed as though the main product were the only product.

(2) *The net proceeds from by-product sales can be treated as cost recoveries and offset against the cost of producing the main product.* When only one main product is manufactured, this method again simplifies accounting proce-

dures by eliminating the need to allocate common processing costs among the multiple outputs.

Example: Demsky Corporation concurrently manufactures two products, Majahs and Minahs. During July, the factory incurs common processing costs of $200,000 and produces 10,000 Majahs that sell for $30 each and 1,000 Minahs that sell for $2 each. Prior to sale, the Majahs require additional separate processing at a cost of $4 per unit. Minahs require 50¢ per unit of additional processing cost. Figure 6–6 illustrates two alternative treatments of by-product costs.

Although treating multiple outputs as by-products simplifies product costing and income measurement, this practice should not be carried to the point that it adversely affects decision making. It can lead to the attitude that by-products are coincidental and unintended and therefore need not be planned for or controlled. If by-products are truly insignificant in quantity and sales value, this outlook may be justified. However, when by-product volume and revenues are regular or material in amount they should be included in the budgetary planning and control process.

Decisions about by-products typically relate to the adequacy of their net contribution or to the method of their disposal. The quantity of by-products

---

FIGURE 6–6

Demsky Corporation
Alternative Treatments of By-Products Costs
Month of July, 19X7

(1) Proceeds from By-Product Sales Treated as Incidental Revenues:

Sales—Majahs (10,000 @ $30)		$300,000
Less: Majahs Processing Costs:		
Basic	$200,000	
Supplemental (10,000 @ $4)	40,000	
		240,000
		$ 60,000
Add: Net Revenue—Minahs:		
[1,000 @ ($2 − $0.50)]		1,500
Total Net Contribution		$ 61,500

(2) Proceeds from By-Product Sales Offset Against the Cost of Manufacturing the Main Product:

Sales—Majahs (10,000 @ $30)		$300,000
Less: Majahs Processing Costs:		
Basic	$200,000	
Supplemental	40,000	
	$240,000	
Less: Net Revenue—Minahs:		
[1,000 @ ($2 − $0.50)]	1,500	
		238,500
Total Net Contribution		$ 61,500

manufactured is determined by production decisions concerning the main products, leaving by-product volume as a given factor rather than a decision variable in its own right. The decision as to whether or not to market a by-product should therefore depend on whether or not the quantity available will generate sufficient revenue to offset the costs of its sale.

When all common processing costs are charged against the main product, there may be a tendency to think of by-products as being cost free, which may in turn encourage the attitude that *any* cash inflow from by-product sales is a net gain. This also can distort decision making, especially when by-product volume and potential revenues are material in amount. There may also be a temptation to misclassify items as by-products simply for convenience in costing and income measurement, when their actual importance justifies their being subjected to decision analysis as joint products.

PRODUCTION IRREGULARITIES IN PROCESS COSTING SYSTEMS

Elementary process costing procedures rest on four assumptions concerning production flows:

1. The output of each process is uniform.
2. Over time, the total number of units leaving a process is the same as the total number entering.
3. The items leaving a process are identifiable and measurable in the same physical terms as the items entering the process.
4. There are no irregularities or discontinuities in the resource conversion process (such as defective units, reworked units, or raw materials scrap).

Because these assumptions are not realistic in most actual production operations, it is necessary to devise accounting methods to deal with production irregularities.

AVERAGING ASSUMPTIONS

The **equivalent unit** concept was introduced in Chapter 5 as a convenient way of expressing unit costs in a continuous production process. It assumes that any number of partially completed units are the cost equivalents of a proportionally smaller number of fully completed units. For example, 2,000 units 60 percent complete are the cost equivalent of 1,200 fully completed units. The equivalent unit concept involves several averaging assumptions. First, it implies that there is a constant rate of resource transformation during the production process. Second, it assumes that all in-process units are at the same average stage of completion. Finally, it assumes that the cost per equivalent unit associates an average and equal amount of cost with every unit subject to the calculation.

Although these averaging assumptions simplify process cost calculations, they can distort cost measurements if they are not appropriate to a particular manufacturing situation. Inaccurate measurements can result when the accounting period is short, when the number of units in process at the end of the period is larger than the number processed during the period, when unit volume is relatively low and unit cost is relatively high, when physical inventories fluctuate significantly in size, or when the input conversion process does not occur at a uniform rate.

SHRINKAGE OR EXPANSION OF UNITS IN PROCESS

The elementary process costing model operates on the assumption that the physical properties of inputs to a process are retained in the outputs from that process. If 10,000 hoe handles enter Department X for processing, 10,000 hoe handles should eventually leave Department X. This assumption is justified only if the same cost object remains physically present in successive stages of production.

But processing sometimes causes major physical changes in partly manufactured items. Shrinkage or expansion often occurs when chemical reactions take place or when ingredients are mixed together after individual processing. Such physical changes require a change in the description of the output unit used as a cost object. Equivalent units and unit product costs must then be calculated in terms of process *outputs,* not process *inputs.* Consequently, the number of units entering a process must be restated in terms of the expected units of output from that process.

Example: Smothers Smelting Company combines steel, titanium ore, and various chemicals to produce a high grade, heat resistant alloy. The refining process results in the fusion of this basic mix into refined alloy, with a leftover waste product of no resale value. During July, 10,000 tons of basic mix were transferred to the final refining department, after incurring prior processing costs of $100 per ton of mix. The normal yield rate is 80 percent; that is, 8,000 tons of refined alloy can be expected from the 10,000 tons of basic mix. Equivalent units in the final refining department should be calculated in terms of expected output of refined alloy. Unit costs should be expressed as cost per ton of refined alloy. The $100 per ton of basic mix therefore becomes $125 per ton of refined alloy [($100 $\times$ 10,000) $\div$ 8,000 = $125].

Assume that $150,000 in conversion costs were incurred in the final refining department during July. There was no work in process at the beginning of the month, but by the end of July, 6,000 tons of refined alloy had been transferred to the next processing department and the remaining 2,000 tons were 75 percent complete with respect to conversion in the refining department. (The change from basic mix to refined alloy is complete at the halfway point of processing in the refining department). The methods demonstrated in Chapter 5 for calculating equivalent units and for process cost transfers between departments produce the solution shown in Figure 6–7.

Refining Department costs are applied to output as follows: 6,000 equivalent units of alloy were completed during July at a unit cost of $20 per ton and a total cost of $120,000. An additional 1,500 equivalent units were in process on July 31 at a unit cost of $20 per ton and a total cost of $30,000.

FIGURE 6–7

Smothers Smelting Company
Process Costs in Final Refining Department
Month of July, 19X3

| | Physi-cal Units | Equivalent Units | | Costs | | |
		Prior Depart-ments	Refining Depart-ment	Prior Depart-ments	Refining Depart-ment	Total Costs
In Process, July 1	—	—	—	—	—	—
Transfers In*	8,000	—	—	$1,000,000	—	$1,000,000
Current Production	—	8,000	7,500	—	$150,000	150,000
Units Processed	8,000	8,000	7,500	$1,000,000	$150,000	$1,150,000
Completions	6,000	6,000	6,000	$ 750,000	$120,000	$ 870,000
In Process, July 31	2,000	2,000	1,500	250,000	30,000	280,000
Units Processed	8,000	8,000	7,500	$1,000,000	$150,000	$1,150,000

* Transfers into the Refining Department are expressed in terms of anticipated tons of output of refined alloy. 10,000 tons of mix = 8,000 tons of expected alloy. Unit costs are calculated as follows:

Prior Department Costs: $\frac{\$1,000,000}{8,000} = \$125$ per ton

Refining Department Costs: $\frac{\$150,000}{7,500} = \$20$ per ton

SPOILED AND DEFECTIVE UNITS IN PROCESS

More common and more critical than physical shrinkage is the tendency for production processes to be less than technically perfect. Production errors and inefficiencies often cause the number of acceptable completed units leaving a process to be smaller than the number that entered that process. Units may be lost because of (1) normal production attrition due to breakage, spoilage, or other physical defects; (2) production inefficiencies (bad materials, poor workmanship, machine malfunctions) leading to defective or unacceptable units; and (3) specific events, such as theft or accidents, that cause loss of output.

Normal Spoilage   When it can be determined that a certain rate of loss among units being processed must be expected under normal operating conditions—*and that this is to be tolerated*—then the output of acceptable units must absorb the cost of this *normal spoilage.* The first step in accounting for normal spoilage is to calculate the total number of equivalent units processed through the department (including both acceptable and spoiled units), so that a unit cost can be derived for *all* items processed. The second step is to revise this unit cost to absorb the cost of normal spoilage into the cost of the acceptable units processed. The normal spoilage rate can best be expressed in relation to the quantity of acceptable output. Accordingly, a 10 percent normal spoilage rate implies that to produce 100 acceptable units, 110 units should be put into process—the normal loss being 10 percent of 100, or 10 units.

Example: Doten Company's Blending Department expects spoilage to occur at the rate of 5 percent of all units passing inspection, which occurs at the end of processing. During August, 21,000 units entered the Blending Department and 20,000 units were passed by the quality control inspectors and transferred to the next department. There were no beginning or ending inventories in the Blending Department. Costs consisted of $52,500 transferred from prior processing departments and $31,500 incurred in the Blending Department.

The unit cost of acceptable outputs is calculated in Figure 6–8. First the $4 unit cost of all units processed is determined. This $4 cost per unit is then used to find the total cost of acceptable units and of normal spoilage. The total cost of processing all units, divided by the number of acceptable units, equals the unit cost of acceptable outputs.

The treatment in Figure 6–8 results in processing costs being assigned only to acceptable units of output. This is appropriate if the defective units provide no revenue and are in effect discarded. The costing of defective outputs that do provide revenues—for example by being sold as scrap or "seconds"—will be discussed later in this chapter in relation to cost recoveries.

Abnormal Spoilage Sometimes more units are lost during processing than is allowed under existing tolerance levels. Such abnormal loss may be caused by continuing production inefficiencies, defects that could have been corrected, or a single unusual occurrence such as a fire or other casualty loss.

FIGURE 6–8

Doten Company—Blending Department
Processing Costs
Month of August, 19X4

Step 1: Total Processing Costs:

From Prior Departments	$52,500
Costs Incurred in Blending Department	31,500
Total	$84,000
Equivalent Units Processed	21,000

Unit Cost of *All* Units Processed: $\dfrac{\$84,000}{21,000} = \$4.00$

Step 2: Cost of Acceptable Units Transferred:

20,000 Units @ $4.00	$80,000
Plus: Cost of Normal Spoilage (5% of 20,000 units @ $4.00)	4,000
Total	$84,000

Unit Cost of Acceptable Units: $\dfrac{\$84,000}{20,000} = \$4.20$

Excessive losses of units in process require different costing methods than are used in handling normal spoilage.

As before, the first step in cost calculation is to determine the total number of equivalent units processed, including both normal and abnormal spoilage. The cost of *normal spoilage* should then be absorbed into the cost of production that has passed inspection. But the cost of *abnormal spoilage* should be isolated and accounted for as a separate item in control reports. This is consistent with the definition of normal spoilage as the amount that will be tolerated as part of acceptable processing activities; any higher rate of loss represents a deviation from the accepted norm. This suggests that there might even be a favorable variance for abnormal spoilage, if total spoilage is less than the predetermined normal amount.

Example: During September, Doten Company transferred to its Blending Department 32,000 units that had prior processing costs of $82,000. The Blending Department produced 30,000 units of acceptable output in September and incurred $46,000 in conversion costs. There were no in-process inventories. The normal spoilage rate is still 5 percent of all units passing inspection, which occurs as the final step in Blending Department processing. Normal and abnormal spoilage costs are calculated in Figure 6–9.

The acceptable Blending Department output absorbs its own processing costs of $120,000, plus the $6,000 cost of normal spoilage, for a unit cost of $4.20. The $2,000 unfavorable variance due to abnormal spoilage is the cost of processing 500 excess spoiled units up to the point of inspection.

In Doten Company, the inspection process occurred at the completion of processing. However, it might have taken place at some intermediate point during production. In that case, it would be necessary to measure the costs of abnormal spoilage and of accepted units in terms of the number of equivalent units processed up to the point of inspection.

Example: During October, Anderson Corporation had the processing costs and production results shown in Figure 6–10. The normal spoilage rate is 10 percent of all units passing inspection, which is performed at the halfway point in processing operations. All materials are added at the start of processing and conversion costs are incurred uniformly during processing. The weighted average cost method is used to account for process costs.

The process costing solution table demonstrated in Chapter 5 can be adapted to help determine total costs of acceptable and spoiled units when inspection occurs halfway through the process. Initial entries in the solution table, using the data given in Figure 6–10, are shown in Figure 6–11.

The normal spoilage rate is 10 percent of all acceptable inspected units. Therefore, the number of *physical units of normal spoilage* is 6,000 (10% × [40,000 + 20,000]), because the ending in process inventory has passed the halfway point in processing, whereas the beginning inventory had not. Given that a total of 10,000 units are defective, *abnormal spoilage* is 4,000 units.

However, in terms of *equivalent units* of processing, spoiled units received only 50 percent of conversion processing, because they were extracted at the midway inspection point and not processed further. Therefore, as shown in Figure 6–12, the 10,000 spoiled units are complete as to materials inputs, but represent only 5,000 equivalent units with respect to conversion costs incurred. Normal spoilage—60 percent of the total spoiled units—is assigned 3,000 of

FIGURE 6–9

Doten Company—Blending Department
Processing Costs
Month of September, 19X4

Step 1: Total Processing Costs:

From Prior Departments	$ 82,000
Costs Incurred in Blending Department	46,000
Total	$128,000
Equivalent Units Processed	32,000

Unit Cost of *All* Units Processed: $\dfrac{\$128,000}{32,000} = \$4.00$

Step 2: Cost of Acceptable Units Transferred:

30,000 Units @ $4.00	$120,000
Plus: Cost of Normal Spoilage	
(5% of 30,000 units @ $4.00)	6,000
Total	$126,000

Unit Cost of *Acceptable* Units: $\dfrac{\$126,000}{30,000} = \$4.20$

Step 3: Cost of Abnormal Spoilage:

Total Units Spoiled (32,000 − 30,000)	2,000
Less: Normal Spoilage (5% × 30,000)	1,500
Abnormal Spoilage	500 units
Cost of Abnormal Spoilage (500 units @ $4.00)	$ 2,000

Step 4: Total Costs Accounted For:

Cost of Acceptable Output (30,000 units @ $4.20)	$126,000
Cost of Abnormal Spoilage (500 units @ $4.00)	2,000
Total Costs Incurred	$128,000

these equivalent units of conversion processing, whereas abnormal spoilage receives the other 2,000 equivalent units.

The following cost calculations are needed to fill in the lower right portion of the solution table, which shows total costs of processing completed units, spoiled units, and ending work in process inventories.

(a) Cost per Unit of Processing All Units:

Materials . . . . . . $\dfrac{\$350,000}{70,000} = \$5$ per unit

Conversion . . . . $\dfrac{\$610,000}{61,000} = \$10$ per unit

FIGURE 6–10

Anderson Corporation
Units Processed and Total Processing Costs
Month of October, 19X8

Units in process, October 1		10,000
Materials (100% complete)	$ 38,000	
Conversion (20% complete)	22,000	
	$ 60,000	
Add: Units Started in Process during October		60,000
Less: Units Completed and Transferred Out		(40,000)
Less: Defective Units		(10,000)
Units in Process, October 31		20,000
Materials (100% complete)		
Conversion (80% complete)		
October Processing Costs:		
Materials	$312,000	
Conversion Costs	588,000	
Total October Processing Costs	$900,000	

FIGURE 6–11

Anderson Corporation
Process Costing Solution Table—Step 1
Month of October, 19X5

	Physical Units	Equivalent Units		Processing Costs		
		Materials	Conver-sion	Materials	Conver-sion	Total Costs
In Process, October 1	10,000	10,000	2,000	$ 38,000	$ 22,000	$ 60,000
Starts	60,000	—	—	—	—	—
Current	—			312,000	588,000	900,000
Units Processed ...	70,000			$350,000	$610,000	$960,000
Completions	40,000					
Spoilage:						
Normal ⎫						
Abnormal ⎬	10,000					
In Process, October 31	20,000					
Units Processed ...	70,000					

FIGURE 6–12

Anderson Corporation
Process Costing Solution Table—Step 2
Month of October, 19X5

| | Physical Units | Equivalent Units | | Processing Costs | | |
		Materials	Conversion	Materials	Conversion	Total Costs
In Process, October 1	10,000	10,000	2,000	$ 38,000	$ 22,000	$ 60,000
Starts	60,000	—	—	—	—	—
Current	—	60,000	59,000	312,000	588,000	900,000
Units Processed	70,000	70,000	61,000	$350,000	$610,000	$960,000
Completions	40,000	40,000	40,000			
Spoilage:						
Normal	6,000	6,000	3,000			
Abnormal	4,000	4,000	2,000			
In Process, October 31 ...	20,000	20,000	16,000			
Units Processed	70,000	70,000	61,000			

(b) Cost of Abnormal Spoilage:

4000 units	—Materials (100%) @ $5	$20,000
	—Conversion (50%) @ $10	20,000
		$40,000

(c) Cost of Normal Spoilage (To Be Absorbed into Cost of Acceptable Output):

6000 units	—Materials (100%) @ $5	$30,000
	—Conversion (50%) @ $10	30,000
		$60,000

Units Passing Inspection:
40,000 + 20,000 60,000

Unit Cost of Normal Spoilage:

$$\frac{\$60,000}{60,000 \text{ units}} \dots\dots\dots\dots\dots\dots\dots\dots\dots\dots \$1 \text{ per unit}$$

(d) Revised Cost of Acceptable Output, Including Normal Spoilage:

(1) Completions — 40,000 units:

Materials (100%) @ $5		$200,000
Conversion (100%) @ $10		400,000
		$600,000
Prorated Normal Spoilage @ $1		40,000
Total Cost		$640,000

Revised Unit Cost $\dfrac{\$640,000}{40,000}$ .... $16 per unit

(2) In Process—20,000 units:
    Materials (100%) @ $5 .... $100,000
    Conversion (80%) @ $10 160,000
                               $260,000
    Prorated Normal Spoilage @ $1 20,000
    Total Cost $280,000

The complete solution table is shown in Figure 6–13.

The calculation of normal spoilage in the following month (November) must exclude the 20,000 units in process on October 31. These 20,000 units passed inspection in October and their recorded cost already includes their share of normal spoilage costs.

But suppose only 5,000 units had been spoiled in October, 45,000 units were satisfactorily completed, and in-process inventory consisted of the same 20,000 inspected units. Normal spoilage would then have been 6,500 units (10% × [45,000 + 20,000]). This would result in *minus* 1,500 units of abnormal spoilage! To be consistent with the concept of a normal amount of spoilage being absorbed into the cost of acceptable output, a *favorable* abnormal spoilage variance would then have to be reported.

FIGURE 6–13

Anderson Corporation
Process Cost Solution Table—Step 3
Month of October, 19X5

	Physical Units	Equivalent Units Materials	Equivalent Units Con-version	Processing Costs Materials	Processing Costs Con-version	Processing Costs Pro-rated Spoilage	Total Costs
In Process, October 1 .	10,000	10,000	2,000	$ 38,000	$ 22,000	—	$ 60,000
Starts	60,000	—	—	—	—	—	—
Current	—	60,000	59,000	312,000	588,000	—	900,000
Units Processed .	70,000	70,000	61,000	$350,000	$610,000	—	$960,000
Completions .	40,000	40,000	40,000	$200,000	$400,000	$40,000	$640,000
Spoilage:							
Normal	6,000	6,000	3,000	30,000	30,000	(60,000)	—
Abnormal ..	4,000	4,000	2,000	20,000	20,000	—	40,000
In Process, October 31	20,000	20,000	16,000	100,000	160,000	20,000	280,000
Units Processed .	70,000	70,000	61,000	$350,000	$610,000	—	$960,000

The positive or negative cost of abnormal spoilage should be highlighted in control reports. Abnormal spoilage can sometimes be explained by the occurrence of an unusual event such as theft, fire, accident, or sabotage. More typically, the abnormal spoilage cost signals management to take remedial action either by correcting the cause of the abnormal spoilage during processing or by recalculating the rate of normal spoilage if results indicate that the rate being used is no longer valid.

THE FIFO COST METHOD AND SPOILAGE

When process costs are accumulated on a first-in, first-out rather than a weighted average basis, the cost of spoilage is calculated only in terms of the current period's processing costs, because the cost of any units in process at the beginning of a period is treated as a separate FIFO cost layer. The use of FIFO also implies that spoiled units come only from the current period's production, because the cost of beginning units in process is always included in the cost of units transferred to the next process.

Example: Using the Anderson Corporation data from Figure 6–13, the FIFO cost per equivalent unit is calculated by dividing the total processing costs incurred during October by the equivalent units produced.

$$\text{Materials} = \frac{\$312,000}{60,000} \quad \cdots\cdots \quad \$\ 5.20$$

$$\text{Conversion} = \frac{\$588,000}{59,000} \quad \cdots\cdots \quad 9.97$$

Cost Per Equivalent Unit $15.17

The cost of *abnormal spoilage,* based on the current period's processing costs up to the inspection point, is found by multiplying these unit costs by the equivalent units of abnormal spoilage.

Abnormal Spoilage—4,000 units:
Materials (100%) @ $5.20 . . . . $20,800.00
Conversion (50%) @ $9.97 . . . .   19,932.20
Cost of Abnormal Spoilage $40,732.20

The cost of *normal spoilage,* to be absorbed into the cost of units that have passed inspection, is determined in the same way.

Normal Spoilage—6,000 units:
Materials (100%) @ $5.20 . . . . $31,200.00
Conversion (50%) @ $9.97 . . . .   29,898.30
Cost of Normal Spoilage $61,098.30

The current processing cost of each of the 60,000 units that passed inspection will be increased by approximately $1.02 ($61,098.30 ÷ 60,000), the prorated cost of normal spoilage. The revised cost of *acceptable output* can then be calculated.

(1)	Completions—40,000 Units:		
	Materials—10,000 @ $3.80	$ 38,000.00	
	—30,000 @ $5.20	156,000.00	$194,000.00
	Conversion—2,000 @ $11.00	$ 22,000.00	
	—38,000 @ $9.97	378,711.88	400,711.88
	Spoilage—40,000 @ $1.02		40,732.20
	Cost of Acceptable Output Completed		$635,444.08
(2)	In Process—20,000 units:		
	Materials (100%) @ $5.20		$104,000.00
	Conversion (80%) @ $9.97		159,457.62
	Spoilage @ $1.02		20,366.10
	Cost of Acceptable Output Still in Process		$283,823.72

The month's *total processing costs* of $960,000 can be summarized as follows:

Completions (40,000 units)	$635,444.08
In Process (20,000 units)	283,823.72
Abnormal Spoilage	40,732.20
Total Processing Costs	$960,000.00

REWORKED UNITS

Units found to be defective are sometimes rerouted through one or more production departments to correct defects. When this is done, it is necessary to (1) report separately the cost of direct materials and productive labor expended on the units being reworked and (2) exclude these reworked units from equivalent unit calculations until they reenter the production stream at the point where they were originally removed.

To avoid distortions in current period unit processing costs, the direct material and labor costs incurred in reworking units should be treated as manufacturing overhead rather than being included in direct materials or direct labor charged to the process. Overhead application rates should allow for anticipated rework costs. To prevent double counting of rework costs, all costs incurred on reworked units up to the point at which processing was interrupted should be held in a separate work in process account until the reworked units resume their passage through the production cycle.

Example: Hatfield Company has two departments: Grinding and Polishing. During November, 19X2, output consisted of 50,000 completed units in Grinding, and 40,000 completed units in Polishing. However, an additional 10,000 units were rejected by quality control inspectors in the Polishing Department because they were found to have been improperly ground. This inspection occurred when the units reached the halfway point in the Polishing Department. They were then returned to the Grinding Department to be reworked and were still there, partly reprocessed, at the end of the month.

Processing costs for November were:

	Grinding	Polishing
Materials	$100,000	—
Direct Labor	50,000	$60,000
Overhead Incurred	62,500*	27,500
Overhead Application Rate......	100% of	50% of
	Direct Labor	Direct Labor

* Includes $17,500 materials and labor reworking costs.

The entire $17,500 of materials and labor cost incurred in reprocessing should be classified as manufacturing overhead, not as direct materials and direct labor. The 10,000 units being reworked should be temporarily accounted for as a separate work in process category. This category should contain all costs incurred in processing the rejected units to the point where they were extracted from the regular process flow. These costs total $50,000, calculated as follows:

		Grinding	Polishing
(1)	Processing Costs:		
	Materials	$100,000	—
	Labor	50,000	$60,000
	Overhead Applied	50,000	30,000
	Total Processing Costs	$200,000	$90,000
(2)	Equivalent Units Produced	50,000	45,000*
(3)	Unit Process Costs	$4.00	$2.00
(4)	Units Being Reworked (10,000 units):		
	Grinding (100%) @ $4		$40,000
	Polishing(50%) @ $2		10,000
	Processing Costs on Units Being Reworked		$50,000

* Includes 40,000 fully complete units, plus 10,000 units half completed.

When these 10,000 units have been satisfactorily reworked, they will resume their former status as half completed units in the Polishing Department. Care should be taken not to count them a second time as output units of the Grinding Department. The $50,000 accumulated costs of grinding and polishing up to the inspection point will be added to work in process costs in the Polishing Department. The rework costs will remain in manufacturing overhead.

COST RECOVERY FROM SPOILED OR DEFECTIVE UNITS

In the earlier discussion of spoiled and defective units, it was assumed that units removed from processing had no recovery value. However, if such units are sold as defective items or "seconds," any revenue received from their sale must be accounted for. Three methods of handling such revenues are as follows:

(1) Incidental Revenue   If the recovery from sales of spoiled units is *immaterial*—only a small percentage of their actual cost—any reprocessing costs should be charged to manufacturing overhead, whereas sales proceeds from spoiled units should be reported separately as incidental revenue.

(2) Cost Offset   If the amount recovered is *material,* sales proceeds should be credited against the cost of spoiled units. The abnormal spoilage variance and the cost of normal spoilage prorated over acceptable units of output then become *net* amounts.

(3) Product Line   If the recovery is *regular* as well as *material* in amount (say, more than the recorded cost of spoilage), it becomes appropriate to consider defective units as a product line and to report separately the net revenues from their sale. No spoilage costs should be assigned to the units passing inspection, because all costs of processing are to be matched with the revenues from units sold separately as part of the spoiled products line.

Example: The January operations of Carroll Corporation's Curing Department resulted in the cost and output results shown in Figure 6–14.

Assume first that the defective units were sold for $2.50 each, that all acceptable units were transferred for further processing, and that there was no abnormal spoilage. Treating the defective units as a *separate product line* results in a net income of $10,000:

Sales (20,000 @ $2.50)	$50,000
Less: Cost of Goods Sold (20,000 @ $2)	40,000
Net Contribution from Spoiled Product Sales	$10,000

In this situation, spoilage does not affect the cost of acceptable units. The 180,000 good units are transferred to the next process at their regular unit cost of $2.

FIGURE 6–14

Carroll Corporation
Curing Department Production and Costs
Month of January, 19X7

Total Equivalent Units Processed:	
Passed Inspection at End of Process	180,000
Units Found to be Defective	20,000
Total Equivalent Units Processed	200,000
Total Cost of Materials and Conversion	$400,000

$$\text{Unit Cost of All Units Processed} = \frac{\$400,000}{200,000} = \$2 \text{ per unit.}$$

But what if the defective units are sold for a smaller but still material amount, say $1.10 each? It is then more appropriate to offset their sales revenues against the cost of spoiled goods. The net cost of spoilage is reduced to $18,000 (20,000 units × [$2.00 − $1.10]) and the cost of good units increases to $2.10 each.

Cost of Processing 180,000 Units @ $2.00	$360,000
Add: Net Cost of Spoilage	18,000
Total Effective Cost of Good Units	$378,000

$$\text{Revised Unit Cost} = \frac{\$378,000}{180,000} \text{ . . . . } \$2.10 \text{ per unit}$$

Finally, if the 20,000 defective units are sold for a nominal amount, say 2¢ apiece, the $400 recovered should be reported as *incidental revenue,* and the cost of the acceptable units is ($400,000 ÷ 180,000 = $2.22) per unit.

In addition to accounting for the revenues from defective items, accountants must analyze the *quantity* of spoilage. Differences between the total number of units spoiled and the number allowed as normal spoilage should be monitored for purposes of control and evaluation.

RAW MATERIALS SCRAP RECOVERY

Similar procedures can be used to account for sales of raw materials that were originally issued to production, but were not used in manufacturing operations. Offcuts of lumber, steel, glass, and rubber may be recycled and sold; so may sawdust, metal filings and shavings, and other scrap items. When the amount recovered is not material, it is preferable to treat the sales proceeds as incidental revenues.

If scrap sales are regular and the proceeds are material in amount, such recoveries should be offset against the total cost of raw materials requisitioned by the department or process. If this is not done, process costs of the main product will be overstated by the amount of cost recovery from unused materials. This error may be compounded if the unadjusted cost figures are then used as a basis for bidding or pricing decisions.

SUMMARY

1. Quite often more than one type of output results from a series of common processing operations. The accumulated costs of common processing cannot be traced directly to any of the joint outputs.
2. For purposes of inventory valuation and income measurement, these common processing costs must somehow be allocated among the joint outputs.
3. The physical units and net realizable value methods are the most commonly used bases for allocation.
4. When one of several joint outputs is of minor importance, it may be classified as a by-product and accounted for separately from the main products.

5. Shrinkage or expansion of materials can cause the number of units leaving a process to be greater or less than the number entering.

6. In other manufacturing situations, the physical basis of the units changes during processing, thereby confusing the relationship between input and output units.

7. Units in process may also be lost due to normal and expected causes (breakage, defects, spoilage, quality rejects), or due to unusual or preventable occurrences (production inefficiencies, accidents, thefts).

8. Units that need reworking often must pass through the same processes more than once, in which case processing costs and the number of equivalent units processed must be adjusted.

9. Costs may be partly or wholly recovered through the sale of spoiled, damaged, or defective units, or from disposal of scrap or surplus materials.

KEY WORDS AND PHRASES

Multiple Outputs (213)
Splitoff Point (213)
Common Processing Costs (214)
Joint or Common Processes (214)
Intermediate Products (214)
End Products (214)
Joint or Common Processing Costs (215)
Physical Units Method of Allocation (216)
Common Physical Input Content Method of Allocation (216)
Market Value of Intermediate Products Method of Allocation (217)
Net Realizable Value Method of Allocation (218)
Multiple Splitoff Points (220)
Main Product (222)
By-Product (222)
Production Irregularities (224)
Equivalent Units (224)
Normal Spoilage (226)
Abnormal Spoilage (227)
Reworked Units (234)
Raw Materials Scrap (237)

Questions

1. What basic accounting problems are created by the presence of joint products that are the output of common processing operations?
2. Explain the following terms: *joint product, intermediate product, end product, splitoff point, common processing costs.*
3. Explain the rationale and method of application of the following techniques for allocating joint or common processing costs:
   a. Physical units of output
   b. Net realizable value
   c. Market value of intermediate products
   d. Common physical input content
   e. No allocation
4. When is the allocation of common processing costs really necessary? Why?
5. When is the allocation of common processing costs potentially misleading and confusing? Why?
6. Differentiate between *by-products* and *main-* or *co-products.*
7. Explain two basic methods of accounting for by-product costs.
8. Should planning and control procedures be applied to by-products even if they are immaterial or insignificant? Why or why not?
9. Explain the implications of the averaging assumptions involved in process costing, especially with regard to calculation of equivalent units of output.
10. What modifications to fundamental process costing procedures are necessary if the inputs to a process are always subject to a regular predictable amount of shrinkage or expansion?
11. Distinguish between *normal spoilage* and *abnormal spoilage.* What alternative accounting treatments are recommended for each?
12. What components should be included in the unit cost of those units of output that survive the effects of spoilage, damage, quality rejection, and so on, and are classified as *acceptable* or *good* units of output? Why?
13. How should the cost of abnormal spoilage be calculated? What disposition of those costs should be made? Why?
14. How does the treatment of costs of spoilage in the weighted average cost method differ from that in the FIFO method?
15. What modifications to process costing procedures should be made for reworked units? Why?
16. Explain the basic alternative treatments of revenues derived from sale of rejected, spoiled or defective units.
17. How may revenue derived from the sale of scrap, waste, or unused raw materials be accounted for?

Exercises

E 6–1   Process Costing—Spoiled Units—Elementary Analysis

Donat Company prepared the following report to summarize processing operations in one of its departments for the month of August, 19X0.

August 1	Units In Process	1,000	
	Materials (100% complete)		$ 950
	Conversion (40% complete)		$ 750
August 30	Units Completed	40,000	
	Units Transferred	36,000	
	Units Spoiled	4,000	
	Units In Process	5,000	
	Materials (100% complete)		
	Conversion (30% complete)		
	Materials Used, August		$44,050
	Conversion Costs, August		$82,250

In this process, inspection occurs when units are fully complete. The cost of all spoiled units is allocated to all completed units that pass inspection. The weighted average cost method is used.

Required:

(a) Prepare a production cost report for the month of August.

(b) Explain the calculation of the cost of the units transferred to the next process.

(c) What is the revised unit cost of one acceptable unit of output of this process for the month of August? Explain its separate components (materials, conversion, etc.).

E 6–2 Process Costing—Spoiled Units—Abnormal and Normal Spoilage

The Assembly Division of McGough Company had the following production and cost figures for its cooking process for February of 19X2. Materials are added at the beginning of the process. Conversion costs occur uniformly throughout the process. Inspection takes place at the end of the process. The normal spoilage rate is 5 percent of all acceptable units that are transferred to the next process. The weighted average cost method is used in assigning costs to output units.

Inventory—February 1	2,400 units
Materials (100% complete)	$ 4,000
Conversion (20% complete)	$ 460
Month of February	
Units Completed	35,000
Units Passing Inspection	33,000
Materials Usage	$53,000
Conversion Costs	$28,500
Inventory—February 28	3,000 units
Materials (100%)	
Conversion (40%)	

Required:

(a) Prepare a production cost report for February.

(b) Explain the various dispositions of costs made for February in the Cooking Department. What accounting treatment does each receive (expense, asset, and so on)?

(c) What is the unit cost of units transferred out of the Cooking Department? What are the components of that amount?

(d) How much of the cost of spoilage for the month is allocated to the 3,000 units in process at the end of the month? Why?

E 6–3   Process Costing—Spoiled Units—Elementary Analysis

The Cutting and Polishing Department of Jaime Company receives rough finished metal extrusions from the Molding Department. Each unit received from Molding is cut into four equal sized lengths in the cutting operation. After the cutting operation, units are inspected for blemishes. Acceptable units are then polished and transferred to Packaging. Half of the conversion activities in the department are accounted for by each operation, cutting and polishing. No materials are added to units in process in the department. An acceptable spoilage rate is 2 percent of units passing inspection.

For May of 19X7, the following information was compiled:

	Units Received from Molding		400,000 units
	Molding Department Costs (for units		
	received by Cutting and Polishing)	$1,200,000	
May 1	Units in Process—Cutting and Polishing		
	(25% complete)		30,000
	Molding Department Costs	$ 90,000	
	Conversion Costs	15,000	
	Units Completed and Transferred to Packaging ...		405,000
May 31	Units in Process		15,000
	Conversion (75%)		
	Cutting and Polishing Department Costs	$ 827,500	
	Units Designated as Defective		10,000

The weighted average costing system is used.

Required:

(a) Prepare a production cost report for May.

(b) Give journal entries for the disposition of (1) costs of units transferred to the Packaging Department and (2) cost of abnormal spoilage.

(c) What was the unit cost of units transferred to Packaging in May? Explain the components of that amount.

(d) What is the cost of the ending work in process composed of? Explain each component.

E 6–4   Cost Flow Diagram—Joint Products and By-Products

Oakmont Company produces a line of commercial fertilizers. Five basic ingredients are used. Materials Z and Y are added to production in Department M when processing begins. An average of 80 percent of the physical output of Department M is good and is transferred to Department N. The other 20 percent has no resale value and is discarded. Sometimes this proportion of good output to waste varies. Materials X and W are inputs at the beginning of processing in Department P. All of the output of Department P is transferred to Department Q, where input material V is also added. Department Q has two outputs—R and S. In Department N, the output of Department M and Product R are processed, resulting in three main marketable products (J, K, and L) and one by-product (B). Finally in Department T, Product S is processed further to generate marketable products G, F, and E.

Required:

(a) Prepare a flow diagram to represent the relationships outlined above.

(b) Explain what components will be included in the manufacturing costs of products J, K, L, G, F, E and B.

(c) From an accounting standpoint, what problems are inherent in this situation? Discuss briefly.

E 6–5 Joint Products—Allocation of Common Processing Costs— Elementary

In the production operations of the Heinen Company, X and Y are joint products. Up to the point of separation, common processing costs in a typical month are $60,000 and the outputs of X and Y are 40,000 and 80,000 units respectively. Beyond this separation point, X requires further processing which costs $60,000. Sales prices of X and Y are $10 and $2 per unit respectively.

Required:

(a) Allocate the common processing costs to Products X and Y using (1) the physical units method and (2) the net realizable value method.

(b) If an inventory of 5,000 units of X and 5,000 units of Y were on hand, how would they be valued (1) using the physical units method and (2) using the net realizable value method?

(c) Which of the two products is more profitable? Explain fully.

E 6–6 Joint Products—Allocation of Common Processing Costs— Alternative Methods

Truax Chemical Company produces two products, Alpha-One and Alpha-Plus from a single key ingredient, Moron. During a typical week, 100,000 tons of Moron are processed at a total common processing cost of $560,000. Output is 120,000 units of Alpha-One and 80,000 units of Alpha-Plus. However, Alpha-Plus is twice as potent as Alpha-One because each unit of Alpha-Plus contains twice as much Moron. Alpha-One can be sold immediately for $4 per unit, but Alpha-Plus requires extra refining at a cost of $2 per unit before it is sold for $12 per unit.

Required:

(a) Allocate the common processing costs to products Alpha-One and Alpha-Plus using (1) the physical units method, (2) the net realizable value method, and (3) the relative input content method.

(b) Inventory of 20,000 units of Alpha-One and 10,000 units of Alpha-Plus are on hand. How would they be costed for income measurement purposes under each of the three methods used in part (a)?

(c) Which of the two products is more profitable? Why?

E 6–7 Joint Products and By-Products—Allocation of Common Processing Costs—Alternative Methods

Consuello Manufacturing Co. produces three outputs from a sequence of common processing operations. Each batch of output usually comprises 80 units of X-1, 200 units of X-2, and 200 units of X-3. Sales prices and weights of the respective products are as follows:

	Sales Price	Weight per Unit
X-1	$ 25	40 lbs.
X-2	$ 60	60 lbs.
X-3	$180	84 lbs.

The cost of processing one batch is $30,000.

Required:
(a) Allocate the common processing costs to the three products using (1) the physical units method, (2) the relative weight of output, and (3) the net realizable value method.

(b) Prepare product-line income statements for the three products under each of the three methods used in part (a).

(c) What conflicting and/or misleading information might be derived from the various results shown in the income statements in (b)?

(d) Assuming that X-1 is treated as a by-product instead of a joint product, calculate the unit costs of the other two products (1) when all by-product revenue is treated as incidental revenue and (2) when all by-product revenue is used to offset common processing costs. Show calculations for each of the three methods of allocating common processing costs as in part (a).

(e) Should X-1 be treated as a by-product or a joint product? Why?

E 6–8 By-Products—Alternative Costing Methods

Sheppard Company uses special ingredients to produce its main product, Super-Gro. The processing of Super-Gro also results in a by-product, Off-Shoot, which can be marketed separately. Each batch of 100,000 pounds of input ingredients results in 80,000 pounds of Super-Gro, 10,000 pounds of Off-Shoot, and 10,000 pounds that are lost to shrinkage. Before being sold for $50 per pound, Super-Gro requires extra processing which costs $10 per pound. Off-Shoot can be sold immediately after separation for $5 per pound. Costs of processing one batch of input are $1,600,000.

Required:
(a) Calculate the cost per pound of Super-Gro if (1) the revenue from Off-Shoot is treated as incidental revenue and (2) the revenue from Off-Shoot is used to offset common processing costs.

(b) Prepare income statements to reflect the production and sale of one batch of 100,000 pounds of inputs under the two alternative approaches used in part (a).

(c) Depending on which of the two alternative methods of accounting for Off-Shoot is used, what will be the difference in income? Show where this difference originates.

(d) If 5,000 pounds of Off-Shoot are on hand at the end of an accounting period, how would they be reported on the balance sheet under each of the two methods?

Cases

C 6–1 Defective and Spoiled Units

(1) "The costs of a process should only be allocated to the acceptable output of that process. No costs should be allocated to products that are discarded because of defects."

Required:
(a) Discuss this statement.
(b) Do you agree? Why or why not?

(2) "It is neither important nor possible to distinguish between those units that are sometimes referred to as 'normal spoilage' and those referred to as 'abnormal spoilage.' If they are spoiled or defective, that's it! Why bother with the charade of calling them different names?"

Required:
(a) Discuss this statement.
(b) Do you agree? Why or why not?

C 6–2 By-Products and Common Processing Costs

(1) "By-products that need no individual processing after their separation from the main product (or products) should be assigned a zero value if held in inventory. Any revenues derived from their sale should be credited against costs of the main products."

Required:
(a) Discuss this statement.
(b) Do you agree? Why or why not?

(2) "Common processing costs should not be allocated among the joint products to which they contribute, because any allocation procedure is necessarily arbitrary."

Required:
(a) Discuss this statement.
(b) Do you agree? Why or why not?

C 6–3 Common Processing Costs

The following information is available for Alda Corporation's production activities during April of 19X3:

Product	Units Produced	Sales Price
A	16,000	$5.00
B	24,000	$6.00
C	8,000	$ .25

Common processing costs totaled $60,000. All output had been sold at the end of the month.

Required:
(a) Allocate the common processing costs. Explain which method you used and why.
(b) Is it possible to determine whether or not production of C should be discontinued? Why or why not?
(c) Is it possible to determine whether or not more units of B should be produced? Why or why not?
(d) Is any of the three products more profitable than the others? If so, why?
(e) What additional information is needed in order to give a more complete answer to parts (b) and (c)?

C 6–4   Allocate Common Processing Costs

Turlock Turkey Company processes turkeys and distributes three products that it derives from its operations. Operating results for November of 19X1 were as follows:

	Output	Sales Price/Lb.
Grade A (Breasts, Thighs)	40,000 lbs.	$1.20
Grade B (Wings, Legs, Backs)......	16,000 lbs.	$0.80
Feathers........................	2,000 lbs.	$3.00

Primary processing costs were $32,000 up to the point of separation of the three products. Additional processing costs were $10,000 for Grade A, $8,000 for Grade B, and $800 for Feathers. All output was sold during the month.

Required:
(a) Prepare an income statement for November.
(b) State which method of common processing cost allocation you chose and which products you treated as joint products and which, if any, as by-products.
(c) Defend your choices in part (b).
(d) If you had used another method in part (b), how would the cost figures differ from those in part (a)?
(e) If not all of the output had been sold in November and there were ending inventories of 2,000 pounds of Grade A, 1,000 pounds of Grade B, and 500 pounds of feathers, what would be the total cost of those inventories?

C 6–5   Normal and Abnormal Spoilage

XYZ Chemical Co. uses a process costing system. During April, production costs in Department X were as follows:

Materials	$ 60,000
Direct Labor	30,000
Variable Overhead......	30,000
Fixed Overhead	30,000
	$150,000

Process output for the month was the equivalent of 50,000 fully complete units.

Required:

(a) What was the cost of one unit processed in Department X during the month (1) on a full cost basis and (2) on a variable cost basis?

(b) How would your answers to part (a) change if you knew that during the month an employee had inadvertently left a drain valve open and 10,000 units of output had been flushed away? This sort of accident does not happen very often. This particular drain valve is located on a tank where the finished product is normally stored. (Output would have been 60,000 units if this had not occurred, but total costs would remain unchanged.) Explain your answers.

(c) Using your answers from part (a), how would you handle the following circumstances? The 50,000 fully completed units included 40,000 that are processed further and sold as Grade A at $6 each. Additional processing costs for these amount to $1.50 per unit. The remaining units are not processed further and are sold as Grade B for $4 each.

    (1) How would you allocate the Department X processing costs to the Grade A and Grade B items in order to make a decision as to whether or not to change the present mix of Grade A and Grade B produced? (It is presently a ratio of 4 to 1. The only difference between Grade A and Grade B is whether or not they have received the "additional" processing.) State all assumptions that you make.

    (2) Should the present mix be changed? Why or why not?

C 6–6   Alternative Costing Methods

Fitzwallace Corporation has built a new chemical processing plant in an area that has rigid environmental control regulations. It is a modern plant with a large amount of computer operated production processing and control equipment. Three major products will be produced and distributed, as well as two minor by-products that will need to be disposed of. One of the by-products is derived very early in processing operations, but the other is not separated until the final production process has been completed. All three major products are processed through four separate production departments. The major products differ as to the composition of inputs that are required, but use the same production facilities.

    Employees of the chemical plant include processing equipment operators, security guards, power plant operators, maintenance crews, and materials handling crews. Because all deliveries are received and products shipped by rail, the plant maintains a rail siding with a crew of switch operators and loaders (these are the materials handlers referred to above). Supervisory personnel are assigned to work with each of these groups as well as with the general factory management staff.

    Materials are purchased in carload lots to take advantage of price discounts for multi-carload shipments. There is no raw material deterioration problem. Deliveries arrive irregularly and shipments are usually made only when a large number of carloads are ready to go. Occasionally, a special order may require a single or partial carload shipment. Materials handling crews are assigned other tasks (maintenance and so on) when there is no work for them to do in the rail siding.

Analysis of total operating costs indicate that the plant, which can process 20,000 tons of major product output per month at full capacity, will incur the following monthly costs:

Direct Raw Materials Cost .... $6 per ton of output
Variable Labor Costs
  (at 75% plant capacity)
    Operators .... $ 45,000
    All others .... $ 30,000
Fixed Labor Costs $125,000
Variable Overhead Items
  (at 75% plant capacity) .... $ 36,000
Fixed Overhead Items .... $ 90,000

The plant must be closed down for an eight-hour period if excessive air pollution is detected. During the shutdown, all operators are to receive full wages.

Required:
(a) What type of cost accounting method would you recommend for this firm? Why?
(b) What major cost objects should be emphasized?
(c) Would the full absorption cost model or the variable cost model be more appropriate here? Why?
(d) Would the wages and salaries of each of the factory worker groups be classified as direct labor or manufacturing overhead? Why?
(e) What special accounting considerations are called for in the following aspects of the situation?
  (1) The plant is shut down on several occasions for pollution violations.
  (2) The rail crews work in the power plant and equipment maintenance departments for periods of time when there are no shipments to handle.
  (3) The first by-product consumes 20 percent of all input raw materials and is separated after the first production operation.
  (4) The second by-product amounts to approximately .50 percent of total output in physical quantity, but has a significant sales value.

Problems

P 6–1   Process Costing—Spoilage—Elementary Analysis

Balboa Company reported the following cost and production data for one of its departments during September of 19X9:

Production Data
  Units in Process—Sept. 1   800
  Units Started during Sept. 5,000
  Units Completed and Transferred 4,800
  Units in Process—Sept. 30   600

Cost Data
Units in Process—Sept. 1
Materials (100%) .... $ 800
Conversion .... $ 475
Materials Usage in Sept. $6,160
Conversion Costs in Sept. $9,255

Inspection occurs when units are complete. Normal spoilage was estimated to be 240 units for this month. Ending work in process was 100 percent complete as to materials and 60 percent complete as to conversion processing. The weighted average cost method is used. Finished goods are transferred for further processing in the Packaging Department.

Required:

(a) Prepare a production cost report for September.

(b) Prepare journal entries for the disposition of costs for the month.

(c) Explain the ending balance in the Work in Process account. What does it represent? Is the cost of any spoilage contained in it? Why or why not?

(d) What action should be taken with regard to the cost of any units that are classified as abnormal spoilage?

P 6–2   Process Costing—Normal and Abnormal Spoilage—Cost Disposition

Sharp Company had the following cost and production results for one of its processes during April of 19X6:

Units in Process .... 47,600 units
Units Transferred Out .... 40,000 units
In Process—April 1 .... 1,000 units
Materials (100%) .... $ 40,000
Conversion (40%) .... $ 22,000
Costs Incurred—April
Materials $154,000
Conversion $210,650
In Process—April 30 .... 8,000 units
Materials (100%)
Conversion (25%)
Normal Spoilage Allowed .... 400 units

Units are inspected halfway through the conversion process. The weighted average cost method is used.

Required:

(a) Prepare a production cost report for April.

(b) Explain the composition of all separately identified elements of cost dispositions for the process for the month.

(c) Discuss the reasons for treating the two components of production spoilage differently.

(d)   What is the unit cost of the output transferred out of this process? What are the separate component amounts?

P 6–3   Process Costing—Spoilage and Shrinkage—Two Departments— Weighted Average Method

The sole product of Morabito Company passes through Departments A and B. In Department A, input X is added at the beginning of processing. There is a consistent amount of shrinkage, in that for every ten tons of X added, only nine tons of output are obtained to be transferred to Department B. This shrinkage occurs at a uniform rate throughout processing (that is, 50 percent of the shrinkage has occurred by the time input tonnage is half processed). Production data in Department A is expressed in batches of 10 tons of input X.

In Department B, input Y is added when processing is half complete and inspection takes place when units are 75 percent complete. The normal rate of spoilage is 5 percent of all output that passes the quality control test.

Production and cost data for August of 19X2 are as follows:

	Department A	Department B
In Process—August 1	200 batches*	5,000 tons
Materials	100%—$2,500	—
Conversion	75%—$4,000	40%—$3,500
Prior Dept. Costs	—	100%—$25,000
Production Starts	5,000 batches	?
Completions (Acceptable)	?	42,000 tons
Costs Incurred		
Materials	$91,100	$168,700
Conversion	$128,300	$66,625
In Process—August 31	400 batches*	2,000 tons
Materials	100%	100%
Conversion	25%	80%
Prior Dept.	—	100%

* Not adjusted for shrinkage.

Required:
(a)   Prepare August production cost reports for Departments A and B.
(b)   Give journal entries (1) for transfers from Department A to Department B, from B to Finished Goods Inventory, and (2) for any other cost dispositions.
(c)   Explain the cost content of the ending work in process inventories.
(d)   Explain the accounting treatment for the shrinkage that occurs in Department A as compared to that for the spoilage in Department B.
(e)   How does the Department B in-process inventory at the beginning of the month differ from that at the end of the month? Of what significance is this difference?

E 6–4   Process Costing—Spoilage and Shrinkage—Two Departments— FIFO

Fuchs Pesticide Company produces a liquid pesticide called Bug-Off, which is passed through two processes: (1) Blending and (2) Dilution and Bottling. In the first process, chemical reactions occur, leading to a 20 percent loss in volume. This loss occurs as soon as processing begins, but is unavoidable and does not vary from one production lot to another. In the Dilution process, water is added in equal parts with the mix obtained from the Blending Department. Quite often bottles are broken or explode, because the mix is occasionally quite volatile. It has been established that five 5-gallon bottles will be lost for every 100 that are filled successfully. Bottles are assumed to explode at the 100 percent conversion point. For May of 19X3, the following product and cost data were obtained:

	Blending	Dilution and Bottling
Costs Incurred		
Materials	$198,000	$76,380
Conversion	$50,250	$80,000
Completions (acceptable)	? gallons	7,500 bottles
Starts	25,000 gallons	? gallons
Breakage	—	500 bottles
In Process—May 1	500 gallons	300 gallons
Materials	100%—$4,950	100%—$600
Conversion	40%—$500	50%—$300
Prior Dept. Costs	—	100%—$2,130
In Process—May 31	400 gallons	500 gallons
Materials	100%	100%
Conversion	50%	30%
Prior Dept. Costs	—	100%

The FIFO cost method is used to account for processing costs in both departments. Units transferred into Dilution and Bottling are accounted for at the average of their FIFO cost from the Blending Department.

Required:
(a) Prepare production cost reports for both the Blending and Dilution and Bottling Departments for May.
(b) Explain the composition of unit processing costs in both departments for the month.
(c) Explain the difference in accounting for shrinkage in the first department as compared to breakage in the second.
(d) What is the cost of one bottle of pesticide that was fully processed during May? What is the composition of this cost?
(e) Were processing costs higher in May than they were in April? Explain.

P 6–5   Process Costing—Units Added During Processing—Shrinkage/ Spoilage—Two Departments—Weighted Average

Arden Corporation produces a household cleaning liquid and has two processing departments, Mixing and Refining. In the Mixing Department, one pound of material X is mixed with one gallon of water. At the 50 percent conversion point, 25 percent of the solution is lost to evaporation. After cooling, the remaining 75 percent becomes the liquid output transferred to the Refining Department. This 25 percent rate of evaporation is constant and occurs every month.

In the Refining Department, the liquid from the Mixing Department is combined with special ingredient Y. The mix ratio is one gallon of Y to every two gallons from the Mixing Department. At the end of the refining process, a quality control inspection occurs. There is no loss of gallonage due to physical reasons in this process, but on an average, output is rejected as being of inferior cleansing strength at the rate of 2 percent of all approved output. Sometimes more or less than this 2 percent allowance is rejected. Rejected output is of no resale value and is dumped. The weighted average cost method is used. Production and cost data for December of 19X0 were as follows:

	Mixing	Refining
In Process—Dec. 1	2,000 gals.	18,000 gals.
Materials	100%—$6,500	100%—$14,250
Conversion	75%—$2,625	25%—$2,750
Prior Dept. Costs	—	100%—$60,000
Completions (approved)	? gals.	90,000 gals.
Production Starts	80,000 gals.	?
Production Costs—Dec.		
Materials	$179,500	$83,050
Conversion	$114,175	$92,870
In Process—Dec. 31	6,000 gals.	4,500 gals.
Materials	100%	100%
Conversion	20%	60%
Prior Dept. Costs	—	100%

Required:
(a) Prepare December production cost reports for the two departments.
(b) Prepare journal entries for all units transferred and any other cost dispositions.
(c) Explain the cost content of all in process inventories on December 31.
(d) What is the difference between the opening and closing inventories in the Mixing Department? Why is this difference important?
(e) Itemize the cost content of units transferred to Finished Goods Inventory during December.

P 6–6 Process Costing—Spoilage—Two Departments—Elementary Analysis

Di Francesco Company operates a chemical distillery to produce a special additive for the food processing industry. There are two departments, Mixing and Blending, but because of the highly perishable nature of the inputs used, quite often batches of spoiled output must be thrown out. For January of 19X2, the following information was obtained:

	Mixing	Blending
In Process—Jan. 1	3,000 gals.	3,600 gals.
Materials	$8,000—100%	—
Conversion	$2,800—50%	$4,272—70%
Prior Dept. Costs	—	$21,240—100%
Costs Incurred—Jan.		
Materials	$109,000	—
Conversion	$40,040	$41,400
Units Started—Jan.	23,000 gals.	20,400 gals.
Units Completed and		
passing inspection	20,400 gals.	18,000 gals.
Normal Loss Allowance	800 gals.	500 gals.

	Mixing	Blending
In Process—Jan. 31	4,400 gals.	5,400 gals.
Materials	100%	—
Conversion	50%	40%
Prior Dept. Cost	—	100%

Inspection of output occurs at the end of each process. The weighted average cost method is in use.

Required:

(a) Prepare production cost reports for the Mixing and Blending Departments for January.

(b) Prepare all journal entries related to units transferred and other cost dispositions.

(c) Explain the balances in the Work in Process accounts at January 31. Is any cost of spoilage included in these amounts? Why or why not?

(d) What should be done about the cost of abnormal spoilage (if it is present)?

P 6–7 Process Costing—Reworked Units—Weighted Average Cost Method

Williamson Company has two manufacturing departments—Machining and Assembly. For May of 19X2, the following cost and production data were available:

	Machining	Assembly
In Process—May 1	20,000	10,000
Materials	$85,000—100%	$6,000—100%
Conversion	$21,000—50%	$5,000—20%
Prior Dept. Costs	—	$60,000—100%
Units Started	?	?
Units Transferred Out	160,000[1]	140,000[3]
Production Costs—May		
Materials	$645,000[4]	$74,000
Labor	$179,500[5]	$228,500
Overhead Incurred	$215,050	$213,050
In Process—May 31	25,000[2]	15,000
Materials	100%	100%
Conversion	60%	80%
Prior Dept. Costs	—	100%

[1] This *includes* 10,000 units that were received from Assembly for rework during the month.
[2] This *excludes* an additional 5,000 units that are on hand awaiting rework. These defective units were returned from Assembly after they had received 40 percent of processing in that Department (but 100 percent of materials had been added).
[3] This *excludes* units returned to the Machining Department.
[4] This *includes* $30,000 for direct materials used in rework operations.
[5] This *includes* $25,000 for labor costs involved in rework operations.

The overhead application rate was 100 percent of direct labor in both departments.

Required:
(a) Prepare a production flow diagram to represent the movement of units through the two departments during May.
(b) Prepare a May production cost report for both departments.
(c) Explain each item in the disposition of costs in the Assembly Department—that is, account for where all production costs in the department were assigned.
(d) What revisions to the production cost data for May were needed? Why?
(e) What accounting treatment is needed for the 5,000 units being reworked (1) at the end of May and (2) when the rework is completed?
(f) Why must reworked units be accounted for separately?

P 6–8   Joint and By-Products—Alternative Methods of Costing of Inventories—Elementary

Murphy Company manufactures products X, Y, and Z in a common processing operation. At present, Z is treated as a by-product and its net realizable value of $50 per pound is subtracted from the common processing costs that are allocable to products X and Y. For September of 19X2, total common processing costs were $340,000 and separate processing costs for Product Y totaled $40,000. Output was 30,000 pounds of X, 10,000 pounds of Y, and 200 pounds of Z. Sales prices are $8, $16, and $150 per pound, for X, Y, and Z respectively.

Required:
(a) Prepare an allocation of common processing costs based on physical units.
(b) Prepare an allocaiton of common processing costs based on net realizable value.
(c) Assume that there were no beginning inventories, but that there were month-end inventories of 5,000 pounds of X, 2,000 pounds of Y, and 50 pounds of Z. Prepare income statements for the firm for the month, using (1) the physical units allocation method and (2) the net realizable allocation method.
(d) Comment on the alternative results obtained in (1) and (2) of part (c).
(e) Should the company continue to treat Z as a by-product? Why or why not?

P 6–9   Joint Products—Net Realizable Value Method—Multiple Splitoff Points

Sparkay Corporation processes sorghum. In the first processing operation, syrup is extracted, leaving a residue of crushed grain and straw. In the second operation, the straw and grain are separated. Finally, the crushed grain is mixed with other ingredients to form cattle fodder. The straw is sold for use in brooms and brushes.

During a typical month, 100,000 pounds of sorghum are processed. The yield is 5,000 gallons of syrup, 50,000 pounds of straw and 75,000 pounds of fodder. The sorghum costs the company 25¢ per pound. The cost of the first syrup extracting process is $15,000; $25,000 is spent in the separation process. The cost of extra ingredients to mix with the grain is $40,000. The mixing process costs another $20,000.

Sales prices are $5 per gallon for syrup, 20¢ per pound for straw, and $2 per pound for fodder.

Required:
(a) Prepare a diagram to show the cost flows and splitoff points in this example.
(b) Prepare an allocation of all purchasing and processing costs using the net realizable value method.
(c) Could the physical units method be used in this example? Why or why not?
(d) Should the straw be treated as a joint product or a by-product? Why?

P 6–10 Joint and By-Products—Two Processes—Alternative Methods

Johnstone Company has two processing departments, A and B, and three outputs, Q, R, and S. R and S are joint products, but Q is treated as a by-product. Production and cost data for August of 19X4 were as follows:

	Department A	Department B
Raw Materials Used	$32,000	$20,000
Direct Labor	$40,000	$60,000
Overhead Incurred	$33,000	$23,250
Production		
Final Product R	1,000 units	—
Intermediate S	2,000 units	—
Final Product S	—	2,000 units
Final Product Q	—	500 units

There were no in process inventories of any partly or fully completed products. Sales prices for products Q, R, and S are $8, $40, and $100, respectively. Overhead is applied at the rate of 80 percent of direct labor in Department A and 40 percent of direct labor in Department B. Revenues from by-product Q are used to offset production costs of the other products. Common processing costs are allocated on a net realizable value basis.

Required:
(a) Prepare a schedule to allocate the processing costs to the three products as directed.
(b) Revise your solution to part (a) using the physical units basis.
(c) What assumptions are needed to make the method in part (b) appropriate?
(d) What decision purposes, if any, does the information in part (a) or part (b) serve? Why?

P 6–11 Joint and By-Products—Inventory Balances—Net Realizable Value Method—Income Calculations

Phillips Company manufactures two main products, B4 and K9, and one by-product, MT. The by-product is accounted for by offsetting the net realizable value of the amount of MT produced during the period against the period's common processing costs. After this, all remaining common processing costs are allocated between B4 and K9 on the basis of their net realizable values.

Production, cost, and sales data for October of 19X3 were as follows:

Inventory October 1
B4   80,000 lbs. @ $1.40 $112,000
K9   40,000 lbs. @ $2.00 $ 80,000
MT   8,000 lbs. @ $1.25 $ 10,000
Production—October
B4   400,000 lbs.
K9   800,000 lbs.
MT   160,000 lbs.
Sales Prices and Sales—October
B4 $4.50   460,000 lbs.
K9 $6.75   800,000 lbs.
MT $1.25   164,000 lbs.

Up to the point of separation of the three products, total common processing costs were as follows: materials $240,000, direct labor $420,000, and manufacturing overhead $800,000. Additional costs incurred to prepare the products for sale are variable and amount to 50¢, 75¢, and 30¢ per unit for B4, K9 and MT, respectively. Selling and administrative expenses of $2,400,000 are divided equally between B4 and K9. The FIFO method is used to account for inventories of finished products of B4 and K9.

Required:
(a) Prepare a schedule to compute the unit costs of production for October.
(b) Prepare a cost of goods sold statement for October.
(c) Prepare an income statement for October.
(d) Explain the balances in all inventory accounts.
(e) Which of the three products was most profitable? Why?

P 6–12   Joint and By-Products—Shrinkage—Multiple Splitoff Points—Net Realizable Value Method

Wallace Company produces three products, Albon, Bakon and Georgon. Bakon is treated as a by-product; Albon and Georgon are considered joint products.

Production operations are arranged as follows: In Department A, raw materials are processed to generate a common output, of which 80 percent is transferred to Department B for further processing, and 20 percent is Georgon, which is transferred to Department C for refining. Due to chemical reactions during the refining process in Department C, the quantity of output effectively achieved is always 80 percent of the number of units transferred in. In Department B, after some common operations, the Albon and Bakon are separated. The output is usually 75 percent Albon and 25 percent Bakon. Before becoming salable, the Albon is run through a final treatment in Department D.

During a typical month, Department A produces 500,000 units and incurs processing costs of $270,000. Processing costs in Departments B, C, and D are $150,000, $60,000 and $40,000, respectively. Per unit sales prices of the end products are $1 for Albon, 10¢ for Bakon, and $3 for Georgon. The net realizable value method is used to allocate common processing costs. The net realizable value of Bakon is offset against the costs of the process during which it is separated.

Required:
(a) Diagram the cost flows and separation points.
(b) Allocate the common processing costs among the three products as directed.

(c) What are the unit costs of the three products?

(d) Prepare an income statement for the month. Assume no beginning inventories, but ending inventories of 10,000, 50,000, and 10,000 units of Albon, Bakon and Georgon respectively.

P 6–13   Joint Products—Multiple Splitoff Points—Shrinkage—Net Realizable Value and Physical Input Content Methods

Francesco Company converts raw materials into intermediate products A1 and A2, and final products A3, A4, and A5. In Department 1, products A1 and A2 are produced. Although the number of units of A1 and A2 are always equal, A2 contains twice as much of the key ingredient, M37, which is the most expensive component of processing costs in Department 1.

In Department 2, product A1 is converted into A3 and A4 in the proportions A3— 70 percent, A4—30 percent. Product A3 is transferred to Department 4 where it receives additional processing before it is ready for sale. Product A4 also requires extra work in Department 5 before it becomes a fully completed product.

Product A2 is transformed into product A5 in Department 3. In Department 6, product A5 is then subjected to further processing during which 20 percent of all units entering the process are lost due to shrinkage.

For April of 19X3, the following production and cost data were available:

	Production	Costs
Dept. 1	400,000 units	$750,000
Dept. 2	200,000 units	$225,000
Dept. 3	200,000 units	$177,000
Dept. 4	140,000 units	$130,000
Dept. 5	60,000 units	$160,000
Dept. 6	160,000 units	$145,500

Per unit sales prices of products A3, A4 and A5 are $4, $8, and $6, respectively. The common processing costs of Department 1 are to be allocated on the basis of the input content of the ingredient M37. The costs at the separation point in Department 2 are to be allocated on the basis of net realizable value. There were no inventories in process at the beginning of April.

Required:

(a) Outline the processing relationships in a flow diagram. Identify separation points, output quantities, costs, and revenues.

(b) Prepare an analysis to allocate all common and separable processing costs among the products as directed.

(c) Calculate the unit costs of each of the three marketable products.

(d) What alternative allocation methods might be appropriate? Why?

(e) Which product is the most profitable? Why?

P 6–14   Process Costing—Joint and By-Products—Comprehensive Review

Derrin Company manufactures three products, Mark-I, Mork-II, and Bye-Bye-III. In Department A, common processing leads to the three basic products from which the end-products are derived. Mark-I is transferred to Department B and Mork-II to Department

C, where they receive additional separate processing. Bye-Bye-III is a residue of Department A and is therefore already available in a disposable form. For August of 19X1, the following data were available:

(1) There were no beginning in process inventories in any department.

(2) Each batch of output from Department A consists of 1,000 units, of which 60 percent are Mark-I, 30 percent are Mork-II, and 10 percent are Bye-Bye-III.

(3) During August, Department A produced 11 fully completed and 2 half-completed batches. All materials and other inputs are added continuously and uniformly in Department A.

(4) By the end of the month, all units transferred to Department C had been fully processed, but 25 percent of the units transferred to Department B were still incomplete. All extra materials had been added to these units in Department B, but they were only 50 percent converted.

(5) August sales included 4,000 units of Mark-I, 3,000 of Mork-II, and 500 of Bye-Bye-III. The remaining Bye-Bye-III was discarded because it is subject to rapid deterioration and cannot be sold.

(6) Mark-I and Mork-II are treated as joint products with the costs of processing in Department A allocated on the basis of their estimated net realizable values at the separation point. Bye-Bye-III is treated as a by-product, but because of the great uncertainty of its salability before it deteriorates, any sales proceeds are treated as incidental revenue and no costs are allocated to the product.

(7) August processing costs were as follows:

	Dept. A	Dept. B	Dept. C.
Materials	$18,000	$16,500	$4,950
Conversion	6,000	5,775	1,650

(8) Per unit sales prices were $7.50, $4.00, and 50¢ for Mark-I, Mork-II, and Bye-Bye-III, respectively.

Required:

(a) Prepare partial production cost reports for Departments B and C. Include only the separable processing costs of those two departments.

(b) Use the information derived in part (a) to determine the net realizable value *per unit* of Mark-I and Mork-II at their point of exit from Department A.

(c) Allocate the common processing costs of Department A between the two joint products.

(d) Complete the production cost reports for Departments B and C, including now the allocated prior departments' costs.

(e) What inventory values will be associated with each of the quantities of completed or in process products? Show all calculations.

(f) Prepare a partial income statement for August. Show sales, cost of goods sold, and gross profit for each of the three products.

(g) Comment on the accounting procedures with regard to the allocation of Department A costs among the three outputs.

P 6–15 Process Costing—Spoilage and Sale of Defective Units— Alternative Accounting Methods

Byner Corporation operates a processing facility from which a single product is derived. The production process is quite sophisticated and a high degree of quality in the end product is desired. Consequently, a significant amount of output that is almost fully completed (100 percent materials content, 80 percent conversion cost) is rejected and must be sold as "seconds." For April of 19X9, the following production, cost, and sales data were available:

	Costs	Units
In Process—April 1		20,000
Materials (100%)	$ 28,500	
Conversion (40%)	$ 15,500	
Full Completions in August..............		240,000
Units Rejected as Defective		60,000
In Process—April 30		30,000
Materials (100%)		
Conversion (60%)		
Processing Costs—April		
Materials	$466,500	
Conversion.........................	$627,100	
Sales—April		
Regular ($8.00 per unit)		250,000
Seconds ($4.00 per unit)		52,000
Finished Products Inventories—April 1		
Regular............................	$ 90,000	25,000
Seconds	$ 3,360	2,000

Required:
(a) Prepare an April production cost report, showing that the defective units absorb their regular share of processing costs up to the point of inspection.
(b) Prepare a partial income statement based on part (a) and showing sales, cost of goods sold, and gross profit. Assume LIFO procedures are followed for finished goods inventories.
(c) Prepare a revised production cost report treating all defective units as normal spoilage. The revenue from the seconds should be used to offset spoilage costs.
(d) Prepare a revised income statement based on part (c). Assume only 240,000 good units were sold.
(e) Which approach (a)/(b) or (c)/(a) do you recommend? Why? Are any alternate approaches worth considering? Explain.

PART TWO

COST INFORMATION FOR PLANNING AND CONTROL

7

THE BUDGETARY PROCESS

LEARNING OBJECTIVES

After studying Chapter 7, you should be able to:

1. Describe the characteristics, scope, structure, contents, and planning purposes of budgets.
2. Distinguish between financial and operating budgets and understand how each is related to a company's accounting data base.
3. Explain the nature and purposes of budget models and use the following modeling techniques in budget preparation:
   a. T-account analysis
   b. Tabular analysis
   c. Algebraic analysis
4. List the sequence in which operating budgets and the master budget are typically prepared.
5. Given the necessary historical and forecast data, prepare the following budgeted financial statements and reports:
   a. Sales budget
   b. Finished goods inventory budget
   c. Production budget
   d. Production cost budgets
   e. Marketing and administrative expense budget
   f. Budgeted cost of goods manufactured
   g. Budgeted cost of goods sold
   h. Budgeted income statement
   i. Cash flow budget
   j. Budgeted balance sheet

Methods of accumulating and using historical costs have been the main concern in previous chapters. But management's role is future-oriented. A business is most likely to achieve its goals when its managers emphasize planning future courses of action. Managers need accounting estimates and forecasts in order to set appropriate objectives and select the courses of action needed to attain those objectives. This planning information then becomes the basis for systems of control, allowing managers to evaluate the organization's performance and to revise plans in the light of operating results.

The accounting system not only enables managers to monitor performance, but also furnishes the data base they need for planning and decision making. Because companies are ongoing entities, much planning data can be derived from accounting information about past performance. Naturally, for planning purposes, historical cost figures need to be adjusted to reflect anticipated changes in the operating environment. Changes may occur in raw materials prices, labor skills, production methods and technology, resource availability, and product research and development—all of which cause variations in costs and related performance measures.

Finally, managers need information about the alternative actions they might take to achieve company goals. Because profit is usually a major business objective, planning data must be structured to measure the profit potential of alternative management decisions, with emphasis on resource requirements, revenues, and costs. The **budgetary process** is the means by which planning information is systematically gathered and plans are developed, communicated, and implemented.

This chapter discusses management's need for predictive accounting data and examines the characteristics and planning purposes of budgets. Demonstrations of three methods of deriving forecast budget figures are followed by descriptions of actual budgets and the sequence in which they are prepared. A case study provides a numerical illustration of budget preparation in a manufacturing company.

THE NEED FOR PREDICTIVE INFORMATION IN DECISION MAKING

HOW MANAGERS MAKE DECISIONS

Figure 7–1 illustrates a general model of the managerial decision making process. The decision making process receives its stimulus (A) when a decision maker notices that performance results do not seem to correspond to stated objectives. He determines this by comparing perceptions (B) of external events (D) with predetermined objectives (C).

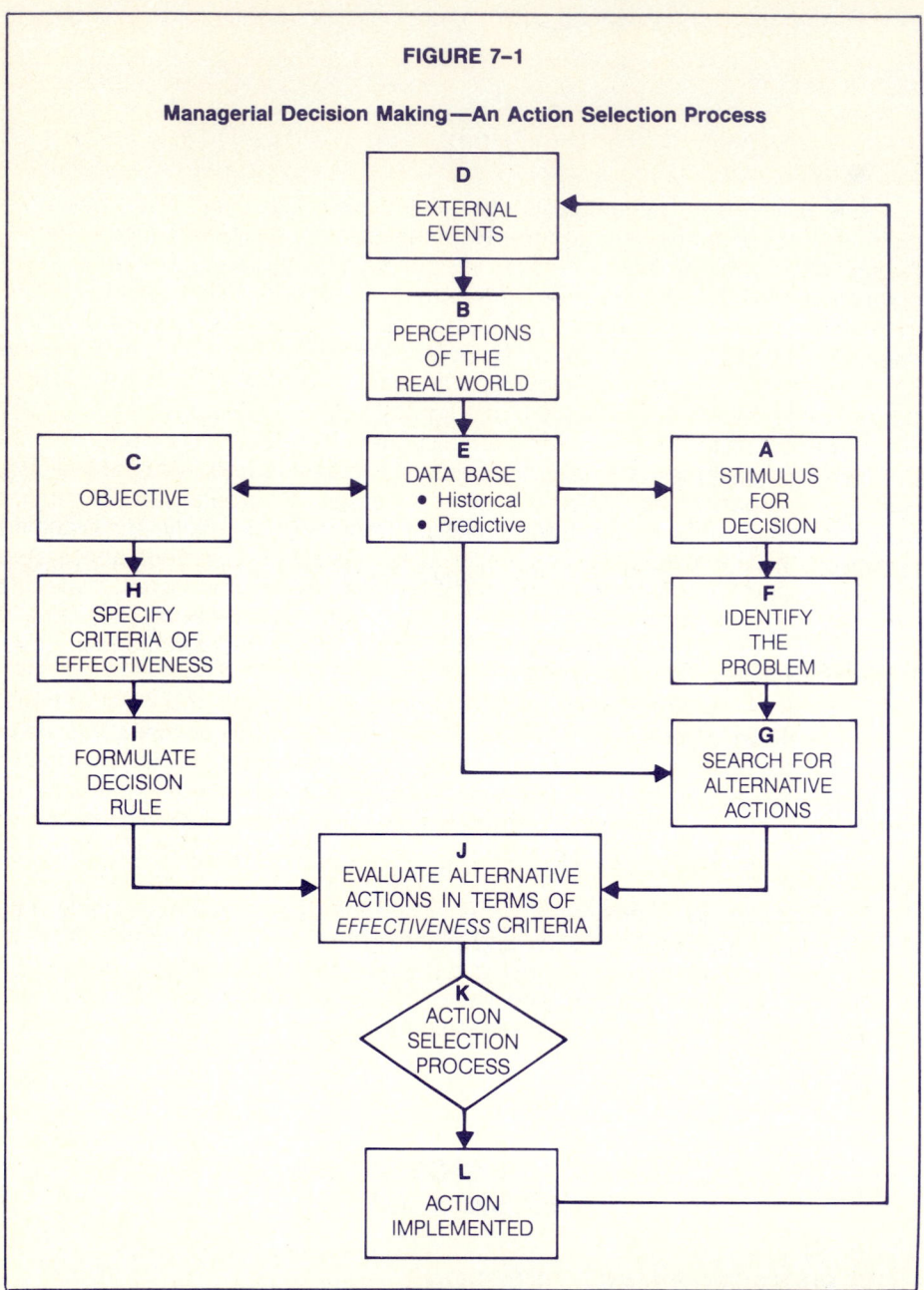

FIGURE 7–1

Managerial Decision Making—An Action Selection Process

When the need for a decision is signaled (A), the decision maker should identify and define the problem fully and accurately (F), making a thorough review of the apparent deviation of actual from planned performance. A response to the wrong problem, or an unnecessary response, wastes managerial effort and company resources.

The decision maker then searches for possible solutions to each problem (G). Before such a search is undertaken, company-wide goals should have been broken down into specific tasks to be achieved by operating managers. This requires specifying the results that must be attained in order to satisfy stated goals (H), and formulating decision rules (I) that will be used in selecting actions to produce those results.

Next, the decision maker evaluates potential courses of action on the basis of the chosen performance criteria (J). This should lead to the selection (K) of the alternative that best satisfies those criteria. Implementing the selected action (L) causes a change in the real world (D), which should be monitored through a process that adds information concerning these changes (B) to the data base.

In a general way, the foregoing model applies to all possible decision situations. The range of possible decisions varies from simple, short-run, almost automatic situations to complex, long-range, multiperiod decisions. Depending on the circumstances, various parts of this decision sequence may be condensed or expanded.

For example, at one extreme, a typical "automatic" decision involves a cash sale in a retail store. The fact that sales prices and operating policies are usually predetermined reduces the action selection process to one of following clearly and narrowly defined instructions.

At the other extreme is a decision to develop a new product line that will materially affect a firm's operations for many years. This is a much more unstructured and challenging situation, involving a wide range of alternatives and complex performance criteria. It requires a variety of long-range forecast data and an evaluation process capable of dealing with many alternative courses of action.

However, both of these examples assume the existence of predetermined goals, policies, or operating procedures. These must have been established as a result of top management's formulation of company-wide objectives.

ACCOUNTING AND DECISION MAKING

Accounting data is needed by decision makers when they

1. Formulate objectives.
2. Search for alternative courses of action.
3. Evaluate these alternatives.
4. Measure performance.
5. Compare performance with objectives.

Formulating objectives and developing and evaluating courses of action relate to management's *planning* function. Measuring and evaluating performance are *administrative* and *control* functions. The accounting system provides budgeted figures for planning purposes, current operating reports for monitoring the results of implementation, and analytical reports for evaluation and control purposes.

Plans must be developed and expressed in terms that reflect the performance levels needed to attain objectives. This requires that broadly defined company-wide objectives be subdivided, expressed in numbers and dollars, and communicated to the firm's operating departments. For example, a company-wide goal of capturing a 20 percent market share might be translated into specific sales quantities and dollar values that each of the company's retail outlets must sell. A retail store manager whose annual sales goal is $2 million needs accounting data in order to help select the product line combinations that are capable of achieving that sales contribution. If the manager's goal has also been formulated to include a profit requirement (for example, a 10 percent net return on sales or a 15 percent return on invested funds), then his decision making must take account of the profit potential of the alternative sales, production, and distribution activities that he coordinates and controls.

CHARACTERISTICS OF BUDGETS

WHAT IS A BUDGET?

Budgets have at least five identifying features:

1. They consist of sets of *forecasts* or *estimates* of the outcomes of future events.
2. They are expressed in *quantitative* terms—money measurements for financial outcomes, attribute measurements for physical outcomes.
3. They are prepared in an iterative sequence that permits *communication* and *negotiation* of the interrelated goals of each organizational segment.
4. They are organized and combined to produce a *coordinated pattern* that results in each part of the enterprise performing consistently with overall objectives.
5. They are primarily *planning* tools, but also serve as a basis for performance evaluation and control analysis.

A budget can therefore be defined as *a statement of expected outcomes of planned future actions, prepared in a coordinated manner that is consistent with attaining the goals of an organization and its sub-units.*

SCOPE OF BUDGETS

A budget may be prepared for any set of activities that has some common purpose. Such activities range from the total long-run operations of a business to the short-run performance of a single employee, machine, or department.

It follows that budget periods may be short (daily, weekly, monthly), or long (quarterly, yearly, or longer). Budgets should be prepared for the time periods over which actual performance is to be monitored and controlled. Predicted and actual performance can then be compared for corresponding time intervals.

The budgets in Figures 7–2 and 7–3 illustrate two extremes of the scope of budgeting. Figure 7–2 shows a corporation's projected five-year income state-

---

FIGURE 7–2

Anson Corporation
Budgeted Income Statement for Five Years
Ending December 31, 19X9
(in thousands)

Sales	$100,000
Cost of Goods Sold	65,000
Gross Profit.....................	$ 35,000
Operating Expenses	15,000
Income Before Tax	$ 20,000
Tax Expense	8,000
Budgeted Net Income.............	$ 12,000

FIGURE 7–3

Anson Corporation
Production Division—Machining Department
Projected Daily Production Schedule
Operator: B.R. Jones   Station No.: 347
Date: July 25, 19X7

			Elapsed Time	
Activity	Start	Finish	Hours	Minutes
Setup Job 743..........................	8:30 A.M.	8:45 A.M.	0.15	
Job 743—100 units	8:45	10:00	1.15	
Break.................................	10:00	10:15	0.15	
Job 743	10:15	12:00 noon	1.45	
Lunch	12:00 noon	12:45 P.M.	0.45	
Job 743	12:45 P.M.	1:30	0.45	
Cleanup and Setup Job 752	1:30	2:00	0.30	
Break.................................	2:00	2:15	0.15	
Job 752—200 units	2:15	4:30	2.15	
			8.00	

---

ment. Figure 7–3 illustrates a daily production schedule for a single machine operator. Note the *aggregation* shown in the first budget and the *detail* shown in the second. Consider also the comparative accuracy and reliability of the two budgets. Because of its narrower scope and shorter time span, the daily plan is much more likely to approximate actual results than is the five-year budget.

STRUCTURE OF BUDGETS

A budget should be organized to reflect the outcomes of anticipated events that are associated with particular **objects of budgeting.** An object of budgeting is a focal point for the budgetary process, similar to the concept of a cost object discussed in Chapter 2. The primary budget objects are *time periods, decision centers,* and *output units.* Figure 7–4 is a budget for Sales Division 275 (decision center), forecasting sales of Products A and B (output units), broken down by weeks for the month of January (time period).

Budgetary projections should be the outcomes of decisions that are feasible within the firm's existing organizational structure. Budgets developed for decision centers as defined in the company's organization chart should reflect established authority–responsibility relationships that will make such budgets relevant for planning and control purposes.

For example, the sales budget for Division 275, shown in Figure 7–4, forecasts unit sales and sales revenues for which decision makers in Division 275 are responsible.

CONTENTS OF BUDGETS

A budget contains quantitative expressions of the projected outcomes of future events. Because profit is usually a primary business objective, the "events" considered in the planning process should be those that will help attain profit goals.

In addition, a budget translates company-wide objectives into operational terms. It should contain information that managers can use to help them achieve their goals and contribute to organizational goals.

Appropriate *performance measures* are needed to specify these local goals. Conventional financial statements contain many performance measures, including measures of periodic revenue, expense, and income, product costs, decision

---

FIGURE 7–4

Anson Corporation
January 19X8
Weekly Sales Forecasts
Division 275

Date	Product A		Product B		Total	
	Units	Dollars	Units	Dollars	Units	Dollars
Jan. 4–10	4,000	$ 40,000	2,500	$ 50,000	6,500	$ 90,000
11–17	5,000	50,000	3,000	60,000	8,000	110,000
18–24	5,500	55,000	3,000	60,000	8,500	115,000
25–31	5,500	55,000	3,500	70,000	9,000	125,000
Total	20,000	$200,000	12,000	$240,000	32,000	$440,000

center costs, return on invested capital, assets employed, liabilities outstanding, and owner's equity.

For example, the budget in Figure 7–4 contains information directly related to divisional sales goals. Clearly the manager of Sales Division 275 needs to know budgeted unit sales and sales revenues in order to measure how well the division's objectives are being accomplished. The specific goals in Division 275 might be maximizing sales revenue, maximizing unit sales, increasing the rate at which sales revenue grows, or reaching a particular combined level of revenues and unit sales.

OPERATING BUDGETS AND FINANCIAL BUDGETS

There are two kinds of budgets: operating and financial. **Financial budgets** are prepared in the same formats as the regular financial statements. Consequently, they feature the same account classifications found in the balance sheet, income statement, and statement of changes in financial position, but contain forecast rather than historical data. They may be prepared for the firm as a whole, or for such company segments as divisions, departments, and product lines.

Operating budgets typically provide more detail than financial budgets, and often include performance measures not found in published financial statements. Examples of operating budgets are:

1. Individual job cost estimates in a job order cost system (shown in Figure 7–5).
2. Forecasts of equivalent units of production and unit costs in a process cost system.
3. Estimates of raw materials acquisition and usage quantities needed to meet forecast production requirements (shown in Figure 7–6).

FIGURE 7–5

Anson Corporation
Manufacturing Division
Schedule N
Job Cost Estimate

Job #3475		
	Starting Date:	June 1, 19X4
	Estimated Completion Date:	July 15, 19X4

	Costs
Materials Requirements (see Schedule M)	$3,425.00
Direct Labor Requirements (see Schedule L)	1,450.00
Total Direct Costs	$4,875.00
Manufacturing Overhead (150% of Direct Labor Cost)	2,175.00
Total Job Cost Estimate	$7,050.00

FIGURE 7–6

Anson Corporation
Schedule M
Materials Requirement Estimate

Job #3475   (See Schedule N)

Part No.	Quantity Required	Unit Cost	Total
24175	200	$12.50	$2,500.00
4378Q	50	11.25	562.50
8317A	145	2.50	362.50
			$3,425.00

FIGURE 7–7

Anson Corporation
Schedule L
Labor Cost Estimates

Job #3475   (See Schedule N)

Labor Category	Hours	Rate	Total
Fitter	50	$12.50	$ 625.00
Welder	50	10.50	525.00
Assistant	50	6.00	300.00
			$1,450.00

4.   Estimates of the inventory levels needed to satisfy forecast sales demand.
5.   Estimates of the labor force required to meet production plans (shown in Figure 7–7).

Figures 7–5, 7–6, and 7–7 also demonstrate the interrelationships among operating budgets.

BUDGETS AS PLANNING DEVICES

The budgetary process serves two major purposes—planning and control. The control applications of budgets will be introduced in Chapter 10 and developed in Chapters 11–13 and 19–22. The discussion in this chapter is limited to the uses of budgets as planning devices.

Budgets serve the following planning purposes:

1. *Budgets help managers influence the course of future events.* The question is sometimes asked: "Why bother to budget when there will always be uncertainty about the future?" In other words, how can *any* budgeting activity be justified? One answer is that the rejection of budgeting implies a fatalistic attitude. In effect, it suggests that no matter what plans are made, the future remains beyond the control of decision makers—clearly an extreme position. Common sense indicates that managers can usually exert some influence on future events by preplanning and by considering possible alternative actions and their consequences.

2. *Budgets help managers understand the activities being budgeted.* In addition to shaping future events, budget preparation has intrinsic merits for the participants. To develop reasonable forecasts, managers must first analyze the system or set of activities being budgeted. Such analysis should increase managerial awareness and understanding of that system in terms of its components, the relationships among those components, the external environment of the system, the other decision makers in the system and their decision rules, and, most critically, the overall goals of the system. Even if a budget is "pigeonholed" and never adopted, those who helped prepare it will usually retain and use some of its information in later decision making.

3. *Budgets focus attention on goals and communicate to managers the performance requirements necessary to reach those goals.* Without a budgeting system, managers would be unaware of the specific performance levels expected of them. To plan without being able to communicate expectations in a way that will direct the efforts of individual decision makers toward common objectives is an invitation to chaos.

4. *Budgets help transform company-wide goals into specific tasks to be performed by operating managers.* Budgets are an important part of a company's communication system. They serve as filters that break down and restate overall objectives in terms of performance measures that operating managers can understand.

5. *Budgets refine decision making.* By forcing executives to quantify their expectations, the budgetary process makes managers more conscious of the effects of their actions. Definite benefits result when the decision maker is required to consider future actions and their possible consequences and to formulate his expectations in an orderly way.

6. *Budgets educate managers about the activities of other company units.* In the course of developing budget data, managers will be exposed to the other company subsystems with which they must interact. This process can help eliminate many of the "black boxes"[1] that might otherwise persist in managerial perceptions of other parts of the company. Budgeting is a negotiative process. The successive revisions needed to arrive at a final budget require that each manager adjust his proposed actions to interact with those of other managers.

7. *Budgets coordinate and integrate the actions taken by individual managers at all levels.* Independently prepared budgets are apt to be inconsistent and suboptimal from the viewpoint of the whole company. Though such

---

[1] The phrase "black box" describes a situation in which managers are aware of the inputs to and outputs from a process or operation, but are unaware of the nature of the activities occurring within that process.

budgets may be accurate and propose valid courses of action for each decision center, they will be inefficient planning tools if they fail to consider the effects of local actions on other parts of the firm. In order to motivate managers to help achieve company-wide goals, the budgets of individual departments should be integrated with the firm's overall financial budgets. Only then will the company-wide budget be a fully effective planning tool.

How much budgeting is feasible? Cost, personnel, time, and other constraints limit the extent of the budgetary process. These limitations must be balanced against the benefits derived from a budgetary system. Unfortunately, as is the case with so many cost–benefit comparisons, the benefits of a budgetary system are much harder to measure than are its costs.

PREPARING THE BUDGET

The remainder of this chapter explains budget preparation techniques. It includes a comprehensive example that outlines the sequence of steps in preparing budgets and illustrates the use of supporting budgets, sources of data, and typical accounting budget models.

The discussion that follows is limited to the procedural aspects of preparing financial and operating budgets. Budget relationships are presented as being singular and invariant. That is, sales forecasts, inventory policies, cash collection and payment patterns, production input requirements, and unit prices are all specified in simple and direct terms, with no consideration given to variations caused by interactions among these factors as operations proceed.

This simplified analysis bypasses the repetitive and negotiative aspects of budgeting and does not address the issues of uncertainty and probabilistic relationships that always affect actual budgeting situations. Refinements of budgetary procedures to deal with these issues are presented in Chapters 15 through 18.

BUDGET MODELS

A *model* is a partial representation of the behavior of a system being studied. The system might be a whole company, a department, a resource category (such as receivables or inventory), or any other company segment. The purposes of modeling are:

1. To *understand* the system being studied and its behavior.
2. To *predict* the system's behavior under various conditions.
3. To *control* the system's performance.
4. To *improve* the system's performance.
5. To *optimize* the system's performance.

A **budget model** is a statement about the relationships among the variable factors that determine a system's predicted performance. A budget model may be as simple as a direct linear relationship. For example, a model may specify that sales revenue equals unit selling price times the quantity sold: $R = SQ$, where S = unit sales price, and Q = quantity sold. Another simple budget model is one that forecasts next period's revenues as being equal to this period's revenues: $R_{t+1} = R_t$.

Budget models may also be quite complex, as in the case of a statistical regression equation that forecasts sales volume as a function of several factors. Another example of a complex budget model is a linear or nonlinear mathematical programming model used to make a complete allocation of resources to all competing uses in order to maximize predicted profits over a particular time period.

MODELING TECHNIQUES

How do planners actually derive the budgeted figures for sales, production, and income? How do they make sure that these figures are compatible with each other?

Account balances change as resources move through the manufacturing process from raw materials to finished goods. Forecasting and reconciling the interrelationships among account balances is a major task in the preparation of financial and operating budgets. Three methods of predicting ledger balance interactions will be demonstrated: *T-account analysis, tabular analysis,* and *algebraic analysis.*

T-account Analysis   This method traces the immediate effects of proposed actions in terms of changes in account balances. T-account analysis can be made on the basis of the usual monetary measures of resource flows (financial budgets) as well as on the basis of physical unit measures (operating budgets). It is helpful to add flow diagrams to the T-account format, using pointers and symbols to indicate the origins and destinations of resource flows.

Example: Strong Corporation forecasts sales of 20,000, 18,000, and 24,000 units for the months of July, August, and September, respectively. It is company policy to maintain finished goods inventories at a level equal to 50 percent of forecast sales for the following month. Therefore 10,000 units of finished goods were on hand on July 1. Each finished unit requires three units of raw material for its manufacture. Raw materials inventories are maintained at an amount equal to 25 percent of the following month's estimated production requirements. There is never any ending work in process inventory.

The following seven-step sequence uses T-account analysis to develop budgets for *finished goods output, raw materials usage,* and *raw materials purchases.*

Step 1: *Enter beginning raw materials and finished goods balances in skeleton T-accounts.* On July 1, 14,250 units of raw materials were on hand. They cost $1 per unit. Finished goods cost $6 per unit, and consisted of three units of raw materials at $1 per unit, plus variable manufacturing costs of $3 per unit of finished product.

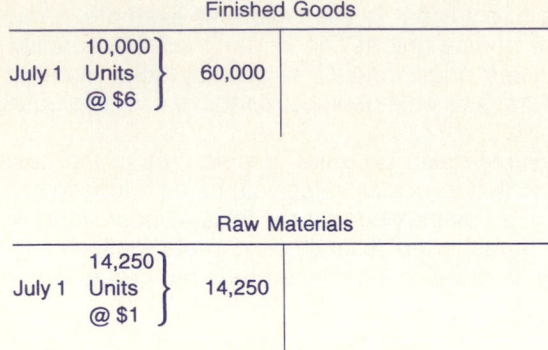

Step 2: *Show the effect on Finished Goods Inventory of the forecast that 20,000 units will be sold during July.*

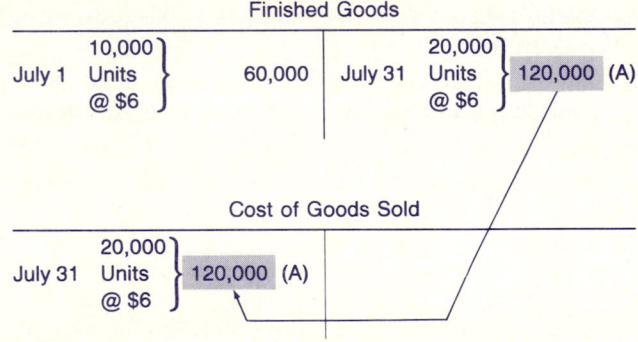

Step 3: *Enter the required ending balance in Finished Goods Inventory* (B), which consists of the August sales forecast (18,000 units) × 50% = 9,000 units at $6 per unit.

Finished Goods			
July 1	60,000	July 31	120,000 (A)
		31 Ending Balance 9,000 @ $6	54,000 (B)
			174,000

Step 4: *Determine how many units must be completed during July to balance the Finished Goods Inventory account* (C). Required completions are 20,000 + 9,000 − 10,000 = 19,000 units.

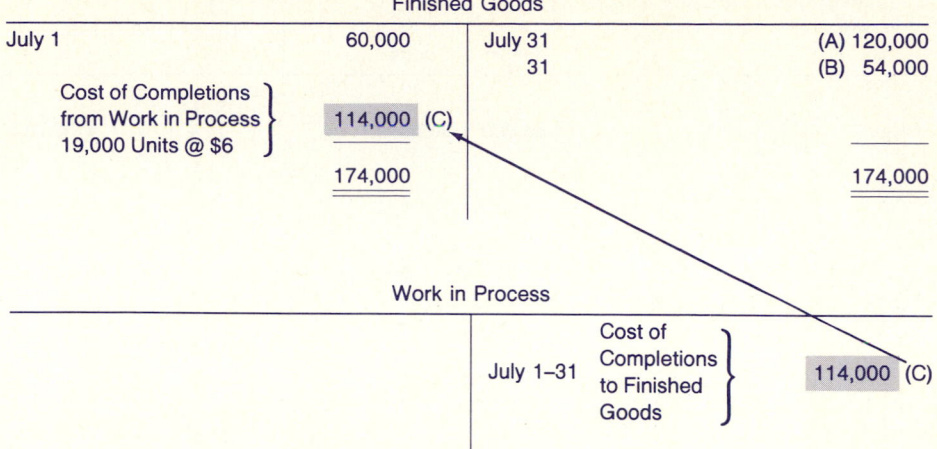

Step 5: *Determine the raw materials used during July* (D), *to produce 19,000 units of finished goods,* if each finished unit requires three units of raw materials. Raw materials usage = 19,000 × 3 = 57,000 units.

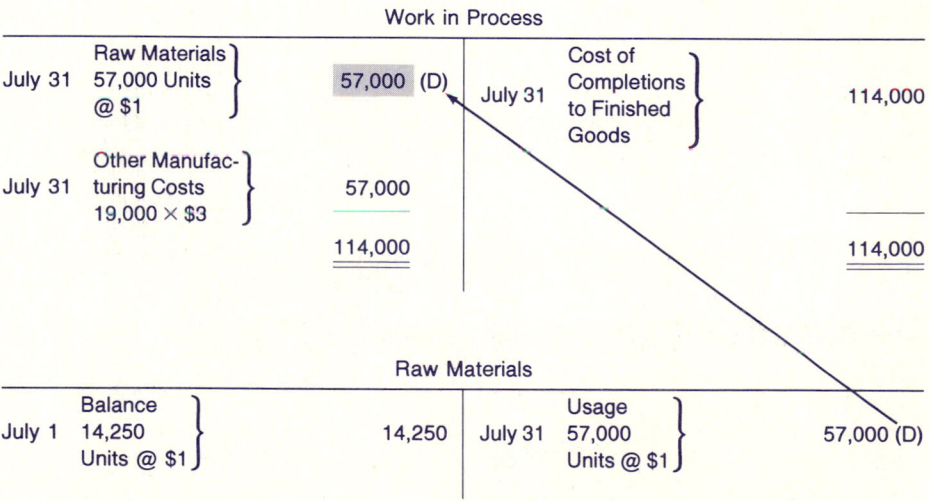

Step 6: *Determine the required amount of raw materials inventory on July 31* by calculating the number of units that must be completed during August.
Step 6A: *Enter the August 1 balance of finished goods inventory:*

Finished Goods

| August 1 | 9,000 Units | 54,000 | |

Step 6B: *Enter the August sales forecast of 18,000 units:*

Finished Goods

| August 1 | 9,000 Units } | | 54,000 | August 31 | To Cost of Goods Sold 18,000 Units @ $6 } | | 108,000 |

Step 6C: *Enter the August 31 finished goods inventory,* which is equal to 50 percent of the September sales forecast of 24,000 units.

Finished Goods

August 1	9,000 Units }		54,000	August 31	To Cost of Goods Sold 18,000 Units @ $6 }		108,000
				August 31	Ending Balance 12,000 Units @ $6 }		72,000
							180,000

Step 6D: *Determine how many units must be completed during August to balance the Finished Goods account.* This is $18,000 + 12,000 - 9,000 = 21,000$ units.

Finished Goods

August 1	9,000 Units }		54,000	August 31	To Cost of Goods Sold 18,000 Units @ $6 }		108,000
August 31	Completions 21,000 Units @ $6 }		126,000	August 31	Ending Balance 12,000 Units @ $6 }		72,000
			180,000				180,000

Step 6E: *Determine raw materials requirements on July 31,* (E), which equal 25 percent of August production requirements:

$$25\% \times (21,000 \times 3)$$
$$= 25\% \times 63,000 \text{ Units}$$
$$= 15,750 \text{ Units}$$

Raw Materials

July 1 Units 14,250 @ $1	14,250	July 31 To Work in Process 57,000 Units @ $1	57,000
		July 31 Ending Balance 15,750 Units @ $1	15,750 (E)
			72,750

Step 7: *Determine July purchases of raw materials* (F), which equal 57,000 + 15,750 − 14,250 = 58,500 Units.

Raw Materials

July 1 Units 14,250 @ $1	14,250	July 31 To Work in Process 57,000 Units @ $1	57,000
July 31 Purchases 58,500 Units @ $1	58,500 (F)	July 31 Ending Balance 15,750 Units @ $1	15,750
	72,250		72,750

Tabular Analysis   This modeling technique has the same purpose as the T-account method. It attempts to derive required budget amounts from a tabular analysis of the underlying ledger account relationships.

Example: Strong Corporation requires budget predictions of (1) *cash collected from customers,* and (2) *cash payments to suppliers of raw materials.* Customers pay, on the average, 25 percent of their accounts during the month of sale and the remaining 75 percent during the following month. No sales discounts are offered. Accounts receivable on July 1 totaled $165,000. July sales were as previously budgeted—20,000 units at $10 per unit.

(1) *Schedule of Cash Collections—July, 19X2*

June Sales—75% × $220,000	$165,000
July Sales—25% × $200,000	50,000
Cash Collections	$215,000

(2) *Analysis of Accounts Receivable—July, 19X2*

Balance, July 1, 19X2	$165,000
Add: Sales—20,000 units @ $10	200,000
	$365,000
Less: Cash Collections [from (1)]	215,000
Balance—July 31, 19X2	$150,000

Strong Corporation pays for 50 percent of its purchases during the month in which they are made, deducting 2 percent cash discounts; it pays the remaining 50 percent in full during the following month. Accounts payable on July 1 were $30,750. July purchases were also as budgeted—58,500 units at $1 per unit.

(3) *Schedule of Cash Payments to Suppliers—July, 19X2:*

June Purchases—50% × $61,500		$30,750
July Purchases—50% × $58,500	$29,250	
Less: 2% Discount	585	28,665
Cash Payments		$59,415

(4) *Analysis of Accounts Payable—July, 19X2:*

Balance, July 1, 19X2		$30,750
Add: Purchases—58,500 units @ $1		58,500
		$89,250
Less: Cash Payments [from (3)]	$59,415	
Purchase Discounts	585	60,000
Balance, July 31, 19X2		$29,250

Algebraic Analysis   A third modeling technique expresses budget relationships as sets of mathematical equations. These equations form a basis for developing formal mathematical budget models and computer simulations. The budget relationships already formulated for Strong Corporation are expressed as mathematical equations in the following example.

(1) Terminology:

t = Current Period
$t+1$ = Next Period
$t-1$ = Previous Period
S^* = Actual Sales—Units
$S^*\$$ = Actual Sales—Dollars
S = Forecast Sales—Units
$S\$$ = Forecast Sales—Dollars
P = Production—Units
RU = Raw Materials Usage—Units
$RU\$$ = Raw Materials Usage—Dollars
RP = Raw Materials Purchases—Units
$RP\$$ = Raw Materials Purchases—Dollars
$OM\$$ = Other Manufacturing Costs—Dollars
FG = Finished Goods Inventory—Units
$FG\$$ = Finished Goods Inventory—Dollars
RM = Raw Materials Inventory—Units
$RM\$$ = Raw Materials Inventory—Dollars
CGM = Cost of Goods Manufactured
CGS = Cost of Goods Sold

AR = Accounts Receivable
AP = Accounts Payable
PD = Purchase Discounts
CR = Cash Receipts
CP = Cash Payments
CD = Cash Discounts Taken

(2) Relationships:
   (a) Finished Goods Inventory
      $FG_t = .5\ S_{t+1}$
      $FG\$_t = \$6 \times FG_t$
   (b) Production
      $P_t = S_t + FG_t - FG_{t-1}$
   (c) Raw Materials Usage
      $RU_t = 3 \times P_t$
      $RU\$_t = \$1 \times RU_t$
   (d) Raw Materials Inventory
      $RM_t = .25\ RU_{t+1}$
      $RM\$_t = \$1 \times RM_t$
   (e) Raw Materials Purchases
      $RP_t = RU_t + RM_t - RM_{t-1}$
      $RP\$_t = \$1 \times RP_t$
   (f) Cost of Goods Manufactured
      $OM\$_t = \$3 \times P_t$
      $CGM_t = RU\$_t + OM\$_t$
   (g) Cost of Goods Sold
      $CGS_t = \$6 \times S_t$
   (h) Cash Receipts
      $CR_t = .75\ S^*\$_{t-1} + .25 S\$_t$
   (i) Cash Payments
      $CP_t = .5RP\$_{t-1} + (.98)(.5RP\$_t)$
      $CD_t = .02\ RP\$_t$
   (j) Accounts Receivable
      $AR_t = AR_{t-1} + S\$_t - CR_t$
   (k) Accounts Payable
      $AP_t = AP_{t-1} + RP\$_t - CP_t - CD_t$

(3) Data Values for Parameters for t = July:
   $S_t = 20,000$ $S_{t+1} = 18,000$ $S_{t+2} = 24,000$
   $S^*_{t-1} = 22,000$
   $AR_{t-1} = \$165,000$ $AP_{t-1} = \$30,750$
   $FG_{t-1} = 10,000$ $FG\$_{t-1} = \$60,000$
   $RM_{t-1} = 14,250$ $RM\$_{t-1} = \$14,250$

(4) Solution
   (a) $FG_t = .5\ (18,000) = \underline{9,000}$
      $FG\$_t = \$6 \times 9,000 = \underline{\underline{\$54,000}}$

(b) $P_t = 20,000 + 9,000 - 10,000 = \underline{\underline{19,000}}$

(c) $RU_t = 3 \times 19,000 = \underline{\underline{57,000}}$

   $RU\$_t = \$1 \times 57,000 = \underline{\underline{\$57,000}}$

(d) $RM_t = .25\ (63,000) = \underline{\underline{15,750}}$

   $RM\$_t = \$1 \times 15,750 = \underline{\underline{\$15,750}}$

(e) $RP_t = 57,000 + 15,750 - 14,250 = \underline{\underline{58,500}}$

   $RP\$_t = \underline{\underline{\$58,500}}$

(f) $OM\$_t = \$3 \times 19,000 = \underline{\underline{\$57,000}}$

   $CGM_t = \$57,000 + \$57,000 = \underline{\underline{\$114,000}}$

(g) $CGS_t = \$6 \times 20,000 = \underline{\underline{\$120,000}}$

(h) $CR_t = (.75)\ \$220,000 + (.25)\ \$200,000$

   $= \$165,000 + 50,000 = \underline{\underline{\$215,000}}$

(i) $CP_t = .5\ (\$61,500) + (.98)\ (.5)\ (\$58,500)$

   $= \$30,750 + \$28,665 = \underline{\underline{\$59,415}}$

(j) $AR_t = \$165,000 + \$200,000 - \$215,000 = \underline{\underline{\$150,000}}$

(k) $AP_t = \$30,750 + \$58,500 - \$59,415 - \$585 = \underline{\underline{\$29,250}}$

All equations can be solved by substituting values for the variables in the model. This modeling technique also permits the creation of a set of generalized equations—a **generalized model**. In this latter form, the model can be solved successfully for subsequent periods or can be used to reevaluate any particular period's data, simply by substituting different values for the key variables in the equation.

Recent developments in computer applications have expanded the capacity of budget models.[2] By building a computer-based model of the firm—a **computer simulation**—planners can refine budget models and test their performance using alternative sets of data and varying the parameters of the models. Such budget models, provided they accurately represent the behavior of the firm or parts of it, are powerful planning tools.

In addition, computer simulation models avoid cost duplications in the budgetary process. They eliminate the cost of developing a model base from scratch each time a budget is prepared. The substantial cost of developing a model need only be incurred once. After the simulation model is created, costs are limited to the data gathering and processing expenditures needed to maintain and revise it.

THE MASTER BUDGET

A **master budget** is an overall plan of future operations. It typically includes a company-wide forecast balance sheet, forecast income statement, and forecast statement of changes in financial position. The master budget is supported

[2] See Richard C. Murphy, "A Computerized Model Approach to Budgeting," *Management Accounting*, vol. 56 (June, 1975), pp. 34–38.

by financial and operating budgets that reduce the contents of these company-wide budgets to the level of detail needed by the firm's operating departments.

Underlying this budgetary structure is the same data base that supports the internal accounting and reporting system. Records of past performance are the main source of forecast data used in financial and operating budgets. Historical figures must of course be supplemented by current information about supply and demand conditions, replacement costs, and so forth, to ensure that accurate predictions can be made.

The content of the budget data base largely depends on the budget model being used. This applies in terms of the *type* of data (quantitative, financial, qualitative), the *detail* of data (from aggregate measures to the results of individual transactions), and the *level of sophistication* of the data (from rule of thumb approximations to the results derived from the use of formal statistical estimation techniques). In each instance, the data that will be needed must possess attributes consistent with the budget model employed.

PREPARING THE MASTER BUDGET

A desirable starting point in preparing the master budget is to forecast the *central variable* in the budget model—that one variable on which most significant parts of the budget depend. In most businesses for which production occurs in anticipation of future sales, the **central planning variable** is *total sales volume.*

This need not always be the case. Some companies treat *total production volume* as the key planning variable, because limited production capacity rather than limited sales potential is the most direct and effective constraint on their operations. Likewise, when firms can assert oligopolistic or monopolistic market powers, they may consider production levels the more useful planning variable on the assumption that they are in a position to sell whatever output they decide to produce.

Based on this forecast of a central planning variable, a network of operating budgets can be prepared. They should be developed in a sequence that reflects the way in which each budget item depends on the items already budgeted. For example, if total sales volume is the central variable, the budgets for finished goods inventory and production, because they are directly dependent on sales levels, should be developed next.

After the overall production budget is prepared, separate budgets are developed for all production and service departments. These individual budgets must then be coordinated to produce company-wide budgets, such as those for raw materials acquisitions, total manpower requirements, processing capacity, and equipment acquisition and maintenance.

Figure 7–8 illustrates the sequence in which a network of operating and financial budgets might be developed. Note how each budget depends on the forecasts already made.

The sales forecast also sets in motion budgeting for nonmanufacturing activities, such as marketing, administrative, and financial functions. Budgets for nonmanufacturing costs are prepared for individual departments and are also combined to form company-wide budgets.

FIGURE 7–8

Network of Operating and Financial Budgets

SALES BUDGET
Forecasts sales volume and total sales revenue

↓

FINISHED GOODS INVENTORY BUDGET
Forecasts finished goods in relation to anticipated sales volume

↓

PRODUCTION BUDGET
Forecasts production quantity needed to satisfy anticipated sales and finished goods inventory requirements

↓

RAW MATERIALS ACQUISITION AND USAGE BUDGET (Quantity and cost)	**DIRECT LABOR BUDGET** (Hours and cost)	**MANUFACTURING COST BUDGET** (Total manufacturing cost)

MARKETING AND ADMINISTRATIVE EXPENSE BUDGET
Forecasts nonmanufacturing costs as a function of total sales revenue

BUDGETED STATEMENT OF COST OF GOODS MANUFACTURED
Forecasts unit cost of goods manufactured based on estimated production quantities and materials, labor, and overhead costs

↓

BUDGETED STATEMENT OF COST OF GOODS SOLD
Forecasts total cost of goods sold based on cost of goods manufactured estimate plus forecast of ending finished goods inventory

↓

BUDGETED INCOME STATEMENT
Combines sales, cost of goods sold, and expense budgets to forecast net income

↓

CASH FLOW BUDGET
Combines data from all previous budgets to forecast cash receipts and disbursements

↓

BUDGETED BALANCE SHEET
Combines data from all previous budgets to forecast assets, liabilities, and capital

Both financial and nonfinancial data appear in these operating budgets. For example, the sales budget contains forecasts of expected unit sales as well as sales revenues. Similarly, manpower budgets will include not only forecasts of wage and salary costs, but also estimates of the number of personnel needed, plus labor hour, experience, and skill requirements and availabilities.

The financial effects of these operating budgets are summarized in a forecast income statement, cash flow statement, and balance sheet. The *budgeted income statement* contains projections of all revenues and expenses as well as expected net income. If historical income statements are normally broken down by departments, divisions, product lines, or other segments, budgeted income statements should be prepared for these same subsystems.

Because the flow of resources and their profitable use need to be considered, the effect of all budgeted operations on cash and working capital balances must also be forecast. Cash flow figures, obtained from the operating budgets already prepared, are used to develop a *budgeted cash flow statement* and a *forecast statement of changes in financial position*. A final summary of budgets can then be made, resulting in a *forecast balance sheet* that shows the projected end results of all budgeted activities.

The foregoing sequence of steps in developing a master budget should be taken as a basic framework—*not* as a rigid formula to be applied in exact detail for all cases. The budgeting environment varies from industry to industry, by size of firm, and according to the depth and breadth of organizational structure. Likewise, the time horizon of budgets varies, as do the nature and extent of activities to be budgeted and, most importantly, the dollar resources available to support the budgetary process. Remember that budgeting causes costs as well as producing benefits. Despite the demonstrated rewards of systematic planning, some attention must be given to the question of how much a company can afford to spend on budgeting.

BUDGETING ILLUSTRATED: NICE AND EEZEE FLOUR COMPANY

The following is a step by step example of the development of a set of operating budgets and the preparation of a master budget. The sequence of budgetary procedures will follow the outline suggested earlier in this chapter. However, the procedures themselves will be simplified in that all the relationships underlying the various sub-budgets will be derived in a direct and deterministic fashion. For example, all input–output relationships will be shown as being fixed and invariant during the budget period. Although unrealistic, these simplifying assumptions highlight the *accounting* aspect of the budgetary process.

HISTORICAL BALANCE SHEET

The Nice and Eezee Flour Company prepares monthly operating budgets for all its major functional areas and coordinates them into a master budget. The company's June 30, 19X6 balance sheet is shown in Figure 7–9.

FIGURE 7–9

Nice and Eezee Flour Company
Balance Sheet
June 30, 19X6

Assets

Current Assets
Cash	$ 34,750	
Accounts Receivable	85,500	
Inventory—Raw Material (650 tons @ $20)	13,000	
Inventory—Finished Goods (440 tons @ $60)	26,400	
		$159,650

Fixed Assets
Land	$ 72,000	
Plant (Net)	245,000	
		317,000
Total Assets		$476,650

Equities

Current Liabilities
Accounts Payable	$ 17,000	
Taxes Payable	34,500	
Total Liabilities		$ 51,500

Stockholders' Equity
Capital Stock	$250,000	
Retained Earnings	175,150	425,150
Total Equities		$476,650

The monthly operating budgets and the master budget for July, 19X6 will be prepared in the following sequence:

A   Sales Budget
B   Finished Goods Inventory Budget
C   Production Budget
D   Raw Materials Acquisition and Usage Budgets
E   Direct Labor Budget
F   Manufacturing Cost Budget
G   Marketing and Administrative Expense Budget
H   Budgeted Statement of Cost of Goods Manufactured
I   Budgeted Statement of Cost of Goods Sold
J   Budgeted Income Statement
K   Cash Flow Budget
L   Budgeted Balance Sheet

FIGURE 7–10

Nice and Eezee Flour Company
Schedule A
Sales Forecast
July, August, September, 19X6

	July	August	September
Total Prior 6 Months Sales	4,800 tons	4,920 tons	5,062 tons
Average Sales Volume per Month	800	820	844
Add: 10%	80	82	84
Forecast Sales	880 tons	902 tons	928 tons
Forecast Sales Revenue ($100 per ton) ...	$88,000	$90,200	$92,800

SALES BUDGET (A)

Because the company operates in a competitive market, it considers *total sales volume* the key planning variable in preparing its monthly operating budgets. As shown in Figure 7–10, sales forecasts are developed by using a formula that estimates each month's sales to be 110 percent of the average sales for the previous six months. Selling prices are predicted to remain constant at $100 per ton of output. August and September sales must also be forecast; for that purpose, it is assumed that the July and August forecasts are accurate. The previous six months' sales were as follows:

January	760 tons
February	760
March	780
April	800
May	840
June	860
Total	4,800 tons

FINISHED GOODS INVENTORY BUDGET (B)

The company requires that each month's ending inventory of finished products be equal to 50 percent of the estimated sales volume of the following month, as shown in Figure 7–11.

PRODUCTION BUDGET (C)

Production budgets—such as the one shown in Figure 7–12—are made after sales and finished goods inventories are budgeted, because the output quantity needed each month is an amount just sufficient to satisfy anticipated sales volume plus inventory level requirements.

FIGURE 7–11

Nice and Eezee Flour Company
Schedule B
Finished Goods Inventory Budget
June, July, and August, 19X6

	June 30	July 31	August 31
Sales of Following Month	880 tons	902 tons	928 tons
Inventory Requirement (50% of Sales Volume)	440 tons	451 tons	464 tons

---

FIGURE 7–12

Nice and Eezee Flour Company
Schedule C
Production Budget
July and August, 19X6

	July	August
Sales Forecast (A)	880 tons	902 tons
Add: Ending Finished Goods Inventory (B)	451	464
Tons of Product Required	1,331	1,366
Less: Beginning Finished Goods Inventory (B)	440	451
Planned Monthly Production Quantities	891 tons	915 tons

PRODUCTION COST BUDGETS (D), (E), (F)

The output quantities budgeted in Schedule C will require the use of raw materials, direct labor, and manufacturing supplies and services. These items are budgeted in separate *Production Cost Budgets* and are coordinated in a budgeted *Statement of Cost of Goods Manufactured*.

Manufacturing operations require the following inputs of direct materials and labor per ton of output:

> *Direct Materials:* 1.75 tons of materials are needed, at $20 per ton, to produce one ton of output.

> *Direct Labor:* 1.25 hours of labor are needed, at $10 per hour, to produce one ton of output.

Analysis of previous months' production activity indicates that manufacturing overhead consists of the following:

> *Variable Items:* $5 per direct labor hour.

> *Fixed Items:* Salaries of $3,000 and depreciation of $3,000 per month.

Raw materials must be purchased in 100-ton lots. It is company policy to maintain monthly ending inventories of raw materials equal to at least 40 percent of the following month's production requirements.

Each of the three budgets that follows—Figures 7–13, 7–14, and 7–15—is an extension of the production budget, because the quantity of output manufac-

---

FIGURE 7–13

Nice and Eezee Flour Company
Schedule D
Raw Materials Usage Requirements
July and August, 19X6

	July	August
Production Forecast (C)	891 tons	915 tons
Input Requirements per Ton of Output	1.75 tons	1.75 tons
Total Input Usage Forecast	1,559.25 tons	1,601.25 tons
Cost per Ton	$20	$20
Total Cost of Materials Used	$31,185	$32,025

Raw Materials Acquisition Forecast
July, 19X6

Total Input Usage Forecast	1,559.25 tons
Add: Minimum Ending Inventory (40% Next Month's Usage)	640.50
Total Raw Materials Requirements	2,199.75
Less: Actual Beginning Inventory	650.00
Purchase Requirements	1,549.75
Actual Purchases (16 lots @ 100 tons)	1,600.00
Revised Ending Inventory (650 + 1,600 − 1,559.25)...............	690.75 tons
Cost of Purchases ($20 per ton)	$32,000

FIGURE 7–14

Nice and Eezee Flour Company
Schedule E
Direct Labor Budget
July, 19X6

Production Requirement (C)	891.00 tons
Labor Hours (1.25 hours per ton)	1,113.75 hours
Labor Cost ($10 per hour)	$11,137.50

FIGURE 7–15

Nice and Eezee Flour Company
Schedule F
Manufacturing Overhead Cost Budget
July, 19X6

Labor Hours (D)	1,113.75 hours
Variable Overhead:	
$5 Per Labor Hour	$ 5,569
Fixed Overhead:	
Salaries..	3,000
Depreciation..	3,000
Total Manufacturing Overhead Cost	$11,569

---

tured directly influences the quantities of materials, labor, and variable overhead inputs that will be acquired and/or consumed during each period.

MARKETING AND ADMINISTRATIVE EXPENSE BUDGET (G)

The sales forecast is also used to generate a budget for *marketing and administrative expenses*. As shown in Figure 7–16, the company forecasts that variable marketing expenses will equal 5 percent of sales revenue during July, that fixed administrative salaries will be $4,000 per month, and that depreciation expense will be $1,000 per month.

FIGURE 7–16

Nice and Eezee Flour Company
Schedule G
Marketing and Administrative Expense Budget
July, 19X6

Sales (A)		$88,000
Variable Expenses:		
Commissions (3% of sales)	$ 2,640	
Delivery Expense (1% of sales)	880	
Supplies (1% of sales)	880	
		$ 4,400
Fixed Expenses:		
Salaries	$ 4,000	
Depreciation	1,000	5,000
Total Expenses		$ 9,400

BUDGETED COST OF GOODS MANUFACTURED AND COST OF GOODS SOLD (H), (I)

Each of the preceding budgets contributes information to the company-wide forecasts of income and cash flows. When the budgets for production, marketing and administrative costs have been prepared, operating performance can be summarized in the projected *income statement* and its supporting *cost of goods sold* and *cost of goods manufactured* budgets (see Figures 7–17 and 7–18).

The budgeted *statement of cost of goods manufactured* brings together all the production costs budgeted for July. The company applies manufacturing overhead costs to production at a predetermined annual rate equal to 100 percent of direct labor cost. The statement of cost of goods manufactured must

---

FIGURE 7–17

Nice and Eezee Flour Company
Schedule H
Budgeted Statement of Cost of Goods Manufactured
July, 19X6

Raw Materials Usage (D)	$31,185.00
Direct Labor (E)	11,137.50
Manufacturing Overhead Applied	
100% Direct Labor	11,137.50
Total Cost of Goods Manufactured	$53,460.00
Units Produced (C)	891 tons
Unit Cost of Goods Manufactured ($53,460 ÷ 891)	$60 per ton

---

FIGURE 7–18

Nice and Eezee Flour Company
Schedule I
Budgeted Statement of Cost of Goods Sold
July, 19X6

Beginning Finished Goods Inventory	$26,400
Cost of Goods Manufactured (H)	53,460
Cost of Goods Available for Sale	$79,860
Less: Ending Finished Goods Inventory	27,060*
Cost of Goods Sold	$52,800

* Average Unit Cost = $79,860 ÷ 1,331 = $60 per ton
 Ending Inventory = $60 × 451 tons = $27,060

therefore contain this *applied* monthly overhead figure, not the budgeted monthly overhead amount from Schedule F. The company uses the weighted average cost method to compute the unit costs of output manufactured and sold each month. Zero balances for ending work in process inventories are forecast for July.

BUDGETED INCOME STATEMENT (J)

The forecast of sales revenues, the cost of goods sold budget, and the budgeted selling and administrative expenses are combined to produce the budgeted *income statement* shown in Figure 7–19. Review of the firm's long-range financing plans reveals that it intends to raise $100,000 by issuing bonds on July 1 to finance the acquisition on July 31 of new equipment costing $90,000. This bond issue will pay 12 percent annual interest. The company is subject to a 50 percent tax on net income; taxes are paid quarterly on January 31, April 30, July 31, and October 31.

CASH FLOW BUDGET (K)

The short-run financial effects of all the transactions and activities repre-sented in the operating budgets are brought together in the *cash flow budget.* This phase of budget preparation therefore highlights the integrative aspect of budgeting by focusing attention on one performance measure—cash flows—that is common to all the supporting sub-budgets.

The company's cash flow budget model includes the following relationships among the budget variables:

1. Collections on sales occur 25 percent in the month of sale, 50 percent in the following month, and 25 percent in the month after that. No cash dis-counts are given.

FIGURE 7–19

Nice and Eezee Flour Company
Schedule J
Budgeted Income Statement
July, 19X6

Sales (A)	$88,000
Less: Cost of Goods Sold (I)	52,800
Gross Profit	$35,200
Selling and Administrative Expenses (G)	9,400
	$25,800
Interest Expense	1,000
Net Income Before Tax	$24,800
Tax Expense (50%)	12,400
Net Income	$12,400

2. Suppliers of raw materials are paid 50 percent in the month of purchase and 50 percent in the following month. Suppliers allow no cash discounts.
3. All wages, manufacturing costs, and marketing and administrative expenses requiring cash outlays are paid in the month of incurrence.
4. As previously noted, income taxes are paid quarterly.
5. Quarterly dividends of $15,000 are declared and paid in January, April, July, and October.
6. As previously noted, $100,000 of long-term bonds will be issued on July 1, and $90,000 of the proceeds will be used to purchase equipment.

As illustrated in Figures 7–20 through 7–23, Schedule K, the cash flow budget, summarizes forecasts of accounts receivable collections (Schedule

---

FIGURE 7–20

Nice and Eezee Flour Company
Schedule K
Cash Flow Budget
July, 19X6

Cash Balance on July 1		$ 34,750.00
Receipts:		
Accounts Receivable (K-1)	$ 86,000.00	
Long-term Borrowing	100,000.00	186,000.00
		$220,750.00
Payments:		
Accounts Payable (K-2)	$ 33,000.00	
Operating Expenses (K-3)	29,106.50	
Income Taxes	34,500.00	
Dividends	15,000.00	
Fixed Asset Acquisitions	90,000.00	201,606.50
Cash Balance on July 31		$ 19,143.50

FIGURE 7–21

Nice and Eezee Flour Company
Schedule K-1
Forecast of Accounts Receivable Collections
July, 19X6

	July
Current Sales (25% × $88,000)	$22,000
Previous Month's Sales (50% × $86,000)	43,000
Two Months' Prior Sales (25% × $84,000)	21,000
Total Accounts Receivable Collections	$86,000

FIGURE 7–22

Nice and Eezee Flour Company
Schedule K-2
Forecast of Accounts Payable Payments
July, 19X6

Current Month Purchases (50% × $32,000)	$16,000
Prior Month's Purchases (50% × $34,000)	17,000
Total Accounts Payable Payments	$33,000

FIGURE 7–23

Nice and Eezee Flour Company
Schedule K-3
Forecast of Operating Expense Payments
July, 19X6

Direct Labor (E)	$11,137.50
Variable Manufacturing Expense (F)	5,569.00
Manufacturing Salaries (F)	3,000.00
Commissions (G)	2,640.00
Delivery Expense (G)	880.00
Supplies (G)	880.00
Administrative Salaries (G)	4,000.00
Interest Expense (J)	1,000.00
Total Operating Expense Payments	$29,106.50

K-1), accounts payable payments (Schedule K-2), and operating expense payments (Schedule K-3).

BUDGETED BALANCE SHEET (L)

The final step in the budget cycle is to prepare a *budgeted balance sheet*. As shown in Figure 7–24, all the amounts that appear on the budgeted balance sheet in Schedule L have already been determined, directly or indirectly, by the relationships expressed in the operating and financial budgets previously presented.

It is the company's practice to eliminate any balance in underapplied or overapplied overhead against the Cost of Goods Sold account at the end of June and December. In all other months, any such balance is carried as an adjustment against Finished Goods Inventory in the balance sheet. The forecast for July 31 is an underapplied overhead balance of $431.50 ($11,569 actual — $11,137.50 applied).

FIGURE 7–24

Nice and Eezee Flour Company
Schedule L
Budgeted Balance Sheet
July 31, 19X6

Assets

Current Assets:

Cash on Hand	$ 19,143.50	
Accounts Receivable	87,500.00	
Inventory—Raw Material	13,815.00	
Inventory—Finished Goods	27,060.00	
Inventory—Overhead Adjustment	431.50	
		$147,950

Fixed Assets:

Land	$ 72,000	
Plant—Net	331,000	403,000
Total Assets		$550,950

Equities

Current Liabilities:

Accounts Payable	$ 16,000	
Taxes Payable	12,400	$ 28,400

Long-term Liabilities:

Bonds Payable		100,000
Total Liabilities		$128,400

Stockholders' Equity:

Capital Stock	$250,000	
Retained Earnings	172,550	422,550
Total Equities		$550,950

The relationships underlying the master budget and the individual operating and financial budgets are presented in simple algebraic form in the study guide that accompanies this text. The collection of these formulas constitutes a basic financial and operating budget model of the Nice and Eezee Company. This model will also be demonstrated in the form of a computer program that allows alternative budgets to be derived by varying the key planning variable—the sales volume forecast—and other parameters.

SUMMARY

1. Budgets are statements of the expected outcomes of planned future actions, prepared to help organizations reach their goals.
2. The planning phase of the budgetary process consists of preparing budgets

and communicating them to managers at all company levels. Budgets also provide a basis for implementing and controlling the operations being budgeted.

3. The planning purposes of budgets include:
   a. Creating awareness of the behavior of any system being budgeted.
   b. Requiring decision makers to consider the possible future effects of their actions.
   c. Focusing attention on goals and alternative means of achieving them.
   d. Communicating performance requirements and expectations to various managerial levels.
   e. Coordinating and integrating the plans of different parts of the organization.

4. The scope and contents of individual budgets vary according to the areas of activity being budgeted. However, all budgets have certain common features: They anticipate the future; they have structural similarities; they are oriented to company goals; they are always based on relationships among planning variables. These relationships are represented by budget models.

5. As the primary financial planning budget, the master budget is supported by a series of financial and operating budgets.

6. Budget preparation follows a pattern established by the network of interrelated planning variables, beginning with a key forecast variable, usually total sales volume.

7. Elementary techniques for constructing financial and operating budgets include:
   a. Account analysis using T-accounts supplemented with flow diagrams.
   b. Tabular analysis of accounts in terms of budget relationships.
   c. Formulation of algebraic equations to represent the relationships among planning variables.

KEY WORDS AND PHRASES

Budgetary Process (265)
Budget (268)
Objects of Budgeting (270)
Financial Budgets (271)
Operating Budgets (271)
Budget Model (274)
T-account Analysis (275)
Tabular Analysis (279)
Algebraic Analysis (280)
Generalized Model (282)
Computer Simulation (282)
Master Budget (282)
Central Planning Variable (283)
Sales Budget (287)
Finished Goods Inventory Budget (287)
Production Budget (287)
Production Cost Budgets (288)
Marketing and Administrative Expense Budget (290)
Budgeted Cost of Goods Manufactured (291)
Budgeted Cost of Goods Sold (291)
Budgeted Income Statement (292)
Cash Flow Budget (292)
Budgeted Balance Sheet (294)

Questions

1. What is the primary purpose of the accounting budgetary process?
2. What are the main accounting data requirements of planning decisions?
3. Explain the need for general organizational goals to be translated into detailed operational directives. How does the accounting budgetary process assist in this regard?
4. What are the five major identifying characteristics of a budget? Why is each important?
5. Why is there a need for highly aggregated budgets and budgets with a great amount of detail as well as for budgets with moderate amounts of both detail and aggregation? Give examples of each.
6. What gives a budget its focus and structure? Give some examples.
7. What principles should be observed when selecting the items to be included in the budget of any given activity center or time period?
8. What role does the concept of performance measurement play in the budgetary process? Why is it so important?
9. Distinguish between financial budgets and operating budgets. What features do they have in common?
10. What supplementary purposes are served by budgets in addition to their use as planning devices?
11. Explain the concept of a budget model. Why is it so critical to the budgetary process?
12. What statements are usually contained in a master budget? What are the advantages and limitations of a conventional, static, financial master budget?
13. Explain the role and importance of a central planning variable in the budgetary process.
14. Explain how a network of operating and financial budgets can be developed around a key planning variable.
15. What sequence should be observed in the development of a network of operating and financial budgets?
16. What is the purpose of budget guidelines?
17. What type of role should the budget staff play in an organization?
18. Why is participative budgeting recommended? Who benefits from it?
19. Why should the budgetary process be treated as an iterative one? What purposes are served by doing so?
20. Why is the approval and communication of budgets so important a step in the total budgetary process?

Exercises

E 7–1 Elementary Sales Budget

The Webster Corporation markets two products—Alphas and Omegas. Forecasts of unit sales for the next three months have been made as follows:

	Alpha	Omega
October.........	16,000	30,000
November......	18,000	34,000
December......	22,000	40,000

Sales prices are $40 for Alphas and $25 for Omegas. Cash sales amount to 40 percent of total sales of each product. Of the remainder, 80 percent is collected in the following month, 20 percent in the month thereafter.

Required:
(a) Prepare a sales budget for the three-month period, showing monthly and quarterly figures for both products individually and in total.
(b) Prepare a schedule of forecast cash receipts relating to the October, November, and December sales.

E 7–2   Elementary Production Budget

Demand for Bradley Company's product reaches its peak during the winter season. Sales are distributed according to the following patterns:

Quarter	Percent
Winter (Jan.–Mar.)..........	50
Spring (Apr.–June)	15
Summer (July–Sept.)	10
Fall (Oct.–Dec.)	25

The inventory policy of the company is to maintain an ending inventory at least equal to 20 percent of the following quarter's sales. Production capacity is 2,400,000 units per year or 600,000 units per quarter. The sales forecasts for 19X7 and 19X8 are 1,500,000 and 1,800,000 units respectively. Inventory on hand at the beginning of Winter, 19X7 was 150,000 units.

Required:
(a) Prepare a schedule of quarterly production requirements for 19X7 and 19X8 (ignoring the production capacity constraint quarter). Assume that the demand for Winter 19X9 will be 1,000,000 units and demand for Spring 19X9 will be 300,000 units.
(b) Revise the production schedule to take account of the limit on productive capacity. If the required production in any quarter exceeds the capacity limit, production must be increased in the *preceding* quarter(s).

E 7–3   Production and Purchasing Budgets

Frances Corporation follows a policy of maintaining an inventory of raw materials equal to production requirements for the following two months. Finished goods inventories are kept at a level equal to 150 percent of the forecast sales for the following month. Each unit of finished output requires 10 pounds of raw material, which costs $1 per pound.

The sales forecasts for the last six months of 19X0 are as follows:

Month	Units	Month	Units
July	25,000	Oct.	40,000
Aug.	30,000	Nov.	35,000
Sept.	25,000	Dec.	50,000

Inventories as of July 1, 19X0 were 550,000 pounds of raw materials and 37,500 units of finished output.

Required:
Prepare schedules of budgeted *production* and *purchases* for the months of July, August, and September.

E 7–4 Budgeting Labor Costs

Thompson Company has generated the following production schedules for the first quarter of 19X4.

	Units of Output	
	Product A	Product B
January	10,000	20,000
February	15,000	25,000
March	12,500	15,000

The labor processing requirements for each product are as follows:

	Product A	Product B
Direct Labor—Class I	50 hours per 100 units	30 hours per 100 units
Direct Labor—Class II	20 hours per 100 units	40 hours per 100 units

Required:
(a) Prepare schedules of the budgeted total labor hour requirements for each class of labor for the months of January, February, and March.
(b) If each employee works an average of 150 regular hours per month and is allowed a maximum of 50 overtime hours per month, what are the budgeted manpower requirements for each month? Assume that minimum levels of 60 Class I and 50 Class II workers must be maintained throughout all months, and that additional part-time employees may only be added when production requirements exceed the capacity available (including allowable overtime) from the base staff. Part-time employees may work up to 150 hours per month.

E 7–5 Cash Flow Budget

Katz Corporation is projecting its cash flow for the month of August 19X2. The following information is available:

(1) Total Sales—June $100,000
           —July $105,000
     Purchases—July .... $ 74,970
     Inventory—August 1 .... $ 30,870
     Cash on Hand—August 1 ..... $ 35,000
     Receivables—August 1 .... $ 78,000
     Payables—August 1 .... $ 37,485
(2) Sales have been forecast to be increasing at the rate of 5 percent per month. Of each month's sales, 40 percent are for cash and 60 percent are credit sales.

(3) Cash collections from receivables follow the pattern of 75 percent of a month's credit sales in the following month and the remaining 25 percent one month later.

(4) The company maintains a constant gross profit margin of 30 percent on all sales. Inventory is maintained at a level equal to 40 percent of the following month's forecast sales.

(5) Purchases are paid for 50 percent in the month of purchase and 50 percent in the following month.

(6) Monthly operating expenses (all those requiring cash are paid during the current month) include:

Wages	$10,000
Advertising	4,000
Depreciation	5,000
Miscellaneous......	1,000
	$20,000

Required:
Prepare a cash flow budget and all supporting schedules for August.

E 7–6   Cash Flow Budget

Muñoz Company has scheduled production of 60,000 units of Product X and 40,000 units of Product Y during May of 19X3. Product specifications call for the following inputs per unit of each product:

Direct Materials	Product X	Product Y
A	5 pounds	10 pounds
B	—	20 pounds
C	10 pounds	—
Direct Labor	2 hours	3 hours

Materials costs are $5, $2, and $3 per pound for A, B, and C respectively. Labor wage rates are $10 per hour.

Indirect labor hours, also at $10 per hour, average 10 percent of total direct labor hours each month. Other variable overhead costs are usually incurred at the rate of $2 per *direct* labor hour and are paid for in the month incurred. Fixed overhead costs include:

Supervisor Salaries	$ 5,000
Depreciation	15,000
Insurance	2,500
Rent	5,000
Total Fixed Overhead Costs	$27,500

Rent is paid six months in advance in January and June, and insurance premiums are paid annually in May each year.

Inventory balances of raw materials are planned to change during May as follows:

A	Increase	50,000 pounds
B	Decrease	100,000 pounds
C	No Change	

Required:
Prepare a budget of cash expenditures for all manufacturing related items for May of 19X3. Show all supporting schedules.

E 7–7   Budgeted Income Statement

Kieland Company had inventories of 80,000 pounds of raw materials and 20,000 pounds of finished output on February 1, 19X6. Sales forecasts for February and the three following months were:

February	40,000 pounds
March	60,000 pounds
April	50,000 pounds
May	50,000 pounds

The company maintains a finished goods inventory equal to 50 percent of the forecast sales of the following month and a raw materials inventory equal to 80 percent of the production requirements of the following month. Each pound of finished output requires 2 pounds of raw material which costs $4 per pound; the sales price of the finished product is $25 per pound.

Direct labor costs are budgeted at $6 per hour. Each 20 pounds of finished output requires 10 hours of direct labor. Variable manufacturing overhead amounts to $4 per labor hour. Fixed manufacturing overhead, including depreciation of $25,000, totals $40,000. Selling and administrative expenses are $75,000 per month, including depreciation of $20,000. Tax expense is accrued each month at the rate of 40 percent of net income.

Required:
Prepare budgeted income statements for the months of February and March of 19X6. (Assume that inventories of finished goods are carried at $15 per pound and raw materials inventories at a purchase price of $4 per pound.) Show all supporting budget schedules.

E 7–8   Elementary Budget Model—Algebraic Formulation

Landry Company wishes to implement a monthly budgeting model as a planning application to make use of its new HAL-4700 computer. The following relationships have been observed among key planning variables.

(1) Sales volume is increasing at the rate of 5 percent per month.

(2) All sales are on credit. Collections are received 30 percent in the month of the sale, 60 percent in the following month, and 10 percent two months later.

(3) Inventory is maintained at a level equal to 150 percent of the following month's forecast sales.

(4) Purchases are paid for 50 percent in the month of purchase and 50 percent in the following month.

(5) Other variable costs average 20 percent of each month's sales revenue. Fixed costs, including depreciation of $30,000, amount to $65,000 each month. All costs requiring a cash outlay are paid in the current month.

(6) The firm's product sells for $20 per unit; its purchase price is $10 per unit.

Required:

Prepare a series of budget equations (in algebraic form) that may be used to represent the following relationships:

(a) Sales for current month in units.

(b) Sales for current month in dollars.

(c) Purchases for current month in units.

(d) Purchases for current month in dollars.

(e) Cost of goods sold (current month)

(f) Cash receipts (current month)

(g) Operating expenses (current month)

(h) Cash disbursements (current month)

(i) Net income (current month)

The following notations should be employed:

S_t	Current period sales (units)
$\$S_t$	Dollar sales
P_t	Current period purchases (units)
$\$P_t$	Dollar purchases
CGS_t	Cost of goods sold
CR_t	Cash receipts
CD_t	Cash disbursements
OE_t	Operating expenses
TE_t	Total expenses
R_t	Revenue
NI_t	Net income
IN_t	Inventory at end of period t
$(t-1)$	Last period
$(t+1)$	Next period
$(t+2)$	Two periods ahead

E 7–9   Comprehensive Operating Budgets—Elementary

Pardee Corporation manufactures and markets a single product, for which quarterly sales for 19X1 have been forecast as follows:

Quarter	Sales (units)
1	40,000
2	50,000
3	60,000
4	55,000

The forecast for 19X2 indicates that sales will be 44,000 units in both quarter 1 and quarter 2. Inventory policies indicate that raw materials sufficient for 40 percent of the next quarter's production be maintained and that finished goods equal to 25 percent of the next quarter's sales be kept on hand. Inventories at the beginning of 19X1 were as budgeted.

Production, marketing, and administrative costs are budgeted at the following amounts:

Materials	10 pounds at $4 = $40 per unit
Labor	4 hours at $8 = $32 per unit
Manufacturing Overhead	$120,000 per quarter plus $6 per labor hour
Marketing and Administrative	$80,000 per month plus 15 percent of sales revenue
Sales Price	$120 per unit

Required:

(a) Prepare the following budget schedules for each quarter of 19X1.
  (1) Sales
  (2) Production
  (3) Purchasing
  (4) Manufacturing costs (Do not include material.)
  (5) Cost of Goods Sold (Assume finished goods inventories are carried at $100 per unit.)
  (6) Net Income

(b) The company hopes to break even in each quarter and earn an annual profit at least equal to 15 percent of sales revenue. Can these goals be met if the conditions specified in the budget are achieved?

Cases

C 7–1   Coordination of Sales and Production Budgets

McCulley Company is preparing its production and profit plans for 19X8 and is attempting to coordinate these with its previously developed sales forecasts.

The company manufactures dolls modeled on four different characters in popular space movies. The company also manufactures a model of a spaceship. Forecast sales for the dolls and the spaceship for 19X8 are as follows:

Model	Demand (units)	Regular Sales Price
Ace Skydriver	100,000	$ 6.00
Princess Mia	80,000	8.00
C-Thru-Me-2	150,000	10.00
Varth Daydar	70,000	7.00
Space Station X99	320,000	20.00

To promote sales, the space station is discounted 20 percent when it is purchased along with one of the dolls. McCulley management estimates that 50 percent of all doll sales will be accompanied by sales of the space station. These sales are included in the unit sales forecasts.

The following production cost information is available regarding input quantities and prices for each of the five products:

Model	Raw Materials	Direct Labor (hours)
Ace Skydriver	$ .75	.25
Princess Mia	.80	.375
C-Thru-Me-2	1.25	.60
Varth Daydar	.80	.50
Space Station X99	4.00	1.00

Direct labor costs $5 per hour and variable manufacturing overhead is normally incurred at the rate of $2 per direct labor hour. Fixed factory overhead is $250,000 per year and productive capacity on a single shift basis is 400,000 labor hours. Should overtime be needed, the variable overhead rate must be adjusted to absorb the total expected overhead premiums. Overtime rates are 150 percent of the normal direct labor rate and a maximum of 125,000 overtime hours is permissible per year.

Variable selling expenses amount to 15 percent of sales revenues. Fixed marketing and administrative expenses total $125,000 per year. Finished goods inventories will be kept at a constant level throughout the year.

Required:

(a) Prepare a detailed sales budget showing unit sales and revenues for each product line.

(b) Prepare a production budget showing input requirements of materials and labor.

(c) Compute the number of overtime hours necessary to attain the required production output within the productive capacity stated.

(d) Recompute the variable overhead rate. Show all calculations.

(e) Prepare a budgeted statement of cost of goods manufactured, showing the direct cost of each product in as much detail as possible.

(f) Prepare a budgeted profit plan for 19X8 with all necessary supporting schedules.

C 7–2 Analysis and Interpretation of Budgets

Several separate budgets have been prepared for Spinks Company for the first three months of 19X8. They are reproduced below:

Cash Receipts Budget
(in thousands)

	January	February	March
Cash Sales	$ 1,000	$ 1,500	$ 2,500
December Sales	1,200		
January Sales		3,000	
February Sales			4,500
	$ 2,200	$ 4,500	$ 7,000

Cash Disbursements Budget
(in thousands)

	January	February	March
Production Costs			
Variable	$ 2,400	$ 3,600	$ 2,100
Fixed	800	800	800
Marketing and Administrative Costs			
Variable			
Current Month	240	360	600
Previous Month	64	160	240
Fixed	1,600	1,600	1,600
	$ 5,104	$ 6,520	$ 5,320

Production Budget
(in units)

	January	February	March
Ending Inventory Planned	9,000	15,000	12,000
Sales	4,000	6,000	10,000
Total Requirements	13,000	21,000	22,000
Beginning Inventory Available	5,000	9,000	15,000
Production Scheduled	8,000	12,000	7,000

Budgeted Income Statement
(in thousands)
January–March 19X8

Sales (20,000 units)		$20,000
Variable Costs		
Manufacturing	$6,000	
Marketing	2,000	8,000
Contribution Margin		$12,000
Fixed Costs		
Manufacturing	$3,600	
Marketing	4,800	8,400
Net Income		$ 3,600

Required:

(a) What are the variable manufacturing costs per unit?

(b) How much are the monthly fixed manufacturing costs not requiring cash outlays?

(c) How much of the monthly fixed marketing and administrative costs is paid in cash?

(d) What collection pattern is present with respect to sales on credit?

(e) How much did credit sales total in December 19X7?

(f) What fraction of variable marketing and administrative costs is paid for in the current month and what fraction in the following month?

(g) What is the balance of accounts receivable at the end of March?

(h) How much are accrued marketing and administrative costs at the end of March?

(i) Assuming the cash balance on January 1, 19X8 was $600,000, what will be the cash balance on March 31, 19X8?

(j) What finished goods inventory policy is the firm following?

(k) What will sales be in April 19X8?

(l) If the firm had sold 4,000 more units during the three-month period, what would net income have been?

C 7–3 Comprehensive Master Budget

Moll Corporation wishes to prepare a master budget and all supporting sub-budgets for the three-month period including April, May, and June of 19X1. It produces three products, L, M, and N, which sell for $12, $14, and $16 respectively. Each product uses a common raw material that costs $2 per pound. Input requirements for L, M, and N are 1 pound, 2 pounds, and 3 pounds respectively. Direct labor costs $7 per hour and one hour of labor can produce either 2 units of L, 4 units of M, or 4 units of N.

Variable factory overhead is incurred at the rate of $1 per direct labor hour and there are no fixed factory overhead costs.

At the end of each month, the company wishes to maintain finished goods inventory equal to 70 percent of the following month's sales of each product and raw materials equal to 120 percent of the current month's production requirements. Raw materials purchases are paid for 25 percent in the current month and 75 percent in the following month.

Other operating costs are sales commissions (5 percent of sales revenues), shipping costs (2 percent of sales revenues), office salaries of $1,200 per month, rent of $800 per month, and depreciation of $2,000 per month. At the end of June, the company plans to pay $38,000 cash for a new office copier.

With the exception of materials purchases, all costs are paid for in the current month. Of all sales, 40 percent are collected in cash and 60 percent in the following month. The company must maintain a minimum cash balance of $10,000. When necessary, money is borrowed at 12 percent per annum in multiples of $1,000. Repayment with interest is made at the end of 30 days.

Sales forecasts in units for the period April–May–June–July of 19X1 were made as follows:

Product	April	May	June	July
L.............	500	500	500	500
M	600	700	800	900
N	900	500	300	100

The company's balance sheet at the beginning of April, 19X1 was as follows:

Assets

Cash		$10,200
Receivables		17,200
Inventory		
Raw Materials: 4,400 lbs. @ $2	$ 8,800	
Product L: 350 units @ $6	2,100	
Product M: 420 units @ $6	2,520	
Product N: 630 units @ $8	5,040	18,460
Office Equipment	$50,000	
Less: Accumulated Depreciation	30,000	20,000
		$65,860

Liabilities and Equity

Payables (March Purchases)	$ 5,400
Owners Equity........................	60,460
	$65,860

Required:

Prepare a master budget for April–May–June 19X1, including separate schedules of:

(a) Forecast sales revenues
(b) Production budget
(c) Purchases budget
(d) Receivables collections

(e) Payments for merchandise
(f) Cash receipts (before loans)
(g) Cash disbursements (before loans)
(h) Loans and loan repayments
(i) Income statement
(j) Balance sheet (inventories are carried at variable cost of production)

Problems

P 7-1   Sales Budgeting

Mammoth Motor Company manufactures four models of automobiles and sells through three different market channels. Budgeted annual sales for 19X6 for these models are as follows:

Model	Total Unit Sales	Market Distribution (percent)		
		Export	Fleet Sales	Regular
Big Mammoth	300,000	30	10	60
Middle Mammoth	800,000	20	15	65
Mini Mammoth.................	600,000	25	10	65
Micro Mammoth	800,000	30	20	50

Quarterly distribution of total unit sales is expected to be:

1.	Fall..........	25%
2.	Winter	40
3.	Spring	15
4.	Summer......	20
		100%

The regular retail sales prices are Big $10,000, Middle $8,000, Mini $5,000, and Micro $4,000. Export sales are made at a 25 percent discount; fleet sales are made at a 15 percent discount and regular unit sales at a 10 percent discount.

Required:
Prepare first and second quarter sales budgets for each model and market, showing unit sales and dollar sales revenue. Show all appropriate totals.

P 7-2   Budgeting Sales

The marketing research division of Noll Corporation has developed sales forecast data for its baby food product, Mishy-Musho. This data includes the following:

Population of Sales Area: 20,000,000
Number of Potential Customers: 10 per 1,000

**Estimated Consumption of All Similar
Baby Food Products by Potential Customers**

Estimated Consumption (cans per year)	Potential Customers (percent of population)
100	20%
80	30
60	20
40	20
20	10
	100%

Sales Plan Alternatives

(1) $1.00 per can—15 percent of total market
(2) $ .75 per can—25 percent of total market
(3) $ .50 per can—30 percent of total market

Required:
(a) Prepare schedules of budgeted sales in cans and in dollar revenue for each of the three sales plans being considered by Noll.
(b) Assume the product cost $.40 per can to produce. Which sales plan should be adopted? Why?

P 7-3 Budgeting Purchases and Production

Miller Company manufactures a single product, using two raw materials, X and Y. When units are started into processing, six pounds of material X are issued for each unit. At the halfway point in processing, three pounds of material Y are added to each unit in process. Information concerning inventories is as follows:

	Jan 1, 19X4 (Actual)	June 30, 19X4 (Budgeted)
Raw Material X	40,000	30,000
Raw Material Y	20,000	15,000
Finished Goods	10,000	20,000
Work in Process (40% complete)	5,000	15,000

Raw materials costs are $4 per pound for material X and $5 per pound for material Y. Unit sales were budgeted at 20,000 from January through June.

Required:
(a) Prepare a schedule of budgeted *production* for the six-month period, January–June, to accommodate the budgeted inventory levels. Show clearly the number of units to be *started* and the number to be *completed*. Show also the number of *equivalent* units produced with regard to (1) material X content and (2) material Y content.
(b) Prepare schedules of budgeted *purchases* of material X and material Y.
(c) In determining the budgeted inventory levels in the preceding data, what factors may have been taken into account and what decision rules might have been used?

P 7-4   Budgeting Production and Purchases

Madden Corporation has made the following sales forecast for its product for the January–June period of 19X2:

Month	Sales (units)	Month	Sales (units)
January	20,000	April	30,000
February	15,000	May	18,000
March	25,000	June	20,000

Because the production process is very short, there are no work in process inventories. Finished goods inventory equal to 80 percent of the following month's sales are to be maintained at all times. Two raw materials are used in production—material K and material L. Because material K is readily available, an inventory equal to 25 percent of the following month's production requirements is considered sufficient. However, material L is sometimes difficult to obtain, and management feels that an inventory amounting to the production requirements of the next two months is necessary. Material K costs $3 per unit and material L is $5. One unit of finished output requires 4 units of material K and 2 units of material L.

Required:

(a) Prepare a budgeted production schedule for February and March of 19X2. Show all supporting calculations. (Assume inventories on February 1 were at the required levels.)

(b) Prepare a schedule of planned purchases of materials K and L for the same two-month period.

(c) Revise the purchase schedule to reflect the fact that material K can only be purchased in lots of 5,000 units and L in lots of 20,000 units.

(d) Revise the production schedule to reflect the fact that productive capacity is only 25,000 units. Where scheduled production would exceed 25,000, the excess must be produced in the previous month.

(e) What alternatives to the revisions made in parts (c) and (d) may be possible? How should a decision among such alternatives and the present action be made?

P 7-5   Production Budget

Phillips Company makes two products, G and H. Sales prices are $24 per unit for G and $50 for H. To manufacture one unit of G, two units of material A and one unit of material B are required. To manufacture one unit of H, two units of B and three units of material C are required. Budgeted direct labor costs are 15 minutes per unit for G and 20 minutes per unit for H. Direct labor rates are $10 per hour. Actual and budgeted inventories for April of 19X2 were as follows:

	Actual Inventory April 1, 19X2 (units)	Budgeted Inventory April 30, 19X2 (units)
Product G	40,000	20,000
Product H	40,000	50,000
Material A	50,000	30,000
Material B	45,000	45,000
Material C	40,000	50,000
Work in Process	–0–	–0–

Sales forecasts for April were for 240,000 units of product G and 100,000 units of product H. Raw material input prices were forecast as follows: A—$2, B—$4, C—$5.

Variable manufacturing costs are budgeted at the rate of $4 per direct labor hour. Fixed manufacturing costs are budgeted at $100,000 per month.

Required:

(a) Prepare a schedule of budgeted production of products G and H for April of 19X2.

(b) Prepare a schedule of budgeted purchases of materials A, B, and C for April of 19X2.

(c) Prepare a schedule of budgeted labor hour requirements for direct labor for April of 19X2.

(d) Prepare a statement of budgeted cost of goods manufactured for April of 19X2.

P 7–6 Production and Expense Budgets

Eubank Corporation produces two types of product and has developed the following sales forecast for the last four months of 19X6:

	Product C	Product D
September	1,800	2,800
October	2,200	3,200
November	2,400	3,600
December	2,600	3,000

No inventories of work in process are maintained, but finished goods inventory equal to 50 percent of the next month's sales is considered necessary. Unit production costs are estimated as follows:

	Product C	Product D
Direct Materials	$35	$30
Direct Labor	$12	$10
Variable Overhead	$12	$10

To manufacture one unit of output, Product C requires 7 units of raw material. Product D uses up to 6 units. The raw material costs $5 per unit, and inventories equal to the production requirements for the following month must be kept on hand at the end of each month. Fixed manufacturing overhead costs are $30,000 per month. Eubank Corporation uses the variable cost model for product costing and income determination. Selling costs are $10 per unit for both products and fixed selling and administrative costs amount to $25,000 per month.

Required:

(a) Prepare a production budget in units for the two products for September and October

(b) Prepare a raw materials purchases budget for September and October.

(c) Prepare a manufacturing overhead budget for September and October.

(d) Prepare a selling and administrative cost budget for September and October.

(e) Prepare schedules of budgeted cost of goods manufactured and budgeted cost of goods sold for September and October. Because the variable cost model is being used, cost of goods manufactured includes only variable manufacturing costs. Fixed manufacturing costs are added directly to cost of goods sold.

P 7–7   Budgeting Labor Hour Requirements

Wilkinson Company operates a vehicle maintenance division that services its customer's fleets of trucks on a contract basis. The facility has three categories of labor—A, B, and C—to perform separate specialized tasks. If during a month there is time available among any group of workers, they may be reassigned to another category, but in such cases their productivity is reduced by 50 percent.

For the month of August, 19X3, the following labor hours are available: A—1,000 hours; B—1,600 hours; and C—400 hours. The average vehicle requires 80 hours of type A labor, 6 hours of type B, and 20 hours of type C, but not all vehicles always require servicing by each category of labor.

The following contracts are due to be serviced during August:

Contract	Number of Vehicles	Work Required A	B	C
776	50	yes	yes	no
777	20	yes	yes	yes
778	30	yes	yes	no
779	20	yes	no	yes
780	10	yes	yes	no

Required:

(a) Prepare a preliminary schedule of the work load requirements for each category of labor for the month.

(b) Calculate the excess hours available or additional hours required for each class of labor for the month.

(c) Make any reassignments possible to allow the contracts to be serviced within the month and with the total labor hours available. Will there be any problems? Why or why not?

P 7–8   Cash Flow Budgeting

Coryell Corporation desires to prepare cash flow budgets for January and February of 19X1. The following forecast data are available:

Sales	January	February	March
(1) Cash	$ 60,000	$ 70,000	$ 90,000
Credit (2/10, n/30)	160,000	180,000	200,000

(2) Of the credit sales, 40 percent are paid within the discount terms, 30 percent by the end of the current month, 20 percent in the following month, 5 percent two months later, and 5 percent are uncollectible. The company uses the allowance method to record the estimated uncollectible amounts in the same month as the related sales are made.

(3) Coryell is a merchandising firm and maintains a constant average gross margin of 40 percent on all sales.

(4) Inventory is maintained at a level equal to a retail value of $200,000.

(5) Purchases are usually paid for 75 percent in the current month and 25 percent in the following month.

(6)   Other operating costs include variable marketing costs equal to 15 percent of sales revenue and fixed costs totaling $35,000 per month. Of these fixed charges, depreciation amounts to $10,000 and prepaid items (insurance, property tax) account for $5,000. All costs requiring cash payments are paid in the current month.

(7)   During January, a cash dividend of $15,000 must be paid; in February, a loan repayment of $10,000 is due.

(8)   In February, the company plans to make a $50,000 deposit on some real estate it intends to acquire.

(9)   Balances at January 1, 19X1 included:

Cash	$ 60,000
Receivables* (net)	58,000
Inventory	120,000
Payables (to suppliers)	30,000

* Credit Sales were $160,000 in November and $200,000 in December.

Required:
(a)   Prepare a schedule of budgeted collections from customers for January and February. Assume that no interest penalties are charged for payments after 30 days.

(b)   Prepare schedules of budgeted purchases and cash payments to suppliers of merchandise for January and February.

(c)   Prepare a schedule of budgeted cash receipts and disbursements for the months of January and February.

(d)   Assuming that a minimum cash balance of $30,000 must always be maintained, can the company make the down payment on the real estate or will it have to resort to borrowing? Why or why not?

P 7–9   Cash Flow Budgeting—Algebraic Budget Model

Clarke Company distributes a single product, which it buys for $16 and sells for $40 per unit. Marketing and administrative costs amount to $4 per unit for variable items and $24,000 per month for fixed items, including $6,000 of depreciation.

Inventory equal to the forecast demand for two months is to be maintained. Clarke pays for 60 percent of its purchases in the current month and 40 percent in the following month. All other costs requiring cash payments are paid for in the current month.

All sales are on credit and collections from customers are estimated to be 60 percent in the month of sale, 30 percent in the following month, and 10 percent in the month thereafter. Monthly sales are budgeted to include a 10 percent increase over the average sales of the previous three months.

Required:
(a)   Formulate a set of equations from the preceding data to represent all the relationships that pertain to budgeted cash flow.

(b)   Evaluate these equations for a month period, using as data the following items:
(1)   Sales in the previous three months: 2,000 units last month, 1,600 units two months ago, 1,800 units three months ago.
(2)   Cash balance at the beginning of the month: $24,000.

(3)   Inventory, receivables, and payables at the beginning of the month correspond to the budgeted amounts previously specified.

P 7–10   Cash Flow Budgeting

Cerf Company is preparing its cash flow budget for the first three months of 19X4 and has developed the following information:

(1)   Sales forecasts for the first six months of 19X4 are as follows:

January	$ 720,000	April	$1,080,000
February	840,000	May	960,000
March	1,200,000	June......	800,000

(2)   Gross accounts receivable on January 1, 19X4 were $760,000. Sales in November and December of 19X3 were $1,200,000 and $1,600,000 respectively. Collections from customers are usually 60 percent of sales in the current month, 30 percent in the following month, and 8 percent two months later. Uncollectible accounts average 2 percent of all sales, are provided for by an allowance for doubtful accounts, and are written off at the end of the second month after the date of sale.

(3)   Inventory is maintained at a level equal to 150 percent of the following month's forecast sales. The standard gross profit margin is 40 percent of sales revenue. Purchases are paid for 25 percent in the month of purchase and 75 percent in the following month. On December 31, 19X3, payables were $126,000.

(4)   Inventory at cost on January 1, 19X4 was $648,000. However, this included items costing $120,000 that were found to be obsolete. Arrangements were made to sell these for cash in January at one half their regular sales price. This transaction is not included in the January sales forecast, but January purchases must account for the inventory decrease involved.

(5)   Fixed marketing and administrative costs amount to $160,000 per month, including depreciation of $20,000. Variable marketing and administrative costs are incurred at the rate of 15 percent of monthly sales. Those costs requiring cash payments are paid for according to the following schedule:

	Variable	Fixed
Prepaid in previous month	0%	50%
Paid in current month	60%	40%
Paid in following month	40%	10%

(6)   Cash dividends of $40,000 are due to be paid quarterly on January 10, April 10, July 10, and October 10.

(7)   Equipment replacements costing $25,000 are scheduled to be purchased for cash in February.

(8)   Taxes due on 19X3 income amount to $150,000 and are to be paid in February.

(9)   To cover anticipated cash requirements for February, a short-term, three-month bank loan of $175,000 has been arranged. The proceeds will be received on January 31.

(10)   The cash balance on January 1, 19X4 was $150,000.

Required:

Prepare cash flow budgets for January, February, and March of 19X4. Show all necessary supporting budget schedules (purchases, receivables, collections, and so on).

P 7–11 Budgeted Income Statement—Algebraic Budget Model

Shula Company wishes to develop formulas for an income statement budget model. The following information has been developed as the basis for this task:

(1) Forecast sales is a weighted average of the previous six months sales. The proportions to be used are as follows:

Previous month	.50
Two months ago	.25
Three months ago	.10
Four months ago	.08
Five months ago	.05
Six months ago	.02
	1.00

(2) Variable manufacturing costs per unit include:

Materials	$10
Direct labor	8
Overhead	12

Fixed manufacturing overhead totals $25,000 per month and the company uses the variable cost model to measure inventory values for income statement purposes.

(3) Inventory of finished goods is kept at a level equal to 120 percent of the following month's forecast sales. Raw materials inventories costing $10 per unit are maintained at a level equal to the next month's production requirements. Work in process inventories are always 0 at the end of the month.

(4) Variable marketing and administrative expenses are $8 per unit sold. Fixed expenses of this type amount to $35,000 per month, including $15,000 depreciation.

(5) Income tax expense is accrued at a rate of 40 percent of net income.

(6) Interest expense is accrued at 12 percent per year on a loan that had an outstanding balance of $500,000 on July 1, 19X5 and is being repaid at $25,000 per month.

(7) The sales price for Shula's sole product is $50 per unit.

Required:

(a) Prepare a set of equations from the preceding data which reflect all of the budget relationships that are relevant to the preparation of budgeted monthly statements of cost of goods manufactured, cost of goods sold, and budgeted monthly income statements.

(b) Evaluate these equations for the month of July 19X5, using the following data:

Sales—January:	30,000 units
February:	20,000 units
March:	30,000 units
April:	25,000 units
May:	36,000 units
June:	30,000 units

Inventory—July 1, 19X5
Finished Goods: 36,600 units
Raw Materials: 30,250 units

Show answers for
(1)   Sales revenue
(2)   Cost of goods manufactured
(3)   Cost of goods sold
(4)   Operating income before tax
(5)   Net income after tax

P 7–12   Budgeted Income Statements

Refer to the data for the Coryell Corporation in P7-8.

Required:
Prepare budgeted income statements and supporting schedules for January and February of 19X1.

P 7–13   Budgeted Income Statements

Refer to the data for the Cerf Company in P7–10.

Required:
Prepare budgeted income statements and supporting schedules for January and February of 19X4.

8

COST–VOLUME–PROFIT ANALYSIS

LEARNING OBJECTIVES

After studying Chapter 8, you should be able to:

1. Understand the basic purposes of short-run cost–volume–profit analysis.
2. Given a sales price, fixed cost, and variable cost per unit, calculate the contribution margin and contribution margin ratio.
3. Calculate the breakeven quantity in terms of units of output.
4. Calculate the breakeven quantity in terms of total sales revenues.
5. Construct a cost–volume–profit graph and derive the breakeven point graphically.
6. Calculate the number of output units that must be sold to earn a specified target profit.
7. Calculate the number of output units that must be sold to earn a specified percentage of total sales revenue.
8. Construct a cost–volume–profit graph showing target profit.
9. Calculate the breakeven point and the target profit when changes occur in sales prices, fixed costs, and variable costs.
10. Convert the cost–volume–profit graph into a profit–volume graph.
11. Discuss five limitations of elementary cost–volume–profit analysis.
12. Calculate the breakeven point and target profit when relevant range limitations are specified.
13. Calculate the breakeven point and target profit for a multiple product firm.
14. Calculate the breakeven point and target profit for a group of products that have uniform contribution margin ratios.
15. Calculate the breakeven point and target profit when multiple outputs are sold in a specified proportion.
16. Calculate the breakeven point and target profit when output units are nonuniform.
17. Understand the differences between the linear accounting cost–volume–profit model and the nonlinear microeconomic cost–volume–profit model.

Thisis the first of seven chapters that describe basic analytical cost accounting techniques. Their emphasis will be on the development and use of cost information for planning purposes. The techniques to be presented assume an understanding of the cost concept, objects of costing, cost classifications, product cost determination, and budgeting, as discussed in Chapters 2–7.

AN OVERVIEW OF COST–VOLUME–PROFIT ANALYSIS

Information about product costs is an essential part of business decision making. **Cost–volume–profit analysis** is an accounting technique that enables a company to achieve its profit goals by permitting managers to take a coordinated approach to the related problems of predicting costs, establishing sales and production levels, and setting prices.

The accounting methods used in elementary cost–volume–profit analysis should be applied to short-run situations only. They are not meant to be used for long-range price and activity-related decision making. These techniques are basically static, because limiting assumptions must be made about the behavior of such key items as sales prices, input costs, capacity levels, technology, and production efficiency. As will be shown, factors that in real life are likely to be variable, probabalistic, or uncertain (especially in the long run), are assumed to be fixed, deterministic, or certain for the purposes of elementary cost–volume–profit analysis.

In order to achieve profit goals, *before production begins,* managers must make decisions about production and sales levels, selling prices of products, and total costs to be incurred. These decisions influence future operations so decisively that cost–volume–profit analysis is sometimes called **profit planning**. However, the former term is preferable; it emphasizes the fact that costs, volume, and sales prices are the primary components of this type of analysis—profit being, as it always is, a residual element.

Predicting how costs will behave in response to activity level changes is central to cost–volume–profit analysis. This requires that costs be classified as either *fixed* or *variable*. Initially it will be assumed that all costs may be separated into these two categories. **Fixed costs** are those for which the total amount remains constant throughout the period of analysis, regardless of variations in activity levels. **Variable costs** are those for which the total amount varies throughout the period in response to changes in production volume or some other measure of activity. It will also be assumed that all variable costs are uniformly variable—that is, that they are incurred at a *constant rate per unit of output*.

The *volume,* or *activity level* in terms of which cost behavior is classified as fixed or variable, should be representative of the *cost object* that is the focus of analysis. For that reason, cost behavior is normally treated as being dependent on a single variable—*the number of units of output*. The finished product manufactured for sale in an external market is the primary cost object in elementary cost–volume–profit analysis. Consequently, the sales price of the finished product is a key aspect of that analysis. The usual assumption is that, in the short run, the *sales price* is a *constant amount per unit of output*.

The **contribution margin** is another key concept in cost–volume–profit analysis. It is defined as the excess of the sales price of a unit of output over the variable cost of that unit. Derived from this is the **contribution margin ratio**, which is the contribution margin per unit divided by the sales price per unit.

Example: Jaime Corporation produces and sells imitation Persian rugs at a market price of $20 per unit. Total fixed costs are $20,000 per month. Variable manufacturing, marketing, and other costs amount to $8 per unit.

The product's contribution margin is $12 per unit, derived as follows:

$$
\begin{array}{lr}
\text{Sales Price per Unit} \dots\dots\dots\dots\dots & \$20 \\
\text{Less: Variable Cost per Unit} \dots\dots\dots & 8 \\
\text{Contribution Margin per Unit} \dots\dots\dots & \$12
\end{array}
$$

The contribution margin ratio is 60 percent (or .60), calculated as follows:

$$
\frac{\text{Contribution Margin per Unit}}{\text{Sales Price per Unit}} = \frac{\$12 \text{ per Unit}}{\$20 \text{ per Unit}} = 60\%
$$

THE BASIC COST–VOLUME–PROFIT MODEL

Suppose that a firm which produces a single type of product is trying to coordinate its sales price, production volume, and costs in order to achieve short-run profit goals. Two criteria used in cost–volume–profit analysis are the breakeven point and target profit. The **breakeven point** is defined as the volume of activity at which total sales revenue exactly equals total costs of the output produced and sold. A **target profit** is a predetermined profit goal, expressed either as an absolute amount (say, $100,000), or as a percentage (10 percent of sales revenue).

CALCULATING THE BREAKEVEN POINT
IN UNITS PRODUCED OR SOLD

The breakeven condition exists when total revenue equals total cost. This condition can be expressed in terms of the *number of output units* that must be produced and sold to break even.

The breakeven condition can be formulated and solved algebraically. Let

$$
\begin{array}{l}
Q_b = \text{Total Number of Units Required to Break Even} \\
F = \text{Total Fixed Cost per Period} \\
S = \text{Sales Price per Unit} \\
V = \text{Variable Cost per Unit} \\
M = S - V = \text{Contribution Margin per Unit}
\end{array}
$$

$$C = \frac{M}{S} = \text{Contribution Margin Ratio}$$

$VQ_b = $ Total Variable Cost of Breakeven Quantity
$T_c = VQ_b + F = $ Total Cost of Breakeven Quantity
$R_b = SQ_b = $ Total Revenue of Breakeven Quantity

The breakeven condition can be written:

$$R_b = T_c \dots\dots\dots\dots\dots\dots\dots\dots\dots\dots\dots\dots\dots\dots\dots\dots\dots \quad [1]$$

which can be simplified and solved as follows:

$$SQ_b = VQ_b + F \dots\dots\dots\dots\dots\dots\dots\dots\dots\dots\dots\dots\dots\dots \quad [2]$$

$$SQ_b - VQ_b = F$$

$$Q_b (S - V) = F$$

$$Q_b = \frac{F}{S - V}$$

However, because $M = S - V$, the *breakeven condition* can also be expressed as follows:

$$Q_b = \frac{F}{M} \dots\dots\dots\dots\dots\dots\dots\dots\dots\dots\dots\dots\dots\dots\dots\dots\dots \quad [3]$$

In other words, the number of units that must be produced and sold to break even can be found by dividing total fixed costs by the contribution margin per unit. The **contribution margin per unit** is the amount that each unit contributes toward meeting fixed costs and, beyond that, toward providing a profit. Therefore, to cover fixed costs exactly, the number of units sold multiplied by the contribution margin per unit must equal total fixed costs ($MQ_b = F$).

Example: Joseph Company manufactures water purifier kits which sell for $10 per unit. The company's variable costs are $6 per unit and its total fixed costs are $12,000 per month. How many units must be produced and sold each month to break even?

$$\left.\begin{array}{l} \textit{Breakeven} \\ \textit{Condition} \end{array}\right\} Q_b = \frac{F}{M} = \frac{\text{Total Fixed Costs}}{\text{Contribution Margin per Unit}}$$

$$= \frac{\$12,000}{(\$10 - \$6) \text{ per unit}}$$

$$= \frac{\$12,000}{\$4 \text{ per unit}}$$

$$= \underline{\underline{3,000 \text{ units}}}$$

The firm must sell 3,000 units at $10 each to generate $30,000 total revenue. This $30,000 exactly equals total costs, which consist of $12,000 in fixed costs and $18,000 in variable costs (3,000 units $\times$ $6).

CALCULATING THE BREAKEVEN POINT IN SALES REVENUES

The following generalized version of the breakeven model permits the calculation of a breakeven point in terms of *total sales revenues* rather than units of output. This approach is often used in analyzing multiple product situations. It can be formulated and solved as follows.

The breakeven condition is first expressed in terms of units of output:

$$Q_b = \frac{F}{M} \quad\quad\quad\quad\quad\quad\quad\quad\quad [3]$$

Multiply through by S:

$$SQ_b = S\left(\frac{F}{M}\right) \quad\quad\quad\quad\quad\quad\quad [4]$$

Rearrange terms and substitute $R_b = SQ_b$:

$$R_b = \left(\frac{F}{(M/S)}\right) \quad\quad\quad\quad\quad\quad [5]$$

Now, because $M/S = C$, the *breakeven revenue condition* may be written as:

$$R_b = \frac{F}{C} \quad\quad\quad\quad\quad\quad\quad\quad\quad [6]$$

This means that the total revenue needed to break even equals the amount of total fixed costs divided by the contribution margin ratio. Each dollar of sales revenue contributes to the coverage of fixed costs and to company profit in proportion to the contribution margin ratio. Consequently, the total contribution needed to cover fixed costs is equal to the number of dollars of sales revenue multiplied by the contribution margin per dollar of sales revenue ($F = R_b C$). **Example:** In the Joseph Company example, the *contribution margin ratio* is ($10 − $6 ÷ $10) = .4. The *breakeven revenue volume* is therefore $F/C = $12,000 ÷ .4 = $30,000. This solution is the same as the one derived in terms of output units, because the breakeven volume of 3,000 units generates revenues of $30,000 (3,000 × $10).

CALCULATING THE BREAKEVEN POINT GRAPHICALLY

Cost–volume–profit analysis can also be presented graphically. In the following diagrams, the horizontal axis represents *units of output*, and the vertical axis represents *total dollars of cost* and/or *revenue*.

In Figure 8–1, C_1F represents *total fixed costs*, which remain constant at $12,000 over all levels of output. Figure 8–2 shows *total variable costs*, OC_3, which are $6 per unit at all levels of output. These two functions are combined

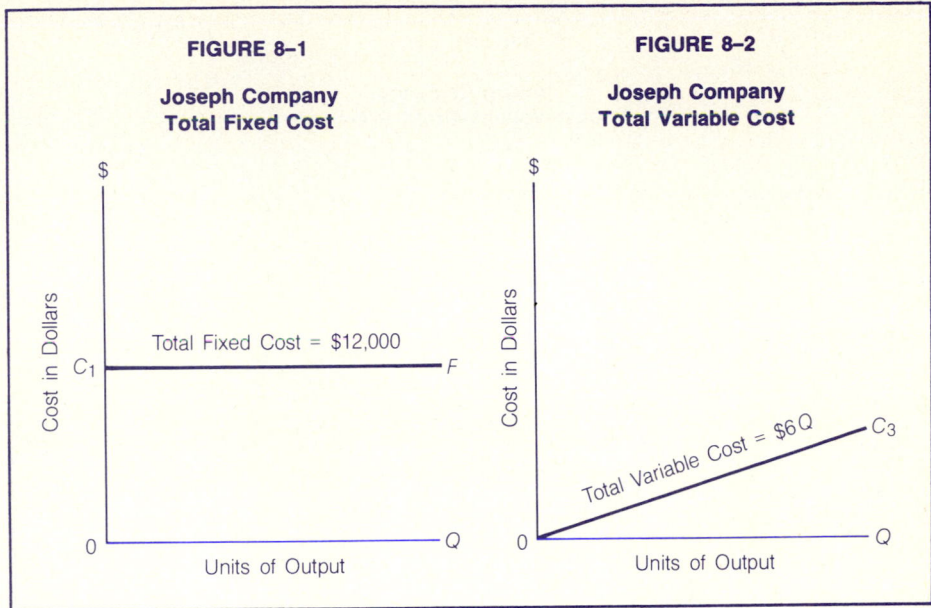

FIGURE 8–1

**Joseph Company
Total Fixed Cost**

Total Fixed Cost = $12,000

FIGURE 8–2

**Joseph Company
Total Variable Cost**

Total Variable Cost = $6Q

in Figure 8–3 to show *total cost,* C_1C_2, composed of fixed costs of $12,000 and variable costs of $6 per unit. *Total revenue* is shown as *OS* in Figure 8–4 and is $10 per unit at all output levels.

Joseph Company's total cost and total revenue functions are combined in Figure 8–5 to produce a *cost–volume–profit graph.* In this graph, the intersection

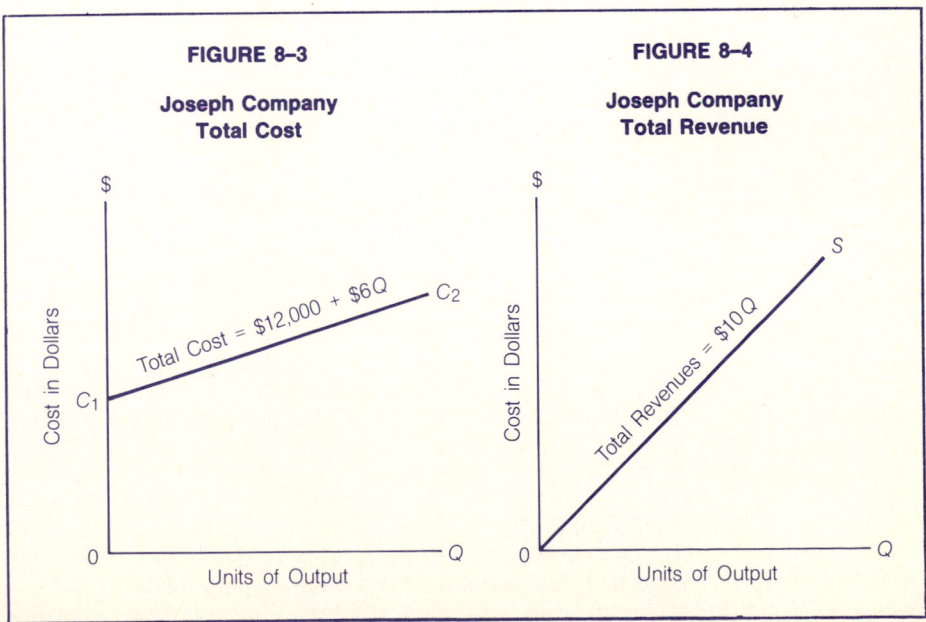

FIGURE 8–3

**Joseph Company
Total Cost**

Total Cost = $12,000 + $6Q

FIGURE 8–4

**Joseph Company
Total Revenue**

Total Revenues = $10Q

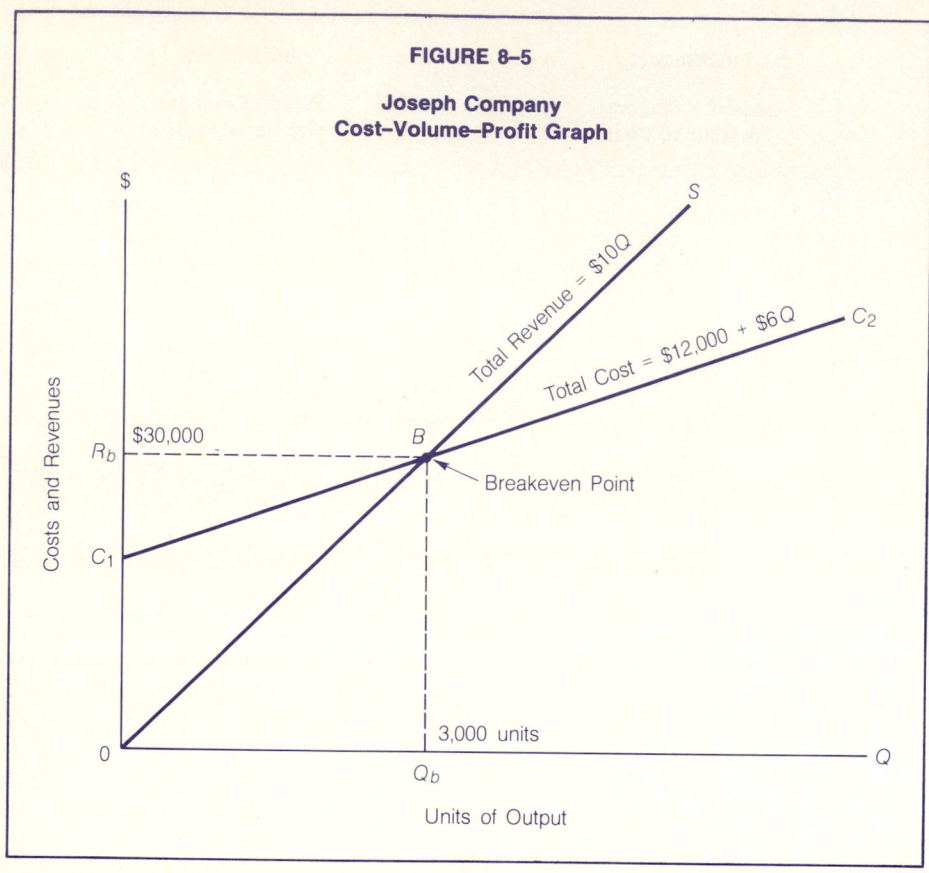

FIGURE 8–5

**Joseph Company
Cost–Volume–Profit Graph**

of the *total cost function, C_1C_2*, and the *total revenue function, OS*, occurs at point B, which establishes the breakeven quantity, OQ_b (3,000 units) and the breakeven revenue OR_b ($30,000). Cost–volume–profit graphs will be used to demonstrate similar relationships throughout this chapter.

CALCULATING TARGET PROFIT IN UNITS PRODUCED OR SOLD

The breakeven point merely indicates the minimum level of activity that must be sustained if the firm is to avoid loss. However, managers want to operate at activity levels that will produce specified profits. Therefore, the *target profit* concept is a useful extension of cost–volume–profit analysis. Target profit requirements are satisfied at the activity level where total contribution margin equals total fixed costs plus the desired profit. The target profit condition can be formulated and solved as follows.

In addition to all foregoing terms defined, let

π_t = Target Profit
Q_t = Units of Output Required to Earn Target Profit
R_t = Sales Revenue Required to Earn Target Profit

The target profit condition is met when

$$R_t = F + VQ_t + \pi_t \dots\dots\dots\dots\dots\dots\dots\dots\dots\dots\dots \quad [7]$$

$$SQ_t = F + VQ_t + \pi_t$$

$$SQ_t - VQ_t = F + \pi_t$$

$$Q_t(S - V) = F + \pi_t$$

$$Q_t = \frac{F + \pi_t}{S - V}$$

Therefore, the equation for the target profit condition can be written as follows:

$$Q_t = \frac{F + \pi_t}{M} \dots\dots\dots\dots\dots\dots\dots\dots\dots\dots\dots \quad [8]$$

The following solution can be used to derive the revenue level required to achieve a target profit:

$$Q_t = \frac{F + \pi_t}{M} \dots\dots\dots\dots\dots\dots\dots\dots \quad [8]$$

Multiply through by S:

$$SQ_t = S\left(\frac{F + \pi_t}{M}\right) \dots\dots\dots\dots\dots\dots \quad [9]$$

Rearrange terms and substitute $R_t = SQ_t$:

$$R_t = \frac{F + \pi_t}{\left(\dfrac{M}{S}\right)} \dots\dots\dots\dots\dots\dots\dots \quad [10]$$

Now, because $M/S = C$, the *target profit revenue condition* may be written as:

$$R_t = \frac{F + \pi_t}{C} \dots\dots\dots\dots\dots\dots \quad [11]$$

Example: Johns Company incurs fixed costs of $20,000 per month and variable costs of $2 per unit in manufacturing five-gallon gasoline cans, which sell for $3 per unit. How many units must be sold to earn a target profit of $10,000?

$$\left.\begin{array}{l} \text{Target Profit} \\ \text{Condition} \end{array}\right\} Q_t = \frac{F + \pi_t}{M} = \frac{\text{Fixed Cost} + \text{Target Profit}}{\text{Contribution Margin per Unit}}$$

$$= \frac{\$20,000 + \$10,000}{(\$3 - \$2) \text{ per unit}}$$

$$= \underline{\underline{30,000 \text{ units}}}$$

The firm must sell 30,000 units at $3 each to generate total revenues of $90,000 and attain its target profit of $10,000. Total costs are $80,000, consisting of fixed costs of $20,000 and variable costs of $60,000 (30,000 units at $2 each).

CALCULATING TARGET PROFIT AS A RETURN ON SALES

Often target profit is expressed as a percentage of total revenue or as a rate of return on sales, rather than as an absolute amount. In such cases a target profit condition can be derived as follows. Let

$$a = \text{Desired Rate of Return on Sales}$$

Now, $\pi_t = aR_t$. But because $R_t = F + VQ_t + \pi_t$ and $SQ_t = R_t$,

$$SQ_t = F + VQ_t + aSQ_t$$

$$SQ_t - VQ_t - aSQ_t = F$$

$$Q_t (S - V - aS) = F$$

$$Q_t = \frac{F}{S - V - aS}$$

Therefore, the *target profit condition as a percentage of sales* can be written as:

$$Q_t = \frac{F}{M - aS} \quad \dots\dots\dots\dots\dots\dots \quad [12]$$

Example: Julie Corporation incurs fixed costs of $25,000 per month and variable costs of $3 per unit in manufacturing sandals that sell for $5 per pair. How many pairs of sandals must be sold to earn a profit equal to 20 percent of sales revenue?

Target Profit Condition Percent of Sales $\Big\}$ $Q_t = \dfrac{F}{M - aS} = \dfrac{\text{Fixed Cost}}{[\text{Contribution Margin} - (\text{Sales Price} \times \text{Target Rate})] \text{ per Unit}}$

$$= \frac{\$25,000}{[\$2 - (.20)(\$5)] \text{ per unit}}$$

$$= \frac{\$25,000}{\$1 \text{ per unit}}$$

$$= \underline{\underline{25,000 \text{ units}}}$$

When the *contribution margin ratio* approach is used, the target profit condition can be formulated as follows:

$$Q_t = \frac{F}{M - aS} \quad \dots\dots\dots\dots\dots\dots \quad [12]$$

Multiply through by S:

$$SQ_t = S\left(\frac{F}{M - aS}\right)$$

Rearrange terms and substitute $R_t = SQ_t$:

$$R_t = \frac{F}{\frac{M}{S} - a}$$

Now, because $M/S = C$, the *target profit condition for sales revenue* can be written as:

$$R_t = \frac{F}{C - a} \quad \dots\dots\dots\dots\dots\dots \quad [13]$$

Example: Jeffrey Company incurs fixed costs of $15,000 per month and has a contribution margin ratio of 50 percent. How much sales revenue is needed to produce a 20 percent return on sales?

$$\left.\begin{array}{l} \textit{Target Profit} \\ \textit{Condition} \\ \textit{Sales} \\ \textit{Revenue} \end{array}\right\} R_t = \frac{F}{C - a} = \frac{\text{Fixed Cost}}{\text{Contribution Margin Ratio} - \text{Desired Rate of Return on Sales}}$$

$$= \frac{\$15,000}{.50 - .20}$$

$$= \$50,000$$

CALCULATING TARGET PROFIT GRAPHICALLY

The **cost–volume–profit graph** can be adapted to represent a target profit instead of a breakeven condition. Using data from the Johns Company example, Figure 8–6 shows a cost–volume–profit graph with a $10,000 target profit, π_t, added to the total cost function to produce the T_1T_2 function. The total revenue function, OS, intersects with this T_1T_2 function at point T^*. Johns Company must manufacture and sell 30,000 units of output, producing $90,000 in sales revenues, to satisfy the $10,000 target profit requirement.

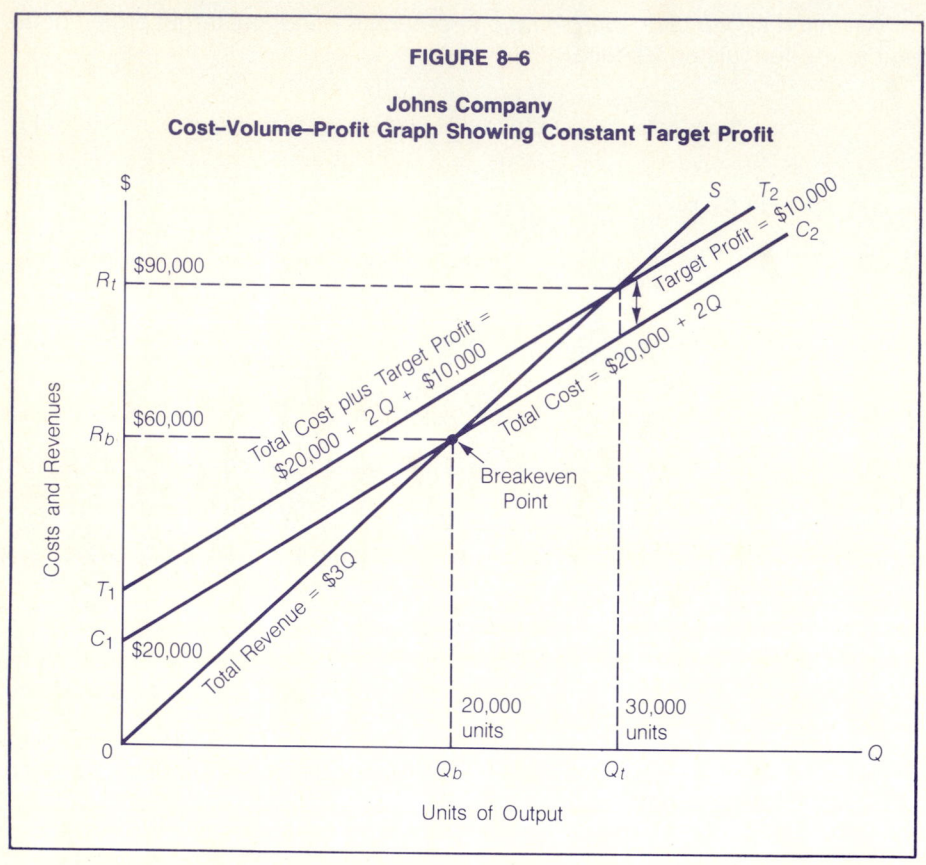

FIGURE 8–6

Johns Company
Cost–Volume–Profit Graph Showing Constant Target Profit

INTERPRETING BREAKEVEN OR TARGET PROFIT SOLUTIONS

Additional information can be obtained from the cost–volume–profit graph after the breakeven quantity or target profit quantity has been determined. In Figure 8–7, note the shaded profit and loss zones. Below OQ_b, the total cost function, C_1C_2, lies *above* the total revenue function, OS, indicating that all activity levels in the range OQ_b are *unprofitable*. Conversely, any activity level larger than OQ_b will be profitable, since in that range total revenue, OS, lies above total cost, C_1C_2.

The same interpretation applies to sales revenue levels above and below the breakeven level of OR_b. The vertical distance between the OS and C_1C_2 functions is the measure of the amount of profit (K_2) or loss (K_1) at each activity level. The amount of this profit or loss at any output level is equal to the contribution margin per unit multiplied by the corresponding number of units above or below the breakeven quantity. This calculation provides a convenient way to analyze the effect of activity level changes on profits. Every unit manufactured and sold beyond the breakeven quantity generates a profit equal to the contribution margin per unit.

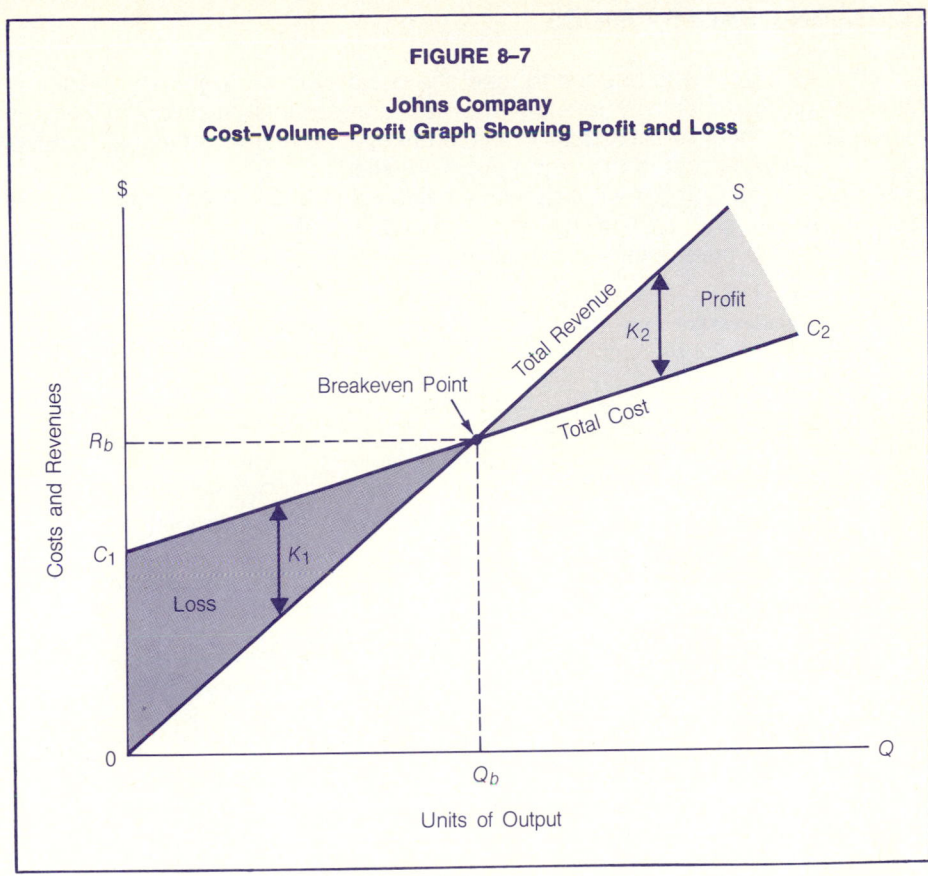

FIGURE 8–7

Johns Company
Cost–Volume–Profit Graph Showing Profit and Loss

Two additional comparisons should be made after the breakeven quantity has been determined. The feasibility of the solution must be established by checking against the firm's production capacity and the sales forecast for the product. If the output level needed to break even is greater than the company's productive capacity, or greater than the sales forecast, the solution is not feasible. When such a situation arises, the next step is to investigate possible variations in one or more parameters of the model in order to determine a set of practical operating conditions.

SENSITIVITY ANALYSIS

Sensitivity analysis is a technique for examining what happens to the output values of a decision model when the input values of that model are changed. The cost–volume–profit model can be adapted to examine the effects of changes in any or all of its key variables: sales prices, fixed costs, variable costs, activity levels, and target profit.

SELECTING SALES PRICES

What selling price is needed to meet the breakeven or target profit requirements at particular activity levels? One can answer this question by setting total revenue equal to total cost in the breakeven situation, or equal to total cost plus desired profit in the target profit situation.

Example: Rand Company anticipates a sales volume of 40,000 units, variable costs of $6 per unit, and fixed costs of $120,000. What *sales price* will (1) allow the firm to break even or (2) allow it to earn a $40,000 profit?

Breakeven Condition

(1)   Total Revenue = Total Cost

Let S_b = Sales Price to Break Even

$$R_b = F + VQ$$

$$S_b Q = F + VQ$$

$$S_b = \frac{F + VQ}{Q}$$

$$S_b = \frac{F}{Q} + V$$

$$S_b = \frac{\text{Fixed Cost}}{\text{Sales Volume}} + \frac{\text{Variable}}{\text{Cost per Unit}}$$

Target Profit Condition

(2)   Total Revenue = Total Cost + Target Profit

Let S_t = Sales Price to Earn Target Profit

$$R_t = F + VQ + \pi_t$$

$$S_t Q = F + VQ + \pi_t$$

$$S_t = \frac{F + VQ + \pi_t}{Q}$$

$$S_t = \frac{F + \pi_t}{Q} + V$$

$$S_t = \frac{\text{Fixed Cost} + \text{Target Profit}}{\text{Sales Volume}} + \frac{\text{Variable}}{\text{Cost per Unit}}$$

Substituting values from the Rand Company example produces the following solutions:

$$S_b = \frac{\$120,000}{40,000} + \$6$$

$$= \$9$$

$$S_t = \frac{\$120,000 + \$40,000}{40,000} + \$6$$

$$= \$10$$

A $9 unit price will enable Rand Company to break even if 40,000 units are sold. To earn the $40,000 target profit at that sales level, a selling price of $10 per unit is needed.

CHANGES IN SALES PRICE

An *increase* in the sales price per unit can be represented by a steeper revenue curve in a cost–volume–profit graph. In Figure 8–8, compare the slope of the OS_1 line to the original OS line. This change allows the breakeven point to be reached at a *lower activity level, OQ_1*. Profits beyond this new breakeven point increase more rapidly per unit of output.

On the other hand, a *decrease* in sales price, as represented by OS_2, will shift the breakeven point to a *higher activity level, OQ_2*, and profit per unit beyond that point will be reduced accordingly.

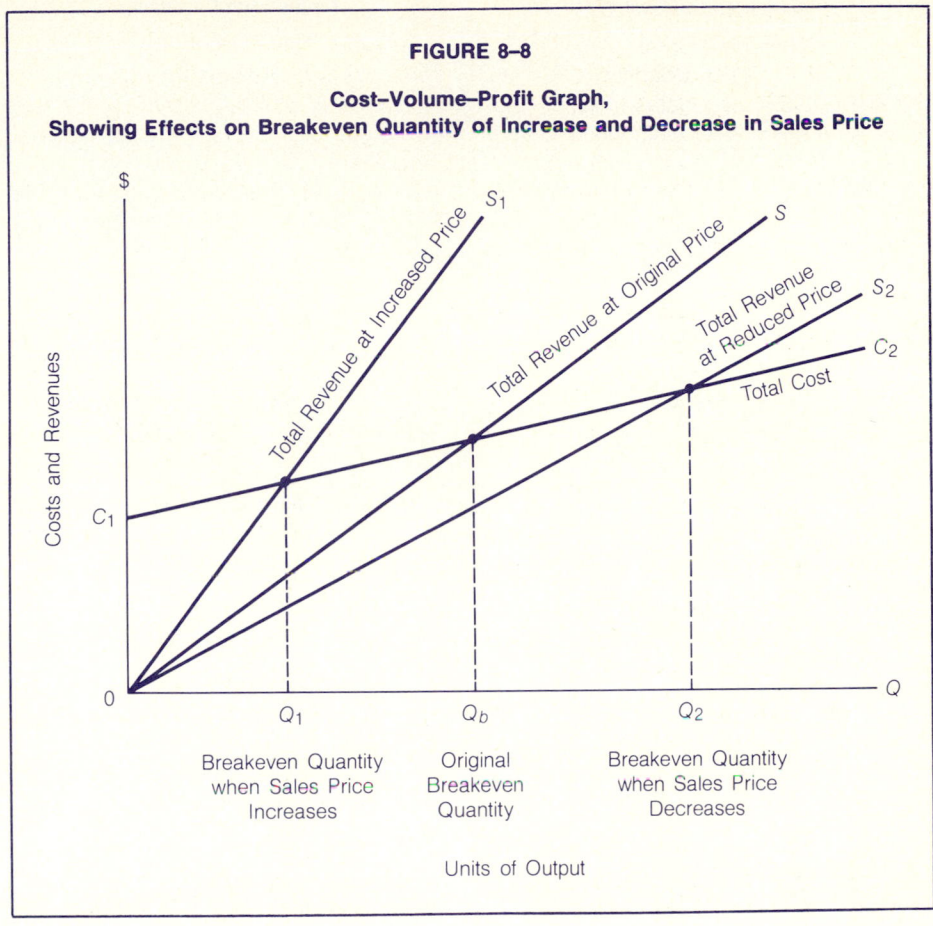

FIGURE 8–8

**Cost–Volume–Profit Graph,
Showing Effects on Breakeven Quantity of Increase and Decrease in Sales Price**

Example: What happens to *breakeven volume* when the sales price is increased to $10 per unit, but fixed costs remain $120,000 and variable costs remain at $6 per unit? Also, what happens to the *target profit quantity* if the target profit is $40,000? The original breakeven output volume for a $9 sales price was 40,000 units, and the original target profit output quantity was 53,333 ⅓ units, calculated as follows:

$$Q_b = \frac{F}{C} = \frac{\text{Fixed Cost}}{\text{Contribution Margin per Unit}}$$

$$Q_t = \frac{F + \pi_t}{VC} = \frac{\text{Fixed Cost} + \text{Target Profit}}{\text{Contribution Margin per Unit}}$$

$$= \frac{\$120,000}{\$3 \text{ per unit}}$$

$$= \frac{\$160,000}{\$3 \text{ per unit}}$$

$$= 40,000 \text{ units}$$

$$= 53,333\tfrac{1}{3} \text{ units}$$

Breakeven Condition

Let Q^*_b = New Break-
even Quantity
$S^* = S + \Delta S$ = New Sales Price
$M^* = M + \Delta S$ = New Contribution
Margin per Unit

$$Q^*_b = \frac{F}{M^*}$$

$$= \frac{F}{M + \Delta S}$$

$$Q^*_b = \frac{\text{Fixed Cost}}{\text{New Contribution Margin}}_{\text{per Unit}}$$

Target Profit Condition

Let Q^*_t = New Target
Profit Quantity

$$Q^*_t = \frac{F + \pi_t}{M^*}$$

$$= \frac{F + \pi_t}{M + \Delta S}$$

$$Q^*_t = \frac{\text{Fixed Cost} + \text{Target Profit}}{\text{New Contribution Margin}}_{\text{per Unit}}$$

Substituting values from the Rand Company example, the following revised breakeven and target profit output quantities are derived:

$$Q^*_b = \frac{\$120,000}{(\$3 + \$1) \text{ per unit}}$$

$$= \frac{\$120,000}{\$4 \text{ per unit}}$$

$$= \underline{\underline{30,000 \text{ units}}}$$

(decrease from 40,000)

$$Q^*_t = \frac{\$120,000 + \$40,000}{(\$3 + \$1) \text{ per unit}}$$

$$= \frac{\$160,000}{\$4 \text{ per unit}}$$

$$= \underline{\underline{40,000 \text{ units}}}$$

(decrease from 53,333⅓)

These solutions correspond to a *decrease* in the breakeven output quantity from OQ_b to OQ_1 in Figure 8–8, and a similar decrease in the target profit output quantity.

CHANGES IN FIXED COST

What activity level change is needed to break even or earn a specified target profit if *total fixed costs* change? These questions can be answered by reformulating the breakeven or target profit equations, finding the new activity levels, then calculating the needed activity level changes.

In Figure 8–9, C_4C_5 represents an increase and C_6C_7 represents a decrease in fixed costs. The direction in which the breakeven point moves is consistent with the direction of change in fixed costs—that is, higher fixed costs require a larger volume of output to break even, whereas lower output volumes are sufficient to break even if fixed costs decrease. Profit per unit beyond the break-even point remains unchanged. The amounts Q_bQ_1 and Q_2Q_b represent the change in volume needed to sustain the breakeven condition as fixed costs increase to OC_4 or decrease to OC_6, respectively.

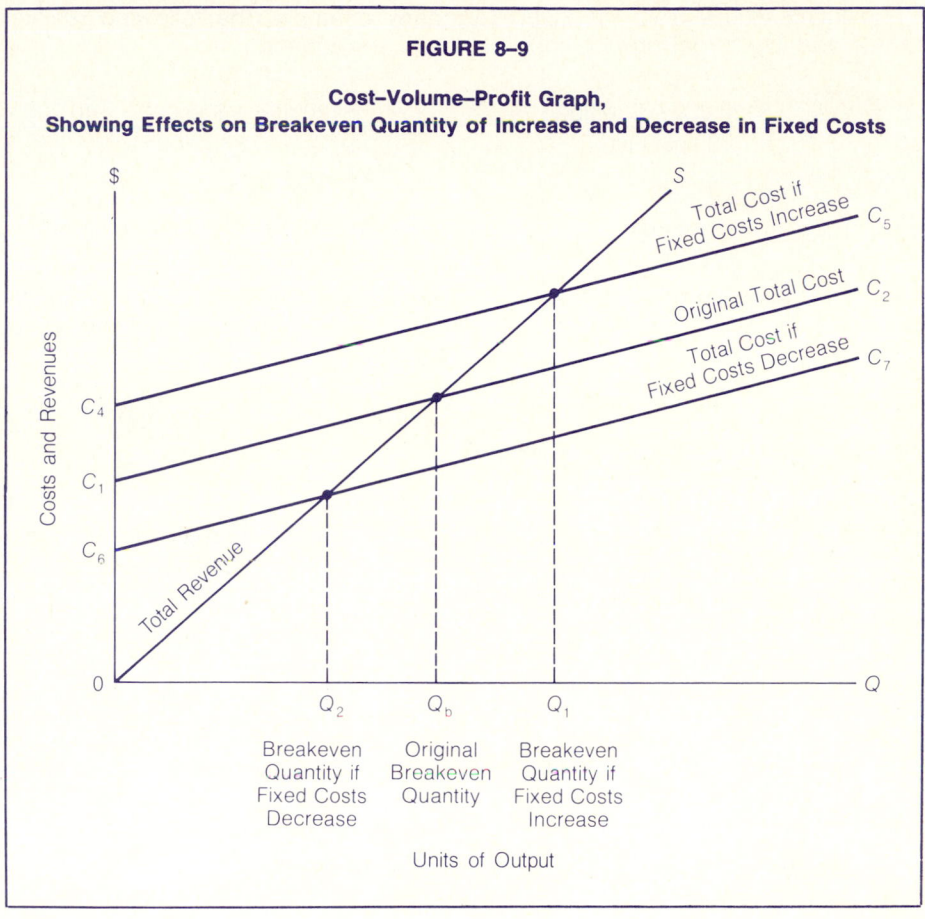

FIGURE 8–9

**Cost–Volume–Profit Graph,
Showing Effects on Breakeven Quantity of Increase and Decrease in Fixed Costs**

Example: Continuing the Rand Company example, how many extra units must be sold to break even or to earn a $40,000 target profit, if *fixed costs* increase from $120,000 to $150,000 but sales prices and variable costs per unit remain at $9 and $6 respectively? Remember, the original breakeven volume was 40,000 units and the target profit volume was 53,333⅓ units.

Breakeven Condition	**Target Profit Condition**

Let Q^*_b = New Breakeven Quantity   Let Q^*_t = New Target Profit Quantity
$F^* = F + \Delta F$ = New Fixed Cost

$$Q^*_b = \frac{F^*}{M}$$

$$Q^*_b = \frac{F + \Delta F}{M}$$

$$Q^*_b = \frac{\text{New Fixed Cost}}{\text{Contribution Margin per Unit}}$$

$$Q^*_t = \frac{F^* + \pi_t}{M}$$

$$Q^*_t = \frac{F + \Delta F + \pi_t}{M}$$

$$Q^*_t = \frac{\text{New Fixed Cost} + \text{Target Profit}}{\text{Contribution Margin per Unit}}$$

Substituting values from the Rand Company example, the following revised breakeven and target profit output quantities are derived:

$$Q^*_b = \frac{\$120,000 + \$30,000}{\$3 \text{ per unit}}$$

$$Q^*_t = \frac{\$120,000 + \$30,000 + \$40,000}{\$3 \text{ per unit}}$$

$$= 50,000 \text{ units}$$

$$= 63,333 \text{ units}$$

(increase from 40,000 units)

(increase from 53,333⅓ units)

These solutions correspond to an *increase* in the breakeven output quantity from OQ_b to OQ_1 in Figure 8–9 and a similar increase in the target profit output quantity.

CHANGES IN VARIABLE COST

What happens to the activity levels needed to sustain breakeven or target profit conditions if the *variable cost per unit* changes? Higher variable costs, as shown by C_1C_8 in Figure 8–10, shift the breakeven point to OQ_1—that is, more units must be produced and sold to break even. Lower variable costs, as in C_1C_9, produce a lower breakeven point at OQ_2, with the result that fewer units are needed to break even.
Example: If Rand Company's *variable cost* increases from $6 to $8 per unit, but fixed costs remain constant at $120,000, and sales price remains constant at $9 per unit, how many additional units must be sold to break even or to earn a $40,000 profit?

Let $V^* = V + \Delta V =$ New Variable Cost per Unit
and $M^* = M - \Delta V =$ New Contribution Margin per Unit

Breakeven Condition	**Target Profit Condition**

$$Q^*_b = \frac{F}{M^*}$$

$$Q^*_t = \frac{F + \pi_t}{M}$$

$$Q^*_b = \frac{F}{M - \Delta V}$$

$$Q^*_t = \frac{F + \pi_t}{M - \Delta V}$$

$$Q^*_b = \frac{\text{Fixed Cost}}{\text{New Contribution Margin per Unit}}$$

$$Q^*_t = \frac{\text{Fixed Cost} + \text{Target Profit}}{\text{New Contribution Margin per Unit}}$$

Substituting values from the Rand Company example, the following revised breakeven and target profit output quantities are derived:

$$Q^*_b = \frac{\$120,000}{(\$2 - \$1) \text{ per unit}}$$

$$Q^*_t = \frac{\$120,000 + \$40,000}{(\$2 - \$1) \text{ per unit}}$$

$$= 120,000 \text{ units}$$

$$= 160,000 \text{ units}$$

(increase from 40,000 units)

(increase from 53,333⅓ units)

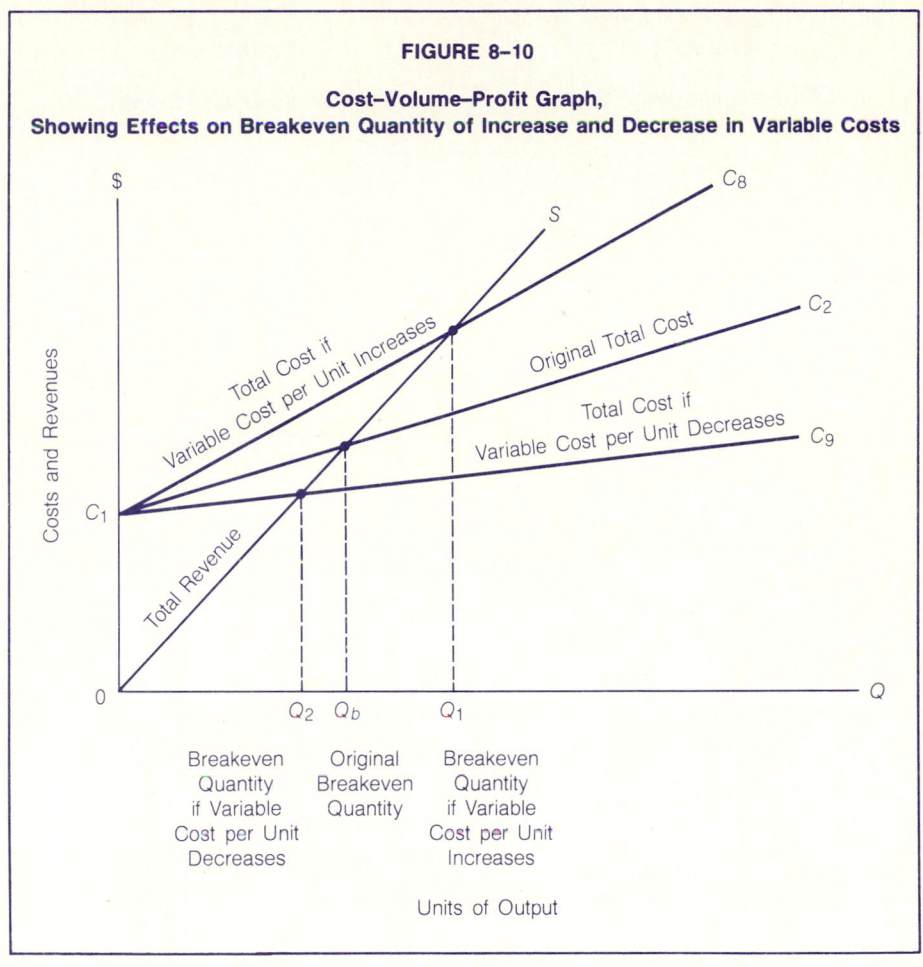

FIGURE 8–10

**Cost–Volume–Profit Graph,
Showing Effects on Breakeven Quantity of Increase and Decrease in Variable Costs**

These solutions correspond to an *increase* in the breakeven output quantity from OQ_b to OQ_1 in Figure 8–10 and a similar type of increase in the target profit output quantity.

THE PROFIT–VOLUME GRAPH

By making dollars of profit the variable on the vertical axis, the cost–volume–profit graph shown in Figure 8–11 can be converted into a **profit–volume graph,** as in Figure 8–12. A profit–volume graph more directly represents the effects of activity level changes on income.

The profit–volume graph in Figure 8–12 is derived by plotting the amount of profit associated with each activity level. This is the same amount of profit that is represented by the vertical distance between the total revenue and total cost curves of the cost–volume–profit graph in Figure 8–11.

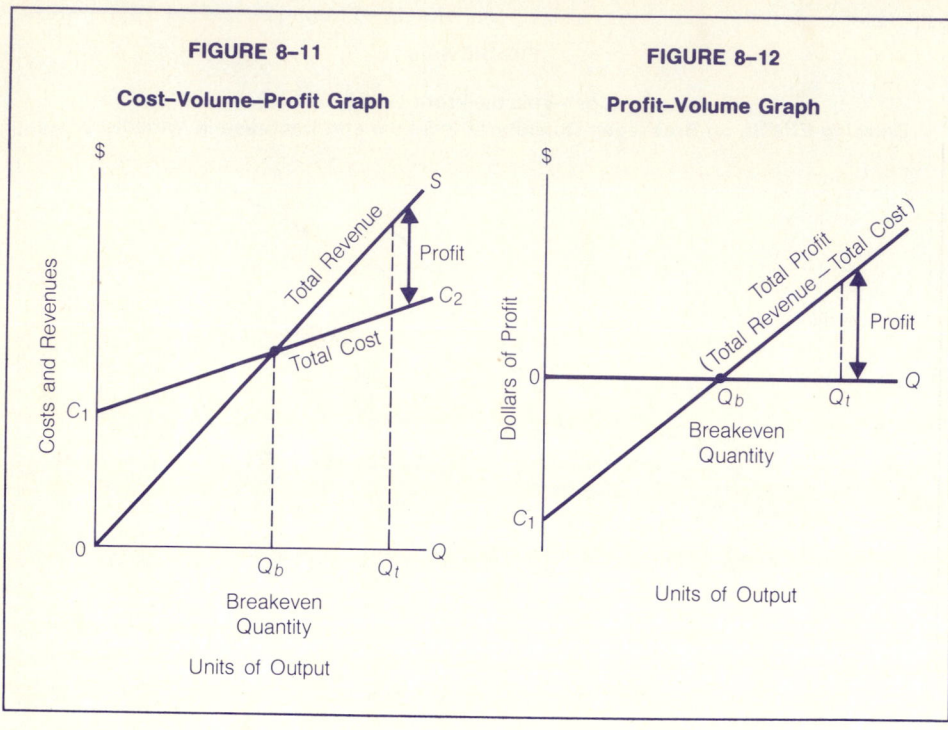

FIGURE 8–11

Cost–Volume–Profit Graph

FIGURE 8–12

Profit–Volume Graph

Algebraically, the profit–volume function is derived as follows:

$R = SQ$ .... Total Revenue
$T_c = VQ + F$ .... Total Cost
$\pi = R - T_c$ .... Profit
$\pi = SQ - (VQ + F)$
$\pi = Q(S - V) - F$

$\pi = MQ - F$ .... Profit–Volume Equation

Example: Figure 8–13 shows the profit–volume graph of Kodiak Company, which has fixed costs of $10,000, a variable cost per unit of $10, and a unit sales price of $15.

Profit–
Volume $\left.\right\}$ $\pi = MQ - F$
Equation   Profit = (Unit Sales Price − Unit Variable Cost) ×
(Units of Output) − Fixed Cost
$\pi = (\$15 - \$10)(Q) - 10,000$
$\pi = \$5Q - \$10,000$

In Figure 8–13, the breakeven point occurs when $Q = 2,000$ units. At that point, profit is zero, calculated as follows: If $\pi = 0$, then

$$5Q_b - 10,000 = 0$$
$$5Q_b = 10,000$$
$$Q_b = 2,000$$

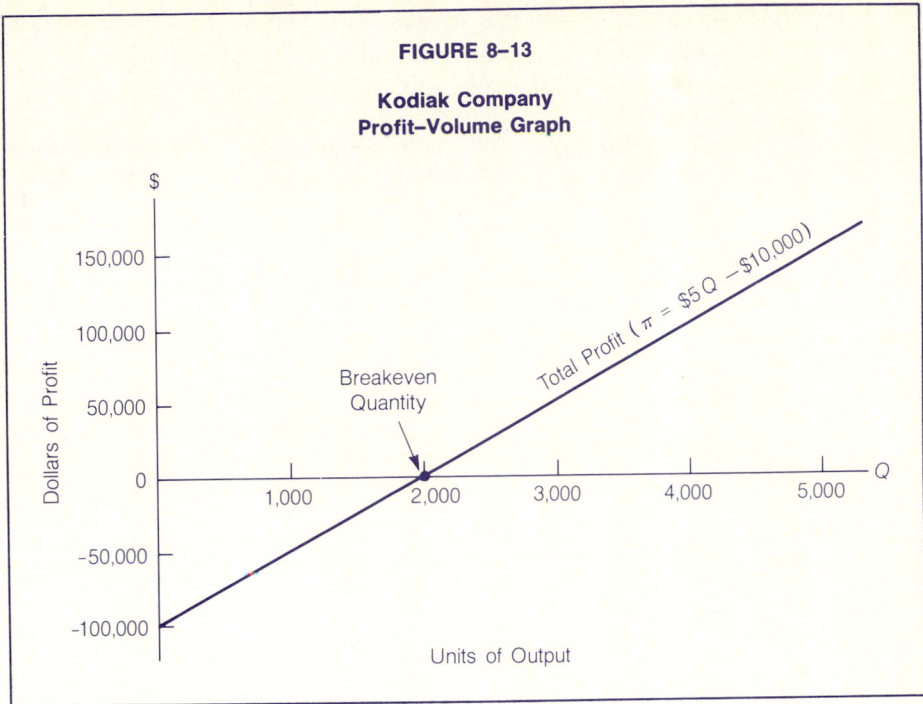

FIGURE 8–13

**Kodiak Company
Profit–Volume Graph**

If Kodiak Company has a breakeven quantity of 2,000 units and a contribution margin per unit of $5 ($15 unit sales price minus $10 unit variable cost), how many units must the company produce and sell to earn a target profit of $4,000?

The profit–volume graph simplifies target profit calculations, because the profit–volume equation ($\pi = MQ - F$) has a slope equal to M, the contribution margin per unit. This means that for each unit increase in volume, profit will increase by an amount equal to the contribution margin per unit. In particular, each additional unit of output beyond the breakeven quantity produces an increase in total profit equal to the contribution margin per unit.

Each unit sold by Kodiak Company adds $5 to profit. An additional 800 units sold will therefore add $4,000 to profit. At the breakeven quantity of 2,000 units, profit is of course zero. Consequently, to earn a profit of $4,000, output must be 2,800 units (2,000 + 800).

LIMITATIONS OF THE BASIC COST–VOLUME–PROFIT MODEL

The preceding discussion of cost–volume–profit techniques is based on five assumptions about costs, sales prices, and activity levels:

1. All costs can be classified as either fixed or variable.
2. All variable costs change at a constant rate per unit of output.

3. Cost behavior depends on a single variable—the number of units produced.
4. The market sales price is a constant amount per unit of output.
5. Cost–volume–profit analysis applies only to short-run situations.

The limitations of these assumptions will now be examined in order to extend cost–volume–profit analysis to more realistic and comprehensive operating situations.

THE FIXED–VARIABLE ASSUMPTION

The assumption that all costs are either fixed in total amount or variable at a uniform rate per unit deserves closer scrutiny. Even in the short run, not all variable costs will be the same amount per unit over a wide range of activity levels. There may be variations in the input costs of raw materials due to price changes or quantity purchase discounts. There may be economies of scale in input resource usage. Labor and other service input costs will probably vary at different activity levels as the efficiency of production changes. On the other hand, many costs that are fixed over a narrow range of activity—for example, the costs of supervision, maintenance, property taxes, and depreciation—will tend to change by step amounts over a broader range of activity.

These variations in fixed and variable costs suggest the use of more flexible cost functions in cost–volume–profit analysis. To this point, the analysis has used a single variable linear function of the form $T_c = F + VQ$ (total cost equals fixed costs plus unit variable cost multiplied by the number of units produced). This **linear cost function** is shown graphically in Figure 8–14.

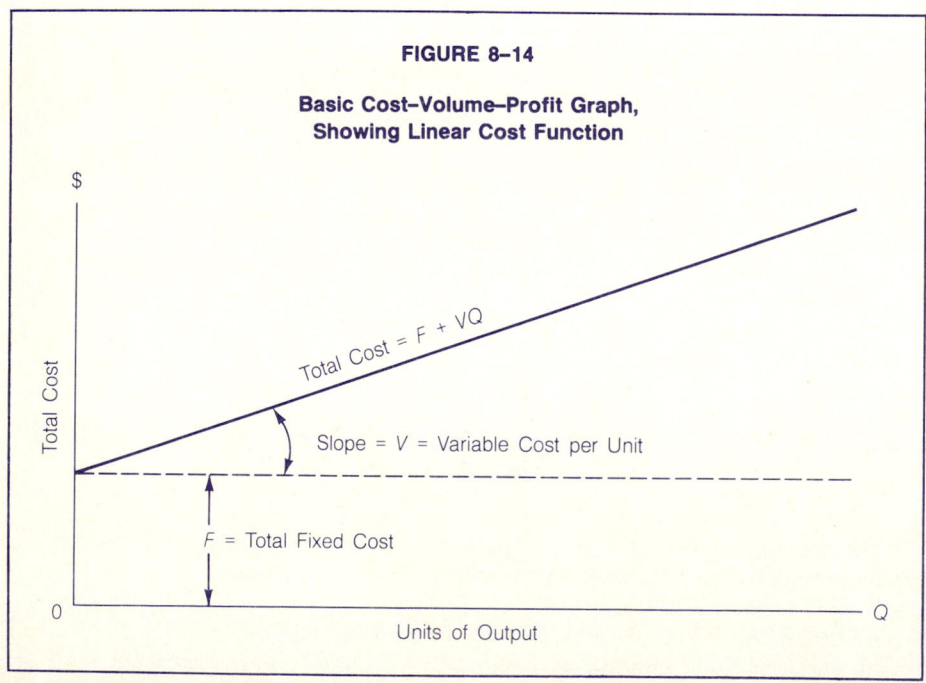

FIGURE 8–14

**Basic Cost–Volume–Profit Graph,
Showing Linear Cost Function**

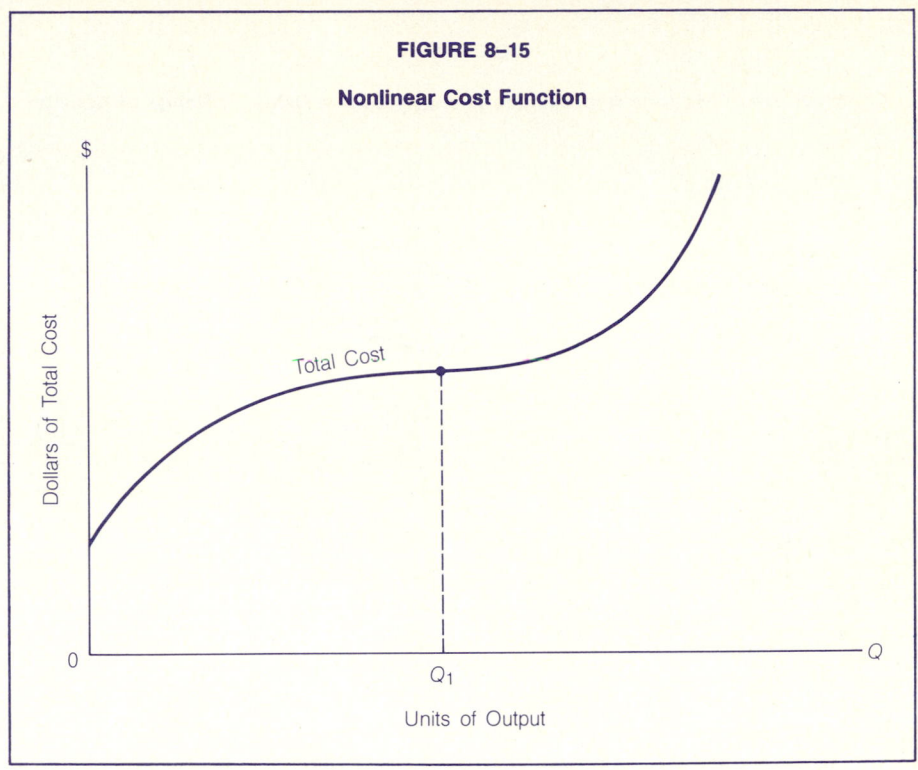

FIGURE 8–15

Nonlinear Cost Function

In microeconomic theory, cost functions are typically shown as being **nonlinear,** displaying successive ranges first of decreasing and then of increasing unit costs. Figure 8–15 shows total cost *increasing* at a *decreasing rate* up to activity level *OQ,* because of increasing returns to scale or economies of scale. Beyond *OQ,* total costs *increase* at an *increasing rate,* due to the presence of diminishing marginal returns or diseconomies of scale.

THE RELEVANT RANGE CONCEPT

The problem of deriving a cost function can also be approached by limiting the function's range to a particular activity level segment, rather than relating it to all possible levels of activity. This approach employs the simple linear cost function originally presented, but also takes account of the irregular cost behavior patterns of individual cost items and the economists' assertions about cost behavior patterns. It does so by specifying a **relevant range** of activity levels within which total fixed costs and unit variable costs will remain constant in the short run.

This *relevant range concept* is realistic for several reasons. In most businesses, internal resource limitations and external market demand limitations create upper limits on the activity levels that operations can possibly sustain. At the other extreme, given the need to recover the costs of invested capital,

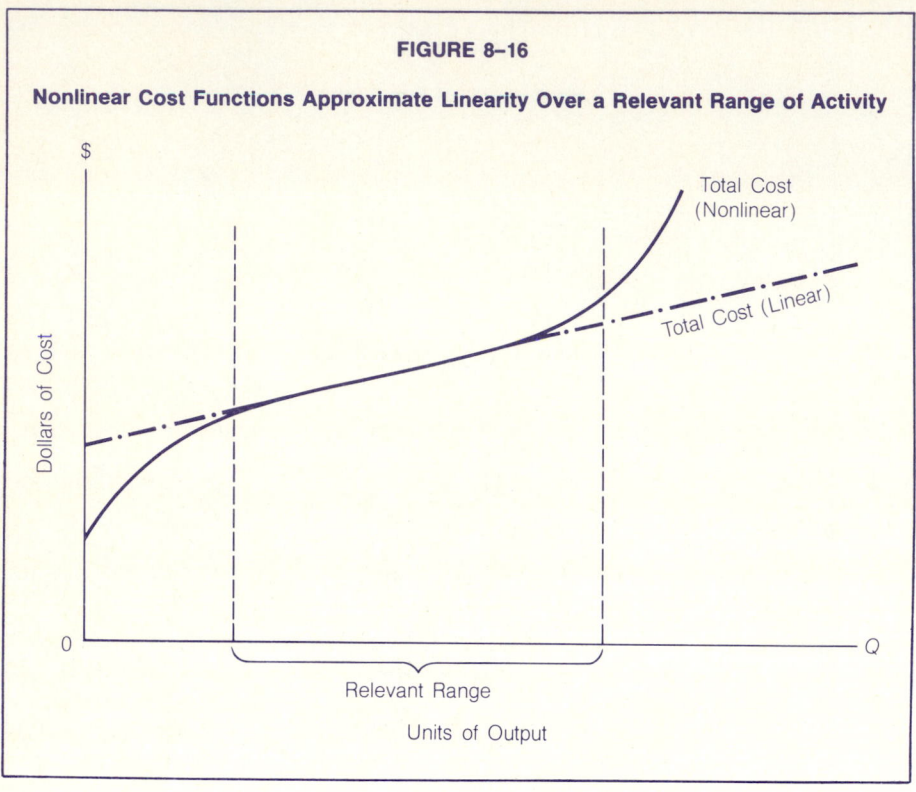

FIGURE 8–16

Nonlinear Cost Functions Approximate Linearity Over a Relevant Range of Activity

firms do not usually plan to operate at very low levels of activity. These two constraints define the relevant range of feasible activity levels.

Moreover, as Figure 8–16 illustrates, the cost curve of microeconomic theory models tends to be nearly linear in some middle range around its inflection point as it changes from increasing to decreasing returns to scale. Finally, empirical studies conducted in various industries have shown that costs do display linear tendencies over intermediate ranges of activity.[1]

Clearly, there is much support for the assumption that cost functions are linear over certain ranges of production and sales volume. Cost–volume–profit analysis should produce useful solutions if the breakeven or target profit level falls within the relevant range of activity levels over which the particular cost function is defined as linear. This idea is illustrated in Figure 8–17

Example: Joanna Company incurs fixed costs of $20,000 per month when operating within the capacity range of 25,000 to 50,000 units of output. Its product incurs variable costs of $2 per unit and sells for $2.50 per unit. What is the company's breakeven point and what is its maximum target profit within the relevant range?

---

[1] J. Johnston, *Statistical Cost Analysis* (New York: McGraw-Hill, 1960) and Joel Dean, *Statistical Cost Estimation* (Bloomington: Indiana Univ., 1977).

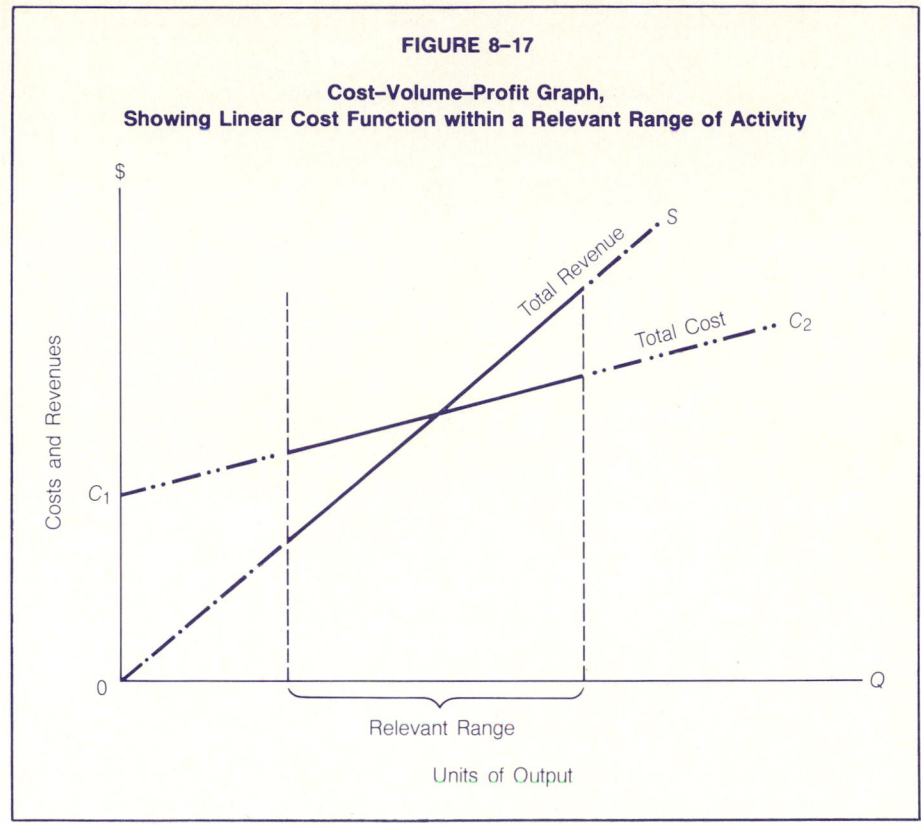

FIGURE 8–17

Cost–Volume–Profit Graph,
Showing Linear Cost Function within a Relevant Range of Activity

The breakeven point is 40,000 units—$20,000 ÷ ($2.50 − $2) per unit. This is a feasible solution because it lies within the relevant range of 25,000 to 50,000 units. The maximum target profit is $5,000 (50¢ contribution margin times 10,000 units). This is the profit obtainable by producing 50,000 units of output at the upper limit of the relevant range.

Any target profit above $5,000 would require an activity level outside the relevant range. Similarly, if the sales price were reduced to $2.25 per unit, the breakeven point would be outside the relevant range [(Q_b = $20,000 ÷ ($2.25 − $2) per unit = 80,000 units)]. In such situations, the target profit and breakeven conditions simply cannot be satisfied within the existing relevant range of 25,000 to 50,000 units. New cost and/or revenue functions extending over a different relevant range must then be derived.

LENGTH OF ACCOUNTING PERIODS IN COST–VOLUME–PROFIT ANALYSIS

The classification of costs as fixed or variable is influenced by the length of the accounting period selected for analysis. Certain costs tend to be more clearly definable as fixed or variable over relatively short periods (weeks, months,

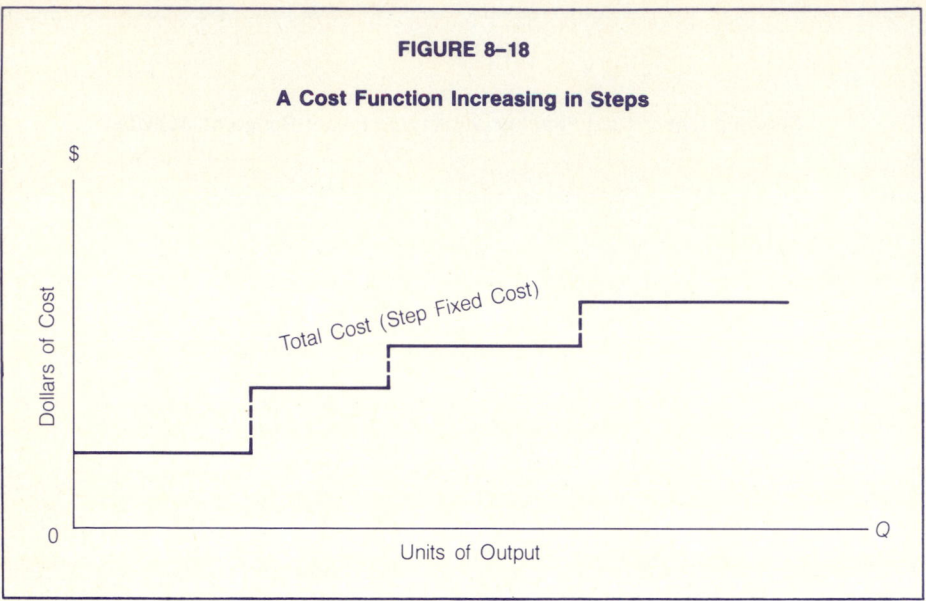

FIGURE 8–18

A Cost Function Increasing in Steps

or quarters). Capacity-related factors that generate fixed costs—such as plant size, number of salaried employees, or amount of equipment—are less subject to short-run change.

In the short run, there will also be less fluctuation in the unit amounts of variable costs. Input prices, physical resource consumption, and labor productivity will be more stable. Consequently, a linear representation of total cost is reasonably valid for short-run analysis.

Longer-run situations, in which larger variations in activity levels occur, may display other cost behavior patterns. Some cost items—such as supervisory salaries, depreciation, insurance, and property taxes—tend to increase in "steps" over an extended range. A typical pattern for **step costs** is shown in Figure 8–18.

Many variable cost items will also occur at non-uniform rates over longer periods. Unit prices of inputs such as raw materials, labor, supplies, and services will change due to economies of scale, discounts, and other savings. Consumption of resources will tend to occur at different rates, due to scale factors, learning curve effects, and technological changes over the wider ranges of volume. Modifications of profit planning techniques to recognize these variations are discussed in Chapters 11 and 22.

THE INDEPENDENT VARIABLE
IN COST–VOLUME–PROFIT FUNCTIONS

The cost function used in elementary cost–volume–profit analysis is assumed to be linear and is depicted as a *function of one independent variable factor;* that is, all cost behavior is represented in terms of changes in the value of a single variable, usually units of output. This allows the mathematics of the analysis to proceed at an elementary level that mainly involves solutions of linear equations with one unknown. But it limits the extent to which cost–volume–profit analysis can realistically depict cost behavior.

Many variable factors in addition to output volume can influence the behavior of total costs. These include plant size, quality of raw materials used, employee skills, degree of mechanization, automation or computerization of operations, size of production lots, inventory replenishment policies, and the number of shifts worked per day. Therefore, some assumption must be made concerning the response of all such variables during the period of analysis.

A convenient assumption is that of *ceteris paribus* (other things being equal). To justify the use of output units as the *only* independent variable in the cost functions used in cost–volume–profit analysis, all other cost-influencing factors must be assumed to remain constant. This is consistent with the relevant range concept, which specifies that in the short run, over a given range of output levels, total cost can reasonably be represented as a linear function of output.

ACTIVITY LEVEL MEASURES IN COST–VOLUME–PROFIT ANALYSIS

In all the preceding examples, units of finished product were used as the volume or activity level measure. Cost–volume–profit analysis requires a variable that can be directly associated with both costs and revenues. When a *uniform product* is manufactured (for example, the homogenous product featured in process costing), then *units of output* is an appropriate measure because revenue per unit and unit product costs are readily available. Elementary cost–volume–profit analysis assumes a single product of that type. But sometimes it is necessary to modify this basic activity level measure to cover more complex situations involving *multiple outputs* or *non-uniform* outputs. The following sections explore several of these possibilities.

COST–VOLUME–PROFIT ANALYSIS FOR MULTIPLE PRODUCT FIRMS

Cost–volume–profit analysis can be used by firms that manufacture several types of products. One approach is to accumulate cost, revenue, and volume measures for each type of product. Breakeven and target profit output quantities can then be calculated and sensitivity analysis performed. However, this approach is appropriate only if all revenues and costs can be traced directly to each of the individual products. Arbitrary assumptions often must be made when fixed costs and joint costs are allocated to particular products. An alternative is to exclude them from the cost–volume–profit calculations, which are then based only on allocations of *separable* costs and revenues.

Example: Green Company manufactures three products, Alpha, Beta, and Gamma, whose individual breakeven points and maximum target profits can be calculated as follows:

	Alpha	Beta	Gamma
Sales price per Unit	$10	$15	$12
Variable Cost per Unit	$5	$10	$10
Separable Fixed Costs	$8,000	$14,000	$12,000
Capacity (units of output)	4,000	6,000	5,000
Contribution Margin per Unit	$10 − $5 = $5	$15 − $10 = $5	$12 − $10 = $2
Breakeven Point (separable fixed costs only)	$\dfrac{\$8,000}{\$5 \text{ per unit}}$	$\dfrac{\$14,000}{\$5 \text{ per unit}}$	$\dfrac{\$12,000}{\$2 \text{ per unit}}$
Breakeven Output Quantity	= 1,600 units	= 2,700 units	= 6,000 units
Maximum Target Profit (at capacity)	($5 × 4,000) − $8,000 = $12,000	($5 × 6,000) − $14,000 = $16,000	($2 × 5,000) − $12,000 = −$2,000

Alpha, Beta, and Gamma require respective sales volumes of 1,600, 2,700, and 6,000 units to cover their separable fixed costs. However, Gamma is not capable of covering its fixed costs because its production capacity is only 5,000 units. Alpha and Beta can satisfy their individual breakeven conditions within their current capacity limits and can therefore make a contribution to company profits if their respective sales volumes can be raised above the breakeven levels of 1,600 and 2,700 units.

The preceding calculations might also be used to evaluate the *relative profitability* of the three products. Because Green Company cannot manufacture enough units of Gamma to break even on sales of that product, management might be wise to consider alternative uses of the plant assets now supporting Gamma's production. The analysis could be extended by examining the possible contributions to profit that could be made if the plant facilities now used to manufacture Gamma were used instead to produce larger volumes of Alpha, Beta, or other products.

PRODUCT GROUPS WITH UNIFORM CONTRIBUTION MARGIN RATIOS

The single product cost–volume–profit model can be adapted to situations in which a group of products has the same contribution margin ratio. Solutions for breakeven and target profit conditions can be obtained, but only in terms of *aggregate sales revenue.*

Example: Hirsch Company manufactures a group of products, all of which have a contribution margin ratio of 40 percent. That is, any item which sells for $10 has variable costs of $6 per unit, items selling for $8 have variable costs of $4.80 per unit, and so on. Total fixed costs are $240,000. What *total sales revenue* is needed (1) to break even, or (2) to earn a 25 percent profit margin on sales?

(1) $\left. \begin{array}{c} \textit{Breakeven} \\ \textit{Condition} \end{array} \right\}$ $R_b = \dfrac{F}{C} = \dfrac{\text{Fixed Cost}}{\text{Contribution Margin Ratio}}$

$$= \frac{\$240,000}{.4}$$

$$= \$600,000 \text{ sales revenue}$$

Any combination of product sales that provides total sales revenues of $600,000 will allow the company to break even.

(2) $\left. \begin{array}{c} \textit{Target Profit} \\ \textit{Condition} \end{array} \right\}$ $R_t = \dfrac{F}{C-a} = \dfrac{\text{Fixed Cost}}{\begin{array}{c}\text{Contribution Margin} \\ \text{Ratio}\end{array} - \begin{array}{c}\text{Desired Rate of} \\ \text{Return on Sales}\end{array}}$

$$= \frac{\$240,000}{(.40 - .25)}$$

$$= \$1,600,000 \text{ sales revenue}$$

Any combination of product sales that generates $1,600,000 in sales revenues will earn a profit equal to 25 percent of sales revenues, calculated as follows:

$$R_t = \$1,600,000 \dots\dots\dots\dots\dots\dots\dots \quad \text{Total Revenue}$$
$$T_c = \$240,000 + (\$1,600,000 \times .6) \dots\dots \quad \text{Total Cost}$$
$$= \$240,000 + \$960,000$$
$$= \$1,200,000$$

$$\text{Profit} = \$1,600,000 - \$1,200,000$$
$$= \$400,000$$
$$= (.25)\,(\$1,600,000)$$

This approach is limited to situations in which all products have the same contribution margin ratio. Because cost–volume–profit analysis is applied to the products collectively, these solutions only indicate the total dollar sales revenue needed to meet specified target profit or breakeven conditions. The contribution margin approach can be combined with the multiple product method described previously. Groups of products with equal contribution margin ratios can be evaluated as to their ability to contribute to the fixed costs directly associated with each group.

MULTIPLE PRODUCT FIRMS—UNALLOCATED FIXED COSTS

Fixed costs are often incurred to support the collective production and sale of a group of products. In such cases, it is logical to analyze fixed costs as part of the total cost of all the products involved, rather than as an allocated cost of particular products.

Example: Curtola Company produces and sells two products: G and H. The following operating information is available:

	G	H
Sales Price	$9	$12
Variable Cost	3	9
Contribution Margin	$6	$ 3
Total Fixed Costs	$36,000	

Curtola Company's breakeven condition can be expressed as follows:

$$G_b = \text{Units of G to break even}$$
$$H_b = \text{Units of H to break even}$$
$$\text{Total Revenue} = \text{Total Variable Cost} + \text{Total Fixed Cost}$$
$$\$9G_b + \$12H_b = [\$3\,G_b + \$9\,H_b] + \$36,000$$
$$\$6G_b + \$3H_b = \$36,000$$

But this is not a particularly helpful solution. Any set of values for G_b and H_b the combined total contribution margins of which are equal to total fixed costs will allow the firm to break even. Additional information about the products and their interrelationships is needed before a meaningful cost–volume–profit analysis can be made.

MULTIPLE PRODUCT FIRMS—CONSTANT SALES MIX

When a firm manufactures several different products—each with a different sales price, variable cost, and contribution margin ratio—elementary cost–volume–profit analysis can still be used if the sales mix of the products remains constant. The **sales mix** is the composition of total sales that reflects the relationship of the sale of one product to another. If the proportion of sales of products among several items remains stable over time, an average sales mix of products can be calculated. For example, cameras and film comprise a significant portion of Kodak's sales. Razors and blades have the same sort of relationship for a company like Gillette. If the sales mix is such that for every camera sold, Kodak sells 10 rolls of film, then managers can identify an average sales mix between the two products and use cost–volume–profit analysis to analyze the company's profit. Other examples of similar sales mix situations are cereal companies that package small, medium, and family size packages of cereal; gasoline stations that sell leaded, unleaded, and premium unleaded gasolines; or a publisher that sells one student guide for every basic text sold. Other sales mix situations may be less obvious, yet still indicate that some stable relationship exists between products. In situations where an established sales mix exists for products, cost–volume–profit analysis is a useful tool.

Example: Assume now that Curtola Company sells one unit of Product G for every two units of Product H. The selling price and contribution margin per unit of sales mix can then be calculated as follows:

	Sales Price	Sales Mix	Dollar Value
G	$ 9	1/3	$ 3
H	12	2/3	8
Selling price per unit of sales mix			$11

	Contribution Margin	Sales Mix	Dollar Value
G	$ 6	1/3	$ 2
H	3	2/3	2
Contribution margin per unit of sales mix			$ 4

What output levels will allow the firm to (1) break even or (2) earn a $24,000 profit?

Let $\overline{Q}_b$ = Breakeven quantity in units of sales mix
$\overline{M}$ = Contribution margin per unit of sales mix
$\overline{Q}_t$ = Target profit quantity in units of sales mix

$$\left.\begin{array}{l}\textit{Breakeven} \\ \textit{Condition}\end{array}\right\} \quad \overline{Q}_b = \frac{F}{\overline{M}} = \frac{\text{Fixed Cost}}{\text{Contribution Margin per Unit of Sales Mix}}$$

$$= \frac{\$36,000}{\$4 \text{ per unit}}$$

$$= \underline{\underline{9,000}} \text{ units of sales mix}$$

This means that 9,000 units of sales mix must be sold to break even. Because the sales mix ratio is one unit of G for every two units of H, these 9,000 units consist of 3,000 units of G and 6,000 units of H. This ratio produces a total contribution margin of $36,000 [(3,000 × $6) + (6,000 × $3) = $18,000 + $18,000] which exactly covers fixed costs.

$$\left.\begin{array}{l}\textit{Target profit} \\ \textit{Condition}\end{array}\right\} \quad \overline{Q}_t = \frac{F+T}{\overline{M}} = \frac{\text{Fixed Cost} + \text{Target Profit}}{\text{Contribution Margin per Unit of Sales Mix}}$$

$$= \frac{\$36,000 + \$24,000}{\$4 \text{ per unit}}$$

$$= \underline{\underline{15,000}} \text{ units of sales mix}$$

Curtola Company must sell 15,000 units of sales mix to earn a $24,000 profit. These 15,000 units include 5,000 units of G and 10,000 units of H. The total contribution margin is $60,000 [(5,000 × $6) + (10,000 × $3) = $30,000 + $30,000] which covers fixed costs of $36,000 plus the target profit of $24,000.

MULTIPLE PRODUCT FIRMS—CONTRIBUTION MARGIN RATIO

The contribution margin ratio for each dollar of sales mix revenue ($\overline{C}$) also provides a useful way of analyzing multiple product situations.

Example: Mateo Company manufactures and distributes three product lines: Uno, Duo, and Tre. The company's total fixed costs are $200,000 per year. The following forecasts have been made for 19X7:

	Uno	Duo	Tre
Contribution Margin Ratio for Each Product	40%	60%	30%
Sales Mix Proportions	.25	.25	.50

This information can be used to calculate the average contribution margin ratio per dollar of sales mix revenue ($\overline{C}$):

$$\begin{aligned} \overline{C} &= .25 \,(40\%) + .25 \,(60\%) + .50 \,(30\%) \\ &= 10\% + 15\% + 15\% \\ &= \underline{\underline{40\%}} \end{aligned}$$

The breakeven revenue in terms of the specified sales mix ($\overline{R}_b$) can then be determined:

$$\bar{R}_b = \frac{F}{\bar{C}} = \frac{\$200,000}{.4} = \$500,000$$

This means that as long as the specified sales mix is produced, total sales revenue of $500,000 will allow the firm to break even. The composition of this $500,000 breakeven revenue is as follows:

Uno (.25) = $125,000
Duo (.25) = $125,000
Tre (.50) = $250,000

MULTIPLE PRODUCT FIRMS—CHANGES IN SALES MIX

Sensitivity analysis can measure the effects of changes in the sales mix of firms that produce multiple products. Each time the sales mix changes, a new average unit of sales mix is created, together with a new contribution margin per unit of sales mix, and a new contribution margin ratio per dollar of sales mix revenue. As a result, the breakeven revenue and the maximum target profit will be higher or lower.

Example: What are the effects of a change in the sales mix of Mateo Company from [.25—.25—.50] to [.50—.30—.20]? This is a favorable change because the mix shifts away from production of Tre, which has the lowest contribution margin ratio, towards Uno and Duo, which have higher contribution margin ratios.

The revised average contribution margin ratio is derived as follows:

$$\begin{aligned}\bar{C} &= .50\,(40\%) + .30\,(60\%) + .20\,(30\%) \\ &= 20\% + 18\% + 6\% \\ &= 44\%\end{aligned}$$

This figure can then be used to determine the revised breakeven revenue condition:

$$R_b = \frac{F}{\bar{C}} = \frac{\$200,000}{.44} = \$454,545.45$$

This breakeven revenue is less than the original amount of $500,000, indicating that the new sales mix allows the company to break even with lower sales revenues. If the original breakeven sales revenue of $500,000 were achieved with this new sales mix, a profit of $20,000 would be earned. This profit is determined as follows:

	Uno	Duo	Tre	Total
Sales Mix	.50	.30	.20	1.00
Sales Revenue	$250,000	$150,000	$100,000	$500,000
Contribution Margin Ratio	40%	60%	30%	44%
Total Contribution Margin	$100,000	$ 90,000	$ 30,000	$220,000

Total profit is therefore $20,000, the amount by which total contribution margin ($220,000) exceeds total fixed costs ($200,000). Note that this $20,000 increase in profit also corresponds to the 4 percent increase in the average contribution margin ratio (from 40 to 44 percent) multiplied by the $500,000 sales volume.

COST–VOLUME–PROFIT ANALYSIS FOR NON-UNIFORM OUTPUT UNITS

When a firm manufactures many dissimilar products (for example, in a job order production setting), the physical units of finished output may not be additive and therefore may not represent a uniform measure of activity. It is then necessary to develop a *substitute measure* to reflect activity levels if cost–volume–profit analysis is to be applied to non-uniform products.

Such a substitute measure should be common to all units of output in measurable amounts and should be directly related to both costs and sales revenues. These are essentially the same criteria required of an activity level index used in setting overhead application rates. Measures such as direct labor hours, machine hours, or direct labor cost are frequently used to represent activity levels.

Example: Cullen Company is in the building maintenance and cleaning business. Its total fixed costs are $100,000 per year. Each of its jobs incurs total variable costs at the rate of $5 per direct labor hour. Jobs are billed at the rate of $15 per direct labor hour worked. What total activity level in terms of direct labor hours must the firm sustain (1) to break even or (2) to earn $50,000 profit?

$$\left.\begin{array}{c} Breakeven \\ Condition \end{array}\right\} Q_b = \frac{F}{M} = \frac{\text{Fixed Cost}}{\text{Contribution Margin per Direct Labor Hour}}$$

$$= \frac{\$100,000}{(\$15 - \$5) \text{ per hour}}$$

$$= \underline{\underline{10,000}} \text{ direct labor hours}$$

Jobs requiring a total of 10,000 direct labor hours must be completed during the year to permit Cullen Company to break even.

$$\left.\begin{array}{c} Target\ Profit \\ Condition \end{array}\right\} Q_t = \frac{F+T}{M} = \frac{\text{Fixed Cost} + \text{Target Profit}}{\text{Contribution Margin per Direct Labor Hour}}$$

$$= \frac{\$100,000 + \$50,000}{\$10 \text{ per hour}}$$

$$= \underline{\underline{15,000}} \text{ direct labor hours}$$

Jobs requiring a total of 15,000 direct labor hours must be completed to permit the firm to earn a $50,000 profit.

INVENTORY LEVELS
IN COST–VOLUME–PROFIT ANALYSIS

The basic cost–volume–profit model refers to "output levels" in a way which assumes that sales volume always equals production volume. Inventory levels are assumed to be either constant or nonexistent. This simplifying assumption detracts from the realism of cost–volume–profit analysis.

If there are no end-of-period inventories, the elementary cost–volume–profit model is justified in equating production levels with sales levels. However, if inventories exist, the model should be modified slightly. It is then necessary to specify *which* units of output make up the independent variable in the cost–volume–profit model. Is it *units of sales* or *units of production?*

If the cost and revenue functions are constructed in terms of units of output *produced,* the cost function will reflect the *current period's costs.* A revenue function can then be derived to represent the revenue to be earned from selling those units in the current period or in some future period, assuming that the same unit price is maintained. This is a reasonable assumption, considering that cost–volume–profit analysis is meant to be used in short-run situations.

If the cost and revenue functions are constructed in terms of units of output *sold,* the revenue function will directly reflect the *current period's sales.* If inventories exist, some of the units sold will have been manufactured in prior periods. The problem then becomes one of specifying an appropriate cost function.

It might be argued that what is needed is a composite function consisting of both prior and current period costs. After all, financial accountants measure income by matching historical costs with revenues. However, for management decision making in the current period, the relevant cost measurement of inventory from prior periods is the *current replacement cost* of those units. This is the cost that must be recovered in order to replace the resources used to manufacture those units. The *current period's variable production costs* are the best approximation of that amount. When they are combined with current fixed production costs, plus all current selling, distribution, and other costs, the resulting total cost function is identical to the total current replacement cost.

The analysis then consists of determining the current *sales level* that will allow the company to break even. The implication is that current production will be supplemented by the inventory already on hand. The breakeven condition is expressed in terms of current replacement costs—that is, the current period's sales must cover the current period's fixed costs plus the current period's variable cost of all units *sold,* regardless of whether those units were produced in the current period or in prior periods. This conforms to the principle of *maintaining real net assets.* In other words, the proceeds from the sale of a physical quantity of output must be sufficient to replace that same physical quantity of output at current period input prices.

Example: At the end of December, 19X1, Claus Company had an inventory of 2,000 units that had been produced when variable costs were $5 per unit. During January, 19X2, fixed costs were $40,000, variable costs were $6 per unit, and sales prices were $10 per unit. How many units must be sold to break even during January, 19X2?

$$\left.\begin{array}{c}\textit{Breakeven} \\ \textit{Condition}\end{array}\right\} Q_b = \frac{F}{M} = \frac{\text{Fixed Cost}}{\text{Contribution Margin per Unit}}$$

$$= \frac{\$40,000}{(\$10 - \$6) \text{ per unit}}$$

$$= \underline{\underline{10,000 \text{ units}}}$$

Sales during January must be 10,000 units in order to break even in terms of the current costs of January production. Only 8,000 units must be manufactured in January in order to have 10,000 units available for sale. Any production in excess of 8,000 units will create an ending inventory, which will then have to be considered in the subsequent period's analysis, but at the variable production cost of that later period.

NONLINEAR COST AND REVENUE FUNCTIONS

The use of linear cost and revenue functions often makes cost–volume–profit analysis less realistic and valid. Nonlinear cost and revenue functions, consistent with microeconomic theory, are shown in Figure 8–19.

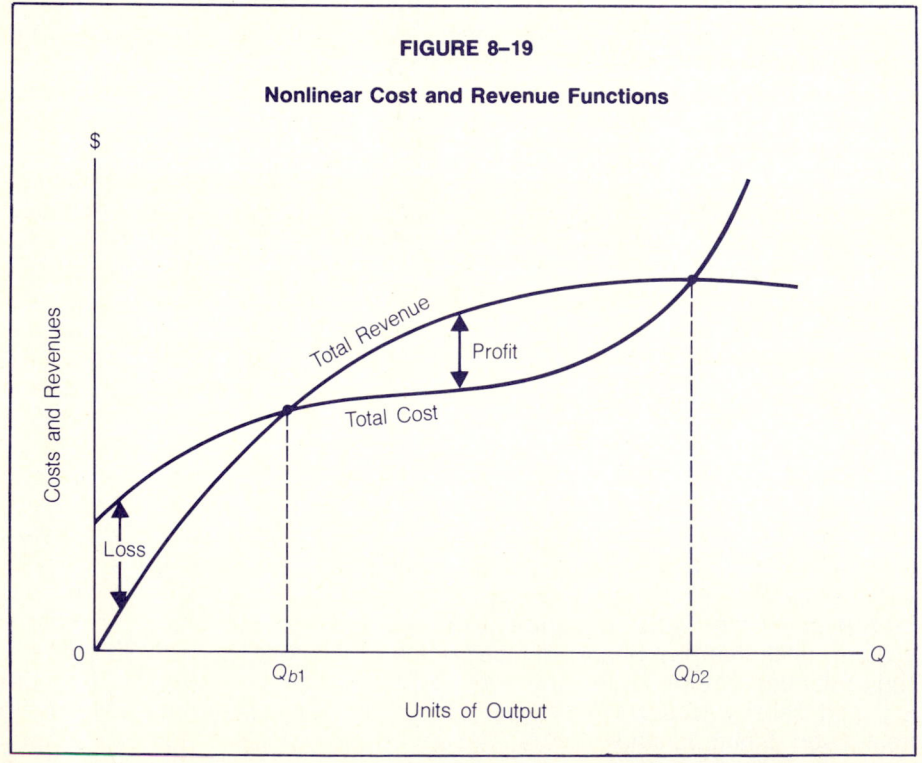

FIGURE 8–19

Nonlinear Cost and Revenue Functions

The cost curve displays successive ranges of increasing and decreasing returns to scale; the revenue function is subject to diminishing marginal revenue. Breakeven points are located at the intersections of the two curves and the vertical distance between the two curves represents the profit (or loss) at each activity level.

In a linear cost–volume–profit model, the point of maximum profit occurs at the upper limit of the relevant range (or, without the relevant range constraint, profits could theoretically be increased indefinitely if volume continued to increase). The nonlinear representation of cost and revenue functions permits a specific determination of a point of maximum profit. Differential calculus is needed to locate the activity level where this maximum profit occurs.

Example: The equations for nonlinear cost and revenue functions are as follows for Kuznets Company:

$$R = 50Q - 5Q^2 \dots \dots \dots \text{Total Revenue (A)}$$

$$T_c = 100 + 10Q - 8Q^2 + \frac{Q^3}{3} \dots \dots \text{Total Cost \quad (B)}$$

$$\pi = (50Q - 5Q^2) - \left(100 + 10Q - 8Q^2 + \frac{Q^3}{3}\right) \dots \text{Profit \quad (C)}$$

$$\pi = -100 + 40Q + 3Q^2 - \frac{Q^3}{3} \dots \dots \text{(D)}$$

For conditions of maximum profit, the first derivative of the profit function is set equal to zero, the second derivative must be negative, and for real economic commodities, the solution value for output must be positive.

$$\frac{d\pi}{dQ} = 0, \quad \frac{d^2\pi}{dQ^2} < 0, \quad \text{and} \quad Q \geq 0$$

This requires the following three conditions:

$$\text{From (D),} \quad \frac{d\pi}{dQ} = 40 + 6Q - Q^2 = 0 \dots \dots \dots \text{(E)}$$

$$(4 + Q)(10 - Q) = 0$$

$$Q = 10$$

$$\text{From (E),} \quad \frac{d^2\pi}{dQ^2} = 6 - 2Q = 6 - 20 = -14 \dots \dots \dots \text{(F)}$$

Clearly, $Q = 10$ is the only feasible solution; it is at this activity level that profit is maximized.

To locate the breakeven points, where profit is zero, the equation (D) must be solved:

$$\pi = -100 + 40Q + 3Q^2 - \frac{Q^3}{3} = 0$$

FIGURE 8–20

Linear versus Nonlinear Cost–Volume–Profit Models

Linear Accounting Model	Nonlinear Microeconomic Model
(1) Static analysis—relevant range assumption—constant sales price, variable cost per unit, and fixed cost.	(1) Dynamic analysis—no restriction on volume—prices and costs may be variable amounts.
(2) Cost and revenue are represented as linear functions of one variable.	(2) Cost and revenue are represented as nonlinear functions of one or more variables.
(3) Implies that maximum profit only occurs at the upper limit of the relevant range.	(3) Allows the determination of a unique maximum profit solution.
(4) Computationally simple. Data requirements and model formulation are feasible in practice.	(4) Computations become moderately complex. Data requirements and model formulation are not usually feasible in practice.
(5) Specifically a short-run analysis.	(5) Applies to short- or long-run analysis.

Approximate solutions to this are $Q \simeq 2.22$ or $Q \simeq 15.5$. These two solution values correspond to points Q_{b1} and Q_{b2} as shown in Figure 8–19.

LINEAR VERSUS NONLINEAR COST–VOLUME–PROFIT MODELS

Figure 8–20 summarizes the major characteristics, advantages, and limitations of the linear accounting cost–volume–profit model as compared to the nonlinear microeconomic approach to cost–volume–profit analysis.

COST–VOLUME–PROFIT ANALYSIS ILLUSTRATED: MERCER MANUFACTURING COMPANY

Mercer Manufacturing Company now produces and sells a single type of electric fan. During 19X7, the company's annual operating costs were as follows:

Fixed Manufacturing Costs	$250,000
Fixed Marketing Costs	$150,000
Variable Manufacturing Costs	$6 per unit
Variable Marketing Costs	$4 per unit
Sales Price	$15 per unit

For each of the following separate situations, determine what *sales volume* would be needed to (1) break even, (2) earn a $100,000 profit, or (3) earn a 10 percent return on sales.

A. *Assume that no changes occur in the preceding cost data and sales price.*

(1) *Breakeven* $\left.\right\} Q_b =$ $\dfrac{\text{Fixed Cost}}{\text{Contribution Margin per Unit}}$
Condition

$$= \frac{\$250,000 + \$150,000}{[\$15 - (\$6 + \$4)]\ \text{per unit}}$$

$$= \frac{\$400,000}{\$5\ \text{per unit}}$$

$$= 80,000\ \text{units}$$

(2) *Target Profit* $\left.\right\} Q_t =$ $\dfrac{\text{Fixed Cost} + \text{Target Profit}}{\text{Contribution Margin per Unit}}$
$100,000

$$= \frac{\$400,000 + \$100,000}{\$5\ \text{per unit}}$$

$$= \frac{\$500,000}{\$5\ \text{per unit}}$$

$$= 100,000\ \text{units}$$

(3) *Target Profit* $\left.\right\} Q_t =$ $\dfrac{\text{Fixed Cost}}{[\text{Contribution Margin} - (\text{Sales Price} \times \text{Target Rate})]\ \text{per Unit}}$
10% of Sales

$$= \frac{\$400,000}{[\$5 - (\$15 \times 10\%)]\ \text{per unit}}$$

$$= \frac{\$400,000}{\$3.50\ \text{per unit}}$$

$$= 114,286\ \text{units}$$

B. *The company intends to modernize its production facilities. This will increase fixed manufacturing costs to $350,000 and reduce variable manufacturing costs to $4 per unit.*

(1) *Breakeven* $\left.\right\} Q_b =$ $\dfrac{\$350,000 + \$150,000}{[\$15 - (\$4 + \$4)]\ \text{per unit}}$
Condition

$$= \frac{\$500,000}{\$7\ \text{per unit}}$$

$$= 71,429\ \text{units}$$

(2) *Target Profit* $\left.\right\} Q_t =$ $\dfrac{\$500,000 + \$100,000}{\$7\ \text{per unit}}$
$100,000

$$= 85,714\ \text{units}$$

(3) *Target Profit* $\left.\right\} Q_t =$ $\dfrac{\$500,000}{(\$7 - \$1.50)\ \text{per unit}}$
10% of Sales

$$= 90,909\ \text{units}$$

C. *The company intends to raise its sales price to $16, increase fixed market-ing costs to $200,000, and reduce variable marketing costs to $3.50 per unit.*

(1) *Breakeven*
     Condition
$$\left.\begin{array}{l}\end{array}\right\} Q_b = \frac{\$250,000 + \$200,000}{[\$16 - (\$6 + \$3.50)] \text{ per unit}}$$

$$= \frac{\$450,000}{\$6.50 \text{ per unit}}$$

$$= 69,231 \text{ units}$$

(2) *Target Profit*
     $100,000
$$\left.\begin{array}{l}\end{array}\right\} Q_t = \frac{\$550,000}{\$6.50 \text{ per unit}}$$

$$= 84,615 \text{ units}$$

(3) *Target Profit*
     10% of Sales
$$\left.\begin{array}{l}\end{array}\right\} Q_t = \frac{\$450,000}{(\$6.50 - \$1.50) \text{ per unit}}$$

$$= \frac{\$450,000}{\$5 \text{ per unit}}$$

$$= 90,000 \text{ units}$$

D. *The company decides to manufacture a second type of electric fan, but to maintain its existing production and distribution facilities. The new fan will sell for $20 and will incur variable manufacturing costs of $8.50 per unit and variable marketing costs of $4 per unit.*

(1) *Breakeven*
     Condition
$$\left.\begin{array}{l}\end{array}\right\} Q_b = \frac{\text{Fixed Cost}}{\text{Contribution Margin per Unit of Sales Mix}}$$

$$= \frac{\$400,000}{[p_1 \times \$5 + (1 - p_1) \$7.50] \text{ per unit}}$$

Here p_1 is the proportion of total unit sales of the original product, $(1 - p_1)$ is the proportion of total unit sales of the new product, and $7.50 is the contribu-tion margin of the new product. Unless the value of p_1 is known, there is no unique solution to this problem. *Any* combination of unit sales of the two products that produces a *total contribution* of $400,000 satisfies the breakeven condition. Consequently, the solution can only be stated as follows:

Total Fixed Cost = Total Contribution Margin

or $400,000 = \$5 \, Q_1 + \$7.50 \, Q_2$

E. *The same change is proposed as in item D, but in addition it is forecast that two units of the new product will always be sold for every three units of the original product. Therefore, the sales mix consists of 60 percent of the original product and 40 percent of the new product.*

(1) $\left.\begin{array}{l}\textit{Breakeven}\\\textit{Condition}\end{array}\right\}$ $\overline{Q}_b = \dfrac{F}{M} = \dfrac{\$400,000}{[(.6)\,(\$5)+(.4)\,(\$7.50)]\text{ per unit}}$

$$= \frac{\$400,000}{(\$3+\$3)\text{ per unit}}$$

$$= \frac{\$400,000}{\$6\text{ per unit}}$$

$$= \underline{\underline{66,666}}\text{ units of sales mix}$$

This breakeven sales volume consists of 40,000 units (.6 × 66,666) of the original product, and 26,666 units (.4 × 66,666) of the new product.

(2) $\left.\begin{array}{l}\textit{Target Profit}\\\textit{\$100,000}\end{array}\right\}$ $Q_t = \dfrac{F+\pi_t}{M} = \dfrac{\$500,000}{\$6\text{ per unit}}$

$$= \underline{\underline{83,333}}\text{ units of sales mix}$$

The \$100,000 target profit is earned on sales of 50,000 units of the original product and 33,333 units of the new one.

(3) $\left.\begin{array}{l}\textit{Target Profit}\\\textit{10\% of Sales}\end{array}\right\}$ $Q_t = \dfrac{F}{M-a\overline{S}} = \dfrac{\$400,000}{\{\$6 - 10\%\,[(.6\times\$15)+(.4\times\$20)]\}\text{ per unit}}$

$$= \frac{\$400,000}{[\$6 - 10\%\,(\$9+\$8)]\text{ per unit}}$$

$$= \frac{\$400,000}{[(\$6 - \$1.70)]\text{ per unit}}$$

$$= \frac{\$400,000}{\$4.30\text{ per unit}}$$

$$= \underline{\underline{93,023}}\text{ units of sales mix}$$

The 10 percent return on sales is earned by selling 55,814 units (.6 × 93,023) of the original product and 37,209 units (.4 × 93,023) of the new product.

SUMMARY

1. Cost–volume–profit analysis is a planning technique that facilitates analysis of the interactions among sales prices, input costs, and operating volume.
2. In its elementary form, cost–volume–profit analysis is a static planning tool, because it involves the assumption that in the short run all parameters of the analysis remain constant within a relevant range of feasible activity.
3. The breakeven point is the activity level at which total sales revenue equals total cost. It may be expressed either in terms of output levels or dollars of sales revenue. The breakeven point is also the activity level at which the total contribution margin is equal to total fixed costs.

4. The activity level required to support a specified target profit can be derived through similar calculations.

5. Sensitivity analysis may be used to determine the effects of changes in the specific values of costs, sales prices, or operating volume, either individually or in combination.

6. Possible extensions of the single product, linear cost–volume–profit model include situations involving separate multiple outputs, multiple outputs with a constant output mix, and nonlinear cost and revenue functions.

7. Cost–volume–profit analysis can also be extended to non-uniform output units and to situations involving beginning and ending inventories.

KEY WORDS AND PHRASES

Cost–Volume–Profit Analysis (319)
Profit Planning (319)
Fixed Costs (319)
Variable Costs (319)
Contribution Margin (320)
Contribution Margin Ratio (320)
Breakeven Point (320)
Target Profit (320)
Contribution Margin per Unit (321)
Cost–Volume–Profit Graph (327)
Sensitivity Analysis (329)
Profit–Volume Graph (335)
Linear Cost Function (338)
Nonlinear Cost Function (339)
Relevant Range (339)
Step Costs (342)
Sales Mix (347)

Questions

1. For what purposes can cost–volume–profit analysis be used?
2. Why is it important to establish cost and revenue behavior patterns for cost–volume–profit analysis?
3. Explain the terms *contribution margin* and *contribution margin ratio.*
4. What is the breakeven condition? What is its meaning for planning purposes?
5. Can the breakeven sales quantity be determined if only the periodic fixed costs and unit variable costs are known? Why or why not?
6. Explain how the typical cost–volume–profit graph is related to the profit–volume graph.
7. How can cost–volume–profit analysis be used in the budgeting and profit planning process?
8. What different ways of expressing target profit can be used with cost–volume–profit analysis?
9. Is cost–volume–profit analysis applicable to situations in which more than one product is involved? Why or why not?
10. Which assumptions of basic cost–volume–profit analysis are least reasonable? Why?
11. What are the major differences between cost–volume–profit analysis as presented in this chapter and the typical microeconomic models of cost and revenue behavior?
12. Explain fully the relevant range concept.
13. Can cost–volume–profit analysis be used for long-range planning? Why or why not?
14. In cost–volume–profit analysis, does the variable that represents "volume" always have to be units of output? Why or why not?
15. How is the concept of output-mix or the *average unit of sales mix* helpful to cost–volume–profit analysis?
16. In cost–volume–profit analysis, does the level of sales during a period always have to equal the level of production in the same period? Why or why not?
17. Will cost–volume–profit analysis be possible even if the cost and revenue curves are not straight lines? Why or why not?
18. Explain the potential usefulness of cost–volume–profit analysis as an elementary control technique. Why is its usefulness relatively limited?
19. "Why bother with breakeven charts? Nobody really wants just to break even!" Discuss these statements fully.
20. "Step-costs don't fit into cost–volume–profit analysis." Discuss this statement.
21. "Some costs are both fixed and variable. For example, repairs and maintenance." Do you agree? Why or why not?
22. "You cannot draw a profit–volume or a cost–volume–profit graph for a multiproduct firm on a single piece of paper." Do you agree? Why or why not?

23. "If we lower prices, the breakeven point should be easier to achieve." Discuss fully.

24. "At present our product prices are so low that we are selling below cost. But when volume picks up, that will all be turned around and we won't even have to raise prices." Is this possible? Discuss.

25. "An increase in fixed costs hurts more than an increase in variable costs." Discuss.

26. "It's better to have $200,000 of fixed costs and a $10 contribution margin, than $100,000 of fixed costs and an $8 contribution margin!" Do you agree? Why or why not?

Exercises

E 8–1   Breakeven Analysis—Single Product

Anderson Corporation manufactures and markets a single product. This product's sales price is now $8 per unit, variable costs are $6 per unit, and fixed costs are $40,000 per month.

Required:
(a) What is the contribution margin per unit?
(b) What is the contribution margin ratio?
(c) What is the monthly breakeven quantity in units?
(d) What is the monthly breakeven quantity in sales revenue?
(e) How many units must be sold to earn a profit of $20,000 per month?
(f) If the sales price is increased to $9, what will happen to the monthly breakeven quantity (in units)?
(g) If fixed costs increase by $10,000, how much must the sales price be increased to keep the breakeven point at the same level as in part (c)?

E 8–2   Breakeven Analysis—Single Product

The following data relate to Reid Corporation, which manufactures a single product.

Annual Fixed Costs	$400,000
Variable Cost per Unit	$15
Sales Price per Unit	$25
Annual Capacity	90,000 units

Required:
(a) What is the contribution margin per unit?
(b) What is the contribution margin ratio?
(c) How many units must be sold to produce a $200,000 annual profit?
(d) How many units must be sold annually to produce a profit equal to 20 percent of sales revenue?
(e) What is maximum profit that can be earned annually, subject to the stated capacity limit?

(f) If the company were forced to reduce its sales price to $18 per unit, but all else remained unchanged, what would you conclude with regard to operating volume?

(g) Suppose fixed costs were reduced to $240,000, but variable costs increased to $17 per unit. How would this affect your answer to part (c)?

E 8–3 Cost–Volume–Profit Analysis–Profit–Volume Analysis—Graphical Methods

FIGURE A

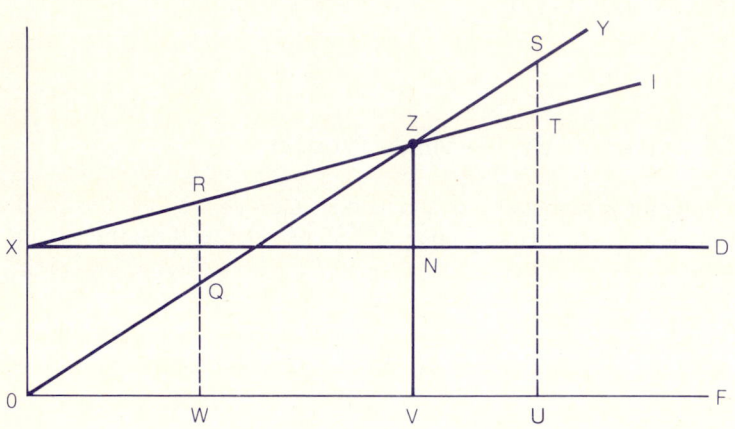

FIGURE B

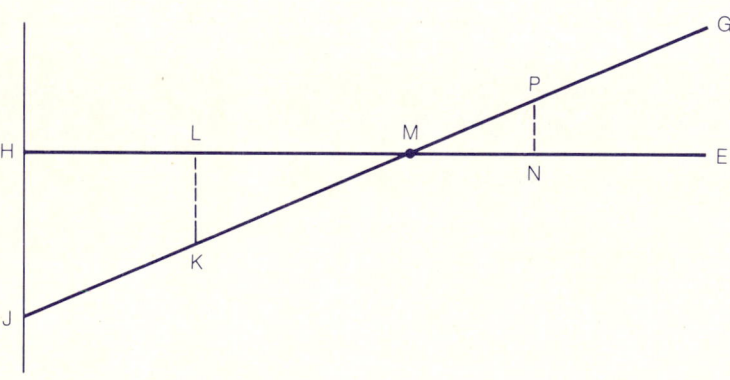

Required:
(a) Identify Figure A and Figure B.
(b) In Figure A, what do the following points, distances, and areas represent?

1. OV	5. ST	9. ZN
2. ZV	6. OY	10. NV
3. XD	7. XI	11. TU
4. WU	8. RQ	12. OU

(c)   In Figure B, what do the following points, distances, and areas represent?
    1.   LN
    2.   HJ
    3.   HM
    4.   PN
    5.   JG
    6.   LK

(d)   Explain the relationship between the two diagrams, assuming that they are based on the same data.

(e)   What assumptions about the variables and relationships are reflected in the way the diagrams are drawn?

(f)   What information can be obtained from Figure A that cannot be obtained from Figure B?

E 8–4   Sensitivity Analysis

Horowitz Company has collected the following data regarding its annual operations in its single product manufacturing plant.

Sales Price per Unit	$10
Variable Costs per Unit	$6
Annual Fixed Costs (total)	$240,000
Average Annual Sales Volume	80,000 units
Maximum Operating Capacity	100,000 units

Required:
(a)   Calculate the following:
    1.   Contribution Margin per Unit
    2.   Contribution Margin Ratio
    3.   Variable Cost Ratio
    4.   Breakeven Quantity (units)
    5.   Breakeven Quantity (revenue)
    6.   Net Profit at Average Annual Volume
    7.   Maximum Potential Net Profit

(b)   Consider each of the following changes independently. For each, compute the breakeven quantity in units, the contribution margin ratio, and the net income at the average annual sales volume:
    1.   10 percent increase in sales price per unit
    2.   10 percent increase in fixed costs
    3.   10 percent increase in variable cost per unit
    4.   Fixed costs decrease by $40,000
    5.   Variable costs decrease by $1 per unit
    6.   Sales price decreases by $2 per unit
    7.   Variable costs increase by $1 per unit and fixed costs decrease by $75,000
    8.   Sales price increases by $1 per unit and fixed costs increase by $200,000

E 8–5   Sensitivity Analysis

Milgram Company manufactures a single type of product. Its sales volume has been steady at 50,000 units per month, with total revenue of $100,000. Its contribution margin ratio is .25 and net income has been $5,000 per month at the present volume. The company wishes to increase monthly net income to $10,000 and proposes to spend an additional $2,000 per month for advertising to promote an increase in sales. Maximum operating capacity is 80,000 units per month.

Required:
(a) What increase in sales volume must result from the advertising campaign if the new profit goal is to be achieved?
(b) If the proposed advertising expenditures are made, what will be the new breakeven quantity? Is this an increase or decrease from the original breakeven quantity? Why?
(c) If the advertising only increases sales volume to 60,000 units, should the $2,000 per month expenditure be made? Why?
(d) Assume that the advertising proposal is rejected, but that the $10,000 profit goal is retained. What increase in sales price will be needed to achieve that profit goal if the sales volume remains unchanged?
(e) What change in fixed costs would be needed to achieve the profit goal, assuming that sales volume and all other prices and costs remain the same?

E 8–6   Cost–Volume–Profit Analysis—Multiple Outputs

Spinks Manufacturing Company makes and sells three types of product, each with its own separate manufacturing and distribution facilities. During 19X8, which was a typical year, average monthly operating results were as follows:

	Product X	Product Y	Product Z	Total
Sales (units)	2,000	3,000	3,000	8,000
Sales Revenue	$80,000	$60,000	$180,000	$320,000
Variable Cost (per unit)	$20	$10	$30	N/A
Fixed Costs	$20,000	$10,000	$30,000	$60,000

Required:
(a) Calculate the *separate* breakeven quantities for each of the three products. Express them in units and in sales revenue.
(b) Calculate the breakeven quantity in *sales revenue for the firm as a whole,* assuming that the 19X8 sales mix holds constant. Also express it in terms of units for each of the three products.
(c) Compare your answer in part (b) to your three answers to the sales revenue breakeven quantities in part (a). Explain the difference between the individual and collective breakeven quantities.
(d) Assume the 19X8 sales mix remains the same. How many units of each product must be sold to earn a total profit of $150,000 per month?
(e) Assume the sales mix changes to X = 20 percent; Y = 30 percent; and Z = 50 percent. What will be the new total breakeven quantity for the firm, in terms of sales revenue and units of the three products?

Cases

C 8–1   Comparing Profit Patterns

Annett Corporation has a plant that can be operated with fixed costs of $20,000 per month. The facilities can be used to produce a product that sells for $10 per unit with variable costs of $7 per unit. The same product has been produced and sold for $10 per unit by Bennett Company, a competitor. The following monthly operating results have been achieved by Bennett Company:

Month	Sales	Net Income
1	$ 60,000	($10,000)
2	100,000	10,000
3	120,000	20,000
4	80,000	0

Required:
(a) Using the high–low method, derive a cost function for Bennett Company.
(b) Use graphs to compare the potential profit patterns of the two companies.
(c) Over what activity range will Annett Corporation be more profitable than Bennett Company? Show an algebraic solution.
(d) If average monthly demand for both companies is 9,000 units, which company will tend to be more profitable? Why?
(e) Should Annett Corporation consider reducing its price to $9? Why or why not?
(f) Which company would be more likely to suffer if a price-cutting war developed between the two? Discuss fully.

C 8–2   Cost–Volume–Profit Relationships

State what assumptions are being made about the behavior of costs, revenues, volume, and profit in each of the following statements. If any of the statements show faulty logic, explain why.

(a) "We went into the red last year because the whole industry was in a recession and everyone was cutting prices to keep their heads above water—but a lot of us got half-drowned anyway."
(b) "Our quarterly net income chart always looks like a roller-coaster ride."
(c) "Too many of our trucks went out on the road less than half-full last month. If we achieve at least a 50 percent load on every truck this month, we'll break even for sure."
(d) "We sold slightly more in total volume this year. Dollar sales were up, too. But profits were off. It must have been because people stopped buying our top-of-the-line model and settled for the less fancy ones."
(e) "Our sales forecast was only 5 percent below our actual sales, which is encouraging. Our contribution margin ratio was pretty close to the estimated amount of 25 percent. But profits still went down."

C 8–3   Cost–Volume–Profit Proposals

Bradman Company's single product production facility can produce 60,000 units per month. Over the last two years, demand has been reasonably consistent but the plant has run at 75 percent of capacity (45,000 units). Analysis of production and distribution costs at this capacity showed the following:

	Cost per Unit
Materials	$ 2
Labor	4
Factory Overhead	8
Selling and Administration	4
	$18

Factory overhead cost includes $2 per unit of variable items. The selling and administration costs are all fixed except for sales commissions, which are 10 percent of sales revenues. The product has been selling for $20 per unit.

The Marketing Division proposes to spend $20,000 per month on a promotion campaign that is forecast to generate an additional 10,000 units of monthly sales. However, the Assistant Controller, Mr. Stan Ford, argues that this is not desirable because the 10,000 units will provide only enough contribution to cover the cost of the promotion.

Mr. Ford favors the alternative proposal of the Production Manager, Mr. Lee Land, which would involve replacing some manual operations with automated equipment. Labor costs of $2 per unit would be avoided, but leasing the equipment would cost $30,000 per month. In addition, Mr. Ford proposes to put all salespeople on fixed salaries (a total of $60,000 per month) instead of paying them a 10 percent commission. Mr. Ford reasons that this will save $4 per unit ($2 in labor costs and $2 in sales commissions), which is more than the average cost of $2 per unit for the additional outlays. Sales volume would not change under this proposal.

Required:

The Controller, Mr. Burke Lee, requests a report on these proposals. Prepare this report making use of cost–volume–profit analysis to demonstrate the relative merits of each proposal. Comment also on the merits (or otherwise) of Mr. Ford's analysis.

C 8–4   Cost–Volume–Profit Analysis

The Nestle-Inn Motel has three separate operations—motel, coffee shop, and bar. An income statement for a typical 30-day month follows:

	Motel	Coffee Shop	Bar	Total
Sales Revenue	$120,000	$60,000	$20,000	$200,000
Cost of Goods Sold	—	$20,000	$10,000	$ 30,000
Wages and Salaries	$ 40,000	20,000	5,000	65,000
Other Direct Costs	10,000	5,000	1,000	16,000
	$ 50,000	$45,000	$16,000	$111,000
Margin	$ 70,000	$15,000	$ 4,000	$ 89,000
Indirect Costs	$ 30,000	$15,000	$ 5,000	$ 50,000
Net Income	$ 40,000	$ 0	$(1,000)	$ 39,000

Analysis of records shows that the average customer spends amounts equal to one-half and one-sixth of his motel bill in the coffee shop and bar respectively. Because the cost of goods sold includes only purchased foodstuffs and beverages, it varies directly with sales volume. The number of employees working in the motel varies from day to day depending on the occupancy rates. However, the coffee shop and bar employees are permanent staff on monthly salaries. The present staff could operate the coffee shop and bar for all levels of occupancy of the motel up to 100 percent full. The direct costs are fixed monthly charges that are needed for each of the three separate operations. The indirect costs are likewise fixed and include managers' salaries, insurance, lighting, depreciation, and property taxes. In the preceding statement, they were allocated on the basis of sales revenues.

The motel has a total of 200 rooms; the average room rental is $25 per night. Management is concerned about the apparently unprofitable operations of the bar and coffee shop. They believe the company is not breaking even on these two operations. A proposal has been made to lease the bar and coffee shop to an independent food and beverage service operation for $24,000 per month ($6,000 for the bar and $18,000 for the coffee shop). All direct fixed costs of these operations would continue, but the food service company would use its own employees. The total indirect fixed costs of the entire operation would also be unchanged.

Required:
(a) Use the techniques of cost–volume–profit analysis to determine the breakeven volume of the whole operation as it is presently being operated. State fully any assumptions you have made.
(b) Evaluate the proposals to lease the bar and coffee shop. Consider whether either, both, or neither should be leased.
(c) If the average room rate were reduced to $24 and the occupancy rate increased to 90 percent, what effect would this have on the total profit performance of the operation? State clearly what assumptions you have made.

Problems

P 8–1   Breakeven Analysis—Single Product

Cavanaugh Corporation manufactures a single product with the following price and cost data:

Sales Price	$20 per unit
Variable Costs	$15 per unit
Fixed Costs	$250,000 per year
Capacity	80,000 units per year

Required:
(a) Prepare a cost–volume–profit graph for all operating levels from 20,000 to 80,000 units per year.
(b) Prepare a profit–volume graph for the same operating levels.
(c) Derive and interpret the solution to the breakeven condition from the two graphs prepared in parts (a) and (b).

(d) Prepare a separate cost–volume–profit graph to show the effect of (1) raising the sales price to $25 and (2) lowering the sales price to $17.50.

(e) Derive and interpret the solutions for the breakeven condition under the revised circumstances in part (d).

(f) What is the effect and the significance of the "20,000 to 80,000 units" operating range in this analysis?

(g) What might be expected to change in this problem (1) beyond 80,000 units per year and (2) below 20,000 units per year?

(h) How many units must be sold to earn a 10 percent return on sales?

P 8–2   Breakeven Analysis—Review of Basic Calculations— Single Product

For each of the following independent situations, fill in the missing information.

	Units Sold	Sales Revenue	Variable Cost	Contribution Margin per Unit	Fixed Cost	Net Income
a.	18,000	$162,000	$ 90,000	$	$40,000	$
b.	16,000	———	80,000	6	———	18,000
c.	———	100,000	———	8	20,000	20,000
d.	6,000	90,000	———	——	36,000	(6,000)
e.	———	180,000	108,000	12	———	12,000
f.	———	———	25,000	5	80,000	(5,000)

P 8–3   Cost–Volume–Profit Analysis—Single Product

Christiansen Corporation has prepared the following estimates of the costs of producing and distributing its product in a proposed new facility.

	Total	Per Unit
Materials	$ 80,000	$4.00
Direct Labor	20,000	1.00
Manufacturing Overhead	30,000	1.50
Selling Expense	15,000	.75
Administrative Expense	5,000	.25
	$150,000	$7.50

These estimates are based on forecast volume of 20,000 units per month. The sales price is expected to be $8 per unit. The new facility can handle a maximum of 30,000 units per month. Administrative expense is all fixed. Manufacturing overhead includes $20,000 of fixed items. Selling expense includes 50¢ per unit of variable items.

Required:
(a) What is the contribution margin per unit? What is the contribution margin ratio?

(b) What is the net income (loss) at the forecast sales volume?

(c) What is the breakeven volume in terms of sales revenue?

(d) What effect has the $7.50 unit cost on the overall profitability of company operations? Does it mean that every unit produced and sold will earn 50¢ profit?

(e) What sales volume (in units) is necessary to generate a profit of $25,000 per month?

(f) What amount of sales revenue will provide a profit equal to 10 percent of sales?

(g) What is the maximum profit possible under the original conditions?

P 8–4   Cost–Volume–Profit Analysis

FIGURE A

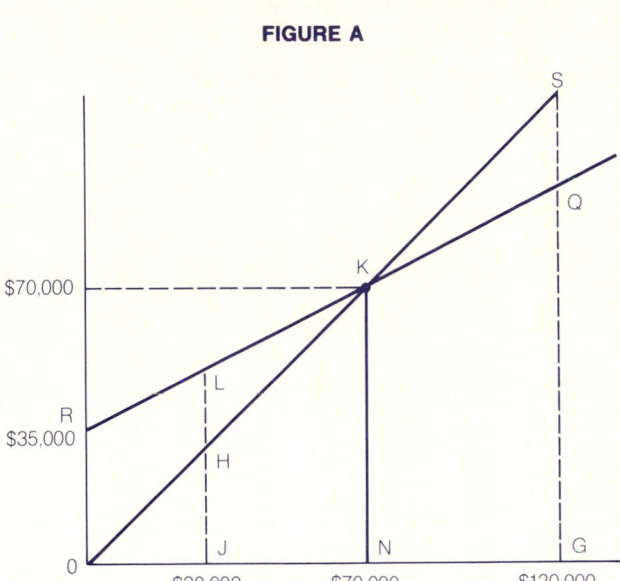

FIGURE B

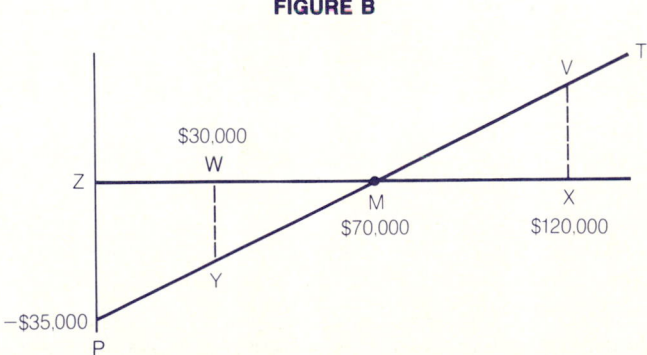

Figure A and Figure B relate to data for the Perkins Corporation. The horizontal axis represents the activity level in terms of sales dollars.

Required:

(a) What is the breakeven quantity? Why can't it be expressed in units from the data contained in the diagrams?

(b) What is the contribution margin ratio? How is the line, PT, in Figure B related to this ratio?

(c)   What do the points J and G, in Figure A, and W and X, in Figure B, probably represent? Why are they important in this type of analysis?

(d)   What are the fixed costs in this case? Explain them numerically and in terms of points and/or lines on these diagrams.

(e)   What does the distance, VX, in Figure B represent? Explain it numerically and show how it is related to Figure A.

P 8–5   Cost–Volume–Profit Analysis—Alternative Cost Structures— Single Product

Bartlett Company manufactures and sells a single type of product. It is considering three alternative methods of conducting its operations, each of which will affect the relative amounts of annual fixed and variable costs.

	Alternative A	Alternative B	Alternative C
Fixed Costs:			
Manufacturing	$160,000	$140,000	$50,000
Selling	$ 50,000	$100,000	$50,000
Variable Costs (per unit):			
Manufacturing	$2	$3	$4
Selling	$2	$1	$2

This product's sales price is $10 per unit. Capacity limits under the three alternatives are: A—45,000 units; B—60,000 units; and C—50,000 units. Annual sales have averaged 40,000 units.

Required: (Answer each part independently, except where indicated.)

(a)   What would be the breakeven quantities under each of the three alternatives? Comment on these solutions.

(b)   If annual demand is not expected to exceed 30,000 units, which of the three alternatives will be preferable? Why?

(c)   If the sales price is increased to $12 per unit, how will the three alternatives be affected with regard to breakeven quantity? Sales revenue? Assume that average annual sales volume will continue relatively unchanged.

(d)   Consider the same price increase as in part (c), but in addition, assume that sales volume is expected to increase by 10,000 units. Comment on the relative effects of these changes on each of the three alternatives.

(e)   Returning to the original data, assume that the market for this product is very uncertain due to the introduction of several competing products. If the sales price is left unchanged, which of the three alternative cost structures will be preferred by a management that adopts a conservative approach aimed at minimizing losses should demand fall off considerably? Why?

(f)   If the future demand for the product is likely to be as much as 50,000 units, which alternative would be preferable, assuming the sales price remains unchanged? Why?

P 8–6   Cost–Volume–Profit Analysis

Solovay Corporation had the following operating results for the first three months of 19X8:

	Sales	Net Income (Loss)
January	$ 800,000	($60,000)
February......	900,000	(30,000)
March	1,200,000	60,000

During this period, the company's sales prices did not vary. Total fixed costs and the variable cost per unit of output remained constant. Production exactly equaled sales in each month and there were no beginning or ending inventories.

Required:
(a) Determine (1) the contribution margin ratio and (2) the amount of fixed cost per month.
(b) What is the breakeven sales level?
(c) April sales revenues are forecast at $1,500,000. What will net income be if all costs and prices remain unchanged?
(d) Show two separate and independent changes that will allow the breakeven quantity to be reduced to a sales volume of $750,000.
(e) Why can't the breakeven quantity be expressed in units in this question?
(f) Is this problem a single product situation? Why or why not?
(g) What simplifying assumptions are implicit in all of the preceding analysis and problems?

P 8–7   Sensitivity Analysis—Single Product

Wendt Corporation produces a single product that sells for $20 per unit. The average unit cost is $22 at the 16,000 unit level, $17 per at the 32,000 unit level.

Required: (Answer each part independently.)
(a) What is the contribution margin ratio?
(b) What is the breakeven quantity in units? What is it in revenue?
(c) Sales revenues are forecast to increase by $100,000 in the coming year. What effect will this have on net income?
(d) By how many units must the sales volume increase if profits are to be increased by $20,000?
(e) Wendt plans an advertising campaign that could increase sales by $80,000 per year. How much can be spent on this campaign without causing profit to decrease?
(f) A one-time order for 5,000 units can be obtained from a discount store. What price should be quoted if the company wishes to earn $10,000 on this one-time transaction?
(g) If fixed costs can be reduced by $40,000 per year, by how much may variable costs change in order to allow the breakeven quantity to remain the same as in the original situation?

P 8-8   Sensitivity Analysis—Single Product

The 19X7 income statement of Hamill Company was as follows:

Sales	$200,000
Less: Variable Costs	120,000
Contribution Margin	$ 80,000
Less: Fixed Costs	60,000
Net Income	$ 20,000

Consider each of the following separate situations independently.

Required:

(a) Marketing management proposes increasing advertising by $10,000 per year to achieve an increase in sales revenue of $40,000. Should this proposal be accepted or rejected? Why?

(b) Production management proposes a rearrangement of facilities that will increase fixed costs by $20,000 but will decrease unit variable costs by one-sixth. If sales volume is unaffected, should this proposal be accepted or rejected? Why?

(c) If both the marketing and the production proposals are considered simultaneously and the sales revenue does increase by $40,000, should the resulting combined project be accepted or rejected? Why?

(d) Assume that neither of the preceding proposals were accepted. In 19X8, sales revenue increased by 30 percent and net income increased by 100 percent. If all input prices and the output sales prices were constant, how efficient is operating management? Why?

(e) What sales level will be necessary to allow a 50 percent increase in profit if, under a rearrangement of operations, variable costs per unit increase by one-sixth and fixed costs decrease by $18,000?

P 8-9   Sensitivity Analysis—Comparison of Two Corporations

Stabler Corporation and Morton Company produce the same product, but have significantly different cost structures due to organizational differences, different sales methods, and varying ages of equipment and facilities. Comparative income statements for the two corporations for the 19X3 year were as follows:

	Stabler	Morton
Sales ($100 per unit)	$200,000	$200,000
Less: Variable Costs	150,000	100,000
Contribution Margin	$ 50,000	$100,000
Less: Fixed Costs	25,000	75,000
Net Income	$ 25,000	$ 25,000

Required:

(a) What is the contribution margin per unit and the contribution margin ratio for each company?

(b) What is the breakeven quantity in units and revenue for each company?

(c) Based on your answers to parts (a) and (b), in which company would you rather own shares if the forecast is for (1) increasing sales levels, or (2) stable or decreasing sales levels?

(d) If the industry sales price increases to $120 in 19X4 and the variable costs increase at the same percentage rate, what profit will each company earn, assuming that the sales volume (1) remains unchanged and (2) increases to 2,500 units.

(e) If the market softened and sales volume fell to 1,000 units, which company would be better off, assuming total fixed costs and unit variable costs remained the same? Why?

P 8–10   Sensitivity Analysis—Alternative Products

The manager of Namath's Department Store is considering alternative uses of one area of floor space. One alternative is to devote the area to packaged panty hose and the other is to devote it to electric popcorn poppers. The following data has been gathered on these two alternatives:

	Panty Hose	Popcorn Poppers
Sales Price (per unit)	$4	$25
Variable Cost (per unit)	$2	$15
Forecast Monthly Sales (units)	4,000	1,000
Shelf Space Available (square feet)	200	200
Maximum Possible Inventory (units)	2,000	200
Fixed Costs (per month)	$7,500	$7,500

Required:
(a) Which product has the higher contribution margin per unit?
(b) Which product has the higher contribution margin ratio?
(c) Which product has the higher contribution margin per square foot of shelf space?
(d) Which of the two products should be carried? Why?
(e) If the company desires to maintain an inventory turnover rate of four times per month, which product would best satisfy this requirement? Why?

P 8–11   Sensitivity Analysis—Alternative Product Decisions

Payton Corporation, which manufactures and sells four independent products, has prepared the following income statements for 19X6.

	Alpha	Beta	Gamma	Delta	Total
Sales	$20,000	$36,000	$25,000	$45,000	$126,000
Cost of Sales	12,000	20,000	20,000	37,000	89,000
Gross Profit	$ 8,000	$16,000	$ 5,000	$ 8,000	$ 37,000
Operating Costs	4,000	2,000	8,000	5,000	19,000
Net Income	$ 4,000	$14,000	($ 3,000)	$ 3,000	$ 18,000
Sales	$20,000	$36,000	$25,000	$45,000	$126,000
Variable Cost	8,000	18,000	15,000	35,000	76,000
Contribution Margin	$12,000	$18,000	$10,000	$10,000	$ 50,000
Fixed Cost	8,000	4,000	13,000	7,000	32,000
Net Income	$ 4,000	$14,000	($ 3,000)	$ 3,000	$ 18,000
Unit Sales........................	2,000	1,800	1,000	5,000	—
Variable Manufacturing Cost	$3	$9	$10	$6	—
Variable Operating Cost per Unit	$1	$1	$ 5	$1	—

All fixed and variable costs have been identified with one or other of the four products. There are no other costs.

Required: (Answer each part independently.)
(a) What will be the effect on net income if product Gamma is discontinued? Should it be discontinued? Why?
(b) If product Gamma is discontinued and has the additional effect of causing 300 units of sales of Alpha to be lost, what is the total effect on net income?
(c) If the sales price for Gamma is reduced to $20 and sales increase to 1,000 units, would this result be acceptable? Why?
(d) Which product was the most profitable in 19X6? Explain your answer.
(e) Some of the productive capacity used for product Gamma can be used to allow more Betas to be produced. To do this, only 800 Gammas will be made (and the sales price will be $26), but 2000 Betas will then be available for sale at $18.50. Should this change be made? Why?
(f) Additional output of Betas is possible if overtime pay is authorized and extra equipment is rented. Variable manufacturing costs will increase to $12 per unit *for the additional output* and fixed costs will go up by $3,000. How many additional units of Beta must be sold at the prevailing price to make this worthwhile?
(g) Consider the same situation as in part (f), except that the increased variable costs will apply to *all* output, including the 1,800 Betas already being produced. How many units must be sold to make the change feasible?
(h) If the price of Deltas is increased to $10 to compensate for an $8,000 increase in fixed costs, how many units must be sold in order to earn the same $3,000 net income?

P 8–12   Sensitivity Analysis—Cost Structure Analysis

Staubuch Company manufactures and distributes a single product. The following estimates have been made of the costs of operating at the upper and lower limits of the company's relevant range of output.

	Lower	Upper
Sales Volume (units)	10,000	20,000
Sales Revenues	$350,000	$700,000
Production Costs:		
Materials	$100,000	$200,000
Direct Labor	80,000	160,000
Indirect Labor	42,000	62,000
Power and Heat	15,000	25,000
Depreciation	24,000	24,000
Other	12,000	14,000
Operating Costs:		
Salaries and Wages	60,000	90,000
Advertising	10,000	10,000
Other	45,000	60,000
	$388,000	$645,000

Required:

(a) Examine each cost item in the preceding schedule and determine its cost behavior pattern. Prepare a list which divides these costs into fixed, variable, and mixed categories. Use the high–low method.

(b) How much is total fixed cost?

(c) What is the total cost function? Show it graphically, indicating the range to which it applies.

(e) What is the breakeven quantity in sales units and in sales revenue?

(f) What is the maximum profit possible under the preceding constraints?

(g) If 16,000 units are sold, what will net income be?

(h) What effect will a 20 percent increase in variable costs have on the breakeven quantity and on net income at the 16,000 unit level?

(i) If fixed costs are reduced by 20 percent *and* sales price also declines by 20 percent, what will be the effect (1) on the breakeven quantity and (2) on net income at the 16,000 unit level?

(j) If sales are forecast to increase to 25,000 units after a price reduction to $32 per unit, what would you recommend? Why?

P 8–13 Sensitivity Analysis—Multiple Outputs

A Simpson Company plant is divided between the production of two items, Os and Js. The following data are forecast for 19X9:

	O	J	Total
Forecast Sales	50,000	100,000	150,000
Sales Price	$6	$12	
Variable Costs	2	9	
Contribution Margin	$4	$3	
Fixed Costs	$120,000	$240,000	$360,000

Required: (Answer all parts independently except where indicated.)

(a) Can the breakeven quantity be computed *separately* for each product? If so, calculate each breakeven quantity.

(b) What are the breakeven quantities of the firm if the forecast sales mix is in effect?

(c) Compare your answers to parts (a) and (b). What explanation can you give for the respective answers?

(d) By spending an extra $40,000 on advertising for Product O, its sales can be increased to 75,000 units. However, sales of Product J will be reduced by 10,000 units. If all other prices and costs remain the same, should this advertising be undertaken? Why?

(e) The company is considering discontinuing one of the two products. All fixed facilities are completely interchangeable between the two products with no effect on costs and sales prices. Under these circumstances,

(1) Which product will have the lower breakeven quantity in units? In sales revenue?

(2) Assuming that the potential sales for each product produced separately are 120,000 of Product O, and 150,000 of Product J, which product should be manufactured? Why?

(3) If the maximum productive capacity is 110,000 of Product O and 150,000 of Product J, which product should be produced? Why?

(4) Combine the assumptions in parts (2) and (3). Which product should be produced? Why?

P 8–14   Sensitivity Analysis—Multiple Outputs

The Honest Cheetahs are a new franchise in a professional sports league. Management is establishing its ticket pricing structure. Three categories of seating are available: (1) courtside, (2) regular, and (3) peanut gallery. Stadium capacity and proposed prices are as follows:

	Capacity	Ticket Prices
Courtside	5,000	$10.00
Regular	30,000	$ 7.50
Peanut Gallery	15,000	$ 5.00
	50,000	

Forecasts show that the average per game attendance will usually provide for occupancy rates as follows:

Courtside—60% of capacity
Regular—83⅓% of capacity
Peanut Gallery—80% of capacity

Customers spend an average of $10 for food, drink, and souvenirs. The club obtains a 20 percent commission on all such sales.

Visiting teams receive a payment equal to 20 percent of gross ticket sales. Fixed costs per game (for salaries, depreciation, insurance, and so on) amount to $211,750. Variable costs are $1.50 per customer.

Required: (Answer each part independently except where indicated.)

(a) If the forecast of average attendance is correct, what will be the profit or loss per game? Explain your answer also in terms of contribution margin per average customer.

(b) If the attendance mix in the forecast average attendance is constant, what will be the breakeven attendance at a single game?

(c) If reducing *all* ticket prices by $1.50 will guarantee a full house for every game, is this reduction a better alternative than the attendance now forecast at the original prices?

(d) What is the breakeven attendance if the $1.50 price reduction is put into effect and the attendance mix is still the same as forecast?

(e) If the franchise pays $1,500,000 (over a 50-game season) to buy the contracts of several star players, 90 percent attendance could be guaranteed for all sections of the stadium. Should this be done? Why or why not?

(f) The original attendance mix forecast proves to be incorrect. The average attendance is courtside 2,500, regular 24,000, and peanut gallery 13,500. How will this change affect average net income per game? Explain your answer also in terms of the contribution margin per "average customer."

P 8–15   Sensitivity Analysis—Multiple Outputs

Lee Corporation manufactures and distributes two different grades of its product, regular and premium. Variable costs per unit of output are as follows:

	Regular	Premium
Direct Materials	$ 4.00	$ 5.50
Direct Labor	4.00	6.00
Factory Overhead	3.00	4.50
Sales Commissions	5.00	7.00
Administrative Cost	2.00	2.00
	$18.00	$25.00

Regular units sell for $25, premium units for $35. Fixed costs are $60,000 per month for manufacturing items and $20,000 per month for selling and administrative costs. Production and sales (in units) for the first months of 19X7 were as follows:

	Regular	Premium	Total
January	7,000	3,000	10,000
February	5,000	5,000	10,000
March	3,000	7,500	10,000
	15,000	15,000	30,000

Required:
(a) What was the net income for each of the three months? Comment on your answer in view of the fact that *total* sales were at the same 10,000-unit level in each month.

(b) Sales commissions are 20 percent of sales revenues. Comment on what appears to be happening to the sales mix. Is this result good for the company? Why or why not?

(c) Taking each month *separately,* what would have been the breakeven quantity for each month? What assumptions did you make in arriving at your answer?

(d) What would have been the monthly breakeven quantity for the three months to-gether? What assumptions did you make in arriving at your answer?

(e) The company wishes to earn a $25,000 profit in April. What sales volume will be necessary to achieve this? What assumptions did you make in arriving at your answer?

(f) Assume that the February sales mix still applies. Should the company change its sales commission from a 20 percent of gross revenue basis to a fixed monthly amount of $72,000? What assumptions did you make in arriving at your answer?

P 8–16   Sensitivity Analysis—Multiple Outputs

Arlette Corporation makes and sells three different varieties of women's exotic sleepwear: the Baby Doll, the Big Momma, and the Grannie. Details of product prices and variable costs are as follows:

	Baby Doll	Big Momma	Grannie
Direct Materials	$ 2	$ 5	$ 6
Direct Labor	4	6	6
Factory Overhead	2	3	3
Selling Expenses	2	1	1
Administrative Expenses	1	1	1
	$11	$16	$17
Sales Prices	$20	$22	$24

Monthly fixed costs amount to $71,000. During the previous year, average monthly sales of $239,800 have been distributed as follows:

Baby Doll	3,300 items (30%)
Big Momma	5,500 items (50%)
Grannie	2,200 items (20%)
	11,000 items

For January, 19X8, total sales were forecast at 12,000 items. Actual sales were 12,500 items—2,000 Baby Dolls, 8,000 Big Mommas, and 2,500 Grannies.

Required: (Answer each part independently except where indicated.)

(a) What was the breakeven quantity during 19X7? What assumptions did you make in deriving your answer?

(b) If the 19X7 sales mix remained constant during January of 19X8 and if the total sales forecast had been achieved, what would be the net income for that month? Assume that all costs behaved as expected.

(c) What was the actual net income for January?

(d) Comment on the relationship between the actual January net income and the forecast amount. Emphasize the fact that total sales were higher than the forecast amount, in terms of both sales revenue and number of items.

(e) Starting in February, the company plans a special advertising promotion of the Baby Doll line that will cost $7,500 per month for the next three months. The promotion is expected to increase sales of the Baby Doll line to 5,000 per month (from the 19X7 monthly average). If sales of the other two lines are unaffected, should this promotion be undertaken?

(f) Refer to part (e). By how much might the sales of the other lines be reduced and still allow the advertising promotion to be worthwhile? What assumptions did you make in answering this question?

P 8–17   Sensitivity Analysis—Multiple Outputs

Vantress Corporation manufactures and distributes residential and industrial air conditioning systems. During 19X4, sales and net income per quarter have fluctuated considerably. In addition, the Residential Systems Division has not earned a positive return after all costs have been allocated to the two divisions. Quarterly income statements (amounts in thousands) were as follows:

Quarter	Sales		Costs		Net Income	
	Residential	Industrial	Residential	Industrial	Residential	Industrial
1	$100	$300	$103	$254	($3)	$46
2	120	200	127	185	(7)	15
3	140	140	151	140	(11)	0
4	120	240	124	212	(4)	28
Total	$480	$880	$505	$791	($25)	$89

Analysis of costs over this period showed that the following relationships were applicable:

Fixed Costs per Quarter:
Directly Traced to Divisions:
Residential $10,000
Industrial $20,000 $30,000

Corporate Fixed Costs per Quarter
(allocated on basis of sales revenues
per quarter) $72,000

Variable Costs (per dollar of sales revenue):

	Residential	Industrial
Manufacturing	$0.40	$0.45
Selling and Administrative	0.35	0.15
	$0.75	$0.60

Required:
(a) Prepare an analysis of quarterly costs and revise the quarterly income statements to incorporate a contribution margin approach.
(b) What statements can be made about the quarterly breakeven sales volume for (1) the firm as a whole and (2) each separate division?
(c) Assuming that its 19X4 performance is indicative of its future earnings, should the Residential Systems Division be eliminated? Why or why not?
(d) If the prices for residential systems are reduced by 20 percent, sales volume for that division is predicted to increase 50 percent over the quarterly average for the previous year. This will be accompanied by a reduction of 33⅓ percent in the rate of variable costs of the residential division, but there will be no change in the total amount of divisional or corporate fixed costs. Should this change be adopted? Why or why not?
(e) How does the presence of corporate fixed costs affect any cost–volume–profit analysis in this type of multiple output situation? Does the allocation of these costs on the basis of sales revenue simplify the analysis, complicate it, or have no effect?

P 8–18   Cost–Volume–Profit Analysis—Income Tax Considerations

Ferguson Corporation makes and distributes a single product that has the following cost and price information:

Sales Price per Unit..................... $40
Variable Manufacturing Cost per Unit...... $24
Variable Selling Cost per Unit $6
Fixed Manufacturing Cost per Year $90,000
Fixed Selling Cost per Year $30,000

Required: (Answer each part separately except where indicated.)
(a)   What is the breakeven quantity in sales volume and in sales revenue, ignoring any income taxes?

(b)   Assume a 40 percent corporate tax rate on all net income. What are the breakeven quantities now?

(c)   How many units must be sold to earn a $48,000 *before-tax* net income?

(d)   How many units must be sold to earn a $48,000 *after-tax* net income?

(e)   On an after-tax basis, would it be better to sell 25,000 units at the regular $40 price or 30,000 units at $38 per unit?

(f)   On an after-tax basis, would it be better to sell 25,000 units at the regular $40 price or spend $40,000 on additional advertising that will enable 30,000 units to be sold at the $40 price?

(g)   At the 30,000 unit level of sales, by how much must variable manufacturing cost be reduced from the original $24 amount to earn $144,000 after taxes, assuming the $40 price is retained?

P 8–19   Cost–Volume–Profit Analysis—Income Tax Considerations

Auerbach Enterprises operates food and drink concessions at a local sports arena. Recent operations have produced the following results:

Variable Costs per Sales Dollar:
Cost of Merchandise	$	0.50
Vendor's Commission	$	0.20
Fixed Costs per Event	$7,200.00	
Income Tax Rate	40%	

Required: (Answer each part independently except where indicated.)
(a)   What is the breakeven sales revenue for each event?

(b)   Average sales per event were $36,000 during the last season. What amount of after-tax income was earned?

(c)   What daily sales revenue would be necessary to earn $3,600 after taxes?

(d)   At the average daily sales level of $36,000, would it be more profitable after taxes to pay vendors the 20 percent commission on sales or to pay them a fixed daily amount of $8,000?

(e)   At what sales level would it be equally profitable to use either the fixed commission arrangement or the variable amount method?

(f)   Sales prices are to be raised 20 percent on all items to compensate for a 10 percent increase in the cost of merchandise and an $800 increase per event in fixed costs. If the average sales volume remains the same as it was for the previous season when sales revenue averaged $36,000 per event, what will be the new after-tax net income?

P 8–20   Cost–Volume–Profit Analysis—Inventory on Hand—Single Product

Weiner Corporation has 5,000 units of its product on hand at December 31, 19X7. These units were produced during 19X7 when variable manufacturing costs were $8 per unit and variable selling costs were $2 per unit. Fixed costs in 19X7 amounted to

$120,000 for manufacturing items and $30,000 for selling and administrative items. In 19X7, the selling price was $15 per unit and sales totaled 45,000 units.

Sales for 19X8 have been forecast at 50,000 units. The sales price will be increased to $18 per unit. All fixed costs will remain the same, but the variable cost per unit will increase by $1 for both manufacturing and selling and administrative items. The company uses the variable cost model (rather than the full absorption cost model) to determine periodic income.

Required: (Answer each part separately except where indicated.)

(a) How much income did Weiner Corporation report in 19X7?

(b) How many units had to be produced and sold in 19X7 to break even, assuming there were zero inventories on January 1 and December 31 of 19X7?

(c) What will the breakeven sales volume be in 19X8? How do the 5,000 units in inventory affect this calculation?

(d) If 19X8 sales volume is exactly equal to the breakeven quantity calculated in part (c), what net income will the company report in 19X8? Comment.

(e) What will be the reported income for 19X8 if the sales forecast of 50,000 units is correct and 45,000 units are produced?

(f) The company sets $90,000 as its 19X8 profit goal. How many units should be *produced* to achieve this goal, assuming that an ending inventory of 8,000 units is planned and that 5,000 units are on hand at the beginning of the year. Show two solutions—one based on replacement cost calculations and a second based on historical cost data. Compare and comment on the two solutions.

9

INCREMENTAL ANALYSIS FOR SHORT-RUN DECISION MAKING

LEARNING OBJECTIVES

After studying Chapter 9, you should be able to:

1. Define sunk cost, committed cost, avoidable cost, and opportunity cost. Explain how these costs affect short-run decision analysis.
2. Calculate whether or not special sales orders should be accepted.
3. Calculate whether or not damaged and obsolete inventories should be disposed of under irregular conditions.
4. Calculate how much the volume of normally priced goods must increase to make up for losses suffered as a result of selling loss leaders.
5. Calculate whether joint outputs can more profitably be sold at the splitoff point or after further processing.
6. Calculate whether firms should produce certain components themselves or purchase them from outside suppliers.
7. Calculate whether a company product line, division, or department should be retained or eliminated.
8. Calculate the most profitable way to allocate scarce resources to competing products.
9. Decide whether a firm should use manual or automated production methods and, in general, whether items of equipment should be retained or replaced.
10. Determine the correct transfer price at which one company sub-unit should sell its outputs to another unit of the same company.

SHORT-RUN DECISION ANALYSIS

In Chapter 7, the typical decision process was outlined. This process involves selecting actions to attain objectives. During this selection process, the accounting system provides a method for measuring and evaluating the outcomes of alternative actions. Accounting information also helps managers set goals and monitor the feedback and control system that reports on actual performance.

As managers evaluate alternatives, they must assemble the data needed to apply the *decision rules* being employed. Moreover, these decision rules must be appropriate for each problem—they must allow managers to select those actions that will help achieve company goals. For example, if cost minimization is a goal, then decision rules must provide solutions whose effects are to minimize costs, rather than, say, to maximize output.

A **problem** may be defined as *a state of nonconformity between actual and planned performance.* Identifying problems is the responsibility of managers in the decision centers where the problems arise. Decision analysis must be based on a correct specification of the **problem space**—the nature of the problem, the relevant goals and decision criteria, the potential decision variables, the problem boundaries, and the "given" or fixed factors. Many decisions occur so repetitively and in such a uniform pattern that they may not seem to be problems at all. Meeting payrolls, paying trade accounts, billing customers, granting credit, and acquiring inventories are such routine problems that decision analysis tends to be automatic and programmable.

More challenging problems that occur less frequently and on an irregular basis involve such matters as idle plant and labor capacity, inventory shortages or surpluses, equipment deterioration and breakdowns, cash flow imbalances, and cost or revenue variances. There are even less frequent, or nonrecurring problems that are often more comprehensive in scope, areas of impact, and the number of decision variables involved. Typical examples are product line selection, fixed asset acquisition policies, long-term financing, and marketing and production strategies.

This chapter is concerned with the second category—relatively infrequent but recurring short-run problems. The decision models needed for these problems are usually easy to specify because the number of decision variables is small, the decision criteria are relatively simple, and the search for alternatives is limited by time and cost constraints. The decision criteria most often used are *cost minimization, profit maximization,* and *contribution maximization.*

For example, if several methods of manufacturing a product component are being compared, a simple decision rule would be to choose the method that is least costly. Comparing the alternative methods requires only basic mathematical calculations. However, the critical part of such an analysis involves deciding *which* costs of each alternative are to be considered and how to measure them. The essential problem is to identify the costs that are relevant in each decision situation and to assess their future amount. This **relevant cost concept** will be discussed more fully later in the chapter.

When the outcomes of alternatives are assumed to be **deterministic** (that is, certain to occur), choosing among these alternatives according to maximization or minimization criteria is easy. For example, assume that X and Y are comparable choices. If alternative X will cost $2,000 and alternative Y will cost $2,500, it is clear that alternative X should be selected.

COST TERMINOLOGY IN DECISION ANALYSIS

Accounting terminology has become overloaded with words and phrases describing different types of costs. Many of these are encountered in discussions of cost information for decision making. This text will acknowledge the existence of such terms, but minimize the use of those which have conflicting or overlapping meanings.

The following cost classification systems have already been introduced:

1. *Unit, total,* and *average* costs
2. *Product* and *period* costs
3. *Fixed* and *variable* costs
4. *Expired* and *unexpired* costs
5. *Direct* and *indirect* costs
6. *Variable* and *full absorption* costs
7. *Marginal* and *incremental* costs
8. *Materials, labor,* and *overhead* costs
9. *Acquisition* and *replacement* costs
10. *Common processing* and *separable* costs

The only additional cost terms that will be used regularly in this chapter are sunk cost, committed cost, avoidable cost, and opportunity cost.

Sunk costs are the acquisition costs of resources that have already been acquired and are usually still available for use or disposition—for example, the purchase prices of fixed assets that have been acquired or the manufacturing costs of inventory items that have been produced. The most important characteristic of sunk costs is that they have already been incurred. Because they cannot be altered by any future action, they should not be directly involved in any decision analysis. However, they may have an indirect effect on certain decisions. Alternative cash flow and tax effects may result from the expensing of sunk costs through depreciation or as a result of converting inventories to cost of goods sold.

In the sense that they indicate whether or not additional alternatives should be sought, sunk costs may also indirectly influence many business decisions. If none of the alternatives under consideration can guarantee a return sufficient to recover sunk costs, then not even nominal capital maintenance is possible—the amount recoverable will not be enough to restore total net assets to their previous level on an historical cost basis. A better method of analysis provides for real capital maintenance by ensuring that at least one alternative will permit recovery of the current replacement cost of the resources that constitute sunk costs.

Committed costs are those costs that will be incurred during the period of decision analysis, regardless of the action chosen. Such costs are committed in the sense that once the decision to incur them has been made, they are unavoidable and invariant with regard to future decisions. Usually they are fixed costs, such as rentals, lease payments, advertising, contracted services, and certain types of salaries.

Avoidable costs (sometimes called escapable or discretionary costs) are those costs that can be avoided in the future as a result of managerial choices. Because management can choose not to incur them, avoidable costs must be treated as relevant costs when particular decision alternatives are compared. Examples of avoidable costs are (1) the current operating costs of a machine, when the decision is being made whether or not to replace that machine and (2) all the direct variable and fixed costs of running a sales outlet, when the decision is being made to continue operating the outlet or close it down.

Opportunity costs measure the resources foregone as a result of choosing one course of action in preference to the other available options. For example, a decision may be required whether to (1) sell a product in its present state for $10 or (2) process it further at an additional cost of $6 and then sell it for $15. In evaluating the second alternative, the opportunity cost of foregoing the first alternative is $10—the revenue lost by choosing not to sell the product in its present form. Likewise, in considering the merits of the first alternative, the opportunity cost of foregoing alternative two is $9 (revenue lost of $15, less cost avoided of $6). Costs incurred in processing the item to the point at which the decision is made are sunk costs and are therefore irrelevant to this particular decision.

EIGHT SHORT-RUN DECISION SITUATIONS

The rest of this chapter demonstrates the following short-run decision situations:

1. Should special sales orders be accepted or rejected?
2. At what stage in processing should a product be sold?
3. Should an item be manufactured or purchased from an outside supplier?
4. Should product lines, divisions, or departments be retained or eliminated?
5. How should scarce resources be allocated among competing products?
6. Should existing equipment be retained or replaced?
7. Should joint outputs be sold at the splitoff point or processed further?
8. How should prices be established when a company's operating units buy from and sell to each other?

These decisions can be made on either a *total* or an *incremental* basis. The simplest approach is to calculate the total cost, total profit, or total profit contribution before the impact of an alternative and compare this figure to the corresponding performance measure after the alternative is adopted. For example, to evaluate a proposal to change from one parts supplier to another, a company might first determine the total cost of purchasing and production using the present supplier, then compare this amount with the total cost that would be incurred if it switched to the new supplier. Multiple alternatives should be considered one at a time. For example, when deciding which of three new products to introduce, decision makers should consider the total profit contributions that would result from adding each of the products to the existing product line and compare it with each of the other two alternatives.

Most short-run decisions involve some form of **incremental analysis.** Incremental costs and revenues are those for which the amounts will change depending on which alternative is chosen. **The alternative selected should have the lowest incremental cost, or the highest incremental profit or contribution margin.** In deciding whether or not to switch parts suppliers, management would compare only the changes in costs between the present and proposed supply situations, excluding from the analysis any costs that will remain the same after the change in suppliers. To choose among three new products, decision makers should assess each product's incremental contribution to profit, leaving out of the calculation all profit contributions from existing products.

SALES VOLUME-RELATED DECISIONS

Acceptance of Incremental, Special, or Extra Sales Orders   Opportunities to increase sales volume sometimes arise under circumstances that differ slightly from the normal marketing pattern. Special orders, one-time quantity sales, and sales to foreign customers are typical examples. If the special transaction will not affect normal sales, the decision to accept or reject it can be based entirely on whether or not the transaction will make a contribution in excess of the incremental costs that it generates.

Example: Newcastle Corporation receives a special, one-time order from a large variety chain store for 50,000 units of a product that usually sells for $10 per unit. The chain store offers $7 per unit for this product, which it intends to feature in its Summer sale. Newcastle Corporation incurs $6 per unit in variable costs to manufacture each item, plus $2 per unit for variable selling costs. Total fixed manufacturing costs are $500,000. Other fixed costs amount to $250,000 per year. Productive capacity is 500,000 units annually and sales volume through normal sales outlets will be about 400,000 units this year. There is no surplus inventory on hand.

Solution: If the order is accepted, revenues will increase by $350,000 ($7 × 50,000). The incremental costs will be only $300,000 ($6 × 50,000)—the variable cost of producing the extra units, assuming that the normal selling costs of $2 per unit need not be incurred in this case. Therefore, the corporation will gain $50,000 ($350,000 − $300,000) by accepting the special order.

This is a qualified and short-run solution. It assumes that this transaction will not affect the product's future sales volume or selling price. However, Newcastle Corporation should avoid using contribution analysis for all of its sales and pricing decisions. Not every transaction that covers its direct and relevant costs is desirable. In this particular situation, a $7 sales price is acceptable because it is larger than the $6 incremental cost. But in the longer run, the company risks being unable to generate sufficient revenues from a $7 sales price to cover its $750,000 of annual fixed costs plus its variable selling costs on regular sales.

However, in the same situation, it would also be wrong to base the decision on a comparison between the $7 sales price and average full cost of $7.50 per unit, consisting of variable cost of $6 plus allocated fixed cost of $1.50 [($500,000 + $250,000) ÷ 50,000]. Such a comparison suggests that the special order should be rejected because a loss of 50¢ per unit ($7.00 − $7.50) is being incurred. The fault in this analysis is that the fixed costs of $750,000 are *committed costs* which will be incurred whether or not the order is accepted. In this case, the fixed costs should be ignored. The variable selling expenses are also disregarded, because they are *avoidable costs* in this special order situation. The only relevant items are the sales price of $7 per unit and the variable production costs of $6 per unit, both of which are directly influenced by the decision taken.

Disposing of Inventories Pricing decisions must take into account the relative marketability of inventories. Often, because of damage, obsolescence, or lack of demand, inventory items cannot foreseeably be sold through normal marketing channels or under normal operating conditions. In such cases, incremental analysis may be appropriate. Whether the items are sold normally or under irregular conditions, all prior costs of producing or acquiring the inventory are *sunk costs* for the purposes of this decision.

Example: Hall Company has on hand 10,000 units of a product that cannot be sold through regular sales outlets because it is an outmoded model. These items were produced at a total cost of $75,000 and would normally have been sold for $10 each. Three alternatives are being considered. The first is to sell the items to a scrap metal dealer for 50¢ each. The second is to repackage them at a cost of $12,000 and sell them as "novelty antiques" for $2 each. Finally, they could be disposed of at the city dump at a cost of $250.

Solution: Assuming these are the only possible alternatives, the most favorable action is the second one. Revenues of $20,000 will be received, and after $12,000 in repackaging costs are incurred, an incremental profit of $8,000 will be earned. This compares to only $5,000 realized from sale to a scrap metal dealer, and a negative return of $250 if the inventory is scrapped. The $75,000 original cost of the inventory can be ignored in making this decision, because it is a *sunk cost* that cannot be altered by any of the three alternatives. Admittedly these three options are not particularly attractive—none of them offers the possibility of recovering even the inventory's acquisition cost. The crucial point is that, for purposes of this decision, the only relevant amounts are the future incremental costs and revenues of these three actions.

This also is a qualified, short-run solution that should be resorted to only when inventories cannot be marketed normally. Moreover, an *opportunity cost* may be involved in alternative two, because the $12,000 outlay needed to repackage the items will probably have to be diverted from other uses in the firm. Any contribution lost as a result of that diversion of funds would reduce the incremental profit from the second alternative.

Loss Leaders A variation of the preceding situation occurs when a product is sold as a **loss leader.** An item may be deliberately priced so low that it incurs short-run losses in the expectation that its sales will generate sufficient additional profitable sales of other products to offset those losses.

Example: McDonald Corporation operates a sales department in which the contribution margin ratio is 40 percent and regular weekly gross sales average

$100,000. Fixed costs are $20,000 per week. To increase turnover in this department, the company plans a one-week sale featuring a special product that will be sold for $2 each. If 16,000 of these items can be purchased for $3 each, by how much must sales volume of normally priced items increase to make this promotion worthwhile?

Solution: The incremental result of offering the loss leader is a loss of $16,000, calculated as follows:

Incremental Revenue:	
16,000 units @ $2	$32,000
Less: Incremental Costs:	
16,000 units @ $3	48,000
Net Incremental Loss	($16,000)

This $16,000 loss must be offset by the contributions derived from increased sales of other products at normal prices. Because the contribution margin ratio is 40 percent, each extra dollar of sales revenue contributes 40¢. Therefore, sales must be increased by $40,000 in order to generate the required additional contribution of $16,000 ($40,000 × .4).

At the new weekly sales level of $140,000, the total contribution margin will be $56,000 ($140,000 × .4), which equals the original contribution margin of $40,000 ($100,000 × .4) plus the amount needed to offset the $16,000 loss on promotional sales. The fixed costs of $20,000 are excluded from this analysis. They are *committed costs* that remain the same whether or not the loss leader is sold. It would also have been incorrect to allocate any of those fixed costs to the loss leader in measuring the incremental loss from the sales promotion.

AT WHAT STAGE IN PROCESSING SHOULD A PRODUCT BE SOLD?

Short-run incremental analysis also applies to many "sell or process further" decisions. When an item in process passes through a series of manufacturing operations, it may become a salable commodity at a number of different points along the way. A company may sell several different products that are actually the same product at various physical stages of completion. It may also sell the product at wholesale or retail distribution levels.

In deciding when to market such a product, identification of *sunk costs* in each decision situation is critical, as is the calculation of incremental returns from the various sales alternatives. All costs incurred before the sell or the process further decision is made must be treated as sunk costs. This is true whether they are fixed or variable costs of the product. The **incremental return** of each alternative is the difference between the costs and revenues that are incurred after the decision point.

Example: Kelleher Corporation manufactures a product that has already accumulated the following processing costs per unit:

Materials	$4
Direct Labor	2
Variable Overhead:	
100% of Direct Labor	2
Fixed Overhead:	
50% of Direct Labor	1
Total Cost per Unit	$9

Normal operating volume is 5,000 units per month. The product can be sold in its present form for $12 or it can be processed further at an additional cost of $6 for materials and $3 for labor and then sold for $25. Overhead costs are allocated to products according to a plant-wide rate based on direct labor cost.

Solution: Selling the product at its current stage of completion will produce revenues of $12 per unit. If the product is processed further and then sold, the return will be $13 per unit, calculated as follows:

Sales Price per Unit		$25
Less: Materials	$6	
Direct Labor	3	
Variable Overhead:		
100% of Direct Labor	3	12
Net Contribution per Unit		$13

Based on this information, the product should be processed further before sale, because further processing yields an incremental return of $1 per unit ($13 − $12). The $9 prior processing costs are not considered—they are *sunk costs*. Nor are any fixed overhead costs allocated to the product's subsequent processing. The only cost taken into account is the variable overhead of $3 per unit. There are two reasons for this treatment. First, because the total fixed overhead cost is a *committed cost* for the purpose of this decision, it will be incurred whether or not additional processing takes place. Second, because unit fixed overhead costs are only arbitrary allocations of *total fixed costs* over some predetermined *total activity level*—both of which are insensitive to incremental changes of the type involved in short-run analysis—fixed costs are not relevant for this decision.

Example: If the fixed resources made idle by avoiding subsequent processing could be diverted to some other use, an *opportunity cost* would enter the analysis. Assume that by expanding output of another product, Kelleher Corporation's idle capacity in the subsequent processing departments can be used to produce a contribution margin of $10,000 per month. That $10,000 then becomes an opportunity cost of the decision to sell the product after additional processing. Consequently, the solution changes in favor of selling at the current stage of completion.

Assuming that the operating volume is maintained at 5,000 units per month, the opportunity cost of going ahead with the additional processing is $2 per unit. This figure is derived by dividing the $10,000 of foregone contribution margin from the alternative use of fixed resources by the 5,000 units of regular output. The return obtained from additional processing is then only $11 per unit, determined as follows:

Sales Price per Unit		$25
Less: Materials	$ 6	
Direct Labor	3	
Variable Overhead	3	
	$12	
Opportunity Cost of		
Diverted Resources	$ 2	14
Net Contribution per Unit		$11

This is less than the $12 per unit that can be earned by selling the product without further processing. Therefore, additional processing should not be undertaken. The same conclusion can be reached in another way. The total contribution from the additional processing is $65,000 ($13 × 5,000). By comparison, $70,000 can be obtained by selling the partly processed items for $60,000 ($12 × 5,000) plus the $10,000 derived from alternative uses of the idle resources. Therefore, if the product receives additional processing, the total contribution will decrease by $5,000 [$65,000 − ($60,000 + $10,000)].

The second method of calculation is preferable because it shows the opportunity cost of the diverted resources as a lump sum ($10,000), rather than an amount per unit of output. This permits managers to make decisions regarding different quantities of output without having to recompute a new opportunity cost per unit in each case.

The preceding alternatives apply specifically to a short-run, one-time solution. If the same type of decision must be made on a permanent basis, the decision analysis will have to include such long-term factors as investment in resources, availability and cost of funds, and projected long-term cash flows. Moreover, it should be based on decision rules appropriate to long-run analysis. These are presented in Chapters 14, 17, and 18.

MAKE OR BUY DECISIONS

Many firms are able to choose between purchasing product components from outside suppliers or manufacturing the components themselves. Incremental analysis can provide short-run solutions to this kind of problem.

Example: In its manufacturing operations, Summers Corporation uses a magneto that can be purchased from a supplier for $20 per unit. The same magneto is now manufactured by Summers at the following unit cost:

Direct Materials	$ 5.00
Direct Labor	6.00
Variable Overhead:	
125% of Direct Labor Cost	7.50
Fixed Overhead:	
75% of Direct Labor Cost	4.50
Total Unit Cost	$23.00

Solution: If the magneto is purchased it will cost $20 per unit. However, that figure should not always be compared with the full cost of internal manufacture, which is $23 per unit. For short-run decision making purposes, fixed overhead costs applied to the product are *committed costs,* the total amount of which will be the same regardless of the alternative chosen. Therefore, the outside purchase price should be compared only with internal manufacturing costs that can be avoided if the outside purchase is made. These *avoidable costs* include the materials cost of $5 per unit, the direct labor cost of $6, and the variable overhead cost of $7.50. Because the total avoidable cost of $18.50 per unit is less than the $20 outside purchase price, Summers Corporation should continue to manufacture the magneto.

Example: Assume that Summers Corporation's excess capacity could be used to generate a contribution of $6,000 per month and that the normal monthly production volume is 1,000 units. The total cost of manufacturing the magneto internally rather than purchasing it will now be $24.50 per unit. This includes the $18.50 of avoidable production costs plus $6 ($6,000 ÷ 1,000) *opportunity cost* of contribution not available from alternative uses of assets when the magnetos are produced internally. Comparing this $24.50 to the $20 outside purchase price, Summers Corporation should buy the 1,000 units from outside suppliers and divert the idle fixed assets to their alternative use.

The same conclusion can be reached in a different way by calculating the total incremental effect of the two options:

Incremental Cost of 1,000 Units Purchased Outside at $20 per Unit . . .		$20,000
Incremental Cost to Produce 1,000 Units at $18.50 per Unit	$18,500	
Plus: Opportunity Cost Foregone by Producing these Units	6,000	24,500
Net Advantage of Outside Purchase		$ 4,500

As before, the preceding decision analysis is meant to be used only for a short-term, one-time situation. Long-term analysis will be needed if a make or buy decision is to apply on a permanent basis.

ELIMINATION OF PRODUCT LINES, DIVISIONS, OR DEPARTMENTS

When a firm maintains multiple sales outlets, product lines, or divisions, it may need to evaluate their individual performances to decide whether or not to continue operating each such segment. Performance reports can be structured to show the contribution margins and segment margins of each product or' company sub-unit, thereby making it easier to measure the absolute and relative amounts that each segment contributes to company-wide costs and profits.

A **segment margin** is calculated by determining a segment's contribution margin and subtracting from it all fixed costs that are directly traceable to that segment. Direct fixed costs include such items as advertising, salaries, maintenance, and insurance, in situations where incurrence of these costs depends on the continuing operation and existence of the segment.

Example: Budge Corporation has three divisions, A, B, and C. Figure 9–1 shows the company's divisional income statement for a typical month of opera-

Budge Corporation
Monthly Divisional Income Statement

	Division A		Division B		Division C		Total
Sales..........................		$100,000		$80,000		$150,000		$330,000
Less: Variable Costs:								
Manufacturing	$50,000		$12,000		$90,000		$152,000	
Marketing	20,000		8,000		10,000		38,000	
Total Variable Costs		70,000		20,000		100,000		190,000
Contribution Margin		$ 30,000		$60,000		$ 50,000		$140,000
Less: Direct Fixed Costs		35,000		25,000		40,000		100,000
Segment Margin		$ (5,000)		$35,000		$ 10,000		40,000
Less: Common Firm-wide Costs ..								33,000
Net Income								$ 7,000

FIGURE 9-2

Budge Corporation
Divisional Income, with Common Firm-wide
Costs Allocated

	Division A	Division B	Division C	Total
Segment Margin	$ (5,000)	$35,000	$10,000	$40,000
Less: Common Firm-wide Costs	10,000	8,000	15,000	33,000
Fully Allocated Net Income	$(15,000)	$27,000	$ (5,000)	$ 7,000

tions. All three divisions have positive contribution margins—their individual revenues exceed their direct variable costs. However, when the fixed costs that can be traced directly to each division are deducted, it is revealed that only Divisions B and C are covering their fixed costs and making any contribution to common firm-wide costs. Division A seems to be a candidate for elimination because it is not able to generate sufficient contribution margin to cover its own fixed costs. In effect, it is being subsidized by the segment margins provided by the other two divisions.

Common firm-wide costs should not be allocated to the divisions for the purpose of making this decision. Any such arbitrary allocation will only confuse the issue and may lead to a wrong decision. For example, if common firm-wide costs were allocated on the basis of sales revenue earned by each division, fully allocated divisional net income would appear as shown in Figure 9-2.

Although Figure 9-2 suggests that Divisions A and C are unprofitable and should be eliminated, these divisional losses result from an arbitrary allocation of common costs that are probably capacity-related and fixed in nature. Moreover, common firm-wide costs are usually *committed costs* that will continue in the short run regardless of a decision to discontinue any of the divisions.

The short-run decision to eliminate a company segment should be based on only those costs and revenues that will cease if the segment's operations are terminated. The *segment margins* shown in Figure 9-1 are more appropriate decision variables because they reveal the amounts of revenue and cost that will be *avoided* by discontinuing one or more divisions. Direct fixed costs should also be examined to ensure that they do not include any items that can be avoided in the short run.

Example: Assume that all of Budge Corporation's firm-wide common costs and 10 percent of its direct fixed costs are committed costs. Figure 9-3 is an analysis of the incremental contribution made by each division, such as might be used by managers in deciding whether or not any of the company's divisions should be discontinued.

Division A has a $1,500 negative incremental segment contribution. Discontinuing Division A would save Budge Corporation $1,500 per month in the short run.

Further analysis is needed to determine what effect the closing of Division A will have on the two remaining divisions. On the positive side, the capacity

---

FIGURE 9–3

Budge Corporation
Incremental Segment Contribution

	Division A	Division B	Division C	Total
Contribution Margin..................	$30,000	$60,000	$50,000	$140,000
Less: Avoidable Direct Fixed Costs	31,500	22,500	36,000	90,000
Incremental Segment Contribution	$ (1,500)	$37,500	$24,000	$ 50,000

---

of Division A may be transferable to Divisions B and C, which might increase their segment margins. However, eliminating Division A may also have harmful effects on the other divisions if their activities or the products they manufacture are interrelated with Division A outputs. These more advanced aspects of divisional performance will be considered in Chapter 19.

The decision to discontinue a product line, division, or department also has far reaching effects not fully covered by short-run analysis. The operations of such large segments need to be treated as potentially continuous in nature, and should be evaluated on a long-term basis, using techniques that will be presented in Chapters 17 and 18.

SHORT-TERM USE OF SCARCE RESOURCES

Incremental analysis can be used to allocate resources that are limited in quantity or in productivity. This requires that alternative courses of action be compared in a way that takes account of resource availability.

Example: O'Rourke Company has only enough machine capacity to produce one of two possible products, X or Y. Unit manufacturing costs for the two products are as follows:

	Product X	Product Y
Direct Materials	$ 6	$ 4
Direct Labor	4	6
Variable Overhead...........	5	10
Fixed Overhead	3	6
Total Cost per Unit	$18	$26

Under normal operating conditions, maximum production capacity is 40,000 machine hours per month. Fixed overhead costs total $60,000 per month. Overhead is applied to products on a machine-hour basis. Product X can be sold for $21 per unit and Product Y for $30 per unit.

The **contribution margin** per unit of output and the *net income* per unit of output for both products are as follows:

	Product X		Product Y	
Sales Price		$21		$30
Variable Costs:				
Materials	$6		$ 4	
Direct Labor	4		6	
Variable Overhead	5	15	10	20
Contribution Margin		$ 6		$10
Fixed Overhead		3		6
Net Income		$ 3		$ 4

Product Y has a contribution margin of $10 per unit and a net income of $4 per unit, compared to only $6 of contribution margin and $3 of net income for Product X. Both these measures seem to indicate that Product Y should be the one produced. However, they fail to consider the firm's limited production capacity in relation to the resources that generate fixed overhead costs. The $6 of fixed overhead allocated to each unit of Product Y is twice the amount allocated to Product X. In other words, each unit of Product Y requires twice as much scarce machine time as each unit of Product X. At the fixed overhead rate of $1.50 per hour ($60,000 ÷ 40,000 hours), Product X requires 2 hours of machine time per unit and Product Y requires 4 hours. Therefore, the total output of Product X can be as much as 20,000 units (40,000 hours ÷ 2 hours per unit), whereas Product Y's maximum output is only 10,000 units (40,000 hours ÷ 4 hours per unit).

Therefore, the *total contribution margin* possible at the firm's maximum production capacity is $120,000 for Product X ($6 per unit × 20,000 units), but only $100,000 for Product Y ($10 per unit × 10,000 units). If only one of the two products can be manufactured, it should be Product X.

This analysis could also be expressed in terms of the *contribution margin per unit of the constrained resource*. For Product X, this is $3 per machine hour; for Product Y, it is $2.50 per machine hour, as calculated in Figure 9–4.

FIGURE 9–4

O'Rourke Company
Contribution Margin per Unit of Products X and Y

	Product X	Product Y
Contribution Margin per Unit	$6	$10
Machine Hours per Unit	2	4
Contribution Margin per Machine Hour	$\frac{$6}{2} = 3	$\frac{$10}{4} = 2.50
Total Contribution Margin at Maximum Capacity of 40,000 Hours	$120,000	$100,000

Product X should be manufactured because its $3 contribution margin per hour of machine time is higher than the $2.50 per hour contribution margin of Product Y. Total contribution margin at maximum capacity will be $20,000 larger if all machine time is used to manufacture Product X. More complex examples of decision making subject to constraints (especially multiple constraints and multiple goals) will be discussed in Chapter 21.

PRODUCTION PLANNING AND EQUIPMENT REPLACEMENT

Short-run analysis can be used as a first approach to production planning and equipment replacement decisions, such as choosing between manual or automated production methods or deciding to keep or replace items of equipment.

Example: Gibson Company has always used a manual manufacturing process in one of its departments. It is now considering a change to automated production methods. This change would reduce operating costs as shown in Figure 9–5.

Figure 9–5 shows that $35,000 per year can be saved by automating the department. By replacing some employees with machinery, Gibson would secure net savings in materials, labor, and variable overhead at the expense of an increase in fixed overhead. In the context of this decision, all the department's costs are *avoidable costs*. Because the scope of the decision makes it possible to change every existing cost, there are no *committed costs*.

Assuming that the equipment to be acquired will cost $250,000, will last for 10 years, and that the annual incremental cost saving of $35,000 will continue for 10 years, Gibson should automate. The total incremental savings of $350,000 over the 10 year period clearly exceeds the new equipment cost of $250,000.

But the analysis must be extended. For each of the 10 years, cost projections should be made that take into account factors that are likely to vary during that time. Costs and savings will probably occur at a different rate and in a different pattern than the flat $35,000 annual rate initially assumed. Money to purchase the needed equipment will have to be borrowed at an interest cost or diverted from other internal uses. Depreciation methods and their tax effects

---

FIGURE 9–5

Gibson Company
Schedule of Annual Operating Costs
at 100,000 Unit Activity Level

	Cost of Manual System	Cost of Automated System	Effect of Change on Costs
Direct Materials	$100,000	$ 95,000	$ (5,000)
Direct Labor	80,000	20,000	(60,000)
Variable Overhead	40,000	30,000	(10,000)
Fixed Overhead	20,000	60,000	40,000
Total Operating Costs	$240,000	$205,000	$(35,000)

must be considered. In combination, all these factors suggest that long-run decision analysis, as presented in Chapters 17 and 18, is needed for this type of decision.

JOINT OUTPUTS OF COMMON PROCESSING OPERATIONS

Further Processing of Joint Outputs Incremental analysis can be applied to certain joint output situations. A common short-run problem involves deciding whether to sell joint outputs at the splitoff point or process them further. The processing plan chosen should maximize the total contribution to common processing costs and profits made by the various joint products. This decision must be made without regard to common processing costs, because at the splitoff point these common processing costs are *sunk costs* that have already been incurred to create the joint products.

Example: Greer Company manufactures two chemical solvents, Gummo and Whummo, in the fixed proportions $1/3:2/3$. During the month of April, 60,000 gallons were produced and $120,000 in common processing costs were incurred. Gummo and Whummo could be sold in their present state for $3 and $4 per gallon respectively. However, Gummo can be sold as Gummo-Plus for $4 per gallon by adding an extra ingredient costing 75¢ per gallon. Whummo can be sold as Super-Whummo for $6 per gallon if it is reprocessed at an additional cost of $2 per gallon plus $20,000 per month for the rental of a special purpose filtering machine with a capacity of 40,000 gallons per month.

Figure 9–6 indicates that the best alternatives are to sell Gummo-Plus after adding the extra ingredient ($65,000 > $60,000), but to sell Whummo in its

---

FIGURE 9–6

Greer Company
Sell or Process Further Decision
Month of April

Sell at Separation Point		Sell After Extra Processing	
(1) Gummo: 20,000 gals. @ $3		Gummo-Plus: 20,000 gals. @ $4	$80,000
		Less: Additive 20,000 gals. @ 75¢	15,000
Contribution	$60,000	Contribution	$65,000
(2) Whummo: 40,000 gal. @ $4		Super-Whummo: 40,000 gals. @ $6	$240,000
		Less: Processing 40,000 gals. @ $2 ...... $80,000	
		Rental 20,000	100,000
Contribution	$160,000	Contribution	$140,000

basic form at the splitoff point ($160,000 > $140,000). This provides the maximum possible contribution of $225,000 ($65,000 + $160,000).

This type of analysis must be used with discretion. A variation in the circumstances of this sell or process further situation may produce a solution that indicates it is not worthwhile to manufacture one of the joint outputs at all.

Example: Assume that there is no immediate market for either the 20,000 gallons of Gummo or the 40,000 gallons of Whummo produced by Greer Company. But extra processing, which costs $2.50 per gallon for all outputs, yields Gummo-Extra and Whummo-Extra, for which there is a market at prices of $2 and $7 per gallon respectively. The incremental effect of additional processing is shown in Figure 9–7.

The extra processing applied to Gummo results in a negative contribution of $10,000. However, it is incorrect to conclude that, because of this negative contribution and the lack of an immediate market, Gummo should not be produced at all. Proposals to eliminate Gummo overlook the nature of the common processing operations which require that *both* Gummo and Whummo be manufactured simultaneously. Because it is profitable to produce Whummo-Extra ($180,000 > $120,000), the essential problem is to dispose of Gummo in a way that will avoid at least some of the $10,000 negative contribution imposed by its only present marketing opportunity. If no method can be found to produce a positive contribution from sales of Gummo-Extra, Gummo should be scrapped at the splitoff point for zero recovery.

Varying Proportions of Joint Outputs   Another type of short-run decision involves choosing among alternative processing plans for joint products when the proportions of the outputs from common processing can be varied. Again incremental analysis is applicable, though in most cases only the total amount of common processing costs are relevant.

Example: Van Loo Company turns out two grades of gaskets—regular and super. Current production capacity is 50,000 gaskets per month and common processing costs are $100,000 per month. Regular and super-grade gaskets are manufactured in a 60:40 ratio. The regular gaskets sell for $3 each, but the super-grade gaskets are processed further at an additional cost of 50¢ apiece and are sold for $4.

FIGURE 9–7

Greer Company
Sell or Process Further Decision
Month of April

Gummo-Extra:			Whummo-Extra:		
Sales: 20,000 @ $2.00	$ 40,000		Sales: 40,000 @ $7.00	$280,000	
Less: Processing Costs			Less: Processing Costs		
20,000 @ $2.50	50,000		40,000 @ $2.50	100,000	
Contribution	$(10,000)		Contribution	$180,000	

FIGURE 9–8

Van Loo Company
Contribution Under Present and Proposed
Production Mixes

Present Net Contribution			Proposed Net Contribution		
Regular Grade:			Regular Grade:		
30,000 @ $3		$ 90,000	10,000 @ $3		$ 30,000
Super Grade:			Super Grade:		
20,000 @ $3.50		70,000	40,000 @ $3.50		140,000
		$160,000			$170,000
Less: Common Costs		100,000	Less: Common Costs		120,000
Net Contribution		$ 60,000	Net Contribution		$ 50,000

Question 1   Assuming that the proportion of regular to super-grade gaskets can be altered without affecting the cost of common processing, in what direction should the mix be changed if there is unlimited demand for both types of gaskets?
Solution: Because contribution per unit is only $3 for regular-grade gaskets but $3.50 ($4.00 − .50) for super grade, the maximum contribution would be achieved by switching the entire production to super-grade gaskets.
Question 2   Given the same basic situation as in Question 1, assume now that maximum monthly demand is 40,000 for regular-grade gaskets, and 35,000 for super-grade. How many of each type should be manufactured?
Solution: Because the maximum contribution per unit comes from the super-grade gaskets, the production mix should include as many of them as possible (35,000 × $3.50). Only the production capacity that remains should be used to manufacture regular gaskets (15,000 × $3). This production mix yields a maximum total contribution of $167,000 ($122,500 + $45,000).
Question 3   Assume further that the ratio of regular to super-grade gaskets can be changed from 60:40 to 20:80, but only if common processing costs are increased from $100,000 to $120,000 per month. Should the production mix bevaried?
Solution: Figure 9–8 indicates that the proposed change is not worthwhile. The increased contribution from the new production mix is only $10,000 ($170,000 − $160,000), which is not sufficient to offset the $20,000 increase in common processing costs. No attempt should be made to allocate the common processing costs among the two products, although in this latter case the change in *total* common processing costs is relevant to the decision.

INTERNAL PRICING DECISIONS

Quite often a firm is organized in such a way that some of its decision centers buy from and sell to each other. Prices in these transactions are usually called **internal prices** or **transfer prices** and the product or service exchanged is referred to as an **intermediate product.** When internal transfers occur, a company's decision centers are acting as profit or investment centers rather than cost centers, because they are held responsible for their performance in terms of some measure of profitability. This arrangement is effective only if the decision centers are allowed to operate independently with a full range of decision making powers. These must include the ability to set prices for their products, and decide whether to deal with other divisions of their own firm or to buy and sell in outside markets.

When a company's decision centers are required to deal only with each other—that is, are not permitted access to outside markets for purchases or sales—transfer pricing is less useful, even if the decision centers have the other characteristics of profit or investment centers. Under such conditions, no real decision making purpose can be served by transfer pricing, because the decision centers cannot choose alternative customers or sources of supply outside the firm. However, transfer prices will still be necessary for performance measurement. This will be discussed fully in Chapters 19 and 20, in which issues relating to divisional performance evaluation are considered.

The following discussion examines transfer prices exclusively from a planning and decision making viewpoint. A transfer pricing policy that serves these purposes must help the various decision centers to attain *overall company objectives*. A price that most benefits the whole company may not always be the price that decision centers would set in order to attain their own profit and performance goals. Assuming that the overriding objective is company-wide profit maximization, the basis for decisions involving transactions among the firm's decision centers must be the minimization of effective total cost to the firm as a whole.

The transfer pricing problem can be approached from either a short-run or a long-range decision perspective. More definite solutions can be arrived at through short-run analysis. It is possible to develop a generalized pricing rule that will minimize firm-wide costs and that can be adapted to various short-term operating capacity conditions. The long-range transfer pricing problem is somewhat like that of long-run product pricing in external markets, in that it involves many alternative approaches, each with its own merits and shortcomings. Long-run transfer pricing is discussed in Chapter 14.

Short-Run Transfer Pricing Situations   Two short-run capacity conditions might apply to an operating division that manufactures a product which may be either sold to the public or transferred to another division of the same firm for further processing. The producing division may (1) have excess capacity, allowing it to manufacture additional units without any change in its fixed costs or (2) already may be selling its total production capacity in external markets. A general purpose short-run transfer pricing rule may be stated as follows: *The correct transfer price to quote to a prospective internal purchaser for decision making purposes is an amount equal to the whole firm's total incremental cost of producing and transferring the outputs in question to that other division.*

When excess productive capacity exists in the producing division, this incremental cost will equal the *directly traceable variable costs* of the output to be produced and internally transferred, up to the division's maximum capacity. These variable costs are the only relevant costs, because in the short-run, fixed costs will remain constant and there will be no opportunity costs, because the production capacity involved would otherwise have been idle.

On the other hand, if the producing division is already working at capacity, it can sell additional units to another division only by curtailing outside sales or by temporarily increasing capacity. The incremental cost to the firm will then be the sum of all *directly traceable variable costs* of producing the item in question, plus any *contribution margin lost* by the division as a result of having to forego some of its external sales.

If the producing division manufactures more than one product and is operating at full capacity, the transfer price must be the *variable cost* of the increased production plus (1) the *lost contribution margin* from whichever product's outside sales are curtailed or (2) the *cost of any other action* taken to facilitate the internal transfer. This might include incremental fixed costs incurred to increase productive capacity or the cost of outside procurement of products needed to meet total demand. If an adjustment of sales is needed, sales of the product with the lowest contribution rate should be reduced in favor of products with higher contribution rates.

A final variation occurs when the proposed internal transfer or the alternative outside transaction has side effects on company units other than the internal buyer and seller. In this case, the correct transfer price is equal to the *variable cost* of producing the intermediate product plus or minus the *net opportunity cost* or gain effect of the internal transfer on all divisions of the firm.

Example: Bowman Corporation has two divisions, Alpha and Baker. Alpha Division manufactures Product A, which has variable manufacturing costs of $6 per unit and variable marketing costs of $1 and can be sold to the public for $10 per unit. Baker Division is also a potential buyer of Product A.

Situation 1   Assume that Alpha Division has the capacity to produce more units of Product A than it is now able to sell to outside customers at $10 per unit. In that case, the correct transfer price is $6 per unit—the effective *incremental cost* to the firm of the additional output. This assumes that the $1 per unit of marketing costs is eliminated when products are sold within the company. If Baker Division cannot buy Product A from any alternative source for less than $6, then the correct decision is to buy it from Alpha Division. But if Product A can be purchased from outsiders for, say, $5 per unit, then it should be, because an outside purchase at that price would reduce the firm's total costs.

Situation 2   Assume that Alpha Division already has committed all its output to external sales at a market price of $10 per unit. To sell any additional units to Baker Division, Alpha must divert sales from the outside market. The contribution margin from a regular sale is $3 per unit and consists of the $10 outside sales price less manufacturing and marketing costs of $7 per unit.

In this case, the correct transfer price is $9 per unit. This price consists of the variable manufacturing cost of $6, plus a lost contribution margin of $3. Bowman Corporation should buy Product A from an outside supplier only if it can do so for less than $9 per unit. An internal transfer at $9 per unit is the proper decision only if the price charged by an outside supplier is greater than $9.

Situation 3   Now assume that Alpha Division also produces Product B, which has a sales price of $12 per unit, variable manufacturing cost of $7, and variable marketing cost of $1. The combined sales of Products A and B require all the production capacity of Alpha Division. Assume also that each unit of Product A requires the same use of fixed resources (say machine-hour capacity) as does each unit of Product B. The transfer price for Product A equals its variable production cost plus the *smaller* of the two products' contribution margins. Because a unit of Product A uses the same amount of constrained capacity (machine hours) as a unit of Product B, it is more economical to sacrifice sales of Product A, which has a contribution margin of $3 per unit, than it is to sacrifice sales of Product B, which has a contribution margin of $4 per unit.

	Product A		Product B	
Sales Price per Unit		$10		$12
Variable Manufacturing Cost	$6		$7	
Variable Marketing Cost	1	7	1	8
Contribution Margin per Unit		$ 3		$ 4

In this situation, the transfer price should be $9 per unit, consisting of the $6 variable manufacturing cost of Product A plus $3, the smaller of the two lost contribution margins.

Situation 4 A further complication may arise if the purchasing division buys from an outside supplier who is in turn dealing with another division of the same firm. Assume that in Situation 2 Baker Division could buy a product similar to Product A for $11 per unit from Ryan Company, an independent supplier. Ryan Company in turn acquires from Bowman Corporation's George Division the materials that it uses to make Product A. In this latter transaction, George Division receives $5 per unit for the materials and earns a contribution margin of $2.50 per unit.

In this situation, the transfer price is $11.50 per unit. This price consists of the variable manufacturing cost of $6, plus the $3 contribution margin sacrificed by Alpha Division when it foregoes some of its outside sales of Product A, plus the $2.50 contribution margin that George Division loses when it is no longer able to supply Ryan Company with raw materials. This $11.50 is the incremental cost to the firm as a whole if Alpha Division manufactures the intermediate product and transfers it to Baker Division, thereby affecting the sales activity of Divisions Alpha and George.

This particular transfer price is relevant for only one purpose—to aid Baker Division in deciding whether or not to buy Product A from Alpha Division or from the outside supplier, Ryan Company. For another supplier that did not have the secondary relationship with George Division, the transfer price would still be $9 per unit as in Situation 2. The solution is for Baker Division to buy Product A from Ryan Company at $11 per unit, because the total cost to the firm of an internal transfer would be $11.50 per unit.

Summary: Internal Pricing Short-run transfer prices should equal the producing division's variable cost plus any contribution margin lost or other cost incurred by any division of the firm as a result of the internal transaction. When sufficient excess capacity exists to manufacture the item for internal use without disturbing its external sales, no contribution margin will be lost and the transfer price will equal the variable cost. When the producing division's outside sales are reduced as the result of an internal transfer, the transfer price should also include the contribution margin lost by foregoing those outside sales. Finally, the transfer price should include any contribution margin lost or other costs incurred by any other division of the firm as a result of the internal transaction.

The preceding situations assume that all information is fully and freely available to participating decision makers. In practice, due to the separation of decision makers into relatively independent managerial groups, decision center managers may have information only about the prices and cost of goods that they produce, buy, and sell. They may be unaware of other relevant data, such as the indirect effects of internal transfers on other divisions. Decision center managers may also tend to pursue their own local profit goals, even at the expense of overall company objectives. These are some of the problems likely to arise when accounting systems are designed to serve the decision making needs of decentralized organizations.

It is also assumed that individual decision center managers will react rationally to the transfer pricing rules and their results. For example, in Situation 3, having set the transfer price at $9, the manager of Alpha Division should know that this price is as attractive as selling to outsiders at $10, because both alternatives produce contribution margins of $3 per unit. There remains the problem of how to induce Alpha Division to sell to Baker Division rather than to the outside market, given that the resulting contribution margins are the same. Theoretically, this can be done by setting the transfer price fractionally (say 1¢) higher than the indifference price. This is one of the practical problems that will be explored in Chapters 19 and 20, in which divisional performance measurements are discussed.

SUMMARY

1. Short-run decision making requires the use of analytical techniques that measure the incremental effects of alternative actions.
2. Accounting information used in this process focuses on those costs and revenues that change as a result of the actions chosen.
3. This general approach, which depends on the identification of relevant incremental revenues and costs, is applicable to a wide variety of short-run decision situations, including:
    a. Decisions to accept or reject special sales orders.
    b. Determining at what stage in processing a product should be sold.
    c. Deciding whether to manufacture a component or purchase it from an outside supplier.
    d. Deciding whether to retain or eliminate product lines, divisions, or departments.
    e. Allocating scarce resources among competing products.
    f. Deciding whether to return or replace equipment.
    g. Establishing internal transfer prices.
4. Avoidable and opportunity costs, as well as the fixed–variable and direct–indirect cost classifications, are important components of incremental analysis.
5. Sunk costs and committed costs should usually be excluded from short-run incremental analysis.

KEY WORDS AND PHRASES

Problem (385)
Problem Space (385)
Relevant Cost Concept (386)
Deterministic Alternatives (386)
Sunk Cost (386)
Committed Cost (387)
Avoidable Cost (387)
Opportunity Cost (387)
Incremental Analysis (388)
Loss Leader (389)
Segment Margin (393)
Contribution Margin (396)
Internal (Transfer) Price (401)
Intermediate Product (401)

Questions

1. Distinguish between *short-run* and *long-run* problems.
2. What *decision criteria* are appropriate for short-run decisions? Why?
3. Briefly explain each of the cost concepts described in conjunction with the ten cost classification systems listed on page 386.
4. Differentiate between *sunk* and *committed* costs. How are costs from each category treated in the analysis of short-run decisions?
5. What is an *avoidable* cost? Under which circumstances would it be important to measure and analyze avoidable costs?
6. What is an *opportunity* cost? When do opportunity costs affect short-run decisions? What accounting problems do opportunity costs involve?
7. Outline the general procedures that comprise *incremental analysis.*
8. What comparisons should be made in deciding whether or not to accept a one-time order at a price different from the regular sales price?
9. In disposing of inventory that has already been manufactured, what costs should be recovered when the product is (1) still marketable in a normal way and (2) obsolete, damaged, or out of fashion?
10. Under what circumstances do sell-or-process-further decisions arise?
11. Explain the role of (1) incremental revenues and (2) subsequent processing costs in sell-or-process-further decisions.
12. Under what circumstances do make-or-buy decisions arise?
13. Explain the role of (1) committed, (2) sunk, (3) avoidable, and (4) opportunity costs in make-or-buy decisions.
14. When the discontinuation of a product line, division, or department is being considered, what short-run analysis can be applied?
15. Why is long-run analysis probably more appropriate for segment discontinuation decisions?
16. What type of analysis is appropriate for decisions involving a single constrained resource that must be allocated among competing uses?
17. What type of analysis is appropriate for decisions involving the further processing of joint outputs?
18. What comparisons should be made concerning possible variations in the mix of outputs from a common processing operation?
19. What is a transfer price? What decisions are transfer prices needed for?
20. What features of organizational structure will require a transfer pricing system?
21. What is the general decision rule regarding proposed intrafirm transactions? Distinguish between cases for which: (1) *excess capacity* exists in the supplying division, (2) *no excess capacity* exists in the supplying division, and (3) third-party divisions are involved.
22. What potential problems must be anticipated when implementing the procedures outlined in Question 21?

Exercises

E 9-1 Special Sales Order—Elementary Analysis

Gutbrod Company produces tennis racquets which it sells under its trade name for $30 each. Although its annual volume has been 300,000 units, it could produce an additional 150,000 units without any change to its cost structure. Unit manufacturing and distribution costs are as follows:

$$
\begin{array}{ll}
\text{Variable Costs} \ldots\ldots & \$16 \\
\text{Fixed Costs} \ldots\ldots\ldots & 8^* \\
\text{Total Cost} \ldots\ldots\ldots & \$24
\end{array}
$$

$$
{}^*\left(\frac{\$2,400,000 \text{ per year}}{300,000 \text{ units}} = \$8\right)
$$

A discount store has offered to purchase one lot of 50,000 racquets for $18 per racquet. The discount racquets will not bear the trade name and will be sold only at retail locations where the regular product is unavailable. This special order would reduce variable marketing costs by $1 per unit on the 50,000 units, but an additional $75,000 of fixed costs would be incurred to produce a die to imprint a different name on each racquet.

Required:
(a) Should the company accept this offer? Show all calculations.
(b) What additional information might be needed? How might it affect the decision?

E 9-2 Special Sales Order—Elementary Analysis

Harris Company has an annual productive capacity of 1,000,000 machine hours. To date, the production of its single product has required only 800,000 hours. Each unit requires two machine hours to produce. Unit costs of production and distribution are as follows:

$$
\begin{array}{ll}
\text{Materials and Labor} \ldots\ldots\ldots\ldots\ldots\ldots\ldots\ldots\ldots\ldots\ldots\ldots\ldots\ldots & \$15 \\
\text{Manufacturing Overhead} & \\
\quad \text{Variable (\$4 per machine hour)} \ldots\ldots\ldots\ldots\ldots\ldots\ldots\ldots\ldots & 8 \\
\quad \text{Fixed (\$2,400,000} \div \text{800,000} = \$3 \text{ per machine hour)} \ldots\ldots\ldots\ldots & 6 \\
\quad \text{Variable Marketing Costs} \ldots\ldots\ldots\ldots\ldots\ldots\ldots\ldots\ldots\ldots\ldots\ldots & 5 \\
\quad \text{Fixed Administrative Costs (\$800,000} \div \text{400,000 units)} \ldots\ldots\ldots\ldots & 2 \\
& \$36
\end{array}
$$

A new customer has offered to buy 75,000 additional units for $30 apiece (75 percent of the normal sales price). If the order is accepted, marketing costs for the additional units will be reduced 50 percent, but all other costs will remain the same.

Required:
(a) Should the offer be accepted? Show all calculations.
(b) If the offer were for 150,000 units, should it be accepted? Why or why not?
(c) What additional information might influence the decisions in parts (a) and (b)?

E 9–3   Elementary Incremental Sales Alternatives

The sales manager of Fagen Coffee Company has proposed that for July, August, and September of 19X9 a promotion be implemented to boost the sales of two-pound cans of coffee. One coupon will be placed in each can; five coupons will be redeemable for one free ticket to a major league baseball game.

The baseball tickets regularly sell for $7, but the company can acquire them for $5 each. A two-pound can of coffee regularly sells for $6, half of which represents variable costs. Monthly fixed costs are $50,000. Sales have recently averaged 40,000 cans per month. Printing and packaging charges for the coupons will add 10¢ to the cost of each can of coffee. It will also cost $1 in handling and postage charges to process each request for tickets. In addition, $10,000 per month will be spent on advertising throughout the promotion. Sales should increase by 15,000 cans per month as a result of the promotion, but only 25 percent of all coupons will be redeemed.

Required:
Should Fagen Company adopt this promotion? Show all supporting calculations.

E 9–4   Sell, Process Further, or Purchase from Outside—Elementary Analysis

One component of Hall Company's final product is processed through three separate departments. The final output is sold for $2 per gallon. Costs for a typical month when 1,200,000 gallons are produced and sold are as follows:

	Department A	Department B	Department C
Materials	$ 72,000	—	—
Labor	168,000	$192,000	$132,000
Variable Overhead	24,000	72,000	84,000
Fixed Overhead	96,000	60,000	60,000
	$360,000	$324,000	$276,000

An outside supplier has offered to supply an item identical to the output of Department C for $1.00 per unit. The company could also sell the 1,200,000 gallon output of Department A for 50¢ per gallon. Should the company decide to rearrange its operations, any idle capacity that results will continue to cause fixed costs to be incurred.

Required:
(a)   Should Hall continue its present operations?
(b)   Should Hall discontinue all production and purchase from outside?
(c)   Should Hall produce the partly processed item and sell it, as well as purchasing the end product from the outside supplier? Show all calculations.

E 9–5   Product Line Discontinuation Decision—Elementary Analysis

Shoan Company prepares income statements for four separate product lines. For a typical month, product line X has produced the following results:

Sales			$120,000
Less: Variable Manufacturing Costs	$47,000		
Equipment Depreciation	18,000		
Salary of Production Manager	5,000		
Fixed Manufacturing Overhead.....	10,000		
Total Manufacturing Costs		$80,000	
Less: Sales Commissions	$ 8,000		
Delivery Charges	6,000		
Advertising	20,000		
Total Marketing Costs		$34,000	
Less: Administrative Costs		$16,000	$130,000
Net Operating Loss			($ 10,000)

The following information is also available:

(1) Special purpose equipment is used, which will become idle if product X is discontinued.

(2) The production manager will be transferred to another division if product X is discontinued.

(3) Fixed manufacturing overhead is allocated to product lines on the basis of direct labor hours of production. If product X is discontinued, manufacturing overhead will not be affected.

(4) Of the advertising costs, $8,000 is specifically for promotion of product X. The remainder represents amounts allocated to each product line based on sales volumes.

(5) Administrative costs are incurred centrally and allocated to products on the basis of sales dollars. Total firm-wide administrative costs will not change if product X is dropped.

Required:

(a) Prepare an analysis to determine whether or not product X should be discontinued.

(b) What assumptions did you make in answering part (a)?

(c) What additional information would be useful in answering part (a)?

E 9-6   Incremental Analysis—Constrained Resource Conditions

Kwon Department Store operates three departments—groceries, clothing, and housewares. The operating results and other data for a typical month are as follows:

	Sales	Variable Costs	Floor Space (Sq. Ft.)
Groceries	$2,000,000	$1,600,000	4,000
Clothing	800,000	400,000	1,600
Housewares......	200,000	150,000	400
	$3,000,000	$2,150,000	6,000

It has been proposed that a hardware department requiring 1,200 square feet be added. Forecast sales for hardware are $600,000 per month, with variable costs of $420,000.

Fixed costs of $450,000 per month are allocated on a floor space basis. The total floor space available in the store cannot be increased in the short run. In all departments, sales revenue is proportional to the amount of floor space occupied.

Required:
(a) Assuming that the necessary floor space has to come from one department (but not housewares), should the hardware department be added? Show calculations.
(b) Assuming that the necessary floor space has to come all from one department *or* from housewares plus part of another department, should the hardware department be added? Show calculations.
(c) What minimum contribution per square foot must any new department provide in order to be added to the store? Explain all assumptions and calculations.

E 9-7 Joint Products—Alternative Sales and Processing Situations

Quale Company produces two products, Masons and Jasons. In Department I, raw materials are processed into two intermediate products from which the end products are eventually obtained. The ratio of output at that point is one unit of Masons for every three units of Jasons. In Department II, the Masons receive subsequent processing, whereas the Jasons are transferred to Department III for additional refining.

For March of 19X3, cost, production, and sales data were as follows:

	Department I	Department II	Department III
Materials	$300,000	—	—
Direct Labor	160,000	$ 60,000	$ 80,000
Variable Overhead	40,000	20,000	40,000
Fixed Overhead	180,000	50,000	70,000
	$680,000	$130,000	$190,000

All fixed overhead costs are incurred on a departmental basis and there are no firm-wide costs.

Production and Sales:
50,000 units of Mason (Sales Price $10)
150,000 units of Jason (Sales Price $5)

An opportunity to sell the two intermediate products has arisen at sales prices of $8 for unfinished Masons and $3 for unfinished Jasons.

Required:
(a) Should the company continue to sell the Masons and Jasons in their processed form or should the two products be sold in their intermediate state? Show all calculations.
(b) What assumptions were necessary to obtain the answer to part (a)?
(c) What additional information would help you reach a solution?

E 9-8 Joint Products—Variation of Output Mix

Terry Company operates four production departments in its manufacture of three outputs, A, B, and C. In Department I, common processing yields A, B, and C in the proportions 3:2:1. Products A, B, and C require additional processing in Departments II, III, and

IV, respectively. Each department is independent and controls all its costs (except for fixed costs, which are allocated on the basis of units of output processed). For August of 19X2, the following operating results were reported:

Production Costs	I	II	III	IV
Materials...............	$200,000	$ –0–	$ –0–	$ –0–
Labor..................	100,000	20,000	32,000	20,000
Variable Overhead	40,000	8,000	12,000	10,000
Fixed Overhead.........	60,000	30,000	20,000	10,000

Output for the month included 120,000 pounds of A, 80,000 pounds of B, and 40,000 pounds of C, which had sales prices of $2, $4, and $6 respectively.

A proposal has been made to purchase a higher grade of raw material for use in Department I. It will cost 25 percent more, but will yield A, B, and C in the proportions 4:3:3. However, total pounds produced will remain the same. Sales prices and all other costs will remain the same (that is, fixed costs will be the same in total, and variable costs will be the same per unit processed).

Required:
(a) Should the proposed change be adopted? Show all calculations.
(b) Explain how each of the costs in Department I were treated in the analysis in part (a).

E 9–9   Joint Products—Alternative Processing and Sales Situations

Grable Company makes decorative chair legs which it sells in prepackaged sets of four for $10. Each set of four legs requires ten board feet of raw lumber, which costs 40¢ per board foot. After being cut and turned on a lathe, the legs are sanded and packaged. Sanding and packaging costs amount to $1.50 per set. The shavings and offcuts from the cutting and turning operations are presently sold for 10¢ per pound in their raw state. Each board foot of lumber produces one-half pound of shavings and offcuts. The variable costs incurred in the cutting and turning process amount to 10¢ per board foot. Fixed costs are $20,000 per month for cutting and turning and $5,000 for sanding and packaging. Currently 8,000 sets of legs are produced and sold each month.

It has been proposed that the company rent equipment to process the shavings into a garden mulch. This equipment will rent for $1,500 per month; chemicals and other processing costs will be 6¢ per pound processed. The processing will yield 8 pounds of mulch for every 10 pounds of shavings and offcuts processed. The mulch will sell for 30¢ per pound.

Required:
(a) Should the company continue to sell the unprocessed shavings or should it rent the equipment and produce the mulch? Show all calculations.
(b) Explain how the cost of lumber, the costs of the cutting and turning operation, and the costs of the sanding and packaging operation were treated in part (a).
(c) In reporting the income from the sale of either the unprocessed shavings or the mulch, should the product be treated as a by-product or a joint product with the table legs? Why?

E 9–10   Internal Pricing—Elementary Analysis

Criss Company has three divisions, X, Y, and Z. The final product which Division Z sells to outside consumers utilizes components produced by Divisions X and Y. The following income statement was prepared for August of 19X0.

Sales (Division Z) (10,000 units @ $80)		$ 80,000
Less: Variable Costs		
Division X (10,000 units)	$120,000	
Division Y (10,000 units)	180,000	
Division Z	100,000	400,000
Contribution Margin		$400,000
Less: Fixed Costs		250,000
Net Income		$150,000

Divisions X, Y, and Z are treated as separate profit centers, and transfer prices of $15 and $25 are presently in effect for the compounds that X and Y respectively provide to Department Z. Fixed costs are allocated among the divisions in proportion to the variable costs of each division.

An outside supplier has offered to provide the components that are presently made by Divisions X and Y for $10 and $20 respectively. Divisions X and Y have no opportunities to sell their output to anyone except Division Z.

Required:
(a) Should the outside supplier's offer be accepted? Show all calculations.

(b) What assumptions were made to arrive at the solution in part (a)?

(c) What additional information would be helpful here? Why?

E 9–11   Transfer Pricing—Incremental Analysis

The Valve Division of Radisch Corporation presently sells all output in a competitive market at $60 per unit. Based on a capacity of 50,000 units, its cost for this product are as follows:

Materials	$20
Direct Labor	10
Variable Overhead	10
Fixed Overhead	12
	$52

Although productive capacity is 50,000 units per month, only 35,000 units are being produced and sold. A new Fabricating Division being added to the corporation will need a component identical to the output of the Valve Division, but is considering purchasing it from an outside supplier for $42.50 per unit. The Fabricating Division expects to need 10,000 units per month.

Required:
(a) Should the Fabricating Division acquire the valves from the outside supplier or from the Valve Division? Show calculations.

(b)   What is the correct transfer price for decisions such as that in part (a)?

(c)   What would be the correct decision if the Fabricating Division needed 20,000 units per month? What transfer price(s) would cause the correct actions to be taken here?

E 9–12   Transfer Pricing—Incremental Analysis

Siebert Company has two divisions, Ajax and Carbine. Ajax sells its product to both outsiders and to Carbine. For the 19X3 year, budgeted operations for Ajax are as follows:

Sales:	
200,000 @ $5	$1,000,000
100,000 @ $4	400,000
	$1,400,000
Less: Variable Costs ($2 per unit)	600,000
	$ 800,000
Less: Fixed Costs	300,000
Net Income	$ 500,000

The sales price to outside customers of Ajax Division is $5. For Carbine Division, an internal transfer price of $4 has been established. Carbine has the chance to buy the same item from an outside supplier for $3.50. Carbine has an annual demand for 100,000 units of the item.

Required:

(a)   From the corporation's point of view, what should the divisions do? Assume that Ajax cannot sell any more than 200,000 units to outside customers and that 300,000 units can be produced.

(b)   What transfer price should be used to make the decision in part (a)? Why?

(c)   In addition to Carbine's original opportunity to buy from an alternative supplier, assume that Ajax has a chance to sell 100,000 units to a chain store for $3.25. These are in addition to its regular sales of 200,000 at $5 per unit. However, 300,000 units is the maximum capacity of Ajax's present facilities. Carbine's outside supply opportunity is still in effect. What should Ajax do?
  (1)   Continue as presently?
  (2)   Accept the chain store's offer?
  (3)   Accept part of the chain store's offer and still sell to Carbine?

Cases

C 9–1   Incremental Sales Alternatives

Krentz Company sells a product for $24 per unit. Variable manufacturing and marketing costs total $10 per unit at normal capacity of 300,000 units per year. The company is considering three alternatives to boost annual sales volume beyond the present 300,000 unit level.

(1)   A department store has offered to purchase 200,000 units to be sold under the store's brand name. The price offered is $20 per unit, but Krentz could reduce

variable marketing costs on this order by $1 per unit. However, to expand capacity to the required 500,000 units per year, additional fixed costs of $1,500,000 would be incurred.

(2) A 10 percent price cut proposed by the Sales Division is expected to increase sales volume by 50 percent. This increase in sales would increase fixed costs by $1,200,000 to expand capacity to 450,000 units.

(3) The Production Division suggests a quality control improvement that will add 80¢ to variable manufacturing costs and $1,200,000 to fixed costs. However, 100,000 additional units of the improved product would be sold.

Required:
Evaluate the three proposals. Which one should be selected? Why? State all assumptions and show all supporting calculations.

C 9–2   Incremental Sales Alternatives

The Bijou Theater has a contract to show the movie, *Mary Poppins Meets Godzilla* for the next two weeks. However, the current feature, *Hot Tub Thrills* has been playing to full houses for four straight weeks. The theater can either (1) show *Hot Tub Thrills* for two more weeks, (2) honor the contract for *Mary Poppins Meets Godzilla,* or (3) extend *Hot Tub Thrills* for one more week only.

Theater capacity is 10,000 customers per week. Admission prices are $4 for adults and $1.50 for children. Sales of soda pop, popcorn, and candy average $1 per customer. It is predicted that *Hot Tub Thrills* would continue to play to a full house (adults only) for one more week and to 75 percent of capacity in the week thereafter. Attendance at *Mary Poppins Meets Godzilla* would be 80 percent of capacity in the first week and 60 percent in the second week. The audience for this movie would include 40 percent children. Rental charges for the movies are $9,000 per week for *Hot Tub Thrills* and $6,000 per week for *Mary Poppins Meets Godzilla.* The contract to rent *Mary Poppins Meets Godzilla* cannot be altered. The contribution margin on concession sales is 40 percent; salaries and other fixed costs amount to $20,000 per week.

Required:
Which alternative should the theater select? Show all calculations.

C 9–3   Special Sales Order

At a time when Quinn Supply Company is operating at full capacity, a regular customer places a special order for 10,000 units. Regular units sell for $13 with variable costs of $8 and monthly fixed costs (of $1 (at full capacity of 30,000 units). The special order will require per unit costs of $4 for materials, $3.50 for labor, and variable overhead of $2. The item will sell for $15, but a special die with no subsequent use will have to be purchased for $4,000. All other fixed costs will be unaffected, but production of regular items will be decreased this month by 50 percent.

Required:
Prepare an analysis to determine whether or not the special order should be accepted. Discuss the full cost, incremental cost, and opportunity cost aspects of the situation. Discuss any other factors that could influence the decision.

C 9-4   Transfer Price Dilemma

Doter Automobile Sales Company has four operating divisions—new cars, used cars, parts, and service. These divisions frequently have transactions with each other. For example, the used car division acquires trade-ins from the new car division and has them repaired by the service division, using parts from the parts division. The new car division often needs optional extra parts for its customers; the service division also uses parts in its work for all of its customers. The service division also does warranty work on cars sold by the new car division.

Required:
Discuss the various transfer pricing problems that are likely to arise in this company. Consider only the decision making aspects of transfer pricing, and do not discuss the evaluation of performance of the various divisions.

C 9-5   Acquire or Retain?

The Upstart Raiders of the B.F.L. have a chance to acquire the services of Ace Riflearm, a star quarterback who has become a free agent in the opposition D.F.L. Having Riflearm on the team should improve attendance by 10,000 admissions per game. The season lasts for 16 games with an equal number of home and away games. The average admission is $10 per person per game, of which the home team collects $7.50 and the visiting team $2.50. Contribution margins earned on concession sales at home games amount to $2 per person per game. Riflearm demands a yearly salary of $600,000, but Fred Fumbly, the current quarterback (whose salary is $50,000 per year), will be released if Riflearm is hired.

Required:
(a)   Should Riflearm be offered the contract?
(b)   What is the minimum increase in attendance necessary to enable the terms of the contract to be worthwhile to the Raiders?
(c)   What if Riflearm is a flop and after half a season, attendance returns to its previous levels?
(d)   What other factors would be pertinent to this decision?

Problems

P 9-1   Special Order Sales Opportunity

Hoglund Company produces bathroom fixtures. One particular product has the following unit costs:

Direct Materials	$32
Direct Labor	18
Variable Overhead ($6 per hour)	6
Fixed Overhead ($18 per hour)	18
	$74

This item is presently sold to wholesale distributors for $90. Variable marketing costs amount to $9 per unit sold. Fixed administrative costs average 10 percent of the sales revenues of all products budgeted to be sold under normal conditions and will not increase if any new orders are accepted.

A department store has offered to purchase 15,000 of these fixtures, provided that Hoglund will reduce the price to $72. However, to meet this increase in volume, annual fixed manufacturing costs will be increased by $120,000, mainly for the rental of extra equipment and facilities.

Required:

(a) Should this special order be accepted on a one-time basis? Show all calculations.

(b) What extra information would be useful in answering part (a)?

(c) Instead of incurring the additional fixed overhead, the order could be filled by reducing sales to wholesale distributors by 5,000 units. Should this alternative be accepted? Show all calculations.

P 9-2 Distress Pricing of Obsolete Inventory Items

Lettam Toy Company began manufacturing yo-yos in anticipation of continued strong sales. In 19X1, the company purchased special-purpose machinery to turn out 5,000,000 yo-yos per year. The machinery cost $800,000 and was expected to have a useful life of four years. During 19X1 and 19X2, 4,000,000 yo-yos were produced with unit costs as follows:

Materials	$.20
Direct Labor	.30
Variable Overhead	.05
Fixed Overhead (including depreciation)	.15
Variable Marketing Costs	.05
Other Fixed Costs	.10
	$.85

Sales prices had been $1.20 throughout 19X1 and 19X2, but toward the end of 19X2, the demand suddenly dropped off. For 19X3, the market outlook was such that similar yo-yos could be purchased for 45¢.

Required:

(a) Should the company continue to manufacture and sell yo-yos in 19X3? Show all calculations.

(b) Assume that on January 1, 19X3, the company had on hand 500,000 yo-yos manufactured in 19X2. Should the company try to sell those for 45¢? Why or why not?

(c) What treatment was given to the cost of the special purpose equipment in the preceding analysis? Why?

(d) What additional information would be useful in this situation?

P 9-3 Special Sales Orders

Weiss Company manufactures water beds. For 19X3, the budgeted income statement for sales at regular prices was as follows:

Sales (9,000 @ $400)............................		$3,600,000
Less: Cost of Goods Sold		
Materials	$675,000	
Direct Labor	900,000	
Overhead	900,000	
		$2,475,000
Gross Margin		$1,125,000
Less: Marketing and Administrative Costs......		585,000
Net Income		$ 540,000

Analysis of these items shows that 50 percent of the budgeted overhead is fixed and that variable marketing and administrative costs are 10 percent of sales revenue. An offer has been received to purchase 2,000 water beds for $300 each, with delivery to be made through 19X3.

Required: (Consider each of the following *separately* and *independently*.)
(a)   Should the offer be accepted? Show calculations and state any assumptions that were made.
(b)   Assume that the special order can be filled only by reducing sales of regularly priced items by 1,000 units. Otherwise, fixed manufacturing costs will increase by $100,000 annually in order to increase output above 10,000 units. Should the offer be accepted under either of these alternative conditions? Show all calculations.
(c)   A separate offer is received to purchase 5,000 units. The negotiated price will be total variable manufacturing cost plus 20 percent. All marketing costs can be avoided on this transaction, but sales to regular customers will have to be reduced by 4,000 units. Should this offer be accepted? Show all calculations and state assumptions.
(d)   Another offer is received from a retail outlet that wishes to purchase 4,000 economy versions of the usual product. To manufacture these, materials costs will be reduced 20 percent per unit, labor costs by 25 percent, and variable overhead by 10 percent. Variable marketing costs will also be reduced by 50 percent on this order. The price offered is $250 per unit. To expand capacity to a new maximum of 13,000 (from the present 10,000) additional fixed overhead of $125,000 will be incurred. Should this offer be accepted? Show all calculations.

P 9-4   Special Sales Order—Alternative Opportunities

Meckfessel Manufacturing Company has recently experienced difficulty in earning profits. For 19X6, the budgeted income statement appeared as follows:

Sales	$6,250,000
Less: Cost of Goods Sold	3,000,000
Gross Profit	$3,250,000
Less: Operating Expenses	3,500,000
Net Loss	($ 250,000)

Cost of goods sold includes $2,000,000 for materials and labor and $1,000,000 for manufacturing overhead. Analysis also showed that manufacturing overhead included $500,000 of fixed costs and that a machine hour rate was in effect, based on a budgeted capacity of 50,000 hours. Maximum capacity is 80,000 hours.

To improve profit performance, the company is considering accepting some additional production of a new product similar to the ones it presently manufactures and distributes. The following information has been developed for the new product:

(1) Materials and labor will amount to $50 per unit.

(2) Each unit of output will require two machine hours of processing.

(3) Fixed manufacturing costs will not change.

(4) Other operating expenses will remain unchanged, except that a 5 percent commission on sales revenue will be paid to the sales manager who coordinated this proposal.

(5) The proposed sales price is $60 per unit for 10,000 units.

Based on the following computation, the company decided to reject the new product:

	Total	Per Unit
Sales (10,000 units)	$600,000	$60
Cost of Goods Sold	700,000	70
Gross Profit	($100,000)	($10)
Operating Expenses	30,000	3
Net Loss	($130,000)	($13)

Required:

(a) Prepare an analysis to determine whether or not the company should accept the special offer. Show all supporting calculations.

(b) Show how the original analysis was prepared. How was the $70 per unit figure for cost of goods sold computed? What was wrong and what was right with that original analysis?

(c) What minimum price should be accepted for this sales offer?

(d) What other factors might influence the decision? Why?

P 9-5   Incremental Sales Alternatives

Mapes Company makes and distributes three brands of laundry detergent, De-Foam, Clean-All, and Sludge-Off. To boost sales, a special three-month promotion of one of the brands is being considered. It will involve putting 25¢ cash refund coupons in boxes of one brand for the three-month period. Current monthly results are as follows:

	De-Foam	Clean-All	Sludge-Off
Sales Price	$2.00	$1.60	$2.40
Unit Cost	$1.76	$1.12	$1.84
Contribution Margin Ratio	20%	40%	30%
Monthly Sales Volume (units)	320,000	240,000	300,000
Forecast Increase in Sales Volume......	200,000	120,000	80,000

It is expected that only 60 percent of all coupons will be redeemed.

The coupons will be placed in all boxes, both the normal monthly sales and the forecast increased sales. Unit cost is a full cost based on normal monthly volume. Each product requires equal amounts of labor and machine processing. A plant-wide overhead application rate is in effect. Advertising of the special promotion will cost an extra $4,000 per month.

Required:

(a) Prepare an analysis to determine whether or not the promotion should be undertaken and to choose the product that will be promoted. Show all calculations.

(b) What assumptions were necessary in order to arrive at the preceding solution?

(c) What extra information would be helpful?

P 9–6 Make or Buy Decisions

Shepard Company is about to introduce a new clothes dryer to its existing product line of home appliances. Motors for the dryer can be acquired from an outside company for $60 each.

The production manager proposes that the company make the motor itself. This will require the rental of some additional equipment and relocation of some existing operations. Equipment rental will cost $75,000 per year. Space now used to store raw materials inventories will become the site of the motor manufacturing operations. The rent allocated to this part of the plant presently amounts to $60,000 per year. To provide storage space for the inventories, a vacant warehouse across the street can be rented for $90,000 per year.

The following preliminary analysis of the motor's manufacturing costs assumes that 15,000 motors per year will be produced:

	Cost per Motor
Materials	$24
Direct Labor	20
Variable Overhead	6
Fixed Overhead	3
Equipment Rental	5
Rent	4
	$62

Required:

(a) Should the company manufacture the motors or purchase them from the outside company? Show all calculations.

(b) Comment on the derivation of the $62 unit cost.

(c) Should the motors be manufactured or purchased if the activity level is (1) 5,000 motors per year or (2) 30,000 motors per year?

P 9–7 Make or Buy Decisions

Alston Company manufactures engines and has been considering the purchase of some component parts that it presently produces. In particular, Part 777 is under review, because it could be acquired for $4.30 per unit from an outside supplier. Purchasing and warehousing costs will increase by $5,000 per month if this is done, regardless of the number of units purchased.

Part 777 is presently produced at the rate of 20,000 units per month with manufacturing costs as follows:

		Costs
Materials	$ 30,000
Direct Labor	20,000
Manufacturing Overhead......	50,000
	$100,000

Direct labor costs $10 per hour and overhead is applied on a labor hours basis. The variable overhead rate is $20 per labor hour.

Required:

(a) Should the company continue to manufacture Part 777 or should it be purchased outside? Show all calculations.

(b) What would be the decision if the monthly volume was (1) 10,000 units or (2) 40,000 units?

(c) Assume that the production facilities idled if Part 777 is not manufactured can be rented for $10,000 per month. How would this affect the decision in part (a)?

(d) What other information would be useful in this situation?

P 9–8   Make or Buy Decisions

Due to substantially increased demand, Wong Corporation must decide whether to continue to manufacture a particularly complex component of its final product or to purchase an identical item from the Wight Corporation. The following information is available:

(1) Wight Corporation will supply up to 20,000 units of the component each month at a price of $24 per unit. The normal monthly production volume has been 10,000 units.

(2) The component is normally processed by the Cutting and Grinding Departments in the Wong Corporation. All raw materials are introduced into production in the Cutting Department, but only labor and overhead are incurred in the Grinding Department. An Assembly Department processes the component once it is completed.

(3) If the component is purchased outside, special cutting equipment will have no immediate use in the Cutting Department. This equipment cost $200,000 five years ago and is being depreciated at the rate of $10,000 per year over an expected 20-year life.

(4) Direct labor costs and any accompanying overhead costs for the component in the Cutting Department will be avoided completely. All capacity related overheads, including the depreciation mentioned in part (3), will be unaffected.

(5) In the Grinding Department, direct labor normally used on the component will be temporarily diverted to indirect labor (60 percent) and idle time (40 percent). Other variable overhead in the Grinding Department will be cut by 90 percent.

(6) Variable manufacturing overhead is allocated to production on a direct labor cost basis in both departments—100 percent in Cutting and 200 percent in Grinding.

(7) If the part is purchased outside, additional storage and handling charges amounting to $10,000 per month will be incurred by the Assembly Department.

(8) For a typical month when 10,000 components were produced, the following manufacturing costs were incurred:

	Cutting	Grinding
Materials	$ 45,000	$ —
Direct Labor	60,000	45,000
Total Overhead......	160,000	190,000
	$265,000	$235,000

(9) The production of this component has amounted to 10 percent of the total activity of the Cutting and Grinding Departments.

(10) Total monthly fixed overheads were $100,000 in the Grinding Department. Both departments are operating well below their potential total capacity.

Required:

(a) Prepare an analysis to determine whether the component should be purchased outside or manufactured by the Cutting and Grinding Departments. Show all calculations and state all assumptions.

(b) Comment on the treatment of the following items in the preceding analysis:
   (1) Depreciation—Cutting Department
   (2) Direct labor—Grinding Department
   (3) Fixed overheads—both departments
   (4) Capacity levels—both departments
   (5) Overhead costs in general
   (6) Assembly Department costs

(c) What additional information could be helpful?

P 9–9   Product Line Discontinuation

Carlone Company has two major product lines and one by-product. Operating results for a typical month were as follows (in thousands):

	Product A	Product B	By-Product C	Total
Sales	$ 640	$840	$ 20	$1,500
Less: Cost of Sales	480	500	20	1,000
Gross Margin	$ 160	$340	$ –0–	$ 500
Less: Operating Costs	178	200	2	380
Net Income	$(18)	$140	$(2)	$ 120

It has been proposed that production and sales of Product A and By-product C be discontinued due to their continued unprofitable operating results. Further analysis shows cost of goods sold included fixed manufacturing overheads totaling $200,000. This amount was allocated equally to Products A and B. Fixed marketing and administrative costs amounted to $150,000 and were allocated to all three products on the basis of net sales revenues. Finally, By-product C has been allocated variable manufacturing costs equal to its sales revenues. By-product C is produced jointly with B and is completely independent of Product A. Variable manufacturing, marketing, and administrative costs are incurred at quite different rates for each of the products.

Required:

(a) Prepare an analysis to determine which, if any, of the two apparently unprofitable product lines should be discontinued. Show all calculations and state all assumptions.

(b) How did the analysis for Product A differ (if at all) from that for By-product C? Why?

(c) What other information would be useful in the preceding analysis?

P 9-10 Product Line Addition

Fred Friendly, the sales manager of Dodge Incorporated, has proposed the addition of a deluxe model to the company's product line. Forecast sales for this model are 40,000 units per month at a sales price of $45. However, there would be a definite side effect on sales of the standard model of the same product. Its volume would fall by 20,000 units to 60,000 units per month.

There is sufficient plant capacity available to manufacture the new model, but additional salary and production support costs will add $80,000 to fixed factory overhead costs. Administrative costs would be increased by $20,000 per month, but marketing costs would continue at the same total amount. Manufacturing overhead is presently allocated on a labor hour basis.

The following preliminary analysis of revenues and costs per unit of the two products has been prepared:

	Standard		Deluxe	
Sales		$35		$45
Less: Materials	$6		$15	
Direct Labor	9		12	
Variable Manufacturing Overhead	3	18	4	31
Contribution Margin		$17		$14
Less: Fixed Manufacturing Overhead Costs	$6		$10	
Marketing Costs	4		4	
Administrative Costs	3	13	3.5	17.5
Net Income (Loss)		$ 4		$ (3.5)

Before a final decision was made to reject the apparently unprofitable proposal, additional review revealed the following information:

(1) Standard items require one hour of direct labor processing.

(2) Deluxe items will require one and one-quarter hours of direct labor processing.

(3) Fixed overhead allocated to the deluxe units includes an amount based on the prevailing application rate plus the additional amounts spread over 40,000 units of output.

(4) Marketing and administrative costs are presently allocated to standard items at a rate per unit of output. These same rates were used as the basis for determining the cost per unit of deluxe items.

Required:

(a) Prepare an analysis to determine whether or not the deluxe model should be introduced. Show all calculations and explain all assumptions.

(b) Criticize the preliminary analysis. Explain any errors or inconsistencies.

(c) What additional information would be useful in this situation?

P 9–11 Product Line Discontinuation and Modifications

Plunkett Company has four major product lines. A summary income statement (in thousands) for a typical month follows:

	A	B	C	D	Total
Sales......................	$ 40	$75	$ 45	$100	$260
Less: Cost of Goods Sold......	28	40	33	64	165
Gross Profit	$ 12	$35	$ 12	$ 36	$ 95
Less: Operating Expenses	14	22.5	13.5	26	76
Net Income	$(2)	$12.5	$(1.5)	$ 10	$ 19

Additional analysis produced the following information:

	A	B	C	D
Units Sold	2,000	2,500	3,000	4,000
Sales Price per Unit	$20	$30	$15	$25
Variable Manufacturing Costs per Unit	$10	$12	$ 7	$12
Variable Marketing Costs per Unit	$ 5	$ 6	$ 3	$ 4

All fixed costs are incurred at the firm-wide level. Fixed manufacturing costs are allocated among the products on the basis of units produced and sold. Fixed marketing costs are allocated on the basis of each product line's sales revenue.

Required:
(a) Revise the summary income statement into a format that is more compatible with the needs of incremental analysis.
(b) Why is the revised statement prepared in part (a) superior to the original?
(c) Should Product A be discontinued? Why or why not?
(d) Should Product C be discontinued? Why or why not?

P 9–12 Constrained Resource Analysis

The management of Harris Company, which presently produces only Product X, is considering a proposal to use its productive capacity to manufacture a new product, Y. A departmental overhead application rate based on machine hours is in effect. Production costs and other operating data for the two products are as follows:

	Product X	Product Y
Sales Price per Unit	$ 3.50	$ 2.50
Production Costs (20,000 pounds of output)		
Direct Materials	$ 7,500	$10,000
Direct Labor	25,000	17,500
Manufacturing Overhead	20,000	10,000
	$52,500	$37,500

Analysis of total manufacturing overhead shows that, based on an expected capacity utilization of 4,000 machine hours, the maximum number of machine hours available, the variable overhead rate was set at $4 per hour and the fixed overhead rate at $6 per hour.

Required:

(a) Which product (or products) should be produced if the demand for both products is 20,000 pounds? Show all calculations.

(b) Which product (or products) should be produced if the demand for both products is 80,000 pounds? Show all calculations.

(c) What production decision should be made if the demand is 60,000 pounds for both products? Show all calculations.

(d) If decisions were made on the basis of contribution margin per pound of output, what problems might arise?

(e) What extra information would be helpful in this analysis?

P 9-13   Incremental Analysis of Constrained Resource Situation

Frazier Company finds that it will probably be unable to manufacture all of the required parts for its product due to a substantial short-term increase in demand. In Department X, monthly capacity is limited to 6,000 machine hours. Two components, R and S, are usually processed in that department. Their normal processing costs per unit are as follows:

	R	S
Materials	$ 80	$10
Labor	20	50
Overhead	50	25
	$150	$85

Overhead is allocated at the rate of $10 per machine hour, and monthly fixed overhead costs total $24,000. If components R and S are not manufactured, they must be purchased from outside suppliers for $145 and $85, respectively. The production schedule calls for monthly volumes of 1,500 units of R and 3,000 units of S.

Required:

(a) Prepare an analysis to determine which product (or products) should be purchased and which should be manufactured. Show all calculations.

(b) How would your analysis change if 8,000 hours were available?

(c) What would be the minimum outside prices that would make it worthwhile to purchase all the required parts from outside suppliers? What assumptions are necessary in answering this question?

(d) How were the fixed overhead costs considered in the foregoing analysis?

P 9-14   Replace or Maintain Existing Facilities—Elementary Analysis

Lindsay Company has production equipment in Department T that was acquired six years ago for $160,000. This equipment has been depreciated on a straight line basis in anticipation of a sixteen-year useful life and zero salvage value. It is special-purpose equipment and has a current cash resale value of only $10,000. The annual operating costs for the only product it is used to manufacture are as follows:

Materials	$ 90,000
Labor	50,000
Variable Overhead Cost.........	65,000
(including depreciation)	45,000
Total Manufacturing Costs	$250,000

In a typical year, 100,000 units are produced. A new machine is now available that will enable materials costs to be reduced by 20 percent, and labor and variable overhead costs by 25 percent. However, fixed overhead (excluding depreciation) will increase by $25,000. This new machine will cost $240,000 and will have a ten-year useful life with no expected resale value. The capacity of the new equipment is 200,000 units per year.

Required:
(a) Prepare an analysis to determine whether or not the existing machinery should be replaced.
(b) What assumptions were necessary to arrive at the answer in part (a)?
(c) What are the shortcomings of the type of analysis used in this problem?

P 9–15   Joint Products—Alternative Processing Configurations

Nelson Company operates a series of manufacturing processes in its plant. At present, all four final products pass through three common processing operations and then pass individually through separate finishing departments. However, the four products could also be sold at the point where they emerge from the third common processing department.

For May of 19X6, the following operating data were available:

Product	Volume (Units)	Unit Sales Price (Final Product)	Unit Sales Price (Intermediate Product)	Separate Finishing Costs
B2.........	20,000	$12	$ 8	$120,000
C3	10,000	8	2	40,000
D4	5,000	16	10	40,000
E5.........	5,000	6	5	10,000

The total cost of operating the three common processing departments was $120,000 for May. The company has been allocating common processing costs to final products on the basis of their net realizable value at the separation point at the end of the third process. "Separate finishing costs" do not include this allocated amount.

Required:
(a) On the assumption that all products must be sold in their intermediate state or in the final product state, prepare an analysis to determine which of these alternatives is preferable.
(b) On the assumption that the further processing decision may be made for each product independently, prepare an analysis to determine which ones should be sold as final products and which ones at the intermediate stage.
(c) Comment on the way in which the joint costs were allocated for the purposes of the decisions in parts (a) and (b).
(d) Which alternative is better for the company, (a) or (b)? Why? Show calculations.

(e) Prepare an income statement for the firm based on the assumption that all four products are subjected to further processing. Comment on the contents of this income statement compared to your answer to part (d).

P 9–16   Joint Products and By-Products—Subsequent Processing Alternatives—Yield Alternatives

Michelle Company produces two separate outputs, Maine and Bye, as a result of a series of common processing operations. There is a facility available in Department W for further refining of the separate products, but its processing capacity is limited to 40,000 gallons per month. Both products can be sold either in their intermediate state at the end of the common processing or after being further refined. Cost and operating data for a typical month are as follows.

	Final		Intermediate	
	Maine	**Bye**	**Maine**	**Bye**
Sales Prices per Gallon.........	$7	$1	$5	$ .50

	Common Process	**Department W**
Processing Costs		
Variable	$2 per gallon	Maine—$1.25 per gallon
		Bye—$ .10 per gallon
Fixed	$150,000	$10,000

The total output of the common processes is now 100,000 gallons of Maine and 50,000 gallons of Bye. For income reporting purposes, the sales proceeds of Bye are treated as an offset to the costs of processing Maine.

Required:
(a) What is the best possible production combination? That is, what is the best use to which the capacity in Department W can be put? Show all calculations.
(b) Assume that the company decides to process as much Maine as possible in Department W and to sell all of Bye in its intermediate state. However, by increasing fixed costs in the common processing operations by $80,000, it will be possible to alter the yield ratio to 125,000 gallons of Maine and 25,000 gallons of Bye. Should this modification be implemented? Show all calculations.
(c) By increasing fixed costs in Department W to $80,000, the capacity there can be increased to 150,000 gallons. Apply this information to part (a). What is the best production combination now?
(d) Consider the alternatives in parts (b) and (c) simultaneously. What is the best production combination now?
(e) What allocation procedure was used for the common processing costs in all the foregoing decision analysis? Why?

P 9–17   Joint Products—Contribution Analysis to Determine Input Price Limits

Galsoud Chemical Company is negotiating the purchase of supplies of an input, Product X, that is used in the manufacture of its two main products, Y and Z. Common processing in Department A involves the mixing of X with all other ingredients to generate Y and

Z in a 4:1 ratio. Production and operating data for a typical month when total output is 100,000 gallons are as follows:

	Department A	Department B	Department C
Variable Manufacturing Costs	$5 per gallon*	$2 per gallon	$3 per gallon
Fixed Manufacturing Costs	$250,000	$160,000	$50,000
Output (gallons)	100,000	80,000	20,000
Variable Marketing Costs	—	$1 per gallon	$2 per gallon
Fixed Administrative Costs	—	$40,000	$30,000

* Excludes the cost of input X.

In addition, firm-wide fixed costs of $100,000 are not allocated to any of the three departments.

For each gallon of output of Department A, one half gallon of output X is required. Products Y and Z are processed individually in Departments B and C, respectively. The firm's profit goal is to earn a profit equal to 5 percent of total sales revenue. Common processing costs are allocated on the basis of physical quantities of output for income measurement purposes. Product Y sells for $15 per gallon and Z for $20 per gallon.

Required:

(a) Prepare an analysis to determine the maximum purchase price that the company should be willing to pay for Product X in order to be able to meet the stated profit goal. Show all calculations.

(b) What would the maximum purchase price be if total output were (1) 50,000 gallons and (2) 200,000 gallons?

(c) What would be the effect on part (a) if the yield of X and Y changed to 3:2, assuming that all other costs and prices remained the same? Show all calculations.

P 9-18 Joint Products—Breakeven Analysis—Alternative Production Combinations—Input Price Decisions

Solestes Company processes soybeans and has a plant capable of processing 200,000 tons per year. The yields of output from one ton of fully processed soybeans are as follows:

	Weight	Market Value per Pound
Meal	800 lbs.*	20¢
Oil	400 lbs.*	50¢
Husks	600 lbs.	10¢
Waste	200 lbs.	—
	2,000 lbs.	

* At the start of Stage II, 1,200 pounds enter the stage.

In the first stage of processing, the husks and waste are separated from the beans. In the second stage, the shelled beans are pressed to separate the oil. Subsequently, in three separate processing operations, (1) the oil is further refined, (2) the meal is ground and mixed with other nutrients, and (3) the husks are separated from the waste.

For a typical month, raw material, processing, and marketing costs are as follows:

	Variable Costs	Fixed Costs (per year)
Stage I	$ 40 per ton of raw beans	$10,000,000
Stage II	$ 90 per ton of shelled beans	10,000,000
Process 1	$150 per ton of oil	10,000,000
Process 2	$ 60 per ton of meal	5,000,000
Process 3	$ 40 per ton of husks and waste	5,000,000

The $30 per ton cost of purchasing raw beans is included in Stage I variable costs. Presently, 160,000 tons are processed per year and all final products are sold. Assume that the products have no sales value until all processing is completed.

Required: (Answer each of the following parts independently, except where indicated.)

(a) At the present level of operations, are all final products profitable? Why or why not? Show all calculations.

(b) At what volume of operations (in terms of tons of beans processed) will the company (1) break even and (2) earn a profit margin of $25,000,000?

(c) By increasing variable costs by 50 percent in Process 3, the waste material can be made into a salable fertilizer with a market value of 5¢ per pound. Yield ratios and fixed costs will not be affected. Is this alternative acceptable or not? Show all calculations.

(d) In order to achieve full capacity of 200,000 tons processed annually, the company is considering reducing prices by 10 percent on all final products. Should this be done?

(e) In Stage II processing, a new production method has been developed. It will re-duce present overall variable costs by one-third, but fixed costs will increase to $15,000,000. The new method will also improve the yield so that 25 percent more oil will be retained from each ton of shelled beans. There will be a corresponding 100-pound decrease in the quantity of meal obtained. Should this new method be introduced? Show all calculations.

(f) What price can be paid for raw beans if the company is to operate at full capacity and earn a $12,500,000 profit?

(g) In each of the foregoing situations, what treatment was given to the common process-ing costs in Stage I and Stage II? Why?

P 9–19   Transfer Prices—Short-Run Decision Analysis

Caulfield Company has two divisions, B and C. Division B manufactures a component that may be sold to outside customers or used by Division C in its production operations. For a typical month, the following cost and operating data apply:

Division B

Sales Price to Outside Customers	$150 per unit
Variable Manufacturing Costs	$90 per unit
Variable Marketing Costs	$20 per unit
Fixed Manufacturing and Marketing Costs......	$500,000
Capacity per month	20,000 units
Outside Sales	10,000 units

Division C

Outside Supplier's Price	$115 per unit
Purchase Requirements	8,000 units

Division C is faced with the alternative of purchasing from the outside supplier or accepting units from Division B. In the past, transfer prices have been set equal to full absorption cost of the producing division, with fixed costs allocated to production on the basis of maximum capacity. However, allowance is made in the internal arrangement for a 50 percent reduction in the usual variable marketing costs. Sales to outside customers have usually accounted for 50 percent of Division B's capacity. Division C has monthly production requirements of 8,000 units of the component produced by Division B.

Required:
(a) Determine whether Division C should buy from the outside supplier or from Division B. Ignore the existing transfer pricing arrangement.

(b) Evaluate the present transfer pricing procedure in terms of its ability to produce correct decisions for the firm as a whole.

(c) What transfer price would allow the correct decision to be made in this situation? Why?

(d) By how much must the outside purchase price be reduced before it will be worthwhile for Division C to purchase from an outside supplier?

(e) What bearing does Division B's sales price of $150 have on this decision? Why?

(f) Repeat steps (a) through (e) assuming that Division B is already selling all 20,000 units of its products to regular outside customers at $150 per unit.

P 9–20   Transfer Pricing—Incremental Analysis of Acquisition Alternatives

Flynn Company's Division J manufactures turntables which it sells to other firms that manufacture stereo systems. For its single product, the division's unit costs are as follows:

Direct Materials	$ 60
Direct Labor	30
Manufacturing Overhead	45
Marketing Costs	20
Administrative Costs	10
	$165

The sales price of the turntable is $200. Current sales volume is forecast to be only 80,000 units for 19X6. Normal capacity is 100,000 units and overhead rates have been set on the basis of that figure. Fixed overhead amounts to $3,000,000 and administrative costs (all fixed) are $1,000,000. Marketing costs are variable and amount to 10 percent of sales revenue.

Division K of Flynn Company has expressed an interest in purchasing turntables from Division J. These turntables will be incorporated in a new type of home entertainment center that Division K proposes to market. Division K presently purchases turntables from an outside supplier for $150. Division K is currently selling a premium quality home entertainment center for $1,250, with a contribution margin of $375. Volume is only 15,000 per year, but the new model will be an economy version. Forecast volume of the new model is 30,000 units with a contribution margin of $200 and a sales price of $995, assuming that turntables are purchased from an outside supplier.

The manager of Division J does not feel that a price below $165 should be considered and is hesitant to try to match the outside price of $150. Division J would incur no marketing costs on turntables sold to Division K.

Required:

(a) Prepare an analysis to determine whether Division K should purchase the turntables from Division J or from the outside supplier. Show all calculations.

(b) What would be the answer to part (a) if Division J were able to sell all 100,000 units of its output to its regular customers?

(c) What would the answer to part (a) be if the sales of Division K's new model were (1) 15,000 units, or (2) 50,000 units?

(d) Assume J can sell 80,000 units to outsiders. Considering the original situation, what outside purchase price (if any) would cause the two alternatives (outside supply or Division J) to be equally attractive? Show all calculations.

P 9–21 Transfer Prices—Production Alternatives— Incremental Analysis

Judson Company has several operating divisions, two of which are the Former and the Latter. The Former Division is operating at full capacity and is able to sell all of its output to external customers. On the other hand, the Latter Division has not been able to use its full capacity of 10,000 units during the past few months. It has been exploring alternative markets and is in the process of bidding on a government contract to supply 2,000 units of an item that it has the capacity and facilities to produce itself with the exception of one component, Component X. This component can be acquired from an outside supplier, but it could also be obtained from the Former Division. Cost and operating data are as follows:

Latter Division—Cost Estimates for Bid

Materials*		$ 34
Component X†		20
Labor		20
Overhead—Variable ($5 per labor hour)		10
Overhead—Fixed ($8 per labor hour)		16
		$100
Margin Allowed in Government Contract—20% of Manufacturing Costs	20	
Bid Price		$120

Former Division—Component X

Sales Price		$25
Variable Costs	$ 10	
Fixed Costs	10	20
Profit per Unit		$ 5

* Excludes Component X.
† Cost of Component X from Outside Supplier.

Required: (Answer each of the following parts independently, except where instructed otherwise.)

(a) Should Component X be acquired from the outside supplier or from Former Division? Show all calculations and state all assumptions. What is the correct transfer price to facilitate this decision?

(b) Assume that Former Division is also operating below capacity. Answer part (a) under these circumstances.

(c) Answer (a) under the assumption that the contract price allows no margin and allows only for the reimbursement of manufacturing costs. State all assumptions.

(d) Besides the original government contract for 2,000 units, Latter Division has an opportunity to sell 4,000 units at a firm price of $110. Only *one* of the alternatives may be accepted. Which one should it be? (Former Division is still operating at full capacity.) Latter Division has 4,000 units excess capacity. Show all calculations.

(e) Explain the treatment of fixed costs in all of the preceding analyses.

P 9-22   Transfer Prices—Incremental Analysis—Alternative Production and Sales Opportunities

Debellis Company has two operating divisions, Michael and Dominic. The output of the Michael Division can either be sold to outside customers or used by the Dominic Division in its end product. One unit of Michael's output is used for each unit Dominic produces. For the current month, the following operating forecasts have been developed:

	Michael	Dominic
Sales Price (to outside customers)	$360	$640
Variable Costs per Unit	$200	$240*
Fixed Costs per Month	$200,000	$80,000
Capacity (units)	2,000	500
Expected Demand in External Markets (units)	1,200	500

* Excludes the cost of the component manufactured by the Michael Division. If the component is purchased outside, it will cost Dominic $225 per unit.

Required: (Answer each of the following questions independently, except where indicated otherwise.)

(a) Under this month's circumstances, should Dominic purchase the item from Michael or from the outside supplier? Show all calculations. What is the appropriate transfer price in this situation?

(b) Should Dominic purchase from Michael or from the outside supplier if the external demand for Michael's product was (1) 2,000 units or (2) 1,800 units? Show calculations.

(c) Michael Division is considering reducing the price of its product to $300 in anticipation of increasing sales to 2,000 units. Answer part (a) under these circumstances. State all assumptions.

(d) An alternative proposal is to reduce the sales price of Michael's product to $320. This is expected to increase demand to 1,600 units. Answer part (a) under these circumstances. State all assumptions.

(e) Which of the alternatives—(a), (c), or (d)—would be best for the firm as a whole? Show all calculations and state all assumptions.

(f) Explain how (1) capacity levels and (2) monthly fixed costs were treated in the preceding analysis.

P 9-23   Transfer Pricing—Incremental Analysis— Constrained Resource Conditions

Kamp Corporation has two manufacturing divisions, Alpha and Beta. Alpha Division produces two grades of output of a single product with cost specifications as follows:

	Premium	Regular
Materials	$ 4	$ 2
Labor and Variable Overhead......	56	14
	$60	$16

Fixed overhead costs of Alpha are $80,000. Each premium grade item requires four hours of labor, whereas regular grade items require only one hour. There are only 40,000 labor hours available in the Alpha Division due to the limited availability of the particular skilled workers needed. The demand for premium grade items is very restricted. No more than 5,000 can be sold at the present price of $100. On the other hand, regular items are very much in demand at $22 per unit.

Beta Division has a single product with the following cost specifications:

Materials (including a $105 part purchased from outside supplier)	$135
Labor and Variable Overhead	65
	$200

This product sells for $250. Beta Division has the capacity to manufacture 6,000 units, but only 3,000 are presently being produced and sold. Fixed overhead of Beta Division is $75,000.

The major component that the Beta Division uses in its manufacturing operations could be replaced by the premium-grade item that Alpha Division produces. This component is presently purchased from an outside supplier for $105. One unit of the component is used for each unit of final output. However, the item produced by the Alpha Division will require minor modification, causing labor and variable overhead costs to increase by 20 percent in the Beta Division.

Required:

(a) Prepare an analysis to determine whether the Beta Division should continue to purchase the component from the outside supplier or from the Alpha Division. Show all calculations and state all assumptions.

(b) What is the correct transfer price for decision making in the situation described in part (a)?

(c) Revise the analysis in part (a) on the basis of Beta Division being able to sell all 6,000 units of its potential output.

(d) Revise the analysis in part (c) on the basis of Alpha Division being able to sell 9,000 premium-grade items to its regular customers.

(e) Explain the principles of transfer pricing that have been used to support your answers in all of the preceding situations.

P 9–24   Transfer Pricing—Short-term Analysis

Williams and Associates is a firm of business consultants, with three separate operating divisions—(1) systems, (2) programming, and (3) personnel. Each division has its own outside clients, but the divisions often perform engagements for each other. Monthly capacity is 10,000 hours in each department. Each division is treated as a profit center. At the present time, the fee structure and operating costs of the three divisions are as follows:

	Variable Cost per Hour	Fixed Cost per Month	Fee per Hour
Systems	$25	$100,000	$50
Programming	18	80,000	40
Personnel	20	50,000	45

Required: (Treat each of the following as *independent* situations, except where otherwise indicated.)

(a) The Systems Group requires programming support on an engagement. The Programming Group has programmers available who are not presently assigned to a project. Programming support can also be obtained from an independent agency for $35 per hour. What should be done? Show calculations.

(b) Same situation as in part (a), except that all programmers are presently engaged on work for outside clients.

(c) The Systems Group needs assistance in personnel planning and placement for one of its clients. The Personnel Division has staff available. What transfer price should be used for their services in order to make comparisons with alternative sources of the same type of aid? Why?

(d) Same situation as in part (c), except that the Personnel Division has no staff unassigned. The Systems Division's only alternative is to use some of its own staff, but they must be diverted from an engagement for another client. Which group should perform the required work—the Personnel Division or the Systems Division? Why?

(e) The Personnel Division has a project which requires Systems Design and Programming. Both these groups have only 1,000 hours of unassigned time in the current month. Programming support can be obtained from an independent agency for $35 per hour, but there is no alternative source of Systems Design assistance. The job in question requires 3,000 programming hours and 1,500 hours of systems design work. Where should the required work be assigned? What is the incremental cost to the firm of this project?

(f) In all of the foregoing, what consideration was given to the monthly fixed costs? Why?

10

ACCOUNTING CONTROL SYSTEMS

LEARNING OBJECTIVES

After studying Chapter 10, you should be able to:

1. Explain the control concept and describe how accounting systems help managers control operations.
2. Describe a control system, its objectives, and its components.
3. Explain the concept of responsibility accounting and relate it to the systems of vertical and horizontal classification found in organizations.
4. Explain how control responsibility might be handled when joint costs and revenues are involved.
5. List and describe four types of responsibility accounting reports.
6. Distinguish between the traditional and modern views of human behavior in organizations. Explain how the modern views affect management accounting procedures.

Every organization must provide for some kind of managerial control over its activities. Failure to do so invites disorder and chaos, the loss of any sense of direction and purpose in the organization, and an abandonment of the principle of goal-oriented decision making. Through the exercise of control, managers can direct attention to organizational objectives, monitor actual performance, and make changes to achieve the desired degree of conformity between actual and planned performance. The **control concept** underlies all the processes through which a firm is organized and managed toward the achievement of its goals.

This chapter examines (1) the basic concepts of control and their application in accounting information systems, (2) the techniques used in accounting control, their applicability and limitations as parts of a firm's overall internal control system, and (3) the important behavioral issues related to the operations of accounting control systems.

WHAT IS CONTROL?

Control refers to the relationship between a system's *actual* performance and its *planned* or *desired* performance. It is usual to speak of a system being "in control" if its performance goals are being achieved. Conversely, a system is "out of control" when observed performance deviates from that which was planned. Because goals need not always be expressed in absolute terms, performance variations can sometimes be tolerated. In defining the limits of acceptable performance, the obvious problem is that there must be guidelines that allow managers to judge whether the system is in or out of control.

For example, a firm might set specific goals such as $100,000 profit per year, a 20 percent return on investment, or a product cost of $200 per unit. The control condition would be violated if actual performance differed *at all* from these specified goals. But if the goals were expressed as ranges—profit between $80,000 and $120,000, rate of return above 15 percent, or unit costs no greater than $240—performance that stayed within these limits would be considered in control.

Goal specifications vary in their strictness and exactness. Production attributes—especially physical requirements such as weights, sizes, pressures, and temperatures—require detailed and rigorous specifications, which usually can be systematically controlled. In contrast, personal and social benefit programs provided by a firm for its employees are much less susceptible to direct, precise measurements.

There are also different interpretations as to what constitutes control. Does control imply attaining optimal performance in an *absolute* sense (maximizing profits, minimizing costs) or does it imply minimizing the *deviation* of actual from planned performance?

FIGURE 10–1

Rebman Company
Budgeted and Actual Performance Under
Alternative Budgets

	Budget	Actual	Variance
Budget A	$2,200	$2,250	$ 50
Budget B	$2,000	$2,150	$150

Example: Rebman Company uses a budgetary control system to plan and evaluate product cost performance. Two alternative budgets have been developed for producing a single product. Budget A specifies a unit cost of $2,200; Budget B projects a unit cost of $2,000. Differences between the two budgets result from different estimates of labor and overhead production efficiencies.

Using Budget A, manufacturing the product results in actual costs of $2,250 per unit. Using Budget B, actual costs are $2,150 per unit. Each of these budgets can be judged to have been "more effective," but on different grounds. As reflected in Figure 10–1, Budget B helped optimize performance in the sense of *minimizing total cost* ($2,150 versus $2,250). Budget A also controlled performance by *minimizing the deviation* of actual costs from budgeted costs ($50 versus $150).

Both these concepts of control have merit. The first interprets control as maximizing or minimizing the *absolute value* of a performance characteristic. The second approach tries to minimize the *difference* between actual and planned performance.

Another interpretive problem involves the assessment of *planned* performance. Usually actual achievements are compared with a budgeted performance plan that was prepared before operations began. Control then becomes a response to deviations from that "before-the-fact" plan.

The basis for comparison might instead be a plan of the results that *should have been achieved*, given complete knowledge of what actually happened during the control period. Often more detailed control information can be obtained by comparing actual performance with an "after-the-fact" plan and relevant parts of the before-the-fact plan.[1] However, the more conventional before-the-fact basis will be used in this chapter.

HOW CONTROL SYSTEMS OPERATE

Systems theory provides a convenient framework for examining the basic mechanisms that permit managers to control operations. A **system** may be defined as a set of activities that proceeds toward common objectives in an orderly way. These objectives give purpose to the system. The participants

---

[1] See Joel S. Demski, "An Accounting System Structured on a Linear Programming Model," *The Accounting Review*, Vol. 42 (October, 1967), pp. 701–12.

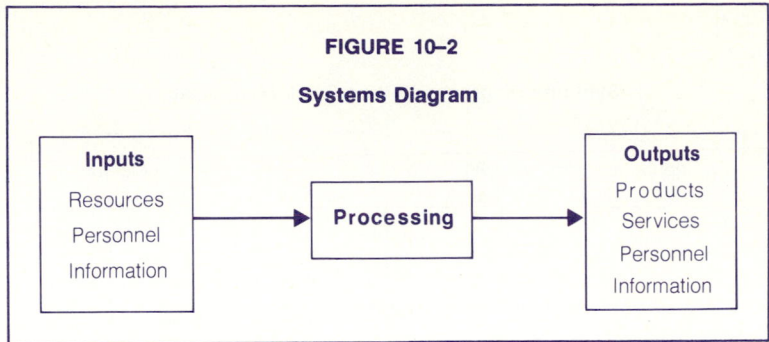

FIGURE 10–2

Systems Diagram

(people, resources, information) interact with each other in the pursuit of those objectives, provoking potential imbalances and conflicts that must be controlled.

Figure 10–2 is a simplified systems diagram. It merely suggests that activities requiring the combination of *inputs* by way of a *processing operation* will result in the production of *outputs*. Other than the path of actions suggested by the ordering of its components, this elementary diagram lacks any suggestion of control. To indicate some sense of purpose, a planning or goal formulation step is added in Figure 10–3. But this still suggests a one-way flow of actions, with no provision for any check on outcomes. Figure 10–4 adds **feedback mechanism** to the systems diagram.

A feedback mechanism relays performance information back to the system's managers. It consists of components designed (1) to perceive, measure, and report performance **(sensor);** (2) to evaluate performance in the light of stated goals (*comparison*); and (3) to modify the inputs, processing, and/or goals (*regulator*). In Figure 10–5, these components are diagrammed in relation to the other parts of the system.

An easily understood real-world system involves the operation of an automobile. The stated *goal* might be to reach a certain destination subject to speed, legal, safety, route, cost, fuel, and comfort requirements. The *inputs* would include the automobile, driver, passengers, luggage, fuel, and information (road

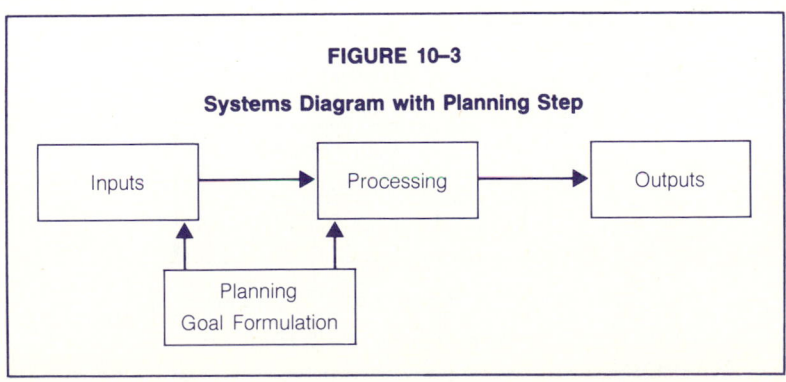

FIGURE 10–3

Systems Diagram with Planning Step

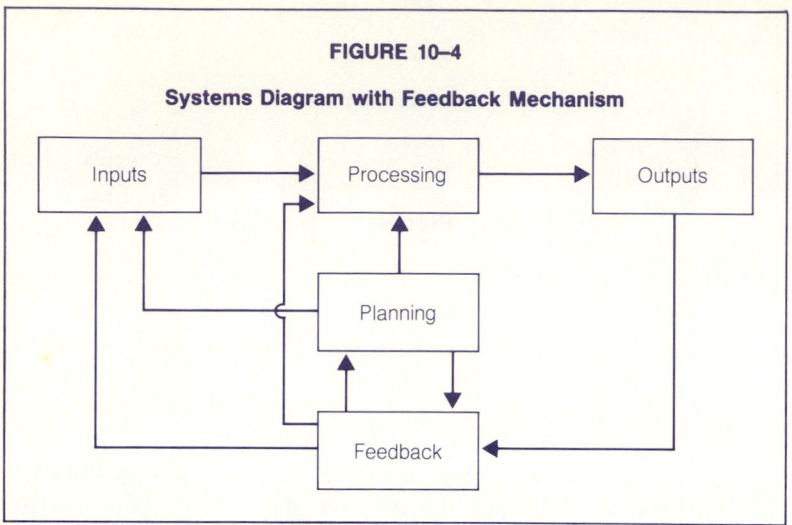

FIGURE 10–4

Systems Diagram with Feedback Mechanism

maps, traffic code, driver's knowledge and experience). The *processing* relates to the interaction of these inputs to obtain the desired result—having the driver, luggage, and passengers arrive at their destination safely and on time.

The feedback control mechanisms include *sensors* (such as the driver's perception of speed, distance, and direction, the fuel gauge, speedometer, rear-vision mirror) that furnish information about the vehicle's performance. Deviations in performance (driving too slow or too fast, taking a wrong turn, running out of gas, getting a speeding ticket) may be discovered by *comparing* these percep-tions with the relevant parts of the stated goals. Required *adjustments* can then be made to various parts of the system—inputs (more fuel, less luggage),

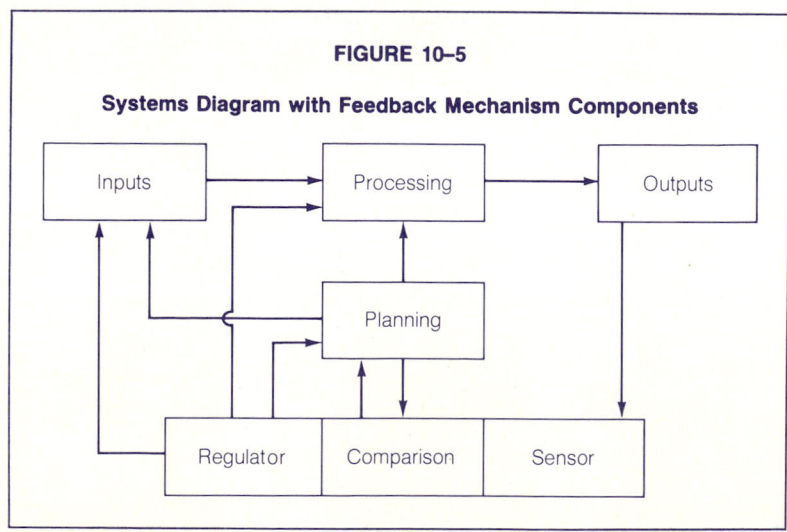

FIGURE 10–5

Systems Diagram with Feedback Mechanism Components

processing (slow down or speed up, get back on the right road), or goals (revise estimated arrival time, change planned destination).

A corresponding business example involves the operations of a budgetary system in a manufacturing firm. The budgeted targets are planned performance objectives. The production system to which the budget applies uses raw materials, money, personnel, and information as *inputs* and *processes* them into the desired *outputs.* To provide feedback data, actual performance must be monitored in terms of equivalent units of output, inputs consumed, and costs. These production and cost measures are then compared to the appropriate budget specifications. The resulting accounting variances can then be used to initiate corrective actions. As will be discussed in Chapter 13, these actions may include modifying the *inputs* (buy materials from other suppliers, hire or fire employees), the *production process* (change production operations, revise schedules, perform more quality control inspections), or the budgetary *goals* (revise variable cost per unit, total fixed costs, input–output relationships).

Accounting control procedures vary in the extent to which they help secure agreement between planned and actual performance. At an elementary level, these procedures may only *report* deviations of actual from planned performance. At an intermediate level, they may include *adjustments of operations* in response to reported deviations for which explanations have been discovered. At the most comprehensive level, they may also encompass *revisions in the planning process* resulting from feedback provided by the control system.

OBJECTIVES OF ACCOUNTING CONTROL SYSTEMS

Internal control objectives include:

1. Protecting the organization's resources.
2. Setting and maintaining information quality standards.
3. Obtaining adherence to policies, guidelines, and procedures stipulated by management.
4. Seeing that the organization works efficiently to achieve its goals.[2]

Protecting Resources   Managers have a basic responsibility to safeguard the resources with which they are entrusted. This responsibility stems from the need for all businesses to maintain capital intact. First of all, control procedures must physically safeguard company assets. This means preventing or minimizing damage, destruction, theft, deterioration, and spoilage due either to deliberate, accidental, or natural causes. Secondly, the firm must be protected against asset mismanagement—the dissipation of company resources by incorrect or inefficient decisions and actions.

Maintaining Information Quality Standards   Control procedures must ensure adequate quality in data processing and reporting. The information to be processed must meet standards of accuracy and reliability so that decision

---

[2] *Statement of Auditing Procedures No. 33* (New York: AICPA, 1963), p. 28. *Statement of Auditing Standards No. 1* (New York: AICPA, 1962), Paragraphs 320–26.

makers can use it confidently. An appropriate quantity of information, neither too much nor too little, must be communicated to decision makers as needed. This information should not be ambiguous to the user, should be presented in a comprehensible form, and should be made available at the proper time. Safety measures, such as backup systems and security procedures, must be observed to protect information from damage or misuse.

Policy Enforcement   Once an organization commits itself to certain planning policies, it must monitor their implementation. Internal control systems should include feedback mechanisms geared to company policies and guidelines. Control can be exercised by observing, supervising, checking, reviewing, and evaluating the performance of managers at all levels. Control can also be maintained by integrating policy guidelines into the decision rules used by managerial decision makers.

Managerial Efficiency   This final category has certain earmarks of a "grab bag" of all the other reasons for keeping management on the track toward achieving its goals. Decisions and actions that may lead away from objectives should be avoided. A wide variety of control procedures must be instituted to help ensure efficient operating performance. As will be discussed, these procedures include planning and decision review techniques, performance measurement and evaluation, and internal audit methods.

RESPONSIBILITY ACCOUNTING

The guiding principle of internal control is that performance should be measured on a basis consistent with the responsibility for that performance. This principle is embodied in the set of practices commonly referred to as **responsibility accounting.**

A system of responsibility accounting is based on an organization's formal authority–responsibility relationships. An accounting control system provides information to help evaluate the performance of both the *decision centers* that are the focal points of authority–responsibility relationships and the *managers* of those decision centers.

CLASSIFICATION IN RESPONSIBILITY ACCOUNTING

Responsibility accounting data may be organized in (1) a **vertical** or **hierarchical classification** according to the level of decision centers or (2) a **horizontal** or **functional classification** according to the decision centers' areas of activity. **Example:**   The organization chart for Citron Corporation in Figure 10–6 illustrates the concept of *vertical classification* for responsibility accounting purposes. The solid line traces out one particular responsibility stream, which runs from the Turlock Assembly Department foreman up to the president of the company.

Performance reports should be prepared for decision centers at each operating level within Citron Corporation. Every decision center's report should include

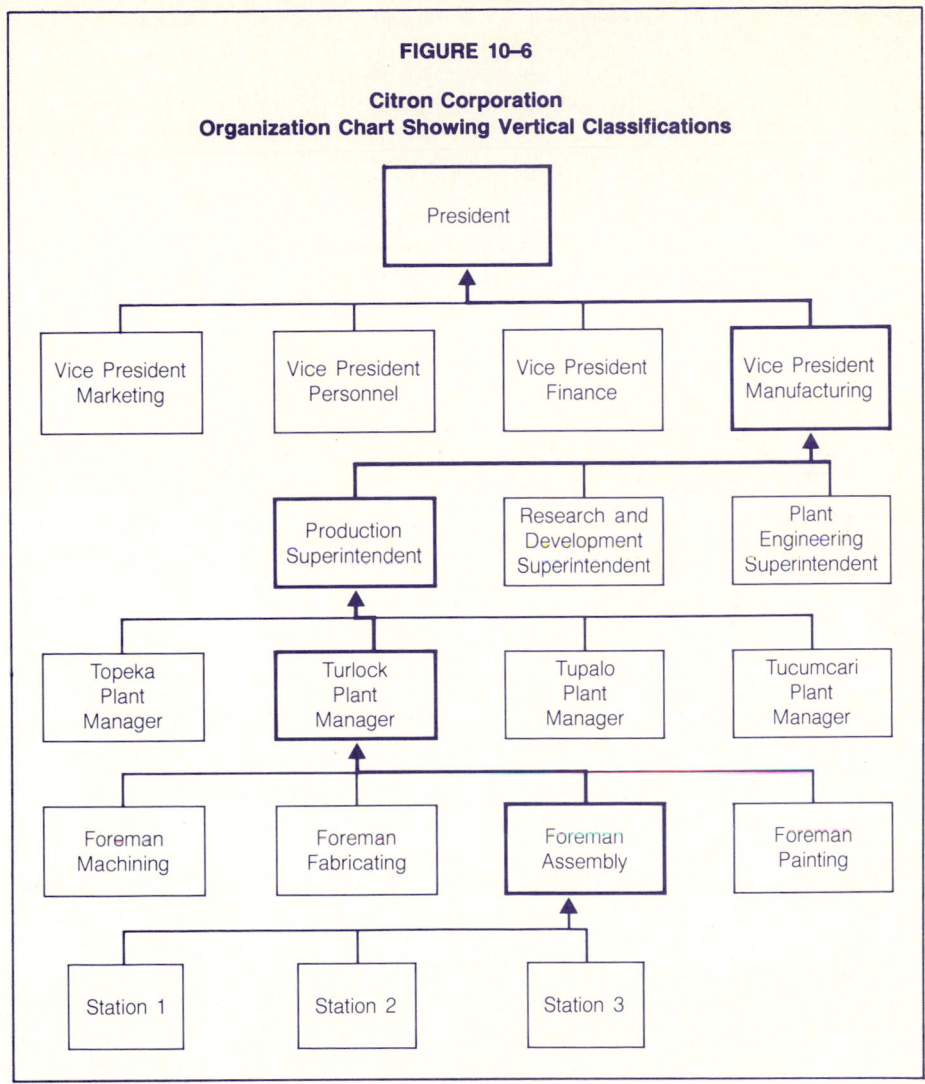

FIGURE 10–6

Citron Corporation
Organization Chart Showing Vertical Classifications

only those items which that decision center can control. The higher in the organization hierarchy the decision center is located, the less detailed the reports become. This reflects differences in the nature and scope of decision making at various reporting levels—broad and comprehensive at the higher levels, specific and detailed at the lower levels.

Horizontal classification describes the separation of performance measurements at the same decision making level within the organizational hierarchy. At that common level, it is necessary to identify performance characteristics with a particular decision center on some systematic basis. For example, in Citron Corporation the various *geographical* plant locations provide a basis for horizontal classification of the Products Division, while the *functional* grouping

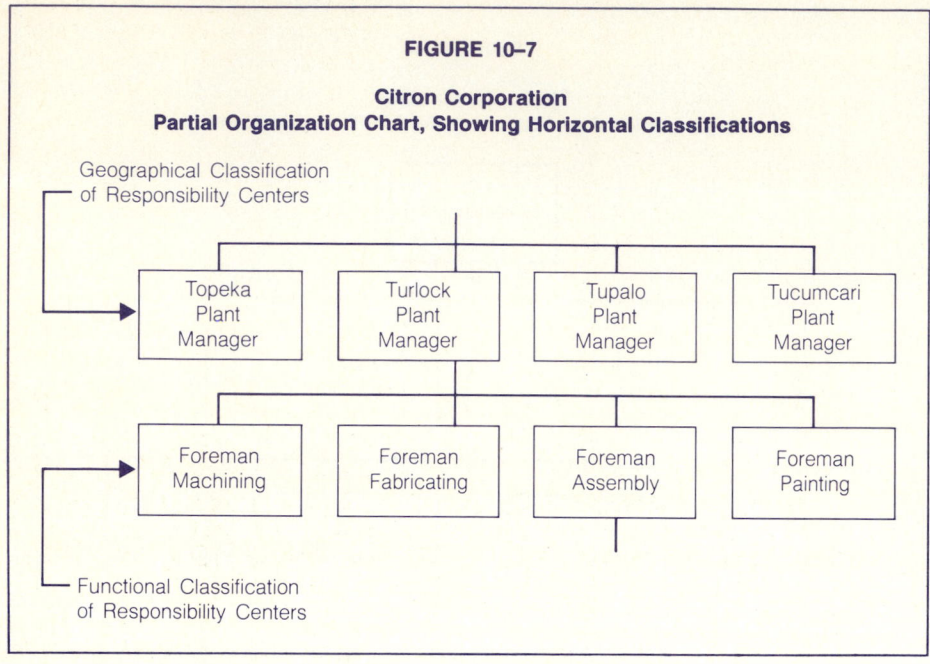

FIGURE 10–7

Citron Corporation
Partial Organization Chart, Showing Horizontal Classifications

Geographical Classification of Responsibility Centers

| Topeka Plant Manager | Turlock Plant Manager | Tupalo Plant Manager | Tucumcari Plant Manager |

| Foreman Machining | Foreman Fabricating | Foreman Assembly | Foreman Painting |

Functional Classification of Responsibility Centers

within the Turlock Plant is the basis for another horizontal classification of performance measures. These two types of horizontal classification are illustrated in Figure 10–7.

Naturally, the *formal* lines of authority and responsibility are effective only to the extent that they correspond to the organization's *real* decision making and command structure. This correlation can best be achieved by ensuring that the organizational structure is designed efficiently and that it operates as planned. Attention to the proper location of decision making authority is critical. At each operating level, authority should be consistent in scope and location with the need for decisions that regulate the flow of resources through the organization.

WHICH ITEMS ARE CONTROLLABLE?

The controllability of costs, revenues, and other performance measures is a pivotal feature of responsibility accounting. To be considered controllable, a performance measure must be capable of being influenced by the decision maker responsible for controlling it. In the case of costs, this requires a definite cause–effect relationship between the decision to incur a cost and the resulting resource transformation. Similar cause–effect relationships must be identified to establish the controllability of revenues, assets, liabilities, and equities by various decision centers as part of a complete responsibility accounting system.

Examples of demonstrated cause–effect relationships include (1) tracing raw materials usage to the specific manufacturing department where the materials are added to work in process, (2) tracing sales commissions to the sales of particular product lines, and (3) tracing plant and equipment items to the company sub-unit in which they are used. But direct cause–effect relationships cannot be established for all items. The controllability of any cost, revenue, asset, or other performance factor depends on each company's organizational structure, its decision hierarchy, and the time horizon of particular decisions.

All performance measures are controllable at some point in time by some decision center. But in the short run, many items will not satisfy the controllability criteria. For example, over a month, a quarter, or a year, the rental costs of property subject to a fixed-term lease agreement cannot be changed by the lessee. However, at some later time, the lease will expire and those rental costs will be controllable by the decision center that has authority to choose among alternative long-term rental properties.

It is also possible for an item to be controllable at certain levels in the organization, but not at others. When control authority is delegated, performance measures remain controllable at all levels *above* the point at which a final operational control decision is made. For example, in the Citron Corporation example, raw materials usage is controllable primarily at the level of a work station within the Assembly Division. But Assembly Division raw materials usage and materials usage in other company divisions are also controllable at the next higher level—raw materials usage within the Turlock Plant. The Vice President for Manufacturing has control authority over all manufacturing raw materials usage throughout the company.

In many cases, especially in the short run, there will be a cutoff level below which an item is not controllable. For example, Citron Corporation's Assembly Division foreman can exercise no direct influence or control over the amount of property tax expense levied on the premises occupied by his division. At his reporting level, property taxes should be treated as a noncontrollable expenditure. Property taxes will become a controllable cost when both the decision time frame and the organizational level are such that the amount of property tax can be affected by actions taken in some decision center, perhaps at the level of top management responsible for making real estate purchase and sale decisions.

Performance items that are noncontrollable at particular reporting levels should not necessarily be excluded from responsibility accounting reports at those levels. Citron Corporation's property tax expense can still be included in performance reports for all levels down to and including the Assembly Division foreman. This is appropriate because property taxes are an indirect operating cost of the Assembly Division and of all higher level sub-units of which that division is a member.

Disclosing noncontrollable costs draws the attention of lower level managers to the existence and extent of those costs. Doing so may create greater cost consciousness throughout the organization if lower level decision centers become more aware of such costs and of the facilities and services that they make available. Disclosure may also encourage lower level managers to more effectively use the resources whose costs they are indirectly responsible for recovering, by increasing the contribution made by activities that they do effectively control. For example, reporting company-wide research and development costs to all manufacturing department levels may encourage managers to make better use of research facilities in their individual areas.

However, the inclusion of noncontrollable items introduces an arbitrary element into responsibility accounting reports. Although the reporting of controllable items is based on directly traceable relationships, noncontrollable items must be *allocated* to lower company levels. This must be remembered when interpreting such reports, because performance measures based on indirect, arbitrary allocations of costs that are only controllable at some higher level in the company have limited control value.[3] Such noncontrollable costs can be distinguished from controllable items in responsibility accounting reports if separate classification and analysis procedures have been established for the noncontrollable items.

CONTROL RESPONSIBILITY FOR JOINT COSTS AND REVENUES

Complex manufacturing operations often lead to situations in which several activity centers at the same decision making level share responsibility for particular costs. This can result from joint production processes in which a sequence of operations results in several types of outputs. The problem is then one of distributing joint product costs among the activity centers that later benefit from those costs. Up to the separation point of the joint outputs, responsibility for performance can be assigned on a direct cause–effect basis. Beyond that point, responsibility reports must somehow reflect the distribution of joint costs among the decision centers responsible for subsequent performance. This may require an arbitrary assessment of joint costs and a consequent lack of controllability.

Example: Groper Company has a production configuration in which its first two manufacturing operations lead to the joint production of three distinct products. These products are then processed separately in three independent product line divisions and are marketed individually. When the joint outputs are transferred to the three product line divisions, can the cost of producing these joint outputs be distributed in a way that preserves the controllability of that cost by the three product line divisions?

In this situation, it seems impossible to establish undivided control responsibility. No method of allocating the joint costs can involve only a single, direct cause–effect relationship. That is, the amount of joint product costs attributed to any one product line division will partly depend on variables over which the division has no control. These variables may include the relative proportions of the joint outputs, the activity levels of other departments to which the joint costs are also allocated, and the method of allocation itself.

Another type of joint cost problem occurs when several decision centers at the same reporting level share responsibility for a performance factor. Examples include general purpose equipment used by several departments, support and supervisory personnel working in more than one division, or simultaneous advertising costs for a range of product lines. Which decision center should be held responsible for which portion of such joint costs? Often it is necessary to arbitrarily allocate an item or reclassify it as a controllable cost at a higher

---

[3] See Joel S. Demski, "Uncertainty and Evaluation Based on Controllable Performance," *Journal of Accounting Research,* Vol. 14 (Autumn, 1976), pp. 230–45.

level of responsibility reporting. Both these steps weaken the control value of responsibility accounting reports at the lower levels.

The same problem often applies to revenues. Several decision centers may claim joint responsibility for the same revenue-producing transaction or series of transactions. When different departments sell complementary products (cameras and film, flashlights and batteries), the revenues from any one such product line may be directly related to decision variables independently controlled by two or more departments. These departments must then share responsibility for decisions affecting the sale of complimentary items.

Similarly, interdivisional sales may require a transfer pricing system. As before, the revenue performance of each division is not necessarily determined only by that division's actions. A good example is the situation of an automobile dealership that operates new car, used car, spare parts, and service divisions. In such a firm, many interdivisional transfers are possible, including sales of trade-ins by the used car division, repairs to trade-ins before sale, spare parts sold as accessories on new cars, spare parts used by the service division, and repair work done on new cars under warranty. All of these interdependencies confuse the issue of unique controllability of cost and revenue items. The problem of evaluating internal profit or investment centers when interdivisional transactions are involved will be examined in detail in Chapters 19 and 20.

Responsibility accounting can also be undermined by political pressures within companies and personal conflicts between managers. Joint technical and physical relationships can lead to "buck passing" and blame fixing. Often resource usage is clearly identified in a physical sense as occurring in one decision center's sphere of activity. But the reason, and therefore the responsibility, for that usage may not be evident. The different viewpoints and conflicting goals of decision makers can easily lead to alternative interpretations of the responsibility for and controllability of certain costs and revenues.

Example: Parker Company's two departments, A and B, perform successive operations in manufacturing the company's product. One machine in Department B jams, causing damage to several units being processed. Some of the damaged units are later reprocessed through Department A to correct the flaws. The other damaged units are scrapped. Idle time occurs in Department B while the machine is out of use. Department A must use additional materials in reworking the damaged units. The Plant Maintenance Department is called in to repair the machine. It is uncertain whether the machine jammed because of (1) defective units processed by Department A, (2) carelessness or error on the part of machine operators in Department B, or (3) faulty machine servicing by the Plant Maintenance Department. The result is a situation ripe for excuses, accusations, and finger pointing with regard to who is responsible for each of the additional costs.

This example reinforces the earlier observation that it is not always easy to determine which decision center has control over a particular cost. It is also presented as a caution that blame fixing should not be allowed to set the tone and emphasis in responsibility accounting. Nor should the pursuit of absolute finality in tracing costs and revenues to specific decision centers be allowed to become an overriding goal. To a considerable extent, effective control requires individualized accounting and reporting for each situation in which vertical levels or horizontal divisions of managerial responsibility are reported on, evaluated, and controlled.

CONTROL REPORTS

The collection of accounting reports generated to provide control information is the most tangible output of an accounting control system. Control reports take various forms and reach every management level. They range from records of routine transactions, through many levels of summarization and analysis, to comparative and evaluative reports. A well designed responsibility accounting system must specify the types of control reports to be prepared, their contents, format, and frequency of preparation and distribution.

Responsibility accounting reports can be divided into four basic types:

1. Enumerative reports
2. Analytical and interpretive reports
3. Comparative and evaluative reports
4. Special purpose, problem solving reports

Enumerative Reports   Some performance measures may be presented in reports that are no more than lists, schedules, or tabulations. Such *scorecards* provide only classified raw data; no explicit reference points or basis for comparison are cited. These reports include *historical* scorecards, such as inventory listings, production cost reports, job order cost tabulations, as well as income statements and balance sheets in their most basic form.

Other scorecards are *predictive*. Budgets, sales forecasts, and production schedules are examples. Such reports are of limited usefulness because the information they present requires further processing before it has any real decision making and control value. But they are necessary building blocks for a responsibility accounting system, providing the raw materials for more powerful evaluation and control reports.

Analytical and Interpretive Reports   Another general category of reports includes those derived through analysis and interpretation. Instead of merely presenting performance measures in dollars and cents, interpretive reports may add *percentage components* of items or display *ratios* between relatable figures. These additions can be made in supplementary rows and columns on the face of reports or they may be depicted graphically in the form of charts and diagrams. Figure 10–8 shows a contribution report (1) in tabular form, with percentages as well as dollar amounts, (2) in bar graph form, and (3) in pie diagram form.

Interpretive reports highlight relationships between figures—for example, the ratios between balance sheet items or the percentage relationship among items in an income statement or a production cost report. Summarized multiperiod reports that include trends and percentage changes, as well as reports with current and period-to-date information highlighted are also interpretive. Note that there is still no external reference point for any of the figures involved.

Comparative and Evaluative Reports   Reports that include comparative and evaluative data are much more useful. They are often called *attention-directing reports,* because they focus on situations that require a decision. In this category are all reports that compare actual and planned performance. For

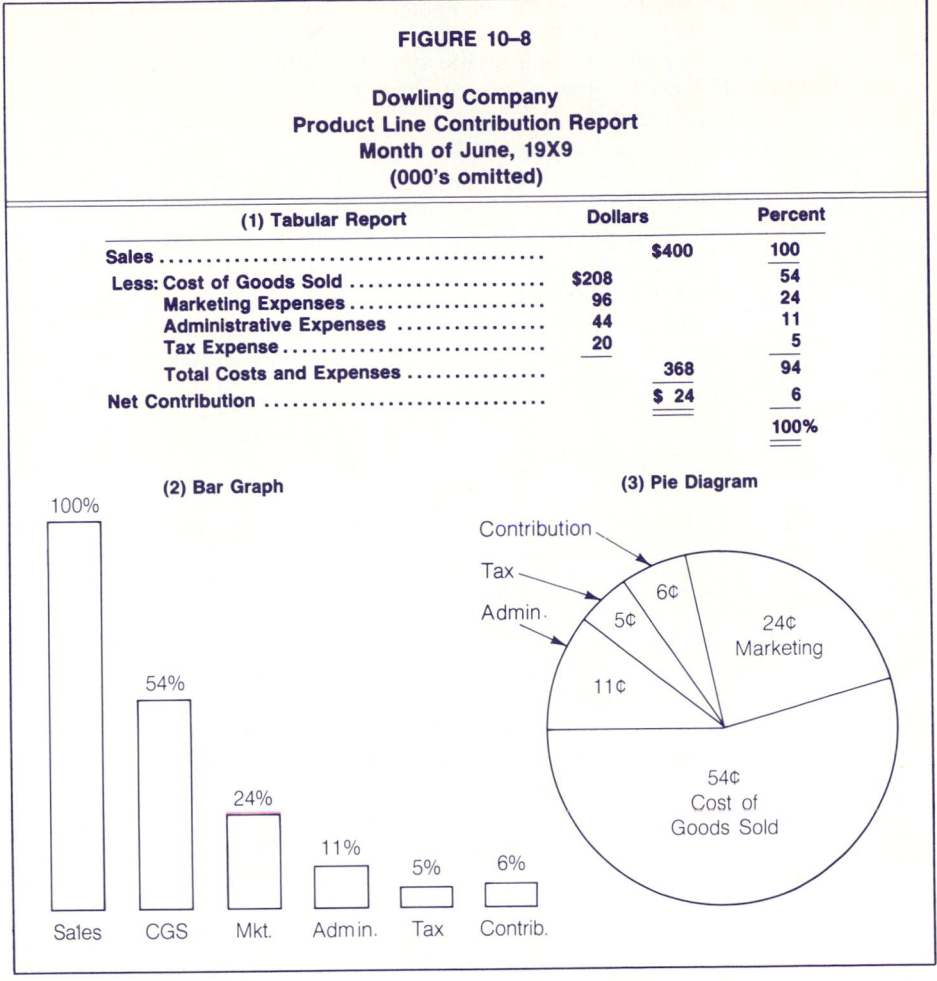

FIGURE 10–8

Dowling Company
Product Line Contribution Report
Month of June, 19X9
(000's omitted)

(1) Tabular Report	Dollars		Percent
Sales		$400	100
Less: Cost of Goods Sold	$208		54
Marketing Expenses	96		24
Administrative Expenses	44		11
Tax Expense	20		5
Total Costs and Expenses		368	94
Net Contribution		$ 24	6
			100%

example, *variance reports* are designed to compare actual results with budgeted amounts.

Control reports are often prepared in accordance with the principle of **management by exception.** All comparative reports implicitly reflect this concept in that they essentially consist of measured deviations from some expected level of performance. But not all variances need be reported, and not all reported variances need be presented in the same amount of detail.

Problem Solving Reports   A final class of reports satisfies the problem solving needs of managers. These range from spontaneous responses to low-level inquiries concerning inventory levels, to extensive, detailed, and long-range problem analyses concerning the best sites for new factories during the next twenty years.

The ability to provide data so that such questions can be answered is an important feedback feature of responsibility accounting systems. Often items such as cash balances, inventory levels, sales, and costs to date require continuous monitoring. In such cases, the answers to inquiries that managers are likely to make must be easily retrievable from the system. (What did that last production run of Product X19 cost? How much of Product Line 87B has been sold in District 11 so far this month?)

Other problem solving reports will be needed for less frequent, but more far-reaching problems. For example, is it worthwhile to continue selling in District 11? Should Product Line 87B be discontinued or expanded? Why are the machinists in Machine Shop Section 16 not consistently able to meet production quotas? Reports on these matters should include comparative and evaluative data drawn from the responsibility accounting system and applied to each specific problem. Capital budgeting analysis of project proposals, long-range sales forecasts, and all types of long-range cost–benefit techniques are useful accounting methods for problem solving reports.

FREQUENCY OF REPORTING

In addition to the form and content of responsibility reports, management must consider their frequency and timing. Feedback reports for evaluation and control must be prepared often enough so that the managers who receive them can make timely control decisions.

The variability of the items reported should affect the frequency of control reports. Revenues, direct materials, and labor, as well as variable manufacturing, marketing, and administrative costs, must be observed and evaluated on a more regular basis than committed or discretionary fixed costs. The latter are better handled by longer-term analysis because they are subject to longer-range performance expectations than are short-term variable costs.

In manufacturing or marketing operations, where the total operating cycle may be days or even hours, cost and revenue reports must *promptly* reflect the results of management's discharge of its responsibilities. Obviously, discovering and reporting cost variances a month after they occur is useless if the production event being evaluated occurs several times in one day. Similarly, cash flow reporting in banks and other financial institutions should be virtually continuous because control of the cash position requires continual decision making attention. At the other extreme, control reporting for a three-year construction project could be much less frequent, but would still need to be performed often enough to permit managers to monitor the progress toward objectives.

INTERNAL REVIEW AND AUDIT

Control systems should include internal review and audit procedures to determine whether or not operating guidelines are being followed. These procedures may be formalized into an internal audit department in which staff employees review managerial effectiveness. Alternatively, an external review may be conducted by a public accounting firm or professional management consultants. Recent developments in this area include the **operational audit,** which expands the traditional CPA audit of accounting procedures to include a review of the management control system and company decision making processes.

COST–BENEFIT ANALYSIS

The internal control system should also be reviewed from a cost–benefit and/or cost-effectiveness viewpoint to ensure that accounting and other internal control techniques are not redundant, burdensome, or unreasonably costly. Organizations are as apt to fall victim to "control system overkill" as they are to suffer from a lack of control procedures. This tendency is evident in the excessive and superfluous paperwork that typifies many business firms and government bureaucracies.

Control techniques should render benefits at least equal to their cost. But such benefits are usually not directly measurable, because they are largely a function of potential losses that are avoided as a result of the control system. Consequently, it is often hard to distinguish between those control procedures that are economically justifiable and those that are not.

ACCOUNTING CONTROL AND HUMAN BEHAVIOR

Planning and control procedures should not be designed or implemented without an awareness that *people* are involved in the activities being considered. Human behavior is probably the most complex phenomenon with which any control system must contend. A major task of the decision makers who act on control information is to secure appropriate responses, decisions, and actions from other individuals in the organization.

Numerous studies have been made of human behavior in business organizations. This chapter will not attempt to summarize or evaluate this extensive body of literature. But it will examine critically the traditional assumptions about the behavior of human participants in organizations, because these assumptions underlie accounting control procedures. Reference to these assumptions is made at appropriate places in other chapters. However, it is also important that these assumptions be considered in an integrated way rather than being treated as an afterthought or a subsidiary issue in the accounting control process.

TRADITIONAL VERSUS MODERN BEHAVIORAL ASSUMPTIONS

Traditional and modern assumptions about human behavior in business organizations differ markedly with regard to:[4]

1. Organizational objectives.
2. Individual goals and needs.
3. The decision making processes of individuals and groups.
4. The nature of authority–responsibility relationships.
5. The information available to people in organizations.
6. The relationship of the management accounting function to the management process.

[4] For a detailed discussion, see Edwin H. Caplin, *Management Accounting and Behavioral Science* (Reading, Mass.: Addison-Wesley, 1971).

ORGANIZATIONAL OBJECTIVES

Profit maximization is the most commonly stated organizational goal. This objective has evolved largely from economists' assumptions concerning business objectives. It has also been widely assumed that the overall company goal of profit maximization translates directly and without any conflict into a set of similar profit maximizing subgoals for company segments. A major result of these traditional assumptions has been to make profit measurement the focal point of most accounting procedures.

However, in recent years there has been a tendency to diversify both the concept of organizational goals and the objects of accounting measurements. The profit motive (often described in terms of *satisficing* or constrained profit achievement) is usually still acknowledged, but company goals are now more often multidimensional. Other frequently specified objectives include desired performance with regard to (1) the physical environment, (2) socio-economic goals, (3) legal, political, and governmental relationships, (4) civic and community goals, and (5) the firm's image and prestige.

The size and complexity of modern businesses has also led to greater emphasis on the goals of divisions or departments. Departmental objectives are generally more understandable, communicable, and implementable than those of the whole organization.

In addition, the *perpetuation* of the organization, especially in the case of corporations, has become a goal in its own right. The sheer size of large corporations often makes them less concerned about profits than they are about economic survival, adaptability to a dynamic business and economic environment, and flexibility to accommodate the changing needs of the corporation's shareholders.

To some extent, management accountants have adapted to these trends. Accounting reports now stress segment performance, in terms of profit contribution and rates of return, as well as deviations of actual performance from budgeted amounts. Often these targeted amounts are specified in a satisficing sense rather than in terms of profit maximization.

Moreover, the recognition that financial survival is a crucial organization goal has led to the more frequent use of reporting procedures that emphasize financial condition, liquidity, solvency, and management of funds flows. The goals of flexibility and adaptability are served by accounting techniques designed to allow continuous review of systems performance, and the revision of a company's plans and those of its sub-units. Variance analysis and investigation, incremental analysis, and cost–benefit analysis are examples of such accounting methods. Added to these are planning and control techniques that deal with the risk and uncertainty of the business environment, with dynamic organization structures and patterns of authority–responsibility relationships, and with continuous evaluation of the performance of company sub-units.

Most goals that are not directly profit-oriented—such as environmental, socio-economic, civic, and prestige objectives—are still largely outside the limits of conventional management accounting measurements. Cost–benefit analysis has been proposed as an approach to situations in which company objectives are not directly measurable in monetary terms. This might involve measuring such things as environmental impact, affirmative action employment, employee welfare, and community public relations.

OBJECTIVES OF INDIVIDUAL AND GROUP PARTICIPANTS

Another traditional assumption is that individuals participating in business firms have strictly economic goals. This has usually been coupled with the assumptions that employees are work averse, tend to be naturally inefficient, and need to be strictly supervised to ensure their productive efficiency. Managerial accounting has tended to emphasize monetary payments (wages, commissions, bonuses) to individuals as the sole reward for their contributions to the firm. The accounting techniques of budgetary planning and control have carried a tone and flavor of imposition, domination, and unilateral determination by management.

This is often the case today. The services of employees are treated like other passive economic commodities, to be purchased at the market price. Improvements in productivity and control of labor and labor-related costs are considered to be attainable only through economic sanctions such as budget requirements, quotas, and monetary penalty–reward systems. Individuals tend to be viewed as appendages to the machinery and other resources used in manufacturing operations. As such, they are subjected to operational and management control techniques similar to those used in controlling a supply of raw materials or a piece of equipment. This is admittedly an extreme version of the traditional approach to control, but much evidence suggests that these types of situations are still widespread.

In contrast to this mechanical, dispassionate, and "time and motion study" assessment of employee motivation, various modern theories of organizational behavior have been proposed to explain the very complex goal structures of individuals as organizational participants. The modern consensus is that:

1. Individuals are motivated to participate in organizations by a wide variety of economic, social, political, and psychological goals and needs.
2. Different individuals have different strengths of preferences and different rank orderings of these personal goals and needs.
3. An individual's continued participation in an organization depends on a balance being maintained between what the individual receives from the organization and what the organization requires of the individual.
4. Individuals do not necessarily find work unattractive and are capable of more constructive roles in a company than those implied by a management approach that emphasizes overt supervision and regulation.

Developments in management accounting methods have accompanied these changed perceptions of individual goals and motives. Nonmonetary rewards sought by individuals are difficult to express in accounting terms and employee remuneration must still be shown only as the dollar amounts of wages, bonuses, and other labor-related benefits. However, planners now give more attention to these multidimensional objectives. Budgeting, standard setting, and establishing target profit goals can be approached in a more personalized and less authoritarian fashion. Top management can pay more attention to choosing the appropriate style, scope, and detail for planning and control procedures and reports. Budgeted or standard levels of performance may be set with consideration for the perceived needs and goals of subordinates. There are, of course, practical limits to any firm's ability to accommodate individual preferences. It is obviously not feasible to develop tailor-made accounting procedures and reports for each employee who is subject to them.

DECISION MAKING PROCESSES OF INDIVIDUALS AND GROUPS

Another traditional behavioral assumption is that decision makers are rational and act with complete and perfect information, free from uncertainty. This allows well-ordered decision rules to be specified, based on rational choices among deterministically valued alternatives. Much of the basic discussion of managerial accounting presented earlier in this text relied heavily on such assumptions. Cost–volume–profit analysis, budgeting, and incremental analysis were initially depicted as occurring in situations where decision makers had complete information concerning the relevant relationships and the values of all decision variables. It was also assumed that these all-knowing decision makers always made logical and consistent choices.

A realistic approach to decision making requires that these assumptions be qualified in several ways. Complete and perfect information is unlikely to be available. Even if it were, individual decision makers would be unable to understand and respond to such large quantities of data. It is more reasonable to assume that decision makers (1) are capable of operating with less than complete information in many situations, (2) have limited ability to make comparisons and choose among alternatives, (3) are frequently biased and inconsistent in their choices, and (4) have varying decision making skills and levels of sophistication.

Because of their human limitations, managers cannot always make optimal decisions. Their ability to make satisficing choices is a more realistic expectation. Managers, their superiors, and their subordinates should recognize the uncertainty present in all decision situations and avoid inappropriate use of deterministic assumptions.

Accounting procedures have been extended to help deal with deficiencies in the decision maker's abilities. The concepts of controllability, attributability, and incrementality have been used to help tailor accounting information to fit the needs of particular decision makers in specific circumstances. In the use of exception reporting, variance analysis, and summarized performance evaluation reports, accounting information is prerefined to narrow the scope of decision making. The accounting system acts as a filter to decrease the quantity and improve the quality of information available to managers.

There is no single or best decision rule to generate the accounting information needed under conditions of uncertainty. Different decision makers will respond differently to given circumstances involving uncertainty, because their attitudes toward risk vary and because the qualitative aspects of decisions—such as prestige, peer approval, acceptance, status, and internal political power—are inherently subjective values.

THE NATURE OF AUTHORITY–RESPONSIBILITY RELATIONSHIPS

Authority–responsibility relationships among managers traditionally have been assumed to derive entirely from the entity's formal organizational structure. Such an assumption implies that these relationships will be accepted without question by the employees on whom they are imposed. It is also assumed that these are one-directional relationships—authority is exercised over subordinates and information flows from the top down in the form of budgets that communicate the requirements of those in charge. Subordinates are held responsible for discharging their duties, and the results of their actions are reported to their superiors. There is no explicit recognition of the need for or existence of informal relationships or for any exchange of information and ideas outside this formal structure.

Responsibility accounting has tended to adapt to and reinforce the authoritarian/submissive roles of superiors and subordinates. Control systems operate on the basis of pressures from the top down. Without consultation with subordinates, budgets are imposed, penalties and rewards are distributed, standards are set, and variances are measured, analyzed, and investigated.

Participative Budgeting The modern consensus is that some interaction between subordinates and superiors is desirable for the effective operation of a firm's authority–responsibility structure. This follows from the idea that authority–responsibility relationships should not be imposed, but should be a matter of mutual acceptance.

Based on these ideas, it has been proposed that *participative budgeting* should be a feature of accounting information and control systems—that is, the budget staff should solicit and obtain managerial inputs to the budgetary process. This does not mean that each manager should be allowed to determine the details of his own area's budget. Rather, the local expertise of each managerial level should be sought to improve the accuracy and insight of budgetary planning. Managers ought to be more familiar than anyone else with the planning variables in their own decision making areas. Accordingly, they are a suitable source for *some* of the required forecasting inputs.

It has been proposed that this type of participation be extended to all employees affected by budgets. Budgets prepared according to this approach should be more effective, if only because the employees participating have become more aware of the interrelationships between their activities and those in other parts of the company. In addition, subordinates who have been given a chance to provide constructive inputs during the budgetary process should be better motivated to contribute to the company's goals.

These advantages may not always be attainable. Some employees seek to avoid participation in budgetary and other planning procedures in order to be able to use the excuse of noninvolvement. This tactic allows them to evade the responsibility that results from having helped to set standards that must later be met. They can say, "Don't blame me for not meeting the budgetary requirements—I had nothing to do with setting them."

The participative approach may also be criticized for being a display of tokenism or ego-stroking. If the participation is not meaningful, the would-be participants will feel that they are being manipulated. A participative approach also runs the risk of provoking counterproductive behavior on the part of employees who are negative toward budgetary procedures. This behavior could range from providing biased or false data to outright sabotage of the planning and control process.

Finally, it has been observed that different employees often require different types of treatment during the budgetary process. This may be true not only of employees at different wage and skill levels, but also of employees in the same work situation. Some prefer to be given explicit budgetary directions and need to be guided with a great deal of information; others demand to set their own goals or standards and prefer to remain relatively unsupervised. Workers on a repetitive production line often fall into the first category, whereas skilled research personnel are more likely to display the characteristics of the second group.

Whether or not participation should be a necessary and universal feature of the budgetary process is clearly a debatable issue. It is impossible to grant each employee his own personally chosen level of participation and interaction in company affairs; to do so would require that the accounting system customize information in the style, form, and content preferred by each individual. The most practical solution is to strive for some degree of coordination in developing accounting information to serve the needs of managers and subordinates at various company levels.

Employee Motivation   Motivation is the second concept dealt with extensively in the literature on the behavioral aspects of accounting control. The traditional view has been that workers are inherently disinclined to work and can only be motivated to perform efficiently by the offer of monetary payments or their direct equivalents. This emphasis on economic incentives underlies much of managerial thinking and practice in the areas of salary negotiations, establishing task standards and job requirements, and formulating penalty–reward systems. Emphasis has usually been placed on money payments (or their denial) as the sole means of encouraging required or improved performance or penalizing inferior performance.

However, it is now widely recognized that subordinates can also be motivated by nonmonetary incentives. These include peer pressures, the need for approval and acceptance, and the desire for personal growth, achievement, and job satisfaction.

As quantitative expressions of desired performance levels, budgets, standards, and quotas also have motivational potential. Their existence is enough to encourage some employees to greater efforts in attaining company objectives. Planning and control reports should be presented in a way that causes employees to associate the company's success with achievement of their personal goals. Management's expectations of employees, as well as the methods of performance evaluation, must be clearly and unambiguously communicated. Employees should be able to understand the degree of control they have over the tasks they are required to perform. They should also be able to relate their work efforts to the tangible and intrinsic rewards that result from those efforts.

Excessive or misdirected attention to employee motivation can be counterproductive. A balance must be maintained between the desire for efficiency on the one hand and competition among company sub-units on the other. As will be shown, decentralized firms are particularly affected by this problem because of the way in which the various segments respond to their different performance requirements.

The human tendency to want to beat the system must be kept in mind when considering questions of motivation. Some employees will allow themselves to be motivated just enough to avoid incurring penalties. They will underproduce to prevent having their performance requirements increased. Similarly, individuals sometimes pad their budgets by providing biased input data so that a margin of slack can be enjoyed. Employees may also manipulate reported results to conceal substandard performance.

Finally, there is the problem of selecting performance levels that achieve the desired motivational effect. Subordinates will quickly see the impossibility of reaching goals when budgets, standards, or quotas are set too high. At the other extreme, easily attained budget requirements will not motivate employees to improve performance, once they understand that they can meet the targeted objectives "with something to spare."

Various theories have been advanced as to how goals should be established and adjusted to achieve desired motivation of subordinates. But experimental results, as well as practical experience, have not shown any single approach to be generally effective. Much as in the famous Hawthorne experiments of the 1920s, different people seem to be motivated positively or otherwise by different approaches to the selection and communication of performance requirements.

THE INFORMATION AVAILABLE TO PEOPLE IN ORGANIZATIONS

Traditional models of economic behavior have assumed the free and complete availability of information. This in turn has led to an assumption of rational behavior on the part of individual and group decision makers. These assumptions are questionable, especially in view of the scale and complexity of modern businesses. Accounting systems should be designed for situations in which complete and cost-free information is *not* available and in which decision makers *cannot* fully understand all the information that is obtainable or make consistently rational decisions.

Limitations on the amount of information available to decision makers may be deliberately imposed by the system's design. Examples include the selective reporting of variances, segment performance analysis, and project planning and control reports. Other, unplanned restrictions on accounting information flows are caused by the cost, volume, speed, accuracy, timeliness, and other attributes of the information processing system.

All these factors influence the behavior of decision makers. One basic response to accounting information is that "if *it* is measured or reported, *it* must be important!" The mere existence of measurement and reporting procedures is sufficient to cause people to pay more attention to the items being reported.

The *purpose* of planning, performance measurement, and control reports must be made clear to all who are affected by them. The more that accounting procedures and reports come to be seen as ambiguous, authoritarian, disciplinary, or threatening, the more likely they will be to evoke unfavorable reactions. Budgets may then be viewed as pressure devices, the subjects of automatic distrust. Both managers and subordinates may interpret budgets and other accounting reports as whipping posts on which to release their frustrations and hostilities.

All this suggests that an individual's ability to reason and make decisions is limited both qualitatively and quantitatively. The concept of **bounded rationality** holds that decision makers can only be expected to respond to a limited quantity of information—and at a level commensurate with their skills and general abilities.

Consequently, whenever possible, accounting information must be refined to reflect its recipient's capabilities, decision style, attitude toward risk, and position in the company.

THE RELATIONSHIP OF THE MANAGEMENT ACCOUNTING FUNCTION TO THE MANAGEMENT PROCESS

The relationship between a firm's accounting control system and the management decision making process could range all the way from "manual" control systems, in which all decisions are made by managers, to fully automated systems, in which decisions are made without human intervention. The accounting system's role can extend to:

1. Being simply a data base.
2. Developing forecasts.
3. Making planning and control decisions.
4. Making and implementing planning and control decisions.
5. Totally absorbing the managerial decision process, including goal and performance criteria specifications.

The role of managerial accounting has traditionally been a passive one, limited to providing accounting data for use by decision makers. This may still be true when the accounting system is used only as a **data base**. The accounting information produced by such a system is analyzed, interpreted, and applied by managers according to their own decision criteria.

A first step in expanding the accounting system's role is to make it provide *forecasts of future events* based on predictive models built into the accounting system itself. This still leaves decision makers free to react to these forecasts. But to the extent that forecasting procedures are internalized in the accounting system, some decision making ability will have been transferred to that system.

Going a step farther, the process of choosing among alternatives can sometimes be made part of the accounting system itself. This is known as *automated* or **programmed decision making.** The lower levels of the decision hierarchy are the most likely environments in which this can occur. At those levels, decision making tends to be repetitive and routine, involving simple decision rules and relatively few decision variables.

It is feasible to make such activities part of the accounting function. Examples include all forms of control reporting and analysis in which the performance measurement, comparison, and evaluation are performed automatically. A specific example is that of inventory control systems, in which usage and availability are continuously monitored and status reports indicating out-of-stock conditions, slow-moving items, or unusually fast-moving items are generated and reported without the personal intervention of a manager. Accounts receivable control systems are another area in which programmed decision making is appropriate. Credit applications, collection procedures, and account activity analysis can also be performed by the accounting system on a preprogrammed basis.

At this level, many decision steps remain in the hands of human decision makers. Determining and reporting imminent inventory shortages, fast-moving items, overdue accounts, or customers' credit ratings would be the limits of the accounting system's role. Control actions beyond that point would continue to be in the manager's domain.

The next step in automated decision making is to allow responses to these programmed decisions to be implemented without further intervention by the manager. The accounting system becomes a **decision taking system,** for example, when it (1) places a purchase order in response to an inventory status report, (2) revises the reorder quantity for an item when its usage rate has increased, (3) sends progressively sterner reminder notices to delinquent customers, or (4) approves or rejects a credit application.

There are obvious practical limits to the automation of decision making. Where decision situations remain relatively complex, unstructured, and nonprogrammable, the decision maker's role tends to be preserved. For example, variances between actual and budgeted costs might be automatically calculated, analyzed, and selectively reported according to predetermined criteria. But the process of interpreting and responding to the variances that are judged to be significant should probably remain part of the managerial decision maker's responsibility. The range and type of explanations and potential responses to a particular situation may be so varied as to prevent complete enumeration and incorporation into programmed decision rules within the accounting system.

These last two stages in the evolution of accounting systems have been enhanced by recent developments in the use of business computer systems. Computers provide a powerful and convenient means of automatically making and implementing decisions. The speed, accuracy, reliability, and comprehensive data access and processing capacities of computers are highly compatible with the data processing requirements of programmed decision making. However, remember that *programmed* decision making need not necessarily be computer-related. The same results can be achieved in accounting systems where manual devices and personnel perform the programmed (that is, prestructured) decision processes.

The ultimate development would be for the accounting system to absorb the entire decision making process, including decision rule selection and decision criteria specification. This is the situation hypothesized under a totally integrated accounting and management information systems approach. It would require continuous evaluation and revision of decision rules and criteria in response to feedback from systems performance as well as the usual adjustment of operational decision and control variables. This is part of the *systemic* information systems philosophy that proposes a *dialectical* approach to systems design and implementation.[5]

Currently most accounting information and control systems are still essentially *data base* systems. Certain subsystems (inventory control, cash control, receivables control, fixed asset control) have been extended up through the *predictive* phase to the *decision making* level. The *decision taking* level is encountered less often, being restricted to routine, low-level, well-defined production and process-oriented decisions. The **total systems approach,** with a completely automated decision making process, appears to exist only in a hypothetical and somewhat speculative form.

Behavioral Conflicts Between Accounting Systems and Management   The relationship between the accounting system and the management

[5] Richard O. Mason, Jr., "Basic Concepts for Designing Management Information Systems," in Alfred Rappaport, *Information for Decision Making,* Second Edition (Englewood Cliffs, N.J.: Prentice-Hall, 1975), pp. 2–16.

process is often beset by behavioral problems and conflicts. Managers sometimes treat the accounting function as a scapegoat for their own failures. Rather than contend with the real causes of their operating problems, they choose to vilify and quarrel with accountants. The accountant—cast in the role of sentry, guard, or overseer, imposing budgetary, reporting, and control procedures— is then characterized through the negative connotation of such words as control, report, investigate, inform, or enforce. An adversary relationship is encouraged if such perceptions and beliefs are allowed to flourish.

These conflicts are not always management's fault. Sometimes it is the accountant, in his planning and control roles, who aggravates the relationship. This can occur whenever accountants seek the credit for improved operating performance, using the argument that it was due to the accounting process that budgetary requirements were exceeded. Trouble is also likely if accountants resort to veiled threats of what the consequences will be for managers who exceed their budgetary spending limits. Such actions should be avoided. It is in the accountant's interest to see that feelings of hostility, rejection, suspicion, or retaliation are not communicated to managers through accounting procedures and reports.

SUMMARY

1. The concept of control is a basic part of the management process through which an organization seeks to achieve its goals.

2. The feedback principle is a central feature of control systems. It involves monitoring operating results and comparing those results with predetermined performance requirements, leading to modification of inputs, operating procedures, and/or objectives.

3. The specific purposes of accounting control systems include (1) protecting resources, (2) establishing and maintaining information quality standards, (3) obtaining adherence to company policies and procedures, and (4) promoting efficiency in all goal-related activities.

4. The most basic accounting control procedure is the preparation and use of responsibility accounting reports. A responsibility accounting system produces planning, performance, and control reports based on measurements of those aspects of operating performance that are controllable by or attributable to particular decision centers.

5. The types of responsibility accounting reports include (1) enumerative reports, (2) analytical and interpretive reports, (3) comparative and evaluative reports, and (4) special purpose reports.

6. Implementing accounting systems for planning and control purposes raises a number of problems regarding the behavior of decision makers. Management accounting procedures have been developed to deal with some of these problems.

7. Major areas of behavioral concern involve (1) organizational objectives, (2) the goals and needs of individuals, (3) the decision processes of individuals and groups, (4) the nature of authority–responsibility relationships, (5) the availability of information to decision makers, and (6) the relationship of the management accounting function to the management process.

KEY WORDS AND PHRASES

Control Concept (437)
Control System (438)
Feedback Mechanism (439)
Sensor (439)
Responsibility Accounting (442)
Vertical or Hierarchical Classification (442)
Horizontal or Functional Classification (442)
Enumerative (Scorecard) Reports (448)
Analytical and Interpretive Reports (448)
Attention-Directing Reports (448)
Management by Exception (449)
Problem Solving Reports (449)
Operational Audit (450)
Participative Budgeting (455)
Employee Motivation (456)
Bounded Rationality (457)
Data Base Accounting System (458)
Programmed Decision Making (458)
Decision Taking Accounting System (459)
Total Systems Approach (459)

Questions

1. What is the basic concept of *control*? Why is it such a critical part of the management process?
2. Explain the role of *objectives* in the control process.
3. Is control a matter of absolutes or relatives?
4. Outline the operation of a system with which you are familiar, showing particularly the feedback mechanism associated with it.
5. What are the objectives of internal control systems?
6. What basic concepts underlie systems of *responsibility accounting*?
7. Explain how a chart of the conventional organizational structure of a firm can be used to design accounting control systems and support the principles of responsibility accounting.
8. How should the controllability of performance measures be identified with specific decision centers? What problems are usually encountered in doing so?
9. What basic control problem is created by the presence of joint, common, or shared resources?
10. Explain the important types of control reports and discuss their usefulness.
11. How often should control reports be prepared? How much control reporting is needed? Discuss these topics in the context of a cost–benefit approach.
12. What problems does the presence of people in organizations present for accounting control systems?
13. Compare (separately) the *traditional* and *modern* assumptions concerning human behavior in organizations with respect to:
    (a) organizational objectives
    (b) individual goals and needs
    (c) individual and group decision making processes
    (d) authority–responsibility relationships
    (e) information available to organizational participants
    (f) the relationship of management accounting to the management process
14. How has contemporary management accounting adapted to the modern assumptions concerning human behavior in organizations?
15. What is meant by the term *participative budgeting*? Why is it proposed as a desirable feature of budgetary control systems?
16. Why is *motivation* such an important basic consideration in designing budgetary control systems? What does *motivate* mean?
17. Why must accounting information be tailored to the needs of specific users?
18. Explain the interface of the management accounting system with an organization's overall system of management.
19. What conflicts between management and accounting systems are likely?
20. Explain how programmed decision making can be implemented with the aid of a well organized and developed management accounting system.

Exercises

E 10-1   Control Systems—Basic Concepts

Discuss each part separately:

(a) Should an accounting control system be based exclusively on the structure and pattern of the authority–responsibility relationships as indicated by a firm's formal organization chart? Why or why not?

(b) Will the absence of a complete feedback loop eliminate any chance of effective control? Consider what elementary controls might be possible without such a mechanism.

(c) What role does planning (goal setting, specification of objectives, action selection) play in the effectiveness of an accounting control system?

(d) Will there be basic differences in the accounting control systems needed for production departments, as compared with those needed for service or administrative departments in a manufacturing organization? Why or why not?

(e) Differentiate between the accounting control systems appropriate to top levels of management and those needed by managers of a product line.

E 10-2   Responsibility Accounting—Basic Conflict in Establishing Controllability of Performance Measures

A typical problem confronting many firms occurs when skilled employees are temporarily transferred to an alternate department to perform less highly skilled tasks at their regular wages. Tinsley Corporation has experienced this problem in the following situation:

During some months of the year there is not enough work to keep all operators of some specialty welding machines fully occupied. However, to prevent having to lay them off, and later rehire and retrain new workers, they are assigned to other departments in the plant where temporary help is needed. Usually they are assigned to work in materials handling, storeroom, tool crib, buildings and grounds, and machine maintenance departments. The average hourly rate paid to regular unskilled workers in those departments is $8 per hour. The welders are paid at their contract rate of $15 per hour for all hours worked.

During July, welders worked a total of 400 hours in the Machine Maintenance Department. The supervisor of that department is unhappy because her performance report for the month includes an unfavorable variance of $2,800 for wages of her maintenance crew.

Required:
(a) Comment on the appropriateness of this treatment from a responsibility accounting point of view.

(b) What are the basic issues involved?

(c) Who is responsible for the costs in question?

(d) Discuss alternative accounting treatments that might be appropriate.

E 10-3   Responsibility Accounting—Assignment of Costs for Control and Evaluation—Behavioral Implications

Findley Corporation has experienced a considerable variation in monthly demand for its equipment repair services. However, rather than terminate the services of key repair mechanics (who are difficult to recruit and expensive to train), the corporation has decided to keep several of them on the payroll even though they will be idle. The corporation also sees this as a good labor relations strategy, because to dismiss the mechanics would be an increased burden on the local community at a time when unemployment is relatively high.

Three alternatives are being considered. The first would be to put the mechanics on a three-day work week during periods of low demand, but to pay them for four work days. The second is to allow the mechanics to go home early on the days when the current work schedule is completed before the end of the regular work day. The final alternative is to dismiss several unskilled general factory maintenance and factory clerical workers and have the mechanics do the jobs of those employees whenever they have completed their own tasks.

Required:
(a) Discuss the possible accounting treatments of the wages paid to the mechanics under each of the three proposed alternatives. Emphasize the issue of how the wages should be reported for planning and control purposes. Who would be held responsible for the mechanics' wages in each situation?

(b) Discuss separately the behavioral implications of each alternative on: (1) the mechanics, (2) department supervisors, (3) plant superintendent, and (4) maintenance and factory clerical workers.

E 10-4   Responsibility Accounting—Assignment of Responsibility for Operating Variances

During July of 19X7, the purchasing manager of Acme Metal Products Company made a large purchase of sheet and coil steel from a steel wholesaler at a price well below the current market. The steel had been subject to heat damage (allegedly minor) when the warehouse where it was stored was partially destroyed by fire.

For July, comparison of actual and budgeted costs of raw materials showed a favorable variance, which was credited to the Purchasing Department. However, in July and August, production costs showed several areas of unfavorable performance, especially in the areas of materials usage in the Metal Stamping and Cutting Departments where the steel is first processed. This poor performance was due to unusual amounts of quality rejects, spoiled items, and machine jams. Labor costs in those departments were also unusually high, with idle time, rework, and overtime well above their budgeted amounts. The average direct labor cost of items stamped and cut was also over budget.

Required:
(a) Explain the basic problems in this situation.

(b) What response could be expected from the supervisor of the Metal Stamping and Cutting Departments? Why?

(c) What alternative accounting treatments of the costs involved could be considered?

(d) Would a responsibility accounting approach help matters? Why or why not?

E 10-5   Internal Control Systems

Discuss separately the internal control concepts that are illustrated in the following situations. Mention both strengths and weaknesses and comment on any pertinent alternatives.

(a) Each employee goes to the materials storeroom and obtains materials as he or she needs them. Materials wastage has been increasing lately. It is suggested that the supervisor of each work crew be the only one allowed to requisition materials.

(b) The production supervisor's office is physically isolated from the main production work area. Productivity and morale are low. If the office is moved, the noise of the work area distracts the supervisor.

(c) Installation of security doors, chain-wire fences, multiple locked doors, and other restrictive devices are viewed as negative aspects of control systems, as also are budgets, quotas, and cost limits. Bonuses, incentive plans, safety devices, guard rails, and lighting systems are viewed as positive aspects.

(d) The perennial problem of the sales manager accepting special orders and promising delivery "immediately" continues to plague production personnel, who seek to stabilize production flows to increase cost savings and efficiency.

(e) Quality control personnel were instructed to "improve the general quality and reliability of finished products shipped to customers." As a result, they instituted procedures that caused production slowdowns, unusual amounts of rework, delays in shipping orders, purchase of sophisticated testing equipment, and extensive retraining programs for their personnel. However, they claim that "not one single defective or suspect product goes out the door now!"

E 10-6   Performance Reports

Classify each of the following performance measures as a *measure of effectiveness* (has a goal been achieved?) or a *measure of efficiency* (how well was the goal achieved?). Indicate also any that are *not* good measures in either context.

(a) Budgeted fixed overhead minus actual fixed overhead.

(b) Number of defective units per 1,000 acceptable units.

(c) Ratio of selling expenses to total sales revenue.

(d) Ratio of indirect materials costs to direct materials costs.

(e) Net sales revenue per product line.

(f) Budgeted sales revenue minus actual sales revenue.

(g) Deviation of actual price of direct material inputs from budgeted prices.

(h) Percentage of sales orders filled within customer's requested time.

(i) Reduction in number of inventory items backordered by customers.

(j) Reduction in number of purchase orders placed per $100,000 of inventory carried.

(k) Increase in monthly average cost to manufacture each unit of output.

(l) Direct labor hours per 1,000 units of output.

(m) Number of units produced per month.

(n) Number of sales calls made per salesman per week.

(o) Total expenditure on advertising per month.

E 10–7   Performance Reporting—Responsibility Accounting System—Elementary Reports

Pietras Company is organized (in part) as shown by the accompanying organization chart:

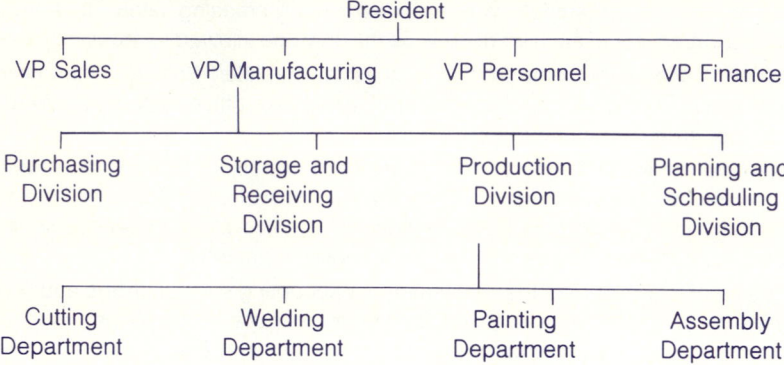

For February of 19X2, the following costs were reported in each of the departments as listed below:

	Actual	Budget
Administrative Costs:		
Manufacturing Division	$ 12,000	$ 13,000
Vice President—Manufacturing	18,000	17,500
President	36,000	35,000
Assembly Department	50,000	49,500
Cutting Department	45,000	46,000
Painting Department	22,500	21,000
Planning and Scheduling Division	29,800	30,000
Purchasing Division	45,800	44,000
Storage and Receiving Division	49,000	48,000
Vice President—Finance	82,500	75,000
Vice President—Personnel	60,500	62,500
Vice President—Sales	128,000	115,000
Welding Department	33,800	35,000

Required:
(a) Utilize responsibility accounting principles as reflected in the organization chart to prepare separate cost reports for the:
   (1) Supervisor of Production
   (2) Vice President—Manufacturing
   (3) President
(b) Explain how the three reports in part (a) articulate with each other.

E 10–8   Performance Reports—Elementary Analysis— Conflict in Performance Criteria

Rochelle Corporation has instructed all of its branch managers that their performance will be evaluated on the basis of maximization of sales revenues. It is implied that sales in excess of budget quotas will lead to bonuses and other rewards for the most successful branch managers. The manager of the Central District branch reviewed his budget for 19X0 and felt that he could easily exceed his sales quota, which was set at $1,600,000. He planned his operation based on his three major product lines as follows:

Budgeted Income Statement
Central District—19X0

	Iotas	Mu-Mu's	Gnuu's	Total
Sales Revenues...............	$400,000	$600,000	$600,000	$1,600,000
Variable Costs	200,000	200,000	400,000	800,000
Contribution Margin	$200,000	$400,000	$200,000	$ 800,000
Direct Fixed Costs				600,000
Segment Profit Contribution....				$ 200,000

Actual sales achieved by the Central District branch for 19X0 were as follows:

Iotas	$ 600,000
Mu-Mu's	300,000
Gnuu's	840,000
Total............	$1,740,000

During 19X0, the actual variable cost ratio for each product line was the same as that budgeted, as were total fixed costs in the Central District branch.

Required:
(a) Prepare a performance report to reflect the achievements of the Central District branch for 19X0.
(b) Evaluate the performance of the Central District branch on the basis of (1) the initially stated criteria and (2) other measures shown in your answer to part (a).
(c) What potential control problem exists here? How might it be resolved?

E 10–9 Motivation and Performance Evaluation in Different Functional Areas and at Different Managerial Levels

In a typical large manufacturing firm, a wide variety of functionally different areas of authority–responsibility usually exist. The Product Research and Development Division and the Spray Painting Department are examples of two quite different functions. Similarly, there are usually substantial differences in the scope and impact of responsibility centers at different *levels* of management. The Vice President in charge of Manufacturing and the foreman of a spray painting work crew are two examples.

Required:
(a) Discuss the similarities and the dissimilarities of each pair of responsibility centers with regard to the measurement and evaluation of their performance for planning and control purposes. (*Hint:* Would you have to budget research and development costs differently than costs in the Spray Paint Department?)
(b) Compare and contrast the needs for, and way of, motivating managers in each of the responsibility centers. (*Hint:* Would a vice president respond to the same type of motivation that a spray painter would?)

E 10–10   Performance Evaluation—Reward Systems— Behavioral and Motivational Considerations and Conflicts

Vinton Corporation distributes two main product lines: *Fabians*, a well-established seller, and *Tormes*, a relatively new product. The sales force has been given sales targets of $40,000 per month per sales representative. Price and cost data are as below:

	Tormes	Fabians
Sales Price	$100	$150
Variable Cost (excluding commissions)	40	100
Contribution Margin	$ 60	$ 50

The present practice is to pay sales representatives a 10 percent commission on gross sales revenue and a 12½ percent bonus, based on commissions earned, if sales exceed the $40,000 target.

Required:

(a) Which product will sales representatives probably try harder to sell? Why?

(b) Which product would the firm prefer to promote? Why?

(c) What change in the sales commission plan could possibly achieve the dual purpose of motivating the sales force to superior performance and improving the contribution margin (after commissions) for the firm?

(d) Could the sales goal be changed in some way to produce the same motivational and profit improving effects?

Cases

C 10–1   Feedback Mechanisms

"In all good control systems, communication is a critical element."

Required:

Discuss this statement in terms of communication directed from managers to subordinates, and vice versa. How does this idea relate to feedback mechanisms?

C 10–2   Control Systems

An investigation of procedures in Makarcyzk Printing Corporation produced the following observations:

(a) Job costs and bid prices are still being estimated on formulas and ratios for labor and overhead established some years ago.

(b) Cost estimates are often prepared separately by cost clerks in the Factory Clerical Department and by product cost engineers in the Production Planning and Scheduling Department.

(c) To arrive at bid prices, a fixed percentage mark-up is added to the estimated manufacturing cost of each job. Monthly profit goals are frequently not achieved.

(d) Materials (paper, ink, supplies, and so on) are accounted for very carefully. Labor costs are not watched too closely. No attempt is made to control overhead costs.

Required:
Evaluate each of these situations, mentioning both the positive and negative aspects of the control systems involved.

C 10–3 Control Systems—Costs

The Tom T. Hall Rope Company has previously specialized in producing one standard line of nylon rope for sailboat suppliers. One major customer expressed an interest in purchasing a variety of high quality rope products in small quantities, but at prices very attractive to the Hall Company.

Hall Company now uses a cost control system oriented to its process type operations. Responsibility for departmental costs is monitored very closely. However, the new activity will present problems because it appears that in each processing department, workers, equipment, and space will have to be assigned to the special orders. The special orders will also make use of the personnel and facilities used in producing the standard nylon rope.

Required:
What problems might arise if the present process cost system is continued? Discuss this from the point of view of (1) income measurement, (2) cost control, and (3) cost information for pricing decisions. What changes in the system would you propose, assuming that cost control is of primary importance?

C 10–4 Establishing an Appropriate Accounting System

A major retail electrical appliance dealer has expanded successfully, establishing four separate operating divisions: (1) Sales—New Appliances, (2) Sales—Used and Reconditioned Appliances, (3) Sales—Spare Parts and Accessories, and (4) Service and Repairs.

Required:
Discuss the problems that will be encountered in establishing an appropriate accounting system based on the principle of responsibility accounting for purposes of control and evaluation of the four divisions. There may be several types of regular transactions among the divisions (for example, trade-ins on new appliances are reconditioned by the Service Division using parts obtained from the Parts Division and eventually sold by the Used Appliance Division). Also, many costs will be incurred for shared resources and services (such as advertising, rent, utilities, administration, clerical, delivery, and so on).

C 10–5 Responsibility Accounting and Control Systems

Typically the responsibility for *purchase,* as distinguished from *consumption* or *use,* of direct materials is separated in most organizations. Tyler Corporation observes this principle, but has encountered some problems. The purchasing manager persists in (1) buying large quantities when a bargain purchase is available or when he believes input prices are about to rise and (2) deferring purchases if he feels that he can get a better deal for larger volume lots or that prices are about to decline.

On the other hand, the production manager is responsible for meeting scheduled production volumes in terms of specified time and cost constraints. Her problems are (1) slowdowns and idle time when materials needed on jobs are not on hand due to purchasing manager's inaction and (2) lost time in locating and handling materials, due to problems of access to the large quantities of those materials that have been purchased.

The production manager proposes that a ceiling be set for the size of any purchase made and that minimum stocks of all materials needed in the foreseeable future be maintained. The purchasing manager protests that these constraints will unnecessarily raise the total cost of materials acquisition and usage.

Required:
(a) Discuss the basic problems in this situation from the viewpoint of responsibility accounting and control systems.
(b) Outline some possible ways of dealing with these problems, both in terms of accounting reports and management policies.
(c) Discuss how organizational objectives are involved in these problems.

C 10-6 Control Systems—Inventory

Monmouth Foundry makes large castings for machine parts, none of which usually weighs less than 600 pounds. At the plant gates, guards check all persons leaving the premises. At a recent meeting of supervisory personnel, where cost savings were being discussed, the suggestion was made to eliminate most of the guards and to restrict inspection to the contents of large vehicles only. "After all, if anyone can carry away one of our castings on their own, they deserve to be able to steal it!" commented one executive.

Required:
Discuss this situation from the viewpoint of control systems concepts. Could a responsibility accounting system provide any assistance in this area? (*Comment:* Remember the story about the new watchman who was instructed to watch out for employees taking tools home with them. On his first day on the job, he noticed one employee going out the gate with a full wheelbarrow. He intercepted the employee, but found there was only wood shavings and scraps inside. The same incident was repeated the next day and the next. After this, the watchman didn't bother to check. At the end of the month, an inventory check showed that twenty wheelbarrows were missing!)

C 10-7 Production Costs as Measures of Efficiency

The production supervisor of Westco Corporation is a firm believer in average unit costs as a measure of production efficiency. Whenever any of his process departments achieves reductions in average unit costs, they are rewarded. Those with increased unit costs are berated and lectured on the need to reduce unit costs. Fred Quimby, one of those in the latter category, has just been chastised for the third consecutive week. His cost reports are as follows:

Week	26	27	28	29
Output (units)	20,000	20,000	18,000	16,000
Total Manufacturing Cost	$80,000	$81,000	$75,000	$72,000
Unit Manufacturing Cost	$4.00	$4.05	$4.20	$4.50

During this period, the price of the major raw material Quimby uses increased 10 percent and his production was cut back due to the inability of the sales force to write sufficient sales orders. Quimby also observes that approximately $40,000 of his weekly costs are fixed costs.

Required:
(a) Discuss the validity of the production supervisor's attitude toward cost performance.
(b) Is Quimby justified in his claim that his performance was really more effective and more efficient than indicated? Explain.
(c) Discuss the relative usefulness of (1) *total* and (2) *average* production costs as measures of effectiveness or efficiency.

C 10–8   Performance Measures

Choosing the correct performance measures for use in planning and control systems is critical for success. Discuss separately the relative merits of each of the following measures being used to evaluate and control related activities:

(a) Long-distance truck drivers are paid on the basis of total trip mileage.
(b) Sales representatives receive a bonus for all sales calls made in excess of their monthly base quota.
(c) Personnel Department employees are evaluated on average number of interviews conducted per day. Total files are reviewed each month.
(d) Production foremen receive bonuses for every favorable weekly cost variance, but receive only a warning for each unfavorable variance.
(e) A print shop, using a job cost format, evaluates its section managers on the basis of jobs completed earlier than the customer's requested delivery date.

C 10–9   Control Systems Procedures

Accounting control system procedures always have behavioral implications. Discuss separately the positive and negative implications of the following situations:

(a) "This responsibility accounting system is terrific. The performance reports it generates always tell exactly who is to blame for things that get out of line."
(b) "We base our budgets on the prior period's achievements in each area, with a flat 5 percent 'tightening-up' factor applied to each item to give the group something to shoot for."
(c) "Budgetary planning is great and we make sure all our managers get involved in the process. However, they are all very highly motivated to achieve, so we don't follow up with any sort of performance review reports."
(d) "Those people in sales are unbelievable! There's no way that we in production can get the jobs out on time when they promise delivery 'yesterday' in a lot of cases!"
(e) "Those people in production are unbelievable! After the two years it took to secure the Acme account, they say they can't produce any of the special items we need to fill the first order for at least six months. Surely they could have geared up in anticipation of our success."

(f) "All variances from budgeted amounts are measured in our system of accounting control, but only the big ones that are unfavorable are followed up."

(g) "We believe in giving all levels of management the opportunity to participate in the budgetary process. But it all boils down to the fact that the budget staff in the controller's department are the only ones who understand the figures enough to put the budget together. Don't tell any of our line managers that, though!"

(h) "Not everyone enjoys getting involved in budgetary procedures, whether it be in setting the budget, administering it, or being evaluated by it. That's human nature for you—some people just don't want to get involved."

C 10–10 Structured versus Flexible Budgeting

The budgetary process usually has to maintain a balance between a formal quantitative, analytical, structured approach and an open, behavioral, political, flexible approach.

Required:
(a) Describe briefly the benefits to be derived from each approach.
(b) Describe briefly the disadvantages associated with each approach.
(c) Should the budgetary process become a compromise composite of the two approaches or should it be one of the two extremes? Why?

C 10–11 Dual Planning and Control Systems

A proposed radical approach to the budgetary process would feature a *dual* system of planning and control. One set of budgets incorporating one level of performance requirements is used for realistic planning purposes and is *not* communicated to lower operative levels of management. Another set, featuring higher levels of required performance, is communicated to managers with the message that it reflects performance expectations.

Required:
(a) What are the apparent objectives of such a dual system of budgeting?
(b) What are the motivational implications (1) if the dual system goes undetected and (2) if lower level managers find out about it?
(c) Discuss the feasibility of such a process from the points of view of (1) cost–benefits, (2) business ethics, and (3) implementation and operation.

C 10–12 Credit and Blame—Responsibility Accounting

"Whenever things go wrong and the budget figures are not met, it's us who have screwed up and are to blame! When things go well and the outcomes are better than were budgeted for, you pencil-pushers take all the credit!" Comment on this complaint made by a production department manager.

C 10–13 Control and the Controller

"The budget always gets put together in a haphazard slap-dash fashion. We never have enough time to get all the information and estimates we need to do a proper job." Comment on this observation by a member of the budget staff of the Controller's Department.

C 10–14   Control

"Budgets are meant to put people in their place, keep them there, and constrain their activities." Evaluate this comment on the budgetary process.

Problems

P 10–1   Designing an Accounting System for Cost Control—Feedback Mechanisms

Fingerhut Corporation has requested assistance in redesigning an appropriate cost accounting control system for its plant. The plant has two main divisions: (1) Machining and Die-Cutting and (2) Molding. The molds that are used to mass produce various plastic kitchen and household aids are made in the Machining and Die-Cutting Division. This involves precision work; skilled tool and die workers are often occupied on a single mold for three to four weeks. Most of this division's output is used by the Molding Division, but contracts are frequently accepted to make molds for outside customers.

In the Molding Division, the molds are used to facilitate production of small kitchen and household aids (soap dishes, spoons, utensils, ashtrays, and so on). Molds are used in the pressing operation where chemical granules are subjected to heat and pressure to form the finished products which are later trimmed, inspected, and packaged.

The following data and procedures apply:

(1)   Both divisions operate on a job order basis: Molds in the first, and batches of particular products in the second.

(2)   There is a central raw materials inventory location, but no record is maintained of issues of steel and supplies to the Machining Division, or plastic granules to the Molding Division.

(3)   Inventories are replenished when it is observed that quantities of any item are "running low."

(4)   All plant employees, except for the salaried supervisors of the two divisions, are paid hourly wages.

(5)   Time cards maintained for all employees show total hours worked each week and time spent on each mold or batch in the respective divisions.

(6)   Sometimes, if their work is slack, the Machining Division workers are allowed to help out in the Molding Division, doing inspection and packaging. They are still paid at their own hourly rate.

(7)   Wages charged to molds or batches on time cards are not balanced with total wages paid.

(8)   There is significant spoilage in the Molding Division (defects, breakages, bad coloration, and so on). Molds are quite often rejected in the course of processing in the Machining Department, due to the high quality standards required there. A simple count of the number of rejects per week is all that is presently maintained.

Required:
(a)   Outline an accounting control system for the monitoring of materials and labor costs in the two manufacturing departments.

(b)   What control deficiencies are present in the existing situation?

(c)   What other control procedures (besides the accounting system controls) would you recommend? Why?

P 10-2   Responsibility Accounting—Assignment of Performance Measures to Departments for Control and Evaluation

Maniatis Distributing Corporation has devised a system of divisional income statements to evaluate the performance of its regional sales territories. All operating costs are charged to territories and a "bottom line" profit figure is used to assess the success of each regional sales manager. Several of the six regional managers have expressed concern over the meaningfulness and fairness of these profit measures, especially because annual bonuses are based on them. In fact, two of the divisions (the ones with highest gross revenues) have shown losses under the present system. Operations are organized as follows:

(1)   Sales orders from each region are forwarded to a central warehouse from which all shipments are made.

(2)   All inventory acquisitions are handled by this centrally administered warehouse.

(3)   Sales orders are shipped from the central warehouse to each region's headquarters, then to customers.

(4)   Credit billing and collection is all done by a central administrative office.

(5)   Regional managers are paid a flat salary plus a profit-sharing bonus based on their region's profit, as shown below.

(6)   Items appearing in each region's profit schedule are calculated or allocated as follows:

> Sales—Actual Revenue Earned
> Cost of Goods Sold—Standard Price at Central Warehouse
> Storage and Handling (central warehouse)—Gross Weight of Sales
> Shipping Costs (from central warehouse)—Sales Revenue
> Delivery Costs (to customers)—Actual Costs Incurred
> Sales Salaries—Actual Costs Incurred
> Sales Representatives' Commissions—Sales Revenue
> Manager's Bonus—Regional Profit
> Credit and Collection—Total Number of Invoices
> Central Administration—Equally

Required:

(a)   Evaluate the regional profit schedules as presently prepared, especially from the viewpoint of their ability to reflect the profit performance for which regional managers are responsible.

(b)   Prepare an alternative schedule of profit performance for a region, indicating and explaining omissions or changes from the basis of calculation and allocation now being used.

(c)   Explain the basic problems that are involved in deciding how to report the costs of each region on the basis of a system of responsibility accounting.

P 10-3 Responsibility Accounting—Assignment of Costs to Cost Centers

Etari Electronics Company prepares quarterly performance evaluation reports as a basis for awarding bonuses to its departmental managers. For the second quarter of 19X8, the manager of the Assembly Department is quite upset when she receives her evaluation, which is summarized below:

Assembly Department
Cost Report—Second Quarter 19X8

Item	Budget	Actual	Variance
Supplies........................	$ 82,000	$ 84,500	$ (2,500)
Direct Labor	348,000	364,000	(16,000)
Indirect Labor	142,000	140,500	1,500
Idle Time	12,000	4,000	8,000
Overtime	34,000	45,000	(11,000)
Utilities........................	14,500	15,000	(500)
General Factory Overhead	95,000	112,500	(17,500)
	$727,500	$765,500	$(38,000)

She admits the budgeted figures were reasonable and do reflect the actual level of activity her department achieved that quarter. She feels, however, that she has been unfairly evaluated because of three specific circumstances.

First, she points out that for three weeks of the first month of the quarter, several of her regular assembly line workers were involved in a work stoppage, requiring the employment of temporary help to maintain output. Because these were inexperienced workers, their output was not up to the levels usually achieved. When the regular employees returned, it took another month to get caught up on the backlog of processing. Secondly, on several occasions, the Sales Department insisted on honoring the tight delivery schedule they had promised some customers. This caused the Assembly Department to work several extra overtime shifts. Finally, because general factory overhead is allocated among departments on the basis of total labor hours, the Assembly Department received a larger allocation than expected. This was partly due to the fact that some other departments worked proportionately fewer total hours than they were budgeted.

Required:
(a) Evaluate the claims of the Assembly Division manager. Has she been treated unfairly? Why or why not?
(b) What responsibility accounting principles and control systems concepts are involved here?
(c) Would you recommend alternative accounting treatment of any of the items included in the above report? Why or why not?

P 10-4 Internal Control Systems—Reporting of Performance

Vicente Company instituted new reporting procedures designed to help control the amount of raw materials that were being wasted. Materials usage had consistently exceeded the amounts allocated for production output. The quantity of scrap material reported as being unusable was greatest on Thursdays and Fridays of each week. Production personnel were advised of this. Subsequently, almost no scrap was reported on those two days.

Required:
(a) How can the cost of scrap material (off-cuts, shavings, broken pieces, off-size or odd shapes, and so on) be controlled?
(b) How might reporting the daily quantity (physical volume) of scrap assist control?
(c) What were the possible reasons for (1) the appearance and (2) the disappearance of the Thursday and Friday scrap?
(d) When should accounting control attention be directed to the issue of scrap and waste?
(e) What should be the objective with regard to the cost of scrap—should it be eliminated, minimized, or what? Discuss with respect to the other costs directly associated with scrap (direct labor, direct materials, utilities, storage, and other overhead costs).

P 10–5 Performance Reports—Separation of Controllable and Noncontrollable Items

The following report is typical of those used to reflect the performance of product line managers in the Sales Division of Lamotta Corporation:

LAMOTTA CORPORATION
Product: Jakos   Manager: E. Scruggs
Month of March, 19X2

Sales (60,000 units)		$1,200,000
Less: Cost of Goods Sold		690,000
Gross Profit		$ 510,000
Less: Operating Expenses		
Sales Commissions	$ 60,000	
Advertising	128,000	
Depreciation	15,000	
Office Expenses	58,000	
Travelling Expenses	16,000	
General Administration	88,000	365,000
Product Line Profit Margin		$ 145,000

The following information is also available:

(1) Cost of goods sold included $90,000 for excess production costs due to problems encountered in the manufacturing division.
(2) Advertising includes $78,000 incurred directly by Scruggs to promote his product. The rest is an allocated share of firm-wide advertising outlays.
(3) Sales commissions are based directly on product line revenues. Travelling expenses are all approved by Scruggs.
(4) Office expenses included $28,000 allocated from the office of the Vice President for Marketing.

(5) General administration costs are shared among product lines on the basis of sales revenues.

(6) Depreciation included $5,000 for items of furniture and equipment in Scruggs' office. The rest was for depreciation on an allocated portion of the firm's general office, sales showroom, and finished goods warehouse.

Required:

(a) Prepare a revised performance report for the Jakos product, emphasizing the principle of controllability.

(b) What problems or conflicts were present in the original report?

(c) Should Scruggs and his product line be evaluated completely independently of any common costs, shared facilities, or joint resources with which they are involved? Why or why not?

P 10–6   Motivational Effects of Performance Evaluation and Reward Systems

Campos Sales Company is considering changes in the way it compensates its sales staff. Presently the sales people receive a sales commission on all sales made and are eligible for quarterly bonuses if their performance exceeds budgeted sales quotas. Sales commissions are paid at the rate of 10 percent on the list price of all items sold. Price concessions on large orders are sometimes approved by the Sales Manager, but full commission is still paid on such sales. Any sales person who exceeds his or her quarterly sales quota receives a bonus of 10 percent of all commissions earned that quarter. Credit applications of new customers are processed centrally, and sales people do not forfeit any commissions on accounts that prove to be slow payers or uncollectible.

The proposed changes must be directed toward the following problems that have caused the sales staff to operate in a way that is counterproductive to the firm's overall profit goals. These include:

(1) Concentrating sales effort on high priced and easy to sell products, rather than on items that have better contribution margins.

(2) Bunching of sales orders so that sales quotas are exceeded in two out of every three quarters.

(3) Selling to high risk, often one-time customers.

Required:

(a) Discuss the favorable and unfavorable motivational effects of the existing sales commission scheme.

(b) Suggest ways to revise the sales commissions procedures so as to maintain employee motivation and also to promote firm-wide profitable operations.

P 10–7   Motivational Impact of Levels at Which Required Performance Levels Are Set

Firms using budgetary controls to improve employee performance and contribute to organizational profit goals face the problem of selecting the appropriate level of required performance to motivate employees in the desired way.

In the Welding Department of Harding Corporation, an analysis of average daily output of eight welders using similar equipment and working on the same product showed the following information for the past six months:

Employee	Average Daily Output
1	150
2	150
3	140
4	130
5	120
6	120
7	100
8	90
Total	1,000
Group Average	125

A difference of opinion develops in setting the budgeted level of required output per day for this operation. The foreman of the Welding Department is hesitant to concede anything higher than 125 units per day per worker. Production scheduling personnel point out that product specification and equipment rating indicate that a rate of 200 per day is technically feasible. The budget officer from the Controller's Department proposes a level of 150 units per day, because he believes that this is attainable.

Required:
(a) Discuss the rationale behind the alternative viewpoints of the three parties, especially with regard to how the three proposed levels would affect cost control, motivation of workers, and performance evaluation.

(b) Comment on the possible effects on employee motivation of a budgeted level of 160 units per day. Discuss this from the point of view of (1) the foreman and (2) each of the eight workers.

(c) What additional information would be helpful in this situation?

(d) Would you consider allowing different budgeted levels for each welder? Why or why not?

(e) If the budgeted level was specified as a group (average) requirement rather than a requirement of each welder, how would this affect the foreman and the various individuals? Discuss.

P 10-8   Service Departments—Motivational Effects of Transfer Prices or Cost Allocations

Helm Corporation operates its own modern data processing facility, complete with programmers, systems analysts, consultants, as well as operators, maintenance staff and the latest in computer hardware. Management wishes to encourage more efficient use of its computer services. One line of attack is to revise the way in which user-departments (customers of the data center) are affected by their use of the center in their own performance reports prepared for budgeting and evaluation purposes. Three proposals were received:

(1) To allow all departments to use the services of the Data Center free of charge. Services would be assigned first to priority items (decided on by top management), then on a first-come, first-served basis.

(2) To have user departments and the Data Center negotiate a price for all services to be performed.

(3) To charge user departments for actual usage with a schedule of fees based on (1) CPU time and (2) key personnel hours. The rates would be set to allow the Data Center to break even at a comfortable level of operations.

Required:

(a) In the light of the firm's goal of achieving more efficient use of the Data Center, discuss the three proposals from the viewpoint of their motivational impact on user department managers.

(b) Discuss the three proposals from the viewpoint of the Data Center Manager and the same firm-wide goal as in part (a).

(c) Discuss possible impact of the three proposals on cost control in the Data Center.

11

FLEXIBLE BUDGETING

LEARNING OBJECTIVES

After studying Chapter 11, you should be able to:

1. Distinguish between static and flexible budgets and explain the planning and control advantages of flexible budgets.
2. Identify the cost and revenue relationships to be used in constructing a flexible budget model.
3. Modify the primary budgetary relationships by using intermediate relationships to allow all budgetary functions to be expressed in terms of a single variable.
4. Prepare a flexible budget that shows expected revenues, costs, contribution margin, and net income over a specified range of activity.
5. Compare budgeted to actual results and calculate the following variances:
   a. Sales price variance
   b. Sales forecast (quantity) variance
   c. Materials price and quantity variances
   d. Labor and overhead efficiency variances
   e. Labor and overhead spending variances
6. Use a flexible budgeting approach to reallocate service department costs to production departments.

Preparation of a master budget and supporting budgets was described in Chapter 7. That discussion emphasized the importance of making the budgetary process responsive to management's need for predictive and future-oriented information. The dynamic, uncertain nature of the business decision making environment was also pointed out. For planning purposes, it is desirable to develop a relatively fixed set of financial and operating budgets. However, it is also necessary to provide for some degree of adaptability to unexpected future events. Only if the outcomes of future actions could be predicted with certainty would there be no need for budgetary flexibility.

When a company prepares an integrated set of budgets, each budget is usually linked to a central planning variable (or variables) such as a sales forecast. It was noted in Chapter 7 that the accuracy of each supporting budget depends to some extent on that key variable. It was also shown that several different budgets, each retaining the same internal structure and interrelationships, can be prepared simply by changing one of the predicted amounts in the sales forecast. Even more dramatic changes can be produced by varying the assumptions underlying the sales forecast. Moreover, any alteration in the budgeted relationships will also produce different budgets. For example, budgeted amounts will change if the inventory policy changes or if the composition of fixed and variable costs is altered.

Given all these possible sources of variation, accountants must develop budgeting methods that can be adapted to a variety of possible outcomes. A type of budget model that permits planning and control analysis of all the variables being budgeted, over a range of possible activity levels is discussed in this chapter.

CONTROL LIMITATIONS OF STATIC BUDGETS

A budget prepared on the basis of a single predicted activity level can be a useful planning tool, because it expresses the goals that the firm and each of its sub-units want to achieve. The master budget is a statement of the financial position to which the company aspires; the supporting financial and operating budgets are statements of the means proposed to achieve that position. Many intrinsic rewards of the budgetary process—cause–effect recognition, future-oriented attention, integrative awareness—can still be attained even if budgets specify only one predicted outcome or set of outcomes.

However, this type of budget is less useful for purposes other than planning, because it does not allow for management's inability to accurately forecast the future. In particular, the usefulness of static budgets for performance evaluation and control is diminished if actual operations produce any variations in the values of the key planning variables or if any of the relationships change after they have been incorporated in the budget model.

FIGURE 11–1

Collins Company
Production Cost Budget
1,500 Units of Output

Materials	$ 6,000
Direct Labor	4,500
Variable Overhead	3,000
Fixed Overhead	1,500
Total Cost	$15,000

Example: Collins Company prepares a static planning budget that calls for the production of 1,500 units of output, and forecasts the costs shown in Figure 11–1.

But what if only 1,200 units are actually produced? Figure 11–2 compares the budgeted estimates for 1,500 units with the costs actually incurred in producing 1,200 units.

No common basis exists for comparing actual and budgeted costs. The $2,400 variation is the difference between the budgeted costs for one set of activities and the actual costs incurred for a different set of activities. At most, Figure 11–2 gives some indication of the accuracy of the forecasting process. It should not be used to evaluate the efficiency or effectiveness of Collins Company's production operations or the decision makers' responsibility for them.

For example, it is not reasonable to claim that the company's materials usage was efficient because its actual cost of $5,000 is less than its budgeted cost of $6,000. The static budget for 1,500 units of output is not an appropriate basis for judging the effectiveness of operations that produce 1,200 units.

Similarly, if 2,000 units had been produced, with materials usage costing $7,500, it would be incorrect to claim that the $1,500 variation ($7,500 actual

---

FIGURE 11–2

Collins Company
Budgeted and Actual Costs

	Budget 1,500 Units	Actual 1,200 Units	Variation
Materials	$ 6,000	$ 5,000	$1,000
Direct Labor	4,500	3,500	1,000
Variable Overhead	3,000	2,500	500
Fixed Overhead	1,500	1,600	(100)
	$15,000	$12,600	$2,400

minus $6,000 budgeted) was a measure of inefficiency in the use of raw materials. These examples merely show that a budget for one level of activity should not be used to assess performance at a higher or lower level.

CONTROL LIMITATIONS OF ELEMENTARY COST–VOLUME–PROFIT ANALYSIS

In the discussion of cost–volume–profit analysis in Chapter 8, several limitations of that technique were described. There too the analysis was basically static. All relationships—unit sales prices, unit variable costs, total fixed costs, and activity levels—were assumed to be constant throughout the period of analysis. The cost object was primarily an output unit. Only single product situations were handled effectively. Strong assumptions were made concerning cost behavior. All costs were assumed to be either fixed or variable with regard to a single planning variable, units of output. To facilitate computation and analysis, a linear relationship among the variables was assumed; to make this assumption, a relevant range of activity had to be specified.

All these constraints make it difficult to use cost–volume–profit analysis as anything more than an elementary, broad based planning tool. Probably the most limiting aspect of the simple cost–volume–profit model is the requirement that it express costs and revenues as *functions of one variable*. These are usually linear functions, and the one variable is a homogenous output unit.

For control purposes, it is necessary to employ budgeting methods that overcome the restrictions of these elementary planning techniques. Costs must be planned and controlled in relation to cost objects other than an aggregate output unit. Multiple output situations, changing activity levels and configurations, variations in input and output prices, complex cost behavior patterns, and the general uncertainty of future operating environments—all must be incorporated into an effective budgetary control process.

THE CONCEPT OF A FLEXIBLE BUDGET

Flexible budgeting involves the development of a **budget model** consisting of a set of functional relationships among the perceived planning variables (the sales forecast, inventory requirements, production plan, cash inflow and outflow projections, and so on). Such a set of relationships was demonstrated when the master budget was derived in Chapter 7. But that budget model was evaluated only once—for a single value of the key planning variable, the sales forecast. Instead of developing a single set of budget measures, the flexible budget specifies a set of functions that explains the behavior of *all* the variables for the activity being budgeted and that can be evaluated over a *range* of possible activity levels.

Flexible budgets are often presented in the form of multicolumn reports, with each column showing the costs and revenues expected at a particular activity level. However, the essential technique in flexible budgeting is to represent the *relationships* that connect each budget variable and that influence the related costs, revenues, and other performance measures.

A **flexible budgeting relationship** may be as simple as a single variable linear equation, such as $Y = \$10X$, in which Y is the total cost of raw materials used and X is the number of output units produced. On the other hand, it could be as complex as the following multivariable, nonlinear function:

$$Y = 5X_1^3 - 2X_2^2 + 3X_3 - 4X_4 + 1,000$$

In this latter case, Y might be the total cost of an activity center and X_1, X_2, X_3, and X_4 might be four variables that influence costs incurred in that center.

ADVANTAGES OF FLEXIBLE BUDGETS

The process of negotiating and coordinating sub-budgets is facilitated when each budget area establishes its own flexible budget *formulas* rather than simply generating a single budget *figure*. Attention is then focused on formulating the set of functions that explains cost and revenue behavior in each budget area. Having the budget formulas in hand also permits a more orderly and efficient integration of the final sets of budgets.

Once the formulas that make up the flexible budget model have been established, costs and revenues can be evaluated at various levels of activity. For control purposes, the relevant budget figures are clearly those that correspond to the actual activity level. By providing these figures, the flexible budget formulas allow managers to compare actual and planned performance at the same activity level.

Example: Using the same data as in the preceding example, Figure 11–3 compares the budgeted costs of producing 1,200 units of output with the actual results. The variations between budgeted and actual costs can be used to assess overall operating efficiency. Either actual expenditures were $300 too high, or costs were budgeted at too low a level. There is now a valid basis for comparison and a starting point to determine *why* variations exist and what can be done to take advantage of favorable variations or eliminate those that are unfavorable.

FIGURE 11–3

Collins Company
Budgeted and Actual Costs
for 1,200 Units

	Budget 1,200 Units	Actual 1,200 Units	Variation
Materials	$ 4,800	$ 5,000	$(200)
Direct Labor	3,600	3,500	100
Variable Overhead	2,400	2,500	(100)
Fixed Overhead	1,500	1,600	(100)
	$12,300	$12,600	$(300)

THE SCOPE OF FLEXIBLE BUDGETS

Flexible budgets can be prepared for the whole firm or for individual subdivisions. They may apply to major functional groupings (production, marketing, administration), local cost centers (Machining Department, Shipping Department), or individual decision makers (one machine operator, one salesperson). In all cases, the objectives of flexible budgeting are the same—to determine the set of relationships among the variables that can be acted on by decision makers in the budget area, and to express those relationships in a convenient form.

The most useful cost object for budgetary control purposes is an *activity center*—a cost center, a profit center, or an investment center—because revenue and cost behavior must be traced directly to those points where the decisions are made that generate the costs and revenues. Cost behavior in particular can best be analyzed as a function of activity levels in the decision center where the costs are incurred.

Of course, it is possible to develop a flexible budget in which *units of final output* are the activity indicator. For example, a firm with fixed costs of $10,000 per month and variable costs of $10 per unit of output would have a highly aggregated flexible budget of the following form:

$$\text{Total Cost} = \text{Fixed Cost} + \text{Total Variable Costs}$$
$$= \$10,000 + \$10Q$$

Here Q equals the number of units of output. This implies that all costs are fixed or vary directly and uniformly with the number of units produced. But, as shown in Chapters 3–6, when there are a number of steps in the production process, measuring the cost of a finished product requires several cost allocations and reallocations, some of them quite arbitrary. Direct relationships between costs and units of final product are the exception rather than the rule.

However, cost reallocations are not needed if cost functions are derived for each activity center rather than for the production process as a whole. As a result, these local cost functions should be more accurate and useful for both planning and control purposes. In general, flexible budgets that apply to decision centers of limited scope (departments, divisions, cost centers) are preferable to budgets that apply to the whole firm.

APPLICABILITY OF FLEXIBLE BUDGETING TECHNIQUES

Although all cost and revenue relationships can be incorporated into flexible budgets, flexible budgeting tends to be most helpful in handling the planning and control of overhead, marketing, and administrative costs, because these costs tend to display irregular patterns of behavior. Revenues, direct materials costs, and direct labor costs are usually easier to predict and analyze because they are directly related to activity levels. However, flexible budgeting will be presented here as a technique that can be used to plan and control all types of costs and revenues.

This general applicability is enhanced by the fact that flexible budgeting does not require that every cost and revenue function be expressed in terms of the same independent variable. As previously mentioned, a flexible budget is most appropriate for localized decision centers. Therefore, a variety of explanatory variables can be used to construct the cost and revenue functions in flexible budgets. In each situation, the variable or variables selected should be those that best explain the behavior of costs and revenues in the particular budget area.

However, there are practical reasons for keeping the number of variables small and the types of functions simple. There is a tendency to acknowledge the variety of possible cost and revenue functions, but to discuss only elementary, single-variable models, using complexity of computation as a justification for neglecting the more complex forms. This chapter will illustrate simple, linear, one-variable models as well as some relatively advanced flexible budget models.

Again, recent developments in computerized data processing should be recognized and applied to this aspect of cost accounting. It is difficult to analyze and manipulate the more complex flexible budgets using only manual methods. However, when appropriate data processing capacity is available, such problems become less important and relatively complex flexible budget models can be employed.

DEVELOPING A FLEXIBLE BUDGET

The preceding examples show only a partial and condensed version of a flexible budget and its preparation. A more detailed description of flexible budget construction will now be presented.

COST AND REVENUE CATEGORIES IN THE FLEXIBLE BUDGET

The **cost and revenue functions** that comprise each flexible budget must reflect the behavior of all costs and revenues identified with the budget area. A first step in developing a flexible budget is to list the cost and revenue items that will appear in the budget.

ESTABLISHING THE COST AND REVENUE FUNCTIONS

The next step is to identify the **functional relationships** that explain the behavior of each of these cost and revenue items. This might be done by observing how each item has tended to behave in the past, and projecting that general pattern into the future. Methods of forecasting costs and revenues are discussed in Chapter 15. These forecasting techniques range from the simple and subjective to the formally mathematical:

1. Account analysis
2. Visual fit or graphic approximations
3. High-low interpolation

FIGURE 11–4

**Christianson Company
Cost Relationships for Flexible Budgets**

Machining Department
Materials .... $25 per item processed
Direct Labor .... $10 per labor hour
Supplies .... $1 per machine hour
Supervision .... $1,500 per month

Buildings and Grounds Department
Labor .... $5 per labor hour
Supplies .... $5 per 1,000 square feet serviced
Power .... 50¢ per equipment operating hour
Depreciation .... $250 per month

Shipping Department
Labor .... $8 per labor hour
Supplies .... $1 per order shipped
Supervision .... $1,500 per 1,000 orders shipped per month
Depreciation .... $200 per month

---

4. Engineering analysis
5. Statistical regression analysis

A major purpose of these forecasting methods is to enable their users to develop functions of one or more variables to explain the behavior of a cost or revenue item. For purposes of exposition, linear, single variable functions, will be used in this chapter. Revenues will be presented as a linear function of the number of units sold. Cost functions usually will be presented as divisible into fixed and variable elements, the variability being a function of a single explanatory variable.

Example: Christianson Company has developed flexible budgets for its Machining Department, Buildings and Grounds Department, and Shipping Department. The functional relationships shown in Figure 11–4 were determined by analyzing the past behavior of each type of cost.

For the Christianson Company, several different variables explain cost behavior in each department. For example, in all three departments, labor cost is measured per labor hour. But the fact that supplies usage is measured on a different basis in each department illustrates the point that flexible budgets need not express all cost and revenue relationships as functions of a common variable.

INTERMEDIATE RELATIONSHIPS

Flexible budgets can be simplified by reducing the number of independent variables. A common practice is to look for **intermediate relationships** that will permit all other functions to be expressed in terms of one key planning variable (say labor hours in the case of an assembly department). Often this is done by simply relating all costs to units of output. However, it is preferable to use an input-related variable such as labor hours, machine hours, or materials used.

Example: Christianson Company, the departmental cost relationships of which were shown in Figure 11–4, has identified the following intermediate relationships for its three departments:

1. *Machining Department*   5 items can be processed per machine hour; every machine hour requires 1½ labor hours.
2. *Buildings and Grounds Department*   Employees can service 10,000 square feet per hour; 2 hours of labor are expended for every hour of equipment use.
3. *Shipping Department*   An average shipment takes ½ hour to process; maximum shipments are 2,000 per month.

A comparison of Figures 11–4 and 11–5 reveals how these intermediate relationships can be used to simplify the flexible budget formulas. Notice that the reduction in the number of independent variables in each department's budget was achieved by using the intermediate relationships to convert each department's budget functions to a common activity basis—machine hours for the Machining Department, labor hours for the Buildings and Grounds Department, and number of shipments for the Shipping Department.

This simplification has the drawback of introducing extra relationships (the intermediate ones) into the budget process. It may also produce additional variability in the analysis, because some degree of variability in the intermediate relationships is probable. The accuracy of the final simplifed cost functions

---

FIGURE 11–5

Christianson Company
Flexible Budget Formulas Using Intermediate Relationships

Machining Department
Materials	$5 per machine hour
Direct Labor............................	$15 per machine hour
Supplies	$1 per machine hour
Supervision	$1,500 per month

Buildings and Grounds Department
Labor	$5 per labor hour
Supplies	50¢ per labor hour
Power	25¢ per labor hour
Depreciation	$250 per month

Shipping Department
Labor	$4 per shipment
Supplies	$1 per shipment
Supervision	$1,500 per 1,000 shipments per month
Depreciation	$200 per month

FIGURE 11–6

Christianson Company
Departmental Flexible Budget Formulas

Machining Department
  Monthly Total Cost   = $1,500 + $21 per machine hour

Buildings and Grounds Department
  Monthly Total Cost   = $250 + $5.75 per labor hour

Shipping Department
Monthly total Cost
$$= \begin{cases} \$1,700 + \$5 \text{ per shipment} \\ \text{(shipments up to 1,000)} \\ \text{or} \\ \$3,200 + \$5 \text{ per shipment} \\ \text{(shipments of 1,000 to 2,000)} \end{cases}$$

FIGURE 11–7

Christianson Company
Flexible Budget—Shipping Department

	800 Shipments	1,000 Shipments	1,200 Shipments	1,500 Shipments
Labor	$3,200	$4,000	$4,800	$ 6,000
Supplies	800	1,000	1,200	1,500
Supervision	1,500	1,500	3,000	3,000
Depreciation	200	200	200	200
Total	$5,700	$6,700	$9,200	$10,700

becomes dependent on the accuracy and stability of these intermediate relationships.

The individual cost functions can be aggregated to produce a single budget formula for each of the three departments, as shown in Figure 11–6.

Figure 11–7 is a flexible budget for Christianson Company's Shipping Department. In it the budget formulas that were derived in Figure 11–6 are evaluated over four activity levels.

Remember that the critical aspect of flexible budget construction is deriving the set of formulas that make up the budget model, rather than producing the tables of numbers found by evaluating the model at various activity levels.

EVALUATING COST AND REVENUE FUNCTIONS: CURRENT REPLACEMENT COST

Future, or at least current, input and output prices must be used when values are attached to the chosen cost and revenue functions. Many input resources that are expected to be consumed during the budget period will also be acquired during that same period—in which case, the relevant measure of cost performance is clearly a *future price*.

The budget may also require the consumption of resources that are already on hand. Although these resources have an historical acquisition price, for planning and control purposes, their relevant price is still a future price—the **current replacement cost** of the resource when its consumption or transformation occurs.

The use of replacement costs is justified by the need for capital maintenance. It is management's responsibility to preserve rather than diminish the real resources of a long-lived business. To do this, management should evaluate the effects of all resource transformations resulting from managerial decisions in terms of what it currently will cost to replace the used up resources. If prospective actions are judged on the basis of past acquisition costs, real resources may be diminished without management's knowledge.

Example: Storrer Company has acquired raw materials inventory for $1,000. Management proposes to convert these raw materials into a product that will sell for $1,500. This will require current outlays of $300 for labor and other production and selling costs. The transaction appears profitable if the cost of raw materials is measured at acquisition prices. Revenue of $1,500 minus costs of $1,000 and $300 produces a net income of $200.

But if the cost to repurchase the same quantity of raw materials has increased from $1,000 to $1,300, the sale at $1,500 will not maintain real capital intact. To regain its position of holding at least the same quantity of real resources, management must make a future outlay of $1,300. Therefore, the relevant cost to be considered in planning future actions is $1,600—the $1,300 future cost of materials plus the $300 manufacturing cost. Because this cannot be offset by the $1,500 of prospective revenues, the proposed sale will not benefit the firm. Looking at it another way, the net future revenue from the proposed sale is only $1,200 ($1,500 revenue minus $300 conversion costs). This is not enough to allow the firm to spend the $1,300 necessary to replenish its raw materials inventory by an amount equivalent to the inventory consumed. Consequently, the company cannot, by making the proposed sale, continue to hold as many real resources as it did before.

Replacement cost of resources at the time of their consumption is therefore the measure that should be used in evaluating cost functions for flexible budgeting purposes. Some prices will remain fairly stable in the short run, thereby reducing this price variability problem. Many resources are consumed shortly after their acquisition—in which case replacement cost should closely approximate acquisition price.

Revenue functions should also be evaluated in terms of anticipated sales prices. Revenues do not pose quite the same acquisition/replacement problem as do cost items, because cash receipts from sales usually are collected during the same accounting period in which sales transactions occur.

TIME PERIODS FOR FLEXIBLE BUDGETING

Flexible budgeting methods are most appropriately applied to short- and medium-length accounting periods. To be effective planning and control devices, the relationships embodied in the budget model must remain valid throughout the budget period. This condition can be readily satisfied when the budget period is as short as a week or a month. Beyond that, the effects of possible changes in activity configurations must be considered. If production methods, supply sources, marketing methods, or product design are varied, the original budget model will lose some of its relevance. Such changes should then be incorporated into a new set of budget formulas. The flexible budget can be meaningfully evaluated and be useful for planning and control only if all underlying relationships remain in effect.

MEASURING AND INTERPRETING VARIANCES

The primary control technique associated with flexible budgeting is analysis of variances. Any deviation of actual performance from planned or budgeted performance is considered a **variance.** Any classification, refinement, explanation, or investigation of a variance is referred to as **variance analysis.**

VARIANCE ANALYSIS USING FLEXIBLE BUDGETS

The independent variables used in flexible budget formulas should be chosen to provide maximum information about the size and causes of variances. As suggested earlier in this chapter, input-related variables such as labor hours, machine hours, or materials consumed may express cost behavior more effectively than units of output measures. This is especially likely when outputs are non-homogenous and when indirect costs such as manufacturing overheads, marketing costs, and administrative costs are involved.

For planning purposes, the *accuracy* of cost estimates produced by use of a particular independent variable is of primary concern to managers. For control purposes, the independent variable must also permit measurement and analysis of the *efficiency* of cost performance. For example, it might be possible to predict indirect labor costs as a function of the number of units produced. But if the number of units produced per indirect labor hour worked tends to vary, or if indirect labor rates change, indirect labor costs budgeted as a function of output units will not be useful for control purposes.

Example: Greenhorn Company budgets indirect labor costs at the rate of $10 per unit of output. As shown in Figure 11–8, actual costs of producing 1,000 units during August, 19X3, are $11,025, which is $1,025 more than the budgeted cost of $10,000.

What caused the $1,025 unfavorable variance? When indirect labor costs are budgeted as a function of output units, the reason for the variance is unclear. However, suppose that two hours of indirect labor at $5 per hour are budgeted to produce each unit of output. Production was 1,000 units but 2,100 hours were actually worked. In Figure 11–9, the flexible budget is based on the number of indirect labor hours worked.

This $525 variance is the difference between the actual cost of working 2,100 hours and the budgeted cost of working the same number of hours ($11,025 − $10,500). Expressed this way, it is evident that the variance is caused by a variation in the wage rate. Instead of the $5 per hour rate anticipated

---

FIGURE 11–8

Greenhorn Company
Indirect Labor Costs as a Function of Output Units
Month of August, 19X3

	Budget 1,000 Units	Actual 1,000 Units	Variance
Budget Formula:			
$10 per unit			
Indirect Labor Costs	$10,000	$11,025	($1,025)
			Unfavorable

---

in the budget formula, indirect labor costs were actually incurred at a rate of $5.25 per hour. The budget in Figure 11–9 provides more information for control purposes than the previous budget based on output units, because the variance can now be traced to a cause—an **input price** or **spending variance.**

Finally, consider a third method of comparing budgeted and actual activity, in which the flexible budget formula for indirect labor cost is expressed as a function of the number of hours that *should have been worked* to attain the output level that was actually produced. This will be referred to as the *required number of hours.*

In Figure 11–10, the flexible budget formula for indirect labor hours is evaluated at two different activity levels: 2,100 actual hours worked and 2,000 hours required to produce the output achieved (2 × 1,000 units).

The data in Figure 11–10 can be used to derive both a *spending variance* and an *efficiency variance,* as shown in Figure 11–11.

The total variance of $1,025 has now been identified with two causes: a variation in the number of hours worked and a variation in the hourly wage rate. The **efficiency** or **usage variance** is $500 (unfavorable), calculated as the 100 hours worked in excess of required hours multiplied by the budgeted hourly rate of $5. The *input price* or *spending variance* is $525 (unfavorable),

---

FIGURE 11–9

Greenhorn Company
Indirect Labor Costs as a Function of Actual
Hours Worked Month of August, 19X3

	Budget 2,100 Hours	Actual 2,100 Hours	Variance
Budget Formula:			
$5 per hour			
Indirect Labor Costs	$10,500	$11,025	($525)
			Unfavorable

FIGURE 11–10

Greenhorn Company
Indirect Labor Costs as a Function of Hours Required,
and of Actual Hours Worked
Month of August, 19X3

	Budget 2,000 Hours Required	Budget 2,100 Hours Worked	Actual Cost
Budget Formula:			
$5 per hour (2 hours required per unit)			
Indirect Labor Costs......................	$10,000	$10,500	$11,025

calculated as the wage rate variation of 25¢ per hour multiplied by the 2,100 hours worked.

This example shows that the extent of variance analysis depends on the basis used in establishing a flexible budget. Different variances were derived in Figures 11–8 and 11–9, because in each case a different independent variable was used as a frame of reference. However, the most useful variance measures were obtained in Figure 11–11, in which the number of indirect labor hours required to produce the actual output was included in the budgetary analysis.

In general, cost functions used in a flexible budget should permit as much detail as possible in the computation of cost variances for control purposes. When the budget is used as a control device, the independent variable must not only allow direct and accurate predictions to be made, but should also permit a clear and complete analysis of why variances occur.

The same considerations apply in selecting an independent variable for budgeting nonmanufacturing costs. Many variables can be used in marketing cost functions, including number of sales orders processed, number of sales visits, labor hours of sales activities, and weight of items shipped. In budgeting

FIGURE 11–11

Greenhorn Company
Flexible Budget Analysis of Indirect Labor Costs
Month of August, 19X3

A Flexible Budget	B Flexible Budget	C Actual Costs	A − B Efficiency Variance	B − C Spending Variance	A − C Total Variance
2,000 Hours Required	2,100 Hours Worked	2,100 Hours Worked	$10,000 − 10,500	$10,500 − 11,025	$10,000 − 11,025
$10,000	$10,500	$11,025	($ 500)	($ 525)	($ 1,025)
			Unfavorable	Unfavorable	Unfavorable

administrative costs, the independent variable could be the number of transactions processed, the number of documents prepared, or the labor hours worked by clerical employees.

SPENDING AND EFFICIENCY VARIANCES

The *spending* (or input price) variance and the *efficiency* (or input usage) variance identified in Figure 11–11 can be measured in the following types of situations:

1. For *individual budget items* such as direct labor, power, repairs, factory supplies, and indirect labor.
2. For fixed or variable cost items in *separate groups* such as manufacturing overhead, marketing costs, and administrative costs.
3. For *all items* in a flexible budget prepared for a single department or for a whole firm.

The spending and efficiency variances for cost items are calculated as follows:

> **Spending Variance** = Budgeted Amount for Actual Input Activity Level – Actual Amount Incurred
>
> **Efficiency Variance** = Budgeted Amount for Required Input Activity Level – Budgeted Amount for Actual Input Activity Level

The following spending and efficiency variances can be calculated using the data from Figure 11–11:

Spending Variance = 2,100 Hours Worked at a Budgeted Rate of $5 per Hour
  – $11,025 Actual Indirect Labor Cost Incurred
 = (2,100 × $5) – $11,025
 = $10,500 – $11,025
 = ($525) (Unfavorable)

Efficiency Variance = 2,000 Hours Required to be Worked at a Budgeted Rate of $5
  – 2,100 Hours Actually Worked at a Budgeted Rate of $5
 = (2,000 × $5) – (2,100 × $5)
 = $10,000 – $10,500
 = ($500) (Unfavorable)

The positive or negative mathematical sign accompanying the results of these calculations is important. When the value of a cost variance is *positive,* actual costs are less than budgeted costs, indicating a **favorable variance.** If

FIGURE 11–12

Greenhorn Company
Flexible Budget Analysis of Factory Supervision Costs
Month of August, 19X3

A Flexible Budget	B Flexible Budget	C Actual Costs	A – B Efficiency Variance	B – C Spending Variance	A – C Total Variance
2,000 Hours Required	2,100 Hours Worked	2,100 Hours Worked		$15,000 – 15,625	$15,000 – 15,625
$15,000	$15,000	$15,625	N/A	($ 625)	($ 625)
				Unfavorable	Unfavorable

the sign is *negative,* actual costs exceed budgeted limits, indicating an **unfavorable variance.**

Two special situations should be noted. First, any item budgeted as a *fixed cost* will have associated with it only a *spending variance.* Because the budgeted amount for a fixed cost will be the same at all activity levels, there cannot be a fixed cost *efficiency variance.* Second, remember that an efficiency variance cannot be computed (1) when budget formulas are expressed in terms of *actual* rather than *required* input usage or (2) when budget formulas are expressed in terms of *units of output.*

Example: Greenhorn Company budgets factory supervision as a fixed cost of $15,000 per month. In August, 19X3, when 1,000 units requiring 2,000 labor hours were produced and 2,100 labor hours were worked, actual supervisory costs amounted to $15,625. Figure 11–12 shows the appropriate flexible budgeting analysis for this situation.

The efficiency variance column is designated "N/A" (not applicable), because there will never be any variation in the budgeted amount of a fixed cost. Therefore, columns A and B, which contain the two flexible budget amounts, will always include the same amount of fixed costs.

The second exceptional circumstance in calculating the efficiency variance is illustrated in Figure 11–8 and 11–10. In Figure 11–8, it was not possible to break down the $1,025 total variance into its spending and efficiency components, because the flexible budget formula was based on units of output. Figure 11–10 could not include any analysis of efficiency, because it contained only information about the actual hours worked and provided no basis for comparison between actual hours and required hours.

SALES AND CONTRIBUTION MARGIN VARIANCES

Flexible budgeting procedures can be applied to activity centers that produce revenues as well as costs. Variations in sales volume and sales prices affect revenues, total contribution margin, and net income. These effects can be identified as a **sales price variance,** caused by variations in unit sales prices, and a **sales forecast variance** (or *sales quantity variance*), caused by variations in the number of units sold.

These variances are calculated as follows:

$$\text{Sales Price Variance} = \frac{\text{(Actual Unit Sales Price} - \text{Budgeted Unit Sales Price)}}{\times \text{Number of Units Sold}}$$

$$\begin{array}{l}\text{Sales Forecast Variance} \\ \text{or} \\ \text{Sales Quantity Variance}\end{array} = \frac{\text{(Actual Sales Volume} - \text{Budgeted Sales Volume)}}{\times \text{Budgeted Contribution Margin per Unit}}$$

The *sales price variance* indicates the extent to which gross sales revenue is affected by differences between actual and budgeted unit sales prices. The *sales quantity variance* measures the effect on total contribution margin of a difference between actual and budgeted sales volume.

Both of these sales-related variances assume the existence of a single homogenous unit of output. Multiproduct firms and non-homogenous output situations call for more complex variance analysis, as discussed in Chapter 13.

As is the case with cost variance calculations, these computations produce positive numbers that represent favorable variances or negative numbers that represent unfavorable variances. However, in the sales variance formulas, the *sequence* of the budgeted and actual amounts used in the cost variance formulas must be reversed to preserve this computational effect.

Example: Morgan Company budgets monthly sales volume of 10,000 units at a sales price of $10 per unit. The company's flexible budget specifies fixed costs of $12,500 per month and variable costs of $7 per unit. Actual sales volume was 9,000 units and the actual sales price was $12 per unit.

$$\begin{aligned}\text{Sales Price Variance} &= \frac{\text{(Actual Unit Sales Price} - \text{Budgeted Unit Sales Price)}}{\times \text{Number of Units Sold}} \\ &= (\$12 - \$10) \times 9,000 \\ &= \$2 \times 9,000 \\ &= \$18,000 \text{ (Favorable)}\end{aligned}$$

$$\begin{aligned}\text{Sales Quantity Variance} &= \frac{\text{(Actual Sales Volume} - \text{Budgeted Sales Volume)}}{\times \text{Budgeted Contribution Margin per Unit}} \\ &= (9,000 - 10,000) \times (\$10 - \$7) \\ &= (-1,000) \times \$3 \\ &= (\$3,000) \text{ (Unfavorable)}\end{aligned}$$

The sum of these two variances, $15,000 (favorable), reconciles with the total variance between the budgeted contribution margin of $30,000 (10,000 units at $3) and the actual contribution margin of $45,000 (9,000 units at $5).

INTERPRETING VARIANCES

The elementary system of variance measurement presented to this point permits the isolation of certain factors that cause actual performance to deviate from planned performance. The names given to these variances indicate their nature: *spending, efficiency, price,* and *quantity.* Each of them is meant to reflect the results of managerial actions taken at different decision points. This is a basic concept of control—to trace responsibility for cost and revenue performance to its points of origin.

Once the size (dollar amount) and direction (favorable or unfavorable) of a variance have been determined, additional analysis may be attempted. For example, if the variance reflects the operations of a whole department or activity center, separate variances for each item of total cost might be calculated. The more aggregated the variance remains, the more likely it is that offsetting variances within it will pass undetected.

After variances have been measured at an appropriate level of detail, a decision must be made as to whether or not to *investigate* the variances. A simple decision rule for this purpose might be to establish control limits, in either absolute dollar or percentage terms. Any variance exceeding those limits will be more fully analyzed to establish its causes and, if possible, to reduce or eliminate the variance. For example, a control limit rule might be stated as follows: "Any variance in excess of $1,000, or greater than 5 percent of the budgeted amount, will be subject to detailed analysis." Control limits and formal methods of setting them will be considered in Chapters 13 and 22.

In summary, many combinations of circumstances lead to variances in cost and revenue performance. Some of the more commonly encountered variance-causing events are:

Spending Variance:
  Input price changes
  Quantity discounts
  Purchases made from alternate suppliers
  Purchases of different quality items
  Purchases of different amounts of fixed cost items
  Price prediction errors

Efficiency Variance:
  Production efficiency or inefficiency
  Changes in yields from input materials
  Changes in labor productivity
  Economies or diseconomies of scale
  Technology variations
  Equipment breakdowns and malfunctions
  Work stoppages, slowdowns, and strikes
  Input quality variations
  Errors in predicting levels of input usage

Sales Price Variance:
  Competitive price adjustments
  Customer demand changes

Product differentiations
Cost changes requiring price changes
Price prediction errors

Sales Quantity Variance:

Customer demand changes
Actions of competitors
Marketing efficiency or inefficiency
Forecasting errors

FLEXIBLE BUDGETING AND SERVICE DEPARTMENT COST REALLOCATIONS

A flexible budgeting approach is appropriate when service department costs are reallocated to production departments. Such an approach lends itself to the dual allocation method introduced in Chapter 3, whereby fixed and variable costs are allocated separately. Flexible budgeting also permits the isolation and analysis of cost variances in the service department where the variances originate.

Budgeted *fixed* service department costs should be allocated according to the *operating capacity* of the service department. Budgeted *variable* service department costs should be allocated according to the *utilization* of service department outputs by user departments. The budgeted allocations can then be expressed in the familiar form of a mixed cost equation ($y = a + bx$). The total budgeted cost allocated to a user department (y) is equal to the constant fixed cost allocation (a) plus the variable cost allocation (bx) in which b is the budgeted variable cost per unit of the activity indicator, x.

Example: The power plant of Carducci Corporation provides electricity to the firm's three production departments, A, B, and C. Budgeted power plant costs for 19X7 include $500,000 for fixed items and $300,000 for variable items. The fixed costs are incurred to support facilities designed to meet estimated peak capacity needs of 100,000 kilowatt hours per year. The variable items relate to expected user needs totalling 60,000 kilowatt hours for the 19X7 year. These capacity and usage requirements are distributed among the producing departments as follows:

Producing Department	Estimated Peak Capacity Needs	Budgeted Requirements (kilowatt hours)
A	30,000	20,000
B	20,000	10,000
C	50,000	30,000
	100,000	60,000

A budgeted variable allocation rate per kilowatt hour can be established as follows:

$$\frac{\$300,000}{60,000 \text{ kilowatt hours}} = \$5$$

FIGURE 11–13

Carducci Corporation
Reallocation of Budgeted Power Plant Costs to Production Departments
for the Year 19X7

Department	Fixed Costs In Proportion to Estimated Peak Capacity	Variable Costs Expected Usage Times Variable Cost per Kilowatt Hour
A	$\frac{30,000}{100,000} \times \$500,000 = \$150,000$	$20,000 \times \$5 = \$100,000$
B	$\frac{20,000}{100,000} \times \$500,000 = 100,000$	$10,000 \times \$5 = 50,000$
C	$\frac{50,000}{100,000} \times \$500,000 = 250,000$	$30,000 \times \$5 = 150,000$
Total	$500,000	$300,000

This rate is used to allocate budgeted variable costs to the producing departments in relation to their expected needs for 19X7. The budgeted fixed costs are allocated as lump sums in proportion to the estimated peak capacity requirements of each producing department as shown in Figure 11–13.

For example, in Department C, the total budgeted allocation of power plant costs is $400,000, consisting of fixed costs of $250,000 plus a variable cost component of 30,000 kilowatt hours of expected usage at $5 per kilowatt hour.

Actual power plant costs during 19X7 included $525,000 for fixed items and $350,000 of variable items. Actual usage of electricity by the three producing departments was as follows:

Department	Actual Usage
A	22,000
B	12,000
C	30,000
	64,000

Figure 11–14 shows the reallocation of actual power plant costs based on the predetermined departmental allocation proportions for fixed items and the predetermined rate for variable items.

Figure 11–14 illustrates how a flexible budgeting approach to service department reallocations permits a separate allocation of the fixed and variable power plant costs, and also insulates the production departments from cost variances originating in the power plant. The *budgeted* costs are reallocated to Departments A, B, and C. The variances of $25,000 in fixed costs and $30,000 in variable costs, which represent the differences between budgeted and actual performance, can be subjected to separate analysis based on input usage within the power plant.

FIGURE 11–14

Carducci Corporation
Reallocation of Power Plant Costs to Production Departments
for the Year 19X7

Department	Fixed Costs Budgeted Allocations	Variable Costs Budgeted Rate × Actual Activity
A	$150,000	$5 × 22,000 = $110,000
B	100,000	$5 × 12,000 = 60,000
C	250,000	$5 × 30,000 = 150,000
Total Budgeted Cost	$500,000	$320,000
Total Actual Cost	525,000	350,000
Power Plant Variances	($ 25,000)	($ 30,000)
	Unfavorable	Unfavorable

FLEXIBLE BUDGETING ILLUSTRATED: WEINSTEIN CORPORATION

A flexible budget is to be prepared for the Ladder Division of Weinstein Corporation. This division manufactures a standard line of six-foot stepladders. Production requires the use of raw materials, employment of production workers and supervisors, use of factory supplies and power, building occupancy, and equipment operation.

A first step in flexible budget preparation is to identify the revenue and cost functions to be used for each budgeted item. Previous data from planned and actual performance have been analyzed and the functional relationships listed in Figure 11–15 have been selected as being representative of anticipated

---

FIGURE 11–15

Weinstein Corporation
Basic Revenue and Cost Relationships
for Flexible Budget Preparation

1. Sales .... $25 per unit sold
2. Raw Materials .... $8 per unit produced
3. Direct Labor .... ½ hour @ $12 per hour per unit produced
4. Factory Supplies .... 25¢ per unit produced
5. Power and Heat .... $500 per month plus 25¢ per machine hour
6. Repairs .... $500 per month plus 50¢ per labor hour
7. Depreciation .... $1,000 per month
8. Rent .... $1,000 per month
9. Supervision .... $2,000 per month

FIGURE 11–16

Weinstein Corporation
Revised Flexible Budget Cost Relationships
Based on Direct Labor Hours per Unit of Output

1.	Sales	$25 per unit sold
2.	Raw Material	$8 per unit produced
3.	Direct Labor	$12 per direct labor hour
4.	Factory Supplies	50¢ per direct labor hour
5.	Power and Heat	$500 per month plus $1 per direct labor hour
6.	Repairs	$500 per month plus 50¢ per direct labor hour
7.	Depreciation	$1,000 per month
8.	Rent	$1,000 per month
9.	Supervision	$2,000 per month

cost and revenue behavior during the budget period of August, 19X5. It has been determined that each unit of output requires 2 machine hours of processing, and that maximum monthly capacity is 4,000 machine hours.

The functions in Figure 11–15 include several different independent variables (units of output, direct labor hours, and machine hours). This is to be expected; these functions are intended to establish the most direct and accurate cost and revenue relationships. But for analytical purposes, it is inconvenient to use functions that include several different variables. A simplifying step is to adopt intermediate relationships in order to allow all functions to be expressed in terms of a single planning and control variable.

In Weinstein Corporation, *labor hours required per unit of output* can serve as an intermediate relationship for all labor and overhead costs. It already appears in several of the individual functions and there are direct relationships between labor hours and other independent variables (machine hours and units of output). Converting all cost functions except sales revenue and materials usage to a direct labor hours basis produces the flexible budget formulations listed in Figure 11–16.

All that remains to be done to produce a flexible budget model for the Ladder Division is to tabulate and sum these individual cost functions. Figure 11–17 is the budget tabulation, from which the flexible budget formula for direct labor and overhead can be summarized as follows: $5,000 per month plus $14 per direct labor hour.

In Figure 11–18, a $10 contribution margin per unit is derived, based on the stated relationship of two units of output per labor hour.

The Ladder Division is expected to require between 1,000 and 1,400 direct labor hours per month. Figure 11–19 shows flexible budgets prepared within this operating range at intervals of 100 direct labor hours.

The Ladder Division predicted 1,200 direct labor hours as its master budget activity level for August of 19X5. It therefore hoped to produce and sell 2,400 ladders. Actual results were as shown in Figure 11–20 (page 506). A variance

FIGURE 11–17

Weinstein Corporation
Flexible Budget Model

		Per Unit
1. Sales		$25
2. Raw Materials		$ 8

Direct Labor and Overhead Costs:	Fixed Cost (per month)	Variable Cost (per direct labor hour)
3. Direct Labor	—	$12.00
4. Factory Supplies	—	.50
5. Power and Heat	$ 500	1.00
6. Repairs	500	.50
7. Depreciation	1,000	—
8. Rent	1,000	—
9. Supervision	2,000	—
Total Direct Labor and Overhead Cost	$5,000	$14.00

FIGURE 11–18

Weinstein Corporation
Contribution Margin Analysis

Sales Price per Unit		$25.00
Less Variable Costs per Unit:		
Raw Materials ($8 per unit)	$8.00	
Direct Labor and Overhead (½ hour per Unit @ $14 per labor hour)	7.00	15.00
Contribution Margin per Unit		$10.00

analysis of actual and budgeted sales activity is shown in Figure 11–21 (page 506). The sales price and sales forecast/quantity variances can also be calculated as follows:

$$\text{Sales Price Variance} = (\text{Actual Price} - \text{Budget Price}) \times \text{Actual Quantity}$$
$$= (\$26 - \$25) \times 2{,}600$$
$$= \$2{,}600 \text{ Favorable}$$

$$\text{Sales Forecast/Quantity Variance} = (\text{Actual Sales Quantity} - \text{Budgeted Sales Quantity})$$
$$\text{(Sales Quantity Variance)} \quad \times \text{Budgeted Contribution Margin per Unit}$$
$$= (2{,}600 - 2{,}400) \times (\$25 - \$15)$$
$$= 200 \times \$10$$
$$= \$2{,}000 \text{ Favorable}$$

FIGURE 11–19

Weinstein Corporation
Flexible Budget Tabulation
Month of August, 19X5
1,000 to 1,400 Direct Labor Hours
(2 Units of output per direct labor hour)

Direct Labor Hours	1,000	1,100	1,200	1,300	1,400
Units of Output	2,000	2,200	2,400	2,600	2,800
1. Sales	$50,000	$55,000	$60,000	$65,000	$70,000
2. Materials	$16,000	$17,600	$19,200	$20,800	$22,400
Direct Labor and Overhead:					
3. Direct Labor	$12,000	$13,200	$14,400	$15,600	$16,800
4. Factory Supplies	500	550	600	650	700
5. Power and Heat	1,500	1,600	1,700	1,800	1,900
6. Repairs	1,000	1,050	1,100	1,150	1,200
7. Depreciation	1,000	1,000	1,000	1,000	1,000
8. Rent	1,000	1,000	1,000	1,000	1,000
9. Supervision	2,000	2,000	2,000	2,000	2,000
	$19,000	$20,400	$21,800	$23,200	$24,600
Total Costs	$35,000	$38,000	$41,000	$44,000	$47,000
Net Income	$15,000	$17,000	$19,000	$21,000	$23,000
Contribution Margin Analysis					
Sales					
($25 per unit)	$50,000	$55,000	$60,000	$65,000	$70,000
Less: Variable Costs					
($15 per unit)	30,000	33,000	36,000	39,000	42,000
Contribution Margin					
($10 per unit)	$20,000	$22,000	$24,000	$26,000	$28,000
Fixed Costs	5,000	5,000	5,000	5,000	5,000
Net Income	$15,000	$17,000	$19,000	$21,000	$23,000

A variance analysis of actual and budgeted labor and overhead costs is shown in Figure 11–22. Actual materials costs were $20,800, which corresponds to the budgeted amount of $8 per unit for 2,600 units. The efficiency and spending variances can also be calculated as follows:

$$\text{Efficiency Variance} = \text{Flexible Budget for Required Hours}$$
$$- \text{Flexible Budget for Actual Hours}$$
$$= \$23,200 - \$24,600$$
$$= (\$1,400) \text{ Unfavorable}$$

Spending Variance = Flexible Budget for Actual Hours
— Actual Costs Incurred
= $24,600 − $25,150
= ($550) Unfavorable

Figure 11–23 illustrates an alternative format for cost variance analysis. The $25,125 of actual costs incurred are first broken down into their fixed and variable components. The variance analysis of labor and overhead costs

---

FIGURE 11–20

Weinstein Corporation
Actual Operating Results
Month of August, 19X5

Ladders Produced	2,600
Direct Labor Hours Worked	1,400
1. Sales (at $26 each)	2,600
Costs Incurred:	
2. Materials	$20,800
3. Direct Labor	17,200
4. Factory Supplies	650
5. Power and Heat	1,750
6. Repairs	1,300
7. Depreciation	1,000
8. Rent	1,000
9. Supervision	2,250

FIGURE 11–21

Weinstein Corporation
Sales Variance Analysis
Month of August, 19X5

	A Actual Sales at Actual Prices 2,600 @ $26	B Actual Sales at Budgeted Price 2,600 @ $25	C Original Master Budget 2,400 @ $25	A − B Sales Price Variance	B − C Sales Forecast/ Quantity Variance
Sales	$67,600	$65,000	$60,000		
Less: Budgeted Variable Costs @ $15 per Unit......	39,000	39,000	36,000		
Contribution Margin	$28,600	$26,000	$24,000	$2,600	$2,000
				Favorable	Favorable

Weinstein Corporation
Variance Analysis of Labor and Overhead Costs
Month of August, 19X5

	A Flexible Budget 1,300 Hours Required	B Flexible Budget 1,400 Hours Worked	C Actual Costs 1,400 Hours Worked	A − B Efficiency Variances	B − C Spending Variances
3. Direct Labor	$15,600	$16,800	$17,200	($1,200) U	($400) U
4. Factory Supplies	650	700	650	(50) U	50 F
5. Power and Heat	1,800	1,900	1,750	(100) U	150 F
6. Repairs	1,150	1,200	1,300	(50) U	(100) U
7. Depreciation	1,000	1,000	1,000	—	—
8. Rent	1,000	1,000	1,000	—	—
9. Supervision	2,000	2,000	2,250	—	(250)
Total	$23,200	$24,600	$25,150	($1,400) U	($550) U

FIGURE 11–23

Weinstein Corporation
Fixed and Variable Distribution of Actual Costs
Month of August, 19X5

	Variable Costs	Fixed Costs	Total Costs
Direct Labor	$17,200	—	$17,200
Factory Supplies	650	—	650
Power and Heat	1,350	$ 400	1,750
Repairs	725	575	1,300
Depreciation	—	1,000	1,000
Rent	—	1,000	1,000
Supervision	—	2,250	2,250
Total Costs	$19,925	$5,225	$25,150

---

is then based on comparisons between the fixed and variable portions of each budgeted and actual cost item, as in Figure 11–24.

Isolating the fixed and variable portions of labor and overhead costs permits a more refined analysis of variances. For example, differences between budgeted and actual *variable* costs may be either efficiency or spending variances. But every difference between budgeted and actual *fixed* costs must be a spending variance, because fixed costs are budgeted at the same amount for all activity levels.

Finally, each of the four variances can be explained in narrative terms:

1. *Sales Price Variance*   There was a favorable sales price variance of $2,600 because all 2,600 units of actual sales volume were sold for $1 per unit above the budgeted amount.
2. *Sales Forecast (Quantity) Variance*   There was a favorable sales quantity variance of $2,000 because sales volume was 200 units higher than the forecast level, with each unit generating a budgeted contribution margin of $10.
3. *Labor and Overhead Efficiency Variance*   There was an unfavorable efficiency variance of $1,400, because 1,400 hours were worked but only 1,300 direct labor hours were budgeted to produce the 2,600 ladders actually made. Each direct labor hour generates variable labor and overhead costs of $14; the 100 extra hours worked produced the $1,400 variance. As Figure 11–24 indicates, this variance pertains only to the variable cost items.
4. *Labor and Overhead Spending Variance*   There was an unfavorable spending variance of $550 because actual labor and overhead costs of $25,150 were incurred, whereas the labor and overhead cost budgeted for the 1,400 hours actually worked was only $24,600 ($14 per hour multiplied by 1,400 hours plus $5,000 in fixed costs). This can be separated into a $325 variance for the variable items ($19,925 actual minus $19,600 budgeted) and a $225

FIGURE 11–24

Weinstein Corporation
Variance Analysis of Labor and Overhead Costs
Month of August, 19X5

	A Flexible Budget 1,300 Hours Required	B Flexible Budget 1,400 Hours Worked	C Actual Costs 1,400 Hours Worked	A – B Efficiency Variances	B – C Spending Variances
Variable Costs:					
Direct Labor	$15,600	$16,800	$17,200	($1,200) U	($400) U
Factory Supplies . . .	650	700	650	($50) U	50 F
Power and Heat . . .	1,300	1,400	1,350	($100) U	50 F
Repairs	650	700	725	(50) U	(25) U
Total Variable					
Costs	$18,200	$19,600	$19,925	($1,400) U	($325) U
Fixed Costs:					
Power and Heat . . .	$ 500	$ 500	$ 400	N/A	$100 F
Repairs	500	500	575	N/A	(75) U
Depreciation	1,000	1,000	1,000	N/A	—
Rent	1,000	1,000	1,000	N/A	—
Supervision	2,000	2,000	2,250	N/A	(250) U
Total Fixed					
Costs	$ 5,000	$ 5,000	$ 5,225	N/A	($225) U
Total Costs	$23,200	$24,600	$25,150	($1,400) U	($550) U

variance for the fixed items ($5,225 actual minus $5,000 budgeted), as shown in Figure 11–24.

SUMMARY

1. The planning and control technique of flexible budgeting overcomes certain deficiencies of static budgets that are based on a single value of some key variable.
2. The essence of flexible budgeting is the establishment of a set of functional relationships—a budget model—which explains the behavior of those performance variables that are the focus of budgetary attention.
3. The budget is "flexible" because, for planning purposes, these functional relationships can be evaluated at different levels of the budgetary variable or variables.
4. Input-related variables, such as labor hours, machine hours, and materials usage, are recommended for use as budgetary variables. They permit the calculation of efficiency variances, which relate to the quantity of input re-

sources used, and spending variances, which relate to the prices paid for those resources.

5. Flexible budgeting can be applied to individual decision centers (departments, divisions, product lines) or to an entire organization.

6. The simpler flexible budget models consist of a single budgetary variable (say, labor hours, machine hours, or materials usage) and linear functions (a fixed cost per period plus a variable cost per unit of the budgetary variable).

7. More complex functional relationships (nonlinear, multivariable, or discontinuous) may also be the basis for flexible budget models.

KEY WORDS AND PHRASES

Static Budget (483)
Flexible Budgeting (485)
Budget Model (485)
Flexible Budgeting Relationship (486)
Cost and Revenue Functions (488)
Functional Relationships (488)
Intermediate Relationships (489)
Current Replacement Cost (492)
Variance (493)
Variance Analysis (493)
Input Price or Spending Variance (494)
Efficiency or Usage Variance (494)
Favorable Variance (496)
Unfavorable Variance (497)
Sales Price Variance (497)
Sales Forecast (Quantity) Variance (498)

Questions

1. What are the major advantages and disadvantages of static budgets?
2. Is a static budget useful for control purposes? Why or why not?
3. How might the use of a static budget lead to invalid conclusions when budgeted and actual performance are compared?
4. What are the advantages and disadvantages of expressing revenues and costs as functions of a single *output* variable?
5. What basic principles underlie flexible budgeting?
6. Discuss the advantages and disadvantages of elementary formulations of cost and revenue functions for flexible budgeting purposes as compared to more complex functions.
7. Why is the *activity level* such an important ingredient of flexible budgeting procedures?
8. What are the advantages and disadvantages of flexible budgets for a firm as a whole as compared with flexible budgets for individual departments or segments of a firm?
9. Why is flexible budgeting more useful for overhead and administrative costs than for direct materials and labor costs?
10. Discuss the relative merits of flexible budgets based on a *single* activity-related variable and those based on multiple activity-related variables.
11. What compromises must be made in order to allow flexible budgets to be expressed in terms of a single variable?
12. What techniques are available to help establish flexible budgeting formulas? What are their limitations?
13. List and give examples of at least six cost behavior patterns that are different from the typical *fixed* and *linearly variable* patterns.
14. What factors should be taken into account when deciding which item should be used as the independent variable in establishing flexible budgeting formulas? Why is this so important?
15. Why should *input-related* variables, rather than *output-related* variables, be used in establishing flexible budgeting formulas?
16. What extra analysis is possible when input-related rather than output-related variables are used in flexible budgeting?
17. Why should *replacement cost* data rather than historical cost data be used in analyses that deal with flexible budgeting?
18. Outline the usefulness of a flexible budgeting approach for *planning* purposes.
19. Outline the usefulness of a flexible budgeting approach for *control* purposes.
20. What control information might be conveyed in (a) price or spending variances and (b) usage, efficiency, or quantity variances?

Exercises

E 11–1 Analysis of Cost Behavior Patterns

The graphs below represent eight different cost behavior patterns. In each case, total cost is on the vertical axis and level of activity (units of output, labor hours worked, or machine hours worked) is on the horizontal axis.

Required:
In each case, suggest a possible cost item the behavior of which fits the pattern shown. Give a brief explanation to support each example.

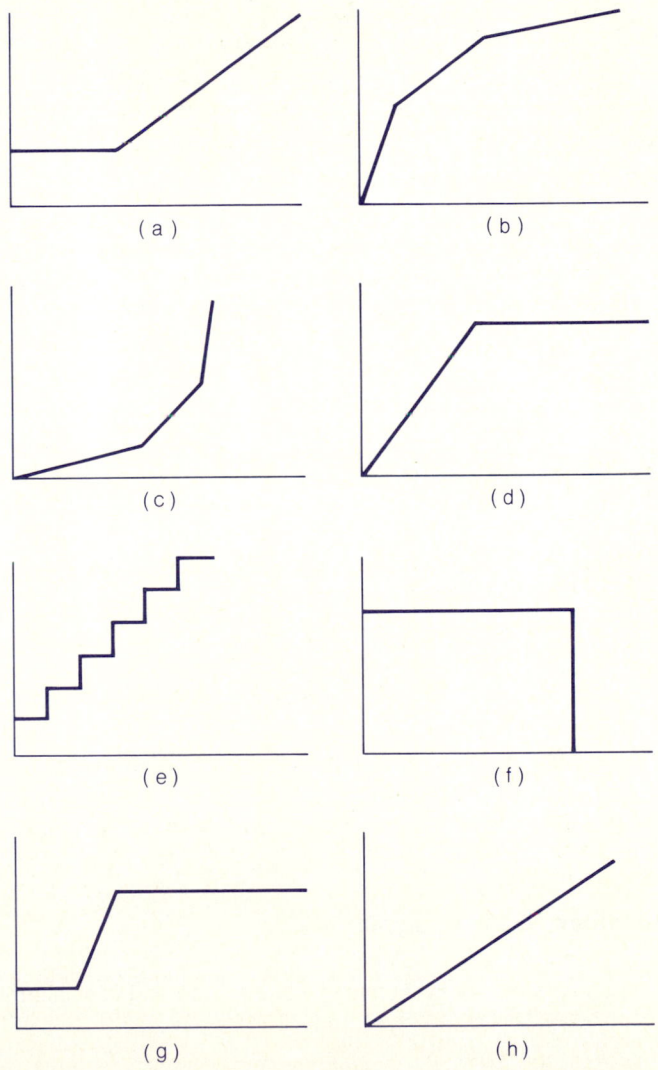

E 11–2   Flexible Budget Preparation

Viva Corporation has established overhead cost functions for one of its departments, as shown below:

Indirect Materials	$1 per Direct Labor Hour
Indirect Labor	$2 per Direct Labor Hour
Maintenance	$2,000 per month *plus* 50¢ per direct labor hour
Depreciation—Equipment	$5,000 per month
Supervision	$7,500 per month
Power and Heat	$2,500 per month *plus* $1 per direct labor hour

Required:
(a) Prepare a flexible budget schedule for the monthly volumes of 5,000, 10,000 and 15,000 direct labor hours. Group all items according to their cost behavior patterns.
(b) Express the flexible budget for overhead of this department as a single formula.
(c) Which answer is more useful, part (a) or part (b)? Why? For what purposes?

E 11–3   Elementary Cost Analysis

Parker Corporation has established the following flexible budget formula for its 19X6 operations: variable items at $5 per machine hour, fixed items at $80,000 per month. During June and July of 19X6, actual performance included the following:

		June	July
(1)	Actual Costs:		
	Variable	$58,000	$53,500
	Fixed	$75,000	$85,000
(2)	Production (units)	5,000	5,000
(3)	Actual Machine Hours	10,500	9,800

According to product specifications, each unit of output should require two hours of machine time.

Required:
(a) Prepare flexible budgets for all activity levels relevant to operations in June and July.
(b) Analyze cost performance for June and July, showing spending and efficiency variances in as much detail as possible.
(c) Comment on the results obtained in part (b). Was cost performance better in June or July? Why?

E 11–4   Elementary Cost Analysis

The following schedule shows relevant manufacturing overhead cost information for four independent companies for the month of August, 19X3.

	W	X	Y	Z
Budgeted Output (units)........................	2,000	3,000	4,000	5,000
Labor Hours per unit	3	2	4	2
Budgeted Overhead Costs:*				
Variable......................................	$24,000	$30,000	$48,000	$40,000
Fixed	$10,000	$20,000	25,000	$30,000
Actual Output (units)	1,500	3,200	4,500	4,500
Actual Labor Hours	4,800	6,000	17,000	9,200
Actual Overhead Costs:				
Variable......................................	$21,000	$31,500	$51,000	$36,500
Fixed	$12,000	$19,500	$26,500	$30,000

* Budgeted Costs are for budgeted output quantity.

Required:

(a) For each company, compute the flexible budget formula for overhead in terms of direct labor hours.

(b) For each company, compute the amount of budgeted overhead costs for (1) the actual hours worked and (2) the hours required for the output actually produced.

(c) For each company, compute the following variances:
    (1) Total overhead variance
    (2) Variable overhead spending variance
    (3) Variable overhead efficiency variance
    (4) Fixed overhead spending variance.

E 11-5   Forecast Variances—Flexible Budget Analysis

Warden Company developed its budgets for 19X2 on the basis of a sales forecast of 100,000 units and zero inventories of finished goods and work in process. The sales price was estimated to be $50 per unit and costs were estimated as follows:

Variable Items (per unit):	
Direct Material	$18.00
Direct Labor	10.00
Manufacturing Overhead	2.00
Marketing Costs	1.50
Administrative Costs	.50
	$32.00

Fixed Items:	
Manufacturing Overhead	$1,200,000
Nonmanufacturing Costs	300,000
	$1,500,000

During 19X2, 90,000 units were produced and sold. Actual revenues and costs were as follows:

```
Sales—90,000 units @ $50 ...........   $4,500,000
Variable Items:
    Direct Materials ....................   $1,400,000
    Direct Labor .......................       900,000
    Manufacturing Overhead ............       170,000
    Marketing Costs ...................       120,000
    Administrative Costs ..............        50,000
                                           $2,640,000

Fixed Items:
    Manufacturing Overhead ............   $1,250,000
    Nonmanufacturing Costs ...........       250,000
                                           $1,500,000
```

Required:
(a) Prepare a table for all revenue and cost items with the following columns:

Item	(A) Original Budget 100,000 units	(B) Revised Budget 90,000 units	(C) Actual Amount	(A-B)	(B-C)
Sales					
Direct Materials					
Etc.					

(b) Comment on the interpretation of the differences between (1) columns A and B and (2) columns B and C.

(c) What combinations of row entries in the table would be useful? Explain.

E 11–6   Flexible Budgeting Variance Analysis—Spending and Efficiency Variances

Refer to Exercise E11–5. The following additional information is available:

(1) The flexible budget formula can be restated as follows:
Sales—$50 per unit sold
Direct Materials—$18 per unit produced
Direct Labor—2 hours per unit @ $5 per hour
Variable Manufacturing Overhead—$1 per labor hour
Variable Marketing—$1.50 per unit sold
Variable Administrative—$0.50 per unit sold
Fixed Manufacturing—$1,200,000 per year
Fixed Nonmanufacturing—$300,000 per year

(2) During 19X2, a total of 160,000 labor hours were used to produce the 90,000 units of output.

Required:
(a) Expand your analysis of the difference between columns B and C in E11–5 to separate the (price related) spending variances from the (usage related) efficiency variances, for (1) direct labor, (2) variable manufacturing overhead, (3) marketing costs, and (4) administrative costs.

(b)   Calculate spending variances for the fixed cost items.

(c)   Given that the actual *amount* of direct materials used per unit of output equaled the budgeted amount, comment on the direct materials variance.

E 11-7   Flexible Budgeting—Variance Analysis—Spending and Efficiency Variances

Vereen Corporation produced 8,400 units of output during January of 19X1. Production specifications called for four direct labor hours per unit, but 34,500 hours were worked at a cost of $179,400. The direct labor rate was budgeted at $5 per hour. Overhead costs incurred, accompanied by the flexible budget formula for each item, are shown in the following table:

Item	Formula	Amount Incurred
1. Supplies	40¢ per direct labor hour	$14,750
2. Power	$2,500 per month plus 25¢ per direct labor hour	11,200
3. Rework	25¢ per direct labor hour	6,500
4. Depreciation . .	$5,000 per month	5,250
5. Supervision . .	$2,500 per month	2,750
6. Repairs	$2,000 per month plus 10¢ per direct labor hour	5,850
		$46,300

Required:

Prepare a performance report for January of 19X1, using the following format:

Item	Flexible Budget — Budgeted Hours (A)	Flexible Budget — Actual Hours (B)	Actual Cost (C)	Efficiency Variance (A) − (B)	Spending Variance (B) − (C)
0. Direct Labor					
1. Supplies					
2. Power					
3. Rework					
4. Depreciation					
5. Supervision					
6. Repairs					
Totals					

E 11-8   Flexible Budgeting— Analysis and Explanation of Variation in Income

Reid Company, which sells its only product for $20 per unit, has a forecast cost structure that allows a contribution margin of 30 percent of sales revenue. Each direct labor hour should produce two units of output, direct material costs are $8 per unit, and variable manufacturing overhead and marketing costs are 50 percent of direct labor costs.

For 19X2, on a budgeted volume of 300,000 units, forecast net income was $600,000. Fixed manufacturing costs were budgeted to be twice the amount of fixed marketing and administrative costs.

Actual results for 19X2 were disappointing to management because net income was only 25 percent of the budgeted amount, even though sales volume was only 10 percent less than the budgeted level. Examination of variances showed that the sales price variance and all direct materials variances were zero. Spending variances on fixed expenses were $80,000 favorable, whereas spending variances on labor and other variable items were $110,000 unfavorable. There were no beginning or ending inventories. Forecast variances are not included in the preceeding items.

Required:

(a) Prepare the budgeted income statement for 19X2.

(b) Prepare an income statement that reflects actual results for 19X2.

(c) Prepare an analysis of the variation between budgeted and actual net income, showing (1) sales forecast variance (in terms of contribution margin), (2) spending variances, and (3) efficiency variances.

E 11–9 Service Department Cost Reallocation—
Flexible Budget—Direct Method

Garcia Corporation uses flexible budgeting procedures to plan and control costs in all its manufacturing departments. The Plant Services Department provides general plant maintenance and repairs. Its cost report for the month of April, 19X5 was as follows:

	Budget	Actual
Variable Items	$ 20,000	$ 26,400
Fixed Items	105,000	105,000
	$125,000	$131,400

Only two production departments, Machining and Assembly, benefit from Plant Services operations. Machine hours relevant to those two departments are:

	Machine Hours		
	Actual April 19X5	Budgeted April 19X5	Annual Capacity
Machining	42,500	40,000	500,000
Assembly	67,500	60,000	1,000,000
	110,000	100,000	1,500,000

It is the company's practice to use a dual allocation method to allocate service department costs to production departments for both planning and control purposes.

Required:

(a) Prepare a schedule to show how much of the Plant Services costs would be allocated to the Machining and Assembly Departments for budgeting purposes at the beginning of 19X5.

(b) Analyze the cost performance of the Plant Services Department for April of 19X5, showing (1) costs charged to the production departments and (2) flexible budget variances reported in the Plant Services Department.

Cases

C 11-1   Static versus Flexible Budgets

The sales manager of Wainwright Corporation is never too happy at budget time. He always feels pressure to produce an accurate sales forecast, because the instructions he receives are always along the lines of "Let us have a single best estimate of sales for next year." He believes that everything else that is planned for the company depends on his sales forecast.

Required:
(a)   Discuss the pros and cons of static versus flexible budgets in relation to the sales manager's position.
(b)   Will flexible budgeting alleviate all of the pressure on the sales manager? Why or why not?
(c)   Will flexible budgeting help the other divisions involved (production, purchasing, finance, and so on) more or less than the Sales Division?
(d)   Will flexible budgeting improve the accuracy of budget figures? Why or why not?

C 11-2   Flexible Budgeting

Hyatt Company uses a flexible budgeting system based on sales volume. For 19X2, the estimated sales volume is 50,000 units, but sales could go as high as 75,000 or as low as 30,000 units. Sales prices are $2 per unit, variable costs are 60 percent of sales revenue, fixed costs are $30,000, and taxes are 50 percent of taxable income.
     The president reads the sales forecasts and says, "Well, what about the 60,000 and 40,000 unit levels? What would be the outcomes there?"

Required:
(a)   Prepare a tabular flexible budget for all five activity levels.
(b)   What are the advantages of the report prepared in part (a) compared with the report that would be prepared for only the 50,000 unit level?
(c)   Discuss the usefulness of the report prepared in part (a) for (1) planning purposes and (2) control purposes.
(d)   Actual sales for 19X2 turn out to be 62,500 units. Was everything that was done in part (a) useless? Discuss.

C 11-3   Budgeting Indirect Labor

During October, production was 200,000 units and indirect labor costs were $132,000. When production dropped to 150,000 units in November, indirect labor costs were $122,000. Budgeted output for December was 160,000 units.

Required:
(a)   Prepare a budget for indirect labor for December. What assumptions did you make?
(b)   Why budget indirect labor costs in the first place, since production for December will probably not be 160,000 units anyway? Discuss fully.

C 11–4   Multiple Activity Bases and Flexible Budgeting

Flexible budgets are intended to deal with the problems caused by different patterns of cost and revenue variability in relation to activity level changes. In Williams Company, direct labor hours has been chosen as the activity index in terms of which flexible budgets are established for overhead items. However, some problems have been experienced with this procedure. Not all indirect costs vary consistently with the levels of direct labor hours worked. Although in the long run there tended to be a general fit, in the short run there were often marked inconsistencies and timing differences. For example, repair costs tended to be very irregular and unpredictable, maintenance work was often performed during slack periods when direct labor hours were relatively low, Receiving Department costs increased and decreased in advance of any effect on direct labor hours, and warehousing and storage costs did the same subsequent to the change in direct labor hours. Other costs like factory clerical, personnel, production planning, and buildings and grounds tend to be almost completely insensitive to any change in direct labor hours.

Required:
(a) Discuss the basic issues here with regard to the flexible budgeting process.

(b) What alternative courses might be taken in response to the apparent problems?

(c) Compare the advantages and disadvantages of flexible budgeting (1) using a single activity base and (2) using multiple activity bases.

C 11–5   Reallocation of Service Department Costs

Harbo Company is considering five alternative procedures to handle the reallocation of service department costs to its production departments. This reallocation will enable overhead rates to be established and budgetary control and analysis to be performed. The alternatives are:

(1) Allocate all fixed and variable budgeted service department costs to user departments in proportion to annual *peak capacity needs* of each user as determined at the beginning of each year.

(2) Allocate all actual fixed and variable service department costs to user departments in proportion to actual usage of services provided *each month*.

(3) Same as alternative (2), except that the allocation is made at the beginning of the year and is based on budgeted costs and budgeted usage.

(4) Allocate actual fixed costs of the service department on the basis of annual peak capacity needs of users; allocate actual variable costs on the basis of actual usage each month.

(5) Select predetermined proportions for fixed costs (based on peak capacity needs) and predetermined rates for variable costs (based on expected annual usage). Allocate costs using these predetermined proportions and rates in conjunction with actual usage each period, possibly leaving variances to be reported in the service department.

Required:
Critically evaluate the advantages and disadvantages of each alternative.

C 11–6   Analysis of Labor Variances—Guaranteed Minimum Wage Provision

Under the terms of its most recent labor contract settlement, Henderson Company must provide a guaranteed minimum monthly salary of $1,500 to all employees who have more than 10 years of service. The current wage rate for employees who qualify is $15 per hour; 200 employees are eligible for this plan.

For 19X7, 800,000 direct labor hours were forecast to be needed at $15 per hour, for a total budget of $12,000,000. Due to the minimum wage requirement, $3,600,000 of this was considered a "fixed" component (200 employees at $18,000 per year). Consequently, a monthly budget formula of $300,000, plus $10.50 per hour, was established for direct labor costs.

For the first three months of 19X7, the following were reported:

	January	February	March
Actual Direct Labor Hours	64,000	44,000	84,000
Actual Direct Labor Cost	$960,000	$660,000	$1,260,000
Budgeted Direct Labor Cost	972,000	762,000	1,182,000
Variances	$ 12,000 F	$102,000 F	($ 78,000) U

The production supervisor responsible for the employees involved is puzzled by this report. She knows that the volume of work expected from the employees was in fact achieved each month—there was no difference between the number of hours actually worked and the number of hours called for in the specifications of the work produced.

"Why is a favorable variance indicated when direct labor hours are low, and an unfavorable one when direct labor hours are high? It just doesn't compute!"

Required:
(a) Discuss the method that must have been used to arrive at the stated budget formula for direct labor costs.

(b) Evaluate the claim by the supervisor that "It just doesn't compute!"

(c) Prepare a revised analysis of the situation, including a new budget formula and analysis of labor cost performance for the three-month period.

Problems

P 11–1   Flexible Budget Formula—Elementary

Based on an estimated annual volume of 250,000 direct labor hours, Bradshaw Corporation has developed the following cost estimates for 19X7:

Variable Items:	
Direct Materials	$3,600,000
Direct Labor	2,000,000
Supplies	400,000
Indirect Labor	300,000
Other Manufacturing Costs	200,000
	$6,500,000

Fixed Items:		
Depreciation	....	300,000
Taxes	....	240,000
Insurance	....	180,000
Other Manufacturing Costs	....	80,000
		$ 800,000
Total	....	$7,300,000

Required:

(a) Express in equation form the flexible budget formula contained in the preceding total cost data.

(b) Express separately the materials, labor, and overhead components of this formula.

(c) Make schedules to show what the total amount of budgeted manufacturing costs for 19X7 will be if the volume is:
   (1) 100,000 labor hours.
   (2) 150,000 labor hours.
   (3) 200,000 labor hours.
   (4) 300,000 labor hours.

(d) What assumptions with regard to the behavior of cost items are implicit in your answers to part (c)?

P 11–2   Flexible Budget—Elementary Analysis

Hottel Company has prepared the following flexible budget for the operation of one of its manufacturing departments during 19X4:

	Machine Hours	
	80 Percent Capacity	100 Percent Capacity
Direct Labor	$ 616,000	$ 770,000
Manufacturing Overhead:		
Indirect Labor	130,000	162,500
Indirect Materials	35,200	44,000
Power and Heat	63,200	74,000
Supervision	74,900	74,900
Depreciation	115,000	135,000
Rent	230,000	230,000
Other Items	40,000	45,000
	$1,304,300	$1,535,400

Required:

(a) Which entries in the table are variable costs? Fixed costs? Mixed costs?

(b) Determine the flexible budget formula for this department, assuming that 100 percent capacity corresponds to 200,000 machine hours per year.

(c) During 19X4, actual operations consumed 175,000 machine hours, but the output actually achieved should have been produced in only 170,000 machine hours. What information from part (b) can be derived that will be useful for control purposes?

(d) Actual manufacturing costs for 19X4 were $1,420,000. What additional analysis is now possible? Explain all calculations.

P 11-3   Analysis of Cost Behavior Patterns

The following is a list of several manufacturing cost items, with descriptions of their likely behavior patterns in relation to volume changes.

Required:
For each item on the list, prepare graphs of the behavior of (1) the *total* cost and (2) the *average* cost per unit of the volume or activity index mentioned. Label each graph carefully.

(a) *Depreciation on buildings*—straight line method. Activity is output units per month.

(b) *Depreciation on equipment*—machine hours method. Activity is machine hours per month.

(c) *Electric power*—a flat fee plus a variable amount beyond a specified number of kilowatt hours. Activity is power usage in kilowatt hours.

(d) *Salaries of quality control staff*—one person required for each 2,000 hours per month of machine time. Activity is machine hours per month.

(e) *Employer's contribution to F.I.C.A. taxes*—8 percent of wages up to a maximum of $15,000 per employee. Activity is labor hours per year.

(f) *Water usage*—cost is a graduated scale with the cost per gallon increasing by 10 percent for each additional 10,000 gallons. Activity is usage of water.

(g) *Raw materials*—price per unit is subject to a 10 percent discount in excess of 100,000 units per month and a 20 percent discount in excess of 200,000 units per month. Activity is production per month up to 300,000 units.

(h) *Incentive bonus plan premiums*—payable per unit of output only when monthly activity exceeds 100,000 units. Activity is monthly production.

(i) *Direct labor cost*—production workers become progressively more efficient as the number of units produced increases up to a levelling off point at 100,000 units. Activity is total production volume.

(j) *Equipment repairs and maintenance*—a preventive maintenance program is in effect, requiring a fixed outlay per month. Repairs are also performed as required due to breakdowns, accidents, and so on. There are significant fluctuations in the number and size of such repairs per month. Activity is machine usage per year.

P 11-4   Flexible Budget Preparation

Having examined the behavior of manufacturing costs in its Machining Department, Hughes Corporation has predicted that the following relationships will be in effect each month during 19X1:

> Direct Materials—$10 per unit produced.
> Direct Labor—2 units produced per hour; $10 per hour.
> Supplies—10 percent of direct materials used.
> Indirect Labor—$40,000 per month plus $2 per direct labor hour.
> Maintenance—$10,000 per month plus $0.50 per direct labor hour
> Power and Heat—$4,000 per month plus $0.75 per direct labor hour.
> Cleaning—$1,000 per month plus $0.25 per direct labor hour.
> Insurance—$2,000 per month.
> Depreciation—$10,000 per month.

Productive capacity is estimated to be 20,000 direct labor hours per month.

Required:
(a) Prepare, in tabular form, a set of budgets for 75, 80, 90, and 100 percent productive capacity. Group all items according to their cost behavior patterns.
(b) What is the overall flexible budget formula? Show how this is made up of materials, labor, and overhead items.
(c) Explain your choice of a volume or activity index in parts (a) and (b). Why is this so critical?

P 11–5 Elementary Flexible Budgeting Variance Analysis— Variable Costs Only

Knox Corporation has established the following budgeted variable overhead rates for its Metal Stamping Department for 19X4:

	$ Per Machine Hour
Factory Supplies	$ .80
Maintenance	.30
Power and Heating	1.20
Rework	.10
Idle Time	.20
Machine Setup	.40
Total Variable Overhead Cost	$3.00

During October of 19X4, 75,000 actual machine hours were worked and 280,000 units were processed. Each hour of machine time is budgeted to allow four units to be processed. Actual variable overhead costs for the month were as follows:

Factory Supplies	$ 60,300
Maintenance	20,350
Power and Heating	85,500
Rework	7,800
Idle Time	14,250
Machine Setup	29,500
	$217,700

Required:
(a) Prepare a performance report for variable overhead costs in the Metal Stamping Department for October.
(b) Comment on any pattern or other significant feature of the variances calculated in part (a).

P 11–6 Flexible Budget Analysis—Fixed and Variable Items

Sharp Company uses a flexible budget for overhead costs. For November of 19X3, the following preliminary report was prepared by a staff assistant in the Costing Department.

	Budget (40,000 Units)	Actual Costs	Variances
Variable Items:			
Indirect Labor	$40,000	$37,000	$3,000 F
Power	12,000	11,500	500 F
Repairs	8,000	8,200	(200) U
Supplies	4,000	4,000	0
Fixed Items:			
Depreciation	20,000	20,000	0
Salaries	10,000	11,000	(1,000) U
	$94,000	$91,700	$2,300 F

Required:

(a) Comment on the shortcomings of this report.

(b) Prepare a revised performance report to incorporate the additional information that actual output was 36,000 units.

(c) Supervisors now learn that each unit is budgeted for two direct labor hours. Actual labor hours worked totaled 75,000. Revise the performance report in the light of this information.

(d) Express the flexible budget formula in terms of (1) units of output and (2) direct labor hours. Explain why you prefer one or the other of these overhead formulas.

P 11–7   Flexible Budgeting—Variance Analysis— Variable, Fixed, and Mixed Items

The overhead budget for Fawcett Corporation's Cutting Department for a typical month is shown in the following table:

Direct Labor Hours	40,000	60,000	80,000
Indirect Materials	$ 40,000	$ 60,000	$ 80,000
Indirect Labor	60,000	90,000	120,000
Power and Heat	30,000	40,000	50,000
Repairs	15,000	20,000	25,000
Supervision	25,000	25,000	25,000
	$170,000	$235,000	$300,000

For May of 19X1, actual overhead costs were as follows:

Indirect Materials	$ 72,000
Indirect Labor	101,500
Power and Heat	47,500
Repairs	22,500
Supervision	26,500
	$270,000

The number of direct labor hours worked was 72,000. Output totaled 210,000 units. The production budget calls for an output rate of three units per direct labor hour.

Required:
(a) Examine each of the cost items in the preceding table and ascertain which ones are being budgeted as (1) fixed, (2) variable and (3) mixed items.
(b) What are budgeted amounts of each individual item and what is the overall flexible budget formula for overhead in the Cutting Department?
(c) Prepare a performance report for May of 19X1, with separate calculations of spending and efficiency variances for the five individual items (where applicable) and for total overhead costs.
(d) Comment on any significant pattern or relationship that is apparent in the analysis performed in part (c).

P 11-8   Flexible Budgeting Analysis—Forecast Variances—Sales Price and Volume Variances—Expense Variances

Hannah Company prepared the following condensed budgeted income statement for 19X3:

Sales (100,000 units @ $8.00)	$800,000
Variable Costs (100,000 @ $6.00)	600,000
Contribution Margin (100,000 @ $2)..........	$200,000
Fixed Costs	100,000
Net Income	$100,000

Actual results for the year included the following:

(1) Sales volume was 10 percent below budget.
(2) Sales prices were increased by 50¢ per unit on all sales.
(3) A total of $601,250 was incurred for variable costs and $110,000 for fixed costs.
(4) Variable costs budgeted at $6 per unit may also have been expressed as $3 per labor hour. During the year, 185,000 labor hours were actually worked.

Required:
(a) Prepare an income statement for 19X3 in a similar format to the budgeted statement.
(b) Compute the following variances:
   (1) Sales quantity (forecast) variance (use sales price basis)
   (2) Sales price variance
   (3) Sales quantity (forecast) variance
        (use contribution margin basis)
   (4) Variable cost spending variance
   (5) Variable cost efficiency variance
   (6) Fixed cost spending variance
   (7) Net income variance
(c) Present a short explanation of the *nature* and possible *cause* of each of the variances calculated.
(d) Explain the usefulness of each of the variances calculated.

P 11–9   Flexible Budgeting Analysis—Forecast Variances—Spending and Efficiency Variances

Pratt Company operates a plant with an annual productive capacity of 200,000 units. Average annual demand of 175,000 units has been forecast over the next 12 years. For 19X1, the master budget was based on a sales forecast of 160,000 units. Production of each unit requires at two direct labor hours. The budgeted labor rate is $8 per hour. Direct materials are estimated to be $10 per unit. Variable overhead is forecast at $4 per direct labor hour and fixed overhead at $400,000 per year. All nonmanufacturing costs are fixed and should amount to $200,000 per year. The budgeted sales price is $50 per unit. Actual results for 19X1 were as follows:

Sales (150,000 units @ $52)	$7,800,000
Production	150,000 units
Direct Materials	$1,600,000
Direct Labor	$2,720,000
Variable Overhead Costs	$1,300,000
Fixed Overhead Costs	$ 410,000
Nonmanufacturing Costs	$ 185,000
Direct Labor Hours	320,000 hours

Required:
(a) Prepare the original budgeted income statement for 19X1. (Assume beginning and ending inventories were zero.)
(b) Prepare an income statement to reflect the actual results for 19X1.
(c) Prepare an analysis of the variances between parts (a) and (b). Show specifically:
   (1) Sales price variance
   (2) Sales forecast variance
      a. Sales price basis
      b. Contribution margin basis
   (3) Total materials variance
   (4) Labor rate and efficiency variances
   (5) Overhead spending and efficiency variances
   (6) Nonmanufacturing cost variance—spending
   (7) Net income variance.
(d) Comment on the results obtained in part (c). What additional analysis might be useful in this situation? Why?

P 11–10   Flexible Budgeting—Variance Analysis—Spending and Efficiency Variances

Reiner Corporation has decided to use a flexible budgeting approach for its manufacturing operations because substantial monthly fluctuations in production levels are frequently experienced. The following data are available for the labor and overhead in one production department:

Normal Capacity—20,000 labor hours per month
Direct Labor—4 hours per unit produced @ $8.00 per hour
Manufacturing Overheads—at normal capacity
    Variable Items:

Indirect Labor	$60,000	
Indirect Materials	6,000	
Power and Heat	8,000	
Repairs	2,000	
Supplies	4,000	$ 80,000
Fixed Items:		
Supervision	$12,000	
Depreciation	8,000	
Property Tax	5,000	$ 25,000
		$105,000

For April of 19X4, the following production and cost data were reported:

Units Produced	4,200 units
Direct Labor (18,000 hours)	$153,000
Indirect Labor	51,000
Indirect Materials	5,800
Power and Heat	7,500
Repairs	3,200
Supplies	1,500
Supervision	12,500
Depreciation	8,000
Property Tax	6,000

Required:

(a) Prepare the flexible budget specifications. Express the labor and overhead (1) as a function of units of output and (2) as a function of direct labor hours.

(b) Will formulation (1) or (2) be more useful for control purposes? Why?

(c) Prepare an analysis of labor and overhead costs for April of 19X4. Show the total flexible budget variances, spending variances, and efficiency variances.

(d) Comment on the results obtained in part (c). Is there any particular pattern or trend evident? What might be its cause?

P 11–11   Flexible Budgeting—Variance Analysis— Multiple Budgeting Relationships

Mull Company has instituted flexible budgeting procedures for planning and control of overhead in its manufacturing departments. The following are the budget relationships for individual items in one production department:

Item	Budget Relationship
Indirect Labor	$5 per direct labor hour
Supplies	$2.50 per machine hour
Supervision	$5,000 per month
Depreciation	$4,500 per month
Repairs	$0.25 per machine hour
Power and Heat	$2,000 per month plus 40¢ per machine hour
Factory Clerical	$1,000 per month plus 10¢ per direct labor hour
Rent	$1,500 per month

Production specifications call for two direct labor hours and three machine hours per unit of output produced by this department. Cost and production data for May of 19X0 were as follows:

Units Produced	7,500 units
Direct Labor Hours Worked	14,000 hours
Machine Hours Worked	25,000 hours
Indirect Labor	$82,500
Supplies	67,500
Supervision	6,500
Depreciation	5,000
Repairs	5,750
Power and Heat	12,600
Factory Clerical	2,800
Rent	1,500

Required:

(a) Develop a monthly flexible budget formula for this department using only direct labor hours and machine hours as budgeting variables for the variable overhead items. Show (1) the budget relationships for each overhead item individually and (2) the total budget relationships.

(b) Assuming the hourly requirements for both labor and machine time per unit remain constant, convert the budget relationship in part (a) to (1) machine hours only and (2) labor hours only.

(c) Compare the relative usefulness of the formulation in part (a) with those in part (b). Which do you prefer and why?

(d) Prepare an analysis of overhead costs for May of 19X0 using the flexible budget formulated in part (a). Show all relevant variances.

(e) Repeat the analysis of the overhead for May using both of the flexible budget formulas developed in part (b).

(f) Comment on the differences between the three sets of variances developed in parts (d) and (e). Which analysis do you prefer and why?

P 11–12 Flexible Budgeting—Comprehensive Review— Spending and Efficiency Variances

Snyder Company has introduced flexible budgeting procedures for planning and control in its manufacturing operations. The following tabulation shows monthly budgets prepared for 75 and 100 percent of normal productive capacity.

	75%	100%
Capacity (percent)	75%	100%
Capacity (labor hours)	7,500	10,000
Indirect Materials	$15,000	$ 20,000
Indirect Labor	30,000	40,000
Rework	7,500	10,000
Setup Costs	12,500	15,000
Power and Heat	9,500	12,000
Depreciation	8,000	8,000
Supervision	7,000	7,000
	$89,500	$112,000

Required:

(a) Examine the cost behavior pattern of each item in the preceding budgets. Rearrange the format of the budgets and prepare a schedule for the 80, 90, and 100 percent capacity levels.

(b) What basic budget formula underlies the preceding tabulation?

(c) For July of 19X8, the company operated at 85 percent of normal capacity. However, for the output produced, only 8,200 labor hours should have been required. Overhead incurred was as follows:

Indirect Materials	$18,500
Indirect Labor	34,000
Rework	7,200
Setup Costs	14,000
Power and Heat	9,800
Depreciation	8,000
Supervision	7,500
	$99,000

With the exception of Supervision, all fixed costs incurred were equal to their originally budgeted amounts. It was also observed that the forecast production level had been for output requiring 9,000 labor hours. Prepare an analysis of overhead costs showing separately the variances due to forecast, spending, and efficiency factors.

(d) Comment on the results of the analysis in part (c).

P 11–13   Flexible Budgeting—Analysis of Overhead and Labor Variances—Multiple Product Situation

Hoaglund Corporation produces products X, Y, and Z, which require two, eight, and four direct labor hours of processing, respectively. Budgeted output for 19X4 was 200,000 units, comprising 100,000 units of X, 25,000 units of Y, and 75,000 units of Z. Budgeted overhead costs for the year included $1,400,000 for variable items and $2,100,000 for fixed items. The budgeted direct labor rate was $8 per hour. To simplify costing procedures, the following calculations were made:

	Budgeted Units	Labor Hours per Unit	Total Labor Hours
X	100,000	2	200,000
Y	25,000	8	200,000
Z	75,000	4	300,000
	200,000		700,000

$$\text{Average Labor Hours per Unit} = \frac{700,000}{200,000} = 3.5$$

$$\text{Total Budgeted Overhead} = \$1,400,000 + \$2,100,000 = \$3,500,000$$

$$\text{Average Overhead Rate} = \frac{\$3,500,000}{700,000 \text{ hours}} = \$5 \text{ per hour}$$

$$\text{Average Labor Cost per Unit} = 3.5 \times \$8 = \$28$$
$$\text{Average Overhead Cost per Unit} = 3.5 \times \$5 = \$17.50$$

For 19x4, the following production and cost data were obtained:

Output: X	70,000 units
Y	40,000 units
Z	90,000 units
	200,000 units

Direct Labor (800,000 hours)	$6,800,000
Variable Overhead Incurred	1,800,000
Fixed Overhead Incurred	2,200,000

The following labor and overhead analysis report was presented:

	Actual	Budget	Variance
Direct Labor	$6,800,000	$5,600,000*	$1,200,000 Unfavorable
Overhead	$4,000,000	$3,500,000†	$ 500,000 Unfavorable

* $5,600,000 = 200,000 units @ $28
† $3,500,000 = 200,000 units @ $17.50

Required:

(a) Evaluate the labor and overhead analysis report as presented. What are its shortcomings?

(b) Prepare a revised cost analysis report using a flexible budgeting approach.

(c) What problems in the original report does your answer in part (b) overcome?

(d) Comment on the relative merits of budgeting on the basis of (1) units of output versus (2) units of input, giving special attention to the problem of multiple output situations.

P 11–14 Flexible Budgeting—Variable, Fixed, Mixed, and Step-Variable Costs—Variance Analysis

Douglass Corporation has adopted flexible budgeting procedures for its manufacturing operations. The following tabulation for three monthly activity levels were prepared for one department:

Units	6,000	8,000	10,000
Labor Hours	12,000	16,000	20,000
Materials (5 lbs. per unit)	$ 60,000	$ 80,000	$100,000
Direct Labor (per hour)	48,000	64,000	80,000
Indirect Labor (per direct labor hour)	24,000	32,000	40,000
Indirect Materials (per lb. input)	15,000	20,000	25,000
Repairs (per direct labor hour)*	9,000	11,000	13,000
Power & Heat (per direct labor hour)*	6,400	7,200	8,000
Depreciation	10,000	10,000	10,000
Supervision †	12,000	24,000	24,000
	$184,400	$248,200	$300,000

* These items are *mixed* costs and contain a fixed element.
  † This is a step-variable cost, with a change occurring from $12,000 to $24,000 at the 15,000 hour level.

For October of 19X2, the following results were obtained:

Output.....................		8,000 units
Labor Hours..................		16,500
Materials used...............		38,500 lbs.
Costs Incurred:		
Materials		$ 84,150
Direct Labor................		70,125
Indirect Labor		33,000
Indirect Materials		18,500
Repairs		11,550
Power and Heat		7,500
Depreciation		12,000
Supervision		25,000
		$261,825

Required:

(a) Prepare an analysis of costs incurred in October compared to a budget based on the actual number of units produced (and the budgeted inputs for that amount of output).

(b) Prepare a flexible budget analysis of October costs, using the information relating to actual hours worked and actual materials used, as well as the results from part (a).

(c) Compare the results obtained in parts (a) and (b). Which is the more useful and for what reasons?

P 11–15   Flexible Budgeting—Analysis of Performance—Revision of Variance Reporting System

K. and 5 Company has adopted a flexible budgeting system for profit planning and performance control. Departmental managers were pleased with the system, but problems were encountered at the level of plant management and above. For example, the following report was prepared for the Machining Department for July of 19X7:

K. and 5 COMPANY
MACHINING DEPARTMENT
July 19X7

	Budget	Actual	Variance
Units Produced	30,000	24,000	
Manufacturing Costs:			
Materials..................	$ 30,000	$ 26,500	$ 3,500 F
Direct Labor	50,000	44,250	5,750 F
Variable Overhead:			
Indirect Labor	15,000	12,000	3,000 F
Utilities	9,000	8,000	1,000 F
Supplies	6,000	5,250	750 F
Fixed Overhead:			
Supervision	12,500	13,000	(500)U
Depreciation..............	2,500	2,500	0
Total	$125,000	$111,500	$13,500 F

When presented with this report, the manager of the Machining Department said, "This is great! Look at the bucks I've saved this month! Don't I deserve a bonus?"

Required:

(a) Is the Machining Department manager's pride justified? Why or why not?

(b) Discuss the basic shortcomings of the preceding report. How should it be redesigned? (Do *not* compute any amounts.)

(c) It is established that each hour of direct labor in the Machining Department, where the hourly rate is $5 per hour, should allow the processing of three units of output. Variable overhead costs are all directly related to direct labor hours. During July, actual direct labor was 8,850 hours. Based on this additional information, prepare a revised flexible budgeting report for the department for July.

(d) Explain the superiority of your report in part (c) over the one originally presented.

(e) Evaluate the performance of the Machining Department manager based on the results in part (c).

P 11–16   Flexible Budgeting—Comprehensive Review— Variance Analysis

The 19X3 budgeted income statement for Kelly Company is as follows:

(1)	Sales (400,000 units @ $15)		$6,000,000
	Variable Costs:		
(2)	Materials	$1,000,000	
(3)	Direct Labor	2,000,000	
(4)	Variable Manufacturing Overhead	400,000	
(5)	Variable Marketing and Administrative Costs	800,000	4,200,000
(6)	Contribution Margin		$1,800,000
	Fixed Costs:		
(7)	Manufacturing	$ 700,000	
(8)	Marketing and Administrative	900,000	1,600,000
(9)	Net Income		$ 200,000

During 19X3, operating results were better than anticipated in terms of volume, but reported income was well off the budgeted amount. In fact, despite production and sales of 480,000 units, Kelly Company reported a *loss* of $50,000.

The following information was also available. Materials prices increased by 20 percent over the budgeted amount, but there was no inefficiency in the amount of materials used per unit produced. Productivity of labor had been planned to be two units per hour. Actual hours worked were 280,000 and there was no change in the labor rate from that planned.

Variable manufacturing overhead costs relate closely to direct labor. An unfavorable spending variance on these items amounted to $210,000. Variable marketing and administrative items are directly related to sales volume. The total amount incurred was $1,120,000. There were offsetting variances with respect to the amounts spent on fixed manufacturing and fixed marketing and administrative costs—$50,000 unfavorable for the former and $50,000 favorable for the latter. Sales prices were increased by $1 per unit on all sales made during the year.

Required:

(a) Prepare an income statement to reflect the actual results for 19X3.

(b) Prepare a complete analysis of all variances to explain the difference between the budgeted income of $200,000 and the actual loss of $50,000. The following schedule should be helpful:

Item	Original Budget 400,000 units 200,000 hours	Revised Budget 480,000 units 240,000 hours	Revised Budget 480,000 units 280,000 hours	Actual
(1) Sales				
(2) Materials				
(3) Direct Labor				
(4) Variable Manufacturing Overhead				
(5) Variable Marketing and Administrative Costs				
(6) Contribution Margin				
(7) Fixed Manufacturing Costs				
(8) Fixed Marketing and Administrative Costs				
(9) Net Income				

P 11–17   Service Department Costs—Flexible Budgeting— Allocation and Variance Calculation

Tinsley Corporation operates its own power generating plant and services four user departments. The 19X3 budget of operating costs for the power plant included $300,000 for fixed items and $900,000 for variable items, based on users' capacity needs and expected demand, respectively. Information concerning the four user departments, their estimated needs, and their usage is as follows:

	Kilowatt Hours		
	Usage—May	Estimated —19X3	Annual Capacity
Dept. I	40,000	480,000	700,000
II	65,000	900,000	1,000,000
III	35,000	480,000	500,000
IV	30,000	300,000	300,000
	170,000	2,160,000	2,500,000

Costs incurred in the power plant during May were $27,500 for fixed items and $84,000 for variable items.

Required:

(a) For budgetary purposes, prepare a schedule to show the allocation of power plant costs to the user departments at the beginning of 19X3.

(b) Analyze the performance of the power plant for May of 19X3, showing costs reallocated and variances.

(c) Comment on the results in part (b), especially with regard to Department IV.

P 11–18   Service Department Cost Reallocations—
Alternative Methods

Darnell Farm Equipment Company has two divisions in its plant, the Tractor Division and the Harvester Division. Each division relies on support services provided by the company's Equipment Maintenance Department. For 19X2, the budgeted costs for the Equipment Maintenance Department were

(1) $1,500,000 for variable items, based on a forecast of 100,000 labor hours of services to be provided.

(2) $600,000 for fixed items, based on the projected capacity needs of the two divisions.

Capacity needs and usage were forecast as follows:

	Forecast Usage, 19x2	Capacity Needs
Tractor Division	50,000 hours	90,000 hours
Harvester Division	50,000 hours	60,000 hours
	100,000 hours	150,000 hours

For the first six months of 19X2, the following operating results were reported:

(1) Equipment Maintenance Department:	
Fixed Costs Incurred	$350,000
Variable Costs Incurred	$825,000
Service Hours Provided	60,000
(2) Tractor Division Service Hours Utilized	36,000
Harvester Division Service Hours Utilized	24,000

Required:

(a)   Allocate service department costs to the user departments on the basis of the forecast information as of the beginning of 19X2.

(b)   Allocate actual costs for the first six months, based on the predetermined amounts set in part (a) and relevant aspects of actual performance.

(c)   Prepare a separate allocation of all actual costs for the first six months based on actual usage of services.

(d)   Comment on the differences between the results obtained in parts (b) and (c).

(e)   Comment on the Harvester Division's estimate of capacity needs and its usage of services in the first six months. What problem may be present? How might it be prevented from recurring or becoming more pronounced?

12

STANDARD COSTS

LEARNING OBJECTIVES

After studying Chapter 12, you should be able to:

1. Distinguish between actual and standard costs. Explain how standards are set and how a standard cost system operates.
2. Describe the uses, advantages, and limitations of standard cost systems.
3. Distinguish between ideal and currently attainable standards and discuss how each might be employed.
4. Distinguish between physical, ideal, normal, and expected capacity. Describe the circumstances in which each might be used appropriately.
5. Calculate the following variances:
    a. Materials price variance (at points of acquisition and usage)
    b. Materials usage variance
    c. Labor rate variance
    d. Labor efficiency variance
    e. Variable overhead spending variance
    f. Variable overhead efficiency variance
    g. Fixed overhead spending variance
    h. Fixed overhead volume variance
    i. Combined overhead spending variance
6. Prepare journal entries to record the acquisition of materials, labor, and overhead inputs, and the accumulation and transfer of costs through the inventory accounts in a standard cost system.
7. Adapt standard cost procedures to equivalent units of output in a process cost system. Prepare a production cost report.
8. Allocate service department costs to production departments using a predetermined standard application rate.

Traditional methods of cost accumulation relied on stores' records of materials requisitions and on foremen's accounts of the time spent by workers on each task. If overhead was added, it was usually calculated as a percentage of the current or previous year's labor or prime costs. The actual costs of materials, labor, and overhead were accumulated to determine the total cost of a job or product.

Only gradually did it become apparent that these actual costs were not very useful for price setting, planning, or controlling operations. There was no agreement as to how materials bought at different prices should be charged to products, how overtime pay should be assigned, what costs should be included in overhead or how it should be allocated. Actual cost data only became available after the goods had been produced. These historical cost summaries not only mixed legitimate costs with avoidable losses that had nothing to do with the final product, but actually impeded attempts to eliminate waste and poor production methods. Although a great deal of repetitive, detailed bookkeeping was required to establish and maintain an actual cost system, the resulting cost figures were affected by so many random factors that they often seemed almost accidental.

Early in this century, a few accountants and industrial engineers proposed an entirely new method of cost accumulation.[1] Why not calculate the cost of a product *before* it is manufactured? These predetermined or *standard costs* could be transferred through the inventory accounts as manufacturing operations proceeded. At each stage in production, actual operating results could be compared with these preset standards and the resulting variances could be analyzed to see why operations did not conform to plan. Knowledge of what costs should be under normal operating conditions would immediately reveal any excess in actual costs and direct managerial attention to substandard performance.

This chapter demonstrates how cost standards are established and used. Journal entries and ledger postings are made to transfer standard costs through the inventory accounts from Raw Materials to Finished Goods. Eight types of variances between standard and actual costs are measured. Financial statements based on standard costs are illustrated.

WHAT ARE STANDARD COSTS?

In everyday usage, the word "standard" means a basis for comparison or a uniform amount. In this chapter, a **standard cost** will be defined initially as *the predetermined cost of a unit of activity*. As the discussion proceeds, this definition will be refined to accommodate various measurement and usage

---

[1] Michael Chatfield, *A History of Accounting Thought,* Revised Edition (Huntington, N.Y.: Krieger Publishing Co., 1977), pp. 169–72.

aspects of the standard cost concept. In particular, it will be used to illustrate how standards are set, administered, and applied as tools of cost analysis and control.

Standards are most frequently established for (1) raw materials used in making a product or one of its components, (2) direct labor needed to perform a manufacturing operation, and (3) manufacturing overhead applied to a unit of output. But they may also be set for the outputs of certain nonmanufacturing activities, such as sales and administration, as well as for the outputs of some service departments in the manufacturing area.

The standard cost of a unit of activity is determined by multiplying the *standard quantities* of inputs required to produce it by the *standard prices* of those inputs. The presence of both unit prices and unit quantity requirements for inputs is therefore central to the standard cost concept.

Standard costs also have an important qualitative dimension. For the moment, it will be assumed that a standard cost reflects *a desired level of achievement consistent with operating objectives.* However, standards cannot be defined on any precise scale that reflects different degrees of success in achieving goals. As will be seen, accounting standards may be described variously as ideal, technical, practical, tight, loose, attainable, or current.

STANDARD COST SPECIFICATIONS

Standard cost specifications include the *prices* that should be paid for individual materials, labor, and overhead inputs, and the *quantities* of those inputs that should be used in producing a specified unit of output. Specifications may be prepared for activity units such as the output of a single production department, a product line, or for certain marketing, service, and administrative departments. A specification will have as many components as there are identifiable raw materials inputs, direct labor categories, and overhead classifications needed to produce the particular unit of output involved. Standard cost specifications are the basis for all planning and control uses of standard costing techniques.

Figure 12–1 shows typical standard cost specifications for a manufacturing company.

The materials, labor, and overhead items in Pearse Corporation's cost specification can be described as follows:

Raw Materials
Quantity   One unit of Product S should require inputs of 10 pounds of Material A and 20 feet of Material B.

Price   Materials inputs should be purchased at unit prices of $2 per pound for Material A and 50¢ per foot for Material B.

Direct Labor
Quantity (*Hours*)   Two hours of direct labor are needed to convert the standard quantities of raw materials into one unit of Product S.

Price (*Rate*)   Direct labor services should be paid at the rate of $10 per hour.

FIGURE 12–1

Pearse Corporation
Standard Cost Specification—Product S

Materials:
    A (10 pounds @ $2 per pound) $20
    B (20 feet @ 50¢ per foot) 10 $30
Labor (2 hours @ $10 per hour)   20

Overhead:
    Variable (2 hours @ $7.50 per hour) $15
    Fixed (2 hours @ $5 per hour)   10   25
Total Standard Cost per Unit of Product S $75

Manufacturing Overhead

Activity Index   A standard amount of overhead is to be applied to each unit of output. This overhead application is based on an **activity index**—in this case, standard labor hours per unit of output. The activity index should be input-related and should also reflect the general behavior of overhead costs in the activity center.

Overhead Rates
Variable Overhead Rate   Variable overhead costs of $7.50 per standard direct labor hour are anticipated under standard operating conditions.

Fixed Overhead Rate   This is the amount of fixed overhead cost per unit of the activity index. It is computed by dividing total budgeted fixed overhead costs by total standard direct labor hours *at some predetermined capacity level.* In Pearse Corporation, the fixed overhead rate is $5 per direct labor hour, based on total fixed overhead of $2,400,000 and an expected capacity level of 480,000 labor hours per year.

SELECTING A CAPACITY LEVEL

The capacity level chosen is critically important because it is used in setting the standard fixed overhead application rate. There are a number of alternative capacity concepts, each with advantages and shortcomings. They include *full capacity, practical capacity, normal capacity,* and *expected capacity.*

There is a **physical** or **technological capacity** limit on the use of productive resources that cause fixed costs. This is also called the **ideal** or **full capacity** level. But it is unlikely that such complete utilization of fixed resources will be sustained for long. Instead, some level of usage less than 100 percent may be the most **practical capacity** level. Practical capacity represents an intensive use of resources, but takes into account the need to avoid the stress of operating at or close to the absolute physical capacity limit and allows for normal down-time, equipment breakdowns, and other anticipated problems. Practical capacity is based on production capabilities alone; it ignores potential market demand for a company's products.

Normal capacity is an average operating level that is expected to be sustained over the long run in response to both market demand and practical productive capacity. Normal capacity can be used to establish a standard fixed overhead rate that will not change over a relatively long period. The establishment of such a long-term rate is a mixed blessing. Because actual capacity utilized per period will tend to vary from this normal capacity level as operating conditions change, the amount of standard fixed overhead applied will differ from the actual amount incurred, thereby creating an underapplied or overapplied overhead balance.

The *expected capacity* is the activity level predicted during the period for which cost standards are being set. In this chapter, **expected annual capacity** will be the basis for setting standard fixed overhead rates. Because expected capacity can be forecast more accurately than the normal capacity level, it should result in smaller underapplied or overapplied overhead costs. The disadvantage of this method is that, if capacity utilization varies much from period to period, the standard fixed overhead rates and the resulting standard product costs will also vary considerably.

SETTING PRODUCT COST STANDARDS

The items to be included in a standard product cost specification are usually easy to identify. They include materials, labor, and overhead costs. The difficulty lies in making appropriate unit measurements of those costs. Because a standard cost serves as a measure of desired performance, the accountant's essential objective is to set standards which quantify that desired level of performance.

Ideal or **theoretical standards** assume operational perfection and the highest possible levels of goal attainment. They suggest that resource acquisition and use occurs under optimal conditions with regard to prices, production efficiency, and capacity utilization. Such a high level of performance can never be achieved, because management cannot control all the related variables. For example, it would be unrealistic to set materials standards to include only the exact amount of materials that are contained in each acceptable unit of output. Allowance must be made in the standard input quantities for evaporation, waste, spoilage, and errors. The only purpose served by ideal standards is to set ultimate goals which may induce greater employee efforts.

Currently attainable standards cover a range of performance levels. For planning, performance measurement, and control, this concept is more useful than that of ideal standards. It allows for a tolerable amount of production inefficiencies, errors, faulty materials, equipment breakdowns, and labor problems.

Establishing currently attainable standards requires a forecast of operating conditions during the period when the standards will be in use. Depending on how far in the direction of ideal standards the currently attainable level is to be positioned, such standards may be described as relatively **tight** or **loose.** Tight currently attainable standards should be difficult, but not impossible to reach; loose standards obviously suggest a greater ease of attainment. Positioning a standard in the range of attainability is a delicate task of managerial judgment. As discussed in Chapter 10, it involves the consideration of behavioral concepts such as motivation, self-actualization, aspiration levels, and penalty–reward systems.

The accounting techniques used to measure cost standards must be as rigorous as possible. Information about material quantities, supplies, and labor and overhead requirements can be obtained from the purchasing, product design, and production planning and scheduling departments. This information is combined with input price data to generate the standard cost specifications. Over time, this information can be supplemented with actual cost performance data. Formal statistical techniques may be used to predict future cost performance and revise standards in the light of past experience. Linear and nonlinear regression are useful methods for this purpose. Learning curves are especially appropriate for cost analysis in those industries where standard costs are most likely to be used (for example, electronics, computers, aircraft manufacture, and shipbuilding). These techniques will be examined in detail in Chapters 15 and 22.

USES OF STANDARD COSTS

The use of predetermined standard costs can simplify cost calculations, the bookkeeping process, and financial statement preparation. Standard costing also permits a refinement of cost data for purposes of planning and competitive bidding. Finally, standards provide a basis for controlling costs and encouraging operating efficiencies.

INVENTORY VALUATION AND INCOME MEASUREMENT

Standard costs can simplify inventory valuation and income measurement. Inventories of raw materials, work in process, and completed products are conveniently priced at amounts that have been determined *before production begins.* Using standard costs for inventory valuation localizes the effects on income of production and purchasing efficiencies or inefficiencies by confining them to the period in which they occur. When inventories are priced at standard cost, the only costs that are capitalized and carried forward to future periods are those which *should have been incurred* under standard production conditions. Any variance between actual and standard production costs is charged to expense in the current period.

Example: Pearse Corporation, which manufactures Product S at a standard cost of $75, recorded the operating results for July of 19X7 shown in Figure 12–2.

In Figure 12–3, these actual sales and cost figures are supplemented by standard inventory costs.

The income statement shown in Figure 12–3 can be easily reformulated to compare actual and standard costs, providing an elementary form of variance analysis as shown in Figure 12–4.

This example shows that standard product costs (1) provide a convenient way to generate data for short-term income statements, (2) permit measurement of variances between standard and actual production costs, and (3) isolate

---

FIGURE 12–2

Pearse Corporation
Operating Data
Month of July, 19X7

Sales (18,000 units @ $120)	$2,160,000
Inventory, July 1 (2,000 units)	
Inventory, July 31 (2,000 units)	
Manufacturing Costs (18,000 units)	
Materials	547,000
Direct Labor	418,000
Manufacturing Overhead	476,000
Marketing Expense	275,000
Administrative Expense	180,000

---

the income effects of these variances in the current period. No part of Pearse Corporation's $91,000 variance is carried forward to future accounting periods. The entire variance is reported as an adjustment to gross profit in July, 19X7.

Because of its convenience, standard costing has sometimes been promoted as a way to reduce bookkeeping costs. It often does so, because it allows short-run financial statements to be prepared without recourse to inventory flow assumptions such as FIFO and LIFO. But the use of standard costs to their

---

FIGURE 12–3

Pearse Corporation
Income Statement
Month of July, 19X7

Actual Sales (18,000 units @ $120)			$2,160,000
Less: Cost of Goods Sold			
Inventory, July 1			
(2,000 units @ Standard Cost of $75)		$ 150,000	
Actual Cost of Goods Manufactured			
Materials	$547,000		
Direct Labor	418,000		
Manufacturing Overhead	476,000	1,441,000	
Cost of Goods Manufactured		$1,591,000	
Less: *Inventory, July 31*			
(2,000 units @ Standard Cost of $75)		150,000	1,441,000
Gross Profit			$ 719,000
Less: Actual Marketing Expense		$ 275,000	
Actual Administrative Expense		180,000	455,000
Net Income			$ 264,000

FIGURE 12–4

Pearse Corporation
Income Statement
Month of July, 19X7

Actual Sales (18,000 units @ $120)		$2,160,000
Less: Standard Cost of Goods Sold (18,000 units @ $75) . .		1,350,000
Standard Gross Profit (18,000 units @ $45)		$ 810,000
Less: Manufacturing Cost Variances		
Actual Costs . . . . , ...	$1,441,000	
Less Standard Costs (18,000 units @ $75)	1,350,000	
Variance Between Actual and Standard Costs		91,000
Adjusted Gross Profit		$ 719,000
Less: Actual Marketing Expense	$ 275,000	
Actual Administrative Expense	180,000	455,000
Net Income		$ 264,000

---

full extent for planning, reporting, and control purposes requires more bookkeeping than if standards were not used. As will be seen, there are many additional procedural steps in an accounting system that is designed to set, administer, and interpret standard costs. However, this is another area in which recent developments in computer data processing have made a standard cost system that includes planning, reporting, and control features a very worthwhile computer-based application.

PLANNING

Standard costs can be effective planning devices. Once established, they facilitate tabulation and comparison of the effects of budgetary alternatives. In particular, standard costs are a means of focusing attention on the *details* of planned operations. Standard cost calculations deal with the amount of material needed to process *one unit of output* in *one activity center* or the amount of labor needed to perform *one processing operation*. This is a much finer level of detail than is emphasized in the more broadly based planning techniques of cost–volume–profit analysis and flexible budgeting.

This emphasis on unit costs makes standard costing especially useful in that part of the planning process which deals with *pricing decisions*. When production is process-oriented and outputs are homogenous, standard product costs are helpful in making long-range pricing decisions, provided that product specifications and activity levels remain relatively constant.

The *variable* components of a standard cost specification are readily adaptable for planning purposes. However, the *fixed* cost element must be handled carefully because the standard product cost concept requires that all costs be expressed as unit amounts. This is contrary to the planning treatment needed for fixed cost items in that it requires choosing a capacity level over which total fixed costs must be spread to derive a unit fixed cost figure. If the expected annual capacity level is used, the fixed overhead component of standard product cost may fluctuate from year to year as the capacity level changes. On the other hand, use of the long-run normal capacity level will tend to stabilize the amount of fixed overhead included in standard product cost per unit, regardless of activity level changes from year to year.

Accountants can avoid this fixed cost/capacity level problem by considering only the variable portions of standard product cost. A standard contribution margin (sales price minus standard variable cost) can be derived, and cost–volume–profit techniques can then be used as a basis for planning decisions.

When finished products are non-homogenous, but have some standardized components, standard costs for those components can be helpful in *developing bids* on similar projects. For example, in custom homebuilding, the initial components built into each house are fairly uniform, but the final interior and exterior construction requires special materials and nonstandard processing.

CONTROL

Standard costs should be viewed primarily as performance evaluation and control tools. Control begins with the setting of future goals in the form of desired performance measures. These performance measures constitute standards with which actual achievements can be compared. Substandard results revealed by such comparisons can then be investigated and corrected.

The principle of **management by exception** can be used effectively when standard costs are adopted. Variances between standard and actual performance can be measured, analyzed, investigated, and reported on a selective basis. When only those variances that violate some criterion of acceptability are reported and investigated, management's attention can be directed first to the more important problems.

MOTIVATION

Standard costs are potentially effective as motivational devices that can be used to improve company performance. As unit measures, standard costs have the advantage of being easily understood. For example, a level of performance expressed in unit terms (10 pounds of material at $1 per pound are required to produce one unit of output), is easier to understand and respond to than is the same performance requirement expressed as a total (8,500 pounds of material costing $8,500 are needed to produce 850 units).

An inherent psychological value in the term "standard" also reinforces its usefulness in promoting efforts to reach goals. "Standard" seems to have more qualitative appeal and impact than the words "budget" or "plan." When a standard is specified, individuals may be expected to associate it with the need for some required effort. Management can use a properly administered system of standard costs as an effective behavior modifier. Participation in standard setting, coordination of standards with penalty–reward systems, goal coordination, self-actualization effects, and group reaction are all behavioral aspects of the use of standards.

LIMITATIONS OF STANDARD COSTS

There are usually significant start-up expenses in establishing a standard cost system. The more often standards have to be revised and new standards set, the larger these expenses will be.

It is always difficult to determine the *correct* standards in a given situation. Standard setting involves all the uncertainties present in any planning process. Previous cost experience usually provides some basis for predicting future costs, leading to forecasts based either on simple approximations or on advanced statistical techniques. But standards need to go beyond projections from past experience. Cost projections require some degree of fine tuning before they can effectively communicate desired achievement levels to the managers subject to those standards. Therefore, it is a real challenge to establish the precise level of achievement that needs to be embodied in a standard in order to evoke the desired response.

The problems of forecasting future performance are increased by the need to determine precise input price and quantity requirements on a *per unit basis*. Full standard product costing requires that fixed costs be expressed as unit amounts. This in turn requires setting a standard fixed overhead application rate based on an expected level of capacity utilization. The fixed overhead component must therefore be viewed more skeptically than the variable components. This fixed overhead element is a reliable unit amount only if the expected capacity level coincides with the capacity level required for the output actually produced.

Because the business environment is dynamic, standards should not be viewed as static indicators. Standards should reflect changes in performance levels, input prices, production technology, and so on. When necessary, standards should be adjusted to encourage stated goals to be achieved. In other cases, the goals themselves must be revised.

MEASURING VARIANCES BETWEEN ACTUAL AND STANDARD COSTS

A standard cost system can help identify the reasons for variations between actual and standard cost performance. This process of **variance analysis** will be illustrated through further examination of Pearse Corporation.

The following *production cost variances* can be calculated from the data in Figure 12–5 and from the standard cost specifications for Pearse Corporation's Product S given in Figure 12–1 (page 541).

MATERIALS PRICE VARIANCE

Prices paid for materials inputs often differ from the standard input prices. The **materials price variance** is the difference between the actual cost of materials purchased and the amount that should have been paid for those materials at standard prices.

FIGURE 12–5

Pearse Corporation
Actual Operating Results
Month of July, 19X7

Sales (18,000 units @ $120)	$2,160,000
Production (18,000 units)	
Raw Materials Purchased:	
A (240,000 pounds @ $2.05)	492,000
B (480,000 feet @ 45¢)	216,000
Materials Used:	
A (190,000 pounds)	
B (350,000 feet)	
Direct Labor (38,000 hours @ $11)	418,000
Manufacturing Overhead Incurred:	
Variable	266,000
Fixed	210,000
Marketing Expense	275,000
Administrative Expense	180,000

$$\text{Materials Price Variance (at point of acquisition)} = \left(\begin{array}{c} \text{Standard} \\ \text{Unit} \\ \text{Price} \end{array} - \begin{array}{c} \text{Actual} \\ \text{Unit} \\ \text{Price} \end{array} \right) \times \begin{array}{c} \text{Actual} \\ \text{Quantity} \\ \text{Purchased} \end{array}$$

$$MPV = (SP - AP) \times AQ$$

Pearse Corporation established standard prices of $2 per pound for Material A and 50¢ per foot for Material B. These materials actually cost $2.05 per pound for Material A and 45¢ per foot for Material B. The materials price variances for Materials A and B are calculated as follows:

$$
\begin{aligned}
MPV(A) &= [\$2.00 - \$2.05] \times 240,000 \\
&= -\$.05 \times 240,000 \\
&= (\$12,000) \text{ Unfavorable}
\end{aligned}
$$

$$
\begin{aligned}
MPV(B) &= [\$.50 - \$.45] \times 480,000 \\
&= \$.05 \times 480,000 \\
&= \$24,000 \text{ Favorable}
\end{aligned}
$$

As explained in Chapter 11, the formulas for calculating cost variances are presented in such a way that *negative results* always indicate **unfavorable variances** and *positive results* correspond to **favorable variances.** The idea that a variance is a deviation of actual from standard is reinforced by always subtracting actual amounts from standard amounts.

CALCULATING MATERIALS PRICE VARIANCE AT THE POINT OF USAGE

Sometimes the materials price variance is calculated when materials are *used* rather than when they are *acquired*. The materials price variance is then the difference between the actual cost of materials used and the amount that should have been paid for those materials at standard prices.

$$\begin{array}{c}\text{Materials Price Variance}\\ \text{(at point of usage)}\end{array} = \left(\begin{array}{ccc}\text{Standard} & & \text{Actual}\\ \text{Unit} & - & \text{Unit}\\ \text{Price} & & \text{Price}\end{array}\right) \times \begin{array}{c}\text{Actual}\\ \text{Quantity}\\ \text{Used}\end{array}$$

$$MPV = (SP - AP) \times AQU$$

Calculating the price variance of materials used causes a lag in reporting the variance. However, it allows the materials price variance and the materials quantity variance to be calculated simultaneously, thereby retaining a symmetrical relationship.

Pearse Corporation's materials price variances at the point of usage are calculated as follows for Materials A and B:

$$MPV(A) = -\$.05 \times 190,000$$
$$= (\$9,500) \text{ Unfavorable}$$

$$MPV(B) = \$.05 \times 350,000$$
$$= \$17,500 \text{ Favorable}$$

Unless stated otherwise, all examples and problem assignments in this text will assume that the materials price variance is calculated at the point of *acquisition.*

MATERIALS USAGE (QUANTITY) VARIANCE

The efficiency with which materials are used is reflected in the **materials usage variance,** which is the difference between the quantity of materials used and the quantity that should have been used to produce the actual output, measured at standard input prices.

$$\begin{array}{c}\text{Materials Usage}\\ \text{Variance}\end{array} = \left(\begin{array}{c}\text{Standard Quantity}\\ \text{of Input Required}\\ \text{to Produce}\\ \text{Actual Output}\end{array} - \begin{array}{c}\text{Actual Quantity}\\ \text{of Input Consumed}\\ \text{to Produce}\\ \text{Actual Output}\end{array}\right) \times \begin{array}{c}\text{Standard}\\ \text{Input Unit}\\ \text{Price}\end{array}$$

$$MUV = (SQ - AQ) \times SP$$

To produce 18,000 pounds of output, Pearse Corporation should have used 180,000 pounds of Material A (18,000 × 10 pounds) and 360,000 feet of Material

B (18,000 × 20 feet). Actual usage was 190,000 pounds of Material A and 350,000 feet of Material B.

$$MUV(A) = [180,000 - 190,000] \times \$2.00$$
$$= -10,000 \times \$2.00$$
$$= (\$20,000) \text{ Unfavorable}$$

$$MUV(B) = [360,000 - 350,000] \times \$.50$$
$$= 10,000 \times \$.50$$
$$= \$5,000 \text{ Favorable}$$

LABOR RATE VARIANCE

The wage rate actually paid may differ from the standard wage rate. The **labor rate variance** is the difference between the actual cost of all labor hours worked and the amount that should have been paid for that same amount of labor at standard hourly rates.

$$\text{Labor Rate Variance} = \left(\begin{array}{c}\text{Standard}\\ \text{Hourly}\\ \text{Rate}\end{array} - \begin{array}{c}\text{Actual}\\ \text{Hourly}\\ \text{Rate}\end{array}\right) \times \begin{array}{c}\text{Total Hours}\\ \text{Actually}\\ \text{Worked}\end{array}$$

$$LRV = (SR - AR) \times AH$$

Pearse Corporation's standard wage rate was \$10 per hour, its actual wage rate was \$11 per hour, and 38,000 hours were worked during July.

$$LRV = [\$10 - \$11] \times 38,000$$
$$= -\$1 \times 38,000$$
$$= (\$38,000) \text{ Unfavorable}$$

LABOR EFFICIENCY VARIANCE

The number of hours actually worked to produce each unit of output may differ from the standard hours required. The **labor efficiency variance** is the difference between the number of hours actually worked and the number that should have been worked to produce the actual output, measured at the standard hourly wage rate.

$$\text{Labor Efficiency Variance} = \left(\begin{array}{c}\text{Standard Hours}\\ \text{Required to Produce}\\ \text{Actual Output}\end{array} - \begin{array}{c}\text{Actual}\\ \text{Hours}\\ \text{Worked}\end{array}\right) \times \begin{array}{c}\text{Standard}\\ \text{Hourly}\\ \text{Rate}\end{array}$$

$$LEV = (SH - AH) \times SR$$

Pearse Corporation employees should have worked 36,000 hours (18,000 × 2) to produce the 18,000 units of actual output, but 38,000 hours were actually worked. The standard wage rate was $10 per hour.

$$LEV = [36,000 - 38,000] \times \$10$$
$$= -2,000 \times \$10$$
$$= (\$20,000) \text{ Unfavorable}$$

VARIABLE OVERHEAD SPENDING VARIANCE

The **variable overhead spending variance** is the difference between variable overhead cost incurred and the amount of variable overhead cost that should have been incurred at the actual level of the activity index used in the variable overhead rate. This variance can be calculated in two ways:

$$\text{Variable Overhead Spending Variance} = \left(\begin{array}{c} \text{Standard} \\ \text{Variable} \\ \text{Overhead} \\ \text{Rate} \end{array} \times \begin{array}{c} \text{Actual} \\ \text{Activity} \\ \text{Index} \\ \text{Level} \end{array} \right) - \begin{array}{c} \text{Actual} \\ \text{Variable} \\ \text{Overhead} \\ \text{Incurred} \end{array}$$

$$VOSV = (SVOR \times AH) - AVO$$

or

$$\text{Variable Overhead Spending Variance} = \left(\begin{array}{c} \text{Standard} \\ \text{Variable} \\ \text{Overhead} \\ \text{Rate} \end{array} - \begin{array}{c} \text{Actual} \\ \text{Variable} \\ \text{Overhead} \\ \text{Rate} \end{array} \right) \times \begin{array}{c} \text{Actual} \\ \text{Activity} \\ \text{Level} \\ \text{Index} \end{array}$$

$$VOSV = (SVOR - AVOR) \times AH$$

Major causes of the variable overhead spending variance are (1) changes in the prices of overhead items and (2) changes in the composition and amount of overhead items consumed per unit of the activity index employed (for example, more supplies or less utilities per labor hour). Therefore, it is not simply a spending variance in the same sense as the materials price variance or the labor rate variance. It reflects not only changes in the prices of variable overhead items, but efficiencies or inefficiencies in the usage of those items compared to the standard usage rates.

Pearse Corporation established a standard variable overhead rate of $7.50 per direct labor hour. During July, 38,000 direct labor hours were worked and $266,000 of variable overhead costs were incurred. The actual variable overhead rate was $7 per hour.

$$\begin{aligned} \text{VOSV} &= [\$7.50 \times 38,000] - \$266,000 \\ &= \$285,000 - 266,000 \\ &= \underline{\underline{\$19,000}} \text{ Favorable} \end{aligned}$$

or

$$\text{VOSV} = \left(\$7.50 - \frac{266,000}{38,000}\right) \times 38,000$$

$$\begin{aligned} &= [\$7.50 - \$7.00] \times 38,000 \\ &= \$.50 \times 38,000 \\ &= \underline{\underline{\$19,000}} \text{ Favorable} \end{aligned}$$

VARIABLE OVERHEAD EFFICIENCY VARIANCE

Variable overhead cost is applied to output based on a standard variable overhead application rate which is expressed in terms of an activity index (often direct labor hours). Any difference between the activity index level actually experienced and the standard activity index level allowed for the output produced results in an efficiency variance.

This **variable overhead efficiency variance** is the difference between the amount of overhead that should have been applied to output according to standard cost specifications and the standard amount of overhead allowed at the actual activity index level. To isolate this efficiency variance from any spending variances, it is calculated at the standard variable overhead rate.

$$\begin{array}{l} \text{Variable Overhead} \\ \text{Efficiency Variance} \end{array} = \left(\begin{array}{c} \text{Standard Activity} \\ \text{Index Level} \\ \text{Required to Produce} \\ \text{Actual Output} \end{array} - \begin{array}{c} \text{Actual} \\ \text{Activity} \\ \text{Index} \\ \text{Level} \end{array} \right) \times \begin{array}{c} \text{Standard} \\ \text{Variable} \\ \text{Overhead} \\ \text{Rate} \end{array}$$

$$\boxed{\text{VOEV} = (\text{SH} - \text{AH}) \times \text{SVOR}}$$

This variance is caused by any deviation in the level of the activity index used in the variable overhead rate. Therefore, it is not purely an overhead efficiency variance, but reflects the variance in overheads that occurs due to efficiency or inefficiency in the usage of the input variable (direct labor hours) which serves as an activity index.

Pearse Corporation's variable overhead efficiency variance is the difference between the standard amount of overhead for the 36,000 hours that were allowed for the 18,000 units actually produced and the standard amount of overhead for the 38,000 hours that were actually worked.

$$\begin{aligned} \text{VOEV} &= [36,000 - 38,000] \times \$7.50 \\ &= -2,000 \times \$7.50 \\ &= \underline{\underline{(\$15,000)}} \text{ Unfavorable} \end{aligned}$$

FIXED OVERHEAD SPENDING VARIANCE

Total fixed costs are budgeted as a lump sum amount, regardless of activity levels. There are usually differences between the budgeted and actual totals for fixed overhead costs. The resulting **fixed overhead spending variance** reflects price differentials and composition changes in fixed overhead items. It is calculated as follows:

$$\text{Fixed Overhead Spending Variance} = \left(\begin{array}{ccc} \text{Total Budgeted} & & \text{Total Actual} \\ \text{Fixed} & - & \text{Fixed} \\ \text{Overhead} & & \text{Overhead} \end{array}\right)$$

$$FOSV = TBFO - TAFO$$

Notice that both actual and budgeted fixed overhead costs are expressed as total amounts, not as unit costs related to activity levels.

Pearse Corporation's annual budgeted fixed overhead cost is $2,400,000, so the monthly budgeted amount is $200,000. However, actual fixed overhead cost totaled $210,000 during July.

$$FOSV = [\$200,000 - \$210,000]$$
$$= (\$10,000) \text{ Unfavorable}$$

FIXED OVERHEAD VOLUME VARIANCE

The expected annual capacity level probably will be different from the level of capacity utilization needed to produce actual output according to the standard specifications. Therefore, applying standard fixed overheads to output can be expected to result in an overapplication or underapplication of fixed overhead costs.

The **fixed overhead volume variance** is the difference between standard fixed overhead cost applied to output at the standard activity index level and the total amount of budgeted fixed overhead cost. This variance can be calculated in two ways:

$$\begin{array}{c} \text{Fixed Overhead} \\ \text{Volume Variance} \end{array} = \left(\begin{array}{ccc} \text{Standard Fixed Overhead} & & \text{Total} \\ \text{Applied to Output at} & - & \text{Budgeted} \\ \text{Standard Activity} & & \text{Fixed} \\ \text{Index Level} & & \text{Overhead} \end{array}\right)$$

$$FOVV = (SFOA - TBFO)$$

or

$$\begin{matrix} \text{Fixed Overhead} \\ \text{Volume Variance} \end{matrix} = \begin{pmatrix} \begin{matrix} \text{Standard} \\ \text{Fixed} \\ \text{Overhead} \\ \text{Rate} \end{matrix} \times \begin{matrix} \text{Standard Activity} \\ \text{Index Required} \\ \text{for Actual} \\ \text{Output} \end{matrix} \end{pmatrix} - \begin{matrix} \text{Total} \\ \text{Budgeted} \\ \text{Fixed} \\ \text{Overhead} \end{matrix}$$

$$\text{FOVV} = (\text{SFOR} \times \text{SH}) - \text{TBFO}$$

The other variances are reasonably attributable to particular decision centers (materials price variance to purchasing, labor efficiency variance to production, and so on). But the fixed overhead volume variance may originate in any of several areas. It could be caused by an error in forecasting the capacity level used in setting the fixed overhead application rate. It might be due to production scheduling that caused more or less utilization of capacity than anticipated. Production problems could have caused idle capacity that contributed to this variance. In the extreme case, marketing operations could lead to an excess or lack of sales orders, which in turn affected production and the expected level of capacity utilization.

Pearse Corporation's standard fixed overhead application rate is $5 per direct labor hour; 36,000 hours were allowed for the 18,000 units actually produced. The total fixed overhead budgeted for July was $200,000.

$$\begin{aligned} \text{FOVV} &= [\$5 \times 36,000] - \$200,000 \\ &= \$180,000 - \$200,000 \\ &= (\$20,000) \text{ Unfavorable} \end{aligned}$$

COMBINED OVERHEAD SPENDING VARIANCE

Sometimes the actual overhead costs incurred cannot be separated into fixed and variable amounts. In such cases, only a **combined overhead spending variance** can be derived by comparing total budgeted and actual overhead costs.

$$\begin{matrix} \text{Combined Overhead} \\ \text{Spending Variance} \end{matrix} = \begin{pmatrix} \begin{matrix} \text{Total} \\ \text{Budgeted} \\ \text{Fixed} \\ \text{Overhead} \end{matrix} + \begin{matrix} \text{Standard Variable} \\ \text{Overhead Cost at} \\ \text{Actual Activity} \\ \text{Index Level} \end{matrix} \end{pmatrix} - \begin{matrix} \text{Total} \\ \text{Actual} \\ \text{Overhead} \\ \text{Incurred} \end{matrix}$$

$$\text{COSV} = [\text{TBFO} + (\text{SVOR} \times \text{AH})] - \text{TAO}$$

or

$$\begin{matrix} \text{Combined Overhead} \\ \text{Spending Variance} \end{matrix} = \begin{pmatrix} \begin{matrix} \text{Total Budgeted} \\ \text{Overhead Cost at} \\ \text{Actual Activity} \\ \text{Index Level} \end{matrix} - \begin{matrix} \text{Total} \\ \text{Actual} \\ \text{Overhead} \\ \text{Incurred} \end{matrix} \end{pmatrix}$$

$$\text{COSV} = \text{TBO} - \text{TAO}$$

Pearse Corporation's budgeted fixed overhead is $200,000 for July, its variable overhead application rate is $7.50 per direct labor hour, and 36,000 hours were allowed for the units actually produced. Actual fixed overhead cost was $210,000 and actual variable overhead cost was $266,000.

$$COSV = [\$200,000 + (\$7.50 \times 36,000)] - (\$210,000 + \$266,000)$$
$$= \$485,000 - \$476,000$$
$$= \underline{\underline{\$9,000}} \text{ Favorable}$$

or

$$COSV = [\$485,000 - \$476,000]$$
$$= \underline{\underline{\$9,000}} \text{ Favorable}$$

FIGURE 12-6

Pearse Corporation
Summary of Materials, Labor, and Overhead Variances

	Materials Price Variance $\left(\dfrac{\text{Standard}}{\text{Price}} - \dfrac{\text{Actual}}{\text{Price}}\right) \times \dfrac{\text{Actual}}{\text{Quantity}}$	*Materials Usage Variance* $\left(\dfrac{\text{Standard}}{\text{Quantity}} - \dfrac{\text{Actual}}{\text{Quantity}}\right) \times \dfrac{\text{Standard}}{\text{Price}}$
Direct Materials		
Material A	$(\$2.00 - \$2.05) \times 240,000$ $\underline{\underline{(\$12,000)}}$ Unfavorable	$(180,000 - 190,000) \times \$2.00$ $\underline{\underline{(\$20,000)}}$ Unfavorable
Material B	$(\$.50 - \$.45) \times 480,000$ $\underline{\underline{\$24,000}}$ Favorable	$(360,000 - 350,000) \times \$.50$ $\underline{\underline{\$5,000}}$ Favorable
	Labor Rate Variance $\left(\dfrac{\text{Standard}}{\text{Rate}} - \dfrac{\text{Actual}}{\text{Rate}}\right) \times \dfrac{\text{Actual}}{\text{Hours}}$	*Labor Efficiency Variance* $\left(\dfrac{\text{Standard}}{\text{Hours}} - \dfrac{\text{Actual}}{\text{Hours}}\right) \times \dfrac{\text{Standard}}{\text{Rate}}$
Direct Labor	$(\$10 - \$11) \times 38,000$ $\underline{\underline{(\$38,000)}}$ Unfavorable	$(36,000 - 38,000) \times \$10$ $\underline{\underline{(\$20,000)}}$ Unfavorable
	Variable Overhead Spending Variance $\left(\dfrac{\text{Standard Variable Overhead Rate}}{} - \dfrac{\text{Actual Variable Overhead Rate}}{}\right) \times \dfrac{\text{Actual}}{\text{Hours}}$	*Variable Overhead Efficiency Variance* $\left(\dfrac{\text{Standard}}{\text{Hours}} - \dfrac{\text{Actual}}{\text{Hours}}\right) \times \dfrac{\text{Standard Variable Overhead Rate}}{}$
Variable Overhead	$(\$7.50 - \$7.00) \times 38,000$ $\underline{\underline{\$19,000}}$ Favorable	$(36,000 - 38,000) \times \$7.50$ $\underline{\underline{(\$15,000)}}$ Unfavorable
	Fixed Overhead Spending Variance $\left(\dfrac{\text{Total Budgeted Fixed Overhead}}{} - \dfrac{\text{Total Budgeted Actual Overhead}}{}\right)$	*Fixed Overhead Volume Variance* $\left(\text{Standard Hours} \times \dfrac{\text{Standard Fixed Overhead Rate}}{} - \dfrac{\text{Total Budgeted Fixed Overhead}}{}\right)$
Fixed Overhead	$(200,000 - 210,000)$ $\underline{\underline{(\$10,000)}}$ Unfavorable	$(36,000 \times \$5) - 200,000$ $\underline{\underline{(\$20,000)}}$ Unfavorable

Here the fixed overhead spending variance, the variable overhead spending variance, and the variable overhead efficiency variance are combined and treated as a composite variance called the *overhead budget variance*. This permits a **two-way analysis** of overhead variances—so called because only the *overhead budget variance* and the *fixed overhead volume variance* are calculated. Two-way analysis is not featured in illustrations or problem assignments in this text; it is simply an aggregation of the more meaningful variances already presented.

SUMMARY OF MATERIALS, LABOR, AND OVERHEAD VARIANCES

Figure 12–6 (page 555) provides an overview of the eight basic cost variances discussed in this chapter. The dollar figures for variances are taken from the Pearse Corporation example. The materials price variance is calculated at the point of acquisition rather than at the point of usage.

JOURNAL ENTRIES FOR STANDARD COSTS

In an accounting system that uses standard costs, Raw Materials, Work in Process, and Finished Goods inventories are recorded at *standard cost.* As costs pass through these inventory accounts, variances between actual and standard costs are extracted, leaving only standard costs to be transferred to the next stage of processing.

For internal reporting purposes, variances removed from the inventory accounts can be treated as adjustments to current period operating expenses. These variances are usually charged or credited to Cost of Goods Sold.

The journal entries for Pearse Corporation are:

Materials Acquisition

Raw Materials Inventory—A	480,000	
Raw Materials Inventory—B	240,000	
Materials Price Variance—A	12,000	
Materials Price Variance—B		24,000
Accounts Payable		708,000

Purchased raw materials and calculated the materials price variance.

Materials Usage

Work in Process—Product S	540,000	
Materials Usage Variance—A	20,000	
Materials Usage Variance—B		5,000
Raw Materials Inventory—A		380,000
Raw Materials Inventory—B		175,000

Issued raw materials to Work in Process and calculated materials usage variance.

Labor Costs Incurred and Applied

Work in Process—Product S	360,000	
Labor Rate Variance	38,000	
Labor Efficiency Variance	20,000	
Wages Payable		418,000

Incurred labor costs, applied them to Work in Process, and calculated labor rate and labor efficiency variances.

Variable Overheads Incurred and Applied

Work in Process—Product S	270,000	
Variable Overhead Efficiency Variance	15,000	
Variable Overhead Spending Variance		19,000
Manufacturing Overhead Control		266,000

Incurred variable overhead costs, applied them to Work in Process, and calculated variable overhead spending and efficiency variances.

Fixed Overheads Incurred and Applied

Work in Process—Product S	180,000	
Fixed Overhead Spending Variance	10,000	
Fixed Overhead Volume Variance	20,000	
Manufacturing Overhead Control		210,000

Incurred fixed overhead costs, applied them to Work in Process, and calculated fixed overhead spending and volume variances.

Production Completed

Finished Goods Inventory	1,350,000	
Work in Process—Product S		1,350,000

Completed units were transferred from Work in Process to Finished Goods.

Sales at Retail and Cost

Accounts Receivable	2,160,000	
Sales		2,160,000

Sold 18,000 units at $120 per unit.

Cost of Goods Sold	1,350,000	
Finished Goods Inventory		1,350,000

Standard cost of 18,000 units sold was $75 per unit.

Variances Charged to Cost of Goods Sold

Cost of Goods Sold	87,000	
Materials Price Variance—B	24,000	
Materials Usage Variance—B	5,000	
Variable Overhead Spending Variance	19,000	
Materials Price Variance—A		12,000
Materials Usage Variance—A		20,000

FIGURE 12–7

Pearse Corporation
Income Statement
Month of July, 19X7

Sales (18,000 units @ $120)		$2,160,000
Less: Standard Cost of Goods Sold		
(18,000 units @ $75)		1,350,000
Standard Gross Profit (18,000 units @ $45)		$ 810,000
Less: Manufacturing Cost Variances		
Materials Price Variance	$ 12,000 F	
Materials Usage Variance	(15,000) U	
Labor Rate Variance	(38,000) U	
Labor Efficiency Variance	(20,000) U	
Variable Overhead Spending Variance	19,000 F	
Variable Overhead Efficiency Variance	(15,000) U	
Fixed Overhead Spending Variance	(10,000) U	
Fixed Overhead Volume Variance	(20,000) U	
Total Variances		(87,000)
Actual Gross Profit		$ 723,000
Less: Actual Marketing Expense.......................	$ 275,000	
Actual Administrative Expense	180,000	455,000
Net Income..		$ 268,000

Labor Rate Variance	38,000
Labor Efficiency Variance	20,000
Variable Overhead Efficiency Variance	15,000
Fixed Overhead Spending Variance	10,000
Fixed Overhead Volume Variance	20,000

July variances eliminated against Cost of Goods Sold.

In Figure 12–7, Pearse Corporation's July income statement shows the results of treating variances as adjustments to Cost of Goods Sold.

In Figure 12–7, total variances are ($87,000)—compared with ($91,000) in Figure 12–4—because the materials price variance is calculated at the point of *acquisition* (net materials variance, ($3,000) unfavorable). In the earlier income statement, the materials price variance was calculated at the point of *usage* (net materials variance, ($7,000) unfavorable). This accounts for the $4,000 differences in the amount of total variances and in net income.

FREQUENCY OF VARIANCE REPORTING

The frequency with which variances are measured and analyzed influences the planning and control effectiveness of a standard cost system. If operations are likely to be materially affected by performance deviations, it is critical that variances be reported promptly enough to allow remedial action to be taken.

Although variances theoretically could be measured for each output unit processed by every worker or machine, this would obviously be impractical and uneconomic. Some amount of aggregation is necessary; the problem lies in deciding how much.

Variances are commonly reported once a month. However, when a product's manufacturing cycle is relatively brief, weekly or even daily variance reports may be needed. Although the nature of each company situation will affect the timing of variance reports, the overriding requirement is that reporting periods be short enough so that managers can make effective, economical responses to variances. The time and cost of more frequent variance analysis must be balanced against the information loss that occurs when the period is longer, especially because of the tendency for individual variances to cancel one another out over that longer period.

STANDARD COSTS IN PUBLISHED FINANCIAL STATEMENTS

Standard costing may be used for external reporting so long as it produces results not materially different from those that would be obtained using actual costs. The AICPA's position is that "Standard costs are acceptable if adjusted at reasonable intervals to reflect current conditions so that at balance sheet date standard costs reasonably approximate costs computed under one of the recognized bases."[2]

The use of standard costs in published financial statements may necessitate (1) a dual system wherein both standard and actual costs are maintained or (2) a proration of variances among the Raw Materials, Work in Process, Finished Goods, and Cost of Goods Sold accounts. This latter method is similar to the proration of underapplied or overapplied overhead costs that was demonstrated in Chapter 3.

STANDARD COSTS IN A PROCESS COST SYSTEM

Some companies can use standard costs more effectively than others. If a firm's technology is fairly stable, and if the sequence and composition of production and other activities remains relatively constant over time, then standard costs will be easier to establish. Moreover, the use of those standards for control purposes will be strengthened because the basis for comparison will remain constant. Any manufacturer who uses a process cost system is a logical candidate to adopt standard costing. Homogenous output, continuous operations, identifiable activity centers, and production of items in a predetermined sequence are characteristic of both process costing and standard costing.

The use of standard costs in a process cost system requires that variances be calculated in relation to the *equivalent number of units produced* during a period for each component of cost. Process cost variances will be measured

[2] *A.R.B. 43.* Accounting Research and Terminology Bulletins, Final Edition (New York: AICPA, 1961), Chapter 4, page 30.

and analyzed as were the basic variances earlier in this chapter, except that there will probably be different equivalent units of output for materials, labor, and overhead.

Example: Knowles Company uses a standard process cost system. Inventory in process at the beginning of January, 19X9, was 2,000 units fully complete as to materials but only 50 percent complete as to labor and overhead. At the end of January, 4,000 units were on hand, 80 percent complete as to materials and 40 percent complete as to labor and overhead. During the month, 20,000 units were completed and transferred to finished goods inventory.

The first step in measuring process cost variances is to determine the number of equivalent units manufactured during January. The **production cost report,** which was used extensively in Chapters 5 and 6, provides a convenient way of making this calculation. Figure 12–8 summarizes the relevant information concerning units in process and percentages of completion.

After the column totals in the bottom half of the production cost report have been determined and transferred to the top half of the table, the missing numbers for equivalent units manufactured during January can be derived as the balancing figures in the columns for materials content and labor and overhead content as shown in Figure 12–9.

The key figures in this production cost report are the 21,200 equivalent units with respect to materials and the 20,600 equivalent units with respect to labor and overhead that were manufactured during January. Variances will be calculated on the basis of these equivalent outputs—not on the basis of the 20,000 units completed and transferred to finished goods. All inventories are recorded at the standard costs of their various inputs. Variances in each process are extracted and reported as the units move from one process to the next. A detailed illustration of standard costs in a process cost system appears at the end of this chapter (pages 564–70).

FIGURE 12–8

Knowles Company
Equivalent Units of Production
Month of January, 19X9

	Physical Units	Equivalent Units — Materials	Equivalent Units — Labor and Overhead
Units in Process—Beginning	2,000	2,000	1,000
Starts	22,000	N/A	N/A
Current Production—Equivalent Units			
Manufactured during January	N/A	?	?
Units Processed	24,000	?	?
Completions	20,000	20,000	20,000
Units in Process–Ending	4,000	3,200	1,600
Units Processed	24,000	?	?

FIGURE 12–9

Knowles Company
Equivalent Units of Production
Month of January, 19X9

	Physical Units	Equivalent Units	
		Materials	Labor and Overhead
Units in Process—Beginning	2,000	2,000	1,000
Starts	22,000	N/A	N/A
Current Production—Equivalent Units			
Manufactured during January	N/A	21,200	20,600
Units Processed	24,000	23,200	21,600
Completions	20,000	20,000	20,000
Units in Process—Ending	4,000	3,200	1,600
Units Processed	24,000	23,200	21,600

STANDARD COSTS IN JOB ORDER AND COMPOSITE COST SYSTEMS

Standard costs are harder to apply in a job order cost environment or in situations where hybrid cost systems are used. Practical problems in these situations include having to determine standards for nonrecurring, unique jobs and having to incur additional costs to reset standards each time a new job goes into production.

Yet even when a manufacturer's final output is not completely uniform, a type of standard costing may still be used. One way to accomplish this is to establish standard cost specifications for each job. This can be done by converting the job-cost estimating process, which is likely to accompany the placing of bids or the quoting of prices, into a process of establishing standard cost specifications. Depending on the frequency and uniqueness of the different jobs being produced, this could either be fairly manageable or time consuming and difficult.

Quite often physical components and manufacturing operations are common to much of a firm's output. This permits the use of composite costing systems—partly process and partly job order. Standard costs may be used in the process-oriented parts of the system and perhaps even in the job order-oriented parts. Modular standard cost systems are quite common. They involve the establishment of standard cost specifications for each standardized physical component or manufacturing operation. Total standard product costs for these standardized components and activities are obtained by adding the individual standard costs. Variances can then be calculated and analyzed for each separate standard component or process.

STANDARD COSTS IN VARIABLE COST SYSTEMS

The **variable cost model** is more compatible with standard costing than is the **full absorption cost model.** The variable cost model treats only variable costs (materials, labor, and variable overhead) as product costs. Inventory is measured in terms of standard variable costs and all fixed production costs are charged to expense as they are incurred. Cost variances for materials, labor, and variable overhead are calculated as they were earlier in this chapter. The standard sales price, minus the standard variable product cost, generates a standard contribution margin, which permits effective use of cost–volume–profit analysis.

The standard cost concept can be modified slightly to accommodate a different treatment of fixed overhead costs. If a *total* standard fixed overhead cost specification is established, a total fixed overhead spending variance can be identified and measured. This variance is the same as the fixed overhead spending variance in the full standard cost model. No other fixed overhead cost variances can be measured, because no activity level comparisons can be made as long as fixed overheads are not treated on a unit cost basis. This treatment of fixed overhead costs is essentially the same as that provided by a flexible budgeting approach.

STANDARD COSTS IN SERVICE DEPARTMENT COST REALLOCATIONS

Establishing cost standards improves both planning and control when service department costs are allocated to production departments. The departments using the services are charged for them at predetermined standard rates. Variances between these rates and actual service department costs can then be measured and analyzed. Cost efficiencies or inefficiencies in the service department are not passed on to the operating departments.

There remains the problem of choosing an activity index that reflects both the behavior of costs within the service department and the volume of services provided. An expected capacity utilization level may be used if the standard rate is to be a measure of full cost, including the fixed costs of the service department. Frequently used indexes include service hours, labor hours, area serviced, and power output.

Example: Carducci Company operates its own power plant.[3] Based on expected utilization of services for 19X7, the company has established a standard rate of $13.33 per kilowatt hour to charge production departments for electricity. This rate is based on annual budgeted power plant costs of $500,000 for fixed items and $300,000 for variable items, and on total expected user needs of 60,000 kilowatt hours. Forecast usage among three production departments is distributed as follows:

[3] See Chapter 11 for the same company situation using a flexible budgeting approach.

Department	Forecast Usage (Kilowatt Hours)
A	20,000
B	10,000
C	30,000
	60,000

$$\text{Standard Service Department Rate} = \frac{\$800,000}{60,000 \text{ Kilowatt Hours}} = \underline{\underline{\$13.33}} \text{ per KWH}$$

Actual power plant costs of $875,000 were incurred during 19X7, including $525,000 of fixed items and $350,000 of variable items. Actual electricity usage was 64,000 kilowatt hours. This usage, distributed among the three production departments, results in the allocation of power plant costs shown in Figure 12–10.

The variances between standard and actual power plant costs include materials, labor, and overhead spending and efficiency variances. In addition, due to the presence of a fixed element in the standard rate, an overhead volume variance can be calculated. The total variance of $21,667 should be analyzed with respect to power plant input prices and quantities, using either a flexible budgeting or full standard cost approach. Notice that the three production departments are insulated from power plant cost variances, because they are charged only for their *actual usage* of electricity at the predetermined *standard rate*.

Developing standard application rates for service department costs is recommended only when (1) the service department's output is homogenous and (2) the fixed cost element is not significant, or the expected activity level can be predicted with reasonable accuracy. If these conditions are not present, a flexible budgeting approach is more appropriate.

FIGURE 12–10

Carducci Company
Allocation of Power Plant Costs to
Production Departments
For the Year 19X7

Department	Power Usage (Kilowatt Hours)		Standard Rate		Allocated Cost
A	22,000	×	$13.33	=	$293,333
B	12,000	×	13.33	=	160,000
C	30,000	×	13.33	=	400,000
Total Allocated	64,000	×	$13.33	=	$853,333
Total Power Plant Cost Variances					21,667 U
Total Power Plant Cost Incurred					$875,000

STANDARD COSTING ILLUSTRATED: VASICEK POWDER COMPANY

Vasicek Powder Company uses standard product costs in its process costing system for manufacturing operations. The company's Milling Department developed standard specifications as shown in Figure 12–11. These specifications involve the production of flashless gunpowder to be used by other departments in manufacturing artillery shells.

Overhead is accounted for on a departmental basis. The Milling Department's annual capacity is 60,000 direct labor hours. The information shown in Figure 12–12 was obtained from the Department's records during August, 19X8.

FIGURE 12–11

Vasicek Powder Company
Standard Cost Specifications

Direct Materials (10 pounds @ $5 per pound)	$ 50
Direct Labor (4 hours @ $10 per hour)	40
Variable Overhead (4 hours @ $6 per hour)	24
Fixed Overhead (4 hours @ $3 per hour)	12
Total Standard Cost per Unit of Output	$126

FIGURE 12–12

Vasicek Powder Company
Operating Data
Month of August, 19X8

Beginning Inventories (August 1, 19X8)

Raw Materials	2,400 pounds
Work in Process	100 units
Materials	100% complete
Conversion Costs	40% complete

Transactions During August:

Raw Materials Purchased	14,000 pounds @ $4.75
Raw Materials Consumed	13,750 pounds
Direct Labor Payroll Costs	5,150 hours @ $10.50
Manufacturing Overhead Incurred	$48,200
Output Completed and Transferred	1,200 units

Ending Inventories (August 31, 19X8)

Work in Process	200 units
Materials	80% complete
Conversion Costs	75% complete

FIGURE 12-13

Vasicek Powder Company
Production Cost Report
Month of August, 19X8

	Physical Units	Equivalent Units		Standard Costs		
		Materials	Conversion	Materials	Conversion	Total
Beginning Balance	100	100	40	$ 5,000	$ 3,040	$ 8,040
Starts	1,300	N/A	N/A	N/A	N/A	N/A
Current Production	N/A	1,260	1,310	63,000	99,560	162,560
Units Processed	1,400	1,360	1,350	$68,000	$102,600	$170,600
Completions	1,200	1,200	1,200	$60,000*	$ 91,200*	$151,200
Ending Balance	200	160	150	8,000†	11,400†	19,400
Units Processed	1,400	1,360	1,350	$68,000	$102,600	$170,600

* Materials: 1,200 units @ $\dfrac{\$68,000}{1,360} = \$60,000$ † Materials: 160 units @ $\dfrac{\$68,000}{1,360} = \$8,000$

* Conversion: 1,200 units @ $\dfrac{\$102,600}{1,350} = \$91,200$ † Conversion: 150 units @ $\dfrac{\$102,600}{1,350} = \$11,400$

Using this data, the equivalent units and standard costs of materials and conversion costs (labor and overhead) can be calculated as shown in Figure 12–13.

MATERIALS AND LABOR VARIANCES

Based on the standard costs and equivalent units of output shown in Figure 12–14, the following materials and labor variances can be calculated:

1. Materials Price Variance
(at point of acquisition)

$$MPV = \left(\begin{matrix} \text{Standard} \\ \text{Price} \end{matrix} - \begin{matrix} \text{Actual} \\ \text{Price} \end{matrix} \right) \times \begin{matrix} \text{Actual Quantity} \\ \text{Purchased} \end{matrix}$$

$$MPV = (SP - AP) \times AQ$$

$$
\begin{aligned}
&= (\$5.00 - \$4.75) \times 14,000 \\
&= \$.25 \times 14,000 \\
&= \$3,500 \text{ Favorable}
\end{aligned}
$$

2. Materials Usage Variance
(based on production of 1,260 equivalent units completed with respect to raw materials inputs)

$$MUV = \left(\begin{matrix} \text{Standard} \\ \text{Quantity} \\ \text{Required} \end{matrix} - \begin{matrix} \text{Actual} \\ \text{Quantity} \\ \text{Used} \end{matrix} \right) \times \begin{matrix} \text{Standard} \\ \text{Price} \end{matrix}$$

$$MUV = (SQ - AQ) \times SP$$

$$
\begin{aligned}
&= (1,260 \times 10) - (13,750) \times \$5.00 \\
&= (12,600 - 13,750) \times \$5.00 \\
&= -1,150 \times \$5.00 \\
&= (\$5,750) \text{ Unfavorable}
\end{aligned}
$$

3. Labor Rate Variance

$$LRV = \left(\begin{matrix} \text{Standard} \\ \text{Rate} \end{matrix} - \begin{matrix} \text{Actual} \\ \text{Rate} \end{matrix} \right) \times \begin{matrix} \text{Actual Hours} \\ \text{Worked} \end{matrix}$$

$$LRV = (SR - AR) \times AH$$

$$
\begin{aligned}
&= (\$10.00 - \$10.50) \times 5,150 \\
&= -\$.50 \times 5,150 \\
&= (\$2,575) \text{ Unfavorable}
\end{aligned}
$$

4. Labor Efficiency Variance
(based on production of 1,310 equivalent units completed with respect to labor and conversion inputs)

$$LEV = \begin{pmatrix} \text{Standard Hours} \\ \text{Required} \end{pmatrix} - \begin{matrix} \text{Actual Hours} \\ \text{Worked} \end{matrix} \times \begin{matrix} \text{Standard} \\ \text{Rate} \end{matrix}$$

$$LEV = (SH - AH) \times SR$$

$$
\begin{aligned}
&= [(1,310 \times 4) - (5,150)] \times \$10.00 \\
&= (5,240 - 5,150) \times \$10.00 \\
&= 90 \times \$10.00 \\
&= \underline{\underline{\$900}} \text{ Favorable}
\end{aligned}
$$

OVERHEAD VARIANCES

For Vasicek Company, separate figures for actual fixed and variable overhead costs are not given—only the figures for *total* actual overheads. Therefore, only a *combined overhead spending variance* need be calculated, although the *variable overhead efficiency variance* and the *fixed overhead volume variance* can also be derived.

FIGURE 12–14

Vasicek Powder Company
Supporting Schedules of Standard Cost Calculations
Month of August, 19X8

Beginning Balances:			
Materials	100 units @ $50 × 100%		$ 5,000
Conversion	100 units @ $76 × 40%		3,040
			$ 8,040
Current Period Costs:			
Materials	1,260 units @ $50		$ 63,000
Labor	1,310 units @ $40	$52,400	
Variable Overhead	1,310 units @ $24	31,440	
Fixed Overhead	1,310 units @ $12	15,720	
Total Conversion Cost	1,310 units @ $76		99,560
			$162,560
Completed Units:			
Materials	1,200 units @ $50		$ 60,000
Conversion	1,200 units @ $76		91,200
Total	1,200 units @ $126		$151,200
Ending Balances:			
Materials	200 units @ $50 × 80%		$ 8,000
Conversion	200 units @ $76 × 75%		11,400
			$ 19,400

Before these variances are determined, the *total standard fixed overhead cost per month* must be derived, because it was not explicitly stated in the previous calculations. The standard fixed overhead rate is $3 per hour. At an expected annual capacity level of 60,000 direct labor hours, total standard fixed overhead cost is forecast at $180,000 per year or $15,000 per month. This monthly figure can now be used to compute the fixed overhead variance.

5. Combined Overhead Spending Variance

$$\text{COSV} = \left(\begin{array}{c} \text{Total} \\ \text{Budgeted} \\ \text{Fixed} \\ \text{Overhead} \end{array} + \begin{array}{c} \text{Standard Variable} \\ \text{Overhead Cost at} \\ \text{Actual Activity} \\ \text{Index Level} \end{array} \right) - \begin{array}{c} \text{Total} \\ \text{Actual} \\ \text{Overhead} \\ \text{Incurred} \end{array}$$

$$\text{COSV} = [\text{TBFO} + (\text{SVOR} \times \text{AH})] - \text{TAO}$$

$$
\begin{aligned}
&= [\$15,000 + (\$6.00 \times 5,150)] - \$48,200 \\
&= [\$15,000 + \$30,900] - \$48,200 \\
&= \$45,900 - \$48,200 \\
&= (\$2,300) \text{ Unfavorable}
\end{aligned}
$$

6. Variable Overhead Efficiency Variance

$$\text{VOEV} = \left(\begin{array}{c} \text{Standard Activity} \\ \text{Index Level} \\ \text{Required to Produce} \\ \text{Actual Output} \end{array} - \begin{array}{c} \text{Actual} \\ \text{Activity} \\ \text{Index} \\ \text{Level} \end{array} \right) \times \begin{array}{c} \text{Standard} \\ \text{Variable} \\ \text{Overhead} \\ \text{Rate} \end{array}$$

$$\text{VOEV} = (\text{SH} - \text{AH}) \times \text{SVOR}$$

$$
\begin{aligned}
&= (5,240 - 5,150) \times \$6.00 \\
&= 90 \times \$6.00 \\
&= \$540 \text{ Favorable}
\end{aligned}
$$

7. Fixed Overhead Volume Variance

$$\text{FOVV} = \left(\begin{array}{c} \text{Standard Fixed Overhead} \\ \text{Applied to Output at} \\ \text{Standard Activity} \\ \text{Index Level} \end{array} \times \begin{array}{c} \text{Total} \\ \text{Budgeted} \\ \text{Fixed} \\ \text{Overhead} \end{array} \right)$$

$$\text{FOVV} = (\text{SH} \times \text{SFOR}) - \text{TBFO}$$

$$
\begin{aligned}
&= (5,240 \times \$3.00 - \$15,000) \\
&= \$15,720 - \$15,000 \\
&= \$720 \text{ Favorable (Overapplied)}
\end{aligned}
$$

These seven variances are summarized in Figure 12–15.

FIGURE 12–15

Vasicek Powder Company
Summary of Variances
Month of August, 19X8

	Favorable	Unfavorable	Percent
Materials Price Variance	$3,500		+5%
Materials Usage Variance		$ 5,750	–9%
Labor Rate Variance		2,575	–5%
Labor Efficiency Variance	900		+2%
Combined Overhead Spending Variance		2,300	–5%
Variable Overhead Efficiency Variance	540		+1%
Fixed Overhead Volume Variance	720		+2%
	$5,660	$10,625	
Net Variance		($4,965) Unfavorable	

The following journal entries are made to record Raw Materials, Work in Process, and Finished Goods inventories at their standard costs and to eliminate August variances against Cost of Goods Sold.

Raw Materials Inventory (14,000 lbs. @ $5)	70,000	
Raw Materials Price Variance		3,500
Accounts Payable (14,000 lbs. @ $4.75)		66,500

Purchased raw materials and calculated the materials price variance.

Work in Process (12,600 lbs. @ $5)	63,000	
Raw Materials Usage Variance	5,750	
Raw Materials Inventory (13,750 lbs. @ $5)		68,750

Issued raw materials to Work in Process and calculated the materials usage variance.

Work in Process (5,240 hrs. @ $10)	52,400	
Labor Rate Variance	2,575	
Labor Efficiency Variance		900
Factory Wages Payable		54,075

Incurred direct labor costs, applied them to Work in Process, and calculated labor rate and labor efficiency variances.

Work in Process (5,240 hrs. @ $9)	47,160	
Overhead Spending Variance	2,300	
Variable Overhead Efficiency Variance		540
Fixed Overhead Volume Variance		720
Manufacturing Overhead		48,200

Incurred overhead costs, applied them to Work in Process, and calculated overhead spending, efficiency, and volume variances.

Finished Goods Inventory (12,000 @ $126)	151,200	
Work in Process		151,200
Completed units were transferred from Work in Process to Finished Goods.		

Materials Usage Variance	5,750	
Labor Rate Variance	2,575	
Combined Overhead Spending Variance	2,300	
Cost of Goods Sold		4,965
Materials Price Variance		3,500
Labor Efficiency Variance		900
Variable Overhead Efficiency Variance		540
Fixed Overhead Volume Variance		720
Eliminated August variances against Cost of Goods Sold.		

The general ledger accounts for Raw Materials and Work in Process appear as follows:

Raw Materials Inventory

Aug. 1	Balance (2,400 @ $5)	12,000	Aug. 31	Usage (13,750 @ $5)	68,750
31	Purchases (14,000 @ $5)	70,000	31	Balance (2,650 @ $5)	13,250
		82,000			82,000
Sept. 1	Balance (2,650 @ $5)	13,250			

Work in Process

Aug. 1	Balance			Aug. 31	Completions		
	Materials	5,000			(12,000 @ $126)		151,200
	Conversion	3,040	8,040	31	Balance		
31	Materials		63,000		Materials	8,000	
	Direct Labor		52,400		Conversion	11,400	19,400
	Overhead		47,160				
			170,600				170,600
Sept. 1	Balance		19,400				

SUMMARY

1. Standard costs are predetermined unit costs of the inputs required to produce an activity center's output.

2. Standards represent a level of desired operating efficiency and are used mainly in manufacturing departments that produce physical outputs. They may also be used for service outputs and in marketing and administrative areas in which activities are sufficiently homogenous.

3. Standard cost specifications detail the quantities of materials, labor, and overhead inputs allowed for each unit of output and the standard prices or rates at which those inputs should be acquired.

4. Direct materials, direct labor, and variable overhead costs are needed to calculate (1) price, rate, or spending variances, and (2) usage or efficiency variances.

5. Price, rate, or spending variances show deviations between actual and standard input prices or rates.

6. Usage or efficiency variances represent differences between the quantities of inputs actually used and the standard quantities allowed according to product cost specifications for the amount of output actually produced.

7. Fixed overhead cost is subject to a spending variance similar to that calculated for materials, labor, and variable overhead costs. However, there is no fixed overhead efficiency variance. Instead, a volume variance is calculated. This volume variance represents underapplied or overapplied fixed overhead and is the difference between fixed overhead applied to output at the standard rate and the total budgeted amount of fixed overhead cost.

8. The variance measurement system described in this chapter permits the isolation of eight types of deviations of actual cost performance from desired performance levels.
   a. Materials Price Variance
   b. Materials Usage (Quantity) Variance
   c. Labor Rate Variance
   d. Labor Efficiency Variance
   e. Variance Overhead Spending Variance
   f. Variable Overhead Efficiency Variance
   g. Fixed Overhead Spending Variance
   h. Fixed Overhead Volume Variance

9. Variances are isolated on a basis consistent with decision center organization, so that each variance reflects cost performance for which a particular manager is responsible.

10. To dispose of variances, they may be (1) absorbed into the Cost of Goods Sold figure, (2) reported as a separate expense or expense adjustment on the income statement, or (3) prorated over the Raw Materials, Work in Process, Finished Goods, or Cost of Goods Sold accounts.

11. Process costing situations are the most favorable for the use of standard cost procedures, although it is sometimes possible to use standard costs in a job order setting.

12. The frequency with which variances are measured and reported is of critical importance. Variance information should be made available promptly enough to permit effective use of the management by exception principle.

KEY WORDS AND PHRASES

Standard Cost (539)
Standard Cost Specification (540)
Activity Index (541)
Physical or Technological Capacity (541)
Ideal or Full Capacity (541)
Practical Capacity (541)
Normal Capacity (542)
Expected Annual Capacity (542)
Ideal or Theoretical Standards (542)
Currently Attainable Standards (542)
Tight or Loose Standards (542)
Variance (543)
Management by Exception (546)
Variance Analysis (547)
Materials Price Variance (547)
Favorable and Unfavorable Variances (548)
Materials Usage Variance (549)
Labor Rate Variance (550)
Labor Efficiency Variance (550)
Variable Overhead Spending Variance (551)
Variable Overhead Efficiency Variance (552)
Fixed Overhead Spending Variance (553)
Fixed Overhead Volume Variance (553)
Combined Overhead Spending Variance (554)
Two-Way Analysis (556)
Production Cost Report (560)
Variable Cost Model (562)
Full Absorption Cost Model (562)

Questions

1. What is a standard cost?
2. For what purposes can standard costs be used?
3. What is a standard cost specification?
4. What qualitative factors should be taken into account when setting standards?
5. Should the standard quantity of materials allowed for one unit of output be exactly equal to the amount physically present in and necessary for the production of each acceptable unit of output? Why or why not?
6. When the standard time to produce one unit of output is computed, what should it include?
7. Why is the selection of a capacity level so critical to the setting of a standard fixed overhead rate? What different capacity levels could be considered for this purpose?
8. Comment on the usefulness and limitations of standard costs.
9. How does a standard costing system complement the procedures of management by exception?
10. What are the potential motivational implications (both positive and negative) of a standard cost system?
11. Discuss the limitations of standard costing procedures.
12. "Measuring and reporting variances is a way of identifying the causes of inferior or superior cost performance." How does a standard cost system contribute to this concept?
13. What purposes are served by reporting several components of manufacturing cost variances, rather than just one single aggregate variance?
14. Why are the variable overhead spending variance and variable overhead efficiency variance not *pure* spending and efficiency variances?
15. Why is the fixed overhead volume variance the "odd man out" in the group of eight basic standard cost variances?
16. Compare the fixed overhead volume variance to the idea of underapplied or overapplied overhead as introduced in Chapter 3.
17. Are standard costs acceptable for use in published audited financial statements? Why or why not?
18. How frequently should cost variances be measured and reported?
19. Why are process costing and standard costing systems compatible?
20. Could standard costs be used in a job cost system?
21. Why is the use of standard costs more likely in a variable cost system than in a full absorption cost system?
22. Why might standard costs be useful for reallocating service department costs?

Exercises

E 12–1   Standard Cost Specifications—Materials, Labor, Variable Overhead

Production requirements for one batch of the main product manufactured by McQuaid Company are as follows:

> Input A: 300 gallons per batch
> Input B: 200 gallons per batch
> Mixing Time: 3 hours per batch
> Mixing Labor: 2 workers per batch
> Boiling Time: 4 hours per batch
> Boiling Labor: 4 workers per batch
> Output Yield: 400 gallons per batch
> Input A: $4 per gallon
> Input B: $2 per gallon
> Mixing Labor: $10 per hour
> Boiling Labor: $8 per hour
> Variable: Manufacturing Overhead: $12 per direct labor hour

Required:

(a)   Determine the total standard cost of one completed batch of output.

(b)   Express the listed amounts in the form of a detailed standard cost specification for one gallon of finished output.

E 12–2   Elementary Standard Cost Variance Analysis— Materials and Labor

Laloma Container Company makes boxes that require the following inputs:

> Materials: 10 square feet of cardboard at $0.25 per sq. ft.
> Direct Labor: 20 minutes per box at $9.00 per hour.

During April of 19X9, the following transactions took place:

> Output: 50,000 boxes completed
> Cardboard Purchased: 600,000 square feet for $144,000
> Cardboard Used: 520,000 square feet
> Labor Hours Worked: 16,500 hours for $156,750

Required:

(a)   Compute all materials and labor variances.

(b)   Briefly interpret each variance.

E 12–3   Standard Cost Variances—Variable Costing System

Johnbeth Company has set the following standard cost specifications for its products:

Materials (4 pounds @ $8)	$ 32
Direct Labor (4 hours @ $12)	48
Variable Overhead (4 hours @ $5)	20
	$100

These standards have usually been attained by production departments over the past year. In October, 19X6, the purchasing department contacted a new supplier of the basic material and acquired 20,000 pounds for $7 per pound on the understanding that similar quantities would be purchased in subsequent months.

Operating results for October were as follows:

Production Scheduled	4,000 units
Actual Output	3,500 units
Materials Used	18,500 pounds
Actual Labor (17,500 hours)	$210,000
Actual Overhead Incurred...........	$ 96,500

Required:

(a) Prepare an analysis of all variances.

(b) Comment on each variance individually. What pattern do you observe?

(c) Comment on the advisability of continuing to purchase from the new supplier.

E 12-4   Standard Cost Variances—Variable Costing System

Santana Corporation has established the following standard variable cost per unit for one of its product components:

Materials	$12
Direct Labor	48
Variable Overhead	24
	$84

During February of 19X1, operations were as follows:

Completed Units	2,000 units
Materials Purchased and Used	12,800 pounds
Cost of Materials.....................	$2.20 per pound
Labor Hours Worked	13,400 hours
Direct Labor Payroll Cost	$106,000
Variable Overhead Incurred	$45,700

The standard price of materials was $2 per pound. Overhead is applied on the basis of direct labor hours and the standard labor rate is $8 per hour.

Required:

(a) Prepare a detailed standard product cost specification for one unit of output.

(b) Compute all variances for materials, labor, and variable overhead.

(c) Interpret each variance. Comment on any interrelationships.

E 12-5   Overhead Variances—Elementary Analysis— Impact of Choice of Denominator Capacity

Cheever Corporation is considering an extension of its standard costing procedures to include analysis of fixed manufacturing overhead. For a typical month's operation, the following data were available:

Budgeted Activity Level	60,000 labor hours
Long Range Average Capacity Level	80,000 labor hours
Practical Capacity Level	100,000 labor hours
Budgeted Fixed Overhead	$480,000
Actual Fixed Overhead Incurred	$525,000
Actual Labor Hours Worked	75,000 hours
Standard Labor Hours Allowed for Actual Output	70,000 hours

Required:
(a) Compute the standard fixed overhead rate per labor hour, based on
    (1) budgeted activity level.
    (2) long-range average capacity level.
    (3) practical capacity level.
(b) Calculate the fixed overhead spending variances and fixed overhead volume variances for each of the three situations specified in part (a).
(c) Explain why some of your answers in part (b) are the same as those in part (a) and why some are different.

E 12–6   Comprehensive Standard Cost System—All Variances

Mackhewn Company uses a full standard product cost system. The results of operations for June of 19X2 are as follows:

(1) *Materials:* Purchased 260,000 pounds at an actual cost of $1,092,000. Usage was 196,000 pounds, but only 10 pounds per unit should have been used. Standard cost of materials per unit of output is $40.
(2) *Direct Labor:* Standard labor rate is $12 per hour, but the actual payroll for 80,000 hours amounted to $980,000. Standard cost of labor per unit of output is $48.
(3) *Overhead:* Standard overhead rates were set at the 100,000 labor hour capacity level. Total budgeted overhead for that level was $500,000. The standard variable overhead rate was $2 per direct labor hour. Actual total overhead costs were $475,000, of which $305,000 was for fixed items.
(4) *Output:* 19,000 units were completed in June.

Required:
(a) Prepare a detailed standard product cost specification.
(b) Compute all standard cost variances.
(c) Comment briefly on the meaning of each variance reported.

E 12–7   Full Standard Product Cost System— Comprehensive Variance Analysis

Renk Corporation produces one product with the following standard product costs per unit of output:

Raw Materials (6 pounds @ $1.50 per pound)	$ 9
Direct Labor (4 hours @ $7 per hour)	28
Variance Overhead (4 hours @ $1 per hour)	4
Fixed Overhead (4 hours @ $5 per hour)	5
	$61

Overhead rates were based on budgeted activities of 56,000 hours per month. During March of 19X3, the following activity was recorded:

Actual Output	14,000 units
Raw Material Purchases ($1.45 per pound)	100,000 pounds
Raw Materials Usage	88,000 pounds
Direct Labor Payroll (58,000 hours)	$402,500
Actual Factory Overhead Incurred	
Fixed	$285,000
Variable	$ 58,250

Required:

(a) Determine the amount of total budgeted fixed overhead.

(b) Compute all variances.

(c) Comment on the overhead variances.

E 12–8   Standard Cost Variance Analysis Review—Reconstruction from Partial Information

Compute all relevant missing items to complete the following table.

1. Standard Variable Product Cost
   - (a) Materials (6 pounds @ $_____ per pound) ..... $_____
   - (b) Direct Labor (_____ hours @ $8 per hour) ..... $ 32
   - (c) Variable Overhead ($6 per direct labor hour) .... $_____
2. Production .... 8,000 units
3. Materials Purchases (60,000 pounds) .... $ 345,000
4. Materials Usage (52,000 pounds @ standard price) .... $_____
5. Direct Labor (actual) (_____ hours) .... $ 236,800
6. Materials Price Variance (at purchase point)................. $ 15,000 F
7. Materials Quantity Variance..................... $_____
8. Direct Labor Rate Variance .... $ (12,800) U
9. Direct Labor Efficiency Variance .... $_____
10. Variable Overhead Spending Variance .... $ (4,800) U
11. Variable Overhead Efficiency Variance .... $_____
12. Actual Variable Overhead .... $_____
13. Materials Price Variance (at usage point) .... $_____

E 12–9   Standard Process Cost System—Equivalent Units— Variance Analysis

Handover Corporation uses a standard process costing system for the variable production costs of its product. Standard costs per unit of output have been established as follows:

Raw Materials (3 tons @ $40)	$120
Direct Labor (4 hours @ $10)	40
Variable Overhead (4 hours @ $4)	16
	$176

On July 1, 19X2, work in process included 2,000 units that were complete with regard to materials but only 50 percent complete as to conversion, which occurs at a uniform rate. During July, the following operating results were reported:

Materials Issued to Processing	12,000 tons
Actual Cost of Materials Issued	$42 ton
Direct Labor Hours Worked	19,500
Actual Variable Overhead	$74,750
Ending Work in Process—July 31	1,000 units
Materials (100% complete)	
Conversion (75% Complete)	
Output Completed and Transferred	
during July	5,000 units

Required:

(a) For July, what were the equivalent units of production with respect to:

   (1) materials?

   (2) conversion?

(b) Prepare a process costing production cost report for July. (For format, see Chapter 5.) *Use standard materials and conversion costs per equivalent unit of output.*

(c) Prepare an analysis of all variable cost variances. The variances should be based on the equivalent units of output *produced during the period* (assuming a FIFO cost flow).

E 12–10 Service Department Reallocation—Standard Cost System

Vernon Company uses standard cost procedures to allocate the costs of operating various factory service departments to its production departments for the purpose of establishing departmental standards.

Overhead Rates: One such service department, the power plant, has had the following standard costs established:

	Standard Cost per 100 Kilowatt Hours
Materials and Supplies	$10
Direct Labor	5
Overhead (All Fixed)	35
	$50

The overhead rate was established in anticipation of a 50,000 kilowatt hour demand by production departments in a typical month. All direct labor in the power plant should be paid at the standard rate of $10 per hour. Materials and supplies requirements are based on a standard amount of 10 gallons per 100 kilowatt hours of energy produced.

During August of 19X7, the power plant operated for 195 hours to provide the power required by production departments. The following costs were incurred in the power plant to generate a total of 40,000 kilowatt hours:

Materials (at $1.05 per gallon)	4,200 gallons	
Labor (195 hours)	$ 2,150	
Overhead	$18,500	

Required:

(a) Based on the predetermined standard rate, what total amount of power plant costs would be passed on to production departments for August?

(b) What will be the total cost variance for the power plant for August?

(c) Prepare an analysis of variances for the power plant for August, showing as much detail as possible.

(d) Comment on the appropriateness of using a standard cost system in this particular situation. Would you recommend an alternative procedure? Why or why not? Which alternatives would you consider?

Cases

C 12–1   Standard Cost Specifications

Wilson Company produces toy airplanes in batches of 100. The present standard variable costs per batch are as follows:

Materials	$20
Direct Labor	48
Variable Overhead	24
	$92

The production supervisor realizes that various changes will affect the standard costs for the coming year. These include:

(1) Material costs will be subject to a 10 percent price increase.

(2) Production workers have a contract calling for an increase in direct labor rates of 12½ percent plus extra fringe benefits equal to 5 percent of direct labor costs.

(3) Improved production methods should allow a reduction in labor hours per unit by one-sixth.

(4) Other variable overhead costs will increase by 50¢ per direct labor hour.

Required:
What will be the new standard cost specification for a 100-unit batch?

C 12–2   Cost Specifications for Planning and Control

Stern Corporation operates a production facility in which raw material X is processed into two intermediate products, Alpha and Iota. However, without further processing, these two products have no market value.

Each of the three processing operations has a separate manager. Every ton of material X, which should cost $800, requires 40 hours of processing labor and should yield 1,000 pounds of Alpha and 800 pounds of Iota, with the remainder a worthless waste product. Based on present levels of attainable performance, Alpha requires 20 hours of additional processing per 1,000 pound batch, and Iota requires 40 hours of additional processing per 800 pound batch. All processing labor costs $10 per hour. A factory-wide variable overhead rate of $6 per direct labor hour is in effect. Sales prices are $2 per pound for Alpha and $2.50 per pound for Iota.

Required:
(a) Calculate whatever standard cost specifications would be useful for cost planning and control.

(b) Discuss the issue of the standard cost of the intermediate products transferred out of the joint processing operation.

(c) Which variances could be calculated in the joint processing department?

C 12–3   Standard Cost Variances

"A very confusing situation surrounds the issue of standard cost variances. The managers who are responsible for such fixed costs as rent, insurance, supervisory salaries, and depreciation often spend too much on these items and thereby cause inefficient use of resources. However, there is no such thing as a fixed overhead efficiency variance. On the other hand, the production manager may cause an excessive number of direct labor hours to be worked, but there is no labor volume variance. Finally, as I have often observed, when supplies and indirect materials are used unnecessarily, they end up in the variable overhead *spending* variance."

Required:

Clarify the misstatements and misconceptions in the preceding passage.

C 12–4   Materials Price Variances

Alphonso Company isolates materials price variances at the time of purchase of each lot of raw materials. During the past two months, the purchasing manager has experienced two quite dissimilar cost variance situations. In June, her total materials price variance was $10,500 *unfavorable*. The manager observed that in that month she was required to make several special purchases to facilitate completion of rush orders that the Sales Department insisted on having expedited. She also recalls that production scheduling was late in processing some of its requisitions for materials. If she had known about these cases in time, she feels she could have purchased the materials in question at least two months in advance at considerable savings.

The following month, July, her materials price variance was $16,400 *favorable*. However, she has received complaints from production, where labor efficiency and variable overhead efficiency variances have shown up unfavorable after several successive months of favorable variances. During July, the purchasing manager made several very favorable purchases of materials from the liquidator of another firm that was going out of business.

Required:

Comment on the circumstances involved in each month's results. What problems are the firm's standard cost system encountering? Comment on the variances of the Purchasing Department in June and in July.

C 12–5   Labor Cost Variances

The production supervisor of Department X, one of four departments in ABC Manufacturing Company, is unhappy about his department's recent labor cost variances. He claims that the person responsible for scheduling work crews to the various departments is displaying favoritism to his friends in the other three departments and is assigning the least experienced and least efficient workers to Department X. The following data are available for a typical week's operations:

Department	Output (units)	Actual Labor	
		Hours	Cost
W	5,000	2,400	$24,500
X	5,200	2,900	27,500
Y	4,800	2,200	24,000
Z	6,000	2,700	58,500

The present standard cost specifications allow for a standard labor rate of $10 per hour and the production of two units per standard labor hour.

Required:
Comment on the claims of the production supervisor of Department X. Do you agree with his point of view? Why or why not? What appears to be the cause of the labor variances in that department? What variances are being experienced in the other three departments?

C 12–6   Overhead Spending Variances

The plant manager of Dowling Corporation was called to explain her apparent overspending on overhead during August of 19X4, when sales and production dropped unexpectedly. The overspending was indicated by the large unfavorable variance shown in the standard cost report presented below:

Plant Overhead—August, 19X4

	Budgeted (90,000 Labor Hours)	Actual (66,000 Labor Hours)	Variance (24,000) U
Total Plant Overhead	$270,000	$240,000	$30,000 F
Total Overhead Applied	$270,000	$198,000	($72,000) U
	$ 0	$ 42,000	($42,000) U

The plant manager has determined that there was no variation between the number of labor hours worked and the standard hours allowed for actual output. The budgeted monthly amounts of overhead have not changed since January, when the standard overhead application rate was set for the year. She does recall some discussion of how the standard overhead rate would be $4 per hour if the total annual level of production were to be reduced to 720,000 labor hours.

Required:
(a) Revise the information in the preceding cost report to produce a more useful format.
(b) Prepare an analysis of variances to support or refute the contention that the $42,000 is an indication of overspending.
(c) What misstatements or misrepresentations were made in the original analysis?
(d) Who is responsible for incurring the variances reported in part (b)?

C 12–7   Labor and Overhead Variance Analysis—Full Standard Cost System

The Assembly Department supervisor of Esco Manufacturing Company prepared the following summary report on his department's activity in June:

	Budget	Actual	Variances
Direct Labor	$ 7,920	$ 8,050	($130) U
Departmental Overhead	11,520	11,895	(375) U
	$19,440	$19,945	($505) U

He took the report to his friend in the Controller's Department and said, "Gee, I hadn't thought I had done so badly last month!" His friend volunteered to check it out for him. The following *budget specifications* were available to the Controller's Assistant:

Labor time: 2 hours per product unit
Labor rate: $2.20 per hour
Overhead rate: $3.20 per labor hour
Normal (long-run average) capacity: 2,000 product units
Overhead budget at normal capacity:

Fixed	$ 4,800
Variable	8,000
	$12,800

Output: 1,750 units
Hours worked: 3,600
Overhead costs incurred:

Fixed	$ 4,750
Variable	7,145
	$11,895

Required:
As the Controller's Assistant, analyze the specifications, compute all relevant variances, and give an appraisal of the supervisor's claim that he hadn't done as badly as the figures indicated.

Problems

P 12–1   Determination of Standard Product Cost Specifications—Materials, Labor, and Variable Overhead

Anderson Metal Stamping Company produces various electrical appliance components from large sections of sheet metal. One particular product, which comes in two sizes, is presently made from sheets measuring 8 feet by 2 feet, weighing 8 pounds and costing $16 each. From each sheet, 25 large products, weighing a total of 7 pounds, or 40 small products, weighing a total of 7.2 pounds, can be fabricated. The remaining scrap metal can be sold for $2 per pound.

Cutting time is 1.2 minutes for a large product and 1 minute for a small product. Polishing and finishing require additional labor, with output rates averaging 100 large or 125 small products per hour. Labor rates are $10 per hour in the Cutting Department and $12 per hour in the Finishing Department. Departmental overhead rates are 150 and 80 percent of direct labor cost in the cutting and finishing departments respectively.

Required:

(a) Determine the total standard cost for a batch of:
(1) 1,000 small products.
(2) 1,000 large products.

(b) Express this information in the form of a detailed standard cost specification for each of the two products.

(c) The purchasing manager has proposed switching to sheets of metal that are twice the size and weight of those presently used. This will allow either 80 small or 60 large products to be produced, with scrap of 1.5 pounds and 1 pound respectively. The larger sheets cost $35 each. Labor processing times would be unaffected. What will be the effect of using the larger sheets on the cost of a batch of 1,000 of either size products? Should the larger sheets be used?

P 12-2   Standard Cost Variances—Elementary Analysis— Materials and Direct Labor

McCullough Company has established the following standard product cost specifications for one of its products:

> Materials: 2 pieces @ $36 per piece
> Direct Labor A: 4 hours @ $10 per hour
> Direct Labor B: 2 hours @ $12 per hour

The following production data were obtained for April of 19X3:

> Completed Units: 1,000
> Materials Purchased: 6,000 pieces @ $35 per piece
> Direct Labor A: 3,500 hours @ $10.50 per hour
> Direct Labor B: 2,200 hours @ $12 per hour
> Materials Used: 1,950 pieces

Required:

(a) Compute all labor and materials variances.
(b) Give a brief explanation of each variance.

P 12-3   Standard Cost Variance Analysis—Materials and Labor

Cleary Company employs a standard cost system. Details for one of its products are as follows for May of 19X0:

(1) Budgeted Output: 25,000 Units
(2) Standard Cost per Unit of Output:

Material P:	$24
Material Q:	15
Direct Labor:	21
	$60

(3) Actual Output: 20,000 units

(4) Materials Purchased:
     P: 40,000 pounds @ $25.00 per pound
     Q: 5,000 gallons @ $80 per gallon

(5) Materials Used:
     P: 21,000 pounds
     Q: 3,900 gallons

(6) Labor Hours Worked: 38,000
     Actual Labor Cost: $427,500

(7) One unit of output requires one pound of material P, one fifth of a gallon of material Q, and two hours of direct labor.

Required:

(a) Prepare a revised statement of product cost specifications, using actual performance to set new standards.

(b) Prepare an analysis of the details of production activities for May to determine all labor and materials variances from the initial standard costs.

(c) Comment on possible reasons for each variance.

P 12–4 Standard Cost Variances—Machine Hour Basis for Labor and Overhead—Variable Costing System

Weiner Corporation operates a highly automated plant in which the wages of all production employees are treated as indirect labor costs and included in manufacturing overhead. Each unit of output requires 20 pounds of raw material at a standard input price of $6 per pound. Processing time includes 40 minutes of machine utilization per unit. Indirect labor costs $12 per machine hour. Other overhead items account for $18 per machine hour.

During July, 19X5, 30,000 units were produced. Material purchases amounted to 750,000 pounds at a total cost of $4,800,000; 640,000 pounds were used during the month. Total indirect labor cost $320,000, while other variable overhead costs were $127,500. During the period, 22,000 machine hours were used.

Required:

(a) Prepare a standard product cost specification.

(b) Calculate all variances for materials and variable overhead.

(c) Comment on the results of part (b).

(d) Comment on the appropriateness of treating all labor costs as part of manufacturing overhead. What additional information would be helpful in this case?

P 12–5 Variable Cost System—Standard Cost Variances— Unit Based Information

Freestone Company manufactures one product for which the following standard costs per unit have been established:

Materials (20 pounds @ $10 per pound)	$200
Direct Labor (30 hours @ $8 per hour)	240
Variable Overhead (30 hours @ $2 per hour) . . .	60
	$500

For January of 19X5, the following unit costs and variances were determined on the basis of 5,000 units actually produced:

	Actual Cost per Unit	Variance per Unit
Materials	$235	($35) U
Direct Labor	220	(20) F
Variable Overhead	75	15 U
	$530	($30) U

The following additional information is available:

(1) In January, materials cost $10.25 per pound; all materials purchased were used during the month.

(2) Labor rates in January were 20¢ per hour above the established standard rate.

(3) Inputs of variable overhead are based on labor hours.

Required:

(a) Prepare an analysis of all variances, showing as much detail as possible.

(b) Develop a revised schedule for the actual results of January operations, showing total quantities and input prices rather than the actual cost per unit of output.

(c) Comment on any inadequacies in the presentation of the original operating performance data.

P 12–6   Overhead Variances—Analysis of Standard Cost Variances

The following factory overhead report was prepared for one of the manufacturing departments of Kelly Company for February of 19X8:

	Actual	Budgeted
Total Departmental Overhead	$135,000	$135,000

The department manager felt very much reassured by the report, especially the part that indicated that the overall variance was exactly zero. However, he later obtained the following additional information:

> Standard Hours per Unit: 2
> Standard Variable Overhead Rate: $5 per Hour
> Budgeted Fixed Overhead: $90,000
> Actual Variable Overhead: $32,500
> Actual Labor Hours: 6,000
> Units Produced: 2,800

Required:

(a) Do you share the manager's feelings about the original report? Why or why not?

(b) Prepare a detailed analysis of standard overhead cost variances for the month.

(c) Comment on the additional information contained in your answer to part (b). Why do your variances in part (b) differ from those in part (a)?

P 12–7   Overhead Analysis—Standard Cost System—Effects of Choice of Denominator Capacity

Clarke Company has been using a standard costing system with a combined standard overhead application rate equal to 125 percent of standard direct labor cost. This rate was based on the following forecast data for a typical year's activities:

> Direct Labor Hours: 144,000
> Direct Labor Cost: $1,440,000
> Manufacturing Overhead:
>   Fixed $ 600,000
>   Variable   1,200,000
> $1,800,000

In February of 19X7, following a similar experience in January, significant overhead variances are experienced as a result of this procedure. February results are summarized below:

> Actual Manufacturing Overhead:
>   Fixed $ 47,500
>   Variable   134,500
> $182,000
>
> Actual Direct Labor Hours: 16,000
> Standard Direct Labor Cost: $174,000
> Standard Overhead Applied: $217,500
> Total Overhead Variance: $35,500 Favorable

Management is puzzled by the *favorable* overhead variance, despite the fact that in January and February actual overhead costs, labor hours, and labor costs exceeded the budgeted monthly averages. All wages were paid at the standard hourly rate.

Required:
(a) Prepare an analysis of the $35,500 favorable total overhead variance, showing as much detail as possible.
(b) Comment on the situation in the light of your answer to part (a).
(c) If the same situation were to continue in subsequent months, what would you recommend be done? What extra information do you feel would be helpful in this case?

P 12–8   Comprehensive Standard Cost System—All Variances

Caldwell Company's product requires five direct labor hours to complete. The standard hourly wage rate is $12.50 per hour. Each unit of output also requires six yards of material at a standard price of $9 per yard. The flexible budget for overhead based on standard direct labor hours showed the following information:

	Standard Direct Labor Hours		
	40,000	60,000	80,000
Variable Cost Items......	$200,000	$ 300,000	$ 400,000
Fixed Cost Items	400,000	400,000	400,000
Mixed Cost Items	300,000	400,000	500,000
Total Overhead	$900,000	$1,100,000	$1,300,000

During September of 19X2, the following production and cost information was reported:

Units Produced................................	14,000
Materials Purchased	100,000 yards @ $8.50
Materials Usage	90,000 yards
Direct Labor Hours	75,000
Direct Labor Cost..........................	$985,000
Actual Overhead Cost	
(including $550,000 fixed overhead)......	$1,250,000

Required:

(a) Compute the standard overhead rate, showing variable and fixed components separately, based on a denominator capacity of:
   (1) 40,000 hours.
   (2) 60,000 hours.
   (3) 80,000 hours.

(b) For the 60,000 hour basis of part (a), compute all standard cost variances.

(c) Recompute all *overhead* variances based on the rates found in parts (a-1) and (a-3).

(d) Comment on the answers in parts (b) and (c) with regard to:
   (1) variable overhead efficiency variances.
   (2) fixed overhead volume variances.
   (3) combined overhead spending variances.

P 12-9 Comprehensive Standard Cost Variance Analysis— Unit and Total Basis

The Milling Department manager of Jolly Miller Flour Company is confused by the following monthly cost report prepared for his department for June, 19X2:

	Costs per Ton of Output		
	Standard	**Actual**	**Variance**
Materials	$ 30.00	$ 29.90	$0.10 F
Direct Labor......	36.00	34.55	1.45 F
Overhead	48.00	54.00	(6.00) U
	$114.00	$118.45	($4.45) U

The manager claims that the report does not adequately reflect what occurred in his department that month. His own records indicate that there were substantial savings in terms of both raw materials inputs processed and total direct labor hours worked.

Further analysis produces the following facts: Budgeted production for the month (consistent with the basis used to set overhead rates) was 12,000 tons. However, only 10,000 tons were produced. Materials totaling 15,000 tons were purchased at $26 per ton. Standard usage was set at 1.2 tons of input per output ton, but the department achieved a yield rate of one output ton for each 1.15 tons of input.

Standards called for three direct labor hours per ton of output. Departmental records show that 2,000 less hours were worked in June than were allowed under the established standards.

Finally, total actual fixed overhead costs were exactly as had been budgeted—$360,000. Variable overhead efficiencies and inefficiencies are assumed to be directly correlated with labor efficiencies and inefficiencies.

Required:
(a) Prepare a detailed standard product cost specification.
(b) Determine all relevant total quantities of inputs purchased and used, actual total input quantity costs, and actual input unit costs.
(c) Prepare a detailed analysis of all standard cost variances.
(d) Do you agree with the manager's complaint? Why or why not?
(e) Comment on the inadequacies of the original report for control purposes.

P 12–10   Standard Product Costs—Multiple Outputs— Analysis of Product Line Variances

A division of Heinen Company is responsible for manufacturing two products, Alpha and Gamma. Standard direct labor times are 30 minutes for one unit of Alpha and 20 minutes for one unit of Gamma. Expected activity level in a normal year is 600,000 direct labor hours. At this activity level, budgeted overhead is $5,400,000, of which $3,600,000 is for fixed items. The standard hourly labor rate is $8. Both products use the same raw material, which has a standard price of $2 per pound. Alpha and Gamma require five and three pounds per unit of this ingredient respectively. For September of 19X2, the following cost and operating data were reported:

	Alpha	Gamma
Units Produced	50,000	50,000
Direct Labor Hours		
(48,500 hours @ $8.25)	29,000	19,500
Materials Used (pounds)	260,000	135,000
Actual Overhead Incurred:		
Fixed	$265,000	
Variable	$232,500	

Required:
(a) Prepare standard product cost specifications for each product.
(b) Prepare an analysis of all standard cost variances, separating the variances for the two products wherever possible.
(c) Comment on the variances determined in part (b).

P 12–11   Full Standard Product Cost System—Comprehensive Variance Analysis—Multiple Inputs and Outputs

Carlone Company has established the following standard product cost specifications for the two products, deluxe and regular, that it produces at its Sierraville plant:

	Standard Price	Standard Quantity	
		Deluxe	Regular
Material A	$ 2.40 per pound	24 pounds	24 pounds
Material B	$ 5.20 per gallon	16 gallons	12 gallons
Direct Labor......	$10.50 per hour	4 hours	3 hours

The standard overhead rates are $4 per hour for variable items and $2 per hour for fixed items. These rates were established on the basis of a budgeted annual activity level of 600,000 hours.

During August of 19X4, the following operating results were reported:

Output:
  Deluxe 5,000 units
  Regular 12,000 units

Raw Materials:	A	B
Purchases	500,000 pounds	250,000 gallons
Purchase Price	$2.50	$5.00
Usage......................	400,000 pounds	235,000 gallons
Deluxe	100,000 pounds	100,000 gallons
Regular	300,000 pounds	135,000 gallons

Direct Labor:
  Deluxe 18,500 hours
  Regular 38,500 hours
  Direct Labor Cost $627,000
  Total Overhead Incurred:
    Fixed: $110,000
    Variable: $235,000

Required:

(a) Prepare standard cost specifications for each product.

(b) Prepare a complete analysis of all standard cost variances, separating the variances for each product whenever possible.

(c) Comment on the various situations reflected in the variances reported in part (b).

P 12–12   Standard Variable Cost System—Reconstruction of Variance Analysis

Tunney Company uses a standard variable cost system. The overhead rate is based on direct labor hours.

Required:

(a) Complete the table below by computing the values of all relevant missing items.

1. Production	_____ units
2. Actual Direct Labor Cost.....................	$184,000
3. Actual Materials Used	6,400 pounds
4. Actual Variable Overhead Incurred	$ 96,000
5. Standard Labor Cost per Unit	$_____
6. Standard Materials Cost per Unit	$ 18
7. Standard Variable Overhead Cost per Unit	$_____
8. Materials Purchased (8,400 pounds)	$ 27,200
9. Material Price Variance (at purchase point)......	$ (2,000) U
10. Material Quantity Variance	$_____
11. Labor Rate Variance	$ (16,000) U
12. Labor Efficiency Variance	$ (8,000) U
13. Variable Overhead Spending Variance	$_____
14. Variable Overhead Efficiency Variance	$_____
15. Direct Labor Hours Worked	42,000 hours

16. Standard Labor Rate .... $_____ per hour
17. Standard Direct Labor Hours per Unit .... 40 hours
18. Standard Variable Overhead Rate .... $ 2.30 per hour
19. Materials Price Variance (at usage point) .... $_____

P 12–13 Full Standard Product Cost System—Reconstruction of Variance Analysis

Complete the tables below for two independent companies. Each company uses a full standard cost system, with overhead based on direct labor hours.

		Company X	Company Y
1.	Total Overhead Variance (fixed and variable)	$_____	$_____
2.	Standard Fixed Overhead Rate (per hour)	$_____	$_____
3.	Standard Variable Overhead Rate (per hour)...........	$_____	$ 1.70
4.	Fixed Overhead Volume Variance	$ 4,000 F	$_____
5.	Fixed Overhead Spending Variance	$_____	$ (5,000) U
6.	Variable Overhead Efficiency Variance...............	$ (2,100) U	$ 2,040 F
7.	Variable Overhead Spending Variance	$_____	$_____
8.	Total Standard Fixed Overhead Applied	$ 84,000	$_____
9.	Total Standard Variable Overhead Applied	$_____	$46,920
10.	Actual Fixed Overhead	$ 81,000	$96,000
11.	Actual Variable Overhead	$ 32,000	$51,840
12.	Total Budgeted Fixed Overhead	$_____	$_____
13.	Actual Hours Worked	11,200	_____
14.	Standard Hours Allowed	10,500	_____
15.	Denominator (budgeted) Hours	_____	13,000
16.	Actual Labor Cost.................................	$114,800	$_____
17.	Materials Usage (pounds)	20,000	_____
18.	Standard Material Price (per pound)	$ 2	$ 5
19.	Materials Required per Unit (pounds)	5	5
20.	Material Price Variance (at usage point)	$ (2,000) U	$_____
21.	Material Quantity Variance	$_____	$ (4,500) U
22.	Labor Rate Variance	$_____	($13,200) U
23.	Labor Efficiency Variance	$_____	$ 6,000 F
24.	Standard Labor Rate (per hour)....................	$ 10	$_____
25.	Units Produced	3,500	_____
26.	Standard Labor Hour (per unit)	_____	4
27.	Actual Materials Cost (per pound)..................	$_____	$ 5.50

P 12–14 Full Standard Process Costing System— Variance Analysis

Schlesinger Corporation uses a standard process costing system for all of its manufacturing departments. The following process cost specifications have been established for one of these departments:

	Standard Cost per Unit
Direct Material	
(4 pounds @ $3 per pound)	$12
Direct Labor	
(2 hours @ $12 per hour)	24
Variable Overhead	4
Fixed Overhead.....................	6
	$46

Overhead costs are applied on the basis of standard direct labor hours. The fixed over-head rate was set in expectation of an annual capacity level of 800,000 standard direct labor hours. All materials are added at the start of processing, but conversion occurs continuously and uniformly. The following cost and operating data were reported for January of 19X2:

(1)	Inventories:	**January 1**	**January 31**
	Raw Materials	50,000 pounds	60,000 pounds
	Work in Process	10,000 units	20,000 units
	Percent Processed	60%	60%
	Finished Goods	10,000 units	15,000 units

(2) Sales: 20,000 units
(3) Raw Materials Purchases: 155,000 pounds @ $3.10 per pound
(4) Direct Labor Costs: 70,000 hours @ $12.50 per hour
(5) Actual Overhead Incurred:
     Variable $140,000
     Fixed 205,000

Required:

(a) For January, what were the equivalent units of production with respect to:
   (1) materials?
   (2) conversion?

(b) Prepare a process cost production report for January. (See Chapter 5 for details of format.) Use standard costs per equivalent unit in all sections of the report.

(c) Prepare an analysis of all cost variances based on the standard cost of equivalent units of production for the month as calculated in part (a).

P 12–15   Full Standard Process Cost System—Comprehensive Review

Morro Company uses a standard processing cost system. Product specifications for processing costs in the Mixing Department are as follows:

Item	**Quantity**	**Standard Price**
Material X	10 gallons per unit	$ 2 per gallon
Material Y	20 pounds per unit	$ 1 per pound
Direct Labor......	4 hours per unit	$10 per hour
Overhead	4 hours per unit	$ 6 per hour

Material X is added at the start of processing in the Mixing Department, but Material Y is not added until processing is half completed. Labor and overhead costs are incurred at a continuous and uniform rate throughout the processing operation. The overhead rate included $2 per hour for variable items. The activity level used for setting the fixed overhead rate was 1,200,000 hours per year. Production operations for October of 19X4 were as follows:

(1) Work in Process (October 1, 19X4)
    20,000 units
    40 percent complete
(2) Materials Purchased
    X (150,000 gallons @ $2.15 per gallon)
    Y (500,000 pounds @ $1.10 per pound)

    (3) Materials Used
          X (135,000 gallons)
          Y (605,000 pounds)
    (4) Direct Labor Cost
          90,000 hours — $875,000
    (5) Actual Overhead Incurred
          Variable $175,000
          Fixed $420,000
    (6) Units Completed and Transferred
          Out of Mixing Department 22,500
    (7) Work in Process (October 31, 19X4)
          10,000 units
          75 percent complete

Required:

(a) For October, what were the equivalent units of production with respect to:
    (1) material X?
    (2) material Y?
    (3) conversion?

(b) Prepare a process cost production report for October of 19X4. (See Chapter 5 for detail and format.) Use standard cost per equivalent unit produced in all calculations.

(c) Compute all cost variances for the month of October, basing the analysis on the standard cost of equivalent units of production with respect to each cost category.

P 12–16   Service Department Reallocations—Standard Cost System

Exacto Company maintains a standard cost system for allocating the costs of its service departments to its production departments. For December of 19X3, the following information was collected regarding the activities of one service department, the cafeteria, which provides free meals to all production line workers under the terms of the most recent contract agreement with employees.

	Production Departments		
	A	B	C
Meals Served—December	10,000	15,000	25,000
Budgeted Meals			
Required Annually	180,000	240,000	300,000

	Factory Cafeteria Costs:	
	December Actual	Annual Budget
Foodstuffs, Supplies	$72,500	$1.50 per meal
Direct Labor	$28,500	$ .50 per meal
Overhead: Variable	$26,500	$ .50 per meal
Fixed	$62,500	$720,000

Standard costs per meal were based on the annual budget for:

(1) cafeteria costs.
(2) meal requirements of the three production departments.

Required:

(a) Prepare a full standard cost specification for the unit output—one meal—of the cafeteria.

(b) Explain the potential usefulness of the standard cost of a meal for:
    (1) the factory cafeteria.
    (2) the production departments, from the points of view of both planning and control.

(c) What will be the total amount of cafeteria costs allocated to the three production departments for December, based on the standard costs calculated in part (a)?

(d) Prepare an analysis of cost variances for the cafeteria for December. Why can the analysis not provide all of the *eight* variances usually associated with a standard cost system?

(e) Comment on the limitations of standard costs for a situation such as this.

13

SALES VARIANCES, COMPLEX PRODUCTION VARIANCES, AND VARIANCE ANALYSIS AND INVESTIGATION

LEARNING OBJECTIVES

After studying Chapter 13, you should be able to:

1. Calculate the following sales-related variances:
   a. Sales price variance
   b. Sales quantity variance (contribution margin basis)
   c. Sales quantity variance (revenue basis)
   d. Sales mix variance
2. Calculate the following complex production-related variances:
   a. Total labor efficiency variance
   b. Materials-related labor efficiency variance
   c. "Pure" labor efficiency variance
   d. Materials price variance for multiple inputs
   e. Input yield variance for multiple inputs
   f. Input mix variance for multiple inputs
3. Describe typical causes of each of the eight basic variances demonstrated in Chapter 12.
4. Distinguish between random and nonrandom variances and describe the type of events that cause nonrandom variances.
5. Construct a control chart and distinguish random from nonrandom variances using sample observations of cost performance.

Eight basic standard cost variances were introduced in Chapter 12. These variances provide planning and control information that helps managers to evaluate particular areas of cost performance—materials acquisition and usage, wage rates and labor productivity, overhead spending and efficiency, and capacity utilization.

This chapter extends the scope of variance measurement through an examination of sales variances and complex cost variances. Whereas Chapters 11 and 12 dealt entirely with single outputs, this chapter explains how variances for multiple output situations are derived, examines the possible causes of the variances calculated in Chapters 12 and 13, and discusses how variances are selected for investigation and possible corrective action.

SALES-RELATED VARIANCES

SINGLE PRODUCT SITUATIONS

Variance analysis can be applied to measures of sales performance. An elementary example appeared in Chapter 11, where sales variances relating to flexible budgeting were introduced. Both **sales price** and **sales quantity** variances can be calculated for sales of individual products. A **sales price variance** measures the effect on total profit of changes in unit sales prices.

$$\text{Sales Price Variance} = \left(\begin{array}{c} \text{Actual} \\ \text{Unit} \\ \text{Sales} \\ \text{Price} \end{array} - \begin{array}{c} \text{Budgeted} \\ \text{Unit} \\ \text{Sales} \\ \text{Price} \end{array} \right) \times \begin{array}{c} \text{Actual} \\ \text{Sales} \\ \text{Quantity} \end{array}$$

A **sales quantity variance** measures the effect on total profit of variations between actual and budgeted sales volume.

$$\text{Sales Quantity Variance} = \left(\begin{array}{c} \text{Actual} \\ \text{Sales} \\ \text{Quantity} \end{array} - \begin{array}{c} \text{Budgeted} \\ \text{Sales} \\ \text{Quantity} \end{array} \right) \times \begin{array}{c} \text{Standard} \\ \text{Contribution} \\ \text{Margin} \\ \text{per Unit} \end{array}$$

These sales variances are similar to production cost variances in that they compare budgeted and actual amounts. The sales quantity variance is derived in terms of the *standard contribution margin per unit* (budgeted sales price minus standard variable cost per unit). It may sometimes be desirable to express the sales quantity variance strictly as a revenue variance, in which case it equals the difference between actual and budgeted sales volume multiplied by the *budgeted sales price.*

To be mathematically consistent with variance calculations in Chapters 11 and 12, budgeted amounts must be subtracted from actual amounts. The sign of each resulting variance can then be interpreted as before: A *positive* sales-related variance is *favorable;* a *negative* sales-related variance is *unfavorable.*
Example: Dasovich Company budgeted sales of 20,000 units at $10 per unit for the month of July. Standard variable cost per unit is $3. Actual sales were 22,000 units at $9 per unit. The company's sales price and sales quantity variances are calculated as follows:

$$\text{Sales Price Variance} = \left(\begin{array}{cc}\text{Actual} & \text{Budgeted} \\ \text{Unit} & \text{Unit} \\ \text{Sales} - \text{Sales} \\ \text{Price} & \text{Price}\end{array}\right) \times \begin{array}{c}\text{Actual} \\ \text{Sales} \\ \text{Quantity}\end{array}$$

$$= (\$9 - \$10) \times 22{,}000 \text{ units}$$
$$= (\$22{,}000) \text{ Unfavorable}$$

$$\begin{array}{c}\text{Sales Quantity Variance} \\ \text{(Contribution Margin Basis)}\end{array} = \left(\begin{array}{cc}\text{Actual} & \text{Budgeted} \\ \text{Sales} - \text{Sales} \\ \text{Quantity} & \text{Quantity}\end{array}\right) \times \begin{array}{c}\text{Standard} \\ \text{Contribution} \\ \text{Margin} \\ \text{per Unit}\end{array}$$

$$= (22{,}000 - 20{,}000) \times \$7$$
$$= \$14{,}000 \text{ Favorable}$$

$$\begin{array}{c}\text{Sales Quantity Variance} \\ \text{(Revenue Basis)}\end{array} = \left(\begin{array}{cc}\text{Actual} & \text{Budgeted} \\ \text{Sales} - \text{Sales} \\ \text{Quantity} & \text{Quantity}\end{array}\right) \times \begin{array}{c}\text{Budgeted} \\ \text{Sales} \\ \text{Price}\end{array}$$

$$= (22{,}000 - 20{,}000) \times \$10$$
$$= \$20{,}000 \text{ Favorable}$$

MULTIPLE PRODUCT SITUATIONS

When a manufacturing process results in multiple outputs, it is sometimes possible to calculate variances that explain variations in the *combined sales performance* of the products. This should not always be done. When the sales of multiple outputs neither complement nor compete with each other, sales results should be analyzed separately for each product; only the usual single product variances should be calculated. However, managers are often held responsible for the joint sales performance of a group of related products. When the products in such a group are interdependent, it is appropriate to measure variances that reflect variations in the proportions or *mix* of the products sold as well as variances in their separate *prices* and *quantities.*

Sales Price Variance   In a multiple product situation, the sales price variance is simply the sum of the sales price variances for each product.

FIGURE 13–1

Evans Company
Budgeted and Actual Sales
Month of June, 19X8

| | Budgeted | | | | Actual | | |
	Sales Price	Units	Contribution Margin	Total Margin	Sales Price	Units	Contribution Margin	Total Margin
Super	$400	1,000	$200	$200,000	$380	1,300	$180	$234,000
Supreme	500	2,000	110	220,000	510	1,800	120	216,000
		3,000		$420,000		3,100		$450,000

$$\text{Sales Price Variance} = \begin{array}{c} \text{Sum for All} \\ \text{Products} \\ \text{of} \end{array} \left[\left(\begin{array}{c} \text{Actual} \\ \text{Sales Price} \\ \text{per Unit} \end{array} - \begin{array}{c} \text{Budgeted} \\ \text{Sales Price} \\ \text{per Unit} \end{array} \right) \times \begin{array}{c} \text{Actual} \\ \text{Sales} \\ \text{Quantity} \end{array} \right]$$

$$SPV = \sum_i [(AP_i - BP_i) \times AQ_i]$$

Example: Evans Company sells two models of stereo sets—Super and Supreme. Budgeted and actual sales performance for the month of June, 19X8, were as shown in Figure 13–1.

Based on these unit selling prices and total sales volumes of each product, the sales price variance for the combined sales of Super and Supreme stereos can be calculated as follows:

$$\text{Sales Price Variance} = \sum_{i=1}^{2} (AP_i - BP_i) \times AQ_i$$

$$= [(AP_1 - BP_1) \times AQ_1] + [(AP_2 - BP_2) \times AQ_2]$$
$$= [(\$380 - \$400) \times 1,300] + [(\$510 - \$500) \times 1,800]$$
$$= (\$26,000) \text{ Unfavorable} + \$18,000 \text{ Favorable}$$
$$= (\$8,000) \text{ Unfavorable}$$

Notice that although this variance applies collectively to the sales of both types of stereos, it can easily be traced to sales of the individual products. The $8,000 unfavorable combined sales price variance is merely the difference between the $26,000 unfavorable variance on Super models and the $18,000 favorable variance on Supremes.

Sales Mix Variance This variance measures the variation in total standard contribution margin caused by the change in the sales mix of multiple outputs, with all other variables held constant (unit prices at standard levels and sales quantities at actual levels). The **sales mix variance** is the difference between (1) the total standard contribution margin that would have been earned if the total actual sales quantity had been sold in the proportions planned in the *stan-*

dard product mix and (2) the total standard contribution margin obtained from the *actual product mix* sold.

To simplify this calculation, compute the standard contribution margins of one average unit of the *standard sales mix* and of one average unit of the *actual sales mix*. The sales mix variance is the difference between these two unit amounts multiplied by the actual number of units sold.

$$
\text{Sales Mix Variance} = \left(\begin{array}{c} \text{Standard} \\ \text{Contribution} \\ \text{Margin per Unit} \\ \text{of Actual Mix} \end{array} - \begin{array}{c} \text{Standard} \\ \text{Contribution} \\ \text{Margin per Unit} \\ \text{of Standard Mix} \end{array} \right) \times \begin{array}{c} \text{Total} \\ \text{Actual} \\ \text{Sales} \\ \text{Quantity} \end{array}
$$

$$
\text{SMV} = \frac{\sum\limits_i (\text{SCM}_i \times \text{AQ}_i)}{\sum\limits_i \text{AQ}_i} - \frac{\sum\limits_i (\text{SCM}_i \times \text{BQ}_i)}{\sum\limits_i \text{BQ}_i} \times \sum\limits_i \text{AQ}_i
$$

Example: The sales mix variance can be demonstrated using the Evans Company data on page 599. Sales of Super stereos were budgeted at 1,000 units with a contribution margin of $200 per unit. Sales of Supreme stereos were budgeted at 2,000 units with a contribution margin of $110 per unit. Actual sales consisted of 1,300 Super models and 1,800 Supreme models.

$$
\begin{array}{ll}
\text{Standard Contribution} \\
\text{Margin per Unit of} & = \dfrac{(\$200 \times 1,300) + (\$110 \times 1,800)}{1,300 + 1,800} \\
\text{Actual Mix}
\end{array}
$$

$$
= \frac{\$458,000}{3,100}
$$

$$
= \$147.74 \text{ per unit}
$$

$$
\begin{array}{ll}
\text{Standard Contribution} \\
\text{Margin per Unit of} & = \dfrac{(\$200 \times 1,000) + (\$110 \times 2,000)}{1,000 + 2,000} \\
\text{Standard Mix}
\end{array}
$$

$$
= \frac{\$434,000}{3,000}
$$

$$
= \$140.00 \text{ per unit}
$$

$$
\begin{array}{ll}
\text{Sales Mix Variance} & = (\$147.74 - \$140.00) \times 3,100 \\
& = \$458,000 - \$434,000 \\
& = \$24,000 \text{ Favorable}
\end{array}
$$

Sales performance improved by $24,000 because more Super models and fewer Supremes were actually sold than were budgeted. Instead of selling 3,100 units in their budgeted proportions to yield an average contribution of $140 and a total contribution of $434,000 ($140 × 3,100), the 3,100 Super and Supreme units were sold in slightly different proportions to yield an average contribution of $147.74 and a total contribution of $458,000 ($174.74 × 3,100). After the sales mix variance is extracted, the total remaining contribution margin of $434,000 reflects the standard contribution margin that would have been earned if the actual quantity had been sold in standard proportions.

Sales Quantity Variance   The remaining sales variance reflects the variation in total standard contribution margin caused by changes in the total number of units sold. Because unit price variations and output mix variations have been accounted for separately, the sales quantity variance equals the difference between the budgeted and actual number of units sold multiplied by the standard contribution margin per unit of standard output mix.

$$\text{Sales Quantity Variance} = \begin{pmatrix} \text{Total} & \text{Total} \\ \text{Actual} & \text{Budgeted} \\ \text{Sales} - \text{Sales} \\ \text{Quantity} & \text{Quantity} \end{pmatrix} \times \begin{matrix} \text{Standard} \\ \text{Contribution} \\ \text{Margin per Unit} \\ \text{of Standard Mix} \end{matrix}$$

$$\text{SQV} = \left(\sum_i \text{AQ}_i - \sum_i \text{BQ}_i \right) \times (\text{SCM/SM})$$

Example: The sales quantity variance for Evans Company can be calculated by subtracting the total budgeted sales quantity from the total actual sales quantity and multiplying the resulting figure by $140, the standard contribution margin per unit of standard output mix.

$$\text{Sales Quantity Variance} = (3,100 - 3,000) \times \$140$$
$$= \$14,000 \text{ Favorable}$$

This $14,000 sales quantity variance can also be determined by subtracting the originally planned standard total contribution margin of $420,000 from the $434,000 revised standard total contribution margin for the actual quantity sold.

Figure 13–2 is a tabular summary of the three multiple product sales variances, using the Evans Company data.

FIGURE 13–2

Evans Company
Sales Variances
Month of June, 19X8

	Actual Contri-bution Margin	Standard Contri-bution Margin	Standard Contri-bution Margin	Standard Contri-bution Margin
	Actual Mix Actual Quantity	Actual Mix Actual Quantity	Standard Mix Actual Quantity	Standard Mix Standard Quantity
Super	1,300 × $180	1,300 × $200 ⎫	3,100 × $140	3,000 × $140
Supreme	1,800 × $120	1,800 × $110 ⎭		
	$450,000	$458,000*	$434,000	$420,000

Sales Price Variance
($8,000) Unfavorable

Sales Mix Variance
$24,000 Favorable

Sales Quantity Variance
$14,000 Favorable

* (3,100 × $147.74 = $458,000)

Combined sales variances should be calculated only when the sales performances of different products are interrelated. The total sales price variance can be broken down into variances for the individual products. The sales mix and quantity variances cannot, because they are computed in terms of the sales mix between different products. When the products sold are interdependent, the sales mix, sales price, and sales quantity variances may themselves be interrelated. These variances often reflect the net effects of simultaneous fluctuations in all three variable factors—sales mix, sales quantity, and sales prices.

COMPLEX PRODUCTION-RELATED VARIANCES

The eight standard cost variances described in Chapter 12 were:

1. Materials Price Variance
2. Materials Usage Variance
3. Labor Rate Variance
4. Labor Efficiency Variance
5. Variable Overhead Spending Variance
6. Variable Overhead Efficiency Variance
7. Fixed Overhead Spending Variance
8. Fixed Overhead Volume Variance

Two additional classes of cost variances will now be examined:

1. *Variances caused by interrelationships among materials, labor, and overhead inputs.* These include:
    a. Materials-Related Labor Efficiency Variance
    b. Pure Labor Efficiency Variance
    c. Materials-Related Variable Overhead Efficiency Variance
    d. Pure Variable Overhead Efficiency Variance
2. *Mix and yield/quantity variances,* resulting from the use in multiple input situations of different types and grades of materials or workers who are paid at different wage rates. These include the following combined variances:
    a. Input Mix Variance
    b. Input Yield Variance

MATERIALS-RELATED LABOR AND OVERHEAD VARIANCES

The standard cost specification for a product or a process output usually lists the standard quantities of *inputs* required to achieve a unit of *output*. However, it may also be possible to set standard usage rates for some *inputs* in terms of the standard usage rates of other *inputs*. For example, it might be possible to specify the standard amount of direct labor and overhead that should be applied to each unit of direct material processed. Establishing this secondary relationship permits a separation of the materials-related portion of labor and overhead variances from the "pure" efficiency portions.

Example: Reid Corporation has set the following standard cost specifications for its product:

Materials (10 pounds @ $1)	$10
Direct Labor (2 hours @ $10)	20
Variable Overhead (2 hours @ $5)	10
Fixed Overhead (2 hours @ $5)	10
(normal capacity: 2,750 hours)	
Total Cost per Unit	$50

It is also specified that each 5 pounds of material used in production should require one hour of labor processing and one hour of variable overhead.

In December 1,000 units were produced. Materials purchased and used totaled 12,000 pounds and cost $1 per pound; 2,500 direct labor hours were worked at $10 per hour. Actual variable overhead costs were $10,500; fixed overhead costs were $15,000.

Materials-Related Labor Efficiency Variance This variance reflects the cost of direct labor hours gained or lost as a result of processing more or fewer materials inputs than were specified to produce the actual output. It is calculated as the standard labor hours required for the amount of output produced minus the standard labor hours required to process the direct materials inputs actually used, measured in terms of the standard labor rate.

$$\text{Material-Related Labor Efficiency Variance} = \left(\begin{array}{c} \text{Standard Hours} \\ \text{Required to Produce} \\ \text{Actual Output} \end{array} - \begin{array}{c} \text{Standard Hours} \\ \text{Required to Process} \\ \text{Actual Materials Inputs} \end{array} \right) \times \begin{array}{c} \text{Standard} \\ \text{Labor} \\ \text{Rate} \end{array}$$

$$LEV_{MR} = (SHR_O - SHR_I) \times SLR$$

Reid Corporation requires 2,000 standard labor hours to produce 1,000 units of output and 2,400 standard labor hours to process 12,000 pounds of materials inputs.

$$\text{Materials-Related Labor Efficiency Variance} = (2,000 - 2,400) \times \$10$$
$$= (\$4,000) \text{ Unfavorable}$$

Pure Labor Efficiency Variance This variance compares the standard cost of actual hours worked to the standard cost of the hours that should have been worked to process the actual input quantities. Therefore, it is strictly a labor-related variance—the standard labor hours required to process direct materials actually used minus the labor hours actually worked, measured in terms of the standard labor rate.

$$\text{Pure Labor Efficiency Variance} = \left(\begin{array}{c} \text{Standard Hours} \\ \text{Required to Process} \\ \text{Actual Materials Inputs} \end{array} - \begin{array}{c} \text{Actual} \\ \text{Hours} \\ \text{Worked} \end{array} \right) \times \begin{array}{c} \text{Standard} \\ \text{Hourly} \\ \text{Rate} \end{array}$$

$$LEV_P = (SHR_I - AH) \times SLR$$

Reid Corporation had budgeted 2,400 standard labor hours to process 12,000 pounds of materials inputs, but 2,500 hours were actually worked.

$$\begin{aligned} \text{Pure Labor Efficiency Variance} &= (2,400 - 2,500) \times \$10 \\ &= (\$1,000) \text{ Unfavorable} \end{aligned}$$

Parallel calculations can be made for a *materials-related variable overhead efficiency variance* and a *pure variable overhead efficiency variance* if the standard variable overhead rate is substituted for the standard labor rate.

Materials-Related Variable Overhead Efficiency Variance   This variance shows the change in variable overhead cost that results when more or fewer materials inputs than were specified are used to produce the actual output. It is calculated as the difference between the standard labor hours required for the amount of output produced minus the standard labor hours needed to process the actual direct materials inputs, measured in terms of the standard variable overhead application rate.

$$\begin{array}{c} \text{Materials-Related} \\ \text{Variable Overhead} \\ \text{Efficiency Variance} \end{array} = \left(\begin{array}{c} \text{Standard Hours} \\ \text{Required to Produce} \\ \text{Actual Output} \end{array} - \begin{array}{c} \text{Standard Hours} \\ \text{Required to Process} \\ \text{Actual Materials Inputs} \end{array} \right) \times \begin{array}{c} \text{Standard} \\ \text{Variable} \\ \text{Overhead} \\ \text{Rate} \end{array}$$

$$VOEV_{MR} = (SHR_O - SHR_I) \times SVOR$$

Reid Corporation specifies that 2,000 hours are needed to produce 1,000 units of output and 2,400 hours are needed to process 12,000 pounds of materials inputs. Variable overhead costs are applied at a rate of $5 per direct labor hour.

$$\begin{aligned} \begin{array}{c} \text{Materials-Related Variable} \\ \text{Overhead Efficiency Variance} \end{array} &= (2,000 - 2,400) \times \$5 \\ &= (\$2,000) \text{ Unfavorable} \end{aligned}$$

Pure Variable Overhead Efficiency Variance   This variance is calculated as the difference between the standard labor hours required to process actual materials inputs and the labor hours actually worked, measured in terms of the standard variable overhead application rate.

$$\begin{array}{c} \text{Pure Variable Overhead} \\ \text{Efficiency Variance} \end{array} = \left(\begin{array}{c} \text{Standard Hours} \\ \text{Required to Process} \\ \text{Actual Materials Inputs} \end{array} - \begin{array}{c} \text{Actual} \\ \text{Hours} \\ \text{Worked} \end{array} \right) \times \begin{array}{c} \text{Standard} \\ \text{Variable} \\ \text{Overhead} \\ \text{Rate} \end{array}$$

$$VOEV_P = (SHR_I - AH) \times SVOR$$

Reid Corporation's standard cost specifications allow 2,400 labor hours to process 12,000 pounds of materials inputs, but 2,500 hours were actually worked. Variable overhead costs are applied at a rate of $5 per direct labor hour.

$$\text{Pure Variable Overhead Efficiency Variance} = (2,400 - 2,500) \times \$5$$
$$= (\underline{\$500}) \text{ Unfavorable}$$

MULTIPLE INPUTS: MIX AND YIELD/QUANTITY VARIANCES

When the manufacture of a product specifies the use of more than one type of raw material or category of labor, deliberate or unintentional substitutions of one input for another may occur. As a result, neither the standard mix of inputs nor the standard quantity of inputs per unit of output is actually used in production. However, materials usage and labor efficiency variances can still be calculated for each input item and for the totals of materials and labor. But it also becomes possible to break these total variances down into a *mix variance* and a *yield (quantity) variance.*

The mix and yield variance analysis explained here should only be applied when management has the ability and the intent to make input substitutions. When multiple inputs are *independent* rather than *interchangeable,* variance analysis should be limited to separate usage or efficiency variances for each type of input. Moreover, in order to calculate mix and yield variances, the input units must be logically and physically additive, so that the concept of an *average unit of input mix* can be meaningfully employed. This is true whether the inputs consist of various grades of raw materials or different classes of labor.

Materials Price Variance   In multiple input situations, the *materials price* and *labor rate* variances can be calculated as the sum of the individual input price and rate variances. Once these variances have been determined and extracted, the input costs remaining to be analyzed represent the total standard cost of inputs actually consumed. The *input mix variance* and *materials yield variance* can then be calculated.

Example: Pincay Company has established the following standard raw materials cost specifications for its product, which requires the blending of two input ingredients.

Standard Cost per 20 Gallon Batch of Output	
Material A (12 gallons @ $2)	$24
Material B (8 gallons @ $3)	24
Total Materials Cost per Batch	$48

Actual output during March was 200,000 gallons. Materials purchased and consumed amounted to 140,000 gallons of Material A at $2.10 per gallon and 70,000 gallons of Material B at $2.75 per gallon. The **materials price variance** is calculated as the difference between the standard and actual unit prices of each type of material multiplied by the actual quantities used.

$$\text{Materials Price Variance} = \begin{array}{c}\text{Sum for}\\\text{Each}\\\text{Material}\\\text{Input of}\end{array}\left[\left(\begin{array}{c}\text{Standard}\\\text{Price}\\\text{per}\\\text{Unit}\end{array} - \begin{array}{c}\text{Actual}\\\text{Price}\\\text{per}\\\text{Unit}\end{array}\right)\times\begin{array}{c}\text{Actual}\\\text{Quantity}\\\text{Used}\end{array}\right]$$

$$MPV = \sum_i [(SP_i - AP_i) \times AQ_i]$$

$$= [(\$2.00 - \$2.10) \times 140,000] + [(\$3.00 - \$2.75) \times 70,000]$$
$$= (\$14,000) \text{ Unfavorable} + \$17,500 \text{ Favorable}$$
$$= \$3,500 \text{ Favorable}$$

Materials Mix Variance   This is the difference between the total quantity of materials used, measured at the standard cost per unit of the *standard mix,* and the same total quantity of materials used, measured at the standard cost per unit of the *actual mix.* This variance measures the effect of any change in the proportions of materials inputs on the total standard cost of production. Therefore, it can also be defined as the difference between the standard cost of *inputs actually used* and the standard cost of the *output that would have been produced* if the actual inputs used had been combined according to the standard mix proportions. This definition emphasizes the way in which the materials mix variance isolates the change in total standard cost that is caused solely by the change in materials input mix, with the quantity of inputs is held constant.

Before the materials input mix variance can be calculated, the standard costs of one unit of the *standard input mix* and one unit of the *actual input mix* must be determined. The standard cost of one unit of standard input mix is calculated by dividing the total standard materials cost of standard inputs required by the total quantity of standard materials inputs required.

$$\begin{array}{c}\text{Standard Unit Cost of}\\\text{Standard Input Mix}\end{array} = \frac{\sum_i (SP_i \times SQ_i)}{\sum_i SQ_i}$$

The standard cost of one unit of actual input mix is calculated by dividing the total standard materials cost of inputs actually used by the total quantity of materials actually used.

$$\begin{array}{c}\text{Standard Unit Cost}\\\text{of Actual Input Mix}\end{array} = \frac{\sum_i (SP_i \times AQ_i)}{\sum_i AQ_i}$$

The **materials mix variance** is then the standard unit cost of the standard mix minus the standard unit cost of the actual mix multiplied by the total actual quantity of materials used.

$$\text{Materials Mix Variance} = (SUC/SM - SUC/AM) \times \sum_i AQ_i$$

or

$$(SUC/SM \times \sum_i AQ_i) - (SUC/AM \times \sum_i AQ_i)$$

Example: For Pincay Company, the materials input mix variance is calculated as follows:

$$\text{Standard Unit Cost of Standard Input Mix} = \frac{\sum_i (SP_i \times SQ_i)}{\sum_i SQ_i}$$

$$= \frac{[(\$2 \times 12) + (\$3 \times 8)]}{12 + 8}$$

$$= \frac{\$48}{20}$$

$$= \$2.40 \text{ per gallon}$$

$$\text{Standard Unit Cost of Actual Input Mix} = \frac{\sum_i (SP_i \times AQ_i)}{\sum_i AQ_i}$$

$$= \frac{(\$2 \times 140,000) + (\$3 \times 70,000)}{140,000 + 70,000}$$

$$= \frac{\$490,000}{210,000}$$

$$= \$2.333 \text{ per gallon}$$

$$\text{Materials Mix Variance} = (SUC/SM - SUC/AM) \times \sum_i AQ_i$$

$$= (\$2.40 - \$2.333) \times 210,000$$
$$= \$504,000 - \$490,000$$
$$= \$14,000 \text{ Favorable}$$

The 210,000 gallons of input mix actually used had a total standard cost of $490,000; but if the standard mix had been maintained, 210,000 gallons would have had a total standard cost of $504,000. Therefore, a cost savings of $14,000 resulted when the input mix was altered to permit greater use of Material A, the less expensive input.

Materials Yield Variance This variance is the difference between the *standard quantity* of materials required for actual output and the *actual quantity* of materials used, both of which are measured in terms of the standard cost per unit of standard input mix. The **materials yield variance** can also be defined as the standard cost of the output actually produced minus the standard cost of the output that should have been produced from the quantity of inputs used, if the expected yield from the standard mix had been achieved.

$$\text{Materials Yield Variance} = \left(\begin{array}{c} \text{Standard Cost of} \\ \text{Outputs } \textit{Achieved} \end{array} - \begin{array}{c} \text{Standard Cost of} \\ \text{Outputs } \textit{Expected} \\ \text{from Actual Quan-} \\ \text{tity of Standard} \\ \text{Input Mix Processed} \end{array} \right)$$

or

$$MYV = \left[\sum_i SQ_i - \sum_i AQ_i \right] \times (SUC/SM)$$

Pincay Company's materials yield variance can be calculated in either of the following ways:

$$\text{Materials Yield Variance} = \left[\sum_i SQ_i - \sum_i AQ_i \right] \times (SUC/SM)$$

$$= (200{,}000 - 210{,}000) \times \$2.40$$
$$= (\$24{,}000) \text{ Unfavorable}$$

or

$$= \left(\begin{matrix} \text{Standard Cost of} \\ \text{Output } \textit{Achieved} \end{matrix} - \begin{matrix} \text{Standard Cost of} \\ \text{Output } \textit{Expected} \end{matrix} \right)$$

$$= (10{,}000 \times \$48) - (10{,}500 \times \$48)$$
$$= (\$480{,}000 - \$504{,}000)$$
$$= (\$24{,}000) \text{ Unfavorable}$$

The first calculation suggests that an unfavorable yield variance occurred because 210,000 gallons of input were processed instead of 200,000 gallons. The resulting unfavorable $24,000 variance reflects the waste of 10,000 gallons of standard materials input mix at $2.40 per gallon.

The second calculation explains the materials yield variance as the cost of output units not manufactured. That is, output from the 210,000 gallons of input should have been 10,500 batches at $48 per batch. But only 10,000 batches requiring 200,000 gallons were actually produced. Therefore, the variance is 500 batches at $48 per batch, or $24,000.

Figure 13–3 summarizes the variance calculations involving input price, mix, and yield. Labor mix and yield variances can be obtained by substituting the appropriate labor-related variables for the materials-related variables in the calculations.

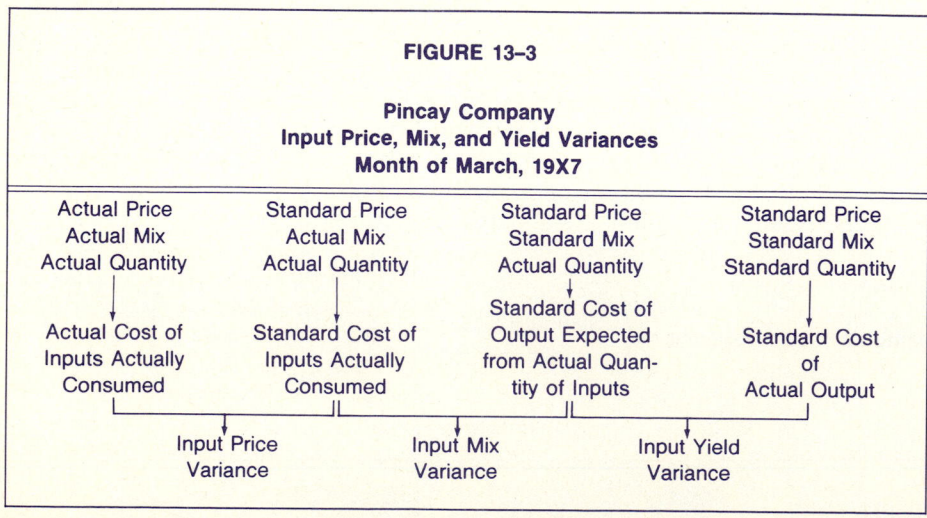

FIGURE 13–3

Pincay Company
Input Price, Mix, and Yield Variances
Month of March, 19X7

Actual Price Actual Mix Actual Quantity	Standard Price Actual Mix Actual Quantity	Standard Price Standard Mix Actual Quantity	Standard Price Standard Mix Standard Quantity
		Standard Cost of	
Actual Cost of Inputs Actually Consumed	Standard Cost of Inputs Actually Consumed	Output Expected from Actual Quantity of Inputs	Standard Cost of Actual Output

Input Price Variance   Input Mix Variance   Input Yield Variance

VARIANCE ANALYSIS AND INVESTIGATION

Once variances have been identified and measured, a follow-up process begins. This process essentially consists of three steps:

1. *The investigation decision*—deciding whether or not to investigate a reported variance.
2. *The investigation process*—finding the causes of those variances that are considered worth investigating.
3. *The adjustment process*—deciding what action to take in response to the ascertained cause of a variance. This could involve:
   a. Taking no action.
   b. Adjusting the plan, budget, or standard that was used to calculate the variance.
   c. Adjusting the operations of the manufacturing system which is the subject of variance analysis.

These last three options correspond to conclusions that the variance has either (1) no decision significance, (2) planning significance, or (3) control significance. The implications of these three alternatives will be discussed in the following sections.

The variance investigation process should be governed by some type of cost–benefit analysis. That is, only those variances that are worth tracking down and remedying should be investigated. Those variances for which investigation and/or correction will cost more than the resulting benefits should be ignored.

In practice, this distinction is not easy to make. Investigation decisions are complicated by the inherent uncertainties surrounding variances and by the problems involved in measuring the costs and benefits of correcting variance causes. A wide variety of procedures—from simple rules of thumb to formal statistical decision models—can be used to decide which variances are worth investigating.

Interpreting Variances for Cause

Variances are deviations of actual performance from planned performance. Therefore, variance measurement presumes that a goal or standard has been established for the activity being analyzed. However, no matter how carefully and explicitly the planning process is conducted, there can be no firm expectation—except in very simple, short-run situations—that those plans will ever be exactly fulfilled. To some degree, the outcomes of planned events will always be uncertain and variable.

The variance measurement process in a standard cost system divides variances into different categories, such as materials price and labor rate. This is only the first step in the interpretation of variances for cause. But before variances can be corrected, more specific reasons for their existence must be determined.

The following are typical events that might cause each of the commonly calculated variances:

Materials Price Variance
    Changes in market prices of inputs.
    Purchases made from an alternate supplier.
    Rush order purchases.
    Extra discounts obtained on quantity purchases.
    Discounts lost on small lot purchases.
    Changes in delivery costs.
    Different grade or type of material purchased.
    Standards are in error, obsolete, or unrealistic.

Materials Usage Variance
    Defective units cause extra scrap, waste, and rework.
    Faulty quality control inspection.
    Materials handling problems cause damage and slowdowns.
    Incorrect product specifications.
    Materials deterioration or obsolescence due to carrying excessive inventory.
    Equipment malfunctions or breakdowns.
    Faulty tools, dies, or jigs.
    Processing by employees is not according to standard specifications.
    Product design changes.
    Standards are in error, obsolete, or unrealistic.

Labor Rate Variance
    Wage rate changes.
    Substitution of one category of labor for another, due to:
        absenteeism, vacations, strikes, illness.
        temporary internal transfers.
        inability to hire the desired categories.
    Standards are in error, obsolete, or unrealistic.

Labor Efficiency Variance
    Quality of materials affects worker productivity.
    Quality control errors.
    Work slowdowns, stoppages, or strikes.
    Equipment malfunctions or breakdowns.
    Power shortages, blackouts, storms, or fires.
    Production scheduling errors.
    Supervision errors.
    Training periods for new employees.
    Using different categories of employees to perform the same job.
    Time spent by employees in learning to manufacture new products.
    Product specifications are incorrect.
    Standards are in error, obsolete, or unrealistic.

Variable and Fixed Overhead Spending Variances
    Changes in market prices of overhead items.
    Overhead items were avoided or unanticipated.
    Indirect materials usage—same factors as affect materials price and usage variances.
    Indirect labor usage—same factors as affect labor rate and efficiency variances.
    Equipment malfunctions or breakdowns.
    Inappropriate activity index used in setting overhead rate.
    Standards are in error, obsolete, or unrealistic.

Variable Overhead Efficiency Variance
   Distorted by the same factors that affect the labor efficiency variance, if labor
      hours is the denominator activity.
   Otherwise, causes of variances are concentrated in the area of the denomina-
      tor activity, including the materials usage variance if the denominator activity
      is materials-related, or equipment-related items if the denominator activity
      is machine hours.
   Standards are in error, obsolete, or unrealistic.

Fixed Overhead Volume Variance
   Errors in estimating expected capacity utilization level.
   Failure to operate at expected capacity level.
   Variation in expected sales volume affects production volume.
   Production shutdowns due to strikes or materials shortages.
   Standards are in error, obsolete, or unrealistic.

The possibility that existing standards were incorrect, obsolete, too tight, or too loose is common to every type of variance in the preceding list of variance-causing events. Consequently, one important remedial action may be the establishment of new and more relevant standards based on experience with the present standards.

Collectively and over longer time periods, certain variances tend to cancel each other out. However, these variances can be measured in the short run and in particular situations. Variations in labor productivity provide an example. Employee productivity may vary from month to month and week to week; it may be different on different days of the week and even at different times during a single day. This may be due to such varied causes as weather, seasons, holidays, health, morale and motivation of employees, as well as social, political, recreational, and economic events external to the firm. Likewise, raw materials are often subject to short-term fluctuations in quality and price, seasonal supply variations, weather and climate effects, as well as the indirect effects of labor productivity variations caused by spoilage, waste, and rework costs.

RANDOM VERSUS NONRANDOM VARIANCES

Variances caused by intrinsic and expected but uncontrollable factors are considered **random variances** that are to be tolerated in a given production situation. In contrast, **nonrandom variances** result from uniquely identifiable and possibly correctable causes.

Nonrandom variances are produced by several types of events, including:

1. Operating or implementation errors
2. Data measurement errors
3. Prediction or forecasting errors
4. Model errors
5. Behavioral side effects

Operating or implementation errors can result from failure to act according to the specifications of the plan or budget. Such deviations may be intentional, as when the materials or labor inputs actually used are different from those called for in the budget or standard specifications. They also may be unintentional, as when price, usage, or efficiency variances are so large that they are outside the range of tolerable (random) operating conditions. Detecting this type of variance requires productivity analysis and internal or operational audit procedures that can be used to evaluate management's ability to adhere to stated plans and budgets.

Data measurement errors can occur when accounting principles (especially the accrual concept) are not adhered to strictly and consistently. They may also result from defective data collection and analysis and from past or present attempts to manipulate performance measurements. Shifting costs from one category to another, from one product or department to another, or from one accounting period to another inevitably leads to some sort of unusual variance. Detecting these errors requires internal accounting control procedures.

Forecasting or prediction errors result from using the wrong values for variables in formulating plans, standards, or budgets. Examples include incorrect unit costs, materials and labor quantity requirements, overhead rates, activity levels, and sales prices. Price variances of this type are easily detected; they are more or less self-evident. However, usage and efficiency variances caused by prediction errors may be more subtle and can require investigation in the form of productivity analysis.

Errors may also be present in the *model* used as the basis for plans and budgets. **Model errors** differ from parameter specification errors in that they relate to the omission of planning variables, the inclusion of irrelevant or redundant variables, or the incorrect formulation of relationships among variables. Detecting these errors in effect requires an invalidation of the original model or a demonstration of the existence of a superior model based on analysis of empirical results.

Those variances produced by budgets but not correctly anticipated at the time of budget formulation involve **behavioral side effects**. Examples include nonacceptance or outright rejection by workers of too tightly set budgetary standards, resulting from employee discouragement, frustration, and suspicion. Also possible, but harder to detect, is a slackening or drop in productivity and efficiency due to too loosely set standards or budgets. Ineffective communication of budgetary data may also contribute to this kind of variance—for example, when workers are unable to understand what performance is expected of them.

FREQUENCY AND TIMING OF VARIANCE INVESTIGATION DECISIONS

The frequency and timing of variance investigation decisions are critical factors in determining whether a variance will be classified as random or nonrandom. In certain cases, very frequent variance analysis and investigation is necessary. When purchases are continually being made, often at rapidly changing prices, materials price variances might even be analyzed each day. Labor rate variances need not be reviewed so often because short-term wage rates are normally fairly stable. Usage and efficiency variances for materials, labor, and variable overhead might also require frequent analysis, depending on the length of production processing cycles. Fixed overhead variances should not require such regular review, because of the long-term nature of the resources involved.

The decision as to how often variances should be analyzed involves, on the one hand, the cost of frequent analysis and investigation and the possible inaccuracy of short-run measurements that may cause random variances to be declared nonrandom. Against this must be considered the economy and greater accuracy of less frequent variance decisions. The timing of variance investigations should also be influenced by the extent to which effective corrective action depends on promptness in detection and reporting. A variance analysis system that reports on significant materials usage variances a month after they begin to occur is not too helpful!

LEVEL OF DETAIL IN VARIANCE ANALYSIS

The *level of detail* in variance analysis must also be considered in some type of cost–benefit framework. The more detailed and individualized the variance, the more control information may potentially be available, although perhaps at prohibitive cost. On the other hand, an aggregate variance (for example, a single materials usage variance for all inputs for all products) may be less expensive to obtain, but could lead to the suppression or distortion of control information due to the offsetting effects of individual variances that are combined in such an overall measure.

Possible interactions among variances should also be considered in deciding on the level of detail in variance investigation. Materials, labor, and overhead variances often cause and affect one another. For example, favorable labor and overhead efficiency variances and unfavorable materials price variances might occur simultaneously due to the use of higher quality materials that permit reductions in processing costs. Or chain reaction effects may occur, as when materials usage and labor and overhead efficiency variances are all unfavorable because inferior grade raw materials were put into process, leading to excess materials waste, spoilage, rework costs, and extra processing time.

Ideally, it is desirable to investigate variances at the most individualized level possible. However, to do so requires detailed performance data that most cost accounting systems are unable to provide. Variance analysis often occurs in departmentalized, process-oriented cost systems in which unit costs of materials, labor, and overhead are determined by averaging total costs over the equivalent units of output of a process or department for a particular period. Individual deviations in cost performance during that period are hidden in these averages, because the only ascertainable accounting variances are those for the results of the whole period. This makes the length of the period of analysis an especially critical factor in variance investigations of process costs.

Sampling techniques offer a possible solution to this problem. Instead of analyzing total or aggregated period variances, the accountant might use samples of cost-related performance measures to distinguish between random and nonrandom variances.

SEPARATING RANDOM AND NONRANDOM VARIANCES

The usual premise is that random variances should not be investigated, because by definition they are unavoidable. Nonrandom variances should possibly, but not always, be investigated. This breaks the investigation decision into two parts: (1) separating random from nonrandom variances, and (2) deciding which nonrandom variances to investigate, in what manner, and to what extent. The first of these is largely an identification and measurement problem; the latter requires the application of cost–benefit analysis in a highly uncertain environment.

A firm could elect to analyze and report all variances, regardless of size and direction, to managers of the activity center to which they relate. This "shotgun" approach has the advantages of simplicity and completeness. However, given any significant scale or complexity of operations, such a variance reporting system would probably communicate a great volume of useless information.

A better type of variance analysis is based on the principle of **management by exception,** which requires selectivity in the investigation and reporting of variances. For example, should a $100 unfavorable materials usage variance be checked out and reported in detail? If not, what about a $1,000 or $10,000 variance? Clearly, the absolute size of a variance is only one consideration managers will apply in deciding whether or not the variance should be investigated. The *relative size* of the variance and its *relative frequency of occurrence* are more important. In general, recurring variances should receive more control attention than variances that do not recur.

Techniques for determining whether or not a variance is *significant* or *material* range from simple rules of thumb to formal statistical procedures. One method is to choose an arbitrary dollar amount (say $1,000) and require that any variance exceeding that amount be investigated in detail—on the grounds that it is *prima facie* nonrandom, because it is unusually large. When this policy is adopted, small variances are still reported, but without detailed analysis or follow-up.

Alternatively, the decision to investigate might be based on some specific percentage of the budgeted or standard amount from which the variance is derived. For example, any variance in excess of 5 percent of standard cost could be investigated.

The *frequency, pattern,* or *trend* of variances over time can also be the basis for classifying them as random or nonrandom. Any compounding or escalation of the variance amount, or any significant pattern of fluctuations, may indicate the presence of nonrandom irregularities. Such judgments must be made somewhat subjectively at this elementary level. How long must a trend continue before being declared nonrandom? How wide, pronounced, or irregular must a fluctuation be to be considered worthy of investigation?

CONTROL CHART TECHNIQUES

Control chart analysis is used to separate random and nonrandom variances. Performance observations are plotted against prespecified **control limits.** Individual deviations, trends, and other patterns can then be observed and highlighted. This is demonstrated in Figure 13–4.

In Figure 13–4, the standard being monitored is a unit cost of $100, with a preset tolerance of $15 in either direction. Actual costs (A, B, C) above $115, or below $85, are considered nonrandom and indicate that an out-of-control situation exists, calling for possible investigation. Observations of cost performance within the control limits are accepted as normal, random variances,

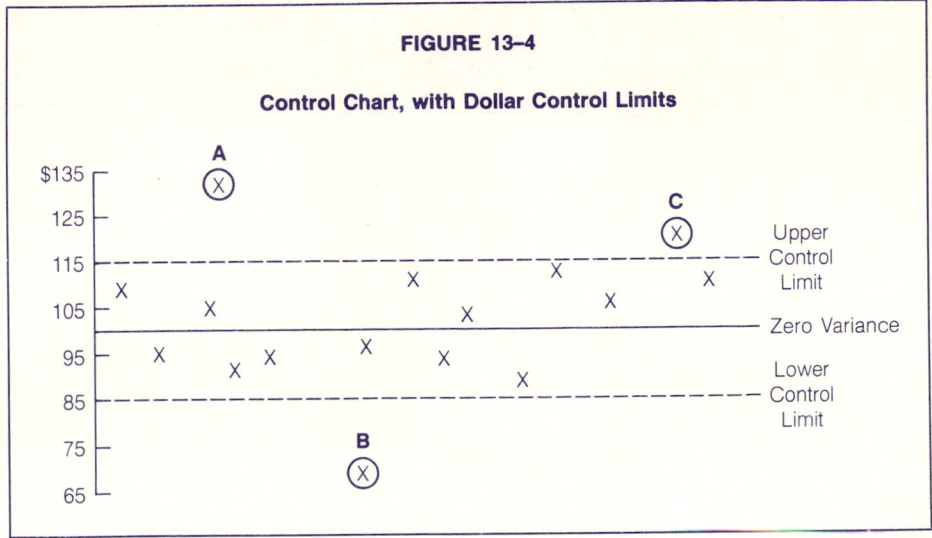

FIGURE 13–4

Control Chart, with Dollar Control Limits

indicating that the activity being monitored is in control. The same interpretations apply to Figure 13–5, in which observations D, E, and F fall outside the control limits, which were set at ±2½ percent of budgeted cost.

Figure 13–6 illustrates the apparent development of a trend, although no unacceptable deviation beyond the control limits has yet been observed. This could be interpreted as a signal that the process is drifting toward an out-of-control state that will require investigation. The pattern of variations may be

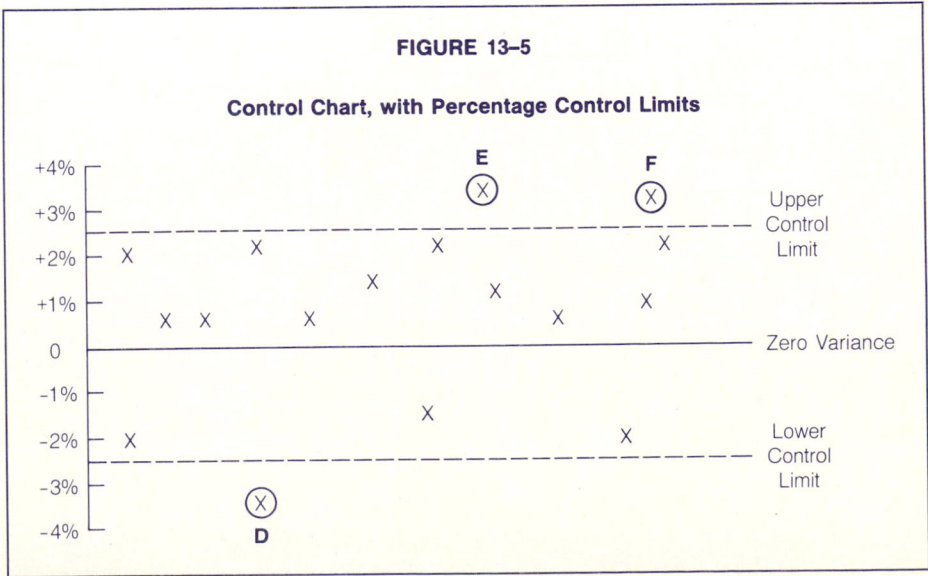

FIGURE 13–5

Control Chart, with Percentage Control Limits

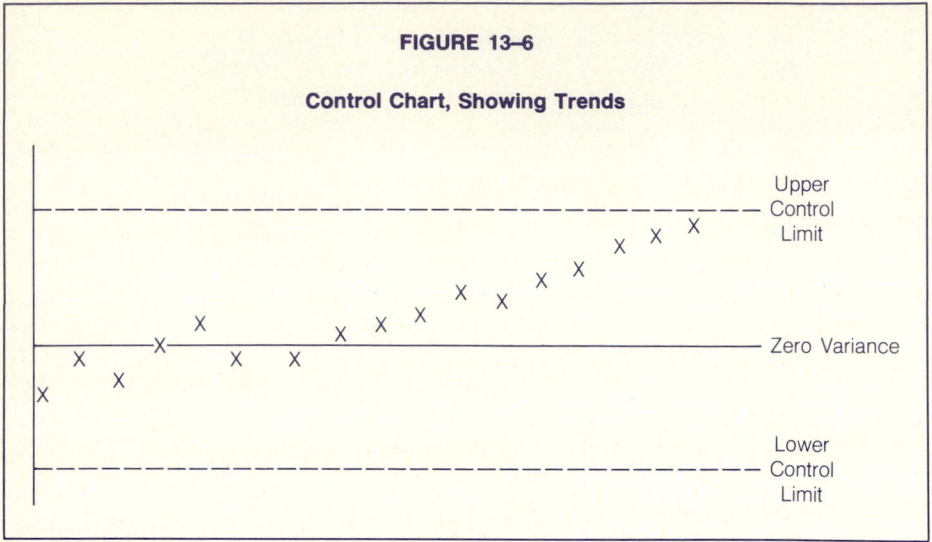

FIGURE 13–6

Control Chart, Showing Trends

caused by faulty performance or by changes in external factors that have made the original standard or budgeted amount irrelevant.

Figure 13–7 shows a pattern of fluctuations that do not violate the control limits, but may indicate some other type of nonrandom variance. For example, this pattern might result if data were manipulated by a manager trying to maximize the number of favorable variances in his department (perhaps because of a

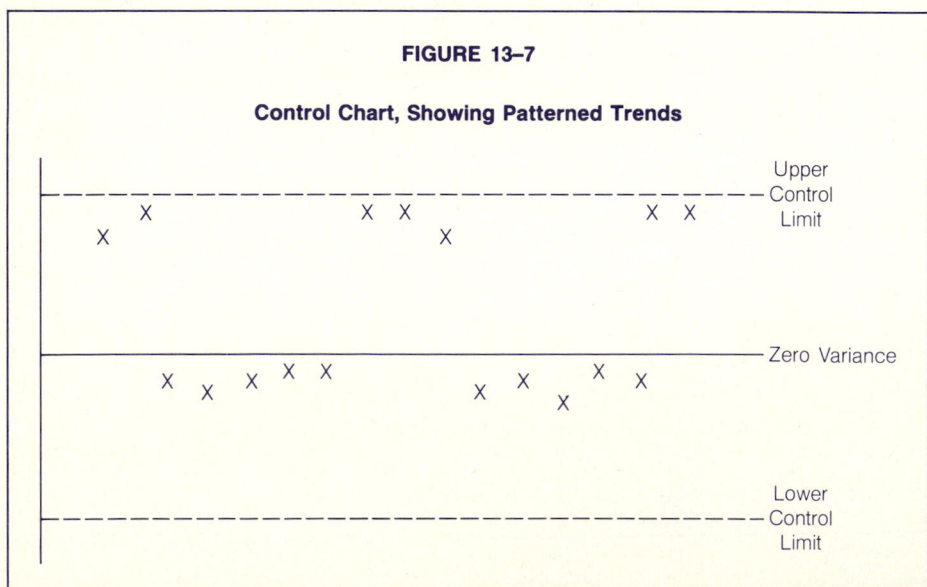

FIGURE 13–7

Control Chart, Showing Patterned Trends

bonus or incentive scheme) and doing so by bunching large unfavorable variances in order to report a series of small favorable variances.

Nonrandom variances in both the upper and lower ranges may require investigation. Managers tend to be preoccupied with unfavorable variances. These may occur more often, because standards and budgets are generally set and administered stringently. However, this does not mean that favorable variances should be ignored or taken for granted. It is also important to identify sources of efficient performance, find why they occur, and use that information to sustain or transfer the favorable performance to other areas.

The control chart approach was borrowed by accountants from the area of industrial quality control, in which the performance measures being monitored are physical attributes such as sizes, weights, temperatures, and rates of flow. In industrial quality control, the goal is always to reset performance to the standard or zero variance state. In accounting, it is more likely that *unfavorable* variances call for adjusting performance back to the zero variance state, but that *favorable* variances imply that the standard itself should be reset.

Control charts should also be interpreted cautiously whenever "expected" or "budgeted" variances are present. That is, if the standard or budget has been set in anticipation of future changes that have not yet occurred, what appear to be significant variances may represent nothing more than a premature comparison between actual and standard costs. Such a situation might arise when the materials price or labor rate standards have been adjusted in anticipation of a pending price change or wage increase or when there is a learning curve effect on labor and overhead costs because standards have been set in terms of the expected steady state level of productivity.

The use of formal statistical decision models to identify variances deserving investigation will be demonstrated in Chapter 22.

SUMMARY

1. Variances in sales performance and production costs can be calculated for multiple as well as single product and input situations.

2. Sales price variances reflect the effect of changes in selling prices on revenue and profit performance.

3. Sales quantity variances, preferably expressed in terms of standard contribution margins, represent the effect on total contribution margins of variations in the level of unit sales.

4. A sales mix variance can be calculated for multiple products that are also interdependent. It shows the effect on profit contribution of variations from the budgeted or standard sales mix of products.

5. When a product's standard cost specifications include labor and overhead amounts as a function of the standard quantity of materials allowed, materials-related labor and overhead efficiency variances can be calculated separately from "pure" labor and overhead efficiency variances.

6. For multiple and interchangeable inputs (different grades of materials or alternate classes of labor), the usage or efficiency variances can be subdivided into an input mix variance and an input yield variance.

7. These two variances are interrelated, because they represent the effect on costs of changes in both the total quantity of inputs used (yield variance), and the combined proportions of inputs used (mix variance).

8. All variance analysis and investigation decisions involve uncertainty. Consequently, the simplified decision models presented in this chapter are at best aids to managerial judgment in identifying variances deserving investigation.

KEY WORDS AND PHRASES

Sales Price Variance (597)
Sales Quantity Variance (597)
Sales Mix Variance (599)
Materials-Related Labor Efficiency Variance (603)
Pure Labor Efficiency Variance (604)
Materials-Related Variable Overhead Efficiency Variance (604)
Pure Variable Overhead Efficiency Variance (604)
Multiple Inputs: Materials Price Variance (605)
Multiple Inputs: Materials Mix Variance (606)
Multiple Inputs: Materials Yield Variance (607)
Variance (609)
Random Variance (611)
Nonrandom Variance (611)
Operating or Implementation Errors (611)
Data Measurement Errors (612)
Forecasting or Prediction Errors (612)
Model Errors (612)
Behavioral Side Effects (612)
Management by Exception (614)
Control Chart (614)
Control Limits (614)

Questions

1. What are the eight basic standard cost variances?
2. What variances can be calculated in regard to the sales performance of a single product firm?
3. Why should sales performance variances be based on different measures of activity than production cost variances?
4. When is it appropriate to compute sales mix and sales quantity variances rather than just a single sales quantity variance? When is it not?
5. What information is conveyed by a materials-related labor efficiency variance? Who is held responsible for such variances?
6. Under what circumstances should the materials quantity variance be divided into a materials mix and a materials yield variance?
7. Should labor substitution (mix) and labor yield variances be calculated and reported when the production manager has no control over the number of workers of each labor category? Why or why not?
8. What procedures should follow variance identification and measurement?
9. What different types of adjustment are possible once the cause of a variance has been established?
10. Identify some of the most likely causes of each of the following types of variances:
    (a)   Materials Price Variance
    (b)   Materials Usage Variance
    (c)   Labor Rate Variance
    (d)   Labor Efficiency Variance
    (e)   Overhead Spending Variance
    (f)   Variable Overhead Efficiency Variance
    (g)   Fixed Overhead Volume Variance
11. Explain the difference between *random* and *nonrandom* variances. Which ones should be investigated? Why?
12. What are the principal causes of nonrandom variances? What is the appropriate type of response to each?
13. How frequently should variance measurements be made and reported?
14. How detailed should variance measurements be?
15. What are some simple techniques for separating random from nonrandom variances?
16. What is a control chart and how is it used in the variance investigation process?
17. Should favorable variances be investigated more or less frequently than unfavorable variances? Why or why not?
18. Is the *amount*, the *frequency*, or the *pattern* of variances most important from the point of view of variance investigation? Why?
19. Explain the variance investigation process in the context of feedback mechanisms and control systems as introduced in Chapter 10.
20. What inherent circularity is present in deciding whether or not to investigate a variance?

Exercises

E 13-1   Sales Variance Analysis—Single Product Situation

Tribune Corporation prepared the following budgetary forecast for July of 19X6:

Sales (24,000 units)	$480,000
Less: Standard Variable Costs	320,000
Standard Contribution Margin	$160,000
Less: Fixed Costs	60,000
Budgeted Net Income	$100,000

Actual operations resulted in the production and sale of 25,000 units at an average sales price of $19 per unit. Total fixed costs were $60,000 and variable costs per unit were exactly the standard amount.

Required:
(a)   Prepare an income statement to reflect the results of operations in July.
(b)   Prepare an analysis of the variances in sales performance, including:
   1.   sales price variance.
   2.   sales quantity variance (contribution margin basis).
   3.   sales quantity variance (revenue basis).
(c)   Comment on the analysis in part (b).

E 13-2   Sales Mix Variance Analysis—Variable Cost System

Saffron Company, which uses a variable cost system, has prepared the following budget for May of 19X3:

	Product M (Regular)	Product N (Economy)	Total
Unit Sales	24,000	16,000	40,000
Sales Revenues	$384,000	$192,000	$576,000
Less: Variable Costs	192,000	128,000	320,000
Contribution Margin	$192,000	$ 64,000	$256,000
Less: Joint Fixed Costs			150,000
Net Income			$106,000

During May of 19X3, the following results of operations were reported:

	Product M (Regular)	Product N (Economy)
Unit Sales	30,000	10,000
Sales Price per Unit	$15	$14
Variable Cost per Unit	$7.50	$7.50
Total Fixed Costs		$160,000

Inventory levels did not change during the month.

Required:

(a) Prepare an income statement for May, using the same format as in the budget shown above.

(b) Prepare an analysis of sales and cost variances for May. Include the following:
   1. sales price variance.
   2. sales mix variance.
   3. sales quantity variance.
   4. total variable cost variance.
   5. total fixed cost variance.

(c) Comment on the analysis in part (b).

(d) What factors must be present to make the sales variance analysis in part (b) meaningful, especially with regard to the market relationship of product M to product N.

E 13-3 Sales Performance Analysis—Multiple Product Situation— Price, Mix, Volume Variances

Irene Company had developed the following sales budget for its two grades of output during February, 19X3:

	Standard	Premium	Total
Sales (units)	240,000	120,000	360,000
Sales Revenues	$2,400,000	$2,160,000	$4,560,000
Standard Variable Costs......	1,200,000	900,000	2,100,000
Contribution Margin	$1,200,000	$1,260,000	$2,460,000

Actual results for the month of February were as follows:

	Standard	Premium	Total
Sales (units)	250,000	100,000	350,000
Sales Revenues	$2,750,000	$1,800,000	$4,550,000
Standard Variable Costs......	1,375,000	750,000	2,075,000
Contribution Margin	$1,375,000	$1,050,000	$2,425,000

Required:

(a) Prepare an analysis of sales performance to explain the variance of actual from budgeted results. Show the following items:
   (1) sales price variances.
   (2) sales mix variance (standard contribution margin basis).
   (3) sales quantity variance (standard contribution margin basis).

(b) Comment on the analysis in part (a).

(c) If actual variable costs for the period's activities were different from the standard amounts, what additional variances could be calculated? Would these variances be based on the actual sales volume or some other level of activity? Why?

E 13-4 Profit Variance Analysis—Single Product Situation

In reviewing the results of the first quarter of 19X1, Alan Company has had the following summary report prepared:

	Budget	Actual	Variance
Sales Revenues	$400,000	$420,000	$ 20,000 F
Less: Variable Costs	240,000	280,500	(40,500) U
Contribution Margin	$160,000	$139,500	(20,500) U
Less: Fixed Costs	120,000	132,500	(12,500) U
Net Income	$ 40,000	$ 7,000	$(33,000) U

Management expresses concern about the failure to earn its targeted profit. However, it notes that the sales price was raised 20 percent to contend with increased labor and materials costs. Sales volume was also down by 5,000 units from the budgeted level of 40,000 units. Variable costs include only materials and labor, the prices of which increased by an average of 10 percent.

Required:

(a) Prepare an analysis of sales performance, showing:
   (1) sales price variance.
   (2) sales quantity variance (from both the sales revenue basis and the contribution margin basis).
(b) Prepare an analysis of costs, showing:
   (1) variable items—price spending variance.
   (2) variable items—efficiency/usage variance.
   (3) fixed items—spending variance.
(c) Reconcile your answers in parts (a) and (b) with the total variance in net income.

E 13–5 Cost Variance Analysis—Multiple Inputs—Mix, Yield, Price Variances

Nelson Company produces a health food product, Super-Granola, by blending various ingredients. The standard input mix calls for the following quantities of items at standard unit prices as indicated:

Input Item	Quantity (pounds)	Price (per pound)
Nuts	200	$4.00
Grain Products...........	700	$0.50
Raisins	100	$2.00
	1,000	

During October of 19X8, the following quantities of inputs were purchased and used in producing a total output of 1,000,000 pounds of Super-Granola.

	Quantity (pounds)	Cost
Nuts	180,000	$ 756,000
Grain Products.........	750,000	360,000
Raisins	120,000	216,000
	1,050,000	$1,332,000

Required:

(a) Prepare an analysis of cost variances for October. Include in your analysis:
   (1) materials price variances.
   (2) materials mix variance.
   (3) materials yield variance.

(b) Interpret each of the variances calculated. To whom will each variance be useful as control information?

E 13–6 Multiple Inputs—Cost Variance Analysis— Rate, Mix, and Yield Variances

Hogan Corporation has developed the following standard cost specifications for the direct labor inputs required for one unit of its major output:

Class I : 5 hours @ $10
Class II: 3 hours @ $15

During August of 19X4, 10,000 units were produced. The following labor costs were incurred:

Class I (60,000 hours)	$ 660,000
Class II (25,000 hours)	400,000
	$1,060,000

Required:
(a) Prepare separate analyses of labor cost variances for each class of direct labor. What is the *total* variance?
(b) Prepare a combined analysis of labor cost variances, including:
   (1) labor rate variances.
   (2) labor substitution (mix) variance.
   (3) labor yield (quantity) variance.
(c) Comment on the answers in parts (a) and (b). Under what circumstances would either be the more acceptable basis of analysis? Why?

E 13–7 Direct Labor Cost Variances—Materials Input-Related Variances

Ace Manufacturing Company produces independent Products X and Y, for which the following standard cost specifications have been established:

	Direct Materials	Direct Labor
X	20 pounds @ $4 per pound	10 hours @ $10 per hour
Y	10 pounds @ $4 per pound	5 hours @ $10 per hour

Standard variable overhead is 75 percent of the standard direct labor cost. Labor costs are more closely related to the quantity of input processed than to the number of units produced. For January of 19X2, during which 6,000 units of X and 4,000 units of Y were produced, the following costs were reported:

Materials Purchased and Used	170,000 pounds	$714,000
Direct Labor	81,000 hours	$845,000
Variable Overhead		$638,500

Required:
(a) Prepare a detailed analysis of all production cost variances. Be sure to include a materials-related labor efficiency variance.

(b) Comment on the analysis in part (a). Are there any patterns present that may cause concern? Why or why not?

E 13–8 Variance Reporting—Control Responsibility—Investigation Decision

The Production Department manager of Wizneski Corporation is a firm believer in management by exception. His policy is to review each week's production cost reports and call for investigation of any variance that is greater than $5,000 or more than 10 percent of the standard cost of the item involved. Because his concern is with production operations, price and rate variances are not his responsibility. However, he is responsible for all aspects of overhead. Standard cost specifications per unit are as follows:

Direct Materials (3 pounds @ $20)	$ 60
Direct Labor (10 hours @ $12)	96
Variable Overhead ($16 per hour)	160
Standard Cost per Unit	$316

For May of 19X6, results of production included:

(1)	Units Produced	3,000
(2)	Materials Used (@ $18.50 per pound)	8,600
(3)	Labor Hours Worked (@ $14 per hour)	32,500
(4)	Overhead Incurred	$515,500

Required:
(a) Prepare an analysis of variances, indicating those for which the production manager is responsible.
(b) Which variances should be investigated on the basis of the criteria specified?
(c) Suggest at least two plausible causes of the variances reported in part (a) and the appropriate response to each.

E 13–9 Sales Performance—Analysis of Variance—Variance Investigation

Dailey Corporation establishes quotas for its sales staff in terms of total sales revenue, total sales units, and number of sales calls per month. Performance reports are then used to evaluate each salesperson, with those sales representatives whose achievements vary more than 10 percent from their quota being subject to review. The following table relates to the February sales activities of Joanne Cunningham, one of the company's top sales representatives:

	Actual	Quota
Sales Revenue	$90,000	$80,000
Sales Units	2,400	2,000
Sales Calls	150	100

Required:
(a) Analyze Joanne's performance during February. Was it acceptable or not? Why?
(b) Does Joanne violate the review criteria on any counts? Explain.

(c) Evaluate the present system with regard to the quotas that are set and the conditions for performance review and investigation.

E 13–10   Control Charts—Variance Investigation

Bryant Corporation uses control chart techniques to monitor production cost performance in its manufacturing divisions. For the Blending Division, an average direct labor conversion cost per batch of $450 has been established as the norm, with control limits of $400 and $500. During the first two weeks of March, the following daily results were observed:

Day	Batches Processed	Total Labor Cost	Day	Batches Processed	Total Labor Cost
1	25	$10,750	6	30	$14,200
2	30	13,800	7	35	17,100
3	25	10,050	8	28	14,750
4	35	15,900	9	40	20,900
5	32	16,600	10	36	16,400

Required:

(a) Prepare a control chart for the Blending Division. Plot the operating data for the first two weeks of March.

(b) Comment on the results of your analysis in part (a).

(c) What are the limitations of the control procedure involved here?

Cases

C 13–1   Changes in Product Mix

The 1973 annual report of Genesco, Inc. contains the following paragraphs:

> Genesco's footwear divisions manufacture and wholesale footwear for men, women, and children in a broad range of styles and prices. Other divisions manufacture uppers, soles, heels, adhesives, finishes, and other footwear components. During 1973, three factors had a major adverse impact on footwear operations.
>
> 1. *The Change in Product Mix.* In fiscal 1972, demand was high for three types of footwear—boots, canvas footwear, and "stitchout/stitchdown" constructions (the casual "jeans shoes"). This consistent demand permitted the plants to operate with high efficiency and low costs. When the product mix shifted in fiscal 1973, the footwear plants made the change-over, but nevertheless experienced start-up costs and temporarily reduced efficiency.
>
> 2. *Major Styling and Construction Changes.* In fiscal 1973, the major fashion change was the emphasis on shoe bottoms: high heels, platforms, and clogs. As the footwear plants shifted, this new fashion emphasis necessitated major expansions of shoe bottom preparation departments and the development of new manufacturing techniques. In men's shoes, the advent of high heels introduced a whole new dimension to the men's shoe factories. These styling and construction changes also complicated the manufacturing changeover.

3. *Rising Hide Prices*. Compounding these two factors was a three-fold increase in hide prices in a year's time caused by rising world demand. The unstable and unprecedented conditions which prevailed throughout fiscal 1973 affected leather operations as well as footwear divisions.

In response to this situation, a significant shift was made to man-made materials. This shift helped hold down costs, although differences between the nature of leather and the synthetic materials created additional manufacturing problems.

Responding to these challenges, footwear manufacturing has been reorganized to reduce the reaction time for future fashion swings. At the same time, the changes and expenses required by these unusual conditions are now largely behind the footwear divisions.

Required:

(a) What are the implications of paragraphs 1, 2, and 3 for standard manufacturing costs in the current year and in future years? Discuss materials, labor, variable overhead, and fixed overhead components of standard cost.

(b) Why would a change in the product mix alluded to in paragraph 1 affect "efficiency"?

(c) What is the significance of the change from hides to man-made materials in paragraph 3?

(d) What are the implications of the change to high heels, platforms, and clogs in paragraph 2?

C 13–2 Labor Variances

Davisson Company employs three grades of production workers. The standard labor rates are as follows:

Grade VI	$7.20 per hour
Grade VII	$8.80 per hour
Grade VIII	$10.00 per hour

In establishing standard costs for production operations, the problem arises of specifying the standard labor rate for each task. One approach would be to use a weighted average standard cost per hour, based on the expected number of workers in each grade. An alternative is to set the standard equal to the rate payable to the least costly labor grade capable of performing the task.

Required:

(a) Which approach would you recommend? Why?

(b) What types of labor variances will be likely to be reported under the two separate approaches? To what department (cost center) would such variances be assigned? Why?

C 13–3 Actual versus Budgeted Costs

The 19X3 budget for Alpine Company predicted a net income of $960,000, after marketing and administrative expenses were deducted from a budgeted gross profit figure of $1,200,000. However, actual results showed a net loss of $264,000 after marketing and administrative expenses of $504,000 were deducted.

Although the unit sales price of $6.40 would only allow a small unit profit, the manager finds it hard to understand such a large variation in reported income.

The budgeted sales volume of 1,200,000 units was attained, and inventories did not vary. To produce 1,200,000 units of output, 1,600,000 units of materials are required, but 1,660,000 units were used up during the year. This should have caused a cost variance of only $36,000.

Labor standards specify 6 units of output per labor hour, but a total of 259,040 labor hours were worked this year. The variable overhead rate is $8.40 per labor hour. Fixed overhead is applied at a standard rate of $1 per unit of output. This rate was set at normal operating capacity. During the year, total overhead incurred amounted to $3,853,600, of which $1,933,600 was for variable items. Actual fixed overhead was the same as the total budgeted amount.

Required:

(a) Prepare separate schedules to show the derivation of the budgeted net income of $960,000 and the actual net loss of $264,000.

(b) Prepare an analysis of all cost variances.

(c) Comment on the analysis in parts (a) and (b).

C 13–4   Variance Analysis and Investigation

Sue Bennett, the new controller of the Fantasy Cup Company, encountered the following response from several production department managers when discussing proposed revisions to the company's system for reporting and analyzing cost performance: "Why should you want to poke around in the cost reports from our departments so much? We never had that happen before when good old Fred was the controller. All we had to do was to be sure that total actual costs didn't exceed total budgeted costs for our department and things ran smoothly. Why are you proposing all this attention to fine detail?"

Required:

Comment critically on the issues involved from the viewpoint of variance analysis and investigation.

C 13–5   Investigating Variances—Alternatives

The controller of Thomas Furniture Company is reviewing the company's variance analysis and investigation procedures. The following alternative rules for deciding whether or not to investigate weekly cost variances have been suggested:

(1) Investigate *all* variances regardless of amount and direction (favorable or unfavorable).

(2) Investigate all unfavorable variances.

(3) Investigate all variances larger than $2,000.

(4) Investigate all variances that exceed 5 percent of the budgeted amount of the item to which they apply.

(5) Investigate all variances that exceed $1,000 and have occurred for three or more consecutive weeks.

(6)   Investigate all variances that exceed $2,000 and have been increasing each week for more than three consecutive weeks.

Required:
Evaluate each of these proposed rules, suggesting circumstances in which they would be appropriate or inappropriate.

C 13–6   Random and Nonrandom Variances

For each of the following possible reasons for deviations from budgeted levels, indicate whether it represents a random or nonrandom variance and, if nonrandom, whether it is due to implementation error, data measurement error, forecasting error, model error, or behavioral side effects.

(1)   Materials were purchased in lots smaller than anticipated when standards were set.
(2)   A labor contract was renegotiated and employees received a 10 percent raise.
(3)   A machine broke down, requiring extraordinary repairs, idle time, rework, overtime, and so on.
(4)   Labor costs were based on time records that a foreman had falsified in order to shift costs from one period to another.
(5)   Factory supplies costs were reported on the basis of amounts purchased, instead of usage as was anticipated.
(6)   Materials usage varied from day to day due to variations in how well employees concentrate on their job.
(7)   Standard materials costs were calculated using product specifications that have since been changed to reflect new product design.
(8)   Although standard labor costs were based on anticipated improvement in productivity of workers, it was subsequently conceded that no further improvements were possible and that standards were already too tight.
(9)   Workers deliberately slowed down activities and disrupted operations to protest the unrealistically tight budget.
(10)   Variations occurred in yield of output per ton of input processed due to differences in the quality of each batch purchased. Such differences are expected due to volatility of input.
(11)   Same as in part 10, except that quality control should reject any inputs that do not meet tolerance limits.
(12)   Labor productivity changes occurred due to variations in temperature—workers were less productive on exceptionally hot or cold days.

C 13–7   Timing and Detail in Variance Analysis

The Slaymaker Corporation has requested a review of its variance reporting and investigation procedures. Two fundamental issues were raised, characterized by the following statements:

(1)   "If materials usage, labor efficiency and overhead efficiency variances as conventionally measured are all we have to go on, we're really in the dark. They are

calculated once a month and represent the aggregate effect of all the events that have occurred in that period. Consequently, a lot of information will be lost, since there will be a cancelling-out effect of all the individual variances. Some of those individual variances that relate to one day's activities or one particular batch of production probably are significant enough to be investigated. However, they get lost in the shuffle if the overall variance for the whole period is within the tolerance range.''

(2) ''It's just not feasible or practical to measure and analyze variances that pertain to individual parts of total output such as each separate batch or short periods of time like one shift or one day or even one hour. It's too expensive and tedious to do that. You just have to go with composite measures of performance for some longer period of time.''

Required:
Critically evaluate these statements as they relate to the problems of timing and detail in the variance analysis and investigation process.

C 13–8 Planning and Control

''Whenever variances are detected and reported, it always seems that it is an automatic assumption that something is wrong with the process or the inputs or the managers involved. Maybe once in a while some thought should be given to the possibility that maybe it's the budget that was wrong. Couldn't it be that sometimes there are inaccuracies and errors in setting the standards?''

Required:
Critically evaluate this statement, discussing the alternative responses to variances that should be considered in the feedback phase of control systems. In particular, discuss the concepts of the *planning significance,* and *control significance* of variances.

C 13–9 Efficiency and Effectiveness—Favorable Variances

''It should be the goal of the managers of all our cost centers to minimize their operating costs at all times. We want variances that are always favorable!''

Required:
Critically evaluate this assertion, especially from the point of view of overall operating efficiency and effectiveness.

C 13–10 Efficiency and Effectiveness–Zero Variance

''What cost centers should achieve is a state where their cost variances are always zero. Then we know everything is under control and no follow-up will ever be needed.''

Required:
Critically evaluate this assertion, especially from the point of view of overall operating efficiency and effectiveness.

Problems

P 13–1 Sales Performance Analysis—Single Product Variances

Bankstown Company produces and distributes a single product. Budgeted and actual results for March, 19X2 were as follows:

	Budget 20,000 Units	Actual 22,000 Units
Sales	$160,000	$168,000
Less: Variable Costs	64,000	76,800
Contribution Margin	$ 96,000	$ 91,200
Less: Fixed Costs	80,000	80,000
Net Income	$ 16,000	$ 11,200

Inventory levels were not budgeted to change during the month and did not do so. Management is concerned that profits were down, even though sales were up in terms of both units and revenues.

Required:
(a) Prepare an analysis of sales performance that includes:
    (1) sales price variance.
    (2) sales quantity variance (revenue basis).
    (3) sales quantity variance (standard contribution margin basis).
(b) What was the total variance with regard to variable cost items? What extra information would be needed to analyze this variance in further detail?

P 13–2 Profit Variance Analysis—Sales Performance and Manufacturing Cost Variances—Single Product Situation

Makarcyzk Company developed the following budget for the first quarter of 19X2:

Sales (10,000 units)			$200,000
Less: Cost of Goods Sold Inventory, January 1			
(2,000 units @ $8)		$ 16,000	
Cost of Goods Manufactured (11,000 units)			
Variable	$88,000		
Fixed	40,000	128,000	
		$144,000	
Less: Inventory, March 31 (3,000 units @ $8)		24,000	120,000
Gross Profit			$ 80,000
Operating Expenses:			
Variable		$ 30,000	
Fixed		20,000	50,000
Net Income			$ 30,000

The company uses a standard variable cost system for its manufacturing costs, and expenses all fixed manufacturing costs in the current period.

During the quarter, actual sales were 11,000 units and total revenue was $231,000. Production totaled 12,000 units with fixed costs of $45,000 and variable costs of

$102,000. Marketing and administrative costs were $34,000 for variable items, $21,000 for fixed items.

Required:

(a) Prepare an income statement to reflect the actual results for the quarter.

(b) Prepare an analysis of sales performance based on standard contribution margin.

(c) What were the *total* variances for (1) variable manufacturing costs, (2) fixed manufacturing costs, (3) variable operating expenses, and (4) fixed operating expenses?

(d) What additional information would be needed to analyze the cost variances in more detail?

(e) Comment on the variances calculated in part (b). Who is responsible for them?

P 13-3   Sales Variances—Multiple Output Situation

Doten Automobile Sales Company distributes three models of a popular vehicle. The following sales budget was prepared for the second quarter of 19X2:

	Vulture	Hawk	Condor
Unit Sales	2,000	4,000	6,000
Sales Price per Unit	$12,000	$10,000	$8,000
Dealer Cost per Unit	$ 9,000	$ 7,500	$6,000
Other Variable Costs per Unit	$ 1,500	$ 1,000	$1,000

All variable costs per unit were as budgeted. Operating results for the second quarter of 19X2 included the following:

	Vulture	Hawk	Condor
Unit Sales	2,500	4,000	6,500
Sales Price per Unit	$12,500	$10,500	$7,500

Required:

(a) Prepare a schedule to show the total budgeted performance results on a contribution margin basis, (1) for each product line, (2) for an average sales unit, and (3) for total performance.

(b) Prepare a similar report to show the results of actual operations.

(c) Prepare an analysis of sales price and sales quantity variances for each separate product line.

(d) Prepare an analysis of sales mix, sales price, and sales quantity variances for the product lines on a combined basis.

(e) Compare the results of parts (c) and (d). Under what circumstances would one particular analysis be more useful? Why?

P 13-4   Sales Performance Analysis—Multiple Product Situation

Johnstone Company sells four products that are to some extent competitive with each other. Budgeted and actual operating results for the month of August, 19X7 were as follows:

	Unit Sales	Total Revenue	Unit Variable Cost
Budget			
Product W......	20,000	$ 400,000	$12
Product X	10,000	600,000	40
Product Y	8,000	400,000	30
Product Z	6,000	300,000	35
	44,000	$1,700,000	
Actual			
Product W......	22,000	$ 440,000	$10
Product X	8,000	520,000	45
Product Y	10,000	450,000	32
Product Z	8,000	440,000	40
	48,000	$1,850,000	

Required:

(a) Prepare schedules of these budgeted and actual results. Show sales revenue, variable cost, and contribution margin amounts in as much detail as possible.

(b) Prepare an analysis of sales and cost variances for the month on an individual product basis.

(c) Prepare an analysis of sales and cost variances for the month on a combined basis. Show (1) total variable cost variance, (2) sales price variance, (3) sales mix variance, and (4) sales quantity variance.

(d) Comment on further possible analysis of the answer to part (c)(1).

(e) Which analysis would be more useful, (c) or (d)? Under what circumstances? Why?

P 13-5   Joint Product Processing—Sales Performance Analysis

El Norte Canning Company purchases fruit for processing and canning. After processing, the fruit is graded with the top grade product being sold under El Norte's own label, the medium grade sold to a national food chain, the broken sections and leftovers sold to a local co-operative.

Each ton of raw fruit (2,000 pounds) should yield 1,800 pounds of salable output, which is usually divided in the following way: 900 pounds of top grade, 600 pounds of medium grade, 300 pounds of broken sections. All processing costs are fixed and amount to $5,000 per week, during which time 10 tons of raw fruit can be processed. Sales prices per pound are budgeted at $2 for top grade, $1.50 for medium, and $1 for broken sections.

During the first week of March, 19X2, ten tons of raw fruit were processed and the following yields and prices were obtained:

> 8,500 pounds of top grade @ $2.25 per pound
> 7,000 pounds of medium grade @ $1.60 per pound
> 2,500 pounds of broken sections @ $.90 per pound

All fixed operating costs were as planned. Raw fruit usually costs 75¢ per pound, but this week, due to plentiful supplies, the price was only 65¢ per pound.

Required:

(a) Prepare a budget for sales and operating costs for the week.

(b) Prepare a similar report to show the results of actual operations.

(c) Prepare an analysis of sales performance showing sales price, sales mix, and sales yield (quantity) variances (based on sales prices) for the week.

(d) Prepare an analysis of cost variances for the week. What level of detail is possible? Why?

P 13–6   Multiple Product Situation—Analysis of Sales, Costs, and Profits

Jayson Paint Sales Company sells premium, standard, and economy paint. Based on previous experience with regard to the total monthly demand for paint and for the various grades, a budget for June, 19X1 was developed as follows:

	Premium	Standard	Economy	Total
Unit Sales (gallons)	20,000	20,000	40,000	80,000
Sales Revenues	$325,000	$180,000	$225,000	$730,000
Variable Costs	230,000	160,000	100,000	490,000
Contribution Margin	$ 70,000	$ 40,000	$100,000	210,000
Fixed Costs				120,000
Net Income				$ 90,000

Actual results of operations for June were as reported below:

	Premium	Standard	Economy	Total
Unit Sales (gallons)	25,000	15,000	50,000	90,000
Sales Revenues	$325,000	$180,000	$225,000	$730,000
Variable Costs	275,000	120,000	100,000	495,000
Contribution Margin	$ 50,000	$ 60,000	$125,000	$235,000
Fixed Costs				125,000
Net Income				$110,000

Required:

(a) Prepare an analysis of June *sales* performance based on the *separate* results for each product.

(b) Prepare an analysis of the results of June operations based on the combined effects of the sales of the three grades of products.

(c) Comment on each of the variances calculated in part (b). Give a brief interpretation of each variance.

(d) What extra information would be needed to allow further analysis of cost variances?

(e) Comment on the relative usefulness of the analysis in parts (a) and (b). When would you recommend the use of one or the other?

P 13–7   Comprehensive Variance Analysis

Standard product cost specifications have been developed for Products Y and Z of KLM Manufacturing Company.

	Y	Z
Direct Materials		
(10 pounds of A @ $8 per pound)......	$ 80	
(10 pounds of B @ $4 per pound)......		$ 40
Direct Labor		
(4 hours @ $10 per hour)	40	40
Overhead		
(4 hours @ $20 per hour)	80	80
	$200	$160

The annual overhead rate was established on the basis of total budgeted fixed overhead of $360,000 and an expected activity level of 36,000 labor hours. For 19X2, the following budgeted income statement was prepared:

	Y	Z	Total
Sales			
Y (4,000 @ $300)	$1,200,000		
Z (5,000 @ $250)		$1,250,000	
			$2,450,000
Less: Standard Cost of Goods Sold			
Y (4,000 @ $200)	800,000		
Z (5,000 @ $160)		800,000	
			1,600,000
Standard Gross Profit	$ 400,000	$ 450,000	$ 850,000
Less: Operating Expenses			
Marketing ($30 per unit) ...		$ 270,000	
Administration (all fixed) ...		280,000	550,000
Net Income			$ 300,000

The following actual results were achieved in 19X2:

	Y	Z	Total
Sales			
Y (3,000 @ $320)	$ 960,000		
Z (5,500 @ $240)		$1,320,000	
			$2,280,000
Less: Standard Cost of Goods Sold			
Y (3,000 @ $200)	600,000		
Z (5,500 @ $160)		880,000	
			1,480,000
	$ 360,000	$ 440,000	$ 800,000
Less: Total Manufacturing			
Variances (unfavorable)			(61,250)
Gross Profit			$ 738,750
Less: Operating Expenses			
Marketing		$ 272,000	
Administration		290,000	562,000
Net Income			$ 176,750

The following additional information was provided:

(1) Purchases:
      A (35,000 pounds @ $8.50 per pound) ... $297,500
      B (65,000 pounds @ $3.75 per pound) ... $243,750

(2) Materials Used:
      A: 32,000 pounds
      B: 56,000 pounds

(3) Direct Labor: 33,000 hours $345,000

(4) Total Overhead Incurred $715,000

(5) Beginning and ending inventories (except Raw Materials) were zero.

(6) Products Y and Z are somewhat competitive, their main difference being that Y is made of a higher quality material than Z.

Required:
Prepare an analysis of all variances—sales performance, manufacturing costs, and operating expenses. Present as much detail as possible. Show sales mix and sales quantity variances separately.

P 13–8 Standard Cost Analysis—Multiple Input Situation— Price, Mix, and Yield Variances

Langer Company blends chemicals to produce a gasoline additive called Blast-Off. The following standard product cost specification has been developed for the direct materials content of each 1,000-gallon batch of the product.

	Standard Input Quantity	Standard Price per Gallon
Methanol	600 gallons	$0.50
Alcohol	500 gallons	$1.00
Ethanol	100 gallons	$4.00
	1,200 gallons	

Due to evaporation and spillage, the standard yield of Blast-Off is expected to be 200 gallons less than the total raw materials input.

During the first week of April, 19X3, 500,000 gallons of Blast-Off were produced and the following production results were reported:

Inputs Consumed	Quantity	Cost
Methanol	325,000 gallons	$146,250
Alcohol	280,000 gallons	266,000
Ethanol	45,000 gallons	191,250
	650,000 gallons	$603,500

Required:
(a) Prepare an analysis of all materials cost variances for the week. Show price, mix, and yield variances.

(b)   Comment on the results in part (a). How useful will these variances be in evaluating the performance in the blending or other departments? Why?

P 13–9   Multiple Inputs—Price, Mix, and Yield Variances

Steerchip Fertilizer Company mixes chemicals with pastoral waste to produce its fast-moving product, Bleeperolio. The standard product mix calls for the following ingredients per 100 tons of output, with some allowance for wastage in mixing:

	Input Quantity (Tons)	Price per Ton
Pastoral Waste	75	$ 5
Phosphates	15	$30
Ammonia Sulphate	10	$40
Tobacco Dust	10	$15
	110	

The manager of the mixing plant can vary the ratio of the mix of inputs within a reasonable range, according to the availability and price of each ingredient each week. In the first two weeks of February, 19X3, the following separate results were reported:

	Week 1 Quantity Used (tons)	Week 1 Total Cost	Week 2 Quantity Used (tons)	Week 2 Total Cost
Pastoral Waste	8,000	$40,000	10,000	$45,000
Phosphate	1,800	$57,600	1,000	$45,000
Ammonia Sulphate	1,000	$42,000	1,800	$64,800
Tobacco Dust	1,100	$17,600	1,300	$20,800
Less: Wastage	(1,900)		(2,100)	
Production	10,000		12,000	

Required:
(a)   Prepare an analysis of price, mix, and yield variances for the two *separate* weeks of operation.

(b)   Prepare a single combined analysis of variances for the entire two-week period.

(c)   Comment on the analysis in parts (a) and (b).

(d)   In which week was the manager of the plant more efficient? Why?

P 13–10   Price, Mix, and Yield Variances—Multiple Inputs—Evaluation of Performance—Materials-Related Labor Variance

Granitella Corporation produces a fuel additive by blending two secret ingredients, Product M and Product N. Product specifications call for the following inputs for each 1,000 gallons of output:

Product M	500 gallons @ $10 per gallon
Product N	500 gallons @ $ 5 per gallon
Direct Labor	50 hours @ $10 per hour

The following results were reported during August:

Output		100,000 gallons	
Purchases:	Product M	45,000 gallons	$495,000
	Product N	80,000 gallons	$320,000
Usage:	Product M	40,000 gallons	
	Product N	65,000 gallons	
Direct Labor		5,750 hours	$ 62,500

Required:

(a) Prepare an analysis of material cost variances, treating Products M and N separately.

(b) Prepare a combined analysis of materials cost variances, showing price, mix, and yield variances.

(c) Prepare an analysis of labor cost variances.

(d) Revise the labor cost variance analysis of part (c) on the assumption that the standard hours required of 50 per 1,000 gallons of output can be restated as 20 hours per 500 gallons of M processed and 30 hours per 500 gallons of N processed.

(e) Comment on the analysis in part (b) and relate those results to the solution to part (d).

P 13–11   Price, Mix, and Yield Variances—Multiple Inputs— Materials, Labor, and Variable Overhead

The following product cost specifications have been established for one of Shoveron Chemical Company's products:

Direct Materials	
A (20 pounds @ $3.25 per pound)......	$ 65
B (30 pounds @ $2.00 per pound)......	60
C (50 pounds @ $1.50 per pound)	75
	$200
Direct Labor	
12 hours @ $12	144
Variable Overhead	
12 hours @ $8	96
Total Standard Cost	
of 100 pounds of Standard Input Mix ...	$440
Standard Yield Rate	
80 pounds of output	
per 100 pounds input mix	

During July, 19X2, the following results were achieved:

Purchases:		
A	50,000 pounds @	$3.20 per pound
B	80,000 pounds @	$2.10 per pound
C	100,000 pounds @	$1.55 per pound
Usage:		
A	45,000 pounds	
B	70,000 pounds	
C	95,000 pounds	

Direct Labor (20,000 hours) $250,000
Variable Overhead Incurred $105,000
Output (160,000 pounds)

Required:

(a) Prepare an analysis of direct materials cost variances, showing price, mix, and yield variances.

(b) Prepare an analysis of direct labor and variable overhead variances. Show the rate, efficiency, and materials yield-related variances separately.

(c) Comment on the usefulness of the variances calculated in parts (a) and (b). When would this level of detail in variance analysis be justified and useful? Why?

P 13–12 Comprehensive Review

Cook Chemical Company uses Material X to produce joint Products A and B. A process costing system is used because manufacturing operations are continuous. Department 1 processes Material X and Department 2 is responsible for subsequent operations on Products A and B. The following information is available:

(1) Standard Input Prices:
   Material X .... 25¢ per pound
   Labor—Department 1 .... $10 per hour
   Labor—Department 2 .... $12 per hour
   Variable Overhead (plant-wide) .. $6 per labor hour

(2) Production Specifications:
   Standard Yield per Ton of Material X:
      Product A .... 900 pounds
      Product B .... 600 pounds
      Waste (no value) .... 500 pounds
                              2,000 pounds

   Direct Labor:
   Department 1   40 hours per ton of Material X *processed*
   Department 2   20 hours per ton of Product A *produced*
                   30 hours per ton of Product B *produced*

(3) Material X is added to processing at the beginning of operations in Department 1. Labor and overhead costs are incurred at a uniform rate in both departments.

(4) Inventories, January 1, 19X3:
   Material X .... 50 tons
   Work in Process, Department 1 .... none
   Work in Process, Department 2 Product A .. 30 tons 50% complete
                                 Product B .. 20 tons 25% complete

(5) Inventories, January 31, 19X3:
   Material X .... 80 tons
   Work in Process, Department 1 .... none
   Work in Process, Department 2 Product A .. 60 tons 75% complete
                                 Product B .. 40 tons 60% complete

(6) Completions, January, 19X3:
      Output transferred to Department 2 ... 450 tons unprocessed A
                                                 350 tons unprocessed B
      Department 2 .... ? tons of A
                                                 ? tons of B

(7) Inputs purchased and used:
    Purchases of Material X
       1,100 tons @ $510 per ton
    Labor—Department 1 42,500 hours $450,000
    Labor—Department 2 21,500 hours $255,000
    Total Variable Overhead Incurred $375,000

(8) The standard costs of unprocessed Products A and B transferred into Department 2 are determined on the basis of the physical units method (see Chapter 6).

Required:

(a) Prepare process production cost reports for Departments 1 and 2 for January. (Department 2 will require separate reports for its two products. See Chapter 5 for format and detail.) Show all items at *standard* cost.

(b) Prepare an analysis of all January cost variances for each department, showing as much detail as possible. Include mix and yield variances where appropriate.

14

VARIABLE AND FULL ABSORPTION COSTING: INCOME MEASUREMENT AND PRICING POLICIES

LEARNING OBJECTIVES

After studying Chapter 14, you should be able to:

1. Distinguish between the full absorption cost and variable cost models, identify the strengths and weaknesses of each, and describe the areas of application for which each model is most appropriate.
2. Calculate the comparative effects on income of the full absorption cost model and the variable cost model when production and sales levels are increasing, stable, or decreasing.
3. Describe long-range pricing policies based on capital maintenance and on attainment of profit goals.
4. Describe long-range pricing policies based on:
   a. Penetration pricing.
   b. Promotional pricing.
   c. Skimming pricing.
   d. Distress or liquidation pricing.
   e. Price differentiation.
   f. Convenience pricing.
   g. Psychological pricing.
   h. Prestige pricing.
5. Calculate a cost-plus selling price for a single type of output using the full absorption cost and variable cost methods.
6. Calculate the sales prices of multiple outputs on a cost-plus basis, when common fixed costs are allocated:
   a. Arbitrarily.
   b. According to the fixed proportions in which the joint outputs are manufactured.
7. Calculate a contractor's bid price in a job cost environment.
8. Calculate the unit sales prices needed to reach profit goals that are defined as
   a. An absolute dollar amount.
   b. A rate of return on sales revenue.
   c. A rate of return on total resources.
   d. A rate of return on equity.
9. Calculate the long-run transfer price and compare it with the unit cost of purchases from outside suppliers.
10. Calculate the long-run total cost of internal transfers at various activity levels and compare it with the total cost of purchases from outside suppliers.

In this chapter, the two major product costing models—*variable cost* and *full absorption cost*—are compared with regard to their effects on income measurement and pricing decisions.

Underlying the **variable cost model** is one basic idea: the separation of *variable costs* from *fixed costs*. This model treats only direct materials, direct labor, and variable manufacturing overhead (the costs that vary directly with activity level changes) as product costs. It requires that fixed manufacturing overhead (the costs of having productive capacity) be charged to expense in the period incurred rather than being capitalized as inventory.

The **full absorption cost model** includes fixed manufacturing overhead in product cost, together with direct materials, direct labor, and variable manufacturing overhead costs.

THE PRODUCT COST MODELS COMPARED

Theoretical arguments for and against the variable and full absorption cost models center around the issues of asset definition and measurement. There are also practical questions concerning the usefulness of the two models.

Assets represent future economic benefits.[1] Inventory items (raw materials, work in process, and finished goods) clearly fit within this definition. But accountants disagree as to how assets should be measured for income reporting, performance evaluation, and decision making purposes. Assuming a cost-based measurement is to be used, the problem becomes one of determining the cost of the service potentials that make the assets valuable.

Financial accountants, applying the matching and realization principles, view assets as unexpired costs[2] to be deferred and matched as expenses against the revenues that will be generated in future periods by the use or sale of the assets. Inventory items are normally held in anticipation of such future sales. Therefore, the costs that should be included in inventory are those which have already been incurred to produce inventory items and which avoid the need to incur future costs. Advocates of variable costing use this argument to support their position that the only relevant costs of inventory items are the variable product costs incurred to produce the inventories. Accordingly, fixed manufacturing costs should be excluded because they would have been incurred whether or not the inventory items were manufactured and because they do not benefit future periods.

The variable cost approach is also supported by the **replacement cost concept** as it relates to inventory measurement. From this viewpoint, the only

---

[1] "Objectives of Financial Reporting and Elements of Financial Statements of Business Enterprises," (Stamford, Conn.: FASB, 1977).

[2] "Basic Concepts and Accounting Principles Underlying Financial Statements of Business Enterprises," *Statement of the Accounting Principles Board No. 4* (New York: AICPA, 1970), paragraph 147.

relevant costs of inventory items are the future costs that are avoided by having already produced or acquired inventories. Similarly, according to the variable cost approach, only future variable product costs should be included in inventory valuations, because future fixed costs will be incurred whether or not inventories are replaced.

Advocates of full absorption costing argue that inventory costs should include *all* manufacturing-related costs that must be incurred directly or indirectly in the production of inventories. These include costs that vary with changes in inventory quantities produced as well as costs that are capacity-related and do not vary. Therefore, fixed manufacturing costs should be capitalized because they provide the capacity without which production could not occur.

This controversy can also be viewed as a disagreement as to whether fixed costs of production are **period costs** or **product costs.** The variable cost approach treats fixed costs as costs of providing productive capacity *for a given period of time.* From this viewpoint, it follows that fixed manufacturing costs should be expensed currently and not be allowed to affect the performance of future accounting periods. On the other hand, the full absorption cost method requires that period costs include only *sales-related items* (Cost of Goods Sold on a full cost basis, marketing costs, and administrative costs). Because fixed manufacturing costs are *production-related,* they are included in the cost of inventories under the full cost approach.

Full absorption costing is presently required in published financial statements and for income tax reporting. The AICPA's position is as follows:

> As applied to inventories, cost means in principle the sum of the applicable expenditures and charges *directly or indirectly* incurred in bringing an article to its existing condition and location.[3]

However, for internal purposes—for analysis, decision making, and reporting to management—variable costing has achieved widespread acceptance and use, especially in recent years.

INCOME MEASUREMENT USING THE VARIABLE AND FULL ABSORPTION COST MODELS

There are practical as well as conceptual issues involved in the variable cost versus full absorption cost controversy. Each model affects income differently under various conditions. The following examples demonstrate these effects and provide a basis for evaluating the practical advantages and disadvantages of the two models.

Example: Wadman Corporation's operating data will be used throughout this analysis. The corporation's unit sales, production, and ending inventory for its first year of operations are shown in Figure 14–1.

The corporation's products sold for $20 per unit throughout the year. Variable manufacturing costs were $8 per unit and variable marketing costs were $2 per unit. Expected annual capacity was 24,000 units. Annual fixed manufacturing costs were $96,000 and annual fixed marketing costs were $48,000.

---

[3] Accounting Research Bulletin No. 43, "Restatement and Revision of Accounting Research Bulletins" (New York: AICPA, 1953), Chapter 4, Statement 3. Emphasis added.

FIGURE 14–1

Wadman Corporation
Quarterly Sales, Production, and Ending Inventories
For the Year 19X9

	Quarter 1	Quarter 2	Quarter 3	Quarter 4
Sales (units)	4,000	4,000	8,000	8,000
Production (units)	6,000	8,000	8,000	2,000
Ending Inventory (units)	2,000	6,000	6,000	0

If all these amounts are held constant during the period of analysis, calculations can be simplified to allow a clearer demonstration of the variable and full absorption cost effects on income. At several points in the following analysis, the phrase "other things being equal" will be used to refer to these simplifying assumptions.

Product costs calculated using the variable cost model are $8 per unit. All inventory and Cost of Goods Sold amounts are measured accordingly. Product costs calculated using the full absorption cost model are $12 per unit— that is, $8 of variable manufacturing cost plus $4 of fixed manufacturing cost ($96,000 ÷ 24,000). Quarterly fixed overhead volume variances will be treated as adjustments to Cost of Goods Sold in the period in which they occur. There will be no spending or efficiency variances because unit costs and prices are assumed to be constant.

Figure 14–2 shows quarterly income statements prepared according to the *variable product cost model.* Quarterly income statements prepared according to the *full absorption product cost model* are shown in Figure 14–3. Ending inventory and net income measures calculated using the two models are compared in Figure 14–4. Wadman Corporation's operating results will now be used to demonstrate specific differences between the effects on income of the variable cost and full absorption cost models.

Inventory Level Increasing—Sales Volume Constant

Compare the results of the first two quarters. Sales were 4,000 units in both periods, but inventory increased from 2,000 to 6,000 units. The variable cost method shows income of $4,000 in both periods, but the full absorption cost method results in $12,000 income in the first quarter and $20,000 in the second quarter. Three general conclusions can be drawn from these differences in reported profits.

First, other things being equal, *full absorption costing results in a higher net income than variable costing when inventory levels are increasing.* As inventory levels increase, full absorption costing causes an increasing amount of fixed overhead cost to be carried forward to future periods as part of ending inventory. When variable costing is used, these fixed overhead costs are charged to expense in the current period. Under full absorption costing, inventory increases result in comparatively higher ending inventory balances, a lower current period cost of goods sold, and a higher net income.

FIGURE 14–2

Wadman Corporation
Quarterly Income Statements—Variable Product Cost Model
For the Year 19X9

	Quarter 1	Quarter 2	Quarter 3	Quarter 4
Sales	$80,000	$80,000	$160,000	$160,000
Cost of Goods Sold:				
Beginning Inventory ($8 per Unit)	$ 0	$16,000	$ 48,000	$48,000
Cost of Goods Manufactured ($8 per Unit)	48,000	64,000	64,000	16,000
	$48,000	$80,000	$112,000	$64,000
Less: Ending Inventory ($8 per Unit)	16,000	48,000	48,000	0
	32,000	32,000	64,000	64,000
	$48,000	$48,000	$ 96,000	$ 96,000
Less: Variable Marketing Costs	8,000	8,000	16,000	16,000
Contribution Margin	$40,000	$40,000	$ 80,000	$ 80,000
Less: Fixed Costs	36,000	36,000	36,000	36,000
Net Income	$ 4,000	$ 4,000	$ 44,000	$ 44,000

FIGURE 14–3

Wadman Corporation
Quarterly Income Statements—Full Absorption Product Cost Model
For the Year 19X9

	Quarter 1		Quarter 2		Quarter 3		Quarter 4	
Sales		$80,000		$80,000		$160,000		$160,000
Cost of Goods Sold:								
Beginning Inventory ($12 per Unit)	$ 0		$ 24,000		$ 72,000		$ 72,000	
Cost of Goods Manufactured ($12 per Unit)	72,000		96,000		96,000		24,000	
Volume Variance	0		(8,000)		(8,000)		16,000	
	$72,000		$112,000		$160,000		$112,000	
Less: Ending Inventory ($12 per Unit)	24,000		72,000		72,000		0	
		48,000		40,000		88,000		112,000
Gross Profit		$32,000		$40,000		$ 72,000		$ 48,000
Less: Marketing Costs		20,000		20,000		28,000		28,000
Net Income		$12,000		$20,000		$ 44,000		$ 20,000

FIGURE 14–4

Wadman Corporation
Quarterly Comparison of Inventory and Income Measurements
Using Variable Cost and Full Cost Models
For the Year 19X9

	Quarter 1	Quarter 2	Quarter 3	Quarter 4
	Inventory Variations			
Ending Inventory (units)	2,000	6,000	6,000	0
Variable Cost Inventory ($8)	$ 16,000	$ 48,000	$48,000	$ 0
Increase during Quarter (ΔVCI)	+16,000	+32,000	0	(48,000)
Full Cost Inventory ($12)	$ 24,000	$ 72,000	$72,000	0
Increase during Quarter (ΔFACI) ...	+24,000	+48,000	0	(72,000)
Net Difference (ΔVCI − ΔFACI)	$ (8,000)	$ (16,000)	$ 0	$+24,000
	Net Income Differentials			
Variable Net Income (VCπ)	$ 4,000	$ 4,000	$44,000	$ 44,000
Full Cost Net Income (FACπ)	12,000	20,000	44,000	20,000
Net Difference (VCπ − FACπ)	$ (8,000)	$ (16,000)	0	$+24,000

Second, other things being equal, *periodic net income is constant under variable costing if the sales volume is unchanged from period to period*. Variable costing insulates net income from inventory level variations. Variable cost income is a function only of current period sales volume, because cost of goods sold is equal to total manufacturing fixed costs (a constant amount) plus the variable costs of the units sold.

Third, *the size and direction of the difference in income shown by the two methods can be reconciled with the size and direction of the change in inventory balances*. For example, Figure 14–4 shows that from Quarter 1 to Quarter 2, full cost inventory increased $48,000 (from $24,000 to $72,000), while variable cost inventory increased $32,000 (from $16,000 to $48,000). The net difference in inventory changes of $16,000 ($48,000 − $32,000) is equal to the difference in income between the two methods ($20,000 − $4,000).

INVENTORY LEVEL CONSTANT—SALES AND PRODUCTION QUANTITIES EQUAL

During Quarter 3, sales and production were both 8,000 units. Net income was $44,000 under both methods. Both methods charge to expense all current period fixed manufacturing costs, but in slightly different ways. The variable cost method expenses each period's fixed manufacturing costs. When production and sales quantities are equal, the full absorption cost method carries forward to the following period in ending inventory exactly the same amount of fixed cost that was brought forward in beginning inventory from the preceding period. Therefore, *when inventory levels are constant, both methods produce the same measures of cost of goods sold and of net income.*

SALES VOLUME CONSTANT—INVENTORY LEVEL DECREASING

Compare the results of Quarter 3 and Quarter 4. Sales were 8,000 units in both periods, but inventory decreased from 6,000 units to zero. Variable cost calculations produced the same net income in both periods. However, the full absorption costing method showed a decrease in net income from $44,000 to $20,000 between the third and fourth quarters. This effect—the opposite of that produced when the inventory level increased—can be attributed to the fact that, because the inventory level is decreasing, less fixed costs will be carried forward to the following period under full absorption costing than were brought forward from the previous period. Cost of goods sold will therefore include more fixed costs than were incurred during the current period and net income will be comparatively smaller. As Figure 14–4 indicates, the $24,000 difference in income between the two costing methods is equal to the difference in the change in inventory values between the third and fourth quarters.

SALES VOLUME FLUCTUATIONS AND NET INCOME

Other things being equal, *the variable costing method allows periodic net income to be measured as a function of one variable, sales volume.* Net income is equal to sales revenues minus total variable costs of products sold, variable marketing and administrative expenses, fixed manufacturing costs, and fixed marketing and administrative expenses. This relationship can be formulated as follows:

Where π = Net Income
Q = Number of Units Sold
S = Sales Price per Unit
V = Variable Manufacturing Cost per Unit
M = Variable Marketing and Administrative Cost per Unit
F = Fixed Manufacturing Costs
A = Fixed Marketing and Administrative Costs

$$\pi = SQ - (VQ + MQ + F + A)$$
$$\pi = Q(S - V - M) - (F + A)$$

In this form, given that F and A are constant total amounts and S, V, and M are constant unit amounts, the only variable is Q—the sales volume. *Therefore, when variable costing is used, net income will always move in the same direction as changes in the level of sales.* The size of the change will be equal to the change in sales volume multiplied by the contribution margin $(S - V - M)$. This is consistent with the cost–volume–profit model discussed in Chapter 8.

FIGURE 14–5

Wadman Corporation
Revised Income Statements—Full Absorption Product Cost Model
For the Year 19X9

	Quarter 3		Quarter 4	
Sales		$150,000		$170,000
Less: Cost of Goods Sold:				
Beginning Inventory	$ 72,000		$ 78,000	
Cost of Goods Manu-				
factured ($12)	96,000		24,000	
Volume Variance	(8,000)		16,000	
	$160,000		$118,000	
Less: Ending Inventory	78,000	82,000	0	118,000
Gross Profit		$ 68,000		$ 52,000
Less: Marketing Costs		27,000		29,000
Net Income		$ 41,000		$ 23,000

When full absorption costing is used, no definite pattern can be predicted for the movement of income in response to sales volume changes. Figure 14–3 shows that although sales volume was constant in Quarters 1 and 2 and in Quarters 3 and 4, under full absorption costing inventory fluctuations caused net income to *increase* in the first half of the year and *decreased* in the second half. When product costs are calculated on a full absorption basis, large inventory fluctuations may even cause income to move in the *opposite* direction from sales volume.

Example: Assume that Wadman Corporation's sales were 7,500 units in Quarter 3 and 8,500 units in Quarter 4. The firm's income statements using full absorption costing would have been as shown in Figure 14–5.

Although sales revenue *increased* from $150,000 to $170,000 and sales volume *increased* from 7,500 to 8,500 units, net income *decreased* from $41,000 to $23,000. This is primarily due to the decrease in inventory from $78,000 in Quarter 3 to zero in Quarter 4. When all existing inventories were sold, all fixed manufacturing costs—those deferred from previous periods plus those from the current period—became part of cost of goods sold in the fourth quarter.

VARIABLE COSTING AND CONTRIBUTION MARGIN ANALYSIS

The variable cost approach allows accountants to use a format for income statements in which all variable manufacturing and marketing costs are subtracted directly from sales revenues to obtain the **contribution margin.**

Example: The Wadman Corporation income statement can easily be recast in a format that facilitates contribution margin analysis. Presenting operating results in the format of Figure 14–6 focuses attention on the *behavior of the*

FIGURE 14–6

Wadman Corporation
Quarterly Income Statements—Variable Product Cost Model
For the Year 19X9

	Quarter 1		Quarter 2		Quarter 3		Quarter 4	
Sales		$80,000		$80,000		$160,000		$160,000
Less: Variable Manufacturing Costs	$32,000		$32,000		$64,000		$64,000	
Variable Marketing Costs	8,000		8,000		16,000		16,000	
		40,000		40,000		80,000		80,000
Contribution Margin		$40,000		$40,000		$ 80,000		$ 80,000
Less: Fixed Manufacturing Costs	$24,000		$24,000		$24,000		$24,000	
Fixed Marketing Costs	12,000		12,000		12,000		12,000	
		36,000		36,000		36,000		36,000
Net Income		$ 4,000		$ 4,000		$ 44,000		$ 44,000

components—sales revenue, variable costs, contribution margin, fixed costs, and net income. Contrast this with the conventional income statement shown in Figure 14–2, which directs attention toward *functional groupings*—sales, cost of goods sold, marketing costs, and net income.

SUMMARY—VARIABLE COSTS VERSUS FULL ABSORPTION COSTS

Five differences usually result from preparing income statements using the variable cost model rather than the full absorption cost model.

1. If fixed manufacturing costs are incurred, the variable cost model will produce lower inventory valuations than the full absorption cost model.
2. When variable costing is used, changes in net income will move in the same direction as changes in sales volume. Under full absorption costing, there will be no predictable pattern; income may even move in the opposite direction from sales volume.
3. When production volume equals sales volume, both models will generate the same net income (although when unit costs change or when actual rather than standard costing methods are used, exact equality may not occur).
4. When sales volume exceeds production volume, thereby causing inventories to decrease, variable costing will tend to produce higher net income than full absorption costing.
5. When production volume exceeds sales volume, thereby causing inventories to increase, variable costing will tend to produce lower net income than full absorption costing.

Remember that the preceding illustrations represent simplified and extreme situations. These examples assume that unit prices, unit costs, and total costs remain constant during the period of analysis. In practice, some variability among these items must be expected, whereas fluctuations in sales, inventory, and production levels normally will be less severe than those shown for Wadman Corporation. Therefore, the preceding examples describe only the general comparative effects of the two product costing models.

THE VARIABLE COST MODEL AND DECISION ANALYSIS

ADVANTAGES OF VARIABLE COSTING

The variable cost model is useful for many planning purposes, because it focuses on cost behavior patterns at various operating levels. *Cost–volume–profit analysis* adopts the variable costing approach by treating all costs according to their pattern of response to activity level changes. Similarly, the chief purpose of *flexible budgeting* is to establish a set of functional relationships that permit accurate prediction of cost behavior over a range of activity levels.

Setting and using *standard product costs* is simplified when only standard variable product costs are included in standard cost formulations. By excluding fixed costs from inventories, the variable cost approach avoids the problems involved in allocating fixed overhead costs to units of output. Variance analysis is then limited to price/spending and usage/efficiency type variances. The potentially confusing volume/capacity type of fixed cost variances cannot be calculated.

Finally, the variable cost model is helpful in many short-term decision situations for which *incremental analysis* is applicable. In order to classify costs as either fixed or variable in relation to activity level changes, the time period of analysis must be specified. When that period is short or when the decision context is by nature incremental, the fixed–variable distinction can be clearly made. The tools of incremental analysis, which rely heavily on the variable cost approach, are therefore most effective in short-run situations.

DISADVANTAGES OF VARIABLE COSTING

Most disadvantages of the variable cost model relate to its application and interpretation—or rather its misapplication and misinterpretation. Typical of such misinterpretation and potential misuse of the variable cost concept is the comment that ''variable costing is great—just concentrate on the variable costs and the fixed costs take care of themselves!''

Although it is proper to use incremental analysis based on variable costs and revenues in solving short-term problems, fixed costs cannot be ignored entirely. To sustain long-run viability, *all* costs must be recovered. If incremental analysis of the contribution margin type is employed continuously and comprehensively throughout a firm, managers will be in danger of making sub-optimal long-run decisions. For example, if a company continues to price its products so that only ''some'' positive contribution margin is obtained, there is no guarantee that the total contribution margin earned will be sufficient to cover total fixed costs, unless fixed costs are somehow integrated into the pricing and order-accepting decision rule.

The variable cost approach may also encourage a tendency toward *improper classification of costs,* which may in turn lead to invalid analysis. It can be tempting to classify all mixed and oddly behaved costs as fixed costs rather than to define their precise behavior pattern. This improperly derived data will distort any analysis in which it is used, because variable costs will tend to be understated and fixed costs and contribution margins will tend to be overstated.

Another wrong impression fostered by variable costing is that there is *a sequence in cost recovery*. The terminology and formats used in cost–volume–profit analysis, contribution margin analysis, and incremental analysis unfortunately tend to strengthen this impression. It is common to hear that a product with a unit sales price of $12 and variable cost of $8 is making a $4 per unit *contribution to fixed cost*. Of course, it is untrue that the directly variable costs are recovered first and that only then, if there is excess revenue, are fixed costs and profits recovered. The matching principle was never intended to apply in this literal sense. There can be only a collective recovery of fixed and variable costs from total revenues.

The variable cost model always shows income moving in the same direction as sales volume changes. This may encourage *overemphasis on sales performance* as the sole determinant of profit performance. Instead, attention should be directed to the coordination of sales, production, and inventories in the pursuit of profit goals.

Finally, remember that in the long run, all costs are potentially relevant to decision making and must be treated accordingly. Use of the variable cost model should be limited to those short-run situations for which it is appropriate.

THE FULL ABSORPTION COST MODEL AND DECISION ANALYSIS

For decision analysis, the strengths and weaknesses of the full absorption cost model tend to be the reverse of those of the variable cost model. Full absorption cost methods are either inappropriate or potentially confusing in cost–volume–profit analysis, flexible budgeting, and standard costing—primarily because full absorption costing requires that fixed overhead costs be expressed as *unit amounts*. The resulting analysis is influenced, and sometimes restricted, by the choice of an activity index on which the calculation of unit fixed costs is based.

Cost–volume–profit analysis and flexible budgeting emphasize the separate behavior of fixed and variable costs in response to activity level changes. If full absorption costing is used, cost–volume–profit analysis cannot provide unique breakeven or target profit solutions. Those analyses then become dependent on (1) the relative amounts and direction of changes in inventory levels and (2) the value assigned to the activity index used as the basis for calculating unit fixed costs.

Full absorption costing is not compatible with flexible budgeting procedures. Its use requires that (1) a new value be calculated for unit fixed costs at each activity level considered or (2) if unit fixed costs are calculated at one particular activity level, a budgeted fixed overhead volume variance (or budgeted underapplied or overapplied fixed overhead amount) must be included in the flexible budget formula for each activity level considered. Analysis of cost variances based on such budget formulations will be less concise and more confusing than the usual flexible budgeting analysis using the variable cost approach.

Although standard full absorption costing is a manageable procedure, the inclusion of fixed overhead as a component of unit standard cost results in a fixed overhead volume variance. This variance can be influenced by such factors as sales performance, production efficiency, or forecasting errors; it is the least useful of the eight basic cost variances in generating control information.

But in principle at least, the shortcomings of a variable cost approach *in long-run situations* are overcome by use of the full absorption cost model. Because full absorption cost systems treat all manufacturing costs (including fixed costs) as product costs, the problem of cost recovery can be approached directly, whereas it may be side-stepped when variable costing is adopted. This approach to cost recovery is particularly useful in cost analysis for pricing decisions that pertain to *long-run regular activities* rather than *short-run incremental decisions.* Pricing policies for incremental short-run decision analysis were discussed in Chapter 9. The remainder of this chapter is a discussion of how managers use cost information to make product pricing decisions in the context of a firm's regular, long-run activities.

OBJECTIVES OF LONG-RUN PRICING POLICIES

A firm's product **pricing strategy** must be compatible with its overall goals. A company may employ a variety of pricing policies, depending on its market structure, its position in the market, its planning horizon, its product distribution channels, and other aspects of its marketing situation. A pricing strategy should also reflect such factors as desired market share, growth and size of the firm, geographical location, product and company image, customer and community relations, as well as legal, social, and ethical constraints.

Product pricing strategies may be based on:

1. Cost recovery, capital maintenance, and profit goals.
2. Product life cycle phases, in particular:
   a. Penetration pricing.
   b. Promotional pricing.
   c. Skimming pricing.
   d. Liquidation pricing.
3. Price differentiation, by way of:
   a. Auctioning.
   b. Volume discounts.
   c. Merchandising methods.
   d. Distribution channels.
   e. Market composition.
4. Convenience, psychological, and prestige pricing tactics.

Capital Maintenance   Economic survival is the primary consideration underlying all pricing decisions. At a minimum, company survival requires that product sales prices must cover costs so that the firm will not incur operating losses. Beyond that, some return must be earned if the company is to offer an incentive to investors. This basic need to earn a profit, as reflected in various company objectives, is sometimes called "profit maximization," "target profits," or "satisficing returns."

Before a firm can earn a profit, it must first recover its costs. **Capital maintenance,** or **cost recovery,** is a basic aspect of pricing decisions. When a firm can establish or influence prices, the price it sets must at least maintain capital intact. When the firm cannot directly influence prices, it must seek a combination of costs, external sales prices, and operating volumes that will meet its capital maintenance requirement. But all pricing decisions ultimately depend on *how* a company measures the cost that must be recovered and the capital that must be maintained.

A firm that is a **price setter** needs cost-plus price calculations to establish the price it will charge for its products. A firm that is a **price taker** also needs cost-plus calculations to determine whether or not it is feasible to continue production under existing market conditions. The illustrations in this chapter assume a price setting context, but they could be reversed and made to apply to price validation by a price taking company. Problem materials at the end of this chapter include both types of situations.

Product Life Cycle Phases A firm's planning horizon is a key factor in its pricing policies. These policies need not be uniform over extended time periods—that is, over the life cycle of one of its products—nor must they be the same for all products at any one time. Although the firm may have a stable long-run goal such as a rate of return on resources employed, this return need not be earned at a uniform annual rate. In fact, the desired rate of return may best be achieved by pricing products differently at different times during their life cycles.

In order to attract customers and establish a market position, a firm sometimes sets the price of a new product fairly low. This is called **penetration pricing.** Note that it requires subjective judgments to assess how low a price is necessary to achieve the desired penetration and how long this low price should be continued before it is increased to a normal, long-run price. A variation of penetration pricing is a **promotional pricing** policy, wherein special offers, cash discounts, refunds, bonuses, gifts, premiums, or sales tie-ins are used to attract buyers who may eventually become steady customers at regular prices.

A **skimming price strategy,** adopted at the start of a product's life cycle, is an attempt to capture or skim off that portion of the market that is relatively insensitive to price. Accordingly, a fairly high initial price is set in an attempt to obtain above normal short-term profits.

Near the end of a product's life cycle, pricing strategies are sometimes quite different than they are in earlier phases of the cycle. For example, it may be necessary to dispose of goods that are becoming unsalable due to obsolescence or deterioration. In that case, a policy of **distress** or **liquidation pricing** may be appropriate. A price will be set that allows the firm to dispose of the products quickly without incurring additional losses. This issue is discussed more fully in relation to incremental analysis in Chapter 9.

Price Differentiation The same product may be sold at different prices to different customers, depending on their willingness to buy. Ideally this would be done by auctioning output units, one at a time, to each successive high bidder. But that is obviously an impractical way to sell most products. Price differentiation is found in such practices as (1) offering quantity discounts for large purchases, (2) packaging, labeling, grading, and sizing differentials (deluxe versus standard, economy size versus giant size, wrapped and boxed versus unwrapped and loose), or (3) setting different prices at different locations, such as specialty stores, department stores, supermarkets, discount houses, and mail order outlets. To some extent, price differentiation is a subtle means of exercising a discriminatory pricing policy; explicit price discrimination is prohibited by various federal laws, including the Robinson–Patman Act and the Miller–Tydings Act.

Pricing policies must sometimes be devised for selling in markets that are *geographically separated* or *functionally different*. Pricing decisions for geographically distinct markets must provide for possible variations in consumers' incomes and preferences, differences in the strength and number of competitors, and different costs of supplies and transportation. If markets are functionally different, the price structure should reflect any cost differences between products sold at the retail and wholesale levels or between name-brands and generic labels.

Customary or Convenience, Psychological, and Prestige Pricing
When sales are paid for in cash, it is common to set prices that correspond to exact coinage and currency denominations. Prices of 5¢, 10¢, 25¢, 50¢, $1.00 and multiples thereof are easy to calculate, are convenient for making change, and facilitate the use of automatic vending machines.

It is also common to set unit prices at a figure that ends in the number nine. Examples include supermarket prices of 29¢, gasoline prices of 1.49\frac{9}{10}$ per gallon, appliance and furniture prices of $299.99, $599.99, and so on. Such prices are a control device in that they force the cashier to ring up cash sales on a cash register in order to make change. Marketers also argue that prices ending in nine are psychologically useful selling devices, because customers sense a bargain in a product priced at say, 99¢ rather than $1.00.

Finally, some products may have upward sloping demand curves over some range of output, indicating that there is a minimum **prestige price** below which the product may tend to be rejected as inferior or suspect.

COST BASED PRICING TECHNIQUES

The pricing policies of most firms give some recognition to the *cost* of items being priced for sale. Therefore, accounting calculations of product cost are critical inputs to the pricing process. The question is, which measure or measures of product cost are relevant for pricing purposes?

COST-PLUS PRICING

Selling prices may be established simply by estimating product costs and adding a profit margin to that cost estimate. This is known as **cost-plus pricing.** This easily understood pricing method is particularly appropriate when the products being priced are unique and readily identifiable, as in job order costing. But it does not directly provide the type of information managers need to make operating level decisions that will help achieve profit goals.

The usual method of applying cost-plus pricing is to determine either the full absorption or variable cost of an output unit and add to that amount a profit margin sufficient to attain some income objective. In pricing a typical manufactured product, *full cost* will include direct materials, direct labor, variable manufacturing overhead, and fixed manufacturing overhead. The "plus" portion—the margin or mark-up—must then be large enough to cover the remaining marketing, administrative, and financing costs and also to provide an after-tax profit.

If the *variable cost* model is the basis for cost-plus pricing, the "cost" part of the price will include only variable expenses—materials, labor, and overhead, and possibly marketing and administrative costs. The "plus" portion must then cover all fixed costs and any desired profit.

To use either method, managers must pose a critical question: *How much fixed cost must be recovered by each unit of output?* Although variable costs are directly traceable to output units, fixed costs by their very nature can only be traced indirectly. In order to set prices at a level that at least recovers production costs, a firm must decide how to unitize fixed costs. Consequently, the firm must establish a fixed cost rate per unit of output, which requires that an activity index be selected to serve as the denominator for that calculation. Both the identity and the value of that activity index are vitally important.

Example: Benston Corporation has developed cost information for its single product, as shown in Figure 14-7.

FIGURE 14–7

Benston Corporation
Operating Costs
For the Year 19X4

Direct Materials	$10 per unit
Direct Labor	$12 per unit
Variable Manufacturing Overhead	$ 8 per unit
Variable Marketing and Administrative Cost	$ 6 per unit
Fixed Manufacturing Overhead	$200,000 per year
Fixed Marketing and Administrative Cost	$300,000 per year

Management wishes to set a sales price that will cover all costs and provide a $100,000 profit before taxes. It forecasts a normal long-range sales volume of 50,000 units per year.

Using the *full absorption cost* approach, Benston's selling price is derived as shown in Figure 14–8. The same $48 sales price is derived using the *variable cost model,* as shown in Figure 14–9. Both solutions depend on the value of the activity index used as the denominator to convert total fixed costs and target profit to unit amounts. As shown in Figure 14–10, when the variable cost approach is used, the unit selling price varies inversely with estimated sales volume (assuming that all unit variable and total fixed costs remain constant).

This example highlights a major shortcoming of any cost-based pricing policy—the need to forecast expected sales volume in order to calculate unit fixed costs, unit target profit, and in turn, a unit sales price. Whenever cost-plus pricing is used, the subjective estimate of anticipated sales volume is likely to affect sales prices and profits. A relatively low estimate of future sales volume will increase unit costs and unit sales prices, which could damage the firm's competitive position. An optimistic forecast of sales volume will have the opposite effect on unit costs and prices, which could contribute to operating losses if the predicted activity level is not achieved.

FIGURE 14–8

Benston Corporation
Cost-Plus Pricing—Full Absorption Product Cost Model
For the Year 19X4

Full Product Cost:

Direct Materials	$10
Direct Labor	12
Variable Manufacturing Overhead	8
	$30
Fixed Manufacturing Overhead ($200,000 ÷ 50,000)	4
Product Cost per Unit	$34

Total Margin Requirement:

Marketing and Administrative Costs:

Variable ($6×50,000)	$300,000
Fixed	300,000
Target Profit	100,000
Nonproduction Costs plus Profit	$700,000

Unit Margin: $700,000 ÷ 50,000 = $14

Sales Price: Full Cost plus Margin = $34 + $14 = $48

FIGURE 14–9

Benston Corporation
Cost-Plus Pricing—Variable Product Cost Model
For the Year 19X4

Variable Costs:

Direct Materials	$10
Direct Labor	12
Variable Manufacturing Overhead	8
Variable Marketing and Administrative Costs	6
Total Variable Cost per Unit	$36

Fixed Costs and Target Profit:

Fixed Manufacturing Overhead	$200,000
Fixed Marketing and Administrative Costs	300,000
Target Profit	100,000
Total Fixed Costs and Target Profit	$600,000

Unit Margin: ($600,000 ÷ 50,000)   12

Sales Price $48

FIGURE 14–10

Benston Corporation
Effect of Sales Volume Changes on Sales Prices
For the Year 19X4

Sales Volume in Units	20,000	30,000	50,000	60,000	75,000
Total Fixed Costs	$500,000	$500,000	$500,000	$500,000	$500,000
Target Profit	100,000	100,000	100,000	100,000	100,000
Total Required Margin	$600,000	$600,000	$600,000	$600,000	$600,000
Unit Margin $= \dfrac{\text{Total Margin}}{\text{Sales Volume}}$ ..	$30	$20	$12	$10	$ 8
Unit Variable Cost	36	36	36	36	36
Sales Price per Unit	$66	$56	$48	$46	$44

PRICING MULTIPLE OUTPUTS

When a firm manufactures several different products, separate prices for each product cannot be uniquely determined using cost-plus pricing, unless the "plus" part of the price is arbitrarily set and does not have to be used to meet target profit or other income objectives on a product-by-product basis. **Example:** Suppose Benston Corporation, using the same plant facilities, also manufactures a second product that has a unit variable cost of $18. What sales prices must be charged for each of the two products in order to recover all fixed costs and earn a target profit of $100,000?

To cover fixed costs of $500,000 and a target profit of $100,000, the total contribution from the two products must be $600,000. But even if a sales forecast is available for each product (say projected sales of 30,000 units of the original product and 20,000 units of the second product), no unique solution is possible. The total contribution condition to be satisfied would be as follows:

$$\$600{,}000 = 30{,}000\,(X - \$36) + 20{,}000\,(Y - \$18)$$

where X represents the sale price of the original product, and Y represents the sale price of the second product. For the two unknowns of this equation there are theoretically an infinite number of solutions. Consequently, cost-plus pricing of multiple outputs cannot provide unique solutions when profit goals are specified.

However, sales prices for each product can be obtained if the joint costs and the desired profit margin are allocated arbitrarily between the two products. Then the problem is reduced to a series of independent single product pricing decisions. For example, any of the following arbitrary joint fixed cost and profit margin allocation bases might be used to help solve the preceding problem:

1. Labor hour content of products
2. Units of output
3. Arbitrary 50–50 percent allocation

Assume that the following information is also known:

	Product 1	Product 2
Forecast Units of Output	30,000	20,000
Labor Hours per Unit	2	1

The resulting allocations of joint fixed costs and profit margins under each of the three possible allocation bases are shown in Figure 14–11 (page 662).

This example is presented only to demonstrate the wide variety of sales prices that could result from arbitrary allocations of joint fixed costs and profit margins among multiple products. None of the solutions suggested in Figure 14–11 is inherently better than another. Each is merely one of a large number of solutions that will allow Benston Corporation to reach its target profit.

Another type of allocation is needed to price joint products that are manufactured in *fixed proportions*.

Example: As shown in Figure 14–12 (page 663), Whitfield Company can manufacture 100,000 units annually of two joint products, Vegys and Mytes, which are produced in a 60:40 ratio. Fixed operating costs are $200,000 per year and variable common processing costs are $6 per unit of output. The company's profit goal of $200,000 per year assumes that production capacity of 100,000 units can be regularly maintained.

If the only pricing constraints are the 60:40 production ratio between Vegys and Mytes and the need to generate sales revenues of $1,000,000, the following pricing formulation can be derived: If V = the price of Vegys and M = the price of Mytes, then $V \geq 0$, and $M \geq 0$, and

$$60,000\ V + 40,000\ M = \$1,000,000$$

This formulation of the pricing problem indicates that a very large number of different prices for Vegys and Mytes will satisfy the above equation.

If additional constraints are imposed, pricing solutions become more definite. For example, if the price of Vegys cannot be more than $15 ($V \leq \$15$), the following solution can be obtained:

Maximum Revenue from Vegys	Minimum + Revenue from Mytes	Total = Revenue Contribution
60,000 ($15) +	40,000 $\bar{M}$	= $1,000,000
	40,000 $\bar{M}$	= $100,000
	$\bar{M}$	= $2.50

The price of Mytes cannot be less than the minimum feasible price ($\bar{M}$) of $2.50.

Still more restrictively, if due to competitive pressures the price of Vegys must be exactly $12, a unique solution can be found. The selling price of Mytes must be $7.

$$60,000\ (\$12) + 40,000\ M = \$1,000,000$$
$$40,000\ M = \$280,000$$
$$M = \$7.00$$

FIGURE 14–11

Benston Corporation
Product Pricing:
Allocation of Joint Fixed Costs and Profit Margins for Two Products
For the Year 19X4

(1) Labor Hours Content	Total Hours	Proportion	Total	Number of Units	Unit Amount	Variable Cost	Sales Price
Product 1	2 × 30,000 = 60,000	¾ × $600,000	$450,000	30,000	$15.00	$36.00	$51.00
Product 2	1 × 20,000 = 20,000	¼ × $600,000	150,000	20,000	$ 7.50	$18.00	$25.50
	80,000		$600,000	50,000			
(2) Units of Output	Number of Units						
Product 1	30,000	⅗ × $600,000	$360,000	30,000	$12.00	$36.00	$48.00
Product 2	20,000	⅖ × $600,000	240,000	20,000	$12.00	$18.00	$30.00
	50,000		$600,000	50,000			
(3) Arbitrary 50–50% Basis							
Product 1		½ × $600,000	$300,000	30,000	$10.00	$36.00	$46.00
Product 2		½ × $600,000	300,000	20,000	$15.00	$18.00	$33.00
			$600,000	50,000			

FIGURE 14–12

Whitfield Company
Annual Profit Plan
For the Year 19X1

Required Cost Recovery:	
Variable Costs (100,000 @ $6)	$ 600,000
Fixed Costs	200,000
Total Costs to be Recovered	$ 800,000
Add: Target Profit	200,000
Required Total Sales Revenue	$1,000,000

There are clearly no easy answers to the problems of pricing joint products, even when a simple approach such as cost-plus pricing is used. The long-range goal of joint product pricing is a *set* of prices that permits the recovery of all common and individual costs and allows a target profit to be earned. Unless sufficient constraints are included in the decision analysis, no unique set of prices can be found to meet these requirements. Determining the profitability of an individual joint product is a futile and frustrating task, involving as it does the unsolvable problem of how to allocate common processing costs to each type of output. Setting prices for joint products is also an arbitrary task beset with complex problems—multiple solution sets, allocation of common costs, and fixed cost/capacity level decisions.

COST-PLUS PRICING IN JOB COST SITUATIONS

Cost-plus pricing is used extensively in pricing job order outputs, especially when such jobs are obtained by competitive bidding. The total cost of each job must be forecast, beginning with directly traceable costs to which is added a fixed cost allocation. Again, choosing an appropriate basis for calculating unit fixed costs requires that a more or less arbitrary allocation basis and activity level be selected. Job order situations also involve nonstandard units of output. Because final output units cannot be totaled meaningfully, the overhead allocation basis must be an intermediate activity measure such as machine hours or labor hours. Therefore, the job bid price must cover variable product costs, a projected fixed cost allocation, marketing and administrative costs, and the desired profit.

Example: Swenson Sauna Corporation specializes in building customized sauna baths for private homes. Its bid price for a job is based on the total cost of direct materials and direct labor for that job, plus manufacturing overhead equal to 50 percent of the direct labor cost, 25 percent markups on materials costs, and 50 percent markups on labor and overhead costs. These markups are intended to cover marketing and administrative costs—and to provide a profit. They are calculated on the basis of previous experience with the relationships between the cost categories and in accordance with competitive policies in the industry, in which most firms tend to prepare bids in a similar way.

For one custom sauna installation, Swenson calculated its bid price as follows:

Materials	$2,500
Direct Labor (120 hours @ $10)	1,200
Manufacturing Overhead (50% of Direct Labor)	600
	$4,300
Markups:	
25% on Materials	625
50% on Labor and Overhead	900
Total Bid Price	$5,825

PRICING ON A COST REIMBURSABLE BASIS

Contract prices are sometimes established under a formula that guarantees the seller reimbursement for all costs incurred in performing his part of the agreement. The accounting measures of cost that are used as a basis for pricing then become vitally important for both buyer and seller. Such contracts typically provide for the reimbursement of all the seller's costs and, usually, a profit margin. The profit margin may be a percentage of the costs incurred or a lump sum amount. In other contracts, the profit margin is a variable amount subject to penalties for time delays and cost overruns or to bonuses for early completion and cost savings.

When a firm works on a cost reimbursable basis, the proper allocation of indirect and fixed costs to each contracted job becomes a particularly sensitive issue. This is especially true when there are differences between the terms of contracts in force at the same time or when the company is filling reimbursable contracts and simultaneously selling some of its output in normal markets at competitive prices. Clearly, a temptation exists to overallocate costs to the contract production in order to increase prices and profits from those contracts.

Government contracting has relied heavily on cost reimbursable pricing, leading to numerous abuses. The notorious "cost overruns" on defense contracts are examples. Deficiencies in accounting for cost reimbursable defense contracts were primarily responsible for the creation of the Cost Accounting Standards Board. Between 1970 and 1980, the CASB formulated eighteen standards for cost measurement by firms performing contract work for the federal government. Its pronouncements concentrated on the problems involved in measuring and allocating indirect, joint, and fixed costs. A complete listing of CASB standards appears in Chapter 1 (page 17).

SPECIFYING PROFIT MARGINS

There have been many references in the preceding discussion to "profit goals" and "target profit." Depending on a company's operating objectives, such amounts can be stated in several ways. They may be expressed as:

1. An absolute dollar amount.
2. A rate of return on sales revenue.

3. A rate of return on total resources.
4. A rate of return on equity.

Example: Benston Corporation, in the single product situation introduced previously, might have considered any of the following profit goals:

1. $100,000 net income per year.
2. A 10 percent return on net sales.
3. A 15 percent return on total assets of $1,000,000.
4. A 20 percent return on owner's equity of $750,000.

Using the variable cost approach, the *unit sales prices* needed to attain each of these profit objectives are calculated as follows:

(1) *Fixed Dollar Amount* $= \$100,000$

$$
\begin{aligned}
\text{Total Desired Contribution} &= \text{Fixed Costs} + \$100,000 \\
&= \$500,000 + \$100,000 \\
&= \$600,000 \\
\text{Unit Contribution} &= \$600,000 \div 50,000 \\
&= \$12 \\
\text{Sales Price} &= \text{Variable Cost} + \text{Unit Contribution} \\
&= \$36 + \$12 \\
&= \$48
\end{aligned}
$$

(2) *10% Return on Net Sales* $= 10\%$ *of Sales Revenue* ($S =$ Sales Price)

$$
\begin{aligned}
\text{Total Revenue} &= \text{Total Cost} + \text{Desired Profit} \\
50,000\ S &= [(50,000 \times \$36) + \$500,000] + (.1)\ 50,000\ S \\
(.9)\ 50,000\ S &= (50,000 \times \$36) + \$500,000 \\
(.9)\ S &= \$36 + \$10 \\
S &= \$46 \div .9 \\
&= \$51.11
\end{aligned}
$$

(3) *15% Return on Total Assets* $= 15\%$ *of $1,200,000*

$$
\begin{aligned}
\text{Total Desired Contribution} &= \$500,000 + (.15)\ (\$1,200,000) \\
&= \$680,000 \\
\text{Unit Contribution} &= \$680,000 \div 50,000 \\
&= \$13.60 \\
\text{Sales Price} &= \$36 + \$13.60 \\
&= \$49.60
\end{aligned}
$$

(4) *20% Return on Owner's Equity* $= 20\%$ *of $750,000*

$$
\begin{aligned}
\text{Total Desired Contribution} &= \$500,000 + (.2)\ (\$750,000) \\
&= \$650,000 \\
\text{Unit Contribution} &= \$650,000 - 50,000 \\
&= \$13 \\
\text{Sales Price} &= \$36 + \$13 \\
&= \$49
\end{aligned}
$$

These alternatives are shown only to demonstrate the results of alternative target profit calculations using cost-plus pricing. None of the preceding methods is inherently "correct" or necessarily superior to any of the others. All are equally feasible ways for a firm to subjectively express its profit goals.

LONG-RUN TRANSFER PRICING

Transfer pricing decisions for incremental situations were discussed in Chapter 9. The techniques outlined there resolved neither the proper treatment of *fixed costs* incurred by the producing and acquiring divisions nor the effect of these fixed costs on the long-run overall profitability of the firm's final product. This problem will be addressed here only from the viewpoint of planning and decision making; questions of divisional performance measurement and control will be discussed in Chapters 19 and 20. In an overall sense, the issue is whether the firm as a whole will be better off *in the long run* as a result of *internal transfers* or as a result of *external purchases and/or sales* of intermediate products. The following analysis assumes that the various decision centers are free to make all related market and activity level decisions, including even the decision to eliminate a division.

The long-run transfer pricing decision should be viewed as a practical problem of deciding how the combined decision centers can best meet company profit goals. This involves determining whether or not the total contribution margins of all the decision centers are sufficient to cover their total fixed costs and to provide the desired profit.

Given a simplified situation in which only two divisions are involved in transfer pricing, the short-run decision rule is to set a transfer price *equal to the variable costs of the producing division,* assuming that it has available capacity. The acquiring division must then price its output to cover only its own variable costs (which include the transfer price of the intermediate product) and its own fixed costs.

Although this variable cost-based transfer price is correct for short-term analysis, it could lead to faulty long-term pricing decisions. For example, in the long run, it may be correct to buy from an outside supplier at a price higher than the producing division's variable cost, if disposing of the producing division's fixed assets or putting them to more profitable alternative uses are feasible alternatives.

Example: Wilbur Company's two divisions, C and D, have the following cost structures:

	Division C	Division D
Fixed Costs	$100,000 per year	$150,000 per year
Variable Costs	$20 per unit	$10 per unit

Division C now produces exclusively for Division D, which sells 10,000 units of final output per year for $50 per unit. The intermediate product manufactured by Division C could be acquired from an outside supplier for $27.50 per unit. Using the short-run rule previously described, the transfer price is Division C's variable cost of $20 per unit. This $20 price would induce Division D to buy from Division C rather than from the outside supplier.

However, if the internal transfers are viewed as a continuing, long-term relationship between the two divisions, the total annual cost to the firm if Division D buys from Division C will include Division C's *fixed costs* as well as its *variable costs*.

Division C:

Variable Costs ($20 × 10,000 units)	$200,000
Fixed Costs	100,000
Annual Long-run Costs of Internal Transfer......	$300,000

If Division D buys the intermediate product from an outside supplier and Division C is abolished, the comparable annual total cost to the firm will be

Division D:

Annual Long-run Costs of Outside Purchase:

$27.50 × 10,000 units	$275,000

Therefore, in the long run it is more economical to abolish Division C and buy from an outside supplier, because doing so reduces total costs by $25,000 per year.

This example demonstrates that short-run incremental transfer prices are inappropriate for long-run decision making. In long-run decision situations, *the transfer price should be equal to the long-run variable and unitized fixed costs of the producing division.*

If Wilbur Company's Division C continues to produce 10,000 units per year, its long-run transfer price will be $30 per unit, derived as follows:

Division C:

Variable Cost per Unit	$20
Fixed Cost per Unit ($100,000 ÷ 10,000)....	10
Total Cost per Unit in Division C	$30

Comparing this $30 transfer price to the outside supplier's price of $27.50 leads to the decision that it is better in the long run to purchase from that supplier and terminate Division C's operations.

An alternative to discontinuing Division C is to seek other uses for its fixed assets. Assuming that the final product's selling price and the costs of Division D cannot be changed, Division C's operations might be allowed to continue if its plant and equipment could be put to some other use.

Example: Suppose that, in the Wilbur Company example, the plant facilities of Division C could be either leased to a tenant for $115,000 a year or used to produce 20,000 units of Product M, which sells for $20 per unit and has variable costs of $14 per unit. Either of these alternatives is acceptable, because each allows Division C to (1) recover its fixed costs and (2) make a direct contribution to the firm's profits—$15,000 ($115,000 − $100,000) in the first case or $20,000 ($400,000 − $280,000 − $100,000) in the second case.

In the original decision situation, no other use of Division C's facilities is possible; the $30 long-run transfer price is compared with the outside supplier's price of $27.50. Any outside price of less than $30 should be accepted by Division D *and* Division C should be abolished. For the two alternative use

---

FIGURE 14–13

Wilbur Company
Long-run Transfer Prices
if Division C Plant is Put to Other Uses

	Lease to Tenant	Produce Product M
Variable Cost	$20.00	$20.00
Fixed Cost ($100,000 ÷ 10,000)	10.00	10.00
Opportunity Cost:	$30.00	$30.00
Profit from Alternate Use:		
Lease: ($115,000 − $100,000) ÷ 10,000	1.50	
Product M: ($400,000 − $380,000) ÷ 10,000		2.00
Long-run Transfer Prices	$31.50	$32.00

---

possibilities, the long-run transfer prices are $31.50 and $32 respectively, as calculated in Figure 14–13.

Because both long-run transfer prices are greater than the outside supplier's price of $27.50, Wilbur Company should purchase Division D's intermediate product from that supplier and take advantage of one of the alternative uses of Division C's fixed assets.

The only drawback to this long-run transfer pricing rule—and to long-run pricing rules in general—is that to apply them toward deriving a unit transfer price, managers must estimate unit fixed costs at some appropriate capacity level. Long-run average (or normal) capacity is a reasonable basis for calculating unit fixed costs. It would be a mistake to omit the fixed cost element just because it is difficult to compute. A transfer price based only on the producing division's variable costs can lead to decisions contrary to the firm's long-run profitability and survival.

FIGURE 14–14

Wilbur Company
Long-run Total Costs of Producing and of
External Purchase

	5,000 Units	10,000 Units	25,000 Units
Total Cost of Outside			
Purchase @ $27.50	$137,500	$275,000	$687,000
Total Cost of Production			
by Division C:			
Variable @ $20	$100,000	$200,000	$500,000
Fixed	100,000	100,000	100,000
Total Cost of Division C	$200,000	$300,000	$600,000

A more useful approach to the long-run pricing problem may be to compare the *total cost* of internal production with the *total cost* of purchasing similar items from outside suppliers. This approach not only sidesteps the perennial problem of calculating unit fixed costs, but allows total cost comparisons to be made for any level of activity.

Figure 14–14 compares Wilbur Company's total purchase and production costs at three activity levels: 5,000, 10,000, and 25,000 units of intermediate output.

If Division C's fixed costs remain at $100,000 per year over the production range from 5,000 units to 25,000 units, the correct long-run decision is to *purchase externally* when Division D requires only 5,000 or 10,000 units annually, but to *produce internally* if demand rises to 25,000 units a year.

SUMMARY

1. Two different approaches to product cost measurement are offered by the variable cost and full absorption cost models.
2. The differences between these two models materially affect income determination and decision analysis, especially pricing decisions.
3. The two models differ in their treatment of fixed manufacturing overhead costs, which are included in product costs under the full absorption cost model but are charged to expense when the variable cost model is used.
4. Variable cost measures of income generally move in the same direction as sales volume changes, but income calculated using full absorption costing will not always follow movements in sales levels.
5. Full absorption cost measures of income are affected by changes in inventory levels and the direction of inventory changes; variable cost income measures are not.
6. Because it emphasizes the separate behavior of fixed and variable costs, the variable cost model is appropriate for basic planning and decision making, including cost–volume–profit analysis, flexible budgeting, and incremental analysis.
7. Full absorption costing is less useful for planning and decision making, because it requires that fixed overhead costs be calculated as unit amounts.
8. When a variable cost approach is used consistently in analyzing the profitability of incremental alternatives, the problem of recovering total costs may not be properly considered.
9. In theory at least, full absorption costing avoids this problem by including fixed manufacturing costs in unit product costs.
10. Therefore, to the extent that long-run planning and pricing decisions require measures of full product costs, there is a better chance that all costs will be recovered when full absorption costing is used.
11. A firm's pricing strategy may include various pricing policies, reflecting differences in products, markets, distribution channels, phases of product life cycles, and traits of consumer behavior.
12. Cost recovery or capital maintenance is facilitated by a cost-plus approach to product pricing, whether the firm is a price setter or a price taker.

13. In cost-plus pricing, when "cost" is full absorption cost, the "plus" must cover marketing and administrative costs as well as profit.

14. In cost-plus pricing, when "cost" is variable cost, the "plus" must cover fixed manufacturing costs, marketing and administrative costs, and profit.

15. The critical problem in cost-plus pricing is the selection of an activity level to be used as the basis for converting fixed costs to unit amounts.

16. Cost-plus pricing of multiple outputs or joint outputs requires an arbitrary allocation of joint costs.

17. Cost-plus price estimates are widely used as a basis for bidding in a job order cost environment.

18. When a firm works on a cost reimbursable basis, the proper allocation of indirect and fixed costs to each contract becomes particularly important if the firm is simultaneously selling some of its output in competitive markets.

19. A target profit may be specified as an absolute dollar amount, a rate of return on sales revenue, a rate of return on total resources, or a rate of return on equity.

20. In long-run decision situations, the transfer price should include the variable and fixed costs of the producing division. The decision as to whether to produce intermediate outputs or purchase them is made by comparing the transfer price with the lowest outside supplier's price.

21. The problem of calculating unit fixed costs in transfer pricing may be avoided by comparing the total cost of internal production with the total cost of purchasing similar items from outside suppliers.

KEY WORDS AND PHRASES

Variable Cost Model (643)
Full Absorption Cost Model (643)
Asset (643)
Replacement Cost (643)
Period Cost (644)
Product Cost (644)
Contribution Margin (650)
Pricing Strategies (655)
Capital Maintenance (655)
Cost Recovery (655)
Price Setter (655)
Price Taker (655)
Penetration Pricing (656)
Promotional Pricing (656)
Skimming Price Strategy (656)
Distress or Liquidation Pricing (656)
Price Differentiation (656)
Customary or Convenience Pricing (657)
Psychological Pricing (657)
Prestige Pricing (657)
Cost-Plus Pricing (657)
Cost Reimbursable Pricing (664)
Long-run Transfer Pricing (666)

Questions

1. How are product costs calculated under (1) the full absorption cost model and (2) the variable cost model?
2. What are the arguments *in favor of* (1) full absorption costing and (2) variable costing?
3. What are the arguments *against* (1) full absorption costing and (2) variable costing?
4. Compare the effects of the two costing models under the following circumstances:
    (a) Physical inventories increase and sales volume remains constant.
    (b) Physical inventories remain constant.
    (c) Physical inventories decrease and sales volume remains constant.
    (d) Sales volume fluctuates.
5. For decision making purposes, when is it more appropriate to use (1) full absorption costing and (2) variable costing?
6. What problems may arise if excessive emphasis is placed on a variable costing approach to decision making?
7. What problems are encountered when the full absorption costing model is applied to decision situations?
8. Outline and describe the four major approaches to product pricing.
9. Describe four pricing methods associated with a product life cycle approach.
10. Describe five pricing methods associated with a price differentiation approach.
11. Explain the concept of *capital maintenance.* What pricing policy must be followed to ensure that capital maintenance is achieved?
12. Explain what the "plus" in a cost-plus pricing policy must include.
13. What problem is inherent in selecting an appropriate cost-plus price in (1) a single product firm and (2) a multiple product firm?
14. What problems are encountered in selecting bid prices on a cost-plus basis in a job order costing environment?
15. What accounting problems are present when a firm secures contracts on a cost reimbursable basis?
16. How does the decision rule for a long-run transfer price differ from a short-run transfer price?
17. What problems are inherent in setting the long-run transfer price referred to in Question 16?

Exercises

E 14-1   Comparison of Full Absorption and Variable Costing— Income Statement Effects

Raihall Corporation has assembled the following data in order to determine its net income for 19X2:

Units Sold	18,000
Units Produced	20,000
Inventory—January 1, 19X2	–0–
Sales Price per Unit	$ 3,000
Manufacturing Costs:	
Materials	$250 per unit
Direct Labor	$300 per unit
Variable Overhead	$100 per unit
Fixed Overhead	$7,200,000 per year
Marketing and Administrative Costs:	
Variable	$150 per unit
Fixed	$1,500,000 per year
Capacity—(Fixed Overhead application rate basis)	20,000 units

Required:
(a) Prepare an income statement for 19X2 using full absorption costing.
(b) Prepare an income statement for 19X2 using variable costing.
(c) Reconcile and explain the difference in net income under the two methods.

E 14–2 Full Absorption Costing and Variable Costing— Income Statement Effects—Fixed Costs*

Dupointe Company's completely automated plant produces organic-ionized-California sunshine. There are absolutely no variable costs; all employees are salaried and customers must provide their own containers. There is unlimited storage space in the company's huge outdoor coverless storage containers located, naturally, in Marin County.

During the first three months of 19X4, the following operating results were reported:

	June	July	August
Production (cubic feet)	1,000,000	200,000	–0–
Sales:			
Cubic feet	200,000	400,000	600,000
Revenue	$200,000	$400,000	$600,000
Fixed Manufacturing Costs	$200,000	$200,000	$200,000
Fixed Marketing and Administrative Costs	$100,000	$100,000	$100,000
Beginning Inventory	–0–	?	?

Required:
(a) Prepare income statements for each of the three months, using full absorption costing, with inventories computed on the weighted average cost basis.
(b) Prepare income statements for each of the three months, using variable costing.
(c) Comment on the results in parts (a) and (b). How much income was earned in March? Why?

E 14–3 Variable and Full Absorption Costing— Standard Cost System

Gazette Company originally developed its quarterly budgeted income statement for the second quarter of 19X4 in expectation of sales of 80,000 units. Subsequently, but prior

* This problem is adapted from the classic article, "Try This On Your Class, Professor," by R.P. Marple, *The Accounting Review*, July 1956, p. 492. It demonstrates the extreme case of a company with no variable manufacturing costs.

to the commencement of the quarter, the budget had to be revised to reflect an expected 10 percent increase in sales volume and a reduction in production by 20,000 units, due to a current shortage of a key raw material. However, management was puzzled by the fact that the revised budget showed a *lower* net income figure, even after the sales increase was accounted for.

A standard full cost system is in use and the fixed overhead rate was based on a total budget amount of $200,000 at the normal capacity of 80,000 units. An inventory of 30,000 units was on hand at the beginning of the quarter.

		Original Budget		Revised Budget
Sales		$800,000		$880,000
Less: Standard Cost of Sales .		500,000		550,000
Standard Gross Profit		$300,000		$330,000
Less: Manufacturing Overhead Volume Variance		–0–		(50,000) Unfavorable
Adjusted Gross Profit		$300,000		$280,000
Less: Operating Expenses				
Fixed	$100,000		$100,000	
Variable	80,000	180,000	88,000	188,000
Net Income		$120,000		$ 92,000

Required:
(a) Explain the derivation and interpretation of the $50,000 unfavorable volume variance in the revised budget.
(b) Prepare budgeted income statements corresponding to both budget situations, using a variable costing approach.
(c) Compare the results in part (b) to the original statements. Which are more representative? Useful? Correct? Why?
(d) Show calculations of the ending inventory amounts under both circumstances and for each costing method. Comment.

E 14–4   Full Cost/Variable Cost—Income Statement Differences—Reconciliation

DePalma Corporation had extracted the following selected general ledger data as of December 31, 19X6:

	Total Debits	Total Credits
Sales		$2,100,000
Cost of Goods Sold	$1,470,000	
Variable Manufacturing Overhead Control	130,000	120,000
Fixed Manufacturing Overhead Control	700,000	720,000
Variable Marketing Expense	168,000	
Fixed Marketing Expense	180,000	
Fixed Administrative Expense	100,000	

The company has been using a full absorption costing system, with overhead costs applied to output at predetermined rates. During 19X6, the company's first year of operations, 240,000 units were produced and 210,000 units were sold. DePalma writes off all overhead variances in the period in which they arise.

Required:
(a) Prepare an income statement based on full absorption costing.
(b) Prepare an income statement based on variable costing.
(c) Reconcile and explain the difference in net income under the two methods.
(d) If sales had been 120,000 units, what would the difference in income have been between the two methods? Why?

E 14–5 Product Pricing—Cost-Plus Calculations— Multiple Products—Alternative Allocations

Saxton Corporation is reviewing its product prices for the coming year. Its existing policy has been to add a mark-up of 40 percent to the total manufacturing cost of each of its three products. Fixed factory overhead is incurred in the amount of $600,000 annually, but cannot be traced to the separate products. Variable manufacturing costs are as follows:

Product	Cost per Unit
A	$20
B	11
C	12

Expected annual sales volumes of products A, B, and C, are 5,000, 4,000 and 3,000, respectively.

Required:
(a) Compute sales prices for the three products to meet the mark-up requirement, allocating fixed costs on the basis of units of sales volume.
(b) Compute sales prices, this time allocating fixed costs on the basis of total variable manufacturing costs of each product.
(c) Repeat parts (a) and (b), assuming that prices are set at variable manufacturing costs plus a 20 percent mark-up.
(d) Compare the results of parts (a), (b), and (c). In each case, what are the mark-ups intended to cover? How would the percentage amount of the mark-ups be determined?

E 14–6 Target Sales Price—Return on Investment Requirement

Chinn Corporation is considering establishing a facility to produce and distribute a new product line. This operation would be almost completely independent of existing operations. The following forecast information has been developed:

Variable Costs (per unit):	
Manufacturing	$24
Marketing and Administration	$6
Fixed Costs (per year):	
Manufacturing	$160,000
Marketing and Administration	$ 80,000
Forecast Sales Volume (per year)	30,000 units
Forecast Investment in Fixed Facilities Required....	$1,500,000
Annual Capacity of New Facility	50,000 units

In this industry, sales prices usually are based on variable manufacturing cost plus a 75 percent mark-up.

Required:
(a) Prepare an analysis to determine the target sales price per unit, including the 75 percent mark-up.
(b) What must the mark-up in part (a) cover?
(c) The corporation has also established a target annual cash-flow rate of return equal to 25 percent of the cost of investment outlays required for new projects. Based on your answer to part (a), can this target rate of return be achieved?
(d) Discuss and demonstrate ways whereby the requirements of the pricing formula and the return on investment rate can be satisfied simultaneously.

E 14–7   Pricing Decision—Multiple Product Situation

Cicero Service Company is in the business of repairing major electrical appliances. During a typical month, it completes jobs requiring a total of 8,000 direct labor hours of work by its service crews, who are paid an average of $10 per hour. The cost of parts and supplies used on jobs usually amounts to $60,000 each month. Monthly fixed overhead costs total $40,000. Other operating expenses (all fixed) amount to $20,000 each month. The company has established a monthly profit goal of $25,000.

Required: (Answer each part independently.)
(a) Assume that it is customary to charge for parts at a price that includes a 40 percent mark-up on cost. What hourly billing rate for labor must be used to allow the company to meet its profit goal?
(b) Assume that an hourly billing rate for labor of $20 has been established. What mark-up on the cost of supplies will allow the company to meet its profit goal?
(c) Assume that *neither* the hourly billing rate nor the mark-up on cost of parts has been set. What combination(s) of rate and mark-up will allow the company to meet its profit goal? Explain your answer(s).
(d) What fundamental multiple product pricing dilemma is highlighted in part (c)?

Cases

C 14–1   Transfer Price for Long-range Decision Analysis—
Alternative Sources of Supply

Gable Company presently manufactures all the components needed to produce its end product. It has received an offer from Lombard Corporation to supply one component that Clark Division of Gable Company presently produces. Lombard offers to supply at least 50,000 units per year for the next five years at a price of $80 per unit. The unit costs presently incurred by Clark Division to produce the component are as follows:

Direct Materials	....	$30
Direct Labor	....	20
Overhead	....	40
		$90

These unit costs pertain to the production of 30,000 units per year, the recent average level of activity. Fixed costs account for two-thirds of the $40 per unit overhead amount. If Clark Division is closed, fixed overhead, with the exception of $200,000 for annual depreciation charges, could be avoided.

Required:

(a) Prepare an analysis to determine the correct transfer price to be quoted for the output of Clark Division in order to allow a correct long-run decision. Assume the long-run average requirements will continue to be 30,000 units per year of Clark's output.

(b) Should the firm purchase from Lombard or from Clark Division? What assumptions are involved in this decision?

(c) Discuss the validity and usefulness of the answer to part (a) if the expected volume were to change to (1) 40,000 units, or (2) 50,000 units per year.

(d) What problem is inherent in this type of pricing situation?

C 14–2 Transfer Pricing—Long-range Considerations

Refer to Exercise 9–10 on page 413. Assume that the fixed costs of $250,000 can be directly associated with the three divisions as follows:

X......	$ 50,000
Y......	100,000
Z......	100,000
	$250,000

Criss Company is considering its long-range source of supply of the two components needed by Division Z. The same outside prices are available on a long-range basis. If either Division X, Division Y, or both divisions are discontinued, 80 percent of the fixed costs associated with any discontinued division can be avoided.

Required:

(a) Should the outside supplier's offer be accepted? Show all calculations.

(b) What transfer prices would be appropriate to allow correct decisions in this long-run context?

(c) What assumptions were made to arrive at the solutions in parts (a) and (b)?

C 14–3 Transfer Pricing—Long-run Decision Analysis

Refer to the data in Exercise 9–11 on page 413. Assume now that the firm is considering its long-run source of supply of the 10,000 valves required by the Fabricating Division. The outside supply price of $42.50 will be reduced to $40 if the firm agrees to a long-term purchase contract for at least 12,000 units per month.

The Valve Division's sales to outside customers at $60 will continue at a 35,000 unit level. The Valve Division could reduce its capacity from 50,000 to 35,000 units by reducing total fixed costs by 25 percent. However, unit variable costs would increase by 10 percent at this lower capacity level, although no fixed assets would need to be disposed of.

Required:
(a) Should the company accept the outside supplier's offer and curtail the operations of the Valve Division, or should it allow the Valve Division to supply the component to the Fabricating Division? Show all calculations.
(b) What long-run transfer price would allow both divisions to come to the same, correct decision? Show how it was derived.
(c) What source of supply should be selected if the external sales of the Valve Division could be permanently increased to 45,000 units per month? Show all calculations. Assume that at a 45,000 unit production level the Valve Division will have $40 per unit variable costs and $600,000 fixed costs.

C 14–4   Transfer Pricing—Long-run Decision Making

Refer to Exercise 9–12 on page 414. Siebert Company is considering alternative long-run sources of supply for the part that Ajax presently supplies to Carbine. The outside supplier is prepared to honor the $3.50 price indefinitely. The annual volume of 100,000 units used by Carbine is also expected to remain unchanged. Ajax Division has the choice of (1) continuing operations with its present capacity of 300,000 units, (2) closing down operations completely, or (3) reducing capacity to 200,000 units. If operations of Ajax Division are terminated, all fixed costs except $50,000 will be avoided. However, if capacity is reduced to 200,000 units, fixed costs can be reduced to $200,000. Outside sales at $5 will continue at the 200,000 unit level.

Required:
(a) What source of supply for Carbine and which of the three preceding alternatives for Ajax will be most beneficial to the firm in the long run? Why? Show all calculations.
(b) Assume that annual sales to external customers at the $5 price will change to (1) 100,000 units or (2) 300,000 units. Now which of the three alternatives would be best for the firm in the long run? What source of supply should Carbine use? Show all calculations.
(c) What long-run transfer price(s) would enable the divisions to arrive at the correct decision(s) in part (a)? In part (b)?

Problems

P 14–1   Variable and Full Costing—Inventory Calculations—Income Statement Effects

Vernon Company, which uses full absorption costing, reported income as follows for its first two quarters of operation:

	1st Quarter	2nd Quarter
Sales	$240,000	$240,000
Less: Cost of Goods Sold	166,400	176,000
Gross Margin	$ 73,600	$ 64,000
Less: Marketing and		
Administrative Expense (all fixed)	40,000	40,000
Net Income	$ 33,600	$ 24,000

Production and sales data for these periods were as follows:

	1st Quarter	2nd Quarter
Production (units)	10,000	8,000
Sales (units)	8,000	8,000
Fixed Manufacturing Overhead	$42,000	$48,000

Required:

(a) Prepare a detailed schedule to show the derivation of cost of goods sold. What is the unit cost of inventory at the end of each quarter, given that the company used the weighted average cost method?

(b) Explain why the income figures for the two quarters are different. Pay specific attention to the fact that the sales volume was the same in both quarters.

(c) Using a variable costing approach, prepare revised income statements for the two quarters. Make schedules to compute the unit cost of inventories at the end of each quarter.

(d) Compare your results in part (c) with the original net income figures. Reconcile the differences and comment.

P 14-2 Full Absorption Costing—"Erratic" Income Results— Inventory Variations

For the first two months of 19X4, Hondo Corporation had the following reported income, based on a standard full absorption costing approach:

	January		February	
Unit Sales		15,000		20,000
Sales Revenues		$1,500,000		$2,000,000
Cost of Goods Sold:				
Beginning Inventory	$ 115,200		$ 475,200	
Cost of Goods Manufactured	1,440,000		1,080,000	
	$1,555,200		$1,555,200	
Less: Ending Inventory	475,200		115,200	
	$1,080,000		$1,440,000	
Volume Variance (unfavorable)	–0–		(250,000)	
		1,080,000		1,690,000
Gross Profit		$ 420,000		$ 310,000
Marketing Expenses	$ 60,000		$ 80,000	
Administrative Expenses	32,000		32,000	
		92,000		112,000
Net Income Before Tax		$ 328,000		$ 198,000
Tax Expense (40%)		131,200		79,200
Net Income After Tax		$ 196,800		$ 118,800

Inventories were deliberately increased during January in anticipation of increased sales in February. Sales volume did increase in February, but the resultant net income as reported was less than in January. Because sales prices and unit costs did not vary from the standard amounts, management has questioned the correctness of the income statements.

Further analysis of operations for the two months showed that although the company operated at normal capacity of 20,000 units in January, due to a shortage of key raw materials, output was only 15,000 units in February. At normal capacity, a unit manufacturing cost of $72 is standard, with $50 of that amount representing fixed manufacturing overhead costs.

Required:
(a) Prepare an analysis of the cost of manufacturing operations for the two months to show why the volume variance was zero in January and $250,000 in February.
(b) Why did net income decrease even though sales revenues increased? Show supporting calculations.
(c) Prepare income statements for the two months on a variable costing basis.
(d) Comment on the solution in part (c). Is it more useful than the original results? Why or why not?
(e) Reconcile the differences between the income statement developed in part (c) and the original results.

P 14–3   Variable Costing and Full Absorption Costing— Income Statement Effects

The first three quarters of operations of Stickney Corporation are reflected in the tabulation of data below:

	1st Quarter	2nd Quarter	3rd Quarter
Sales (units)	80,000	100,000	120,000
Production (units)	120,000	140,000	50,000
Unit Sales Price	$20	$20	$20
Variable Costs per Unit:			
Manufacturing	$8	$8	$8
Marketing	$2	$2	$2
Fixed Costs per Quarter:			
Manufacturing*	$260,000	$260,000	$260,000
Marketing	$140,000	$140,000	$140,000

* Absorbed into cost of units produced each quarter under full absorption costing. FIFO inventory method is assumed when computing the value of ending inventory.

Required:
(a) Prepare income statements for each of the three quarters on a full absorption cost basis.
(b) Prepare income statements for each of the three quarters on a variable cost basis.
(c) Reconcile and explain the differences between the respective quarterly results developed in parts (a) and (b).
(d) If sales and production in the fourth quarter are 100,000 units, what will net income be under (1) full absorption costing and (2) variable costing? What assumptions did you make in reaching your conclusion?
(e) Compare your answers in part (d) to the results for the second quarter. Comment.

P 14–4   Full Absorption Costing versus Variable Costing—
Income Statement Effects—Standard Costing System

Brinkley Company has developed the following operating and cost data for the first four months of 19X6:

Month	Units Produced	Units Sold
January	32,000	28,000
February	40,000	24,000
March............	28,000	28,000
April	16,000	36,000

During these four months, there were no price, rate, efficiency, spending, or materials quantity variances. The standard product cost specifications, based on an expected annual output of 360,000 units, were as follows:

	Standard Cost Per Unit
Direct Materials	$25
Direct Labor	15
Variable Overhead	10
Fixed Overhead	20
	$70

The sales price per unit was $100. Monthly marketing and administrative costs (all fixed) amounted to $600,000. There were no beginning inventories.

Required:
(a)   Prepare monthly income statements for the four-month period, using the full standard product costs specified. Fixed overhead volume variances are to be adjusted against the cost of goods sold amount each month.

(b)   Prepare monthly income statements for the four-month period, using a variable cost approach.

(c)   Prepare a schedule to compare the monthly net income figures developed in parts (a) and (b). Comment on the results of this comparison.

(d)   Which method, (a) or (b), presents a more (1) accurate, (2) realistic, (3) useful analysis of monthly operating results? Why?

P 14–5   Full Absorption Costing versus Variable Costing—
Process Costing—Standard Product Costs

Waterview Corporation is concerned that its present method of product costing—standard full absorption cost—does not accurately reflect its operating performance from month to month. Although the information concerning various price rate, spending, and efficiency variances is understandable and useful, the fixed overhead volume variance is often puzzling, particularly with regard to its effect on monthly reported income.

The following standard product cost specification is in effect:

Direct Materials (4 pounds @ $5 per pound)	$20
Direct Labor (2 hours @ $12.50 per hour)	25
Variable Overhead (2 hours @ $4.50 per direct labor hour)	9
Fixed Overhead (2 hours @ $10.50 per hour)	21
	$75

For May of 19X8, the following operating results were reported:

	May 1	May 31
Inventories:		
Finished Goods	40,000 units	10,000 units
Work in Process	20,000 units	5,000 units
Percent Complete	80%	20%
Raw Materials (@ $5 per pound)	10,000 pounds	20,000 pounds
Units Completed		50,000
Units Sold..............................		80,000
Materials Purchased (160,000 pounds).....		$ 825,000
Direct Labor Costs (72,000 hours)		$ 895,000
Variable Overhead Incurred		$ 315,000
Fixed Overhead Incurred		$1,100,000

All direct materials are added when processing starts, but labor and overhead costs are incurred uniformly and continuously. The fixed overhead rate was based on an expected annual capacity of 1,200,000 direct labor hours. The sales price is $90 per unit. All marketing and administrative costs are fixed, amounting to $50,000 per month.

Required:
(a) Prepare a process costing production report for May of 19X8. Use standard full absorption product costs throughout.
(b) Prepare an analysis of all manufacturing cost variances for May of 19X8.
(c) Prepare an income statement for May, using standard full absorption product costs, with *all* variances shown as an adjustment against Cost of Goods Sold.
(d) Prepare a revised income statement for May, using standard *variable* product costs, also with *all* variances shown as adjustments against Cost of Goods Sold. (Assume for this purpose that the opening inventory is carried at a standard variable cost of $54 per unit.)
(e) Reconcile and comment on the difference between your results in parts (c) and (d). Which method would you recommend and why?

P 14–6   Full Absorption Costing and Variable Costing— Inventory, Tax, and Income Effects

Carducci Company produces farm machinery. For January of 19X2, the following income statement was prepared based on a full absorption costing approach:

Sales (220 units)	$2,200,000
Less: Cost of Goods Sold	1,100,000
Gross Profit	$1,100,000
Less: Marketing and Administrative Expenses......	300,000
Taxable Income	$ 800,000
Tax Expense (40%)	320,000
Net Income.....................................	$ 480,000

It was also established that the fixed portion of marketing and administrative expenses amounted to $190,000 for the month. Variable manufacturing costs were $3,500 per unit. Fixed overhead is applied on the basis of a predetermined rate of $1,500 per unit. This rate was set in anticipation of a monthly output of 250 units. Any monthly amount of underapplied or overapplied overhead is carried forward and only adjusted against Cost of Goods Sold in December of each year. In January of 19X2, 160 units were produced. January 1 inventory was 100 units. Total fixed overhead incurred for January was as predicted.

Required:

(a) Prepare a schedule to show the derivation of (1) the cost of goods manufactured and (2) the cost of goods sold.

(b) What was the amount of underapplied or overapplied fixed overhead for January, 19X2?

(c) Prepare a revised income statement for January, 19X2, using a variable costing approach. (Assume for this purpose that the January 1 inventory was carried at its variable cost per unit.) Show tax expense based on taxable income as determined under the variable costing method.

(d) Assuming that full absorption costing must be used for tax reporting purposes, comment on the difference between the amounts of tax expense in the original statement and in the solution to part (c). What accounting treatment will be required to account for this difference?

(e) Reconcile and comment on the differences between the amounts of *taxable income* in the original statement and in the solution to part (c).

P 14–7 Variable Costing and Full Absorption Costing— Multiple Products—Income Statement Effects— Inventory Measurement

Bellanca Corporation manufactures a single, premium quality product, which sells for $10 per unit. Its costs, based on average annual capacity of 120,000 units, are as follows:

	Cost per Unit
Materials	$2.00
Direct Labor	1.50
Variable Overhead	1.00
Fixed Overhead	2.50
Variable Marketing Cost	1.00
Fixed Administrative Cost	0.50
	$8.50

The company proposes to introduce a lower grade product which will sell for $7.50 per unit and use the same basic ingredients and facilities. However, materials costs per unit will be 25 percent less and labor and variable overhead will be 20 percent less. Variable marketing costs for all sales are 10 percent of sales revenue. With minor modifications, the firm's present production and administrative facilities could manufacture 120,000 units of the new product in addition to the present capacity of premium grade items. These modifications would increase both total annual fixed overhead and total annual fixed administrative costs by 10 percent.

An analysis based on full absorption costing at the 120,000 unit level of production (annually) produced the following report, which indicates that the new product might not be all that profitable.

	Cost per Unit
Materials	1.50
Direct Labor	1.20
Variable Overhead	0.80
Fixed Overhead	2.75
Variable Marketing Cost	0.75
Fixed Administrative Cost	0.55
	$7.55

The management is confused by this result and requests further study.

Required:
(a) Comment on the $7.55 cost of producing the new product. Do you agree with it? Why or why not?
(b) Prepare an alternative analysis of the feasibility of the new product. Should it be introduced? Why or why not?
(c) The company decides to proceed with the introduction of the new product. During the first month (January, 19X1) of operations, 10,000 units of each product are produced. However, only 8,000 of the premium grade and 6,000 of the standard grade are sold. (Assume there were no beginning inventories of either product.) Prepare income statements for the month based on (1) full absorption costing and (2) variable costing. State any assumptions you are making. Comment on the results.
(d) In the second month, production is cut back to 5,000 units of each product. Sales are 7,000 of the premium grade and 9,000 of the standard grade. Repeat the requirements of part (c).

P 14–8   Cost-Based Pricing—Alternative Mark-up Procedures

Rosevita Company is investigating alternative price setting procedures for its major product. For 19X7, the following cost predictions have been made:

	Per Unit
Direct Materials.............	$16
Direct Labor	32
Variable Overhead	12
Fixed Overhead	20
Variable Operating Cost	4
Fixed Operating Cost	8
	$92

These amounts are based on an expected annual volume of 50,000 units. However, there is some uncertainty about the demand for this product; forecasts as high as 80,000 units and as low as 30,000 units were considered in the planning discussions.

Required:
(a) Assume that only the 50,000 unit sales forecast is used. Prepare estimates of the required sales price per unit based on:
(1) A 60 percent mark-up on all variable costs.
(2) A 25 percent mark-up on full manufacturing costs.

(b)   What amounts of income (loss) would be reported if all of the forecasts in (a)(1) and (a)(2) held true?

(c)   What income will be reported (under *both* pricing formulas) if both production and sales volume (1) fall to 30,000 units or (2) increase to 80,000 units with prices remaining the same as calculated in part (a).

(d)   Comment on the basic pricing dilemma involved here. Which pricing procedure would you recommend? Why?

P 14–9   Pricing Procedures—Cost Feasibility— Target Income Requirements

Gluschenko Company is preparing an analysis of the feasibility of a new product and has obtained the following cost estimates:

	Per Unit
Direct Materials	$ 90
Direct Labor	25
Variable Overhead	15
Fixed Overhead	25
Variable Marketing Costs	10
Fixed Marketing Costs	35
Fixed Administrative Costs	25
	$225

These figures were based on a projected annual volume of 10,000 units. In addition, new manufacturing and distribution facilities will require the outlay of $1,800,000. All fixed costs in the preceding schedule are directly associated with the proposed product. No firm-wide, allocated costs are involved.

Because the market for this proposed new product is quite competitive, the sales price probably cannot exceed $255 per unit. In addition, the company requires that all new projects anticipate at least a 20 percent rate of return on required investment outlays.

Required:
(a)   If the company charges $255 per unit, will it be able to meet its rate of return requirement? Show calculations. What assumptions were made?

(b)   What is the minimum sales price that would allow the rate of return requirement to be satisfied (1) at the 10,000-unit level, (2) at the 15,000-unit level, (3) at the 8,000-unit level?

(c)   What adjustments to the targeted cost amounts would have to be made to meet the rate of return requirement, assuming the 10,000-unit level is achieved? Comment separately and independently on (1) the fixed costs, (2) the variable costs, and (3) the cost of investment required.

(d)   Refer to the solution to part (b)(1). If that price is set, will the company be sure to meet its target profit goal? Why or why not?

(e)   Outline and discuss the three types of conflict that make the pricing decision difficult in this situation.

P 14–10 Pricing Decisions—Multiple Outputs— Common Fixed Costs

Marlene Company operates a plant in which two types of products are manufactured. The separate costs of the two products are as follows:

	Alpha	Gamma
Direct Materials......	$50	$20
Direct Labor	$20	$30

The direct labor rate is $10 per hour and a plant-wide variable overhead rate of $8 per direct labor hour has been established. Total fixed manufacturing overhead is $120,000 per month. Variable marketing costs are $20 per unit for both products. Other fixed marketing and administrative costs amount to $80,000 per month. The company has established a profit goal of $50,000 per month.

Required: (Answer each part independently except as indicated.)
(a) Given only the preceding information, solve the problem of setting prices for the two products to meet the profit goal. Explain the solution.
(b) Assume that the demand for Alpha will be exactly 5,000 units. How will this affect the solution to part (a)?
(c) Assume that the demand for Gamma will be at least 4,000 units. How will this affect the solution to part (a)?
(d) Assume the company arbitrarily decides to divide all fixed costs and target profits equally between the two products. How will this affect the solution to part (a), if 4,000 units of Alpha and 5,000 units of Gamma will be sold?

P 14–11 Multiple Outputs—Pricing Decisions— Alternative Pricing Strategies

McCulley Company presently operates in a relatively competitive industry, manufacturing and distributing two grades of its product. For 19X6, the following budget was developed:

	Deluxe		Standard		Total	
Sales (units)		10,000		30,000		40,000
Sales Revenues		$900,000		$1,800,000		$2,700,000
Less: Variable Costs:						
Manufacturing	$300,000		$750,000		$1,050,000	
Marketing	200,000		600,000		800,000	
		500,000		1,350,000		1,850,000
Contribution Margin ..		$400,000		$ 450,000		$ 850,000
Less: Fixed Costs:						
Manufacturing					$ 300,000	
Marketing					400,000	
Administrative					200,000	$ 900,000
Net Loss						$ (50,000)

Following this loss, these alternatives were proposed:

1. By *reducing* sales prices by 10 percent, unit sales volume would increase by 20 percent on deluxe and 15 percent on standard models.
2. By *increasing* sales prices by 10 percent, unit sales volume would decrease by 15 percent on deluxe and 5 percent on standard models.
3. By *increasing* fixed marketing costs by $100,000, unit sales volume of both products would improve by 10 percent.
4. By *reducing* fixed marketing costs by $50,000, unit sales volume of both products would be reduced by 5 percent.

Required:
(a) Evaluate each of the four alternatives. Which one should be chosen? Why?
(b) Assume that the unit sales of the two products remain in the same relative proportions as in the original budget. What increase in unit sales volume will allow the company to earn a profit of $100,000?
(c) Again assume that the sales mix and relative sales prices as mentioned in part (b) do not change. What change in *sales prices* would be necessary to allow the company to earn a profit of $100,000, given that the unit sales volume (1) remains as budgeted, (2) increases by 5 percent, (3) decreases by 10 percent? Show all calculations and state all assumptions.

P 14–12   Joint Outputs—Pricing Decisions— Common Processing Cost Allocation Procedures

Lerch Company produces two products, Webers and Demezas, using common processing facilities. For a typical month when 100,000 pounds of basic material inputs are processed, manufacturing costs and production results are as follows:

Manufacturing Costs	
Direct Materials (100,000 pounds)	$200,000
Direct Labor	100,000
Variable Overhead	100,000
Fixed Overhead	200,000
	$600,000

Output (in pounds)	
Webers	400,000
Demezas	200,000

Marketing and Administrative Costs (all fixed)	$200,000

Required:
(a) Using the physical units of output method, prepare a schedule to allocate common processing costs to the two products.
(b) Based on their share of manufacturing costs as allocated, plus a 50 percent markup to cover other costs and a contribution to profit, what *prices* should be charged for the two products?
(c) What are the advantages and limitations of the pricing method offered in part (b)?
(d) If the market price of Webers cannot exceed $1.50 per pound, what are the implications for the pricing and marketing of Demezas?

(e)   If the market price of Demezas is fixed at $2 per pound, what are the implications for the pricing and marketing of Webers?

(f)   What alternative treatment of the common processing costs for pricing purposes could be considered?

(g)   What purpose (if any) is served by allocating common processing costs when pricing decisions are involved?

P 14–13   Pricing of Job Order Contracts—
Cost-Based Negotiated Prices—Allowable Costs

Cassidy Company contracted with a federal agency to supply 20 closed-circuit surveillance systems over a two-year period. The terms of the contract included the following:

(1)   Maximum Adjusted Price $2,200,000
       Target Contract Price   1,800,000
       Target Contract Cost   1,550,000

(2)   Adjusted Contract Price:

Total Allowable Costs	Total Allowable Profit
1. Equal to Target Cost	Target Profit
2. Less than Target Cost	Target Profit *plus* 15% of Cost Underrun*
3. Greater than Target Cost	Target Profit *less* 15% of Cost Overrun**

　　 * Cost Underrun = Target Cost − Allowable Cost
　 ** Cost Overrun = Allowable Cost − Target Cost

During the first year, 10 systems were completed and delivered. The following cost data were then developed:

	Actual Costs to Date	Estimated Costs to Complete
Materials	$ 300,000	$ 310,000
Direct Labor......	330,000	340,000
Overhead	400,000	430,000
	$1,030,000	$1,080,000

It was noted that, on average, 5 percent of allocated overhead costs are usually disallowed by the agency's auditors. In addition, actual costs include $10,000 for nonrecurring set-up and training costs and $5,000 per year for depreciation on idle equipment. It is expected that these, together with $5,000 for purchase discounts that were not taken advantage of, will also be disallowed.

Required:

(a)   Prepare a schedule to determine the *estimated* total adjusted contract price.

(b)   Prepare an income statement for the first year.

(c)   Assuming that the company has other customers and other products, discuss the accounting problems involved in determining the amount of overhead for this federal agency contract. Mention also the impact of C.A.S.B. pronouncements on this procedure.

P 14–14   Contract Bid Pricing—Continuing Basis versus One-time Situation—Cost Recovery Requirements

Shogun Company presently manufactures and distributes one major product called Amoroso. Production capacity exceeds the sales level the firm has been able to maintain. A search for alternative products has resulted in the receipt of a sales order for a new product, Imparato. The new product can be produced in the existing facilities using some of the same ingredients as are used to make Amoroso (namely, Materials J, K, and L).

The initial contract calls for 40,000 pounds of Imparato to be delivered during December, 19X3. The order can be filled without affecting the present regular volume of production of Amoroso (160,000 pounds per month). Inputs required to produce each ton (2,000 pounds) of Imparato are as follows:

Material J	1,000 pounds
Material K	600 pounds
Material L	600 pounds
Direct Labor	50 hours

Presently the inventory of raw materials includes:

	Inventory (in pounds) Dec. 1, 19X3	Acquisition Cost per Pound	Replacement Cost per Pound
J......	30,000	$2.00	$2.20
K......	5,000	0.75	0.80
L......	10,000	0.55	0.60
M......	20,000	1.00	2.50

Material M, which has zero salvage value, was acquired some time ago for use in another product, Defuncto. However, it is substitutable for Material J on a pound for pound basis. The direct labor hourly rate is $12. Variable overhead costs are $8 per direct labor hour. Monthly fixed overhead costs are $100,000. All other operating costs, which are also fixed, total $80,000. These latter amounts will not be affected by the acceptance of this contract. Monthly capacity is 5,000 direct labor hours, of which Amoroso presently uses 4,000.

Required:
(a) Prepare an analysis to determine the minimum contract bid price that would allow all costs of the December order to be recovered. State all assumptions.

(b) Assume that orders for at least 40,000 pounds of Imparato per month are forthcoming for the following year. What base price will allow all costs to be recovered? Again, state all assumptions. Assume that if the firm uses over 5,000 direct labor hours, fixed costs will increase by $20,000.

(c) Discuss the basic problems involved in setting the price for a continuing sales arrangement as compared to a one-time contract.

P 14–15   Pricing Policies—Product Introduction Decisions

Chamberlain Company is considering introducing a new product created by its Research and Development Department. A stable demand of 100,000 units per year has been confidently predicted. None of the firm's competitors has developed a comparable product.

Two product introduction and pricing policies have been proposed. The first involves a limited volume operation for the first two years, during which time output would be limited to 20,000 units annually and the price per unit would be set at $1,500 in anticipation of "skimming" the market. At that level of output, variable costs would be $600 per unit and total fixed costs would be $2,500,000 annually, with an initial outlay of $25,000,000 for investment in fixed facilities and required working capital items.

Alternately, an annual output level of 100,000 units can be implemented immediately. This would reduce variable costs to $500 per unit, but fixed costs would increase to $10,000,000 per year and an additional $55,000,000 would have to be invested in fixed facilities and working capital support items.

Assume a ten-year life on fixed facilities, zero salvage value, and straight line depreciation. Working capital items constitute 25 percent of the total investment outlay.

Required: (Answer each part independently.)

(a) Assuming that competitors will not be able to develop a similar product for at least two more years, what price must the company charge for the product at the 100,000-unit volume to make it equally profitable, in terms of rate of return on investment, as would be the "skimming" policy for the first two years. Show all calculations and state all assumptions.

(b) Assume that a $1,000 sales price per unit has been selected to be compatible with the 100,000-unit volume. However, the company is not sure that competitors will not be able to develop a comparable product within two years. Should the company manufacture and sell: (1) 100,000 units at $1,000 apiece or (2) 20,000 units at $1,500 apiece? Why? State all assumptions.

(c) Assume that the company decides to pursue the "skimming" alternative and sets its price at $1,500. After one year, a competitive product priced at $995 threatens the second year sales of the Chamberlain Company's product. However, it will take a full year to acquire and make operational additional facilities to increase volume to the 100,000-unit level. What price should the company set in the second year? State all assumptions.

(d) Based on part (c), what price should the company charge in the third year and beyond, given that total market demand for the product will not exceed 100,000 units? Assume that the competitor's product is as attractive as Chamberlain's and that the competitor will match any price reduction by Chamberlain. The only alternative capacity configuration would be a 60,000 unit set-up under which variable costs would be $560 per unit, fixed costs would be $8,000,000 per year, and investment outlay would be $60,000,000. State all assumptions and show all calculations.

P 14–16   Contract Bid Pricing—Problems in Cost Estimation and Allocation—Multiple, Nonuniform Outputs

Alviso Corporation produces a variety of custom-made specialty products. Three production departments usually perform part of the work, but in varying proportions, on each job passing through the plant. Recently several jobs that were successfully bid on turned out to be relatively unprofitable, while several other apparently competitive bids did not succeed in securing an order from the potential customer. The following information has been obtained:

1. Materials used by Alviso on most jobs are standard items for which purchase prices are quite stable and freely available to Alviso's competitors.
2. Direct labor rates are also comparable to those paid by competitors, since all are subject to the same union contract settlements.
3. The firm is well-established and its record for efficiency, spoilage, wastage, and productivity is better than average relative to its competitors.
4. Overhead costs include mostly labor-related items, some variable and some fixed. However, due to its recent experiences, the company has decided to include a very liberal allowance for idle time and set-up time in the total of overhead costs, rather than anticipate higher direct labor hours.
5. Department Z, where direct labor rates are relatively lower than in other departments, has the highest concentration of equipment, facilities, and space occupancy. Departments X and Y use less fixed facilities, but their direct labor rates are higher due to the higher skilled manual work performed there.
6. An analysis of a typical bid that was *not* successful showed the following labor and overhead cost components:

Direct Labor		
Dept. X (500 hours @ $15 per hour)		$ 7,500
Dept. Y (300 hours @ $10 per hour)		3,000
Dept. Z (50 hours @ $5 per hour)		250
		$10,750
Overhead		
80% of Direct Labor Cost		8,600
Total Labor and Overhead		
Components of Job Cost		$19,350

7. For the current year, the estimates upon which the overhead rate was based were as follows:

Direct Labor		
Dept. X (60,000 hours)		$ 900,000
Dept. Y (80,000 hours)		800,000
Dept. Z (110,000 hours)		550,000
		$2,250,000
Manufacturing Overhead		
Variable Items		500,000
Fixed Items		1,300,000
		$1,800,000

8. Analysis of the costs of jobs that have been successfully bid on indicated that they have tended to require considerable amounts of work in Department Z.

Required:
(a) Based on the information provided, discuss the probable reasons for the company's lack of success in securing the contracts for jobs such as the one outlined in point 6.

(b)   Outline the probable reasons for the nonprofitability of jobs that were successfully bid on.

(c)   Based on the information provided, what revision in costing procedures would you recommend to respond to the problems outlined? Show computations and state all assumptions.

(d)   Discuss the fundamental problems that the company faces with respect to basing its bid prices on the estimated costs of individual jobs.

P 14–17   Transfer Pricing Decisions—Long-run Analysis

Gilligan Corporation operates two divisions, X and Y, with cost and production details as follows:

	X	Y
Capacity per Year	20,000 units	10,000 units
Variable Costs per Unit	$10	$12
Fixed Costs per Year	$200,000	$300,000

Division X presently operates at only half its potential capacity and sells all of its output to Division Y. Presently a transfer price of $30 per unit (on a full absorption cost basis) has been set for the item transferred by Division X to Division Y.

An outside supplier has offered to supply the requirements of Division Y for this same item at a long-term firm price of $24 per unit for 10,000 units annually. The following alternatives for Division X are being considered:

1.   Continue present operations with existing capacity level.

2.   Discontinue Division X completely and have Division Y purchase outside.

3.   Discontinue production in Division X, but use its facilities (no change in total fixed costs) to manufacture a new product with an estimated demand of 40,000 units per year and a contribution margin of $2 ($7 selling price − $5 variable cost) per unit. Capacity production of the new product would be 40,000 units.

4.   Continue production in Division X, but reduce capacity to 10,000 units per year by reducing total fixed costs to $100,000, while increasing variable cost to $12 per unit.

Required:

(a)   Prepare an analysis to determine the long-run course of action that should be taken with regard to Division X and the source of supply for Division Y.

(b)   What long-run transfer price(s) for Division X's product would allow both Division X and Division Y to arrive at the same correct decision independently?

(c)   If Division X were to locate a customer who was prepared to pay $25 apiece for 15,000 units of the product Division X now provides to Division Y, how would this affect the analysis in part (a)? Show all calculations and state all assumptions.

P 14–18   Transfer Pricing Decisions—Long-run Analysis

Refer to Problem 9–19 on page 429. Consider the question from the point of view of what Divisions B and C should do in the long run. Assume that Division B can (1) maintain capacity, costs, and outside sales as originally stated or (2) reduce capacity to 10,000 units and reduce fixed costs to $300,000 per month.

Required:

(a) What action by Divisions B and C will be best for the firm as a whole in the long run? Show all calculations and state all assumptions.

(b) Assume that monthly outside sales for Division B's product change to (1) zero units or (2) 20,000 units. Again, what is the best long-run solution for the firm as a whole?

(c) What long-run transfer price(s) would enable the divisions to arrive independently at the correct decisions in parts (a) and (b)?

P 14–19   Transfer Pricing Decisions—Long-run Analysis

Refer to Problem 9–21 on page 431. Latter Division must make a permanent decision as to (1) the capacity level to maintain, (2) the source of Component X, and (3) the choice between the government contract on a recurring basis or the sales to the private customer, also on a continuing basis.

Latter Division can either (1) maintain its current capacity of 10,000 units with costs unchanged or (2) reduce capacity to 6,000 units, which will reduce fixed costs to $5 per labor hour. Former Division's costs will not be affected and it will continue to have potential external customers for all of its output at $25 per unit. Finally, Latter Division's sales to regular customers are made at $125 per unit.

Required:

(a) Prepare an analysis to resolve the decisions facing Latter Division from the viewpoint of what actions are in the long-run best interest of the firm. (*Note:* If the government contract is taken, none of the 4,000-unit special order can be filled.)

(b) How does the solution to part (a) affect Former Division?

(c) What long-run transfer price(s) would allow the divisions to arrive at the same correct decision(s)?

P 14–20   Transfer Pricing Decisions—Long-run Analysis

Refer to Problem 9–22 on page 432. The long-run external demand for the product of the Michael Division is now not expected to exceed 700 units per month. Consequently, a decision is to be made to either continue producing at the present capacity level, to discontinue operations altogether, or to reduce capacity to 1,200 units per month. Demand for the product of the Dominic Division is expected to continue at 500 units per month. If Michael's capacity is reduced to 1,200 units, fixed costs of $60,000 per month can be avoided.

Required:

(a) Prepare an analysis to determine which actions should be taken with regard to the capacity level in the Michael Division and the source of supply for the Dominic Division. Show all calculations and state all assumptions.

(b) Is there a long-run transfer price that will allow the divisions to arrive independently at the same correct decision?

(c) Suppose that the external demand for Michael's products falls to zero. Revise your analysis in part (a).

PART THREE

COST INFORMATION FOR SPECIALIZED DECISION MAKING

15

FORECASTING COSTS AND REVENUES

LEARNING OBJECTIVES

After studying Chapter 15, you should be able to:

1. Forecast costs and revenues using the methods of
   a. Individual account analysis.
   b. High–low interpolation.
   c. Visual fit.
   d. Engineered estimates.
   e. Single variable least squares regression.
   f. Multiple variable least squares regression.
2. Forecast sales volume using a constant growth or decline model, moving cumulative averages, and weighted moving averages.
3. Compare and contrast these elementary forecasting methods with linear regression analysis. Explain the advantages and disadvantages of the latter method.
4. Understand the preconditions and data requirements for use of least squares regression.
5. Interpret the results of least squares regression with regard to
   a. The regression coefficients.
   b. The coefficient of determination.
   c. The correlation coefficient.
   d. The standard error of the regression estimate.
   e. The standard error of the regression coefficients.
   f. t-statistics for the regression coefficients.
6. Interpret the results of time series regression analysis.
7. Interpret the results of multiple regression analysis.

To be effective, managers must estimate the outcomes of future actions. This is especially true in planning and budgeting, for which prediction is the essential accounting task. Cash flow estimates and forecasts of sales, inventories, production costs, and marketing and administrative expenses are basic ingredients of operational planning. Accountants need accurate forecast information to establish predetermined overhead rates. Cost–volume–profit analysis and short-term incremental analysis also depend on projections of the effects of future alternative actions. Flexible budgeting and capital budgeting involve similar forecasting procedures.

In this chapter, methods of forecasting costs and revenues for planning and control purposes are demonstrated. The relative usefulness and limitations of elementary and formal statistical forecasting procedures are considered, along with some qualitative and subjective aspects of the forecasting process.

ELEMENTARY FORECASTING METHODS

Most decision making involves answering questions about activity levels, such as: How many items should be manufactured and sold? Which input resources should be consumed and in what quantities? Consequently, costs and revenues are usually forecast in relation to the anticipated level of some activity-related variable—for example, expected units of output or anticipated units of input.

A cost accountant will typically use elementary forecasting methods to establish a simple linear relationship between expected activity levels and forecast costs and revenues. In the following examples, the total value of each forecast cost is expressed in terms of a constant fixed amount per period plus a variable amount per unit of an influencing, activity-related variable. The general forecast equation is:

$$y = a + bx$$

Here y is the forecast cost, a is the constant amount per period, and b is the variable amount per unit of the influencing variable, x.

Four elementary forecasting methods are based on observations of past performance.

1. Individual Account Analysis
2. High–Low Interpolation
3. Visual Fit
4. Engineered Estimates

INDIVIDUAL ACCOUNT ANALYSIS

The simplest forecasting procedure is best used in a preliminary investigation of cost and revenue behavior. As its name implies, **individual account analysis** involves analyzing the contents of cost and revenue accounts in the general ledger. Based on this analysis, the entries in particular ledger accounts can be classified as fixed or variable, depending on whether or not they appear to be influenced by activity level changes.

This classification process is subjective, arbitrary, and limited. If it relates only to a single accounting period, it permits no comparison between the behavior of costs at different activity levels. These limitations are increased if the fixed–variable analysis is restricted to the total of each account rather than applied to individual entries in the accounts.

Appropriate use of this method requires (1) examination of several periods of account data covering a wide range of activity levels, (2) detailed analysis of entries in each account, made on a consistent basis over those periods, and (3) relatively stable input prices, technology, production configurations, and total operating capacity.

Example: Cox Company has made a fixed–variable analysis of the entries in its accounts for Department A for the three months ended March 31, 19X9, during which the department produced 10,000 units of output. The total fixed cost per quarter is $60,000 and the total variable cost is $250,000—$25 per unit of output ($250,000 ÷ 10,000 units). Department A's estimated cost function is as follows:

$$y = \$60,000 + \$25x$$

Here y represents total cost per quarter and x represents the number of units manufactured each quarter. Assuming that this cost function will remain the same in future periods, Department A's quarterly costs can be forecast simply by multiplying the anticipated number of output units by $25 and adding $60,000 for the fixed cost component.

HIGH–LOW INTERPOLATION

Another method of estimating the fixed and variable elements of a cost function is called **high–low interpolation.** It involves interpolating cost behavior over a range of activity levels, on the assumption that a linear relationship exists between total cost and activity levels. This can be done algebraically or geometrically by solving for the fixed and variable components of total cost at two different activity levels.

Usually the two observations chosen are the *extreme high and low points of observed activity levels.* However, this method can be challenged on the grounds that such extreme observations may not be truly representative of the relationship that exists between the two variables at other activity levels. Just as the extreme high and low scores are disregarded in judging gymnastic and diving competitions, perhaps the highest and lowest pairs of costs and output quantities should be discarded when an interpolation approach is used to develop a cost function.

But this only raises the issue of how many extreme values should be discarded. Obviously, any decision concerning which pair of observations to use will be an arbitrary choice, either of extreme high and low points or of intermediate points.

Example: Findlay Company has compiled monthly totals for manufacturing overhead cost and number of products processed in one of its manufacturing departments during the past 20 months. Figure 15–1 shows the resulting distribution.

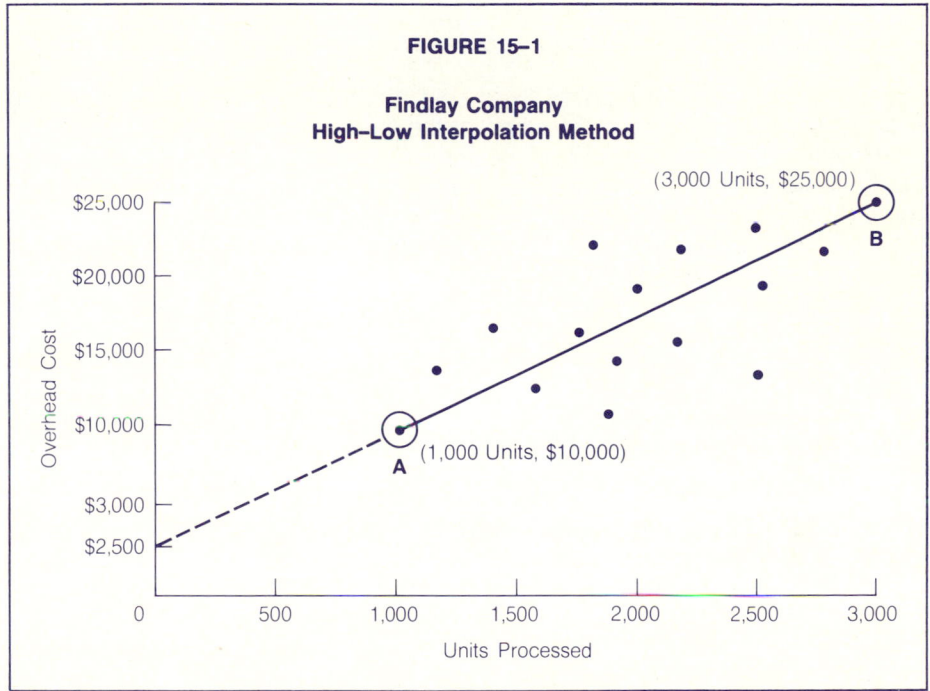

FIGURE 15–1

Findlay Company
High–Low Interpolation Method

The high and low observed values are represented by points B (3,000 units, $25,000) and A (1,000 units, $10,000). The solid line joining these two points has an equation that can be determined as follows:

	Units	Total Cost
High (B)	3,000	$25,000
Low (A)	1,000	10,000

Let F = Total Fixed Costs and V = Unit Variable Cost. Then:

$$3,000\,V + F = 25,000 \quad \ldots\ldots\ldots\ldots\ldots\ldots\ldots\ldots\quad [1]$$
$$1,000\,V + F = 10,000 \quad \ldots\ldots\ldots\ldots\ldots\ldots\ldots\ldots\quad [2]$$

Subtract Equation 2 from Equation 1:

$$2,000V = 15,000$$
$$V = 7.5 \ \dots\dots\dots\dots\dots\dots\dots\dots\dots\dots\dots\dots[3]$$

Substitute Equation 3 in Equation 1:

$$3,000 \ (7.5) + F = 25,000$$
$$F = 2,500 \ \dots\dots\dots\dots\dots\dots\dots\dots\dots[4]$$

This can be stated in equation form as follows:

$$\text{Total Cost} = \$2,500 + \$7.50 \text{ per unit}$$

In other words, the total monthly fixed cost (the intercept on the vertical axis) is \$2,500; the variable cost (the slope of the line) is \$7.50 per unit.

However, this solution should be interpreted and used cautiously. Fixed overhead costs are not the same at all activity levels. The \$2,500 is only their apparent value, obtained by extrapolating the high–low line back to the y-axis. It should be inferred that these figures will hold true only over the observed range of from 1,000 to 3,000 units.

The limitations of high–low interpolation include:

1. The cost function is based on the arbitrary choice of two possibly extreme pairs of observations.
2. The assumption of linearity over the observed range of operating levels disregards the distribution pattern of cost/activity combinations at each activity level.

Although its simplicity and directness give high–low interpolation some measure of acceptability, these two weaknesses detract from its predictive reliability. Its results can be inspected graphically by plotting the high–low curve to see how well it fits the set of observed data. The results can also be evaluated by measuring how far each observed value of the forecast variable varies from the plotted line. However, no formal mathematical or statistical tests can be applied to these results. The forecaster can only judge subjectively whether or not the deviations of observed data from the high–low line are significant.

VISUAL FIT OR GRAPHIC APPROXIMATION METHOD

Rather than rely on a single set (account analysis) or pair (high–low interpolation) of observations, a more representative cost function can be derived by making use of all available observations of costs and activity levels. One convenient way to do this for cost items is by inspecting the scattergraphs of observed sets of cost/activity level combinations. Figures 15–2 to 15–5 illustrate typical patterns of observed cost/activity level combinations.

Once a scattergraph has been prepared and inspected, a subjective, visual method can be used to fit a representative line to the collection of data points. There is nothing rigorous about this process. To the person drawing it, such a line merely appears to be representative of the general pattern of data observa-

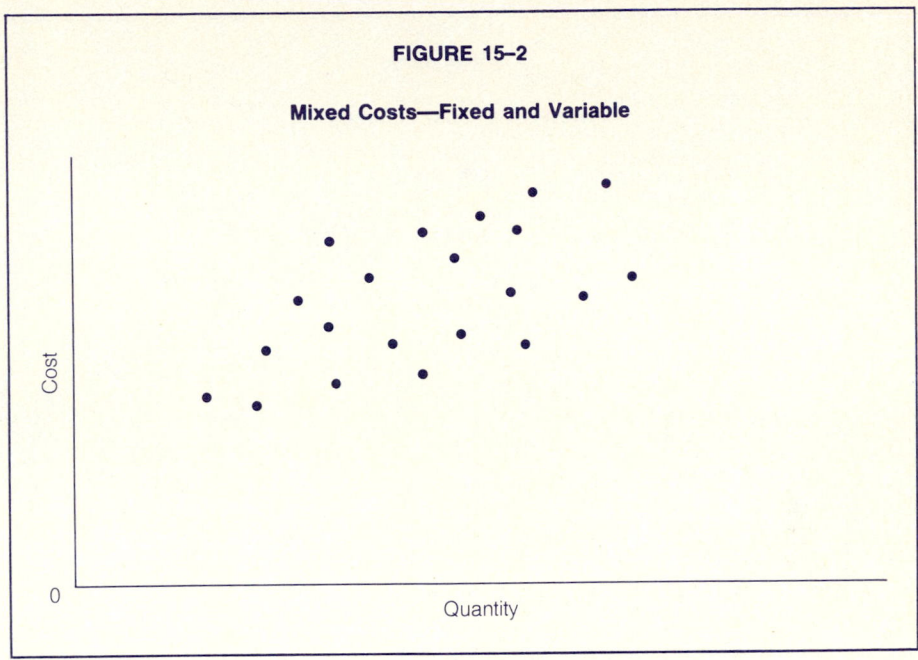

FIGURE 15–2

Mixed Costs—Fixed and Variable

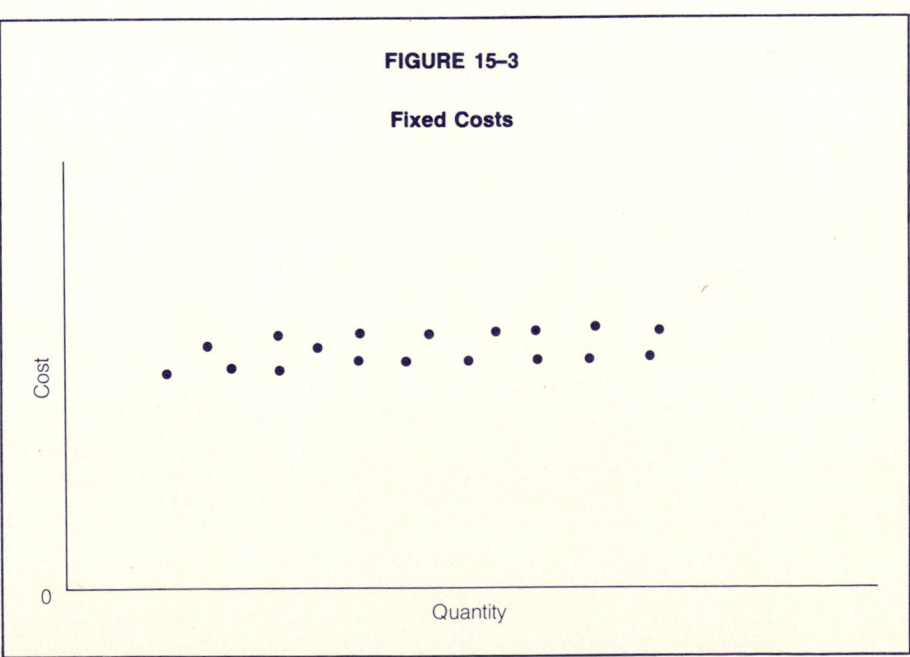

FIGURE 15–3

Fixed Costs

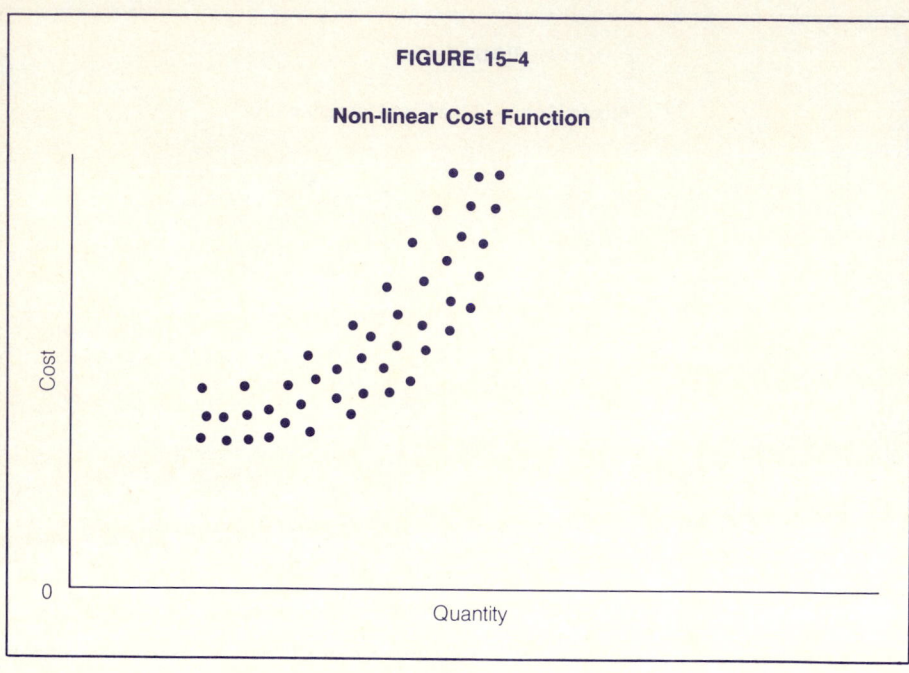

FIGURE 15–4

Non-linear Cost Function

Cost

0

Quantity

FIGURE 15–5

No Determinable Pattern

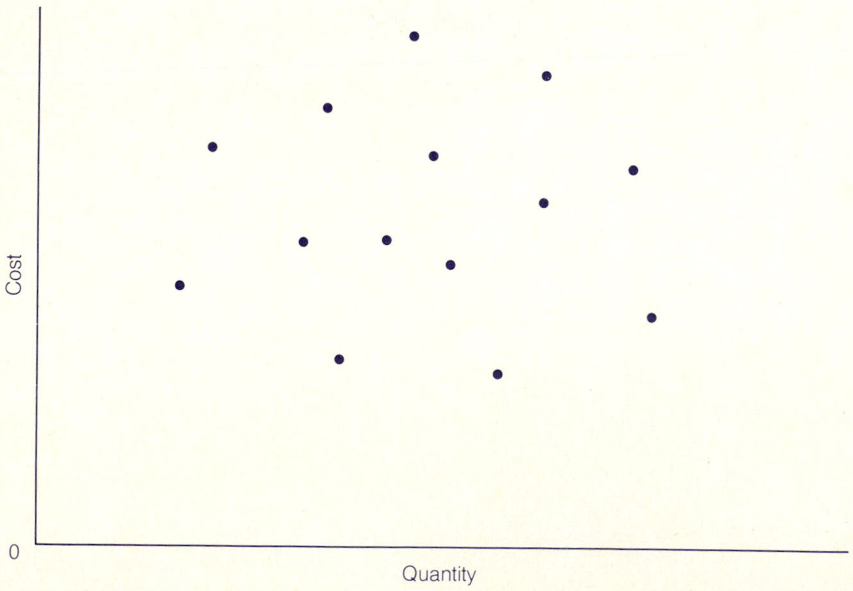

Cost

0

Quantity

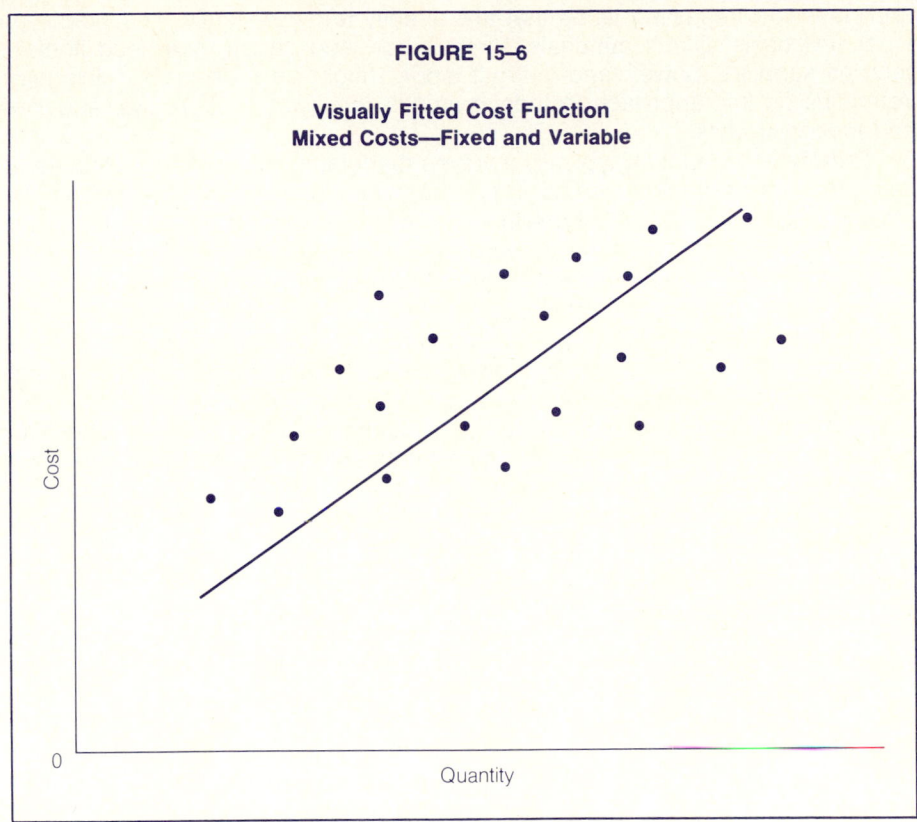

FIGURE 15–6

Visually Fitted Cost Function
Mixed Costs—Fixed and Variable

Cost

0

Quantity

tions. After this line is drawn, the equation that defines it must be established by geometric inspection. Figure 15–6 shows a visually fitted cost function based on the data presented in Figure 15–2.

Except in extreme cases, for which a pattern is very well defined, different observers are likely to disagree as to which is the proper line for a particular set of data. Hence the likelihood of obtaining different results, even when this method is applied repeatedly to the same set of facts. Unlike the previously described methods, visual fitting does not have the defect of being based on too few observations. However, no specific degree of precision or reliability can be associated with its results.

ENGINEERED ESTIMATES

The three preceding methods require at least some data representing actual performance. However, forecasts are often needed for situations that have never been experienced—for example, costs of new products. When no historical results are available, forecasts must be based on other information.

Product specifications and preproduction **engineered estimates** can sometimes be used to generate cost and revenue forecasts. This method is most applicable to forecasting items that are directly and physically measurable on a per unit basis. Direct materials, direct labor, and certain overhead items—such as supplies, power, and indirect labor—might be measured in this way. Variations on this approach include *prototype production, test runs,* and *time and motion studies.*

Prototype production typically involves manufacturing one or several items before regular production begins. This is often helpful in establishing or confirming estimated material quantity requirements. However, the resulting labor and overhead costs may not have forecast value because of the unusually small scale of operations, first-time learning experiences for employees, and the difficulty of applying labor and overhead costs to a single unit of output.

Although **test runs** have most of the same limitations, differences of scale can sometimes be overcome by having the test run approximate the volume of intended production.

Controlled observations of actual production operations are another way to determine what costs should be, thereby establishing a basis for predicting future costs. **Time and motion studies** are intended to measure performance under "ideal" or "technically efficient" conditions.

The cost estimates that result from these methods are of limited usefulness, except as a basis for further planning and review. Engineered estimates based solely on blueprint specifications are necessarily subjective and speculative, because they are not founded on actual performance. The time and motion study, test run, and prototype production approaches are also affected by biases that prevent them from being completely representative of actual production conditions. The irregular environments in which they occur may well produce atypical results, leading to poor forecasts of future operations. Cost performance may seem to be unusually good or unusually poor because of the contrived, experimental, and pressured nature of the situations from which the data are drawn. The results may also be distorted by low operating volumes, the degree of skill and experience of the workers observed, the quality of materials used, and the condition of equipment.

ELEMENTARY TIME-DEPENDENT FORECASTING TECHNIQUES

The preceding methods used measures of *activity levels* as the basis for forecasting costs and revenues. Another type of elementary forecast uses *time periods* as the basis for prediction. Figure 15–7 illustrates a typical cyclical pattern of sales behavior in relation to consecutive monthly time periods.

The following discussion involves three *time series* forecasting methods:

1. Constant growth or decline models
2. Moving cumulative totals and averages
3. Weighted moving averages

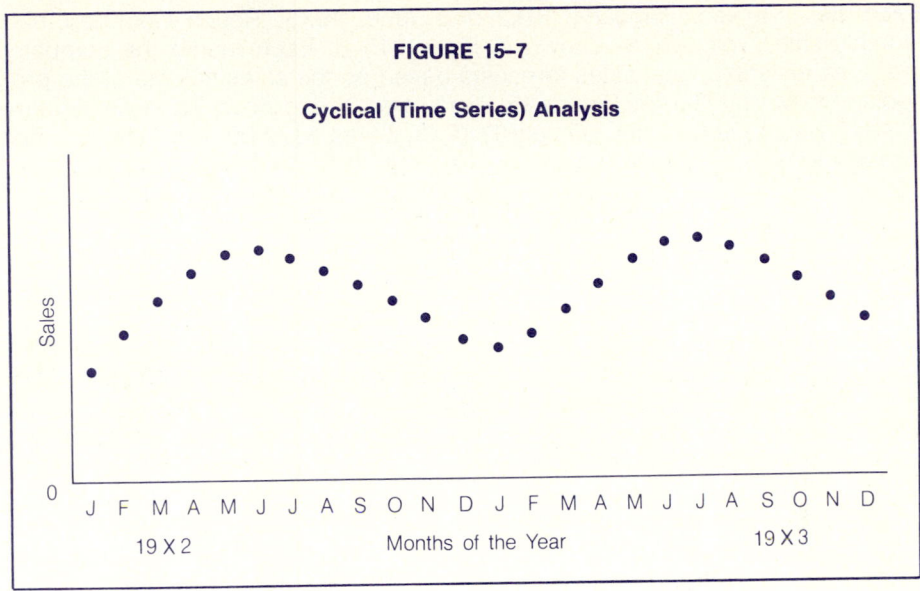

FIGURE 15–7

Cyclical (Time Series) Analysis

CONSTANT GROWTH OR DECLINE MODELS

In the simplest form of time series forecast, the estimate of the next period's performance is based directly on the results of the current period. For example, next month's sales volume might be estimated at 105 percent (or 90 or 100 percent) of this month's sales volume. This can be expressed:

$$S_{t+1} = (1 + \alpha) \, S_t$$

Here S = sales volume, t = time period, and α is a constant growth or decline factor.

This method has the merit of simplicity, but its usefulness obviously depends on the accuracy and reliability of the α term. The implication is that the value of the forecast variable is affected only by the prior period value of that same variable weighted by some constant rate of growth or decline.

MOVING CUMULATIVE TOTALS AND AVERAGES

Various cumulative and average performance measures can be used to reflect the forecast variable's behavior over an extended time period rather than merely over the preceding period. Moving cumulative annual totals and moving monthly averages based on the preceding year are typical examples of this type of forecast. A forecast based on data from a twelve-month period absorbs seasonal fluctuations, but still reflects trends over the entire year.

Example: Between January, 19X2 and June, 19X3, Rauch Company had monthly sales volumes as shown in Figure 15–8. Each month the company prepares revised annual sales forecasts based on the sales volume of the preceding twelve months. As Figure 15–8 indicates, the forecast basis on January 1, 19X3 was 108,000 units. On July 1, 19X3, it was 112,500 units. The forecast formula is:

$$S_{t+1} = 1.05 \frac{\sum\limits_{i=0}^{11} S_{t-i}}{12}$$

Therefore, the forecast for the year beginning January 1, 19X3 is (1.05) (108,000) = 113,400 units. The forecast for the year starting July 1, 19X3 is (1.05) (112,500) = 118,125 units. Thus, the annual budget as of January 1, 19X3 is based on a sales volume forecast of 113,400 units. By July 1, 19X3, the budget will have been updated to reflect a forecast of 118,125 units for the next twelve-month period.

The unadjusted moving average of the preceding twelve months (or some other number of months) can also be used to forecast *monthly* costs and revenues. This allows the *trend effect* over the averaging period to be reflected in the forecast. The fewer periods over which the average is computed, the faster will be the adjustment to recent trends in the forecast variable. A four- or six-month average will be more sensitive to current changes than a twelve-month average. However, any moving average will tend to retain some of the effects of earlier periods.

Example: Rauch Company's forecast basis for January of 19X3 is 9,000 units (108,000 ÷ 12) and for July of 19X3 is 9,375 units (112,500 ÷ 12). Assuming that a 5 percent growth rate is reflected in the monthly forecast, the sales volume estimate for January of 19X3 will be 9,450 units (9,000 × 1.05), and for July,

---

FIGURE 15–8

Rauch Company
Sales Volumes by Months
January, 19X2 to June, 19X3

19X2	Units	19X2	Units	19X3	Units
Jan.	8,000	July	10,500	Jan.	8,500
Feb.	7,500	Aug.	11,000	Feb.	8,000
March	7,000	Sept.	12,000	March	7,500
April	8,000	Oct.	9,000	April	8,500
May	9,000	Nov.	8,500	May	10,000
June	10,000	Dec.	7,500	June	11,500
Six-month Subtotals	49,500		58,500		54,000
Twelve-month Subtotals		108,000		112,500	

19X3 will be 9,844 units (9,375 $\times$ 1.05). Note that the 9,450 unit sales volume *estimate* was not a good prediction of actual sales, which are 8,500 units.

WEIGHTED MOVING AVERAGES

To improve the forecast basis, a moving average that already reflects a trend effect can be weighted to include monthly, cyclical, or seasonal influences. Multipliers or constants can be derived for each month, cycle, or season that is to be differentiated from the total period effect. This multiplier or constant reflects the ratio of the observed value of the forecast variable for the particular period to the average observed value of the forecast variable over the total averaging period. For one year's data, a monthly constant (CM_i) can be derived as follows:

$$CM_i = \frac{12 \, x_i}{\sum\limits_{j=1}^{12} x_j}$$

Here x_j represents all 12 observed values of the forecast variable; x_i is the observed value for a particular month.

Example: For Rauch Company, the monthly constant for January of 19X3, derived from 19X2 data, is as follows:

$$CM_{\text{Jan.}} = \frac{12 \, x_{\text{Jan.}}}{\sum\limits_{j=1}^{12} x_j} = \frac{12 \, (8,000)}{108,000} = .88888$$

The forecast for January of 19X3, calculated at 105 percent of the weighted moving monthly average as of December of 19X2 is that 8,400 units will be sold [(1.05) (.88888) (9,000)]. Notice the improvement in forecasting by using the weighted moving average. The forecast of 8,400 units compares quite favorably with actual sales of 8,500 units.

Summary   The major limitation of these time-based methods is that the forecast must be based on previously observed values of the forecast variable. The implication is that the value of the cost or revenue being forecast is strictly time dependent and is not influenced by any other factor, except perhaps a constant rate of growth or decline. This approach may be justified by the presence of cyclical or trend effects which are not directly controllable by the forecasting entity.

FORMAL STATISTICAL FORECASTING METHODS

Formal statistical forecasting procedures offer a solution to some of the problems caused by the lack of precision and testability in the simpler forecasting techniques. One popular statistical method is **linear regression,** which uses the procedure called *least squares analysis.* This involves determining the equation of a linear function which is based on observations of prior events and which can be formally evaluated to assess the strength of some of its predictive attributes.

Least squares regression provides the equation for the straight line that gives a "best fit" to the supporting set of data. This "best fit" condition is satisfied when the sum of the squares of the vertical distances separating all data points from the resultant line are minimized—hence the name, least squares regression.[1]

THE REGRESSION EQUATION

The elementary form of least squares regression involves making a simple one variable linear regression of the **dependent variable** (the one being forecast) on another single **independent variable** (the one being used as the basis of the forecast). For example, to derive a linear function for overhead cost, it would be reasonable to regress overhead costs (the dependent variable) on machine hours (the independent variable).

The general form of the regression equation that is derived from least squares analysis is:

$$y = a + bx + u$$

Here *y* is the *dependent variable*, the value of which is being estimated;
  x is the *independent variable*, the behavior of which is being used to predict the value of the dependent variable;
  b is the mean value estimate of the *slope of the regression* line along which values of *y* lie;
  a is the mean value estimate of the *intercept* that the true regression line makes with the *y* axis;
  u is the **error or disturbance term,** with a mean value of zero and a constant variance over all observed values of *x*.

PRECONDITIONS FOR USE OF LEAST SQUARES REGRESSION

Appropriate use of least squares regression can only be made if a *logical, linear,* and *continuous* relationship exists between the dependent and independent variables.

A preexisting and apparent *logical connection* should be established between two items before conclusions based on a statistical relationship between them are drawn. It is reasonable to regress overhead costs only on a variable that under normal circumstances can logically be expected to directly affect overhead costs—such as labor hours, machine hours, output units, or materials usage. Classic misuses of statistical inference occur when impressive relationships are discovered by regressing church attendance and alcohol consumption, or the birthrate and the number of storks sighted on chimney tops.

---

[1] Computational details of least squares regression are described in the appendix to this chapter, beginning on page 740.

Linear regression is based on the assumption that a *linear relationship* exists between the dependent and independent variables. For example, if overhead cost is being forecast, the independent variable used should be one with which overhead costs may reasonably be expected to vary directly and proportionately. In other words, the variable portion of overhead cost should be a constant amount per unit of the independent variable.

Finally, any use of regression results for forecasting requires that all relationships present in the historical data be present in the future situations being forecast. This *continuity* must include the physical, technological relationships between the dependent and independent variables: Physical production processes must remain the same, as must product specifications, grades of materials, classes of labor, and plant capacity. Although unit input prices are also assumed to continue unchanged, as will be shown, price changes and inflationary influences can be incorporated into the analysis. However, any changes in the physical relationships will tend to invalidate the regression's predictive usefulness.

Some indication as to whether the assumptions of linearity and continuity are justified may be obtained by applying the visual fit method before the linear regression is calculated. Inspection of a scattergraph of data observations may reveal whether or not a stable, linear relationship appears to exist between the dependent and independent variables proposed for regression analysis. For example, Figure 15–9 shows a reasonably stable, linear relationship between

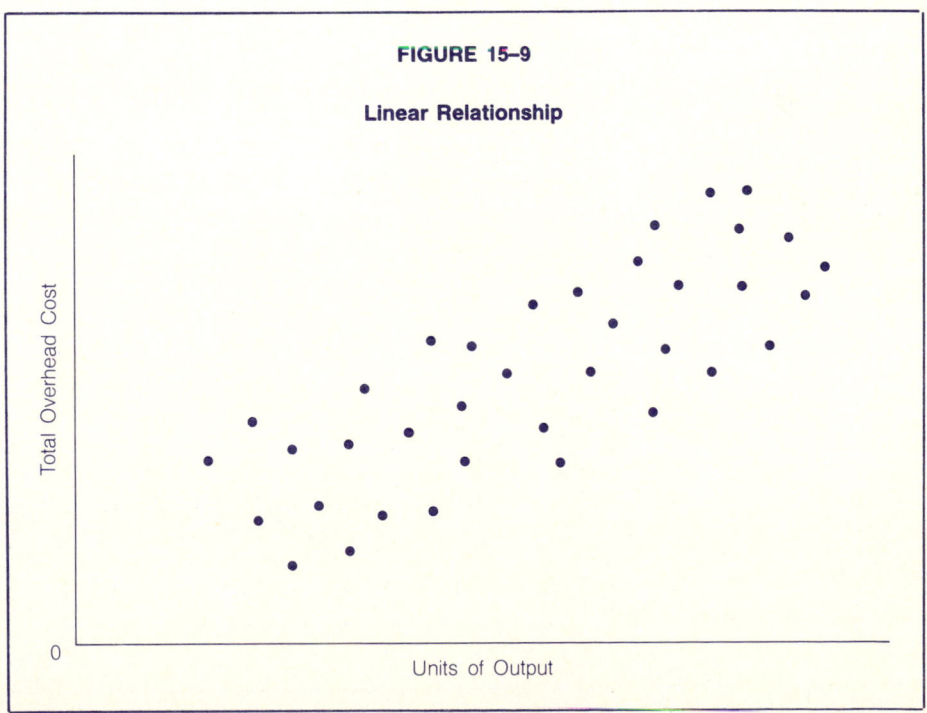

FIGURE 15–9

Linear Relationship

Total Overhead Cost

0

Units of Output

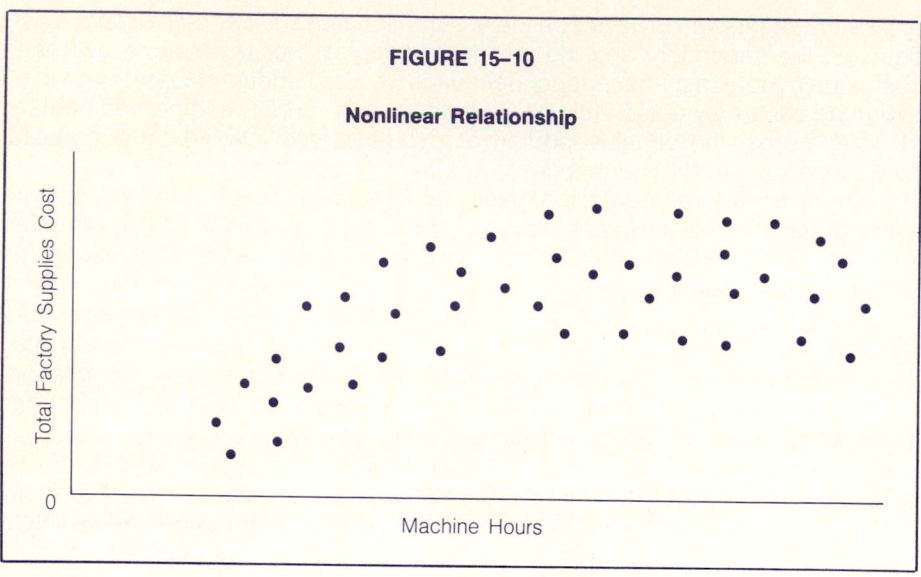

overhead cost and units of output, whereas Figure 15–10 exhibits a nonlinear relationship between factory supplies cost and machine hours and Figure 15–11 shows a discontinuous relationship between plant supervision cost and direct labor hours.

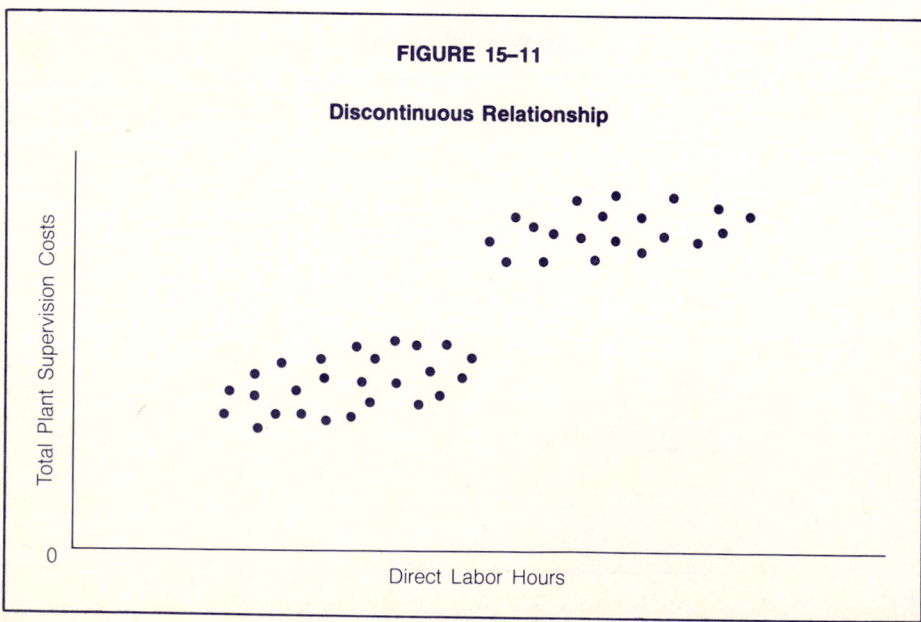

DATA REQUIREMENTS FOR USE OF LEAST SQUARES REGRESSION

Certain data requirements must be satisfied before least squares analysis can appropriately be applied. These pertain to:

1. Quantity of data
2. Accuracy and reliability of data
3. Statistical attributes of data

Quantity of Data To solve for the regression equation coefficients (a and b), there must be at least one more set of observations than there are independent variables in the proposed regression analysis. This means that at least two sets of observations are needed in the single variable situation. If only one observation is available, any number of lines can be drawn through the observed point. It should also be apparent that as more sets of observations are used, the regression results will become more representative. Figure 15–12 shows a regression line, C_1C_2, that is obtained if only a small number

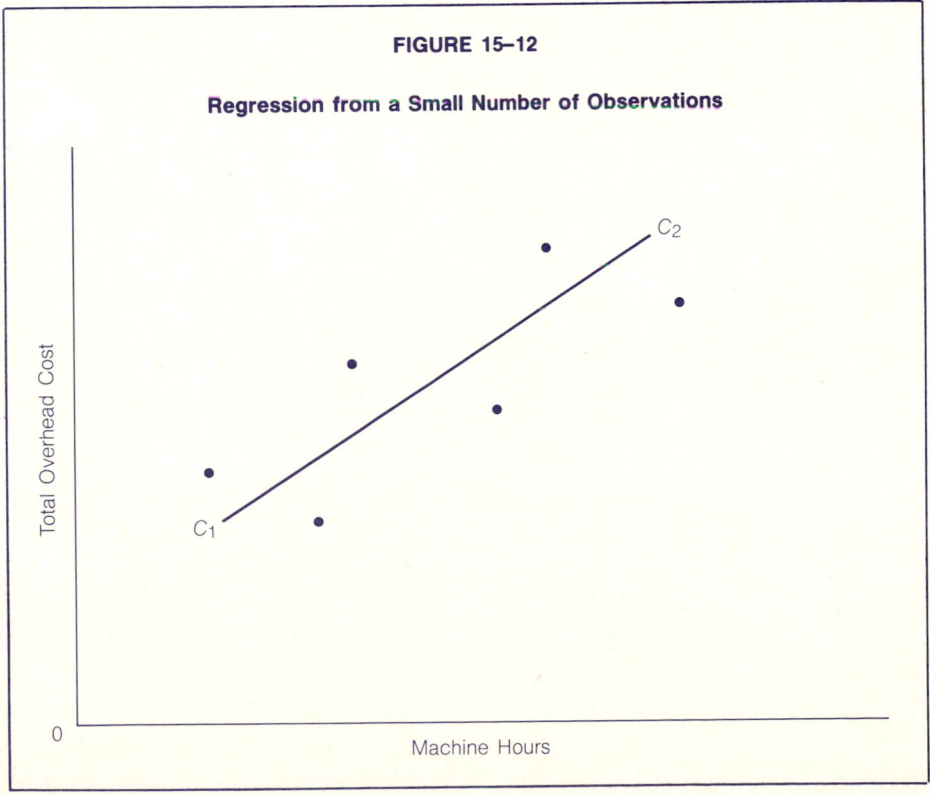

FIGURE 15–12

Regression from a Small Number of Observations

of data sets are used. Figure 15–13, with the original data points circled, shows the new solution, C_3C_4, based on a larger number of observations.

In addition to the number of sets of data observations to be used, consideration must be given to (1) the *total time period* and *range of activity levels* covered by the observations and (2) the *time intervals* at which the observations are made.

The total period of analysis must be long enough to permit a significant range of fluctuations in the values of observed variables. If the observation period is too short, the resulting regression equation may not be adequately representative of the relationship among the variables over a meaningful range of values. If the observation period is too long, it may include changes in production configurations, technology, plant capacity, and/or managerial methods. These features must be relatively uniform throughout the total period of analysis.

Observations of the variables should be made often enough so that fluctuations in their values are not hidden by compensating or averaging effects. On the other hand, the shorter the intervals between observations, the more difficult and expensive it will be to obtain accurate data. It is not possible to specify one best length for the total period of analysis or one best frequency of observations of values. Both of these are influenced by the characteristics of each activity being analyzed.

It would be uneconomical and time-consuming to use regression analysis to establish patterns of behavior for every attribute of performance. Moreover, doing so would probably produce more information than could be assimilated

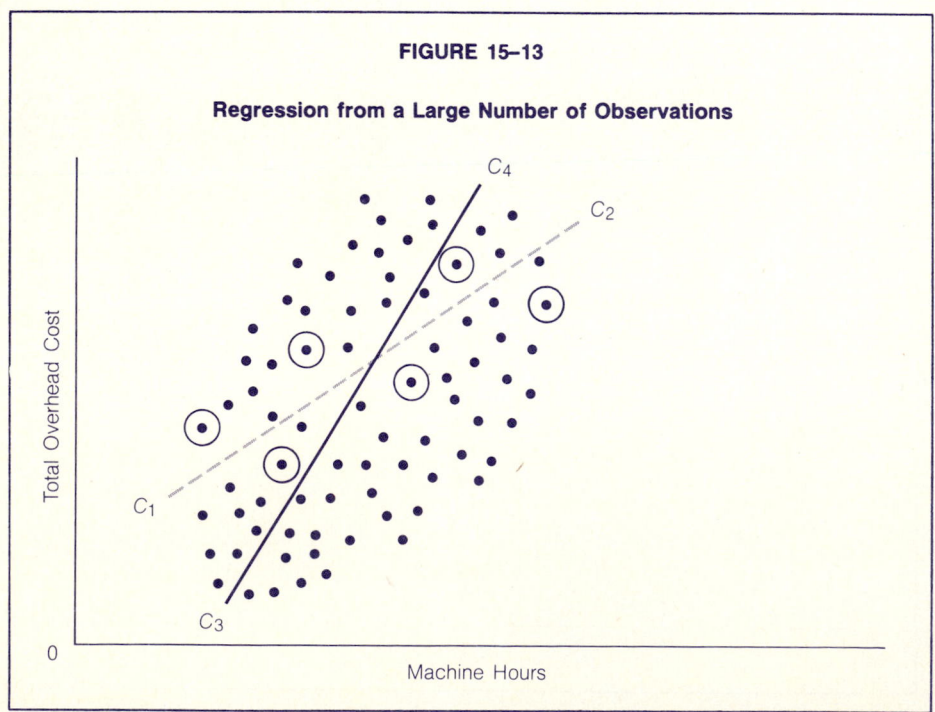

FIGURE 15–13

Regression from a Large Number of Observations

and used. Compromises are necessary for the sake of economy and understandability. Such compromises generally involve aggregation in the dependent variable—a tendency to analyze departmental costs or activity center costs, rather than individual cost items.

Accuracy and Reliability of Data   The data used in regression analysis must satisfy certain standards of accuracy and reliability. Information should be derived on a consistent basis and be free from error and bias. Because the regression analysis is performed in an accounting environment, it is especially important that the results be objective and consistent from an accounting measurement viewpoint.

One simple test involves inspecting all data sets in an attempt to detect any unusual observations, or *outliers,* that may be present. For example, in Figure 15–14, points A and B appear to be distinctly outside the pattern indicated by the other data. If a specific explanation, such as data error, strike, fire, theft, or accident can be found to explain these outliers, data points A and B should be excluded from the regression analysis.

Because regression analysis usually pertains to costs, revenues, and activity level measures from a series of different accounting periods, the *accounting period* and *accrual* principles should be strictly observed. Therefore, if monthly operating costs are being analyzed, the data should reflect as accurately as possible actual monthly outlays on an accrual and usage basis, not on a cash or acquisition basis. This problem of accounting data inaccuracies is more acute

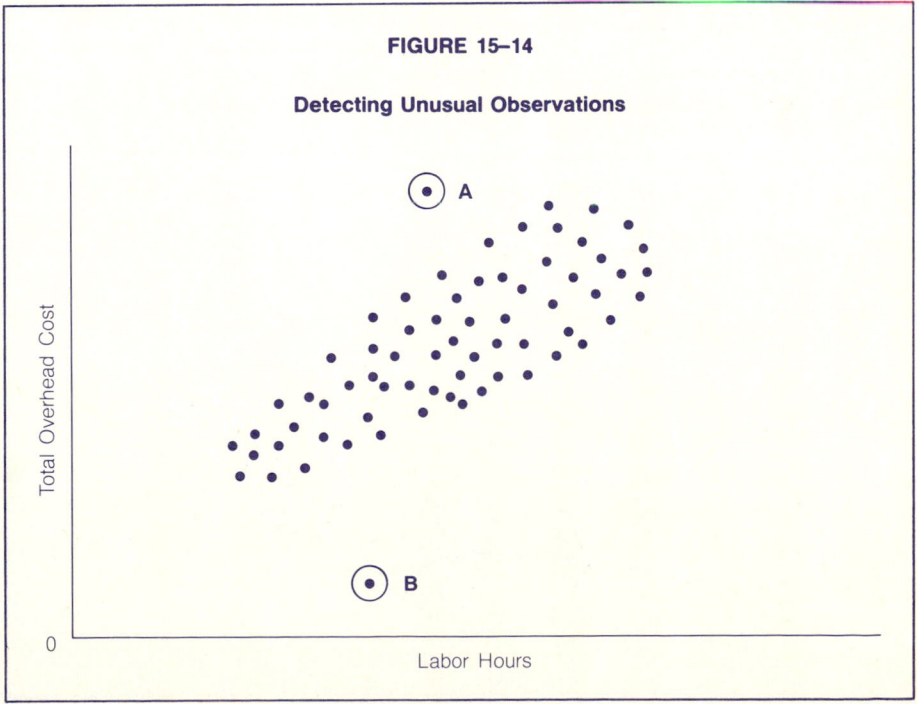

FIGURE 15–14

Detecting Unusual Observations

when the forecasting interval is short. But lengthening the time period only creates additional problems, because the variability of cost behavior tends to smooth out over longer forecasting periods.

Only *actual costs* should be used in regression analysis. Estimated amounts determined by overhead application procedures should be excluded. For example, regressing applied overhead costs against machine hours when a machine hour-based overhead rate is being used will simply create a circularity in the results. Using applied costs instead of actual costs will also make depreciation, rent, property taxes, and other fixed costs appear to be variable costs, because they will have been reduced to unit amounts within the total overhead application rate.

Price level changes make historical costs less useful for predictive purposes. Historical data should be restated using replacement costs or price level adjusted costs. In addition, the regression results should be adjusted to reflect anticipated future input prices.

Statistical Attributes of Data   Least squares regression requires that certain formal statistical attributes be present in the data. For the single variable regression it is assumed that, for each particular value of the independent variable (x_i), the corresponding values of the dependent variable (y_i) are normally distributed around their mean value (μ). In addition, all the mean values of the dependent variable (μ) are assumed to lie on a straight line—the regression line. These requirements are satisfied in Figure 15–15, but not in Figure 15–16.

The condition of **homoscedasticity** is also required. This means that, for each value of the independent variable, the variance of the dependent variable has a constant value, or alternatively, that the variance of u, the disturbance term, is a constant. In Figure 15–17, this condition seems to be met; the cost values are relatively evenly distributed around the regression line for all values of labor hours. This condition is not met in Figure 15–18 in which the dispersion of cost measurements is clearly larger for higher values of labor hours.

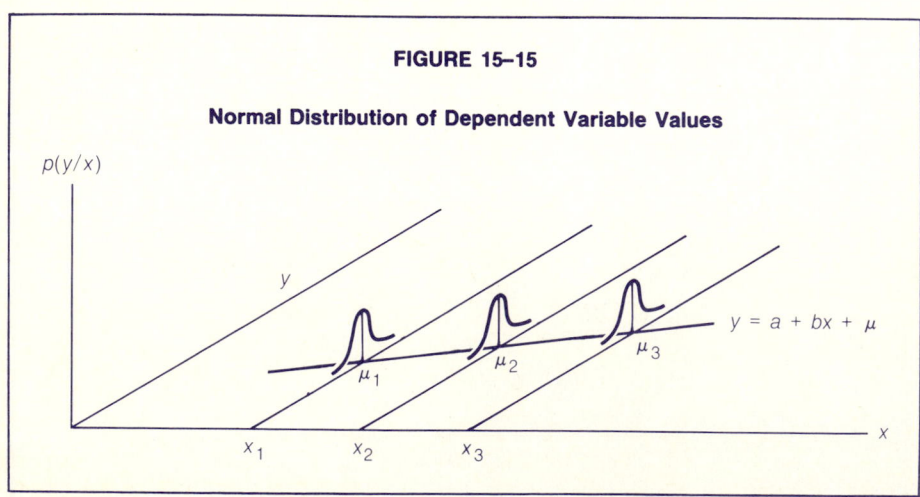

FIGURE 15–15

Normal Distribution of Dependent Variable Values

$p(y/x)$

$y = a + bx + \mu$

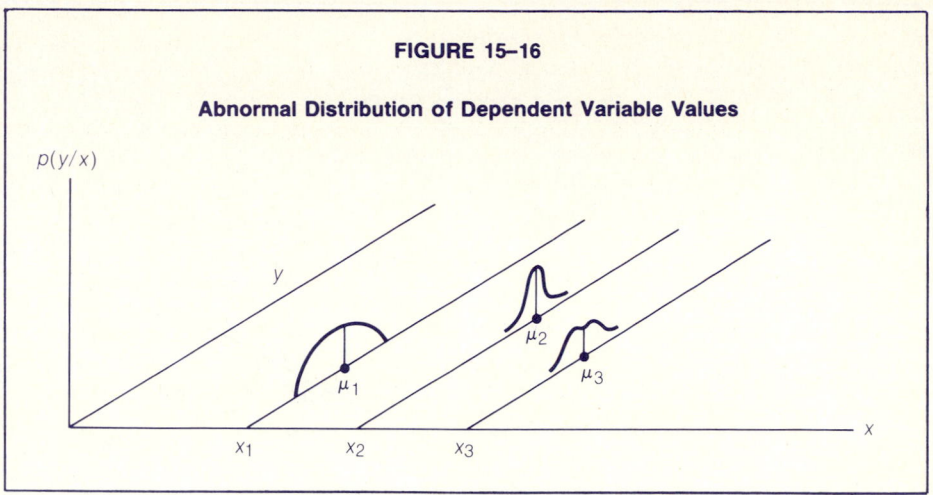

FIGURE 15–16

Abnormal Distribution of Dependent Variable Values

FIGURE 15–17

Constant Variance Condition

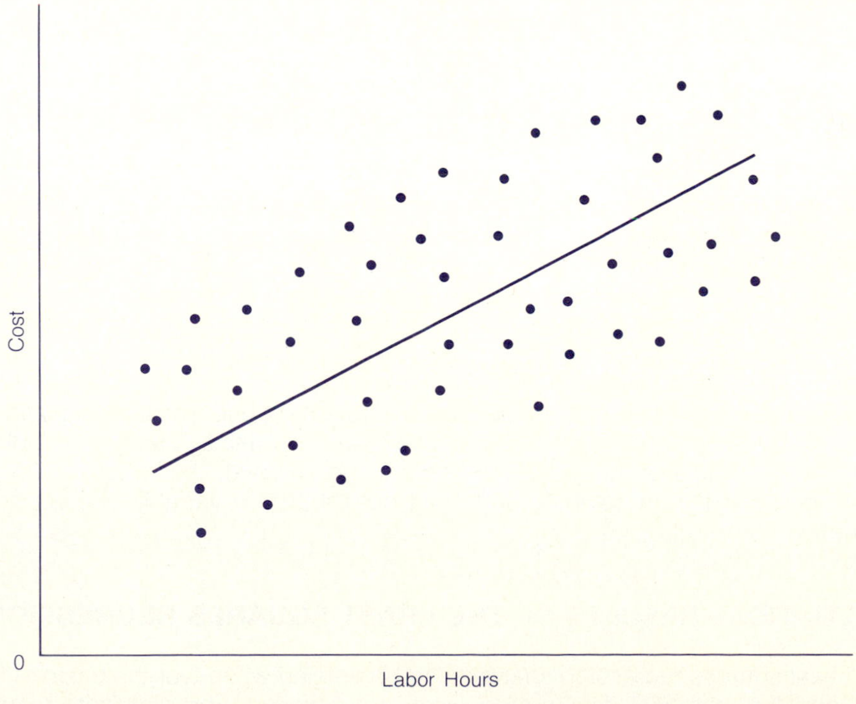

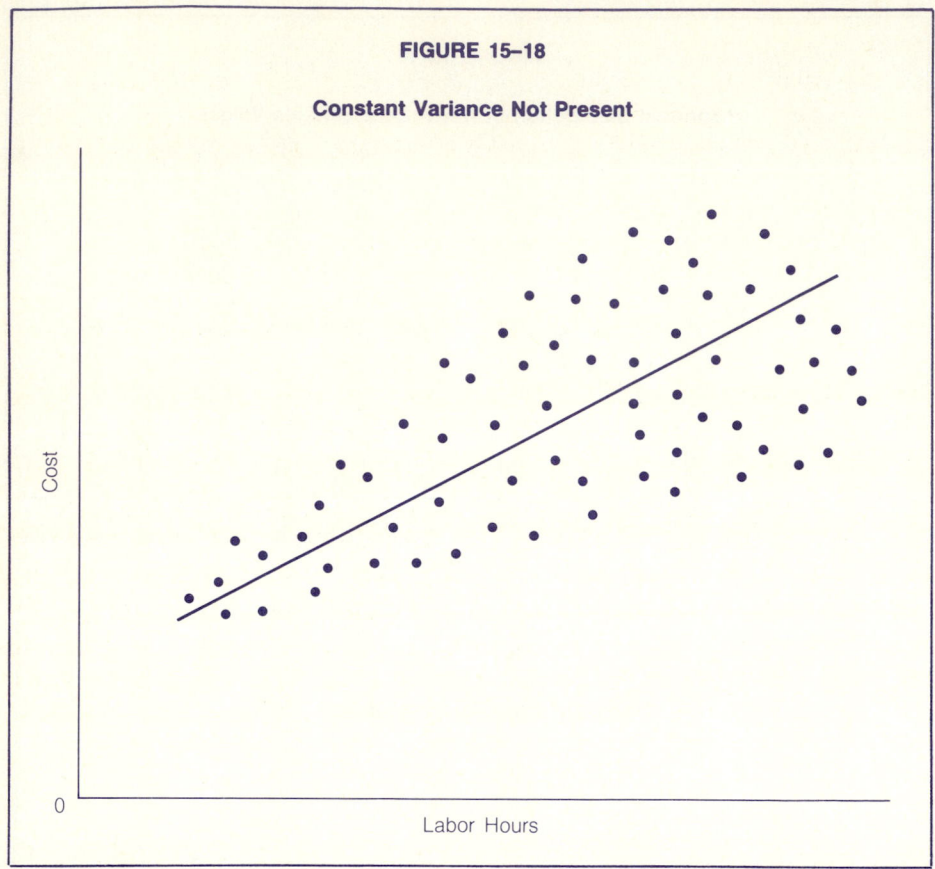

FIGURE 15–18

Constant Variance Not Present

Cost

0

Labor Hours

Serial correlation or **autocorrelation** must not be present. For each value of the independent variable, x, the corresponding value of the dependent variable, y, must not be influenced by any other observed values of the dependent variable. This is often not the case when costs from successive periods are being observed. There is sometimes a "ratchet" effect (or cost stickiness) that causes costs to increase as the activity level increases, but not to decrease in the same proportions when activity levels decrease.

Finally, the independent variable must be capable of being assigned a unique value as a mathematical variable. For example, in order to forecast shipping costs as a function of the weight of items to be shipped, the weight of items must be specifiable in advance and must not itself be a variable subject to a distribution function.

STATISTICAL RESULTS OF THE LEAST SQUARES REGRESSION

Least squares regression analysis can be applied whenever the basic rationale and the statistical data prerequisites are satisfied. The statistical results of the regression include:

1. The *regression coefficients, a* and *b*, in the regression equation, $y = a + bx + u$.
2. The coefficient of determination, r^2, and the *correlation coefficient, r*.
3. The *standard error of the regression estimate, s_e*.
4. The *standard error of the regression coefficients, s_b* and *s_a*.
5. *t-statistics* for the regression coefficients, t_b and t_a.

Regression calculations become tedious for any significant sized set of data. Fortunately, standard computer routines are readily available to perform this task. In this text, the emphasis, as it should be for accountants, will be placed on the interpretation of the results rather than on their computational derivation.

Example: Gogetter Company has recorded the following monthly overhead cost data and machine hour activity in its Machining Department:

Month	Machine Hours	Overhead Costs
1	1,600	$ 4,000
2	2,400	5,000
3	3,200	6,800
4	1,500	3,600
5	2,000	4,500
6	1,200	2,900
7	1,800	4,200
8	1,400	3,600
9	1,000	2,700
10	2,900	6,700
	19,000	$44,000

Regression Coefficients[2]   The regression coefficients that result from this data are:

$$a = 755.67 \qquad\qquad b = 1.918$$

The regression equation is:

$$y = 755.67 + 1.918x$$

The proper interpretation of this regression equation is that (1) total overhead cost per month can be expected to have an average value equal to $755.67 plus 1.918 times the number of machine hours per month; and (2) average variable overhead costs per machine hour are equal to $1.918 per machine hour. However, both these conclusions should be restricted to situations in which machine hours per month fall between the upper and lower bounds (3,200 and 1,000 hours respectively) of the observed data used as the basis for the regression.

These regression results should be examined for logical consistency and numerical reasonableness. In particular, the mathematical sign (+ or −) of the *b* term should correspond to the direction of the anticipated relationship between the dependent and independent variables. For example, if an *increase* in Goget-

[2] For derivation of regression coefficients, see pages 740–49 of the appendix to this chapter.

ter Company's independent variable (machine hours) would logically be expected to cause an *increase* in the value of the dependent variable (overhead costs), then the sign of *b* in the regression should be *positive,* indicating a positive correlation.

Negative values of *b* may occur; this is sometimes an acceptable or at least a logical result. For example, if weekly vehicle repair costs were regressed against weekly total vehicle mileage, the regression equation might be of the form:

$$y = 4,000 - .75x$$

This seems to suggest that vehicle repair costs can be *reduced* by *increasing* the number of miles driven! Such an answer does not appear to make sense. The explanation probably lies in the fact that repairs tend to be made during those weeks when vehicles are off the road, thereby producing an inverse relationship between repair costs and miles driven. Such a statistical anomaly might be corrected by increasing the forecast interval from a week to a month. However, as long as all factors pertaining to the original situation remain unchanged, this regression equation will continue to provide an acceptable basis for forecasting weekly vehicle repair costs.

Negative values of *a* suggest that the fixed component of total cost is a negative amount. Figure 15–19 demonstrates this implied relationship. It is invalid

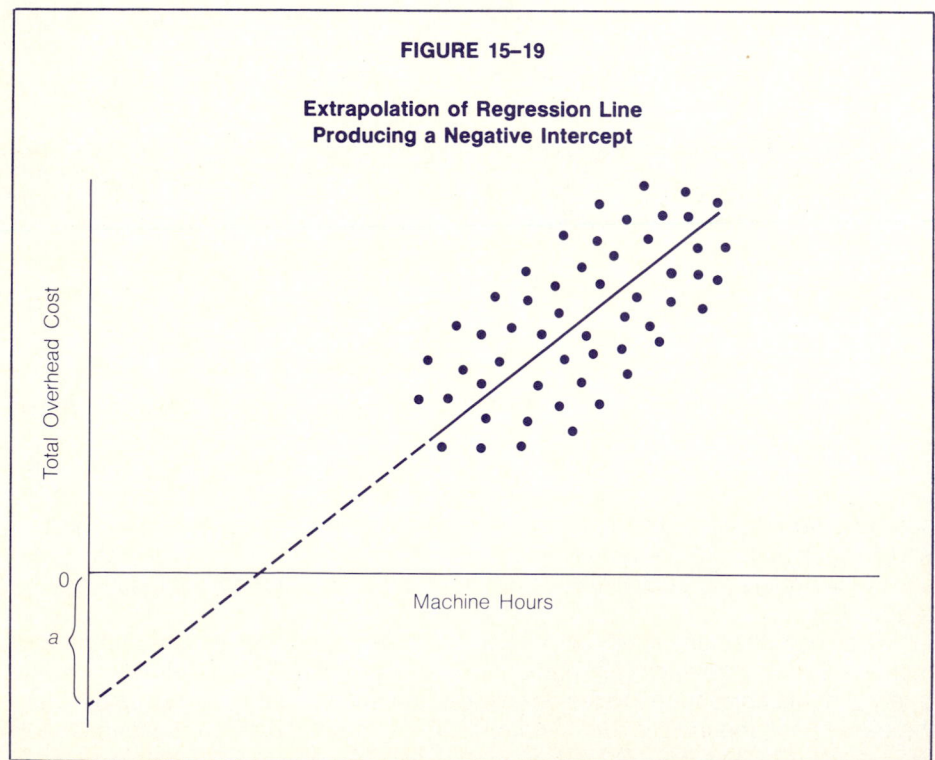

FIGURE 15–19

**Extrapolation of Regression Line
Producing a Negative Intercept**

to conclude that fixed costs are a negative amount, because the regression coefficient for *a* is obtained by extrapolating the regression line back to the *y*-axis. If doing this involves passing over a wide range of values for which no data were used in the analysis, the answer for *a* may be suspect. At most, the value for *a* should only be construed as a factor that contributes to the behavior of total overhead costs within the relevant range from 1,000 to 3,200 machine hours.

If more observations are obtained for total overhead costs and machine hours, extending back to (or at least close to) the origin, the result may be a positive value for *a,* as shown in Figure 15–20.

Figures 15–19 and 15–20 demonstrate that the value of *a* in the regression equation is not always a reliable estimator of the fixed cost component of a cost function. In Gogetter Company, the value of $755.67 for *a* is not a valid estimate of fixed costs because the lowest value of machine hours in the data set was 1,000, which is significantly far from the origin.

The same caution applies to extrapolating above or below the range of values used as the basis for the regression analysis. It is not possible to make unqualified forecasts of the total, fixed, or variable components of the dependent variable for values of the independent variable that lie significantly outside the relevant range. The behavior pattern outside the relevant range is likely to be

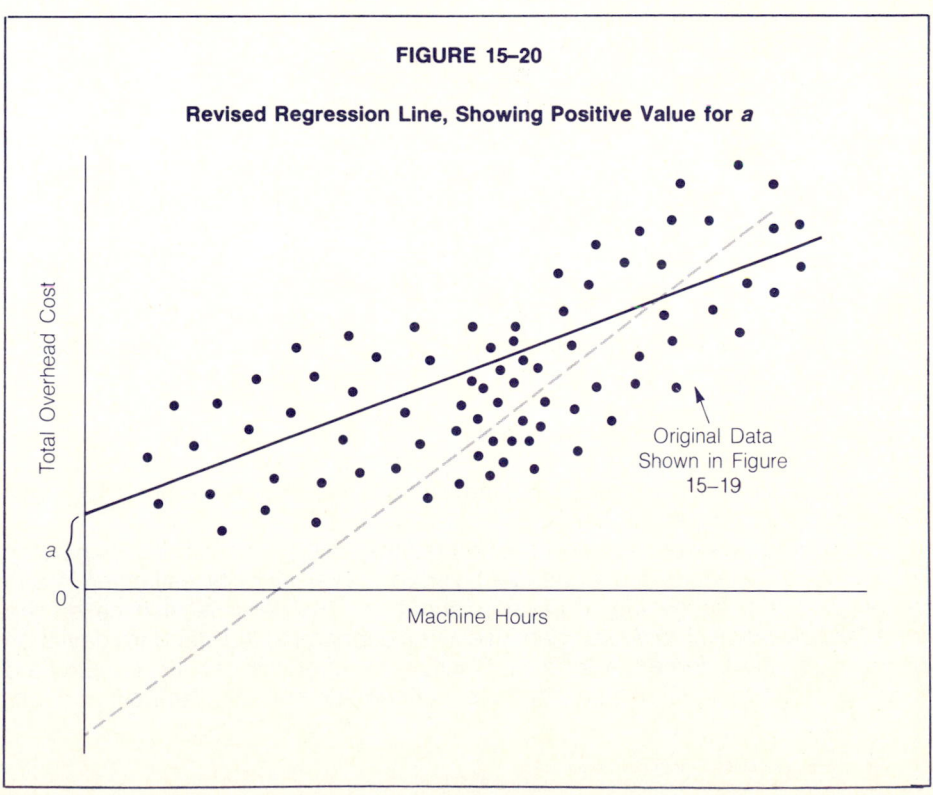

FIGURE 15–20

Revised Regression Line, Showing Positive Value for *a*

different than that which applies within the range of observed values. If forecasts are needed for values beyond the relevant range, it is reasonable to resort to the engineered estimates described earlier in this chapter.

Correlation Coefficient (r) and Coefficient of Determination (r²)   The equation of a line that satisfies the least squares regression conditions can be found for any set of data, no matter how the observations are dispersed. How strong a relationship exists between the dependent and independent variables is harder to determine. To assess their relative predictive strength or "goodness of fit," it is necessary to test the results of the regression analysis.

The **coefficient of determination** (r^2) and the **correlation coefficient** (r) are two statistics that provide evaluative information about a regression. The r^2 term ($0 \leq r^2 \leq 1$) indicates what proportion of the value of the dependent variable is statistically explained by changes in the value of the independent variable.

In Gogetter Company, $r^2 = .971$, which means that 97.1 percent of the variation is overhead costs is explained by the changing values of machine hours. Note the use of the phrase "explained by" rather than "caused by" or "due to." The test being applied is statistical, not physical or causal.

The correlation coefficient r, ($-1 \leq r \leq 1$), is a measure of the extent of linear relationship between the dependent and independent variables. Values of r close to 1 indicate a strong positive linear relationship, as in Figure 15–21. Values of r close to -1 show a strong but inverse relationship, as in Figure 15–22. Where no significant linear relationship exists, as in Figures 15–23 and 15–24, the value of r is close to zero.

The tests that can be applied to the values of r and r^2 are judgmental rather than absolute. In Gogetter Company, $r = .985$, and $r^2 = .971$.[3] This indicates that a strong positive relationship exists between the variables and suggests that approximately 97.1 percent of the variability in the dependent variable is explained by the behavior of the independent variable. There is no defined cut-off point for r or r^2 below which the relationships can be stated to be insignificant. However, the r and r^2 terms can be used for comparative analysis, as when the results of alternative regressions using different independent variables are to be evaluated. The regression that provides the higher r and r^2 values will be preferable, though other tests should be applied before a definitive choice can be made.

Standard Error (Deviation) Terms   The values of a and b, as well as the estimate of the dependent variable, y, are mean values in the regression equation. Because it is assumed that the distributions involved are normal, these variables have normal standard deviations.

The **standard error of the regression estimate** (s_e) indicates the dispersion of observed values of the dependent variable y around its estimated mean value, as specified by the regression equation. This term is also called the *standard deviation of residuals* because it corresponds to the standard deviation of the error or disturbance term u. Confidence intervals can be constructed using the 1-, 2-, or 3- sigma limits as defined for normal distributions.[4] For

---

[3] For derivation, see chapter appendix, page 743.
[4] See page 746 for tables of areas under the normal distribution curve.

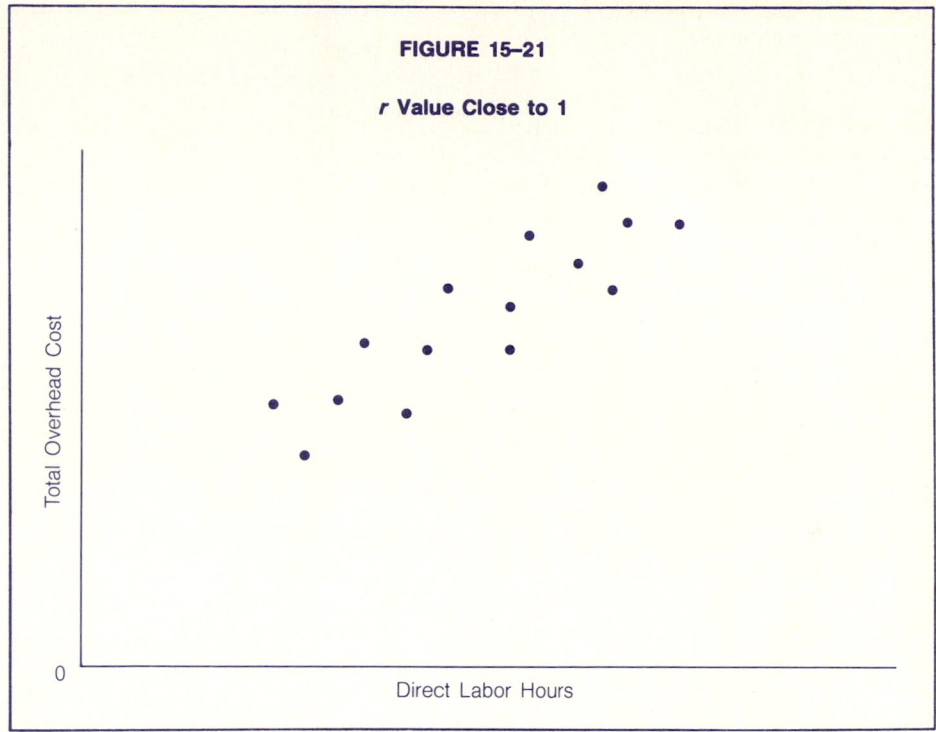

FIGURE 15–21

r Value Close to 1

example, there is approximately a 95 percent probability that the estimated value of the dependent variable is within 2 standard deviations of the estimated mean value for any particular value of the independent variable.

The following table of confidence intervals[5] can be prepared for Gogetter Company, after it is established that $s_e = 256.92$.

n	$n \cdot s_e$	$E(y) - n \cdot s_e$	$E(y) + n \cdot s_e$	Confidence Interval
1	256.92	$E(y) - 256.92$	$E(y) + 256.92$	67%
2	513.84	$E(y) - 513.84$	$E(y) + 513.84$	95%
3	770.76	$E(y) - 770.76$	$E(y) + 770.76$	99%

The interpretation for the case $n = 2$ is that there is approximately a 95 percent probability that the estimated total overhead cost lies within ± \$513.84 of its mean value as specified by the regression equation for any value of machine hours within the relevant range. Therefore, if a 2,000 machine hour operating level is being considered, the 95 percent confidence interval would be found from the modified regression equation as follows:

$$E(y) = 755.67 + 1.918x \pm 513.84$$
$$= 755.67 + 3,836 \pm 513.84$$
$$= [4,077.83, \quad 5,105.51]$$

[5] For derivation, see chapter appendix, page 744.

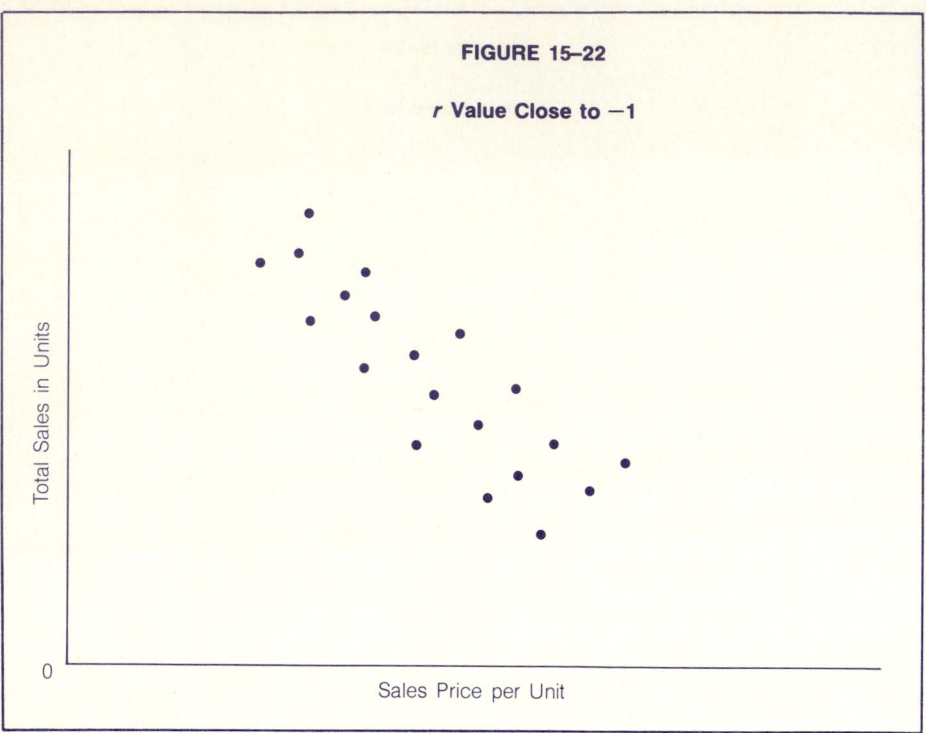

FIGURE 15–22

r Value Close to −1

Total Sales in Units

0

Sales Price per Unit

This indicates that if 2,000 machine hours are worked there is a 95 percent probability that overhead costs will be between $4,077.83 and $5,105.81.

The **standard error of the regression coefficients** (s_b and s_a) indicates the dispersion of observed values of those variables around their respective mean values as specified in the regression equation. Confidence intervals for those variables can be constructed in the manner previously described.

For Gogetter Company, where $s_b = .118$, the 95 percent confidence interval[6] is 1.918 ± .336, or from 1.582 to 2.254. This indicates a 95 percent probability that variable overhead cost is between $1.582 and $2.254 per machine hour.

t-Statistics The standard error terms of the regression estimate and of the regression coefficients can be tested to determine the regression's predictive power. In general, the standard error terms should not be too large relative to the mean value of the variable to which they pertain. This comparison makes use of a *t-statistic* ($t_b = b \div s_b$), which is the ratio of the mean value of the variable to its standard error.

If the regression results are to be statistically significant, it must be shown that it is not merely by chance that b has the estimated mean value specified by the regression equation. The *t*-statistic can be used to test the null hypothesis

[6] For derivation, see chapter appendix, page 744.

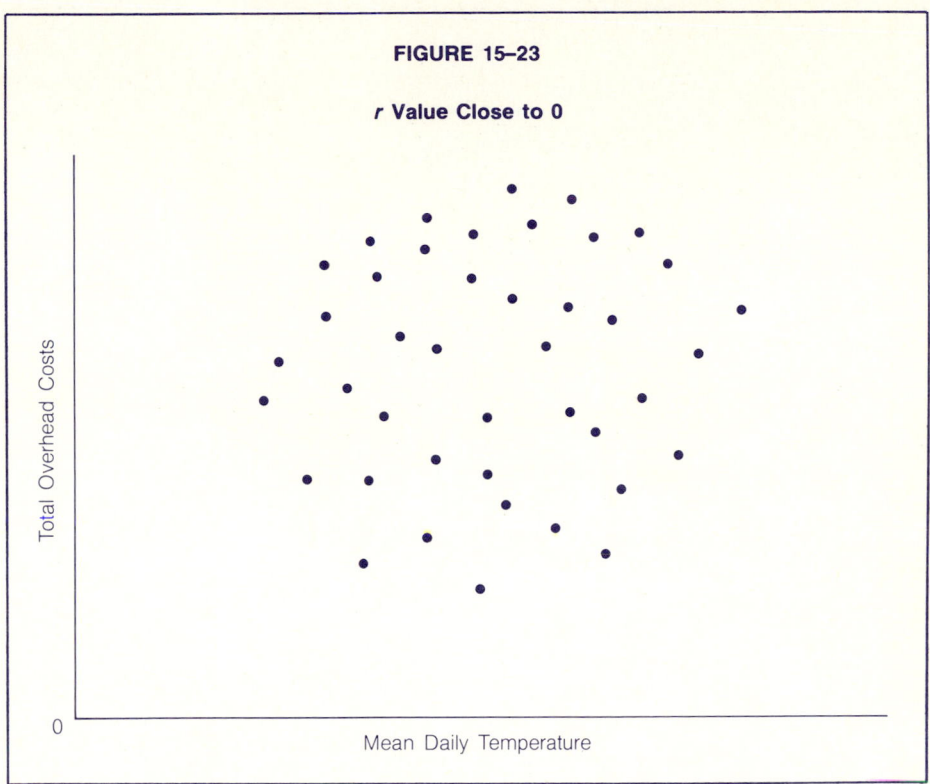

FIGURE 15–23

r Value Close to 0

Total Overhead Costs

0

Mean Daily Temperature

that $b = 0$. This is done by determining whether t_b exceeds the relevant *t*-table value. Entries in a *t*-table are minimum values that a *t*-statistic must satisfy to allow rejection of the stated null hypothesis. The entries are specified for combinations of (1) the confidence level of the test (for example, 99 percent significant) and (2) the number of degrees of freedom (the number of observations minus the number of variables in the regression).

A less precise test simply requires that the *t*-statistic be greater than 2. This is only an approximate comparison. However, as can be seen from the *t*-tables in the appendix to this chapter, it is valid for situations in which the required confidence level is 95 percent or less and in which the number of degrees of freedom is relatively large.

Gogetter Company's *t*-statistic for *b* is 16.29 (1.918 ÷ .118).[7] This exceeds the *t*-table value of 5.041 for 8 degrees of freedom (10 minus 2), at the 99.9 percent confidence level.[8] This supports the conclusion that there is a greater than 99.9 percent probability that the regression line does not have a slope of zero and that a significant linear relationship therefore exists between the dependent and independent variables.

[7] For derivation, see chapter appendix, page 745.
[8] See *t*-tables on pages 748–49.

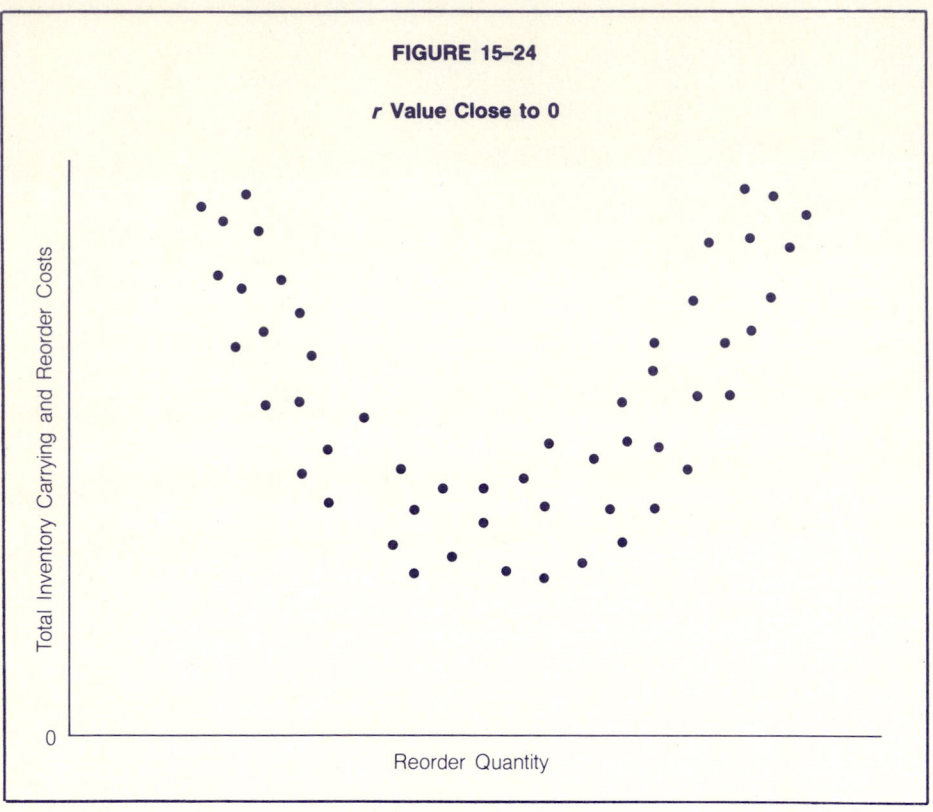

FIGURE 15–24

r Value Close to 0

Total Inventory Carrying and Reorder Costs

0

Reorder Quantity

COMPARING THE RESULTS OF THE VISUAL FIT, HIGH–LOW, AND LINEAR REGRESSION METHODS

How different are Gogetter Company's linear regression results from the estimates that could be obtained using the simpler visual fit and high–low interpolation methods? If applied independently, these three methods will usually produce different answers for the slope and intercept of a given set of data. How different the answers will be depends on the tightness (possibly quite similar results) or dispersion (possibly quite divergent results) of the data being analyzed. But to some extent the three methods can support and verify each other. For example, the visual fit method can be used as a first test for the possible presence of a linear relationship, before the regression results are calculated. High–low results can also be evaluated through use of the visual fit method. In Figure 15–25, the results of the three methods are compared using Gogetter Company's overhead costs and machine hours.

Visual Fit Method   The solid line in Figure 15–25 represents one person's estimate of the line that best fits the data. From geometric inspection, it was found that this line has the equation, $y = 800 + 1.933x$.

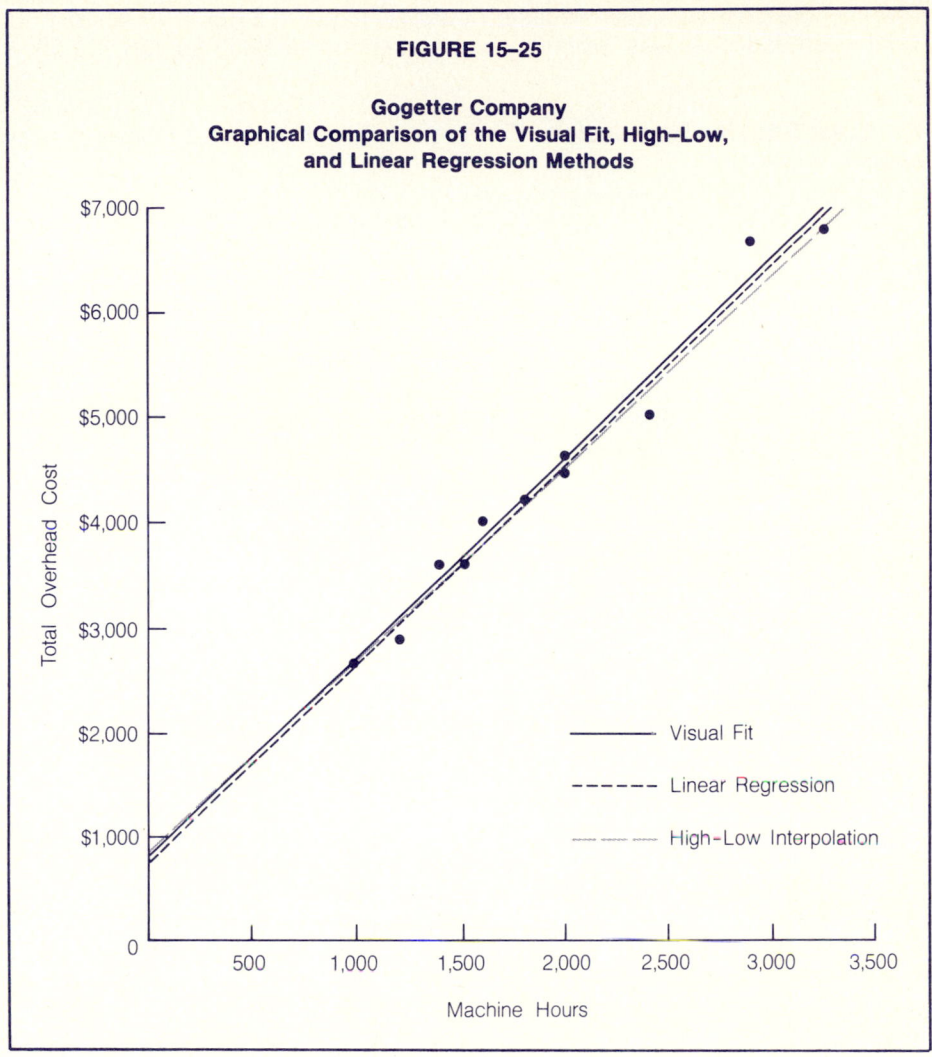

FIGURE 15–25

Gogetter Company
Graphical Comparison of the Visual Fit, High–Low,
and Linear Regression Methods

High–Low Method   High–low interpolation produces a line with the equation, $y = 853.20 + 1.864x$. This line is shown as a series of long dashes in Figure 15–25. The equation was derived as follows:

	Machine Hours	Overhead Cost
High	3,200	$6,800
Low	1,000	2,700
Increment	2,200	$4,100
Slope	$\dfrac{\$4,100}{2,200} =$	1.864

The variable cost of 3,200 machine hours is 3,200 × $1.864, or $5,964.80. Total overhead cost was $6,800, so the intercept is $853.20 ($6,800.00 − $5,964.80).

Least Squares Regression   The previously derived results for regression analysis were:

$$y = 755.67 + 1.918x$$

This line is shown as a series of short dashes in Figure 15–25.

The results of the three methods can be summarized as follows:

	Intercept	Slope
Visual Fit	800.00	1.933
High–Low	853.20	1.864
Regression.....	755.67	1.918

This comparison is not intended to represent any general relationship among these results. However, in this particular case, all three methods produce equations that are reasonably similar in terms of slope and intercept and give very similar *total* results over the interior range of, say, 1,500 to 3,000 machine hours.

TIME SERIES REGRESSION ANALYSIS

The previously explained regression techniques can also be used when the independent variable is a time period rather than an activity level. **Time series regression** establishes a relationship between a performance measure and a series of successive, equal valued time intervals (days, weeks, months, years). The limitations that apply to elementary time series forecasting also apply here.

Example: Edwards Company has recorded the following sales volumes during the past seven years:

x Year	y Sales Volume
19X1	25,000
19X2	28,000
19X3	32,000
19X4	36,000
19X5	34,000
19X6	43,000
19X7	47,000

Before least squares analysis is applied to this data, the values of the year numbers can be normalized to simplify computations. This is done by subtracting the mean value of all the years (19X4 in this case) from each individual year. The resulting data set then appears as follows:

$\bar{\bar{x}}$ Revised Year	y Sales Volume
−3	25,000
−2	28,000
−1	32,000
0	36,000
1	34,000
2	43,000
3	47,000

Regression analysis applied to this revised data produces an equation[9] of the following form:

$$y = 35,000 + 3,500\bar{\bar{x}}$$

This means that sales volume equals 35,000 plus 3,500 times the current year minus 19X4. Therefore, the 19X8 sales volume estimate based on this regression is:

$$y = 35,000 + (3,500)(19X8 - 19X4)$$
$$= 35,000 + (3,500)(4)$$
$$= 49,000$$

MULTIPLE REGRESSION ANALYSIS

Relating the behavior of a cost or revenue to a single variable (units produced, time periods, labor hours, machine hours, materials usage) involves the assumption that all other factors remain constant. In reality, nearly every cost or revenue item is responsive to changes in more than one variable.

For example, the cost of materials used is likely to be affected not only by the number of units manufactured, but by the size of production lots, the skill and experience of production workers, the operating efficiency of equipment, the season of the year, the shift during which items are produced, and so on. Although units of output manufactured may still be the primary determinant of materials costs, it is unlikely that all these other variables will remain constant and have no effect on the cost of raw materials usage. It would also be unusual for sales volume to depend entirely on the passage of time from one period to another, as is assumed when sales are forecast by a simple time series method.

For these reasons, more representative and possibly more accurate estimates of performance measures can be obtained if **multiple regression analysis** is used, rather than a single variable regression. The procedures for multiple regression are basically similar to those used in single regression analysis. The results will include an additional regression coefficient and standard error term for each independent variable used, as well as a matrix of the correlation coefficients for the interrelationships between the dependent variable and all of the independent variables.

[9] Solution derived as demonstrated on pages 740–45.

The multiple regression equation is of the form:

$$y = a + b_1 x_1 + b_2 x_2 + b_3 x_3 \ldots + b_n x_n + u$$

where n is the number of different independent variables used in the regression. As with single variable regressions, logical, linear, and continuous relationships are assumed to exist between the dependent variables and *all* of the independent variables. Also, requirements for quantity, accuracy, and reliability of data must be satisfied, as must the statistical attributes of normal distributions, constant variance, homoscedasticity, and autocorrelation.

Multiple regression analysis also requires avoiding multicollinearity in the data. **Multicollinearity** indicates that the independent variables are influencing each other. If the independent variables are not truly independent, the regression results, particularly the interpretation of the various b_i coefficients, will not be reliable. The values of the regression coefficients (b_i) of the interrelated variables are then not accurate indicators of cost variability with respect to any individual variable, because a change in one independent variable will tend to cause a change in the other independent variable, as well as to induce a change in the dependent variable. In other words, b_i will not be a reliable indicator of variable or marginal cost with respect to the variable x_i, if x_i is in some way interrelated with one or more of the other independent variables.

The presence of multicollinearity can be detected through inspection of the **correlation matrix,** which is a matrix of the correlation coefficients (r) of the dependent variable (y) and all independent variables (x_i).

Figure 15–26 illustrates a correlation matrix. In this matrix, x_1 and x_2 show a high positive correlation ($r = .97$). This is a greater degree of correlation than exists between the dependent variable, y, and either of those two independent variables ($.97 > .91$, and $.97 > .87$). On the other hand, all other independent variables appear to be only moderately or slightly correlated (r values are relatively low). In all other cases, the relationship between the dependent variable,

FIGURE 15–26

Correlation Matrix

	y	x_1	x_2	x_3	x_4
y	1.0	.91	.87	−.85	.26
x_1	.91	1.0	.97	−.42	.05
x_2	.87	.97	1.0	−.31	.13
x_3	−.85	−.42	−.31	1.0	.20
x_4	.26	.05	.13	.20	1.0

y, and each of the other independent variables is stronger than the relationships among those variables themselves.

The solution to this problem of multicollinearity is either to drop one of the apparently interrelated variables from the regression or to construct a new composite variable. For example, in a joint product situation in which two of the proposed independent variables are output units of separate joint products, it is highly probable that those variables are *not* independent, especially when the output mix is a constant proportion of the two products. A new variable might be devised and substituted in the regression. It might consist of aggregate units of output or, if the products are not additive, of units of aggregate common content of the joint products.

Even if multicollinearity is present, the total results of the regression may still be useful if the other tests of r, r^2, s_e, s_{b_i}, and t-statistics are satisfied. It is the interrelated b_i coefficients of those variables that must not be used. For example, consider the case in which a joint product cost function has been derived by multiple regression, with this solution:

$$y = 2,000 + 5x_1 + 10x_2$$

$$(s_e = 145) \quad (s_a = 177) \quad (s_{b_1} = 0.5) \quad (s_{b_2} = 1.2) \quad (r^2 = .82)$$

where x_1 is output units of the first product, and x_2 is output units of the second product. However, the correlation coefficient of x_1 and x_2 is .98. Although the estimate of total cost will still be valid, the variables $b_1 = 5$ and $b_2 = 10$ should not be used as estimates of total cost *variability* with respect to independent changes in the individual variables x_1 and x_2. The marginal cost of one joint product cannot be determined without reference to its effect on the production of other joint products.

DUMMY VARIABLES

Multiple regression analysis allows the inclusion of **dummy variables** (or zero–one variables), together with continuously valued variables. These dummy variables can be used to represent attributes, conditions, or states of the world that are either present (dummy variable = 1), or absent (dummy variable = 0). Typical applications of dummy variables are:

1. *Quarterly or seasonal variables*—four dummy variables corresponding to the first, second, third, and fourth calendar quarters, or to Fall, Winter, Spring, and Summer seasons.
2. *Monthly, weekly, or daily variables*—as many as are needed to correspond to the divisions of a total time period being analyzed.
3. *Increase/decrease variables,* to signal increases or decreases in key variables such as inventory quantities, output levels, or sales volume.
4. *Shift variables,* corresponding to the particular shifts being worked each day.

These dummy variables sensitize the regression analysis to the presence or absence of particular attributes or conditions that are relevant to the forecast variable's behavior. For example, the behavior of power and heating costs is most likely to be influenced by the season of the year and the number of shifts worked each day. Similarly, dummy variables can be added to the regression analysis to reflect the tendency of certain costs to respond differently depending on whether activity levels rise or fall from one period to the next.

A CHECKLIST EVALUATION OF ALTERNATIVE REGRESSION FORMULATIONS

Forecasters must often choose the best of several alternative regression formulations. Various tests and decision rules exist to aid in this selection process, but none of them is universally correct or completely descriptive of particular decision situations. Neither is there any generally accepted, formal procedure for judging a set of alternative regression formulations.

However, a checklist approach may help to eliminate those regressions that fail to meet acceptability criteria or are dominated by other regression formulations. Each proposed single variable or multivariate least squares regression might be subjected to the following tests:

1. *Basic Rationale*
    a.   Are the variables logically related? Is there likely to be a causal relationship that can be confirmed statistically?
    b.   Is the assumption of linearity plausible? Can it be expected that the dependent variable actually varies in proportion to changes in the independent variable(s) over the relevant range of observations?
    c.   Will the same relationships that are present in the historical data continue between the variables during the future periods to which the regression results are to be applied?
2. *Data Prerequisites*
    a.   Assuming the forecaster has collected enough data to perform the regression, are these data accurate, reliable, and free from bias? Have extraordinary observations (outliers) been explained or excluded?
    b.   Does the source data satisfy all the tests and assumptions relating to the statistical attributes of normal distribution, constant variance, homoscedasticity, autocorrelation, and multcollinearity?
3. *Regression Results*
    a.   Does the regression equation make sense? Are the signs of the regression coefficients consistent with what is to be logically expected? Are the numerical values of the coefficients reasonable? Exclude the regression formulation if it does not pass these tests.
    b.   What are the values of the r and r^2 terms? Exclude any regression that has significantly low r^2 values.
    c.   What is the value of s_e? Exclude any regression that has an excessively high s_e value relative to other regressions.
    d.   Examine the s_{b_i} terms and the corresponding t-statistics ($b_i \div s_{b_i}$). Exclude any regression in which the t-statistics are too low, either because they fail to meet formal t-table tests or because they equal less than two if the approximation method is used.

e. For multiple regressions, inspect the correlation matrix. When the r value among pairs of independent variables is relatively large and is greater than the r value for the independent variables calculated individually with the dependent variable, avoid using that regression for situations in which use of the corresponding b_i coefficients was intended.

After this series of comparisons and evaluations has been made, some pattern may become apparent. One regression formulation may have emerged dominant on all or almost all tests, or all regressions except one may have been rejected. However, all regressions might prove deficient or none might appear superior in a majority of tests. The forecaster should then seek a regression that rates best with respect to that aspect which is most central to the intended use of the regression results. For example, if a total cost estimate is being made, a high r^2 value and a low s_e are desirable. In making marginal cost estimates, the forecaster should look for large t-statistics and an absence of multicollinearity. If none of these options exists, a choice should not be forced by picking the best of a bad lot. It may then be necessary either to consider new regression formulations with different independent variables or to abandon the use of formal linear regression techniques altogether.

FORECASTING ILLUSTRATED: EVALUATING ALTERNATIVE REGRESSION FORMULATIONS

Near the end of July, 19X8, the management of Ray Company noticed that 1,000 hours of machine time were unassigned and could be used to complete either of two production orders. The following unit cost estimates were developed to help decide which of the two orders to accept:

	Order #1 600 Units Product X	Order #2 400 Units Product Y
Materials	$40	$60
Labor	12	16
Overhead	?	?
Total Costs	$?	$?

The firm has been using a combined annual overhead application rate of $15 per machine hour, but management feels that in this case it would be more appropriate to forecast the incremental amount of variable overhead likely to be incurred on either job. Product X requires three hours of machine time per unit and Product Y requires four hours per unit. The orders were for 600 units of Product X at $85 per unit and 400 units of Product Y at $120 per unit.

To assist the forecasting process, the company accountant assembled the following data on overhead costs, units manufactured of Products X and Y, and machine hours usage for the past six months:

Month	(1) Total Overhead	(2) Units of X Produced	(3) Units of Y Produced	(4) Machine Hours Used
1	$63,642	742	906	11,894
2	41,026	750	332	6,972
3	25,870	338	82	2,558
4	63,472	516	1,026	11,474
5	51,836	608	732	9,118
6	52,734	540	960	10,090

Several linear regressions were attempted on the basis of this information, using the three independent variables separately and also all their possible combinations. Figure 15–27 shows the results of these regressions.

The next step is to evaluate these regression results in order to choose the regression formulation that is most appropriate to Ray Company's decision situation. Inspection of the regression results in Figure 15–27 suggests the following conclusions:

Logical Relationships   It is reasonable to suppose that linear relationships may exist between overhead costs and any of the three proposed independent

---

FIGURE 15–27

Ray Company
Linear Regressions

Regression Equation	Dependent Variable	Independent Variable	Regression Coefficient	Standard Error	t Value	r^2
1	1	Intercept	22,588.80			.2514
		2	46.66	40.27	1.16	
2	1	Intercept	25,667.12			.8995
		3	35.80	5.99	5.98	
3	1	Intercept	14,117.11			.9827
		4	4.10	0.27	15.07	
4	1	Intercept	14,808.20			.9491
		2	21.76	12.74	1.71	
		3	33.11	5.17	6.40	
5	1	Intercept	16,342.98			.9857
		2	−6.03	7.72	−.78	
		4	4.25	0.34	12.37	
6	1	Intercept	14,181.98			.9827
		3	0.27	9.78	0.02	
		4	4.07	1.07	3.80	
7	1	Intercept	18,141.36			.9980
		2	−32.86	8.27	−3.97	
		3	−34.15	9.55	−3.57	
		4	8.49	1.20	7.10	

variables. However, because management must estimate the incremental overhead cost of manufacturing Product X or Product Y, but not both, it might be anticipated that any regression which includes the two products together will not be useful.

Reasonableness of Numerical Results   The results of equation 7 are unusual, showing negative values of regression coefficients but an exceptionally high r^2 value. Together with the fact that autocorrelation might be expected between machine hours and the number of units manufactured, this gives reason to discard equation 7. Equation 5, which also has a negative regression coefficient and probably autocorrelation, should also be discarded.

r^2 Values   Only equation 1 has a relatively low r^2 value, .2514. It should be discarded.

Standard Error Terms and t-Values   Of the remaining equations, 4 and 6 have low t-values for key independent variables (1.71 and 0.02 respectively). These equations may also be discarded.

The Remaining Regression Equations   Only equations 2 and 3 satisfy all four of the preceding tests. However, equation 2 should also be discarded, not only because it is dominated by equation 3 on the key tests of r^2 and t-values, but because it would not allow overhead costs to be predicted as a function of manufacturing either Product X or Y.

The key element in the equation 3 solution is the regression coefficient for variable 4—machine hours. The logical interpretation is that the mean value of variable overhead cost is $4.10 per machine hour. In Figure 15–28, this

Figure 15–28

Ray Company
Contribution of Products X and Y

	Product X Cost per Unit	Product Y Cost per Unit
Direct Materials	$ 40.00	$ 60.00
Direct Labor	12.00	16.00
Variable Overhead:		
X (3 hrs. @ $4.10)	12.30	
Y (4 hrs. @ $4.10)		16.40
Total Variable Cost		
per Unit	$ 64.30	$ 92.40
Sales Price per Unit	$ 85.00	$ 120.00
Contribution Margin		
per Unit	$ 20.70	$ 27.60
Volume (units)............	600	400
Total Contribution	$12,420.00	$11,064.00

estimate of variable overhead cost results is used to compare the predicted contributions of Product X and Product Y. Ray Company should accept the Product X order, because its estimated contribution margin of $12,420 is greater than the $11,064 contribution margin of Product Y.

APPLYING THE RESULTS OF FORMAL REGRESSION ANALYSIS

Formal statistical estimating procedures can be applied to a wide variety of situations, including:

1. Forecasting sales volumes and revenues.
2. Forecasting cash inflows from cash sales and/or customer receipts as part of cash planning.
3. Developing departmental cost functions for flexible budgeting systems.
4. Establishing departmental or plant-wide overhead application rates—especially their variable portions.
5. Incremental and marginal analysis, when estimates are needed of the relevant incremental items.
6. Estimating the costs of functional activities in the marketing and administrative areas.
7. Developing forecasts of product cost components for standard cost specifications.
8. Estimating joint product cost functions when common processing costs are involved, especially when the product mix is not a fixed proportion.
9. Generating cash flow forecasts in relation to multiperiod capital budgeting analyses.

LIMITATIONS OF FORMAL REGRESSION ANALYSIS

Before applying the results of a regression analysis, the forecaster must test the model and data preconditions and assumptions and evaluate the statistical results of the regression using the tests described in this chapter.

The formal mathematical atmosphere of regression analysis should not be thought to guarantee accuracy and conclusiveness. Regression results are not valid simply because the method is rigorous. If all preconditions are not met or if the results are not tested, resorting to these formulations provides only a false security.

Remember that multiple rather than single regression analysis adds independent variables to the problem, thereby increasing the data requirements for any future use of the results. Forecasting the dependent variable then requires information about several independent variables instead of just one.

Another common error involves the unwarranted extrapolation of results. This is true regarding both extremes of the range of observations on which the regression is based. At the lower end, no strong conclusions should be drawn about the value of the intercept, especially when no observations were used from anywhere near the zero activity level. At the upper end, extension of the regression equation into ranges where no observations were available assumes the continuation of the same linear relationship that was present within the range of actual observations. This is clearly inappropriate in view of the probability that nonlinear and/or discontinuous patterns of total cost behavior will emerge as activity levels increase.

Price level changes pose a different type of problem. The use of unadjusted regression results assumes that unit prices are constant in relation to the source data. If price movements can be predicted for the forecasting period, the regression results should be adjusted. Likewise, technological changes, productivity fluctuations, and equipment deterioration may disturb the results of the regression. The only remedy in such cases may be to use subjective judgment or an engineered cost approach to modify forecasts according to the expected impact of those changes on the performance measures involved.

Finally, as discussed in Chapter 10, many behavioral and organizational factors can influence the ways in which formal forecast data should be interpreted and modified before being used in specific applications. This is especially true when these modified forecasts attempt to induce a particular type of performance on the part of managers who are subject to the performance specifications and requirements. An example is the setting of standard cost specifications and budgetary objectives, based primarily on past performance but adjusted to reflect desired levels of future performance.

SUMMARY

1. Business decision making is future oriented and requires information about anticipated outcomes of actions.
2. Apparent causal relationships should be the basis for forecasts.
3. Prior experience provides a foundation for most forecasting procedures. However, in developing useful forecast information, allowance must be made for anticipated changes in the relationships and/or the values of the variables involved.
4. Elementary forecasting methods include account analysis, high–low interpolation, visual fit, and engineered estimates. These methods typically use expected changes in activity levels as the basis for predicting costs and revenues.
5. Other elementary forecasting procedures use time periods as the basis for prediction. Forecasts of this type usually involve cumulative moving or weighted averages.
6. Formal statistical estimating methods can also be used if certain data requirements are met. These requirements include the presence of a logical relationship among the variables analyzed, sufficient data, accuracy and reliability of data, and certain statistical properties of the data.
7. Least squares regression is the most commonly employed of the formal statistical methods. It provides a linear, best-fit solution based on sets of observed values of the dependent and independent variables.

8. Elementary forecasting procedures (especially the visual fit method) should be used to pretest whether or not the formal statistical techniques are appropriate.

9. Although it is relatively more difficult and expensive, formal regression analysis provides information that is not available when simpler and less rigorous methods are used. This extra information allows evaluation of the relative strength of the statistical relationship among the variables being analyzed, as well as the specification of range and confidence limit type estimates.

10. Multiple regression analysis, in which several independent variables are used to explain the dependent variable's behavior, is an extension of the single variable regression method.

KEY WORDS AND PHRASES

Individual Account Analysis (700)
High–Low Interpolation (700)
Visual Fit Method (702)
Engineered Estimates (705)
Prototype Production (706)
Test Run (706)
Time and Motion Study (706)
Constant Growth or Decline Model (707)
Linear Regression (709)
Least Squares Regression (710)
Linear Regression Equation (710)
Dependent Variable (710)
Independent Variable (710)
Error or Disturbance Term (710)
Homoscedasticity (716)
Serial Correlation or Autocorrelation (718)
Regression Coefficient (719)
Coefficient of Determination (722)
Correlation Coefficient (722)
Standard Error of the Regression Estimate (722)
Standard Error of the Regression Coefficients (724)
t-Statistic (724)
Time Series Regression (728)
Multiple Regression Analysis (729)
Multicollinearity (730)
Correlation Matrix (730)
Dummy Variables (731)

Appendix: Regression Analysis— Method of Least Squares

The least squares method of regression analysis provides the equation of a line that satisfies the condition of best fit for a given set of values for the dependent and independent variable(s). The condition to be satisfied is that the sum of the squares of the vertical distances of all observations from the solution line is minimized.

The behavior of the *dependent variable* (*y*) is represented by this line; the variable used to explain that behavior is the *independent variable* (*x*) (or independent variables x_1, x_2, . . . x_n in the case of multiple regression). The *regression equation*—the equation of the solution line—is written:

$$y = ax + b + u$$

with *a* and *b* referred to as the *regression coefficients*. The slope of the regression line is given by the value of *b*, and the intercept with the *y* axis by *a*. The disturbance term, *u*, has a mean value of zero.

REGRESSION COEFFICIENTS

The values of *a* and *b* are derived from the solution of the following two simultaneous equations:

$$\Sigma y = na + b\Sigma x \ldots \ldots \quad [1]$$
$$\Sigma xy = ax + b\Sigma x^2 \ldots \ldots \quad [2]$$

The following notation and terminology apply:

$n =$ the number of sets of observations used in the analysis.
$\Sigma y =$ the sum of all values of *y*.
$\Sigma x =$ the sum of all values of *x*.
$\Sigma xy =$ the sum of the cross products of all corresponding *x* and *y* values.
$\Sigma x^2 =$ the sum of all squared values of *x*.
$\Sigma y^2 =$ the sum of all squared values of *y*.

Example: Using the data for Gogetter Company presented on page 727, the following table of values can be constructed:

Month	x Machine Hours	y Overhead	x^2	xy	y^2
1	1,600	4,000	2,560,000	6,400,000	16,000,000
2	2,400	5,000	5,760,000	12,000,000	25,000,000
3	3,200	6,800	10,240,000	21,760,000	46,240,000
4	1,500	3,600	2,250,000	5,400,000	12,960,000
5	2,000	4,500	4,000,000	9,000,000	20,250,000
6	1,200	2,700	1,440,000	3,240,000	7,290,000
7	1,800	4,200	3,240,000	7,560,000	17,640,000
8	1,400	3,600	1,960,000	5,040,000	12,960,000
9	1,000	2,900	1,000,000	2,900,000	8,410,000
10	2,900	6,700	8,410,000	19,430,000	44,890,000
	19,000	44,000	40,860,000	92,730,000	211,640,000
	Σx	Σy	Σx^2	Σxy	Σy^2

Substituting the appropriate values from this table in equations 1 and 2 gives the following:

$$44,000 = 10a + b \cdot 19,000 \qquad [1]$$
$$92,730,000 = a \cdot 19,000 + b \cdot 40,860,000 \qquad [2]$$

Rearranging terms, from equation 1

$$10a + 19,000b = 44,000 \qquad [3]$$

and from equation 2

$$19,000a + 40,860,000b = 92,730,000 \qquad [4]$$

from equation 3

$$10a = 44,000 - 19,000b$$
$$a = 4,400 - 1,900b \qquad [5]$$

Substituting equation (5) in equation (4),

$$19,000 (4,400 - 1,900b) + 40,860,000b = 92,730,000$$
$$83,600,000 - 36,100,000 + 40,860,000b = 92,730,000$$
$$4,760,000b = 9,130,000$$

$$b = \frac{9,130,000}{4,760,000}$$

$$b = 1.9180672 \qquad [6]$$

Substituting equation (6) in equation (5),

$$a = 4,400 - 1,900 (1.9180672)$$
$$a = 755.6724 \qquad [7]$$

The regression equation is therefore:

$$y = 755.6724 + 1.9180672b$$

ALTERNATIVE SOLUTION FOR REGRESSION COEFFICIENTS

To simplify some of the preceding calculations, it is convenient to adjust the source data values as follows:

1. Let $\bar{\bar{x}} = x - \bar{x}$, so that $\Sigma\bar{\bar{x}} = 0$. That is, subtract the mean value of x, ($\bar{x}$), from all observed values of x to give the new set of normalized values, $\bar{\bar{x}}$.
2. This will not affect the value of b, but since the above modification corresponds to moving the y-axis to the right by an amount equal to $\bar{x}$, there will be a different value of the intercept, $\bar{\bar{a}}$, in the new situation. This will be $\bar{\bar{a}} = a + b\bar{x}$.

Because $\Sigma\bar{\bar{x}} = 0$, the original source equations 1 and 2 are simplified as follows:

Revised Equation 1 $\Sigma y = n\bar{\bar{a}}$ .... [8]
Revised Equation 2 $\Sigma\bar{\bar{x}}y = b\Sigma\bar{\bar{x}}^2$ .... [9]

Example: For Gogetter Company, the following revised table of data can be constructed:

Month	$\bar{\bar{x}} = x - \bar{x}$	$\bar{\bar{x}}^2$	$\bar{\bar{x}}y$	$\bar{\bar{y}} = y - \bar{y}$	$\bar{\bar{y}}^2$
1	−300	90,000	−1,200,000	400	160,000
2	500	250,000	2,500,000	−600	360,000
3	1,300	1,690,000	8,840,000	−2,400	5,760,000
4	−400	160,000	1,440,000	800	640,000
5	100	10,000	450,000	−100	10,000
6	−700	490,000	−1,890,000	1,700	2,890,000
7	−100	10,000	−420,000	200	40,000
8	−500	250,000	−1,800,000	800	640,000
9	−900	810,000	−2,610,000	1,500	2,250,000
10	1,000	1,000,000	6,700,000	−2,300	5,290,000
	0	4,760,000	9,130,000	0	18,040,000
	$\Sigma\bar{\bar{x}}$	$\Sigma\bar{\bar{x}}^2$	$\Sigma\bar{\bar{x}}y$	$\Sigma\bar{\bar{y}}$	$\Sigma\bar{\bar{y}}^2$

Substituting the appropriate values from this table and from the preceding one in equations 8 and 9 results in the following:

Equation 8
$$\Sigma y = n\bar{\bar{a}}$$
$$44,000 = 10\bar{\bar{a}}$$
$$\bar{\bar{a}} = 4,400$$

Equation 9
$$\Sigma\bar{\bar{x}}y = b\Sigma\bar{\bar{x}}^2$$
$$9,130,000 = b \cdot 4,760,000$$

$$b = \frac{9,130,000}{4,760,000}$$

$$b = 1.9180672$$

But, because $\bar{\bar{a}} = a + b\bar{x}$

$$a = \bar{\bar{a}} - b\bar{x}$$
$$= 4,400 - (1.9180672)(1,900)$$
$$= 4,400 - 3644.3276$$
$$a = 755.6724$$

CORRELATION COEFFICIENT (r) AND COEFFICIENT OF DETERMINATION (r^2)

The coefficient of determination (r^2) describes the degree of linear relationship between the dependent and independent variables. It is defined as the ratio of the amount of explained variation to the amount of total variation. It can be calculated as follows:

$$r^2 = \frac{b\Sigma xy}{\Sigma y^2} \quad \dotfill \quad [10]$$

Example: Substituting the appropriate values from the above tables in equation 10 produces the following *coefficient of determination:*

$$r^2 = \frac{(1.9180672)(9,130,000)}{18,040,000}$$

$$= .9707291$$

The *correlation coefficient* (r) is found by taking the square root of r^2 and adjusting the mathematical sign ($+$ or $-$) to correspond to that of the regression coefficient b. Consequently, for Gogetter Company, the result is:

$$r = \sqrt{.9707291}$$
$$= \pm.9852558$$

Because the value of b is *positive* ($+1.9180672$), the value of r is .9582558.

STANDARD ERROR OF ESTIMATE (s_e)

The standard error (standard deviation) of the regression estimate, s_e, is a measure of the dispersion of the observed values of the dependent variable (y) around the regression line. The equation that is the source of this measure is:

$$s_e = \sqrt{\frac{\Sigma(y - y')^2}{n - 2}} \quad \dotfill \quad [11]$$

Here y' is the value of the dependent variable based on the equation of the regression line and the divisor $(n - 2)$ is the number of sets of observations minus two for the degrees of freedom lost due to the presence of two variables, (x and y). The following table shows the derivation of the values of: (1) y', (2) $y - y'$, (3) $(y - y')^2$, and (4) $\Sigma(y - y')^2$:

x	y	y' $(755.67 + 1.91820x)$	$y - y'$	$(y - y')^2$
1,600	4,000	3,824.47	175.53	30,810.78
2,400	5,000	5,358.87	−358.87	128,767.67
3,200	6,800	6,893.27	−93.27	8,699.29
1,500	3,600	3,632.67	−32.67	1,067.33
2,000	4,500	4,591.67	−91.67	8,403.39
1,200	2,700	3,057.27	−357.27	127,641.85
1,800	4,200	4,208.07	−8.07	65.12
1,400	3,600	3,440.87	159.13	25,322.36
1,000	2,900	2,673.67	226.33	51,225.27
2,900	6,700	6,317.87	382.13	146,023.33
			$\Sigma(y - y')^2 =$	528,046.39

For Gogetter Company, the *standard error of the regression estimate* is as follows:

$$s_e = \sqrt{\frac{528,046.39}{10 - 2}}$$

$$= \sqrt{\frac{528,046.39}{8}}$$

$$= \sqrt{66,005.80}$$

$$s_e = 256.9159$$

STANDARD ERROR OF REGRESSION COEFFICIENT (s_b)

The standard error of the regression coefficient, b, is a measure of the sampling error that may be present in the value of b as derived from the regression equation. It is defined by the following equation:

$$s_b = \frac{s_e}{\Sigma(x - \bar{x})^2} \quad \dots \dots \dots \dots \dots \dots \dots \dots \dots \quad [12]$$

For Gogetter Company, the *standard error of the regression coefficient* is calculated as follows:

$$s_b = \frac{256.9159}{\sqrt{4,760,000}}$$

$$= \frac{256.9159}{2,181.7424}$$

$$s_b = 0.1177572$$

t-STATISTICS

The ratio of the mean value of a regression coefficient to the value of its standard error is called a *t-statistic*. When compared to predetermined *t*-table values, *t*-statistics permit an evaluation of the hypothesis that a significant statistical relationship exists between the dependent and independent variables. For the regression coefficient b, the *t*-statistic t_b is equal to $b \div s_b$.

In Gogetter Company, the *t*-statistic is calculated as follows:

$$t_b = \frac{1.9180672}{.1177572}$$

$$t_b = 16.288322$$

The test employed involves determining whether the *t*-statistic derived from the regression results is greater than the predetermined *t*-value which corresponds to the number of degrees of freedom pertaining to the sets of observations used in the analysis and the percentage significance level being tested. The formal statement of the hypothesis being evaluated is that "the null hypothesis that $b = 0$" is rejected if the regression *t*-statistic exceeds the predetermined *t*-table value. A general rule of thumb is that *t*-statistics greater than 2.00 indicate the presence of a significant statistical relationship. However, Table 15–3 should be used for greater precision.

In Gogetter Company, the *t*-statistic $t_b = 16.288322$ exceeds all listed entries in the *t*-value table for 8 degrees of freedom. This can be interpreted to mean that there is less than .001 probability that the two variables (machine hours and overhead cost) are not statistically related.

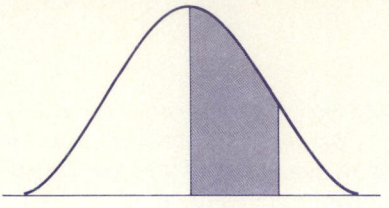

TABLE 15–1

Areas Under the Normal Curve

Z	.00	.01	.02	.03	.04	.05	.06	.07	.08	.09
0.0	.0000	.0040	.0080	.0120	.0160	.0199	.0239	.0279	.0319	.0359
0.1	.0398	.0438	.0478	.0517	.0557	.0596	.0636	.0675	.0714	.0753
0.2	.0793	.0832	.0871	.0910	.0948	.0987	.1026	.1064	.1103	.1141
0.3	.1179	.1217	.1255	.1293	.1331	.1368	.1406	.1443	.1480	.1517
0.4	.1554	.1591	.1628	.1664	.1700	.1736	.1772	.1808	.1844	.1879
0.5	.1915	.1950	.1985	.2019	.2054	.2088	.2123	.2157	.2190	.2224
0.6	.2257	.2291	.2324	.2357	.2389	.2422	.2454	.2486	.2517	.2549
0.7	.2580	.2611	.2642	.2673	.2704	.2734	.2764	.2794	.2823	.2852
0.8	.2881	.2910	.2939	.2967	.2995	.3023	.3051	.3079	.3106	.3133
0.9	.3159	.3186	.3212	.3238	.3264	.3289	.3315	.3340	.3365	.3389
1.0	.3413	.3438	.3461	.3485	.3508	.3531	.3554	.3577	.3599	.3621
1.1	.3643	.3665	.3686	.3708	.3729	.3749	.3770	.3790	.3810	.3830
1.2	.3849	.3869	.3888	.3907	.3925	.3944	.3962	.3980	.3997	.4015
1.3	.4032	.4049	.4066	.4082	.4099	.4115	.4131	.4147	.4162	.4177
1.4	.4192	.4207	.4222	.4236	.4251	.4265	.4279	.4292	.4306	.4319
1.5	.4332	.4345	.4357	.4370	.4382	.4394	.4406	.4418	.4430	.4441
1.6	.4452	.4463	.4474	.4485	.4495	.4505	.4515	.4525	.4535	.4545
1.7	.4554	.4564	.4573	.4582	.4591	.4599	.4608	.4616	.4625	.4633
1.8	.4641	.4649	.4656	.4664	.4671	.4678	.4686	.4693	.4700	.4706
1.9	.4713	.4719	.4726	.4732	.4738	.4744	.4750	.4756	.4762	.4767
2.0	.4773	.4778	.4783	.4788	.4793	.4798	.4803	.4808	.4812	.4817
2.1	.4821	.4826	.4830	.4834	.4838	.4842	.4846	.4850	.4854	.4857
2.2	.4861	.4865	.4868	.4871	.4875	.4878	.4881	.4884	.4887	.4890
2.3	.4893	.4896	.4898	.4901	.4904	.4906	.4909	.4911	.4913	.4916
2.4	.4918	.4920	.4922	.4925	.4927	.4929	.4931	.4932	.4934	.4936
2.5	.4938	.4940	.4941	.4943	.4945	.4946	.4948	.4949	.4951	.4952
2.6	.4953	.4955	.4956	.4957	.4959	.4960	.4961	.4962	.4963	.4964
2.7	.4965	.4966	.4967	.4968	.4969	.4970	.4971	.4972	.4973	.4974
2.8	.4975	.4975	.4976	.4977	.4978	.4978	.4979	.4980	.4980	.4981
2.9	.4981	.4982	.4983	.4983	.4984	.4984	.4985	.4985	.4986	.4986
3.0	.4987	.4987	.4987	.4988	.4988	.4989	.4989	.4989	.4990	.4990
3.1	.4990	.4991	.4991	.4991	.4992	.4992	.4992	.4992	.4993	.4993
3.2	.4993	.4993	.4994	.4994	.4994	.4994	.4994	.4995	.4995	.4995
3.3	.4995	.4995	.4996	.4996	.4996	.4996	.4996	.4996	.4996	.4997
3.4	.4997	.4997	.4997	.4997	.4997	.4997	.4997	.4997	.4998	.4998
3.5	.4998	.4998	.4998	.4998	.4998	.4998	.4998	.4998	.4998	.4998
3.6	.4998	.4999	.4999	.4999	.4999	.4999	.4999	.4999	.4999	.4999
3.7	.4999	.4999	.4999	.4999	.4999	.4999	.4999	.4999	.4999	.4999
3.8	.4999	.4999	.4999	.4999	.4999	.4999	.4999	.5000	.5000	.5000
3.9	.5000	.5000	.5000	.5000	.5000	.5000	.5000	.5000	.5000	.5000
4.0	.5000	.5000	.5000	.5000	.5000	.5000	.5000	.5000	.5000	.5000

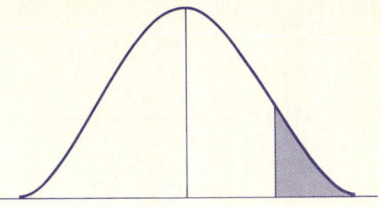

TABLE 15–2

Areas in One Tail of the Normal Curve

z	.00	.01	.02	.03	.04	.05	.06	.07	.08	.09
0.0	.5000	.4960	.4920	.4880	.4840	.4801	.4761	.4721	.4681	.4641
0.1	.4602	.4562	.4522	.4483	.4443	.4404	.4364	.4325	.4286	.4247
0.2	.4207	.4168	.4129	.4090	.4052	.4013	.3974	.3936	.3897	.3859
0.3	.3821	.3783	.3745	.3707	.3669	.3632	.3594	.3557	.3520	.3483
0.4	.3446	.3409	.3372	.3336	.3300	.3264	.3228	.3192	.3156	.3121
0.5	.3085	.3050	.3015	.2981	.2946	.2912	.2877	.2843	.2810	.2776
0.6	.2743	.2709	.2676	.2643	.2611	.2578	.2546	.2514	.2483	.2451
0.7	.2420	.2389	.2358	.2327	.2296	.2266	.2236	.2206	.2177	.2148
0.8	.2119	.2090	.2061	.2033	.2005	.1977	.1949	.1921	.1894	.1867
0.9	.1841	.1814	.1788	.1762	.1736	.1711	.1685	.1660	.1635	.1611
1.0	.1587	.1562	.1539	.1515	.1492	.1469	.1446	.1423	.1401	.1379
1.1	.1357	.1335	.1314	.1292	.1271	.1251	.1230	.1210	.1190	.1170
1.2	.1151	.1131	.1112	.1093	.1075	.1056	.1038	.1020	.1003	.0985
1.3	.0968	.0951	.0934	.0918	.0901	.0885	.0869	.0853	.0838	.0823
1.4	.0808	.0793	.0778	.0764	.0749	.0735	.0721	.0708	.0694	.0681
1.5	.0668	.0655	.0643	.0630	.0618	.0606	.0594	.0582	.0570	.0559
1.6	.0548	.0537	.0526	.0515	.0505	.0495	.0485	.0475	.0465	.0455
1.7	.0446	.0436	.0427	.0418	.0409	.0401	.0392	.0384	.0375	.0367
1.8	.0359	.0351	.0344	.0336	.0329	.0322	.0314	.0307	.0300	.0294
1.9	.0287	.0281	.0274	.0268	.0262	.0256	.0250	.0244	.0238	.0233
2.0	.0227	.0222	.0217	.0212	.0207	.0202	.0197	.0192	.0188	.0183
2.1	.0179	.0174	.0170	.0166	.0162	.0158	.0154	.0150	.0146	.0143
2.2	.0139	.0135	.0132	.0129	.0125	.0122	.0119	.0116	.0113	.0110
2.3	.0107	.0104	.0102	.0099	.0096	.0094	.0091	.0089	.0087	.0084
2.4	.0082	.0080	.0078	.0075	.0073	.0071	.0069	.0068	.0066	.0064
2.5	.0062	.0060	.0059	.0057	.0055	.0054	.0052	.0051	.0049	.0048
2.6	.0047	.0045	.0044	.0043	.0041	.0040	.0039	.0038	.0037	.0036
2.7	.0035	.0034	.0033	.0032	.0031	.0030	.0029	.0028	.0027	.0026
2.8	.0025	.0025	.0024	.0023	.0022	.0022	.0021	.0020	.0020	.0019
2.9	.0019	.0018	.0017	.0017	.0016	.0016	.0015	.0015	.0015	.0014
3.0	.0013	.0013	.0013	.0012	.0012	.0011	.0011	.0011	.0010	.0010
3.1	.0010	.0009	.0009	.0009	.0008	.0008	.0008	.0008	.0007	.0007
3.2	.0007	.0007	.0006	.0006	.0006	.0006	.0006	.0005	.0005	.0005
3.3	.0005	.0005	.0004	.0004	.0004	.0004	.0004	.0004	.0004	.0003
3.4	.0003	.0003	.0003	.0003	.0003	.0003	.0003	.0003	.0002	.0002
3.5	.0002	.0002	.0002	.0002	.0002	.0002	.0002	.0002	.0002	.0002
3.6	.0002	.0001	.0001	.0001	.0001	.0001	.0001	.0001	.0001	.0001
3.7	.0001	.0001	.0001	.0001	.0001	.0001	.0001	.0001	.0001	.0001
3.8	.0001	.0001	.0001	.0001	.0001	.0001	.0001	.0000	.0000	.0000
3.9	.0000	.0000	.0000	.0000	.0000	.0000	.0000	.0000	.0000	.0000
4.0	.0000	.0000	.0000	.0000	.0000	.0000	.0000	.0000	.0000	.0000

TABLE 15–3

Student's *t*-Distribution*

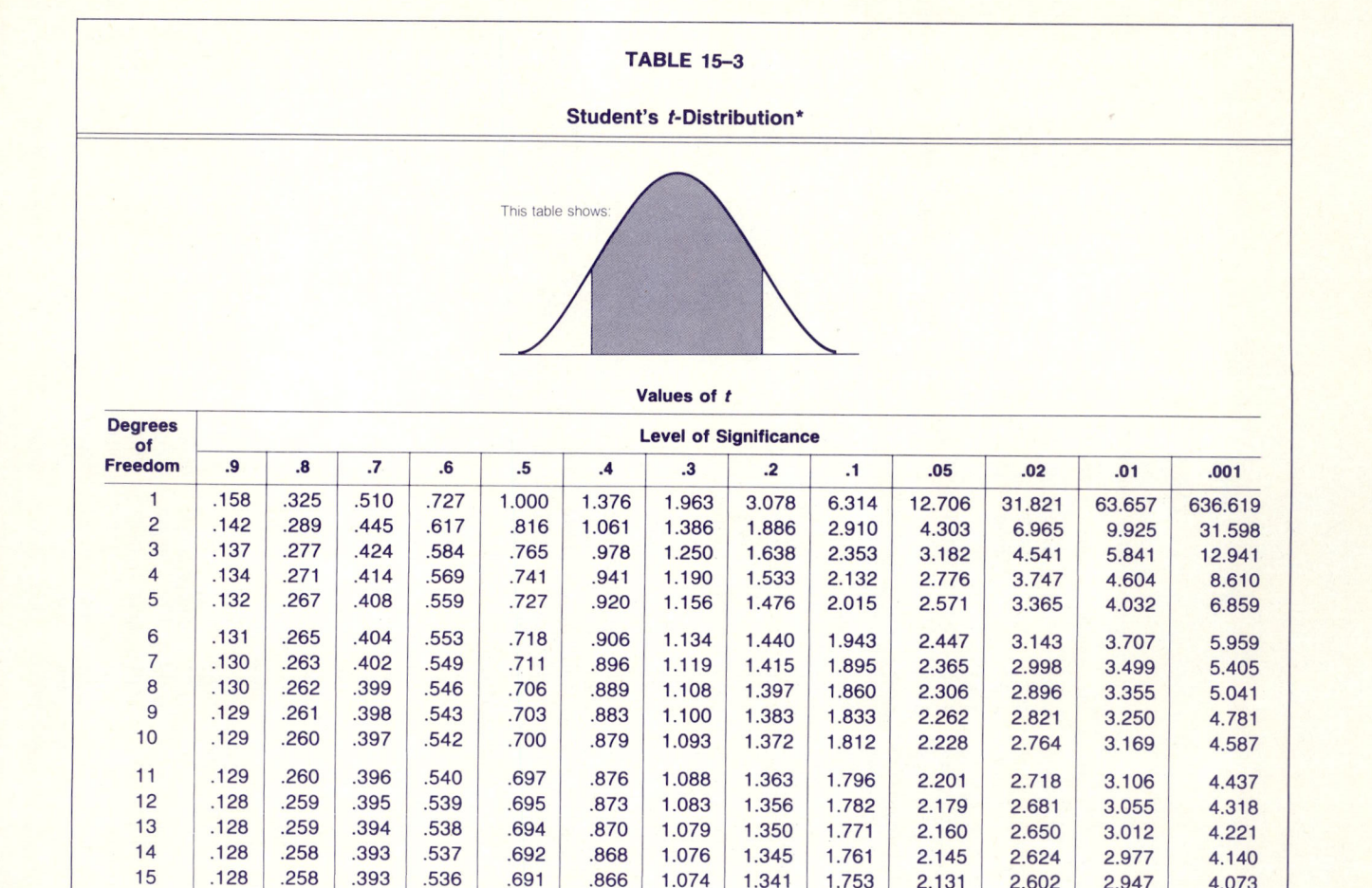

This table shows:

Values of *t*

Degrees of Freedom	Level of Significance												
	.9	.8	.7	.6	.5	.4	.3	.2	.1	.05	.02	.01	.001
1	.158	.325	.510	.727	1.000	1.376	1.963	3.078	6.314	12.706	31.821	63.657	636.619
2	.142	.289	.445	.617	.816	1.061	1.386	1.886	2.910	4.303	6.965	9.925	31.598
3	.137	.277	.424	.584	.765	.978	1.250	1.638	2.353	3.182	4.541	5.841	12.941
4	.134	.271	.414	.569	.741	.941	1.190	1.533	2.132	2.776	3.747	4.604	8.610
5	.132	.267	.408	.559	.727	.920	1.156	1.476	2.015	2.571	3.365	4.032	6.859
6	.131	.265	.404	.553	.718	.906	1.134	1.440	1.943	2.447	3.143	3.707	5.959
7	.130	.263	.402	.549	.711	.896	1.119	1.415	1.895	2.365	2.998	3.499	5.405
8	.130	.262	.399	.546	.706	.889	1.108	1.397	1.860	2.306	2.896	3.355	5.041
9	.129	.261	.398	.543	.703	.883	1.100	1.383	1.833	2.262	2.821	3.250	4.781
10	.129	.260	.397	.542	.700	.879	1.093	1.372	1.812	2.228	2.764	3.169	4.587
11	.129	.260	.396	.540	.697	.876	1.088	1.363	1.796	2.201	2.718	3.106	4.437
12	.128	.259	.395	.539	.695	.873	1.083	1.356	1.782	2.179	2.681	3.055	4.318
13	.128	.259	.394	.538	.694	.870	1.079	1.350	1.771	2.160	2.650	3.012	4.221
14	.128	.258	.393	.537	.692	.868	1.076	1.345	1.761	2.145	2.624	2.977	4.140
15	.128	.258	.393	.536	.691	.866	1.074	1.341	1.753	2.131	2.602	2.947	4.073

16	.128	.258	.392	.535	.690	.865	1.071	1.337	1.746	2.120	2.583	2.921	4.015
17	.128	.257	.392	.534	.689	.863	1.069	1.333	1.740	2.110	2.567	2.898	3.965
18	.127	.257	.392	.534	.688	.862	1.067	1.330	1.734	2.101	2.552	2.878	3.922
19	.127	.257	.391	.533	.688	.861	1.066	1.328	1.729	2.093	2.539	2.861	3.883
20	.127	.257	.391	.533	.687	.860	1.064	1.325	1.725	2.086	2.528	2.845	3.850
21	.127	.257	.391	.532	.686	.859	1.063	1.323	1.721	2.080	2.518	2.831	3.819
22	.127	.256	.390	.532	.686	.858	1.061	1.321	1.717	2.074	2.508	2.819	3.792
23	.127	.256	.390	.532	.685	.858	1.060	1.319	1.714	2.069	2.500	2.807	3.767
24	.127	.256	.390	.531	.685	.857	1.059	1.318	1.711	2.064	2.492	2.797	3.745
25	.127	.256	.390	.531	.684	.856	1.058	1.316	1.708	2.060	2.485	2.787	3.725
26	.127	.256	.390	.531	.684	.856	1.058	1.315	1.706	2.056	2.479	2.779	3.707
27	.127	.256	.389	.531	.684	.855	1.057	1.314	1.703	2.052	2.473	2.771	3.690
28	.127	.256	.389	.530	.683	.855	1.056	1.313	1.701	2.048	2.467	2.763	3.674
28	.127	.256	.389	.530	.683	.854	1.055	1.311	1.699	2.045	2.462	2.756	3.659
30	.127	.256	.389	.530	.683	.854	1.055	1.310	1.697	2.042	2.457	2.750	3.646
40	.126	.255	.388	.529	.681	.851	1.050	1.303	1.684	2.021	2.423	2.704	3.551
60	.126	.254	.387	.527	.679	.848	1.046	1.296	1.671	2.000	2.390	2.660	3.460
120	.126	.254	.386	.526	.677	.845	1.041	1.289	1.658	1.980	2.358	2.617	3.373
∞	.126	.253	.385	.524	.674	.842	1.036	1.282	1.645	1.960	2.326	2.576	3.291

* From Table III of Fisher and Yates: STATISTICAL TABLES FOR BIOLOGICAL, AGRICULTURAL AND MEDICAL RESEARCH, published by Longman Group Ltd., London (previously published by Oliver & Boyd, Ltd., Edinburgh) and by permission of the authors and publishers.

Questions

1. Explain the role of forecasting techniques in the various aspects of company management.
2. Describe the forecasting method known as account analysis. What are its advantages and limitations?
3. Explain the forecasting method referred to as high–low. What are its advantages and limitations?
4. What are the advantages and disadvantages of the visual fit method of forecasting?
5. When there are no empirical data from actual experience, what forecasting procedures must be adopted?
6. When are time-dependent (time series) forecasting methods useful? What are the implications of the use of this type of forecasting technique?
7. Explain the advantages and disadvantages of the constant growth, moving average, and weighted moving average forecasting techniques.
8. What condition is satisfied by solutions from the least squares regression method?
9. List and briefly explain what *preconditions* should be satisfied before a least squares regression analysis is attempted?
10. What *prerequisites* should be satisfied by data that are to be used in a least squares regression analysis?
11. What *statistical attributes* must be satisfied by the data to be used in a least squares regression analysis?
12. What results of a least squares analysis are most useful for forecasting purposes? Why?
13. Give an interpretation of the regression coefficients that would be found by regressing total manufacturing overhead per month against total machine hours per month.
14. Why should the value of the intercept (*a*) be used carefully, if at all?
15. Why is *extrapolation* not recommended for estimating the value of the dependent variable relevant to a value of the independent variable much larger or smaller than the upper and lower bounds or the relevant range?
16. What information is provided by the *correlation coefficient* and the *coefficient of determination* derived from a least squares regression analysis? For what is it useful?
17. How should the *standard error of a regression estimate* be interpreted and used?
18. How should the *standard error of a regression coefficient* be interpreted and used?
19. What is a *t-statistic* and how should it be interpreted and used?
20. What is the purpose of using the visual fit and/or the high–low methods preliminary to attempting least squares regression analysis?
21. When would time-series regression analysis be useful for forecasting purposes?
22. What are the advantages and disadvantages of multiple variable regression analysis?

23. What extra statistical attributes of data must be evaluated before the results of multiple variable regression analysis are used?
24. What is a dummy variable and how does it help regression analysis and forecasting?

Exercises

E 15-1 Analysis of Accounts—Estimating Costs—Setting Overhead Rate

Royce Corporation's accountant has analyzed the entries in the Machining Department's overhead accounts for October of 19X2. The balances have been assigned to variable and fixed categories based on inspection of the nature of each account entry. The following tabulation was derived:

Variable Items		Fixed Items	
Machining Supplies	$ 850	Supervision	$1,800
Electricity	3,110	Rent	300
Tool Replacements	1,260	Property Tax	500
Machine Repairs	2,760	Preventive Maintenance	1,400
Rework and Idle Time	1,020	Depreciation	2,000
	$9,000		$9,000

During October, 2,000 machine hours were worked in this department.

Required:
(a) Develop a forecast formula for the overhead costs of the Machining Department.
(b) What will this formula forecast be for November, when it is expected that 2,500 hours will be worked?
(c) Discuss the advantages and limitations of this method of forecasting overhead costs.

E 15-2 Visual Fit—Estimating Costs

Ajax Manufacturing Company has developed the following information concerning manufacturing overheads for its plant in Poughkeepsie:

Year	Quarter	Overhead	Units of Output
19X5	1	$1,600,000	36,000
	2	1,720,000	44,000
	3	1,850,000	47,000
	4	1,650,000	41,000
19X6	1	1,660,000	42,000
	2	1,890,000	47,500
	3	2,370,000	55,000
	4	2,050,000	51,000
19X7	1	2,200,000	52,000
	2	2,450,000	61,000
	3	2,650,000	67,500
	4	2,370,000	59,000

Required:

(a) Plot the above data (1) all on the same scattergraph, and (2) on four separate quarterly scattergraphs.

(b) What cost estimates could be developed from inspection of the above graphs?

(c) What limitations are inherent in this approach?

(d) What additional information would be useful in developing cost estimates in this situation?

E 15–3 High–Low Method—Cost Estimation

Over the past year, the following quarterly cost data pertaining to the overhead costs of the Manufacturing Division of Gnasso Company has been collected:

	Quarter 1	Quarter 2	Quarter 3	Quarter 4
Machine Hours	100,000	150,000	120,000	130,000
Repairs	$ 60,000	$ 87,000	$ 72,000	$ 78,400
Janitorial Services	48,000	62,000	56,000	58,000
Supervision	12,000	12,000	12,000	12,000
Rent	15,000	15,000	15,000	15,000
Power and Heat	75,000	108,000	90,000	96,000
Supplies and Lubricants ..	5,150	7,500	6,000	6,550
	$215,150	$291,500	$251,000	$265,950

The company has decided to use the high–low approach to estimate cost variability relationships based on machine hours per quarter.

Required:

(a) Using the high–low method, develop a cost estimating formula for total overhead costs.

(b) Using the high–low method, develop cost estimating formulas for each individual item of overhead.

(c) What would be the forecast of costs for quarters in which the number of machine hours are: (1) 125,000, (2) 140,000, and (3) 160,000?

(d) What problems may be encountered in part (c)?

(e) What are the limitations of this approach to estimating costs?

E 15–4 Visual Fit—High–Low Method—Comparative Analysis

The following cost data have been collected concerning the use of factory supplies in the manufacturing divisions of Hussein Corporation during 19X3.

Month	Machine Hours	Labor Hours	Supplies Costs
January	48,000	170,000	$12,000
February	36,000	120,000	16,800
March	33,000	120,000	19,200
April	42,000	140,000	24,000
May	45,000	150,000	16,000
June...........	45,000	140,000	16,800
July	45,000	160,000	32,000

Month	Machine Hours	Labor Hours	Supplies Costs
August	39,000	140,000	18,800
September	36,000	200,000	14,000
October	24,000	20,000	20,000
November	30,000	100,000	12,000
December	30,000	120,000	16,000

Required:
(a) Prepare separate scattergraphs of the preceding data—one on the basis of machine hours and one on the basis of labor hours.

(b) Inspect the diagrams you produced in part (a) and comment on any unusual items.

(c) Use a visual fit method to estimate the cost relationship based on (1) machine hours, and (2) labor hours. Use your conclusions from part (b) in this regard. Would you rather base your estimate on machine hours or labor hours?

(d) Use the high–low method in conjunction with conclusions from part (b) to develop cost estimating formulae, based on (1) machine hours and (2) labor hours.

(e) Compare the results of parts (c) and (d). Which is preferable? Why?

E 15–5 Sales Forecast—Constant Growth Model—Seasonal Adjustments

Part 1: Anderson Corporation has experienced steady and increasing growth in its sales over the past several years. It feels that the current growth rate of 6 percent experienced in 19X3 will continue to increase by 1 percent per year for the next five years. Sales in 19X3 were $12,500,000.

Required:
(a) Develop sales forecasts for the years 19X4 to 19X8.

(b) State the forecast formula in general terms.

(c) What are the advantages and limitations of this approach to forecasting?

Part 2: Raun Company bases its quarterly sales forecasts on (1) a yearly estimate of industry sales and (2) an index to weight sales performance in each quarter. The annual sales of the company are projected on the basis of the following formula:

$$\text{Company Sales} = 8,000,000 + .05 \text{ Industry Sales}$$

The four quarters of the year are weighted as follows:

Winter	87.5*
Spring	101.5
Summer	112.0
Fall	99.0

* 87.5 means sales in this quarter are 87.5% of those in an average quarter.

Required:

(a) Develop sales forecasts for each quarter of 19X3, when industry sales are estimated to be $400,000,000.

(b) Discuss the merits and weaknesses of this method of forecasting.

E 15-6 Linear Regression—Single Variable Model—Revenue Forecasts

Over the past ten years, the Silver State Samurai, a professional basketball team, has seen its fortunes fluctuate in the won–lost column. Management has noticed that gross revenues also appear to follow the team's pattern of success or failure. For this period, the following data are available:

Year	Revenue*	Games Won
1	$6,250,000	62
2	5,950,000	56
3	2,600,000	30
4	5,450,000	48
5	7,100,000	72
6	3,850,000	36
7	4,050,000	46
8	5,150,000	52
9	3,450,000	36
10	4,050,000	42

* Assume that this data has been adjusted for price level changes.

Required:

(a) Use least squares regression to establish a linear equation relating sales revenue to games won.

(b) Evaluate the statistical results of this regression.

(c) By spending an additional $800,000 on fixed costs (player salaries, training and conditioning costs, and so on), the management expects to field a super team capable of winning 80 games next year. Variable costs are expected to continue to average around 25 percent of sales revenue. The existing team can expect to win only 50 games at the most. Should management pay $800,000 for the super team?

(d) What are the limitations of this forecasting method? What other variables besides games won may influence total receipts?

E 15-7 Time Series Analysis—Linear Regression Analysis—Sales Forecast

Kidder Company has recorded the following annual sales revenues during the last ten years:

19X0	$16,500,000	19X5	$23,750,000
19X1	21,250,000	19X6	26,250,000
19X2	19,750,000	19X7	27,150,000
19X3	20,150,000	19X8	28,450,000
19X4	22,250,000	19X9	30,350,000

Required:

(a) Use linear regression methods to forecast sales for the next year, 19Y0, using time series analysis.

(b) Interpret the result in part (a) and discuss the limitations of this method of forecasting.

E 15–8* Cost Estimating—Multiple Regression with Dummy Variables

Refer to the information provided in Exercise 15–2.

Required:

(a) Using dummy variables for each of the four separate quarters, derive a regression equation for overhead costs as a function of output and the quarter of the year.

(b) Statistically evaluate the equation derived in part (a). Interpret the results from a forecasting point of view.

(c) Compare the answer to those derived in part (b) of Exercise 15–2. Comment on the relative merits of each set of results.

(d) What purpose does the use of the dummy variable serve?

E 15–9 Visual Fit—Regression Analysis—Comparison of Results

Brickford Company is attempting to select the best basis for forecasting plant overhead costs. For the past six months, the following data are available:

Month	Machine Hours	Labor Hours	Direct Materials Used (tons)	Total Overhead
January ...	12,000	13,500	1,800	$44,000
February ..	9,000	7,500	1,100	28,000
March	6,000	13,500	2,000	43,000
April	4,000	10,500	1,400	35,500
May	10,000	12,000	1,500	31,500
June......	6,000	6,000	1,100	24,500

Required:

(a) Prepare three separate diagrams to plot overhead costs against each of the three possible independent variables. Fit linear functions to each diagram, using the visual fit method.

(b) Use linear regression to determine the relationship between overhead costs and each of these three variables *independently* (one at a time, that is).

(c) Determine geometrically the parameters (slope and intercept) of the lines drawn in part (a). Compare these results to those in part (b). Comment on your findings.

(d) Comment on the relative strengths and weaknesses of these two forecasting methods.

---

* This problem cannot be solved unless students have access to a computer system and a linear multiple regression program.

Cases

C 15–1   Estimating Overhead Costs

Conrad Company's new assistant controller presented the following analysis of overhead costs in the Polishing Department.

Month	Direct Labor Hours	Overhead Cost
1	34,600	$4,400
2	37,000	6,100
3	25,000	5,400
4	32,000	4,000
5	38,000	5,800
6	42,000	6,200
7	49,000	7,800
8	48,000	6,600

"Estimated overhead costs will be $2,900 plus 10¢ per direct labor hour, based on inspection of the high–low observations in this data," the assistant claims.

Required:
Critically evaluate this analysis and its conclusions.

C 15–2   Linear Regression as a Forecasting Tool

An assistant in the Controller's Department of Sloan Manufacturing Company was assigned the task of developing a monthly overhead forecast for the Machining Department. Because the assistant understood a little statistics, he decided to use linear regression. After several trials, the following results were presented as being the best available:

$$y = 50,000 + 21.15x$$
$$r^2 = .982$$

where y = overhead in Machining Department and x = indirect labor hours in Machining Department.

The manager of the Machining Department was puzzled, because indirect labor was only an incidental item in her department. She had expected her overhead costs to be related to some other central activity.

Required:
Discuss the situation with respect to:
(a)   the validity or otherwise of the regression as a forecast basis.
(b)   the choice of the independent variable.
(c)   the manager's expectations.
(d)   the usefulness of the regression for forecasting in (1) incremental situations and (2) monthly situations.
(e)   what additional information would be useful.

C 15–3   Forecasting Maintenance and Repair Costs

An analysis of the cost of equipment maintenance and repairs in the operating divisions of Greene Company was requested in order to assist in forecasting those costs. The person assigned this task used linear regression, and chose daily activity levels in terms of machine hours of operation as the independent variable.

The results obtained from analysis of daily data for a three-month period were as follows:

$$y = 875.50 - 4.165x$$

where y = equipment maintenance and repairs costs and x = machine hours.

It was noted that r^2 equalled .785 for the set of data analyzed. However, in performing the analysis, data for eight days were omitted. These were judged to be unusually high costs (three times more than that for any other day) and were therefore not representative of the true relationship. The analyst also supported his conclusions by saying, "It was clear that maintenance costs were caused by machine usage."

Required:
Critically analyze this situation from the viewpoint of the technique used, assumptions made, and results achieved. If necessary, suggest an alternative approach.

C 15–4   Establishing Standard Overhead Rates

Walters Cabinet Company was studying its overhead costs with a view to (1) establishing a predetermined overhead rate and (2) forecasting overheads for future periods. As a result of examining two years' data and listing 26 different relationships, the quantity of raw materials scrap per month was found to support a regression equation with the highest r^2 term. Accordingly, it was proposed that the factory overhead allocation rate be based on materials scrap amounts and that total overhead cost also be forecast on the basis of materials scrap amounts.

Required:
Critically analyze the preceding case. Point out the possible shortcomings of the approach used. Identify the major data gathering problems in this type of situation.

C 15–5   Regression Analysis as a Forecasting Tool

Arlington Corporation has several manufacturing divisions, one of which is Terrace Division. The output of Terrace Division includes six different products which are produced with the use of common processing operations, equipment, and facilities. The only data available are the total manufacturing costs per month over an eight-month period for Terrace Division and the monthly output of each of the six products.

			Units of Output				Total
Month	P₁	P₂	P₃	P₄	P₅	P₆	Costs
1	220	800	400	900	400	400	$22,500
2	420	800	450	700	500	450	21,500
3	350	800	600	600	700	600	24,200
4	400	800	750	550	600	750	38,500
5	450	800	500	600	550	500	38,750
6	350	800	600	700	600	600	46,500
7	400	800	700	500	700	700	48,500
8	350	900	750	400	900	750	52,700

Further investigations show that:

1. Total manufacturing overhead of the division includes plant-wide items (rent, supervision, property taxes, and so on) that are allocated to each division each month on the basis of total units of output of the whole plant.

2. Some of the products use identical raw materials and processing operations in their initial stages of processing.

3. In the last three months, the price of one key input, used in four of the products, increased 100 percent due to a temporary shortage.

4. Wage rates paid to production workers increased 10 percent in the fourth month.

5. No costing procedures are presently available to trace either raw materials or direct labor costs directly to any of the six products being manufactured.

Required:

Evaluate this situation with regard to the potential usefulness of regression analysis as a means of forecasting costs (a) for the division and (b) for each individual product. Indicate any shortcomings that may be involved in such a procedure. If necessary, suggest alternative courses of action that may lead to a more reliable forecasting procedure.

Problems

P 15–1   Account Analysis—Cost Estimating

The following is a cost of goods manufactured statement for Tarry Company for 19X3. There were no beginning or ending work in process inventories.

Direct Materials		$350,000
Direct Labor		200,000
Overhead Costs:		
Depreciation	$50,000	
Utilities	15,000	
Indirect Labor	20,000	
Supervision	35,000	
Supplies	15,000	
Repairs	45,000	
Property Tax	20,000	200,000
		$750,000

During 19X2, 100,000 units were manufactured. A 25 percent increase in output is scheduled for 19X3. Materials and supplies prices will increase an average of 5 percent over 19X2, and on July 1, 19X3 all employees will receive a 10 percent pay raise. Inspection of overhead accounts showed that 75 percent of the 19X2 utilities costs varied with output. Repairs in 19X2 included $25,000 for the annual overhaul of machines; but of the remainder, 50 percent was for preventive maintenance and the rest related directly to the amount of equipment usage. Depreciation is on a straight-line basis and no additions are planned for either depreciable assets or property subject to property tax. Supplies and indirect labor costs both vary directly with output levels.

Required:

(a) Prepare an account analysis for 19X2 to separate manufacturing costs into fixed and variable categories.

(b) What forecast formula could be based on this analysis?

(c) Prepare a revised forecast for 19X3, taking into account activity level and input price changes.

(d) What is the revised forecast formula for 19X3?

(e) What are the advantages and limitations to this approach to forecasting?

P 15–2   Visual Fit—Cost Estimation by Inspection

Freeley Company is concerned about estimates of communications costs (telephone, telex, postage, and so on). The following table of costs and production levels for the past eight months was prepared.

Month	Communications Costs	Production Volume (units)
March	$14,700	38,000
April	19,200	46,000
May	21,000	50,000
June	11,700	34,000
July	17,850	42,000
August	16,500	60,000
September	18,600	43,000
October	24,600	56,000

Required:

(a) Prepare a scattergraph to plot all observed combinations of costs and production volume.

(b) Fit a linear curve to the plotted points. Estimate its slope and intercept.

(c) What is the budget formula for communications costs that would be derived in this way?

(d) Estimate costs for the following activity levels: 40,000, 60,000, 80,000.

(e) What problems are involved in part (d)?

(f) Discuss the limitations and advantages of this technique for estimating costs.

(g) What basic problem probably underlies the fact that there is a great deal of uncertainty in all of the answers proposed to the above questions?

P 15–3   Cost Estimation—High–Low Method

Boyd Corporation has a very equipment-intensive operation that requires considerable maintenance outlays. Preventive maintenance is scheduled to be performed once every 400 hours of operating machine time. This involves outlays of $750 per operation. In addition to these items, the following maintenance costs have been incurred over the past eight months:

Month	Maintenance Costs	Machine Hours
1..........	$3,500	3,400
2..........	4,600	4,800
3..........	4,450	4,600
4..........	3,600	3,600
5..........	3,850	4,000
6..........	3,750	3,900
7..........	4,120	4,200
8..........	4,250	4,400

Required:

(a) Use the high–low method to develop a forecast formula for maintenance costs, excluding preventive maintenance.

(b) Prepare forecasts for total maintenance costs for the following activity levels: (1) 3,500, (2) 4,000, (3) 4,500, and (4) 5,000.

(c) What problems may be encountered in part (b)?

(d) What are the limitations of this approach to cost estimation?

P 15–4   Visual Fit—High–Low Method—Comparative Analysis—
Evaluation of Estimates

Stewart Company is interested in developing cost estimates in its Packaging Department. For the last nine months of 19X5, the following cost and operating data were observed:

Month	Output (units)	Labor Costs	Other Packaging Costs
1	80,000	$28,000	$13,500
2	128,000	38,000	21,000
3	196,000	55,000	30,300
4	138,000	43,500	19,200
5	124,000	37,000	20,100
6	136,000	40,000	21,750
7	60,000	20,000	10,800
8	68,000	22,000	12,300
9	64,000	21,000	11,700

For the coming year, 19X6, a new union contract will be in effect which will increase labor costs by 20 percent. Also a new packaging machine will be installed which will increase fixed costs by $4,500 per month, but will reduce variable costs by 5¢ per unit.

Required:
(a) Use the high–low method to develop separate cost estimating functions for labor and for other packaging costs, based on the observed data.

(b) Prepare two scattergraphs and use the visual fit method to locate what appear to be representative cost estimating functions.

(c) Compare the results of parts (a) and (b) and comment.

(d) Use the results from part (a) to compare the other seven actual observations to the corresponding amounts that would be predicted by the high–low cost function.

(e) Revise the results in part (a) to reflect the changes for 19X6 with regard to wage rates and the new equipment.

(f) If output in January, 19X6 is forecast to be 75,000 units, what will the estimated costs be based on in the answer in part (e)?

P 15–5   Moving Average Forecasts

Downes Company maintains a monthly sales forecasting procedure based on the moving average of sales of its products over the previous four months. For the past twelve months, sales revenues were as follows:

Month	Sales	Month	Sales
January	$600,000	July	$700,000
February	640,000	August	740,000
March	580,000	September	620,000
April	660,000	October	740,000
May	700,000	November	660,000
June	600,000	December	840,000

Required:
(a) Assuming the company uses an unadjusted four-month moving average to forecast monthly sales, what would the forecasts have been for the months May to November?

(b) Compare the forecasts to the actual results. Comment.

(c) What are the advantages and disadvantages of this forecasting technique? In what sales situations would it be an appropriate method?

(d) Compute forecasts for the months July to November using (1) a six-month and (2) a two-month moving average. Comment on these forecasts after comparing them to actual sales.

P 15–6   Sales Forecasting—Moving Average—Seasonal Adjustments

Refer to the information in Problem 15–5. Downes Company has decided to use a three-month moving average as the basis of its sales forecast and to add an index to weight each month. For example, the index for the month of January would be the sales for January divided by the total sales for the whole year, and so on. Base this monthly index on the actual results for each month.

Required:
(a) What would the forecasts have been for the months April to December?

(b) Compare the forecasts to the actual results. Comment.

(c) Compare the answer to part (b) with the answer to Problem 15–5, part (b).

P 15–7   Cost Estimation—Linear Regression—Single Variable Model

Winslow Company has developed monthly data for total overhead costs and labor hours in its Manufacturing Division. The following table shows monthly results for 19X3.

Month	Labor Hours	Overhead	Month	Labor Hours	Overhead
January	24,000	$520,000	July	27,000	$640,000
February	24,200	540,000	August	26,900	632,000
March	25,500	564,000	September	25,400	608,000
April	26,100	596,000	October	24,900	592,000
May	26,400	624,000	November	26,000	598,000
June	26,800	632,000	December	25,700	568,000

Required:
(a) Use least squares regression to develop a cost estimating formula based on labor hours.
(b) Evaluate the statistical results of the regression. Interpret the regression equation from a forecasting point of view.
(c) Forecast labor hours for January and February, 19X4 are 26,500 and 29,500, respectively. Make forecasts of total overhead costs for those months. Comment.
(d) Revise your answers to part (c) so that the forecasts are in the form of a range which corresponds to 95 percent confidence intervals.
(e) What preconditions should be tested to assist in the validation of this forecasting procedure? Why?

P 15–8   Cost Estimation—Linear Regression—Single Variable— Alternative Bases

Adams Company is developing its overhead budget for 19X7. One item of concern is power and heating costs. For 19X6, the following monthly data were collected.

Month	Power and Heating Cost	Labor Hours	Machine Hours
January	$20,800	9,400	6,000
February	20,000	11,000	5,600
March	23,600	11,200	6,700
April	22,800	10,200	7,500
May	24,400	13,500	8,000
June	22,800	10,700	8,700
July	26,400	15,300	9,550
August	26,900	15,400	10,500
September	26,400	12,500	10,250
October	24,100	16,200	9,350
November	24,500	10,500	9,550
December	26,000	13,000	9,650

Required:
(a) Use linear regression to develop a forecasting formula for power and heating based on labor hours.
(b) Repeat part (a), using machine hours in place of labor hours.
(c) Evaluate the statistical results of the regressions in parts (a) and (b). Interpret the resulting forecasts.

(d) Which is the better forecasting relationship, labor hours or machine hours? Why?

(e) From the answers to parts (a) and (b), comment on the marginal cost of power and heating with regard to (1) labor hours and (2) machine hours. Express these in the form of 95 percent confidence intervals

P 15–9 Cost Estimation—Linear Regression—Single Variable— Alternative Basis

Soupee Sales Company is attempting to develop a forecast relationship for salespersons' travelling expenses. They believe that it is a mixed cost, with both fixed and variable components; but they wish to establish a sound basis for estimating the variable portion. For the previous year, 19X0, the following data were collected.

Month	Travelling Expenses	Orders Received (number)	Sales Revenue	Sales Visits (number)
January	$40,000	450	$ 730,000	615
February	44,000	465	850,000	630
March	36,000	390	680,000	570
April	48,000	470	930,000	690
May............	42,000	505	840,000	645
June	44,000	450	870,000	675
July	38,000	500	800,000	585
August	46,000	470	960,000	705
September......	50,000	550	1,020,000	720
October	48,000	580	820,000	735
November	44,000	480	840,000	660
December	48,000	510	1,000,000	690

Required:

(a) Prepare separate linear regression analyses for travelling expenses based on (1) orders received, (2) sales revenue, and (3) sales visits.

(b) Evaluate each of the sets of the statistical results of the regressions. Interpret the results as forecasts.

(c) Which basis would be best for forecasting travelling expenses in the future? Why? What will be the forecast for January, 19X2 if sales visits are estimated to be 700, orders received 500, and sales revenue $960,000? Express the answer in terms of a 95 percent confidence interval.

(d) Explain what might contribute to the superior forecasting results of the basis you have proposed and to the less favorable results of the other two.

(e) Discuss any data gathering and analysis problems that may influence the results in part (a).

P 15–10 Linear Regression—Time Series Forecasting of Sales

Jeremy Corporation has experienced the following annual sales revenues over a twelve-year period.

19X3	$ 600,000	19X9	$1,990,000
19X4	780,000	19Y0	2,250,000
19X5	1,140,000	19Y1	2,420,000
19X6	1,450,000	19Y2	2,660,000
19X7	1,400,000	19Y3	2,650,000
19X8	1,950,000	19Y4	2,640,000

Required:
(a) Use linear regression methods to derive a sales forecasting relationship based on time series analysis.
(b) Interpret the results for 19Y5, 19Y6, and 19Y7. Comment.
(c) Comment on the relative strengths and weaknesses of this method of forecasting.

P 15–11*   Cost Estimation—Multiple Regression—Comparison with Single Variable Results

Refer to Problem 15–9 and to the solutions in part (a) of that problem.

Required:
(a) Prepare regression analysis of travelling costs (1) on all three variables simultaneously, and (2) on each possible pair of variables.
(b) Evaluate the statistical results of the regressions in part (a) of this problem. Which of the four provides the best forecast basis for travelling costs?
(c) Compare the selection in part (b) of this problem to that in part (c) of Problem 15–9. Which of these should be used as the forecast basis and why?
(d) Explain the relative advantages and disadvantages of the analysis in part (a) of this problem to that in part (a) of Problem 15–9.

P 15–12*   Cost Estimation—Multiple Regression—Alternative Basis

Olympia Company has observed that its overhead costs are somewhat difficult to predict. It has assembled the following data for the last 10 quarters of 19X3–19X5.

Quarter		Materials Usage (pounds)	Labor Hours	Output (units)	Overhead Costs
19X3	3	54,000	5,000	70,000	$41,000
	4	96,900	6,120	85,000	43,800
19X4	1	88,800	5,760	80,000	41,600
	2	52,500	3,500	50,000	32,500
	3	59,400	3,840	60,000	33,200
	4	45,000	3,000	50,000	30,000
19X5	1	38,800	2,605	45,000	27,650
	2	30,000	8,080	40,000	26,400
	3	37,500	2,500	50,000	27,500
	4	36,450	2,250	45,000	27,200

Required:
(a) Use multiple and single variable linear regression analysis to find forecasting formulas for overhead costs based on all seven possible combinations of independent variables.
(b) Evaluate each statistical result. Interpret the results from a forecasting point of view.
(c) Which forecasting formula derived in part (a) is preferable?
(d) What information about marginal costs is contained in the answer to part (c)?
(e) What problems result from using (1) too many independent variables and (2) too few independent variables in a linear regression?
(f) Inspect the correlation matrix of the independent variables. Comment.

* Problems 15–11 through 15–15 cannot be solved without access to a computer system and a linear multiple regression program.

P 15–13* Cost Estimation—Multiple Regression—Alternative Bases

Grambling Repair Company has contracts to perform contracted maintenance and overhauls on equipment of various manufacturers. In the past, records of total hours worked by employees and number of machines serviced have been the only records kept. All maintenance workers are paid $12.50 per hour and variable overhead costs are estimated to be $7.50 per labor hour. The following data are available for the first ten months of 19X3:

| | | Machines Serviced | | | |
Month	Hours Worked	Drill Press	Turret Lathe	Cropping Machine	Total
1........	490	10	40	20	70
2........	530	20	40	30	90
3........	570	35	35	30	105
4........	510	25	30	30	85
5........	540	40	28	30	98
6........	530	50	20	30	100
7........	640	55	36	30	121
8........	640	75	28	30	133
9........	620	70	20	30	120
10........	630	65	30	35	130

Required:
(a) Use multiple regression analysis to develop forecasting formulas for total hours worked each month as a function of the number of each type of machine serviced.
(b) Evaluate the statistical result of the regression developed in part (a). Interpret the results from a forecasting point of view.
(c) Discuss any information contained in the regression results that concerns (1) fixed costs and (2) marginal costs.
(d) For months 11 and 12, the numbers of machines to be serviced will be as follows:

	11	12
Drill Press	75	72
Turret Lathe	25	27
Cropping Machine	35	40

Make forecasts of the number of hours of work required.
(e) Besides the one in part (c), what alternative regression equations might be useful in this situation? Discuss the possible shortcomings of the equation derived in part (a).

P 15–14* Cost Estimation—Multiple Regression—Use of Dummy Variables

Cooper Company has experienced problems in developing forecasts of overhead costs for one of its departments in which output levels fluctuate significantly from month to month. For the previous nine months, the following information was collected:

Month	Total Overhead Cost	Output (units)
1	$22,000	2,000
2	29,000	3,000
3	33,000	4,000
4	36,000	5,000
5	34,000	4,000
6	32,000	3,000
7	35,000	3,500
8	30,000	2,500
9	38,000	5,000

Required:

(a) Use linear regression to determine a forecast relationship between output and total overhead cost.

(b) Repeat your analysis in part (a), but include a dummy variable to represent the direction of the change in output levels from month to month. (Let the dummy variable equal 0 for months when the change is positive, and equal 1 in months when it is negative.)

(c) Evaluate the statistical results in parts (a) and (b).

(d) Explain the purpose served by use of the dummy variable. Does it provide a better forecast in this instance? Why or why not?

(e) Suggest some other dummy variables that might be examined in expectation of improving the forecast in this situation.

(f) If the expected output level in month ten is (1) 34,000 units and (2) 38,500 units, what will be the 95 percent confidence interval bounds on the forecast of overhead costs based on the results of part (b)?

P 15–15*   Sales Forecasting—Multiple Regression Analysis

Galaxy Can Company maintains a forecasting procedure to estimate the potential demand for its aluminum beer cans. The model used features the following variables:

x_1 = personal disposable income per year.
x_2 = number of sales outlets per 1,000 persons.
x_3 = percentage of population of legal drinking age.
x_4 = percentage of cans reclaimed at recycling centers.
x_5 = index of beer prices relative to other alcoholic beverage prices.

The following data were collected for the past eight years.

Year	x_1	x_2	x_3	x_4	x_5
1	$18,500	23	.64	.03	.85
2	21,750	24	.63	.08	.92
3	23,450	23	.62	.12	.73
4	24,350	27	.67	.11	.84
5	26,500	28	.69	.15	.95
6	28,700	25	.71	.18	1.03
7	29,200	28	.73	.19	1.05
8	31,300	26	.74	.22	1.21

The company has made a separate estimate of its share of the total beer can market. Beer can sales in the eight years were as follows:

Year	Volume	Year	Volume
1	3,900,000,000	5	4,875,000,000
2	4,000,000,000	6	4,915,000,000
3	4,250,000,000	7	4,960,000,000
4	4,300,000,000	8	4,985,000,000

For the ninth year, the company estimates its share of the total market will be 40 percent.

Required:

(a) Based on Galaxy's data, develop a forecasting equation for the total market demand for beer cans. Use multiple variable regression analysis.

(b) Interpret and evaluate statistically the results of the regression analysis.

(c) What is the company's forecast demand for the ninth year? Express it (1) as a mean expected value and (2) as a 95 percent confidence interval.

(d) Comment on the choice of independent variables used in the analysis. Suggest some additional independent variables.

(e) Comment on the correlation matrix. Does it indicate any problems? If so, how might they be resolved?

P 15–16 Cost Estimation—Alternative Forecasting Procedures

Over the past nine months, the Rocky Mountain Spring Company has experienced considerable fluctuation in activity levels and total manufacturing overhead costs. It has collected the following data:

Month	Labor Hours	Overhead Costs
1	24,500	$130,000
2	31,800	330,000
3	40,900	630,000
4	41,000	690,000
5	47,000	790,000
6	45,000	730,000
7	36,000	430,000
8	31,500	180,000
9	33,000	240,000

Required:

(a) Use a scattergraph to plot the preceding sets of observations. Use the visual fit method to establish a forecasting equation.

(b) Use the high–low method to find the equation of a forecasting formula for this set of data.

(c) Use linear regression analysis to determine the equation of the cost function for overhead costs with respect to labor hours.

(d) Compare the results of parts (a), (b) and (c). Comment on the results of the comparison. Which basis would you say is most relevant in this instance? Why?

(e) Discuss the relative merits of each of the three methods of developing forecast formulas.

(f) Explain how any of the three methods may be used in conjunction with the others.

P 15–17   Cost Estimation—Alternative Forecasting Procedures

Campbell Manufacturing Company has assembled the following data relating to the cost of factory supplies, labor hours, and machine hours of operation during 19X3.

Month	Factory Supplies	Labor Hours	Machine Hours
January	$ 9,800	6,900	2,700
February	11,200	7,600	2,750
March	10,000	7,000	2,500
April	10,800	7,400	2,400
May	9,800	7,900	2,250
June	9,400	7,700	2,100
July	14,000	9,000	1,000
August	7,600	6,800	1,650
September	6,800	6,400	1,700
October	7,200	7,600	1,750
November	12,000	10,000	2,000
December	4,000	7,500	2,500

Required:

(a) Prepare two separate scattergraphs to plot the observed values of supplies costs against (1) labor hours and (2) machine hours. Determine geometrically the parameters of linear functions that are derived from these graphs using the visual fit method.

(b) Use the high–low method to derive equations for the relationship between supplies cost and (1) labor hours and (2) machine hours.

(c) Use linear regression to derive equations for the relationship between supplies cost and (1) labor hours and (2) machine hours.

(d) Compare the results of the estimating methods used in parts (a), (b), and (c). Comment on any significant relationship.

(e) Recommend the most appropriate basis and method for forecasting supplies costs. Support your choice.

(f) For January, 19X4, it is estimated that labor hours will be 8,000 and machine hours 3,000. Use the method selected in part (e) to make as full and detailed a forecast of supplies cost as possible.

P 15–18   Linear Regression—Multiple Variable Analysis—Interpretation of Results

Chester Company has used regression analysis to develop a forecast relationship for monthly manufacturing overhead costs. The basis used was the following.

$$\text{Manufacturing Overhead} = a + b_1x_1 + b_2x_2 + b_3x_3 + b_4x_4 + b_5x_5$$

where:

$x_1 =$ machine hours
$x_2 =$ labor hours
$x_3 =$ direct materials usage
$x_4 =$ scrap recovery
$x_5 =$ dummy variable for direction of monthly output change
(0 = increase, 1 = decrease)

Based on twelve months of data, the statistical results of the analysis were as follows:

Variable	Regression Coefficient	Standard Error	t-Statistic
x_1	17.00	2.00	8.5
x_2	20.00	4.00	5.0
x_3	3.00	0.50	6.0
x_4	−0.25	0.01	−25.0
x_5	350.00	50.00	7.0
Intercept	2,500.00	1,000.00	2.5
$r^2 = .996$			
$S_e = 500$			

Correlation Matrix (r)				
	x_2	x_3	x_4	x_5
x_1	.675	.575	−.125	.275
x_2		.895	−.225	.315
x_3			−.925	.245
x_4				−.155

Required:
(a) Interpret and evaluate the results of the regression as presented.
(b) What are the positive aspects of the regression results? What are the questionable aspects of the results?
(c) How might the problems noted in part (b) be dealt with?
(d) To what valid forecasting use could the original regression results be put?
(e) For what forecasting purposes should the original regression results not be used?
(f) Explain how, after the corrections suggested in part (c) are made, the resulting regression may give better results than the original.

P 15–19 Cash Flow Forecasting—Combined Analysis—Linear Regression, Simple Constant Growth, and Time Series Methods

Lucas Merchandising Company has developed a technique for estimating its short-term cash flow position, based on the following relationships:

(1) Sales are increasing at the rate of 1 percent per month.
(2) All sales are on credit and customers pay 25 percent of their accounts in the month of sale and 75 percent in the following month.

(3) Cost of sales are all variable and amount to 40 percent of sales revenue.

(4) A fixed inventory of $250,000 (at purchase prices) is always carried.

(5) Payments for inventory purchases are made 50 percent in the month of purchase and 50 percent in the month thereafter.

(6) Other expenditures for marketing and administrative items are estimated from the following regression based on forecast monthly sales.

$$y_t = 140,000 + .325\, x_t$$

where x_t = forecast sales in month t, and y_t = marketing and administrative costs. The regression also reveals the following statistical data: $r^2 = .924$, $s_e = 12,500$, and $s_b = .025$. The regression was based on observations of data for 16 months. For May of 19X3, sales totalled $1,500,000.

Required:

(a) Forecast the cash inflows for the months of June and July of 19X3. For marketing and administrative costs, use the mean value of the regression estimate.

(b) Revise your answer to (a) so that it is in the form of range estimates, based on a 95 percent confidence interval on the amounts of marketing and administrative costs.

(c) Assume that the company wishes to use simple, one-variable linear regression to forecast (1) sales, (2) cash collections from customers and (3) cash paid to suppliers. Suggest some independent variables that might logically be used in those three regressions. Explain your choices.

(d) Comment on the statistical results of the regression presently used for marketing and administrative costs.

(e) Discuss what might be gained by using regression for all four variables in the forecast, as well as the problems that might arise.

P 15–20   Cost Estimating—Evaluation and Interpretation of Results of Alternative Regression Formulations

Oriole Company is studying the results of analysis of the overhead costs in its Metal Stamping Division. Using least squares regression analysis, the following results have been obtained, based on observations for the previous 24 weeks.

Dependent Variable	*Independent Variables*
1. Overhead Costs	2. Machine Hours
	3. Number of Jobs Processed
	4. Usage of Supplies (pounds)

Regression Results

Independent Variable	Regression Coefficient	Standard Error	*t* Value	r^2	Standard Error of Estimate
A. 2	21.95	4.45	4.93	.66	3,293
a	32,640	4,840	6.74		
B. 3	346.72	185.32	1.87	.10	7,436
a	72,876	22,532	3.23		

Regression Results

Independent Variable		Regression Coefficient	Standard Error	t Value	r²	Standard Error of Estimate
C.	4	21.73	6.55	3.32	.45	4,154
	a	37,453	5,980	6.26		
D.	2	18.13	7.32	2.48	.51	4,372
	3	305.16	104.13	2.18		
	a	62,137	8,347	7.44		
E.	2	17.85	3.72	4.80	.78	2,524
	4	15.01	4.29	3.50		
	a	25,213	4,572	5.51		
F.	3	321.47	137.24	2.34	.42	3,579
	4	18.81	6.13	3.07		
	a	47,325	6,215	7.6		
G.	2	17.11	3.75	4.56	.78	2,537
	3	313.87	124.41	2.52		
	4	13.21	14.52	.91		
	a	42,037	4,572	5.26		

Correlation Matrix (r)				
	1	2	3	4
1.	1.000	.813	.314	.672
2.		1.000	.367	.243
3.			1.000	.115
4.				1.000

Required:

(a) Evaluate the seven separate sets of regression analysis results. Give reasons for those eliminated in arriving at a choice of the most appropriate basis for estimating overhead costs in the Metal Stamping Division.

(b) Interpret each component item of the statistical results of the regression formulation you have chosen as the most appropriate.

(c) For what particular forecasting purpose (or purposes) will these regression results be useful? For what forecasting purposes might they be unreliable, misleading or inappropriate? Why?

P 15–21 Cost Estimation—Evaluation and Interpretation of Results of Alternative Regression Formulations

Blyleven Company has analyzed data pertaining to its overhead costs and the three products that it manufactures. The results of this are the following regression analyses, based on data for the preceding twelve months.

Dependent Variable
1. Manufacturing Overhead

Independent Variables
2. Units of Production—D
3. Units of Production—E
4. Units of Production—F

Regression Results

Independent Variable	Regression Coefficient	Standard Error	*t* Value	r^2	Standard Error of Estimate
A. 2	327.59	300.38	1.09	0.239	6,437.25
a	7,229.38	2,839.05	2.55		
B. 3	102.70	9.23	11.13	0.937	527.86
a	514.67	239.02	1.76		
C. 4	88.46	87.23	1.01	0.137	8,376.26
a	1,403.92	4,127.06	0.34		
D. 2	21.75	74.36	0.29	0.813	725.86
3	95.67	9.87	9.72		
a	427.43	971.62	0.44		
E. 2	−174.37	175.21	−1.00	0.145	7,743.29
4	61.25	67.31	0.91		
a	3,147.27	1,742.43	1.81		
F. 3	97.26	8.27	11.76	0.874	1,011.72
4	21.32	17.43	1.22		
a	675.43	721.36	0.94		
G. 2	−32.47	257.82	−0.13	0.938	499.55
3	119.72	11.16	10.73		
4	−20.31	47.31	−0.43		
a	973.43	1,943.25	0.50		

Correlation Matrix (*r*)

	1	2	3	4
1	1.000	−0.489	0.968	0.370
2		1.000	−0.387	−0.500
3			1.000	0.416
4				1.000

A sampling of monthly data for the third and ninth months showed the following:

Month	Overhead	Product D	Product E	Product F
3	$76,855	82	737	17
9	$87,989	14	857	46

Required:
(a) Evaluate the seven separate sets of regression analysis results. Give reasons for those eliminated in arriving at a choice of the most appropriate basis for estimating total overhead for the company.

(b) Interpret each component item of the statistical results of the regression formulation you have chosen as the most appropriate.

(c) Comment on how the sample data for the third and ninth months support (or do not support) your choice of the best regression formulation.

(d) For what particular forecasting purpose (or purposes) will these regression results be (1) useful and (2) misleading or unreliable?

(e) Comment on the problems of forecasting overheads for a month during which total output is likely to be (1) 50 percent *greater* than any previous month's total, and (2) 60 percent *lower* than any previous month's total?

16

ACCOUNTING INFORMATION FOR DECISION MAKING UNDER UNCERTAINTY

LEARNING OBJECTIVES

After studying Chapter 16, you should be able to:

1. Distinguish between deterministic and probabilistic decision techniques and describe the advantages of the latter.
2. Given a probability distribution over the outcomes of a proposed action, calculate the expected value of each outcome.
3. Distinguish between the expected value of monetary outcomes and the expected value of utility.
4. Given probability distributions, use heuristic decision rules to select among actions according to
   a. the most likely outcome.
   b. the least favorable outcome.
   c. the most favorable outcome.
5. Calculate the standard deviation and coefficient of variation and use these as decision criteria in choosing among alternative actions.
6. Use discrete probability forecasts of sales volume and other budget variables for decision purposes.
7. Use continuous probability forecasts of sales volume and other budget variables for decision purposes.
8. Incorporate considerations of uncertainty into cost–volume–profit calculations of breakeven quantity and target profit sales level.
9. Use a decision tree approach to choose among alternative actions.
10. Use a game theory matrix to choose among alternative actions.
11. Calculate the gross benefits and the net value of information.

DETERMINISTIC OR PROBABILISTIC DECISION TECHNIQUES?

The decision techniques described in previous chapters have been almost exclusively *deterministic*. That is, they were formulated in terms of variables and relationships with fixed values which guaranteed certain solutions for each particular application. In cost–volume–profit problems, the linear, one-product model was based on given sales prices, fixed costs, and variable costs, and specified a single solution for the breakeven point or target profit. Budgeting models developed unique cost functions with specific fixed and variable components. Sales forecasts and cash flow forecasts produced point estimates of future activity. Incremental analysis of short-run decision situations provided single-valued measures of the incremental effects of each decision.

In each case, decision making was simplified by the assumptions that all relationships remained constant during the period of analysis and that all decision variables could be expressed as single values. But the apparent precision of point estimates involved in these situations is deceptive. There will always be some uncertainty regarding most components of any decision situation—the variables in decision models, their values and interrelationships. **Probabilistic decision models** are needed to deal with these uncertainties. Such decision models can be formulated to incorporate uncertainty and provide for the possible variability of outcomes due to that uncertainty. Probabilistic decision techniques and their implications for accounting information and control systems are described in this chapter.

EXPECTED VALUE DECISION MODELS

One of the simplest and most common ways of dealing with uncertainty involves the use of **expected values.** To compute the expected value of an action, the set of all possible outcomes and their associated probabilities of occurrence must be known. The expected value is then calculated as the sum of the products of the probability of each outcome multiplied by the payoff value of each outcome:

$$E(X) = \sum_i p_i x_i$$

Here p_i = probability of outcome i, x_i = payoff value of outcome i, and $E(X)$ = expected value.

Example: Figure 16–1 shows the quantity of raw materials consumed per production batch in Hearst Corporation's Process A.

FIGURE 16–1

Hearst Corporation
Materials Consumed per Production Batch

Process A		
Payoff Value (x_i)	Probability (p_i)	Expected Value $(p_i x_i)$
80 lbs.	.1	8.0
85 lbs.	.2	17.0
90 lbs.	.2	18.0
95 lbs.	.3	28.5
100 lbs.	.1	10.0
105 lbs.	.1	10.5

$$E(X) = \sum_i p_i x_i = 92.0$$

The *expected* (mean or average) *value* of the quantity of materials consumed in this process is 92.0 pounds. This assumes that enough batches will be manufactured to allow the stated distribution of possible outcomes to take effect and that the specified probabilities and payoff values will continue in effect.

Both these conditions are necessary for the expected value of 92.0 pounds to have *general* decision relevance. For example, it would be incorrect to predict that the materials consumed in the *next* production batch will weigh 92.0 pounds. Moreover, assuming that the probability distribution continues as specified, there is zero probability that the weight of materials consumed in any single production batch will *exactly* equal 92.0 pounds. This means that expected values will not be useful in all prediction situations.

USING EXPECTED VALUES AS DECISION CRITERIA

Expected value analysis assumes that all actions for which monetary outcomes have the same expected value are equally desirable, regardless of the composition of their probability distributions and the range of values of their possible outcomes. Therefore the decision maker whose choices are based solely on the expected values of monetary outcomes is said to be **risk neutral**.

For example, consider the following three alternative actions, A, B, and C:

Action	Values of Outcomes	Probability of Outcomes	Expected Value of Outcome
A	$ 500	1.0	$ 500
B	$1,000	0.5	$ 500
	$ 0	0.5	0
			$ 500
C	$5,000	0.4	$2,000
	($2,500)	0.6	(1,500)
			$ 500

All three actions have expected values of $500, which is the mean value of possible monetary outcomes in each of the probability distributions. A decision maker who responds only to these expected values will not prefer any of the three alternatives. The decision maker's risk neutrality is evidenced by the fact that he gives no explicit consideration to the absence of risk in alternative A, which pays a sure return of $500, as compared to the presence of risk in alternative C, with which he has a 60 percent chance of losing $2,500 and only a 40 percent chance of gaining a $5,000 return.

To emphasize this point with a more extreme example, suppose a decision maker must choose between (1) an action that assumes a sure return of $1,000,000 and (2) an action the possible outcomes of which are a $10,000,000 return with a probability of 25 percent, and a loss of $2,000,000 with a probability of 75 percent. The expected value of each alternative is $1,000,000, calculated as follows:

(1) $1,000,000 \times 1.0 = $1,000,000
(2)   ($10,000,000 \times .25) + (-$2,000,000 \times .75) = $1,000,000

To the risk neutral decision maker, both alternatives are equally attractive. His basis for judgment disregards the fact that the second alternative is obviously much more risky than the first because it includes a 75 percent chance of a $2,000,000 loss, whereas the first alternative assures him of a $1,000,000 profit.

EXPECTED VALUE OF MONETARY OUTCOMES AND EXPECTED VALUE OF UTILITY

The preceding discussion assumed that decision makers based their decisions entirely on the expected value of monetary outcomes. However, decision makers often make choices which reflect their personal preferences and which are different from the choices that would result solely from the use of expected monetary value analysis. In such cases, decision makers may still behave consistently if they respond to the expected utility of the outcomes of alternatives. **Expected utility** can include not only monetary outcomes, but factors such as the range in the possible values of different outcomes, the risk associated with the distribution of expected outcomes, and other nonmonetary considerations.

Figure 16–2 shows a linear utility function in which the expected utility of outcomes is directly proportional to the *expected value* of the monetary outcomes of actions over the entire range of monetary amounts for all possible actions, regardless of their risks. This type of utility function is associated with the behavior of risk neutral decision makers who respond only to expected monetary value amounts.

The linear behavior of the utility function in Figure 16–2 is its important feature. To simplify the presentation, it is assumed that the utility of a zero monetary outcome is also zero. This is not always true. Some decision makers may associate a negative or positive amount of utility with a zero monetary outcome.

Figure 16–3 shows two types of nonlinear utility functions. Function U_2 reflects the tendency of **risk seeking decision makers** to place a *higher* value on the expected utility of an action than would risk neutral decision makers.

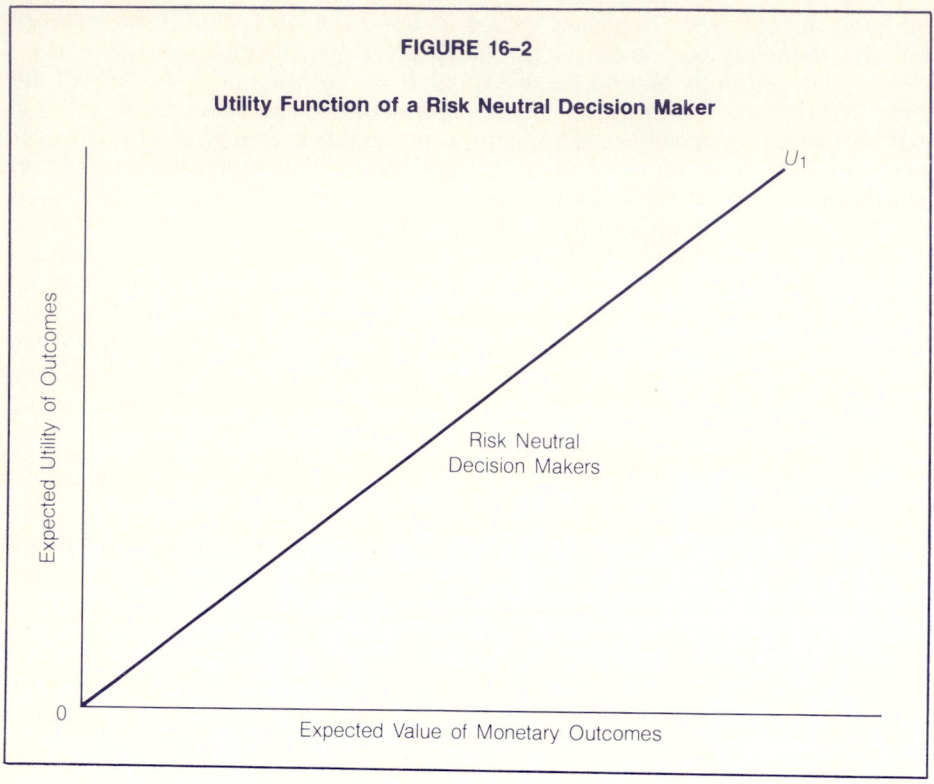

FIGURE 16–2

Utility Function of a Risk Neutral Decision Maker

Expected Utility of Outcomes

U_1

Risk Neutral
Decision Makers

0

Expected Value of Monetary Outcomes

-unction U_3 reflects the tendency of **risk averse decision makers** to place a *lower* value on the expected utility of an action than would risk neutral decision makers.

Notice that the concave (downward sloping) utility function of the risk averse decision maker corresponds to the concept of diminishing marginal utility. The higher the monetary payoffs to such a risk averse decision maker, the less per unit he values those payoffs.

Example: The sales manager of Tully Company is considering two new products, only one of which can be added to the firm's product line. Product X is a sure seller. It is certain that 20,000 units of Product X (the firm's maximum capacity) can be manufactured and sold each month, with a contribution margin of $5 per unit. Product Y, with a contribution margin of $10 per unit, is potentially more profitable. However, there is uncertainty about its marketability, and the following sales forecast has been prepared:

Sales of Y	Probability
5,000	.25
10,000	.50
15,000	.25

With fixed costs at $60,000 per month, Product X will generate a certain profit contribution of $40,000 [(20,000 @ $5) − $60,000]. Product Y will also

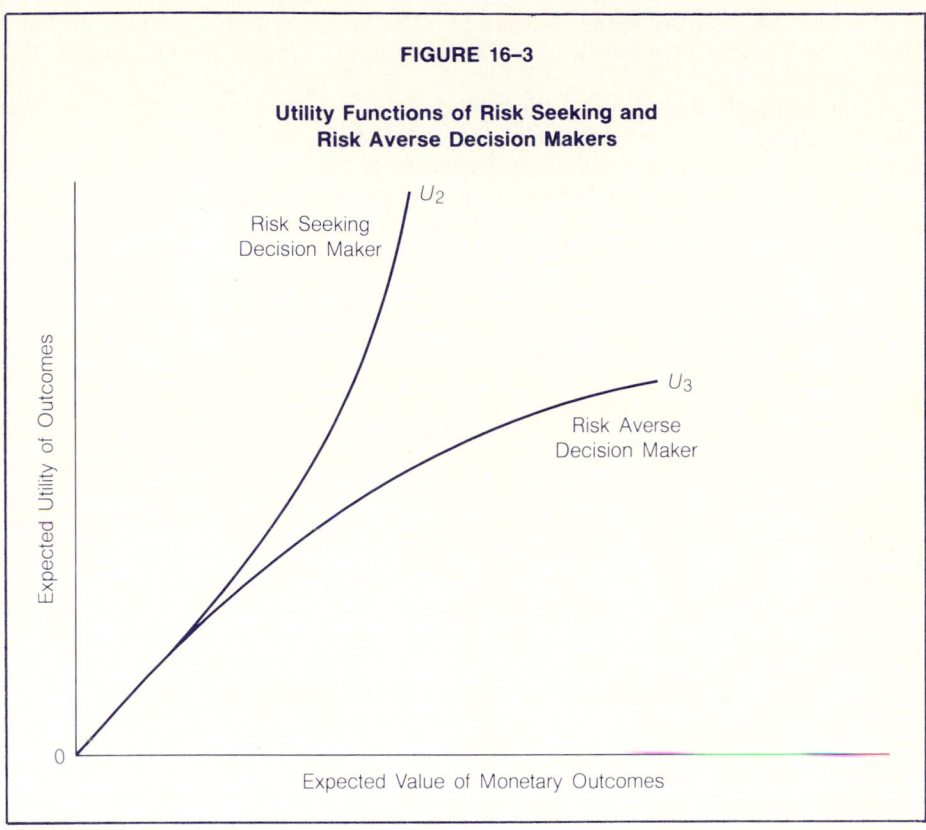

FIGURE 16–3

**Utility Functions of Risk Seeking and
Risk Averse Decision Makers**

produce an expected value profit contribution of $40,000, as shown in Figure 16–4.

Risk neutral decision makers are apt to consider the two products equally desirable, because both have an expected value profit contribution of $40,000. Risk averse decision makers may prefer Product X with its guaranteed profit contribution of $40,000. They will seek to avoid the 25 percent probability of

FIGURE 16–4

Tully Company
Product Y: Expected Value Profit Contribution

Sales	Contri-bution Margin	Fixed Cost	Profit Contri-bution	Proba-bility	Expected Value
5,000	$ 50,000	$60,000	($10,000)	.25	($ 2,500)
10,000	100,000	60,000	40,000	.50	20,000
15,000	150,000	60,000	90,000	.25	22,500
				$E(PC) =$	$40,000

a $10,000 loss. Risk seekers may prefer Product Y. They will tend to be attracted by the 25 percent probability of a $90,000 profit, despite the possibility of a $10,000 loss.

This suggests that utility functions should be developed separately for each decision maker, to take account of the wide variety of factors that appear to influence each person's decision preferences. In addition to expected monetary outcomes, these factors include attitude toward risk, intensity of profit motive, and ability to absorb losses. Unique solutions can be derived for risk neutral decision makers; their utility functions are linearly proportional to expected values. But one can only generalize about the tendencies of risk averse and risk seeking decision makers unless their utility functions can be definitely established. Instead of maximizing or minimizing the *expected values* of monetary outcomes, they seek to maximize or minimize *expected utility* in relation to their individual utility preference functions.

Risk averse and risk seeking patterns of decision making behavior are likely when potential gains and losses are large, or when the decision is nonroutine and represents a situation of a type not previously experienced. In large organizations, decision making tends to be routinized and there is a greater tendency to respect the expected value criteria and to be risk neutral. This is accompanied by the tendency to observe a linear utility function, even to the extent of contradicting the economic concept of diminishing marginal returns.

HEURISTIC DECISION RULES

In reacting to decision criteria other than the expected monetary value of outcomes, decision makers often use **heuristic decision rules** that approximate the value systems of risk seeking or risk averse decision makers. These heuristics include:

1. Most likely outcomes
2. Least favorable outcomes (*minimax* or *maximin*)
3. Most favorable outcome (*maximax*)

A *most likely outcome* criterion involves choosing actions in which the outcome with the highest probability of occurring is the most favorable. This strategy is often used for one-of-a-kind decisions. In such cases, the decision maker displays risk averse behavior by choosing on the basis of the greatest likelihood of a single occurrence. The race track bettor who, on the assumption that they are the most likely to win, always bets on favorites is displaying this type of behavior. Quite often the most likely outcome will be the same as the expected value outcome, if the probability distribution is symmetrical or if the most likely outcome dominates the other alternatives.

The **minimax** decision criterion involves choosing the action for which the worst possible outcome is the least unfavorable of those available to the decision maker. Similarly, the **maximin** decision criterion involves choosing the action for which the least favorable outcome is the best available. In other words, these two options involve selecting the best of the worst possible outcomes or the worst of the best possible outcomes. These strategies also represent

FIGURE 16–5

Hearst Corporation
Materials Consumed per Production Batch

Process A			Process B			Process C		
Quantity	Probability	$p_i x_i$	Quantity	Probability	$p_i x_i$	Quantity	Probability	$p_i x_i$
80	.1	8.0	75	.1	7.5	85	.1	8.5
85	.2	17.0	80	.1	8.0	90	.4	36.0
90	.2	18.0	85	.1	8.5	95	.3	28.5
95	.3	28.5	90	.2	18.0	100	.2	20.0
100	.1	10.0	95	.3	28.5			
105	.1	10.5	110	.2	22.0			
	$E(X) = 92.0$			$E(X) = 92.5$			$E(X) = 93.0$	

pessimistic or risk averse behavior; they are often used when complete and accurate information is not available about the probability distribution applicable to outcomes.

The **maximax** criterion involves choosing the best of the most favorable outcomes. This is an extreme form of risk seeking behavior because the decision maker chooses the action for which the best possible individual outcome is also the most favorable.

Example: The following is an extension of the Hearst Corporation example introduced previously. In addition to the original Process A, the company is considering adding two other processes, B and C. Materials usage per production batch would then be distributed as shown in Figure 16–5. The possible decision criteria are:

	A	B	C
Expected Value	92.0	92.5	93.0
Most Likely Outcome	95.0	95.0	90.0
Least Favorable Outcome	105.0	110.0	100.0
Most Favorable Outcome	80.0	75.0	85.0

If the goal is to minimize materials usage, a decision maker using any of these four criteria would choose the boxed values corresponding to the strategy he prefers. The *expected value strategy* indicates that Process A will make the most economical use of materials. A decision based on expected value will give demonstrably superior long-run results—that is, it will ensure that a long-run average materials usage of 92.0 pounds per batch will be achieved in Process A. However, depending on their risk preferences, decision makers might prefer any of the other three options.

1. *Most Likely Outcome* A cautious decision maker chooses Process C, because the most economical of the most likely outcomes for a single production run will be the use of 90 pounds of material.

2. *Minimax Strategy*   A cautious decision maker selects Process C in order to ensure that no more than 100 pounds of material will ever be used to produce a batch of output.
3. *Maximax Strategy*   An adventurous decision maker chooses Process B, hoping for the most favorable possible outcome—to produce a batch of output using only 75 pounds of material.

DISPERSION OF OUTCOMES AS DECISION CRITERIA

In addition to the expected value and other individual values derived from probability distributions, the amount of *dispersion* in values of outcomes may also be used as a decision criterion. The outcomes of two alternative actions may have identical expected values, but the dispersion (or spread) of the individual payoffs under each alternative may be quite different. This becomes particularly important when the decision situation is nonrecurring or infrequent. In such cases, a wide variability of possible outcomes becomes an additional risk to be avoided if possible.

STANDARD DEVIATION

The amount of dispersion in an action's possible outcomes can be expressed in terms of the **standard deviation.** This is calculated as the square root of the sum of the products of the probability of each outcome and the squared deviation of each outcome from the value of the average outcome. It is written:

$$\sigma = \sqrt{\sum_i p_i \, (x_i - \bar{x})^2}$$

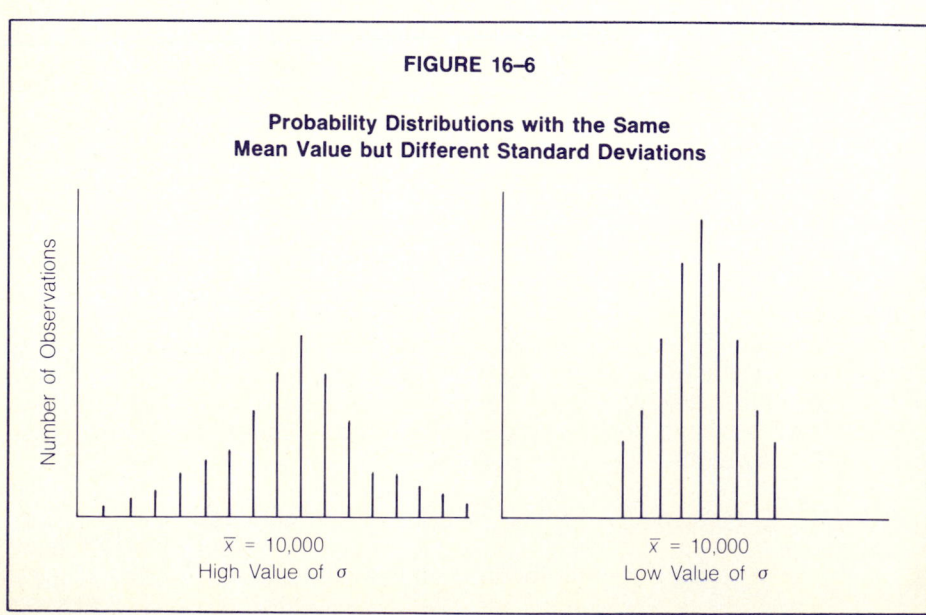

FIGURE 16–6

Probability Distributions with the Same Mean Value but Different Standard Deviations

Number of Observations

$\bar{x} = 10{,}000$
High Value of σ

$\bar{x} = 10{,}000$
Low Value of σ

Figure 16–6 illustrates two probability distributions with the same mean value ($\bar{x} = 10,000$). The distribution on the left has a larger standard deviation ($\sigma = 2,000$), which is evidenced graphically by the greater dispersion or variability in the values of possible outcomes. The distribution on the right has a smaller standard deviation ($\sigma = 400$), which is reflected in the tighter distribution and smaller variability in the values of its possible outcomes.

The standard deviation by itself is not always a reliable basis for comparing and evaluating alternative actions. It should be considered together with other measurements of outcomes, especially the mean or expected value. Suppose a manager must choose between two projects, each with a standard deviation of $1,000, but one of which has an expected value of $25,000, while the other has an expected value of $500. Clearly, the fact that the standard deviations are identical is not an appropriate basis for concluding that the two projects are equally desirable.

COEFFICIENTS OF VARIATION

Sometimes it is more revealing to measure the *relative dispersion* rather than the *total dispersion* of the outcomes of an action. This can be done by use of the **coefficient of variation,** which is equal to the ratio of the standard deviation to the expected value: ($\sigma \div \bar{x}$).

This measure gives some indication of the *relative risk* associated with the possible outcomes of a particular action. Events with high coefficients of variation have relatively higher degrees of risk. Events with low coefficients of variation involve relatively less risk. The extreme case is an outcome that is certain to occur and therefore has a zero value for both its standard deviation and its coefficient of variation.

Example: Shogun Corporation is considering two production configurations, M and N. The possible cost distributions per 1,000 units processed, the *expected value* of cost per 1,000 units, the *standard deviation,* and the *coefficient of variation* are derived in Figure 16–7.

Production configurations M and N have the same expected value of cost per 1,000 units processed ($\bar{x} = \$1,000$). However, alternative N may be preferred because of its lower risk of extreme cost performance, as evidenced by its lower standard deviation ($89.44 < 252.98), and more importantly, its lower coefficient of variation (.08944 < .25298).

The expected value measures and the relative dispersion measures often produce conflicting results. A certain alternative may have a favorable mean value, but a comparatively large standard deviation and coefficient of variation. Figure 16–8 illustrates this situation. The distribution of the payoffs X_1 is closely centered around the mean value $E(X_1)$, whereas the distribution of the payoffs X_2 is more widely dispersed around the higher valued mean, $E(X_2)$.

Some risk averse decision makers may prefer the greater certainty of the narrow range of outcomes offered by the X_1 alternative, together with a lower probability of less favorable returns at the bottom of the scale, even though the expected value of X_1 is less than that of X_2. Risk seeking decision makers and those who are responsive to expected value criteria will tend to choose X_2, with its greater probability of higher returns at the top of the scale and its higher mean value.

FIGURE 16-7

Shogun Corporation
Coefficients of Variation

Alternative M			Alternative N		
Cost per 1,000	Proba- bility	Expected Value	Cost per 1,000	Proba- bility	Expected Value
$ 600	.15	$ 90	$ 900	.2	$ 180
800	.2	160	1,000	.6	600
1,000	.3	300	1,100	.2	220
1,200	.2	240	—	—	—
1,400	.15	210	—	—	—
	$\bar{X}=$	$1,000		$\bar{X}=$	$1,000

$(x_i - \bar{x})$	$p_i(x_i - \bar{x})^2$	Expected Value	$(x_i - \bar{x})$	$p_i(x_i - \bar{x})^2$	Expected Value
(600 − 1,000)	.15 (160,000)	$24,000	(900 − 1,000)	.2 (20,000)	$4,000
(800 − 1,000)	.2 (40,000)	8,000	(1,000 − 1,000)	.6 (0)	–0–
(1,000 − 1,000)	.3 (0)	–0–	(1,100 − 1,000)	.2 (20,000)	4,000
(1,200 − 1,000)	.2 (40,000)	8,000	—	—	—
(1,400 − 1,000)	.15 (160,000)	24,000	—	—	—
	$\sigma^2 =$	$64,000		$\sigma^2 =$	$8,000
	$\sigma =$	$252.98		$\sigma =$	$89.44

$$\text{Coefficient of Variation} = \frac{\sigma}{\bar{X}} = \frac{\$252.98}{\$1,000} = .25298$$

$$\text{Coefficient of Variation} = \frac{\sigma}{\bar{X}} = \frac{\$89.44}{\$1,000} = .08944$$

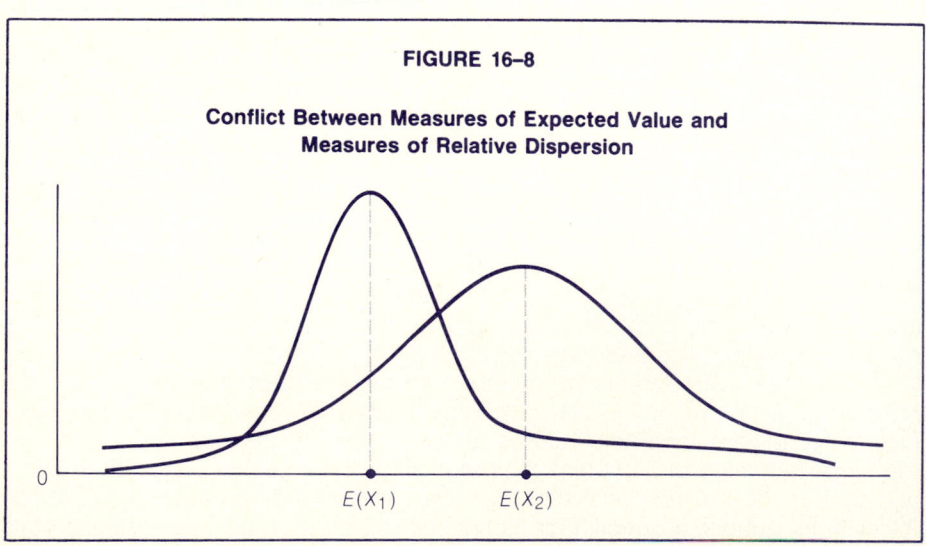

FIGURE 16-8

Conflict Between Measures of Expected Value and Measures of Relative Dispersion

$E(X_1)$ $E(X_2)$

INCORPORATING UNCERTAINTY INTO ACCOUNTING PLANNING AND CONTROL TECHNIQUES

The preceding general discussion of decision making under uncertainty has several specific accounting applications. For example, *budgeting* and *cost-volume-profit analysis,* are areas in which it is necessary to contend with uncertainty.

The earlier discussion of these accounting techniques presented them from an essentially deterministic viewpoint. In Chapter 7, *budgetary planning* was shown to involve the preparation of a single, static set of financial statements, based on one value of a key planning variable, usually sales. There was no suggestion that variations might occur in the forecast sales volume, in the values of any other budgetary variables (input prices, production specifications), or in any of the budget relationships (cost functions, cash flow functions).

Similarly, the discussion of *cost-volume-profit analysis* in Chapter 8 assumed constant values for the sales price, fixed costs, unit variable costs, capacity ranges, and sales demand. Sensitivity analysis was introduced, but only in terms of discrete changes that were certain to occur in one or more of the variables.

PROBABILISTIC BUDGETS: UNSPECIFIED DISTRIBUTION FUNCTION

The simplest departure from these deterministic, point estimate planning and control reports involves allowing for variations in the values of one or more planning variables. This might begin with the sales forecast because it is central to the budgetary process. Several alternative sales forecasts could be developed, perhaps anticipating the upper and lower bounds of a range of possible sales volumes and thereby conveying a sense of what the best and worst outcomes might be.

Example: Hartell Company projects that sales volume will be somewhere between 200,000 and 300,000 units during the coming year. The company's product sells for $10 per unit. Variable costs are $6 per unit and fixed costs are $500,000 per year. Budgeted income statements have been prepared to show expected profits under the highest and lowest sales volume forecast.

Figure 16–9 forecasts that net income will be between $300,000 and $700,000, assuming that sales volume is within the projected range of 200,000 to 300,000 units.

Going one step further, a three-level sales forecast might be prepared: *high* (optimistic), *most likely* (realistic), and *low* (pessimistic). This approach fosters awareness of the *range* of likely outcomes. When operating and cash flow budgets are based on these three different forecasts, the effect of possible sales volume variations on other budget variables can be observed.

Example: Hartell Company forecasts its sales for the coming year according to the following categories:

Optimistic	300,000 units
Most Likely	250,000 units
Pessimistic	200,000 units

FIGURE 16–9

Hartell Corporation
Budgeted Income Statements Based on Range of
Projected Sales for 19X8

	Upper Bound	Lower Bound
Unit Sales Volume	300,000	200,000
Sales ($10 per Unit)	$3,000,000	$2,000,000
Variable Costs ($6 per Unit)	$1,800,000	$1,200,000
Fixed Costs	500,000	500,000
Total Costs	$2,300,000	$1,700,000
Net Income	$ 700,000	$ 300,000

Based on these sales forecasts, Figure 16–10 shows the likely range of sales revenues, total costs, and net income for the three anticipated sales levels. These three sets of measurements correspond to the *most favorable outcome, most likely outcome,* and *least favorable outcome* described in the earlier sections on decision making under uncertainty.

PROBABILISTIC BUDGETS: DISCRETE PROBABILITY DISTRIBUTION FUNCTION

The next step in probabilistic budgeting is to estimate the probability that different values of planning variables will occur. This can be done by subjectively assessing the discrete probability that each of a limited number of possible values will occur—for example, the three sales volume forecasts in Figure 16–10.

FIGURE 16–10

Hartell Company
Budgeted Income Statements Based on
Three-Level Sales Forecast for 19X8

	Optimistic	Most Likely	Pessimistic
Unit Sales Volume	300,000	250,000	200,000
Sales ($10)	$3,000,000	$2,500,000	$2,000,000
Variable Costs ($6)	$1,800,000	$1,500,000	$1,200,000
Fixed Costs	500,000	500,000	500,000
	$2,300,000	$2,000,000	$1,700,000
Net Income	$ 700,000	$ 500,000	$ 300,000

FIGURE 16–11

Hartell Company
Budgeted Income Statement Based on
Expected Value of Forecast Sales for 19X8

Sales (247,500 units @ $10)		$2,475,000
Variable Costs (247,500 units @ $6)	$1,485,000	
Fixed Costs	500,000	1,985,000
Net Income		$ 490,000

Example: Hartell Company assigns the following probabilities to each of its three sales forecasts:

Optimistic	10%
Most Likely	75%
Pessimistic	15%

Now, an *expected value* of the number of units which will be sold can be derived as follows:

Sales (units)	Probability	Expected Value
300,000	10%	30,000
250,000	75%	187,500
200,000	15%	30,000
	$E(S) =$	247,500 units

A budgeted income statement including this information (see Figure 16–11) can then be prepared and used independently or in conjunction with the three individual forecasts already derived.

PROBABILISTIC BUDGETS: CONTINUOUS PROBABILITY DISTRIBUTION FUNCTION

At a higher level of sophistication, a continuous distribution function specified over all possible values of a planning variable can be incorporated into the budgetary process.

Example: Hartell Company estimates that its sales volume is normally distributed, with a mean value of 250,000 units per year and a standard deviation of 25,000 units. Using this information, a budgeted income statement based on the mean sales volume can be prepared with budgeted income statements based on other sales levels corresponding to particular points over the range covered by this normal distribution of the sales volume—that is, 2-sigma and 3-sigma intervals that approximately correspond to the 95 and 99 percent confidence limits.

Figure 16–12 shows budgeted income statements for sales volume levels at the mean and at two and three standard deviations around the mean. These

---

FIGURE 16–12

Hartell Company
Budgeted Income Statement Based on a
Normally Distributed Sales Forecast for 19X8

	Mean −3σ	Mean −2σ	Mean	Mean +2σ	Mean +3σ
Unit Sales Volume	175,000	200,000	250,000	300,000	325,000
Sales ($10)	$1,750,000	$2,000,000	$2,500,000	$3,000,000	$3,250,000
Variable Cost ($6) .	$1,050,000	$1,200,000	$1,500,000	$1,800,000	$1,950,000
Fixed Costs	500,000	500,000	500,000	500,000	500,000
Total Costs	$1,550,000	$1,700,000	$2,000,000	$2,300,000	$2,450,000
Net Income	$ 200,000	$ 300,000	$ 500,000	$ 700,000	$ 800,000

---

figures suggest that there is a 95 percent probability that net income will be between $300,000 and $700,000 and a 99 percent probability that it will be between $200,000 and $800,000.

PROBABILISTIC BUDGETS: SEVERAL VARIABLES SUBJECT TO PROBABILITY DISTRIBUTIONS

What if several planning variables are simultaneously subjected to probability distributions? Independent distribution functions might be specified for the values of the forecast sales volume, the unit variable cost, the total fixed cost, and even the unit sales price. As before, the analysis based on these forecasts could be handled at several levels of sophistication, ranging from a two- or three-level set of estimates with no specific probability values, through a set of discrete probability estimates, to continuous distribution functions.

Although this is conceptually clear, its practical application becomes unwieldy if several probabilistic independent variables are considered at the same time. Even if only three variables are valued probabilistically, and if only three different values of these independent variables are considered, there will be 27 (3× 3 × 3) sets of results to be analyzed. Similarly, if several independent variables are involved, the interrelationships that must be calculated in order to generate a continuous probability distribution, mean value, and standard deviation become computationally complex. However, such calculations are manageable, especially given the availability of electronic computers.

COST–VOLUME–PROFIT ANALYSIS UNDER UNCERTAINTY

In Chapter 8, cost–volume–profit analysis was demonstrated as a deterministic technique. Sales prices, variable costs, fixed costs, capacity levels, and sales demand were assumed to remain constant during the budget period. However, this elementary analysis can be expanded to incorporate some of the uncertainties that always exist in real world situations.

First, consider how the results of basic cost–volume–profit analysis are interpreted and used. These results include the breakeven sales volume and revenue, the amounts of sales volume and revenue necessary to reach target profits, and profit and loss ranges. If the sales volume forecast is considered not as a single number but as a range of values subject to a probability distribution, it is possible to forecast the likelihood of breaking even, earning a specified target profit, or avoiding losses of a certain size.

Example: Dean Company has developed the sales volume forecast and probability distribution shown in Figure 16–13, along with cost, sales price, and profit estimates. Based on this probability distribution, the sales volume needed to (1) break even, (2) earn a target profit of $60,000, and (3) incur a $50,000 loss, can be derived as shown in Figure 16–14 (page 792).

Comparing these results to the sales forecast data in Figure 16–13 indicates that:

1. There is an 80 percent probability of at least breaking even. In other words, the cumulative probability of sales volumes equal to or greater than the 25,000 unit breakeven volume is 80 percent (10% + 20% + 30% + 10% + 10%).
2. There is a 50 percent probability of earning the target profit of $60,000 or more, because the cumulative probability of sales greater than 32,500 units is 50 percent (30% + 10% + 10%).
3. There is a 20 percent chance of incurring a loss (equal to the cumulative probability of sales being less than 25,000 units) and a 10 percent chance of incurring a loss greater than $50,000 (equal to the cumulative probability that sales will be less than 18,750 units).

Example: In Figure 16–15 (page 793), Dean Company has developed an alternative sales volume forecast that shows sales demand to be normally distributed with a mean value of 30,000 units and a standard deviation of 4,000

FIGURE 16–13

Dean Company
Sales Volume Forecast Using Discrete
Probability Distribution

Unit Sales Price	$20	Total Fixed Cost	$200,000
Unit Variable Cost	$12	Target Profit	$ 60,000

Sales Volume Forecast

Quantity	Probability
15,000	10%
20,000	10%
25,000	10%
30,000	20%
35,000	30%
40,000	10%
45,000	10%

FIGURE 16–14

Dean Company
Breakeven Quantity and Target Profit and Loss Quantities

Breakeven Quantity	$60,000 Target Profit	$50,000 Target Loss
$Q_b = \dfrac{F}{M}$	$Q_{t_1} = \dfrac{F + \pi t_1}{M}$	$Q_{t_2} = \dfrac{F + \pi t_2}{M}$
$= \dfrac{\text{Fixed Cost}}{\text{Contribution Margin per Unit}}$	$= \dfrac{\text{Fixed Cost} + \text{Target Profit}}{\text{Contribution Margin per Unit}}$	$= \dfrac{\text{Fixed Cost} + \text{Target Profit}}{\text{Contribution Margin per Unit}}$
$= \dfrac{\$200,000}{(\$20 - \$12) \text{ per Unit}}$	$= \dfrac{\$200,000 + \$60,000}{(\$20 - \$12) \text{ per Unit}}$	$= \dfrac{\$200,000 - \$50,000}{(\$20 - \$12) \text{ per Unit}}$
$= \dfrac{\$200,000}{\$8 \text{ per Unit}}$	$= \dfrac{\$260,000}{\$8 \text{ per Unit}}$	$= \dfrac{\$150,000}{\$8 \text{ per Unit}}$
$= 25,000 \text{ Units}$	$= 32,500 \text{ Units}$	$= 18,750 \text{ Units}$

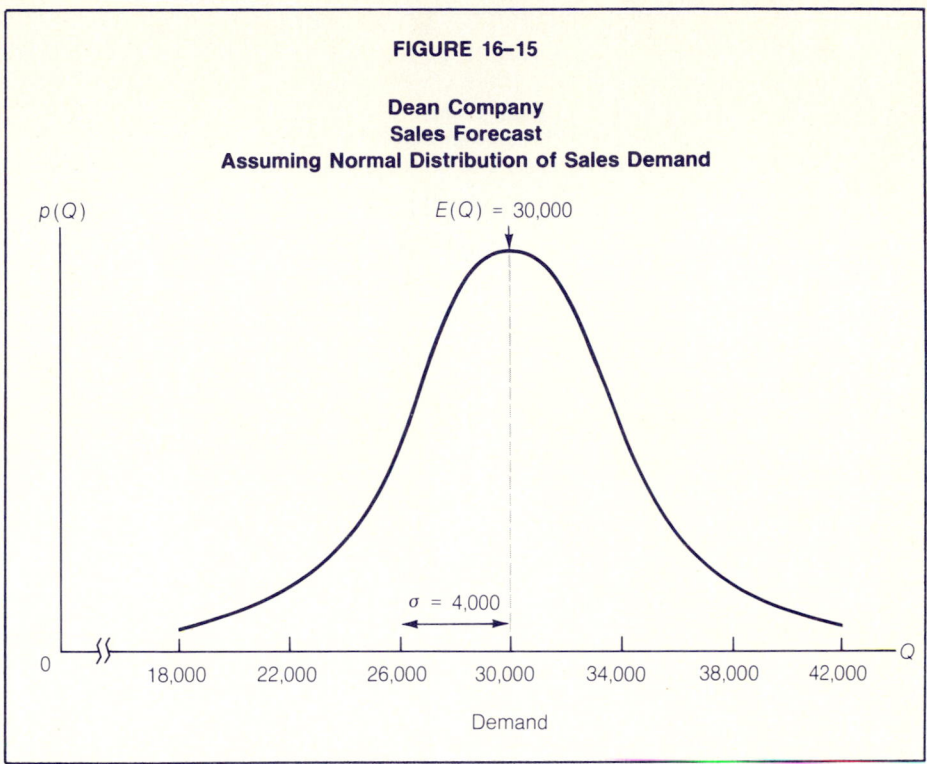

FIGURE 16–15

Dean Company
Sales Forecast
Assuming Normal Distribution of Sales Demand

units. Assuming the same sales price, cost structure, and target profit as in the preceding example, the following statements can be made, based on characteristics of the normal distribution function:

1. *The expected value of net income, $E(\pi)$,* can be determined for the forecast mean sales level of 30,000 units:

Sales (30,000 @ $20)		$600,000
Less: Variable Costs	$360,000	
Fixed Costs	200,000	560,000
Net Income		$ 40,000

2. *The standard deviation of net income, σ_π,* will be equal to the standard deviation of sales volume multiplied by the contribution margin per unit ($4,000 \times \$8 = \$32,000$).
3. *The breakeven point* (25,000 units) is located 1.25 standard deviations [$(30,000 - 25,000) \div 4,000 = 1.25$] below the mean sales value. Tables for ordinates of the normal curve (see page 746) show that 1.25σ corresponds to the .1056 level. There is accordingly an 89.44 percent probability ($1.0 - .1056 = .8944$) that Dean Company will at least break even. This is demonstrated in Figure 16–16. The darker area to the left of the 25,000 unit breakeven quantity accounts for .1056 of the occurrences of Dean

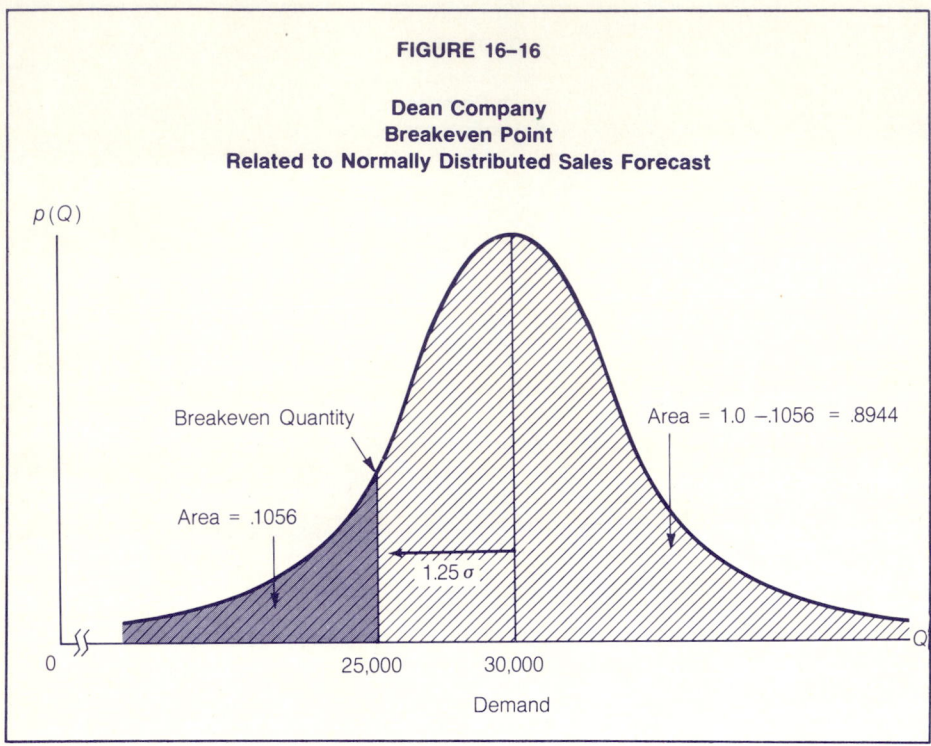

FIGURE 16–16

**Dean Company
Breakeven Point
Related to Normally Distributed Sales Forecast**

$p(Q)$

Breakeven Quantity

Area = 1.0 –.1056 = .8944

Area = .1056

1.25 σ

0   25,000   30,000   Q

Demand

Company's sales volume. This leaves .8944 of the occurrences of forecast sales volume in the paler area to the right, representing the probability that sales volume is likely to satisfy the breakeven condition.

4. *The $60,000 target profit* is located .625 standard deviations [(32,500 − 30,000) ÷ 4,000 = .625] above the mean sales volume. This corresponds to a .2661 level on the normal curve, indicating a 26.61 percent probability that Dean Company will earn as much or more than the target profit. This is shown in Figure 16–17. The shaded area to the right of the 32,500 unit sales level accounts for .2661 of the occurrences of Dean Company's sales volume, representing the probability that sales volume is likely to satisfy the target profit requirement.

5. *The 2-sigma and 3-sigma confidence limits* can be calculated as follows:

$E(Q) \pm 2\,\sigma = 30,000 - 2(4,000)$ and $30,000 + 2(4,000) = 22,000$ and $38,000$
$E(Q) \pm 3\,\sigma = 30,000 - 3(4,000)$ and $30,000 + 3(4,000) = 18,000$ and $42,000$

In other words, there is approximately a 95 percent chance that sales volume will be between 22,000 and 38,000 units and approximately a 99 percent chance that sales volume will be between 18,000 and 42,000 units.

6. *Income statements* can be constructed with sales revenues and costs corresponding to the 2σ and 3σ intervals, as in Figure 16–18, which indicates that there is approximately a 95 percent probability that net income will be between ($24,000) and $104,000, and a 99 percent probability that income will be between ($56,000) and $136,000.

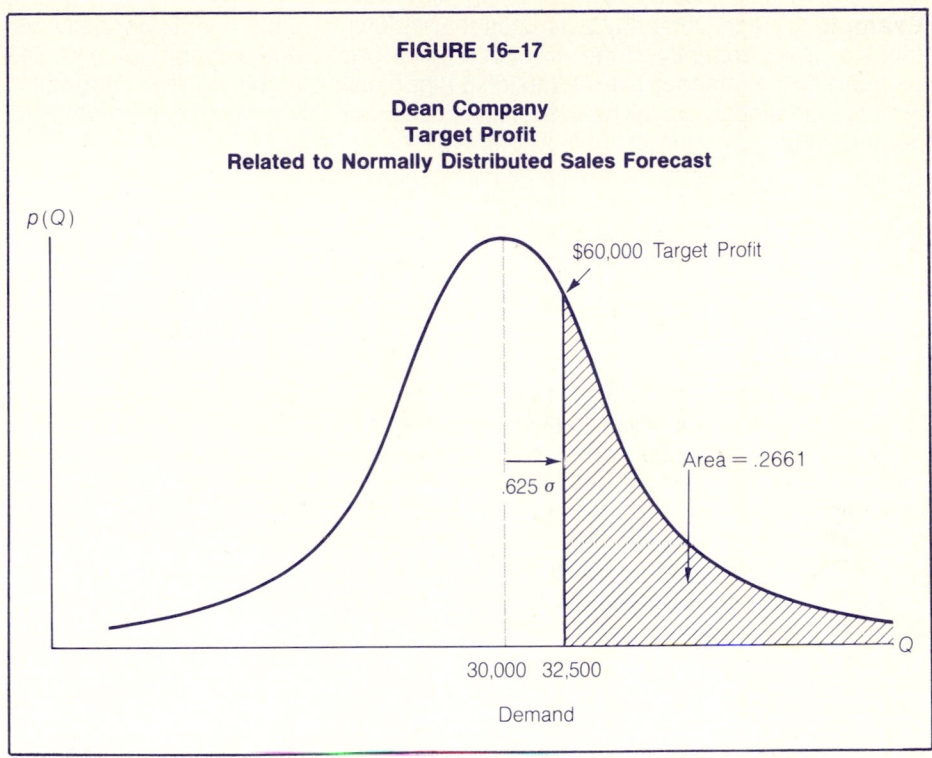

FIGURE 16–17

Dean Company
Target Profit
Related to Normally Distributed Sales Forecast

$p(Q)$

$60,000 Target Profit

Area = .2661

.625 σ

30,000 32,500

Demand

It is also possible to evaluate the effects of variability on the values of each of the other decision variables in the cost–volume–profit model. This can be done as previously described, one variable at a time (fixed costs, variable costs, sales price) or it can be done for all variables simultaneously. But to make statements about the probability distribution of net income based on such analysis, all the variables must be distributed independently of each other.

FIGURE 16–18

Dean Company
Budgeted Income Statements for Two and Three Sigma Levels
Above and Below the Mean Value of the Sales Forecast

	Mean -3σ	Mean -2σ	Mean $+2\sigma$	Mean $+3\sigma$
Unit Sales Volume	18,000	22,000	38,000	42,000
Sales	$360,000	$440,000	$760,000	$840,000
Variable Costs	$216,000	$264,000	$456,000	$504,000
Fixed Costs	200,000	200,000	200,000	200,000
	$416,000	$464,000	$656,000	$704,000
Net Income	($ 56,000)	($ 24,000)	$104,000	$136,000

Example: Dean Company estimates that its unit variable cost is normally distributed, independently of the product's sales price, with a mean value of $12 per unit and a standard deviation of $1 per unit. Combining this information with the previously developed data produces the following expected value of net income:

$$\begin{aligned} E(\pi) &= E(Q)(\$20) - E(Q) \cdot E(V) - \$200,000 \\ &= (30,000)(\$20) - (30,000)(\$12) - \$200,000 \\ &= \$600,000 - \$360,000 - \$200,000 \\ &= \$40,000 \end{aligned}$$

The same expected value of net income was derived in the earlier version of this example, in which sales volume was the only variable subject to a probability distribution. However, when additional variables are subject to probability distributions, the standard deviation of net income must increase. In this case, the standard deviation increases from $32,000 in the preceding example to $56,746. This increase in standard deviation increases the spread of particular confidence intervals for which decisions concerning profit values might be made. The 95 percent (2-sigma) and 99 percent (3-sigma) confidence ranges now become:

$$E(\pi) \pm 2\sigma_\pi = \begin{cases} 40,000 - 2(56,746) = (\ 73,492) \\ 40,000 + 2(56,746) = \ 153,492 \end{cases}$$

$$E(\pi) \pm 3\sigma_\pi = \begin{cases} 40,000 - 3(56,746) = (130,238) \\ 40,000 + 3(56,746) = \ 210,238 \end{cases}$$

The expected value of the breakeven quantity is now located .705 standard deviations [($40,000 − 0) ÷ $56,746 = .705] below the mean, making the probability of breaking even only .7596 (compared to the .8944 of the previous example in which sales volume was the only probabilistically valued variable).

The inclusion of additional probabilistic variables will not always have a negative effect on all aspects of the analysis. An increased dispersion of possible profits often *increases* the probability of reaching the target profit. In the Dean Company example, the target profit of $60,000 is now located .3524 standard deviations [($60,000 − $40,000) ÷ $56,746 = .3524] above the mean profit level of $40,000. This corresponds to a .3622 probability on the normal curve, so there is now a 36.22 percent chance of being able to meet or exceed the target profit requirement (compared to only 26.61 percent for the previous example in which sales volume was the only probabilistically valued variable).

Figure 16–19 illustrates this situation, in which the mean value is the same for two distributions, but the standard deviations are different. The *darker* areas represent the relatively smaller probabilities of (1) not breaking even or (2) earning the target profit under the original distribution function, in which sales volume was the only variable. The *paler* areas represent the larger probabilities of these two occurrences under the second distribution, in which unit variable cost is also treated as a variable. Similarly increased dispersion effects would be obtained from a probability distribution over the estimated values of fixed costs and possibly also over the values of the sales price.

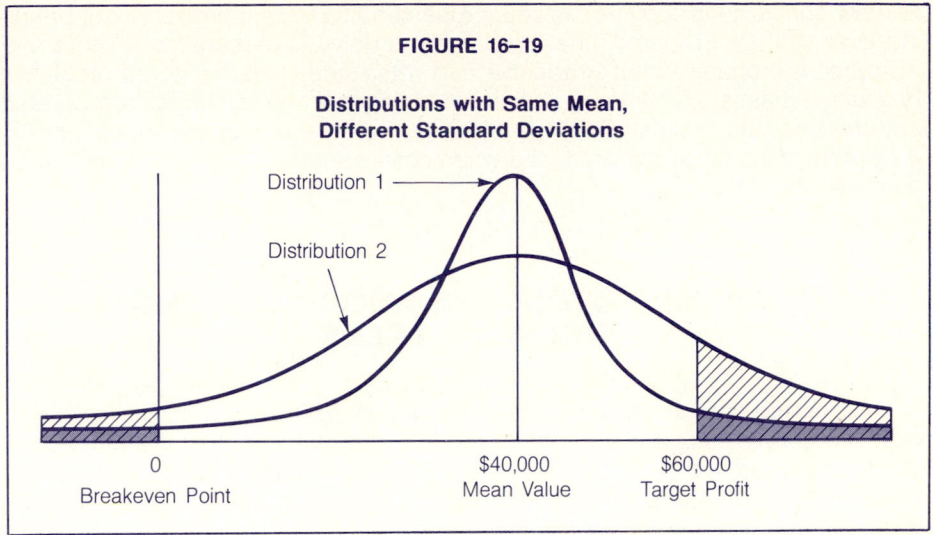

FIGURE 16–19

Distributions with Same Mean, Different Standard Deviations

Distribution 1

Distribution 2

| 0 | $40,000 | $60,000 |
| Breakeven Point | Mean Value | Target Profit |

Another effect of the probability distribution on the values of variable cost per unit is that the breakeven quantity will now have an expected value and a standard deviation. Because variable cost per unit has a mean value of $12 and a standard deviation of $1, contribution margin per unit has a mean value of $8 per unit ($20 − $12) and a standard deviation of $1. Using these figures, 2-sigma confidence intervals for the breakeven quantity can be calculated as follows:

$$E(Q_b) = \frac{F}{E(c)} = \frac{\$200,000}{\$8 \text{ per Unit}} = 25,000 \text{ Units}$$

$$\sigma_v = \sigma_c = \$1$$

$$E(Q_b) + 2\sigma_{Q_b} = \frac{F}{E(c) + 2\sigma_c} = \frac{\$200,000}{\$10} = 80,000 \text{ Units}$$

$$E(Q_b) - 2\sigma_{Q_b} = \frac{F}{E(c) - 2\sigma_c} = \frac{\$200,000}{\$6} = 33,333\tfrac{1}{3} \text{ Units}$$

These equations indicate that the breakeven quantity has a mean value of 25,000 units and will fall between 20,000 and 33,333⅓ units approximately 95 percent of the time.

However, each situation must be analyzed individually to determine the results of treating cost–volume–profit factors as variables with independent probability distributions. No general statement can be made about these possible effects, because so much depends on the locations of mean values, breakeven points, and target profit levels.

Summary   Consideration of uncertainty adds an important dimension to cost–volume–profit analysis, especially when decisions must be made regarding alternative products. It provides additional information to strengthen the necessarily subjective evaluations involved. This type of analysis permits decision makers to draw conclusions such as "Product A has an 80 percent probability of breaking even, but for Product B that probability is only 35 percent" or "There is a 25 percent probability that Product A can return the required target profit, but Product B has a 75 percent chance of doing so." When it is incorporated into the decision process, this information creates a richer and more realistic environment than the data produced when cost–volume–profit factors are valued deterministically.

MULTISTAGE DECISIONS AND UNCERTAINTY: DECISION TREES

When decisions must be made in sequence, with each decision involving independently distributed outcomes of alternative actions, it is useful to know the results of the various combinations of choices open to the decision maker. A **decision tree** technique[1] permits a convenient graphic representation of the possible options. Each **branch point** or **node** in the decision tree corresponds to a decision leading to possible alternative outcomes which are represented by the **branches** or **arcs** that emanate from each branch point.

In Figure 16–20, decisions occur at branch points A, B, C, and D. Branches A_1, A_2, and A_3 lead from branch point A to decisions B, C, and D and will have associated with them probabilities $p(A_1)$, $p(A_2)$, and $p(A_3)$. Decisions B, C, and D, each with its separately distributed sets of outcomes, lead in turn to final outcomes designated X_1 through X_7. Because decisions A, B, C, and D are independent events, the likelihood of reaching any of the final outcomes is equal to the product of the probabilities of each of the outcomes (branches) that lead to it. For example, in Figure 16–20, $p(X_6) = p(A_3)$ times $p(D_2)$. Consequently, if values are given for the final payoffs and for the probabilities of outcomes of all intervening actions, decision rules can be specified that will allow decision makers to select a preferred course of action, using criteria such as expected value of payoff, most likely payoff, or best payoff.

Example: Harnden Company is considering hiring a geological survey service to assist it in making oil well drilling decisions. This assistance will cost $50,000 for each potential oil well site surveyed and analyzed. The survey company has advised drilling on 60 percent of the sites it has analyzed. However, only 80 percent of the sites receiving favorable survey reports have actually produced oil. On the other hand, Harnden's management has proceeded with drilling in 70 percent of potential sites considered, relying solely on the intuition of their field manager. Of these sites drilled, only 50 percent have produced oil. The average cost of drilling a well is $200,000; producing wells provide an average return of $500,000. Harnden Company decides to use the survey service for half of its sites over the next six months, to compare its performance with that of their field manager. This problem is formulated in the decision tree shown in Figure 16–21.

---

[1] For a comprehensive discussion of decision trees, see Howard Raiffa, *Decision Analysis* (Reading, Mass.: Addison–Wesley Publishing Co., 1970).

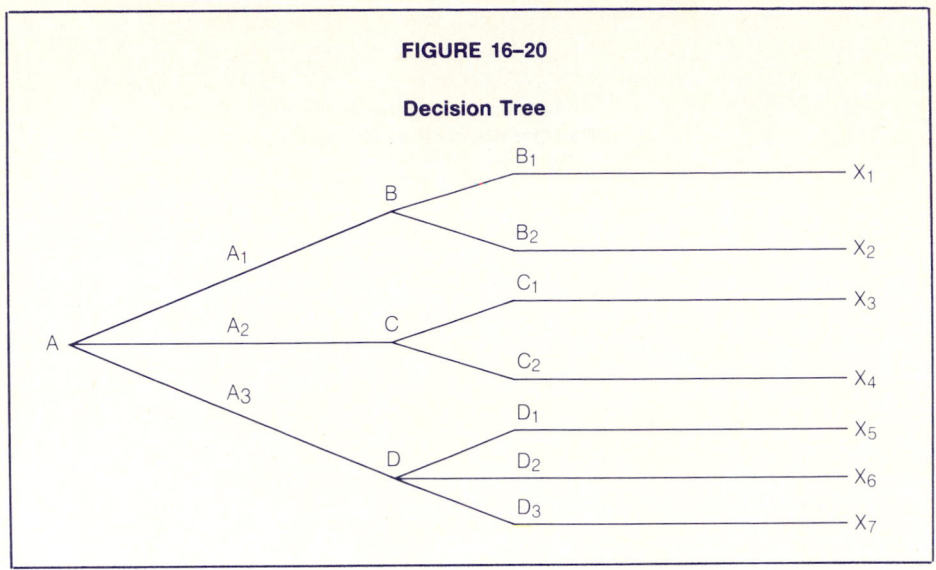

FIGURE 16–20

Decision Tree

FIGURE 16–21

Harnden Company
Decision Tree Comparing Survey Service with
Field Manager

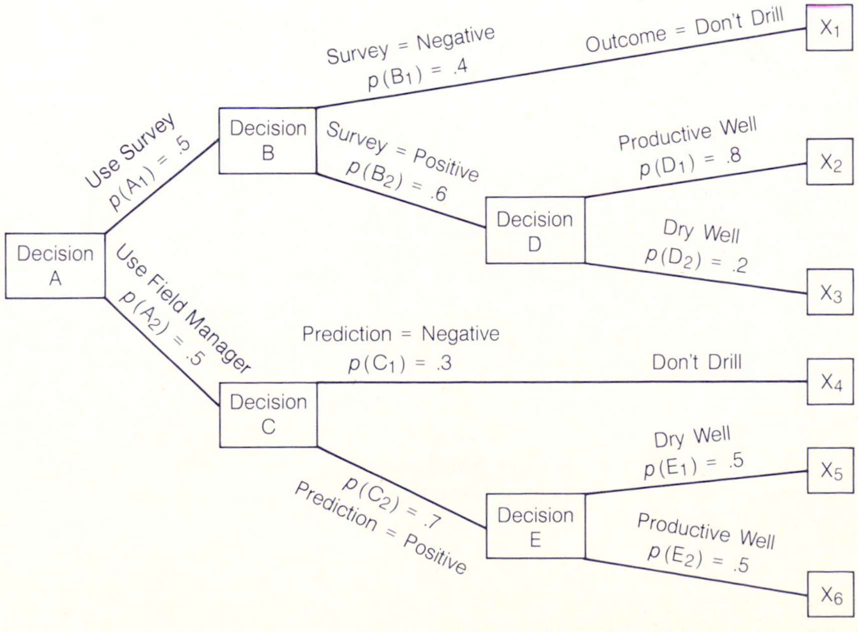

FIGURE 16–22

Harnden Company
Payoffs from Alternative Strategies

End State	Revenues	Expenses	Net Payoff
X_1	–0–	$ 50,000	($ 50,000)
X_2	$500,000	250,000	250,000
X_3	–0–	250,000	(250,000)
X_4	–0–	–0–	–0–
X_5	–0–	200,000	(200,000)
X_6	500,000	200,000	300,000

The Figure 16–22 shows the computation of the value of payoffs X_1 through X_6. The probabilities of reaching each of these payoffs are computed as follows:

$$p(X_1) = p(A_1)p(B_1) \qquad\quad = (.5)(.4) \qquad = .2$$
$$p(X_2) = p(A_1)p(B_2)p(D_1) = (.5)(.6)(.8) = .24$$
$$p(X_3) = p(A_1)p(B_2)p(D_2) = (.5)(.6)(.2) = .06$$

$$p(X_4) = p(A_2)p(C_1) \qquad\quad = (.5)(.3) \qquad = .15$$
$$p(X_5) = p(A_2)p(C_2)p(E_1) = (.5)(.7)(.5) = .175$$
$$p(X_6) = p(A_2)p(C_2)p(E_2) = (.5)(.7)(.5) = .175$$

Harnden Company's strategy is to use the survey company half the time and the field manager's intuition the other half, and to follow the recommendations of each with regard to drill/no drill decisions. The expected value of the payoff of this decision strategy, calculated using the preceding information, is shown in Figure 16–23.

FIGURE 16–23

Harnden Company
Expected Value of "Half and Half" Strategy

	Payoff	Probability	Expected Value
X_1	($ 50,000)	.2	($10,000)
X_2	250,000	.24	60,000
X_3	(250,000)	.06	(15,000)
X_4	–0–	.15	–0–
X_5	(200,000)	.175	(35,000)
X_6	300,000	.175	52,500
			$52,500

FIGURE 16–24

Harnden Company
Expected Value of Using the Survey Service Only

	Payoff	Probability	Expected Value
X₁	($ 50,000)	(.4)(1) = .4	($ 20,000)
X₂	250,000	(.6)(.8) = .48	120,000
X₃	(250,000)	(.6)(.2) = .12	(30,000)
			$ 70,000

Expected Value of Using the Field Manager Only

	Payoff	Probability	Expected Value
X₄	–0–	(.3)(1) = .3	–0–
X₅	($200,000)	(.7)(.5) = .35	($ 70,000)
X₆	300,000	(.7)(.5) = .35	105,000
			$ 35,000

This strategy will result in an expected value payoff of $52,500 per drilling site considered. An alternative is to consider separately the two halves of the decision tree corresponding to using the survey service or the field manager exclusively. The results of this analysis are shown in Figure 16–24.

If the decision is to use either the survey service or the field manager exclusively, an *expected value* decision criterion would favor the survey service, because it has a mean value payoff of $70,000 compared to only $35,000 for the field manager. The criterion of *maximum value of the most likely outcome* would also favor the survey company, because the payoff from its most likely outcome—$p(X_2) = .48$—is $120,000, which is greater than the $105,000 for X_6, the most likely outcome using the field manager approach. The *pessimistic* decision maker would prefer the field manager, whose worst possible outcome is only the X_5 loss of $200,000 compared to the X_3 loss of $250,000 for the survey service. Finally, an *optimistic* approach would also lead to using the field manager, where the best possible outcome (X_6) promises $300,000, compared to only $250,000 for the survey service (X_2).

GAME THEORY MODELS

Certain decision situations involving uncertainty can be formulated in a game-type framework. When a decision maker must choose actions in anticipation of the choices of another decision maker (competitor, customer, supplier, or "nature"), some of the decision techniques of **game theory** can be employed.[2]

[2] For a comprehensive discussion of game theory, see R.N. Luce and Howard Raiffa, *Games and Decisions* (New York: John Wiley and Sons, 1957).

FIGURE 16–25

Game Theory Matrix

		Opponent	
		State 1	State 2
Decision Maker	Action 1	Z_{11}	Z_{12}
	Action 2	Z_{21}	Z_{22}

The situation confronting a game playing decision maker can be represented in the format of a payoff matrix. As suggested in Figure 16–25, the contents of each matrix location represent the payoffs to the decision maker resulting from each possible combination of actions taken by the decision maker and his opponent. Entries in a particular horizontal row correspond to the decision maker's payoffs for each alternative action, assuming that his opponent chooses the "state" shown in the vertical columns.

The decision criteria introduced earlier in this chapter can be employed here. If no specific values have been assigned to the probability that the opponent will choose either State 1 or State 2, the decision maker might seek to ensure that he takes the best possible action by adopting a *maximin strategy* when the payoffs are positive (profits, sales revenues, contribution margin) or a *minimax strategy* when the payoffs are negative (costs, expenses, losses). This requires the decision maker to evaluate each of his two alternative actions in terms of the worst outcome that could occur as a result of his opponent's choosing either State 1 or State 2. Then, from the set of worst outcomes for State 1 or State 2, the decision maker must decide which is most favorable to him and choose the action that corresponds to it. By doing this, the decision maker is assured of maximizing his minimum gain (maximin) or of minimizing his maximum loss (minimax).

Example: Jones Company is considering two advertising campaigns, one more intensive and costly than the other. However, it anticipates that its major competitor will retaliate with some form of advertising. On the assumption that each firm has a choice between *low key* or *intensive* advertising campaigns, the payoff table in Figure 16–26 has been constructed in terms of incremental returns (contribution margin minus advertising expense) to Jones Company.

If Jones Company chooses the intensive advertising program, the worst possible outcome will be a $30,000 return, whereas if the low key program is adopted, the least favorable payoff will be $15,000. A *minimax strategy* dictates choosing the intensive program, which assures at least a $30,000 payoff regardless of what Jones' opponent does.

However, a risk seeker might prefer a *maximax strategy*. This involves choosing the action whose best outcome is a maximum return, regardless of what the opponent does. This strategy would lead Jones Company to choose

FIGURE 16–26

Jones Company
Game Theory Matrix for Low Key and
Intensive Advertising Campaigns

		Competitor	
		Intensive	Low Key
Jones Company	Intensive	$40,000	$30,000
	Low Key	$15,000	$50,000

the low key advertising campaign because it would be attracted by the possible return of $50,000, which is higher than the $40,000 maximum return from the intensive advertising campaign.

When it is known or can be predicted that an opponent will choose a particular action, an *expected value approach* can be adopted. If Jones' competitor is expected to alternate between the low key and intensive advertising campaigns, giving each equal emphasis, then the expected value payoffs for Jones' alternatives are:

$$E(\text{Intensive}) = (.5)(40,000) + (.5)(30,000) = \$35,000$$
$$E(\text{Low Key}) = (.5)(15,000) + (.5)(50,000) = \$32,500$$

By consistently choosing the intensive advertising campaign, while its competitor alternates between the two strategies, Jones Company will achieve a long-run average payoff of $35,000, which is $2,500 better than the $32,500 average payoff that would result from adopting the low key campaign.

If it applies the criterion of *maximum value of the most likely outcome,* Jones Company will prefer the low key advertising campaign. Although there is no single most likely outcome for either of Jones' options, the $50,000 payoff with a 50 percent probability is preferable to the $40,000 payoff with the same probability.

Finally, a *risk averse* decision maker might prefer an opportunity cost-flavored strategy known as the **minimum regret strategy.** This requires the calculation of a revised payoff matrix—Figure 16–27—showing the opportunity costs of choosing the less desirable action for each of the opponent's alternative actions. For example, under State 1, which assumes the competitor chooses an intensive advertising campaign, the opportunity cost to Jones Company of choosing Action 2, the low key campaign, is zero—because that was the correct act, given that the opponent chose State 1. However, the opportunity cost to Jones Company of choosing the intensive campaign (Action 1) is $25,000 ($40,000 − $15,000), which is a measure of how much better it would have been to have chosen the low key campaign (Action 2). Similarly, the opportunity costs to Jones Company if its competitor conducts a low key campaign are

---

FIGURE 16–27

Jones Company
Game Theory Matrix Showing Opportunity Costs

		Opponent	
		Intensive	Low Key
Jones Company	Intensive	$25,000	0
	Low Key	0	$20,000

---

zero ($30,000 − $30,000) if Jones opts for an intensive campaign, and $20,000 ($50,000 − $30,000) if Jones chooses a low key campaign.

In this case, the decision rule is to choose the action for which the **maximum regret** (opportunity cost) is the smallest. Therefore, Jones Company should adopt the low key advertising campaign, because the most "regret" it can cause is $20,000, if the competitor also mounts a low key campaign.

MEASURING THE COSTS AND BENEFITS OF INFORMATION

Most business decision making takes place under conditions of uncertainty. It is reasonable to expect that decision makers will use information to reduce that uncertainty whenever they can. This implies a cost–benefit analysis, in which the cost of information is compared to the benefits it produces. The cost of information can usually be determined in a fairly objective manner. It might include payment for a market research study, subscribing to a forecasting service, preparing accounting reports, or conducting investigations and surveys. However, measuring the benefits of information is a more challenging task.

The benefits obtainable from a piece of information can be defined as the improvement in payoffs resulting from the use of that information. For example, knowing exactly what the demand for a product will be can eliminate losses due to manufacturing or buying too much or too little of that product, especially if it is perishable or non-inventoriable.

The **gross benefits** and the **net value** of information can be defined as follows:

$$\text{Gross Benefits of Information} = \frac{\text{Payoff with the information } minus}{\text{Payoff without the information}}$$

$$\text{Net Value of Information} = \frac{\text{Gross benefits of information } minus}{\text{Cost of the information}}$$

These definitions are based on the assumption that both costs and benefits are expressed in terms of the expected value of monetary amounts.

The highest possible benefits of information would result from comparing outcomes for which decision makers had perfect information to outcomes for which they had no information. However, some information is available in nearly all business decision making, either inherently in the data concerning the variables and relationships that comprise the decision situation or in explicitly developed data bases of past experiences. Therefore, the typical decision involves determining how much *more* information it is worthwhile to acquire.

Example: Critchfield Company forecasts the following probable daily demand for its product:

Quantity	Probability
1,000	10%
2,000	30%
3,000	30%
4,000	20%
5,000	10%

The product is non-inventoriable (such as fresh cut flowers, packaged sandwiches, racetrack programs), so it is critical that the right quantity be available each day. Excess purchases have no resale value and must be thrown away at the end of the day. The sales price is $10 per unit, variable costs are $4 per unit, and fixed costs are $8,000 per day.

This information permits use of the following decision rule: Purchase the quantity that maximizes the expected value of the daily contribution margin. Figure 16–28 (page 806) compares the expected values of the total contribution margin for each forecast purchase quantity.

The expected value is maximized by purchasing 3,000 units daily. This produces a long-run average daily contribution margin of $13,000 and a net income of $5,000 ($13,000 contribution margin − $8,000 fixed costs).

This $13,000 payoff might be improved if additional information were available. If the amount of each day's demand could be forecast exactly, the correct amount of inventory could be purchased each day, leading to the expected value payoff shown in Figure 16–29. This perfect forecast promises gross benefits of $4,400, which is the difference between $17,400 (the new payoff) and $13,000 (the best payoff available without this information). The $4,400 benefit must then be compared to the cost of obtaining this perfect forecast. This additional information will have a positive *net value* if it can be obtained for less than $4,400.

Because such perfect information is rarely available, a more usual problem involves calculating the net value of less than perfect information. Suppose a forecasting service can accurately predict the probability that Critchfield Company's daily demand will be either more than 3,000 units (30 percent) or less than or equal to 3,000 units (70 percent). Management can then use this incomplete information to determine the best inventory buying policies under either of the two signals that it may receive from the forecasting service.

Figure 16–30 (page 807) shows the payoffs from purchasing 4,000 or 5,000 units when the forecasting service predicts that demand will exceed 3,000 units per day. The best action is to buy 4,000 units, which allows an expected value contribution margin of $24,000. But because sales demand above 3,000 units per day is only encountered 30 percent of the time, this action contributes only $7,200 (30% × $24,000) to the expected value of the payoff for the whole decision.

FIGURE 16–28

Critchfield Company
Expected Values of Product Contribution Margins

Purchases	Sales	Revenue	Variable Costs	Contribution Margin	Proba-bility	Expected Value
1,000	1,000	$10,000	$ 4,000	$ 6,000	1.0	$ 6,000
					E(CM) =	$ 6,000
2,000	1,000	$10,000	$ 8,000	$ 2,000	.1	$ 200
	2,000	20,000	8,000	12,000	.9	10,800
					E(CM) =	$11,000
3,000	1,000	$10,000	$12,000	($ 2,000)	.1	($ 200)
	2,000	20,000	12,000	8,000	.3	2,400
	3,000	30,000	12,000	18,000	.6	10,800
					E(CM) =	$13,000
4,000	1,000	$10,000	$16,000	($ 6,000)	.1	($ 600)
	2,000	20,000	16,000	4,000	.3	1,200
	3,000	30,000	16,000	14,000	.3	4,200
	4,000	40,000	16,000	24,000	.3	7,200
					E(CM) =	$12,000
5,000	1,000	$10,000	$20,000	($10,000)	.1	($ 1,000)
	2,000	20,000	20,000	–0–	.3	–0–
	3,000	30,000	20,000	10,000	.3	3,000
	4,000	40,000	20,000	20,000	.2	4,000
	5,000	50,000	20,000	30,000	.1	3,000
					E(CM) =	$ 9,000

FIGURE 16–29

Critchfield Company
Expected Values of Profit Contribution Margins,
Assuming Perfect Knowledge

Purchases	Sales	Revenue	Variable Costs	Contribution Margin	Proba-bility	Expected Value
1,000	1,000	$10,000	$ 4,000	$ 6,000	.1	$ 600
2,000	2,000	20,000	8,000	12,000	.3	3,600
3,000	3,000	30,000	12,000	18,000	.3	5,400
4,000	4,000	40,000	16,000	24,000	.2	4,800
5,000	5,000	50,000	20,000	30,000	.1	3,000
					E(CM) =	$17,400

FIGURE 16–30

Critchfield Company
Expected Values of Profit Contribution Margins,
Assuming 30 Percent Probability of Demand More than 3,000 Units

Signal–Demand > 3,000 Occurs with Probability = .3

Purchases	Sales	Revenue	Variable Costs	Contribution Margin	Proba- bility	Expected Value
4,000	4,000	$40,000	$16,000	$24,000	1.0	$24,000.00
					E(CM) =	$24,000.00
5,000	4,000	$40,000	$20,000	$20,000	.6667	13,333.33
	5,000	50,000	20,000	30,000	.3333	10,000.00
					E(CM) =	$23,333.33

Figure 16–31 shows the payoffs from purchasing 1,000, 2,000, or 3,000 units when the forecasting service predicts that demand will be equal to or less than 3,000 units per day. In this case, the best action is to buy 3,000 units, which provides an expected value payoff of $10,857.28. Because the probability of this level of demand is 70 percent, the action will contribute $7,600.10 ($10,857.28 × 70%) to the expected value of the payoff for the whole decision.

FIGURE 16–31

Critchfield Company
Expected Value of Profit Contribution Margins,
Assuming 70 Percent Probability of Demand Less than 3,000 Units

Signal–Demand ≤ 3,000 Occurs with Probability = .7

Purchases	Sales	Revenue	Variable Costs	Contribution Margin	Proba- bility	Expected Value
1,000	1,000	$10,000	$ 4,000	$ 8,000	1.0	$ 8,000.00
					E(CM) =	$ 8,000.00
2,000	1,000	$10,000	$ 8,000	$ 2,000	.1428	$ 285.60
	2,000	20,000	8,000	12,000	.8572	10,286.40
					E(CM) =	$10,572.00
3,000	1,000	$10,000	$12,000	($ 2,000)	.1428	($ 285.60)
	2,000	20,000	12,000	8,000	.4286	3,428.80
	3,000	30,000	12,000	18,000	.4286	7,714.80
					E(CM) =	$10,858.00

Combining the results for the "less than 3,000 units" forecast and the "over 3,000 units" forecast gives the following total contribution margin:

$$E(CM) \text{ when signal} > 3,000 = \$24,000.00 \times .3 = \$ \ 7,200.00$$
$$E(CM) \text{ when signal} \leq 3,000 = \$10,858.00 \times .7 = \$ \ 7,600.00$$

Combined Values of Expected Contribution Margins $14,800.00

This imperfect and incomplete information provided by the forecast service produces an expected gross benefit of $1,800 ($14,800 − $13,000). If this information can be obtained at a cost of less than $1,800, it will have a positive net value and be worth acquiring.

SUMMARY

1. Decision criteria must take account of the fact that business decision making occurs in an environment of uncertainty.

2. When a probability distribution can be developed over the outcomes of an action, the expected (mean) value of an action can be calculated. Rational decision makers who are risk neutral will make decisions strictly on the basis of maximizing or minimizing the expected monetary value of outcomes.

3. The amount of variability in possible outcomes of actions often causes decision makers to modify their expectations of the value of those outcomes to reflect the risk represented by this potential variability. Although they may still choose rationally, they try to maximize expected utility and thereby display risk averse or risk seeking tendencies. Therefore, each decision maker develops personal utility preference functions that modify the expected value of monetary outcomes according to his perceptions of and attitudes toward the risk represented by the distribution pattern and the range of possible outcomes.

4. Heuristic decision rules approximate decision makers' risk averse or risk seeking tendencies. Use of maximax criteria reflects a risk seeking approach. Risk aversion is reflected by decisions made on the basis of most likely outcomes, or minimax or maximin criteria.

5. The amount of dispersion in possible outcomes can be measured in terms of the standard deviation or the coefficient of variation—the ratio of the standard deviation to the mean value. These measures reflect the absolute and the relative variability of outcomes, respectively. They should be used together with expected value decision criteria.

6. Probabilistic decision methods can be applied in budgeting and in cost–volume–profit analysis. Expected value, dispersion, and range analysis can be used in budgetary planning when probability distributions are available over the values of budgetary variables.

7. Probability distributions specified for sales volume forecasts, fixed costs, variable costs, and/or sales prices allow the extension of cost–volume–profit analysis to include predictions of the likelihood that the breakeven condition will be satisfied or target profit levels achieved.

8. Decision tree and game theory formulations of business decisions use expected values and other probabilistic decision criteria to compare alternative actions.

9. The value of information in business decision making can be assessed by determining the expected value of the best actions when information is available and when it is not. The difference between these two amounts is the gross value of information. By subtracting the cost of information from its gross value, the net value of information can be calculated and used to determine the economic desirability of obtaining and applying the information in question.

KEY WORDS AND PHRASES

Deterministic Decision Techniques (777)
Probabilistic Decision Models (777)
Expected Value Decision Models (777)
Risk Neutral Decision Maker (778)
Expected Utility (779)
Risk Seeking Decision Maker (779)
Risk Averse Decision Maker (780)
Heuristic Decision Rules (782)
Most Likely Outcomes (782)
Least Favorable Outcomes (782)
Most Favorable Outcomes (782)
Minimax Strategy (782)
Maximin Strategy (782)
Maximax Strategy (783)
Standard Deviation (784)
Coefficient of Variation (785)
Discrete Probability Distribution Function (788)
Continuous Probability Distribution Function (789)
Decision Tree (798)
Branch Point or Node (798)
Branches or Arcs (798)
Game Theory (801)
Minimum Regret Strategy (803)
Maximum Regret Strategy (804)
Gross Benefits of Information (804)
Net Value of Information (804)
Perfect Information (805)
Imperfect Information (805)

Questions

1. Distinguish between *deterministic* and *probabilistic* decision situations.
2. Explain what is meant by the *expected value* of the outcome of an event.
3. What is the relationship between the expected value decision criteria and the decision maker's attitude toward risk? Why is this important?
4. What are the limitations of the use of expected value criteria in decision making under conditions of uncertainty?
5. Explain the following concepts: (1) risk neutral, (2) risk averse, and (3) risk seeking.
6. Explain the concept of expected utility as it pertains to decision making under conditions of uncertainty.
7. Contrast some of the prominent heuristic decision criteria to the expected value approach. Which would you use and why?
8. How can the dispersion of possible outcomes of an action be included in decision criteria? Why is this important?
9. Explain the relative usefulness of (1) the standard deviation, and (2) the coefficient of variation as decision criteria.
10. What advantages, if any, does a probabilistic budget, expressed in terms of ranges and/or dispersion of estimates, have over a deterministic budget, expressed as a set of point estimates?
11. Explain how probabilistic budgets might be prepared when the values of the sales forecast are (1) normally distributed, (2) discretely distributed, or (3) distributed over a range but according to some unknown distribution pattern.
12. What problem is encountered when several budgetary variables are each subject to separate, independent probability distributions?
13. How can cost–volume–profit analysis techniques be modified to allow for probability distributions over the values of some of the key variables (for example, sales forecast, fixed costs, and variable cost per unit)?
14. Explain how conflicts might be resolved in choosing between (1) alternatives with the same expected value but different standard deviations and (2) alternatives with different expected values as well as different standard deviations?
15. What purposes does decision tree analysis serve?
16. Explain the basic formulation of a problem in a game theory format.
17. What is a minimax strategy and what type of decision maker would tend to use it?
18. Explain the concept of the "value of information." Why is it a useful idea?
19. How might the value of information be calculated? What problems will be encountered in obtaining the data needed to make such calculations?
20. How can uncertainty of outcomes be introduced into the calculation of the value of information?

Exercises

E 16–1   Expected Value Analysis

Rosen Company is examining the possible effects of alternative sales prices on the profitability of a new product. The product has variable costs of $6 per unit. The company has conducted a survey and has projected sales volume and probabilities as follows:

		Sales Price	
Sales Volume (Units)	$10	$12	$15
10,000	—	.1	.75
20,000	.2	.3	.25
30,000	.3	.4	—
40,000	.5	.2	—

Required:
(a) Calculate the expected value of unit sales for each of the three alternative sales prices. Explain fully the meaning of this type of answer.
(b) Prepare a schedule to show the expected total contribution margin to be derived for each of the three prices, based on the solutions to part (a).
(c) Which sales price would you recommend, based on an expected value criteria? Why?

E 16–2   Budgeting under Certainty—Alternative Criteria

Hector Company has developed the following forecast data for its 19X6 operations:

	Total Revenue
1. Most Optimistic Forecast ...	$500,000
2. Liberal Forecast	400,000
3. Most Likely Forecast	300,000
4. Conservative Forecast	200,000
5. Least Optimistic Forecast...	100,000

The corporation has fixed costs of $100,000 and a contribution margin ratio of 60 percent.

Required:
(a) Prepare a columnar budgeted income statement that includes each of these five forecasts. Explain the possible usefulness and also the limitations of such a report.
(b) Assume that probabilities are assigned to the forecasts as follows: (1) .05, (2) .25, (3) .3, (4) .25, (5) .15. Using this data, prepare a budgeted income statement based on the expected value of annual sales revenue.
(c) Why is the expected value forecast different from the most likely forecast?
(d) Compare the potential usefulness of the report prepared in part (b) to that prepared in part (a). Which would you, as a manager, prefer? Why?

E 16–3   Expected Value Analysis and Other Decision Criteria

Holl Corporation has developed the following forecast of monthly sales of a new product line:

Monthly Sales (Units)	Probability
20,000	.2
40,000	.4
60,000	.3
80,000	.1

Required:
(a)   Using the expected value criteria, what is the expected value of monthly unit sales? Explain fully what this answer represents and what type of decision maker would be likely to use it.
(b)   After reviewing the forecast data, three independent analysts have proposed that decisions should be based on a sales forecast of (1) 20,000, (2) 80,000, and (3) 40,000 units, respectively. Identify each of the three analysts' attitudes toward uncertainty in this situation.
(c)   Which of the three forecasts do you feel is (1) the most appropriate, and (2) the least appropriate? Explain.

E 16–4   Expected Value and Standard Deviation Analysis

The time it takes a bus to cover the route between two cities is normally distributed with a mean value of ten hours and standard deviation of one hour. Operating costs are $200 per hour of operating time.

Required:
(a)   What is the expected value of the cost per run?
(b)   What is the standard deviation of the cost per run?
(c)   How frequently (what percent of the time) will operating costs per run be more than (1) $2,200, (2) $2,500, (3) $1,900?
(d)   What is the probability that the elapsed time will be (1) less than 9 hours, (2) more than 10.5 hours, (3) more than 9.75 hours?

E 16–5   Cost–Volume–Profit Analysis under Uncertainty

Stoner Corporation has developed the following estimates of its key planning variables for the 19X7 year.

Fixed Costs per Year		Variable Cost per Unit	
$100,000	.5	$4	.3
$120,000	.5	$5	.6
		$6	.1

Sales Price per Unit			
$10	.2		
$12	.6		
$15	.2		

Required:

(a) What are the expected values of these three planning variables?

(b) What is the expected value of the breakeven quantity based on your answer to part (a)? (Assume all three variables are independent.)

(c) How might your answer to part (b) be interpreted and used?

(d) What is the (1) most optimistic and (2) most pessimistic value of the breakeven quantity? What are the probabilities of each of those two events?

(e) Discuss other ways in which the type of data presented here could be analyzed, presented, and interpreted for planning purposes. (Include, for example, the decision tree approach, most likely outcome approach, and range estimates.)

E 16–6   Decision Tree Analysis—Budgetary Analysis

Kamp Company is concerned that its present budgetary procedures, based on single-valued estimates of each key variable, are not sufficiently realistic. Management proposes to include information relating to the probability of alternative values of (a) sales volume, (b) unit variable costs, and (c) fixed costs.

Sales volume is estimated to be either 160,000 units ($p = .3$), 200,000 units ($p = .5$), or 220,000 units ($p = .2$). Variable costs will be either $10 per unit ($p = .6$) or $12 per unit ($p = .4$). Fixed costs are estimated at $600,000 ($p = .7$) or $800,000 ($p = .3$). Selling Price per unit is $20.

Required:

(a) Prepare a decision tree diagram to show all possible outcomes, their payoff values (net income), and their probabilities.

(b) What is the expected value of net income? Show how it can be derived from the decision tree.

(c) Besides the expected value result, what other information does the decision tree provide? How can this information be used for planning and decision making?

E 16–7   Game Theory—Decision Analysis

Acme Machine Company is trying to decide whether to purchase replacement parts for one of its key operating machines immediately or to defer the purchase until the need to replace occurs. A parts manufacturer has quoted a special price of $80,000 for the desired items. This price is only good for the next month, after which time the parts will be available only at their regular price of $120,000.

If the company decides to purchase the parts, it will cost an extra $20,000 to store and insure them until they are needed or disposed of. If they are not needed, the manufacturer has agreed to repurchase them for $30,000. On the other hand, if the parts are not purchased now and a need for them later arises, it is estimated that other expenses and losses due to temporary interruption of production while they are obtained will amount to $30,000. (For the purposes of this question, do *not* attempt to perform any multiperiod analysis involving use of present value calculations.)

Required:

(a) Identify the two *actions* available to the company and the two possible *states of the world* that may transpire.

(b) Prepare a payoff matrix to show the values associated with each action/state combination.

(c) What action should the manufacturer take? Why? Explain the attitude toward risk that is implied in your solution.

(d) Assume that the probability of replacement parts being needed is forecast to be (1) .25 or (2) .8. What actions would you recommend in each case? Why? Again explain the attitude toward risk that is implied in your solution.

(e) Suggest an alternative decision criteria to the one that you used in part (d). What action would have been recommended using this criteria?

E 16–8   Value of Information—Decision Analysis

Refer to Exercise 16–7. Assume that a firm of engineering consultants has offered its services and guarantees its ability to predict the likelihood of the failure of the machine.

Required:
(a) What would be the value of the information the consultants offer, assuming (1) that an expected value criterion is being used and (2) that the probability of machine failure is .4?

(b) Discuss the appropriateness of using an expected value criterion in a decision situation such as this. Can you suggest alternative criteria that would be more appropriate?

E 16–9   Decision Making under Uncertainty—Value of Additional Information

Chidi Company is reviewing its inventory policy for the forthcoming year. Three alternative strategies have been proposed, each with different total annual costs. Each strategy will also have different costs depending on whether a strong, medium, or weak market exists for the firm's product. The following table of predicted costs has been developed:

	Market Conditions		
Strategy	Strong	Medium	Weak
A	1,300,000	1,000,000	900,000
B	1,200,000	1,100,000	1,000,000
C	1,500,000	1,000,000	750,000

Required:
(a) In the absence of any indication as to what the market situation will be, which strategy would you recommend? Why? Describe the decision criteria you have used.

(b) From past experience, the company knows that the probabilities of the market conditions prevailing are as follows:

Strong   .3
Medium   .5
Weak   .2

Using an expected value criteria, which strategy should be used?

(c) What criteria (other than the expected value) could be used in conjunction with the data provided in part (b)? Explain.

(d) If an accurate prediction of the market condition were available (that is, perfect information), what would be the value of that piece of information?

Cases

C 16–1   Point and Range Estimates

Required:
Discuss the relative advantages and disadvantages of using (1) a budgetary process based on a single, *point estimate* of sales volume as compared to (2) one based on a *range estimate* of sales volumes, expressed in terms of most likely, pessimistic, and optimistic sales outlooks. As a *controller,* which would you prefer and why? As a *manager,* which would you prefer and why?

C 16–2   Sales Forecasts

Elias Company has been using the following regression equation as the basis for its annual sales forecast:

$$Y = \$50,000,000 + .225X$$

where Y represents the company's sales and X represents forecast sales of the total industry. However, conflicting information is usually present concerning the forecast level of industry sales. The company's own marketing group forecasts industry sales for the next year at $330,000,000. A recent article in the financial section of a prominent daily newspaper forecast mild recessionary conditions leading to industry sales of only $300,000,000. Finally, the industry's leading trade journal has optimistically published a sales forecast of $380,000,000.

Required:
Discuss the possible approaches to developing budgetary information for the Elias Company. Which sales forecast(s) would you recommend? Why? How would you incorporate information from the three separate forecasts into the budgeting process? What other information would be helpful in such a situation?

C 16–3   Decision Criteria

Required:
(a) Discuss the rationale that supports the use of an expected value criteria for decision making.

(b) Compare and contrast an expected monetary value criteria with an expected utility criteria.

(c) Evaluate the relative usefulness and validity of heuristic decision criteria, such as maximin/minimax, most likely, and maximax.

(d) What criteria would you adopt in (1) one-time decision situations, and (2) recurring decision situations? Why?

C 16–4   Expected Value and Dispersion of Payoff Amounts

Two alternative actions being considered both have the same expected value of their payoff (profit) amount. However, alternative A has a much larger amount of variability (dispersion) in the values of the possible payoffs than does alternative B.

Required:
Assuming that both actions have payoffs that are normally distributed, discuss the factors that are relevant to choosing between the two. What if A and B had equal dispersions of their payoff amounts, but different expected values?

C 16–5   The Value of Information

It has been proposed that the value of information can be measured in terms of the potential change in the payoff (profit, return, contribution, and so on) that may occur as a result of using that information (compared to the payoff that would be possible without that information).

Required:
(a)   Discuss the problems likely to be encountered in making measurements consistent with this concept (that is, in measuring the incremental payoff associated with the information provided).
(b)   What role does the cost of information play in this approach?
(c)   How is the uncertainty of outcomes of alternative actions provided for in this analysis?
(d)   What decision criteria are assumed to be used by decision makers in this analysis?

Problems

P 16–1   Expected Value Analysis

Willis Company is examining the potential profitability of three new products. It only has capacity to introduce one of them. Sales forecasts and other operating data are shown below:

		Proposed Products				
	Alpha		**Sigma**		**Gnu**	
	Units	**Probability**	**Units**	**Probability**	**Units**	**Probability**
Forecast Unit	10,000	.1	20,000	.2	5,000	.2
Sales and	20,000	.1	30,000	.6	10,000	.3
Probabilities	30,000	.3	40,000	.1	15,000	.5
	40,000	.4	50,000	.1		
	50,000	.1				
Sales Price per Unit.....	$20		$30		$50	
Variable Cost per Unit ...	$ 5		$10		$15	

Required:
(a)   Calculate the expected value of unit sales for each of the three proposed products. Explain fully the correct interpretation of this type of answer.

(b) Prepare a schedule to show the expected values of the contribution margins from each of the three products, based on the solution to part (a).

(c) Which product would you recommend and why?

P 16–2   Expected Value Analysis and Alternative Decision Criteria

Wise Novelty Company is investigating two proposed new products. Because the acceptance of new products in this market is subject to a great deal of uncertainty, the forecasting of sales must provide for both the extremes of success and of failure. Accordingly, the following data have been developed:

	Item R		Item S	
Forecast Unit Sales	Units	Probability	Units	Probability
Successful..........	25,000	.1	30,000	.25
Average	20,000	.6	20,000	.4
Failure	15,000	.3	10,000	.35

Both novelty items sell for $2 and have variable costs of $1 per unit. Fixed costs amount to $12,000.

Required:
(a) Prepare columnar budgeted income statements to show the complete range of possible outcomes for both products.
(b) Using the expected value criteria, prepare budgeted income statements based on the expected values of unit sales of the two products.
(c) Which product should be produced? Why? Explain the relative advantages and disadvantages of an answer based on part (a) as compared to one based on part (b).

P 16–3   Expected Value Analysis and Alternative Decision Criteria

Laird Company is interested in improving the profit performance of one of its product lines. The item sells for $20 and has variable costs of $4 per unit. However, fixed costs are quite high, especially those for the monthly rental on specialized equipment that turns out this product. The three different machines available have rental charges and capacities as follows:

Machine	Capacity	Monthly Rental
A	10,000	$100,000
B	15,000	135,000
C	20,000	150,000

Excluding the machine rental, monthly fixed costs amount to $50,000. Forecast monthly sales are as follows:

Units	Probability
10,000	.2
15,000	.5
20,000	.3

Assume that for cases in which the potential monthly sales volume exceeds available capacity, there is no effect other than the loss of sales in that same period (that is, backorders are impossible and sales will not be lost in subsequent periods).

Required:
(a) Prepare budgeted income statements for all nine possible combinations of circumstances (for the three sales levels with each of the three possible machines). Comment on the resulting information.
(b) Using expected value criteria, prepare budgeted income statements for each of the three machines.
(c) What is the best course of action for the firm for the next twelve months? Why?
(d) What criteria did you use in part (c)? Why? Why did you reject other decision criteria?

P 16–4   Expected Value Analysis and Alternative Decision Criteria

The plant manager for the Eastern Division of Gibb Company is considering some alterations to her production setup. The proposed changes would add $30,000 to monthly fixed costs, but would reduce variable costs by 40¢ per unit produced. There would be no setup costs and no outlays for machinery would be required. However, demand for the product involved varies quite significantly from month to month, but without any apparent cyclical or predictable pattern. The best sales forecast data obtained are as follows:

Probability	Monthly Unit Sales
.25	50,000
.30	80,000
.35	120,000
.10	140,000

Required:
(a) What minimum monthly sales volume will justify the changeover?
(b) What is the maximum possible monthly savings from the changeover?
(c) Should the changeover be made? Why or why not?
(d) Discuss some alternative criteria to that used in part (c). Why did you reject those criteria?

P 16–5   Expected Value Analysis—Expected Utility Analysis

Woolfe Company is considering introducing a controversial new product, but finds considerable disagreement as to whether it will be accepted in the market. The product will sell for $50, with variable costs of $30 per unit. Fixed costs directly traceable to the new product amount to $650,000 per year, including $100,000 for promotion and advertising. Marketing Research Associates, Inc. has provided the following survey data for the company:

Forecast Unit Sales per Year	Probability
10,000	.4
40,000	.4
70,000	.2

The general manager expressed the point of view that "the utility from the loss of one dollar is twice as much as the utility of the earning of a dollar." On this basis, she requested further analysis of a preliminary report that showed the product to be profitable. The preliminary report had used an expected monetary value criteria.

Required:
(a) Prepare an analysis of the product's profitability based on an expected monetary value criteria.
(b) Repeat the analysis using an expected utility criteria based on the assertion made by the general manager.
(c) Which analysis would you recommend? Why?

P 16–6   Expected Value and Standard Deviation Decision Criteria

Based on analysis of sales performance, it has been forecast that the monthly sales volume of product Amigo by Arroyo Corporation is normally distributed with a mean value of 100,000 units and a standard deviation of 20,000 units. The product sells for $20, has variable costs of $12 per unit, and monthly fixed costs of $640,000.

Required:
(a) What is the expected value of monthly income from this product?
(b) Develop a 2-sigma confidence interval for the sales forecast. What are the net income (loss) boundaries of this range?
(c) What is the probability that the firm will break even each month?
(d) What is the probability of a monthly income of *at least* $250,000?
(e) What are the chances of losing more than $100,000 per month?
(f) Is this a potentially profitable product? Why or why not?

P 16–7   Expected Value Analysis and Other Decision Criteria—Discrete Probability Distribution

Acme Real Estate Agency has analyzed the performance of its sales staff. It finds that the property sales made each week by any individual member of the sales staff are distributed as follows:

Probability	Number of Sales
.40	Zero
.25	One
.15	Two
.10	Three
.05	Four
.05	Five

Each sale costs the agency a commission fee of $5,000. The agency earns gross commissions of $8,000 on each sale and has no other variable costs.

Required:
(a) How many sales is a salesperson most likely to make in one week? What is the expected value of the weekly number of sales? Why are these two results different?

(b) Referring only to the discrete probability distribution listed, what is the likelihood that a salesperson will make at least a $6,000 per week contribution toward the firm's fixed costs?

(c) Should a salesperson be retained if a target of $9,000 of net contribution per salesperson per week is put into effect? Why or why not?

(d) What is the probability of a salesperson having four consecutive weeks that do *not* meet the performance criteria mentioned in part (c)?

P 16-8 Expected Value—Standard Deviation— Coefficient of Variation—Alternative Decision Criteria

Concorde Corporation has four alternative investment projects under review. Their forecast outcomes are shown in the tables below:

Proposal A		Proposal B	
Monthly Income	**Probability**	**Monthly Income**	**Probability**
$30,000	.4	$20,000	.2
50,000	.2	40,000	.6
70,000	.4	60,000	.2

Proposal C		Proposal D	
Monthly Income	**Probability**	**Monthly Income**	**Probability**
$10,000	.1	($ 20,000)	.3
50,000	.8	40,000	.4
90,000	.1	100,000	.3

The projects are comparable in all respects other than the amounts and distribution of monthly income.

Required:
(a) For each of the four proposals, calculate (1) the expected value of monthly income, (2) the standard deviation of monthly income, and (3) the coefficient of variation.

(b) Which proposal would you select if the criteria were (1) to maximize expected value or (2) to minimize the variability of returns?

(c) Discuss the problems you encountered in answering part (b). How did you resolve them?

(d) Discuss how useful the answers derived in part (a) were in resolving the problems mentioned in part (c).

(e) Which of the four proposed projects would you select? Why? What decision criteria did you use?

P 16-9 Expected Value Analysis, Uncertainty, and Analysis of Dispersion of Payoffs

Radisch Corporation manufactures a product with a variable cost of $16 per unit. Proposed sales prices of $20, $22, and $24 are being evaluated. It is known that the total output capacity of the plant—12,000 units per month—can be sold at the $20 price. However, for the higher prices, the following forecasts have been developed:

Price = $22		Price = $24	
Probability	Unit Sales	Probability	Unit Sales
.20	12,000	.05	12,000
.60	11,000	.20	11,000
.15	10,000	.50	10,000
.05	8,000	.15	8,000
		.10	6,000

Required:

(a) Using an expected value approach, prepare an analysis of how the three alternative prices affect total contribution margin.

(b) Which price would be selected on the basis of part (a)? Why?

(c) What factors limit the answer provided in part (b)? How might they be overcome?

(d) Present an analysis of the three alternative prices that incorporates the dispersion of the values of the possible outcomes. Use the standard deviation and coefficient of variation in your analysis. Which alternative price would you select based on this analysis? Why?

(e) Discuss the problem from the points of view of three different decision makers: (1) one who is risk neutral, (2) one who is risk averse, and (3) one who is a risk seeker.

P 16–10   Cost–Volume–Profit Analysis under Conditions of Uncertainty

Whisler Company is preparing its operating budget for 19X2. Data relating to sales prices and costs are as follows:

Sales Price	$20 per unit
Variable Costs......	$ 8 per unit
Fixed Costs	$2,400,000 per year

Sales forecasts have been prepared which disclose the following:

Unit Sales	Probability
100,000	.10
150,000	.20
200,000	.40
250,000	.25
300,000	.05

Required:

(a) What is the breakeven quantity?

(b) How many units must be sold to earn a profit of (1) $240,000, (2) $600,000, (3) $1,000,000?

(c) Based on the sales forecast, what is the probability that the firm can break even?

(d) What are the probabilities of achieving each of the sales volumes involved in part (b)?

(e) What is the probability that a loss greater than $600,000 will be incurred?

(f) Comment on other ways in which the information in this problem could be analyzed and reported for planning purposes.

P 16–11   Cost–Volume–Profit Analysis under Conditions of Uncertainty

Refer to the data presented in Problem 16–10. The firm has obtained a second sales forecast which predicts that the sales volume is likely to be normally distributed with a mean value of 210,000 units and a standard deviation of 30,000 units.

Required:
Answer the same questions (a) to (e) as in Problem 16–10, using this second sales forecast rather than the original.

P 16–12   Cost–Volume–Profit Analysis under Uncertainty—Alternative Products

Ostenberg Company is comparing the relative profitability of two products. It only has capacity to produce and market one of these. Forecast data on sales prices, sales volumes, and costs are as follows:

	Product A	Product B
Sales Price per Unit	$50	$40
Variable Cost per Unit......	$30	$15
Fixed Costs per Year	250,000	250,000

Sales Forecast

Units	Probability	Units	Probability
8,000	.1	6,000	.1
10,000	.2	8,000	.2
12,000	.3	10,000	.5
14,000	.2	12,000	.1
16,000	.2	15,000	.1

Required:
(a) Prepare schedules to show all possible net income results for each product using the respective sales forecasts.
(b) What is the breakeven sales volume for each product?
(c) What is the expected value of (1) the sales volume and (2) the net income for each product?
(d) Which product is more likely to break even? Why?
(e) Which product is more likely to earn a target income of $50,000? Why?
(f) Which product should the firm produce? Why? Explain the type of approach to uncertainty that you used in this answer.

P 16–13   Decision Tree Analysis

Ferguson Company is investigating the profitability of a proposed new product. If the product is introduced, minimum production must be 20,000 units per month. Sales have been forecast as follows:

Units	Probability	Units	Probability
10,000	.2	30,000	.3
20,000	.4	40,000	.1

It is possible that variable costs will be either $8, $7, or $6 per unit, with probabilities of .2, .5, and .3, respectively. Fixed costs are likely to be $100,000 with a probability of .6 or $120,000 with a probability of .4. The sales price has been set at $15 per unit. Any unsold units must be disposed of because they deteriorate rapidly.

Required:
(a) Prepare a decision tree analysis of the profit potential of this product.
(b) What is the expected value of the profit from this product? Show how this can be derived from the decision tree.
(c) What is the value of the most likely outcome in this analysis? How likely is this event? Why does this event have a different value than the expected value?
(d) A risk averse decision maker is reviewing your analysis in part (a). What parts of the analysis would be of most interest to such a decision maker? Why?
(e) Should the product be introduced? Why or why not? Explain what attitude toward risk is reflected in your decision.

P 16–14   Decision Tree Analysis—Product Innovation Decision

Hodgson Corporation is planning to introduce a new product line. Initial estimates of product research and development costs are $200,000. However, there is only a 75 percent probability that the project will be successful. If this first stage is not successful, a further $100,000 may be allocated. In that case, there will be an 80 percent probability that the project will be successful after additional costs of $300,000. At this point, the project will be abandoned if it is still unsuccessful.

Assuming that a successful product can be developed, sales forecasts show the following:

	Unit Sales	Probability
Highly Successful	1,200,000	.3
Moderately Successful	800,000	.4
Unaccepted Product	200,000	.3

The product will have a market life of only three months because it can only be sold to persons attending a convention that is held every ten years. Fixed manufacturing and distribution costs (excluding product development costs) will be $600,000. Variable costs of manufacture and distribution will be $3.50 per unit. The anticipated sales price will be $5 per unit.

Required:
(a) Prepare a decision tree analysis to represent all possible outcomes of this situation.
(b) What is the expected value of the net income from this venture? Show how it can be derived from the decision tree analysis.
(c) Based on the expected value analysis, should the project be undertaken? Why or why not?
(d) Two decision makers, one who is quite risk averse and one who is a risk seeker, evaluate the project. What information in the decision tree analysis would each be most interested in?
(e) Would you undertake this project? Why or why not? Explain the attitude towards uncertainty that influenced your choice.

(f) If an additional $600,000 is spent on advertising, it is predicted that the sales forecast will be affected as follows:

Units	Probability	Units	Probability
1,500,000	.3	400,000	.1
1,200,000	.5	200,000	.1

Should the project be undertaken under these circumstances? Why or why not? Discuss fully.

P 16–15 Game Theory—Decision Analysis

Valley Gold Fruit Company is trying to decide how to market a fruit crop which is subject to possible damage from severe temperature fluctuations. A local canning company is prepared to purchase the entire crop immediately, which is two months prior to the normal harvest time. The canner's price will assure the fruit company of a $200,000 return if the crop meets quality specifications. However, if the crop is affected by weather conditions, the contract stipulates that the return to the fruit company will only be $100,000.

The alternative is to market the crop in the fresh fruit market after it is harvested. At forecast market prices, this will give the company a return of $350,000 if the fruit is in top condition. However, if the crop is damaged the market probably will only accept the fruit as inferior grade, in which case the return will be $50,000.

Required:
(a) Prepare a payoff matrix to show the outcomes of all the possible combinations of actions and states.
(b) What action would you recommend that the fruit company take? Why?
(c) Analysis of weather in previous years shows that the probability of the type of weather likely to damage the crop prior to the harvest date is (1) .25, or (2) .5. What action would you recommend now? Why?
(d) Discuss any differences in your answers to parts (b) and (c). If the answers are the same, explain why they are. Discuss specifically the attitude toward risk that is implied in your answer.

P 16–16 Value of Information—Decision Analysis

Refer to Problem 16–15. Assume that a meteorological consultant has offered to forecast the weather for the critical period. Results of the forecast can be assumed to be correct. It has been noted that good weather conditions occur with a probability of .7.

Required:
(a) What would be the value of the forecast information to the fruit company (assuming that it is always correct as stated above)?
(b) Assume now that the records of the consultant show that, in such situations, a favorable weather prediction is made 75 percent of the time and an unfavorable weather prediction 25 percent of the time. However, although all the unfavorable predictions prove to be correct, only 80 percent of the favorable predictions turn out to be correct. Revise your analysis of the value of this information, based on the assumption that an expected value criterion is used to make the decision.

(c)   Discuss the appropriateness of expected value criteria for decisions of this type. What alternative criteria would be more appropriate? Which ones would be inappropriate? Why?

P 16–17   Decision Making under Conditions of Uncertainty—Value of Information

The *Daily Bugle* is reviewing its production volume decision making process. It has been printing 1,000,000 copies per day. Sales results have been as follows:

Sales	Probability
1,000,000	.75
800,000	.15
600,000	.10

In addition, when all 1,000,000 copies are sold, there is sometimes unfilled demand. It is estimated that under those circumstances 200,000 extra copies could have been sold 25 percent of the time.

The paper sells for 25¢ per copy, of which variable production and distribution costs account for 15¢ per copy. Unsold copies are worth 2¢ each as recyclable paper.

Required:
(a)   Using expected value criteria, what is the best production level for the company? (Assume that printing must be done in lots of 200,000.)
(b)   If it were possible to predict exactly what the sales volume would be on each day, by how much could the company improve its profits *over what it is achieving presently?*
(c)   In relation to the solution to part (a), what is the value of the perfect prediction mentioned in part (b)?
(d)   What is the expected value of daily sales volume? What is the expected value of the contribution margin under those circumstances? Is this the same as the optimal solution you derived in part (a)? Why or why not? State the assumption about the production decision that was necessary to answer this question.

P 16–18   Decision Making under Conditions of Uncertainty—Value of Information

Santa Albany Corporation produces and sells racetrack programs for each day of its racing season. Predicting daily sales is a problem, because unsold programs are a complete loss and unhappy potential patrons who don't get a program sometimes decide not to attend that day. Programs sell for $1.50 each and cost $1 to print and distribute. Daily sales over the past few seasons have been distributed as follows:

Sales (units)	Probability
6,000	.25
8,000	.20
10,000	.30
12,000	.25

Required:

(a) Prepare a table of payoff values for each of the four possible production volumes. (Assume that there is no cost associated with being out of stock.)

(b) Based on this analysis, what is the best number of programs to print?

(c) Assuming the company never wants to have an unsatisfied patron, how many should it print each day? Relative to your solution to part (b), what is the cost of this policy?

(d) What is the expected value of the number of programs sold each day? How much is the contribution associated with that number? Is this the same as your solution to part (b)? Why or why not?

(e) A sportswriter in the area offers to forecast daily attendance. Relative to your solution to part (b), if he is able to do an errorless job, what will his services be worth to the company?

(f) Referring to the original data, assume that whenever there are not enough programs, there is a probability that one customer in ten who misses out on a program decides not to attend the track that day. The lost contribution margin per customer is estimated to be $50. Prepare a revised payoff table to reflect this extra information. What is the best number of programs to print based on this analysis?

P 16–19 Decision Making under Conditions of Uncertainty— Comprehensive Review

Renk Company's single product is subject to rapid deterioration if not sold within one week of manufacture. Because production time is also one week, the decision concerning how many to produce each week is critical. The sales price is $100 per unit. Variable manufacturing costs are $40 per unit and variable marketing costs are $20 per unit. All other costs are fixed and amount to $150,000 per week. During the past two years, weekly sales have fluctuated around a steady 10,000 units per week as follows:

Unit Sales per Week	Number of Weeks
8,000	10
9,000	20
10,000	50
11,000	10
12,000	10
	100

When there is not enough inventory on hand to meet sales orders in any week, the company makes up the deficiency by buying the units needed from a competitor. The purchase price is $105 per unit, but Renk still incurs the same amount of variable marketing costs on these units. Excess units on hand at the end of any week have a resale value as scrap of $5 per unit.

The company has adhered to a policy of producing 11,000 units each week. It is interested in investigating alternative production and sales strategies.

Required:

(a) Prepare a schedule to show the weekly net income to be earned at each sales level under the present production plan.

(b) What is the expected value of weekly net income at the present time?

(c) Prepare a payoff table for each of the other four possible production levels to show their respective expected weekly net incomes.

(d) Based on your answers to parts (a), (b), and (c), is the company presently pursuing the best production strategy? Why or why not?

(e) If Renk Company cuts its price by $10, the firm's customers can be induced to order one week earlier. This will allow the company to know exactly how many units to produce each week. Is this an acceptable alternative to the present best strategy as selected in part (d)? Why or why not?

(f) As another alternative, an agency that specializes in negotiating sales of this product has made the following proposal. For a weekly fee of $50,000, the agency will agree to purchase any of the company's excess production at the market price of $100. It will also make up any deficit in production for the company at a cost of $60 per unit delivered to customers. Is this an acceptable alternative to the present best strategy selected in part (d) or to the proposal in part (e)? Why or why not?

17

BASIC CAPITAL BUDGETING ANALYSIS

LEARNING OBJECTIVES

After studying Chapter 17, you should be able to:

1. List the sequence of steps that a manager might take in planning the acquisition and use of long-term assets.
2. Define the terms project, project life, investment outlay, net benefit flows, cost of capital, rate of return, operating cash flows, and reinvestment assumption.
3. Distinguish between accept–reject decisions and ranking–rationing decisions.
4. Given an income statement and information about operating costs and revenues, calculate cash flow after taxes.
5. Distinguish between nondiscounting and discounting methods of capital budgeting analysis and explain the circumstances in which each type is useful. Explain the advantages and limitations of the various capital budgeting methods.
6. Evaluate capital investment projects using the following nondiscounting methods:
   a. Accounting rate of return
   b. Payback period
   c. Payback reciprocal
   d. Bailout factor
7. Evaluate capital investment projects using the following discounting methods:
   a. Net present value
   b. Net present value ratio
   c. Internal rate of return
   d. Discounted payback period

Many business decisions have significant long-run effects on company operations. Decisions to buy new or replacement fixed assets, to establish a product line, to open a factory, or to set up a sales outlet—to suggest a few examples—need to be analyzed on a long-term, multiperiod basis because of their far-reaching effects.

The definition of *long-term* must be somewhat arbitrary, because multiperiod analysis might be applied to groups of short periods (weeks or months). The important identifying characteristics of long-term investment decisions are that the relevant decision variables (costs, revenues, resources acquired and supplied, capacity levels, and so on) affect *successive* accounting periods and that their amounts *vary* from period to period.

The accounting-related decision techniques that are applied to such long-run investments are referred to collectively as **capital budgeting analysis.** Emphasis is placed both on the term *capital,* suggesting that the resources involved are long-term and often fixed in nature, and on the term *budgeting,* indicating that the analysis serves control as well as planning purposes. This chapter explores the general class of problems to which capital budgeting applies, demonstrates capital budgeting calculations, and assesses the usefulness and limitations of commonly used capital budgeting methods.

THE CAPITAL BUDGETING SYSTEM

Short-term budgeting was demonstrated in connection with the preparation of master financial and operating budgets, the development of incremental analysis for short-run decision making, and the preparation and use of flexible budgets. A firm's total budgetary system should also include planning and control procedures for the acquisition and use of long-term resources. A **capital budgeting system** consists of two separate but related aspects—*financing* (securing funds) and *investing*(applying funds).

Accounting data are needed for decision making in both these areas, in order to measure the *costs* of funds secured for investment purposes and the *returns* that will be generated when those funds are invested. For example, if the problem involves deciding whether or not to establish a new sales outlet, the decision maker needs information concerning the expected cost of operating the sales outlet, its expected revenues, and the amount and cost of funds needed to acquire and operate its assets.

THE TIME HORIZON IN CAPITAL BUDGETING

Capital budgeting should be viewed as a continuous process. A firm's long-range plans need not be reviewed and reformulated every day, but long-term projects should be continually monitored, and at appropriate points in time specific problem-solving procedures should be initiated. Capital budgeting analysis may become a feature of annual master budget preparation, but it need not be restricted to that time frame. In capital budgeting terms, the annual budget is only an installment in the firm's total long-range planning commitments.

Philosophies of long-term budgeting range from an ambitious, whole-life, total systems approach to a limited, finite time horizon approach (for example, a five-year plan) to ad hoc practices useful only in reacting to emergencies. This latter approach is unfortunately typical of many businesses in which long-range commitments are made in response to breakdowns, obsolescence, the wearing out of fixed assets, or the financial difficulties of company segments.

The more deliberate the planning and the longer the company's time horizon, the more likely sophisticated capital budgeting methods are to be used. On the other hand, when little planning is done, budgetary tools tend to be rudimentary. For example, suppose a firm's policy is to allow its motor vehicles to wear out completely before being replaced. When a truck does break down, management's alternatives will be necessarily limited because of the urgent need to obtain a replacement, the difficulty of acquiring funds on short notice, and the limited range of replacement choices. These problems can be avoided if the company adopts a formal vehicle replacement policy. Such a policy might include establishing vehicle maintenance guidelines, projecting usage requirements, planning to have funds available for replacement purchases, selecting methods of financing, and comparing beforehand the available replacement vehicles.

A recommended approach involves developing and implementing a *finite time horizon capital budgeting system.* This allows a firm to progressively revise its plans for asset acquisition and use over some definite time period—perhaps five or ten years into the future. Such a system might include the following sequence of steps:

1. Identify overall company goals for the total time period.
2. Estimate when major fixed asset acquisitions will be required during that period.
3. Determine the potential sources of the funds needed to acquire those assets.
4. Evaluate periodically the firm's long-term investing and financing requirements and coordinate these with annual financial and operating budgets.
5. Select particular long-term projects to be implemented and identify sources of funds to finance them.
6. Integrate the immediate effects of long-term project decisions into current financial and operating budgets.
7. Evaluate progress on long-term projects in a manner consistent with the techniques used in selecting the projects.
8. Revise the first three steps, based on feedback obtained from step 7, to provide for continuity in the capital budgeting system.

The accounting function is important in performing steps 4 through 7, especially in evaluating proposals for sources and uses of funds; coordinating capital budgeting plans with current budgets; and measuring, evaluating, and reporting the performance of ongoing capital budgeting projects. Procedures for the first three steps in this sequence should parallel those outlined in Chapter 7 with respect to budget preparation in general. These include considering organizational goals in developing budgets, using appropriate budget models, integrating the budgets of interrelated areas, and using participative and coordinative budgetary techniques.

Ordinary budget procedures must be adapted to the special circumstances of long-term planning. There is a great deal of difference between budgeting for one month's operations of a single department in a standardized manufacturing process, and budgeting for the total plant and equipment requirements of a large corporation for a five-year period. The differences between normal and capital budgeting include the following:

1. The broader scope of the long-term budgeting process.
2. The greater uncertainties involved in long-term planning.
3. The more highly aggregated planning variables in long-term budgeting.
4. The greater importance of the timing of events in long-term planning.
5. The greater degree of commitment and permanence involved in long-term projects.

ACCOUNTING TERMINOLOGY IN CAPITAL BUDGETING ANALYSIS

A specialized accounting vocabulary is used in capital budgeting analysis. Terms requiring definition include project, project life, investment outlay, net benefit flows, cost of capital, and rate of return.

PROJECT

The word **project** describes any long-term transaction or set of transactions to which capital budgeting analysis is applied. A project may involve the acquisition of a new motor vehicle, the replacement of a machine, the establishment of a sales outlet, or the discontinuance of a product or product line. A project is defined in terms of its expected economic duration (*project life*), the amount of funds needed to make it operational (*investment outlay*), and the net operating returns it will produce during that project life (*net benefit flows*). The cost of funds needed to support a project over its life is the *cost of capital*.

PROJECT LIFE

Project life is the length of time during which the project continues to have some measurable effect on company performance. It begins with the first acquisition outlays and ends when operating revenues and costs cease and the project's assets have been disposed of. If company policy is to replace vehicles at five-year intervals, the life of such a project can be set precisely at five years. For the more common situation in which a project's lifespan cannot be exactly forecast (for example, a new product line), the project life must be estimated by marketing research and product planning experts.

INVESTMENT OUTLAY

The **investment outlay** (or investment base) is the net cost of acquiring a project and getting it into normal operating condition. This outlay includes the purchase price of items that comprise the *physical substance* of the project (buildings, equipment, vehicles), as well as its *legal substance* (licences, franchise fees, patents). It also includes costs of installing and testing physical assets and any recruiting and training costs of the workers who operate them. When new products or production methods are introduced, the investment outlay may also include research, development, and testing costs.[1]

When an acquisition involves the sale, trade in, or other disposal of existing assets, the net proceeds from such dispositions must be deducted from the cost of the new assets to arrive at the effective investment outlay. The undepreciated book values of the assets being disposed of do not directly affect the amount of the investment outlay. They represent sunk costs because they were incurred in the past and are not influenced by the investment decision. However, the income tax effects of dispositions (capital gains and losses) do affect investment outlays, as do any related tax effects of the acquisition (investment tax credits). Finally, when a capital budgeting project requires an increase in current assets (for example, increased inventories, receivables, or cash balances), these amounts must also be considered part of the investment outlay.

NET BENEFIT FLOWS

Net benefit flows are the results obtained from operating the project over its life, excluding financing costs. There will usually be both positive flows (returns, revenues, or inflows) and negative flows (costs or outflows). Measurement should be in terms of the performance criteria used by the company to express its own objectives. If this can be done in monetary terms, the relevant measures are of cash inflows and cash outflows.

Most outflows can be measured directly in terms of the monetary cost of operating a project. Inflows typically include additional revenues received as a result of project operations, such as increased sales from a new product line or market outlet. Reductions in cash outflows, such as cost savings from the use of a more efficient machine, really amount to net cash inflows.

When the inflows associated with a project are less tangible, measurement becomes a problem. For example, it should be feasible to measure a new product's benefits in terms of the sales revenue it will generate. However, if the project involves the installation of a new computerized data processing system, the benefits will not be directly measurable in terms of increased revenues. Although "improved decision making" and "more profitable operations" may characterize the planned outputs of the computer installation, it is difficult to place a monetary value on such vaguely defined benefits.

It is often convenient to assume that the benefits derived from a proposed project will be at least equal to those present in the existing situation. For exam-

---

[1] For internal capital budgeting analysis, research and development costs may properly be capitalized as investment outlays. For external reporting purposes, research and development costs must normally be charged to expense. See "Accounting for Research and Development Costs," *Statement of Financial Accounting Standards No. 2* (Stamford, Conn.: FASB, 1974).

ple, a new delivery truck will normally be capable of performing the same functions and providing the same benefits as the present truck. This assumption simplifies capital budgeting analysis by allowing projects to be evaluated entirely in terms of their required cash outflows.

In this chapter, net benefit flows will be expressed in terms of cash inflows and outflows that occur as a result of operations throughout the project's life. The timing of these cash flows materially affects the results produced by most of the capital budgeting methods that will be demonstrated. Care should also be taken to identify and measure net benefit flows on a basis consistent with the project's intended purpose. For example, if a project involves replacing one machine with another, the *incremental* net benefits that result from the replacement must be analyzed. The basic techniques of incremental analysis presented in Chapter 9 can be used in such situations, with the difference that they apply to changes that occur over a series of time periods.

It is particularly important that a project's *after-tax operating cash flows* be measured accurately. These will be different from its *after-tax income,* which includes depreciation and other noncash expenses.

Example: Myeve Corporation has annual sales of $400,000 and operating expenses of $150,000, excluding depreciation of $50,000. The income tax rate is 40 percent of taxable income.

Figure 17–1 shows the derivation of the company's after-tax net income. The $120,000 after-tax net income is a deceptive indicator of both net benefit flows and the change in Myeve Corporation's spending power. Items C and F are the only net cash flows in the income statement. The company's after-tax cash flow can be derived directly from them.

Cash Flow before Taxes (C)	$250,000
Less: Income Tax @ 40% (F)	80,000
Cash Flow after Taxes	$170,000

The after-tax cash flow can also be determined by adding depreciation cost to the after-tax net income.

FIGURE 17–1

Myeve Corporation
Income Statement
For the Year Ended December 31, 19X7

(A)	Sales	$400,000
(B)	Less: Operating Expenses (cash)	150,000
(C)	Cash Flow before Taxes	$250,000
(D)	Less: Depreciation	50,000
(E)	Taxable Income	$200,000
(F)	Less: Income Tax @ 40%	80,000
(G)	Net Income after Taxes	$120,000

Net Income after Taxes (G)		$120,000
Add: Depreciation (noncash item) (D)		50,000
Cash Flow after Taxes		$170,000

The $170,000 after-tax cash flow can also be derived by adjusting the cash flow before taxes (item C) to reflect income tax payments and the tax shield from depreciation:

Cash Flow before Taxes (C)	$250,000	
Less: Income Tax @ 40%	100,000	$150,000
Add: Tax Shield from Depreciation		
($50,000 × 40%)		20,000
Cash Flow after Taxes		$170,000

COST OF CAPITAL

Cost of capital is the term used to describe the effective cost of funds needed to support a project over its life. The investment outlay needed to finance a project requires a commitment of funds that are then unavailable for other uses, but are gradually recovered as net benefit flows are generated. Therefore, the amount of funds needed to support a project over its remaining life will always equal the unrecovered portion of the investment outlay.

There are several ways to measure cost of capital. One conventional approach is to calculate the *weighted average cost of all available funds,* both from equity and debt sources. This includes the effective interest costs of borrowed funds (loans, notes, bonds, mortgages) and the implicit cost of equity funds (capital stock and retained earnings).

An alternative is to measure the *incremental cost of the funds actually spent on each project.* Because it is applied both to the investment outlay and to the net benefit flows, this allows the concept of incrementality to be preserved throughout the capital budgeting analysis. However, this approach is often complicated by the difficulty of identifying the sources of funds used for a particular project. It may also produce inconsistent decisions when the incremental cost of funds varies. For example, suppose that two equally profitable projects are evaluated against two different incremental costs of capital. The first would be evaluated against the more cheaply available funds and might be accepted. The second would be more apt to be rejected, because it would have to be evaluated against the higher cost of capital of the scarcer funds.

A third approach to measuring cost of capital is the generalized **opportunity cost** concept, which assumes that there is a universally available risk-free rate of return that can be earned on invested funds. This return is effectively foregone by the commitment of funds to *any* project. A variation on this approach involves specifying, before the investment is made, some subjectively chosen minimum acceptable rate of return and calling this the cost of capital. A refinement of these opportunity cost approaches is to define the cost of capital as the rate of return available on other projects that have similar characteristics (project life, investment outlay, and certainty of receipt of net benefit flows). The practical problem is to decide how similar these characteristics have to be. Must they be exactly equal, or can they fall within some reasonable range?

In this chapter, *the cost of capital will be assumed to equal the opportunity cost of alternative projects that involve similar types of assets, with similar lives and outlays and a similar certainty of receiving net benefit flows*—that is, projects involving about the same amount of risk.

RATE OF RETURN

In its most general form, a **rate of return** is defined as the ratio of the amount of a return to the base that supports or produces that return—that is,

$$\text{Rate of Return} = \frac{\text{Return}}{\text{Base}}$$

Because there are many acceptable ways of calculating rates of return, care must be taken to define exactly *which return* and *which base* are involved in any particular calculation. Here are several different rates of return:

1. $\text{Net Income Rate} = \dfrac{\text{Net Income}}{\text{Net Sales}}$

2. $\text{Gross Profit Ratio} = \dfrac{\text{Gross Profit}}{\text{Net Sales}}$

3. $\text{Contribution Margin Ratio} = \dfrac{\text{Contribution Margin}}{\text{Net Sales}}$

4. $\text{Return on Common Stockholder's Equity} = \dfrac{\text{Net Income Available to Common Stockholders}}{\text{(Average) Total Common Stockholder's Equity}}$

5. $\text{Return on Total Assets or Return on Total Investment} = \dfrac{\text{Operating Income}}{\text{(Average) Total Assets or Investment}}$

Several variations of the rate of return on total assets, typically referred to as **return on investment** ratios (R.O.I.), will be examined in this chapter. Emphasis will be on measuring the ratio numerator and denominator—operating income and investment outlay—and on the uses of this ratio as a capital budgeting tool.

AN OVERVIEW OF CAPITAL BUDGETING ANALYSIS

Capital budgeting analysis involves a set of procedures used to select courses of action involving projects that extend over several accounting periods. As in all decision analysis, the capital budgeting decision should begin with a precise definition of the problem to be solved. This definition should include specification of the goals to be attained, the performance criteria relevant to those goals, the decision rules to be applied in the selection process, the set of alternatives to be evaluated, and the separation of the relevant decision variables from those that are to be treated as external to the decision situation.

These are largely management tasks. The accounting function is to evaluate a project or group of projects according to specified performance criteria, using the tools of capital budgeting analysis. To do this, accountants must first ensure that the **decision perspective** is properly established. For example:

1. If the capital budgeting problem involves comparing two new projects, the analysis should focus on the separate *performance measures* of each project (investment outlays, net benefit flows, and so on).

2. If the problem is whether or not to change from an existing project to an alternative, the *incremental effects* of the change are the central features of any analysis.

3. If only one project is being considered, it may be compared to the alternative of taking no action.

4. Deciding whether or not to discontinue an existing project also involves the alternative of taking no action.

Each of these four general decision perspectives is in effect a variation of the incremental perspective, because every capital budgeting project must be compared with some other alternative, even if that alternative is to do nothing.

The decision perspective will be affected by the availability of support funds for the proposed project or projects. When funds sufficient to finance the project are readily available, the only decision necessary is whether to accept or reject the project. When funds are insufficient to undertake all proposed projects, a means of *ranking* the competing projects and a cutoff system for screening out unacceptable projects are necessary.

Most examples in this chapter will demonstrate the criteria for accept–reject capital budgeting decisions. These are usually easy to apply and they produce consistent results if the decision criteria themselves are consistent. However, when rankings are required, the various decision criteria used in capital budgeting analysis may not always produce *consistent* rankings.

Example: Frances Company is considering expansion of its facilities to produce and distribute a new type of water purifier. The total outlay needed to buy the necessary manufacturing and support equipment is $400,000. This equipment will have a useful life of eight years—the same as the market life of the new product—but will have no residual value thereafter. Annual sales of the water purifiers are estimated at 20,000 units. The product will sell for $10 per unit. Variable manufacturing and marketing costs will total $4 per unit. Increased fixed manufacturing and administrative costs, not counting depreciation of new equipment, will amount to $20,000 per year. Because demand is expected to remain stable over the eight-year period, production will be maintained at 20,000 units per year. Straight line depreciation will be taken. The tax rate is 40 percent of taxable income. Frances Company has specified a 10 percent cost of capital for investment projects of this size, risk, and duration.

For purposes of capital budgeting analysis, this project can be assessed as follows:

1. *Problem Perspective*   This is an incremental decision situation because the new product will be manufactured in addition to existing outputs. Therefore, analysis should be restricted to the incremental effects of this new product on the assumption that it will have no side effects on any of the company's existing operations.

2. *Project Life*   The product's expected economic life of eight years should be the period of capital budgeting analysis.

3. *Cost of Capital*   Frances Company has decided that 10% is the effective cost of capital to be used in evaluating this project's profitability. To be acceptable, the project must earn a return on investment of at least 10 percent.

4. *Investment Outlay*   The project's only required cash expenditure is

---

FIGURE 17–2

Frances Company
Income Statement and Schedule of Operating Cash Flows

(A)	**Income Statement**	
	Sales (20,000 units @ $10)	$200,000
	Less: Variable Costs (20,000 units @ $4)	80,000
	Contribution Margin	$120,000
	Less: Fixed Costs	20,000
	Cash Flow Before Taxes	$100,000
	Less: Depreciation ($400,000 ÷ 8)	50,000
	Taxable Income	$ 50,000
	Less: Income Taxes (40%)	20,000
	Net Income	$ 30,000
(B)	**Cash Flow Analysis**	
	Derivation Method 1	
	Cash Flow before Taxes	$100,000
	Less: Income Taxes	20,000
	Operating Cash Flow after Taxes	$ 80,000
	Derivation Method 2	
	Net Income after Taxes	$ 30,000
	Add: Depreciation	50,000
	Operating Cash Flow after Taxes	$ 80,000
	Derivation Method 3	
	Cash Flow before Taxes $100,000	
	Less: Income Taxes (40%) 40,000	$ 60,000
	Add: Tax Shield from Depreciation ($50,000 × 40%)	20,000
	Operating Cash Flow after Taxes	$ 80,000

$400,000, the cost of the new production and support equipment. This investment outlay will occur at the start of the project life. Because these assets have no salvage value, the depreciation basis will also be $400,000.

5. *Net Benefit Flows*   This project's purpose is to produce and market a new product. Therefore, the benefit flows to be analyzed are the operating cash flows from the product's manufacture and sale. Because the same sales volume and other performance measures are anticipated each year, the operating cash flows for all eight years will be identical to those shown in Figure 17–2.

The first method of deriving operating cash flow is preferable because it is the most direct method and because it emphasizes the fact that net operating cash flow is influenced not by depreciation charges themselves, but by the tax effect of the depreciation expense on the amount of cash outflow. The second method is a shortcut technique that converts net income into after-tax cash flows. The third method shows separately the effects of depreciation expense in reducing taxes.

EVALUATING CAPITAL BUDGETING PROPOSALS

The preceding data concerning problem perspective, project life, cost of capital, investment outlay, and net benefit flows must now be analyzed using capital budgeting decision criteria. There are two general types of capital budgeting decision rules—nondiscounting methods and discounting methods.

Nondiscounting methods are fairly simple evaluation procedures that do not take into account the time value of money. *Discounting methods* are more rigorous in that they do account for the time value of money. In recent years, as a more scientific and comprehensive approach to capital budgeting analysis has replaced previously used rule-of-thumb methods, the use of discounting procedures has been increasingly accepted.

NONDISCOUNTING METHODS

Three nondiscounting methods of evaluating capital budgeting proposals will be demonstrated: accounting rate of return, payback period, and bailout factor.

ACCOUNTING RATE OF RETURN

The **accounting rate of return** is a commonly used capital budgeting rule. It compares a project's accounting rate of return to a predetermined cost of capital. In practice, no universal form of this rule exists, because the project returns, project investment base, and cost of capital can be defined and measured in various ways.

This method measures the average annual rate (per dollar of the investment base that supports it) at which a project generates returns. In accrual accounting terms, returns are measured as net average annual income from the project. This should be an operating income measure that excludes financing costs. Returns may be calculated either before or after income tax expense, but the tax assumptions must be specified when calculating or using a rate of return rule.

Example: In the Frances Company example shown in Figure 17-2, both the average annual income before taxes ($50,000), and the net average annual income after taxes ($30,000) can be used as numerators in accounting rate of return calculations.

The total investment base of $400,000 is the acquisition cost of the project's assets. Using this figure as the denominator in a rate of return calculation implies that the whole investment outlay is needed to support the project over its life, even while returns are being generated. An alternative assumption is that the investment outlay is recovered at a uniform rate throughout the project's life. The denominator is then the average of the project's book value at the outset of the project life and at its termination. For Frances Company, this average investment base is $200,000 [($400,000 + 0) ÷ 2].

Combining the preceding income figures and investment bases produces *four* possible measures of the accrual accounting rate of return for this project, as shown in Figure 17–3. These rates of return are measures of the project's *average operating profitability.*

A parallel series of calculations can be made to measure the project's *cash flow generating rate.* Frances Company's average annual operating cash flow is $100,000 before taxes and $80,000 after taxes. Figure 17–4 shows the results of using these average cash flows as numerators in rate of return calculations in which the full and average investment bases are the denominators.

It should now be apparent that many different rates of return can be calculated for a single project. None of them is necessarily a correct measure of the project's profitability. The most one can say is that a series of projects can be *ranked consistently* if the same rate of return calculation is applied to each of them. If a number of alternative projects are evaluated on the basis

---

FIGURE 17–3

Frances Company
Accrual Income Rates of Return

	Total Investment Base	Average Investment Base
Before-tax Rate	$\frac{\$50,000}{\$400,000} = 12.5\%$	$\frac{\$50,000}{\$200,000} = 25\%$
After-tax Rate	$\frac{\$30,000}{\$400,000} = 7.5\%$	$\frac{\$30,000}{\$200,000} = 15\%$

FIGURE 17–4

**Frances Company
Cash Flow Rates of Return**

	Total Investment Base	Average Investment Base
Before-tax Rate	$\dfrac{\$100,000}{\$400,000} = 25\%$	$\dfrac{\$100,000}{\$200,000} = 50\%$
After-tax Rate	$\dfrac{\$\ 80,000}{\$400,000} = 20\%$	$\dfrac{\$\ 80,000}{\$200,000} = 40\%$

---

of one particular rate of return, an elementary screening procedure can be applied in which all projects that fail to meet a specified minimum rate of return are immediately rejected.

If this cutoff point or target rate of return is to be compared with the average accounting rate of return, it should reflect the *average cost* of funds used in a project. Moreover, this average cost should include more than just interest charges and other explicit financing costs. A project with an operating cash flow rate of return that exceeds its average cost of funds is assured of covering only those explicit financing costs. The target rate of return should include the weighted average cost of *all* funds, both explicit and implicit, including funds from debt and equity sources.

Many methods have been proposed to measure the average cost of total funds. One popular technique[2] involves the following definitions:

$$C_d = \text{Average cost of borrowed (debt) funds}$$
$$C_e = \text{Average cost of equity funds}$$
$$p_1 = \text{Proportion of borrowed funds}$$
$$1 - p_1 = \text{Proportion of equity funds}$$
$$D = \text{Dividend per share}$$
$$P = \text{Market price of one share}$$
$$g = \text{Expected annual growth rate of dividends}$$
$$C_a = \text{Average cost of all funds}$$

Accordingly, if

$$C_e = \frac{D}{P} + g$$

then

$$C_a = p_1 C_d + (1 - p_1) C_e$$

Measured in this way, the average cost of total funds approximates the opportunity cost of capital as defined earlier in the chapter. It does so because the key variables (market price of stock, dividend rate, and expected growth

[2] James C. Van Horne, *Financial Management and Policy,* Fourth Edition (Englewood Cliffs, N.J.: Prentice Hall, 1977).

of dividends) tend to reflect the firm's earnings expectations. Such expectations are based on the general type and risk class of investment opportunities normally available to Frances Company. Therefore, this calculation of the cost of equity funds approximates the opportunity cost of funds which is implied by the relationship between the market price of stock and dividends paid or expected to be paid.

Example: The average cost of total funds is calculated as follows if Frances Company obtains funds from these debt and equity sources:

	Amount	Proportion
Total Borrowed Funds......	$ 2,500,000	.25
Total Equity Funds.........	7,500,000	.75
	$10,000,000	1.00

Average After-tax Interest Rate on Borrowed Funds = 8%
Dividends per Share = $5
Market Price per Share = $20
Expected Growth Rate of Dividends = 15%

Then the average cost of equity funds can be calculated as follows:

$$C_e = \frac{D}{P} + g$$

$$= \frac{\$5}{\$20} + .15$$

$$= .25 + .15$$

$$= .40$$

Therefore, the average cost of total funds is 32 percent, calculated as follows:

$$C_a = p_1 C_d + (1 - p_1)\, C_e$$
$$= (.25)\,(.08) + (.75)\,(.40)$$
$$= .02 + .30$$
$$= .32$$

When this average cost of funds is used as a target or cutoff rate of return, it should be compared to the project's *after-tax cash flow rate of return*. The project is acceptable and should be undertaken if its rate of return exceeds the average cost of funds. Otherwise it should be rejected. By this test Frances Company's project is acceptable—its average cost of funds is 32 percent and its cash flow rate of return, calculated on an *average* investment base, is 40 percent. However, if the 32 percent average cost of funds is compared to the 20 percent cash flow rate of return calculated on the *full* investment base, the project will be rejected.

Limitations of Accounting Rates of Return   Accounting rates of return measure *average returns* over a project's life. Projects with the same lifespans and equal total returns will have the same average returns. If investment outlays for such projects are also equal, they will have identical average rates of return and will be ranked equally. Such rankings ignore the fact that some projects pay off more quickly than others and that, other things being equal, the sooner returns are obtained during a project's life, the more desirable that project is. In other words, by giving equal weights to returns from different time periods in calculating average rates of return, this method ignores the time value of money.

Accounting rates of return also fail to consider the earning power of operating cash inflows. Total operating returns are identified with the project that generates them, but these funds are implicitly treated as merging into a general pool of funds available for later use. The reinvestment or other use of cash inflows is ignored in calculating a project's profitability.

Finally, there is the problem of standardizing accounting rate of return calculations. As was noted, there are income rates of return, cash flow rates of return, and before- and after-tax rates of return. In addition, the investment base may be a total or an average measure. The cost of capital or target rate with which the accounting rate of return is to be compared can also be calculated in various ways, some of which are quite subjective. The existence of so many variations diminishes the usefulness of this method as a capital budgeting tool.

PAYBACK PERIOD

Because the recovery of funds invested in a project is of major importance, the length of time that a project takes to pay for itself is another indicator of its acceptability. When operating cash flows are assumed to occur at a constant rate during the project's life, this **payback period** is calculated as follows:

$$\text{Payback Period (in years)} = \frac{\text{Investment Outlay}}{\text{Average Annual Operating Cash Flows}}$$

In the Frances Company example, the payback period is five years ($400,000 ÷ $80,000). The project's operating cash inflows will repay its cost in five years. But when operating cash inflows vary from period to period, a table of cumulative cash inflows is needed to find the point at which the total cash flow recoveries exceed the investment outlay.

Example: Convey Company is considering a project that requires an investment outlay of $200,000 and has the annual cash inflows shown in Figure 17–5. This project will pay back its total cost during the *sixth year,* when the cumulative cash inflows first exceed $200,000.

The payback period calculation can also be used to compare and screen alternative projects. Decision rules may arbitrarily specify a minimum payback period. Projects with payback periods exceeding that length of time will then be excluded from further consideration.

Like the accounting rate of return, the payback period should not be the only basis for project evaluation. Suppose a project has an investment outlay of $100,000 and operating cash flows of $25,000 per year, but a project life of only three years. Payback analysis is invalid here because the four-year payback period ($100,000 ÷ $25,000) is longer than the project life. Yet if a five-year minimum payback period is specified as a screening test and if payback

FIGURE 17–5

Convey Company
Cumulative Operating Cash Inflows

Year	Annual Operating Cash Inflows	Cumulative Cash Inflow
1	$35,000	$ 35,000
2	40,000	75,000
3	40,000	115,000
4	40,000	155,000
5	30,000	185,000
6	20,000	205,000
7	20,000	225,000
8	15,000	240,000

calculations are the only type of analysis made, this project would appear to be acceptable.

The **payback reciprocal** is also sometimes used as a ranking and evaluation test. For projects with constant annual cash flows, the payback reciprocal equals the average annual operating cash flow divided by the investment outlay.

$$\text{Payback Reciprocal} = \frac{\text{Average Annual Operating Cash Flow}}{\text{Investment Outlay}} = \frac{1}{\text{Payback Period}}$$

In the Frances Company example, the payback reciprocal is calculated as follows:

$$\frac{\$80,000}{\$400,000} = 20\% \quad \text{or} \quad \tfrac{1}{5} = 20\%$$

The payback reciprocal calculation gives the same result as the cash flow rate of return based on total investment outlay, as shown in Figure 17–4.

Summary   The payback period method is a conservative approach to capital budgeting analysis. It suggests that the recovery of investment outlays is more important than a project's overall profitability. For this reason, the payback period approach may be particularly appropriate in a high-risk decision making environment such as industries that have speculative characteristics (mining and fashion goods) or investments in countries or regions where the political and economic climate is volatile.

If used independently, the payback period may result in illogical decisions, as illustrated in the earlier example in which a five-year minimum payback period was used to screen a three-year project. This method may also cause certain projects with short payback periods to be ranked higher than more profitable projects with longer payback periods. To ensure that projects are adequately evaluated, the payback method should be supplemented by other capital budgeting techniques.

BAILOUT FACTOR

A variation of the payback period method is known as the bailout factor. This is also a time period measure, but instead of assuming that the project continues over its expected life, the bailout method compares the investment outlay with the project's cash cumulative inflows plus the amount that would be recovered if the project were terminated at the end of each period. The **bailout factor** is defined as the minimum number of periods necessary to allow cumulative operating cash flows plus terminal recovery value to exceed the

---

FIGURE 17-6

Convey Company
Projected Recovery Values from Project Disposal

End of Year	Recovery Value	End of Year	Recovery Value
1	$140,000	5	$35,000
2	90,000	6	20,000
3	70,000	7	10,000
4	55,000	8	0

FIGURE 17-7

Convey Company
Bailout Period
Operating Cash Inflows Plus Project Recovery Values

Year	Annual Operating Cash Inflow	Cumulative Operating Cash Inflow	Recovery Value	Total
1	$35,000	$ 35,000	$140,000	$175,000
2	40,000	75,000	90,000	165,000
3	40,000	115,000	70,000	185,000
4	40,000	155,000	55,000	210,000
5	30,000	185,000	35,000	220,000
6	20,000	205,000	20,000	225,000
7	20,000	225,000	10,000	235,000
8	15,000	240,000	0	240,000

investment outlay. Continuing the Convey Company example, assume that the projected recovery values from disposal of the project are as shown in Figure 17–6.

These terminal recovery values, combined with the operating cash inflows in Figure 17–5, are used to produce a table from which the bailout factor can be determined by inspection. In Figure 17–7, recovery of the $200,000 investment outlay occurs during the *fourth year*.

Summary   The bailout factor method of project evaluation has all the limitations of the payback period technique. In fact, it implies an even more conservative approach, because it assumes that a project may be abandoned at the end of any reporting period. Moreover, it does not permit comparison of the overall or relative profitability of different projects. It is chiefly useful in ranking competing projects and in screening out those for which expected cash flows plus recovery values will not equal the original investment outlay during some specified minimum time period.

DISCOUNTING METHODS

The more sophisticated capital budgeting methods adjust for the time value of money by basing calculations on the discounted present values of a project's cash flows.[3]

A major shortcoming of nondiscounting methods is that they fail to measure the present value of the future cash flows associated with a project. In fact, the accounting rate of return, payback period, and bailout factor methods may give equal rankings to projects with very dissimilar cash flow patterns.

Example: Tanoury Corporation is examining three projects with investment outlays and operating cash flows as shown in Figure 17–8.

Because average cash flow per period is the same for each project, all three projects have identical accounting rates of return. However, it should be intuitively clear that Project B is the most desirable of the three, because it promises the highest cash inflows in its early years. There is usually a better chance of actually receiving the returns that are predicted for early periods. Also, the sooner operating cash flows are received, the sooner they will be available for reinvestment or other use.

Four discounting methods of evaluating capital budgeting proposals will be demonstrated: net present value, net present value ratio, internal rate of return, and discounted payback period.

NET PRESENT VALUE

The discounting technique used most frequently in capital budgeting analysis is the **net present value** method. This method requires that all cash flows associated with a project be discounted at a predetermined rate equal to the project's

---

[3] It is assumed that students understand the basic rationale and the computational techniques of present value analysis. Appendix A, pages 867–72, provides a review of this material for those who need it.

FIGURE 17–8

Tanoury Corporation
Accounting Rate of Return Analysis of
Three Alternative Projects

	Project A	Project B	Project C
Investment Outlay	$120,000	$120,000	$120,000
Operating Cash Flows:			
Year 1	$ 10,000	$ 60,000	$ 40,000
Year 2	30,000	60,000	40,000
Year 3	30,000	30,000	40,000
Year 4	60,000	30,000	40,000
Year 5	70,000	20,000	40,000
	$200,000	$200,000	$200,000
Average Annual Cash Flow	$ 40,000	$ 40,000	$ 40,000
$\dfrac{\text{Accounting}}{\text{Rate of Return}} = \dfrac{\text{Average Annual Cash Flow}}{\text{Investment Outlay}} =$	33⅓%	33⅓%	33⅓%

---

cost of capital. The resulting amount is referred to as the net present value of the project. If this amount is *positive* (present values of inflows exceed present values of outflows), the project is acceptable. If it is *negative* (present values of inflows are less than present values of outflows), the project should be rejected.

Example: For Tanoury Corporation, which has specified a 16 percent cost of capital for projects of the type being evaluated, the net present value of its three proposed capital investment projects is calculated as shown in Figure 17–9.

Project A should be rejected because its net present value is negative, whereas Projects B and C are acceptable because their net present values are positive.

The net present value method assumes that operating cash inflows are reinvested at a rate equal to the prespecified cost of capital. Reinvestment is a necessary assumption that allows a project to be evaluated as an independent entity throughout its life. This reinvestment assumption does not disturb the mathematical solution of the net present value, because any amount reinvested and compounded forward at a given interest rate will still have a discounted present value equal to that original amount, provided that the discounting and compounding rates are the same.

The *size* of a project's net present value is also significant. This net present value represents the immediate savings in investment outlay on a project, over and above the investment needed to sustain a rate of return equal to the prespecified cost of capital. For example, Figure 17–9 shows that Project B can be financed with an investment outlay of $120,000, whereas an outlay of $141,610 would be required if a 16 percent rate of return is to be earned throughout the project's life.

FIGURE 17–9

Tanoury Corporation
Net Present Value Analysis of Three Alternative Projects

Item	Amount	Periods	Discount Factor	Present Value
Project A				
Investment Outlay	($120,000)	0	1.000	($120,000)
Operating Cash Flows	10,000	1	.862*	8,620
	30,000	2	.743	22,290
	30,000	3	.641	19,230
	60,000	4	.552	33,120
	70,000	5	.476	33,320
Net Present Value of Project A				($ 3,420)
Project B				
Investment Outlay	($120,000)	0	1.000	($120,000)
Operating Cash Flows	60,000	1	.862	51,720
	60,000	2	.743	44,580
	30,000	3	.641	19,230
	30,000	4	.552	16,560
	20,000	5	.476	9,520
Net Present Value of Project B				$ 21,610
Project C				
Investment Outlay	($120,000)	0	1.000	($120,000)
Operating Cash Flows	40,000	1–5	3.274†	130,960
Net Present Value of Project C				$ 10,960

* Tables for the present value of amounts to be received (or paid) in the future are shown inside the back cover of this book. The present value of $1 at the rate r per period and located n periods in the future are designated as p_n^r.

† The present value of a series of regular installments (an annuity) of $1 at the rate r per period located at the end of each of the next n periods is designated as pA_n^r.

Uneven Cash Flows and Working Capital Requirements   Projects often have uneven cash flows per period, which complicates net present value calculations. In addition, the required cash inflow should include any funds needed to finance a project's working capital requirements.

Example: Cosenza Corporation is considering the purchase of a new pipe-bending machine. The machine will cost $200,000, to be paid immediately, and will require a major overhaul costing $100,000 at the end of the third year of its five-year life. Management anticipates the following net operating cash inflows before taxes:

Year	Net Operating Cash Inflow
1	$ 60,000
2	80,000
3	100,000
4	120,000
5	100,000

Cosenza Corporation uses the straight line depreciation method, and this machine has an expected cash resale value of $50,000 after its five years of use. The cost of the overhaul is considered an asset improvement and will be capitalized and depreciated during the fourth and fifth years. Increased cash, receivables, and inventories, averaging $60,000 per year, will need to be carried to support the project over all five years. The company is subject to a 40 percent income tax rate and has decided that 10 percent is the appropriate cost of capital rate for projects of this type.

As Figure 17–10 shows, the $60,000 needed in the first year to fund the increase in cash, receivables, and inventories must be treated as part of the project's investment outlay. It will be released at the end of the project life and should be shown as a cash inflow at that time. In other words, the amount committed to working capital is handled as an *outflow* at the inception of the project and as an *inflow* at the project's termination.

Working capital commitments reduce the project's net present value by the difference between the original outlay and the discounted value of the inflow at the end of the project life. In Cosenza Corporation this is $22,740, the difference between the $60,000 working capital outlay and $37,260, the discounted value of the $60,000 inflow five years hence at 10 percent. This $22,740 can be reconciled with the opportunity cost of lost income that results because the $60,000 is unavailable for alternative uses during the project life. If the $60,000 could be invested at a rate equal to the 10 percent cost of capital, then $6,000 of net cash inflow is foregone each year. The present value of that series of inflows over five years is also approximately $22,740 ($6,000 × 3.791).

A complete analysis of the cash flows associated with this project is presented in Figure 17–11. This analysis indicates that the pipe-bending project has a net present value of $8,638 and is therefore acceptable.

FIGURE 17–10

Cosenza Corporation
Schedule of Annual After-tax Operating Cash Flows

Year	1	2	3	4	5
Operating Cash Flow					
(before taxes)	$60,000	$80,000	$100,000	$120,000	$100,000
Less: Depreciation*	30,000	30,000	30,000	80,000	80,000
Taxable Income	$30,000	$50,000	$ 70,000	$ 40,000	$ 20,000
Less: Income Tax Expense ..	12,000	20,000	28,000	16,000	8,000
Net Income After Tax	$18,000	$30,000	$42,000	$24,000	$12,000
After-tax Operating					
Cash Flow	$48,000	$60,000	$ 72,000	$104,000	$ 92,000

* Depreciation:

$$\text{Years 1–3} = \frac{\$200,000 - \$50,000}{5} = \$30,000 \text{ per year}$$

$$\text{Years 4–5} = \frac{\$200,000 + \$100,000 - \$50,000 - \$90,000}{2} = \$80,000 \text{ per year}$$

FIGURE 17–11

Cosenza Corporation
Net Present Value Analysis of Pipe-Bending Machine Acquisition

Item	Amount	Period	Discount Factor	Present Value
Cost of Machine	($200,000)	0	1.000	($200,000)
Working Capital	(60,000)	0	1.000	(60,000)
After-tax Operating Cash Flows:				
Year 1	48,000	1	.909	43,632
Year 2	60,000	2	.826	49,560
Year 3	72,000	3	.751	54,072
Year 4	104,000	4	.683	71,032
Year 5	92,000	5	.621	57,132
Machine Overhaul	(100,000)	3	.751	(75,100)
Working Capital Released	60,000	5	.621	37,260
Resale of Machine	50,000	5	.621	31,050
Net Present Value of Pipe-Bending Machine Project				$ 8,638

Projects with No Direct Cash Inflows   Some projects have no operating cash inflows associated directly with them. For example, the purchase of a new or replacement automobile, building, or machine may only cause changes in operating cash outflows. Net present value analysis can sometimes be applied in such cases by comparing the total discounted cash outflows associated with each alternative. If the benefits provided by the alternative projects are equivalent, then the project with the *smallest discounted cash outflows* is the most desirable.

Example: Calvert Company must decide whether or not to replace one of its delivery trucks. A new truck can be purchased for $20,000 and would be used for five years, at which time it could be sold for $5,000. The present delivery truck cost $12,000 three years ago. It could also be used for another five years, but only if it is completely overhauled in two years' time at a cost of $9,000. This truck could be sold now for $10,000, but will have no resale value after five more years.

The new truck would cost $4,000 per year to operate as compared to $6,500 per year for the present truck. All fixed assets are depreciated on a straight line basis. The truck now in use has a book value of $7,500. The cost of overhauling this truck would be spread over the last three years of its life for tax purposes. The company is subject to a 40 percent income tax rate. A 15 percent cost of capital has been established for vehicle acquisitions.

In Figure 17–12, the cash outflows associated with the old and the new truck are discounted to find the net present values of keeping the old truck and of buying the new truck and selling the old one.

Assuming that each truck provides equivalent benefits, it is preferable to buy the new truck because the $12,537 present value of outflows associated with purchasing the new truck is less than the $15,794 present value of outflows associated with keeping the old truck.

FIGURE 17–12

Calvert Company

Schedule of After-tax Cash Outflows

		Old Truck		New Truck
		Years		Years
		1–2	3–5	1–5
(A)	Annual Operating Cash Outflows	$ 6,500	$ 6,500	$4,000
(B)	Add: Depreciation	1,500	4,500	3,000
(C)	Total Taxable Deductions	$ 8,000	$11,000	$7,000
(D)	Tax Effects of Deductions (40% Tax Rate) .	$3,200	$ 4,400	$2,800
(A − D)	Net Cash Outflows	$ 3,300	$ 2,100	$1,200

After-tax Proceeds of Sale of Old Truck

Cash Proceeds of Sale $10,000

Less: Tax Effect of Gain on Sale
    Tax Rate × Book Gain
    40% ($10,000 − $7,500) 1,000

Net Proceeds of Sale after Tax .... $ 9,000

Net Present Value Analysis

Item	Amount	Period	Discount Factor	Present Value
Keep the Old Truck:				
Operating Costs	($ 3,300)	1–2	1.626	($ 5,366)
Operating Costs	(2,100)	3–5	(2.283)(.756)	(3,624)
Overhaul Cost	(9,000)	2	.756	(6,804)
Net Present Value of Keeping the Old Truck				($15,794)
Purchase a New Truck and Sell the Old Truck:				
Investment Outlay	($20,000)	0	1.000	($20,000)
Sale of Old Truck	9,000	0	1.000	9,000
Operating Costs	(1,200)	1–5	3.352	(4,022)
Resale of New Truck	5,000	5	.497	2,485
Net Present Value of Buying a New Truck and Selling the Old One ...				($12,537)

* The old truck's operating costs in years 3–5 consist of a three-period annuity of $2,100, where present value at the beginning of period 3 is found by multiplying $2,100 by $(pA._3{}^{15})$, or 2.283. This amount must then be discounted to its present value at the beginning of the project, by multiplying it by $(p._2{}^{15})$, or .756.

NET PRESENT VALUE RATIO

Certain limitations of the net present value method as a basis for comparing projects can be overcome by converting the net present value *amount* to a *ratio.* Expressing a project's discounted cash inflows as a percentage of its

FIGURE 17–13

Tanoury Corporation
Net Present Value Ratio Analysis
of Three Alternative Projects

	Project A	Project B	Project C
$\dfrac{\text{Discounted Cash Inflows}}{\text{Discounted Cash Outflows}}=$	$\dfrac{\$116,580}{\$120,000}$	$\dfrac{\$141,010}{\$120,000}$	$\dfrac{\$130,960}{\$120,000}$
Net Present Value Ratio	.9715	1.175	1.091

discounted cash outflows provides a measure of the *relative size* of its net present value. Any project with a **net present value ratio** equal to or greater than 1.00 is acceptable. The net present value ratio can also be used to improve the ranking of competing projects.

Example: Net present value ratios for Tanoury Corporation's three projects are calculated in Figure 17–13. Project A should be rejected, because its net present value ratio is less than 1.00. Projects B and C are acceptable, because their net present value ratios are greater than 1.00.

Comparison of these results with those in Figure 17–9 shows that the net present value and net present value ratio methods produce the same accept–reject decisions and the same rankings of these three projects. However, as will be shown in Chapter 18, when competing projects have unequal investment outlays or unequal lives, the net present value ratio method can produce different and superior results.

INTERNAL RATE OF RETURN

By taking into account the distribution of cash flows over time, it is possible to measure a project's rate of return as a function of its unrecovered investment outlays. This can be done by finding the rate of return that equates the discounted amount of all cash inflows to the discounted amount of all cash outflows. This rate is known as the **internal rate of return** or the *time adjusted rate of return.* It may also be defined as the effective cash flow generating rate of the project, measured in relation to the amount of unrecovered investment outlays.

Uniform Operating Cash Flows The operating cash inflows for Project C in the Tanoury Corporation example consist of a five-period annuity of $40,000 per period. To determine this project's internal rate of return, it is necessary to find a discount rate which will equate the present value of that five-period annuity of $40,000 per year to the investment outlay of $120,000. The present value of annuity table in Appendix B contains the factor (pA_n^r), which is the present value of a $1 per period annuity, discounted for n periods at an interest rate of r per period. A discount rate must be found in this present value of annuity table that satisfies the following equality condition:

$$\text{Present Value of} \atop \text{Cash Outflows} = {\text{Present Value of} \atop \text{Cash Inflows}}$$

$$\$120{,}000 = \$40{,}000 \ (pA_{\overline{5}})$$

$$(pA_{\overline{5}}) = \frac{\$120{,}000}{\$\ 40{,}000} = 3.000$$

The present value table factor $(pA_{\overline{5}}^{.20})$ is 2.991, which closely approximates 3.000 and indicates that an interest rate very close to 20 percent equates the present values of cash inflows and cash outflows. Project C therefore has an internal rate of return of approximately 20 percent.

This means that the unrecovered investment outlay generates cash flows at a constant rate of about 20 percent per year throughout the project's life. This solution implies that the project's cash inflows are reinvested at the same 20 percent internal rate of return for the remainder of the project's life. This assumption permits the project and all its cash flows to be evaluated as a total package for its entire duration. This assumption also provides a convenient explanation of what happens to net cash inflows after they are received. The assumption that cash inflows are reinvested at the internal rate of return does not affect the calculation of that rate. The net present value method involves a similar reinvestment assumption, except that reinvestment is assumed to occur at the firm's cost of capital rate.

The internal rate of return can also be calculated by finding an interest rate that equates the future value of all cash inflows and the future value of all cash outflows, with the reference point being the end of the project life. Project C has a $120,000 investment outlay. If invested at 20 percent, this amount will accumulate to about $298,560 at the end of five years.[4] If each net cash inflow is invested at 20 percent, each will also amount to about $298,600 at the end of the project life.[5]

Non-uniform Operating Cash Flows   The internal rates of return for Projects A and B are harder to calculate because their cash inflows are unevenly distributed over the projects' lives. A process of trial and error, conducted manually or with computer assistance, is needed to find the internal rate of return that equates the present value of these cash inflows to the amount of the investment outlay. For example, a rate of 20 percent produces a present value of $131,532 for Project B; a 30 percent rate produces a $111,199 present value. Because the investment outlay of $120,000 lies between these two amounts, the internal rate of return for Project B is somewhere between 20 and 30 percent. By progressively reducing the spread between the two proposed rates, it is possible to find a rate that approximates the equality condition. For Project B, the internal rate of return is approximately 25 percent and for Project A it is slightly less than 16 percent.

---

[4] From Appendix B, Table 3; 2.488 × $120,000 = $298,560.
[5] From Appendix B, Table 3; 7.465 × $40,000 = $298,600.

Decision Rules Using the Internal Rate of Return   A project's internal rate of return may be compared to the internal rates of return of competing projects and/or compared to a predetermined cost of capital. When there is no scarcity of investment funds and the decision is simply to accept or reject a project, the internal rate of return is a reasonably valid decision criterion. Any project with an internal rate of return that is higher than the predetermined cost of capital is acceptable. Any project with a rate that is lower than the cost of capital should be rejected.

Suppose Tanoury Corporation sets a minimum 16 percent cost of capital rate, based on management's evaluation of the potential returns from comparable projects that involve a similar degree of risk. Project A has an internal rate of return below 16 percent; Projects B and C have internal rates of return above that cutoff figure. On that basis, Projects B and C are acceptable, but Project A is not.

When not enough money is available to finance all the projects with a rate of return that exceeds the target rate, it may be necessary to screen the competing projects for acceptability. The internal rate of return might then be used to *rank* such projects. In the Tanoury Corporation example the rankings would be as follows:

Project	Approximate Internal Rate of Return	Rank
B	25%	1
C	20%	2
A	16%	3

In this example, because the three projects have equal lives and equal investment outlays, ranking offers a reasonably valid basis for comparison. However, as will be shown in Chapter 18, it is often a mistake to use the internal rate of return to rank projects that have unequal project lives and/or unequal investment outlays.

Limitations of the Internal Rate of Return   The internal rate of return has several shortcomings as a tool of capital budgeting analysis. Its derivation can be tedious (though less so when computer routines are available). If a project generates an alternating series of positive and negative operating cash flows, several different rates of return solutions are mathematically possible. Indeed, some projects may have such unusual patterns of cash inflows and outflows that there is no mathematical solution for the internal rate of return.[6]

Cash inflows are assumed to be reinvested at a rate equal to the project's own internal rate of return. However, the fact that each project is a unique endeavor suggests that its internal rate of return is also uniquely valued. Therefore, it is not reasonable to assume that the internal rate of return earned by a particular project will be freely available elsewhere.

It is usual to calculate a single internal rate of return for a project, on the assumption that this rate remains constant throughout the project life. Comparisons between rates of return and a predetermined cost of capital can be made

---

[6] Richard Brealey and Stewart Myers, *Principles of Corporate Finance* (New York: McGraw-Hill, 1981), pp. 70–76.

more conveniently if both the cost of capital and the internal rate of return are assumed to be constant over the life of the project. However, these factors do not always remain constant. If their variations are taken into account, innumerable internal rate of return combinations applied to *segments* of the project life will satisfy the condition of equality between the present values of cash inflows and cash outflows.

The net present value, net present value ratio, and internal rate of return methods often produce conflicting rankings for a group of projects. When there is no shortage of investment capital, any project may be accepted if it satisfies the following criteria:

Net Present Value > 0
Net Present Value Ratio > 1.0
Internal Rate of Return > Cost of Capital

When funds are scarce, some form of capital rationing must be adopted to allocate resources among competing projects. As will be shown in Chapter 18, capital allocation procedures often use one or a combination of these discounting methods in evaluating capital budgeting projects.

DISCOUNTED PAYBACK PERIOD

A project's **discounted payback period** can be determined by calculating the number of periods required for the cumulative present value of operating cash inflows to exceed the investment outlay.

FIGURE 17–14

Tanoury Corporation
Discounted Payback Period Analysis of Two Alternative Projects

Period	Operating Cash Inflow	Discount Factor	Present Value of Cash Inflows	Cumulative Present Value of Cash Outflows
Project A				
1	$10,000	.862	$ 8,620	$ 8,620
2	30,000	.743	22,290	30,910
3	30,000	.641	19,230	50,140
4	60,000	.552	33,120	83,260
5	70,000	.476	33,320	116,580
Project B				
1	$60,000	.862	$51,720	$ 51,720
2	60,000	.743	44,580	96,300
3	30,000	.641	19,230	115,530
4	30,000	.552	16,560	132,090
5	20,000	.476	9,520	141,610

Example: The discounted payback periods for Tanoury Corporation's Projects A and B are shown in Figure 17–14.

Project B has a discounted payback period of slightly more than three years, because it is not until the fourth year that the $132,090 cumulative present value of cash flows exceeds the $120,000 investment outlay. Project A does not have a feasible discounted payback period, because even at the end of its project life the $116,580 cumulative present value of its cash inflows is less than its $120,000 investment outlay. In present value terms, Project A will never return its cost and should be rejected.

The discounted payback period calculation overcomes certain deficiencies of the nondiscounted payback period method. However, it does not directly measure project profitability and should only be used as a supplement to other capital budgeting methods.

CAPITAL BUDGETING ILLUSTRATED: GIBSON COMPANY

The Gibson Company example, which was introduced in Chapter 9, will now be used to demonstrate and summarize the basic techniques of capital budgeting analysis. The company's problem is whether to replace a manual production facility with an automated one. This is an *incremental* investment decision. The pertinent data to be analyzed therefore include the proposal's *project life,* its *cost of capital,* the *incremental investment outlay* needed to make the change, and the *incremental benefit flows* produced by the change.

INVESTMENT OUTLAY

The project's *incremental investment outlay* includes the effective cost of acquiring the new equipment plus any additional costs or savings related to the acquisition or disposal of the old equipment. Figure 17–15 shows that in addition to the $140,000 paid for the new equipment, it will cost $15,000 for installation and testing, $10,000 to train operators, and $20,000 in severance pay for terminated employees. The old equipment can be sold for $5,000 cash. Because this old equipment has an undepreciated book value of $25,000, its sale will result in a $20,000 capital loss, which can be deducted for income tax purposes at a 30 percent rate. Training costs and severance pay are tax deductible at a 40 percent rate, but installation and testing costs must be added to the depreciable basis of the new equipment. Management has decided that 10 percent is the appropriate cost of capital to be used in evaluating projects of this type.

The $162,000 net investment outlay is a measure of the amount of cash effectively committed to this project at its inception. Over the project's life the incremental benefit flows, measured as net operating cash inflows, should allow for the recovery of the investment outlay and, if possible, for a profit as well.

FIGURE 17–15

Gibson Company
Net Investment Outlay

Acquisition Cost			$140,000
Add: Installation & Testing		$ 15,000	
Training Costs	$10,000		
Severance Pay	20,000		
	$30,000		
Less: Income Tax (40%)	12,000	18,000	33,000
			$173,000
Acquisition Cost and Additional Expenses			
Less: Sale of Equipment		$ 5,000	
Tax Savings on Capital Loss			
(30% × $20,000)		6,000	
Recovery from Sale of Old Equipment			11,000
Net Investment Outlay			$162,000

FIGURE 17–16

Gibson Company
Alternative Annual Operating Costs

	Manual System	Automated System	Incremental Amount
Materials	$100,000	$ 95,000	($ 5,000)
Labor	80,000	20,000	(60,000)
Variable Overhead	40,000	30,000	(10,000)
Fixed Overhead	20,000	60,000	40,000
	$240,000	$205,000	($35,000)

NET BENEFIT FLOWS

The schedule of operating cash flows shown as Figure 17–16 was presented in the original Chapter 9 example. These operating costs did not include financing expenses, depreciation, or income taxes. The example will now be expanded to account for these additional items. The original equipment was to be depreciated over the remaining ten years of its life at $2,500 per year. The new equipment, also with a ten-year life, has an expected disposal value of $20,000 at the end of that time and will be depreciated on a straight line basis. The annual depreciation on this equipment will be $13,500, calculated as follows:

FIGURE 17-17

Gibson Company
Incremental Annual Net Income

	Manual Equipment		Automated Equipment		Increment from Automation	
Sales		$300,000		$300,000		–0–
Less: Operating Costs	$240,000		$205,000		$35,000	
Depreciation	2,500	242,500	13,500	218,500	(11,000)	$24,000
Taxable Income		$ 57,500		$ 81,500		$24,000
Income Tax Expense (40%)......		23,000		32,600		(9,600)
Net Income		$ 34,500		$ 48,900		$14,400

Depreciation Basis $= $ Acquisition Cost $+$ Installation Costs $-$ Disposal Value
$= \$140,000 + \$15,000 - \$20,000$
$= \$135,000$

Annual Depreciation Charge $= \dfrac{\$135,000}{10} = \underline{\underline{\$13,500}}$

Therefore, the incremental depreciation cost is an increase of $11,000 ($13,500 depreciation on the new equipment minus $2,500 depreciation on the old equipment). But this is not a cash flow. The relevant cash flow for capital budgeting analysis results from the *income tax effects* of the change in depreciation cost. Because $11,000 additional depreciation cost would result from the changeover to automated equipment, cash outflows for taxes would be reduced by $4,400 (40 percent $\times$ $11,000).

A complete schedule of after-tax operating cash flows can now be developed. It takes into account the pre-tax operating cash flows, depreciation charges, and income tax expense. Assuming that sales revenues of $300,000 per year will continue under both production methods, the project's annual net benefit flow, expressed in terms of incremental after-tax cash flows, is $25,400. This consists of $35,000 of pre-tax incremental operating cash flows minus $9,600 of incremental income tax expense. The same $25,400 benefit flow can be calculated by adding $14,400 incremental after-tax income to $11,000 incremental noncash charges or by adding the tax shield of $4,400 (40 percent of $11,000 incremental appreciation) to the pre-tax operating cash flows minus the tax, $21,000 ($35,000 $-$ 40 percent $\times$ $35,000).

Figure 17–17 shows annual net income using manual or automated equipment and the incremental annual income if the automated system is adopted.

In Figure 17–19, the same net operating cash inflow is derived by adding noncash items, such as depreciation, to the after-tax income figures.

In Figure 17–18, the net operating cash inflows are calculated as the differences between cash inflows from sales and cash outflows for operating costs and income taxes.

In Figure 17–20, the same net cash inflows are derived by adding the tax shield from depreciation to the pre-tax operating cash flows minus the income tax expense.

This data will now be used to evaluate Gibson Company's investment proposal using six nondiscounting and discounting methods of capital budgeting analysis:

1. Accounting Rate of Return
2. Payback Period
3. Discounted Payback Period
4. Net Present Value
5. Net Present Value Ratio
6. Internal Rate of Return

FIGURE 17–18

Gibson Company
Incremental Annual After-tax Cash Flow

	Manual Equipment		Automated Equipment		Increment from Automation	
Cash Inflows:						
Sales		$300,000		$300,000	–0–	
Cash Outflows:						
Operating Costs . . .	$240,000		$205,000		$35,000	
Income Tax						
Expense	23,000	263,000	32,600	237,600	(9,600)	$25,400
Net Operating						
Cash Inflow		$ 37,000		$ 62,400		$25,400

FIGURE 17–19

Gibson Company
Incremental Annual After-tax Cash Flow

	Manual Equipment	Automated Equipment	Increment from Automation
Net Income after Taxes	$34,500	$48,900	$14,400
Add: Noncash Items:			
Depreciation	2,500	13,500	11,000
Net Operating Cash Inflow	$37,000	$62,400	$25,400

FIGURE 17–20

Gibson Company
Incremental Annual After-tax Cash Flow

	Manual Equipment	Automated Equipment	Increment from Automation
Cash Inflows:			
Sales	$300,000	$300,000	–0–
Cash Outflows:			
Operating Costs	240,000	205,000	$35,000
Pre-tax Operating Cash Flows	$ 60,000	$ 95,000	$35,000
Less: Income Tax at 40%	24,000	38,000	14,000
	$ 36,000	$ 57,000	$21,000
Add: Tax Shield from Depreciation			
(40% × Depreciation Charge)	1,000	5,400	4,400
Net Operating Cash Inflow	$ 37,000	$ 62,400	$25,400

ACCOUNTING RATE OF RETURN

(a) *Accrual Income Rates of Return:*

$$\text{Rate of Return} = \frac{\text{Income}}{\text{Investment Base}}$$

	Total Investment Base	Average Investment Base
Before-tax Rate	$\dfrac{\$24,000}{\$162,000} = 14.81\%$	$\dfrac{\$24,000}{\$91,000^*} = 21.84\%$
After-tax Rate	$\dfrac{\$14,400}{\$162,000} = 8.89\%$	$\dfrac{\$14,400}{\$91,000} = 15.82\%$

*Average Investment Base = [Outlay + Disposal Value] ÷ 2
= [$162,000 + $20,000] ÷ 2
= $91,000

(b) *Cash Flow Rates of Return:*

$$\text{Rate of Return} = \frac{\text{Incremental Cash Flow}}{\text{Investment Base}}$$

	Total Investment Base	Average Investment Base
Before-tax Rate	$\dfrac{\$35,000}{\$162,000} = 21.60\%$	$\dfrac{\$35,000}{\$91,000} = 38.46\%$
After-tax Rate	$\dfrac{\$25,400}{\$162,000} = 15.68\%$	$\dfrac{\$25,400}{\$91,000} = 27.91\%$

To evaluate this project's acceptability, one or the other of these rates must be compared to the corresponding rates of return for alternative projects, or to predetermined target rates such as the 10 percent cost of capital.

PAYBACK PERIOD

$$(a) \quad \text{Payback Period} = \frac{\text{Investment Outlay}}{\text{Average Annual Cash Inflow}}$$

$$= \frac{\$162,000}{\$25,400 \text{ per year}}$$

$$= 6.38 \text{ years}$$

$$(b) \quad \text{Payback Reciprocal} = \frac{1}{\text{Payback Period}}$$

$$= \frac{1}{6.38}$$

$$= 15.68\%$$

This project satisfies the payback criteria, provided that a payback period of more than 6.38 years is acceptable.

DISCOUNTED PAYBACK PERIOD

Year	Net Cash Inflow	Discount Factor	Cumulative Present Value
1	$25,400	.909	$ 23,089
2	25,400	.826	44,070
3	25,400	.751	63,145
4	25,400	.683	80,493
5	25,400	.621	96,266
6	25,400	.565	110,617
7	25,400	.513	123,571
8	25,400	.467	135,433
9	25,400	.424	146,203
10	45,400	.386	163,803

The discounted payback period is more than nine years, because it is not until the tenth year that the cumulative discounted value of cash inflows exceeds the $162,000 investment outlay.

NET PRESENT VALUE

Item	Amount	Period	Discount Factor	Present Value
Investment Outlay	($162,000)	0	1.000	($162,000)
Operating Cash Inflows	25,400	1–10	6.145	156,083
Disposal Value	20,000	10	.386	7,720
Net Present Value				$ 1,803

The project is acceptable because its net present value is positive.

NET PRESENT VALUE RATIO

$$\text{Net Present Value Ratio} = \frac{\text{Discounted Cash Inflows}}{\text{Discounted Cash Outflows}}$$

$$= \frac{\$163,803}{\$162,000}$$

$$= 1.011$$

The project is acceptable because its net present value ratio is greater than 1.

INTERNAL RATE OF RETURN

Present Value of Cash Outflows = Present Value of Cash Inflows

$$\$162,000 = (\$25,400)\,(pA_{\overline{10}|}^{r}) + (\$20,000)\,(p_{\overline{10}|}^{r})$$

An internal rate of return slightly higher than 10 percent equates the present value of cash outflows and cash inflows ($r = 10.2$ percent). If Gibson Company's management will accept an internal rate of return of 10.2 percent or less, then this project is acceptable.

SUMMARY

1. Capital budgeting involves planning for investment and disinvestment decisions, the effects of which extend over several accounting periods in a non-uniform pattern.
2. The critical capital budgeting decision variables are the project life, the cost of capital, the investment outlay, and the net cash benefit flows.
3. Capital budgeting decisions are either accept–reject decisions or ranking–rationing decisions.
4. In accept–reject decision situations, it is assumed that sufficient funds are available to finance all acceptable projects. The decision maker must then judge whether or not a project satisfies some target criterion of acceptability.
5. In ranking–rationing decisions, when not enough funds are available to undertake all acceptable projects, there is the additional problem of selecting the most acceptable projects that the firm can afford to implement.
6. Nondiscounting and discounting criteria may be used to evaluate capital investment projects.
7. Nondiscounting methods include accounting rate of return, payback period, and bailout factor analysis. These methods do not take account of the time value of money and usually involve the averaging of cash flows and net income. These methods often serve as screening tests prior to the application of more rigorous discounting procedures.
8. Discounting methods include net present value, net present value ratio, internal rate of return, and discounted payback period.
9. Net present value and net present value ratio are the preferred methods, because (1) the discounted payback period calculation does not measure income and (2) the internal rate of return is subject to computational ambiguities and includes questionable assumptions about the reinvestment rate for funds recovered during the project's life.
10. The net present value and net present value ratio methods require that a cost of capital be specified. From an opportunity cost viewpoint, the cost of capital is defined as the rate of return available on projects of a similar type, duration, investment outlay, and risk class.

KEY WORDS AND PHRASES

APPENDIX A:
THE TIME VALUE OF MONEY

COMPOUNDING AND DISCOUNTING PROCEDURES

Amounts of money to be received or paid at different points in time may be initially expressed in terms of their nominal amounts: for example, $10,000 to be received at the end of two years, or $10,000 to be paid at the end of five years. However, computational analysis that involves combining or comparing such nominal amounts with other amounts occurring at different points in time will not always produce valid results. For example, the two patterns of cash flows mentioned above might be considered equivalent because they both involve a total nominal amount of $10,000. In fact, these amounts are not equivalent because of the timing difference in the incidence of their cash flows. Money attracts a return—interest—when in use and incurs an implicit or opportunity cost when unavailable for use. Valid comparisons of monetary amounts that are receivable or payable at different times require that those amounts be converted to some common basis. This is achieved by *compounding* and *discounting*. Nominal amounts may be adjusted to their effective compounded value at some future time by adding the interest to be earned. Alternatively, nominal amounts may be discounted back to their present value by taking account of the discount (or interest foregone) during the intervening period.

COMPOUNDING OF SINGLE AMOUNTS

The compounded amount (F) of a single amount (P) at a point n periods into the future, at a per period rate of interest r is calculated as follows:

$$F_n^r = P(1 + r)^n \qquad \text{\textit{Compounded Value of a Single Amount}}$$

Example: If $1,000 is invested for 5 years at an interest rate of 10 percent per annum, its compounded future value would be $1615.10:

$$F_5^{.1} = 1{,}000\ (1 + .1)^5$$
$$= 1{,}000\ (1.61051)$$
$$= \$1{,}615.10$$

DISCOUNTING OF SINGLE AMOUNTS

The present value (P) of an amount (F) that is paid or received n periods in the future at the per period interest rate r is calculated as follows:

$$P_n^r = \frac{F}{(1 + r)^n} \qquad \begin{array}{l} \textit{Present Value} \\ \textit{of a Single Amount} \end{array}$$

Example: The present value of $10,000 to be received in four years' time at an 8 percent per annum interest rate is $7350.24:

$$P_4^{.08} = \frac{10,000}{(1 + .08)^4}$$

$$= \frac{10,000}{1.3605}$$

$$= \$7,350.24$$

This could also be interpreted as showing that an amount of $7,350.24 received immediately is the equivalent of $10,000 to be received in four years' time, given that an 8 percent interest rate is in effect. This type of calculation is basic to analysis of the cash flows from long-term projects, for which all amounts must be converted to their present values at the outset of the project.

REGULAR SEQUENCES OF AMOUNTS—ANNUITIES

In some situations, the same nominal amount may be receivable or payable at regular intervals. Such an *annuity* requires the calculation of the sum of the compounded or present values of each individual amount. Formulas are available to reduce this to a single calculation.

The compounded amount (FA) of an amount (R) to be received or paid at the end of each period for n periods at a per period interest rate of r, is calculated as follows:

$$FA_n^r = \left(\frac{(1 + r)^n - 1}{n} \right) R \qquad \begin{array}{l} \textit{Compounded} \\ \textit{Value of} \\ \textit{an Annuity} \end{array}$$

Example: If $1,000 is deposited in a savings account each year for three years at 6 percent interest per year, it will accumulate to $3183.60:

$$FA_3^{.06} = \left(\frac{(1 + .06)^3 - 1}{.06} \right) 1,000$$

$$= \left(\frac{.191016}{.06} \right) 1,000$$

$$= (3.1836) \, 1,000$$

$$= \$3,183.60$$

The present value (PA) of an amount (R) to be received at the end of each period for the next n periods at an interest rate of r per period is calculated as follows:

$$PA_n^r = \left(1 - \frac{1}{(1+r)^n}\right)\frac{R}{r} \qquad \begin{array}{l}\textit{Present Value}\\ \textit{of an Annuity}\end{array}$$

Example: Suppose a cash dividend of $1,000 is to be received each year for four years. At an interest rate of 12 percent, the present value of those cash receipts is $3,037.35:

$$PA_4^{.12} = \left(1 - \frac{1}{(1.12)^4}\right)\frac{1{,}000}{.12}$$

$$= (1 - .6355181)\, 8{,}333.33$$
$$= (.3644819)\, 8{,}333.33$$
$$= \$3{,}037.35$$

COMPOSITE CALCULATIONS AND COMPARISONS

Any sequence of single amounts and/or annuities can be subjected to compounding or discounting in order to reduce them to a common basis by applying the appropriate conversions separately to each amount in the sequence. For example, consider the following four alternative patterns of cash receipts, each totaling a nominal amount of $10,000:

A. $10,000 received at end of Year 4
B. $2,500 received at end of each year for four years
C. $5,000 received at the end of Years 2 and 4
D. $5,000 received at the end of Year 2, and $2,500 at the end of Years 3 and 4

Using present value analysis and assuming that the interest rate is 10 percent, the following calculations would be made:

A. This is the present value of a single amount:

$$P_4^{.1} = \frac{\$10{,}000}{1.1^4} = \frac{\$10{,}000}{1.4641} = \underline{\underline{\$6{,}830.13}}$$

B. This is the present value of an annuity:

$$PA_4^{.1} = \left(1 - \frac{1}{1.1^4}\right)\frac{2{,}500}{.1}$$

$$= (.3160)\, 25{,}000 = \underline{\underline{\$7{,}900.00}}$$

C. This is the sum of the present values of two separate single amounts:

$$P_2^1 + P_4^1 = \frac{\$5,000}{1.1^2} + \frac{\$5,000}{1.1^4}$$

$$= \$4,132.23 + \$3,415.07$$

$$= \$7,547.30$$

D. This is the sum of the present value of a single amount and the present value of an annuity occurring at a later time. First, the present value of the two-period annuity must be calculated at the outset of its own cycle. Then that present value amount must be treated as a separate single amount and discounted back to the outset of the total four-year cycle. First,

$$PA_2^1 = \left(1 + \frac{1}{(1.1)^2}\right)\frac{\$2,500}{.1}$$

$$= (.1735)\ 25,000$$

$$= \$4,337.50$$

Then,

$$P_2^1 + P_2^1 = \frac{\$5,000}{(1.1)^2} + \frac{\$4,337.5}{(1.1)^2}$$

$$= \$4132.23 + \$3584.71$$

$$= \$7,716.94$$

The four patterns of cash receipts can now be compared on a present value basis:

Alternative	Present Value
A	$6,830.13
B	7,900.00
C	7,547.30
D	7,716.94

Alternative B is the most attractive of the four because it offers the equivalent of $7,900 at the present time, an amount larger than the present values of the other three. Another interpretation pertinent to investment decision making is that, given that a 10 percent rate of return is to be earned continuously on each over the four-year period, the outlays required for each of the four alternatives would be the respective present value amounts in the preceding table.

USE OF TABLES

Fortunately, it is not necessary to resort to the formulas each time discounting or compounding calculations are needed. The availability of (1) precalculated tables of discounting and compounding factors, (2) computer programs, and

(3) hand calculators with built in functions, simplifies computations. It will be assumed that students have access to one or more of these computational aids. The relevant tables are provided on pages 874–81 of this text. These tables give compound and discount factors for various combinations of n (number of periods) and r (interest rate per period). The factors are for the cases where the single amount (F) is $1 and the annuity amount (R) is $1. To differentiate these table factors from the notation used in the preceding formulas, the following modifications will be made:

Table 1 (pages 874–75): p_n^r = Present value of $1 to be received after n periods, discounted at r% per period.

Table 2 (pages 876–77): a_n^r = Future value of $1 by the end of n periods, compounded at r% per period.

Table 3 (pages 878–79): pA_n^r = Present value of $1 per year for each of n periods, discounted at r% per period.

Table 4 (pages 880–81): sA_n^r = Sum of an annuity of $1 per period, compounded at r% per period for n periods.

Calculations are simplifed to the following steps:

1. In the appropriate table, locate the factor corresponding to the correct combination of number of periods (row) and interest rate (column).
2. Multiply that factor by the value of the single amount or annuity amount.

REINVESTMENT ASSUMPTIONS IN PRESENT VALUE ANALYSIS

When present value analysis is applied to a series of cash receipts occurring over a period of time, it is necessary to make some assumption about the reinvestment of those amounts in order that the total impact of all amounts received be included in the analysis. It is convenient to assume that any amount of cash received in the course of a project's life is reinvested until the end of the project's life at a rate equal to the interest rate used for calculating the present value of the cash flows of the project. Doing this will *not* alter the present value of the cash flows originating in the project as initially calculated. **Example:** Able Company projects cash receipts from Project Capricorn as follows:

Year 1	$100,000
Year 2	200,000
Year 3	300,000
Year 4	200,000

The present value of those receipts can be calculated using Table 1 (pages 874–75) and assuming a 10 percent interest rate:

Present Value $= (.909) \$100,000 + (.826) \$200,000 + (.751) \$300,000 + (.683)$

$$\$200,000$$
$$= \$90,900 + \$165,200 + 225,300 + \$136,600$$
$$= \underline{\underline{\$618,000}}$$

Observe that each of the first three amounts is available for use once received. Let each be invested for the remainder of the project life (to Year 4) at a 10 percent interest rate. The total compound value of these three amounts at the end of Year 4 (plus the final receipt of $200,000 in Year 4) is calculated using Table 2 (pages 876–77):

Compound Value $= (1.331) \$100,000 + (1.210) \$200,000 + (1.1) \$300,000 + \$200,000$
$$= \$133,100 + \$242,000 + \$330,000 + \$200,000$$
$$= \underline{\underline{\$905,100}} \text{ (approx.)}$$

Now compute the revised present value, at the project outset, of the $905,100 which is the accumulated amount of all cash flows generated by the project, including interest from reinvestment.

Present Value $= 905,100 \times .683$
$$= \underline{\underline{\$618,000}} \text{ (approx.)}$$

This revised present value amount, based on reinvestment, is no different than the original amount based on the primary cash flows.

APPENDIX B:
PRESENT AND FUTURE VALUE TABLES

TABLE 1

Present Value of $1
Discount Factors: Present Value of $1 to Be Received
after n Periods, Discounted at r% per Period.

$$p_n^r = \frac{1}{(1+r)^n}$$

r = Interest Rate per Period

n = Number of Periods	1%	2%	3%	4%	5%	6%	7%	8%	9%	10%	11%	12%	13%	14%	15%
1	.990	.980	.971	.962	.952	.943	.935	.926	.917	.909	.901	.893	.885	.877	.870
2	.980	.961	.943	.925	.907	.890	.873	.857	.842	.826	.812	.797	.783	.769	.756
3	.971	.942	.915	.889	.864	.840	.816	.794	.772	.751	.731	.712	.693	.675	.658
4	.961	.924	.888	.855	.823	.792	.763	.735	.708	.683	.659	.636	.613	.592	.572
5	.951	.906	.863	.822	.784	.747	.713	.681	.650	.621	.593	.567	.543	.519	.497
6	.942	.888	.837	.790	.746	.705	.666	.630	.596	.564	.535	.507	.480	.456	.432
7	.933	.871	.813	.760	.711	.665	.623	.583	.547	.513	.482	.452	.425	.400	.376
8	.923	.853	.789	.731	.677	.627	.582	.540	.502	.467	.434	.404	.376	.351	.327
9	.914	.837	.766	.703	.645	.592	.544	.500	.460	.424	.391	.361	.333	.308	.284
10	.905	.820	.744	.676	.614	.558	.508	.463	.422	.386*	.352	.322	.295	.270	.247
11	.896	.804	.722	.650	.585	.527	.475	.429	.388	.350	.317	.287	.261	.237	.215
12	.887	.788	.701	.625	.557	.497	.444	.397	.356	.319	.286	.257	.231	.208	.187
13	.879	.773	.681	.601	.530	.469	.415	.368	.326	.290	.258	.229	.204	.182	.163
14	.870	.758	.661	.577	.505	.442	.388	.340	.299	.263	.232	.205	.181	.160	.141
15	.861	.743	.642	.555	.481	.417	.362	.315	.275	.239	.209	.183	.160	.140	.123
16	.853	.728	.623	.534	.458	.394	.339	.292	.252	.218	.188	.163	.141	.123	.107
17	.844	.714	.605	.513	.436	.371	.317	.270	.231	.198	.170	.146	.125	.108	.093
18	.836	.700	.587	.494	.416	.350	.296	.250	.212	.180	.153	.130	.111	.095	.081
19	.828	.686	.570	.475	.396	.331	.277	.232	.194	.164	.138	.116	.098	.083	.070
20	.820	.673	.554	.456	.377	.312	.258	.215	.178	.149	.124	.104	.087	.073	.061

n = Number of Periods	16%	17%	18%	19%	20%	21%	22%	23%	24%	25%	26%	27%	28%	29%	30%
															r = Interest Rate per Period
1	.862	.855	.847	.840	.833	.826	.820	.813	.806	.800	.794	.787	.781	.775	.769
2	.743	.731	.718	.706	.694	.683	.672	.661	.650	.640	.630	.620	.610	.601	.592
3	.641	.624	.609	.593	.579	.564	.551	.537	.524	.512	.500	.488	.477	.466	.455
4	.552	.534	.516	.499	.482	.467	.451	.437	.423	.410	.397	.384	.373	.361	.350
5	.476	.456	.437	.419	.402	.386	.370	.355	.341	.328	.315	.303	.291	.280	.269
6	.410	.390	.370	.352	.335	.319	.303	.289	.275	.262	.250	.238	.227	.217	.207
7	.354	.333	.314	.296	.279	.263	.249	.235	.222	.210	.198	.188	.178	.168	.159
8	.305	.285	.266	.249	.233	.218	.204	.191	.179	.168	.157	.148	.139	.130	.123
9	.263	.243	.225	.209	.194	.180	.167	.155	.144	.134	.125	.116	.108	.101	.094
10	.227	.208	.191	.176	.162	.149	.137	.126	.116	.107	.099	.092	.085	.078	.073
11	.195	.178	.162	.148	.135	.123	.112	.103	.094	.086	.079	.072	.066	.061	.056
12	.168	.152	.137	.124	.112	.102	.092	.083	.076	.069	.062	.057	.052	.047	.043
13	.145	.130	.116	.104	.093	.084	.075	.068	.061	.055	.050	.045	.040	.037	.033
14	.125	.111	.099	.088	.078	.069	.062	.055	.049	.044	.039	.035	.032	.028	.025
15	.108	.095	.084	.074	.065	.057	.051	.045	.040	.035	.031	.028	.025	.022	.020
16	.093	.081	.071	.062	.054	.047	.042	.036	.032	.028	.025	.022	.019	.017	.015
17	.080	.069	.060	.052	.045	.039	.034	.030	.026	.023	.020	.017	.015	.013	.012
18	.069	.059	.051	.044	.038	.032	.028	.024	.021	.018	.016	.014	.012	.010	.009
19	.060	.051	.043	.037	.031	.027	.023	.020	.017	.014	.012	.011	.009	.008	.007
20	.051	.043	.037	.031	.026	.022	.019	.016	.014	.012	.010	.008	.007	.006	.005

* If the interest rate is 10 percent per period, the present value of $1 received at the end of period 10 is $0.386. Alternatively, $0.386 invested now at 10 percent per period will amount to $1.00 at the end of 10 periods.

TABLE 2

Amount of $1
Future Value of $1 by the End of n Periods, Compounded at r% per Period

$$a_n^r = (1 + r)^n$$

$n =$ Number of Periods	$r =$ Interest Rate per Period														
	1%	2%	3%	4%	5%	6%	7%	8%	9%	10%	11%	12%	13%	14%	15%
1	1.010	1.020	1.030	1.040	1.050	1.060	1.070	1.080	1.090	1.100	1.110	1.120	1.130	1.140	1.150
2	1.020	1.040	1.061	1.082	1.102	1.124	1.145	1.166	1.188	1.210	1.232	1.254	1.277	1.300	1.323
3	1.030	1.061	1.093	1.125	1.158	1.191	1.225	1.260	1.295	1.331	1.368	1.405	1.443	1.482	1.521
4	1.041	1.082	1.126	1.170	1.216	1.262	1.311	1.360	1.412	1.464	1.518	1.574	1.630	1.689	1.749
5	1.051	1.104	1.159	1.217	1.276	1.338	1.403	1.469	1.539	1.611	1.685	1.762	1.842	1.925	2.011
6	1.062	1.126	1.194	1.265	1.340	1.419	1.501	1.587	1.677	1.772	1.870	1.974	2.082	2.195	2.313
7	1.072	1.149	1.230	1.316	1.407	1.504	1.606	1.714	1.828	1.949	2.076	2.211	2.353	2.502	2.660
8	1.083	1.172	1.267	1.369	1.477	1.594	1.718	1.851	1.993	2.144	2.305	2.476	2.658	2.853	3.059
9	1.094	1.195	1.305	1.423	1.551	1.689	1.838	1.999	2.172	2.358	2.558	2.773	3.004	3.252	3.518
10	1.105	1.219	1.344	1.480	1.629	1.791	1.967	2.159	2.367	2.594*	2.839	3.106	3.395	3.707	4.046
11	1.116	1.243	1.384	1.539	1.710	1.898	2.105	2.332	2.580	2.853	3.152	3.479	3.836	4.226	4.652
12	1.127	1.268	1.426	1.601	1.796	2.012	2.252	2.518	2.813	3.138	3.498	3.896	4.335	4.818	5.350
13	1.138	1.294	1.469	1.665	1.886	2.133	2.410	2.720	3.066	3.452	3.883	4.363	4.898	5.492	6.153
14	1.149	1.319	1.513	1.732	1.980	2.261	2.579	2.937	3.342	3.797	4.310	4.887	5.535	6.261	7.076
15	1.161	1.346	1.558	1.801	2.079	2.397	2.759	3.172	3.642	4.177	4.785	5.474	6.254	7.138	8.137
16	1.173	1.373	1.605	1.873	2.183	2.540	2.952	3.426	3.970	4.595	5.311	6.130	7.067	8.137	9.358
17	1.184	1.400	1.653	1.948	2.292	2.693	3.159	3.700	4.328	5.054	5.895	6.866	7.986	9.276	10.761
18	1.196	1.428	1.702	2.026	2.407	2.854	3.380	3.996	4.717	5.560	6.544	7.690	9.024	10.575	12.375
19	1.208	1.457	1.754	2.107	2.527	3.026	3.617	4.316	5.142	6.116	7.263	8.613	10.197	12.055	14.232
20	1.220	1.486	1.806	2.191	2.653	3.207	3.870	4.661	5.604	6.727	8.062	9.646	11.523	13.743	16.366

n = Number of Periods	r = Interest Rate per Period														
	16%	17%	18%	19%	20%	21%	22%	23%	24%	25%	26%	27%	28%	29%	30%
1	1.160	1.170	1.180	1.190	1.200	1.210	1.220	1.230	1.240	1.250	1.260	1.270	1.280	1.290	1.300
2	1.346	1.369	1.392	1.416	1.440	1.464	1.488	1.513	1.538	1.563	1.588	1.613	1.638	1.664	1.690
3	1.561	1.602	1.643	1.685	1.728	1.772	1.816	1.861	1.907	1.953	2.000	2.048	2.097	2.147	2.197
4	1.811	1.874	1.939	2.005	2.074	2.144	2.215	2.289	2.364	2.441	2.520	2.601	2.684	2.769	2.856
5	2.100	2.192	2.288	2.386	2.488	2.594	2.703	2.815	2.932	3.052	3.176	3.304	3.436	3.572	3.713
6	2.436	2.565	2.700	2.840	2.986	3.138	3.297	3.463	3.635	3.815	4.002	4.196	4.398	4.608	4.827
7	2.826	3.001	3.185	3.379	3.583	3.797	4.023	4.259	4.508	4.768	5.042	5.329	5.629	5.945	6.275
8	3.278	3.511	3.759	4.021	4.300	4.595	4.908	5.239	5.590	5.960	6.353	6.768	7.206	7.669	8.157
9	3.803	4.108	4.435	4.785	5.160	5.560	5.987	6.444	6.931	7.451	8.005	8.595	9.223	9.893	10.604
10	4.411	4.807	5.234	5.695	6.192	6.728	7.305	7.926	8.594	9.313	10.085	10.915	11.805	12.761	13.786
11	5.117	5.624	6.176	6.777	7.430	8.140	8.912	9.749	10.657	11.642	12.708	13.862	15.111	16.462	17.922
12	5.936	6.580	7.288	8.064	8.916	9.850	10.872	11.991	13.214	14.552	16.012	17.605	19.342	21.236	23.298
13	6.886	7.699	8.599	9.596	10.700	11.919	13.264	14.749	16.386	18.190	20.175	22.359	24.758	27.395	30.287
14	7.988	9.007	10.147	11.420	12.839	14.421	16.182	18.141	20.319	22.737	25.420	28.396	31.691	35.339	39.373
15	9.266	10.538	11.973	13.590	15.407	17.450	19.742	22.313	25.195	28.422	32.030	36.063	40.564	45.587	51.186
16	10.748	12.330	14.129	16.172	18.488	21.114	24.086	27.446	31.242	35.527	40.358	45.799	51.923	58.807	66.541
17	12.467	14.426	16.672	19.244	22.186	25.548	29.384	33.759	38.740	44.409	50.851	58.165	66.461	75.862	86.504
18	14.462	16.879	19.673	22.900	26.623	30.913	35.849	41.523	48.038	55.511	64.072	73.869	85.070	97.862	112.455
19	16.776	19.748	23.214	27.252	31.948	37.404	43.736	51.074	59.567	69.389	80.731	93.814	108.890	126.242	146.192
20	19.460	23.106	27.393	32.429	38.338	45.259	53.358	62.821	73.864	86.736	101.721	119.145	139.370	162.852	190.050

* If the interest rate is 10 percent per period, the investment of $1 today will be worth $2.594 at the end of 10 periods.

TABLE 3

Present Value of an Ordinary Annuity of $1
Annuity Table: Present Value of $1 *per Year*
for Each of *n* Periods, Discounted at *r*% per Period

$$pA_n^r = \frac{1}{r}\left(1 - \frac{1}{(1+r)^n}\right)$$

r = Interest Rate per Period

n = Number of Periods	1%	2%	3%	4%	5%	6%	7%	8%	9%	10%	11%	12%	13%	14%	15%
1	.990	.980	.971	.962	.952	.943	.935	.926	.917	.909	.901	.893	.885	.877	.870
2	1.970	1.942	1.913	1.886	1.859	1.833	1.808	1.783	1.759	1.736	1.713	1.690	1.668	1.647	1.626
3	2.941	2.884	2.829	2.775	2.723	2.673	2.624	2.577	2.531	2.487	2.444	2.402	2.361	2.322	2.283
4	3.902	3.808	3.717	3.630	3.546	3.465	3.387	3.312	3.240	3.170	3.102	3.037	2.974	2.914	2.855
5	4.853	4.713	4.580	4.452	4.329	4.212	4.100	3.993	3.890	3.791	3.696	3.605	3.517	3.433	3.352
6	5.795	5.601	5.417	5.242	5.076	4.917	4.767	4.623	4.486	4.355	4.231	4.111	3.998	3.889	3.784
7	6.728	6.472	6.230	6.002	5.786	5.582	5.389	5.206	5.033	4.868	4.712	4.564	4.423	4.288	4.160
8	7.652	7.325	7.020	6.733	6.463	6.210	5.971	5.747	5.535	5.335	5.146	4.968	4.799	4.639	4.487
9	8.566	8.162	7.786	7.435	7.108	6.802	6.515	6.247	5.995	5.759	5.537	5.328	5.132	4.946	4.772
10	9.471	8.983	8.530	8.111	7.722	7.360	7.024	6.710	6.418	6.145*	5.889	5.650	5.426	5.216	5.019
11	10.368	9.787	9.253	8.760	8.306	7.887	7.499	7.139	6.805	6.495	6.207	5.938	5.687	5.453	5.234
12	11.255	10.575	9.954	9.385	8.863	8.384	7.943	7.536	7.161	6.814	6.492	6.194	5.918	5.660	5.421
13	12.134	11.348	10.635	9.986	9.394	8.853	8.358	7.904	7.487	7.103	6.750	6.424	6.122	5.842	5.583
14	13.004	12.106	11.296	10.563	9.899	9.295	8.745	8.244	7.786	7.367	6.982	6.628	6.302	6.002	5.724
15	13.865	12.849	11.938	11.118	10.380	9.712	9.108	8.559	8.061	7.606	7.191	6.811	6.462	6.142	5.847
16	14.718	13.577	12.561	11.652	10.838	10.106	9.447	8.851	8.313	7.824	7.379	6.974	6.604	6.265	5.954
17	15.562	14.292	13.166	12.106	11.274	10.477	9.763	9.122	8.544	8.022	7.549	7.120	6.729	6.373	6.047
18	16.398	14.992	13.754	12.659	11.690	10.828	10.059	9.372	8.756	8.201	7.702	7.250	6.840	6.467	6.128
19	17.226	15.679	14.324	13.134	12.085	11.158	10.336	9.604	8.950	8.365	7.839	7.366	6.938	6.550	6.198
20	18.040	16.351	14.878	13.590	12.462	11.470	10.594	9.818	9.129	8.514	7.963	7.469	7.025	6.623	6.259

$n =$ Number of Periods	$r =$ Interest Rate per Period														
	16%	17%	18%	19%	20%	21%	22%	23%	24%	25%	26%	27%	28%	29%	30%
1	.862	.855	.847	.840	.833	.826	.820	.813	.806	.800	.794	.787	.781	.775	.769
2	1.605	1.585	1.566	1.547	1.528	1.509	1.492	1.474	1.457	1.440	1.424	1.407	1.392	1.376	1.361
3	2.246	2.210	2.174	2.140	2.106	2.074	2.042	2.011	1.981	1.952	1.923	1.896	1.868	1.842	1.816
4	2.798	2.743	2.690	2.639	2.589	2.540	2.494	2.448	2.404	2.362	2.320	2.280	2.241	2.203	2.166
5	3.274	3.199	3.127	3.058	2.991	2.926	2.864	2.803	2.745	2.689	2.635	2.583	2.532	2.483	2.436
6	3.685	3.589	3.498	3.410	3.326	3.245	3.167	3.092	3.020	2.951	2.885	2.821	2.759	2.700	2.643
7	4.039	3.922	3.812	3.706	3.605	3.508	3.416	3.327	3.242	3.161	3.083	3.009	2.937	2.868	2.802
8	4.344	4.207	4.078	3.954	3.837	3.726	3.619	3.518	3.421	3.329	3.241	3.156	3.076	2.999	2.925
9	4.607	4.451	4.303	4.163	4.031	3.905	3.786	3.673	3.566	3.463	3.366	3.273	3.184	3.100	3.019
10	4.833	4.659	4.494	4.339	4.192	4.054	3.923	3.799	3.682	3.571	3.465	3.364	3.269	3.178	3.092
11	5.029	4.836	4.656	4.486	4.327	4.177	4.035	3.902	3.776	3.656	3.543	3.437	3.335	3.239	3.147
12	5.197	4.988	4.793	4.611	4.439	4.278	4.127	3.985	3.851	3.725	3.606	3.493	3.387	3.286	3.190
13	5.342	5.118	4.910	4.715	4.533	4.362	4.203	4.053	3.912	3.780	3.656	3.538	3.427	3.322	3.223
14	5.468	5.229	5.008	4.802	4.611	4.432	4.265	4.108	3.962	3.824	3.695	3.573	3.459	3.351	3.249
15	5.575	5.324	5.092	4.876	4.675	4.489	4.315	4.153	4.001	3.859	3.726	3.601	3.483	3.373	3.268
16	5.668	5.405	5.162	4.938	4.730	4.536	4.357	4.189	4.033	3.887	3.751	3.623	3.503	3.390	3.283
17	5.749	5.475	5.222	4.990	4.775	4.576	4.391	4.219	4.059	3.910	3.771	3.640	3.518	3.403	3.295
18	5.818	5.534	5.273	5.033	4.812	4.608	4.419	4.243	4.080	3.928	3.786	3.654	3.529	3.413	3.304
19	5.877	5.584	5.316	5.070	4.843	4.635	4.442	4.263	4.097	3.942	3.799	3.664	3.539	3.421	3.311
20	5.929	5.628	5.353	5.101	4.870	4.657	4.460	4.279	4.110	3.954	3.808	3.673	3.546	3.427	3.316

* If the interest rate is 10 percent per period, the present value of $1 received at the end of each of the next 5 periods is $6.145.

TABLE 4

Amount of an Ordinary Annuity of $1
Sum of an Annuity of $1 per Period,
Compounded at r% per Period for n Periods

$$sA_n^r = \frac{(1+r)^n - 1}{r}$$

$n =$ Number of Periods	$r =$ Interest Rate per Period														
	1%	2%	3%	4%	5%	6%	7%	8%	9%	10%	11%	12%	13%	14%	15%
1	1.000	1.000	1.000	1.000	1.000	1.000	1.000	1.000	1.000	1.000	1.000	1.000	1.000	1.000	1.000
2	2.010	2.020	2.030	2.040	2.050	2.060	2.070	2.080	2.090	2.100	2.110	2.120	2.130	2.140	2.150
3	3.030	3.060	3.091	3.122	3.153	3.184	3.215	3.246	3.278	3.310	3.342	3.374	3.407	3.440	3.473
4	4.060	4.122	4.184	4.247	4.310	4.375	4.440	4.506	4.573	4.641	4.710	4.779	4.850	4.921	4.993
5	5.101	5.204	5.309	5.416	5.526	5.637	5.751	5.867	5.985	6.105	6.228	6.353	6.480	6.610	6.742
6	6.152	6.308	6.468	6.633	6.802	6.975	7.153	7.336	7.523	7.716	7.913	8.115	8.322	8.536	8.754
7	7.214	7.434	7.663	7.898	8.142	8.394	8.654	8.923	9.200	9.487	9.783	10.089	10.404	10.730	11.066
8	8.286	8.583	8.892	9.214	9.549	9.898	10.259	10.636	11.028	11.435	11.859	12.299	12.757	13.232	13.726
9	9.369	9.755	10.159	10.582	11.026	11.491	11.978	12.487	13.021	13.579	14.164	14.775	15.415	16.085	16.785
10	10.462	10.949	11.463	12.006	12.577	13.180	13.816	14.486	15.192	15.937*	16.722	17.548	18.419	19.337	20.303
11	11.566	12.168	12.807	13.486	14.206	14.971	15.873	16.645	17.560	18.531	19.561	20.654	21.814	23.044	24.349
12	12.682	13.142	14.192	15.025	15.917	16.869	17.888	18.977	20.140	21.384	22.713	24.133	25.650	27.270	29.001
13	13.809	14.680	15.617	16.626	17.713	18.882	20.140	21.495	22.953	24.522	26.211	28.029	29.985	32.088	34.351
14	14.947	15.973	17.086	18.291	19.598	21.015	22.550	24.214	26.019	27.975	30.094	32.392	34.883	37.581	40.504
15	16.096	17.293	18.598	20.023	21.578	23.276	25.129	27.152	29.360	31.772	34.404	37.279	40.418	43.842	47.580
16	17.257	18.639	20.156	21.824	23.657	25.672	27.888	30.324	33.003	35.949	39.189	42.753	46.672	50.980	55.717
17	18.430	20.012	21.761	23.697	25.840	28.212	30.840	33.750	36.973	40.544	44.500	48.883	53.739	59.117	65.075
18	19.614	21.412	23.414	25.645	28.132	30.905	33.999	37.450	41.301	45.599	50.395	55.749	61.725	68.394	75.836
19	20.810	22.840	25.116	27.671	30.539	33.760	37.379	41.446	46.018	51.159	56.939	63.439	70.765	78.969	88.211
20	22.019	24.297	26.870	29.778	33.066	36.785	40.995	45.762	51.160	57.275	64.169	72.052	80.962	91.024	102.440

n = Number of Periods	16%	17%	18%	19%	20%	21%	22%	23%	24%	25%	26%	27%	28%	29%	30%
1	1.000	1.000	1.000	1.000	1.000	1.000	1.000	1.000	1.000	1.000	1.000	1.000	1.000	1.000	1.000
2	2.160	2.170	2.180	2.190	2.200	2.210	2.220	2.230	2.240	2.250	2.260	2.270	2.280	2.290	2.300
3	3.506	3.539	3.572	3.606	3.640	3.674	3.688	3.743	3.778	3.813	3.848	3.883	3.918	3.954	3.990
4	5.067	5.141	5.215	5.291	5.368	5.446	5.504	5.604	5.684	5.766	5.848	5.931	6.016	6.101	6.187
5	6.877	7.015	7.154	7.296	7.442	7.590	7.719	7.893	8.048	8.207	8.368	8.532	8.700	8.870	9.043
6	8.978	9.207	9.442	9.682	9.930	10.184	10.422	10.708	10.980	11.259	11.544	11.836	12.135	12.442	12.756
7	11.413	11.772	12.141	12.522	12.915	13.322	13.719	14.171	14.615	15.073	15.546	16.032	16.533	17.050	17.583
8	14.240	14.773	15.327	15.901	16.499	17.119	17.742	18.430	19.122	19.842	20.588	21.361	22.163	22.995	23.858
9	17.518	18.284	19.085	19.922	20.798	21.714	22.650	23.669	24.712	25.802	26.941	28.129	29.369	30.664	32.015
10	21.321	22.392	23.521	24.707	25.958	27.274	28.637	30.123	31.643	33.253	34.946	36.724	38.592	40.557	42.619
11	25.732	27.199	28.755	30.402	32.150	34.002	35.942	38.039	40.237	42.566	45.031	47.639	50.398	53.318	56.405
12	30.850	32.823	34.931	37.179	39.580	42.142	44.854	47.788	50.894	54.208	57.739	61.501	65.510	69.780	74.327
13	36.786	39.403	42.218	45.243	48.496	51.992	55.726	59.779	64.109	68.760	73.751	79.107	84.852	91.016	97.625
14	43.672	47.102	50.818	54.839	59.195	63.911	68.990	74.528	80.496	86.949	93.926	101.465	109.610	118.411	127.912
15	51.659	56.109	60.965	66.259	72.035	78.332	85.172	92.669	100.810	109.687	119.346	129.861	141.300	153.750	167.285
16	60.925	66.647	72.939	79.849	87.442	95.782	104.914	114.982	126.010	138.109	151.376	165.924	181.860	199.337	218.471
17	71.673	78.977	87.068	96.021	105.930	116.896	129.000	142.428	157.250	173.636	191.734	211.723	233.790	258.144	285.012
18	84.140	93.403	103.740	115.265	128.110	142.444	158.384	176.187	195.990	218.045	242.585	269.888	300.250	334.006	371.516
19	98.603	110.282	123.410	138.165	154.740	173.357	194.233	217.710	244.030	273.556	306.657	343.758	385.320	431.688	483.971
20	115.370	130.030	146.620	165.417	186.680	210.761	247.591	268.784	303.600	342.945	387.388	437.572	494.210	558.112	630.163

* If $1 is invested at the end of each period for the next 10 periods and compounded at the rate of 10 percent per period, it will accumulate to $15.937.

Questions

1. What important characteristics of a decision situation require the use of capital budgeting analysis?

2. What are the two important parts of the overall capital budgeting process?

3. Why is the length of the planning period (the planning horizon) important to capital budgeting analysis?

4. Describe the recommended steps in an overall capital budgeting system for a firm.

5. Define the following terms as they refer to capital budgeting situations:
   a. Project
   b. Project life
   c. Investment outlay
   d. Net benefit flows
   e. Cost of capital
   f. Rate of return on investment

6. Why is *rate of return* or *return on investment* such an elusive concept? What are the difficulties encountered in measuring it?

7. Explain the *accounting rate of return* method. What are its advantages and disadvantages?

8. How can the explicit average cost of capital from all sources be calculated?

9. Explain the *payback period* method. What are its advantages and limitations?

10. What is the *payback reciprocal?* How should it be interpreted?

11. Explain the *bailout factor* method. When would it be appropriate to use this method to evaluate proposed projects? Why?

12. Why are *discounting* methods preferable to nondiscounting methods for project evaluation purposes?

13. Explain the *net present value* method. What are its advantages and limitations?

14. How should working capital requirements of a project be included in capital budgeting analysis?

15. What does the *net present value ratio* show that the *net present value amount* does not?

16. Explain the *internal rate of return* method. What are its advantages and limitations?

17. What does the *discounted payback period* method show that the *simple payback period* method does not?

18. What is the real impact of depreciation charges on capital budgeting analysis when the following methods are used?
   a. Payback method
   b. Accounting rate of return method
   c. Net present value method
   d. Internal rate of return method

Exercises

E 17-1   Payback Period—Accounting Return on Investment— Elementary Analysis

Salvatore Simone Corporation is planning to purchase additional sales equipment for its retail outlet. This planned expansion will require the outlay of $100,000 for equipment with an expected life of nine years and expected disposal value of $10,000. The use of this equipment is expected to produce annual operating results as follows:

Increased Sales Revenues	$80,000
Increased Operating Expenses (excluding depreciation)	$50,000

Straight-line depreciation will be used and the corporation is subject to a 50 percent income tax rate.

Required:

(a) *Ignoring income taxes,* compute (1) the payback period, (2) the accounting rate of return based on the total outlay, and (3) the accounting rate of return based on the average outlay.

(b) Repeat all the steps in part (a) on an after-tax basis.

E 17-2   Payback Period—Accounting Rate of Return—Incremental Analysis

Hazzard Company is evaluating a proposal to replace one of its stamping machines that possibly could be used for another six years. A new model is now available that could reduce operating costs. The company is subject to a 40 percent income tax rate. A comparison of costs and other aspects of the two machines follows.

	Old Machine	New Machine
Original Cost	$26,000	$31,000
Remaining Useful Life	6 years	6 years
Salvage Value—Now	$ 2,000	$ 2,000
Salvage Value—6 Years	$ -0-	$ 1,000
Operating Costs per Year	$70,000	$63,000
Depreciation per Year	$ 2,000	$ 5,000
Current Book Value	$12,000	N/A

Required:

(a) Prepare a schedule of *all* operating cash flows associated with the proposal to purchase the new machine and replace the old one, rather than to continue to use the old machine, (1) before taxes and (2) after taxes.

(b) What is the incremental investment outlay associated with the purchase of the new machine (1) before taxes and (2) after taxes?

(c) Compute the payback period for the new machine (1) before taxes and (2) after taxes.

(d) Compute the accounting rate of return based on the initial outlay as computed in part (b) (1) before taxes and (2) after taxes.

E 17-3 Payback Period—Accounting Rate of Return—Alternative Decision Criteria

Waite Equipment Company has not established any firm criteria for its managers to use in making capital project investment decisions. Both the payback period and the accounting rate of return have been used to evaluate proposals.

Presently two department managers have submitted requests for $100,000 machines for their respective departments. Projected annual operating cash flows are as follows:

	Department A	Department B
Years 1–10	$20,000	—
Years 1–4	—	$0
Years 5–10	—	$40,000

Neither machine will have any salvage value at the end of the tenth year.

Required:
(a) Evaluate each project on the basis of its payback period.
(b) Evaluate each project on the basis of its accounting rate of return on average investment outlay.
(c) Which criterion would each department manager choose, assuming that they are each aware of the other's proposal? Why?
(d) Which is the better proposal? Why?

E 17-4 Net Present Value Method—Elementary Analysis—Before-tax Basis

Jude Company is considering the acquisition of a new drilling machine. The price of the new machine is $90,000, but it will replace an existing machine that can be sold for $10,000. The effect of the use of the new machine will be to reduce the outlay for indirect materials, supplies, and maintenance by $24,000 per year. However, the fact that more highly skilled operators will be needed will increase labor costs by $4,000 annually, and the new machine will require a major overhaul costing $12,000 after six years of operation. At the end of eight years, the machine can be sold for $6,000. The company considers 15 percent to be the appropriate before-tax cost of capital for projects of this type.

Required:
(a) Prepare a schedule of all cash flows associated with the project.
(b) Compute the net present value of the project.
(c) Should the project be undertaken? Why or why not?

E 17-5 Net Present Value Method—Elementary Analysis—After-tax Basis

Refer to the data in Exercise 17–4. Assume that the company is subject to a 40 percent tax rate. The straight-line depreciation method is used and, for depreciation purposes, the new machine is assumed to have no salvage value. The old machine had a book value of $25,000 when the new machine was purchased. An after-tax cost of capital of 10 percent is relevant to this type of project. Assume the overhaul is charged to expense in year six.

Required:
(a) Prepare a schedule of all after-tax cash flows associated with the project.
(b) Compute the net present value of the project.
(c) Should the project be undertaken? Why or why not?

E 17-6 Net Present Value Analysis—Total Project and Incremental Analysis

Travolta Enterprises, Inc. is considering the replacement of the sound system in one of its downtown discos. The present sound system could last for another five years if extensive maintenance is performed on it in three years' time. The new system is quite expensive, but will not require such extensive maintenance.

The company considers 20 percent to be the appropriate before-tax cost of capital rate for projects of this type. The following estimates and information have been developed:

	Keep Existing System	Acquire New System
Original Acquisition Cost	$200,000	$450,000
Book Value	80,000	N/A
Overhaul—Now	100,000	N/A
Overhaul—3 Years	80,000	N/A
Annual Operating Costs	160,000	120,000
Resale Value Old Machine—Now	N/A	50,000
Resale Value—5 Years	5,000	50,000

Required:
(a) Using net present value analysis, *compare* the two alternatives on the basis of their respective total costs. Ignore tax effects.
(b) Use an incremental approach, based on the *net* effect of making the change, to evaluate the proposal on the basis of net present value analysis.
(c) Should the new equipment be acquired? Why or why not?

E 17-7 Net Present Value Method—Project Evaluation—Sensitivity Analysis—Internal Rate of Return

Butts Timber Company is considering the replacement of the lumber processing equipment at its Padstow facility. Existing equipment will have no net recovery value due to the costs of removal and disposal. New equipment will make use of laser technology and will cost $1,000,000. This new equipment is attractive because it could save $200,000 in annual operating costs. The company believes that a 20 percent cost of capital rate before taxes is appropriate to this project. The laser equipment will have no salvage value whenever its use is discontinued. In all the following cases, ignore income tax effects.

Required:
(a) Compute the net present value of the project, assuming an eight-year project life and using a before-tax cost of capital rate of (1) 8, (2) 10, (3) 15, and (4) 20 percent. Comment on the results.

(b)   Compute the net present value of the project, using a before-tax cost of capital rate of 12 percent and assuming a project life of (1) 6, (2) 10, (3) 12, and (4) 15 years. Comment on the results.

(c)   Assuming a project life of eight years and a before-tax cost of capital rate of 10 percent, compute the net present value of the project for situations where the operating cash flows per year are (1) $100,000, (2) $200,000, and (3) $300,000. Comment on the results.

(d)   Assume a project life of eight years and operating cash flows of $200,000 per year. What internal rate of return is implicit in the project under those conditions? Repeat the calculation for project lives of (1) 5 and (2) 12 years. Comment on the results.

E 17-8   Net Present Value Analysis—Comparison of Alternative Projects—Payback Period and Accounting Rate of Return

Holbrook Company is considering two alternative investment opportunities. Both require an initial outlay of $100,000 and are to be evaluated relative to a before-tax cost of capital rate of 10 percent. Project A will return $20,000 per year for the next ten years; Project B will have no return for the first five years, then $40,000 per year for the next five years.

Required:
(a)   Use (1) net present value analysis and (2) discounted payback period to evaluate the two projects. Which project would be preferred on each of these bases? Why?

(b)   Use (1) payback period and (2) the accounting rate of return on average investment outlay to evaluate the two projects. Which project would be preferred on each of those bases? Why?

(c)   Compare your answers in parts (a) and (b). Comment on the relative merits of the three different criteria.

(d)   A third alternative is to invest in a ten-year term deposit with a Savings and Loan Bank which pays 12 percent interest.
(1)   Is this any more or less attractive than Projects A or B? Why or why not?
(2)   Would it make any difference if the interest were paid out in cash each year rather than being compounded? Why or why not?

(e)   What are the limitations of the type of analysis used in parts (a) and (d)? What other factors might need to be considered in the analysis of alternative investment projects?

E 17-9   Net Present Value Analysis—Comparison of Alternative Projects

Rhode Corporation is considering the purchase of duplicating equipment for its new administrative headquarters. Three alternative suppliers have submitted proposals, but each proposal varies with regard to initial cost, operating costs and expected lives. However, each proposal meets the minimum requirements of expected volume, service warranty, and reliability. Details of the three suppliers' proposals are as follows:

	Yerox	B.B.M.	A.D. Pick
Initial Cost	$1,000,000	$750,000	$500,000
Useful Life	6 years	4 years	3 years
Resale Value—End of Life	$ 100,000	$100,000	$ 50,000
Annual Cash Operating Costs	$ 80,000	$120,000	$160,000

The company wishes to analyze the proposals over a 12-year period and considers that a 15 percent before-tax cost of capital rate is appropriate to this type of project. Ignore income tax effects.

Required:
(a) Compute the net present value of the total outlays and operating costs associated with each of the three proposals.
(b) Which proposal should be accepted? Why?
(c) What factors, besides the basic financial ones previously noted, should be considered in the selection process? Why?

Cases

C 17–1   Cost of Capital Rate

Gordon Company has the following composition of its capital sources:

Common Stock (1,000,000 shares)......	$ 50,000,000
Retained Earnings	110,000,000
Bonds (coupon rate 10%)	40,000,000
	$200,000,000

Similar bonds would need to be sold presently at a discount to provide a yield to the purchaser of 12 percent per annum (after tax). The market price of common stock is $200. Dividends are always distributed in an amount equal to 50 percent of current earnings. Earnings have been increasing at the rate of 10 percent per year, and the current year's dividend was $10 per share. The company is subject to a 50 percent corporate tax rate.

Required:
(a) Compute the company's weighted average after-tax cost of capital rate. Show all calculations and state all assumptions.
(b) How should this cost of capital rate be interpreted and used? What are its limitations?

C 17–2   After-tax Cash Flows

(a) Inberg Corporation has acquired a new truck that will require $8,000 per year in cash outlays for operating costs. If the company is subject to a 35 percent tax rate, what will be the annual after-tax cash flows resulting from operating the truck?
(b) The truck mentioned in part (a) has a purchase price of $15,000 and will last for five years, at the end of which time it will have a resale value of $3,000. It will be depreciated on a straight-line basis. What will be the effects of these depreciation charges on after-tax cash flow per year?
(c) What will be the after-tax cash flow per year resulting from the operating costs in part (a) and the depreciation charges in part (b)? Show two different ways of arriving at the correct answer.

C 17–3   After-tax Cash Flows

(a)   Kam Company can acquire one of two machines to assist in the manufacture of a new product line. The first costs $200,000 and will generate after-tax operating cash flows of $40,000 per year for ten years. The second will cost $300,000 and its after-tax operating cash flows will be $55,000 per year, also for ten years. Using the net present value method, which machine will be more desirable if the relevant cost of capital is 10 percent?

(b)   What other factors that need to be considered in this decision are not mentioned in part (a)?

(c)   Should the net present value method be the only decision criterion in this case? Why or why not?

C 17–4   After-tax Cash Flows

(a)   Lowenthal Incorporated presently spends $80,000 each year on advertising, but is considering an increase in this amount to $140,000 annually. If the company is subject to a tax rate of 45 percent, what effect will the change in advertising expenditures have on the after-tax cash flow per year?

(b)   Instead of an increase, Lowenthal is considering reducing its advertising outlays by $30,000 annually. What will be the new annual after-tax cash flow for advertising?

(c)   Assume that the increase in advertising proposed in part (a) causes sales to increase by $600,000 per year. If the company has a contribution margin ratio of .25, what will be the net effect of the change in sales revenues and advertising expenses on the annual after-tax operating cash flows?

C 17–5   Keep or Replace Equipment

Gottschalk Corporation has two pieces of equipment of basically the same productive capacity and ability. One was purchased eight years ago and has a book value of $500. The other machine was purchased twelve months ago at a cost of $48,000. However, a revolutionary new machine, which will reduce variable operating costs by more than half, has just become available. Although both of the old machines are functional and could go on producing the same standard product for several years, they cannot compete favorably with the new machine in terms of variable cost per unit of manufacture. Management has decided that the eight-year-old machine will be replaced with one of the new models, which costs $80,000. However, management feels that they "cannot afford to dispose of the newer one because of the considerable loss that will be incurred." The only viable alternative use of both old machines is to sell them to a scrap metal dealer for $750 each.

Required:
(a)   Comment on the validity of the management's decision to keep the twelve-month-old machine.

(b)   How should the two existing machines be incorporated into the decision to purchase new machines?

(c)   What other quantitative factors besides the reduction in variable cost per unit to manufacture should be included in the analysis? What nonquantitative factors?

C 17–6   Alternative Investments

Gaspardone Corporation is considering two alternative projects, both of which will require $100,000 initial outlay and generate cash inflows of $30,000 per year for five years. Project A involves acquisition of equipment that will have a resale value of $10,000 at the end of the fifth year. Project B involves acquisition of inventories. At the end of the fifth year, all inventory will have been disposed of and all funds initially invested will have become available for other purposes.

Required:
(a) Compare and contrast the two investment projects.
(b) Demonstrate how several different capital budgeting methods could be applied to this decision. Do they produce consistent results? Why or why not?

C 17–7   Capital Budgeting Misconceptions

(1) "Any project with an economic life that is *longer* than its payback period must be a profitable one."
(2) "Any project with an economic life that is *shorter* that its payback period must be an unprofitable one."
(3) "All projects have a point of no *return*—once you have committed yourself so far, you have to go through with it."
(4) "I have all the money I need for the outlays on this project in my checking account. Since it is earning no interest there, I don't have to consider any sort of cost of capital in regard to the project's profitability."

Required:
Comment separately on each of the preceding assertions. Do you agree with each of them? Why or why not? What fallacies, half-truths, or misconceptions are involved?

C 17–8   Capital Budgeting Methods

"The net present value ratio and the internal rate of return serve as common denominator type measures of capital investment projects. So does the discounted payback period method. The net present value method provides answers that are quite sensitive to the size of a project. Therefore, it is a biased measure of the profitability of an investment."

Required:
Critically evaluate this assertion. Do you agree? Why or why not?

Problems

P 17–1   Accounting Rate of Return—Project Evaluation

A division of Ulferts Corporation has proposed the addition of a new product line. Some manufacturing facilities are available, but special equipment costing $600,000 would need to be purchased. This equipment has a five-year useful life with zero scrap value.

Production would take place in an area of the plant presently used as an inventory storage area, requiring the rental of an adjoining vacant warehouse at an annual cost of $80,000. Additional information related to the project is as follows:

Estimated Annual Sales	$2,000,000
Cost of Sales (excluding depreciation and rent)	1,400,000
Marketing and Administrative Expenses	220,000

The existing manufacturing facilities to be used in this project have a remaining useful life of five years, will have a zero scrap value, and have a current book value of $400,000. Straight-line depreciation is taken on all plant assets. The corporation considers 12 percent to be an acceptable after-tax accrual income accounting rate of return, based on average investment for projects of this type. The company is subject to a 40 percent tax rate.

Required:

(a) Prepare a statement to show the average annual effect of this project on net income after tax.

(b) Should this proposal be accepted? Why or why not?

(c) What minimum increase in annual net income would the project need to promise to meet the company's investment requirements?

(d) What are the limitations of this type of analysis?

P 17–2 Payback Period—Accounting Rate of Return—Comparative Analysis

Martin Corporation is considering the replacement of one of its major equipment items, a metal stamping machine. Two replacement models are available, each with approximately identical technical operating specifications. A schedule of comparative aspects of the three machines follows.

	Old Machine	New Machine A	New Machine B
Annual Capacity (units)	10,000	10,000	12,000
Selling Price (per unit)	$15	$15	$15
Annual Labor Costs	$75,000	$30,000	$20,000
Annual Maintenance Costs	$10,000	$ 5,000	$ 4,000
Annual Supply Costs	$ 4,000	$ 1,000	$ 1,000
Annual Indirect Materials,			
Waste, and so on	$12,000	$ 4,000	$ 2,000

Machines A and B have acquisition costs of $300,000 and $400,000, respectively. The existing machine has a book value of $100,000, but could be sold now for $20,000. All three machines will last for five years and will have no scrap value at the end of that time. The company is subject to a 40 percent tax rate.

Required:

(a) Prepare a schedule to show the incremental effect on annual after-tax net income of: (1) acquiring Machine A and (2) acquiring Machine B.

(b) Prepare a schedule to show the incremental effect on annual operating after-tax cash flows of (1) acquiring Machine A and (2) acquiring Machine B.

(c) Compute the after-tax payback period for each alternative. Which would be preferred on this basis?

(d) Compute the after-tax accounting rate of return based on average investment outlay for each alternative. Which would be preferred on this basis?

(e) Comment on the answers to parts (a) and (d).

(f) What are the (1) limitations and (2) advantages of the analysis used in parts (c) and (d)?

P 17-3   Net Present Value Analysis—Project Evaluation

Davis Corporation is planning to introduce a new product with a projected life of eight years. Equipment to manufacture the product will cost $6,000,000, and additional equipment costing $1,000,000 will be needed in three years' time. At the end of eight years, the original equipment will have no resale value, but the supplementary equipment can be sold for $120,000. Sales volume over the eight-year period has been forecast as follows:

Year 1	80,000 units
Year 2	120,000 units
Years 3–5	300,000 units
Years 6–8	200,000 units

A sales price of $40 per unit is predicted and variable expenses will amount to 60 percent of sales revenues. Fixed operating costs (excluding depreciation, which is computed on a straight-line basis) will amount to $1,600,000 per year. In addition, an extensive advertising campaign will be implemented, requiring annual outlays as follows:

Year 1	$3,000,000
Years 2–3	1,500,000
Years 4–8	400,000

The corporation is subject to a 30 percent tax rate and considers 12 percent to be an appropriate after-tax cost of capital rate for this type of project. In addition, the company will receive a one-time tax-free payment of $10,000,000 at the end of Year 4 from the government, because the new product is related to pollution control.

Required:

(a) Prepare a schedule of all after-tax cash flows associated with this project.

(b) Compute the net present value and the net present value ratio for this project. Should it be accepted? Why or why not?

(c) *Without computations,* comment on the possible effect of an overestimation of the cost of capital rate for this project.

(d) *Without computations,* comment on the possible effect of (1) overstating the useful life of the product or (2) understating the ratio of variable expenses to sales revenue.

(e) Referring to your decision in part (b), what additional information might be useful in the analysis of this proposal?

P 17–4   Net Present Value Analysis—Comparison of Alternative Proposals

Elliot Enterprises, Inc., acquired a set of blending machines four years ago for $700,000. They will last for another ten years and should have a disposal value at that time of $10,000. Computer-controlled machines are now available that will perform the same tasks as the existing ones. However, these will cost $1,000,000 to acquire and will last for ten years, after which they can be sold for $100,000. The new machines will increase production volume by 25 percent. The present sales volume is 100,000 units per year at full capacity. There are indications that as many as 140,000 units could be sold annually at the normal sales price of $20 per unit. Additional operating, cost, and revenue data are as follows:

	Existing Machine	New Machine
Variable Cost per Unit	$15	$10
Fixed Cost per Year (excluding depreciation)	$150,000	$500,000

The existing machines could be sold now for $250,000. The straight-line depreciation method is used, with zero salvage values assumed. The company is subject to a 40 percent tax rate on all operating income, as well as on gains or losses from disposal of assets. The after-tax cost of capital rate for this project has been set at 15 percent.

Required:
(a)   Prepare schedules of all after-tax cash flows associated with this project, (1) showing the *total* effect of the two alternatives separately and (2) showing the incremental effect of making the changeover.
(b)   Use the net present value method to evaluate the proposed changeover of equipment. Should it be adopted? Why or why not?
(c)   What is the net present value ratio for the changeover project? In what decision situation could this piece of information be used?
(d)   Comment on other factors that might influence the decision as to whether or not to make the equipment changeover.

P 17–5   Net Present Value Analysis—Evaluation of Alternative Projects

Refer to the data in Problem 17–2. Assume that the company observes an 8 percent after-tax cost of capital rate for this type of project.

Required:
(a)   Use net present value analysis to determine whether *either, both,* or *neither* of the new machines is acceptable. Which machine, if any, would you recommend and why?
(b)   Compare your solution in part (a) to that in part (d) of Problem 17–2. Comment.

P 17–6   Net Present Value Analysis—Evaluation of Alternative Projects— Net Present Value Ratio

Nimitz Corporation anticipates increased demand for one of its major product lines and is interested in expanding its productive capacity. It presently operates one Model XL-700 and is considering two alternatives: *Plan A:* Acquire an additional Model XL-700 to operate in tandem with the existing one. *Plan B:* Acquire the newly-introduced Model XL-1500, which has double the output capacity of an XL-700, but keep the old XL-700 for emergencies, since tests have shown that the XL-1500 is a very sensitive machine. The following information has been developed for the two alternatives:

	Model XL-700	Model XL-1500
Acquisition Cost	$50,000	$80,000
Operating Costs per Unit:		
Materials	40¢	80¢
Labor	80¢	30¢
Overhead	20¢	10¢
Annual Operating Fixed Costs per Machine		
(excluding depreciation)	$ 5,000	$ 8,000
Resale Value in 10 Years	–0–	–0–

The existing Model XL-700 was purchased four years ago for $40,000. If operated, it will have to be replaced six years from now at an estimated cost of $60,000. This replacement machine will have a market value of $30,000 after four years. If the XL-1500 is acquired, it will cost $2,000 per year to maintain the existing XL-700 on standby status. However, if the XL-700 is kept on standby, it will not need to be replaced at the end of six years. The company believes that a 20 percent before-tax cost of capital rate is appropriate to this decision. Forecast sales at $2 per unit over the next ten years are as follows:

Years	Units
1–2	45,000
3–5	50,000
6–10	70,000

Required:

(a) Prepare schedules of all before-tax cash flows associated with the two proposed plans.

(b) Use (1) net present value analysis, (2) the net present value ratio, and (3) the discounted payback period to evaluate the two plans. Which plan would you recommend? Why?

(c) What other factors should be considered in making the choice between Plan A and Plan B?

(d) *Without computations,* indicate separately which plan would be made *relatively* more acceptable by (1) increases in labor rates, (2) decreases in materials costs per unit, (3) increases in sales demand, and (4) proportional increases in the prices of the two new models. Explain your answer in each case.

(e) Resolve parts (a) and (b) of this problem on an after-tax basis, observing a 12 percent after-tax cost of capital. The company is subject to a 40 percent tax rate.

P 17–7 Net Present Value Analysis—Net Present Value Ratio— Accelerated Depreciation

Frances Corporation plans to install automated equipment to perform tasks presently done manually by production line workers. Acquisition cost of the equipment is $450,000; installation and testing will amount to $50,000. For tax purposes, installation and testing will be allowable deductions in Year 1. The sum-of-the-years'-digits depreciation method will be used, based on a five-year useful life and a zero resale value. Annual operating and maintenance costs for the five-year period will increase as follows:

Year	Operating and Maintenance Costs
1	$ 40,000
2	75,000
3	120,000
4	150,000
5	200,000

The workers who will be displaced are now earning a total of $300,000 annually. Wage rates are forecast to increase by 10 percent in Year 2 and by another 10 percent in Year 4. The corporation is subject to a 45 percent tax rate and uses a 10 percent after-tax cost of capital rate to evaluate such proposals.

Required:

(a) Prepare a schedule of all after-tax cash flows associated with the project.
(b) Use net present value analysis to evaluate the proposal. Should it be accepted? Why or why not?
(c) What is the net present value ratio of the project? Interpret the meaning of this ratio.
(d) What is the discounted payback period for this project? Interpret its meaning.
(e) What other factors might be relevant to the decision to accept or reject this project?

P 17–8   Net Present Value Analysis—Payback Period—Accounting Rate of Return—Alternative Criteria

Powers Corporation has found that its present production facilities, although working at their full capacity of 10,000 units per year, are unable to keep pace with the continued growth in demand for its product. Sales forecasts indicate that at least 12,000 units can be sold annually over the next four years. In order to expand productive capacity sufficiently, equipment costing $320,000 must be acquired. This equipment has a useful life of four years and can be sold for $20,000 at the end of that time. Current operating data has been analyzed to provide the following information:

	Dollars per Unit	
Sales Price		$160
Variable Costs:		
Manufacturing	$84	
Marketing	12	$96
Fixed Costs:		
Manufacturing	$20	
Administrative......	28	48
		144
Net Profit		$ 16

The new equipment will not affect variable costs, but additional fixed manufacturing costs (excluding depreciation) of $15,000 will be incurred annually. The company is subject to a 30 percent tax rate.

Required:
(a) Prepare schedules to show the incremental effect of the acquisition of the extra productive capacity on (1) annual net income and (2) annual operating cash flow, both on an after-tax basis.

(b) Evaluate the proposed acquisition in relation to:
   (1) a payback requirement of three years.
   (2) an accounting rate of return on average investment of 20 percent.
   (3) net present value, based on a cost of capital rate of 15 percent.
   (4) net present value ratio, based on a cost of capital rate of 15 percent.
   (5) a discounted payback requirement of 3.5 years.

(c) Comment on the answers to part (b). Are there any conflicts? Which method would you use? Why?

P 17-9   Expansion of Facilities—Capital Budgeting Analysis

Bedrock Gravel Corporation is considering an expansion of its presently successful quarry operations. A new site, containing an estimated 8,000,000 cubic yards of rock and gravel, can be purchased for $2,000,000. It will take eight years to extract, process, and sell the rock and gravel—800,000 cubic yards per year in the first four years and 1,200,000 cubic yards per year in the latter four. Equipment and facilities costing $2,400,000 must be installed before operations begin. Working capital of $250,000 will be needed throughout the life of the project.

The equipment is estimated to have a resale value of $400,000 at the end of the eighth year. The site can be sold at that time for $600,000, but only after being resurfaced and rehabilitated to satisfy environmental protection laws. This process will cost $600,000, half of which will be spent at the end of the seventh year and half at the end of the eighth.

The sales price of gravel is expected to be $2.40 per cubic yard in the first four years and $2.50 in the second four. Labor and other variable costs of processing will be 75¢ per cubic yard. Other fixed costs (excluding depreciation) will be $400,000 per year. Straight-line depreciation will be used for the equipment; depletion charges will be based on the cubic yards of gravel produced. The company is subject to a 40 percent tax rate and considers 12 percent to be an appropriate after-tax cost of capital rate.

Required:
(a) Prepare schedules showing (1) net income after tax and (2) cash flow after tax for the project. Show two columns—one for Years 1–4 and one for Years 5–8.

(b) Does the project satisfy the stated cost of capital requirement when it is evaluated using the net present value method? Show all calculations.

(c) What is the after-tax discounted payback period?

P 17-10   Evaluation of New Product Proposal—Net Present Value Method—Irregular Operating Cash Flows

Bing Wong Corporation is evaluating its proposed introduction of a new product. Research, development, and testing will require an immediate outlay of $800,000. Production facilities for the new product are available in the existing plant. The equipment and building facilities to be used for the new product now have a book value of $2,100,000.

Forecasts indicate that the new product will have a market life of five years, with unit sales of 800, 1,000, 1,200, 1,000, and 600 in Years 1–5, respectively. The sales price will be $3,000 per unit. Variable costs will be $1,000 for manufacturing and $300 for marketing. Fixed costs (requiring cash outlays) will amount to $160,000 per year. The company is subject to a 40 percent tax rate. For tax purposes, the research and development costs will be written off in the first year; the equipment and building will be depreciated over these five remaining years of life, using the sum-of-the-years'-digits method and assuming zero resale value. If the new product is not introduced, the equipment and building involved could be sold immediately for $2,100,000. Also assume that the company will have significant amounts of taxable income from its other products over all five years under review.

Required:
(a) Remembering that the alternative is to dispose of the existing building and equipment, develop schedules showing (1) the change in net income after taxes and (2) the incremental after-tax operating cash flow, for each of the five years of its life, if the project is accepted.
(b) Develop a net present value analysis for the project, assuming that 15 percent is the appropriate cost of capital.

P 17–11   Net Present Value Analysis—Project Evaluation—Working Capital Considerations—Complementary Effects

Christensen Inc. proposes to introduce a new product that will sell for $40 and have variable costs of $21 per unit. Fixed costs of operating a facility with capacity of 150,000 units will average $4 per unit at that level of capacity (exclusive of depreciation). Equipment to manufacture the product can be acquired for $4,000,000. These machines have a useful life of ten years and zero recovery value. Depreciation charges are computed on the straight-line method. The company is subject to a 40 percent tax rate, and a 16 percent after-tax cost of capital rate is to be observed.

It has been proposed that manufacturing activities be located in a section of existing premises owned by the corporation, but which are presently sublet to another firm as a storage facility for $850,000 per year. The lease on this area is presently subject to renewal for the coming ten years and the present lessee has indicated an interest in renewal at the same annual rate that presently applies.

Introducing the new product line will mean that an average inventory of $1,000,000 has to be maintained and that receivables amounting to one month's sales will always be outstanding. Accounts payable will increase by $400,000 as a result of the additional volume of materials being handled. These changes are to be included in the analysis of the proposal.

Required:
(a) Prepare a schedule to show the proposal's effects on all after-tax cash flows involved. Assume that 150,000 units can be sold annually.
(b) Evaluate the proposal using net present value analysis. Should it be accepted? Why or why not?
(c) In addition to all of the foregoing, assume that the introduction of the new product will also increase sales of an existing product by 50,000 units annually over the ten-year period. This product sells for $12 and has variable costs of $8 per unit. However, this increase in volume will require an additional $150,000 of inventories and receivables and an extra $50,000 per year of fixed costs.

Using net present value analysis, evaluate this additional consideration (1) as a completely separate incremental project and (2) in terms of its overall effect on the original proposal.

P 17–12   Sell-or-Process Further Decision—Long-run Situation—Capital Budgeting Analysis—Incremental Analysis

Wubdeiser Corporation is reviewing the alternatives of producing and selling a new product either at the wholesale or at the retail level. The product is expected to have a market life of five years and will sell for $7.50 wholesale or $12 retail. At the wholesale level, volume will be 100,000 units per year; at the retail level, it will be 120,000 units per year.

The immediate outlays required to facilitate production and distribution of the product on a wholesale basis will amount to $150,000 for equipment and other depreciable items. However, an additional $100,000 will be required for similar items to allow expansion of operations to the retail level. These items will be depreciated using the straight-line method, with expected disposal values of $30,000 and $20,000 respectively at the end of five years.

In addition, there will be start-up costs of $80,000 for the wholesale operation and a further $40,000 for the retail operation. These must be paid in cash at the outset, but can be expensed for tax purposes in the first year. The company is subject to a 40 percent tax rate and observes a 14 percent cost of capital on similar investment proposals. Operating costs requiring current outlays each year are forecast as follows:

	Wholesale*	Retail†
Variable costs (per unit)	$5.00	$7.50
Fixed costs (per year)	$150,000	$300,000

* Includes costs to manufacture and distribute at the wholesale level.
† Includes total costs to manufacture and distribute at the retail level.

Required:
(a) Prepare schedules of (1) net income after tax and (2) operating cash flow for the five-year period. Show columns separately for (1) the *wholesale project,* (2) the *retail project,* and (3) the *incremental effect* of switching from wholesale to retail.
(b) Evaluate the acceptability of the wholesale project, using net present value analysis.
(c) Evaluate the acceptability of the retail project, using net present value analysis.
(d) Evaluate the acceptability of changing from the wholesale to the retail project, using the incremental data from part (a) (3).
(e) Reconcile your answer in part (d) with your answers to parts (b) and (c). Comment.

P 17–13   Net Present Value Analysis—Sensitivity Analysis—Internal Rate of Return Approximation

Alpha–Beta–Gamma Corporation is considering the installation of a new machine to replace an existing one. The existing machine has a book value of $80,000, annual depreciation of $10,000, and a current salvage value of $32,000. Operating costs amount to $60,000 per year.

The new machine would cost $200,000 and would have an expected life of eight years. It would also cost $20,000 to train employees to operate the new machine, but this amount may be written off immediately for tax purposes. Operating cost of the new machine will be $10,000 per year. Both machines will have zero salvage value at the end of eight years. Straight-line depreciation is used, and the company is subject to a 40 percent tax rate.

Required:

(a) Prepare schedules showing (1) the after-tax operating cash flows associated with the two alternatives and (2) the incremental after-tax operating cash flows associated with the switch to the new machine.

(b) Use net present value analysis to evaluate the two alternatives, using after-tax cost of capital rates of (1) 8, (2) 10, (3) 12, (4) 15, and (5) 20 percent.

(c) Comment on the results in part (b), indicating which alternative would be preferred under each cost of capital rate.

(d) At approximately what cost of capital rate would the company be indifferent between the two alternatives? Explain how this rate might be considered the internal rate of return when the changeover of equipment is treated in terms of its incremental effects.

P 17–14   Net Present Value Analysis—Sensitivity Analysis—Alternative Cost of Capital Rates

Trezevant Corporation is about to introduce a new product projected to have a sales volume of 40,000 units in the first year, followed by increases of 20,000 per year until the seventh year, when it will stabilize at 160,000 units per year.

    Two proposals regarding manufacturing facilities have been prepared. The first involves purchasing a single machine with the capacity to produce 200,000 units per year. This machine will last for ten years and will cost $2,000,000. It will have a zero salvage value. The second proposal involves buying a single machine with a 120,000-unit capacity. This will cost $500,000 and will last for five years. After that time, the machine will have no resale value and will have to be replaced by two similar machines also costing $500,000 each and having five-year useful lives. These machines will also have no resale value at the end of their useful lives. Operating costs are projected as follows:

	Large Machine	Small Machine
Materials (per unit)	$10	$12
Labor (per unit)	$8	$10
Other Variable Overheads (per unit)	$2	$3
Property Tax and Insurance (per machine per year)	6% of Original Cost	6% of Original Cost
Repairs and Maintenance (per machine per year)	$25,000	$15,000

The company is subject to a 40 percent tax rate. The product is scheduled to sell for $45 per unit.

Required:

(a) Prepare schedules to show the effects of the two proposals on after-tax cash flows.

(b) Use net present value analysis to evaluate the two proposals, based on after-tax cost of capital rates of (1) 10 and (2) 20 percent. Which proposal would be preferred in each case and why?

(c) Assume that sales volume will stabilize at 120,000 units after five years and not go higher in the remaining years. How will this affect your analysis in parts (a) and (b)? What alternative would you recommend and why? Use both the 10 and 20 percent cost of capital rates.

(d) Assume that sales volume continues to increase in Years 8–10 as follows:

Year	Units
8	170,000
9	190,000
10	200,000

How will this affect your analysis in parts (a) and (b)?

P 17–15   Net Present Value Analysis—Alternative Cash Flow Patterns—Project Evaluation

Macewan Corporation has one main product that sells for $40 per unit. Its plant is presently operating at full capacity with 30 employees scheduled to work three 8-hour shifts per day, 7 days per week, with 10 employees per shift. Hourly wage rates are $8 for regular time, $10 for second shift, and $12 for third shift. On Saturdays and Sundays, all wage rates are subject to an additional 50 percent premium. Assume there are 104 Saturdays/Sundays in every year and 261 weekdays.

Production volume depends on one critical piece of equipment with a production capacity of only 10 units per hour. This machine cost $720,000 three years ago. It has a remaining useful life of five years and is being depreciated on the basis of the sum-of-the-years'-digits method assuming a zero scrap value. The current resale value of this machine is $400,000.

A more efficient machine has been developed with an output rate of 12 units per hour. This machine will cost $1,000,000, but will have a resale value of $100,000 at the end of five years. The sum-of-the-years'-digits method will also be used to depreciate this asset. Materials costs are presently $12 per unit, and variable overhead is $4 per direct labor hour. The new machine will allow savings of $2 per unit on material costs, but will increase variable overhead costs by $1 per labor hour. Fixed costs will be unchanged except for depreciation.

Sales forecasts indicate that the annual sales volume can be increased by 20 percent if the sales price is reduced to $36 per unit. Alternatively, retaining the sales price at $40 per unit would still allow the annual sales volume to increase by 5 percent. The company observes a policy of ensuring that every employee works at least 40 hours per week, but the total number of employees can be adjusted as needed. The company is subject to a 40 percent tax rate and observes a 15 percent after-tax cost of capital rate on projects of this nature.

Required:
(a) Identify at least *three* alternatives available to the company.
(b) Prepare schedules to show the effects of each alternative on after-tax cash flows.
(c) Use net present value analysis to evaluate the alternatives. Which would you choose and why?
(d) What other factors might affect the decision in this situation?

18

SPECIAL PROBLEMS IN CAPITAL BUDGETING

LEARNING OBJECTIVES

After studying Chapter 18, you should be able to:

1. Adjust project investment outlays for the tax effects of sales and trade-ins of old equipment.
2. Calculate the effects of alternative depreciation methods on after-tax cash flows.
3. Rank competing projects consistently using a variety of capital budgeting methods.
4. Select the best combination of projects when investment funds are rationed.
5. Make the necessary calculations to compare capital investment projects that have unequal project lives.
6. Make the necessary calculations to compare capital investment projects that have unequal investment outlays.
7. Evaluate alternative sources of project financing.
8. Decide whether to continue to operate a project or close it down and dispose of its assets.
9. Decide whether to keep an existing bond issue outstanding or refinance it with a new issue of bonds.
10. Prepare a three-level forecast of capital investment projects and develop net income and cash flow forecasts at high, most likely, and low levels for competing projects.
11. Add a subjective probability distribution to these outcomes and derive the expected value of net income and cash flows for each competing project.
12. Prepare a cash flow forecast that treats the cost of capital as a variable rather than a constant factor over the life of the project.
13. Use sensitivity analysis to vary capital budgeting parameters in order to refine evaluations of competing projects.

Several extensions of the basic capital budgeting analysis presented in Chapter 17 will now be considered. These are

1. Income tax aspects of capital budgeting analysis.
2. Ranking competing projects.
3. Evaluating projects with unequal lives.
4. Evaluating projects with unequal investment outlays.
5. Evaluating alternative sources of project funding.
6. Evaluating disinvestment and refinancing proposals.
7. Capital budgeting under uncertainty.

INCOME TAX ASPECTS OF CAPITAL BUDGETING ANALYSIS

TAXES AND INVESTMENT OUTLAYS

In capital budgeting analysis, the calculation of investment outlays and operating cash flows must take account of income tax effects. When existing assets are sold for cash in the course of developing a new project, their disposal usually involves a taxable gain or loss. The tax effects of such gains or losses must be treated as increases or decreases in the project's investment outlay. When existing assets are traded in, the depreciation basis for tax purposes of the newly acquired assets is nearly always affected by the trade-in; the tax effects will result from incremental depreciation charges on the new assets. Investment credit provisions in the tax code can also change a project's investment outlay. The timing of all these tax effects is important, because there is often a time lag between the start of a project and the incidence of tax-related cash flows.

Example: Sottomayor Corporation is considering replacing an old machine that has an undepreciated value of $90,000. It can be traded in for $60,000 on a new machine of a similar type which has a list price of $320,000, or it can be sold for $10,000 cash, with the resulting loss deducted as a capital loss for tax purposes at a 25 percent rate. The new equipment is eligible for an investment tax credit equal to 10 percent of the purchase price. The acquisition will occur on January 1, 19X2. To simplify calculations, it is assumed that the tax effects will influence cash flows on January 1, 19X3. The cost of capital is considered to be 10 percent.

If the old machine is *traded in,* the **effective investment outlay** is calculated as shown in Figure 18–1.

FIGURE 18–1

Sottomayor Corporation
Investment Outlay Adjusted for Trade-In of Old Machine

List Price of New Machine	$320,000
Less: Trade-In Allowance on Old Machine	60,000
Cash Paid for New Machine	$260,000
Less: Investment Tax Credit	
($320,000 × 10% × .909)*	29,088
Effective Investment Outlay, January 1, 19X2	$230,912

* Discounted for one year at 10 percent.

If the old machine is *sold for cash,* the effective investment outlay is calculated as shown in Figure 18–2. In both cases, the disposal of the old machine reduces the effective investment outlay needed to acquire the new machine. However, the offsetting effect of a $60,000 trade-in allowance is more beneficial to Sottomayor Corporation than is the $10,000 received from a cash sale of the old machine.

Note also that the depreciation basis of the new machine will be different depending on the method of disposing of the old machine. If the old machine is sold for cash, the depreciation basis will be $320,000—the total purchase price. If the old machine is traded in on a new similar machine, the new machine's depreciation basis for tax purposes will be $350,000—the $260,000 cash paid plus the $90,000 book value of the old machine.

FIGURE 18–2

Sottomayor Corporation
Investment Outlay Adjusted for Cash Sale of Old Machine

List Price of New Machine	$320,000
Less: Sales Proceeds from Old Machine	10,000
	$310,000
Less: Investment Tax Credit	
($320,000 × 10% × .909)	29,088
	$280,912
Less: Tax Reduction for Capital Loss	
(25% × [$90,000 − $10,000] × .909)	18,180
Effective Investment Outlay, January 1, 19X2	$262,732

TAXES AND OPERATING CASH FLOWS

The depreciation methods used for tax purposes can affect capital budgeting decisions. The choice of a depreciation method influences periodic depreciation expense, which, in turn, changes net income, income tax expense, and cash flows. This can be demonstrated by comparing the results of using *straight-line* and *sum-of-the-years'-digits* depreciation.

Example: Glueck Corporation is investigating a manufacturing process that requires the purchase of new equipment costing $160,000 and that promises pre-tax operating cash inflows of $50,000 each year for the next five years. The equipment will have a $10,000 resale value at the end of that time. The cost of capital is 12 percent. Depreciation expense under the straight-line and the sum-of-the-years'-digits methods is shown in Figure 18–3.

These depreciation figures can be combined with the company's $50,000 per year pre-tax cash inflow to produce the after-tax cash flows shown in Figure 18–4, which assumes that the firm is subject to a 40 percent income tax rate.

Although total after-tax cash flows are $210,000 under both depreciation methods, the *discounted values* of those cash flows differ, due to variations in the annual amounts of straight-line and sum-of-the-years'-digits depreciation over the five-year period. This is shown in Figure 18–5.

When the sum-of-the-years'-digits method is used, after-tax cash flows are higher during the early years of the project's life, because of the lower tax expense resulting from the accelerated depreciation charges during those years. In addition, the present value of future cash inflows decreases as the period over which they are to be discounted increases. Consequently, the sum-of-the-years'-digits method, which produces larger cash inflows than the straight-line method during the project's early years, will result in a higher present value of operating cash inflows over the project's life.

FIGURE 18–3

Glueck Corporation
Depreciation Expense During Five-Year Project Life

Year	Straight-Line		Sum-of-the-Years'-Digits	
1	$\left(\frac{1}{5}\right)$	$ 30,000	$\left(\frac{5}{15}\right)$	$ 50,000
2	$\left(\frac{1}{5}\right)$	30,000	$\left(\frac{4}{15}\right)$	40,000
3	$\left(\frac{1}{5}\right)$	30,000	$\left(\frac{3}{15}\right)$	30,000
4	$\left(\frac{1}{5}\right)$	30,000	$\left(\frac{2}{15}\right)$	20,000
5	$\left(\frac{1}{5}\right)$	30,000	$\left(\frac{1}{15}\right)$	10,000
		$150,000		$150,000

FIGURE 18–4

Glueck Corporation
After-tax Operating Cash Flow

Year	(A) Pre-tax Cash Flow	(B) Depreciation Expense	(C) Taxable Income	(D) Tax Expense	(E) After-tax Net Income	(F) = (A − D) After-tax Cash Flow
Straight-Line Depreciation:						
1	$ 50,000	$ 30,000	$ 20,000	$ 8,000	$12,000	$ 42,000
2	50,000	30,000	20,000	8,000	12,000	42,000
3	50,000	30,000	20,000	8,000	12,000	42,000
4	50,000	30,000	20,000	8,000	12,000	42,000
5	50,000	30,000	20,000	8,000	12,000	42,000
	$250,000	$150,000	$100,000	$40,000	$60,000	$210,000
Sum-of-the-Years'-Digits Depreciation:						
1	$ 50,000	$ 50,000	$ 0	$ 0	$ 0	$ 50,000
2	50,000	40,000	10,000	4,000	6,000	46,000
3	50,000	30,000	20,000	8,000	12,000	42,000
4	50,000	20,000	30,000	12,000	18,000	38,000
5	50,000	10,000	40,000	16,000	24,000	34,000
	$250,000	$150,000	$100,000	$40,000	$60,000	$210,000

FIGURE 18–5

Glueck Corporation
Discounted After-tax Cash Flows

Year	Straight-Line Depreciation			Sum-of-the-Years'-Digits Depreciation		
	Cash Flows	12% Discount Factor	Discounted Amount	Cash Flows	12% Discount Factor	Discounted Amount
1	$ 42,000	.893	$ 37,506	$ 50,000	.893	$ 44,650
2	42,000	.797	33,474	46,000	.797	36,662
3	42,000	.712	29,904	42,000	.712	29,904
4	42,000	.636	26,712	38,000	.636	24,168
5	42,000	.567	23,814	34,000	.567	19,278
	$210,000		$151,410	$210,000		$154,662

Summary   Although the amount of depreciation expense does not directly affect cash flows, it has an important indirect effect resulting from the impact of depreciation charges on income tax payments. Specifically, after-tax cash flows are sensitive to the depreciation method used. When projects are evaluated using one of the discounting methods (net present value or internal rate of return), the result of that evaluation may be affected by the choice of depreciation

FIGURE 18–6

Glueck Corporation
Net Present Values
Under Two Depreciation Methods

	Straight-Line		Sum-of-the-Years'-Digits	
Investment Outlay		$160,000		$160,000
Discounted Operating Cash Flows (from Figure 18–3)	$151,410		$154,662	
New Equipment Resale Value in Year 5 ($10,000 × .567)	5,670	157,080	5,670	160,332
Net Present Value		($2,920)		$ 332

methods. Figure 18–6 indicates that Glueck Corporation's project would be acceptable ($332 positive net present value) if sum-of-the-years'-digits depreciation is taken, but would be rejected ($2,920 negative net present value) if straight-line depreciation is taken.

RANKING COMPETING PROJECTS

When funds are available to finance all acceptable projects, only accept–reject decisions are required. However, there are usually limits on the amount of funds available for investment in acceptable projects. Ranking procedures must be applied to projects that compete for the use of limited or rationed funds. The basis for ranking should be one or more of the capital budgeting methods demonstrated in Chapter 17.

Although discounting methods of capital budgeting analysis are preferable to nondiscounting methods, the latter can be useful as screening devices. Projects that fail to pass simple nondiscounting tests, such as having a payback period less than some predetermined length, can immediately be eliminated from further analysis under the more sophisticated discounting methods. Surveys of corporate investment policies have shown that this type of screening is quite common.[1]

Example: Fischer Company is evaluating seven alternative projects on the basis of payback period and net present value. Each of the projects has an eight-year project life. Management has specified a 15 percent cost of capital.

The company has two decision criteria: The project payback period must not exceed five years, and total net present value of accepted projects must be maximized. A total of $2,000,000 is available for investment.

---

[1] James M. Fremgen, "Capital Budgeting Practices: A Survey," *Management Accounting*, Vol. 54 (May, 1973), pp. 19–25.

FIGURE 18–7

**Fischer Company
Alternative Capital Investment Projects**

Project	Payback Period (years)	Net Present Value	Investment Outlay
A	4.5	$15,000	$600,000
B	3.7	30,000	500,000
C	6.2	18,000	300,000
D	4.8	29,000	800,000
E	4.2	42,000	700,000
F	5.7	16,000	400,000
G	3.9	12,000	500,000

As can be seen in Figure 18–7, Projects C and F can immediately be eliminated because they do not pay back their investment outlays within five years. The remaining projects are then ranked as shown in Figure 18–8.

The three most highly ranked projects—E, B, and D—exactly account for the $2,000,000 of available funds. However, because certain *combinations* of projects may be more desirable than the projects selected *individually* according to the ranking criteria, it is often useful to apply some form of sensitivity analysis to projects that fall just above or just below the cutoff point in terms of funds available. This should be done whether or not the supply of funds is exactly used up. This analysis can be performed by tabulating and then comparing all potentially feasible combinations of projects.

Example: Assume that Fischer Company now has $2,400,000 instead of $2,000,000 available for capital investments. On the basis of the original net present value rankings, only Projects E, B, and D are still feasible, because neither Project A nor Project G can be added within the $2,400,000 funds constraint. However, if various feasible groups of projects are examined, a

FIGURE 18–8

**Fischer Company
Ranking of Projects**

Rank	Project	Net Present Value	Project Investment Outlay	Cumulative Investment Outlays
1	E	$42,000	$700,000	$ 700,000
2	B	30,000	500,000	1,200,000
3	D	29,000	800,000	2,000,000
4	A	18,000	600,000	2,600,000
5	G	17,000	500,000	3,100,000

FIGURE 18–9

Fischer Company
Evaluating Combinations of Projects

Combination	Projects	Investment Outlay	Net Present Value
	E	$ 700,000	$ 42,000
1	B	500,000	30,000
	D	800,000	29,000
		$2,000,000	$101,000
	B	$ 500,000	$ 30,000
2	D	800,000	29,000
	A	600,000	18,000
	G	500,000	17,000
		$2,400,000	$ 94,000
	E	$ 700,000	$ 42,000
3	D	800,000	29,000
	A	600,000	18,000
		$2,100,000	$ 89,000
	E	$ 700,000	$ 42,000
4	B	500,000	30,000
	A	600,000	18,000
	G	500,000	17,000
		$2,300,000	$107,000

combination that yields a higher total net present value than Projects E, B, and D may be found. Figure 18–9 demonstrates this evaluation of feasible project combinations.

Combination 4, which includes Projects E, B, A, and G, generates the highest total net present value and still satisfies the funds constraint. Choosing this combination requires omitting Project D, which was *individually* preferable to either Projects A or G. The general conclusion is that, when funds are rationed, projects may need to be evaluated on a basis other than their primary rank ordering. Moreover, a preferable combination of projects can sometimes be found by substituting a lower-ranked project or projects for investment opportunities that have higher individual rankings.

EVALUATING PROJECTS WITH UNEQUAL LIVES

The methods of capital budgeting analysis described in Chapter 17 do not always give consistent rankings of projects with different durations.
Example: Scotten Company is evaluating two alternative investment proposals, Project M and Project N. Pertinent data for both projects are summarized in Figure 18–10.

FIGURE 18–10

Scotten Company
Comparing Projects with Unequal Lives

	Project M	Project N
Project Life	1 year	4 years
Investment Outlay	$30,000	$30,000
Operating Cash Flows:		
Year 1	$48,000	0
Year 2	0	0
Year 3	0	0
Year 4	0	$85,715
Accounting Rate of Return:		
$\dfrac{\text{Average Cash Flow}}{\text{Total Outlay}}$	$\dfrac{\$48,000}{\$30,000} = 160\%$	$\dfrac{\$21,429}{\$30,000} = 71.4\%$
Payback Period	7.5 months	4 years
Discounted Cash Flows:		
(10% Cost of Capital)	$43,636	$58,545
Net Present Value	$13,636	$28,545
Net Present Value Ratio	1.4545	1.9515
Internal Rate of Return	60%	30%

Figure 18–10 indicates that neither project is superior in all aspects. The accounting rate of return, payback period, and internal rate of return methods favor Project M. The net present value and net present value ratio indicators favor Project N. Unless the decision maker arbitrarily insists on using one method or the other, no clearcut decision is possible.

The essential difficulty is that Projects M and N are not strictly comparable— M has a project life of one year and N has a project life of four years. Instead of comparing Project M with Project N, the problem can be redefined to compare Project N with a hypothetical Project M*, which includes the one-year life of Project M plus the reinvested proceeds from Project M for the second, third, and fourth years. This requires specifying how these proceeds are to be reinvested over that three-year period and at what rate of return.

Arguments can be made in support of several alternative reinvestment rates. These include

1. The cost of capital used to evaluate Projects M and N.
2. Project M's internal rate of return.
3. Project N's internal rate of return.
4. Some other rate of return available during periods two, three, and four.

The fact that a particular *cost of capital* has already been specified for Projects M and N can be interpreted to mean that this rate is the opportunity cost of alternative investments. Therefore, it is logical to assume that proceeds reinvested from Project M will earn a return at least equal to this opportunity cost rate.

From another viewpoint, it can be argued that if Project M is available for a one-year period, equally profitable projects might be available later. Consequently, *Project M's internal rate of return* may be the appropriate reinvestment rate.

From an incremental opportunity cost viewpoint, it can be argued that *Project N's internal rate of return* should be the reinvestment rate, because it is the specific rate that is foregone in periods two, three, and four as a result of the investment in Project M.

Finally, a more general approach could consider that Projects M and N are unique events which depend on time and circumstance and therefore cannot be duplicated. Consequently, their internal rates of return are irrelevant to alternative investments. Instead, it might be contended that the correct reinvestment rate is the *opportunity cost of the best independent alternative project* available during periods two, three, and four.

The calculations for each of these approaches are presented in Figure 18–11. Alternatives O, P, and Q represent three alternative projects available during periods two, three, and four. Comparisons are made among the possible results of reinvesting the $48,000 proceeds from Project M in each of these projects for another three years. Project O involves reinvestment of the $48,000 at 10 percent—the cost of capital originally used to evaluate Projects M and N. Alternative projects P and Q promise internal rates of return of 21.4 percent and 40 percent respectively.

These comparisons indicate that Project N is preferable if the reinvestment rate is less than 21.4 percent. For example, funds reinvested in Project O at the 10 percent cost of capital rate will accumulate to only $63,888 (compared to $85,715 for Project N). A reinvestment rate of about 21.4 percent is the point of indifference, at which the accumulated proceeds of Project P, $85,881,

---

FIGURE 18–11

Scotten Company
Comparing Projects on the Assumption that Project M
Proceeds are Reinvested

Project N   Accumulated Proceeds at the End of Year 4 $85,715

Project M   Accumulated Proceeds at the End of Year 1 $48,000

Project M* $48,000 Proceeds of Project M Reinvested for Three Years at Five Different Rates of Return:

	Alternative O	Alternative P	Internal Rate of Return Project N	Alternative Q	Internal Rate of Return Project M
Reinvestment Rate ..	10%	21.4%	30%	40%	60%
Accumulated Proceeds at End of Year 4	$63,888	$85,881	$105,456	$131,712	$196,608

are close to the proceeds from Project N. When proceeds are reinvested at rates above 21.4 percent, Project M* is superior to Project N.

It is not possible to generalize about the likely outcomes of comparisons when project lives are equalized in this way. The amounts and distribution of operating cash flows, the cost of capital, the relative internal rate of return for each project, and the possible reinvestment rates are too complexly interrelated to allow any universally valid conclusions to be drawn. Each set of projects must be evaluated on the basis of particular reinvestment assumptions to determine which projects deserve to be funded.

EVALUATING PROJECTS WITH UNEQUAL INVESTMENT OUTLAYS

Problems also arise when projects with different investment outlays must compete for a limited supply of funds. It is not certain that such a group of projects will be ranked consistently by all the methods discussed in Chapter 17.

Example: Murphy Company, which has specified a 10 percent cost of capital and has only $60,000 available for investment, has prepared an evaluation of three projects, Q, R, and S, as shown in Figure 18–12.

Based on all the methods shown—except net present value—the projects would be ranked: (1) Q, (2) S, and (3) R. Under the net present value method, the rankings would be: (1) S, (2) Q, and (3) R. These rankings not only fail to agree, but fail to take account of the fact that Project Q's investment outlay is $20,000 less than the outlay required for Projects R and S.

One way to refine these rankings is to determine whether or not the incremental outlay of $20,000 required for Projects R and S is justified in terms of the additional benefits that outlay will produce. Specifically, the **incremental invest-**

FIGURE 18–12

Murphy Company
Comparing Projects with Unequal Investment Outlays

	Project Q	Project R	Project S
Project Life	3 years	3 years	3 years
Investment Outlay	$40,000	$60,000	$60,000
Operating Cash Flows:			
Year 1	$20,000	$27,500	$29,000
Year 2	$20,000	$27,500	$29,000
Year 3	$20,000	$27,500	$29,000
Payback Period	2 years	2.18 years	2.07 years
Discounted Cash Flows	$49,740	$68,393	$72,123
Net Present Value	$ 9,740	$ 8,393	$12,123
Net Present Value Ratio	1.244	1.114	1.202
Internal Rate of Return	23%	17.5%	21.5%

ment outlay involved in changing from Project Q to Project R or S must be considered in relation to the **incremental operating cash flows** that would result from the same changes. These incremental cash flows are $7,500 ($27,500 − $20,000) for Project R and $9,000 ($29,000 − $20,000) for Project S. Figure 18–13 shows the detailed results of this incremental analysis.

Figure 18–13 shows that Project S, which has a $20,000 incremental investment outlay relative to Project Q, is acceptable according to the following capital budgeting criteria:

> Net Present Value > 0
> Net Present Value Ratio > 1
> Internal Rate of Return > 10%

Project R, which also has a $20,000 incremental investment outlay relative to Project Q, is not acceptable on the basis of these same capital budgeting tests:

> Net Present Value < 0
> Net Present Value Ratio < 1
> Internal Rate of Return < 10%

Valid comparisons between the three projects can also be made by equalizing their investment outlays. In Figure 18–14, Projects R and S are compared to Project Q*, which includes Project Q plus an additional $20,000 invested at a rate equal to the cost of capital. Thus Project Q*'s third year operating cash flows of $46,620 include the original $20,000 plus the proceeds from investing $20,000 for three years at 10 percent.

Four capital budgeting tests indicate that the returns from Project S are superior to those from Project Q plus an additional $20,000 investment at the

---

FIGURE 18–13

Murphy Company
Effects of $20,000 Incremental Outlay on Projects R and S

	Project R	Project S
Project Life	3 years	3 years
Incremental Outlay	$20,000	$20,000
Incremental Operating Cash Flows:		
Year 1	$ 7,500	$ 9,000
Year 2	$ 7,500	$ 9,000
Year 3	$ 7,500	$ 9,000
Payback Period	2.67 years	2.22 years
Discounted Cash Flows	$18,653	$22,383
Net Present Value	($ 1,347)	$ 2,383
Net Present Value Ratio	0.933	1.119
Internal Rate of Return	6.25%	16.5%

FIGURE 18–14

Murphy Company
Comparing Three Projects with Equalized Investment Outlays

	Project Q*	Project R	Project S
Project Life	3 years	3 years	3 years
Investment Outlay	$60,000	$60,000	$60,000
Operating Cash Flows:			
Year 1	$20,000	$27,500	$29,000
Year 2	$20,000	$27,500	$29,000
Year 3	$46,620	$27,500	$29,000
Discounted Cash Flows	$69,740	$68,393	$72,123
Net Present Value	$ 9,740	$ 8,393	$12,123
Net Present Value Ratio	1.162	1.114	1.202
Internal Rate of Return	18%	17.5%	21.5%

---

10 percent cost of capital rate. The same bases of comparison show that Project R is inferior to Project Q*, because the incremental investment in Project R is less profitable than allowing the $20,000 to remain invested at the 10 percent cost of capital.

Equalizing the investment outlays permits a consistent ranking of the projects under all four capital budgeting methods: (1) S, (2) Q*, and (3) R.

If identifiable uses exist for the incremental investment outlays, these uses may be given the status of separate projects which can be grouped as needed to equalize total investment outlays. Assume that Murphy Company has two additional investment opportunities, Project T and Project U, which require outlays of $20,000 each and will provide cash flows of $29,791 and $34,560 respectively at the end of three years. Combining each of these projects with

---

FIGURE 18–15

Murphy Company
Comparing Project S with Two Combined Projects
with Equalized Investment Outlays

	Project QT	Project QU	Project S
Investment Outlay	$60,000	$60,000	$60,000
Operating Cash Flows:			
Year 1	$20,000	$20,000	$29,000
Year 2	$20,000	$20,000	$29,000
Year 3	$49,791	$54,560	$29,000
Discounted Cash Flows	$72,123	$75,705	$72,123
Net Present Value	$12,123	$15,705	$12,123
Net Present Value Ratio	1.202	1.262	1.202
Internal Rate of Return	21.5%	22.75%	21.5%

Project Q to form Project QT and Project QU permits comparisons to be made on the basis of equalized investment outlays, as shown in Figure 18–15.

This comparison indicates that Project QU is superior to Project QT and Project S. On the other hand, Project QT and Project S are equally desirable investment opportunities, because all their indicators are equal.

As was noted in analyzing projects with unequal lives, no firm generalizations can be made about projects with unequal investment outlays. To be correctly ranked, each group of competing projects must be analyzed individually, using the techniques previously demonstrated.

EVALUATING ALTERNATIVE SOURCES OF PROJECT FINANCING

All previous examples have assumed that sufficient funds were available to finance approved projects. However, the *sources* of those funds were not specified. Another aspect of capital budgeting analysis involves choosing among alternative sources of financing for acceptable projects. For example, a project's investment outlay might be secured from currently available cash balances, from a bank loan, from the proceeds of stock or bond issues, or from the lease rather than purchase of the project's assets.

The *net present value method* provides an appropriate basis for evaluating alternative financing arrangements. The most desirable method of financing is the one that maximizes a project's net present value.

Example: Gryczk Corporation proposes to install vending machines in its plant cafeteria. It can purchase the machines outright for $100,000 or lease them for five years at $25,000 per year. If purchased, the machines will have a cash resale value of $10,000 at the end of five years. Projected cash revenues from the machines, after operating costs have been deducted, are $40,000 per year. The company depreciates machinery on a straight-line basis and is subject to a 40 percent income tax rate. Company management considers that 10 percent is the appropriate cost of capital rate for this type of project.

FIGURE 18–16

Gryczk Corporation
Schedule of Annual After-tax Operating Cash Inflows

		Self-Financed	Bond Issue	Lease
	Net Revenue	$40,000	$40,000	$40,000
	Less: Interest Cost	—	10,000	—
	Rental Cost	—	—	25,000
(A)	Cash Inflow before Depreciation and Tax ...	$40,000	$30,000	$15,000
	Less: Depreciation	18,000	18,000	—
	Taxable Income	$22,000	$12,000	$15,000
(B)	Income Tax Expense (40%)	$ 8,800	$ 4,800	$ 6,000
(A − B)	After-tax Operating Cash Inflow	$31,200	$25,200	$ 9,000

FIGURE 18–17

Gryczk Corporation
Net Present Value Analysis

	Amount	Years	Discount Factor	Present Value
Self-Financed:				
Investment Outlay	($100,000)	–0–	1.000	($100,000)
Operating Cash Inflows	31,200	1–5	3.791	118,279
Resale Value at End				
of Year 5	10,000	5	.621	6,210
Net Present Value				$ 24,489
10% Bond Issue:				
Investment Outlay	($100,000)	–0–	1.000	($100,000)
Bond Issue Proceeds	100,000	–0–	1.000	100,000
Operating Cash Inflows	25,200	1–5	3.791	95,533
Repay Bonds at Maturity	(100,000)	5	.621	(62,100)
Resale Value at End				
of Year 5	10,000	5	.621	6,210
Net Present Value				$ 39,643
Lease:				
Operating Cash Inflows	$9,000	1–5	3.791	$ 34,119
Net Present Value				$ 34,119

Gryczk Corporation can acquire these machines by:

1. Buying them with its own money.
2. Issuing $100,000 of 10 percent five-year bonds at par to finance the purchase.
3. Leasing them for five years at $25,000 per year with payments due at the end of each year.

Figure 18–16 shows the projected annual after-tax cash inflows from each of these alternatives.

Figure 18–17 shows the derivation of the net present value of each alternative's after-tax cash inflows over the five-year project life.

These three financing alternatives are ranked as follows on the basis of maximizing net present value:

		Net Present Value
1.	Bond Issue	$39,643
2.	Lease	34,119
3.	Self-Financing	24,489

Of course, this ranking will be different if changes occur in interest rates, payment terms, or rental amounts. Similarly, other projects with different compositions of these key variables will also have a different ordering of results. The only general observation that can be made is that those financing alternatives with the lowest interest costs and the longest deferment of payments will tend to be the most attractive. Note that in this case the self-financing alternative is the least acceptable, provided that borrowed money is available at a rate less than the cost of capital.

EVALUATING DISINVESTMENT AND REFINANCING PROPOSALS

Capital budgeting analysis can also be applied to the following types of decision situations:

1. *Disinvestment in a project*—for example, the discontinuation of a production division, product line, or sales outlet.
2. *Refinancing of a project*—for example, the redemption of a bond issue and the sale of new bonds.

The net present value method is most appropriate to analyze these types of problems.

PROJECT DISINVESTMENT

Example: Livnat Corporation is considering what to do with its Joshua Division, which has performed less profitably than expected. Joshua Division's average annual income for the last three years is shown in Figure 18–18.

Livnat Corporation is considering two alternatives to continuing Joshua Division's operations. The first involves complete closure of Joshua Division and the sale of all its facilities for $3,000,000 cash. These plant assets have a current book value of $1,800,000 and are being depreciated on a straight-

---

FIGURE 18–18

Joshua Division
Income Statement
Averages for the Three Years Ended December 31, 19X2

Sales	$2,000,000
Costs (including depreciation of $360,000)	1,050,000
Income before Taxes	$ 50,000
Income Taxes @ 40%	20,000
Net Income after Taxes	$ 30,000

line basis. They have five years of expected useful life remaining, after which they will be worthless and the division will have to be closed or completely reequipped.

The second alternative is to sell half of Joshua Division's assets for $600,000 cash and to transfer the other half to Livnat Corporation's Sasoon Division. In Sasoon Division, these transferred assets will be used to generate increased annual sales revenue of $1,400,000, with a contribution margin ratio of 60 percent. Continuing fixed costs of operating the plant assets, excluding depreciation, will be $160,000 per year.

Livnat Corporation is subject to a 40 percent income tax on operating income and a 25 percent capital gains tax on gains from the sale of plant assets. A 15 percent cost of capital rate has been used by management in evaluating the feasibility of projects similar to Joshua Division's operations.

Net present value analysis will be used to evaluate Livnat Corporation's three alternatives:

1. Continue to operate Joshua Division.
2. Close Joshua Division and sell all its assets.
3. Close Joshua Division, sell half its assets, and transfer the rest to Sasoon Division.

Figure 18–19 shows the projected annual after-tax cash inflows from continued use of Joshua Division's assets. Figure 18–20 shows the derivation of the net present value of each alternative's after-tax cash inflows over the five-year remaining life of Joshua Division's plant assets.

Figure 18–20 indicates that the best choice would be to liquidate Joshua Division and sell all its assets, because that alternative has the highest net present value. Note that this analysis considers only *future* cash flows and

---

FIGURE 18–19

Joshua Division
Schedule of Annual After-tax Operating Cash Inflows

		Continue Joshua Division Operations	Transfer Partial Facilities to Sasoon Division
	Net Sales Revenue	$2,000,000	$1,400,000
	Less: Expenses Paid in Cash	1,590,000	720,000
(A)	Cash Inflow before Depreciation and Taxes	$ 410,000	$ 680,000
	Less: Depreciation	360,000	180,000
	Taxable Income	$ 50,000	$ 500,000
(B)	Less: Income Tax Expense (40%)	20,000	200,000
	Net Income after Taxes	$ 30,000	$ 300,000
(A − B)	After-tax Operating Cash Inflow	$ 390,000	$ 480,000

FIGURE 18–20

Joshua Division
Net Present Value Analysis

Item	Amount	Years	Discount Factor	Present Value
Continue to Operate Joshua Division:				
Operating Cash Inflows..................	$390,000	1–5	3.352	$1,307,280
Net Present Value				$1,307,280
Close Joshua Division and Sell its Assets:				
Sale Proceeds	$3,000,000			
Less: Capital Gain Taxes on Sale				
[($3,000,000 − $1,800,000) × 25% ..	300,000			
After-tax Sale Proceeds	$2,700,000	–0–	1.000	$2,700,000
Net Present Value				$2,700,000
Partial Sale and Transfer Assets to Sasoon Division:				
Sale Proceeds	$ 600,000			
Add: Tax Savings from Loss on Sale				
[($900,000 − $600,000) × 25%]	75,000			
After-tax Sale Proceeds	$ 675,000	–0–	1.000	$ 675,000
Operating Cash Inflows..................	480,000	1–5	3.352	1,608,960
Net Present Value				$2,283,960

ignores outlays already made and cash inflows already received. The point of reference is the present time; past transactions have no direct bearing on this disinvestment decision.

DEBT REFINANCING

The net present value method can also be used to decide whether to allow existing debt to remain outstanding or to refinance it with new borrowings.

Example: Fernandes Company presently has outstanding a $5,000,000 issue of 12 percent bonds that were sold five years ago at par. The bonds mature in ten years and are presently quoted at 72. Due to increases in bond interest rates, it would be necessary to issue replacement bonds at a 16 percent rate at par. The company is subject to a 40 percent income tax rate. This tax rate also applies to gains or losses on bond redemptions. A 10 percent after-tax cost of capital rate is deemed relevant to projects financed from the proceeds of the original bond issue.

Figure 18–21 shows the net present value of after-tax cash outflows that will result if the company continues to keep the original bond issue outstanding or retires it and issues new bonds.

FIGURE 18–21

Fernandes Corporation
Net Present Value Analysis of Refinancing Proposal

	Amount	Years	Discount Factor	Present Value
Keep Original Bond Issue Outstanding:				
Interest Payments	$ 600,000			
Less: Income Tax Expense (40%)	240,000			
After-tax Interest Cost	$ 360,000	1–10	6.145	$2,212,200
Maturity Value of Bonds	$5,000,000	10	.386	1,930,000
Net Present Value of Cash Outflows				$4,142,200
Retire Original Bonds and Issue New Ones:				
Bond Redemption Cost				
($5,000,000 × 72)	$3,600,000			
Add: Taxes on Redemption Gain				
[($5,000,000 − $3,600,000)				
× 40%]	560,000			
After-tax Redemption Cost	$4,160,000	–0–	1.000	$4,160,000
Proceeds of New Bond Issue	($5,000,000)	–0–	1.000	(5,000,000)
Interest Payments on New Bond Issue ..	$ 800,000			
Less: Income Tax Expense (40%)	320,000			
After-tax Interest Cost	$ 480,000	1–10	6.145	2,949,600
Maturity Value of Bonds	$5,000,000	10	.386	1,930,000
Net Present Value of Cash Outflows				$4,039,600

This analysis indicates that the refinancing alternative is preferable because it has the lower net present value of expected cash outflows.

CAPITAL BUDGETING UNDER UNCERTAINTY

The relatively long time horizon involved in capital investment projects suggests that they are likely to involve considerable uncertainty. The projections of periodic cash flows, residual values of project assets, and cost of capital are all prone to variability, as are the capital budgeting indicators derived from them—accounting return on investment, payback period, net present value, and internal rate of return. Techniques similar to those previously demonstrated for dealing with uncertainty in budgeting and cost–volume–profit analysis can be applied to capital budgeting problems.

The **"three-level" approach,** without quantification of probabilities, can be used to introduce a **range concept** into the results of capital budgeting analysis. By developing *optimistic, most likely,* and *pessimistic* forecasts of operating cash flows, accountants can obtain three separate results for each of the capital budgeting indicators.

Example: Freeman Company has prepared forecasts of sales and costs for two similar proposed products, as shown in Figure 18–22. Each product has a projected life of five years and will require a $200,000 investment outlay for fixed assets. The company uses straight-line depreciation. The fixed assets involved will have no resale value at the end of their lives. Freeman Company is subject to a 40 percent income tax rate and applies an 8 percent cost of capital rate to projects of this type.

Based on these forecast data, income and cash flow projections can be developed for high, most likely, and low levels of projected sales volume, as shown in Figure 18–23.

In Figure 18–24, these results are compared under four capital budgeting methods: payback period, accounting rate of return, net present value, and internal rate of return.

Although Products A and B have identical "most likely" results, the range of possible outcomes shows Product A to be less risky because its high and low indicators are less widely dispersed. In addition, under the pessimistic sales forecast there is a possibility that Product B will incur a loss, whereas a breakeven situation is the worst outcome projected for Product A. On the other hand, the optimistic sales forecast favors Product B over Product A on all four capital budgeting indicators.

A subjective probability distribution can be combined with these outcomes to add an *expected value* solution to the preceding analysis:

| | Subjective Probability | |
Forecast	Product A	Product B
High	.2	.3
Most Likely	.5	.6
Low	.3	.1

The expected values of net income and operating cash flows for each product can now be calculated, as shown in Figure 18–25 (page 924).

FIGURE 18–22

Freeman Company
Sales and Costs Forecasts

	Product A	Product B
Sales Price per Unit	$20	$50
Variable Cost per Unit	$10	$30
Annual Fixed Costs (excluding		
depreciation)	$60,000	$60,000
Sales Forecast in Units:		
Optimistic	15,000	10,000
Most Likely	12,000	16,000
Pessimistic	10,000	4,000

FIGURE 18–23

Freeman Company
Income and Cash Flow Projections

		Product A			Product B		
		High	Most Likely	Low	High	Most Likely	Low
	Sales Revenues	$300,000	$240,000	$200,000	$500,000	$300,000	$200,000
	Less: Variable Costs	$150,000	$120,000	$100,000	$300,000	$180,000	$120,000
	Fixed Costs (excluding depreciation) ...	60,000	60,000	60,000	60,000	60,000	60,000
		$210,000	$180,000	$160,000	$360,000	$240,000	$180,000
(A)	Before-tax Operating Cash Flows	$ 90,000	$ 60,000	$ 40,000	$140,000	$ 60,000	$ 20,000
	Less: Depreciation	40,000	40,000	40,000	40,000	40,000	40,000
	Taxable Income	$ 50,000	$ 20,000	–0–	$100,000	$ 20,000	($20,000)
(B)	Less: Tax Expense	20,000	8,000	–0–	40,000	8,000	(8,000)
	Net Income	$ 30,000	$ 12,000	–0–	$ 60,000	$ 12,000	($12,000)
(A–B)	After-tax Operating Cash Flows	$ 70,000	$ 52,000	$ 40,000	$ 80,000	$ 52,000	$ 28,000*

*Tax effect is a saving of $8,000. Therefore, the after-tax cash flow is $20,000 + $8,000 = $28,000.

FIGURE 18–24

Freeman Company
Capital Budgeting Assessment of Income and Cash Flow Projections

	Product A			Product B		
	High	Most Likely	Low	High	Most Likely	Low
Payback Period	$200,000 / $70,000	$200,000 / $52,000	$200,000 / $40,000	$200,000 / $80,000	$200,000 / $52,000	$200,000 / $28,000
	= 2.86 yrs.	= 3.85 yrs.	= 5 yrs.	= 2.5 yrs.	= 3.85 yrs.	= 7.14 yrs.
Accounting Rate of Return (total outlay basis)	$30,000 / $200,000	$12,000 / $200,000	–0– / $200,000	$60,000 / $200,000	$12,000 / $200,000	($12,000) / $200,000
	= 15%	= 6%	= 0%	= 30%	= 6%	N/A
Net Present Value						
Present Value of Cash Inflows......	$279,510	$207,636	$159,720	$319,440	$207,636	$111,804
Present Value of Cash Outflows	200,000	200,000	200,000	200,000	200,000	200,000
Net Present Value ...	$ 79,510	$ 7,636	($ 40,280)	$119,440	$ 7,636	($ 88,196)
Internal Rate of Return (approximate)	22%	9.5%	0%	29%	9.5%	N/A

FIGURE 18-25

Freeman Company
Expected Values of Net Income

Product A			Product B		
Net Income	Probability	Expected Value	Net Income	Probability	Expected Value
$30,000	.25	$7,500	$60,000	.30	$18,000
12,000	.50	6,000	12,000	.60	7,200
–0–	.25	–0–	(12,000)	.10	(1,200)
		$13,500			$24,000

Expected Values of Operating Cash Inflows

Product A			Product B		
Cash Inflow	Probability	Expected Value	Cash Inflow	Probability	Expected Value
$70,000	.25	$17,500	$80,000	.30	$24,000
52,000	.50	26,000	52,000	.60	31,200
40,000	.25	10,000	28,000	.10	2,800
		$53,500			$58,000

The final step is to apply capital budgeting analysis to these expected values of net income and operating cash inflows, as shown in Figure 18–26.

Earlier comments on decision criteria under uncertainty apply here. The *risk neutral decision maker* who relies solely on expected value criteria will prefer Product B, which produces superior results under all four capital budgeting methods. The cautious, *risk averse decision maker* might choose Project A because of the less desirable income and operating cash flows possible at the "low" end of the Project B forecast. A *risk seeker* might be attracted to Project B because of the possibility of very favorable income and operating cash flows at the "high" end of the forecast.

VARIABILITY OF COST OF CAPITAL

Specifying a cost of capital is critical in both the net present value and internal rate of return methods of capital budgeting analysis. Although the elementary discussion in Chapter 17 assumed that cost of capital was constant over the life of a project, it may reasonably be treated as a variable. This treatment can be justified in several ways:

1. The acceptable rate of return on assets of similar risk classes may tend to vary over time, as the productivity of resources changes. It is natural for managers to hope that overall operating productivity will increase from year to year.

FIGURE 18–26

Freeman Company
Capital Budgeting Analysis
Based on the Expected Values
of Products A and B
Net Income and Operating Cash Inflows

	Product A	Product B
Payback Period	$\dfrac{\$200,000}{\$53,500}$	$\dfrac{\$200,000}{\$58,000}$
	= 3.77 years	= 3.45 years
Accounting Rate of Return	$\dfrac{\$13,500}{\$200,000}$	$\dfrac{\$24,000}{\$200,000}$
	= 6.75%	= 12%
Net Present Value		
Present Value of Cash Inflows		
A ($53,000 × 3.993)	$213,626	
B ($58,000 × 3.993)		$231,594
Present Value of Cash Outflows	200,000	200,000
Net Present Value	$ 13,626	$ 31,594
Internal Rate of Return		
(approximate)	10.5%	13.75%

2. An increasing cost of capital per period allows future cash flows to be more conservatively evaluated, because there is less certainty about cash flows forecast to occur in more distant time periods.

3. If inflation is expected to continue, increases in the cost of capital rate from period to period compensate for the decreasing real value of cash flows that will be received in future periods.

A variable cost of capital increases the computational difficulty of capital budgeting analysis, but not to any insurmountable extent, given the availability of electronic computers. The more important issue is whether or not realistic cost of capital measures can be estimated over a project's life.

Example: As shown in Figure 18–27, Kwon Company anticipates four-year cash inflows from a project that will require an investment outlay of $200,000. The company estimates that cost of capital will increase each year during the project life because of a projected 2 percent annual increase in the profitability of projects in this risk class and an estimated 5 percent annual compound rate of inflation.

Figure 18–28 shows the effect on net present value of using these graduated cost of capital rates, compared to using a constant 20 percent rate.

FIGURE 18–27

Kwon Company
Variable Cost of Capital Forecast

Year	Cash Inflows*	Cost of Capital
1	$100,000	20% = 20%
2	120,000	[20% + 2%] × 1.05 = 23.1%
3	150,000	[20% + 4%] × 1.05^2 = 26.46%
4	150,000	[20% + 6%] × 1.05^3 = 30.1%

* In dollars of future years.

FIGURE 18–28

Kwon Company
Variable Versus Constant Cost of Capital Rates

Year	Cash Inflow	Present Value at 20%		Present Value at Graduated Rates	
1	$100,000	(.833)	$ 83,333	(.833)	$ 83,333
2	120,000	(.694)	83,280	(.660)	79,200
3	150,000	(.579)	86,850	(.495)	74,250
4	150,000	(.482)	72,300	(.349)	52,350
			$325,763		$289,133

Failure to adjust the cost of capital rate for anticipated inflation and productivity increases will overstate the present value of cash inflows by $36,630 ($325,763 − $289,133). In this case, the $300,000 investment outlay required for the project lies between the two present values of cash inflows. The project would be accepted if a constant cost of capital were used. It would be rejected on a variable cost of capital basis.

SENSITIVITY ANALYSIS IN CAPITAL BUDGETING

Sensitivity analysis techniques can also be used to evaluate the responsiveness of capital budgeting methods to changes in parameter values. By holding all values constant except one, tolerance limits for each variable can be estimated. For example:

1. By varying its *operating cash flow* forecasts, management can determine the minimum average cash flow per period needed to satisfy various capital budgeting indicators.

2. By varying the *discount rate,* management can determine the minimum or maximum possible cost of capital that satisfies net present value criteria.

3. By varying *sales prices, variable costs, sales volumes,* and *fixed costs,* individually or together, management can determine their effect on operating cash flows and, in turn, on various capital budgeting indicators.

Example: Penman Corporation is considering an investment proposal that requires an investment outlay of $20,000 and is expected to generate cash inflows of $8,000 each year for four years. Management seeks answers to the following questions:

1. To what average amount can the annual operating cash flow decline and still allow the investment to be acceptable on the basis of the following separate decision criteria?

a. *Payback Period:* 3 years
b. *Accounting Rate of Return:* 12½%
c. *Net Present Value:* 14% Cost of Capital

a. For a Payback Period of 3 years:

$$\frac{\text{Investment Outlay}}{\text{Average Cash Flow}} = 3$$

$$\frac{\$20,000}{\text{Cash Flow}} = 3$$

$$\text{Cash Flow} = \frac{\$20,000}{3}$$

$$\text{Minimum Acceptable Annual Cash Flow} = \$6,666.67$$

b. For a 12½% Accounting Rate of Return:

$$\frac{\text{Average Net Income}}{\text{Investment Outlay}} = 12\tfrac{1}{2}\%$$

$$\frac{y}{\$20,000} = .125$$

$$y = \$2,500$$
$$\text{Cash Flow} - \text{Depreciation} = \text{Net Income}$$
$$\text{Cash Flow} - \$5,000 = \$2,500$$
$$\text{Minimum Acceptable Annual Cash Flow} = \$7,500$$

c. For Net Present Value ≥ 0:

Discounted Cash Flows ≥ Investment Outlay
Cash Flows × Discount Factor ≥ $20,000
Discount Factor for 4-year annuity at 14% = 2.9137
Cash Flow × 2.9137 ≥ $20,000
Cash Flow ≥ $6,864.12

Therefore, $6,864.12 is the minimum acceptable annual cash inflow that will satisfy a 14 percent cost of capital requirement.

2.   What is the maximum cost of capital rate that this project will satisfy in relation to the net present value criteria?

> For Net Present Value ≥ 0,
> Present Value of Cash Inflows ≥ Investment Outlay
> $8,000 × Discount Factor ≥ $20,000
> Discount Factor ≥ 2.5

Therefore, for a four-period annuity, a discount factor of 2.5 corresponds to a 21.86 percent cost of capital rate.

SUMMARY

1.   Complete cash flow analysis of projects requires accounting for the tax effects of asset acquisitions (investment tax credits), asset dispositions (taxes on capital gains and losses), and operating performance (taxes on operating income).

2.   The effects of alternative depreciation methods on cash flows must be considered. Capital investment projects may even receive different evaluations and/or rankings depending on which depreciation methods are adopted.

3.   Capital often must be rationed; this requires the use of ranking procedures to select the most desirable projects. Although discounting methods of capital budgeting analysis are recommended for ranking purposes, they may be supplemented by tests that use such nondiscounting methods as payback and return on investment as screening devices.

4.   Because capital budgeting projects are indivisible, it is advisable to reevaluate all feasible combinations of projects that fall close to the cutoff point of available funds. Combinations of projects other than the group selected by the original ranking sequence may prove to be the most desirable.

5.   Competing projects with unequal lives should be made comparable. This can be done by making appropriate assumptions about the reinvestment of funds generated by the shorter-lived project. Use of a reinvestment rate equal to the cost of capital is recommended, but if other identifiable projects are available during the reinvestment period, their rates of return may be used.

6.   Competing projects with unequal investment outlays should be made comparable. This can be done by adding to the less costly project the incremental returns from an amount equal to the difference between the investment outlays of the two projects. Such incremental returns should be calculated at a rate equal to the cost of capital or the rate available on an alternative project requiring the same investment outlay.

7.   There are usually various ways of financing investment outlays—self-financing, bank borrowing, issuing stock or bonds, or leasing the assets instead of buying them. The most desirable financing method is the one that maximizes the project's net present value.

8. Managers often must decide whether to continue operating a project or discontinue it and dispose of its assets. This decision can best be made by comparing the net present values of the future cash inflows from the various alternatives.

9. The net present value method can also be used to decide whether to keep a bond issue outstanding or to refinance it with a new issue of bonds. The preferable financing alternative is the one that minimizes the present value of expected cash outflows.

10. Because capital budgeting projects typically extend over several accounting periods, they are likely to involve a greater amount of uncertainty than is found in single period budgetary analysis. There are several ways to incorporate this uncertainty into the decision model. By developing high, most likely, and low estimates of key planning variables, the results of capital budgeting analysis can be presented in range-type formats. By introducing probability distributions over those key variables, the results can be extended to include expected value, maximax, maximin, and most likely outcomes.

11. The cost of capital measure can be augmented, either over a portion or the whole of the project life, by an amount that reflects the increasing uncertainty of future cash flows. As the cost of capital is increased, the resulting present values of future amounts are reduced, thereby contributing to a more rigorous set of capital budgeting criteria.

12. Sensitivity analysis can be used to vary the values of key capital budgeting parameters. The responsiveness of the results of capital budgeting analysis to such changes can be used as a supplement to the basic evaluation and ranking procedures.

KEY WORDS AND PHRASES

Effective Investment Outlay (903)
Ranking Competing Projects (907)
Unequal Project Lives (909)
Unequal Investment Outlays (912)
Incremental Investment Outlay (912)
Incremental Cash Flow (913)
Project Disinvestment (917)
Project Refinancing (917)
Three-Level Approach to Uncertainty (920)
Range Concept (920)
Variable Cost of Capital (924)
Sensitivity Analysis (926)

Questions

1. What likely tax-related aspects resulting from the initiation and acquisition of a project will affect the amount of the investment outlay for purposes of capital budgeting analysis?

2. How can the choice of depreciation methods affect the outcome of capital budgeting analysis?

3. Is there one *best* method of accounting for depreciation in the evaluation of alternative investment projects? Discuss fully.

4. What basic problems are encountered when there are more acceptable investment projects than there are available funds?

5. What alternative criteria can be used in ranking competing investment projects? What problems, conflicts, and contradictions may be encountered in applying some of those criteria?

6. Explain how the technique of incremental analysis may be helpful in solving problems that involve the ranking of alternative investment projects.

7. What basic problem is involved when projects with unequal lives are compared using capital budgeting methods of analysis?

8. Evaluate some of the alternative approaches suggested for dealing with the problem cited in Question 7.

9. What basic problem is involved when projects with unequal investment outlays are compared using capital budgeting methods of analysis?

10. Evaluate the alternative approaches suggested for dealing with the problem cited in Question 9.

11. Explain how alternative sources of financing can be evaluated using capital budgeting methods of analysis.

12. Outline the aspects of a disinvestment decision that should be included in a capital budgeting analysis of such a situation.

13. Outline the aspects of a refinancing decision that should be included in a capital budgeting analysis of such a situation.

14. Describe how the use of a "three-level" approach can provide a way of incorporating uncertainty into capital budgeting analysis. What are the advantages and limitations of such an approach?

15. Outline the way in which probability distributions of the values of variables in capital budgeting analysis can be used to incorporate uncertainty with regard to those variables.

16. How should the expected value of net income and cash flow per period be interpreted in the context of capital budgeting analysis of a project?

17. What can the cost of capital be considered to include? Should the cost of capital for any particular project necessarily be the same rate for every future period? Why or why not?

18. How can sensitivity analysis be applied to the capital budgeting process?

Exercises

E 18–1   Tax Effects of Alternative Depreciation Methods—Net Present Value Analysis

Thomas Corporation is reviewing a proposed plant addition. The equipment involved will cost $400,000 and has a useful life of four years. At the end of that time, it will have an estimated resale value of $130,000. The new equipment will allow the company to reduce operating costs and to increase sales volume so that an overall increase of $145,000 per year in before-tax operating cash flows will result in all four years. The company is subject to a 40 percent tax rate. A 10 percent after-tax cost of capital rate is appropriate.

Required:
(a) Prepare schedules of annual after-tax operating cash flows (1) when the straight-line method is used and (2) when the sum-of-the-years'-digits method is used.
(b) Using the net present value method, evaluate the project under each of the depreciation methods cited in part (a).
(c) Comment on the results obtained in part (b).

E 18–2   "To Pollute or Not to Pollute"—Acquisition of Control Devices—Disposition of Old Facilities—Tax Effects of Alternative Actions

Chemco Corporation may be fined if it does not replace certain equipment to meet environmental control requirements. The new equipment will cost $2,000,000 and have a ten-year life with no salvage value. The polluting equipment is still functional for ten years, but has a zero book value because it is already fully depreciated for tax purposes. If replaced, the old equipment can be sold for $10,000 cash.

   Two other alternatives have been suggested. Under the first, the old equipment could be modified at a cost of $500,000. This would allow minimal compliance with the environmental controls. However, annual operating costs would be $350,000 per year higher with the renovated but inferior equipment, as compared to the new equipment. These fixed-up items would have no salvage value at the end of ten years. The second alternative is to make no modifications, keep the old equipment, and incur whatever fines and penalties are assessed. Under existing and proposed legislation, estimated fines would be $100,000 per year for the first five years and $200,000 per year thereafter. In addition, operating costs would be $50,000 per year cheaper than with the new equipment.

   For tax purposes, the straight-line method is used for all depreciable assets, fines are *not* allowable as tax deductions, and the company is subject to a 40 percent tax rate on all operating profits and losses and 25 percent on capital gains or losses. The company estimates its cost of capital at 10 percent.

Required:
(a) Prepare schedules to show the effect on after-tax operating cash flows of the latter two proposals, as compared to the original proposal to purchase the new equipment. [*Hint:* Use an incremental approach.]
(b) Prepare schedules to determine the relative desirability of the three alternatives

using a net present value approach—that is, determine which alternative minimizes the present value of cash outflows.

(c) Would you propose that the solution indicated in part (b) be adopted? Why or why not? What is the nature of the problem involved? Why is conventional capital budgeting probably inadequate in this situation?

E 18–3   Alternative Financing Sources—Lease, Buy, or Borrow

Rosso Corporation is investigating alternative ways of acquiring and operating an aircraft to speed up deliveries of supplies and products between its two plants and its three sales outlets located throughout California. The alternatives are as follows:

(1) Purchase the aircraft outright for $4,000,000. Estimated resale value after six years will be $400,000 and the straight-line depreciation method will be used.

(2) Issue six-year bonds with a total face value of $4,000,000 at par. Interest of 12 percent per annum is payable annually at the end of each year. The proceeds of the bond issue will be applied directly to the purchase of the aircraft.

(3) Lease the aircraft at an annual rental of $1,000,000 payable at the beginning of each year for six years. The lease does *not* qualify as a capital lease because title to the aircraft reverts to the leasing company at the end of the sixth year.

The company is subject to a 40 percent tax rate and uses a 12 percent after-tax cost of capital rate.

Required:
(a) Prepare schedules to show the impact of each of the three alternatives on after-tax cash flows per year.

(b) Using net present value analysis, ascertain which form of financing is most attractive. (Assume that the cash needed for the first alternative is available from funds already held by the company.)

(c) Comment on other aspects of the financing decision not directly included in the analysis in parts (a) and (b).

E 18–4   Alternative Financing—Lease or Borrow

Merrion, Inc. is trying to decide whether to acquire a new limousine for its chief executive officer. It can be purchased outright for $45,000, but this would require a bank loan for the full amount, with 10 percent interest payable annually and the principal repayable in full at the end of five years. Alternatively, the limousine could be leased for five years with annual rentals of $12,000 payable at the beginning of each year.

The company is subject to a 40 percent tax rate and uses the straight-line depreciation method. If purchased, the limousine will have a resale value of $10,000 after five years. If leased, the limousine reverts to the leasing company at the end of the lease. The company uses a 12 percent cost of capital in evaluating projects of this type.

Required:
(a) Prepare schedules to show the annual after-tax cash flows associated with (1) the purchase/borrow alternative and (2) the lease alternative.

(b)   Use the net present value method to ascertain which alternative is preferable—that is, which one minimizes the present value of cash outflows.

(c)   Comment on other factors that would influence a decision of this type, but were not mentioned.

E 18–5   Disinvestment Decision—Net Present Value Analysis

Caldwell Corporation operates two production facilities, Eastern and Western, and has a central sales and administrative facility. The Eastern plant is owned outright, but all facilities at Western are leased. The plants ship directly to their own customers. Analysis of current operating results follows:

	Eastern	Western	Total
Sales (@ $20 per unit)	$6,000,000	$4,000,000	$10,000,000
Variable Expenses:			
Manufacturing	$3,000,000	$2,400,000	$ 5,400,000
Marketing	600,000	400,000	1,000,000
Fixed Expenses:			
Rent (plant)		800,000	800,000
Depreciation (plant)	600,000		600,000
Marketing and			
Administrative	1,500,000	1,000,000	2,500,000
	$5,700,000	$4,600,000	$10,300,000
Net Income (Loss)	$ 300,000	$ (600,000)	$ (300,000)

The lease on the Western plant facility expires at the end of this year, but could be renewed for another six years, subject to a $200,000 increase in rentals after the third year. Average annual sales volume is expected to increase by 20 percent after Year 2 and remain at the higher level through Year 6. If the lease is not renewed, all current manufacturing will be transferred to the Eastern plant. However, this will require outlays amounting to $2,000,000 to acquire additional equipment plus $300,000 per year for additional fixed administrative costs. This equipment will last for six years and have a $200,000 resale value at the end of that time. Variable costs at the Eastern plant will continue at the same rate as before. However, if the additional equipment is not acquired, Eastern will have enough idle capacity to produce sufficient output to supply half of the current sales volume presently produced at the Western plant. The marketing and administrative fixed costs are all committed fixed items and will not change in total if the Western plant is closed. They have been allocated to the two plants on the basis of sales revenue. The company believes that 15 percent is the appropriate before-tax cost of capital rate for this type of business venture.

Required:

(a)   Prepare schedules to show the incremental effects on operating cash flows of the three alternatives—(1) to renew the lease, (2) to acquire the extra equipment for Eastern, and (3) neither to renew the lease nor acquire the equipment.

(b)   Use net present value analysis to evaluate the three alternatives. Which would you recommend? Why?

(c)   What other factors could be considered in a decision of this nature?

(d)   Under what circumstances would it undoubtedly be correct to terminate operations at the Western plant? Why?

E 18–6   Make-or-Buy Decision—Long-range Situation—Capital Budgeting Analysis

Campodonico, Inc. is investigating the feasibility of manufacturing one of the components needed for its finished product rather than purchasing it from an outside supplier. Its present supplier has just announced that it intends to raise its price from $35 to $50 per unit, but will guarantee the $50 price for the next six years provided that Campodonico will purchase at least 6,000 units per year.

The equipment needed by Campodonico can be purchased for $600,000 and should have a salvage value of $60,000 at the end of the sixth year. Fixed costs (excluding depreciation) are $150,000 in Year 1 and will increase by $30,000 each year. Variable costs of manufacturing each component will be $15 per unit. Straight-line depreciation will be used, the company is subject to a 40 percent tax rate, and 10 percent is the appropriate cost of capital rate for this project. The company projects annual needs at 7,500 units per year for the six-year period.

Required:
(a)   Prepare schedules showing the annual after-tax cash flows for the two alternatives: (1) to continue to buy outside and (2) to begin manufacturing operations.
(b)   Use net present value analysis to determine which alternative is preferable.
(c)   What other important factors should be considered in this decision?
(d)   Which alternative will tend to become more desirable if annual volume (1) increases above 7,500, (2) falls between 7,500 and 6,000, or (3) falls below 6,000 units per year?

E 18–7   Inflationary Impact on Operating Cash Flows—Capital Budgeting Analysis

Garfinkel Company is exploring the possibility of expanding its operations by adding a new product line. This will require additional equipment costing $2,000,000, but based on 19X5 prices, should result in annual sales revenues of $1,000,000 and operating costs (excluding depreciation) of $400,000. The company is subject to a 40 percent tax rate and uses straight-line depreciation. The new product has a projected life of five years, after which the special equipment will have a zero value.

Over the next five years, the rate of inflation, affecting all products and services, will increase by 10 percent per year. The company has decided that 20 percent is an appropriate cost of capital that will allow for the expected inflation. Depreciation charges can only be computed on an historical cost basis.

Required:
(a)   Prepare a schedule of annual operating cash flows without adjustments for the expected inflation.
(b)   Prepare a schedule showing operating cash flows adjusted for the expected inflation.

(c) Use net present value analysis to evaluate the project on the basis of the inflation—adjusted cash flows in part (b).

(d) Comment on the solution to part (c).

E 18–8   Ranking Projects—Alternative Criteria

Crossan Corporation is analyzing the desirability of four alternative investment projects. The following data have been prepared.

Project	Year 0	Year 1	Year 2	Year 3	Year 4	Year 5
			Outlays and Cash Flows (All After-tax)			
R	$(200,000)	$ –0–	$ –0–	$ –0–	$ –0–	$300,000
S	(200,000)	60,000	60,000	60,000	60,000	60,000
T..........	(225,000)	75,000	75,000	75,000	–0–	–0–
U	(150,000)	75,000	75,000	–0–	–0–	–0–

Required:

(a) Rank the four projects according to (1) payback period, (2) net present value (cost of capital is 10 percent), (3) net present value ratio, and (4) accounting rate of return (based on total investment outlay).

(b) Comment on the rankings in part (a).

(c) Assume that only $400,000 is available for investment outlays at this time. Which projects would you recommend? Why?

E 18–9   Capital Budgeting—Uncertainty Analysis—Expected Values

Nelnotes Incorporated is investigating the possibilities of introducing a new line of X-rated greeting cards (for adults only). Three different strategies are being considered: (1) introduce nationwide, (2) introduce in California only, and (3) introduce in Marin County only.

The costs of the original artwork and typesetting will be $200,000. To advertise and promote the product line will cost $600,000 nationally, $300,000 for California only, or $100,000 for Marin County only. These amounts are one-time outlays and must be incurred immediately. Annual sales revenues for the three plans have been forecast as follows:

National		California		Marin	
Sales	Probability	Sales	Probability	Sales	Probability
$ 200,000	.4	$400,000	.3	$200,000	.1
900,000	.4	600,000	.3	300,000	.6
1,200,000	.2	800,000	.4	400,000	.3

The company anticipates a contribution margin ratio of 50 percent on the production, distribution, and sale of these cards. All initial costs of the product line will be amortized equally over the four-year product life. The company is subject to a 30 percent tax rate and regards 15 percent as its cost of capital on new product lines.

Required:

(a) Prepare schedules to show the annual net income and operating cash flow for all possible outcomes for each of the three marketing plans.

(b) Using net present value analysis, evaluate the feasibility of the *high* and *low* sales estimates for each of the plans. Comment on the results.

(c) Use expected net present value analysis to evaluate each of the three plans.

(d) Based on your solution to part (c), which of the plans should be adopted? Why?

E 18–10 Sensitivity Analysis in Capital Budgeting—Alternative Evaluation Criteria

Fitzgerald Company has the following project under consideration:

Project:	Plant Expansion
Project Life:	5 years (initial estimate)
Investment Outlay:	$150,000 (all fixed assets)
After-tax Operating Cash Flows:	$40,000 per year
Cost of Capital:	14%
Depreciation:	Straight-line—zero salvage value
Tax Rate:	40%

Required: (Answer all questions independently and based upon the original data in the problem.)

(a) Is the project acceptable on a net present value basis?

(b) What must the annual after-tax operating cash flows be in order to make the project acceptable if the cost of capital is: (1) 10, (2) 20, or (3) 25 percent?

(c) What must the life of the asset be in order to make the project acceptable if the cost of capital is (1) 10, (2) 20, or (3) 25 percent?

(d) What must the investment outlay be in order to make the project acceptable if the cost of capital is (1) 10, (2) 20, or (3) 25 percent?

E 18–11 Project Evaluations—Unequal Project Lives

Crosby Corporation is considering the acquisition of a new copying machine for its office. Two proposals have been received, but the expected lives of the two machines are not the same. The following schedule shows the after-tax cash flows associated with operating each machine, including acquisition costs and resale proceeds. Both machines will have equal capacity during their respective lifetimes.

	Cash Outflows	
Year	Machine 1	Machine 2
0	$24,000	$32,000
1	8,000	6,000
2	(2,000)	4,000
3	–0–	(8,000)

Machine 1 will only last for two years, whereas Machine 2 is good for three years. Cash inflows are shown in parentheses in the preceding table. The relevant cost of capital is 12 percent.

Required:

(a) Use net present value analysis to determine the discounted value of the cash outflows associated with each machine.

(b) Why is the data provided in part (a) insufficient to allow a clear decision to be made?

(c) What assumptions must be made to resolve the problem of the machines' having unequal lives?

(d) Which machine should Crosby Corporation buy? Why?

E 18–12 Comparison of Projects with Unequal Lives—Alternative Criteria

The following schedule shows the values of the key variables relating to three investment projects being evaluated by Busch Corporation. The company observes a 25 percent cost of capital on projects of this general type.

	Project X	Project Y	Project Z
Investment Outlay	$500,000	$500,000	$500,000
After-tax Operating Cash Flows			
Year 1	200,000	300,000	250,000
Year 2	200,000	300,000	250,000
Year 3	200,000	300,000	250,000
Year 4	200,000	–0–	250,000
Year 5	200,000	–0–	–0–
Residual Value			
(at end of life)	–0–	–0–	–0–
Net Income after Tax			
Year 1	100,000	133,333	125,000
Year 2	100,000	133,333	125,000
Year 3	100,000	133,333	125,000
Year 4	100,000	–0–	125,000
Year 5	100,000	–0–	–0–

Required:

(a) Compute the payback period for each project.

(b) Compute the accounting rate of return based on the average investment outlay for each project.

(c) Compute the payback reciprocal (or the cash flow accounting rate of return) based on the total investment outlay for each project.

(d) Compute (1) the net present value and (2) the net present value ratio for each project.

(e) Compute the (approximate) internal rate of return for each project.

(f) Rank the projects separately according to each of the criteria specified in parts (b), (c), (d), and (e).

(g) What conclusion, if any, can you reach based on part (f)?

(h) What further analysis would you suggest to resolve the problem of choosing one of the three projects?

Cases

C 18–1 Net Present Value Analysis—Trade-In or Sell Alternative— Project Evaluation

Pastorini Company is considering replacing one of its machines with a similar but more modern machine. Details concerning the present machine include:

Original Cost	$1,000,000
Current Book Value	600,000
Annual Depreciation (straight-line)	60,000
Current Resale Value.................	350,000
Resale Value (10 years)	–0–
Annual Cash Operating Costs	200,000

The replacement machine will cost $750,000, will have a useful life of ten years, and will incur annual cash operating costs of $100,000. Two machinery sales organizations have made proposals. One will accept the old machine as a trade-in and will charge only $400,000 for the new machine. The second dealer will only sell the replacement machine for cash, but has located a third party who is interested in purchasing the old machine for $350,000.

Present tax regulations specify that any book losses resulting from trade-ins of similar assets are *not* allowable as deductions for tax purposes. In such cases, the carrying value and depreciation basis of the new asset must be treated as the sum of the book value of the asset traded-in plus any cash consideration given. On the other hand, if an asset is sold for cash, any resulting book loss is deductible for tax purposes.

The new asset will be depreciated over its ten-year life using the straight-line method with a zero salvage value. The company is subject to a 40 percent tax rate, and an after-tax cost of capital rate of 15 percent is in effect.

Required:
(a) Prepare schedules to show the effect on after-tax cash flows of acquiring the new machine on the basis of (1) the trade-in alternative and (2) the sale alternative.
(b) Use net present value analysis to evaluate the alternative disposal methods. Should the new machine be acquired? Why or why not? If the new machine should be acquired, how should the old machine be disposed of?

C 18–2 Company Relocation Proposal

The City of Bankstown has drafted a proposal to present to Sutherland Enterprises Incorporated, in an effort to induce it to move its manufacturing operations to Bankstown. The city will build a $40,000,000 plant to Sutherland's specifications and rent it to Sutherland for $1,000,000 per year for twenty years on the condition that at least 2,000 unemployed residents of Bankstown are given jobs at the new plant. Projections of the impact on the city of the plant and its operations are as follows:

Increased annual retail sales	$60,000,000
Increased property tax base	$45,000,000
Increased annual cost of city services (police, fire, school, administration)	$10,000,000

Reduced annual unemployment
benefits paid by city
(per unemployed resident) .... $ 2,000

It was projected that, in addition to the jobs directly provided by Sutherland, another 3,000 unemployed persons will find new jobs created by the presence of the Sutherland plant. The city collects a 1 percent sales tax on all retail sales, and the property tax rate is 8 percent of assessed property values per year.

Required:
(a) Prepare a capital budgeting-type analysis to help decide whether or not the city should go ahead with the offer to Sutherland. Use a 10 percent discount rate for any present value calculations.
(b) Based only on the preceding analysis, should the offer be made? Why or why not?
(c) What are the limitations of conventional financial analysis in a case like this? What other factors should be considered?

C 18–3   Plant Closing Proposal

Collingwood Company has one of its plants on the Yarra River. The company has a 40 percent tax rate, a 14 percent cost of capital, and uses straight-line depreciation. Due to newly enacted environmental protection laws, the company must either close this plant or install extensive decontamination devices.

The plant could be sold for $2,000,000, an amount equal to its book value. Severance payments of $4,000,000 would be required under the terms of the current labor contract. If the Yarra River plant were closed, its manufacturing operations would be transferred to the Bendigo plant. Production costs would not change, but additional shipping and storage costs of $4,500,000 per year would be incurred.

The new control equipment would cost $10,000,000 and would have a ten-year useful life with no estimated salvage value. Operating costs would increase by $1,000,000 annually if the new equipment were installed.

Required:
(a) Prepare a capital budgeting-type analysis to assist in the decision of closure or purchase of the equipment. Based only on this analysis, what action should be taken?
(b) What other factors that are not included in the preceding analysis should be considered?
(c) Comment on the limitations of conventional financial capital budgeting analysis in situations such as this.

C 18–4   Ranking Capital Investment Alternatives

McGlone Corporation has proposed a $16,000,000 program of capital outlays for 19X3 based on funds available. The following projects with estimated outlays and operating cash flows are under consideration:

Project	Outlay	Operating Cash Flow	Life (years)
Z	$ 8,000,000	$2,500,000	8
Y	8,000,000	2,000,000	6
X	4,000,000	1,400,000	8
W..........	6,000,000	1,600,000	6
V	10,000,000	4,000,000	6

The company observes 12 percent as its cost of capital rate.

Required:
(a) Calculate the net present value and net present value ratio of all five projects.
(b) Rank the projects on the basis of both sets of results in part (a).
(c) How should the $16,000,000 be allocated? What assumptions did you make and what complicating factors are present?

C 18–5 Net Present Value Analysis

A project with a $70,000 required investment outlay is being considered. It is expected to generate after-tax operating cost savings of $20,000 per year. However, the useful life of the project could be either five, six, or seven years. The company observes a 20 percent cost of capital.

Required:
(a) Use a range-type analysis to present a net present value solution to this proposal. Should it be accepted? Why or why not?
(b) Assume probabilities are associated with the possible lives as follows: (1) 5 years: $p = .2$; (2) 6 years: $p = .5$; (3) 7 years: $p = .3$. Develop an expected net present value analysis to this problem. Should it be accepted? Why or why not?
(c) Comment on your solutions to parts (a) and (b).

Problems

P 18–1 Tax Effects of Disposal of Capital Assets—Capital Budgeting Analysis

Darnell Corporation proposes to purchase a new warehouse and shipping facility for the Bay Area market. A suitable building has been located and can be purchased for $3,000,000. Of the total cost, $1,200,000 attributable to the land is not subject to depreciation for tax purposes. The building will be depreciated on a straight-line basis over ten years with zero resale value. The use of this new facility will save the company $750,000 per year in shipping, storage and handling costs when compared to the present antiquated warehouse located over 500 miles to the south.

The old warehouse can be sold now for $275,000, of which $250,000 applies to the land and $25,000 to the building. These have existing book values for tax purposes of $150,000 and $60,000 respectively. It is anticipated that the new site and building will have a market value of $160,000 after ten years. The old building would have a zero value if kept for ten more years, but the land would be worth $300,000.

The company is subject to a 40 percent tax rate on regular earnings and a 25 percent rate on losses or gains on disposals of fixed assets. The relevant cost of capital rate is 12 percent.

Required:

(a) Prepare an analysis to show the after-tax proceeds of the immediate sale of the old premises and the net cost of acquiring the new premises.

(b) Prepare an analysis to show the after-tax proceeds of the sale of the new premises in ten years.

(c) Use the net present value method to determine whether or not the new premises should be acquired.

P 18–2   Alternative Methods of Asset Disposal—Trade-In or Sell-and-Buy—Capital Budgeting Analysis

Becker Company is considering the acquisition of a new pizza oven to enable it to expand its operations at its highly successful Pizza-Video Palace. The existing oven could either be sold for cash or traded in as partial payment for the new oven. Another nearby pizza parlor is willing to pay $50,000 for the old oven. Alternatively, the vendor of the new oven, which has a cash purchase price of $200,000, will allow a $66,000 trade-in allowance on the old oven.

The old oven originally cost $160,000, but has been written down to $96,000. If kept for another five years, as previously intended, it would have a resale value of only $16,000. If acquired, the new oven will have an estimated resale value of $24,000 at the end of five years.

Volume can be increased from 16,000 to 20,000 pizzas per year if the new oven is acquired. Operating revenues and costs are forecast as follows:

	Old Oven	New Oven
Sales Revenue	$10 per pizza	$10 per pizza
Variable Costs......	$5 per pizza	$4.50 per pizza
Fixed Costs	$15,000 per year	$4,000 per year

The company observes a 10 percent cost of capital on an after-tax basis. It is subject to a 40 percent tax rate on operating income and a 30 percent tax rate on capital gains or losses. In the event that the old oven is traded in, no gain or loss can be reported and the depreciation basis of the new oven will be adjusted accordingly. If the old oven is sold, the gain or loss is taxable at the previously noted rates. Straight-line depreciation will continue to be used for the old oven, but the sum-of-the-years'-digits method will be used if the new oven is acquired.

Required:

(a) Determine any capital gains or losses that will apply to any of the possible asset dispositions mentioned.

(b) Prepare schedules to show net income and after-tax cash flow per year for the following situations:
   (1) The old oven is kept
   (2) The old oven is sold and a new one purchased
   (3) The old oven is traded in and a new one acquired

(c) Prepare a net present value analysis to determine which of the three alternative courses of action should be taken.

P 18–3   Lease-or-Buy Decision—Net Present Value Analysis—Sensitivity Analysis

Blues Brothers, Inc. presently has a policy of reimbursing employees at the rate of 27¢ per mile for use of personal automobiles while on official company business. Management is reviewing a proposal to either purchase or lease company cars. The following data have been developed:

(1) Mileage driven:

Employee 1	15,000 miles per year
Employee 2	25,000 miles per year
Employee 3	40,000 miles per year

(2) New vehicles cost $7,500 each. The cars will be retained for three years at which time they can be sold for $3,000 each.

(3) Operating costs are projected as follows:

Gasoline	8¢ per mile
Tires	1¢ per mile
Maintenance	1¢ per mile
Insurance	$350 per year per car
Licenses, Registration, and so on	$150 per year per car

(4) Terms of the leasing arrangement call for an annual prepaid rental fee of $4,000, plus 7½¢ per mile in excess of 30,000 miles per year, payable at the end of each year. The lease covers all normal operating costs except gasoline. The lease specifies an option to purchase the leased vehicles at the end of three years for $2,500 per vehicle. The leased vehicles will also have a resale value of $3,000 at that time. (Treat the lease as an operating lease.)

(5) The company is subject to a 40 percent tax rate and observes an after-tax cost of capital rate of 12 percent. Straight-line depreciation is used.

Required:

(a) Prepare schedules for each employee to show the effects on after-tax cash flows of the three alternatives: (1) purchase the automobiles, (2) lease the automobiles, or (3) pay mileage.

(b) Use net present value analysis to evaluate the three alternatives for each of the three employees. Which would you choose and why?

(c) What other factors would influence the choice?

(d) What purchase price would make the purchase alternative as attractive as the lease alternative? Ignore any effects on depreciation or salvage value.

(e) What change in the present mileage allowance rate would make that alternative as attractive as the lease alternative?

(f) If all three employees drove their cars 50,000 miles per year, how would this change your answers to part (b)?

P 18–4   Alternative Financing of Project—Lease or Purchase/Borrow

Buttigan Company is considering the acquisition of an additional computer to supplement its capability to provide time-shared computer services to its clients. It has two opportunities:

(1) To purchase the computer outright for $460,000.

(2) To lease the computer for three years from a vendor for $100,000 annually plus 10 percent of gross time-share service revenue. This alternative also requires a payout of $150,000 at the end of the third year. Rentals are payable at year-end and the computer reverts to the vendor after the payout settlement.

The company realizes that at the end of three years a new, more modern computer will be needed. It estimates that the computer under review now will be worth $200,000 at that time. Revenues are forecast to be $450,000, $500,000, and $550,000 in the three years of operation. Annual operating costs (*excluding* depreciation or rental of the new computer) should be $175,000, with an additional $25,000 for start-up and training costs at the beginning of the first year.

If purchased, $400,000 of the price must be borrowed from a bank with interest at 10 percent and repayments made according to the following schedule:

	Principal	Interest
End of Year 1......	$100,000	$40,000
End of Year 2......	150,000	30,000
End of Year 3......	150,000	15,000
	$400,000	$85,000

The company intends to use the sum-of-the-years'-digits method for depreciation and is subject to a 40 percent tax rate. The cost of capital for projects of this type has been set at 14 percent.

Required:

(a) Prepare schedules of net income and after-tax cash flows for the three years (1) under the purchase/borrow arrangement and (2) under the lease arrangement.

(b) Use the net present value method to evaluate the two alternatives.

(c) Which alternative would you recommend? Why? What other factors would be relevant to this decision?

P 18–5 Make-or-Buy Decision—Long-Range Situation—Possible Disinvestment in Facilities—Capital Budgeting Analysis

Kingsley Corporation currently manufactures all components of its final product, but Garcia Company, an independent firm, has offered to provide one of the main subassemblies needed by Kingsley at what appears to be a very attractive price. However, Kingsley is hesitant to buy from Garcia because quite a lot of special purpose equipment that will no longer be needed will have to be sold at a considerable loss. The following information is available:

(1) Garcia will supply the subassembly in any quantity needed for $45 per unit. Forecast demand is 10,000 units per year for the next six years.

(2) Presently the costs incurred by Kingsley to produce 10,000 subassemblies per year are as follows:

Materials	. . . .	$100,000
Direct Labor	. . . .	200,000
Variable Overhead	. . . . . .	100,000
Fixed Overhead	. . . .	225,000
		$625,000

Because of previously negotiated contracts, materials prices will rise by 25 percent after three years and labor rates by 10 percent after each of the next two years. Overhead rates are not expected to increase.

(3) If the subassemblies are purchased from Garcia, all variable manufacturing costs can be avoided. Of the fixed overhead, $25,000 cannot be avoided because it relates to plant-wide administrative costs (all paid in cash) that were being allocated to the subassemblies.

(4) The other $200,000 is for depreciation charges on the special purpose equipment usable only to manufacture the subassemblies. This equipment has a book value of $1,200,000 and would be depreciated on a straight-line basis. The only opportunity to dispose of this equipment would generate an immediate cash return of $200,000 before taxes. If kept, the equipment would have no resale value after six years.

(5) The company is subject to a 40 percent tax rate on operating income and 25 percent on capital gains and losses. The cost of capital appropriate for projects of this type is considered to be 12 percent.

Required:

(a) Prepare schedules to show the annual after-tax cost for the next six years of (1) purchasing the subassemblies and (2) continuing to manufacture the subassemblies.

(b) Use net present value analysis to determine which alternative should be chosen.

(c) Discuss the treatment of the loss on disposal of the special purpose equipment. Was the management's original apprehension warranted? Why or why not?

(d) What other factors should be considered in the decision in part (b)?

(e) What price would Garcia have to quote in order for Kingsley to be indifferent between the two alternatives?

P 18–6   Research Project—Continue-or-Abandon Decision—Capital Budgeting Analysis

Hi-Tek Corporation pursues a comprehensive program of product research and development to maintain its position in its highly competitive and dynamic market environment. Projects are evaluated at several points once the initial research commitment is made.

Project 247 was approved two years ago, and $2,000,000 has already been spent on supplies, test materials, salaries, special purpose equipment, and other services needed specifically for the project. Although all items of expenditure qualify for immediate expensing, the research department is still hesitant to treat them as being "written off." This often leads to arguments and confusion among the various parties involved, especially concerning decisions as to whether or not to persevere with a project. The outlook is as follows:

(1) If the project is terminated at its present stage, the equipment and some unused supplies and materials, could be sold for $500,000. All work would be terminated and no direct product benefits would be obtained.

(2) The project could be funded for one more year. This would require immediate outlays of another $1,500,000. The results of this stage of development should produce operating cash inflows of $1,200,000 per year for four years starting in one year.

(3) The project could be funded for a total of two more years, requiring $2,000,000 now and another $1,000,000 in one year. This advanced level of the project is forecast to be capable of producing operating cash inflows of $1,800,000 per year for four years starting in one year.

All expenditures and recepts are subject to a 40 percent tax rate and the company observes a 12 percent cost of capital for this class of project.

Required:
(a) Prepare an analysis, using the net present value method, to determine which of the three alternatives should be adopted.
(b) Comment on the treatment of the original outlay of $2,000,000 in the foregoing analysis.
(c) Assume that all of the preceding data had been available when the original decision to initiate Project 247 was being made. What would the decision have been then?
(d) Comment on the solutions to parts (a) and (c). Are there any problems or inconsistencies involved? Explain.

P 18–7   Product Line Discontinuation—Long-range Effects—Capital Budgeting Analysis

Refer to Exercise 9–5 on pages 409–10. The decision to discontinue product line X is now being addressed from a long-range view, with the following additional and revised information:

(1) The results of a typical month as originally presented remain the same. They should be revised to present data on an annual basis by multiplying all items by 12.
(2) The special purpose equipment, instead of remaining idle, can be sold for $200,000 immediately. This equipment has a book value of $1,080,000 at this time and a remaining useful life of five years.
(3) The production manager will be permanently transferred to another division and will receive a $10,000 per year bonus.
(4) Fixed manufacturing overhead will be reduced by $50,000 per year, but total firm-wide advertising expenditures allocated among product lines will remain the same. The administrative costs will be reduced by $60,000 per year.
(5) Sales of other products will decline by $500,000 per year. An average contribution margin ratio of 40 percent was being generated by those other products.
(6) If the product line had not been discontinued at this point, it would have been in five years' time when the special purpose equipment was worn out.
(7) The company is subject to a 30 percent tax rate and a 15 percent cost of capital rate.

Required:
(a) Prepare a schedule of the annual after-tax operating cash flow effects that will result from the discontinuation of product line X.

(b)   Use net present value analysis to evaluate the discontinuation decision. Based on that analysis, what should be done?

(c)   What other considerations are relevant to a decision of this type?

P 18–8   Product Line Rearrangement—Long-range Effects—Capital Budgeting Considerations

Refer to Problem 9–9 on pages 422–23. Management is considering a permanent change in the product lines of Carlone Company. The proposal calls for (1) discontinuation of production of Product A and (2) the introduction of a new item, Product D, which will be obtained by reprocessing Product C rather than selling it as an intermediate by-product.

If Product A is discontinued, fixed manufacturing overhead costs can be reduced by one half of their original amount, but Product D will require additional fixed manufacturing overhead costs of $800,000 per year. Both these overhead changes include depreciation amounts. When Product A is discontinued, equipment used to produce it, having a book value of $4,000,000, will be sold for $800,000. This equipment would otherwise have lasted ten more years and would have had a zero salvage value. New equipment to manufacture Product D will cost $2,500,000, and will have a useful life of ten years and a disposal value of $100,000. Straight-line depreciation is used in all cases.

Projected sales for Product D are $5,000,000 per year for the next ten years. Variable manufacturing costs are expected to be $1,000,000, and variable marketing and administrative costs equal 10 percent of sales revenue per year. Total fixed marketing and administrative costs will not change but will now be allocated two-thirds to B and one-third to D. The variable cost of producing Product B and the item that used to be Product C (but which is now part of Product D) will remain unchanged. Sales of Product B for the next ten years will not be affected by these changes. The company is subject to a 40 percent tax rate and considers 12 percent to be the cost of capital relevant to this type of venture.

Required:

(a)   Prepare schedules to show the effect of all the preceding changes on (1) net income per year and (2) after-tax operating cash flow per year.

(b)   Use net present value analysis to evaluate the acceptability of the proposed product line rearrangement. Based on this analysis, should it be undertaken?

P 18–9   Project Analysis—Expected Inflation—Capital Budgeting Analysis

Milgram Company is considering the acquisition of a new machine that will increase output by 10,000 units per year. The company's product sells for $20 and incurs variable costs of $8 per unit. In addition to the extra depreciation charges, annual fixed costs will increase by $20,000. The machine costs $240,000 but will only be used for five years, at which time it will be sold for $40,000. The company is subject to a 40 percent tax rate.

Over the next five years, inflation is projected to increase at a rate of 10 percent per year. A 20 percent cost of capital has been chosen to include an allowance for the rate of inflation expected over the life of the project.

Required:

(a) Prepare schedules of operating cash flows from the project (1) without any consideration of inflation and (2) after allowing for the inflationary effect. Assume that depreciation charges can only be calculated on an historical cost basis, but that all other operating costs and revenues are subject to the specified inflation rate.

(b) Evaluate the project using the net present value method (1) on the basis of cash flows unadjusted for inflation and (2) on the basis of cash flows adjusted for inflation.

(c) Comment on the answers to part (b).

P 18–10   Project Analysis—Expected Inflation—Graduated Cost of Capital—Capital Budgeting Analysis

Refer to Problem 18–9 on page 947. In place of a constant 20 percent cost of capital over the life of the project, the company decides to observe a graduated cost of capital over the five years as follows:

Year	Percent
1	16%
2	18%
3	20%
4	22%
5	25%

This schedule takes into consideration the fact that inflation is increasing at a 10 percent rate and that the cost of capital is currently about 15 percent. All operating cash flows should be adjusted according to the original instructions concerning inflation.

Required:

(a) Evaluate the project using the net present value method on the basis of the graduated cost of capital schedule and the inflation-adjusted operating cash flows.

(b) Comment on the results of part (a), and compare them to part (b) of Problem 18–9.

P 18–11   Project Ranking—Capital Rationing—Alternative Criteria

Baker Company is performing a preliminary screening of several proposed capital investment projects. The following projects are under consideration:

Project	Outlay	Life (years)	Annual After-tax Operating Cash Flows
M	$ 500,000	10	$ 80,000
N	2,000,000	10	500,000
O	2,000,000	10	400,000
P	600,000	10	120,000
Q	1,400,000	10	280,000

Required:

(a) Rank the projects according to (1) payback period, (2) net present value, (3) net present value ratio, and (4) internal rate of return. A 12 percent cost of capital is in effect.

(b) Assume at this time that the corporation has decided to outlay no more than (1) $2,000,000, (2) $2,500,000, or (3) $3,000,000. Which projects should be accepted under the four separate criteria for each of the three levels of expenditure?

(c) Comment on the answers to part (b).

P 18–12 Ranking Competing Projects—Alternative Criteria—Capital Rationing

Sutherland Company is reviewing requests for capital outlays on projects submitted by its three operating divisions. The company uses a 10 percent cost of capital rate for evaluation of all investment proposals. Details of the requests are partly analyzed and summarized below:

	Outlay	Annual Operating Cash Flows	Present Value of Operating Cash Flows
Division D:			
Project 1	($400,000)	$160,000	$507,200
Project 2	(300,000)	120,000	454,920
Division W:			
Project 3	(160,000)	55,000	208,505
Project 4	(680,000)	185,000	805,675
Division S:			
Project 5	(200,000)	60,000	261,300
Project 6	(520,000)	165,000	625,515

Required:
(a) Determine the expected life of each of the projects.
(b) Rank the projects on the basis of (1) net present value, (2) net present value ratio, and (3) payback period.
(c) Assume that only $800,000 is available for new project outlays. How should it be allocated? What criteria did you use to decide the allocation and why?
(d) What complicating factors are present in part (c)?

P 18–13 Project Profitability with Uncertainty—Multiple Independent Probabilistic Variables—Capital Budgeting Analysis

Joe Six Productions, Inc., is in the process of planning its next movie extravaganza, a musical adaptation of a best-selling novel, *Nancy! Oh! Nancy!* Although the company has previously completed several successful movie, television, and stage ventures, it still experiences considerable uncertainty with regard to production costs, performers' salaries, and box office revenues. The following forecasts have been made for various aspects of the project:

(1) *Production Costs* (Uncertain because of usual problems in coordinating production details, efficiency of staff, delays, temperamental actors, and so on.)

Estimated Amount	Probability
$ 6,000,000	.3
$ 8,000,000	.5
$10,000,000	.2

(2) *Performers' Salaries*   (Uncertain because of terms in contracts of performers that adjust salaries to current box-office ratings of performers.)

Estimated Amount	Probability
$ 5,000,000	.6
$ 7,500,000	.3
$10,000,000	.1

(3) *Box Office Revenue*   (Uncertain because of its sensitivity to public response to movie, reviews, and so on.)

Estimated Amount		Probability
$10,000,000	("Flop")	.1
$30,000,000	("Average")	.7
$40,000,000	("Big Hit")	.2

(4) *Marketing and Distribution Costs*   These include $2,000,000 of fixed items plus variable items that amount to 10 percent of gross revenues.

(5) *Television Residuals*   At the end of its life as a movie, the television rights to the movie can be sold for $2,500,000 cash. This amount must be reported as revenue in the first six-month period.

The film is expected to have an effective revenue-generating life of two-and-a-half years from the date of its release, divided into five six-month periods for ease of calculation. All production costs and performers' salaries will be considered incurred at a point six months before release. The fixed marketing costs are one-time promotion costs incurred when the film is released. All operating costs and revenues occur at the end of each six-month period.

The company is subject to a 30 percent tax rate and observes a 40 percent per annum cost of capital on projects of this type. For tax purposes, the production, salary and fixed promotional costs will be written off on a modified sum-of-years'-digits basis (5/15 in first six months, 4/15 in second six months, and so on). Box office revenues are distributed over the 30-month period according to the following patterns: (30, 25, 25, 10, and 10 percent). The film will be released on July 1, 19X4. The variables subject to probability distributions are to be considered independent of each other for the purposes of expected value calculations.

Required:

(a) Prepare schedules of the net income and operating cash flows for each of the six 6-month periods beginning January 1, 19X4, (1) on an expected value basis, (2) on a best-of-all-possible-outcomes basis, and (3) on a worst-of-all-possible-outcomes basis.

(b) Use net present value analysis to evaluate each of the three scenarios outlined in part (a).

(c) Should the film be made? What basis did you use for your decision?

(d) Comment on the problems of applying capital budgeting analysis to a situation such as this.

P 18–14   Product Introduction—Uncertainty Analysis—Expected Value and Range Considerations

Kleerex Incorporated is about to introduce a new product to its line of kitchen detergents. The product, "Schmearoff," has already been developed at a cost of $10,000,000 for product production and marketing research and development. Three alternate marketing strategies, each involving different advertising programs, promotions, and pricing strategies, are under consideration. A summary of the expected impact of each strategy follows.

	Plan I		Plan II		Plan III	
Initial Promotional Outlays	$4,000,000		$ 7,000,000		$10,000,000	
Contribution Margin Ratio	50%		55%		60%	
Annual Sales Forecast (with probability):						
Optimistic	$8,000,000	(.3)	$10,000,000	(.1)	$14,000,000	(.2)
Realistic	5,000,000	(.6)	6,000,000	(.7)	8,000,000	(.6)
Pessimistic	2,000,000	(.1)	2,000,000	(.2)	–0–	(.2)
Fixed Operating Costs per Year (excluding depreciation)	$ 500,000		$ 600,000		$ 800,000	

Promotional outlays will be amortized over the expected five-year life of the product. No outlays for new plant or equipment are needed for the new product. The company is subject to a 35 percent tax rate and a 12 percent cost of capital requirement.

Required:
(a) Prepare schedules of annual operating cash flows and net income for all possible sales levels under each of the three plans.
(b) Use net present value analysis to examine the feasibility of the *high* and *low* sales volumes of each plan. Comment on these results.
(c) Determine the expected net present value of each of the plans. Which should be chosen on the basis of this analysis?
(d) Comment on the information found in part (b) with the results of part (c).

P 18–15   Sensitivity Analysis in Project Evaluation

Komatsu Corporation has an old machine with a book value of $50,000 and a current resale value of $28,000. Cash operating costs with this machine are $40,000 per year. The machine is good for five more years of use but will then be worthless. It could be replaced now with a new machine costing $120,000 that will cost $10,000 to operate, last five years, and have a zero resale value thereafter. The tax rate is 40 percent. The company uses straight-line depreciation and observes a 20 percent cost of capital.

Required:
(a) Evaluate the proposal using the net present value method.
(b) Comment on the effects of the cost of capital being (1) 10, (2) 15, (3) 25, or (4) 40 percent.

(c) Comment on the effects of the life of the machine being (1) three, (2) six, or (3) ten years.

(d) Refer to the original data. What must the cost of operating the new machine be in order to make the proposal acceptable at a 20 percent cost of capital?

P 18–16 Project Evaluation—Sensitivity Analysis

Pietras Company is considering expanding its facilities to increase operating volume. Proposed outlays include:

Working Capital	$ 250,000
Buildings	1,200,000
Plant	550,000
	$2,000,000

Initial operating estimates are as follows:

Sales Volume	1,500,000 units
Sales Price	$2 per unit
Variable Costs	50¢ per unit
Fixed Costs	$800,000 per year
Project Life	10 years
Disposal Values (in 10 years):	
Plant	–0–
Buildings	$200,000
Tax Rate	30%
Cost of Capital	12%

Required: (Answer each part independently.)

(a) Evaluate the project using net present value analysis and the original operating estimates.

(b) Present an analysis of the effects of the sales price being (1) $1.50, (2) $2, or (3) $2.50.

(c) Present an analysis of the effects of the sales volume being (1) 1,000,000, (2) 1,500,000, or (3) 2,000,000 units.

(d) Present an analysis of the effects of (1) a sales price of $1.50 and volume of 2,000,000 units, (2) a sales price of $2.50 and volume of 1,000,000 units, and (3) the original sales price and volume.

P 18–17 Project Evaluation—Unequal Lives—Unequal Outlays

Casey, Inc., is considering two sets of investment projects. Set 1 projects have different project lives; Set 2 projects have different investment outlays. The estimates for the key cash flow measures for the various projects are as follows:

	Projects			
	Set 1		Set 2	
	A	B	C	D
Investment Outlay	$100,000	$100,000	$200,000	$500,000
Project Life	6 years	3 years	2 years	2 years
After-tax Operating Cash Flow per Year	$ 27,000	$ 46,000	$140,000	$310,000

The corporation observes a 10 percent cost of capital for Set 1 projects and 12 percent for Set 2 projects.

Required:

(a) For each separate set of projects, calculate (1) the net present value, (2) the net present value ratio, and (3) the (approximate) internal rate of return.

(b) For each separate set of projects, comment on the problems present in choosing between the two alternative projects.

(c) What assumptions must be made to resolve these problems?

(d) Assume that with regard to Set 1, Project E is also available. It will require an outlay of $150,000 at the end of the third year and will generate after-tax cash flows of $70,000 per year for the *following* three years. Reevaluate Set 1 using this information in conjunction with the net present value method. Which alternative(s) should be selected? Why?

(e) Assume that with regard to Set 2, Project F is also available. It will require an initial outlay of $300,000 and will generate after-tax operating cash flows of $160,000 per year for the next two years. Reevaluate Set 2 using this information in conjunction with the net present value method. Which alternative(s) should be selected? Why?

P 18–18   Project Evaluation—Unequal Investment Outlays—Cash Flow, Earnings, and Dividend Considerations—Evaluation of Alternative Separate Capital Budgeting Criteria

Watanabee Corporation is comparing two alternate investment projects. Only one can be financed and it will constitute the corporation's major source of earnings for the next five years. Estimates of cash flows and other considerations are as follows:

	Project MT7	Project PK9
Investment Outlay	$10,000,000	$9,000,000
Project Life	5 years	5 years
After-tax Operating Cash Flows:		
Year 1................	($ 1,000,000)	$4,000,000
Year 2................	(500,000)	3,000,000
Year 3................	4,000,000	2,500,000
Year 4................	8,000,000	2,000,000
Year 5................	8,000,000	1,000,000

The company observes a 10 percent cost of capital for its investment projects. Several available projects requiring a $1,000,000 outlay meet this requirement.

Required:

(a) Evaluate the two projects using the net present value method. Which project appears to be preferable on that basis?

(b) How did the information about the available $1,000,000 projects affect your answer? What other information might be useful to resolve that same problem?

(c) Compute (1) the payback period (cumulative method) and (2) the accounting rate of return (average income related to average book value of investment) for each project. Comment on the results.

(d) Review the operating cash flow projections of the two projects with regard to their impact on the company's ability (1) to show earnings each year and (2) to pay dividends each year. Comment on the problem involved.

(e) Discuss the need for methods of capital budgeting analysis to be multidimensional. Mention the limitations of each individual method of analysis, especially with regard to the information obtained in the solutions to parts (a), (c), and (d) of this problem.

19

SEGMENT PERFORMANCE EVALUATION: PROFIT CENTERS

LEARNING OBJECTIVES

After studying Chapter 19, you should be able to:

1. Discuss the possible bases for company segmentation, its advantages and disadvantages, and the purposes of segment evaluation.
2. Analyze the nine account categories in a segmented income statement and evaluate company segments according to these criteria.
3. Evaluate segment performance in terms of decisions to expand, contract, initiate, or discontinue company segments.
4. Calculate transfer prices based on the market price or the net realizable value of the intermediate product.
5. Calculate transfer prices based on variable production cost, variable cost with margin, full production cost, and full production cost with margin.
6. Calculate transfer prices based on incremental cost, for short-run and for long-run evaluation purposes.
7. Assess the usefulness of negotiated transfer prices and the indicated segment profit contributions for producing and acquiring divisions.
8. Calculate structured transfer prices for producing and acquiring divisions.
9. Calculate dual transfer prices for producing and acquiring divisions.
10. From the standpoint of performance evaluation and decision making, evaluate the strengths and weaknesses of the six transfer pricing methods demonstrated in this chapter.

Preceding chapters have emphasized the need for planning and control techniques for separate components of a company's total activities. However, the centralized, single product firm is a rarity. Multiple output, divisionalized, and decentralized companies are so prevalent that *segmented accounting* is frequently required.

Accounting procedures for segmented firms have already been introduced. Departmental flexible budgeting, standard product costing, product line cost–volume–profit analysis, and capital budgeting project analysis are used to develop information for the managers of company sub-units. The concept of responsibility accounting—and the controllability, traceability, and attributability of performance measures—underlies the accounting methods used by such sub-units. In this chapter, the procedures for evaluating the profit performance of departments, divisions, product lines, and other organizational segments are described in detail.

THE BASIS FOR ORGANIZATIONAL SEGMENTATION

Segmentation describes various ways in which an organization's total activities can be divided for managerial and operating purposes. **Decentralization**—the diffusion of corporate decision making authority and responsibility among sub-units or the geographical or physical separation of company activities—is a frequently encountered form of segmentation. Both types of decentralization are not always found in the same company. For example, although nationwide retail chains are geographically decentralized, much of their decision making remains highly centralized. On the other hand, within a single factory, operating departments are often subject to local control and decision making by foremen, supervisors, and other managers.

For purposes of planning, evaluation, and control, performance might also be segmented according to *products or product lines, sales territories, customers or customer groups,* and *functional activity groupings*—such as production, marketing, and administrative units.

ADVANTAGES AND DISADVANTAGES OF DECENTRALIZATION

Advocates of corporate decentralization support it for many reasons. In general, it is claimed that decentralization improves managerial decision making. Managers are brought closer to actual operations. Their expertise is enhanced by the task specialization permitted in a decentralized firm. The chain of command is shortened, the span of decision making is narrowed, and managerial creativity is encouraged.

Management's responsibilities tend to be more specifically defined in decentralized businesses. Performance measures for each responsibility center can be developed in a more understandable and communicable form. Group motivation and individual aspiration can be improved; an atmosphere of independence, responsibility, and healthy competition can be fostered. Better training opportunities are possible, together with chances for more rapid advancement, more direct participation in decision making, a reduction in the burdens of management, and an increase in the speed and responsiveness of decision making.

Physical necessity, the scale of operations, and legal and financial convenience may also cause a firm to decentralize its operations. These influences may be especially important when raw materials are produced at one location and processing of the final product occurs elsewhere. Diversified parent–subsidiary operations and corporations organized to claim the tax advantages of multiple-entity activities may find decentralization particularly attractive.

On the negative side, decentralization obviously makes coordination and control of operations more difficult. Internal competition among decentralized units may become unduly severe, local goals may be pursued at the expense of overall company objectives, and conflict and disharmony between segments may result. Because no company can ever be completely decentralized, interdependencies among segments are inevitable and can confuse and frustrate segment performance measurement.

Decentralization can cause duplication of managerial functions. Segmenting a company's operations sometimes becomes an end in itself, leading to ungainly organizational structures that defeat attempts to clarify and streamline a firm's total activities.

PURPOSES OF SEGMENT PERFORMANCE EVALUATION

If company operations are decentralized, accounting information systems must permit managers to evaluate the performance of individual segments. The reasons for assessing segment performance are similar to those for evaluating the whole company:

1. *Measuring Segment Profit Contribution.* Because profit is typically the main goal of a company and its sub-units, the **profit contribution** made by each segment toward its own or the firm's profit goals is an essential element of segment performance evaluation. As will be seen, segment profit contribution can be measured and expressed in several ways.

2. *Control.* Comparing actual performance with standards, budgets, or other prespecified performance criteria is particularly urgent in segmented companies, because decentralization tends to produce conflict, lack of coordination, and decisions detrimental to the achievement of firm-wide goals.

3. *Evaluation.* The interpretation of operating results is the link between the final phase of control and the continuation of planning activities. Therefore, evaluation of segment performance provides the basis for the replanning of future actions. This is especially important in planning for a segment's

continuation or discontinuance or for the expansion, contraction, or modification of segment operations.

4. *Penalty–Reward Systems.* The performance of segment management must also be evaluated. Segment performance measurement must be coordinated with any system established to provide rewards (money, promotion, prestige) and penalties (demotion, termination) for managerial achievements.

5. *Motivation.* Some of the advantages claimed for decentralization relate to its potential for improving the efficiency of local managers. Budgets and standards that express desired segment performance, together with the evaluation of results, should be used to motivate and influence managers of decentralized units. Individuals can more easily be stimulated to improve their performance when recognizable segment goals are emphasized.

6. *Comparisons and Rankings.* Healthy competition between segments is a potential advantage of decentralization. However, overemphasis on the comparative and competitive aspects of performance can be counterproductive. For example, using scarce resources in Division A when they could be used more profitably in Division B may enhance Division A's performance but be detrimental to the performance of the entire firm. Segment evaluations that involve comparisons and rankings are useful in resource allocation and in incentive and reward systems, but should not be adopted when there is no common basis for comparison, or when there are no dominant criteria for performance evaluation.

THE SCOPE OF SEGMENT PERFORMANCE EVALUATION

A basic principle of evaluation and control is that performance attributes subject to these procedures should be controllable by the unit being evaluated. This **controllability concept** is also important when a segment's managers are being evaluated. Because managers must operate within the scope of authority defined for their particular segment, they should be evaluated only in terms of the results of such actions.

The managers of a department, division, product line, or sales region do not always directly control all aspects of their segment's performance. Consequently, a segment should also be evaluated in terms of those performance characteristics that are attributable to it. In this case, **attributability** refers to outcomes that are directly associated with or directly traceable to the existence and operations of a segment. It includes items that are necessary to a segment's continuing operation but are beyond the direct and immediate control of segment management. For example, the salary of a divisional manager would be attributable to the segment's performance if that salary could be avoided by closing the division. However, the same salary cost would be excluded from evaluations of segment management if it is not controllable by the divisional manager.

There remains the problem of evaluating **common firm-wide costs** that are neither directly controllable by particular segments nor attributable to them. For example, corporate administrative salaries, property taxes, and depreciation on general purpose buildings and other plant assets are usually excluded from the measurement of segment performance because they do not satisfy the conditions of controllability and attributability and because, if included, they would have to be allocated arbitrarily among segments.

Against this is the argument that segments should not escape the burden of these common costs, which are incurred to provide shared facilities, services, and other resources. Segments are collectively responsible for earning a total profit contribution sufficient to allow the recovery of these costs.

A delicate balance between the two viewpoints must be preserved if common firm-wide costs are to be included in segment performance evaluation. Segment managers should be informed about the presence and amount of these common costs. However, they should be reported and interpreted separately from the controllable and attributable aspects of segment performance.

SEGMENT PERFORMANCE VERSUS SEGMENT MANAGEMENT PERFORMANCE

The distinction between *segment performance* and *segment management performance* is important in determining which costs and revenues are to be evaluated and also in interpreting and using the resulting evaluations. The major purpose of *segment* evaluation is to provide information about the segment's contributions to company objectives so that a decision can be made as to whether or not segment operations should be continued. During the evaluation, the decision maker is likely to compare the performance of different segments of the same firm, different firms, and even other industries.

Evaluation of *segment management* attempts to measure how efficiently each manager has discharged his duties within his sphere of segment authority. The basis for such managerial evaluation is largely internal and relates to the goals, budgets, and standards established for the particular segment management.

This contrast suggests that a universally applicable process of segment performance evaluation may not be possible. The various bases for segmentation, the divergent and potentially conflicting goals of different segments, and the variety of purposes for which evaluative information is needed, combine to prevent the use of uniform procedures.

PROFIT CENTER PERFORMANCE EVALUATION

The scope of evaluation will vary depending on whether the segment is treated as a **cost center,** a **profit center,** or an **investment center.** Cost center evaluation techniques include variance analysis used in flexible budgeting and standard cost systems, elementary job order systems, and process costing systems. These methods can be applied directly to the particular manufacturing department, product line, marketing function, or other segment. Because cost control and evaluation have been discussed extensively in Chapters 10–13, there will be no direct coverage of these techniques here, except to note that they can also be used in profit center and investment center evaluation.

Profit center evaluation requires an income statement approach. The conventional income statement format can be recast to highlight various subcategories of segment performance. A segmented income statement should begin with revenues, followed by costs arranged according to the criteria of variability, controllability, and attributability. The nine major subcategories that might appear in a segmented income statement are

1. Sales and Other Major Revenues
2. Controllable Variable Costs
3. Controllable Contribution Margin
4. Controllable Fixed Costs
5. Controllable Segment Margin
6. Attributable Segment Costs
7. Segment Profit Contribution
8. Common Firm-wide Costs
9. Segment Net Income

Sales and Other Major Revenues   Revenues earned by a particular segment are usually easy to identify and measure. This is the case when (1) the segment sells only to customers outside the company, (2) market transactions determine the amounts of sales revenues, and (3) the products or services sold by one segment are clearly distinguishable from those of other segments.

When any of these three conditions is not met, it may be difficult to objectively measure the amount of revenue controllable by or attributable to a segment. Transactions involving transfer prices between segments may cause problems, particularly if the segment has no sales outside the company. The transfer price problem is discussed later in this chapter.

To evaluate segment sales revenues, they must be compared with other performance measures, such as prior period sales of the same segment, sales volumes of comparable segments of the same firm, sales of other companies in the same industry, or the segment's predetermined, budgeted sales volumes. These comparisons may be made in terms of total dollar amounts, physical units, rates of change, or deviations from budgeted amounts.

Evaluation should not necessarily be limited to current period or short-run performance. For example, if the intent is to evaluate the continuing progress of the segment and its management, a single period's results should not be used to draw strong conclusions about the effectiveness of the segment's sales activities. Bunching sales in particular periods, pursuing increased sales volume without regard for credit risks, accepting rush orders that create production bottlenecks, and concentrating sales efforts on easy to sell but low contribution margin items are all practices that may produce superior short-run sales results. But in each case, once the countereffects begin to be felt, the longer-run results may be quite different. Therefore, short-run sales data should not be used indiscriminately as a basis for segment performance evaluation. Trend and comparative measures are more useful for this purpose.

Example: Ultan Company maintains budgetary control and performance measures on a segmented basis for its product line Divisions X and Y. The evaluation reports in Figures 19–1 and 19–2 show budgeted and actual sales figures for the month of May and for the year to date.

FIGURE 19–1

Ultan Company
Sales Analysis
Month of May, 19X9
(in thousands)

Product Line	Unit Sales			Sales Revenues				Sales Variances	
	Budget	Actual	Variance	Budget	Actual	Variance	Percent	Volume	Price
X	10	12	+2	$100	$120	$20F	+20%	$20F	–0–
Y	20	20	–0–	100	120	20F	+20%	—	$20F
Total				$200	$240	$40F	+20%	$20F	$20F

FIGURE 19–2

Ultan Company
Sales Analysis
Year to Date

Product Line	Budget	Actual	Variance	Percent
X	$500,000	$520,000	$20,000F	4%F
Y	500,000	460,000	40,000U	8%U
	$1,000,000	$980,000	$20,000U	4%U

Sales revenues from product line X exceeded the current month's budgeted expectations and cumulative goals. Product line Y performed exceptionally well during the current month, apparently because of a price increase, but its year-to-date performance is still below budgeted levels.

Controllable Variable Costs   All of the costs in this group are directly controllable by segment managers and vary according to the segment's activity levels. Items such as the segment's variable cost of goods sold (direct materials, direct labor, and variable overheads) and the segment's variable marketing and administrative costs are **controllable variable costs;** they can usually be measured objectively, except when transfer prices for interdivisional acquisitions are involved. The evaluation methods to be used include variance analysis based on flexible budgeting and standard costing systems, trend analysis, cost to sales ratio analysis, and comparisons with other segments.
Example: Ultan Company has established the following standard unit variable costs for its product line divisions:

$$X = \$4 \quad Y = \$12$$

FIGURE 19–3

Ultan Company
Analysis of Controllable Variable Costs
Month of May, 19X9

Product Line	A Original Budget at Budgeted Sales Volume	B Sales Forecast Related Variance	C Revised Budget at Actual Sales Volume	D Spending and Efficiency Variances	E Actual Costs Incurred
X	$40,000	$8,000U	$48,000	$6,000F	$42,000
Y	40,000	0	40,000	8,000U	48,000
Total	$80,000	$8,000U	$88,000	$2,000U	$90,000

To simplify this illustration, assume that these costs represent all manufacturing costs and that there were no beginning or ending inventories. Actual variable manufacturing costs during May were $42,000 and $48,000 for X and Y respectively. In the analysis of segment controllable variable costs shown in Figure 19–3, these budgeted and actual figures are compared.

Column D is the most important part of the analysis in Figure 19–3. It indicates whether or not variable costs have deviated from budgeted levels. In this case, product line X has a favorable variance and product line Y an unfavorable one. Column B indicates how the deviation of actual sales volume from forecast sales volume affects the expected amounts of segment controllable variable costs.

Controllable Contribution Margin   Sales revenues minus controllable variable costs equals segment **controllable contribution margin.** This contribution margin measures the profitability of a segment's sales. It can be used to evaluate the segment's ability to sustain itself and, beyond that, to provide a contribution to the costs of other segments, firm-wide common costs, and company profits. **Example:**   The two preceding analyses can be combined to produce Figure 19–4, a schedule of controllable contribution margins for product line Divisions X and Y.

Controllable Fixed Costs   Fixed costs of a period, incurred directly as a result of segment management's decisions, and related exclusively to resources consumed by the segment are **controllable fixed costs.** Examples include rental charges for equipment and property, executive salaries, and advertising costs—provided that these items meet the conditions of controllability and uniqueness of impact as previously specified. Interest costs that result from borrowing decisions made by segment managers should also be included in evaluating segment management's performance. However, the segment's operating results should be expressed on a before-interest basis because it is more reasonable to evaluate segment operating performance independently of the way in which the segment is financed.

FIGURE 19–4

Ultan Company
Controllable Contribution Margins
Month of May, 19X9
(in thousands)

	Product Line X			Product Line Y			Total		
	Budget	Actual	Variance	Budget	Actual	Variance	Budget	Actual	Variance
Sales	$100	$120	$20F	$100	$120	$20F	$200	$240	$40F
Controllable Variable Costs	40	42	2U	40	48	8U	80	90	10U
Controllable Contribution Margin	$ 60	$ 78	$18F	$ 60	$ 72	$12F	$120	$150	$30F
Contribution Margin Ratio	.60	.65	.05F	.60	.60	–0–	.60	.625	.025F

Controllable Segment Margin   The excess of a segment's controllable contribution margin over its controllable fixed costs is its **controllable segment margin.** Maximizing controllable segment margin is usually but not always a desirable objective. Undue emphasis should not be placed on ranking segments according to the size of their controllable segment margins. A firm's segments usually have too many dissimilarities in sales volumes, cost structures, and product types to make this type of comparison meaningful. Instead, the controllable segment margin should be compared to previous periods' results and to predetermined budgeted amounts, preferably through a flexible budgeting approach that recognizes the various patterns of revenue and cost behavior.

Attributable Segment Costs   Some costs incurred as a result of the existence and operations of a segment are not directly controllable by the segment's management. These **attributable segment costs** can also be defined to include all costs which are not controllable by segment management and which could have been avoided if the segment had been discontinued. They may include segment managers' salaries that were set by another management level, or depreciation, rent, and insurance on facilities used exclusively by the segment but acquired as a result of decisions made at higher management levels. Also in this category are interest charges on debt that was incurred specifically to support the segment's operations but which was authorized in a decision made outside the segment.

Although these costs are not directly controllable by segment managers, they are an important factor in overall segment performance and should be evaluated through comparison with the segment's budgeted amounts and with its prior period results.

Segment Profit Contribution   Deducting attributable segment costs from the controllable segment margin leaves an amount known as the **segment profit contribution.** All components of this measure are either controllable by segment managers or are directly attributable to segment activities. Variance analysis of flexible budgets, percentage analysis of individual costs and revenues, and trend and time period analyses can be used to evaluate the various components of segment profit contribution.

Measures of external performance are also appropriate in this evaluation. For example, it may be possible to make comparisons with industry or product line standards, if the segment is comparable to others and if the necessary data are available. However, maximizing a segment's short-run profit contribution should not become an overriding goal, nor should a ranking of segments on that basis necessarily be attempted, unless the earning power of different segments is truly comparable.

Example: Ultan Company's budgeted and actual controllable fixed costs and attributable segment costs for May are shown in Figure 19–5.

The information in Figure 19–5 on actual performance during May can be incorporated into the summary report of segment profit contribution shown in Figure 19–6.

Common Firm-wide Costs   Decentralized companies usually incur costs that cannot be traced *directly* to particular segments. Because such costs must be allocated arbitrarily, they should not be included in single period evaluations

Ultan Company
Controllable Fixed Costs and Attributable Segment Costs
May, 19X9
(in thousands)

	Product Line X			Product Line Y			Total		
	Budgeted	Actual	Variance	Budgeted	Actual	Variance	Budgeted	Actual	Variance
Controllable Fixed Costs	$10	$11	$1U	$10	$13	$3U	$20	$24	$4U
Attributable Segment Costs	$20	$22	$2U	$30	$32	$2U	$50	$54	$4U

FIGURE 19–6

Ultan Company
Segment Profit Contribution Statement
Month of May, 19X9

	Product Line X	Product Line Y	Total
Sales	$120,000	$120,000	$240,000
Less: Controllable Variable Costs	42,000	48,000	90,000
Controllable Contribution Margin............	$ 78,000	$ 72,000	$150,000
Less: Controllable Fixed Costs	12,000	12,000	24,000
Controllable Segment Margin	$ 66,000	$ 60,000	$126,000
Less: Attributable Segment Costs	22,000	32,000	54,000
Segment Profit Contribution	$ 44,000	$ 28,000	$ 72,000
Percentage of Sales	37%	23%	30%

of segments or their managements. This is why segment profit contribution, which is calculated before common firm-wide costs are allocated to segments, is usually considered a better measure of short-term segment performance than is segment net income. Segment profit contribution is also a primary indicator of the immediate effect on a firm of the addition or discontinuation of a segment, assuming such changes will not affect common firm-wide costs or the profit contributions of other segments.

However, if common firm-wide costs are *not* allocated, attention is not properly drawn to the need for each segment to contribute to the recovery of those costs. Ultimately, all costs must be covered by total segment revenues if the firm is to remain in business.

When common firm-wide costs are assigned to segments, it may be difficult to determine an appropriate basis for allocation and to avoid incorrect interpretations of the results. Depending on the allocation method chosen, a particular segment may be made to absorb larger or smaller amounts of firm-wide costs, quite independently of any actions taken by the segment manager. For example, assume that firm-wide costs are allocated on the basis of sales revenues and that the sales revenues of one segment remain constant while the sales revenues of all other segments decline. The segment with constant revenues must then bear a larger proportion of total firm-wide costs. Consequently, its performance will appear to have deteriorated when it actually did better than the other segments.

Care must also be taken to avoid drawing incorrect conclusions when firm-wide costs are allocated among segments. For example, if the amount allocated to a particular segment exceeds that segment's profit contribution, it is not necessarily correct to conclude that the segment is unprofitable and should therefore be abolished. In the short run, a segment justifies its existence when it generates a positive *controllable contribution margin,* regardless of its share of firm-wide costs. This assumes that all controllable fixed costs and attributable segment costs will remain unchanged in the short run. However, if these latter cost items are avoidable when the segment is discontinued, then the **segment profit contribution** is the appropriate indicator of the short-run feasibility of a segment's operations. Of course, in the long run, segments must collectively generate sufficient total profit contribution to allow the recovery of all firm-wide costs and the achievement of corporate profit goals. Consequently, it is often difficult to decide how much firm-wide cost each segment must bear in order to justify its long-run existence.

Segment Net Income   If firm-wide costs are arbitrarily allocated to segments, **segment net income** figures can be derived. However, such measures should be used judiciously for evaluation and decision making purposes, in view of the previously noted cautions regarding the allocation of firm-wide costs. Segment net income measures tend to give a false sense of conclusiveness. The apparent mathematical precision of fully allocated firm-wide costs and segment net incomes does not make these measures any more useful or accurate as tools for segment performance evaluation.

Example: The preferred treatment of Ultan Company's common firm-wide costs, with no allocation made to product lines X or Y, is shown in Figure 19–7.

Figure 19–8 shows the net income of each segment, with firm-wide costs allocated on the basis of segment sales revenues.

FIGURE 19–7

Ultan Company
Income Statement by Segments—Firm-wide Costs Unallocated
Month of May, 19X9

	Product Line X	Product Line Y	Total
Segment Profit Contribution	$44,000	$28,000	$72,000
Less: Common Firm-wide Costs			48,000
Corporate Net Income			$24,000

FIGURE 19–8

Ultan Company
Income Statement by Segments—Firm-wide Costs Allocated
Month of May, 19X9

	Product Line X	Product Line Y	Total
Segment Profit Contribution	$44,000	$28,000	$72,000
Less: Common Firm-wide Costs	24,000	24,000	48,000
Net Income	$20,000	$ 4,000	$24,000

The weakness of Figure 19–8 is that segment net income figures are too dependent on the method by which firm-wide costs are allocated to segments. The use of a different allocation basis (say, number of employees per segment) might completely alter the distribution of common firm-wide costs. For example, assume that product line Division X has 20 employees and product line Division Y has 40. If the allocation is made on an employees per segment basis, product line X will have to bear only $16,000 of the firm-wide costs (20 ÷ 60 × $48,000), whereas product line Y will have to absorb $32,000 (40 ÷ 60 × $48,000). This allocation changes the net income of product line Division Y to a *loss* of $4,000. However, it does not necessarily follow that Division Y is unprofitable. All that can be concluded is that Division Y was unable to generate sufficient profit contribution in relation to the firm-wide costs that were allocated to it on this particular basis.

USES OF PROFIT CENTER PERFORMANCE MEASURES

Profit center performance measures may be used (1) for evaluation and ranking of profit centers and (2) as a basis for decisions to modify operations of profit centers.

EVALUATION AND RANKING OF PROFIT CENTERS

Profit centers may be evaluated on the basis of their performance in relation to various types of profit goals. Typical criteria incorporated into profit center goals are controllable contribution margin, controllable segment margin, segment profit contribution, contribution margin ratio, segment profit contribution rate, and possibly segment net income. Evaluation procedures may involve assessing whether or not individual segments achieve their targeted objectives, or ranking the comparative performance of segments.

Example: Mighetto Company operates three product line divisions as profit centers. Quarterly bonuses are awarded to divisional managers according to rankings of segment profit contributions earned by their divisions. Figure 19–9 shows segment profit contributions for the quarter ended June 30, 19X3.

Based on their profit contributions, the three divisions would be ranked (1) Z, (2) X, and (3) Y. The negative segment contribution shown for Division Y indicates that division's inability to recover all of its fixed and attributable costs.

However, further analysis is needed before a decision can be made to continue or discontinue Division Y operations. For example, assume that all Division Y's direct fixed costs and attributable segment costs could be avoided by closing the division. Abolishing Division Y will then eliminate the $20,000 deficit now incurred by the division. But if, in the short run, more than $20,000 of Division Y's direct fixed costs and attributable segment costs are unavoidable, then management should allow the division to continue operating. Its closure would result in a deficit larger than the present $20,000.

Ranking Divisions X, Y, and Z according to their segment profit contributions might be unfair because of the dissimilarities among the three divisions. Figure

FIGURE 19–9

Mighetto Company
Segment Income Statement
For the Quarter Ended June 30, 19X3
(in thousands)

	Division X	Division Y	Division Z	Total
Sales	$300	$400	$500	$1,200
Less: Controllable Variable Costs	100	200	300	600
Controllable Contribution Margin...............	$200	$200	$200	$ 600
Less: Direct Fixed Costs	50	100	50	200
Controllable Segment Margin	$150	$100	$150	$400
Less: Attributable Segment Costs	70	120	40	230
Segment Profit Contribution....................	$ 80	$ (20)	$110	$170
Less: Firm-wide Costs				70
Corporate Net Income				$100

19–9 shows significant differences in sales volumes, contribution margin ratios, fixed costs, and attributable costs. The differences between actual and budgeted segment profit contributions might be a better basis for ranking these divisions.

Alternative Bases for Segment Analysis and Reporting   The same collection of company activities can be evaluated simultaneously on several different bases of segmentation. For example, a firm's profit performance might be analyzed according to product lines, sales territories, or wholesale or retail distribution channels, so long as these segments are consistent with the firm's operating structure. Similarly, multiple levels of segment evaluation can be performed at the same time, as when a major segment such as a sales territory is further analyzed on the basis of its component product lines or sales representatives.

Example: Mighetto Company divides its operations into Northern and Southern sales territories. Sales (in thousands) of the company's three product lines were distributed as follows:

Division	Northern	Southern	Total
X	$120	$180	$ 300
Y	200	200	400
Z	300	200	500
	$620	$580	$1,200

Each product line's contribution margin ratio is a constant amount (.667 for X, .5 for Y, and .4 for Z). Costs (in thousands) were directly identified with sales territories as follows:

	Northern	Southern	Total
Direct Fixed Costs	$50	$100	$150
Attributable Costs	$70	$120	$190

The remaining costs, totaling $160,000, must be classified as common firm-wide costs. Note that when the basis of segmentation is altered, the classification of many costs changes. Some items that were directly attributable or traceable to product line Divisions X, Y, or Z, are not directly traceable to either the Northern or Southern sales territories. In Figure 19–10, Mighetto Company's income statement is segmented on a sales territory basis.

Alternative Measures of Profit Center Performance   Various indicators are appropriate for analyzing profit center performance, depending on the purpose of the analysis and the time period involved. For short-run evaluation, assuming that direct fixed costs and attributable costs do not vary with changes in segment activity levels, *controllable contribution margin* is an appropriate measure. *Controllable segment margin* is a suitable measure of the longer-run use of resources by segment managers. *Segment profit contribution* is the preferred long-run measure of a segment's ability to sustain itself as a separate company sub-unit.

Profit centers should not be judged solely on their ability to maximize sales revenues. To do so may encourage the production and sale of products that generate higher sales revenues but smaller profit contributions than would otherwise be possible.

Example: Miller Company's president has instructed his divisional sales managers to maximize total sales revenues and to achieve certain specified divisional sales objectives. Alpha Division has been given a monthly sales goal of $100,000, with the product breakdown shown in Figure 19–11.

FIGURE 19–10

Mighetto Company
Segmented Income Statement
For the Quarter Ended June 30, 19X3
(in thousands)

	Northern Sales Territory	Southern Sales Territory	Total
Sales	$620	$580	$1,200
Less: Controllable Variable Costs	320	280	600
Controllable Contribution Margin	$300	$300	$ 600
Less: Direct Fixed Costs.............................	50	100	150
Controllable Segment Margin	$250	$200	$ 450
Less: Attributable Segment Costs......................	70	120	190
Segment Profit Contribution	$180	$ 80	$ 260
Less: Firm-wide Costs................................			160
Corporation Net Income			$ 100

FIGURE 19–11

Miller Company—Alpha Division
Budgeted Divisional Income Statement
For the Month Ended March 30, 19X4

	Product P	Product Q	Product R	Total
Sales	$25,000	$35,000	$40,000	$100,000
Less: Variable Costs	15,000	24,500	16,000	55,500
Contribution Margin	$10,000	$10,500	$24,000	$ 44,500
Contribution Margin Ratio	(.4)	(.3)	(.6)	(.445)
Less: Segment Direct Fixed Costs and Attributable Costs				24,500
Segment Profit Contribution				$ 20,000

As Figure 19–12 shows, Alpha Division's actual sales revenues exceeded the budgeted amount by $20,000. However, the divisional income statement revealed that the segment's profit contribution was only $19,500, $500 less than the budgeted amount.

The division's sales goal was exceeded, but in such a way as to reduce its segment profit contribution. This reduction was due to the shift in sales away from the more profitable line (Product R, with contribution margin ratio of .6) to the less profitable lines (Products P and Q, with contribution margin ratios of .4 and .3 respectively). The decline in the average contribution margin ratio from .445 (budgeted) to .3667 (actual) is further evidence that management's policy of maximizing sales revenues did not maximize segment contributions to company-wide profits.

FIGURE 19–12

Miller Company–Alpha Division
Actual Divisional Income Statement
For the Month Ended March 30, 19X4

	Product P	Product O	Product R	Total
Sales	$50,000	$60,000	$10,000	$120,000
Less: Variable Costs	30,000	42,000	4,000	76,000
Contribution Margin	$20,000	$18,000	$ 6,000	$ 44,000
Contribution Margin Ratio	(.4)	(.3)	(.6)	(.3667)
Less: Segment Direct Fixed Costs and Attributable Costs				24,500
Segment Profit Contribution				$ 19,500

DECISIONS TO MODIFY OPERATIONS OF PROFIT CENTERS

Decisions to modify profit center operations should take account of the *incremental effect* on overall company profits of proposed segment expansions, contractions, additions, or closings. In the immediate short run, assuming that all attributable segment costs are fixed, the effect of expanding or contracting a profit center's operations is usually limited to changes in its controllable contribution margin. From a longer-run viewpoint, changes in direct fixed costs and/or attributable segment costs may also have to be accounted for in deciding whether or not to expand or contract a profit center's operations. Analysis of segment profit contribution is usually the best basis for deciding whether or not to add or discontinue an entire segment, provided that the addition or closing does not affect common firm-wide costs or the profit performance of other segments.

Example: Boyd Corporation has experienced losses on product line 77 during the past year. The company's most recent product line income statement is shown in Figure 19–13.

Assuming that all attributable segment expenses are fixed, any decrease in sales of this product line will, in the short run, reduce income at the rate of 66 ⅔ percent of the amount of reduced sales revenue. This is the contribution margin ratio ($100,000 ÷ $150,000 = 66⅔%). However, if the product line is discontinued, there will be a $20,000 *decrease* in overall company income. This is the amount of segment profit contribution that will be lost as a result of closing out the product line, assuming that all direct fixed costs and attributable segment costs are avoidable. In this case, the allocated firm-wide costs will not be part of the incremental effect of discontinuing product line 77. They will continue to be incurred and will have to be absorbed by other divisions.

A more complex situation arises when the effects of discontinuing a segment include (1) changes in firm-wide costs, (2) the diversion to other divisions of some of the segment's direct fixed and/or attributable costs, and (3) changes in activity levels of other divisions.

FIGURE 19–13

Boyd Corporation
Product Line Income Statement
Product 77
For the Year Ended December 31, 19X8

Sales	$150,000
Less: Controllable Variable Costs	50,000
Controllable Contribution Margin	$100,000
Less: Direct Fixed Costs	45,000
Segment Contribution Margin	$ 55,000
Less: Attributable Segment Costs	35,000
Segment Profit Contribution	$ 20,000
Less: Allocated Firm-wide Costs	30,000
Net Loss	$ (10,000)

FIGURE 19–14

Boyd Corporation
Analysis of Proposed Discontinuance of Product Line 77

Loss of Controllable Contribution Margin (product line 77)		$100,000
Add: Loss of Contribution Margin (Product 66)		10,000
		$110,000
Less: Costs Avoided and Other Gains:		
Fixed Costs Avoided		
($45,000 − $15,000)	$30,000	
Attributable Segment Cost Avoided		
($35,000 − $10,000)	25,000	
Firm-wide Costs Decreased.	10,000	
Increased Contribution Margin (product line 55)	20,000	85,000
Net Loss Due to Discontinuing Product Line 77		$ 25,000

Suppose Boyd Corporation experiences the following additional effects from discontinuing product line 77:

1. Total firm-wide costs decrease $10,000.
2. Facilities and personnel now absorbing $15,000 of product line 77's direct fixed costs and $10,000 of its attributable segment costs are transferred for use in product line 55.
3. These transfers generate additional sales of $50,000 in product line 55, which has an average contribution margin ratio of 40 percent.
4. Product 66 complements product line 77. When product line 77 is discontinued, sales of Product 66, which has a contribution margin ratio of 25 percent, drop by $40,000. The other fixed costs of Product 66 are not affected.

Figure 19–14 shows the complete effect of discontinuing product line 77 under these circumstances.

The immediate effect of discontinuing product line 77 is a reduction of $25,000 per year in company-wide profits. Therefore, from a short-run viewpoint, product line 77 should not be eliminated. This type of decision situation can also be approached from a long-run point of view by evaluating the cumulative incremental effects on profits over a number of years. Moreover, as will be demonstrated in Chapter 20, capital budgeting techniques can be applied if the product line is treated as an investment center, because the discontinuation decision then becomes a long-run disinvestment decision.

TRANSFER PRICES
AND SEGMENT PERFORMANCE EVALUATION

Segment performance evaluation is affected by purchases and sales between segments that create a need for **transfer prices.** In Chapters 9 and 14, transfer pricing was discussed essentially as a problem of formulating decision rules to ensure that only rational intrafirm transfers are made. The **incremental cost,** including opportunity costs, of an intermediate product to the whole firm was shown to be the correct transfer price for short-run decision making. For long-run, continuing intrafirm transactions, the correct transfer price was shown to be the **full cost** of the intermediate product, including the opportunity cost of any profit lost as a result of the internal transaction.

However, these decision rules assume that complete information is available to all parties. This is not always possible, especially when the information required includes the effects of potential intrafirm transactions on company segments other than those directly involved in the transfer.

These decision rules sometimes produce results that are unfair or unacceptable to the segments involved. When a producing division had excess capacity, the short-run transfer price was shown to equal that division's variable cost. To use the producer's variable cost as the measure of both the acquiring division's costs and the producing division's revenues would (1) give the producing division no contribution margin and (2) give the acquiring division the full benefit of any cost savings resulting from the acquisition of the intermediate product from the firm's own division rather than from an external supplier.

Similarly, the transfer price sometimes included an opportunity cost element equal to the contribution margin lost in a third division due to the disruption of operations caused by the internal transfer. It may seem unreasonable to the acquiring division that it should have to reimburse the producing division for an imaginary transaction to which neither is directly a party. Even less equitable is the fact that, in this situation, the producing division rather than the third party division receives credit for the lost contribution margin.

These preliminary observations concern the problems involved in establishing a transfer pricing system for use in segment performance evaluation. Because such evaluations are often based on profit-related measures, conflicts arise as divisions try to obtain more favorable evaluations of their own performance. Transfer prices are not only the result of accounting calculations, but reflect power relationships among competing company segments. The acquiring division will want relatively low transfer prices, whereas the producing division will seek relatively high transfer prices.

Many solutions to this dilemma have been proposed. Each has merits as well as defects and limitations. The more important proposals will be examined here expressly in terms of their usefulness in segment performance evaluation, not as substitutes for the decision rule transfer prices discussed in Chapters 9 and 14. However, consideration will be given to a possible method for simultaneously solving both the decision making and evaluation problems.

CRITERIA FOR USING TRANSFER PRICING IN EVALUATION SYSTEMS

Three criteria will be used to determine the validity and acceptability of each transfer pricing proposal:

1. The transfer price should be objective and impartial and, to the extent possible, should simulate the conditions of an external, arms-length transaction.
2. The transfer price should reward the producing division and charge the

acquiring division commensurately with the value of the functions performed and/or the value of the products exchanged.

3. The transfer price should not encourage either division to act in a way that is inconsistent with company-wide objectives, but it should allow each division to act in accordance with the criteria applied in segment performance evaluation.

Six transfer pricing systems will be examined:

1. Market Based Prices
2. Cost Based Prices
3. Incremental Cost Based Prices
4. Negotiated Prices
5. Structured Prices
6. Dual (Two-Way) Prices

MARKET BASED PRICES

If an external market for the intermediate product exists, and if the buying and selling divisions have access to that market, the price in that market is an objective measure of the value of the product being exchanged. When the price is that of an equivalent product, it represents the amount the acquiring division would otherwise have to pay if it could not purchase internally. This price also represents the revenue that the producing division foregoes by engaging in the internal transaction.

Sometimes this market price must be adjusted to a net figure by deducting any marketing and administrative costs that are avoided as a result of the internal transaction. This is often referred to as a **market price minus rule,** because the transfer price reflects only those parts of the transaction that actually occur (production plus internal delivery).

Example: Alphonse Division of the Chevalier Corporation manufactures a part which it transfers to Gaston Division for inclusion in the firm's final product. The same product is sold by Alphonse Division to external customers for $20. Variable manufacturing costs are $10 per unit. The product costs $2 per unit to package and distribute when it is sold outside the firm.

Because Alphonse and Gaston are being evaluated as profit centers, the transfer price for internal transactions has been set at the *net market price* of the product transferred. This means that Alphonse receives credit at the rate of $18 per unit and Gaston is charged $18 per unit. This is the product's effective value—its $20 market price minus $2 for the costs of those portions of an external market transaction that do not occur.

If no external market exists for the intermediate product, a variation of this method involves deriving the product's *net realizable value.* This is done by working backward from the market price of the final product. A problem arises in deciding what to deduct from the end product's market price to arrive at its net realizable value. Possible deductions include (1) variable cost in the acquiring division, (2) full cost in the acquiring division, (3) variable cost plus a margin, and (4) full cost plus a margin.

Net realizable value can be supported on the grounds that it approximates the intermediate product's value at the transfer point. However, this method cannot assure a truly objective and independent result. As was just shown, there are alternative interpretations as to how much should be deducted to arrive at the net realizable amount. Also, the amount so deducted may be influenced by the costs incurred in the acquiring division. This favors the acquiring division, which is guaranteed some measure of cost recovery by this method.

Example: Reed Company has two divisions, Howard and James. Howard manufactures and sells a subassembly to James, which markets the completed product for $100 per unit. Annual volume is 10,000 units, with fixed costs of $100,000 in the Howard Division and $50,000 in James. Variable costs are $50 per unit for manufacturing by Howard and $25 per unit for assembly and finishing work performed by James. Management has specified margins of 60 percent on variable cost and 50 percent on full cost. Net realizable value of the subassembly under the four assumptions previously described is calculated in Figure 19–15.

Figure 19–16 demonstrates that each of these four interpretations of net realizable value has a different effect on the profit contributions reported for Howard and James Divisions.

Each division will tend to prefer transfer prices at one of the two extremes. Howard Division will opt for NRV_a, which maximizes its profit contribution, whereas James Division will prefer NRV_d for the same reason.

FIGURE 19–15

Reed Company
Four Interpretations of Net Realizable Value

(1) NRV_a = Final Sales Price − Variable Cost in Acquiring Division
   = $100 − $25
   = $75

(2) NRV_b = Final Sales Price − Full Cost in Acquiring Division
   $= \$100 - \left(\$25 + \dfrac{\$50,000}{10,000}\right)$
   = $100 − ($25 + $5)
   = $70

(3) NRV_c = Final Sales Price − Variable Cost in Acquiring Division − Margin
   = $100 − $25 − (60% × Variable Cost)
   = $100 − $25 − $15
   = $60

(4) NRV_d = Final Sales Price − Full Cost in Acquiring Division − Margin
   = $100 − $30 − (50% × Full Cost)
   = $100 − $30 − $15
   = $55

FIGURE 19–16

Reed Company
Segment Profit Contributions Using Alternative Transfer Prices

Howard Division—Segment Profit Contribution

	NRV_a	NRV_b	NRV_c	NRV_d
Sales	$750,000	$700,000	$600,000	$550,000
Less: Variable Cost	500,000	500,000	500,000	500,000
Contribution Margin.................	$250,000	$200,000	$100,000	$ 50,000
Less: Fixed Cost..................	100,000	100,000	100,000	100,000
Segment Profit Contribution	$150,000	$100,000	$ –0–	($ 50,000)

James Division—Segment Profit Contribution

	NRV_a	NRV_b	NRV_c	NRV_d
Sales	$1,000,000	$1,000,000	$1,000,000	$1,000,000
Less: Variable Cost (including internal transfer) ..	1,000,000	950,000	850,000	800,000
Contribution Margin	$ –0–	$ 50,000	$ 150,000	$ 200,000
Less: Fixed Cost	50,000	50,000	50,000	50,000
Segment Profit Contribution ...	($ 50,000)	$ –0–	$ 100,000	$ 150,000

COST BASED PRICES

When no market price exists for an intermediate product, the transfer price can be based on some measure of the *costs* incurred by the producing division. The implication is that production costs reflect the value of the intermediate product. Cost measures that have been used as transfer prices include variable cost, full cost, variable cost-plus, full cost-plus, standard cost, and incremental cost. Except for standard cost, all these are usually assumed to be actual rather than predetermined costs.

Variable Cost and Full Cost Based Prices   Variable cost and full cost transfer prices are measured as those terms are conventionally defined, with full cost including some allocation of the producing division's fixed costs. The variable **cost-plus** and full cost-plus measures include a margin, expressed either as an amount per unit transferred, or as a lump sum subsidy. In both cases the effect is to allow the producing division to receive some return over and above its variable or full costs.

The main deficiency of these cost methods is that the producing division is guaranteed reimbursement for its costs—and for more in the cost-plus situations. This is likely to be counterproductive to any company-wide efforts at overall performance improvement, especially if the producing division tends not to exercise appropriate cost control. At the same time, the acquiring division, because it is required to reimburse the producing division in this way, may be placed at a disadvantage. This will happen if the "plus" part of the transfer

---

FIGURE 19–17

Reed Company
Four Interpretations of Cost Based Transfer Prices

(1) TP_a = Variable Cost in Producing Division
= $50

(2) TP_b = Variable Cost Plus Margin
= $50 + (15\% \times$ Variable Cost)
= $57.50

(3) TP_c = Full Cost in Producing Division
= $50 + \left(\dfrac{\$100{,}000}{10{,}000}\right)$
= $60

(4) TP_d = Full Cost Plus Margin
= $60 + (10\% \times$ Full Cost)
= $66

---

price is so large that it gives the producing division too much of the profits that result from the combined activities of the two divisions. The logical response is to set the "plus" part of the transfer price at a level that permits an equitable distribution of profits.

There is also considerable leeway in determining the "cost" portion of the transfer price. Here also, the producing division has an advantage. For example, it can adopt costing procedures that allocate proportionally larger costs to products it sells internally under a cost-plus arrangement and away from products it sells externally. This is similar to the possible manipulation of cost data when external cost-reimbursable contracts are involved.

Example: Using the information from the Reed Company example and assuming margins of 15 percent on variable cost and 10 percent on full cost, variations of cost-based transfer prices can be derived as shown in Figure 19–17.

Considerable variations will occur in the profit contributions of the two divisions, depending on which type of cost based transfer price is adopted. Howard's profit contribution will be ($100,000), ($25,000), $0, or $60,000 respectively for the four prices considered in Figure 19–17. The corresponding results for James will be $200,000, $125,000, $100,000, and ($40,000).

Standard Cost Based Prices Predetermined standard costs can be used to overcome some of the inconsistencies and inequities of actual cost based transfer pricing systems. The main advantage of a standard cost based price is that it is a prespecified amount, which permits a fairer evaluation of performance. A transfer price equal to this preset standard cost may increase the producing division's incentive to control its costs, which is its chief method of improving performance. Revenue manipulation is not possible for a producing division, and recovery of actual production costs is not guaranteed when items are transferred at standard costs. Moreover, the acquiring division is no longer burdened by cost inefficiencies in the producing division, as it may be when actual cost based pricing systems are used.

Although in principle this is an attractive alternative, the obvious question is: How should the standard cost be established? In long-run situations, it should ideally represent the standard full cost of the intermediate product, with fixed costs allocated at a normal long-run activity level (plus possibly an equitable per unit amount of profit contribution allowed to the producing division). The determination of these amounts in practice clearly represents a considerable challenge.

INCREMENTAL COST BASED PRICES

When transfer prices are based on the incremental cost of the internal transfer to the whole firm, the acquiring division must absorb costs equal to the total company-wide effect of the intrafirm transaction. This might seem unjust to the producing division. It could force the producing division into a breakeven situation in the case where the transfer price is equal to the producing division's variable cost. Or, if the transfer price includes the lost profit contribution of a third division, the producing division could receive credit for an imaginary transaction to which it is only a third party.

Situation 1:

In a one-time transaction, Damian Division of Hess Company sells 1,000 units of the monthly output of its only product to Cheryl Division. These units were produced to make use of idle capacity in Damian Division, which can usually sell its total monthly output of 4,000 units to outside customers for $20 per unit. Damian's variable costs are $9 per unit for manufacturing and $4 per unit for marketing and administration. Damian's monthly fixed costs are $15,000.

The **incremental cost transfer price** for this one-time transaction is $9 per unit. This price represents only incremental manufacturing cost and assumes that variable marketing and administrative costs can be avoided. The transfer price is favorable to Cheryl Division, because the $9 purchase price is well below the external market price of $20. The loser from this transaction is Damian Division, which receives no contribution margin on the sale because its incremental cost will exactly offset its incremental revenue. In addition, its rate of return on sales will decline, because it will earn the same amount of profit but on an increased sales volume.

Situation 2:

Now assume that the same transaction occurs, except that the internal sale to Cheryl Division requires Damian Division to forego 1,000 units of its normal sales of 4,000 units to outside customers. The incremental cost transfer price is now $16 per unit, determined as follows:

$$\text{Variable Cost} + \text{Foregone Contribution Margin} =$$
$$\$9 + [\$20 - (\$9 + \$4)] = \$9 + \$7 = \$16$$

As demonstrated in Figure 19–18, this $16 per unit transfer price allows Damian Division to earn the same total profit contribution as it would have from a sale to outside customers.

FIGURE 19–18

Damian Division of Hess Company
Incremental Cost Based Transfer Prices

Original Segment Profit Contribution (outside sales only)
= Contribution Margin − Fixed Costs
= $4,000 \times (\$20 - \$13) - \$15,000$
= $\$28,000 - \$15,000$
= $\$13,000$

Revised Segment Profit Contribution (including internal transaction)
= Contribution Margin (external) + Contribution Margin (internal) − Fixed Costs
= $3,000 \times (\$20 - \$13) + 1,000 \times (\$16 - \$9) - \$15,000$
= $\$21,000 + \$7,000 - \$15,000$
= $\$13,000$

This $16 transfer price also seems fair to Cheryl Division, because it is below the external market price of $20.

Situation 3:

Finally, to introduce a more complex situation, assume that Cheryl Division has an alternate external supplier that usually buys some of its supplies for the product in question from Rufus Division, also part of Hess Company. Each unit sold by Rufus generates a contribution margin of $3, which will be included in total incremental cost if Cheryl decides to buy the product from Damian. The revised incremental cost is now $19 per unit, as determined in Figure 19–19.

FIGURE 19–19

Damian Division of Hess Company
Incremental Cost Based Transfer Price

Incremental Cost = Variable Cost + Lost Contribution Margins
= $\$9 + [\$20 - (\$9 + \$4)] + \$3$
= $\$9 + \$7 + \$3$
= $\$19$

This $19 per unit price still seems equitable from Cheryl's viewpoint because it reflects the transaction's incremental cost to the firm as a whole. However, Damian Division gets more than it deserves, because the sales revenues of $19 per unit with which it is credited include the $3 of contribution margin diverted from Rufus Division.

Situation 4:

As discussed in Chapter 14, long-run continuing relationships call for a revision of the decision making transfer pricing rule based on incremental costs. The structure of the pricing rule remains the same, but the *variable cost* component is replaced by *full cost per unit,* and the **lost contribution margin** component is replaced by a **lost profit contribution.**

In the Hess Company case, assume now that all 4,000 units of Damian Division's output are to be sold to Cheryl Division on a regular, continuing basis and that no outside sales are possible. The long-run transfer price for decision making is $12.75 per unit, as determined in Figure 19–20.

FIGURE 19–20

Damian Division of Hess Company
Long-run Incremental Cost Based Transfer Price

Transfer Price = Full Cost per Unit + Lost Profit Contribution per Unit

$$= [\text{Variable Cost per Unit} + \text{Fixed Cost per Unit}] + \text{Lost Profit Contribution per Unit}$$

$$= \left[\$9 + \frac{\$15,000}{4,000}\right] + 0$$

$$= [\$9 + \$3.75]$$

$$= \underline{\underline{\$12.75}}$$

When this price is used for performance evaluation, Damian Division breaks even, with total revenue exactly equal to total costs. Cheryl Division pays a transfer price which reflects the long-run incremental cost to the firm of having Damian produce the item and maintain the necessary fixed facilities.

If allocating Damian Division's capacity exclusively to production for Cheryl Division precludes potential outside sales of 4,000 units at $20, the decision making transfer price would be $15.25, as calculated in Figure 19–21.

In this case, Cheryl Division pays a $15.25 transfer price that includes the full production cost to Damian Division and to the whole firm as well as the potential profit from the outside sales. For these reasons, assuming that this transfer price is lower than the external market price, both Cheryl and Damian Divisions should be agreeable to this arrangement.

FIGURE 19–21

Damian Division of Hess Company
Long-run Incremental Cost Based Transfer Price

Transfer Price = Full Cost per Unit + Lost Profit Contribution per Unit

$$= \$12 + \left[\frac{(\$20 \times 4{,}000) - (\$13 \times 4{,}000) - \$15{,}000}{4{,}000}\right]$$

$$= \$12 + \left[\frac{\$80{,}000 - \$52{,}000 - \$15{,}000}{4{,}000}\right]$$

$$= \$12 + \$3.25$$

$$= \$15.25$$

NEGOTIATED PRICES

The idea of using predetermined standard cost-based transfer prices, together with the earlier observation that transfer prices should reflect arm's length transactions to simulate an external purchase and sale, suggest the possibility of setting transfer prices by a process of negotiation between company segments. Divisions might establish transfer prices following a procedure similar to that used in reaching agreement on price in dealings with an outside customer.

Such negotiations do not necessarily ensure fair or reasonable transfer prices. For example, differences in bargaining strengths and skills among divisional negotiators may result in a transfer price that does not properly reflect the intermediate product's real value.

It can be argued that there is nothing wrong with such an outcome. The ability to bargain and negotiate transactions is an aspect of managerial performance that should be reflected in any evaluation system, even if the other party involved happens to be another division of the same firm.

Example: Howard and James Divisions of Reed Company, introduced on page 977, agree to negotiate the transfer price at which Howard sells subassemblies to James.

Situation 1:

Both divisional managers, being reasonable and fair-minded, agree that the total profit contribution available from their combined production and sales activities should be shared equally. The transfer price so negotiated is determined in Figure 19–22.

Therefore, the transfer price must allow both Howard and James Divisions to earn a $50,000 segment profit contribution. Howard Division's transfer price is calculated as shown in Figure 19–23. James Division's share of profit contribution will also be $50,000, based on a $65 transfer price, as shown in Figure 19–24. A negotiated transfer price of $65 allows each division to show segment profit contribution of $50,000.

FIGURE 19–22

Howard and James Divisions of Reed Company
Negotiated Transfer Price—Profit Contribution Shared Equally

$$\text{Total Sales Revenue} = 10{,}000 \times \$100$$
$$= \$1{,}000{,}000$$

$$\text{Total Combined Segment Costs} = \text{Total Variable Costs} + \text{Total Fixed Costs}$$
$$= [(10{,}000 \times \$50) + (10{,}000 \times \$25)]$$
$$+ [\$100{,}000 + \$50{,}000]$$
$$= \$900{,}000$$

$$\text{Total Profit Contribution} = \$1{,}000{,}000 - \$900{,}000$$
$$= \$100{,}000$$

FIGURE 19–23

Howard Division of Reed Company
Determination of Negotiated Transfer Price
That Shares Segment Profit Contribution Equally

$$\text{Segment Profit Contribution} = \text{Revenue} - \text{Variable Cost} - \text{Fixed Cost}$$
$$\text{SPC}_H = \$50{,}000 = 10{,}000 \times \text{Transfer Price} - (10{,}000 \times \$50) - (\$100{,}000)$$
$$\$50{,}000 = 10{,}000 \times \text{Transfer Price} - \$600{,}000$$
$$10{,}000 \times \text{Transfer Price} = \$650{,}000$$
$$\text{Transfer Price} = \$65$$

FIGURE 19–24

James Division of Reed Company
Reconciliation of Segment Profit Contribution

$$\text{SPC}_J = (\$100 \times 10{,}000) - (\$25 \times 10{,}000) - (\$65 \times 10{,}000) - \$50{,}000$$
$$= \$1{,}000{,}000 - \$250{,}000 - \$650{,}000 - \$50{,}000$$
$$= \$50{,}000$$

Situation 2:

The manager of James Division exerts bargaining pressure during negotiations, threatening that unless the transfer price is set at $55 per unit, James Division will buy the subassembly from an outside supplier at that price.

If this threat (or bluff) is successful, the resulting transfer price will favor James Division. The total profit contribution of $100,000 will be credited to

James, and Howard Division will just break even. This is only one of many inequitable results that may occur if political or power pressures are applied during the price negotiation process.

For example, Howard Division may counter by refusing to sell to James Division at this $55 transfer price, thereby forcing James to seek an outside source of supply. If the outside price is above the $55 incremental cost to the firm of the internal transaction, Howard's action will be disadvantageous to James and to the whole firm. In addition, Howard Division then has the problem of finding an alternate use for its now idle resources. Depending on the contribution that can be obtained from the use of these resources, relative to the outside supply price now paid by James Division, this could be either favorable or unfavorable to Howard Division and/or the firm.

Situation 3:

There are other ways in which negotiated prices can lead to internal conflicts and suboptimal decisions, especially when later opportunities arise for external purchases and sales. This is the typical dilemma created by the need for transfer prices to serve two purposes—performance evaluation and decision making.

Assume that the "equitable" price of $65 per unit determined in situation 1 has been agreed to by both Howard and James Divisions. Subsequently, an offer is received from an outside firm to supply James Division with the same product for $55 per unit. If Howard Division insists on the previously negotiated price of $65, James will probably buy from the outside supplier at $55. This will be in James Division's best interest, because it increases their divisional profit contribution by $10 per unit purchased ($65 − $55). However, it is not in Howard Division's interest, nor would it be the correct action from the firm's short-run viewpoint. In the short run, the company stands to lose $5 ($55 outside price − $50 internal incremental cost) for each unit purchased from the independent supplier. Howard Division's profit contribution is reduced by $15 per unit, the amount of that division's potential contribution margin ($65 − $50).

From a long-run viewpoint, and assuming that there is no alternative use for Howard Division's resources that generates the fixed costs of $100,000, a prenegotiated transfer price of $65 per unit may cause the right thing to happen, but for the wrong reason! The correct transfer price for a long-run decision is $60—Howard Division's full unit cost ($50 + $100,000 ÷ 10,000), assuming the activity level remains at 10,000 units per year. Because James Division will tend to resist any transfer price above the external price of $55, it will probably reject the negotiated price of $65. An opposite situation arises if the external price is between $60 and $65, in which case James Division will still prefer to buy from an outside supplier. This would be an incorrect decision, because the $60 full cost to the whole firm is less than an outside purchase in the $60–65 range.

Refereed or Arbitrated Prices   This variation on negotiated prices requires company segments to submit proposed transfer prices to an arbitrator or referee (logically at some higher management level) who will then resolve any differences. The arbitrator's power to dictate prices may be an advantage, if he makes use of information concerning the company-wide impact of interseg-ment transactions. Alternatively, his power could be detrimental if he insists on prices that are unfair to one segment or the other.

A centrally and unilaterally determined and imposed price is the most ex-treme type of arbitrated transfer price. Although this procedure may lead to firm-wide optimal solutions, it will undermine the autonomy of segment managers, who will no longer be free to make such decisions.

A compromise solution might permit the arbitrator to set transfer prices, yet allow segment managers to react to those prices by making their own pur-chase and sale decisions. This approach could improve segment evaluations, if segments which made decisions contrary to the arbitrator's "master plan" were penalized by means of a variance analysis system based on his optimal solutions. Discipline might also be achieved through specific charges and credits applied to segments the managers of which took actions contrary or favorable to optimal company-wide solutions.

STRUCTURED PRICES

Transfer prices may also be calculated as two separate components, a fixed amount per period and a variable amount per unit of output transferred. These **structured prices** are most appropriate when the purchasing and selling divisions have a long-term, continuing relationship. The variable portion of the transfer price should be based on the incremental costs of the product being transferred. The fixed portion of the transfer price should be based on the capacity-related costs of the producing division. This procedure parallels the structured approach to the allocation of service department costs that was dem-onstrated in Chapters 3, 11, and 12.

Specifying two separate components of the transfer price does not solve the problem of determining how much each of these components should be. Moreover, it still must be decided whether each component should be an actual cost, a standard cost, or a cost-plus amount. In addition, whenever the producing division also sells to outside customers, an allocation of fixed costs must be made to determine the amount of fixed cost per period to be included in the transfer price.

DUAL (TWO-WAY) PRICES

All the preceding proposals assume that the same transfer price should be applied to both parties in an intrafirm transaction. However, it was noted that several of these solutions are more appropriate and acceptable for one division than for the other. Another possibility is to establish a **dual** or **two-way pricing** system for segment performance evaluation: The producing division receives credit at one price, but the acquiring division is charged at a different price. Such an arrangement would eliminate the potential conflict caused by a single transfer price, in which one division receives relatively less profit contri-bution because the price-setting process entitles the other division to receive relatively more.

The *acquiring division* should pay what it costs the firm as a whole to produce and distribute the intermediate product internally under normal conditions. The appropriate transfer prices are *incremental cost* in nonrecurring situations and *full standard cost* for long-run, continuous relationships. These prices reflect the effective cost of the resources consumed to the firm and to the division. Consequently, this is an appropriate basis for evaluating the performance of the user of those resources.

The *producing division* should receive the *market price* for the intermediate product, if this price can be established through reference to the price of an equivalent product. When no market price exists for an intermediate product, a negotiated price, based on the market price of the final product, should be used to approximate the net realizable value of the intermediate product. This price represents the best possible assessment of the intermediate product's exchange value.

When dual prices are adopted, segment profit measures will not reconcile with total company profits. This should not be a deterrent to the use of dual prices, because they are intended only for segment performance evaluation, not for decision making, where their use would obviously create confusion. A dual pricing system removes some of the interdependencies and conflicts that would otherwise be present in segment performance evaluation; it also permits a more objective assessment of segments as individual entities.

Example: Assume that Reed Company decides to adopt a dual pricing arrangement to resolve its transfer pricing problem. James Division is to be charged for the products it buys from Howard Division at a transfer price equal to Howard's full standard cost. This will be $50 of variable cost plus allocated fixed costs of $10 ($100,000 ÷ 10,000), for a total of $60. Howard Division will receive $75 credit, an amount equal to the prevailing market price for an equivalent product. Segment profit contributions will then be $150,000 for Howard Division and $100,000 for James Division.

THE TRANSFER PRICING SYSTEMS COMPARED

Each of these transfer pricing methods satisfies some, but not necessarily all, of the criteria for a valid system of performance evaluation. A transfer price should be

1. Objectively determinable.
2. Equivalent to the value of intermediate products being transferred.
3. Compatible with decision making that maximizes attainment of company goals and evaluation of segment performance.

Market price comes closest to satisfying all these criteria. It is an objectively determined price and, as such, reflects value exchanged. However, it depends on the existence of an accessible market for an equivalent product. Moreover, a transfer price exactly equal to market price implies that a segment will not care whether it deals with another segment or with an independent company. As was demonstrated, firm-wide suboptimal actions may result if segments respond to a transfer price equal to market price.

In general, *cost based prices* do not satisfy the criteria of impartiality and arm's length transactions. They are unilaterally determined and depend on the producing segment's incurrence and measurement of costs, as well as on the selection of any added margin (cost-plus). They are only substitutes for value exchanged, because they have no relationship to any external measure of value (that is, market price of the intermediate product). With the exception of incremental costs, they are no more likely to encourage better decision making than are the other transfer pricing methods. Incremental cost is demonstrably superior for short-run company-wide decision making purposes. However, it sometimes leads to conflict between the transfer pricing objectives of decision making and performance evaluation.

Negotiated prices simulate objectively determined prices. They also allow segments to act rationally and consistently with the criteria used to evaluate their performance. However, they are subject to the pressures and possible inequities of the negotiation process. They do not ensure a proper representation of value exchanged, nor do they guarantee that firm-wide optimal decisions will be made.

The use of *dual prices*—the compromise solution intended to "keep everyone happy"—sidesteps the issue of a universally useful and uniquely determinable price. Dual prices contradict the concept of divisional autonomy, because the existence of two prices for the same transaction suggests that the segments are not acting independently and that some "supervision" is present. In addition, duality of prices suggests that each party has a different idea of the intermediate product's value. The arm's length transaction requirement is also violated, because a single price is necessary in any exchange transaction between independent parties.

MISUSES AND LIMITATIONS OF TRANSFER PRICE SYSTEMS

The use of transfer pricing systems—and the accompanying treatment of segments as profit or investment centers—should be avoided if the segments involved lack the power to make independent decisions. When the divisions involved in intrafirm transactions have no access to alternative sources of supply or alternative outlets for their intermediate products, transfer prices serve no decision making purpose. There are simply no choices involving the intermediate product that can be made by either division.

Similarly, when external transactions are prohibited, only an artificial profit measure results from the use of transfer prices. The resulting contrived profit centers serve little purpose, except perhaps to create the impression that the center is contributing to profits rather than merely incurring costs. In situations such as this, when external market prices do not exist or are not pertinent, it is better to adopt a cost center approach. Preferably, a predetermined standard full cost should be charged to the acquiring division, just as would be done in a standard process costing system. A possible alternative for long-run situations is a standard variable cost that reflects the volume of actual intrafirm transactions plus a standard lump-sum subsidy to cover the fixed costs of the producing division.

SUMMARY

1. Company segments may be established for various managerial and operating purposes. Decentralization of decision making and/or physical activities is a particularly important reason for segmentation.

2. When decentralized units are treated as profit centers, profit-related performance measures must be developed for planning and control purposes, as well as to permit evaluations and comparisons to motivate management and to facilitate penalty–reward procedures.

3. The traditional income statement format can be recast to provide useful measures of profit center performance. The key categories in this revised income statement are (1) controllable contribution margin, (2) segment contribution margin, (3) segment profit contribution, and (4) segment net income.

4. Segment profit contribution is the best direct measure of profit performance attributable to and controllable by a segment. Segment net income may also be a useful measure because it focuses attention on a segment's long-run ability to contribute to company-wide profits.

5. Segment profit contribution and segment net income may be used for (1) evaluating segment performance in relation to predetermined objectives, (2) competitive ranking of segments, and (3) decisions relating to the expansion, contraction, addition, or discontinuation of segments.

6. Transfer prices often become a critical aspect of profit center performance evaluation. A dilemma is created by the need for transfer prices to serve two distinct purposes—decision making and performance evaluation. The transfer price that results in optimal firm-wide decisions will often be unacceptable to segment managers trying to achieve divisional profit goals. Conflicts may occur and suboptimal decisions may result if segment goals are allowed to dominate company-wide objectives. Certain of these conflicts can be avoided by not using a profit center approach when transfer price arrangements are forced on participating segments in an artificial context.

7. Alternative transfer prices for performance evaluation include market based prices, cost based prices, incremental cost based prices, negotiated prices, structured prices, and dual prices. All of these lack one or more of the desired transfer pricing criteria of (1) objectivity and impartiality, (2) equivalence to values exchanged, and (3) compatibility of decision making with firm-wide and segment goals.

8. The market price of a product that is equivalent to the intermediate product being transferred between segments is in most cases the preferred basis for segment performance evaluation, although it has limited value for decision making purposes.

KEY WORDS AND PHRASES

Questions

1. Define *decentralization.* Compare and contrast geographical decentralization with managerial decentralization.
2. List the main advantages of geographical decentralization and comment briefly on each.
3. List the main disadvantages of managerial decentralization and comment briefly on each.
4. Describe the purposes of evaluating the performance of the separate segments of a decentralized organization.
5. What aspects of the responsibility accounting concept are most directly applicable to the evaluation of segment performance?
6. Differentiate between the evaluation of segment performance and the evaluation of segment management performance. Why is this differentiation important?
7. Explain the appropriate conceptual basis for evaluating a profit center.
8. When should a decision center be treated as a profit center rather than as a cost center? Why?
9. List and briefly explain the nine suggested elements of profit center performance.
10. Differentiate between *controllable segment margin* and *segment profit contribution.* In what situations is each an appropriate performance measure?
11. What problems exist with regard to firm-wide, common costs when segments are treated and evaluated as profit centers? What alternative treatments are available?
12. What are the dangers of reporting allocated common firm-wide costs? What purpose (if any) is served by such allocations?
13. Why must profit centers be evaluated and/or ranked? What problems result when undue emphasis is placed on the comparison of segments' profit performance?
14. When comparing the profit performance of segments, what general principles should be observed?
15. Explain why an incremental approach is most useful in making decisions that involve possible modification of the operations of profit center segments.
16. What basic dilemma in profit center performance evaluation usually arises when a transfer pricing system is present?
17. Why are transfer prices that lead to correct (optimal) short- and/or long-run decisions not always useful for performance evaluation?
18. What three basic criteria must be satisfied by a transfer price system used for performance evaluation?
19. List the cost based transfer pricing systems suggested in this chapter and explain briefly their strengths and weaknesses for performance evaluation purposes.
20. Evaluate the proposed solution to intrafirm pricing offered by negotiated transfer prices.

21. What are the potential merits of a dual (two-way) transfer pricing system? What are its limitations?

22. "Transfer prices must always be equal to externally determined market prices of comparable products or services." Comment fully.

23. Do structured prices create more problems (allocation, and so on) than they solve? Discuss fully.

24. What is wrong with a refereed or arbitrated transfer pricing arrangement?

Exercises

E 19–1   Segment Profit Contribution Reporting—Elementary Analysis

Wheaton Corporation operates local and out-of-state sales divisions. The local sales staff is paid a fixed salary, whereas out-of-state sales are handled by various agents who are paid a commission based on total sales revenue. For 19X7, the following operating results were reported:

	Local	Out-of-State
Unit Sales	60,000	120,000
Sales Price (per unit)	$40	$45
Variable Manufacturing Cost (per unit)	$24	$25
Marketing Expenses:		
Fixed (per year)	$200,000	—
Variable (percent of sales)	—	10%

Total fixed manufacturing costs amount to $800,000 per year and relate to facilities used to manufacture products for both local and out-of-state markets. Administrative expenses of the firm's corporate headquarters amount to $1,200,000 per year.

Required:

(a) Prepare an income statement for the firm for 19X7, showing the separate profit contributions of the two market segments.

(b) Which market segment was the more profitable? Why?

(c) If output can be increased by 20,000 units without affecting any of the present unit or total costs, in which market segment should the company attempt to sell those units? Why?

(d) Discuss your treatment of (1) the fixed marketing expenses and (2) the fixed manufacturing and administrative costs.

E 19–2   Segment Profit Contribution Analysis

McGuigan Corporation has the following total operating results for 19X3:

Sales	$560,000
Less: Variable Costs	372,000
	$188,000
Less: Fixed Costs	100,000
Net Income	$ 88,000

The following additional information concerning the performance of each of the firm's three operating departments has been provided:

	Department X	Department Y	Department Z
Sales	$240,000	$200,000	$120,000
Contribution Margin Ratio	.3	.4	.3
Direct Fixed Costs	$ 32,000	$ 28,000	$ 20,000

Required:

(a) Prepare an income statement showing the profit contribution of the three separate departments.

(b) Comment on the relative profitability of the three departments.

(c) A proposal to increase advertising expenses by $10,000 is expected to generate a 10 percent increase in sales in all three departments. Analyze the effect of this proposal on the firm as a whole and on each department. Assume that the cost of the campaign will be allocated to divisions according to each division's percentage of total sales.

(d) Comment on the treatment of the $100,000 of fixed costs in parts (a), (b), and (c).

E 19–3   Profit Center Performance—Alternative Bases of Evaluation

The following is the partially completed income statement for Delphi Corporation for 19X3 (amounts in thousands):

	Foreign		Domestic		
	Product X	Product Y	Product X	Product Y	Total
Sales	$320	$280	$400	$600	$1,600
Variable Costs	160	112	200	240	712
	$160	$168	$200	$360	$ 888
Direct Fixed Costs	24	64	40	120	248

An additional $480,000 of costs still must be accounted for. Of this amount, $120,000 can be traced to domestic operations and $80,000 to foreign operations, but neither amount can be traced to Product X or Y. Moreover, amounts of $40,000 and $60,000 are associated with Products X and Y respectively, but cannot be directly associated with either of the market areas. The remaining $180,000 represents items that cannot be attributed to either the individual products or the separate market areas.

Required:

(a) Revise Delphi's income statement so that the information concerning the $480,000 of fixed costs is best reflected. (*Hint:* Prepare two separate reports.)

(b) Comment on the relative profitability of (1) the two products and (2) the two market areas.

(c) Discuss possible treatments of the $180,000 of common fixed costs. Should these costs be allocated to the products and/or the market areas for the purpose of segment performance analysis?

E 19-4   Segment Performance Analysis—Order Size and Sales Personnel

Sahara Company produces a single product which sells for $50 per unit. Variable manufacturing costs are $25 per unit and fixed manufacturing costs are $50,000 per month. Sales representatives are paid commissions based on the number of sales orders received and the dollar value of sales orders—$25 per order and 5 percent of sales revenue respectively. Other marketing and administrative costs include variable processing costs of $15 per sales order, $30,000 per month for fixed items, and variable items that amount to 5 percent of total sales revenue. For April of 19X1, the following operating results were reported:

Order Size	Sales Representative J Number of Orders	Sales	Sales Representative K Number of Orders	Sales
1–10 units	400	$100,000	500	$125,000
11–20 units	100	75,000	100	75,000
21–30 units	40	50,000	30	75,000
	540	$225,000	630	$275,000

Required:

(a) Prepare an analysis to compare and evaluate the performance of the two sales representatives.

(b) Prepare an analysis to evaluate the relative profitability of each of the three order size groups.

(c) Comment on the items (if any) that were excluded from your evaluation in parts (a) and (b).

(d) Comment on the advisability of the present sales commission arrangement. What actions might it encourage the sales representatives to take that might not be in the company's best interests? How could that situation be remedied?

E 19-5   Divisional Performance Measurement—Intrafirm Transactions— Elementary Analysis

Pud and Eid T.V. Sales and Repair Company has been in operation for one year, following its expansion from what was previously a repair and spare parts operation. The company's 19X2 income statement was as follows:

	Repairs	Sales	Total
Sales and Service Revenue	$ 600,000	$1,400,000	$2,000,000
Less: Variable Costs	450,000	560,000	1,010,000
Contribution Margin	$ 150,000	$ 840,000	$ 990,000
Less: Direct Fixed Costs	100,000	280,000	380,000
	$ 50,000	$ 560,000	$ 610,000
Less: Common Fixed Costs	205,000	205,000	410,000
Net Income (loss)	$(155,000)	$ 355,000	$ 200,000

Prior to the addition of the sales division, the repairs and spare parts operation was quite profitable. The manager of the Repair Department is particularly upset because of two factors. First, she is upset about the arbitrary division of common fixed costs on a 50/50 basis. These costs relate to general management and space occupancy and resulted from the addition of the Sales Division. Second, her division received no credit for work done on new sets sold by the company and covered by the company's sales promise, "We fix it free within the first year!"

The Repair Division manager believes she should receive credit for this work on the same basis as repair work is billed to regular customers. This is done at the rate of variable costs plus 100 percent. However, the Sales Division manager argues that he is not prepared to accept any charges in excess of the actual variable cost of work done on sets sold carrying the sales promise of free repairs. However, the sales manager does agree that the allocation of the common costs is arbitrary and should be discontinued.

Required:
(a) Determine the variable cost of work done by the Repair Division on sets sold by the Sales Division.

(b) Prepare an income statement based on the Sales Division manager's claims.

(c) Prepare an income statement based on the Repair Division manager's requests.

(d) Which (if either) of the income statements in parts (b) or (c) would you recommend for performance evaluation purposes? Why?

E 19–6   Transfer Pricing and Divisional Performance Reporting— Decision Making and Reporting Conflicts

All of the operating and service departments of Miekno Company are considered profit centers for planning and performance evaluation purposes. The manager of one department has proposed some changes for its production operations that will cost $2 per unit for additional direct variable overhead costs. This department usually produces 8,000 units per month. However, the change will allow this department to reduce its use of the services of the firm's power plant (another profit center) by one-half hour per unit produced. Costs in the power plant are presently $96,000 per month for fixed items and $3 per hour for variable items. The power plant had previously been authorized to charge $5 per hour for its services, and is presently operating at 48,000 hours per month. The $5 per hour rate was chosen because it approximates what user departments would have to pay outside suppliers of the same services.

Required:
(a) Analyze the proposal from the viewpoints of the following personnel: (1) the product line manager, (2) the power plant manager, and (3) the manager of the firm. What problem do you see?

(b) How does the present transfer pricing arrangement affect departmental planning decisions of the type involved here?

(c) How does the present transfer pricing arrangement affect departmental performance evaluations?

(d) How can the conflicts in parts (a), (b), and (c) be resolved? Would the use of the generalized transfer pricing rules outlined in Chapters 9, 14 and 19 be of any help? Why or why not?

E 19–7   Transfer Pricing—Divisional Performance Evaluation Analysis

Still Appliance Corporation is a multidivision operation in which each division is established as a profit center for planning and performance evaluation purposes. A problem has arisen with respect to the Electric Motor and the Washing Machine Divisions. In the past, the Washing Machine Division has acquired 6,000 motors per month for its products from the Motor Division at a price of $90 per unit. An alternate supplier has offered to supply a similar motor for $85 per unit, which is $10 below the regular market price of $95. The low price is being offered due to the potentially large number of motors that Still Corporation might purchase. Still's Motor Division also sells some of its motors for $100 to customers in the external market and has a monthly capacity of 10,000 motors.

An analysis of the costs incurred directly by the Electric Motor Division of Still Corporation follows:

Variable Costs per Unit:

Direct Materials	$30
Direct Labor	20
Variable Overhead	10
Variable Marketing Costs	10
	$70

Monthly Fixed Costs:

Overhead	$100,000
Administration	50,000

Required:

(1) Assume that sales by the Motor Division to outside customers total 4,000 per month. What transfer price would allow each division to make the correct decision as to the source of supply of the motors for the Washing Machine Division, (1) in the short run and (2) in the long run?

(b) What problems would be likely to arise in reporting the profit contribution results of the two divisions based on the price(s) specified in part (a)? How would you attempt to resolve them?

(c) Assuming that the sales of motors to outside customers are (1) zero units per month and (2) 10,000 units per month, what are the correct short-run and long-run transfer prices in these situations?

E 19–8   Divisional Performance Evaluation—Profit Centers or Cost Centers?

Gallego Corporation must decide whether to operate some of its divisions as cost centers or as profit centers. Of particular concern are the firm's electric power generating plant and its fleet of delivery trucks operated by the Transportation Division. The only users of the services of these two divisions are other departments of the corporation. For 19X3, the following *budgeted* information applied to the two divisions:

	Power Plant	Transportation
Total Fixed Costs	$ 360,000	$ 480,000
Total Variable Costs	900,000	320,000
	$1,260,000	$ 800,000
Total Estimated Mileage	N/A	2,000,000
Total Estimated Kilowatt Hours Needed	6,000,000	N/A
Total Capacity Available (kilowatt hours)	9,000,000	N/A

For 19X4, the following *actual* results pertaining to the two departments were reported:

	Power Plant	Transportation
Total Fixed Costs	$ 350,000	$ 500,000
Total Variable Costs	1,120,000	270,000
	$1,470,000	$ 770,000
Power Usage (kilowatt hours)	7,000,000	N/A
Mileage Driven	N/A	1,800,000

The cost of electricity from the local utility company was 24¢ per kilowatt hour during 19X3. Also, a local truck rental firm was charging 40¢ per mile for the use of trucks similar to those owned by the firm.

Required:
(a) Prepare an analysis of the performance of the two divisions of the firm, treating them as cost centers. Compute all relevant cost variables.
(b) Prepare an analysis of the performance of the two divisions of the firm, treating them as profit centers and using transfer prices equal to competitive market prices for their services.
(c) Comment on the problems that may be involved in implementing part (b).
(d) Should the centers be treated as cost or profit centers? Why? Discuss fully.

Cases

C 19-1   Segment Revenue and Cost Allocations

The general manager of a large diversified corporation is concerned with the need for reports that reflect the profit performance of each principal segment or line of activity. His suggestion is to develop a system wherein *all* revenue and cost items will be allocated to each territorial sales division *and* to each product line.

Discuss the problems that are likely to arise in implementing a system of this nature. What purpose (if any) would such a system serve?

C 19-2   Profit Centers

It has been suggested that each production and service department of XYZ Company be operated as a profit center. Included in the departments under consideration for such treatment are (1) legal services, (2) computer center, (3) buildings and grounds, (4) machining, and (5) production scheduling.

Discuss the techniques and procedures necessary to implement such a system. Comment on the advisability of treating these five departments as profit centers.

C 19-3   Segment Profit Maximization

A proposal has been made that all divisional managers of product line operations of Diversified Conglomerate International, Inc. be instructed to maximize the profits of each of their individual divisions.

Comment on the advantages and disadvantages of this proposal, from (1) management's viewpoint and (2) the viewpoint of the Controller's Department.

C 19–4   Segment Profit Contribution

"Evaluation of the profit contribution made by segments of a firm is no easy task."

Evaluate this statement. Discuss especially the problems of choosing an appropriate basis of evaluation. Discuss some of the alternative bases of evaluation, as well as the identification, classification and measurement problems involved.

C 19–5   Transfer Prices

A special problem in transfer pricing exists when the costs of the producing department are largely fixed in nature.

Discuss this issue from the point of view of transfer prices for (1) decision making and (2) divisional performance evaluation. Comment on both short-run (one-time) and long-run (continuous) situations.

Problems

P 19–1   Segment Profit Performance Analysis

Zick Company reports the following income for 19X7:

	Division I	Division II	Total
Sales	$160,000	$220,000	$380,000
Less: Variable Costs:			
Manufacturing	$ 64,000	$110,000	$174,000
Other	8,000	11,000	19,000
	$ 72,000	$121,000	$193,000
Contribution Margin	$ 88,000	$ 99,000	$187,000
Less: Direct Fixed Costs	30,000	40,000	70,000
Segment Profit Contribution	$ 58,000	$ 59,000	$117,000
Less: Common Fixed Costs			50,000
Net Income			$ 67,000

Division II sells three products, A, B, and C, for which the following analysis has been made:

	A	B	C
Sales	$80,000	$80,000	$60,000
Contribution Margin Ratio	.35	.55	.45
Direct Fixed Costs	$10,000	$10,000	$10,000

Division II sells Product A in both a local and a regional market, for which the following analysis is available:

	Regional	Local	Total
Sales.........................	$20,000	$60,000	$80,000
Contribution Margin Ratio	.26	.38	.35
Direct Fixed Costs	$ 4,000	$ 4,000	$ 5,000
Common Divisional Fixed Costs			$ 2,000

Required:

(a) Prepare a segmented income statement for Division II showing profit contribution by product lines. Do not allocate *corporate* common fixed costs.

(b) Prepare a segmented income statement for Product A, showing profit contribution by market areas. Do not allocate *corporate* common fixed costs.

(c) Comment on the common fixed costs in parts (a) and (b).

(d) An advertising campaign costing $2,000 has been proposed for Product A. If it is placed in the local market, sales of A will increase by $6,000. If it is placed in the regional market, sales of A will increase by $7,000. Where should the campaign be placed? Why? Assume that other fixed costs will be unaffected by the increased volume.

P 19-2 Segment Profit Performance Analysis

Concordia Company operates in three sales territories—north, south and central—selling Products X, Y and Z. For 19X2, the following results were obtained:

	X	Y	Z	Total
Unit Sales............................	40,000	80,000	60,000	180,000
Sales Price per Unit	$30	$24	$15	N/A
Variable Cost per Unit	$18	$18	$11	N/A
Product Line Supervision*	$96,000	$112,000	$80,000	$288,000
Depreciation—Production Equipment**	$24,000	$ 32,000	$16,000	$ 72,000
Manufacturing Overhead	—	—	—	$ 80,000
Administrative Cost......................	—	—	—	$100,000
Fixed Marketing Cost	—	—	—	$240,000

* A direct fixed cost.
** An attributable segment cost.

Further analysis of sales performance and traceable expenses in the three territories showed the following:

	North	South	Central	Total
Sales Distribution:				
Product X	40%	10%	50%	100%
Product Y	40%	20%	40%	100%
Product Z	20%	60%	20%	100%
Traceable Fixed Costs:				
Manufacturing Overhead				
and Administrative Costs.....	$40,000	$ 80,000	$40,000	$160,000
Marketing Costs	$56,000	$120,000	$64,000	$240,000

Required:

(a) Prepare a segmented income statement on a product line basis.

(b) Prepare a segmented income statement on a territorial basis.

(c) Comment on the relative profitability of (1) sales territories and (2) product lines.

(d) Comment on the treatment of fixed costs throughout parts (a), (b), and (c).

(e) Should the common nontraceable fixed costs be allocated to product lines or territories on some arbitrary basis? What purposes would be served, and/or what problems would be created by such allocations?

P 19–3   Segment Performance Reporting—Alternative Reporting Bases

Weiner Distributing Corporation had the following income statement prepared for 19X4:

	Retail	Wholesale	Total
Sales (units).......................	300,000	250,000	550,000
Sales (dollars)	$1,500,000	$1,000,000	$2,500,000
Less: Cost of Goods Sold............	$1,000,000	$ 800,000	$1,800,000
Sales Commissions	150,000	100,000	250,000
Managers' Salaries	20,000	20,000	40,000
Advertising	15,000	10,000	25,000
Other Marketing Expenses......	80,000	40,000	120,000
Administrative Expenses........	30,000	20,000	50,000
	$1,295,000	$ 990,000	$2,285,000
Net Income	$ 205,000	$ 10,000	$ 215,000

In preparing the preceding statement, the following relationships and allocations were observed:

(1) The same product is sold by both divisions, but prices in the wholesale division are 20 percent below those in the retail division.

(2) Cost of sales is a variable cost, because the company buys directly from manufacturers.

(3) Sales commissions are based on sales revenue.

(4) Each division has a manager on a fixed salary.

(5) Advertising has been allocated on the basis of sales revenues and consists mainly of newspaper and radio advertisements.

(6) Other marketing expenses are largely order filling, delivery, and credit checking expenses. These were allocated on the basis of the number of sales orders processed. However, a large proportion of these items are fixed expenses.

(7) Administrative expenses are all fixed items and represent general firm-wide management expenses.

Required:

(a) Comment critically on the basis of allocation for each expense item in the income statement.

(b) Revise the statement in order to provide more useful information concerning the performance of the two divisions as separate areas of responsibility.

(c) Comment on the dilemma that is posed in this problem—that is, to allocate or not to allocate.

P 19–4   Segment Performance Reporting

The following divisional income statement was prepared by the new assistant controller of Leyland Corporation:

Sales—Capacitors	$800,000	
Sales—Transistors	850,000	$1,650,000
Labor and Materials Costs:		
Materials—Transistors	$175,000	
Labor—Transistors ($10 per hour)	300,000	
Labor—Capacitors ($10 per hour)	200,000	
Materials—Capacitors	150,000	825,000
Permanent Fixed Costs:		
Transistor Division—Depreciation......	$ 85,000	
Depreciation—Capacitors	215,000	300,000
Capacitor Division:		
Supervision.........................	$ 20,000	
Advertising	15,000	
Administration	15,000	
Other Factory Overhead	120,000	170,000
Transistor Division:		
Supervision.........................	$ 25,000	
Advertising	15,000	
Administration	15,000	
Other Factory Overhead	120,000	75,000
Net Income		$ 180,000

Management was dissatisfied with this report because they were aware of the following additional information:

(1) Production facilities are shared. Special purpose equipment for the Capacitor Division accounted for depreciation of $130,000. Other depreciation was on general purpose equipment shared by both divisions.

(2) Each division has its own supervisor.

(3) Advertising expenses are for the firm's entire product line.

(4) Administrative expenses are for the central administrative office.

(5) Factory overhead items are largely labor-related.

Required:
(a) Comment critically on the statement as originally prepared, both in terms of form and content.

(b) Prepare a revised report that better reflects the separate performance of the two divisions.

(c) Discuss the problems involved in assessing the profit performance of divisions that share the same facilities.

P 19–5 Product Line Profitability Analysis

Hefner Doll Company has a product line consisting of four models: Farah, Bo, Cheryl, and Suzanne. The following analysis of sales prices, gross margins, and cost of goods sold has been prepared on a per unit basis:

	Farah	Bo	Cheryl	Suzanne
Sales Price	$32.00	$24.00	$20.00	$15.00
Cost of Goods Sold:				
Materials	$ 8.00	$ 5.50	$ 4.00	$ 5.00
Labor	8.00	7.00	6.00	3.00
Overhead	4.00	3.50	3.00	1.50
	$20.00	$16.00	$13.00	$ 9.50
Gross Margin	$12.00	$ 8.00	$ 7.00	$ 5.50

The standard direct labor rate is $10 per hour and overhead is applied to products on a labor hours basis, assuming an annual capacity of 100,000 direct labor hours. Fixed manufacturing costs relating to facilities used to produce all dolls amount to $400,000 per year. The plant has operated consistently at close to the 100,000-hour annual level and sales volume has kept pace with this amount of production. Sales analysis shows that Farah and Bo are the best sellers by far and the sales staff acknowledges that it has been concentrating its efforts on these two because of their higher gross margins. Because sales commissions are paid at the rate of 15 percent of sales revenue, it is clear that the sales staff is not anxious to push the Cheryl and Suzanne dolls. Apart from commissions, all other sales and administrative costs are fixed and amount to $450,000 annually. Sales volume in the past year, 19X2, was distributed as follows: Farah, 55,000 units; Bo, 50,000 units; Cheryl, 25,000 units; and Suzanne, 20,000 units.

Required:
(a) Prepare a product line profit report for 19X2 using a conventional format (sales—cost of goods sold—gross profit—operating expenses—net income). Allocate fixed sales and administrative costs on the basis of sales volume (in units).
(b) Prepare a revised product line profit report for 19X2, stressing controllable aspects of product line performance.
(c) Compare the results in parts (a) and (b).
(d) Which of the four dolls is the *most profitable?* Why? Show all supporting figures and state any assumptions made.
(e) What steps could be taken to improve overall profitability of the firm's product line?

P 19–6 Profit Center Performance Analysis—Budgeted versus Actual Performance

Maxwell Corporation's two sales divisions are treated as separate profit centers. For 19X3, the following *budgeted* income statements were prepared:

	Western Division	Eastern Division	Total
Sales	$800,000	$600,000	$1,400,000
Less: Variable Manufacturing Costs	$160,000	$120,000	$ 280,000
Fixed Manufacturing Costs	200,000	150,000	350,000
Sales Commissions	80,000	60,000	140,000
Sales Promotions	40,000	30,000	70,000
Other Marketing Costs	80,000	60,000	140,000
Divisional Administration	25,000	25,000	50,000
Central Administration	160,000	120,000	280,000
	$745,000	$565,000	$1,310,000
Net Income	$ 55,000	$ 35,000	$ 90,000

Divisional budgets were based on the following relationships and allocations:

(1)   The two divisions sell the same product, which is manufactured in a single production facility.

(2)   Fixed manufacturing costs are divided between the two divisions on the basis of budgeted sales volume.

(3)   Sales commissions are paid as a percentage of sales revenue.

(4)   Sales promotion expenses are exclusively related to a nation-wide campaign administered by the company's headquarters and intended to promote the firm's total image and product line.

(5)   Other marketing costs are largely order filling costs; $105,000 of their total amount is fixed in nature. These costs, along with promotional costs, are allocated on the basis of budgeted divisional sales revenues.

(6)   Each division has its own general management staff and facility.

(7)   The headquarter's administration incurs costs that are allocated on the basis of budgeted sales revenues of the divisions.

In 19X3, the following actual results were reported, based on the same relationships and allocations as were used in the budget:

	Western Division	Eastern Division	Total
Sales	$1,000,000	$500,000	$1,500,000
Less: Variable Manufacturing Costs	$ 200,000	$100,000	$ 300,000
Fixed Manufacturing Costs	233,333	116,667	350,000
Sales Commissions	100,000	50,000	150,000
Sales Promotions	46,667	23,333	70,000
Other Marketing Costs	95,000	47,500	142,500
Divisional Administration	25,000	25,000	50,000
General Administration	186,667	93,333	280,000
	$ 886,667	$455,833	$1,342,500
Net Income	$ 113,333	$ 44,167	$ 157,500

The manager of the Western Division was pleasantly surprised (profits up 106 percent, whereas sales were up only 25 percent). The general manager and the manager of the Eastern Division were somewhat puzzled by some of the results as reported (sales down 16.7 percent, profits up 26.2 percent).

Required:

(a) Comment on the appropriateness of the type of divisional income statement used for budgetary and performance evaluation purposes. Especially, comment on the allocations of costs to the divisions.

(b) How did the Eastern Division manage to increase its reported net income, even though its sales were decreasing?

(c) Prepare a revised set of statements, budgeted and actual, that will be more useful in projecting and evaluating divisional profit performance in this case.

(d) Explain the rationale behind the proposal in part (c).

(e) Based on part (c), comment on the relative performance of the two profit centers.

P 19–7   Profit Center Performance Reports—Budgetary Control and Performance Evaluation

Stilwell Corporation treats its two sales divisions, local and out-of-state, as profit centers. For 19X7, the *budgeted* income statement for the firm was as follows:

	Local	Out of State	Total
Sales	$100,000	$80,000	$180,000
Less: Cost of Goods Sold	$ 50,000	$40,000	$ 90,000
Commissions	8,000	6,400	14,400
Advertising	11,000	9,000	20,000
Administration	21,500	19,000	40,500
	$ 90,500	$74,400	$164,900
Net Income	$ 9,500	$ 5,600	$ 15,100

In 19X7, *actual* results were as follows:

	Local	Out of State	Total
Sales	$116,000	$64,000	$180,000
Less: Cost of Goods Sold	$ 58,000	$32,000	$ 90,000
Commissions	9,280	5,120	14,400
Advertising	13,600	6,400	20,000
Administrative	25,320	15,180	40,500
	$106,200	$58,700	$164,900
Net Income	$ 9,800	$ 5,300	$ 15,100

The following information is also available:

(1) Sales division managers have control over all variable items included in their budgets.

(2) Fixed advertising and administrative expenses are allocated equally between the two divisions. There was no variation in the total amount of these expenses this year.

Required:

(a) Prepare a revised product line profit report, emphasizing controllable items of product line performance. Include both budgeted and actual figures.

(b) Comment on the deficiencies of the original report.

(c) Which product line was more profitable in 19X7? Why?

P 19–8 Divisional Performance Reporting—Performance Evaluation— Profit Centers or Cost Centers

Part A: Garvey Company operates its own power plant. During 19X3 it generated 12,000,000 kilowatt hours of electricity for user departments. Total operating costs were

Direct Variable Production Costs......	$ 720,000
Direct Fixed Production Costs	1,800,000
Allocated Firm-wide Costs	600,000
	$3,120,000

The power plant has been treated as a cost center and its cost performance compared to budgeted amounts. The utility company that supplies electricity in the area charges 22¢ per kilowatt hour.

Required:

(a) Evaluate the power plant as a profit center. Comment on the results.

(b) Would you recommend that the power plant be evaluated as a cost center or profit center? Discuss fully and state any important assumptions needed.

Part B: Valenzuela Corporation maintains a fleet of 40 delivery trucks. For 19X3, budgeted operating expenses were 36¢ per mile of operations plus $240,000 for fixed maintenance, insurance, and other costs (including depreciation of $180,000). During 19X6, total mileage amounted to an average of 25,000 miles per truck. Actual costs were $372,500 for operating costs and $265,000 for fixed costs. A nation-wide rental organization charges $180 per truck per month and 50¢ per mile for similar trucks.

Required:

(a) Prepare an analysis to evaluate the delivery truck fleet operation as a cost center.

(b) Prepare an analysis to evaluate the delivery truck fleet operation as a profit center.

(c) Which basis of evaluation do you prefer? Why? What assumptions were needed or what extra information would be useful in this situation?

P 19–9 Divisional Performance Measurement and Evaluation—Transfer Pricing Situations—Three Division Involvement

Agee Corporation has several divisions that operate as autonomous profit centers. Three of these are Divisions X, Y, and Z. Division X is presently considering the acquisition of components needed to complete an order. The items can be produced by Division Y, but outside bids were also solicited.

Division Y submits a suggested price of $10 per unit for the 10,000 units required. This price is equal to Division Y's full unit cost to produce the component. Division Y is presently operating at 75 percent capacity per month with total monthly fixed costs of $160,000. This order would allow Division Y to achieve full operating capacity. Its other present output requires proportionally the same use of fixed facilities per unit as the order being considered.

Two other corporations also submit bids: Blumenthal Corporation for $8 per unit and Lanny Corporation for $8.50. Blumenthal is a completely independent company. Lanny, on the other hand, deals with Division Z of Agee Corporation. Division Z will supply Lanny with materials that will be used in the component Lanny proposes to supply to Division X. Division Z charges $2 per unit for this item, a price which will include a contribution margin of 40 percent.

Required:

(a) As manager of *Division X,* which bid should be accepted, given that each division is expected to maximize its own contribution to corporate profit? Show calculations.

(b) Would this decision be correct from the viewpoint of the firm as a whole? Why or why not?

(c) What transfer price(s) on the part of Division Y will allow the correct decisions to be made by all divisions independently?

(d) Evaluate the impact of this price on the performance reports of the various divisions, assuming that Division X decides to buy from Division Y.

(e) What problem is inherent to the conflict suggested in parts (c) and (d)? How might it be resolved?

(f) Comment on the preceding situation, assuming that the order in question is a recurring, rather than a one-time order.

P 19–10 Divisional Performance Evaluation—Transfer Pricing Situation

Genutech Corporation operates several divisions as profit centers. Two of these, Eastern and Western, have in the past been engaged in an arrangement whereby Eastern supplied Western with all of its requirements of product A.N.D., which total 2,000,000 pounds per month.

Each division is free to choose its source of supply and to select the customers it sells its products to. At the moment, Eastern charges Western $2 per pound for A.N.D. This price is 10¢ in excess of Eastern's variable cost of producing A.N.D. Eastern also sells the same product to external customers for $2.25 per pound.

Eastern now finds that the demand by its regular external customers has grown to the point that it could sell its total output of 10,000,000 pounds per month at the $2.25 per pound price. Consequently, it has proposed raising its price to Western to $2.25 per pound. Western is not pleased with this, especially because the only other source of supply for A.N.D. charges $2.20 per pound. Western notes that the increase in price for A.N.D. will significantly reduce its potential monthly profit. At its present level of operation, purchasing from Eastern at $2.00 per pound, Western has shown a monthly profit of $450,000.

Required:

(a) Is Eastern's request to increase its transfer price reasonable? Why or why not?

(b) What should Western do? Why?

(c) Will the $2.25 transfer price maximize overall company profits?

(d) What are the transfer pricing and divisional performance evaluation implications of parts (a) and (b)?

(e) Discuss the original situation from the point of view of divisional performance evaluation, assuming that Eastern were *not* able to sell all of its output to external customers.

P 19–11   Divisional Performance Evaluation—Transfer Pricing Situation

Victoria Corporation has two divisions, Belmont and Swansen. Belmont is operating at full capacity, selling all of its output of electric motors to outside customers for $75 per unit. Its variable manufacturing costs are $35 per unit and its variable marketing costs are $25 per unit.

Swansen is operating below full capacity and is anxious to secure new customers. It has received an order for 1,000 units of a small machine that requires a motor similar to that produced by Belmont. The cost estimates for this machine (excluding the motor) are as follows:

	Cost per Machine
Materials	$ 60
Direct Labor	50
Variable Overhead	25
Fixed Overhead	25
	$160

The customer will place the order for 1,000 machines only if the price is $200 or less per unit. Consequently, Swansen Division is prepared to offer no more than $40 per unit to Belmont for the motors. Comparable motors from outside suppliers would cost Swansen at least $72. If Belmont supplies the motors, it can avoid the variable marketing costs.

Required:
(a) If both divisions seek to maximize their own profit contributions, what will their reactions be to the proposed $40 price?
(b) From the firm's point of view, where should Swansen acquire its motors?
(c) Is there a transfer price that would lead both divisions independently to that correct decision? If so, what is it?
(d) Swansen presently earns a profit of 10 percent on sales. How will the divisions respond to the price determined in part (c) when it comes to divisional performance evaluation?
(e) Comment on the possible resolution of the problems in parts (a) and (d).

P 19–12   Divisional Performance Evaluation—Transfer Pricing Situation

Abendroth Corporation is decentralized and has instructed its division managers to maximize their divisional profit contributions. The report for Divisions R and S for a typical month was as follows:

	R	S	Total
Sales:			
To Division S: 5,000 units	$ 80,000		$ 80,000
To Outside Customers:			
5,000 units		$150,000	150,000
10,000 units	200,000		200,000
	$280,000	$150,000	$430,000
Variable Costs:			
15,000 units	$180,000		$180,000
5,000 units		$100,000*	100,000
	$180,000	$100,000	$280,000
Direct Fixed Costs	60,000	40,000	100,000
	$240,000	$140,000	$380,000
Divisional Profit Contribution	$ 40,000	$ 10,000	$ 50,000

* Includes cost of units purchased from Division R at $16 per unit.

An alternate supplier of the items now purchased from Division R has quoted Division S a price of $14 per unit. However, the manager of Division R argues that she cannot reduce the transfer price below the present $16, which, she points out, is already her "breakeven price."

Required:

(a) How did the manager of Division R determine the "breakeven price"? Is it valid? Why or why not?

(b) What is the correct decision (with regard to the source of supply for Division S) from the firm's point of view? What transfer price would enable the firm's divisions to arrive at that decision independently?

(c) From the point of view of performance evaluation, what conflicts are evident in parts (a) and (b)? Why will everyone be unhappy?

(d) What is the basic cause of these conflicts? How can these conflicts among the divisions, and between the divisions and the firm, be resolved?

P 19–13   Divisional Performance Evaluation—Profit Centers—Transfer Price Implications

Refer to Problem 14–17 on page 692.

Part A: Consider only the original situation, wherein Division X was selling all of its 10,000 units of output to Division Y for $30 per unit. Assume that Division Y sells its product for $80, with unit variable costs totaling $42, including the component acquired from Division X.

Required:

(a) Discuss the effects of the existing transfer pricing arrangement on the evaluation of the two divisions as separate profit centers.

(b) How might the existing transfer price have been determined? What problems does it pose for performance evaluation?

(c)   What complications from the viewpoint of performance evaluation are created by the possibility of having to change the transfer price to $24 to match the offer of the outside supplier?

Part B: Assume that only two alternatives are available to Division X: It can continue as presently and supply Division Y or manufacture the new product as outlined in item (3) of Problem 14–17. Likewise, assume that Division Y also has two alternatives: It can purchase the component from Division X or from the independent outside supplier.

Required:
(d)   Discuss the problems that the two divisions, acting as separate profit centers, will encounter in arriving at a solution that is compatible with their own goals of maximizing segment profit contribution.

(e)   From the viewpoint of the firm's overall profitability, what are the relative advantages and disadvantages of adopting a profit center approach in a situation such as this?

P 19–14   Divisional Performance Evaluation—Profit Centers—Transfer Price Implications

Refer to Problem 14–18 on page 692.

Required:
(a)   Discuss the problems that may arise in preparing and interpreting segment profit contribution measurements based on the transfer prices specified for the various situations in part (c) of Problem 14–18.

(b)   How might these problems be resolved?

P 19–15   Profit Center Evaluation—Transfer Price Implications

Refer to Problem 14–20 on page 693.

Required:
(a)   Discuss the problems that may arise in preparing and interpreting segment profit contribution measurements based on the transfer price specified in part (b) of Problem 14–20.

(b)   How might these problems be resolved?

20

SEGMENT PERFORMANCE EVALUATION: INVESTMENT CENTERS

LEARNING OBJECTIVES

After studying Chapter 20, you should be able to:

1. Define an investment center, distinguish it from cost and profit centers, and identify the criteria that are relevant to evaluating investment center performance.
2. Calculate segment return on investment on a total asset and a net asset basis.
3. Discuss the usefulness of dividing segment return on investment into its two parts—asset turnover rate and rate of return on sales.
4. Discuss evaluation, calculation, and measurement problems involving the numerator and denominator of the return on investment figure.
5. Calculate return on investment using implicit interest depreciation and discuss this figure's relevance for performance evaluation.
6. Calculate segment residual income and use the resulting figure to analyze segment profitability.
7. Discuss the effects of transfer prices on segment and company-wide return on investment and investment center performance evaluation techniques.

When company segments are treated as **investment centers,** they are held responsible for the acquisition, use, and disposal of their *resources,* as well as for the *revenues* and *costs* that they generate. To evaluate investment centers, the interrelationships among these three basic aspects of segment performance must be assessed. Previously described techniques of cost evaluation, profit evaluation, and control, as well as investment analysis procedures, are useful in making such an evaluation.

The principles of controllability and attributability of performance characteristics are important in accounting for investment centers. A center's investment base includes all assets that are controllable by or attributable to that segment and its management. As will be shown, a segment's *operating performance,* which is determined independently of financing considerations, must be distinguished from its net *overall profitability,* which takes account of financing costs.

RETURN ON INVESTMENT ANALYSIS

In Chapter 17, rate of return calculations were introduced as decision making aids in capital budgeting analysis. A **rate of return** is the ratio between some measure of returns and the base that produces or supports those returns:

$$\text{Rate of Return} = \frac{\text{Return}}{\text{Base}}$$

An appropriate rate of return for investment center performance evaluation expresses the rate at which the segment generates a profit contribution in relation to its resources:

$$\frac{\text{Segment Return}}{\text{on Investment}} = \frac{\text{Segment Profit Contribution}}{\text{Segment Resources}}$$

$$\text{SROI} = \frac{\text{SPC}}{\text{SR}}$$

The rate of return on investment incorporates all relevant aspects of investment center operating performance—revenues, costs, and resources. Consequently, return on investment reflects in a single number the relationship between profit contribution and the investment base that supports it. When used as a performance measure for planning, evaluation, and control purposes, return on investment forces segment managers to emphasize control of the *relative* profitability of segment resources, as well as control of the absolute amounts of costs and revenues.

RETURN ON INVESTMENT:
OPERATING PERFORMANCE OR MANAGEMENT PERFORMANCE?

Segment profit contribution is calculated as shown in Chapter 19. It should not include any arbitrarily allocated firm-wide costs. Interest costs are included only if the segment has specific authority to incur debt and if the intent of the evaluation is to assess the segment's net performance. Segment resources include only those assets that meet the tests of controllability or attributability. Evaluation of *operating performance* requires a measure of *total resources,* whereas a review of the segment's net profitability employs a measure of *net resources* (net assets, net investment, or owner's equity). Therefore, the two commonly encountered variations of segment return on investment are

$$\underset{\text{(operating)}}{\text{SROI}_o} = \frac{\text{Segment Profit Contribution (before interest)}}{\text{Total Assets}}$$

$$\underset{\text{(net)}}{\text{SROI}_n} = \frac{\text{Segment Profit Contribution (after interest)}}{\text{Net Assets}}$$

The operating return on investment ratio is useful in evaluating the total earning power of all assets directly employed by a segment, regardless of how they are financed. The net return on investment ratio is a better indicator of a segment's ability to generate profit contributions in excess of the direct cost of financing its operations.

Example: Able Division of Patterson Corporation has directly traceable assets of $1,000,000 and liabilities of $400,000. The division's annual after-tax profit contribution is $150,000. This includes $30,000 of interest charges calculated on an after-tax basis.

$$\text{SROI}_o = \frac{\$150,000 + \$30,000}{\$1,000,000} = 18\%$$

$$\text{SROI}_n = \frac{\$150,000}{\$1,000,000 - \$400,000} = 25\%$$

These ratios show that (1) every dollar invested in gross resources generates an operating profit contribution of 18¢ and (2) the division earns 25¢ for every dollar of resources that is supported by firm-wide equity funds.

COMPARISONS AMONG SEGMENTS

Segment return on investment figures are often used to compare and rank company units. Return on investment calculations eliminate some of the bias that would occur if segments were ranked according to the total dollar amounts of their profit contributions. Larger divisions tend to have an advantage in such rankings because they can usually generate larger profit contributions. However, use of a ratio shifts the emphasis to the *rate* at which profit contribution is earned, thereby providing a fairer basis for comparing differently sized divisions.

Segment return on investment figures can be used to differentiate among segments on the basis of relative productivity of their assets. Such differentiation may facilitate the allocation and rationing of incremental resources among competing segments. However, using return on investment measures for evaluation purposes does not automatically make segment results fully comparable. Comparisons and rankings of segments based solely on return on investment measures should not be overemphasized, especially when dissimilar segment results are anticipated.

Example: Baker Division is another segment of Patterson Corporation. It has directly traceable assets of $2,000,000, liabilities of $200,000, and makes a segment profit contribution of $380,000 after interest charges of $20,000. Figure 20–1 compares the performance of Able and Baker Divisions.

Baker Division outperforms Able in terms of total segment profit contribution, which may be expected because Baker's investment base is twice the size of Able's. However, segment return on investment comparisons show that Able's performance is almost as profitable as Baker's per dollar of total resources employed (18 to 20 percent) and superior in terms of return per dollar of net assets (25 to 21.1 percent).

One reason for Able's superior return on net assets is that it has been more successful in financing its activities. Whereas Able used $400,000 of funds borrowed at a cost of $30,000, (7½ percent), Baker has used only $200,000 at a cost of $20,000, (10 percent). Although both divisions are successfully leveraged (that is, their cost of borrowing is less than their operating rate of return on total assets), Able is more highly and more favorably leveraged.

The preceding comparisons demonstrate that when investment center performance is evaluated on several different bases, the results may not be consistent due to variations in the size, asset and debt structure, and cost structure of different segments.

FIGURE 20–1

Patterson Corporation
Comparative Returns of Able and Baker Divisions
For the Year Ended December 31, 19X7

	Able	Baker
Segment Profit Contribution	$ 150,000	$ 240,000
Segment Profit Contribution (before interest)	180,000	250,000
Segment Return on Investment (operating) . .	$\frac{\$180,000}{\$1,000,000} = 18\%$	$\frac{\$400,000}{\$2,000,000} = 20\%$
Segment Return on Investment (net)	$\frac{\$150,000}{\$600,000} = 25\%$	$\frac{\$380,000}{\$1,800,000} = 21.1\%$

TARGET RATES OF RETURN

Return on investment analysis may also be used to compare actual results to predetermined segment goals. A budgeted or target return on investment might be established for each segment, which the segment management would be responsible for achieving through its decisions relating to the amount and composition of resources and the costs and revenues resulting from the use of those resources. This approach can be employed whether or not a comparison of segments is made. Indeed, it is more appropriate when segments cannot be equitably compared due to differences in their sizes, age of resources, product lines, cost structures, or market situations. These differences accentuate the need for different target rates of return for each segment.

COMPONENTS OF RETURN ON INVESTMENT

The composite nature of the segment return on investment measure permits an integrated evaluation of both a division's *profit performance* and the *resource productivity* or revenue generating power of its assets. This can be demonstrated by separating the return on investment measure into its component parts:

$$\text{SROI} = \frac{\text{Segment Profit Contribution}}{\text{Segment Resources}}$$

$$= \frac{\text{Segment Profit Contribution}}{\text{Segment Sales Revenue}} \times \frac{\text{Segment Sales Revenue}}{\text{Segment Resources}}$$

The first part of this expanded return on investment ratio represents the rate of segment profit contribution as a function of sales revenue. This rate of return on sales summarizes all elements of the segment's cost structure and its ability to generate profit per dollar of sales revenue. For example, if other factors remain constant, the segment can increase its return on investment by increasing sales revenues relative to costs or by decreasing costs relative to sales revenues.

But because fixed costs are usually present, the rate of return on sales revenue is not always a reliable indicator of the effects of changes in a segment's volume of operations. The rate of return on sales will increase as sales volume increases, if unit sales prices, unit variable costs, and total fixed costs remain constant. However, changes in any of these factors will influence the direction and size of the change in the rate of return on sales.

The second part of the return on investment ratio represents the rate at which sales revenues are generated per dollar of investment in segment resources. Often called the **asset turnover rate,** this is a gross measure of asset productivity. To improve return on investment, sales must increase relative to total assets or fewer assets must be used to produce an equal or greater amount of sales revenue.

Because of the dual nature of segment return on investment, comparisons among segments should not be limited to the total return on investment measure. Analysis should also include the component elements previously defined. Figure

20–2 depicts the interrelationships of these elements as they influence rate of return on total assets.

Segments that display similar returns on investment may have quite different revenue generating abilities and/or cost structures. Performance evaluation (especially incremental analysis) and subsequent decision making should take account of all components of the segment return on investment measure.

Example: The current year operating results of Tracy Company's three divisions, David, Jonathan, and Goliath, are shown in Figure 20–3. Different returns

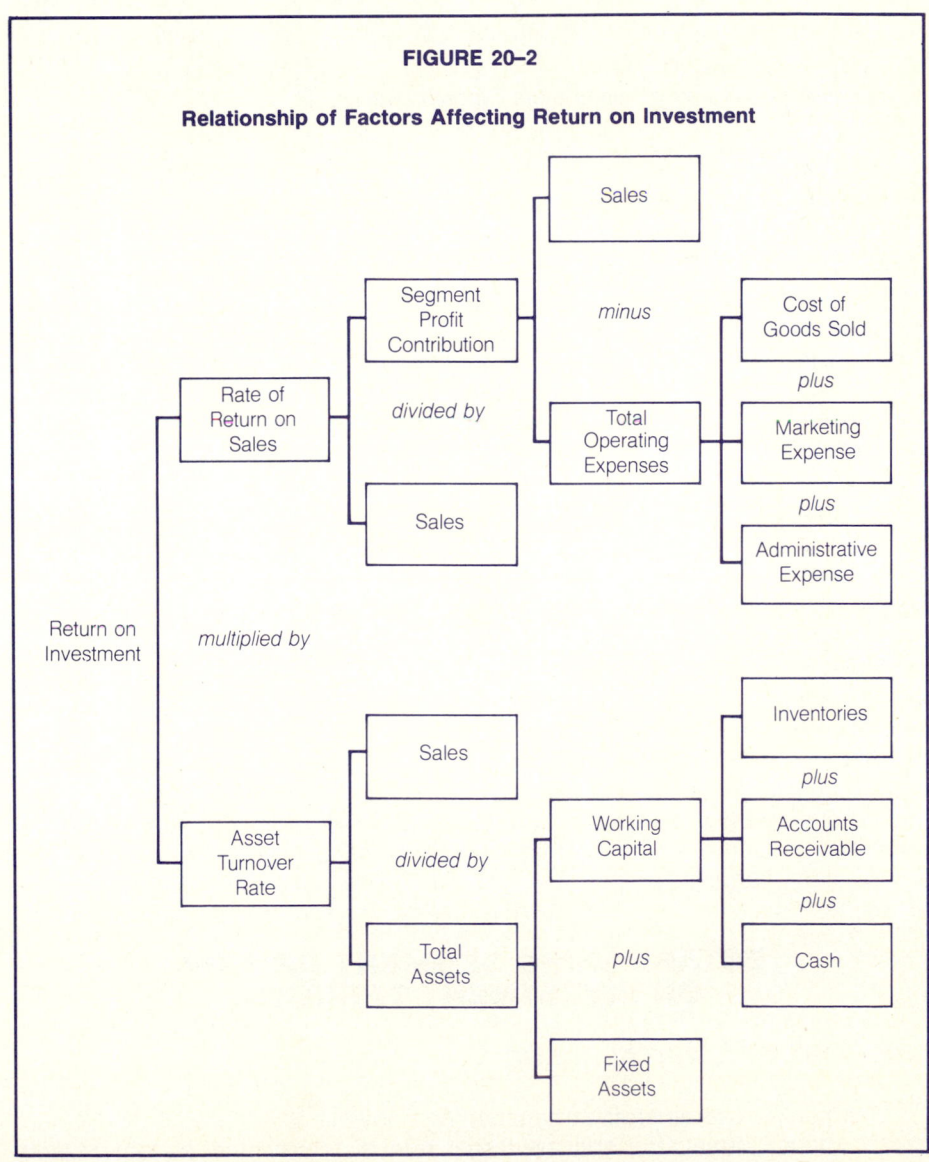

FIGURE 20–2

Relationship of Factors Affecting Return on Investment

FIGURE 20-3

Tracy Company
Annual Divisional Operating Results
(in thousands)

		David	Jonathan	Goliath
A.	Sales	$200	$200	$1,000
B.	Expenses	180	100	900
C.	Segment Profit Contribution.......................	$ 20	$100	$ 100
D.	Segment Assets	$100	$400	$2,000
E.	Return on Sales (C ÷ A)	10%	50%	10%
F.	Revenue Generating Rate or Asset Turnover Rate (A ÷ D)	2.0	0.5	0.5
G.	Return on Investment (C ÷ D)	20%	25%	5%

on investment are earned by divisions with similar rates of return on sales (David and Goliath) or similar revenue generating rates (Jonathan and Goliath). Jonathan and Goliath achieved the same segment profit contribution ($100,000) and had the same revenue generating rate (0.5). However, Jonathan had a higher return on investment (25 percent) than Goliath (5 percent) because its rate of return on sales was 50 percent compared to 10 percent for Goliath. Although David and Goliath both had 10 percent rates of return on sales, David earned a 20 percent return on investment compared to 5 percent for Goliath, because David's revenue generating rate was 2.0, whereas Goliath's was only 0.5.

UNDERSTANDABILITY AND COMMUNICABILITY

Evaluations based on return on investment criteria are consistent with investor assessments of a firm's profit performance. Because so many analyses produced by the investment community are expressed in rate of return terms, it is appropriate that businesses evaluate their activities in like fashion. Despite various deficiencies, segment return on investment is still widely used for performance evaluation and analysis. Managers of small divisions often rely on its equalizing tendencies to show that their performance can be competitive with that of other, larger divisions.

ESTABLISHING SEGMENT RETURN ON INVESTMENT TARGETS

THE COST OF CAPITAL ISSUE

Segment or overall profit targets can be conveniently expressed in a return on investment format. But first the target rate of return must be determined. The cost of capital concept, introduced in Chapter 17, is useful for this purpose.

Cost of capital is a measure of the cost of funds employed in a project or segment. It can be defined either as an explicit out-of-pocket cost or as an implicit opportunity cost. In Chapter 17, the opportunity cost interpretation was shown to be preferable for decision making purposes. It represents the rate of return that is foregone as a result of investing in that particular project or segment rather than another with similar characteristics. Once the cost of capital has been determined, actual profit performance can be compared with the results that would be expected from alternate use of the segment's resources.

DETERMINING SEGMENT COST OF CAPITAL

The target rate of return might be calculated by referring to the performance of similar entities, provided that information concerning comparable industries, product lines, and geographical areas is available. If such information is unavailable, management must use its judgment as to what constitutes a satisfactory rate of return relative to stockholder and creditor expectations, explicit financing costs, alternative investment opportunities with known returns, and subjective estimates of the relative uncertainty inherent in each segment's activities.

SINGLE OR MULTIPLE COST OF CAPITAL MEASURES?

The target return on investment rate need not be the same for all of a company's segments. A firm-wide target rate is appealing because of its simplicity and understandability, as well as for the competitiveness it engenders between divisions. However, it may be unfair to expect each segment to achieve a similar profit rate, especially when segments operate in different markets or geographical areas, manufacture different products, or sell through different distribution channels. Different rates of return can also be expected when cost structures, scale of activity, age of assets, and scope of decentralized authority differ among segments.

These variations require that separate target segment return on investment rates be established for each segment. Because each segment usually has a collection of assets of different risk classes and profit potentials, it can be argued that each segment's rate of return on investment should be calculated as a weighted average of the rates of return identified for each class of resource. Alternatively, the performance of each resource class held by a segment might be evaluated against its own target rate of return on investment. However, this would require a much more refined measure of segment profit contribution, which would then have to be subdivided according to the various resource classes involved.

One advantage of a single target rate of return on investment is that decisions to dispose of, reduce in size, or expand or add new segments must have reference to some common indicator of profitability, such as a return on investment measure. However, a single company-wide return on investment rate should not be the only basis for such decisions. Using a standard return on investment rate in that way might lead to decisions that reduce the firm's overall profitability or even to such extreme actions as discontinuing all segments except the most profitable one.

Segment activities are often diversified in an attempt to reduce operating variability and the risks involved in "putting all one's eggs in one basket." Corporations often establish separate segments that complement each other's activities, offer a wide range of different products, or extend the firm's outputs to a wide variety of customer groups and service areas. In such cases, the individual segments typically have quite different rates of return and cannot appropriately be evaluated using a single firm-wide return on investment rate.

Summary   The reasons for establishing and maintaining decentralized activities include organizational, behavioral, security, efficiency, growth, and risk dispersion factors. Although these motives may appear to be nonquantitative, their collective effect must ultimately be evaluated in economic terms. Consequently, for performance evaluation purposes, there is a place for both segment and firm-wide target return on investment rates. In practice, businesses commonly adopt the single rate approach and are reluctant to come to grips with the more conceptually correct, but more complex, separate rate procedures.

RETURN ON INVESTMENT EVALUATION PROBLEMS

EXCESSIVE COMPETITION

Knowing that they are being evaluated, particularly when comparisons and rankings are involved, often leads segment managers to devise ways to improve their "score" by manipulating reported measures of performance. This can be detrimental both to the segment and to the firm as a whole.

The use of segment return on investment measures for *short-run* evaluation purposes may lead to this type of ratio manipulation. The numerator of the return on investment ratio—segment profit contribution—can be boosted in the short run by postponing discretionary costs (repairs, advertising, management training, employee benefits), concentrating sales efforts on easy to sell or high margin items, or by extending credit to high-risk customers in order to increase sales volume. The denominator—segment resources—can be lowered by reducing inventories at year-end, selling idle assets, keeping old assets that have low recorded values, or deferring expenditures for replacement and expansion. The segment manager who resorts to these methods can show inflated current profits and resource productivity. However, the longer-run effects of such actions may be exactly the reverse!

SUBOPTIMAL INVESTMENT DECISIONS

Using return on investment criteria to encourage competitiveness among segment managers can be harmful to the organization as a whole. Assuming that maximizing segment return on investment is a stated goal, segment management may not only be enticed into the manipulative practices just noted, but may also be influenced to make incorrect decisions that benefit segment performance at the expense of the firm's overall performance.

Example: Lisa Division of Roberts Company earns a segment return on investment of 25 percent—the best rate of return of any division. Roberts Company has set 17.5 percent as a target goal for all its divisions and has promised a bonus to the managers of the three top performing divisions. Lisa Division, which now earns $1,000,000 on an asset base of $4,000,000, has the chance to make an additional investment of $1,000,000 that will generate profits of $200,000. Lisa Division rejects this opportunity because acceptance would reduce its segment return on investment to only 24 percent ($1,000,000 + $200,000) ÷ ($4,000,000 + $1,000,000). Because several other divisions presently earn nearly 25 percent, this reduction from its present 25 percent return on investment might cause Lisa Division to lose its first place ranking. Note that the incremental rate of return on the proposed investment is 20 percent ($200,000 ÷ $1,000,000), which is above the 17.5 percent firm-wide target rate. Accepting the project would have furthered attainment of the company's overall profit objectives.

This example illustrates how return on investment criteria can encourage an emphasis on segment goals at the expense of firm-wide objectives. Companies may promote a controlled competitive spirit for motivational purposes, but all-out competition among divisions quickly becomes counterproductive. Besides leading to suboptimal decision making and possible manipulation of return on investment components, intense competition to achieve short-run return on investment targets diverts attention from more basic managerial tasks, such as cost control, quality control, customer service, up-keep of facilities, and employee development.

RETURN ON INVESTMENT CALCULATION PROBLEMS

Return on investment criteria may also be deficient because of the way in which they are calculated. There is no standardized method for measuring either the numerator or the denominator. Because many variations of the return on investment calculation exist, the intended version or interpretation should be specified in each situation.

SEGMENT PROFIT CONTRIBUTION IN RETURN ON INVESTMENT

In Chapter 19, the discussion of the measurement of **segment profit contribution** introduced several subcategories, all of which qualify as possible numerators in the return on investment equation. Segment profit contribution, controllable segment margin (either before- or after-tax), and before or after interest expense are all variations on the *return* earned by a segment. Even segment net income, including fully allocated company-wide costs, unfortunately finds its way into the list of possible interpretations.

It is vitally important that the return on investment numerator (return) be determined under the same controllability/attributability conditions that are applied to the denominator (investment base). The return must reflect the results of using only those resources that are included in the investment base. If a segment's *operating performance* is being evaluated, the numerator should be the segment profit contribution, excluding financing charges, and the denominator should be total segment resources. However, if *managerial performance* is being evaluated, and if segment management is responsible for financing decisions, the numerator should be segment profit contribution after interest charges are deducted, and the denominator should be net resources (total assets minus total liabilities).

THE INVESTMENT BASE: IDENTIFICATION PROBLEMS

It is even more difficult to determine a correct measure of the return on investment denominator. When geographically separate or functionally differentiated segments are involved, when the lines of authority and responsibility among segments are clearly defined, and when there is no confusion regarding the controllability or attributability of segment assets, assets can easily be traced to specific segments.

However, when several segments have access to the same assets, the distinction between directly attributable resources and allocated common resources often becomes blurred. Each segment obviously needs cash to operate, but cash balances are often administered centrally. Also held in common are raw materials inventory, general purpose buildings and equipment, and shared research and development programs. Even accounts receivable may be difficult to attribute to separate segments if several divisions have the same firm as a customer.

Arbitrary allocations of resources to segments to measure segment return on investment should be avoided whenever possible. Just as segment profit contribution is not intended to be a "bottom line" measure, segment return on investment should not be considered a final and definitive measure of segment performance. It should only be used to reflect the rate at which the directly controllable and attributable aspects of a segment's resource usage contribute to the remaining unallocable company-wide costs and to company profit.

IDLE ASSETS AND THE INVESTMENT BASE

It might seem desirable to exclude idle resources from the investment base. Although they are controlled by or traceable to a segment, they remain unused during the evaluation period. Excluding them will make segment return on investment more representative of effective resource productivity, because only the returns on those assets that were actively used by the segment will be measured. On the other hand, it can be argued that because a segment is responsible for earning a return on *all* its resources, the investment base should include idle resources.

In practice, the reason why the resources are idle should determine the matter. The investment base should include idle resources if segment management caused them to remain unused. If they are idle because of the actions of other segments or higher levels of management, then it is fairer not to hold the segment responsible for generating returns on those assets.

ASSETS OMITTED FROM THE INVESTMENT BASE

Often the investment base derived from conventional accounting reports excludes assets which are part of the pool of resources that allow a segment to operate. For example, when significant amounts of leased assets are employed, their capitalized value should be included in the investment base for return on investment calculations unless they are already capitalized as long-term assets.

Financial accounting rules generally require or permit research and development costs, sales promotion expenditures, and training and personnel development costs to be charged immediately to expense. However, these costs represent a part of the investment base that allows a segment to earn profits over extended periods of time. This is also true of implicit (nonpurchased) goodwill and the value of human resources (management skills, expertise, teamwork) that are not recognized as assets in conventional balance sheets.

The omission of these items requires either subjective revision of the investment base or acknowledgement that the return on investment measures are overstated. More critically, inconsistent comparisons of segments must be avoided. Suppose two divisions of a firm are the same size and use similar equipment, but one division leases rather than owns its assets. Their investment bases should be equalized before segment return on investment is calculated and before their net profitability is evaluated, when alternative financing costs (interest expense versus leasing charges) are included in income.

THE INVESTMENT BASE: MEASUREMENT PROBLEMS

Measurement of the investment base also causes problems. Because the return on investment measure applies to a *period of time,* it is logical that the *average amount* of resources held during that period be calculated, not just the balance at year-end. This average is often of the simple "beginning plus ending divided by two"-type, but, to avoid possible end of period distortions, it could also be derived from the average of a larger number of observations.

NET BOOK VALUE IN THE INVESTMENT BASE

More importantly, the accounting basis for measuring average resources must be established. To be consistent with the accounting derivation of segment profit contribution, a "book value" approach is usually adopted. Segment assets are represented by the average amount of their accounting carrying values.

However, this causes a gradual reduction in the book value of a segment's investment base as assets are depreciated. Unless the earnings from the use of these resources decrease at least as fast as their book value declines, segment return on investment will automatically increase. The reasonable expectation would be for resource productivity to decrease as the age of assets in the investment base increases. However, separate trends in the numerator and the denominator cause the opposite effect. When either straight-line or accelerated depreciation is used, the segment profit contribution tends to be a constant

---

FIGURE 20-4

Chance Division of Kennedy Corporation
Five-Year Segment Profits

Year	Segment Profit Contribution	Average Investment Base*	Segment Return on Investment
1	$100,000	$500,000	20%
2	90,000	400,000	22½%
3	80,000	300,000	26⅔%
4	80,000	200,000	40%
5	75,000	100,000	75%

* Average of beginning and ending balances. For example, Year 1 = ($550,000 + $450,000) ÷ 2 = $500,000.

---

or increasing amount over time, assuming that operating cash flows per period do not decrease. At the same time, if no new assets are purchased, the accumulated depreciation will cause the investment base to decline. When a ratio's numerator is constant or increasing and its denominator is decreasing, the ratio *must* increase in size.

Example: After allowing for depreciation of $100,000 per year, Chance Division of Kennedy Corporation has reported the five-year segment profit results shown in Figure 20–4. The investment base was originally $550,000, including fixed assets of $500,000.

Segment return on investment increases dramatically in Years 4 and 5, even though segment profit contribution declined during that period. More extreme examples are possible. Segment operating cash flows might be constant, or the investment base could consist entirely of fixed assets. However, these extreme escalations of return on investment figures are usually dampened somewhat, because a segment's assets are generally at different stages in their life cycles.

What are the practical implications of this built-in bias which exists when segments are evaluated on a return on investment basis using book values of assets and conventional depreciation methods? Divisions with newer assets will be at a disadvantage because their segment return on investment will be depressed, whereas divisions with older assets will report relatively inflated return on investment figures. The threat of reduced return on investment performance could make segment managers reluctant to dispose of older assets or to embark on expansion and asset replacement programs.

GROSS BOOK VALUE IN THE INVESTMENT BASE

Several solutions to this problem have been proposed. The bias in segment return on investment can be reduced if the denominator is kept equal to the original total outlay for resources in the investment base. Eliminating accumulated depreciation will cause the denominator to remain constant, assuming that the physical quantity of segment assets neither increases nor decreases. The numerator may still be a constant or increasing amount over time, if conventional depreciation methods are used and segment operating cash flows do not decrease.

The rationale for this approach is that a segment is expected to earn a return on its total outlay for resources over all periods in which those resources are used. However, this rationale can be criticized on the grounds that (1) funds invested in assets are recovered gradually throughout the asset's life and (2) the amount of the investment base should be progressively reduced to reflect the expected decline in asset productivity.

CASH FLOW GENERATING RATE

Another alternative is to adopt a cash flow approach, excluding the effects of depreciation charges from *both* the numerator and the denominator. The return on investment measure then would indicate the rate of cash recovery of segment asset outlays.

This approach eliminates any distortion caused by depreciation methods. It also eliminates the tendency for segment return on investment to escalate over time because of the mathematical effects previously discussed. It allows segments with newer and more productive assets to receive fairer evaluations than they would get under conventional return on investment methods. Applied consistently, it should also produce better measures of asset productivity in terms of the segment's ability to generate cash flows.

CURRENT REPLACEMENT COSTS AND RETURN ON INVESTMENT

General price levels and the costs of particular assets are likely to change over time. When these changes are significant, any segment return on investment measure based on book values may become distorted and potentially misleading. In one sense, return on investment becomes an internally inconsistent measure; in another sense, it does not adequately represent asset productivity as measured in current output prices and market values of input resources.

This internal inconsistency results from the fact that conventional measures of segment profit contribution, because they are derived from accounting income, include many items measured in terms of asset prices and transaction amounts from different time periods. This is especially true for cost of goods sold, depreciation charges, and other deferred and amortized items. An investment base calculated in terms of book values is also a conglomeration of assets acquired at different price levels. The resulting segment return on investment is not based on uniformly determined or current values in either numerator or denominator.

To achieve uniform valuation, all components of segment return on investment must be translated into units of common purchasing power. Price level adjusted figures are one alternative, but current replacement costs are more useful for segment evaluation purposes. This reinforces the earlier observation that planning decisions should always anticipate replacement costs. It follows that actual operating results should be evaluated similarly, to determine how productive management's decisions have been when the results are calculated

	Book Value (Historical Cost)			Current Replacement Cost	
	Segment Profit Contribution	Depreciation	Net Assets	Depreciation	Net Assets
Delta	$200,000	$100,000	$1,000,000	$150,000	$1,500,000
Gamma	360,000	150,000	2,400,000	180,000	2,750,000

FIGURE 20–5

ABC Company
19X7 Operating Results

in current resource values—that is, to determine whether capital has been maintained in terms of current purchasing power.

Example: Current year operating results for ABC Company's Delta and Gamma Divisions are shown in Figure 20–5.

When depreciation costs are restated on a replacement cost basis, the following revised segment contribution margins are obtained:

$$\text{Delta:} \quad \$200,000 + (\$100,000 - \$150,000) = \$150,000$$
$$\text{Gamma:} \quad \$360,000 + (\$150,000 - \$180,000) = \$330,000$$

Segment return on investment figures on a book value basis and on a replacement cost basis would be

	Historical Cost	Replacement Cost
Delta	$\dfrac{\$200,000}{\$1,000,000} = 20\%$	$\dfrac{\$150,000}{\$1,500,000} = 10\%$
Gamma	$\dfrac{\$360,000}{\$2,400,000} = 15\%$	$\dfrac{\$330,000}{\$2,750,000} = 12\%$

When book values based on historical cost are used, Delta returns 20 percent on its assets, compared to only 15 percent for Gamma. However, after operating results are revised to reflect replacement cost depreciation and the replacement cost of assets in the investment base, the return on investment is 10 percent for Delta, 12 percent for Gamma. This is not only a material change in the size of the return on investment measures, but a change in the rankings of segment performance. Segment return on investment now relates the current exchange values of resources sold and consumed to the current replacement value of assets employed. Because Delta's replacement cost revisions are proportionally larger than Gamma's, further analysis might reveal that Delta has comparatively older assets.

ACQUISITION COST—A COMPROMISE SOLUTION

The use of asset **acquisition costs** in the investment base avoids certain problems inherent in the net book value and replacement cost approaches. Using original acquisition costs somewhat offsets the tendencies for net book values to cause return on investment to rise automatically over time and for increases in replacement costs to require return on investment to be restated downward. Acquisition cost involves less computation than the other methods, which require adjustment of the investment base. On the other hand, this method's ability to properly reflect *current* productivity of resource use is weakened as the segment's assets grow older and as current replacement costs diverge more and more from acquisition costs.

CONFLICT BETWEEN THE USE OF RETURN ON INVESTMENT TECHNIQUES FOR PLANNING AND EVALUATION

Another criticism of conventional return on investment measures is that they are applied strictly as single period indicators. This conflicts with the ongoing nature of segment operations, which cut across accounting periods. Moreover, these single period return on investment calculations often differ from the return on investment concepts used in decision making and planning for the segment's long-term activities. This may not be true if long-term analysis employs simple decision rules such as the average accounting rate of return, or the payback period. However, if time-dependent discounting methods of capital budgeting analysis are used to plan segment activities, they will be inconsistent with the short-run accounting return on investment measures described to this point.

This conflict between planning methods and evaluation methods becomes acute when net present value or internal rate of return methods are used to allocate resources and plan the segment's multiperiod activities, whereas single period return on investment ratios based on accounting book values are used to evaluate performance. In that situation, no meaningful control comparisons can be made between the results of the two methods.

Example: The Quadraphonic Division of Marengo Corporation plans its activities four years in advance, using a net present value approach to select a set of resources that will earn a return of exactly 20 percent per year over the next four years. In this highly simplified example, Figure 20–6 shows the analysis of forecast cash flows.

FIGURE 20–6

Marengo Corporation—Quadraphonic Division
Four-Year Forecast of Operating Cash Flows

Investment Base:
Fixed assets with a four-year life, no salvage value, and acquisition cost of $517,600

Forecast Operating Cash Flows (discounted at 20%):

Year 1	$200,000 × .833 =	$166,600
Year 2	200,000 × .694 =	138,800
Year 3	200,000 × .579 =	115,800
Year 4	200,000 × .482 =	96,400
Total Present Value of Operating Cash Flows		$517,600

FIGURE 20–7

Marengo Corporation—Quadraphonic Division
Segment Return on Investment

		Year 1	Year 2	Year 3	Year 4
A.	Operating Cash Flow	$200,000	$200,000	$200,000	$200,000
B.	Less: Depreciation ($517,600 ÷ 4) .	129,400	129,400	129,400	129,400
C.	Segment Profit Contribution	$ 70,600	$ 70,600	$ 70,600	$ 70,600
D.	Investment Base (book value at the start of each year)	$517,600	$388,200	$258,800	$129,400
E.	Segment Return on Investment (C ÷ D)	13.64%	18.19%	27.28%	54.56%

Assuming that all cash flows occur as forecast, conventional accrual accounting using straight-line depreciation will produce the operating results shown in Figure 20–7. But what has happened to the 20 percent rate of return planned for this division? Although each year's cash flows and profit contributions are identical, segment return on investment shows a considerable increase in Years 3 and 4. Interpreted literally, these figures suggest that the division was four times as productive in Year 4 as in Year 1 (54.56 percent compared to 13.64 percent). The more likely reason for this increased return on investment is that accumulated straight-line depreciation has reduced the investment base (see item D).

RETURN ON INVESTMENT AND IMPLICIT INTEREST DEPRECIATION

The implicit interest method of depreciation will allow period to period return on investment measures to be reported on a basis consistent with the uniform rate of return that was anticipated from the present value analysis used in planning the investment. **Implicit interest depreciation** is an increasing charge procedure that makes the annual depreciation cost equal to the net decrease in the present value of expected cash flows from the asset. Implicit interest depreciation can also be calculated as the difference between the amount of cash flow received from the asset per period and the growth during the period of the present value of the asset's cash flow.

Example: Figure 20–8 shows how implicit interest depreciation is calculated for Marengo Corporation's Quadraphonic Division.

These depreciation costs can be incorporated into a conventional income statement, and the period to period return on investment can be determined as shown in Figure 20–9.

Implicit interest depreciation allows period to period segment profit contribution to be determined on a basis consistent with the methods used when the segment's multiperiod activities were planned. Therefore, performance evalua-

FIGURE 20–8

Marengo Corporation—Quadraphonic Division
Implicit Interest Depreciation

		Year 1	Year 2	Year 3	Year 4
A.	Beginning Investment Base	$517,600	$421,120	$305,344	$166,413
B.	Add Income: Growth of				
	Present Value at 20%	103,520	84,224	61,069	33,587*
		$621,120	$505,344	$366,413	$200,000
C.	Less: Operating Cash Flow	200,000	200,000	200,000	200,000
D.	Ending Investment Base	$421,120	$305,344	$166,413	$ –0–
E.	Depreciation Cost (A − D)	$ 96,480	$115,776	$138,931	$166,413

* Adjusted for rounding error in calculation.

FIGURE 20–9

Marengo Division—Quadraphonic Division
Segment Return on Investment
Using Implicit Interest Depreciation

		Year 1	Year 2	Year 3	Year 4
A.	Operating Cash Flow	$200,000	$200,000	$200,000	$200,000
B.	Less: Depreciation (see				
	Figure 20–8)	96,480	115,776	138,931	166,413
C.	Segment Profit Contribution	$103,520	$ 84,224	$ 61,069	$ 33,587
D.	Beginning Investment Base	$517,600	$421,120	$305,344	$166,413
E.	Segment Return on				
	Investment (C ÷ D)...........	20%	20%	20%	20%

tion is better able to reflect *variations* from those plans. Because depreciation charges are predetermined on the basis of the original set of cash flow forecasts and the original investment outlay, the only performance characteristic that will vary once the investment has been made is the amount of operating cash flows.

Example: Consider the following variation on the Marengo Corporation example. Assuming that actual cash flows were $200,000, $220,000, $200,000, and $180,000 respectively during the four years, calculating *straight-line depreciation* results in the annual returns on investment shown in Figure 20–10.

Note the inconsistent relationship between operating cash flow performance (the only controllable variable) and segment return on investment (the proposed performance evaluator). In Years 3 and 4, when cash flows decline and even

FIGURE 20–10

Marengo Corporation—Quadraphonic Division
Segment Return on Investment
Using Straight-Line Depreciation

		Year 1	Year 2	Year 3	Year 4
A.	Operating Cash Flow	$200,000	$220,000	$200,000	$180,000
B.	Less: Straight-Line Depreciation	129,400	129,400	129,400	129,400
C.	Segment Profit Contribution	$ 70,600	$ 90,600	$ 70,600	$ 50,600
D.	Beginning Investment Base	$517,600	$388,200	$258,800	$129,400
E.	Segment Return on Investment (C ÷ D)	15.95%	23.34%	27.28%	39.16%

fall below the forecast level, the segment return on investment continues to increase!

However, if implicit interest depreciation is calculated on the segment's investment base, return on investment for each of the four years will be consistent with the movement of cash flows, as shown in Figure 20–11.

Use of implicit interest depreciation allows return on investment to move in the same direction as the period to period change in the only control variable, operating cash flows. For example, operating cash flows declined during Years 2, 3, and 4, and the implicit interest return on investment followed that trend (24.75, 20, 8.16 percent), whereas the conventional return on investment results in Figure 20–10 suggested improved performance (23.34, 27.78, 39.16 percent). In Year 2, when operating cash flow increased, the implicit interest return on investment increased from 20 to 24.75 percent. In Year 4, a decline in operating cash flow was accompanied by a decline in return on investment, from 20 to

FIGURE 20–11

Marengo Corporation—Quadraphonic Division
Segment Return on Investment
Using Implicit Interest Depreciation

		Year 1	Year 2	Year 3	Year 4
A.	Operating Cash Flow	$200,000	$220,000	$200,000	$180,000
B.	Less: Implicit Interest Depreciation	96,480	115,776	138,931	166,413
C.	Segment Profit Contribution	$103,520	$104,224	$ 61,069	$ 13,587
D.	Beginning Investment Base	$517,600	$421,120	$305,344	$166,413
E.	Segment Return on Investment (C ÷ D)	20%	24.75%	20%	8.16%

8.16 percent. This example is simplified and portrays an extreme contrast between straight-line and implicit interest depreciation. When operating cash flow fluctuations over time are more mixed, results may not be as dramatic as in the Marengo Corporation case. However, the general superiority of implicit interest depreciation over conventional depreciation methods will remain.

Despite the fact that implicit interest depreciation permits more consistent and effective evaluation of a segment over time, it is not widely used. As an increasing charge method, it defers depreciation expense to the later periods in a product's life cycle. This may be undesirable because it contradicts the usual expectation that a long-term asset's value will decline more rapidly in the early years of its use and because it conflicts with cash flow maximization goals, which favor the use of accelerated depreciation to obtain tax reductions in the early years of an asset's life.

DUAL MEASUREMENT

A final alternative is a **dual measurement system.** Planning and decision making could be based on a net present value or internal rate of return approach. Once a set of segment activities was decided on, the forecast accrual accounting results of that set of activities would be prepared. This would comprise an independent, multiperiod budget against which actual segment results could be evaluated, also on an accrual accounting basis. The original long-range capital budgeting projections would not be compatible with the company's period-to-period operating performance reports; each would have to be used for its own specialized purposes.

MULTIPLE AND NONACCOUNTING EVALUATION CRITERIA

Segment performance evaluation systems based on accounting data tend to focus on segment profit contribution measures and their derivatives. Emphasis is placed on specific financial performance characteristics—costs, revenues, assets, and combined measures derived from them. An alternative is to develop composite evaluation measures that consider other performance characteristics, including nonaccounting characteristics. Sales growth, market share, product innovation, rate and change in productivity, public image, personnel development, employee and union relations, social responsibility, and environmental responsibility are among the many variables that are relevant to a multiple criteria system.

Obviously, significant problems are involved in developing measurement scales and establishing performance goals for the factors involved, either individually or collectively. In practice, the easily understandable and measurable profit-related measures still tend to dominate management's decision making.

RESIDUAL INCOME

The residual income concept offers another way to evaluate segments and encourage segment managers to achieve company-wide goals. **Residual income** is the amount by which actual profit contribution exceeds a predetermined target amount. This latter amount is usually calculated as a function of a desired rate of return on resources. Preferably, this targeted rate should reflect the opportunity cost of capital appropriate to each segment, in order to permit equitable evaluation of segment performance.

$$\begin{array}{c}\text{Segment} \\ \text{Residual} = \\ \text{Income}\end{array} \begin{array}{c}\text{Segment} \\ \text{Profit} \\ \text{Contribution}\end{array} - \left(\begin{array}{c}\text{Desired} \\ \text{Segment} \times \\ \text{ROI}\end{array} \begin{array}{c}\text{Segment} \\ \text{Resources}\end{array}\right)$$

$$\text{SRI} = \text{SPC} - (\text{SROI} \times \text{SR})$$

RESIDUAL INCOME AS A PERFORMANCE EVALUATOR

The use of residual income to measure segment performance may help segment managers avoid errors that can result from preoccupation with maximizing return on investment. Residual income measures a segment's ability to exceed profit goals established in terms of a desired return on resources used. It is a composite measure of performance because it refers to both the *rate* at which profit contribution is achieved and the *total dollar amount* of profit contribution. As a result of its use, management's temptation to maximize return on investment by manipulating the size of the numerator and denominator can to some extent be avoided.

If the same target rate of return is specified for all segments, residual income evaluations may favor segments with larger asset bases. Other things being equal, larger segments can usually generate larger amounts of residual income. On the other hand, if the differences among segments—size of investment base, cost structure, and risk class—are reflected in separate target rates of return for each segment, residual income can provide more equitable segment performance evaluations. In the final analysis, the choice between residual income, return on investment, or other evaluation criteria must be made by management, based on their formulation of company objectives.

Example: Sharp Corporation has two divisions, Prince and Princess. Figure 20–12 shows a tabulation of their current year operating results. A 12 percent target return on investment rate has been specified for both divisions.

Princess Division earns the higher return on investment (25 to 20 percent), but Prince Division contributes more profit in excess of its 12 percent target

FIGURE 20–12

Sharp Corporation—Prince and Princess Divisions
Residual Income Analysis

		Prince	Princess
A.	Segment Profit Contribution	$ 200,000	$125,000
B.	Segment Resources	$1,000,000	$500,000
C.	Segment Return on Investment (A ÷ B)	20%	25%
D.	Target Profit Contribution (12% × B)	$ 120,000	$ 60,000
E.	Segment Residual Income (A − D)	$ 80,000	$ 65,000

FIGURE 20–13

Sharp Corporation—Prince and Princess Divisions
Residual Income Analysis

		Prince	Princess
A.	Segment Profit Contribution	$ 200,000	$125,000
B.	Segment Resources	$1,000,000	$500,000
C.	Segment Return on Investment (A ÷ B)	20%	25%
D.	Target Profit Contribution:		
	Prince Division (15% × B)	$ 150,000	
	Princess Division (10% × B)		$ 50,000
E.	Residual Income (A − D)	$ 50,000	$ 75,000

---

rate ($80,000 to $65,000). Neither division is conclusively more profitable than the other. However, assuming that target income is representative of the opportunity cost of operating each division, segment residual income does show that Prince Division is currently making the larger contribution in terms of earnings beyond the target requirement.

On the other hand, if the two divisions have significantly different asset bases and cost structures, they should be assigned separate target rates of return, reflecting their different opportunity costs of capital. Assume that Prince and Princess Divisions have been assigned target rates of return of 15 and 10 percent respectively. The resulting residual income calculations are shown in Figure 20–13. With these particular combinations of target profit requirements and actual operating results, Princess Division provides significantly more residual income than Prince Division.

RESIDUAL INCOME AND INCREMENTAL INVESTMENTS

The *total* amount of segment residual income is useful only for evaluating the results of *past* performance. For decisions involving *future* resource allocation among segments, the potential *change* in residual income is more important. Residual income criteria tend to encourage segment managers to pursue company-wide goals in judging incremental investment opportunities. Because emphasis is not on the maximization of the average return on all investments undertaken, projects that promise *any* positive contribution to a segment's residual income should be acceptable to management. These may include projects that would have been rejected using return on investment criteria because they would have reduced the segment's average return on investment. Therefore, segment decision making on a residual income basis should conform more closely to firm-wide profit maximization goals.

Example: Lisa Division of Roberts Company has a 17.5 percent target rate of return on investment. If maximization of residual income replaces maximization of segment return on investment as an operating goal of Lisa Division, the analysis of a new investment opportunity would be as shown in Figure 20–14. In this case, the investment opportunity should be accepted because it will

---

FIGURE 20–14

Lisa Division of Roberts Company
Residual Income Analysis

		Before New Project	After New Project	Increment
A.	Segment Profit Contribution	$1,000,000	$1,210,000	$ 210,000
B.	Segment Resources	$4,000,000	$5,000,000	$1,000,000
C.	Segment Return on Investment (A ÷ B)	25%	24.2%	21%
D.	Segment Target Profit Contribution (17.5% × B)	$ 700,000	$ 875,000	$ 175,000
E.	Residual Income (A − D)	$ 300,000	$ 335,000	$ 35,000

---

increase segment residual income from $300,000 to $335,000 and will also benefit the firm as a whole. This project might have been rejected if the basis for judgment had been return on investment maximization. Although the project's incremental rate of return is 21 percent (better than the 17.5 percent target rate), it will reduce Lisa Division's average return on investment from 25 to 24.2 percent.

RESIDUAL INCOME AS A VARIANCE MEASURE

If each segment's profit contribution is set accurately and fairly, residual income can be used to measure the efficiency of individual segments and their managers. Because segment residual income is a residual amount, it may be interpreted as a deviation or *variance* of actual from planned performance. The size and direction of such variances are easily understandable and communicable—advantages that support the use of residual income as a control and evaluation device.

On the other hand, segment residual income is less widely understood and accepted than is return on investment. Every decision maker has a "feel" for the meaning of a 10 or 20 percent rate of return because these measures are so widely used in analysis and decision making. It can be argued that although residual income is a specialized, tailor-made measure with localized applications, return on investment affords more general comprehension and comparability.

RESIDUAL INCOME AND THE COST OF CAPITAL

The use of residual income requires that the amount of target profit contribution and/or the desired return on investment rate be determined beforehand. The observations concerning target rates of return and the cost of capital in the segment return on investment context also apply to residual income calculations. If a target return on investment is used, it should be set in terms of the anticipated opportunity cost of funds employable in segment resources of a comparable risk class.

Should each segment have its own target profit contribution rate or should separate rates be established for each subclass of segment assets? Alternatively, should a single firm-wide target rate be established? Separate target rates are desirable in order to reflect the different characteristics of each segment's activities and resources—their cost structure, markets, products, size, and age. In practice, the tendency is still to establish a single firm-wide target profit contribution rate.

A segment's target profit contribution can be determined by applying the target return on investment rate to the assets for which segment management is responsible. Or a target residual income could be specified simply as a predetermined dollar amount. The segment could be allowed to select the size of its own investment base and then try to achieve that target residual income. Under this latter approach, segment management could be evaluated for its investment as well as its operating decisions.

Example: The operating results for Albatross Company's two divisions, Enko and Ixxon, are shown in Figure 20–15.

When a target return on investment rate above 13.75 percent is applied to both divisions, Enko has a larger residual income than Ixxon. At the 13.75 percent level, the two segments earn the same residual income; below that level Ixxon performs better. However, as noted previously, the target rate of return need not be the same for each division. If Enco and Ixxon Divisions had individual target return on investment rates, their residual incomes might be quite different.

FIGURE 20–15

Albatross Company—Enko and Ixxon Divisions
Residual Income Analysis

	Enco	Ixxon
Segment Resources............................	$2,000,000	$10,000,000
Segment Profit Contribution	$ 400,000	$ 1,500,000
Actual Segment Return on Investment...........	20%	15%
Target Profit Contribution:		
1. 10% Return on Investment	$ 200,000	$ 1,000,000
2. 13.75% Return on Investment	275,000	1,375,000
3. 15% Return on Investment	300,000	1,500,000
4. 20% Return on Investment	400,000	2,000,000
Residual Income:		
1. 10% Return on Investment	$ 200,000	$ 500,000
2. 13.75% Return on Investment	125,000	125,000
3. 15% Return on Investment	100,000	0
4. 20% Return on Investment	0	(500,000)

The important conclusion suggested by this example is that, with a given set of resources, the total amount of segment residual income is sensitive to the target return on investment rate used in calculating residual income. Therefore, any segment comparisons based on residual income data should be preceded by careful specification of each division's target return on investment rate.

RESIDUAL INCOME AND IMPLICIT INTEREST DEPRECIATION

Because it is derived from accrual accounting measures of segment profit contribution and investment base, residual income is subject to the same inconsistencies as the return on investment figure. Residual income, like return on investment based on accounting book values, will usually escalate over the life of a project or set of segment activities.

Example: Using the data from Marengo Corporation cited previously, assume that a target return on investment rate of 15 percent has been established. A conventional income statement approach, using straight-line depreciation, would report the increasing amounts of residual income shown in Figure 20–16. But use of the implicit interest depreciation method results in the residual incomes shown in Figure 20–17. The residual income now *declines* each year. This is consistent with the expectation that an asset base will produce progressively smaller earnings in the latter years of its economic life. In this case, the residual income is 5 percent of the asset base per year. This is a mathematical necessity, because reported income and target income were 15 percent and 10 percent of the asset base, respectively. Finally, when cash flows diverge from their budgeted amounts, residual income under the implicit interest depreciation method increases or decreases with operating cash flows, as shown in Figure 20–18.

FIGURE 20–16

Marengo Corporation—Quadraphonic Division
Segment Residual Income
Using Straight-Line Depreciation

		Year 1	Year 2	Year 3	Year 4
A.	Operating Cash Flow	$200,000	$200,000	$200,000	$200,000
B.	Less: Straight-Line Depreciation ($517,600 ÷ 4)	129,400	129,400	129,400	129,400
C.	Segment Profit Contribution	$ 70,600	$ 70,600	$ 70,600	$ 70,600
D.	Beginning Investment Base	$517,600	$388,200	$258,800	$129,400
E.	Target Income Requirement (15% × D)	$ 77,640	$ 58,230	$ 38,820	$ 19,410
F.	Residual Income (C − E)	($ 7,040)	$ 12,370	$ 31,780	$ 51,190

FIGURE 20–17

Marengo Corporation—Quadraphonic Division
Segment Residual Income
Using Implicit Interest Depreciation

		Year 1	Year 2	Year 3	Year 4
A.	Operating Cash Flow	$200,000	$200,000	$200,000	$200,000
B.	Less: Implicit Interest Depreciation ..	96,480	115,776	138,931	166,413
C.	Segment Profit Contribution	$103,520	$ 84,224	$ 61,069	$ 33,587
D.	Beginning Investment Base	$517,600	$421,120	$305,344	$166,413
E.	Target Income Requirement (15% × D)	$ 77,640	$ 63,168	$ 45,802	$ 24,962
F.	Residual Income (C − E)	$ 25,920	$ 21,056	$ 15,267	$ 8,625

FIGURE 20–18

Marengo Corporation—Quadraphonic Division
Segment Residual Income
Using Implicit Interest Depreciation

		Year 1	Year 2	Year 3	Year 4
A.	Operating Cash Flow	$200,000	$220,000	$200,000	$180,000
B.	Less: Implicit Interest Depreciation ..	96,480	115,776	138,931	166,413
C.	Segment Profit Contribution	$103,520	$104,224	$ 61,069	$ 13,587
D.	Beginning Investment Base	$517,600	$421,120	$305,344	$166,413
E.	Target Income Requirement (15% × D)	$ 77,600	$ 63,168	$ 45,802	$ 24,962
F.	Residual Income (C − E)	$ 25,920	$ 52,608	$ 15,267	($ 11,375)

TRANSFER PRICING AND INVESTMENT CENTER EVALUATION

Transfer prices for short-run decision making should be set at the incremental cost to the firm as a whole. However, such prices may produce discord among divisions seeking to achieve investment center goals such as return on investment or residual income. The essential problem is to specify a single transfer pricing procedure that satisfies both decision making and performance evaluation needs.

Example: The Switch Division of Eastco, Incorporated produces a switch used by manufacturers of electrical appliances. The division's annual fixed costs are $210,000. The variable cost per switch is $6. At present, the division is responsible for productive assets of $300,000 and has been instructed to maximize its rate of return on investment subject to a target rate of 10 percent. Sales to external customers amount to 60,000 units per year at a price of $10 per unit. Production capacity is 60,000 units per year. Under these conditions, operating at full capacity, the Switch Division can achieve its 10 percent target return on investment.

The Appliance Division of Eastco has an annual demand for 30,000 switches, which it purchases from an outside supplier for $9 each. Capacity in the Switch Division can be increased by 30,000 units annually if assets costing $150,000 are acquired. The additional production would also require annual increases in fixed costs of $82,500.

Should Eastco's Switch Division supply the 30,000 switches to the Appliance Division at $9 per unit? From the standpoint of performance evaluation, the Switch Division will probably *reject* the $9 transfer price because it would reduce the Division's return on investment below the 10 percent target level, as shown in Figure 20–19. This $9 transfer price offers only a 5 percent incremental rate of return to the Switch Division and reduces the division's average return on investment to 8⅓ percent. Because the division's goal is to earn at least a 10 percent target return on investment, this proposal is not acceptable to the Switch Division.

On the other hand, from a company-wide viewpoint, the proposal should be accepted. The decision making transfer price, which represents the incremental cost to the whole firm of producing the additional 30,000 switches for the Appliance Division, is calculated as follows:

$$
\begin{aligned}
\text{Decision Making Transfer Price} & \\
\text{(for 30,000 additional units)} &= \text{Incremental Cost per Unit} \\
&= \text{Variable Cost per Unit} \\
&\quad + \text{Incremental Fixed Cost per Unit} \\
&\quad + \text{Lost Contribution Margin} \\
&= \$6 + \frac{\$82,500}{30,000} + \$0 \\
&= \$6 + \$2.75 \\
&= \$8.75
\end{aligned}
$$

Because this $8.75 transfer price is less than the $9 outside purchase price, the firm as a whole would benefit from the internal transaction. However, at the proposed $9 transfer price, the Appliance Division will be indifferent as to whether it buys from the Switch Division or from its present outside supplier. Furthermore, the Switch Division will probably resist the transaction because, although its segment profit contribution would *increase* from $30,000 to $37,500, its return on investment would *decrease* from 10 to 8⅓ percent.

If the Switch Division refuses the $9 price—which is logical in view of its 10 percent return on investment goal—the Appliance Division's performance will not be affected. It will continue to purchase switches from the outside supplier for $9 each. However, suppose the Switch Division is offered a $10 transfer price to supply switches to the Appliance Division. This price will be attractive to the Switch Division, as demonstrated in Figure 20–20.

FIGURE 20-19

Switch Division of Eastco, Incorporated
Present and Proposed Return on Investment—
$9 Transfer Price

	Present Position		Proposed Position		Incremental	
Sales................		$600,000		$870,000		$270,000
Variable Costs........	$360,000		$540,000		$180,000	
Fixed Costs..........	210,000	570,000	292,500	832,500	82,500	262,500
Segment Profit Contribution		$ 30,000		$ 37,500		$ 7,500
Asset Base		$300,000		$450,000		$150,000
Return on Investment ..	$\dfrac{\$30,000}{\$300,000} = 10\%$		$\dfrac{\$37,500}{\$450,000} = 8\frac{1}{3}\%$		$\dfrac{\$7,500}{\$150,000} = 5\%$	

A $10 per unit transfer price will increase the Switch Division's average return on investment to 15 percent, with an incremental return on investment of 25 percent. However, the Appliance Division, which is now buying switches for $9 per unit, will not want to purchase them from the Switch Division for $10 per unit. The proposed internal transfer would benefit the whole firm in savings on acquisition costs of $7,500 (30,000 units at $9 versus 30,000 units at $8.75). But if the Switch Division holds out for a $10 transfer price (the price it obtains in the external market) or if the Appliance Division insists on a $9 price (its cost from the outside supplier), interdivisional conflicts will result. As noted in Chapter 19, situations like this call for negotiations, or even for higher level arbitration, to avoid incorrect company-wide decisions and disharmony among divisional managers.

FIGURE 20-20

Switch Division of Eastco, Incorporated
Present and Proposed Return on Investment—
$10 Transfer Price

	Present Position		Proposed Position		Incremental	
Sales................		$600,000		$900,000		$300,000
Variable Costs........	$360,000		$540,000		$180,000	
Fixed Costs..........	210,000	570,000	292,500	832,500	82,500	262,500
Segment Profit Contribution		$ 30,000		$ 67,500		$ 37,500
Asset Base		$300,000		$450,000		$150,000
Return on Investment ..	$\dfrac{\$30,000}{\$300,000} = 10\%$		$\dfrac{\$67,500}{\$450,000} = 15\%$		$\dfrac{\$37,500}{\$150,000} = 25\%$	

SUMMARY

1. Complex and frustrating problems arise when attempts are made to evaluate the performance of company segments that are treated as investment centers. There is no shortage of proposed solutions to these problems, but each solution has shortcomings as well as advantages. In reviewing the major points raised in this chapter, remember that no single method is a conclusive or all-purpose solution to the investment center evaluation problem.

2. *Short-term Measurements of Long-term Operations*   Most conventional methods of evaluating the performance of investment centers are essentially single period measures, focusing only on the results of segment activities during the current period. This is an unfortunate side effect of accounting systems designed primarily to measure periodic accounting income. Its worst result is a tendency for segment management to seek to improve its own short-term periodic performance measures at the expense of firm-wide performance, both short- and long-term, and at the expense of its own long-term performance. Manipulation of accounting results, suboptimal operating and investment decisions, and other types of gamesmanship were cited as examples.

3. *Emphasis on Single Performance Characteristics*   When segment profit contribution, segment return on investment, or segment residual income are used as evaluation criteria, they foster some degree of preoccupation with a single dimension of segment performance. Although such specific, understandable, and measurable goals are helpful, management tends to focus on that single aspect of achievement at the expense of efficient overall performance. Consequently, exclusive use of a single performance measure should be discouraged.

4. Likewise, preoccupation with the absolute results of a single period should not be encouraged. Instead, more attention should be given to variances from predetermined performance measures during the period, to trends and changes in performance over time, and to cumulative results. Also, because most of the suggested performance criteria are composite and integrated measures, there will be a tendency to seek combinations of activities that maximize segment return on investment and segment residual income. This may be less beneficial to the segment and to the whole firm than are measurements that emphasize control and improvement of the basic operating variables, such as sales growth, production mix, and cost minimization.

5. *Accounting Measurement Problems*   Most evaluation methods involve a variety of possible accounting interpretations and alternative accounting methods. Segment profit contribution requires that controllable and/or attributable revenues be traced to segments. The same issue of traceability arises in connection with segment resources used in segment return on investment and residual income calculations. The identification and measurement of assets to be included in the investment base requires choosing among various accounting options—total or net assets; book value of assets, acquisition cost, or replacement cost; conventional depreciation methods

or implicit interest depreciation; and the treatment of idle resources and unrecorded assets.

6. Reference to a cost of capital concept in most evaluation methods introduces a measurement problem, as well as the issue of whether to use single or multiple rates for each segment or a single firm-wide rate. When target rates or target profit amounts are needed, it is always difficult to decide what constitutes an appropriate level of segment achievement.

7. *Misemphasis on Comparisons and Rankings*   Segment performance evaluation should not be viewed exclusively as a process of comparing the results of various segments. Instead of ranking segments on the basis of common criteria (that is, by size of segment, profit contribution, return on investment, or residual income), it is more appropriate to assess each segment's performance against separate targets or goals, using variance analysis techniques.

8. Comparative evaluation, if carefully controlled and used in appropriate situations, can improve a firm's overall performance by encouraging internal competitiveness. However, if used to excess, it may lead to a breakdown of coordination within the company as segments strive to optimize their local achievements. Also, if comparisons are made when no equitable basis for such comparisons exists, the result may be frustration, conflict, and deteriorating total performance as certain managers realize that their units are not able to compete effectively with other segments.

9. *Suboptimization and Goal Incongruence*   The misuse of segment performance evaluation often results in suboptimal performance from the viewpoint of the firm as a whole. This is typically caused by setting segment goals that are incompatible with firm-wide objectives. In a decentralized firm, a delicate balance must be sought between reaching organizational goals and maintaining coordination, control, and effectiveness. Once the balance shifts toward allowing divisional managers to make decisions that improve their own standing at the organization's expense, the value of decentralization becomes questionable. A segment performance evaluation system must provide controls to prevent this from happening, but at the same time must give the divisions incentives to participate at a satisfactory level of overall effectiveness.

KEY WORDS AND PHRASES

Investment Center (1013)
Rate of Return (1013)
Segment Return on Investment Ratio (1013)
Target Rate of Return (1016)
Asset Turnover Rate (1016)
Cost of Capital (1019)
Suboptimization (1020)
Segment Profit Contribution (1021)
Investment Base (1022)
Cash Flow Generating Rate (1025)
Current Replacement Cost (1025)
Acquisition Cost (1026)
Implicit Interest Depreciation (1028)
Dual Measurement System (1031)
Residual Income (1031)
Incremental Investments (1033)
Segment Transfer Prices (1037)

Questions

1. Define an investment center. What aspects of segment performance must be evaluated if a segment is to be treated as an investment center?

2. What concepts of responsibility accounting are important for investment center evaluation?

3. What do rates of return measure?

4. Explain the advantages of return on investment as a measure of the performance of investment centers.

5. Outline some of the shortcomings of the use of return on investment as a measure of the performance of investment centers.

6. Differentiate between segment return on total assets and segment return on net assets (or net investment, or owners equity).

7. Outline the situations in which the two return on investment measures mentioned in Question 6 will be useful.

8. "Each segment should maximize its own return on investment." Critically evaluate this assertion.

9. Explain how the decomposition of return on investment into the two separate measures of profit performance and resource productivity is useful in evaluating investment center performance.

10. What purposes are served by segment target rates of return (segment cost of capital rates)?

11. "All investment center segments should be evaluated in relation to a single, uniform, cost of capital rate." Critically evaluate this assertion.

12. Evaluate the usefulness of (1) *multiple* segment cost of capital rates and (2) *structured* segment cost of capital rates.

13. What important items are omitted from measures of the investment base developed from conventional accounting records?

14. List several different ways in which the segment investment base may be measured. Briefly explain the usefulness of each.

15. Why is it so critical that current replacement cost information be incorporated in segment return on investment measures?

16. What built-in bias of return in investment measures based on accounting book value of assets and net income causes them to favor segments with relatively old assets?

17. What is the relevance of the implicit interest method of depreciation for segment return on investment purposes?

18. Explain the concept of segment residual income. What does it measure?

19. Compare residual income and return on investment as measures of segment performance for evaluation purposes.

20. What different cost of capital rates might be used in measuring segment residual income? Which one(s) do you prefer? Why?

21. "Residual income resolves all the decision making dilemmas and performance evaluation confusion that return on investment generates." Critically evaluate this assertion.

22. How do transactions among a company's segments confuse the procedures of investment center evaluation?

23. Assess the overall complexity of attempting to evaluate the period-to-period performance of investment centers committed to the operation of multi-period projects.

24. What aspects of investment center performance cannot conveniently be included in accounting measures of performance?

Exercises

E 20–1   Return on Investment—Elementary Analysis

Required:
Determine the missing amounts in each of the following independent situations. Return on investment is based on average assets for the year.

	A	B	C	D
Sales	$400,000	$1,800,000	$	$ 300,000
Cost of Goods Sold	150,000		200,000	
Gross Profit	$250,000	$ 600,000	$ 300,000	$ 200,000
Operating Expenses	200,000			220,000
Net Income	$ 50,000	$ 200,000	$ 200,000	$
Assets—January 1	$150,000	$	$	$1,800,000
Assets—December 31	250,000	400,000	1,200,000	
Rate of Return on Sales				
Revenue Generating Rate		3		$\frac{1}{3}$
Return on Investment..........	%	%	20%	%

E 20–2   Ranking Divisional Performance

Cook Company's three sales divisions are treated as investment centers. Their operating results for the first quarter of 19X1 were as follows:

	Purtell Division	Munro Division	Pike Division
Sales	$360,000	$400,000	$500,000
Segment Assets	$120,000	$320,000	$280,000
Segment Profit Contribution	$ 14,400	$ 16,000	$ 33,600
Target Rate of Return	10.5%	7.5%	12.5%

Required:
(a) Rank the three divisions' performance as investment centers for the first quarter of 19X1 based on (1) segment profit contribution, (2) segment return on investment, and (3) segment residual income.

(b) Comment on the results in part (a).

(c) Why do the divisions have different target rates of return?

(d) An incremental project is available and could be implemented by any of the three divisions. It has a potential profit return of $4,400 and requires an outlay of $40,000.

How would each of the sales division managers respond to this proposal if they have been told to (1) maximize segment return on investment or (2) maximize segment residual income?

E 20-3   Asset Base—Alternative Measures

Selkrig Division of Thompson Corporation had the following operating results for 19X2:

Sales	$3,600,000
Operating Expenses	(2,400,000)
Depreciation	(800,000)
Divisional Profit	$ 400,000
Average Assets (at cost)	$4,000,000
Average Assets (at book value)	3,200,000
Average Assets (at current replacement cost)	5,000,000
Depreciation (current cost basis)	1,000,000

Divisional management expresses concern over the number of different ways in which divisional return on investment can be calculated.

Required:
(a)   Calculate the division's return on investment for 19X2, based on:
   (1)   Divisional profit and assets at book value
   (2)   Divisional operating cash flow and assets at acquisition cost
   (3)   Divisional profit on a current cost basis and assets at current replacement costs
(b)   Compare the results in part (a) and comment fully on the interpretation of each.
(c)   Which of the three return on investment figures do you prefer? Why?

E 20-4   Return on Investment—Elementary Incremental Analysis

Hanover Corporation is about to add a new item to its product line. Projected sales of the new product are 10,000 units per year at a price of $3,000 per unit. Anticipated variable production and distribution costs are $1,000 per unit; annual fixed costs attributable to the product will amount to $10,000,000. Assets directly traceable to the production and distribution activities for the new product will be $50,000,000. The new product will make use of existing production facilities and an estimated $2,000,000 per year will be allocated to the new product for their use. The facilities involved have a book value of $14,000,000.

The new product introduction has been held up because, based on an analysis of the information, it apparently will not satisfy the firm's required 18 percent return on all new investments. The projected rate of return is only 12½ percent—($8,000,000 ÷ $64,000,000). Presently the firm is generating an overall rate of return of 16 percent. However, this includes, on the one hand two product lines that are generating returns in excess of 30 percent, and on the other hand, a substantial amount of idle plant assets, some of which will be utilized by this new product.

Required:
(a)   Prepare an analysis to show how the 12½ percent rate of return figure was apparently derived.

(b)   Prepare a revised analysis based on an incremental approach to this problem. Should the product line be added? Why or why not?

(c)   Decisions of this type have both incremental and long-run average implications. Discuss the problems involved.

E 20–5   Residual Income—Elementary Analysis

Required:
For each of the following situations, determine the missing amounts. The target rate of return is 20 percent in all cases.

	1	2	3	4	5
Profit Contribution	$100,000	$200,000			$500,000
Assets	$100,000		$2,000,000	$3,000,000	
Return on Investment		25%	30%		
Residual Income				$ 100,000	($30,000)

E 20–6   Residual Income—Return on Investment—Elementary Analysis

Bowmer Corporation has four operating divisions—Baker, Logan, Rooney, and Fenton. For 19X7, results of their operations included the following:

	Baker	Logan	Rooney	Fenton
Divisional Assets	$360,000	$280,000	$840,000	$160,000
Divisional Profit Contribution	$ 60,000	$ 50,000	$120,000	$ 34,000
Sales	$180,000	$560,000	$420,000	$480,000

Required:
(a)   Calculate return on investment for each division. Decompose return on investment into its two components: rate of return on sales and revenue generating rate.

(b)   Calculate residual income for each division, assuming a target rate of return of (1) 10, (2) 15, and (3) 20 percent.

(c)   Comment on the results of part (b).

(d)   Which division was most profitable? Why?

E 20–7   Investment Center Performance Evaluation— Alternative Depreciation Methods

Rice Corporation encourages its division managers to pursue profitable new opportunities by rewarding the top three managers each year. The rankings are determined on the basis of maximum return on investment, calculated on the basis of divisional controllable profit and book value of divisional net assets. Anne, the manager of the Stanley Division, is currently in the top three with recent results of 18 percent return on investment on an asset base of $600,000. She is presently considering a project that requires a $150,000 outlay and will generate operating cash flows of $50,000 for each of the next five years. This project would satisfy a 20 percent cost of capital requirement using net present value analysis. (For purposes of this question, treat the present value of a five-period annuity of $1 at 20 percent as being equal to 3.000.)

Required:

(a) Prepare an analysis to show the impact of accepting the project on the Stanley Division's return on investment for each of the next five years, using (1) straight-line depreciation, (2) sum-of-the-years'-digits depreciation, and (3) implicit interest depreciation. Assume that other operations continue to generate the same results and that the $600,000 asset base remains unchanged. Use beginning of the year asset base balances for all rate of return calculations.

(b) Comment on the results of part (a).

(c) Which depreciation method should Anne use? Why?

(d) Should Anne accept the project? Why or why not?

E 20–8 Divisional Performance Evaluation—
Alternative Return on Investment Formulations

Divisional profit reports and balance sheets for Carioca Corporation are as follows:

	Eudare Division	Sportster Division
Divisional Profit Reports		
Sales	$400,000	$600,000
Controllable Divisional Costs	310,000	470,000
Controllable Divisional Profit	$ 90,000	$130,000
Allocated Common Costs	50,000	65,000
Divisional Net Income	$ 40,000	$ 65,000
Divisional Balance Sheets		
Current Assets	$120,000	$190,000
Plant Assets (net)	240,000	390,000
	$360,000	$580,000
Liabilities	$230,000	$320,000
Owners' Equity	130,000	260,000
	$360,000	$580,000

Controllable divisional costs include interest expense of $15,000 for Eudare and $20,000 for Sportster. Accumulated depreciation was $60,000 for Eudare and $130,000 for Sportster. Depreciation expense was $20,000 for Eudare and $40,000 for Sportster.

Required:

(a) Calculate return on investment for the two divisions using the following combinations:
  (1) Controllable profit and net assets
  (2) Net income and net assets
  (3) Total assets (book value) and the most appropriate income measure
  (4) Total assets (acquisition cost) and operating cash flow (excluding interest)

(b) Discuss the relative usefulness for evaluation purposes of the four sets of measures developed in part (b).

(c) Which division was more profitable? Why?

Cases

C 20–1   Comparing Cost of Capital Rates

The corporate level cost of capital requirement for Mundakal Company is 10 percent. Two investment center divisions, Sellwood and Mulley, generated the following operating results for 19X3:

	Sellwood	Mulley
Segment Profit Contribution	$120,000	$ 80,000
Segment Net Assets	750,000	375,000

Required:
(a) Which division was most profitable? What basis of comparison did you use, and why?
(b) Would your answer change if (1) the corporate cost of capital rate was 20 percent or (2) the cost of capital rate was 12 percent for Sellwood and 13⅓ percent for Mulley? Explain.
(c) Comment on the difficulties of specifying a cost of capital rate for investment center evaluation.

C 20–2   Comparing Return on Investment Rates

Trevillian Corporation has two divisions—Dalvaney and Tungston. For 19X8, Dalvaney reported a 15 percent return on investment, whereas Tungston returned only 10 percent.

Required:
(a) Is Dalvaney's performance superior to Tungston's? Why or why not?
(b) What additional information should be obtained to help clarify this issue?
(c) Should the corporation close down Tungston because of this situation? Why or why not?
(d) Assume that the Dalvaney Division is a grocery distributor and Tungston is a wholesale jeweller. Review the answers to parts (a) and (c) based on this information.

C 20–3   Ranking Investment Centers

Meredith Corporation has four divisions, with operating results for 19X3 as follows:

Division	Segment Profit Contribution	Segment Assets
W.........	$120,000	$500,000
X	60,000	200,000
Y	100,000	400,000
Z	60,000	300,000

Required:
(a) Rank these four divisions based on the following criteria:
    (1) Absolute segment profit contribution
    (2) Return on segment assets
    (3) Residual income (target return on investment is 20 percent for all segments)

(b)   Comment on the results of the evaluations of the divisions as shown in part (a).

(c)   Assume that the target return on investment is (1) 15 percent or (2) 25 percent. How would these changes affect the rankings? Comment.

C 20–4   Evaluate Rates of Return on Investment

Williams Corporation encourages its division managers to "operate as efficiently as possible and maximize the rate of return on income in relation to divisional assets." Conventional accounting measures (divisional profit contribution and book value of divisional assets) are used to measure return on investment. Aileen Division's manager purchases replacement assets only when absolutely forced to by the breakdown of existing assets. In addition, the replacement assets are always the cheapest available. Consequently, this division's rate of return has lately been considerably higher than that of divisions with managers who have recently purchased modern plant assets.

Required:
Discuss this situation from the point of view of (1) return on investment as a basis for evaluating operating efficiency and (2) the impact of return on investment measures on managerial decision making.

C 20–5   Evaluate Return on Investment Criteria

The new manager of the Berry Division of Hayes Company noted that the corporation's divisional managers were rewarded on the basis of the rate of return of divisional profit contribution in relation to divisional assets. Consequently, during his first few months on the job, he sold for cash several plant assets that were not currently in use and acquired a small portfolio of stocks that he believed would appreciate in market value within the year. He also made a $1,000,000 reduction in inventory levels of all major product lines. Finally, he negotiated a sale and lease-back of the division plant premises. The premises were sold for $6,000,000 cash and leased back for 50 years at $400,000 per year. Half of the sale proceeds was invested in 15 percent ten-year certificates of deposit and the remainder was held to "help make financing of current operating transactions more convenient."

Required:
(a)   Comment on the effect of these actions on the return on investment of Berry Division *for the current year*. Assume that all other aspects of operations were the same as in previous years.

(b)   Comment on the effect of these actions from a *long-run point of view*.

(c)   Evaluate the manager's actions *from the corporation's point of view*, commenting on the relative merits of return on investment as a measure of divisional performance.

C 20–6   Evaluate Return on Investment Criteria

"Return on investment has reached an inordinately exalted position in our organization! It is the one magic number that supposedly tells everything about efficiency of operations, whether it be one division or the whole firm! But what about its obvious flaws? It is usually far overstated because it fails to take into account so many things. Everyone is fooled into believing things are much better than they really are! What about assets used under operating leases? What about research and development costs? What about recruitment, training, and personnel development program costs? What about our firm's goodwill? None of those is included in the investment base. And, on the other hand, everyone knows that book assets are understated because conventional accounting only uses historical cost measures. Think how current replacement cost measures would turn this around!''

Required:
Critically evaluate this tirade delivered by a cynical manager. Do you agree or disagree? Why?

C 20–7   Evaluate Return on Investment Effects

For Contreras Company, the implementation of return on investment criteria for investment center evaluation led to dramatically improved profit and return on investment results for the first four years of its use. In subsequent years, return on investment has declined. This latter effect was accompanied by noticeable increases in cash and marketable securities balances and decreases in inventory and plant asset balances.

Required:
Comment on the possible causes of this development. What problems may have been created or accentuated by the emphasis on return on investment as a basis for performance evaluation and managerial remuneration? Discuss fully.

C 20–8   Evaluate Return on Investment Effects

A corporate executive of Blumenthal Company contends, ''Minimization of inventory levels and disposal of idle assets are favorable side effects of implementing divisional objectives that stress maximizing return on investment.''

Required:
Critically evaluate this assertion. Do you agree? Why or why not?

C 20–9   Return on Investment Asset Base

A divisional manager for Suribachi Company asserts, ''Only controllable assets should be included in the investment base for return on investment and residual income calculation purposes. This implies that divisions are not required to earn any return on shared or corporate-wide resources.''

Required:
Critically evaluate this conclusion. Do you agree? Why or why not?

C 20–10   Cost Center or Investment Center?

Novick National Bank has seventeen branch offices. A centralized computer division services all the data processing needs of the branches and, in addition, provides consulting and data processing services to outside clients who are mostly regular bank customers.

The computer division is now accounted for as a cost center. Revenues from customer services are reported as separate income and are not reflected in reports of the performance of the computer division. Therefore, the division's budgeted and actual operating reports contain only expense items. For various reasons—including prestige, motivational impact, and responsibility—the computer division manager has requested that in the future her division be treated as an investment center.

Required:
(a) Evaluate the proposed change. Is it appropriate to treat the computer division as an investment center? Comment specifically on the issues of proportion of outside business, authority for investment decisions, and transfer prices.

C 20–11 Qualitative Evaluation of Investment Centers

Besides profitability, decentralized units of large corporations often need to be evaluated in terms of performance criteria in areas such as

1. Market share
2. Employee relations
3. Community relations
4. Environmental issues
5. Innovation and creativity
6. Personnel development
7. Productivity improvement
8. Long-range growth and stability
9. Customer relations
10. Public image

Required:
(a) What aspects, if any, of these ten areas can be included in traditional accounting reports of performance of a firm's independent investment center divisions?
(b) Do return on investment or residual income evaluation techniques include consideration of any of the ten items? If so, which ones and how?
(c) Comment on the limitations of accounting-type evaluations of divisional performance in relation to these diverse criteria.

Problems

P 20–1 Investment Center Evaluation—Alternative Return on Investment Formulations

Shannon Corporation has developed the following divisional profit reports for its two divisions, Flight and Blue Legend, which are treated as investment centers:

	Flight	Blue Legend
Sales	$1,000,000	$1,500,000
Operating Expenses	$ 550,000	$ 850,000
Interest	40,000	100,000
Depreciation	60,000	100,000
	$ 650,000	$1,050,000
Controllable Divisional Income	$ 350,000	$ 450,000
Common Firm-wide Costs	150,000	200,000
Net Income	$ 200,000	$ 250,000
Current Assets	$ 250,000	$ 350,000
Plant Assets (cost)	1,900,000	3,400,000
Accumulated Depreciation	(450,000)	(650,000)
Total Assets	$1,700,000	$3,100,000
Current Liabilities	$ 200,000	$ 300,000
Long-term Debt	500,000	1,200,000
Owners' Equity	1,000,000	1,600,000
Total Equities	$1,700,000	$3,100,000

Required:
(a) Calculate return on investment for each division using
   (1) Net assets (book value) and net income
   (2) Total assets (book value) and the appropriate controllable income measure
   (3) Total assets (acquisition cost) and operating cash flow
(b) Assuming sales volume, productivity, maintenance costs, and price levels remain approximately constant over time, what will happen to return on investment based on book value of net assets? Explain.
(c) Assuming sales volume, productivity, and maintenance costs remain approximately constant over time, but price levels increase, what will happen to return on investment based on book value of net assets? Explain.
(d) What revised measures of the asset base and periodic income would help overcome some of the problems noted in parts (b) and (c)? Explain.

P 20–2   Lease-or-Purchase Decision—Return on Investment Implications

Callaghan Division of Deviney Corporation is considering acquisition of equipment that has the potential to reduce annual operating costs by $28,000. This equipment can be purchased for $80,000 and will have a five-year life with no resale value. However, the division manager is hesitant to approve the purchase because the immediate impact in the first year would appear to reduce his division's return on investment below its present level of 22 percent. He supports this view with the following calculations:

$$\frac{\text{Cost Savings} - \text{Depreciation}}{\text{Outlay}} = \frac{\$28,000 - \$16,000}{\$80,000}$$

$$= \frac{\$12,000}{\$80,000}$$

$$= \underline{\underline{15\%}}$$

The equipment sales company responds to the apparent loss of a sale by offering to lease the equipment to Callaghan for five years for $24,000 annually under a noncancellable lease agreement.

Callaghan's current period results show divisional profit of $44,000 on an asset base of $200,000. Deviney Corporation observes a 16 percent target rate of return on all proposed new projects.

Required:
(a) Evaluate the division manager's decision not to purchase the equipment. Was it correct? Why or why not?
(b) Will the incremental rate of return on the purchased assets continue to be 15 percent in later years? Why or why not? Show calculations. Use average assets for the year in the investment base.
(c) What will be the effect of leasing on the division's return on investment? Should the equipment be leased? Why or why not?
(d) Comment on the implications of operating leases (not shown on balance sheet) for return on investment calculations and for performance evaluation in general.

P 20-3 Return on Investment—Residual Income— Evaluation of Performance—Incremental Analysis

Blackhawk Manufacturing Company, a decentralized producer of building materials, has a firm-wide goal of 18 percent return on investment. The following data relate to the company's operating divisions:

	Income	Investment
Division D	$15,000	$100,000
Division E	$25,000	$125,000
Division F	$10,000	$ 40,000

Blackhawk is currently considering a new venture that would be placed in one of the existing operating divisions. The project will have assets of $15,000 and earn $3,000 per year.

Required: (Answer parts (a), (b), and (c) without reference to the proposed venture.)
(a) Compute the return on investment for each division.
(b) Compute the residual income for each division.
(c) Rank the divisions according to performance. Comment on what method of evaluation you used and why.
(d) Should the new venture be undertaken? Why?
(e) Which division should receive the project? Why?

P 20-4 Incremental Analysis—Residual Income— Return on Investment

The Food Products Distribution Division of Meadowlands Corporation has budgeted 19X6 revenues of $160,000,000, expenses of $150,000,000, and net assets of $30,000,000. A cost of capital of 10 percent is being observed.

An opportunity has arisen to acquire the Apmat Food Chain, which would be operated as an additional division. The price to purchase Apmat outright is $20,000,000 and forecasts indicate that it will generate revenue of $72,000,000 and expenses of $68,-000,000 (including $1,000,000 interest on a $6,000,000 loan needed to help finance the acquisition of Apmat).

Required:
(a) Analyze this proposal from the viewpoint of its effect on the budgeted rate of return on net assets.
(b) Analyze this proposal from the viewpoint of its effect on budgeted residual income.
(c) Should the Apmat Food Chain be acquired? Why or why not?

P 20–5   Investment Center Evaluation—Incremental Project Analysis—Return on Investment and Residual Income

Esperanza Corporation has three operating divisions, Hannah, Marti, and Gini. Results of their activities for 19X2 are as follows:

	Hannah	Marti	Gini
Sales	$4,000,000	$2,000,000	$3,000,000
Operating Expenses	1,800,000	1,300,000	1,200,000
Operating Income	$2,200,000	$ 700,000	$1,800,000
Interest (10%)	200,000	60,000	400,000
Income before Tax...........	$2,000,000	$ 640,000	$1,400,000
Taxes (50%)	1,000,000	320,000	700,000
Income after Tax	$1,000,000	$ 320,000	$ 700,000
Total Divisional Assets	$8,800,000	$5,000,000	$7,500,000

Each year the manager whose division reports the highest rate of return on total assets on an after-tax basis is rewarded with an expense-paid vacation to Sydney, Australia. Competition for this award has led to noticeably improved results in all three divisions.

As of January 1, 19X3, the corporation has secured a new project that is compatible with all three divisions. The project requires an outlay of $2,000,000, of which $1,000,000 must be financed from additional external borrowing at 10 percent per year. Annual operating income generated by the project will be $400,000.

Required:
(a) What rate of return on investment (calculated according to the previously stated evaluation criteria) was earned by each division in 19X2? Who got the trip Down Under?
(b) What response would each division manager have to the proposed project? Who, if anyone, would accept it? Why?
(c) From the corporation's viewpoint, should the project be accepted? By which division? Why?
(d) Assume that instead of the original evaluation criteria, divisions were instructed to maximize their residual income based on a target rate of return of 15 percent on net assets. Answer parts (b) and (c) under this revised assumption.

P 20–6 Investment Center Performance Evaluation—Measurement of Divisional Assets and Income—to Allocate or not to Allocate?

Harding Corporation has three divisions, Annette, Leslie, and Patricia. Results of operations for 19X3 were reported as follows:

	Annette	Leslie	Patricia
Sales	$400,000	$600,000	$1,000,000
Cost of Goods Sold	200,000	280,000	660,000
Gross Profit	$200,000	$320,000	$ 340,000
Marketing and			
Administrative Expenses	80,000	180,000	160,000
Net Income	$120,000	$140,000	$ 180,000
Plant Assets (net)	$450,000	$600,000	$ 750,000
Current Assets	$ 80,000	$140,000	$ 120,000
Current Liabilities	$ 60,000	$ 40,000	$ 20,000

Further investigation revealed the following:

1. Cost of goods sold includes $360,000 of joint production costs that were allocated to the divisions on the basis of sales revenue. All other components of cost of goods sold can be traced directly to the divisions.

2. Marketing and administrative expenses includes $215,000 of firm-wide expenses allocated to divisions in proportion to divisional gross profits as previously reported. All other marketing and administrative expenses are directly traceable to divisions.

3. Plant assets which are used jointly by all three divisions amount to $600,000 and were assigned arbitrarily to the divisions as follows: Annette, $150,000; Leslie, $200,000; and Patricia, $250,000.

4. All current assets and liabilities are directly traceable to divisions, except for $60,000 in cash which was divided equally among the divisions.

Required:

(a) Calculate the return on investment for each division, using divisional net income and divisional net assets as originally specified.

(b) Calculate residual income for each division, using the same original reports and assuming a target rate of return of 15 percent.

(c) Rank the divisions based on the results of (1) part (a) and (2) part (b).

(d) Repeat parts (a), (b), and (c), restricting the analysis to controllable divisional profit contribution and controllable divisional net assets.

(e) Comment on the differences in the performance measures used in the two sections of part (c). Which is more appropriate, the fully allocated approach or the controllable items only approach? Why?

P 20–7 Evaluating Divisional Performance—Investment Rate of Return

Darby Products, Inc., consists of three independent divisions—Household Products, Jewelry Products, and Pharmaceutical Products. The household products market is very large, but competition is extremely keen. Therefore, the margin earned by the Household

Products Division tends to be small in comparison with the other two divisions. Condensed income statements of the three divisions for 19X5, the most recent year, follow:

	Household	Jewelry	Pharmaceutical
Sales	$12,000,000	$8,000,000	$4,000,000
Less: Variable Costs	9,000,000	5,000,000	1,500,000
Contribution Margin	$ 3,000,000	$3,000,000	$2,500,000
Less: Fixed Costs:			
Direct to the division	$ 2,400,000	$1,800,000	$2,000,000
Allocated from corporate headquarters*	480,000	320,000	160,000
Total Fixed Costs	$ 2,880,000	$2,120,000	$2,160,000
Net Operating Income	$ 120,000	$ 880,000	$ 340,000

* Allocated on a basis of sales dollars.

Top management treats the divisions as if they were separate companies, allowing the divisional managers great discretion to make investment, operating, and borrowing decisions. In a recent management development course, the executive vice-president learned that a popular way of evaluating divisional performance under these circumstances is by the rate of return formula. After asking the accounting department to compute the rate of return generated by each division during 19X5, he has received the following data:

Household Products	3.20%
Jewelry Products	13.75%
Pharmaceutical Products	17.00%

The executive vice-president is shocked when he sees that the Household Products Division has earned a rate of return of only 3.2 percent during the year. He is all the more perplexed when he learns that the industry average rate of return for household products is about 7 percent. As the executive vice-president walks toward the president's office, he mutters to himself, "I'll give two-to-one odds that there's a new manager in that division by the end of the week."

Required:

(a) Show how the Accounting Department computed the rate of return figures given to the executive vice-president. Assume that average total assets for 19X5 were

Household Products	$3,750,000
Jewelry Products	$6,400,000
Pharmaceutical Products	$2,000,000

(b) What possible criticism can you make of the way the Accounting Department computed the rate of return figures?

(c) Assume that direct fixed costs of each division included interest expense as follows:

Household Products	$120,000
Jewelry Products	200,000
Pharmaceutical Products	20,000
	$340,000

In addition, borrowings directly traceable to each division were as follows:

Household Products...............	$1,500,000
Jewelry Products	2,000,000
Pharmaceutical Products	200,000
	$3,700,000

Using the foregoing information, recompute the rate of return figures as you think they should appear. Comment on the results of your computations.

(d) Should these three divisions be expected to generate comparable rate of return figures? Why or why not?

P 20-8 Structured and Multiple Target Rates of Return in Return on Investment and Residual Income Analysis

Macdougal Corporation is exploring the possibility of establishing separate structured target rates of return for its two investment center divisions, Baystone and Toparoa. This would replace the present procedure, whereby the divisions are evaluated against a firm-wide target rate of 20 percent. The structured rates are intended to reflect the relative profitability and riskiness of investments in different categories of assets. Because the compositions of asset holdings, product lines, and marketing areas of the two divisions are quite different, this change is considered appropriate. The proposed structured target rates of return are as follows:

Cash and Receivables	10%
Inventory	16%
Plant	25%

Budgeted operations for the coming year are as follows:

	Baystone	Toparoa
Divisional Income	$ 550,000	$ 670,000
Divisional Assets:		
Cash and Receivables	$ 400,000	$ 240,000
Inventories	750,000	360,000
Plant Assets (net)	1,250,000	2,000,000
	$2,400,000	$2,600,000

Required:
(a) Calculate the return on investment for each division.
(b) Calculate the residual income for each division, based on the original firm-wide target of 20 percent.
(c) Calculate the targeted divisional profit requirements based on the structured target rate previously specified.
(d) Calculate the residual income for each division, using the target requirements based on the structured rates.
(e) Comment on the advantages and the disadvantages of using structured rate of return requirements for evaluation purposes.

P 20–9   Alternative Depreciation Methods—Incremental Analysis— Investment Center Decisions

Fettle Division of Caduceus Corporation is considering an opportunity to expand operations. Using net present value analysis, it has found that the project will satisfy a cost of capital requirement well in excess of the present 20 percent specified by corporate management. However, the following schedule shows that the project will have some unpleasant effects on the division's annual profit projections and other measures over its three-year duration. The project will require outlays of $300,000 and will generate annual operating cash flows of $150,000 for each of the three years. The company uses sum-of-the-years'-digits depreciation, and assets required for this project will have no resale value. The following table shows a comparison of projected results *without* the project and projected results *with* the project.

Fettle Division
Budgeted Performance Report
(thousands of dollars)

	19X0 Without Project	19X0 With Project	19X1 Without Project	19X1 With Project	19X2 Without Project	19X2 With Project
Sales	$1,300	$1,550	$1,450	$1,700	$1,750	$2,000
Operating Expenses	$ (550)	$ (650)	$ (625)	$ (725)	$ (850)	$ (950)
Depreciation	(250)	(400)	(200)	(300)	(150)	(200)
Divisional Profit	$ 500	$ 500	$ 625	$ 675	$ 750	$ 850
Divisional Assets (beginning of year)	$2,000	$2,300	$2,200	$2,400	$2,500	$2,600
Return on Investment	25%	21.7%	28.4%	28.1%	30%	32.8%

The manager of Fettle Division is particularly concerned because his annual bonus depends on his division's return on investment relative to other divisions.

Required:
(a) Comment on the report as originally prepared. What would the manager of Fettle Division be inclined to do?
(b) Revise the parts of the schedule that apply to the acceptance of the project, using reverse sum-of-the-years'-digits depreciation.*
(c) Comment on the results of part (b).
(c) Should the project be accepted? Why or why not?
(e) Discuss the basic conflicts that arise between decision making using net present value analysis and performance evaluation based on conventional accounting reports.

P 20–10   Alternative Depreciation Methods—Effect on Return on Investment and Residual Income

Schumacher Division of Moore Corporation is preparing budgeted reports of its anticipated operations for the next four years. Budgeted divisional profit contribution before depreciation is $2,000,000 for each year. The division is responsible for assets of

* In reverse sum-of-the-years'-digits depreciation, the yearly fractions for a four-year asset are (1/10, 2/10, 3/10, 4/10) instead of (4/10, 3/10, 2/10, 1/10).

$5,000,000, including current assets of $2,000,000 and plant assets of $3,000,000. These plant assets will be acquired at the beginning of the first year of operations and will last for four years with no salvage value.

Divisions of the Moore Corporation are evaluated on the basis of annual rate of return on book value of divisional assets at the beginning of each year. Schumacher Division has not yet decided which depreciation method to use in reporting its earnings. Three methods are being considered: (1) straight-line, (2) sum-of-the-years'-digits, and (3) reverse sum-of-the-years'-digits. Ignore income taxes.

Required:
(a) Prepare schedules to show (1) divisional profit contribution and (2) book values of divisional assets, for all four years under each of the three depreciation methods.

(b) Calculate annual divisional return on investment for all four years under each of the three depreciation methods.

(c) Which depreciation method should be used? Why? Discuss fully.

P 20–11   Investment Center Evaluation—Impact of Price Level Changes

The management of Wisneski Corporation has noticed that the return on investment results of its Dalray and Akbar Divisions have diverged significantly in the last two years after having shown consistent and comparable results for several previous years. The following table summarizes this situation, using results for the most recent year:

	Dalray	Akbar
Operating Cash Flow	$400,000	$ 500,000
Depreciation	100,000	200,000
Divisional Income..............	$300,000	$ 300,000
Divisional Assets (net)	$600,000	$2,400,000
Return on Investment	50%	15%

Eight years ago, when the general price level was 100, Dalray's plant was acquired for $1,000,000. One year ago, when the price level was 180, Akbar's plant was acquired at a cost of $2,500,000. Besides these plant items, divisional net assets include working capital of $400,000 for Dalray and $100,000 for Akbar. The current price level is 200 and all components of operating cash flows reflect resource transfers within the current period. It has been suggested to management that price level adjusted measures of those assets and related expenses that are subject to price level changes will cause performance reports to approximate current resource exchange values. Assume that neither company has any long-term debt.

Required:
(a) Revise the schedule of operating results for the two divisions, restating depreciation charges and divisional assets to reflect the current price level.

(b) Recompute divisional income and return on investment for each division based on the results of part (a).

(c) Considering the price level adjusted statements that purport to represent current exchange values of resources, comment on the revised evaluation of the two divisions. Is the revised analysis better than the original? Why or why not?

P 20–12   Investment Center Performance Evaluation—
Replacement Cost Analysis

Bernborough Corporation has two divisions, Todman and Tulloch, that are operated as investment centers. The manager of the Tulloch Division complains that her division's unfavorable results are mainly due to the fact that most of her plant assets are much newer than Todman Division's. Consequently her asset base is higher, reflecting increased replacement costs, and her depreciation charges are higher for the same reason. The manager of Todman Division refutes this claim, saying that Tulloch's almost brand-new assets are more productive than his older assets, thus cancelling out the effect Tulloch is complaining about. Tulloch's manager also alleges that the larger amount of borrowed funds used by her division reacts unfavorably against her because of the higher interest costs involved. Results for the most recent year are as follows:

Divisional Income Statements

	Todman	Tulloch
Sales	$600,000	$400,000
Operating Expenses	$470,000	$170,000
Depreciation	40,000	70,000
Interest Expense	22,000	46,000
	$532,000	$286,000
Profit Contribution	$ 68,000	$114,000

Divisional Balance Sheets

	Todman	Tulloch
Current Assets	$150,000	$240,000
Plant Assets (net)	320,000	650,000
	$470,000	$890,000
Current Liabilities	$ 80,000	$150,000
Long-term Debt	200,000	400,000
Owners' Equity	190,000	340,000
	$470,000	$890,000

The following revised amounts show items restated on a current replacement cost basis:

	Todman	Tulloch
Plant Assets (net)	$500,000	$700,000
Current Assets	175,000	280,000
Depreciation	60,000	75,000
Operating Expenses	500,000	180,000

Required:
(a) Calculate the divisional return on investment from the original reports (1) based on total assets and (2) based on net assets.
(b) Comment on the results in part (a). Which division appears to be more profitable? Why?
(c) Calculate the divisional return on investment from the estimated current replacement cost data (1) based on total assets and (2) based on net assets.

(d)   Which division appears to be more profitable? Why?

(e)   Which set of performance measures is more useful for evaluation purposes? Why? Discuss fully.

P 20–13   Investment Center Evaluation—Transfer Price Implications

Maier Electronic Products Corporation has taken over the Allen Transistor Company and has established it as a separate division to be operated as an investment center. Marlene Division of Maier Corporation is a potential customer of the new Allen Division because it requires transistors for its own products.

Allen Division has an established market with outside customers for 1,200,000 transistors annually at a competitive market price of $1.50 each. Allen's annual production capacity is 1,500,000 units, which has no impact on fixed costs. Based on an annual volume of 1,200,000 units, the per-unit cost to produce transistors is as follows:

Variable Items	$ .90
Fixed Items	.20
	$1.10

Marlene Division now acquires its transistors from an independent supplier for $1.45 per unit and requires 250,000 units per year. Divisional assets of Allen Division are $3,000,000, but will increase to $3,050,000 due to the need for extra inventories if transistors are produced for Marlene Division.

Required:

(a)   What transfer price should be quoted by Allen to allow the correct decision to be made by Marlene as to where it should acquire the required transistors?

(b)   What effect would the use of this price have on the divisional income and return on investment of Allen Division (as compared to the same amounts without the transactions with Marlene)?

(c)   What response would the manager of Allen Division make to the use of this transfer price, assuming the division's goal is to maximize its return on investment? Why?

(d)   What response would the manager of Allen Division make to the use of this transfer price, assuming the division's goal is to maximize residual income, with a target rate of return of 15 percent? Why?

(e)   How might any conflicts evidenced in parts (b), (c), and (d) be resolved?

(f)   If Allen were able to sell all 1,500,000 transistors to outside customers for $1.50, how would this affect the answer to part (a)?

P 20–14   Investment Center Performance Evaluation— Transfer Price Implications

DiFrancesco Division of Mintz Corporation now sells all of its output to independent outside customers. Results of the most recent year's operations are as follows:

	DiFrancesco
Sales (10,000 units)	$400,000
Variable Costs	250,000
	$150,000
Fixed Costs	100,000
Profit Contribution	$ 50,000
Net Assets	$250,000

Langer Division of Mintz Corporation is seeking a supplier of a new product component it proposes to manufacture and distribute. It is similar to the product produced by DiFrancesco Division, but DiFrancesco has capacity available to expand its output without increasing its fixed costs significantly.

Langer requires 2,000 units annually and could acquire them from an independent supplier for $30. When this price is mentioned to the manager of DiFrancesco Division, he reacts negatively. He asserts that he can't afford to sell to Langer at such a low price, because doing so would adversely affect his overall return on investment. The units needed could be produced by DiFrancesco at $2.50 per unit less than the variable cost of the units it presently manufactures for outside sale. Annual fixed costs would increase to $110,000, and there would have to be an increase in net assets (extra inventories) of $20,000. The corporation presently observes a 17.5 percent target return on investment for all divisions.

Required:

(a) Prepare a schedule to show the effect of the proposed expansion of activities on DiFrancesco's divisional profit, assets, and return on investment.

(b) What is the correct source of supply for the component required by Mintz? Show calculations.

(c) What transfer price would allow the correct decision to be made?

(d) Assuming that maximization of divisional return on investment is a goal of the corporation, what would DiFrancesco's manager be likely to do? Was his original claim valid? Why or why not?

(e) What basic conflict is present here? How might it be resolved? Explain.

21

ACCOUNTING INFORMATION FOR QUANTITATIVE DECISION MODELS: PLANNING

LEARNING OBJECTIVES

After studying Chapter 21, you should be able to:

1. Define a quantitative decision model and describe its purpose and methodology.
2. Describe five goals of inventory management.
3. Use the A–B–C method to determine inventory purchasing procedures.
4. Use the economic order quantity model, including stockout costs and safety stocks, to determine inventory purchasing procedures.
5. Identify and derive the accounting data needed for inventory models.
6. Interpret the results of inventory planning models for budgetary purposes.
7. Formulate a linear programming problem.
8. Identify and derive the accounting data needed for a linear programming problem.
9. Derive a graphical and corner-point solution to a two-variable linear programming problem.
10. Formulate a dual program to derive shadow prices for the variables involved in a linear programming model.
11. Interpret the primal and dual solutions to a linear programming problem, and use the solutions for management decision making purposes.
12. Explain the PERT and critical path methods used in controlling long-term projects.
13. Given a PERT network diagram, determine the critical path and the costs to complete the project.
14. Evaluate the advantages and disadvantages of quantitative decision models.

During the past three decades there has been significant growth in the use of formal quantitative decision models by businesses and non-profit organizations. These models may be classified as belonging to the areas of *management science* techniques (M.S.), *operations research* (O.R.), or *quantitative business methods* (Q.B.M.).

Quantitative decision models use mathematical and statistical procedures to formulate and solve business decision problems. They provide a formal structure to decision processes and add precision to the computational process. Many quantitative decision models have direct accounting implications—they include planning and control techniques that can be incorporated into accounting information and control systems, and their implementation usually creates demands for accounting-related data.

Accountants need to understand (1) the general framework and purposes of quantitative decision models, (2) model formulation procedures, (3) data requirements, (4) interpretation and use of results, and (5) limitations and possible misuse of quantitative decision models.

This chapter demonstrates three common types of quantitative decision models that are particularly useful for planning purposes:

1. Inventory planning and control models
2. Linear programming models
3. PERT/CPM models

These models will be examined in terms of their formulation, their accounting data prerequisites, and their interpretation, uses, and limitations in the context of accounting planning and control systems. Minimal reference will be made to the detailed computations used in some of these models (for example, matrix algebra, calculus, and the simplex algorithm). These techniques are fully and more appropriately covered in mathematics, statistics, and operations research texts. In addition, there exist standard computer programs and routines to perform the necessary calculations.

THE SCOPE AND COMPONENTS OF QUANTITATIVE DECISION MODELS

Models can be defined as partial representations of real-world systems. All accounting reports are models. A *balance sheet* represents a company's financial position at a specific time. An *income statement* represents the production and sales activities that have caused revenues to be earned and expenses to be incurred over a period of time. A departmental *operating budget* represents the inputs required to achieve a certain level of activity. A *standard cost specifica-*

tion is a model of the inputs that should make up a particular unit of output.

Models exist in various forms: *mental* (ideas, concepts), *verbal* (descriptions, narrations), and *symbolic* (written reports, checklists, flowcharts, diagrams, accounting statements, sets of mathematical relationships and equations, computer programs). Models also take a variety of *modes,* including *descriptive* (an historical income statement), *predictive* (a budgeted balance sheet), and *normative* (a standard cost specification). Models can be used for many purposes, beginning with increased *understanding* of a system's behavior, proceeding through the *prediction, control,* and *improvement* of the system's performance, and ultimately aiming at *optimization* of system behavior.

Quantitative decision models can be used for all these purposes. They provide structure to the managerial decision environment. The following terms are used to describe the components of this environment:

1. Objective functions
2. Actions
3. States
4. Payoffs
5. Outcomes

6. Constraints
7. Parameters
8. Decision rules
9. Algorithms
10. Solution sets

Objective functions specify the criteria for choosing actions that are consistent with an organization's objectives. If the decision criterion is constrained profit maximization, the objective function will be a profit or contribution margin function, the value of which the firm will try to maximize by making an appropriate choice of values for the decision variables in that function. For example, suppose that in a short-run profit maximization situation, Products X and Y have contribution margins of $3 and $5 respectively. The relevant objective function would then be

$$\underset{\text{max}}{Z} = 3X + 5Y$$

Actions result from the choices of decision makers. They correspond to the selection of values for the decision variables controlled by a decision maker. In the preceding example, this would involve choosing values for X and Y, the number of units of each product to be manufactured and sold.

States are external factors that are not currently under the decision maker's control but are a part of the environment in which the decision model operates. In the preceding example, this would include the market demand for Products X and Y, prices set by competitors, and the firm's long-run production capacity.

Payoffs are values assigned to the **outcomes** of results of action–state interactions. Payoffs should be the basis for rational decision making, because they should be reflected in the objective function that serves as the basis for selecting actions. For example, values of $X = 1,000$ and $Y = 3,000$ will result in a payoff (value of Z) equal to $18,000 [$3 (1,000) + $5 (3,000) = $18,000].

Constraints limit the possible actions that can be chosen. They emanate from the states that are known or are postulated to exist. These constraints are specified in terms of *relationships* among the decision variables, with particular **parameter** values assigned to the variables and states in those relationships. In the preceding example, assume that there are only 10,000 machine hours of available processing capacity per month (a state) and that Product X requires 4 machine hours per unit, whereas Product Y requires 5 machine hours per unit (a constraint relationship among decision variables). This constraint would be expressed in a quantitative decision model as follows:

$$4X + 5Y \leq 10,000$$

The mechanism for selecting actions is referred to as a **decision rule.** It is used to evaluate alternative actions with respect to the impact of their payoffs on the objective function. At one extreme, this may be a simple ranking procedure to find which alternative satisfies a single criterion. For example, assuming that the criterion is sales maximization and alternatives A, B, and C promise to generate sales of $200,000, $350,000, and $300,000 respectively, the order of ranking would be B, C, A.

At the other extreme, a complex **algorithm** may be needed to find the optimal **solution set** to a problem mathematically formulated in terms of a large number of decision variables and constraining relationships. The *simplex algorithm* for linear programs is a commonly encountered example.

INVENTORY PLANNING AND CONTROL MODELS

INVENTORIES AS BUFFERS

The way in which raw materials, work in process, and finished goods inventories are managed will materially affect company profits. A firm's inventory acquisition and carrying policies are vitally important because inventories serve as a *buffer.* The existence of inventory stocks absorbs some of the uncertainties of sales performance and permits more efficient production and acquisition procedures. Without inventories, managers would face the almost impossible task of exactly matching sales with acquisitions and production.

FIVE GOALS OF INVENTORY MANAGEMENT

Although cost–benefit considerations dominate inventory management decisions, inventory policies are also subject to other constraints. Ideally, an inventory management policy should

1. Minimize inventory acquisition, production, carrying, and stockout costs.
2. Ensure that all sales orders are filled in exact conformity with customer specifications.
3. Eliminate internal control problems related to the physical and financial management of inventories.
4. Optimize financial performance in all aspects of inventory management, including profit and return on investment maximization, turnover rate optimization, and tax minimization.

5. Provide the best possible economic and technological inventory operations through optimally sized and timed inventory purchases and production runs and by avoiding back orders, rush orders, stockouts, and production bottlenecks.

Clearly many potential conflicts exist among the various objectives that an inventory management strategy must attempt to attain.

ELEMENTARY INVENTORY MODELS

A wide range of possible models is available for use in inventory planning and control. The simplest models involve various "eyeball" techniques, such as the intuitive judgment of a manager who places orders as a result of "looking over the shelves." Somewhat more sophisticated are two-bin, reserve tank, red line, or tag systems that cause orders to be placed when inventory stocks decline to some arbitrarily specified minimum level. The effectiveness of such methods depends largely on how well the inventory decision points—reorder level and reorder quantity—are established. More formal inventory models are designed to select optimal values for these decision points.

Most inventory decision models implicitly assume that inventory items are fairly standardized and are in constant demand. Most models ignore items that are required only sporadically or for specific, one-time situations. The practical way to stock such items is to purchase them in response to ascertained demand on an item-by-item basis.

COMPONENTS OF INVENTORY COST

The usual objective of quantitative decision models for inventory management is to minimize cost. The solution sets for such models specify quantities to be purchased or produced at particular times—the reorder quantity or production lot size and the reorder or set-up point, respectively. This is done subject to constraints relating to physical production and storage capacity, demand for the inventory item, and financial considerations (amounts and costs of funds, inventory turnover, and return on investment).

Inventory costs may be divided into four major categories: acquisition–production costs, inventory carrying costs, reorder and set-up costs, and stockout costs.

Acquisition–Production Costs   These are the costs of buying inventories of raw materials or finished goods and of manufacturing finished goods inventories. Planning and controlling these costs has been the major subject of the preceding chapters. Because most inventory models adopt a short-run approach, it is reasonable to treat the total fixed costs and the unit variable costs of acquisition or production as constant amounts. The unit cost of purchased inventory items is not very responsive to the quantity purchased, unless volumes are large enough to permit quantity discounts. For production lot decisions, the only relevant costs are variable manufacturing costs; these can reasonably be assumed to be constant in the short run. Each period's fixed costs are, of course, invariant to the quantities manufactured or purchased. Consequently, inventory models treat unit variable and total fixed costs of production–acquisition as insensitive to reorder quantity and reorder point decisions. Such costs affect reorder decisions only indirectly, because carrying costs are usually a function of the cost of inventories held.

Inventory Carrying Costs   These are costs incurred as a result of holding inventories, both in a physical and in a financial sense. In physical terms, carrying costs include the direct cost of handling and storage, insurance, and property tax. Additional inventory carrying costs are often incurred because of theft, spoilage, damage, deterioration, and obsolescence.

Inventory carrying costs include a financial component, in addition to the explicit cost of funds borrowed to invest in inventories. The financial carrying cost should be calculated as an opportunity cost—the rate of return foregone as a result of using funds to support existing inventory balances rather than employing those funds in comparable alternative investments.

It is usually convenient to measure most carrying costs as a percentage of the cost of inventory held, although as will be shown later, it is sometimes necessary to convert this measure to a per unit cost for computational purposes. Only those carrying costs that vary *incrementally* with the quantity of inventory held should be included in decision models. Fixed costs, such as rent, depreciation, and salaries, which do not vary in relation to inventory levels, cannot affect this type of decision and should be excluded.

Reorder and Set-up Costs   Associated with each inventory acquisition are certain reorder costs. These may include costs of supplies, stationery, postage, and data processing, as well as receiving, handling, quality control, and inspection costs. Clerical costs may also be included, but like all other costs, they will only be relevant to inventory model analysis if they are incremental in relation to acquisition decisions.

When inventory items are manufactured rather than purchased, the corresponding category for production decisions consists of **set-up costs**. These include outlays for such items as supplies, tools, dies and jigs, cleaning and maintenance, and the direct labor cost of set-up activities. Supervision, depreciation, and other fixed manufacturing costs should not be included if they do not vary with the number of production set-ups.

Stockout Costs   These include all costs incurred as a result of not having inventory on hand when required. As a first approach, they may be measured in terms of the contribution margin foregone as a result of inventory shortages. However, there may also be longer-range stockout effects, such as subsequent lost sales caused by customer dissatisfaction. In addition, costs are sometimes incurred to avoid out-of-stock conditions. Overtime premiums, premium purchase prices for rush orders, and other special handling and delivery costs can be considered stockout costs. So can idle time costs resulting from production delays caused by inventory shortages. This type of cost is difficult to measure because of the variety of indirect and opportunity costs resulting from lost sales.

INVENTORY CONTROL MODELS

Seldom will uniform management procedures be applicable to all items in a company's inventory. There will almost certainly be significant differences in the rate and frequency with which inventory items are used, the cost per unit, and the relative storability of inventories. This, together with the complex and conflicting objectives of inventory management, suggests the need for a variety of acquisition–production decision rules.

THE A–B–C METHOD

The A–B–C method of dealing with variations in the cost and frequency of inventory usage involves dividing inventory items into three (or sometimes four) categories, so that each category can be managed according to a different set of decision rules. Inventory items are ranked according to the total cost of usage of each item per period. Then the ranked items are somewhat arbitrarily allocated to categories A, B, and C. The resulting categories often tend to approximate an inverse ranking of inventory items according to the quantity of each item used per period.

Class A usually comprises 70 or 80 percent of the total cost of inventory usage but includes only a small percentage of the total number of units used. Tight inventory controls and restrictive reorder policies are appropriate for Class A items. Because of the high carrying cost of these relatively expensive items, they are sometimes stocked on an almost "hand to mouth" basis.

At the other extreme, Class C items, which may comprise only 10 percent of the total cost of inventory usage, usually represent the majority of units used. Their carrying costs are less critical because the cost of capital investment in these items will be relatively low. Therefore, reorder costs should be minimized by making large but less frequent purchases.

Finally, Class B items have neither relatively high nor relatively low unit costs. It is usually suggested that a balanced policy be adopted toward these items, taking account of both carrying costs and reorder costs.

Example: Hastings Auto Supply has adopted an A–B–C inventory policy to determine the purchasing procedures for its auto parts inventory. A schedule of the annual forecast of transaction volumes and unit costs for one of the company's departments is shown in Figure 21–1.

From this information, the following percentage analysis and ranking by total cost of usage can be obtained. Inventory items are then assigned to Class A, B, or C (as shown in Figure 21–2) according to the following arbitrarily specified 70:20:10 percent division:

Inventory Class	Percentage of Total Cost
A	70%
B	20%
C	10%

FIGURE 21-1

Hastings Auto Supply
Parts Usage and Unit Cost Forecast

Item	Units of Usage	Cost per Unit	Total Cost of Usage
123	2,000	$193.50	$387,000
124	75,000	.20	15,000
125	22,000	2.00	44,000
126	16,000	3.00	48,000
127	6,000	50.00	300,000
128	12,000	2.50	30,000
129	60,000	.10	6,000
130	7,000	10.00	70,000
	200,000		$900,000

FIGURE 21-2

Hastings Auto Supply
Division into Inventory Classes by Total Cost of Usage

Item	Units	Percent of Inventory	Total Cost	Percent of Cost	Class
123	2,000	1.0	$387,000	43.0	A
127	6,000	3.0	300,000	33.3	A
130	7,000	3.5	70,000	7.8	B
126	16,000	8.0	48,000	5.3	B
125	22,000	11.0	44,000	4.9	C
128	12,000	6.0	30,000	3.3	C
124	75,000	37.5	15,000	1.7	C
129	60,000	30.0	6,000	.7	C
	200,000	100.0	$900,000	100.0	

The items assigned to each class are then subjected to the different inventory policies previously described in order to minimize the inventory balance in Class A and minimize the number of purchases of Class C items. Judgment must be used to decide the classification of marginal items 125, 126, and 130. Arbitrary choices must be made in setting class sizes and in specifying policies to be applied to each class. Nevertheless, this strategy is effective and is frequently used, even when the resulting decision rule consists simply of reordering weekly for Class A, monthly for Class B, and quarterly for Class C.

ECONOMIC ORDER QUANTITY
AND ECONOMIC LOT SIZE MODELS

The most commonly cited quantitative decision model for inventory planning and control is known as the EOQ **(Economic Order Quantity)**, or ELS **(Economic Lot Size)** Model. It is intended to determine an inventory acquisition–production pattern that will minimize total inventory costs. It uses the following terminology:

Q = Order Quantity
$\overline{Q}$ = Economic Order Quantity
D = Total Demand (usage per period)
R = Reorder Cost (cost to place one purchase order *or* make one production set-up)
C = Carrying Cost (cost to hold one unit in inventory for the period)
K = Stockout Cost (opportunity cost of one lost unit of sales)
T = Total Inventory Costs per Period

The elementary **EOQ Model** assumes that demand/usage occurs at a constant rate throughout the period, that inventory replenishment occurs instantaneously (with no waiting for delivery) and that no inventory items are ever out of stock. The behavior of the inventory level over time is shown in Figure 21–3.

Purchases of size Q are made each time the balance falls to zero, with usage continuing at a uniform linear rate. The average inventory on hand will therefore be $Q + 0/2 = Q/2$, and the number of orders per period will be D/Q. Therefore, the total cost of placing orders will be equal to the number of orders placed multiplied by the cost per order (RD/Q). The total carrying cost will be the average number of units in inventory multiplied by the carrying cost per unit ($QC/2$). In Figure 21–4, these cost functions are compared with the total inventory cost function, which is

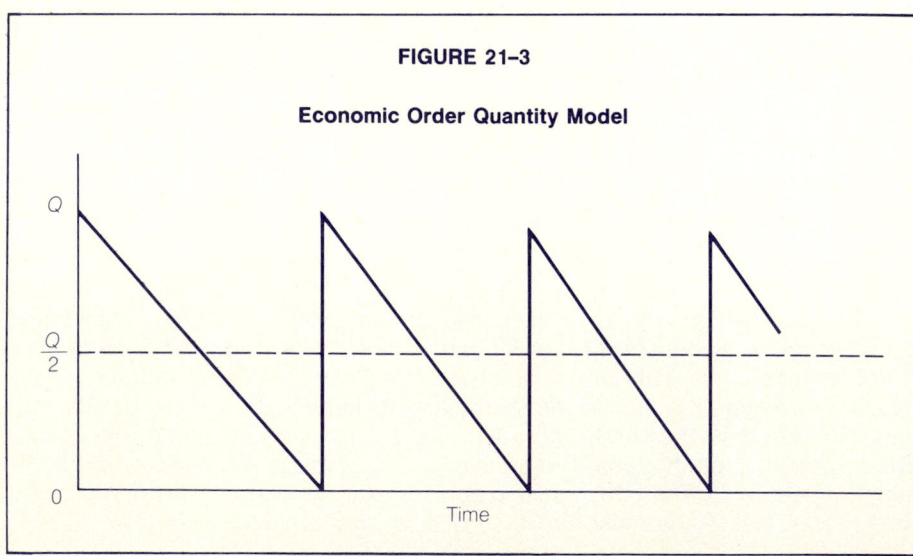

FIGURE 21–3

Economic Order Quantity Model

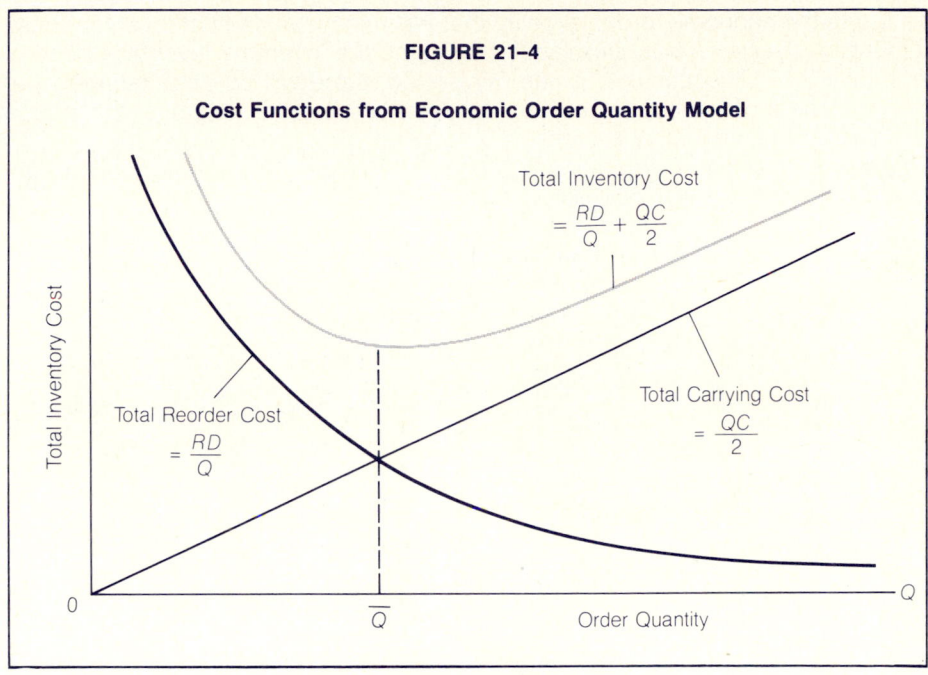

FIGURE 21–4

Cost Functions from Economic Order Quantity Model

$$T = \frac{RD}{Q} + \frac{QC}{2}$$

To minimize T, using elementary calculus, the first derivative with respect to Q is found and the condition $dT/dQ = 0$ is applied.

$$\frac{dT}{dQ} = \frac{-RD}{Q^2} + \frac{C}{2}$$

For minimization,

$$\frac{dT}{dQ} = 0$$

Therefore,

$$\frac{-RD}{Q^2} + \frac{C}{2} = 0$$

$$-2RD + CQ^2 = 0$$

$$CQ^2 = 2RD$$

$$Q^2 = \frac{2RD}{C}$$

Consequently,

$$\overline{Q} = \sqrt{\frac{2RD}{C}}$$

$\overline{Q}$ is the economic order quantity that will minimize the total inventory cost, T. Orders of size $\overline{Q}$ must be placed each time the inventory level falls to zero. Because this will occur $D/\overline{Q}$ times per period, there will be $D/\overline{Q}$ reorders per period. The length of time between reorders will be the length of the period divided by the number of reorders.

Example: Bandvik Corporation has developed the following information concerning one of its main inventory items:

Annual Demand = 10,000 units
Cost per Unit = $25
Carrying Cost = 20% of Inventory Cost
Cost to Reorder = $10

Using the economic order quantity model, the following results will be obtained:

$$\overline{Q} = \sqrt{\frac{2RD}{C}}$$

$$= \sqrt{\frac{2 \times 10 \times 10,000}{(.2 \times \$25)}}$$

$$= \sqrt{\frac{200,000}{5}}$$

$$= \sqrt{40,000}$$

$$= \underline{200} \text{ (Reorder Quantity)}$$

Also,

$$\frac{D}{\overline{Q}} = \frac{10,000}{200} = 50 \text{ (Number of Reorders)}$$

And,

$$T = \frac{RD}{\overline{Q}} + \frac{C\overline{Q}}{2}$$

$$= \frac{(\$10)\,(\$10,000)}{200} + \frac{(\$5)\,(200)}{2}$$

$$= \$500 + \$500$$

$$= \underline{\$1,000} \text{ (Total Inventory Cost)}$$

ECONOMIC ORDER QUANTITY MODEL WITH STOCKOUT COST

To incorporate stockout costs, the EOQ model is modified as follows: Let S be the maximum inventory level after purchasing quantity Q. Therefore, the stockout quantity is $Q - S$. Let the length of time out-of-stock be equal to t_2,

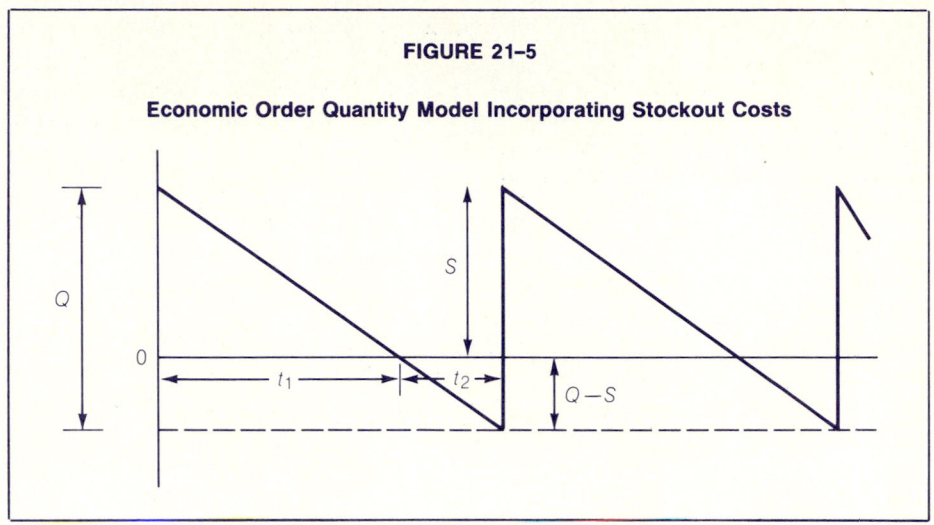

FIGURE 21–5

Economic Order Quantity Model Incorporating Stockout Costs

the length of time in stock be t_1, and the stockout cost be K. These relationships are shown in Figure 21–5.

Total inventory cost now includes three elements: reorder cost, carrying cost, and stockout cost. Reformulating the total cost function ($\overline{T}$) results in the following equation:

$$\overline{T} = \frac{RD}{Q} + \frac{CS^2}{2Q} + \frac{K(Q-S)^2}{2Q}$$

The conditions necessary for cost minimization are $d\overline{T}/dQ = 0$ and $d\overline{T}/dS = 0$. These requirements are satisfied by the following values:

$$\overline{\overline{Q}} = \sqrt{\frac{2RD}{C}} \cdot \sqrt{\frac{C+K}{K}}$$

$$\overline{\overline{S}} = \sqrt{\frac{2RD}{C}} \cdot \sqrt{\frac{K}{C+K}}$$

Example: Bandvik Corporation estimates that its stockout cost will be $15 per unit of lost sales. Therefore:

$$\overline{\overline{Q}} = \sqrt{\frac{(2)(10)(10,000)}{5}} \cdot \sqrt{\frac{5+15}{15}}$$

$$= \sqrt{40,000} \cdot \sqrt{\frac{4}{3}}$$

$$= (200)\,(1.155)$$

$$= \underline{231} \text{ (Reorder Quantity)}$$

$$\overline{\overline{S}} = \sqrt{\frac{(2)(10)(10,000)}{5}} \cdot \sqrt{\frac{15}{5+15}}$$

$$= \sqrt{40,000} \cdot \sqrt{\frac{3}{4}}$$

$$= (200)(.861)$$

$$= \underline{172} \text{ (Maximum Inventory Level)}$$

These calculations suggest that total cost will be minimized by purchasing lots of 231 units, and by allowing maximum inventory to be 172 units and maximum back-order (out-of-stock) level to be 59 units ($231 - 172 = 59$).

Total cost, $\overline{T}$, is equal to $866.09, derived as follows:

$$\overline{T} = \frac{(172)^2(5)}{(2)(231)} + \frac{(231 - 172)^2(5)}{(2)(231)} + \frac{(10)(10,000)}{231}$$

$$= 320.17 + 113.02 + 432.90$$

$$= \underline{\$866.09}$$

In this example, permitting stockouts reduces total inventory cost because the savings in reorder costs (fewer orders) plus the savings in carrying costs (lower average inventory) more than offset the stockout costs. However, this will not always be true, because the values of C, R, K, and D can take on various combinations. In particular, as the value of K gets very large, representing the fact that no stockouts are to be permitted, the solution reverts to the original $\overline{Q} = \sqrt{2RD/C}$.

THE ECONOMIC ORDER QUANTITY MODEL AND SENSITIVITY ANALYSIS

The results of the EOQ model, like those of any algorithmic decision rule, are sensitive to changes and/or errors in estimates of the values of the model's parameters—demand, reorder cost, carrying cost, and stockout cost. The nature of the total cost function tends to make total inventory cost (T) insensitive to changes in the value of the reorder quantity (Q). The variable Q appears in the denominator of one term and in the numerator of the other in the total cost function, $T = RD/Q + CQ/2$. Consequently, there is an internally offsetting effect of changes in the value of Q, particularly around the optimal solution point, $\overline{Q}$. This can be seen in the relative flatness of the total inventory cost function in that region, as shown in Figure 21–6.

Example: Bandvik Company has prepared the analysis in Figure 21–7 of the effects of variations in the value of the reorder quantity (Q) on total inventory cost (T).

In this case, as the size of the reorder quantity increased from 100 (half the optimal amount) to 400 (double the optimal amount), total inventory cost remained at $1,250. Of course, given different values for the key parameters (R, C, and D), total inventory cost might have increased or decreased as reorder quantities increased.

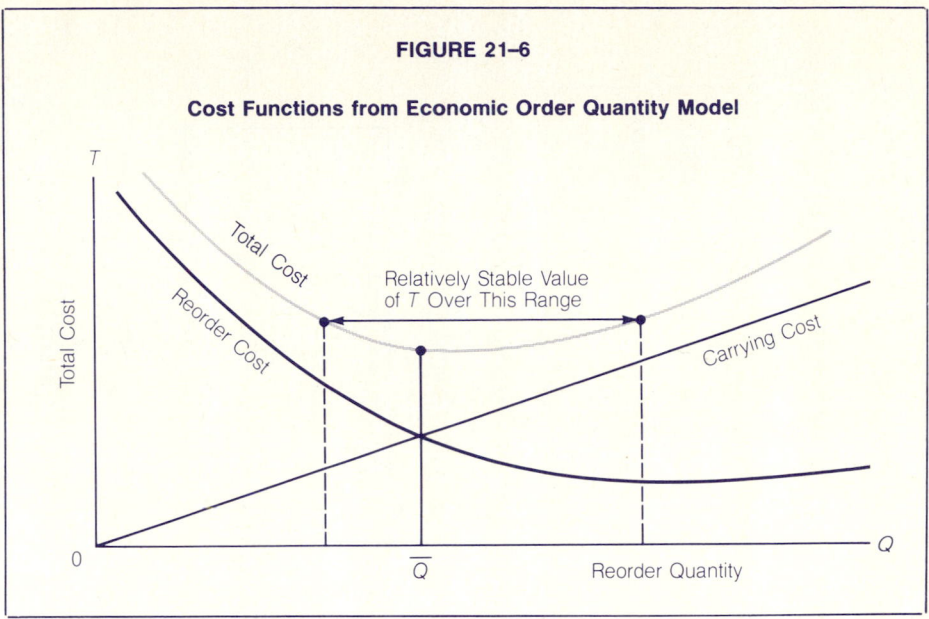

FIGURE 21–6

Cost Functions from Economic Order Quantity Model

It can also be shown that the value of the total cost function is not particularly sensitive to errors in the estimated values of the reorder cost (R) and the carrying cost (C). In Figures 21–8 and 21–9, a range of possible values of R and C are used to determine optimal values of $\overline{Q}$. The total inventory cost (T) is then measured, based on each separate value of $\overline{Q}$ but keeping the values of R and C at their originally specified amounts.

FIGURE 21–7

Bandvik Company

**Analysis of the Sensitivity of Total Inventory Cost
to Changes in Reorder Quantity**

$(R = \$10; C = \$5; D = 10,000)$

Reorder Quantity (Q)	100	150	200	300	400
Reorder Cost (RD/Q)	$1,000.00	$ 666.67	$ 500.00	$ 333.33	$ 250.00
Carrying Cost ($CQ/2$)	250.00	375.00	500.00	750.00	1,000.00
Total Inventory Cost (T)	$1,250.00	$1,041.67	$1,000.00	$1,083.33	$1,250.00

FIGURE 21–8

Bandvik Company
Total Inventory Cost, Based on Reorder Quantity
Derived from Incorrect Estimates of R,
but with the Actual Value of R Remaining at $10

Economic Order Quantity ($\overline{Q}$) (in units)	142	173	200	245	283
Number of Orders ($D/\overline{Q}$)	70	58	50	41	35
Estimated Reorder Cost (R)	$5.00	$7.50	$10.00	$15.00	$20.00
Total Inventory Cost [$T = RD/\overline{Q} + C\overline{Q}/2$]					
(based on R = $10)	$1,055.00	$1,012.50	$1,000.00	$1,022.50	$1,057.50

FIGURE 21–9

Bandvik Company
Total Inventory Cost, Based on Reorder Quantity
Derived from Incorrect Estimates of C,
but with the Actual Value of C Remaining at $5

Economic Order Quantity ($\overline{Q}$) (in units) ..	283	224	200	182	142
Number of Orders ($D/\overline{Q}$)	35	45	50	55	70
Estimated Carrying Cost (C)	$2.50	$4.00	$5.00	$6.00	$10.00
Total Inventory Cost [$T = RD/\overline{Q} + C\overline{Q}2$]					
(based on C = $5)	$1,057.50	$1,010.00	$1,000.00	$1,005.00	$1,055.00

Note that in estimates of the reorder cost (R) or carrying cost (C), even errors as large as 100 percent caused only minor variations in the total inventory cost, assuming that the actual values of R and C were the same as the values posited in the original example. This has been called a weakness of the EOQ model, as is the fact that the solution for $Q = \sqrt{2RD/C}$ is in most cases likely to be dominated by the value of total demand (D) rather than by R or C, which will usually be small relative to the value of D.

DELIVERY LEAD TIMES, SAFETY STOCKS, AND REORDER POINTS

It is often unrealistic to assume that all inventory items can be replenished immediately. If they cannot, a **reorder point** must be established that allows replenishments to be obtained early enough to avoid stockouts (or to satisfy an optimal stockout level, S). Assuming a constant demand/usage rate and a constant **delivery lead time,** the reorder point in days will equal the average daily demand multiplied by the delivery lead time. Therefore, if the inventory supplier in the Bandvik Company example can guarantee a five-day delivery period from the receipt of order, the optimal reorder point occurs when the inventory level reaches 137 units [(10,000 ÷ 365) × 5 = 137].

It is also doubtful that the inventory usage rate will be uniform throughout the period. If it varies, the reorder point must be located so as to include a **safety stock** to provide for demand fluctuations, as well as the normal delivery lead time. Given some probability distribution over the demand/usage rate per day, an expected value approach can be used to find the safety stock level that will minimize the total expected value of stockout costs plus the cost of carrying the safety stock. Alternatively, a tolerance limit rule might be adopted, by specifying that there can only be a limited (say 5 percent) probability that an out-of-stock condition may occur.

Example: Bandvik Company estimates that the five-day demand for its inventory item is likely to be distributed as follows, with a mean value of 137:

Demand	Probability	Cross Product
110	10%	11
120	10%	12
130	20%	26
140	30%	42
150	20%	30
160	10%	16
		$\Sigma(D)$ 137

This means that stockouts are possible if the five-day demand is 140 units or more, assuming that orders are to be placed only when the inventory level falls to 137 units.

Figure 21–10 shows the expected value of the additional total cost of purchasing before the 137-unit inventory level is reached, in order to maintain a safety stock. Only the 140-, 150-, and 160-unit levels are considered. As before, the carrying cost is $5 per unit and the stockout cost is $15 per unit.

FIGURE 21–10

Bandvik Company
Cost of Maintaining a Safety Stock

Reorder Point	Safety Stock	Demand	Stockout Quantity	Probability	Individual Stockout Costs	Expected Value of Stockout Cost	Extra Carrying Cost
137	0	140	3	.3	$ 45.00	$13.50	$ 0.00
		150	13	.2	190.00	39.00	
		160	23	.1	345.00	34.50	
						$87.00	$ 0.00
140	3	150	10	.2	$150.00	$30.00	$ 15.00
		160	20	.1	300.00	30.00	
						$60.00	$ 15.00
150	13	150	10	.1	$150.00	$15.00	$ 65.00
160	23	160	0			$ 0.00	$115.00

Expected total costs are then as follows:

Reorder Point	Expected Stockout Cost	+	Carrying Cost	=	Total Cost of Safety Stock
137	$87		$ 0		$ 87
140	60		15		75
150	15		65		80
160	0		115		115

Therefore, using an expected value approach, a reorder point of 140 will mini-mize the total extra inventory costs. This means the optimal safety stock is 3 units, and reorders (still equal to 200, the EOQ size) should be placed when the inventory level reaches 140 units.

Example: Bandvik Company prepares an alternative forecast which shows the five-day demand to be normally distributed, with a mean value of 137 units and standard deviation of 12 units. The company wishes to reduce the possibility of a stockout to no more than 2½ percent. To ensure this, the reorder point must be set at a level equal to the mean demand in the lead delivery time *plus* 1.96 standard deviations. This is equal to 161 [137 + (1.96) (12) = 160.52]. Therefore, the safety stock is 24 units (161 − 137).

   In some cases, the lead time may be greater than the time between sched-uled reorder points. As a result, orders may overlap. In that case, the reorder level is equal to the demand during the lead delivery period plus the safety stock minus the quantity already ordered.

Example: Bandvik Company's supplier must have 12 days' notice before making deliveries. If the reorder quantity is 200 units, safety stock is 3, and daily demand averages 27 units, then the reorder point is 127 units [(12 × 27) + 3 − 200].

CONCLUSIONS

No single inventory model will be applicable to all firms or even to all inventory items carried by one firm. Differences in demand for inventory items, in inventory values and turnover rates, in the standardization or uniqueness of the items handled, and in the cost of related information processing and control systems all combine to make the designing of inventory planning and control systems quite complex. Although the economic order quantity model appears to provide precise solutions, it should not be thought of as a panacea for all inventory planning and control problems. More elaborate inventory models, which introduce many more variables, more complicated relationships, and more sophisticated solution procedures,[1] have been developed. However, these also have specific and selective, rather than general applicability.

LINEAR PROGRAMMING MODELS

Mathematical programming models are another class of quantitative decision models. These include linear, nonlinear, integer, stochastic, and dynamic programming models. They provide a mathematically optimal solution to a program, consisting of an objective function that is to be maximized or minimized subject to some set of constraints on the decision variables involved. Only **linear programming models** will be discussed here. The general principles governing linear programming formulation, accounting data requirements, interpretation, use, and limitations of results also apply to the other, more advanced models.

LINEAR PROGRAMMING:
ASSUMPTIONS, FORMULATION, APPLICABILITY

Resource allocation problems lend themselves to the use of linear programming analysis. These include product line selection; production scheduling; warehousing, storage, and transportation; investment portfolio selection; and allocation of fixed capacity resources. All such problems involve a need to maximize or minimize some criterion (profit, contribution, cost) subject to limitations imposed on the amount of available resources (space, labor hours, machine hours, market demand, or money). The presence of *multiple constraints* usually requires

[1] G. Hadley and T.M. Whitin, *Analysis of Inventory Systems* (Englewood Cliffs, N.J.: Prentice-Hall, 1963).

that the problem be approached in terms of maximizing the contribution margin (or minimizing the variable cost) per unit of constrained resources, rather than per unit of output. This is an extension of the elementary incremental analysis introduced in Chapter 9, which included a discussion of how to maximize the contribution margin per unit of a single constrained resource.

Formulating a planning decision as a linear program requires

1. Identifying a set of *decision variables* (such as quantities of output of a group of products).
2. Specifying an *objective function* (such as the sum of the contribution margins from the group of products).
3. Specifying the availability of the set of *constraining factors* (such as amounts of machine time, storage space, or customer demand).
4. Specifying the *technical relationships* among the decision variables and the constraining factors (such as machine time required for each product and storage space required for each product).

The linear programming model also includes a number of specific assumptions. First, the mathematical condition of *linearity* is assumed to apply to all functions and relationships in the model. This means that all values, costs, and requirements expressed in the program must always be constant amounts per unit of the related decision variable. For example, an objective function consisting of the sum of the contribution margins of a set of products must increase or decrease at a constant rate per unit of each product. Z (total contribution margin) $= 3X_1 + 4X_2 + 5X_3$, where the contribution margins per unit of products X_1, X_2, and X_3 are \$3, \$4, and \$5 respectively. The constraint requirements for each decision variable must also be a constant amount per unit. For example, $2X_1 + 3X_2 + 5X_3 \leq 10,000$, where 2, 3, and 5 are the respective machine hour requirements per unit for products X_1, X_2, and X_3, and 10,000 total hours are available.

Second, the objective function must be unique and nonambiguous, so that there is a single-valued solution for each set of decision variable values. In general linear programming problems, the decision variables are assumed to be continuously valued (able to assume fractional values). However, it is clearly impossible to build exactly 2.475 blast furnaces or produce 34,768.287 automobiles. Fortunately, the integer programming model, which provides integer-valued solutions, is available for such cases.

Third, to ensure that a finite and unique solution is possible, there must be at least as many constraints as there are variables. Finally, because business problems typically involve real economic variables, all decision variables must have nonnegative values (it is not possible to produce $-10,000$ units of a product).

Example—Formulation: Loureiro Company wishes to produce a combination of its two products, X and Y, that will allow it to maximize net profit, subject to operating resource and market demand constraints. The following table lists various performance characteristics related to the two products:

	Product X	Product Y
Sales Price (per unit)	$20	$15
Materials Cost (per unit)	$ 6	$ 4
Labor Hours (per unit)	2	1
Machine Hours (per unit)	2	2.5

The hourly labor rate is $5, and 6,000 labor hours are available. Total available machine hours are 10,000. All overhead costs are fixed and amount to $8,000 per month. There is a contractual requirement that at least 1,000 units of Product X be produced and delivered each month. Total demand for Product Y will never be more than 3,000 units per month.

Objective Function: The total contribution margin (Z) is the sum of the total contribution margins of the individual products. Fixed costs need not be included in the objective function because they are invariant to the solution set. Therefore, the company's objective function is

$$\underset{max}{Z} = 4X + 6Y$$

	Product X	Product Y
Sales Price (per unit)	$20	$15
Materials	$ 6	$ 4
Labor	10	5
Variable Cost (per unit)	$16	$ 9
Contribution Margin (per unit)	$ 4	$ 6

Constraint Relationships:

(a) *Labor Capacity:* Total labor hours used cannot exceed 6,000: $2X + 1Y \le 6,000$

(b) *Equipment Capacity:* Total machine hours used cannot exceed 10,000: $2X + 2.5Y \le 10,000$

(c) *Demand Constraints:* $X \ge 1,000$ and $Y \le 3,000$

(d) *Nonnegativity Constraints:* $X \ge 0$ and $Y \ge 0$

Accounting Data Requirements: Critical data requirements in this type of model include the *coefficients* of the decision variables in these constraint relationships (labor hours required per unit), as well as the *values* assigned to the constrained *resource availabilities* (total number of available machine hours). Similarly, the solution is materially affected by the coefficients of decision variables in the objective function (contribution margin per unit). In estimating these items, their supporting technological, physical, spatial, and financial relationships must be analyzed as fully and accurately as possible. The source of such accounting data is in flexible budgeting procedures which produce the functions that represent the causal relationships between input and output variables.

When the program is formulated as a maximization problem, the objective function typically involves a profit or contribution margin and the primary accounting data requirements are *unit sales prices* and *unit variable costs*. If the problem is one of cost minimization, *unit variable costs* are needed. This assumes that the linear programming model is to be used for short-run, single-period planning situations. In that case, fixed costs are appropriately excluded from the solution process, although their later impact on the controllable part of the problem must eventually be reviewed to ensure that the optimal total contribution margin is sufficient to cover fixed costs.

LINEAR PROGRAMMING SOLUTION PROCEDURES

Graphical Method   When only two decision variables are involved, the solution process can be demonstrated graphically with constraint relationships (equations and/or inequations) represented as lines and areas on a coordinate axis system. The shaded portions of Figures 21–11 and 21–12 define an area called the **feasible region,** which consists of all points with coordinates that satisfy each of the individual constraint requirements. Figure 21–13 (page 1086) also shows the feasible region (ABCDE) that satisfies all of the constraint requirements simultaneously.

Example: In its general form, the objective function can be represented by a *family* of parallel lines, given that the value of Z is not yet specified. Figure 21–14 (page 1087) demonstrates this in the case of Loureiro Company, where $Z = 4X + 6Y$.

A solution is established by locating that member of the family of objective functions which intersects with at least one point of the feasible region and, in

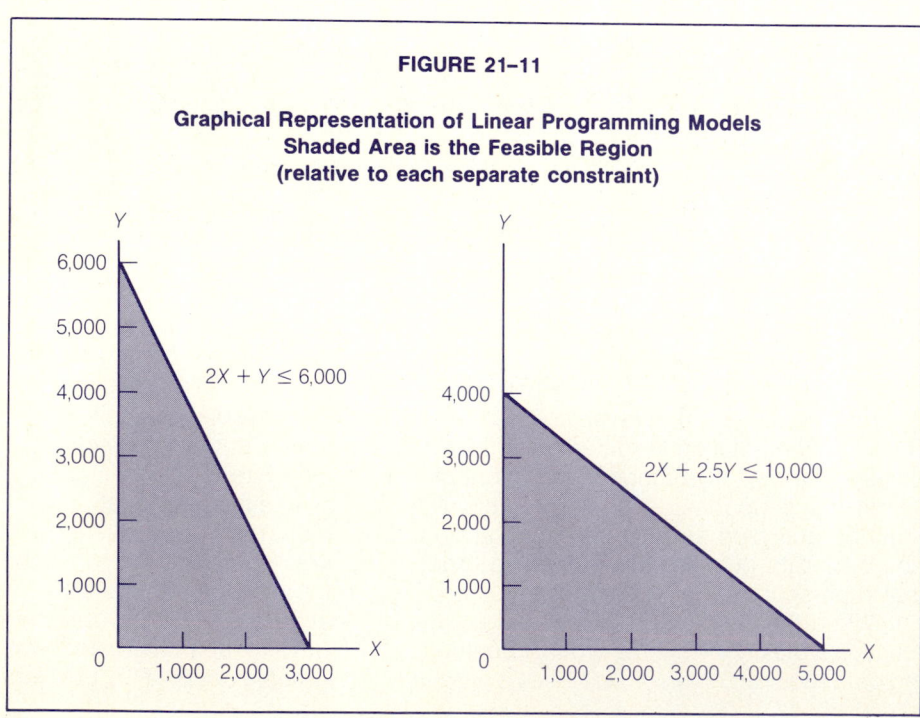

FIGURE 21–11

**Graphical Representation of Linear Programming Models
Shaded Area is the Feasible Region
(relative to each separate constraint)**

$2X + Y \leq 6,000$

$2X + 2.5Y \leq 10,000$

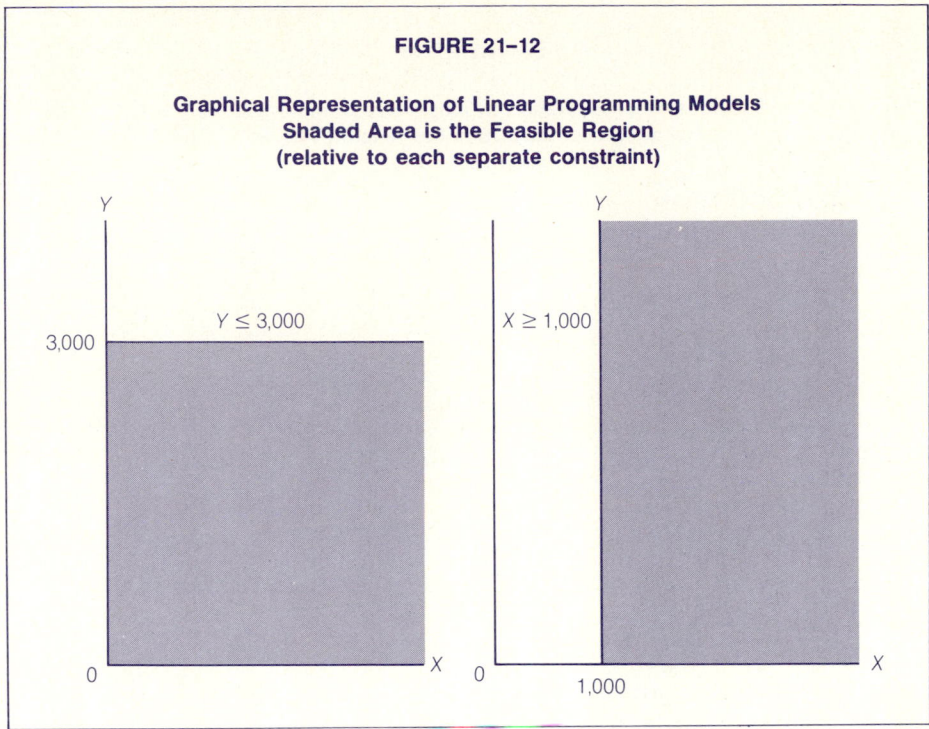

FIGURE 21–12

**Graphical Representation of Linear Programming Models
Shaded Area is the Feasible Region
(relative to each separate constraint)**

doing so, provides the maximum (or minimum) possible value of Z. In Loureiro Company, this occurs at the point where the objective function $4X + 6Y = Z = 23,000$ intersects the feasible region. This point's coordinates, 1,250 and 3,000, correspond to the optimal solution values for the decision variables X and Y, respectively.

This solution is demonstrated graphically in Figure 21–15 (page 1088), in which the line corresponding to the objective function $4X + 6Y = Z = 23,000$ is tangential to the shaded feasible region at point C.

One important attribute of the linear programming solution process is that an optimal solution occurs at a *corner point* of the feasible region, unless the objective function is parallel to one of the constraint boundary lines. This can be proven mathematically and provides a convenient way to find or verify an optimal solution.[2] The coordinates of each corner point may be substituted in the objective function to find the one that gives the optimal value. Figure 21–16 (page 1088) verifies the result for the preceding example.

Algebraic Solution Method   In general, algebraic solution methods must be used in linear programming problems when more than two decision variables are involved. The simplex method (or **simplex algorithm**) is the process most often used for this purpose. It consists of a series of steps taken to examine feasible solutions until one is found that provides an optimal value in the objective

[2] George B. Dantzig, *Linear Programming and Extensions* (Princeton, N.J.: Princeton University Press, 1963), pp. 154–55.

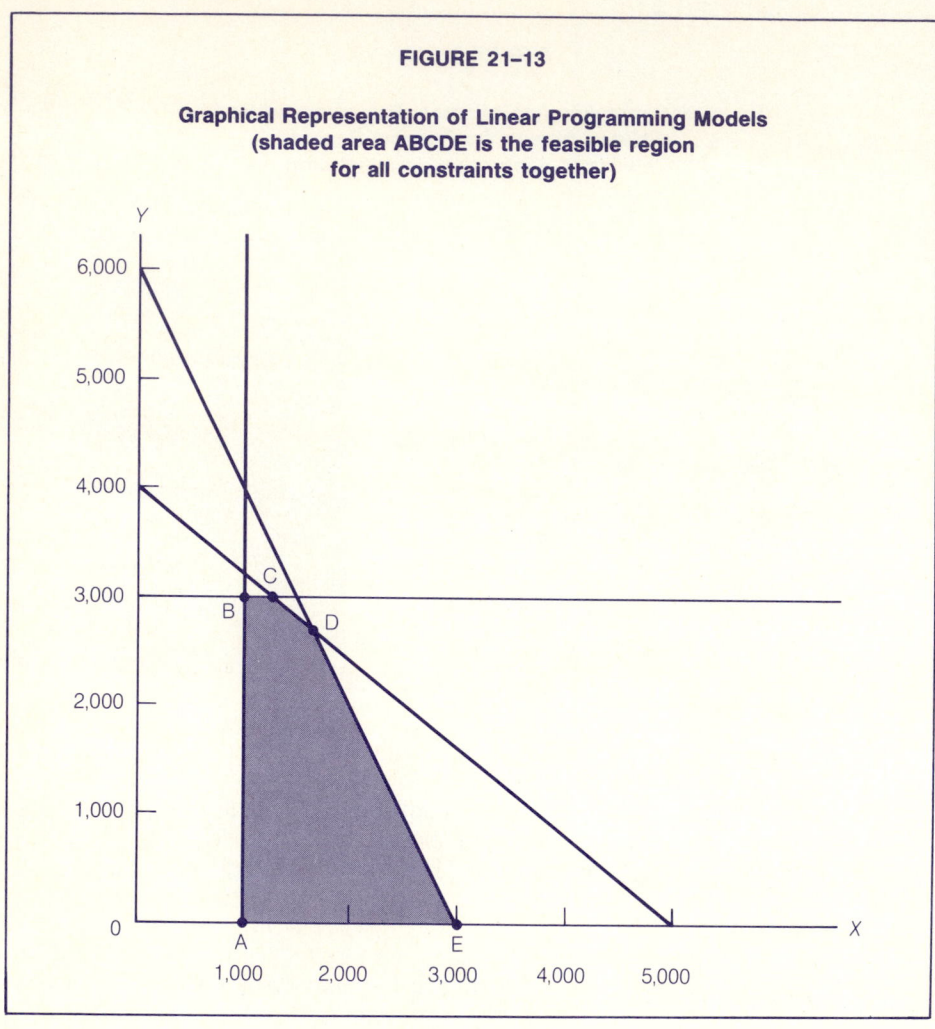

FIGURE 21–13

**Graphical Representation of Linear Programming Models
(shaded area ABCDE is the feasible region
for all constraints together)**

function. This algorithm is readily available in computer program form and is fully explained in quantitative business methods and operations research texts.[3] Therefore, the mechanics of the procedure will not be discussed here, but certain aspects of the simplex method that relate to accounting data requirements will be explained, as will the interpretation and use of the solution.

The **primal solution** to a linear programming problem specifies the values of the decision variables that will optimize the objective function while satisfying the constraint requirements. This information can be immediately applied to planning decisions made by segment managers whose activities are subject to linear programming analysis. However, the more extensive the coverage of the linear programming model, the more this implies a centralized style of management. As the number of decision variables and constraint relationships is

[3] Ibid.

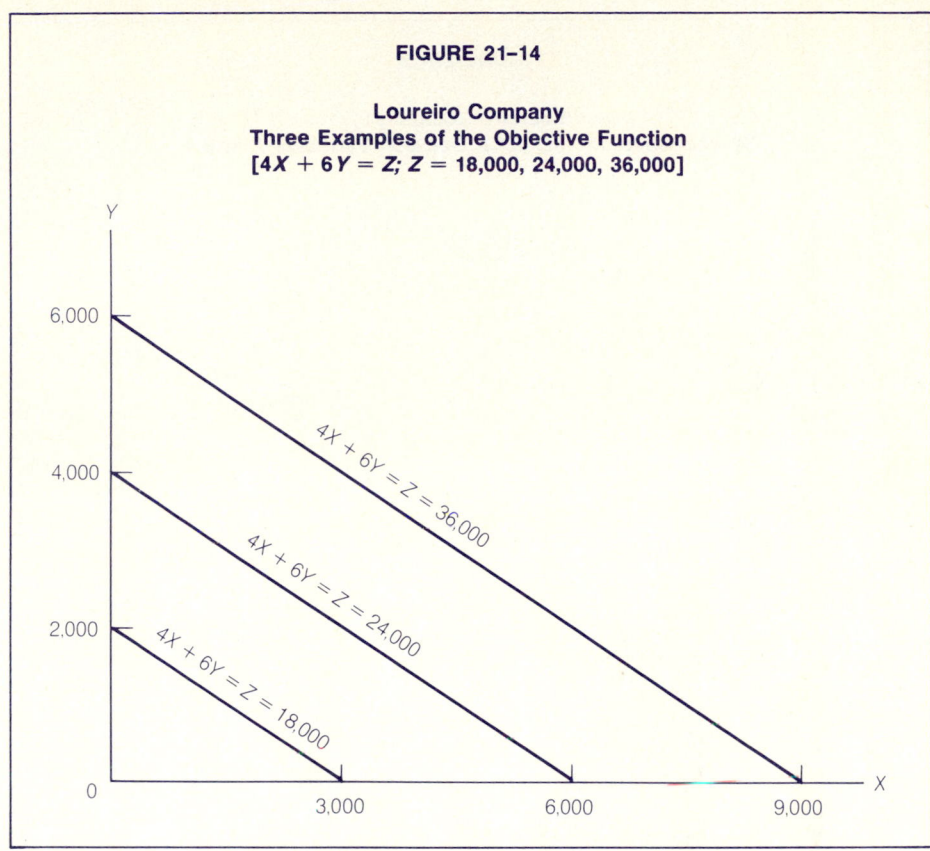

FIGURE 21-14

Loureiro Company
Three Examples of the Objective Function
[4X + 6Y = Z; Z = 18,000, 24,000, 36,000]

expanded, this technique becomes a tool that allows management to coordinate and integrate plans for the company's various segments. Of course, linear programming can also be used for localized planning, for example when the activities of a single segment are subjected to a linear planning model.

SHADOW PRICES: THE DUAL PROBLEM

The solution obtained from the simplex method includes not only the primal solution but also some important secondary information. Each linear programming problem has associated with it a mathematical mirror image or **dual problem**. The solution to this dual problem is a set of variables called **shadow prices** (opportunity costs). They correspond to the effects of a one-unit change in the solution values of each constrained resource on the value of the objective function.[4]

[4] For a mathematical explanation of this, see Dantzig, *op. cit.*, pp. 241–53.

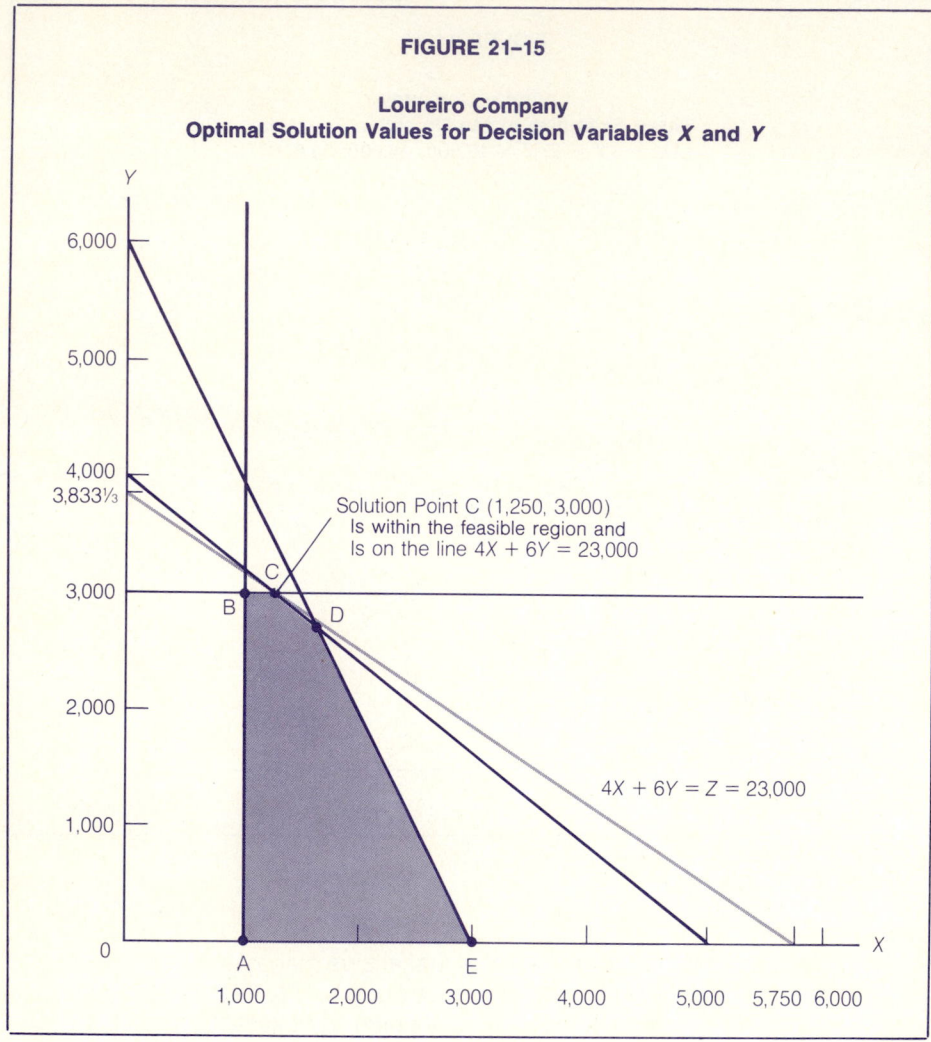

FIGURE 21–15

Loureiro Company
Optimal Solution Values for Decision Variables *X* and *Y*

Solution Point C (1,250, 3,000)
Is within the feasible region and
Is on the line $4X + 6Y = 23,000$

$4X + 6Y = Z = 23,000$

FIGURE 21–16

Loureiro Company
Corner Point Method of Locating Optimal Value

Corner Point	Coordinates	Z
A	(1,000, 0)	4,000
B	(1,000, 3,000)	22,000
C	(1,250, 3,000)	23,000
D	(1,666⅔, 2,666⅔)	22,666⅔
E	(3,000, 0)	12,000

Example: For Loureiro Company, the dual program would be formulated as follows:

$$A = \text{Shadow Price per Labor Hour.}$$
$$B = \text{Shadow Price per Machine Hour.}$$
$$C = \text{Shadow Price per Unit of Product X.}$$
$$D = \text{Shadow Price per Unit of Product Y.}$$

Objective Function: $\underset{\min}{V} = 6{,}000A + 10{,}000B - 1{,}000C + 3{,}000D$

Constraints: $2A + 2B + 2C \geq 4$
$$A + 2.5B + D \geq 6$$
$$A \geq 0$$
$$B \geq 0$$
$$C \geq 0$$
$$D \geq 0$$

The solution of this dual problem is

$$A = 0$$
$$B = 2$$
$$C = 0$$
$$D = 1$$

Therefore, $V = 6{,}000 \ (0) + 10{,}000 \ (2) - 1{,}000 \ (0) + 3{,}000 \ (1) = 23{,}000.$

This solution may then be interpreted as follows. At the point of the optimal solution, the opportunity cost of one extra machine hour is $2 ($B = 2$) and the opportunity cost of one extra unit of demand for Product Y is $1 ($D = 1). An extra unit of either labor hours or demand for Product X has zero opportunity cost ($A = 0$, $C = 0$). Alternatively, the potential marginal increase in the value of the objective function is $2 for an additional unit of available machine time and $1 for an additional unit of demand for Product Y. At the present optimal solution point, an additional unit of labor hours or demand for Product X will have no effect on the value of the objective function.

These results are significant for budgeting and planning purposes. When a dual variable, such as B or D, has a nonzero value, the present optimal solution to the primal problem can be improved if an additional unit of the resource corresponding to that dual variable is obtained. If this marginal change can be made at a cost less than the shadow price of that resource, it is worthwhile to do so.

However, this is strictly a marginal technique, which applies only to changes of one unit. Larger incremental changes in resource availability probably must be evaluated by resolving the whole linear program, because it is likely that the interdependencies among the decision variables and constrained resources will eventually cause some change in the shadow prices at the original optimal solution point.

The resources with zero-valued shadow prices have no present marginal effect on the optimal solution. They are often called **nonbinding resources.** A marginal change in their availability will have no effect on the optimal solution, but a significantly large change could have some effect.

SENSITIVITY ANALYSIS IN THE LINEAR PROGRAMMING MODEL

Although the linear programming model is essentially short-run and static, planning and control information other than that derived from an analysis of shadow prices may be obtained by applying other methods of sensitivity analysis. **Sensitivity analysis,** in general, involves investigating how changes in the values of parameters of a model affect the solution. A further step is model testing and verification, which evaluates the effects of changes in the structure of a model—for example, by adding, deleting, or modifying functions and relationships. It is most important to be able to determine the relative sensitivity of the original optimal linear programming solution (both the value of the objective function and the values of the decision variables) to changes in the values of the coefficients in the objective function, the coefficients in the matrix of constraint relationships, and the available quantities of resources.

The linear programming model has been applied to problems that have very large numbers of variables and constraints. Companies in the petroleum, chemical, and food processing industries, as well as banks and other financial institutions, have successfully used large scale linear programming models. However, it remains basically a deterministic, short-run model. When discounted present value measurements are incorporated into the objective function and the constraints, it can be made to emulate a long-range, multiperiod, planning model. But the inclusion of probabilistic analysis is not possible, except to the extent that sensitivity analysis may be used to examine the responsiveness of the solution to changes in model parameters. However, stochastic programming techniques exist that do permit consideration of probabilistically valued parameters of a model.

In addition, the strict assumption of linearity is a significant restriction on the practical relevance of the linear programming model. This is theoretically a valid criticism, because it is hard to imagine a business environment of any scale or degree of complexity in which all relationships are strictly linear and where there is no variability in the rate of change. On the contrary, experience with large scale applications has shown that these assertions of linearity are sometimes realistic. Linear relationships are most likely to occur when the activities subjected to the linear programming model are production-related and involve a high degree of technology and equipment utilization. Linearity is also promoted by a short-range planning horizon, during which economies and diseconomies of scale and productivity effects are less likely to have time to take effect.

PERT/CPM ANALYSIS

Planning and control of long-term projects that involve sequences of complex, time-dependent segments, is facilitated by the use of **PERT** (Program Evaluation Review Techniques) and **CPM** (Critical Path Method). Both methods have been used in the construction industry, computer manufacture, shipbuilding, automobile and aircraft manufacture, and in performing services such as building maintenance, education, medicine, and auditing.

PERT planners develop a network that represents the time and spatial relationships among the various events comprising the total project. The time needed to complete each segment can be specified either deterministically, with single point estimates, or as a probabilistic range. A frequently used formula specifying the PERT time estimate for the completion of a segment is defined as follows:

$$t_e = \text{estimated time to complete}$$
$$t_o = \text{optimistic estimate}$$
$$t_m = \text{most likely estimate}$$
$$t_p = \text{pessimistic estimate}$$
$$t_e = \frac{t_o + 4t_m + t_p}{6}$$

It is suggested that corresponding cost estimates be generated along with these time estimates, so that the estimated PERT cost to complete each segment will be available for analysis.

Example: Figure 21–17 shows a typical PERT network diagram for a construction project being considered by Alfredo Company.

Nodes A, B, C, D, E, F, and G represent activities that are required to complete the total project. The values associated with each arc (the path between each pair of nodes) represent the PERT estimates of time needed to complete the activity. The **critical path** is the longest necessary continuous path from start to finish of a project. It is determined by ranking the lengths of all continuous start-to-end paths in the network. In Alfredo Company, the critical path would be determined as shown in Figure 21–18. In this case, the critical path is the one containing the sequence A–B–E–F–G, which represents the shortest possible completion time for the total project.

Two other time concepts are useful in project planning—slack time and float time. **Slack time** exists on all paths except the critical path. It corresponds to the amount of unconstrained time that is present in the sequence of activities

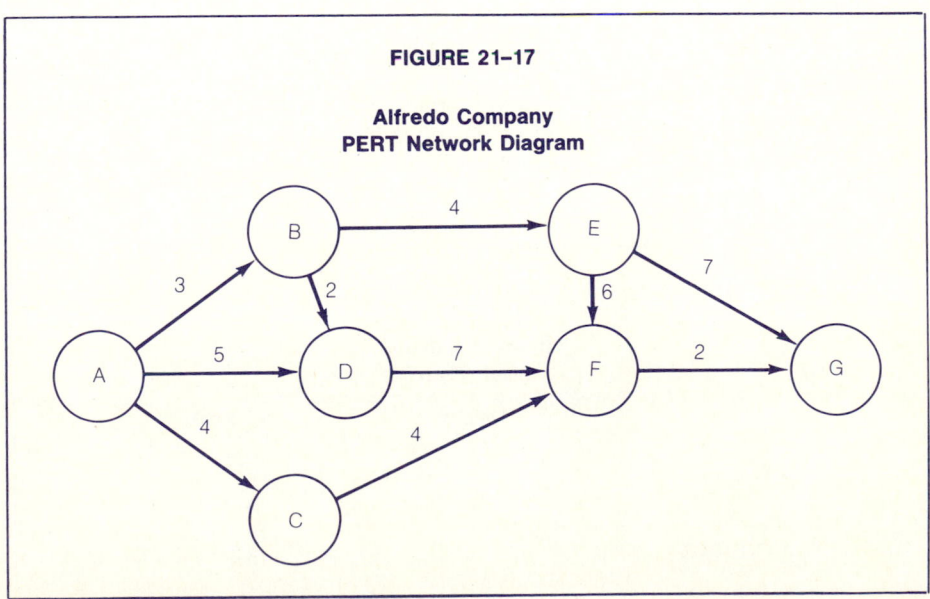

FIGURE 21–17

**Alfredo Company
PERT Network Diagram**

FIGURE 21–18

Alfredo Company
The Critical Path

Path	Sequence	Length (in weeks)
1	A–B–E–G	$3+4+7 \quad = 14$
2	A–B–E–F–G	$3+4+6+2 = 15$
3	A–C–F–G	$4+4+2 \quad = 10$
4	A–D–F–G	$5+7+2 \quad = 14$
5	A–B–D–F–G	$3+2+7+2 = 14$

---

on those noncritical paths. Slack time is calculated as the difference between the length of each path and the length of the critical path. Figure 21–19 shows the amount of slack time in each of the paths in Alfredo Company's network.

It is sometimes possible to determine exactly where the slack time in a path is located in relation to individual activities. This specific slack time is referred to as **float time.** It is the difference between the earliest possible starting time and the latest allowable starting time for each activity. Figure 21–20 summarizes the time and spatial relationships among all activities in the Alfredo Company proposal.

The critical path (A–B–E–F–G) establishes both the latest allowable starting time and the earliest possible starting time for events A, B, E, and F, because they lie on the critical path. These activities are at time points 0, 3, 7, and 13 respectively (denoted by the four downward pointing arrows in the diagram). Indirectly, this establishes time point 5 as the earliest possible starting time for D, which is dependent on the prior completion of B on the critical path. On the other hand, event C appears on only one path and therefore has only its earliest possible starting time (4) determined there. The shaded areas are float times, indicating periods when the earliest possible start time of an activity allows that activity to be completed before the earliest possible start time of the next activity on that particular path. Figure 21–20 shows that a float time

---

FIGURE 21–19

Alfredo Company
Slack Time

Path	Length	Slack
A–B–E–G	14	$15 - 14 = 1$
A–B–E–F–G	15	$15 - 15 = 0$
A–C–F–G	10	$15 - 10 = 5$
A–D–F–G	14	$15 - 14 = 1$
A–B–D–F–G	14	$15 - 14 = 1$

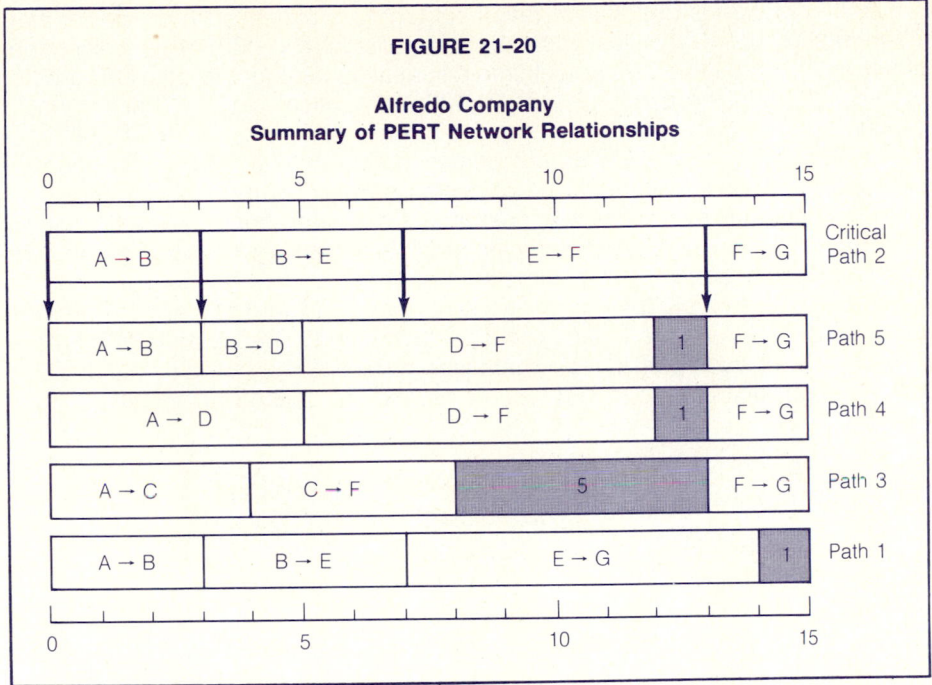

FIGURE 21-20

Alfredo Company
Summary of PERT Network Relationships

of one unit exists for the completion of the D → F segment and the E → G segment, and five units on the C → F segment.

Knowledge of the existence and location of slack and float times gives project managers added flexibility in their planning and control decisions. Project planning and control must focus on these time/sequence relationships to ensure that all activities making up the total project are completed on time and in the proper order. Cost considerations are always present; in this case, they are particularly evident in terms of possible time/cost tradeoffs. Assuming that alternative project networks are feasible, two overall objectives might be pursued: (1) to minimize total project time subject to a cost constraint, such as maximum allowable cost level or (2) to minimize total project cost subject to a time constraint such as maximum allowable project time. Attaining these goals requires evaluation of the alternatives, using PERT-time estimates and PERT-cost estimates to determine the time-cost network that optimizes whichever criterion is most desired.

Example: Van Loo Construction Company is considering four alternative project schedules for which the following PERT-cost and critical path estimates have been prepared:

Proposal	Critical Path	PERT Cost Estimate
A	21 weeks	$2,500,000
B	19 weeks	2,750,000
C	18 weeks	3,000,000
D	16 weeks	3,250,000

If the criterion is cost minimization subject to a critical path no longer than 20 weeks, proposal B (critical path 19 weeks, cost $2,750,000) would be chosen. However, if the criterion is project time minimization subject to costs no greater than $3,000,000, proposal C (cost $3,000,000, critical path 18 weeks) would be chosen. When the duration of the project is significant, the PERT cost estimates should be calculated as discounted present values, to reflect possible timing differences in the incidence of costs between competing proposals.

Once projects are underway, cost analysis is often needed to adjust time/cost relationships. For example, it may become necessary to shorten the critical path to allow a project to be completed to meet a contract deadline. In that case, incremental cost–benefit analysis is needed to find the arc (or arcs) in the network that are the least expensive to shorten. The **differential cost per unit of time** for each possible segment time reduction may be a useful decision aid. Cost per unit of time in this type of situation is defined as follows:

$$\begin{array}{c}\text{Differential}\\ \text{Cost per Unit}\\ \text{of Time}\end{array} = \dfrac{\begin{array}{c}\text{Accelerated Cost}\\ \text{to Complete}\end{array} - \begin{array}{c}\text{Normal Cost}\\ \text{to Complete}\end{array}}{\begin{array}{c}\text{Length of Normal}\\ \text{Arc}\end{array} - \begin{array}{c}\text{Length of}\\ \text{Shortened Arc}\end{array}}$$

All segments in which time reductions are possible can be compared on the basis of this measure. The project should be revised whenever the total differential cost of time reduction of the segment with a minimum cost per unit is less than the penalty cost of not meeting a time deadline. Such a revision may change the critical path if the time revision is greater than the slack on an unadjusted path.

Example: Alfredo Company is subject to a $200,000 penalty clause if its project is not completed within 14 weeks. This means that some way must be found to shorten the critical path A–B–E–F–G. Management has developed the information shown in Figure 21–21 concerning possible adjustments to segments of the critical path.

FIGURE 21–21

Alfredo Company
PERT Revised Time and Cost Estimates

Segment	Original PERT Time Estimate	Original PERT Cost Estimate	Revised Time Estimate	Revised Cost Estimate
A–B	3	$ 500,000	2	$ 675,000
B–E	4	700,000	3	800,000
E–F	6	1,000,000	5	1,250,000
F–G	2	200,000	1	350,000

The differential cost per unit of time for each possible segment reduction can then be calculated as follows:

$$A\text{–}B: \quad \frac{\$675,000 - \$500,000}{3 - 2} = \frac{\$175,000}{1} = \$175,000$$

$$B\text{–}E: \quad \frac{\$800,000 - \$700,000}{4 - 3} = \frac{\$100,000}{1} = \$100,000$$

$$E\text{–}F: \quad \frac{\$1,250,000 - \$1,000,000}{6 - 5} = \frac{\$250,000}{1} = \$250,000$$

$$F\text{–}G: \quad \frac{\$350,000 - \$200,000}{2 - 1} = \frac{\$150,000}{1} = \$150,000$$

This shows that the least expensive alternative *per week of time* is to reduce the time spent on segment B–E by one week to meet the contract deadline. Such a revision is acceptable because its total differential cost of $100,000 is less than the $200,000 penalty cost that would otherwise be levied.

PERT/CPM cost planning and control procedures should be supplemented by an accounting and reporting system that employs job order costing for the total project and process costing for any compatible elements. Variance reports should emphasize accounting cost variances and project time variances. This will facilitate the type of incremental analysis and interim revisions previously described. Accounting techniques of budgeting, performance measurement, control, and evaluation are all relevant for these purposes.

SUMMARY

1. Quantitative decision models permit a formal and rigorous analysis in support of planning decisions. The purpose of these models is to specify optimal decision rules for planning purposes. Much of the input data required by users of these models must be provided by the management accounting system.

2. An inventory management policy should minimize costs, ensure that adequate inventory stocks are maintained, that orders are filled promptly and correctly, and that adequate internal control of inventories exists.

3. The A–B–C method of inventory management involves dividing inventory items into three or four categories and managing each category according to a different set of decision rules.

4. Economic order quantity and economic lot size models are used to determine an inventory acquisition or production pattern that will minimize total inventory costs.

5. When inventory items cannot be replenished immediately, it is necessary to calculate delivery lead times, safety stocks, and inventory reorder points.

6. Linear programming models, which can be solved graphically or algebraically, are particularly applicable to situations in which resources must be allocated among several types of inventories.

7. PERT (Program Evaluation Review Techniques) facilitate the planning of sequential, time-related projects, by developing a network that represents the completion times of different project segments. Cost estimates should be developed to go with the estimated completion times.

8. CPM (Critical Path Method) traces the longest necessary continuous path from start to finish of a project. It can be used to determine the shortest possible completion time for the project.

KEY WORDS AND PHRASES

Quantitative Decision Model (1065)
Objective Functions (1066)
Actions (1066)
States (1066)
Outcomes (1066)
Payoffs (1066)
Constraints (1066)
Parameters (1067)
Decision Rules (1067)
Algorithms (1067)
Solution Set (1067)
Inventory Acquisition–Production Costs (1068)
Inventory Carrying Costs (1069)
Inventory Reorder Costs (1069)
Inventory Set-up Costs (1069)
Stockout Costs (1069)
A–B–C Method (1070)
Economic Order Quantity Model (1072)
Economic Lot Size Model (1072)
Reorder Point (1079)
Delivery Lead Time (1079)
Safety Stock (1079)
Linear Programming Model (1081)
Feasible Region (1084)
Simplex Algorithm (1085)
Primal Solution (1086)
Dual Problem (1087)
Shadow Prices (1087)
Nonbinding Resources (1089)
Sensitivity Analysis (1090)
PERT (Program Evaluation Review Techniques) (1090)
CPM (Critical Path Method) (1090)
Nodes (1091)
Arc (1091)
Critical Path (1091)
Slack Time (1091)
Float Time (1092)
Differential Cost per Unit of Time (1094)

Questions

1. In what ways can quantitative decision models be of assistance in the managerial accounting process?
2. List and briefly explain the different *forms* in which models can be prepared and presented. Do the same for the different *modes* of models.
3. List and briefly explain the basic components of quantitative decision models.
4. What are the major objectives of an inventory control system?
5. List and explain the components of inventory costs. What is an appropriate goal with regard to total inventory cost? Explain.
6. Briefly outline the A–B–C method of inventory control. In what situations would this method be appropriate?
7. What general inventory acquisition and holding policies should be applied to each separate inventory category under the A–B–C method?
8. What is the objective function in the EOQ (ELS) inventory model?
9. What are the key parameters in the EOQ inventory model? What are the decision variables (solutions)?
10. How can the results of an EOQ inventory formulation be used for planning and control purposes in the managerial accounting process?
11. How can sensitivity analysis be incorporated into the EOQ model?
12. Explain the role of stockout costs and safety stocks in the EOQ model.
13. What are some typical managerial accounting applications of linear programming models?
14. What is the typical objective function in some of the applications mentioned in Question 13?
15. Explain the role of the *linearity assumption, constraining factors,* and *technical relationships* in linear programming models that have managerial accounting applications.
16. What simple (not simplex!) solution methods are possible for small-scale (two-variable) linear programming problems?
17. What are the accounting data requirements for linear programming models?
18. Give an interpretation of the primal solution to a linear programming problem.
19. What is the dual problem and what extra information does its solution provide? What is a shadow price? What are nonbinding and binding resources?
20. What are PERT time and PERT cost estimates? How can they be useful to the managerial accounting and control process?
21. What information can be obtained from a PERT network diagram?
22. What is *slack time?* What is *float time?*
23. How can incremental analysis be applied to situations that are conducive to PERT–CPM techniques?
24. What accounting techniques can be applied to projects that are conducive to PERT–CPM techniques?

Exercises

E 21-1   Economic Lot Size—Elementary Analysis

Rainbird Company sells 12,000 units per year of a product that costs $30 per unit to purchase. Reorder costs are $90 per transaction and the annual cost to carry one unit of this item in inventory is 20 percent of its purchase price. Delivery is instantaneous.

Required:
(a) Determine the economic order quantity for this item. How often must orders be placed?
(b) What will total inventory costs, including requisition costs, be under this method?
(c) Assume that the reorder cost increases to $120. How will this affect the EOQ and total inventory cost?
(d) Assume that the carrying cost decreases to 10 percent of acquisition cost. How will this affect EOQ and total inventory cost?

E 21-2   EOQ Analysis—Cost Savings

Jason Corporation purchases its requirements of item P247 in 6,000-item lots ten times each year. This has resulted in total reorder costs of $1,000 and total inventory carrying costs of $9,000. The annual usage requirement for this item is distributed uniformly throughout the year. The item costs $20 per unit.

Required:
(a) Assuming that the corporation adopted an EOQ approach, what would be the reorder quantity and the number of reorders per year?
(b) What cost savings, if any, would be obtained from this change in inventory procedures?
(c) What effect has the unit purchase price of the item on this example? Why?

E 21-3   EOQ Model—Differential Analysis

DeYoung Corporation makes frequent purchases of an ingredient that it uses in several of its products. Annual demand for this ingredient is 100,000 tons. If purchased in lots of fewer than 5,000 tons, the cost is $12 per ton; but if lots of 5,000 or more are purchased, the cost is only $10 per ton. The cost of reordering is $200 per transaction and the cost to carry one ton of inventory for a year is 15 percent of its purchase price.

Required:
(a) Determine the EOQ for both possible purchase lot sizes.
(b) What are the total inventory costs under the two alternative optimal EOQ solutions?
(c) What inventory replenishment policy should the firm observe? Why?

E 21-4   Linear Programming—Resource Allocation— Elementary Analysis

Valerius, Incorporated makes beer steins in two styles—Grosse and Humungous. Two raw materials are used to produce both styles. These materials, as well as direct labor hours, are limited in supply in the short run. Grosse steins need 20 ounces of Material A, 10 ounces of Material B, and ½ hour of labor. Humungous steins require 10 ounces of Material A, 20 ounces of Material B, and ¾ hours of labor.

Material A costs 10¢ per ounce, Material B costs 20¢ per ounce, and direct labor is $4 per hour. Sales prices are $10 for Grosse steins and $14 for Humungous steins. All expenses other than materials and labor are fixed in amount and total $10,000 per month. Supplies available each month are limited to 60,000 ounces of Material A and 50,000 ounces of Material B, and labor hours cannot exceed 3,500.

*Required:
(a) Formulate this situation as a linear programming problem.
(b) Prepare a diagram to represent this formulation, indicating the feasible region and all corner points.
(c) Determine, by inspection or algebraic solution, the coordinates of the corner points.
(d) Determine the optimal solution from part (c).
(e) Interpret this solution and indicate how it could be used for planning purposes.

E 21–5   Linear Programming—Resource Allocation— Elementary Analysis

Adrian and Dominica are operating the Wong-Leung Won-Ton Corporation. Two different varieties of won-ton are produced and both use shared facilities, the same employees, and one common ingredient—all of which are limited in supply in the short run. The following schedule shows the monthly production and sales data for the two varieties:

	Requirements (per 1,000 pounds Won-Ton)		
	Grade A Won-Ton	Grade B Won-Ton	Resource Availability
Labor Hours	40	40	400
Machine Hours	80	120	960
Material X (pounds)	140	400	2,800
Sales Price (per 1,000 pounds)	$480	$800	
Variable Costs (per 1,000 pounds) ...	$280	$560	

*Required:
(a) Formulate the situation as a linear programming problem with the objective of maximizing the combined contribution margin from the two products.
(b) Prepare a diagram to show this formulation, indicating the feasible region and all corner points.
(c) Determine, by inspection or algebraic solution, the coordinates of the corner points.
(d) Determine the optimal solution from part (c).
(e) Interpret the solution. How could it be included in managerial accounting procedures?

E 21–6   PERT/CPM—Elementary Analysis

Ferguson Construction Company has developed the following network diagram for its next project. All time periods are in terms of weeks needed to complete each phase.

* Parts (b), (c), and (d) may also be solved by use of the simplex algorithm, which is generally available in computer program form.

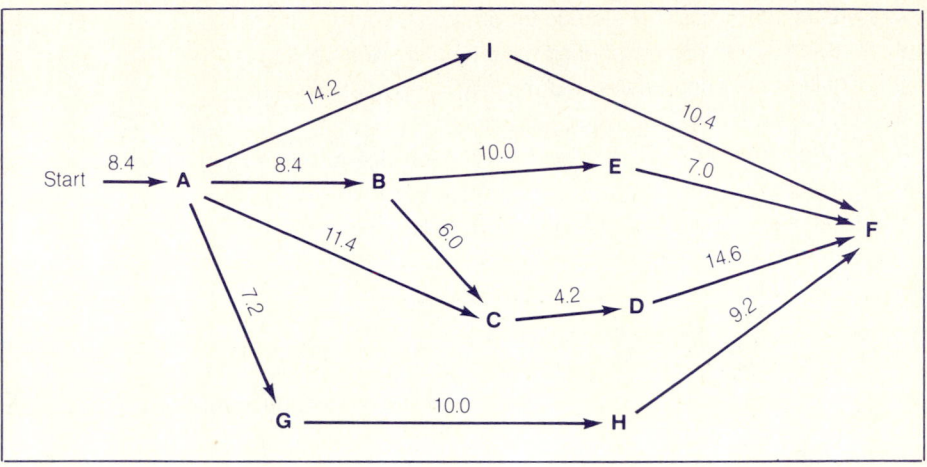

Required:

(a) Determine the *critical path*. Explain its significance for planning and control purposes.

(b) How much slack time is available on the A–I–F path? Explain the planning and control significance of this component of the analysis.

(c) What are the earliest and latest times for reaching event F on the A–B–E–F path? What do these times mean for planning and control purposes?

(d) Will the project's completion time be affected by any of the following delays or time savings?
   (1) 8 weeks on path A–G–H–F—time savings
   (2) 4 weeks on path A–I–F—time savings
   (3) 2 weeks on path A–B–C–D–F—delay
   (4) 6 weeks on path A–B–E–F—delay
   Explain each effect.

Cases

C 21–1 Inventory Costs and Methods of Analysis

The following is a list of inventory-related costs. Indicate whether they are pertinent to:

(a) EOQ inventory techniques
(b) A–B–C inventory techniques
(c) Inventory control techniques in general

Discuss briefly the reasons for the classification chosen. Mention also any possible measurement problems.

1. Purchase price of an item per unit.
2. Volume of usage of an item per period.

3. Annual rental costs of storage facilities.
4. Losses due to breakage, theft, deterioration, and spoilage.
5. Costs of checking quality and quantity at point of receipt.
6. Telephone bill in purchasing department.
7. Lost contribution margin on sales not made due to out-of-stock conditions.
8. Total cost of inventory purchases per period.
9. Total cost of purchases of one inventory item per period.
10. Interest cost of funds used to finance inventory holdings.
11. Quantity discounts lost by purchasing in small lots.
12. Quantity discounts gained by purchasing in large lots.
13. Fire insurance premiums on inventory.
14. Labor costs of employees involved in readying production facilities for next production run.
15. Dissatisfied customers whose orders are not filled.
16. Delivery charges on shipments received.
17. Salary of production schedules, purchasing agents, and factory clerical personnel.
18. Depreciation on storage buildings.

C 21–2   Production and Inventory Quantities

Angles, Incorporated has experienced a series of confrontations between its sales and production departments concerning the availability of products to meet sales orders. The controller's department often gets dragged into the fray because both sides use financial "facts" to support their positions.

The sales manager contends that out-of-stock conditions are intolerable and that inventories of all salable products should be maintained at levels which allow ample time to replenish them from a current production run and which prevent sales orders from being filled and delivered late or lost altogether.

The production manager argues that the only way she can minimize the cost and inconvenience of frequent production set-ups of her general purpose equipment is to produce large quantities of each regular product. The purchase of supplies is also more economical if large quantities of only those items needed for current production runs are held. The effect is "double-barreled" because the costs of reordering are similar to the costs of production set-ups.

The controller is concerned with all of these issues but must also appease financial managers who insist that the cost of funds tied up in inventories be kept to a minimum.

Required:

Evaluate the viewpoints of all parties involved. Discuss how inventory control methods (specifically EOQ methods, A–B–C methods, and rule-of-thumb methods) can be used to resolve these problems and differences of opinion.

C 21–3   The A–B–C Method

Ted Harris, the new controller of Ken Howard Company, is a firm believer in inventory control procedures. Fred Tupper, the purchasing agent, had been in the habit of purchasing only when the production supervisor, Robert Gunn, advised him that stocks of certain items were "running low." Harris suggests the use of an A–B–C method. Tupper and Gunn are skeptical because they insist that no one method can fit the peculiarities and irregularities of demand for the various items used by the company. Some items are used in large quantities almost continuously, some are used infrequently and irregularly in moderate amounts, and still others are used only occasionally in small quantities.

Required:
Draft a report to be presented by Harris, explaining how the A–B–C method operates and how it might resolve certain problems inherent in a haphazard system such as the existing one.

C 21–4   Product Mix

The following is a formulation of the product mix problem of Redcraze Corporation:

$$\text{Maximize } Z = 6X_1 + 4X_2 \quad \dots \quad \text{Contribution Margin}$$

Subject To:
$$4X_1 + 2X_2 \leq 24{,}000 \quad \dots \quad \text{Process 1 Capacity}$$
$$X_1 + 2X_2 \leq 12{,}000 \quad \dots \quad \text{Process 2 Capacity}$$
$$X_2 \leq 5{,}000 \quad \dots \quad \text{Demand Constraint}$$
$$X_1, X_2 \geq 0 \quad \dots \quad \text{Nonnegativity of Product Quantities}$$

Required:
(a) Explain the problem as formulated.

(b) Determine the optimal solution. Use graphical, algebraic, or computer program methods.

(c) If the fixed costs of this company are $40,000, will a breakeven condition be possible? Explain.

(d) Assume that the capacity of Process 1 can be expanded by 50 percent without affecting costs. How would this affect the original solution? Explain.

(e) Assume that the capacity of Process 2 is *reduced* by 25 percent without affecting costs. How would this affect the original solution? Explain.

Problems

P 21–1   EOQ Model—Differential Analysis

James Scott Company currently purchases one of its principal inputs in quantities of 10,000. Annual needs are 80,000, spread uniformly throughout the year. To place an order and have it delivered, inspected, and stored costs $3,000, irrespective of the quantity involved. Carrying costs are $8 per unit of inventory per year. The item costs James Scott Company $45 per unit.

Required:
(a) Calculate the EOQ for this situation and the total inventory cost, including acquisition costs.

(b) Was this more or less than the total costs in the original situation? Why?

(c)   What change in reorder costs would make the original arrangement optimal?

(d)   What change in the carrying costs would make the original arrangement optimal?

(e)   What effect does the purchase price of the item have on any of the preceding solutions? Why?

P 21–2   EOQ Model—Determination of Amounts of Key Parameters— Incremental Cost Analysis

Hiraji Corporation employs unsophisticated inventory acquisition procedures. It purchases new supplies when someone observes that there is an actual or imminent shortage. A newly hired executive proposes the use of EOQ techniques. For that purpose, the following data for one key item of inventory are developed by the controller using figures supplied by the purchasing, receiving, and storage departments:

Purchasing and Receiving Departments:

Salaries	$50,000 per year
Stationery	$20 per purchase order
Inspection Supplies	$54 per shipment received
Receiving Costs	$8 per hour per employee (2 hourly rate employees work 6 hours on each shipment received)

Storage Costs:

Rent	$10,000 per year allocated for space occupied by inventory
Inventory Insurance	$1,000 per year plus $2 per unit of inventory carried for a full year
Taxes	2% of cost of average inventory
Deterioration	4% of average inventory will spoil each year and have to be discarded

Controller's Department:

Cost of Capital	Investments in inventory are required to generate a 12% annual rate of return
Sales Projections	200,000 units per year
Purchase Price	$10 per unit

Required:

(a)   Prepare an analysis to determine the cost of placing a purchase order and the cost of carrying one unit of inventory for the whole year.

(b)   Use this information to compute the EOQ, the number of orders per year, and the total cost of acquiring and holding inventory.

(c)   Review each inventory cost component and indicate the circumstances that would lead to each one's being either *included* or *excluded* from the analysis in part (a).

P 21–3   EOQ Model—Sensitivity Analysis—Variations in Estimated Parameter Values

Gough, Incorporated uses 80,000 tons per year of the major ingredient of its single product. This ingredient is expected to cost $50 per ton during the coming year. Reorder costs are forecast at $4,000 per transaction, and the cost of carrying one ton of inventory for the year is expected to be 15 percent of its purchase price.

Required:

(a) Determine the EOQ, number of orders per year, and total inventory cost (excluding cost of purchases of materials).

(b) Assume that the solution to part (a) is acted on and purchases occur as scheduled. However, the actual reorder cost is (1) 100 percent larger or (2) 50 percent smaller than forecast. Determine what effect each of these changes will have on total inventory costs (excluding cost of purchases of materials). Comment.

(c) Again assume that the solution to part (a) is implemented. However, the carrying cost turns out to be (1) 10 percent or (2) 25 percent of the purchase price. Determine what effect each of these will have on total inventory costs. Comment.

(d) Again assume the solution to part (a) is implemented. However, the purchase price is actually $60 per ton. Determine what effect this will have on total inventory costs (excluding cost of purchases of materials). Comment.

P 21-4 EOQ Analysis—Stockout Cost Considerations— Lead Time in Delivery

McGrath Company requires 60,000 units per year of a particular item. Usage in production occurs at a uniform rate throughout the year. The total cost of executing one purchase order is $600. The cost of holding one unit of this item in inventory for the whole year is 16 percent of its acquisition cost. The purchase price of the item is expected to be $400 per unit.

Required:

(a) Determine the EOQ for this item. How many orders per year will be placed?

(b) What will total inventory costs, including acquisition costs, be for the whole year?

(c) Assume that delivery occurs ten days after an order is placed. How does this affect the solution in part (a)? Why?

(d) Refer to the original situation. Assume the company is prepared to incur stockout costs by allowing inventory to be depleted to zero and have some customers' orders go unfilled. The stockout cost associated with having an item back-ordered for a customer is $150 per unit. Recompute the EOQ based on this extra information. What is the maximum inventory level and the maximum back-order quantity?

(e) What is the total inventory cost under the solution to part (d)? Compare this to the solution in part (b) and comment.

P 21-5 Inventory Replenishment Decisions—Safety Stock— Probabilistic Demand Distribution

Barnham Company uses an EOQ approach to determine the quantities it purchases of its most regularly consumed inputs. For product MNOP, which is used at the average rate of 65,000 per year, a reorder quantity of 5,000 has been established, with purchase orders placed once every four weeks. It usually takes one week from the date of the order for a shipment to arrive.

In the original analysis, the carrying cost applicable to one unit of MNOP in inventory for a whole year was $25. However, it is estimated that it costs the company $100 for each unfilled sales order. Therefore, the company seeks to minimize the combined cost of carrying either too much or too little inventory by establishing a safety stock over and above that required for the normal delay in delivery. It has been observed that demand for product MNOP averages 1,250 per week, with variations as follows:

Weekly Demand	Percentage of Occurrence
1,000	15%
1,200	20%
1,250	30%
1,300	20%
1,500	15%
	100%

Required:
(a) What would be the lead time (safety interval) and safety stock level if only the normal delay in delivery is taken into account?
(b) Prepare a schedule to show the effect of establishing a safety stock to allow for the delivery delay *and* for the variations in weekly demand. Show the total cost (extra carrying costs and out-of-stock costs) associated with each possible level of total safety stock relevant to the preceding considerations (that is, 1,000, 1,200, 1,250, 1,300, or 1,500).
(c) Use expected value analysis to determine the expected total cost associated with each of the five possible safety stock levels.
(d) Which safety stock level should be used, based on part (c)? Why?

P 21–6 EOQ Model—Sensitivity Analysis—Probabilistically Distributed Demand

Hoysted, Incorporated has established EOQ procedures for several of its continuously used components. For part number F375K, the reorder quantity was calculated based on annual demand of 200,000 units, a reorder cost of $500, and a carrying cost of $8 per unit of inventory per year. A delay occurs between the placing of an order and the receipt of materials. During this lead time, demand for the component is normally distributed with a mean value of 2,000 units and a standard deviation of 400 units.

Required:
(a) Determine the EOQ according to the specified data.
(b) Based on the solution to part (a) and the average value of the observed demand during the delivery lead time, what is the delivery lead time?
(c) What is the probability of incurring stockout costs if no safety stock is carried? (Reorders are placed when the inventory level falls to 2,000 units.)
(d) Assume the cost of being out of stock is $25 per unit back-ordered. What is the average cost of stockouts per delivery period if the policy of carrying no safety stock is continued?
(e) How large a safety stock must be carried to reduce the probability of being out of stock to (1) 1, (2) 2½, and (3) 25 percent?

(f) What extra costs will be incurred if the policies in (1), (2), or (3) of part (e) are implemented? (That is, examine the effect on carrying costs and stockout costs.) Comment.

P 21-7 Linear Programming Model—Formulation and Solution— Elementary Analysis—Dual Program

Rising Fast Baking Company produces two fast-selling lines of cakes—Winkies and Binkies. Each variety uses a special common ingredient, Supergoo, that is in limited supply. Each variety must also share total baking time available in the company's ovens. Total oven hours available each week are 4,000. Only 2,500 pounds of Supergoo can be purchased each week. Details of requirements and contribution margin (per 1,000 cakes) are as follows;

	Winkies	Binkies
Pounds of Supergoo	10	20
Hours of Oven Time	30	20
Contribution Margin	$300	$250

Required:
(a) Formulate this situation as a linear programming problem.
(b) Represent it in graphical form.
(c) Determine the optimal solution, using graphical, algebraic, or computer program methods.
(d) Interpret the solution and indicate how it could be used for managerial planning and control purposes.
(e) Formulate and solve the dual to this problem. Interpret the solution to the dual.

P 21-8 Linear Programming Model—Resource Allocation—Primal and Dual Problems

Temeraire Corporation processes fruit and vegetables. The Peach Canning Division purchases two grades of fresh peaches and processes them to produce canned peach halves and canned sliced peaches. The current crop available consists of 800 tons of grade A peaches and 640 tons of grade B. The contribution margin on peach halves is $600 per ton; on sliced peaches, it is $400 per ton. Possible yields from each grade are shown as follows:

	Tons Required for One Ton of Peach Halves	Tons Required for One Ton of Sliced Peaches
Grade A	4	6
Grade B	6	3

Required:
(a) Formulate and solve this as a linear programming problem. (Use either graphical, algebraic, or computer program methods.)
(b) Interpret the solution and indicate how it should be used in the managerial planning process.

(c) Formulate the dual problem and solve it. What are the shadow prices of grade A and grade B peaches?

(d) If an extra ton of grade B peaches were available for $70, should the company purchase it? Why?

(e) What maximum price can the company afford to pay for an extra ton of grade A peaches? Why?

P 21-9   Linear Programming Model—Cost Minimization—Resource and Yield Constraints

The Flying Fling Dog Food Company has determined that the best balanced dog food is one that contains at least 40 units of Vitamin A and 60 units of Vitamin B per two-pound box. Two key ingredients are blended to form the main nutrient content of their product. The first, called Yelpo, costs 50¢ per pound and contains 20 units of Vitamin A and 40 units of Vitamin B per pound. The second ingredient, called Woofah, costs 20¢ per pound and contains 10 units of Vitamin A and 30 units of Vitamin B per pound. The company has plant capacity to process and blend a total of 200,000 pounds of input per week to produce 100,000 boxes of output.

Required:
(a) Formulate this situation as a linear program with the objectives of minimizing total cost of inputs, utilizing all available plant processing capacity, and satisfying the minimum vitamin requirements.

(b) Determine the optimal solution (using graphical, algebraic, or computer program methods).

(c) Interpret the solution. How can it be used to assist the managerial accounting planning and control process?

(d) Formulate and solve the dual to this problem. Give an accounting interpretation of this solution.

P 21-10   Linear Programming Model—Basic Analysis—Sensitivity Analysis—Planning Implications

Geordash, Incorporated manufactures two styles of women's jeans—Brook and Stream. Brook jeans earn a contribution of $14 each, but Stream jeans earn only $4. Direct labor hours needed for Brook jeans are twice those for Stream, which require only one hour. Under a long-term contract, the supply of the special embroidery on Brook jeans cannot exceed the requirements for 2,000 of this style per week. Also, the total supply of special zippers used for both styles is limited to 4,000 per week. Stream jeans are made with belts, of which only 1,500 per week are available. Total weekly supply of buttons is 30,000, with 10 needed for each Brook and 15 for each Stream. Total labor hours available are 3,500 per week.

Required:
(a) Formulate this situation as a linear programming problem.
(b) Prepare a graph to demonstrate the feasible region and all corner points.
(c) Determine the optimal solution (using either graphical, algebraic, or computer program methods).

(d) Interpret the solution and explain its relevance for managerial planning and control purposes.

(e) Which resource (or resources) are binding and which are nonbinding at the point of the optimal solution? What significance has this for planning purposes?

(f) Consider each resource individually. Specify a change (that is, available labor hours decrease to 3,000). Discuss the planning and control significance of each change and the possible effect of each change on the optimal solution.

P 21–11   PERT/CPM Analysis—Developing Time and Cost Estimates

Kwiatkowski Construction Company uses PERT methods to assist planning and control of each of its major projects. The following estimates were prepared for an upcoming project:

Activity	Immediately Preceding Activity	Time Estimates (days)		
		Optimistic	Most Likely	Pessimistic
1	Start	8	10	16
2	1	8	12	18
3	1	4	10	14
4	2	16	18	24
5	3	2	4	8
6	4, 5	4	10	12

Activity	Cost Estimates		
	Optimistic	Most Likely	Pessimistic
1	$ 80,000	$100,000	$150,000
2	100,000	150,000	220,000
3	30,000	80,000	100,000
4	240,000	300,000	400,000
5	20,000	30,000	40,000
6	50,000	80,000	100,000

Required:
(a) Prepare a PERT network diagram for this project.
(b) Determine PERT time and cost estimates for each activity path.
(c) Which is the critical path and how long is it? What planning significance does it have?
(d) Indicate where slack time exists (if at all) on any of the paths. What planning significance does this have?
(e) Refer to the following table which shows estimates of accelerated costs to complete each activity phase in the shortened time as indicated:

Activity	Estimated Accelerated Cost	Estimated Shortened Time to Complete (days)
1	$160,000	8.0
2	210,000	10.0
3	120,000	7.5
4	350,000	17.5
5	45,000	4.5
6	120,000	8.0

Which activity paths should be allowed to incur the accelerated completion costs in order to reduce completion time by five days from the original estimated time calculated in part (b)?

(f) Discuss the accounting control techniques that should be applied to the cost aspects of a project of this type.

P 21-12 PERT/CPM Analysis

Robinson Corporation has identified two critical paths on its next project. Data relating to each are as follows:

	Path 1 Days	Path 1 Probability	Path 2 Days	Path 2 Probability
Shortest Time	160	.2	150	.2
Most Likely Time	180	.5	180	.5
Longest Time	210	.3	240	.3
Cost per Day to Shorten	$5,000		$4,000	

The two paths are relatively separate, making each set of probable time estimates independent of the other. A $30,000 per day penalty will be assessed if the project is not completed within 180 days.

Required:

(a) Based on the stated probability distributions, what is the expected time to complete each path? What is the expected time to complete the project?

(b) Is there a possibility that penalty costs will be incurred? If so, how much and why? If not, why?

(c) As a precaution, the company is considering incurring the extra costs to accelerate the project, making the longest expected completion time 180 days for both projects. How much extra cost will be incurred to achieve this?

(d) Should the extra costs referred to in part (c) be incurred and completion times shortened or should the original plan be followed? Why?

(e) What other course of action would you recommend? (*Hint:* Consider what might be done after 30 days, 60 days, 75 days, and so on.) What accounting control techniques would be useful here?

P 21-13 PERT/CPM Analysis—Time and Cost Analysis

Kane, Incorporated has a contract to manufacture a complex electronic guidance system for which the following time and cost estimates were prepared:

Activity	Optimistic	Time Estimates Most Likely	Pessimistic	Variable Costs (per week)	Total Fixed Costs
A	12	14	16	$15,000	$37,000
B	4	6	20	16,000	16,000
C	6	8	10	56,000	8,000
D	8	10	24	36,000	24,000
E	6	10	14	9,000	5,000
F	8	12	16	9,600	2,400
G	2	4	6	8,000	4,000

The following network diagram was also prepared:

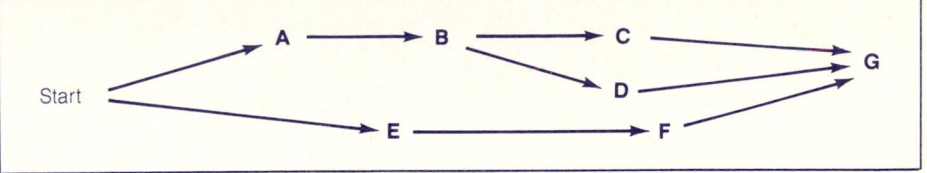

After 22 weeks, the following cost and completion data were reported:

Activity	Weeks	Cost	Percent Complete
A	12	$206,000	100
B	9	141,000	100
C	2	120,000	25
D	3	78,000	$16\frac{2}{3}$
E	2	16,000	20

Required:
(a) Determine the critical path. How long is it, based on the PERT cost estimate to complete the project?
(b) Prepare an analysis to determine how the project stands relative to the PERT time and PERT cost estimates.
(c) Comment on the current status of the project. Are any problems apparent? Discuss.

P 21-14 PERT/Cost Analysis—Incremental Analysis—Acceleration to Complete

The following schedule shows projections of completion times and costs for the next project scheduled by Clampett Corporation:

Phase	Immediately Preceding Activity	Normal Time (days)	Cost	Accelerated Time (days)	Cost
1	Start	10	$2,400	6	$4,000
2	1	8	3,200	6	5,600
3	1	16	4,000	10	7,600
4	1	6	3,200	4	5,600
5	2	6	2,400	4	3,200
6	4	8	2,400	4	3,200
7	3, 5, 6	10	3,200	8	4,200

Required:
(a) Prepare a PERT network diagram for this project. Identify and determine the length of the critical path.
(b) Assume that the maximum time allowed to complete the project is 26 days. Ascertain which phases should be shortened to accomplish this at the least cost. Show all calculations.
(c) What would be the cost of implementing all phases on an accelerated basis?
(d) How can the information in part (c) be used for planning purposes?

22

COST INFORMATION FOR QUANTITATIVE DECISION MODELS: CONTROL

LEARNING OBJECTIVES

After studying Chapter 22, you should be able to:

1. Describe the learning curve effect and the manufacturing situations to which it applies.
2. Calculate the learning curve ratio and use it to derive cumulative and incremental production costs.
3. Calculate learning curve production costs when cumulative output doubles.
4. Calculate expected variances during the learning period.
5. Use control charts to distinguish random from nonrandom variances, based on sample observations of performance, when the total population is known or assumed to be normally distributed.
6. Use the central limit theorem to distinguish random from nonrandom variances, based on sample observations of performance, when the total population is not known to be normally distributed.
7. Construct control limits using Chebyshev's inequality together with sample observations of cost performance.
8. Using an expected value approach, determine the costs of investigating and not investigating nonrandom variances.
9. Use Bayesian statistics to reassess the probability that a process is out of control.

An efficient internal control system permits managers to monitor and evaluate performance, compare planned and actual results, and initiate appropriate corrective action when variances are detected. This chapter demonstrates quantitative decision methods—learning curve analysis and variance investigation techniques—that can be incorporated into accounting information and control systems.

LEARNING CURVE ANALYSIS

Labor cost estimates should be systematically adjusted when it is reasonable to expect that worker performance of repetitive tasks will improve with practice. Improvement of this type is known as the **learning curve effect**. It is particularly applicable to complex, labor-intensive manufacturing activities. Aircraft manufacture and assembly operations in the electronics and computer industries are typical environments in which major improvements in employee proficiency are likely to occur.

The learning curve effect exists during a worker's start-up and familiarization period on a particular job, after which the limits of experiential learning are reached, productivity tends to stabilize, and no further improvement is possible. The rate at which learning occurs is influenced by many factors, including the relative unfamiliarity of workers with the task, the relative novelty or uniqueness of the job, the length and complexity of the process, the stability of the work group, and the impact of incentive plans, supervision, and union pressure on worker productivity.

THE LEARNING CURVE RATIO

The learning curve is based on the assumption that a constant rate of change, or **learning curve ratio,** applies to labor-related cost performance. This ratio is derived as follows:

$$\text{Learning Curve Ratio (LCR)} = \frac{\text{Average Labor-Related Cost of First } 2N \text{ Units Produced}}{\text{Average Labor-Related Cost of First } N \text{ Units Produced}}$$

Here N is the size of the first production lot, batch, or run. Therefore, if the first unit of output incurs labor costs of \$100 and the first two units cost \$160, the learning curve ratio would be .8 (or 80%), calculated as follows:

$$\text{Learning Curve Ratio} = \frac{\$160 \div 2}{\$100}$$

$$= \frac{\$80}{\$100}$$

$$= \underline{\underline{.8}}$$

The *learning curve effect* based on this ratio is then defined in terms of the following relationship:

$$Y_x = ax^b$$

Here,

> x is the cumulative number of units or lots produced to date
> y_x is the cumulative average unit cost of those x units or lots
> a is the average cost of the first unit or lot
> b is the ratio $\dfrac{\log \text{LCR}}{\log 2}$

Figure 22–1 illustrates the type of curve derived from this function.

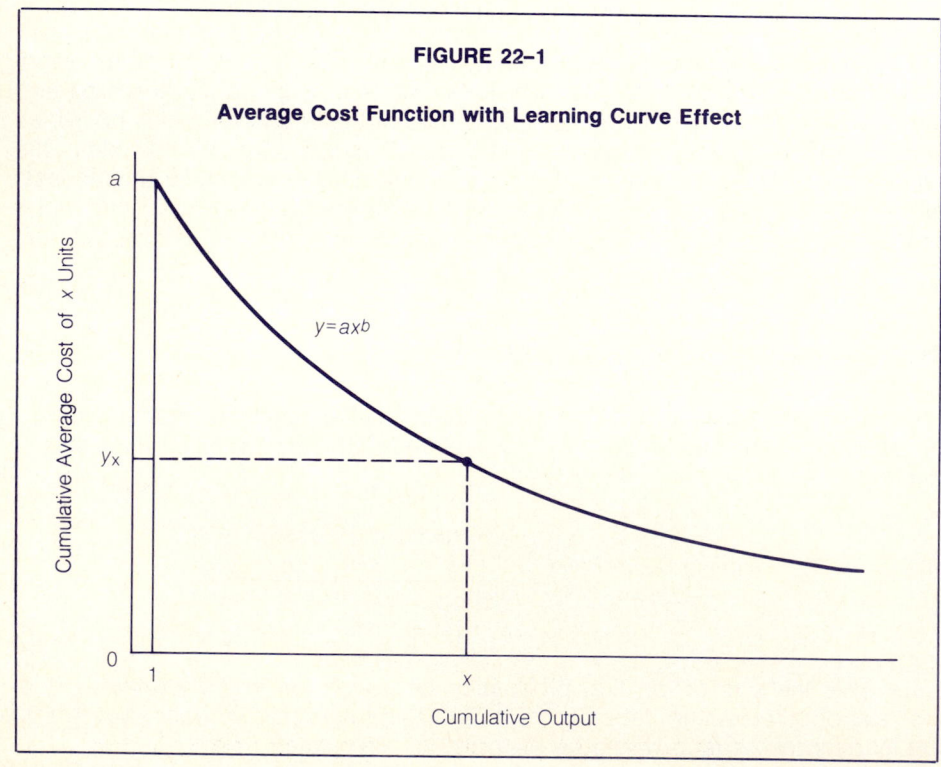

FIGURE 22–1

Average Cost Function with Learning Curve Effect

In the preceding example, where the learning curve ratio equals .8 and $a = \$100$ for the first unit manufactured, the cumulative average cost for the first 32 units produced would be derived as follows:

$$y_{32} = (100)(32^{\log .8/\log 2})$$
$$= (100)(32^{-.322})$$

Therefore,

$$\log y_{32} = \log 100 + (-.322 \log 32)$$
$$= 2.00 + (-.322)(1.5051)$$
$$= 2.00 - .4846$$
$$= 1.5154$$
$$y_{32} = \$32.768$$

In other words, by the time 32 units have been produced, the *average cost per unit* is \$32.768. However, this is not a measure of the marginal cost of the thirty-second unit. That cost is derived as follows:

Cumulative Average Cost of First 31 Units:
$$y_{31} = (\$100)(31^{\log .8/\log 2})$$
$$\log y_{31} = \log 100 + (-.322 \log 31)$$
$$= 2.0 - .4802$$
$$= 1.5198$$
$$y_{31} = \$33.10$$

Now let T_x be the total cumulative cost of x lots—that is, the number of lots (x) times the average cost of x lots $(y_x) = T_x$.

$$T_{32} = (32)(\$32.768) = \$1048.576$$
$$T_{31} = (31)(\$33.10) = \$1026.10$$

Therefore,

$$T_{32} - T_{31} = \$1048.576 - \$1026.10 = \$22.476$$

The *marginal cost* of the thirty-second unit is \$22.476. The *incremental cost* of the next five units beyond the thirty-second unit is equal to $(T_{37} - T_{32})$—the difference in total cost of the two quantities at each end of the increment.

$$y_{37} = (\$100)(37^{-.322})$$
$$\log y_{37} = 2.0 - 0.5050$$
$$= 1.495$$
$$y_{37} = \$31.262$$

$$T_{37} = (37)(\$31.262) = \$1156.694$$
$$T_{37} - T_{32} = \$1156.694 - \$1048.576$$
$$= \$108.118$$

The incremental cost of the next five units would therefore be \$108.118.

An alternative method of performing learning curve cost calculations avoids the use of logarithmic computations. However, it only provides solutions for production situations in which the cumulative output has *doubled*. This simplified calculation is based on the fact that *as the cumulative total output doubles, the cumulative average unit cost decreases proportionally to the learning curve ratio*. Therefore, if the learning curve ratio is .8 and the first unit produced costs $100, by the time output doubles (to 2 units) the average cost has become $80 (80% × $100). Figure 22–2 shows five successive steps in this progression.

Because this method only provides solutions for quantities that correspond to an exact doubling of the cumulative output, incremental costs can be calculated only for these "doubled" quantities of output. The marginal costs of particular incremental units of output cannot be determined by using this logarithmic computation.

Note that the learning curve equation $y = ax^b$, when rewritten in its logarithmic form, becomes a linear equation:

$$\log y = \log a + b \log x$$

By converting observed values of actual average costs over a range of outputs to a logarithmic scale, as in Figure 22–3, accountants can estimate individual values of the learning curve ratio. By finding the values of log a (intercept) and log b (slope), the value of the learning curve ratio can be estimated using the relationship:

$$b = \frac{\log \text{LCR}}{\log 2}$$

Therefore,

$$\log \text{LCR} = (b)(\log 2)$$

FIGURE 22–2

Learning Curve Effect when Production Doubles

A	B	C	D	E
Incremental Quantity	Cumulative Quantity	Cumulative Average Cost	Total Cumulative Cost	Incremental Cost
$A_t = (B_t - B_{t-1})$	$B_t = 2B_{t-1}$	$C_t = .8C_{t-1}$	$D_t = (B_t \times C_t)$	$E_t = (D_t - D_{t-1})$
1 1	1	100	100	100
1 2	2	80	160	60
2 4	4	64	256	96
4 8	8	51.2	409.6	153.6
8 16	16	40.96	655.36	245.76
16 32	32	32.768	1048.576	393.216

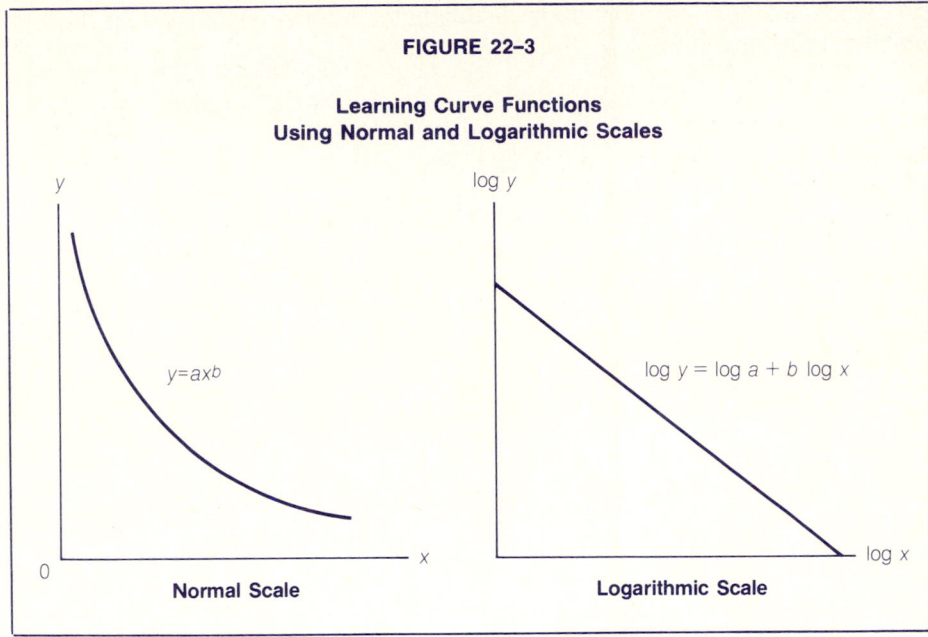

FIGURE 22–3

**Learning Curve Functions
Using Normal and Logarithmic Scales**

$y=ax^b$

Normal Scale

$\log y = \log a + b \log x$

Logarithmic Scale

A visual fit method can be used to approximate the linear function with which the data appears to coincide, or the curve can be fitted using the formal statistical method of linear regression analysis described in Chapter 16.

USES OF LEARNING CURVE ANALYSIS

The cost data provided by learning curve analysis can be used to refine standard cost specifications, to analyze cost variances in greater detail, and to improve the budgetary process and cost-related decision making.

Standard costs will tend to be set too high if the costs incurred early in a product's life cycle are used as a basis for judging labor productivity. The result will be favorable labor efficiency variances which merely indicate that workers are becoming more proficient at their jobs, as expected.

This problem might be avoided by decreasing standard labor cost and variable overhead cost specifications as production increases. However, this may be confusing and not worth the computational time and effort. Another alternative is to set the standard cost permanently at the level where the learning curve effect is expected to cease and the steady state of productivity to commence. This should be accompanied by the reporting of **expected variances,** which represent the difference between the stabilized standard cost and the cost that would be in effect for the actual cumulative level of output.

Example: Ryan Company anticipates that the labor costs in one of its assembly departments will be subject to a 90 percent learning curve effect, but that a steady state condition will apply beyond the 10,000-unit level on each new product. The labor cost of the first unit was $20. Based on this, the following projection of $5 per unit (rounded) was made for the average cost at the 10,000-unit level.

$$Y_x = ax^b$$
$$Y_{10,000} = (\$20)(10,000^{\log .9/\log 2})$$
$$= (\$20)(10,000^{-.1518})$$
$$\log Y_{10,000} = \log 20 + (-.1518 \log 10,000)$$
$$= 1.3010 + (-.1518)(4)$$
$$= 1.3010 - .6072$$
$$= .6938$$

Therefore,

$$Y_{10,000} = \underline{\underline{4.944 \cong 5}}$$

This is demonstrated in Figure 22–4, where 0S is the standard cost per unit, based on the rounded average cost per unit at the 10,000-unit level.

Ryan Company's labor cost variances are calculated as the difference be-

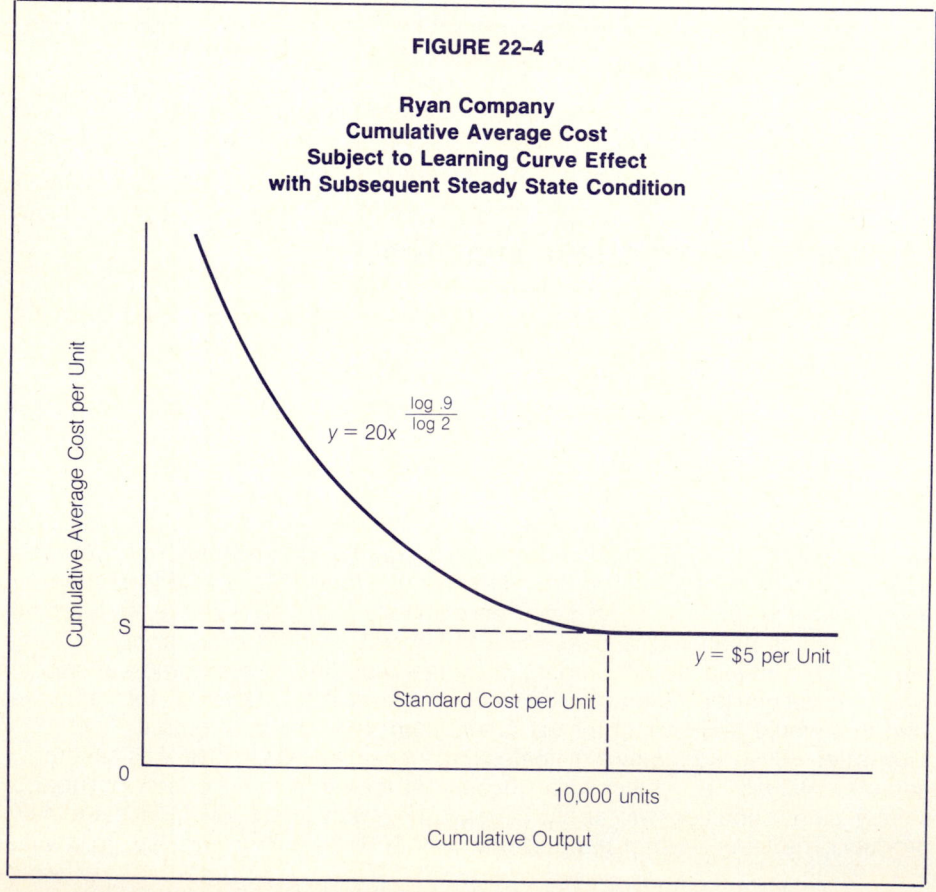

FIGURE 22–4

Ryan Company
Cumulative Average Cost
Subject to Learning Curve Effect
with Subsequent Steady State Condition

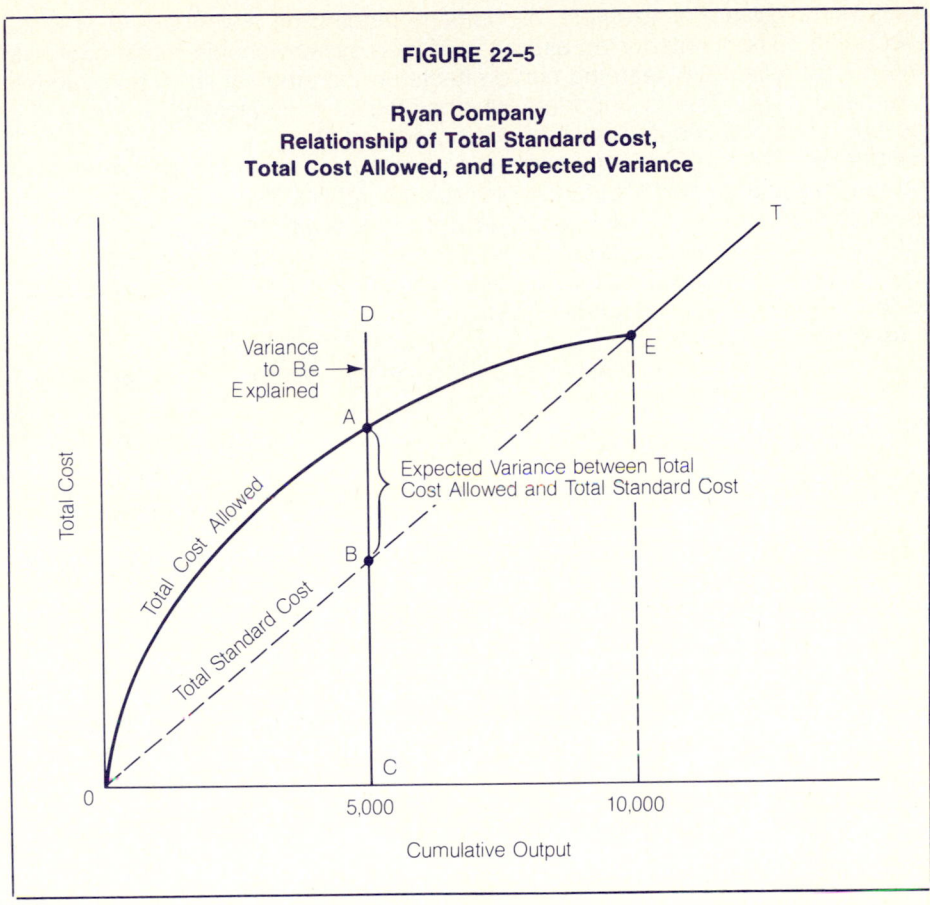

FIGURE 22–5

**Ryan Company
Relationship of Total Standard Cost,
Total Cost Allowed, and Expected Variance**

tween estimated and standard costs at each activity level. In Figure 22–5, the total estimated cost of producing 5,000 units is shown by the vertical distance AC. The total standard cost of those 5,000 units, based on the $5 per unit amount projected as the stabilized cost, is shown by the interval BC. An expected variance (AB) is present because total estimated cost at that level will be less than total standard cost. This will be true for all activity levels below 10,000 units, at which point the steady state condition begins. In addition to variances based on the learning curve effect, there will usually be other variances that require analysis and investigation. They will correspond to the difference between total actual cost and total estimated cost, which is shown in Figure 22–5 by the distance DA.

ESTIMATING INCREMENTAL COSTS
SUBJECT TO LEARNING CURVE EFFECTS

Estimates of the incremental costs of manufacturing particular units of output are often required. Where learning curve effects apply, such estimates must take account of the levels of cumulative output to which the incremental output units correspond. For example, a company bidding on a contract to produce electronic components for an aircraft guidance system should make cost estimates that reflect any learning curve effects on incremental labor and variable overhead costs. This is important whether the unit in question is the first to be produced, the twenty-first, or the hundred-and-first.

Example: Stewart Company assembles computer circuitry. Management has observed that a 90 percent learning curve ratio applies to all labor-related costs each time a new model enters production. It is anticipated that 320 units of HAL 1984 will be manufactured. Direct labor for the first lot of 10 units amounted to 1,000 hours at $8 per hour. Variable overhead cost is assigned to products at the rate of $2 per direct labor hour.

Questions:

1.   What will be the *total labor and labor-related costs* to manufacture 320 units of output?

2.   What will be the *average cost* of (a) the first 40 units produced?   (b) the first 80?   (c) the first 100?

3.   What will be the *incremental cost* of (a) units 41–80, and (b) units 101–200?

Solution: Using labor hours as the measure of cost, Figure 22–6 provides some of the answers.

The following cost measures can be derived directly from the data in Figure 22–6:

$$\text{Total Cost} = 18{,}895.68 \times \$10 \text{ per hour} = \$188{,}956.80$$
$$\text{Average Cost of First 40 Units} = 81 \times \$10 \text{ per hour} = \$810 \text{ per unit}$$
$$\text{Average Cost of First 80 Units} = 72.9 \times \$10 \text{ per hour} = \$729 \text{ per unit}$$
$$\text{Incremental Cost of Units 41–80} = 2{,}592 \times \$10 \text{ per hour} = \$25{,}920$$

The basic learning curve formula must be used to derive the average cost of the first 100 units and the incremental cost of units 101–200.

FIGURE 22–6

Stewart Company
Cost Projections Based on 90 Percent Learning Curve

Incremental Quantity	Cumulative Quantity	Cumulative Average Hours per Unit	Cumulative Total Hours	Incremental Hours
10	10	100	1,000	1,000
10	20	90	1,800	800
20	40	81	3,240	1,440
40	80	72.9	5,832	2,592
80	160	65.61	10,497.6	4,665.6
160	320	59.049	18,895.68	8,398.08

$$Average\ Cost\ of\ First\ 100\ units[1]:$$
$$y_x = ax^b$$
$$y_{10} = (1,000)(10^{log\ .9/log\ 2})$$
$$= (1,000)(10^{-.1518})$$
$$\log y_{10} = \log 1,000 + (-.1518 \log 10)$$
$$= 3.0 - .1518$$
$$= 2.8482$$
$$y_{10} = \underline{\underline{705}}$$

The solution $y_{10} = 705$ means that the average processing time for the first 10 lots of output was 705 hours per lot. Because each lot includes 10 units of output, the average processing time for each of the first 100 units is 70.5 hours. At a cost of $10 per hour, this means the average cost of the first 100 units was $705 per unit.

The *incremental cost of units 101–200* corresponds to the incremental cost of lots 11–20. This, in turn, is equal to the total cost of the first 20 lots minus the total cost of the first 10 lots.

$$y_{10} = 705$$
$$y_{20} = (1,000)(20^{-.1518}) = 634.5$$

Therefore,

$$T_{20} = 20(634.5) = 12,690 \text{ hours}$$
$$T_{10} = 10(705) \quad = \quad 7,050 \text{ hours}$$
$$T_{20} - T_{10} \quad = \quad \underline{5,645 \text{ hours}}$$

This means that 5,645 hours are required to process lots 11–20. At $10 per hour, the incremental cost is $56,450.

STATISTICAL TECHNIQUES FOR VARIANCE ANALYSIS

When sufficient cost and performance data are available, decisions as to whether a process is in control (**random variance**) or out of control (**nonrandom variance**) can be based on formal statistical analysis. This involves setting control limits on the basis of sample observations of costs and cost related measures, the mean values and standard deviations of which can be calculated or estimated.

In this case, the decision whether or not to investigate a particular variance is based only on the dispersion of observations in relation to prespecified statistical criteria—the control limits. Such criteria do not usually consider the likely costs or benefits of investigation. The implicit assumption is that all observations outside the control limits should be investigated.

---

[1] Because the first production lot contained 10 units, $a = \$1,000$ (the cost of the first lot) and $x = 10$ (the number of lots needed to produce 100 units).

PERFORMANCE MEASURES NOT KNOWN TO BE NORMALLY DISTRIBUTED

Often it is not known whether or not the cost or other performance measure being monitored is normally distributed. Similarly, the population mean and standard deviation of the performance measure may be unknown. In such cases, sampling techniques based on the **central limit theorem** may be useful. This theorem specifies that the mean values of sample means tend to become normally distributed as the sample size and the number of samples increase. Thirty samples is usually considered an adequate number to approximate a normal distribution.

The procedure is to collect sample sets of cost performance data, compute sample means, and apply control limit criteria to distinguish random, in control samples from apparently nonrandom, out of control samples. In place of a known population mean, the central measure is the grand mean ($\bar{\bar{X}}$), which is the mean of all sample means observed. The population standard deviation (σ) is replaced by the mean of the sample ranges ($\bar{R}$). The control limits are then specified as follows:

$$\bar{\bar{X}} \pm A_2\bar{R}$$

Because the total population may not be normally distributed, the control limits cannot be set in terms of the characteristics of the normal population. Instead, a separate conversion table (see Appendix, Table 22–2) provides a factor (A_2) that is a function of the number of items in each sample (n) and the desired tolerance limits.

Example: Milne Company has a production process in which materials usage per batch is closely monitored, with regular sampling of quantities consumed. Figure 22–7 shows the results of samples drawn over a ten-day period, with five observations taken each day.

To construct control limits around the grand mean, $\bar{\bar{X}}$, find the value of the expression $\bar{\bar{X}} \pm A_2\bar{R}$, using the appropriate A_2 values from Appendix Table 22–2. For Milne Company, where $\bar{\bar{X}} = 279.8$ and $\bar{R} = 16$, based on a sample size of five and with control limits corresponding to the 3σ range (approximately 99 percent), the results are as follows:

$$\bar{\bar{X}} - A_2\bar{R} = 279.8 - (.58)16 \qquad \bar{\bar{X}} + A_2\bar{R} = 279.8 + (.58)16$$
$$= 279.8 - 9.28 \qquad\qquad = 279.8 + 9.28$$
$$= \underline{\underline{270.52}} \qquad\qquad\qquad = \underline{\underline{289.08}}$$

Any sample with a mean ($\bar{X}$) that falls outside the range (270.52 to 289.08) is considered to represent an out of control situation warranting investigation. Samples 4 and 8 violate these control limits.

A further test that should be applied to sample cost data relates to the range of dispersion *within* each sample. This test is intended to guard against the "smoothing out" of performance measures that occurs when the sample mean is used as a basis for analysis. For example, two samples—(10, 30, 50) and (30, 30, 30)—have identical means of 30 but are clearly dissimilar with regard to internal consistency of individual values.

		FIGURE 22–7					

Milne Company
Sample Observations of Raw Materials Inputs

	Observation (pounds per batch)					Sample Mean $\bar{X}$	Range R
Day	1	2	3	4	5		
1......	270	290	290	282	272	280.8	20
2......	274	274	286	288	290	282.4	16
3......	280	282	282	272	282	279.6	10
4......	286	298	296	284	286	290.0	14
5......	287	282	276	272	269	277.2	18
6......	282	270	282	280	280	279.2	12
7......	280	268	280	282	276	277.2	14
8......	262	272	262	262	270	266.4	10
9......	276	288	268	302	278	282.4	34
10......	282	292	286	284	280	284.8	12

$\Sigma\bar{X} = 2798.0$ $\Sigma R = 160$
$\bar{\bar{X}} = 279.8$ $\bar{R} = 16$

Upper and lower control limits against which the value of the range (R) of individual samples must be tested are specified as $D_4\bar{R}$ and $D_3\bar{R}$. The factors D_4 and D_3 are obtained from conversion tables and are functions of the number of items per sample and the desired percentage tolerance limits. Samples with a range that exceeds the upper limit ($D_4\bar{R}$) or is less than the lower limit ($D_3\bar{R}$) are classified as out of control and become candidates for investigation.

Example: Using the data from the preceding Milne Company example, the following range control limits can be established, using values for D_4 and D_3 from Appendix Table 22–2, again corresponding to the 3σ level:

$$D_4\bar{R} = (2.11)(16) = 33.76$$
$$D_3\bar{R} = (0)(16) = 0$$

Any sample with a range outside these limits is considered to represent an out of control situation. Sample 9, with a range of 34, violates the control limits (although its mean, 282.4, is close to the grand mean).

NORMALLY DISTRIBUTED COST PERFORMANCE MEASURES

If the cost-related performance measures of a process are known to be, or are assumed to be, normally distributed with a mean (μ) and standard deviation (σ), control limits can be set in relation to the characteristics of the standard normal distribution. When it is known that the total population of observations should conform to the normal distribution, the mean and standard deviation can be used in specifying upper and lower control limits. For example, if control limits are to be set at the 95 percent confidence level, the range beyond which variances are to be investigated will be the mean ±1.96 standard deviations. In practice, there is a tendency to set control limits based on a 3-standard deviation range, the interpretation being that there is 1 percent or less chance that any random observation will occur outside that range. The implication is that those observations outside this 3-sigma range limit are the most likely to need investigation.

Example: Frates Company's usage of raw materials is 1,000 pounds per batch and the standard deviation is 25 pounds. The company prepares control charts to record and analyze daily materials usage, with a tolerance range of ±3 standard deviations, as shown in Figure 22–8.

The circled observations A, B, and C in Figure 22–8 fall outside the control limits, which were set at 925 and 1,075 pounds per batch:

$$1,000 + 3(25) = 1,075$$
$$1,000 - 3(25) =   925$$

These three observations would be classified as potentially nonrandom variances requiring further investigation.

Often performance data can only be obtained conveniently and economically on a sampling basis. If the total population is assumed to be normally distributed, control limits can be set in terms of the grand mean, $\overline{\overline{X}}$ (which approximates

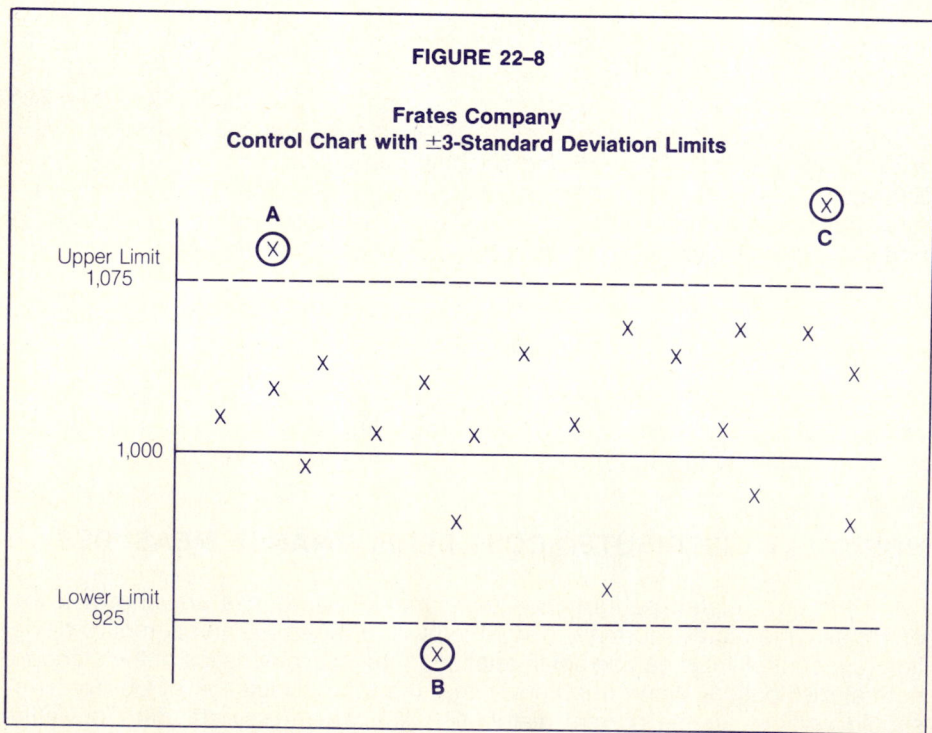

FIGURE 22–8

Frates Company
Control Chart with ±3-Standard Deviation Limits

the population mean), and the standard deviation of the sample means. Because sample data are used, t-distribution tables (see Table 15–2, page 747) should be used to provide the appropriate factors (t_α) for specifying the tolerance ranges around the grand mean.[2] The standard deviation of sample means, ($\sigma_{\bar{x}}$), is equal to $\sigma/\sqrt{n}$, where σ is the population standard deviation and n is the sample size. The control limits are therefore defined:

$$\bar{\bar{X}} \pm t_\alpha \sigma_{\bar{x}}$$

Example: Frates Company still assumes a normally distributed materials usage rate with a mean value of 1,000 pounds per batch and a standard deviation of 25 pounds. Using a sample size of 16, performance is monitored on the basis of control limits set at the 1 percent exception level. Therefore, the control limits are

$$\text{Range} = \bar{\bar{X}} \pm t_\alpha \sigma_{\bar{x}}$$

$$= 1{,}000 \pm (2.947)\frac{25}{\sqrt{16}}$$

$$= 1{,}000 \pm (2.947)(6.25)$$
$$= 1{,}000 \pm 18.41875$$
$$= (981.58125,\ 1{,}018.41875)$$

This means that there is less than a 1 percent probability that any sample of 16 observations will have a mean value less than 981.58125 or greater than 1,018.41875. If the statistical control limits are selected in this way, any sample with a mean that falls outside this range becomes a candidate for investigation.

CHEBYSHEV'S INEQUALITY AND VARIANCE ANALYSIS

Fairly large samples must be collected before the preceding method can be used. However, by using **Chebyshev's inequality,** statistical control limits can be constructed in situations where the number of observations of cost-related performance is relatively small. This formula states that, for any set of observations, the proportion $(1 - 1/t^2)$ of all sample means will fall within the range $\pm t\sigma_{\bar{x}}$ of the grand mean. For example, for $t = 3$, 88.89 percent $(1 - \frac{1}{3^2} = 1 - \frac{1}{9} = \frac{8}{9})$ of all sample means will fall within the range $\pm 3\sigma_{\bar{x}}$ of the grand mean.

Example: Assume that Frates Company's Manufacturing Division still uses raw materials at an average rate of 1,000 pounds per batch, with a standard deviation of 25 pounds per batch. Setting 99 percent confidence limits using Chebyshev's inequality and samples of size 9, requires the following calculations:

---

[2] t_α is a "multiplier" which is a function of degrees of freedom (sample size −1) and the specified tolerance range.

$$1 - \frac{1}{t^2} = .99$$

$$\frac{1}{t^2} = .01$$

$$t^2 = 100$$

$$t = 10$$

Therefore, the control limits would be

$$\bar{\bar{X}} \pm t\sigma_{\bar{x}}$$
$$1{,}000 + (10)(25) = 1{,}250$$
$$1{,}000 - (10)(25) = 750$$

Note that this range (750, 1250) is much wider than the control limits established for a 99 percent significance level under the previous methods, (925, 1075) and (981, 1018), where the existence of a normal distribution was assumed.

INVESTIGATING CHANGES IN MEAN VALUES

When a mean value and standard deviation are estimated rather than known, a further application of statistical decision theory involves testing to see whether or not these estimates are being validated by actual observations. If they are not, the result may be a "drift" of actual observations toward and beyond the previously estimated control limits, as shown in Figure 22–9.

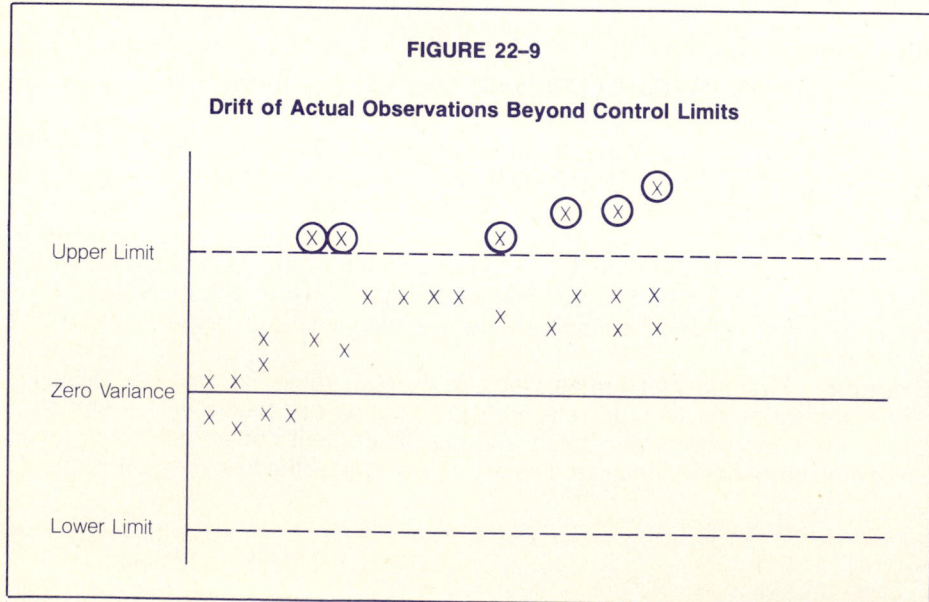

FIGURE 22–9

Drift of Actual Observations Beyond Control Limits

If the true standard mean has shifted upward, as this figure suggests, two types of errors can result. Although all observations falling within the present control limits will still be considered in control, some of those in the lower zone may actually be out of control. Similarly, several of the circled out of control observations may actually be in control in terms of the process's new mean and standard deviation.

To test for "drift," it is necessary to compute the deviation of the distribution of actual costs from the presumed distribution pattern of standard or budgeted costs. If this actual deviation does not fall within allowable limits,[3] it must be concluded that there has been a change in the mean and standard deviation of the population from which the observations were obtained.

INVESTIGATING NONRANDOM VARIANCES

The final stage in the variance analysis cycle involves investigating those variances that have been classified as nonrandom. All random variances should have been eliminated from consideration, leaving only those variances that deserve to be investigated. However, there is still a chance that an unneeded investigation will be undertaken if a variance has been incorrectly classified as nonrandom. Likewise, if variances classified as random are explainable and correctable, some needed investigations will not be performed.

Although in principle a cost–benefit approach is required to decide which nonrandom variances to investigate, the decision situation does not lend itself to a straightforward application of that technique. Before the decision to investigate is made, there is apt to be uncertainty about the cost of investigation, because the nature and extent of the needed analysis presumably are not known. Nor is it known what benefits will result when the variance is corrected. These benefits will depend on the cause of the variance and on the costs of taking corrective action. Therefore, a great deal of circularity exists. Both costs and benefits depend on the results of the variance investigation and cannot be known until the investigation is completed.

A STATISTICAL DECISION THEORY MODEL
FOR VARIANCE INVESTIGATION DECISIONS

One commonly cited elementary decision model includes the assumption that several key parameter values are known. The decision table in Figure 22–10 explains the possible action–state combination as follows: The possible *actions* are to *investigate* or *not to investigate,* and the possible *states* involve the existence of a *correctable cause* (out of control) or of *no correctable cause* (in control).

To this formulation are added the following variables:

C = Cost to inspect
M = Cost to correct if cause is discovered

[3] See F.S. Luh, "Controlled Cost: An Operational Concept and Statistical Approach to Standard Costing," *The Accounting Review,* Vol. 43, Jan. 1968, pp. 123–32.

FIGURE 22–10

Variance Investigation Decision Table

State / Action	Correctable Cause (Out of Control)	No Correctable Cause (In Control)
Investigate	Yes	No
Not Investigate	No	Yes

$L =$ Loss if cause exists and remains uncorrected

or

Savings if cause exists and is corrected

$p =$ Probability that the out of control state exists

Using an expected value approach, the expected *cost to investigate* can be expressed as follows:

$$E(INV) = p(C + M) + (1 - p)C$$
$$= pC + pM + C - pC$$
$$= pM + C$$

In other words, every time a decision is made to investigate, the cost to inspect (C) is incurred, and in addition, with probability p, the cost to correct (M) will be incurred in those cases where a correctable cause is discovered.

The *cost of not investigating* may be expressed as follows:

$$E(NOT\ INV) = pL + (1 - p)0$$
$$= pL$$

This means that when no investigation occurs, there is no cost of inspection or correction. However, with probability p, the opportunity cost of not having investigated will be incurred in those cases where a correctable cause does exist.

The decision rule is therefore *to investigate if $pL > pM + C$* and *not to investigate if $pL < pM + C$.*

Example: Coffey Company has determined that there is a 95 percent probability that one of its production processes remains in control. The company estimates that when correctable variances occur, if the process continues out of control until the next investigation, the extra cost will be $5,000. It will cost $150 to inspect the process at the investigation point and, if a correctable cause is discovered, it will cost $1,000 to make the necessary adjustments.

Solution:

$$E(INV) = pM + C$$
$$= (.05)(\$1,000) + \$150$$
$$= \$50 + \$150$$
$$= \underline{\underline{\$200}}$$

$$E(NOT\ INV) = pL$$
$$= (.05)(\$5,000)$$
$$= \underline{\underline{\$250}}$$

Because E(INV) is \$50 less than E(NOT INV), the variance should be investigated.

For given values of C, L, and M, an indifference condition can be determined in terms of p^*, the probability of the process's being out of control. When the expected cost of not investigating is equal to the expected cost of investigation, the following condition holds:

$$E(NOT\ INV) = E(INV)$$
$$p^*L = p^*M + C$$
$$p^*L - p^*M = C$$
$$p^*(L - M) = C$$

Consequently, a decision rule can be constructed in the following form:

$$p^* = \frac{C}{L - M} \text{ (the indifference condition)}$$

Then, if the posited value of p (the probability that the process is out of control) is greater than p^*, the process should be investigated. On the other hand, if the probability p is less than p,* the process should not be investigated.
Example: This can be demonstrated using the previous data from Coffey Company.

$$p^* = \frac{C}{L - M}$$

$$= \frac{\$150}{\$5,000 - \$1,000}$$

$$= \frac{\$150}{\$4,000}$$

$$= \underline{\underline{.0375}}$$

Presently it is asserted that the probability that the process is out of control is .05. Because p (.05) > p^* (.0375), the process should be investigated. This is consistent with the decision to investigate based on the previous comparison between the expected costs of investigating and not investigating.

LIMITATIONS OF THE COST–BENEFIT MODEL

Although the preceding model is conceptually sound, several limitations make its practical implementation difficult. The following discussion reviews the problems of obtaining values for the key parameters C, M, L, and p.

Cost to Inspect (C)   This might be defined as the incremental cost of determining the causes of variances. However, measurement problems exist if the only relevant costs are the arbitrarily allocated fixed costs of maintaining a quality control or internal audit staff that uses permanent facilities. The cost to inspect also depends on the cause of the variance. Realistically, C is likely to be a different amount for each inspection, because a series of investigative steps usually must be taken before a variance's cause is discovered or the search for a cause is abandoned.

Cost to Correct the Process (M)   This should also be measured incrementally because it represents the cost of restoring control to the process. However, this cost can only be predetermined if it is assumed that both the type of required adjustment and its cost are known in advance. This is seldom the case. If the correction consists simply of revising standards or budgets, and if this work is done by the existing accounting staff at minimum incremental cost, the cost to correct the process could be immaterial or even zero. On the other hand, the cost could be substantial if the production process requires a major technical adjustment.

Cost Savings (L)   These stem from a correctable cause that is corrected or from a correctable cause that remains uncorrected, in which case they are termed *Lost Cost Savings*. This is usually considered a measure of the discounted present value of excess costs that will go on being incurred if an out of control process is allowed to continue until the next investigation occurs. Cost savings are difficult to specify in particular cases, because of (1) uncertainty about the cause of the variance, (2) uncertainty about what correction is needed and/or possible, and (3) uncertainty as to what change in costs will be possible when the correction is made. The cost saving could be zero if a variance was caused by a wrongly set standard because the only required control action would be to revise the standard. Alternatively, large cost savings could result if the correction removed an implementation error or other cost-inducing factor. For example, to eliminate a usage variance, a firm might change suppliers, use different grades of material or categories of labor, revise production methods and schedules, or replace equipment.

Probability that the Process is Out of Control (p)   Determining the probability that a nonrandom correctable cause exists involves a fairly subjective estimate as to what percentage of the time a variance falls into the nonrandom, out of control, correctable category. Managerial judgment based on prior experience with the process would be a logical starting point for making such a probability estimate.

A further limitation of this type of model is that it is essentially a single stage model. Only performance within a single specified period is subject to analysis. This same limitation applies to all the other variance investigation methods examined in this chapter. However, it is possible to view performance variances as parts of a continuous, multistage process. Therefore, it can be argued that dynamic analysis, applied to *cumulative* rather than single period performance measures, is more appropriate. Various sophisticated statistical techniques have been proposed, based on the cumulative aspects of performance variances and using a multistage decision approach.[4]

VARIANCE INVESTIGATION AND BAYESIAN STATISTICS

A more sophisticated approach to variance analysis reassesses the probability that a process is out of control, using the methods of **Bayesian statistics.** This involves computing a **posterior probability** that the process is still in control, based on estimated and/or observed **prior probabilities** to that effect, together with probability measures related to the distributions of the cost measure or variance being monitored.

Example: Assume that there is an estimated prior probability that a production process is in control 85 percent of the time and that, when it is in control, the performance measure is a unit cost, normally distributed, with a mean of $100 and standard deviation of $20. Assume also that the system is out of control the other 15 percent of the time, with a normally distributed mean cost of $150 per unit and a standard deviation of $20.

$$p(\text{IC}) = .85$$
$$p(\text{OC}) = .15$$

This relationship is expressed in Figure 22–11. Now assume that the actual observed unit cost is $130. Should the variance between prior estimate and actual cost be investigated? Does it belong to the in control population or the

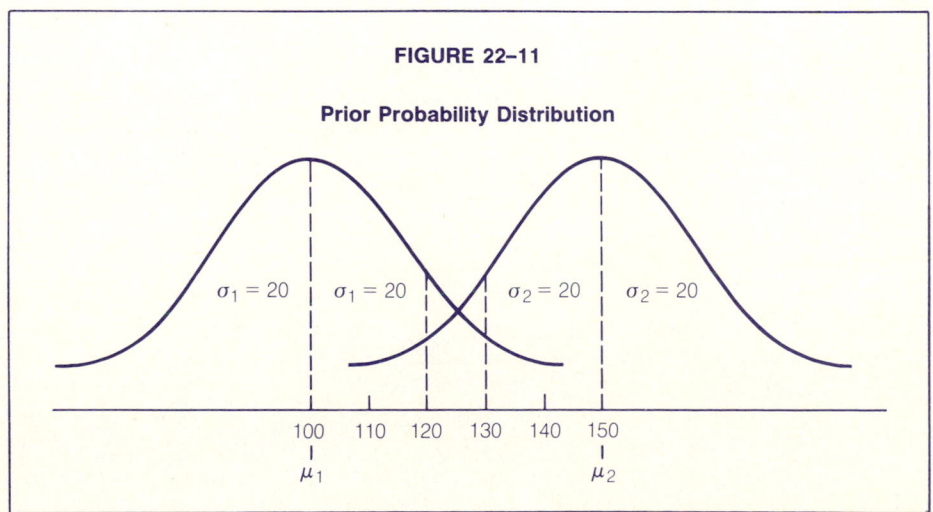

FIGURE 22–11

Prior Probability Distribution

$\sigma_1 = 20$ $\sigma_1 = 20$ $\sigma_2 = 20$ $\sigma_2 = 20$

100   110   120   130   140   150

μ_1 μ_2

---

[4] Robert S. Kaplan, "The Significance and Investigation of Cost Variances: Survey and Extensions," *Journal of Accounting Research*, 1975, pp. 311–17 and "Optimal Investigation Strategies with Imperfect Information," *Journal of Accounting Research*, 1975, pp. 32–43.

out of control population? If it belongs to the in control population, the calculated probability of a cost observation of $130 is .1295 (see Appendix, Table 22–3).

If the actual cost belongs to the out of control population, the probability of a cost observation of $130 is .242. This can be written

$$p(X/IC) = .1295$$
$$p(X/OC) = .242$$

These values, together with $p(IC) = .85$ and $p(OC) = .15$, can be substituted in the equation from Bayes' Theorem as follows:

$$p(IC/X) = \frac{p(X/IC)\, p(IC)}{p(X/IC)\, p(IC) + p(X/OC)\, p(OC)}$$

$$= \frac{(.1295)(.85)}{(.1295)(.85) + (.242)(.15)}$$

$$= \frac{.110075}{.110075 + .0363}$$

$$= \frac{.110075}{.14705}$$

$$= .7485549$$

This value represents the posterior probability that the process is still in control, based on the cost observations and the postulated prior probabilities that it was in control. This value has a complement, $p(OC/X)$, the posterior probability that the process is out of control, equal to $1 - p(IC/X)$. In this example, $p(OC/X) = 1 - .7485549 = .2514451$.

The next step is to compare the posterior probability that the process is out of control $[p(OC/X)]$ with the probability value that corresponds to the indifference point in the expected cost of investigation model ($p^* = C/L - M$). If $p^* > p(OC/X)$, the process should not be investigated. If $p^* < p(OC/X)$, the process should be investigated.

Example: Assume that the values of L, C, and M in the preceding illustration are $2,500, $400, and $500 respectively.

$$p^* = \frac{C}{L - M}$$

$$= \frac{\$400}{\$2,500 - \$500}$$

$$= \frac{\$400}{\$2,000}$$

$$p^* = .2$$

$$p(OC/X) = 1 - p(OC/X)$$
$$= 1 - .7485549$$
$$= .2514451$$

Therefore,

$$p^* < p(OC/X)$$

The decision should be to investigate, because the posterior probability $[p(OC/X)]$ that the process is out of control is greater than the investigate/not investigate indifference probability level (p^*). In other words, there is a significant chance that the process is out of control and that investigation will be worthwhile.

SUMMARY

1. The learning curve effect derives from the tendency for labor and variable overhead costs in certain industries to decrease as worker experience and cumulative output increase.
2. A precise pattern applies to the behavior of cumulative average unit costs in these industries. Cumulative average cost per unit decreases as a function of the cost of the initial unit of output and the learning curve ratio. From this relationship, measures can be derived for total cumulative cost and incremental cost.
3. Learning curve analysis may be used when cost information is needed about particular incremental quantities of output (for example, project cost estimation or bid price selection).
4. Learning curve analysis may also be used to help set standard costs that will apply when a steady state condition of the learning curve effect is achieved.
5. Over intermediate ranges of cumulative output, cost standards may be progressively tightened in accordance with the cost reduction tendencies associated with the learning curve effect. Expected variances can then be calculated as the difference between the steady state standard cost and the expected cost at prior levels of cumulative output.
6. Sample observations of performance can be plotted on control charts to distinguish random from nonrandom variances, when the total population is known to be or assumed to be normally distributed.
7. The central limit theorem can be used to distinguish random from nonrandom variances, when the total population is not known to be normally distributed.
8. Control limits can be constructed using Chebyshev's inequality together with sample observations of cost performance.
9. An expected value approach can be used to determine the cost of investigating and the cost of not investigating nonrandom variances.
10. Bayesian statistics can be used to reassess the probability that a process is out of control. This involves calculating a posterior (after the fact) probability that the process is still in control, based on prior (before the fact) assessments of the data being monitored and the probabilities that the process is in control.
11. All variance analysis and investigation decisions necessarily involve dealing with uncertainty. Consequently, the simplified decision models presented

in this chapter are at best partial solutions and aids to managerial judgment in such decision situations.

12. Whatever method is used to identify variances deserving investigation—from simple rules of thumb, to control charts and control limits, to expected value minimization models using formal statistical decision theory—the same limitations apply due to the prevailing uncertainty.

13. There is also considerable circularity and interdependence in the variance analysis and investigation environment. This results from the interrelatedness of variance causes, the cost of investigation, the costs of correction, and the benefits of investigation and correction. All these factors, plus the uncertainty inherent in any error detection system, add to the difficulty of specifying clearly defined, objective, and conclusively testable decision models.

KEY WORDS AND PHRASES

Learning Curve Effect (1115)
Learning Curve Ratio (1115)
Expected Variances (1119)
Random Variance (1123)
Nonrandom Variance (1123)
Central Limit Theorem (1124)
Chebyshev's Inequality (1127)
Control Chart (1128)
Control Limits (1128)
Variance Investigation Decision (1129)
Bayesian Statistics (1133)
Posterior Probability (1133)
Prior Probability (1133)

Appendix: Statistical Tables*

TABLE 22–1											
Common Logarithms of Numbers											
Number	**0**	**1**	**2**	**3**	**4**	**5**	**6**	**7**	**8**	**9**	**Average Difference**
1.0	0.0000	0043	0086	0128	0170	0212	0253	0294	0334	0374	
1.1	0414	0453	0492	0531	0569	0607	0645	0632	0719	0755	
1.2	0792	0828	0864	0899	0934	0969	1004	1038	1072	1106	
1.3	1139	1173	1206	1239	1271	1303	1335	1367	1399	1430	
1.4	1461	1492	1523	1553	1584	1614	1644	1673	1703	1732	
1.5	1761	1790	1818	1847	1875	1903	1931	1959	1987	2014	
1.6	2041	2068	2095	2122	2148	2175	2201	2227	2253	2279	
1.7	2304	2330	2355	2380	2405	2430	2455	2480	2504	2529	
1.8	2553	2577	2601	2625	2648	2672	2695	2718	2742	2765	
1.9	2788	2810	2833	2856	2878	2900	2923	2945	2967	2989	
2.0	0.3010	3032	3054	3075	3096	3118	3139	3160	3181	3201	21
2.1	3222	3243	3263	3284	3304	3324	3345	3365	3385	3404	20
2.2	3424	3444	3464	3483	3502	3522	3541	3560	3579	3598	19
2.3	3617	3636	3655	3674	3692	3711	3729	3747	3766	3784	18
2.4	3802	3820	3838	3856	3874	3892	3909	3927	3945	3962	17
2.5	3979	3997	4014	4031	4048	4065	4082	4099	4116	4133	17
2.6	4150	4166	4183	4200	4216	4232	4249	4265	4281	4298	16
2.7	4314	4330	4346	4362	4378	4393	4409	4425	4440	4456	16
2.8	4472	4487	4502	4518	4533	4548	4564	4579	4594	4609	15
2.9	4624	4639	4654	4669	4683	4698	4713	4728	4742	4757	15
3.0	0.4771	4786	4800	4814	4829	4843	4857	4871	4886	4900	14
3.1	4914	4928	4942	4955	4969	4983	4997	5011	5024	5038	14
3.2	5051	5065	5079	5092	5105	5119	5132	5145	5159	5172	13
3.3	5185	5198	5211	5224	5237	5250	5263	5276	5289	5302	13
3.4	5315	5328	5340	5353	5366	5378	5391	5403	5416	5428	13
3.5	5441	5453	5465	5478	5490	5502	5514	5527	5539	5551	12
3.6	5563	5575	5587	5599	5611	5623	5635	5647	5658	5670	12
3.7	5682	5694	5705	5717	5729	5740	5752	5763	5775	5786	12
3.8	5798	5809	5821	5832	5843	5855	5866	5877	5888	5899	11
3.9	5911	5922	5933	5944	5955	5966	5977	5938	5999	6010	11

* See Chapter 15, page 747–48 for table concerning Student's t-Distribution.

Common Logarithms of Numbers (*continued*)

Number	0	1	2	3	4	5	6	7	8	9	Average Difference
4.0	0.6021	6031	6042	6053	6064	6075	6085	6096	6107	6117	11
4.1	6128	6138	6149	6160	6170	6180	6191	6201	6212	6222	10
4.2	6232	6243	6253	6263	6274	6284	6294	6304	6314	6325	10
4.3	6335	6343	6355	6365	6375	6385	6395	6405	6415	6425	10
4.4	6435	6444	6454	6464	6474	6484	6493	6503	6513	6522	10
4.5	6532	6542	6551	6561	6571	6580	6590	6599	6609	6618	10
4.6	6628	6637	6646	6656	6665	6675	6684	6693	6702	6712	10
4.7	6721	6730	6739	6749	6758	6767	6776	6785	6794	6803	9
4.8	6812	6821	6830	6839	6848	6857	6866	6875	6884	6893	9
4.9	6902	6911	6920	6928	6937	6946	6955	6964	6972	6981	9
5.0	0.6990	6998	7007	7016	7024	7033	7042	7050	7059	7067	9
5.1	7076	7084	7093	7101	7110	7118	7126	7135	7143	7152	8
5.2	7160	7168	7177	7185	7193	7202	7210	7218	7226	7235	8
5.3	7243	7251	7259	7267	7275	7284	7292	7300	7308	7316	8
5.4	7324	7332	7340	7348	7356	7364	7372	7380	7388	7396	8
5.5	7404	7412	7419	7427	7435	7443	7451	7459	7466	7474	8
5.6	7482	7490	7497	7505	7513	7520	7528	7536	7543	7551	8
5.7	7559	7566	7574	7582	7589	7597	7604	7612	7619	7627	8
5.8	7634	7642	7649	7657	7664	7672	7679	7686	7694	7701	7
5.9	7709	7716	7723	7731	7738	7745	7752	7760	7767	7774	7
6.0	0.7782	7789	7796	7803	7810	7818	7825	7832	7839	7846	7
6.1	7853	7860	7868	7875	7882	7889	7896	7903	7910	7917	7
6.2	7924	7931	7938	7945	7952	7959	7966	7973	7980	7987	7
6.3	7993	8000	8007	8014	8021	8028	8035	8041	8048	8055	7
6.4	8052	8069	8075	8082	8089	8096	8102	8109	8116	8122	7
6.5	8129	8136	8142	8149	8156	8162	8169	8176	8182	8189	7
6.6	8195	8202	8209	8215	8222	8228	8235	8241	8248	8254	7
6.7	8261	8267	8274	8280	8287	8293	8299	8305	8312	8319	6
6.8	8325	8331	8338	8344	8351	8357	8363	8370	8376	8382	6
6.9	8388	8395	8401	8407	8414	8420	8426	8432	8439	8445	6
7.0	0.8451	8457	8463	8470	8476	8482	8488	8494	8500	8506	6
7.1	8513	8519	8525	8531	8537	8543	8549	8555	8561	8567	6
7.2	8575	8579	8585	8591	8597	8603	8609	8615	8621	8627	6
7.3	8633	8639	8645	8651	8657	8663	8669	8675	8681	8686	6
7.4	8692	8698	8704	8710	8716	8722	8727	8733	8739	8745	6
7.5	8751	8756	8762	8768	8774	8779	8785	8791	8797	8802	6
7.6	8808	8814	8820	8825	8831	8837	8842	8848	8854	8859	6
7.7	8865	8871	8876	8882	8887	8893	8899	8904	8910	8915	6
7.8	8921	8927	8932	8938	8943	8949	8954	8960	8965	8971	6
7.9	8976	8982	8987	8993	8998	9004	9009	9015	9020	9025	5

$\log \pi = 0.4071$ $\log \pi/2 = 0.1961$ $\log \pi^2 = 0.9943$ $\log \sqrt{\pi} = 0.2486$

$\log e = 0.4343$ $\log(0.4343) = 0.6378 - 1$

Common Logarithms of Numbers (*continued*)

Number	0	1	2	3	4	5	6	7	8	9	Average Difference
8.0	0.9031	9036	9042	9047	9053	9058	9063	9069	9074	9079	5
8.1	9085	9090	9096	9101	9106	9112	9117	9122	9128	9133	5
8.2	9138	9143	9149	9154	9159	9165	9170	9175	9180	9186	5
8.3	9191	9196	9201	9206	9212	9217	9222	9227	9232	9238	5
8.4	9243	9248	9253	9258	9263	9269	9274	9279	9284	9289	5
8.5	9294	9299	9304	9309	9315	9320	9325	9330	9335	9340	5
8.6	9345	9350	9355	9360	9365	9370	9375	9380	9385	9890	5
8.7	9395	9400	9405	9410	9415	9420	9425	9430	9435	9440	5
8.8	9445	9450	9455	9460	9465	9469	9474	9479	9484	9439	5
8.9	9494	9499	9504	9509	9513	9510	9523	9528	9533	9538	5
9.0	0.9543	9547	9552	9557	9562	9566	9571	9576	9581	9586	5
9.1	9590	9595	9600	9605	9609	9614	9619	9624	9628	9633	5
9.2	9638	9643	9647	9652	9657	9661	0666	9671	9675	9680	5
9.3	9685	9689	9694	9699	9703	9708	9713	9717	9722	9727	5
9.4	9731	9736	9741	9745	9750	9754	9759	9763	9768	9773	5
9.5	9777	9782	9786	9791	9795	9800	9805	9809	9814	9818	5
9.6	9823	9827	9832	9836	9841	9845	9850	9854	9859	9863	4
9.7	9868	9872	9877	9881	9886	9390	9894	9899	9903	9908	4
9.8	9912	9917	9921	9926	9930	9934	9939	9943	9948	9952	4
9.9	9956	9961	9965	9969	9974	9978	9983	9987	9991	9996	4

TABLE 22–2

Factors for Determining the
3-Sigma Control Limits for $\bar{X}$ and $\bar{R}$ Charts

Number of Observations in Subgroup n	Factor for $\bar{X}$ Chart A_2	Factors for R Chart	
		Lower Control Limit D_3	Upper Control Limit D_4
2	1.88	0	3.27
3	1.02	0	2.57
4	0.73	0	2.28
5	0.58	0	2.11
6	0.48	0	2.00
7	0.42	0.08	1.92
8	0.37	0.14	1.86
9	0.34	0.18	1.82
10	0.31	0.22	1.78
11	0.29	0.26	1.74
12	0.27	0.28	1.72
13	0.25	0.31	1.69
14	0.24	0.33	1.67
15	0.22	0.35	1.65
16	0.21	0.36	1.64
17	0.20	0.38	1.62
18	0.19	0.39	1.61
19	0.19	0.40	1.60
20	0.18	0.41	1.59

TABLE 22-3

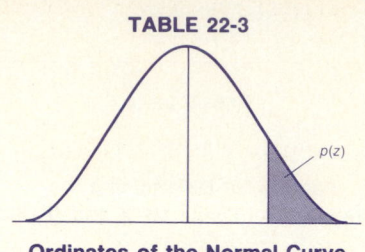

Ordinates of the Normal Curve

Z	.00	.01	.02	.03	.04	.05	.06	.07	.08	.09
0.0	.3989	.3989	.3989	.3988	.3986	.3984	.3982	.3980	.3977	.3973
0.1	.3970	.3965	.3961	.3956	.3951	.3945	.3939	.3932	.3925	.3918
0.2	.3910	.3902	.3894	.3885	.3876	.3867	.3857	.3847	.3836	.3825
0.3	.3814	.3802	.3790	.3778	.3765	.3752	.3739	.3726	.3712	.3697
0.4	.3683	.3668	.3653	.3637	.3621	.3605	.3589	.3572	.3555	.3538
0.5	.3521	.3503	.3485	.3467	.3448	.3430	.3411	.3391	.3372	.3352
0.6	.3332	.3312	.3292	.3271	.3251	.3230	.3209	.3187	.3166	.3144
0.7	.3123	.3101	.3079	.3056	.3034	.3011	.2989	.2966	.2943	.2920
0.8	.2897	.2874	.2850	.2827	.2803	.2780	.2756	.2732	.2709	.2685
0.9	.2661	.2637	.2613	.2589	.2565	.2541	.2516	.2492	.2468	.2444
1.0	.2420	.2396	.2371	.2347	.2323	.2299	.2275	.2251	.2227	.2203
1.1	.2179	.2155	.2131	.2107	.2083	.2059	.2036	.2012	.1989	.1965
1.2	.1942	.1919	.1895	.1872	.1849	.1827	.1804	.1781	.1759	.1736
1.3	.1714	.1691	.1669	.1647	.1626	.1604	.1582	.1561	.1540	.1518
1.4	.1497	.1476	.1456	.1435	.1415	.1394	.1374	.1354	.1334	.1315
1.5	.1295	.1276	.1257	.1238	.1219	.1200	.1182	.1163	.1145	.1127
1.6	.1109	.1092	.1074	.1057	.1040	.1023	.1006	.0989	.0973	.0957
1.7	.0941	.0925	.0909	.0893	.0878	.0863	.0848	.0833	.0818	.0804
1.8	.0790	.0775	.0761	.0748	.0734	.0721	.0707	.0694	.0681	.0669
1.9	.0656	.0644	.0632	.0620	.0608	.0596	.0584	.0573	.0562	.0551
2.0	.0540	.0529	.0519	.0508	.0498	.0488	.0478	.0468	.0459	.0449
2.1	.0440	.0431	.0422	.0413	.0404	.0396	.0387	.0379	.0371	.0363
2.2	.0355	.0347	.0339	.0332	.0325	.0317	.0310	.0303	.0297	.0290
2.3	.0283	.0277	.0270	.0264	.0258	.0252	.0246	.0241	.0235	.0229
2.4	.0224	.0219	.0213	.0208	.0203	.0198	.0194	.0189	.0184	.0180
2.5	.0175	.0171	.0167	.0163	.0158	.0154	.0151	.0147	.0143	.0139
2.6	.0136	.0132	.0129	.0126	.0122	.0119	.0116	.0113	.0110	.0107
2.7	.0104	.0101	.0099	.0096	.0093	.0091	.0088	.0086	.0084	.0081
2.8	.0079	.0077	.0075	.0073	.0071	.0069	.0067	.0065	.0063	.0061
2.9	.0060	.0058	.0056	.0055	.0053	.0051	.0050	.0048	.0047	.0046
3.0	.0044	.0043	.0042	.0040	.0039	.0038	.0037	.0036	.0035	.0034
3.1	.0033	.0032	.0031	.0030	.0029	.0028	.0027	.0026	.0025	.0025
3.2	.0024	.0023	.0022	.0022	.0021	.0020	.0020	.0019	.0018	.0018
3.3	.0017	.0017	.0016	.0016	.0015	.0015	.0014	.0014	.0013	.0013
3.4	.0012	.0012	.0012	.0011	.0011	.0010	.0010	.0010	.0010	.0009
3.5	.0009	.0008	.0008	.0008	.0008	.0007	.0007	.0007	.0007	.0006
3.6	.0006	.0006	.0006	.0005	.0005	.0005	.0005	.0005	.0005	.0004
3.7	.0004	.0004	.0004	.0004	.0004	.0004	.0003	.0003	.0003	.0003
3.8	.0003	.0003	.0003	.0003	.0003	.0002	.0002	.0002	.0002	.0002
3.9	.0002	.0002	.0002	.0002	.0002	.0002	.0002	.0002	.0001	.0001
4.0	.0001	.0001	.0001	.0001	.0001	.0001	.0001	.0001	.0001	.0001

Z = Number of standard deviations from the mean.
$p(Z)$ = Probability of a single observation at the location Z standard deviations from the mean.

Questions

1. Explain the learning curve effect. What costs might be associated with it? Why?
2. What factors are likely to cause a learning curve effect?
3. Might there be such a thing as a reverse or negative learning curve effect? (A "forgetting curve" effect!) Comment.
4. What factors determine the behavior of the learning curve in a particular situation?
5. Explain the usefulness of the following cost measurements obtained in a learning curve analysis:

    (1) cumulative average cost
    (2) total cost
    (3) incremental cost
    (4) marginal cost

6. How can the values of the key parameters of the learning curve be determined?
7. Explain the potential impact of learning curve analysis on job cost estimating and bid prices.
8. Explain the potential impact of learning curve analysis on standard cost systems, in terms of (1) setting standards and (2) measuring and interpreting variances.
9. Explain the steady state assumption or phenomenon as it relates to the learning curve effect.
10. Which variances should be investigated? Why is this such a difficult problem to resolve?
11. What role do *control limits* play in variance investigation situations?
12. What techniques based on the central limit theorem can be helpful in variance investigation situations?
13. Why should the range of sample observations be examined as well as the mean of sample observations in a control situation?
14. What does the test based on Chebyshev's inequality have to offer with regard to variance analysis?
15. If a population of performance measurements is known or asserted to be normally distributed, what type of control limits can be specified for variance analysis purposes?
16. When variance investigation decisions are based on sample data from a normally distributed population of performance measurements, what control limit criteria can be specified? Explain.
17. Explain how cost–benefit analysis, in the general sense, could be applied to the decision whether or not to investigate a variance. What specific problems will be encountered in applying this type of analysis?
18. What types of costs may be incurred in investigating a variance? What measurement problems are involved?

19. What types of costs may be involved if a variance is not investigated? What measurement problems are involved?

20. What is the importance of the probability that a correctable cause of a variance exists?

21. What additional analysis of variance investigation situations is possible if a Bayesian approach is employed? What situations will allow the use of this technique?

Exercises

E 22-1   Learning Curve Effects—Elementary Analysis—Labor Costs

Acme Machine Company produces complex process control devices, which require the use of a significant amount of skilled labor. Each new model developed is subject to an 80 percent learning curve effect with regard to direct labor costs. Model P4900 has just been introduced and the first batch of ten items required 10,000 labor hours at a cost of $12 per hour.

Required:
(a) Prepare a table to show the cumulative, incremental, and average labor costs at the following total output levels: 10, 20, 40, 80, 160, 320.
(b) What is the incremental cost of items 41–80?
(c) What is the total cost of the first 160 items? The second 160?
(d) What is the average cost of the first 320?
(e) Explain the usefulness of the answers to parts (b), (c), and (d).

E 22-2   Learning Curve Effect—Labor Cost Analysis—Contract Bid Estimation

Eagle Instrument Company produces precision measuring devices. It has been observed that each new product is subject to a 75 percent learning curve effect in relation to labor and variable overhead costs, due to improved worker productivity, less waste, less rework, and fewer delays and disruptions.

The latest model, the LT-ACCORD-9, has just been produced in a first-off batch of 40. Subsequent production is to be scheduled in multiples of 40 as follows: 40, 80, 160, 320. This first batch required 2,400 man-hours to complete.

Required:
(a) Prepare a schedule to show the total, cumulative, average, and incremental cost of these batches in terms of direct labor hours.
(b) In terms of direct labor hours, what is the total cost of the first 640 devices produced?
(c) In terms of direct labor hours, what is the average cost of the first 320 devices produced?
(d) If it took 2,000 hours to produce the third batch (items 81–160), what comment would you make on labor efficiency? Why?

E 22-3   Learning Curve Effects—Labor and Overhead Costs—Cost Estimates—Bid Prices

Faircloud Electronics Corporation is preparing to bid on a contract to produce 32 high performance, long-range tape recording devices for military surveillance purposes. The cost of materials and supplies for these devices is estimated at $200,000 for each unit. Over the two-year period that it is anticipated these devices will be manufactured, fixed costs are forecast to be $2,500,000 per year.

The company's previous experience in manufacturing sophisticated systems such as these is that direct labor and variable overhead costs are subject to an 80 percent learning curve effect. This project is likely to be subject to the same effect, and will also be small enough so that the steady state condition will not be reached. Direct labor costs are $12.50 per hour and variable overheads are incurred at the rate of 60 percent of direct labor cost. Production of the first unit of output will require 40,000 hours of direct labor.

The company has a policy of setting contract bid prices equal to manufacturing costs plus 40 percent, with a sufficient margin added to cover marketing and administrative costs and to allow an adequate profit.

Required:
(a) Prepare a schedule to show the total, average, and incremental labor and overhead costs of the components of the 32-unit order, based on the learning curve effect as outlined.

(b) Prepare a schedule to show the total estimated cost of manufacturing the 32 devices.

(c) What will be the bid price, based on the company's present policy with regard to bidding?

(d) Assume that a second contract for an additional 32 devices may also be secured. If the company feels that a steady state condition will apply after the first 32 units have been produced, what will the bid price be on this second contract?

E 22-4   Learning Curve Analysis—Contract Bid Price Setting

Fitzgerald Construction Company has just completed its first production batch of 10 units of a new product. The government has ordered 400 units of the same item. Costs of the first batch were as follows:

Direct Materials	$25,000
Direct Labor (2,500 hours © $10)	25,000
Variable Overhead ($6 per direct labor hour)	15,000
Fixed Overhead ($3 per direct labor hour)	7,500
	$72,500

Fitzgerald Company will produce the product in batches of 10 and has found that labor and related costs of similar products are subject to an 80 percent learning curve effect.

Required:
(a) Prepare an estimate of the cost of the units needed to fill the government contract.

(b) Can a learning curve effect apply to materials costs? Discuss.

E 22–5   Variance Investigation—Analysis of Sample Means and Ranges

Reseck Corporation has collected the following sample data relating to output per hour on one key machine in its manufacturing operation. This machine is felt to be critical because variations in its rate of output have a significant impact on labor and overhead costs. The current standard rate specified for the machine is 280 units per hour.

Sample Number	Output per Hour Observation Number				
	1	2	3	4	5
1............	170	200	190	160	200
2............	270	220	250	300	320
3............	280	240	260	220	220
4............	260	300	200	280	250
5............	240	330	310	360	300
6............	280	300	240	260	270
7............	200	180	260	280	300
8............	240	260	220	240	220

Required:
(a) Compute the mean ($\overline{X}$) and range (R) of each sample.
(b) Compute the grand mean ($\overline{\overline{X}}$) and the mean of the ranges ($\overline{R}$).
(c) Use the appropriate A_2, D_3, and D_4 factors in the tables provided to establish control limits at the 3-sigma level.
(d) Compare the sample data to these control limits. What comments do you have? What investigation recommendation would you make? Comment on the existing standard rate of output expected (280 units per hour).

E 22–6   Variance Investigation—Statistical Control Analysis— Normal Distribution

Higa Corporation has observed that one of its production processes consumes a key material at an average rate of 4,000 pounds per batch. However, usage per batch has been observed to be normally distributed with a standard deviation of 400 pounds per batch.

Required:
(a) Compute control limits for observations of the amount of this material consumed per batch (1) at the 2-sigma level, (2) at the 3-sigma level, and (3) at the 70 percent confidence interval level.
(b) Explain how the control limits corresponding to the 3-sigma level, as calculated in part (a), could be used for control and variance investigation.
(c) What assumptions and/or analyses are necessary before this situation is subjected to statistical control analysis?
(d) What actions remain to be taken after the control limits specified in part (b) are applied to observations of actual materials usage? What problems may still remain? Discuss.

E 22–7   Variance Investigation—Statistical Control Analysis—Sample Data—Normal Distribution

Refer to Exercise 22–6. Assume that Higa Corporation measures the amount of materials used on a random sampling basis by taking samples of nine batches of output each shift. The grand mean (the mean of all observed sample means) is also 4,000 pounds. The population standard deviation is still 400 pounds per batch.

Required:

(a) Compute control limits for the value of the mean of a sample of nine observations of quantities of materials consumed per batch (1) at the 1 percent exception level, (2) at the 2 percent exception level, and (3) at the 5 percent exception level.

(b) Explain how the control limits corresponding to the 1 percent exception level, as calculated in part (a), could be used for control and variance investigative purposes.

(c) Compare the results of part (a) of this exercise with those from part (a) of Exercise 22–6. Comment.

(d) What circumstances would make the use of this type of statistical control technique appropriate? Explain.

E 22–8   Variance Analysis—Statistical Control Analysis— Chebyshev's Inequality

Refer to Exercise 22–6. Assume that Higa Corporation has observed that the mean rate of usage of materials is 4,000 pounds per batch with a standard deviation of 400 pounds. However, the population of observed values of materials usage is not known to be normally distributed.

Required:

(a) Use Chebyshev's inequality in conjunction with this data to construct (1) 99 percent control limits, (2) 2-sigma control limits, and (3) 3-sigma control limits for the amount of usage of materials per batch.

(b) Explain how the 99 percent control limits, as calculated in part (a), could be used for control and variance investigation purposes.

(c) Compare your answers in part (a) of Exercise 22–6 and part (a) of Exercise 22–7 to those in part (a) of this question. Comment.

(d) Under what circumstances would this type of statistical control analysis be most appropriate? Explain.

E 22–9   Variance Investigation—Cost–Benefit and Expected Value Analysis

Required:

(a) For each of the following sets of data, use the expected value of cost of investigation method to decide whether or not an investigation is needed.

	Cost of Correction	Cost of Inspection	Cost Savings from Correction	Probability of Presence of Correctable Cause
1.........	$1,000	$ 200	$2,000	.4
2.........	2,000	800	5,000	.5
3.........	1,000	1,000	8,000	.6
4.........	1,000	1,500	4,000	.4

(b) For each of the preceding sets of data, determine the indifference probability with regard to the investigative decision.

(c) Comment on the types of production situations in which this analysis might be most helpful.

E 22–10   Statistical Control Procedures—Bayesian Analysis

Madigan Company uses a great deal of automated production and production control equipment. The performance of one machine that is prone to minor problems, leading to defective products, is as follows:

Machine Within Tolerance Limits

Rate of Occurrence of Defects per 1,000 processed	Probability of Occurrence
20	0.1
16	0.2
10	0.4
6	0.3

Machine Outside Tolerance Limits

Rate of Occurrence of Defects per 1,000 Processed	Probability of Occurrence
40	0.3
30	0.3
20	0.2
16	0.2

At the start of the current period, it was established that the machine was within tolerance limits with a probability of 75 percent. During the period's operations, the rate of defects actually experienced was 20 per 1,000.

Required:

(a) Use Bayesian analysis to revise the probability that the machine is still within tolerance limits.

(b) In what decision models could the information from part (a) now be used? Explain, including all necessary assumptions.

(c) What are the relative merits of this approach to statistical quality control? When is it most appropriate?

Cases

C 22–1   Learning Curve Effects

The Hughes Corporation is preparing a bid on a contract for 64 helicopters. The labor costs on a project such as this are expected to be subject to a learning curve effect, but the steady state condition will not be reached before the completion of this contract. A schedule of estimated costs was begun, but has not been completed.

Batch Number	Units per Batch	Cumulative Materials Cost	Cumulative Labor and Variable Overhead Costs	Total Cost per Unit	Cumulative Average Cost per Unit
1	1	$ 800,000	$1,200,000	$2,000,000	$2,000,000
2	1	1,600,000	1,920,000	1,520,000	1,760,000
3	2				
4	4				
5	8				
6	16				
7	32				

Complete the schedule and point out the key pieces of information it contains for cost estimating, cost control, and bid pricing purposes.

C 22–2   Learning Curve Effects

Selby Company operates in an industry where an annual model changeover is routine. In the Assembly Department, operations are complex and it has been observed that a 90 percent learning curve applies to labor and labor-related costs. (It is expected that steady state conditions apply after 400,000 labor hours.) Production scheduled for the current year amounts to 500,000 units of output. The first production lot of 10,000 units is forecast to require 20,000 direct labor hours. Monthly capacity in the Assembly Department in terms of direct labor is 60,000 hours. The hourly labor rate is set at $8.

Required:
(a) Discuss the preceding situation in terms of forecasting labor hour requirements for the year, for each quarter, and for each month. Show calculations to support your analysis.
(b) Discuss the problems of setting labor cost standards for this product. What standard would you recommend? Why?
(c) What variances are likely to be experienced in the first and second quarters but possibly not in the third and fourth quarters? Why?

C 22–3   Variance Analysis and Investigation

Ultimate Corporation has several production departments in which standard costing procedures are in effect and variances are reported weekly. Managers frequently complain that these reports arrive too late for them to do anything about such things as materials usage rates and direct labor productivity, which really call for almost constant monitoring. In addition, only the large variances (in dollar amounts) are presently subjected to follow-up procedures, and these variances usually have obvious explanations. On the other hand, frequent follow-ups of smaller variances might cause production disruptions and extra costs. Finally, because no follow-ups are presently applied to variable or fixed overhead costs, it is contended that the whole system is of questionable value.

Required:
(a) Discuss fully all the problems that appear to exist here in regard to the issues of variance measurement, reporting, and investigation.
(b) What alternative measurement, reporting, and investigation procedures would you recommend? Why?

(c) Discuss the possible application of statistical control techniques and cost–benefit analysis in this case.

C 22–4   Statistical Control Methods

Room service operations of the Wyatt Wegency Hotel (in Wochester) have been criticized for haphazard management. The new manager, Joseph Koppel, has requested reports on the length of time taken by staff to clean and make up rooms. Industry statistics in a recent trade journal article show that it should take 22 minutes to clean and make up an average hotel room. The following sample data were collected:

Day	Minutes Taken per Room				
1	24,	20,	28,	18,	22
2	28,	22,	23,	27,	24
3	20,	24,	28,	18,	20
4	20,	30,	28,	24,	26
5	22,	26,	20,	30,	24
6	24,	22,	18,	20,	16
7	28,	20,	16,	22,	24
8	22,	22,	22,	22,	22

Required:
(a) Compute the mean and range of each sample, the grand mean, and the mean of the ranges.
(b) Use these results to establish 3-sigma control limits for this situation.
(c) Evaluate the sample data in relation to (1) these control limits and (2) the industry average. Comment.
(d) Discuss the appropriateness of using statistical control techniques in this particular situation. Do you agree or disagree with their use? Why? What problems might be involved? What other control techniques might be useful?

C 22–5   Variance Investigation Decision—Cost–Benefit Analysis

Rodriguez Corporation uses a control chart technique to evaluate reported daily materials usage variances. Any such variance in excess of $2,000 (favorable or unfavorable) has been designated a potential candidate for investigation. These apparent out of control variances occur 5 percent of the time.

It has also been determined that these out of control variances are almost always associated with processing machinery that gets out of tolerance, requiring recalibration and resetting. Inspecting the machinery costs $400; if it is found that resetting is required, this costs an additional $800. If the inspection is not performed, estimated excess production costs (spoiled units, rework costs, and so on) of $4,500 will be incurred before the whole production setup is taken down and set up again for the next production run. When variances of this magnitude have occurred in the past, there has been a 75 percent probability that the machine requires resetting to correct an otherwise continuing problem.

Required:
(a) Prepare a matrix to show the outcomes of all possible combinations of events and actions relevant to this situation.

(b)   Use an expected value approach to determine whether or not this variance should be investigated with a view to correction. Show all calculations.

(c)   Determine the particular value of the probability that a variance in excess of $2,000 really does indicate a correctable cause of deviation such that the firm will be indifferent as to whether or not it should investigate. Show all calculations.

(d)   Discuss the sources of data for the key cost variables and the various probability estimates in this analysis. What problems are probably present in developing these measures? What assumptions may be necessary?

C 22–6   Statistical Quality Control—Bayesian Analysis

Mertz Auto Rental Company has observed that keeping its vehicles tuned up is critical to economical operations. Gasoline consumption rates are used as an indicator of whether a vehicle is "in-tune" or "out-of-tune." It is presumed that there will be separate probability distributions over the rate of gasoline consumption per vehicle, depending on whether the vehicle is in-tune or out-of-tune. A flat fee is incurred each time a vehicle is inspected. Vehicles found to be out-of-tune incur an additional fixed tune-up cost. Out-of-tune vehicles left to operate incur excess gasoline consumption costs.

Required:
(a)   Outline how Bayesian analysis could be used to help in this situation.
(b)   With what decision rule could the results of Bayesian analysis be used?
(c)   What are the relative strengths and weaknesses of such an approach to a problem of this nature? Discuss.

Problems

P 22–1   Learning Curve Effects—Cost Forecasting

Alizing Company operates in a highly specialized, technologically oriented industry and has found that its new products are subject to a 90 percent learning curve effect with respect to labor and variable overhead costs.

A new product line has just been put into production. The first batch of 200 units required 40,000 labor hours and a total labor cost of $400,000. Variable overhead costs associated with these units amounted to $150,000.

Required:
(a)   Prepare a schedule to show the cumulative average cost and the total cost of labor and variable overhead for output up to the 6,400-unit level.
(b)   Prepare a graphical diagram to show the behavior of *total* and *average* labor costs over the range from zero to 6,400 units of output.
(c)   From the graph prepared in part (b), estimate the cost of *each* 400 units of output from the 800-unit to the 4,000-unit level.

P 22–2   Learning Curve Analysis—Labor Cost Analysis—Budgetary and Control Uses

XYJ Computer Company has observed that an 80 percent learning curve applies to the direct labor costs on each of its new product lines. In January of 19X9, the company introduced the Mark-69, the latest addition to its line of computing devices. Manufacture and assembly of the first production lot of 10 of these models required 4,000 labor hours at an average cost of $10 per hour.

Production for the months of January, February, and March is scheduled (in lots of 10) as follows:

Month	Units per Month
January	200
February	350
March	450

Required:

(a) Assuming that the learning curve effect will still be operative at the end of March, prepare an analysis to determine the total labor cost budget for each of the three months. (Note that the table approach cannot be used here because production quantities are not in the "multiples-of-two" form.)

(b) What will be the estimated direct labor costs of the lots consisting of units 301–400 inclusive.

(c) What other costs may display the same pattern as the direct labor costs?

(d) If a steady state condition is found to apply after 750 units, what effect will this have on the labor cost budget for March?

(e) How would the information derived in parts (a) and (d) be used for control purposes?

P 22–3 Learning Curve Analysis—Cost Estimation—Bid Price Estimation—Special Contract Termination Provisions

The R.A.U.T. (River Area Urban Transit) Authority contracted with the Eastinghome Electronic Company for the manufacture of 320 electronic subway cars for its new urban transit system. The contract price agreed to was $200,000,000. However, a special provision written into the contract allowed the transit authority to reduce the total number of cars that they would accept, conditional on their receiving adequate public bond financing of the system and to the cars' meeting all operating performance requirements. If this provision was invoked, the contract price was to be adjusted as follows:

The price of the cars will equal the actual total manufacturing costs of all units delivered and accepted, *plus* an amount equal to the average profit per unit (if the full contract had been completed) times the number of units delivered and accepted.

However, if the completion of *all* 320 units would result in a loss to the company, the contract price would be revised for the number actually delivered and accepted as follows:

The price of the cars will equal the actual total manufacturing costs of all units delivered and accepted *less* an amount equal to the average loss per unit (if all 320 were completed) times the number of units delivered and accepted.

Cost information on the production of the first two lots of cars was as follows:

Lot Number	Number of Cars	Materials	Labor and Overhead
1	10	$2,000,000	$4,000,000
2	10	2,000,000	3,200,000

In addition, variable distribution and administrative costs amounted to $50,000 per car. Fixed overhead and administrative costs are $1,250,000 per month.

Required:

(a) What learning curve ratio appears to be in effect with regard to labor and overhead costs? Show calculations.

(b) Prepare an analysis of the total estimated cost of the contract, assuming that it will take 20 months to complete.

(c) Prepare an analysis of the total cost of completing the project based on the foregoing, assuming that it takes 24 months to complete and that materials costs of the second group of 160 cars increased to $250,000 per car. What would be the profit or loss on the contract? Show all calculations.

(d) Assume that only 160 cars are completed before the contract is terminated. Prepare an analysis of costs incurred on the basis of the foregoing, assuming that it took 15 months to produce this number of cars.

(e) What revision would be made to the contract price based on your answer to part (d)? Show all calculations. What would be the profit or loss on the contract?

P 22–4 Regression Analysis—Cost Estimation—Learning Curve Effect

Darnell Electronics Company has observed that the behavior of its direct labor costs does not appear to be linearly related to the number of output units produced. It has been suggested that a learning curve effect may be operative. The following cost data were recorded for the first eight months of 19X3, during which time a new model was first being manufactured:

Month	Labor Cost	Units of Output per Month
January	$120,000	100
February	140,000	125
March	152,000	150
April	125,000	120
May	145,000	150
June	132,500	140
July	148,000	160
August	158,000	180

Required:

(a) Prepare a graphical analysis of the data, showing the apparent relationship of total labor cost to the number of units of output. Can a linear cost function be fitted to this data using the visual fit method?

(b) Use log–log paper and prepare an analysis of the data, based on (1) the logarithm of cumulative average labor cost and (2) the logarithm of the cumulative number of units of output. Does a linear relationship appear to exist?

(c) Use least squares regression to prepare an estimate of the relationship between the two logarithmic variables in part (c).

(d) Translate your results into an estimate of the learning curve ratio and the cost of producing the first unit of output.

(e) If 200 units are forecast for September, estimate their total labor cost based on parts (c) and (d).

P 22–5   Cost Estimate of Special Production Order Subject to Learning Curve Effect on Labor and Overhead Costs

Tacoma Equipment Company is considering whether or not to accept a sales order for a specialty product that it has never produced before. The customer has requested prices for (1) 200 units and (2) 400 units.

Materials for the product are also highly specialized. The following price quotations were obtained from the only available supplier:

Total Units	Cost per Unit
200	$50
400	40
800	35

Production studies have shown that Tacoma is subject to an 80 percent learning curve ratio with regard to direct labor hours on products of this general type. The labor rate is $10 per hour. The estimate for time required to produce the first 200 units is 2,500 hours.

Based on a normal monthly capacity of 20,000 labor hours, the following standard overhead rates are in effect:

> Variable Overhead: $4 per hour
> Fixed Overhead: $3 per hour

During the current month, regular output requiring 16,000 labor hours has already been scheduled. If overtime has to be worked, it must be paid for at the rate of time-and-a-half, but the previously specified overhead rates do not include any allowance for anticipated overtime. A special nonreusable die costing $8,000 must be purchased to manufacture this special product.

Required:
(a) Prepare an analysis of the estimated total labor hours needed for the production of either 200, 400, or 800 units during the current month.

(b) Prepare an analysis of the total cost to produce either (1) 200 units or (2) 400 units in this special, one-time order.

(c) The Sales Department also requests that the cost of an 800-unit order be prepared in the hope that the customer will increase his order to that amount. Develop the necessary cost estimates.

(d) Sales prices per unit are quoted on the basis of the average manufacturing cost of the special order plus 50 percent to cover selling and administrative costs plus a profit margin. What will be the unit sales prices for an order of (1) 200 units, (2) 400 units, and (3) 800 units?

P 22–6   Cost Estimation—Learning Curve Effects on Labor and Overhead Included in Cost Basis of Contract Price

Conroy Equipment Company has received an order for 200 specially engineered lathes from a major manufacturing concern for installation in its various nationwide plants. Conroy's initial quote of $3,000 per machine is rejected by the customer, who in turn proposes to reimburse Conroy for the full cost to manufacture the total order plus a 50 percent markup on all materials, labor, and labor-related costs.

Based on completion of a first production lot of 100 lathes, the following cost information was prepared:

Materials	$600 per lathe	$60,000
Direct Labor	7,500 hours @ $12 per hour	90,000
Variable Overhead	7,500 hours @ $6 per hour	45,000
Fixed Overhead	7,500 hours @ $4 per hour	30,000
Labor and Overhead Costs . .	Initial setup—200 hours @ $22	4,400
Tools, Dies, and Jigs	(nonreusable)	15,600

The order can be filled comfortably within the capacity level used to set the fixed overhead rate. However, materials costs will be reduced to $500 per unit after the first 100 lathes are produced. Production will continue to be scheduled in lots of 10 lathes per lot. An 80 percent learning curve effect applies to labor and variable overhead costs.

Required:
(a) Use the learning curve cost formula ($y = ax^b$) to estimate the total number of hours required to produce 100, 200, 300, and 400 lathes.

(b) Prepare a schedule to show the total cost of producing the order of 200 lathes on a full cost basis.

(c) What amount will the customer pay to Conroy under the revised contract terms? What contribution margin will be generated by that amount, assuming all marketing and administrative costs are fixed?

(d) Repeat the analysis in part (b) for the cost of (1) 100 lathes and (2) 300 lathes. Assume that no further reduction in materials costs beyond the $500 per unit amount is possible.

(e) Comment on the relative profitability of the original bid for 200 lathes as compared to the revised arrangements.

P 22–7 Cost-Reimbursable Contract Pricing—Learning Curve Effects— Price Renegotiation

Morning Corporation has been awarded a government contract to supply 32 weather satellite signal recording systems. The original bid price which resulted in the contract award was as follows:

Bid Price per Recording System	
Direct Materials	$400,000
Direct Labor (10,000 hours @ $12.50)	125,000
Variable Overhead (10,000 hours @ $7.50)	75,000
Fixed Overhead (10,000 hours @ $10.00)	100,000
	$700,000
Plus: Markup for Administrative Costs and Profit (40%)	280,000
Total Bid per System	$980,000

The contract was awarded subject to the following provisions:

1. The government would pay for the full bid price only on the first batch of four systems produced and delivered.
2. The bid price on the remaining 28 systems would be revised to reflect the fact that Morning Company was subject to a 90 percent learning curve effect on its labor and variable overhead costs.
3. The allowable fixed overhead rate would be increased by 25 percent on the remaining 28 systems, due to the lower capacity utilization level implied by the learning curve effects.
4. The margin for administrative costs and profits would be kept at the same percentage level (40 percent of all manufacturing costs).

Required:
(a) Prepare an analysis to show the computation of the revised contract price for the 32 systems.
(b) Discuss fully the accounting issues involved in the contract price renegotiation (1) from the viewpoint of the government and (2) from the viewpoint of Morning Corporation.

P 22–8   Learning Curve Analysis—Clerical Activities—Cost Estimation and Control

Inouye Insurance Company has observed that new clerical employees become more proficient in processing insurance claims the longer they have been on the job. It has been estimated that a 90 percent learning curve effect applies to this type of activity, relative to the processing of batches of 20 claims. A new employee usually takes 60 hours to process the first batch of 20 claims routed to him.

Required:
(a) Develop a table to show the time it will take to process the following number of claims: 40, 80, 160, 320, 640. Show the total cost, average cost, and incremental cost for each level.
(b) Comment on how the information developed in part (a) can be useful for planning and control purposes.
(c) Discuss the appropriateness of using learning curve analysis in a clerical and administrative context. Can the same effects expected in a manual production work environment also be expected in a clerical office work environment? Why or why not?

P 22–9   Variance Investigation—Sample Mean and Range Analysis

Morton Company has collected the following sample data regarding usage rates of the principal ingredient per batch of the company's main product:

Sample Number	Usage in Pounds per Batch Observation Number					X̄	R
	1	2	3	4	5		
1	67.5	73.5	72.5	69.5	68.0	70.2	6.0
2	68.5	68.5	71.5	72.0	72.5	70.6	4.0
3	70.0	71.0	70.5	67.5	70.5	69.9	3.5
4	71.5	74.5	72.0	71.0	71.5	72.1	3.5
5	72.0	70.5	69.0	68.0	67.0	69.3	5.0
6	71.0	67.0	71.0	71.0	70.0	70.0	4.0
7	70.0	66.5	70.0	71.0	69.0	69.3	4.5
8	69.5	70.0	68.0	67.5	68.0	68.6	2.5
9	69.0	72.0	68.5	74.0	69.5	70.6	5.5
10	70.5	73.0	71.5	71.0	70.0	71.2	3.0

Required:

(a) From this set of data, determine the values of $\overline{\overline{X}}$ (the grand mean) and $\overline{R}$ (the mean of the ranges).

(b) Use these results to establish 3-sigma control limits.

(c) Examine the sample data in light of these control limits. Comment. What suggestions do you have? Why?

P 22–10   Variance Investigation—Sample Mean and Range Analysis

The director of the Data Processing Division of Etter Computer Services Corporation is concerned about variations in the rate at which documents are encoded for computer processing by her staff of terminal operators. To help analyze the situation, the following random sample of output per 15-minute intervals was taken:

Sample Number	Documents Encoded per 15 Minutes Observation Number				
	1	2	3	4	5
1	30	32	33	29	31
2	49	26	43	39	40
3	42	32	38	42	42
4	34	36	38	38	34
5	45	47	43	41	48
6	39	39	37	43	45
7	32	45	33	37	39
8	34	34	35	40	42

Required:

(a) Calculate the mean and range of each sample, the grand mean, and the mean of the ranges.

(b) Use these results to calculate 3-sigma control limits for this operation.

(c) Evaluate the sample data in relation to these limits.

(d) Discuss the appropriateness of using statistical control techniques in a situation such as this.

(e) What actions might be considered based on your analysis in part (c)?

P 22-11 Variance Investigation—Sample Data—Chebyshev's Inequality

Lager Corporation has one processing operation in which materials usage occurs at an average rate of 200 pounds per batch, with a population standard deviation of 45 pounds. The population is not known to be normally distributed.

Required:
(a) Based on samples of size 9, use the method of Chebyshev's inequality to construct control limits corresponding to the (1) 75, (2) 90, (3) 95, and (4) 99 percent control levels.
(b) Explain how these control limits can be used.
(c) A sample of 9 batches has an actual average usage rate of 218 pounds. Comment.

P 22-12 Variance Investigation—Statistical Control Techniques— Sampling Techniques—Alternative Criteria

The production manager of Esposito Corporation requested data on the machine time required to perform one of the key operations in the Machinery Department. it was reported to her that the mean value of observed machine times, based on observations of production runs over the last four months, was 120 minutes, with a standard deviation of 12 minutes.

Required: (Answer each part independently except where indicated otherwise.)
(a) Develop 3-sigma control limits for the process, based on the assumption that the population of machine processing times for this operation is normally distributed and has the parameters previously stated.
(b) Develop 3-sigma control limits for the process, assuming that it is not known whether or not the machine processing time is normally distributed but that the grand mean of all observed samples is 120 minutes and the mean of the ranges of the samples is 12 minutes. Sample size is 20.
(c) Develop 99 percent control limits for the process using the method of Chebyshev's inequality. Assume that the grand mean of samples of observed processing time was 120 minutes, with a standard deviation of 4 minutes, based on samples of size 4.
(d) Comment on the answers obtained in parts (a), (b), and (c). Under what circumstances would each be most appropriate?
(e) Apply the previously derived control limits to each of the following related observations:
   Part (a): Observed individual machine times of (1) 80, (2) 100, (3) 120, and (4) 160.
   Part (b): Observed samples of size 20: (1) mean 80, range 10; (2) mean 100, range 12; (3) mean 120, range 20; (4) mean 120, range 6.
   Part (c): Observed samples of size 4: (1) mean 80, (2) mean 100, (3) mean 120, (4) mean 160.
(f) Comment on the overall appropriateness of the use of statistical control techniques in a situation such as this.

P 22–13   Variance Investigation Decisions—Expected Value of Costs and Benefits

Sharon Corporation has estimated that it will cost $4,000 to inspect one of its production operations to determine whether or not it is still in conformity with original specifications. If it is found that original specifications are not still in effect, it will cost $20,000 to make the necessary adjustments. If the operation is allowed to continue unadjusted, and if it is in an out-of-specification condition, an estimated $15,000 of excess costs will be incurred annually over the next four years. Cost of capital for Sharon is 16 percent.

Required:

(a) If the chances of the system's being in an out-of-specification condition are 50 percent, should the investigation be conducted? Show all calculations.

(b) What minimum probability of the system's being out-of-specification would justify an investigation?

(c) Assume now that, after making the $20,000 outlay, there is only an 80 percent chance that the correction will be successful in avoiding the $15,000 of excess annual costs. Answer parts (a) and (b) on this basis.

(d) Discuss the sources of data for the cost estimates and probability measures in this problem.

(e) Compare this decision situation to one in which a daily inspection is made of a production process. Discuss both situations from the viewpoint of using statistical decision techniques.

P 22–14   Variance Investigation Decisions—Expected Value Analysis

At the start of each five-day work week, Ellen Corporation completely resets and tests all stations on its automated assembly line. If the line operates smoothly, average daily operating costs are $100,000. But when problems occur on the line due to variation from specifications, average daily costs are $140,000. If problems do arise and are not corrected, they will continue for the rest of the week. On any one day, the chances of a problem arising are 10 percent. Inspecting the system costs $10,000. If a problem is found, an extra $40,000 will be required to remedy it. Once the process is reset, it will remain that way for the rest of the week.

Required

(a) Prepare a schedule to show the costs relevant to this problem: (1) the cost to inspect, (2) the cost to readjust, and (3) the cost of allowing the assembly line to remain unadjusted. Show calculations for each of the five days of the week, assuming that no inspection or readjustment has occurred on any of the prior days.

(b) Given all stated costs and probabilities, determine whether or not the assembly line should be inspected on any one of the five days of the week (assuming that no inspection has already occurred on a prior day). Show all calculations.

(c) If the decision has been made *not* to inspect on one day (say Monday), should the assembly line be inspected on any subsequent day? Explain.

(d) Assume now that the probability of a problem arising with the assembly line is 20 percent on Monday but increases by 10 percent each day for the rest of the week. Answer part (b) based on this alternative information. Comment.

P 22–15   Variance Investigation—Partial Information— Cost–Benefit Analysis

Jackson Company has one production department where relatively frequent cost variances have recently occurred due to machine malfunctions. The trouble has been traced to one very sensitive piece of equipment which must be kept within very precise tolerance limits. Based on the firm's own observations, experience, and estimates, it is predicted that (1) the cost to inspect this machine is $1,000 per inspection, (2) the cost to make adjustments if the machine is found to be outside tolerance limits is $3,000, and (3) a cost savings of $20,000 will come from correcting a tolerance deviation.

The firm has a policy of making inspections whenever the average rate of out-of-tolerance situations reaches 40 percent. A pretest can be conducted to help determine whether or not the machine is out of tolerance. The pretest will always predict correctly if the machine is operating properly, but is only 80 percent correct if the machine is out-of-tolerance. The average out-of-tolerance rate is still 40 percent for all cases considered for inspection.

Required:
(a) Determine whether to inspect or not inspect if only the original information were available.

(b) If the pretest can be performed at no cost, what savings in costs of inspection, correction, and noncorrection will it produce? All inspection and correction costs will still need to be incurred if the decision to inspect is made.

(c) What is the maximum amount that the firm could pay for the pretest and be as well off as under the original situation?

(d) Refer to the original situation. What would be the value of the pretest if it could predict both out-of-tolerance and in-tolerance situations with perfect reliability? All inspection and correction costs would still be incurred if the decision to inspect were made.

P 22–16   Statistical Quality Control—Bayesian Analysis

Hepburn Corporation has compiled the following data regarding one of its automated stamping machines:

Machine Within Tolerance Limits Number of Defects per 1,000	Probability	Machine Out of Tolerance Limits Number of Defects per 1,000	Probability
8	.05	15	.10
10	.10	18	.10
12	.20	20	.20
14	.30	24	.30
16	.20	26	.10
18	.10	30	.10
20	.05	32	.10

At the start of the current period, it was asserted that there was a 75 percent chance the machine was still operating within tolerance specifications. During the current period, defects were experienced at the rate of 18 per 1,000.

Required:

(a) Using Bayesian analysis, determine the revised probability of the machine's still being within tolerance limits.

(b) The company has a policy of considering the machine a candidate for inspection if the probability of its being out of control rises above 50 percent. Comment, relative to your solution to part (a).

(c) What further decision will be required once it is found that the probability of the machine's being out of control is above 50 percent? Comment.

INDEX

W

Z